EDUCATIONAL PSYCHOLOGY

A DEVELOPMENTAL APPROACH

SIXTH EDITION

Norman A. Sprinthall

North Carolina State University

Richard C. Sprinthall

American International College

Sharon N. Oja

University of New Hampshire

McGraw-Hill, Inc.
New York St. Louis San Francisco Auckland Bogotá Caracas
Lisbon London Madrid Mexico City Milan Montreal New Delhi
San Juan Singapore Sydney Tokyo Toronto

This book was developed by Lane Akers, Inc.

EDUCATIONAL PSYCHOLOGY
A Developmental Approach

Photo Credits appear on pages 661–662, and on this page by reference.

This book is printed on acid-free paper.

1 2 3 4 5 6 7 8 9 0   DOW   DOW   9 0 9 8 7 6 5 4 3

ISBN 0-07-060547-5

This book was set in Palatino by Monotype Composition Company.
The editors were Lane Akers and Sheila H. Gillams; the production supervisor was Paula Keller.
The cover was designed by Wanda Lubelska.
The photo researcher was Mira Schachne.
R. R. Donnelley & Sons Company was printer and binder.

Cover art: HERBIN, Auguste.
Composition on the Word "Vie," 2. 1950.
Oil on canvas, $57\frac{1}{2} \times 38\frac{1}{4}''$.
The Museum of Modern Art, New York. The Sidney and Harriet Janis Collection.
Photograph © 1993   The Museum of Modern Art, New York.

Library of Congress Cataloging-in-Publication Data

Sprinthall, Norman A., (date).
   Educational psychology: a developmental approach / Norman A. Sprinthall, Richard C. Sprinthall, Sharon Oja.—6th ed.
       p.   cm.
   Includes bibliographical references (p.   ) and index.
   ISBN 0-07-060547-5
   1. Educational psychology.   I. Sprinthall, Richard C., (date).   II. Oja, Sharon Nodie.   III. Title.
LB1051.S6457   1994
370.15—dc20   93-31230

INTERNATIONAL EDITION

Copyright 1994. Exclusive rights by McGraw-Hill, Inc. for manufacture and export. This book cannot be re-exported from the country to which it is consigned by McGraw-Hill. The International Edition is not available in North America.

When ordering this title, use ISBN 0-07-113669-X.

ABOUT THE AUTHORS

Norman A. and Richard C. Sprinthall were born and grew up in Pawtucket, Rhode Island, graduating from the same public high school and undergraduate college, Brown University. After completing his doctorate in psychology at Boston University, Richard took an assistant professorship at American International College in Springfield, Massachusetts, and soon rose to department head in psychology and a full professorship. He currently serves as director of graduate studies.

Norman completed his doctorate in counseling psychology at Harvard and, upon graduation, remained there to eventually rise to the position of program head in counseling. He eventually left Harvard to accept a position as chair of the counseling psychology program at the University of Minnesota. More recently, he accepted a position at North Carolina State University.

Both Norman and Richard have been prolific writers throughout their careers. In addition to being a regular contributor to professional journals, Richard has authored other texts in the field of statistics and research design. Likewise, Norman has co-authored another successful McGraw-Hill text, *Adolescent Psychology: A Developmental View*, as well as other books and numerous journal articles. Finally, both have received Outstanding Teacher Awards for their classroom teaching.

Sharon Oja grew up in St. Paul, Minnesota, where she graduated from Central High School and Macalester College. While teaching high school mathematics, she completed a master's degree at the University of Minnesota in mathematics education. There she co-founded a school-university peer-teaching program in mathematics and science for disadvantaged junior and senior high school students (including African Americans, Native Americans, Spanish Americans, and Euro-Americans). Her interest in teacher development grew, and she completed her doctorate in developmental education at the University of Minnesota. As a professor at the University of New Hampshire, she teaches courses in educational psychology and is director of field experiences in teacher education. She is co-author of *Collaborative Action Research: A Developmental Approach*.

To children

Ye are better than all the ballads
That ever were sung or said
For ye are living poems
And all the rest are dead.

H. W. Longfellow

CONTENTS
IN BRIEF

CONTENTS

SPECIAL FEATURES

PREFACE

As we have just completed the revisions for our sixth edition, the temptation is simply too strong not to say, "We're back." At the same time, as we'll note shortly, we'll also say, "But with significant changes."

The most obvious is that we've been joined by a third author, Professor Sharon N. Oja from the University of New Hampshire. This has had the obvious advantage of bringing on a professional who has been using the text over the years and who has been able to provide important new perspectives to the current edition. She has been particularly helpful in strengthening our information in two critically important areas, the gender issue and the question of multiculturalism. She took major responsibility to revise and expand our treatment of those issues in the unit on teaching effectiveness (Chapters 12–14). You'll find the latest recommendations from the new work on *Women's Ways of Knowing* as well as a significant outline of how to expand classroom atmospheres in a way which genuinely accommodates and values cultural diversity.

Since educational psychology as a discipline so closely related to practice continues to grow apace, we've made many other changes to incorporate the new material. In the first unit on fundamentals, the new research has been included as well as implications. We've added the importance of social interaction from the work of Lev Vygotsky. The outstanding research of Robbie Case and his team from Stanford provides, in our view, a major cross-validation for the Piaget stage and sequence for children of all cultures. So too the new research on Eriksonian identity formation validates the stages for ethnic minority teenagers. The unit ends with the latest on the Kohlberg stages of moral reasoning, behavior, and the recent research that casts major doubts on the charges of Carol Gilligan.

In the sections on learning, there has been a major increase in the formation processing framework of meta cognition, episodic memory, schemata, and attention deficits. In fact, one reviewer commented that this chapter was the best single chapter on cognitive psychology she had ever seen. In the testing chapter we introduce new graphing procedures, including the stem-and-leaf and coverage of virtually all scoring systems—from normal curve equivalents to z scores, T scores, stanines, SATs, and IQ scores. A new table has been constructed to allow the student to quickly and easily convert from one scoring system to another. Also included is new material on computer-assisted testing, curriculum testing, and the portfolio approach.

Another new slant, especially for teachers, is the inclusion of the action-research framework as well as teacher narratives as methods for reflection. This emphasis encourges teachers' work in schools with colleagues to be viewed as a context for continuing teacher development and also for the organizational development of the schools. These are a few of the most striking changes.

For continuity, we've retained and expanded the other features from previous editions, namely the chapter summaries, the extensive glossary descriptions, many new spotlight boxes on contemporary issues, extensive biographies, and end-of-the-chapter theory to practice assignments. For students we've also prepared a supplemental *Student Study Guide* to aid in learning and retention.

For faculty, we've expanded our *Test Bank* to over 1500 items. A new feature will be a separate *Instructor's Manual*. At first we were ambivalent over such a project. Our editor, Lane Akers, finally convinced us to do it. We've all had extensive experience in teaching educational psychology (a euphemism for aging?), and he felt it was time to share some of our techniques. So with hubris aside we went to work and describe in some detail a wide variety of our own approaches such as lectures, small group exercises, and experiential activities that can improve both student motivation and learning.

Naturally there are a great number of colleagues to acknowledge for their assistance. The Minnesota

Twins, Jim Rest and Jim Ysseldyke, continued to provide input. In North Carolina, Don Locke, Cortland Lee, and now joined by Tracy Robinson helped with the multicultural issues, Barbara and Tom Parramore aided on the search for the "Lost Colony," and "Bo" Page from Duke continued to make suggestions in his most gracious way. Less well known, but nonetheless most valuable, is the feedback we received from a large number of experienced school teachers who use the work as a basis for the systematic induction of beginning teachers. This group, now numbering over 700, comments repeatedly on the usefulness of the work for practice. We appreciate their compliments and the ideas for improvement.

In Massachusetts, valuable contributions were made by Lee Sirois, Greg Schmutte, and Art Bertrand. We thank them for adding their expertise to the measurement chapter. Also, we thank Toni Spinelli-Nannen, Nancy Hayes, and Tom Noland for their valuable suggestions for both the information processing and motivation chapters, and to Gerry Weaver for his excellent outline on Grade-Equivalent Scores. We thank Gus Pesce for his important additions to the growth and development chapter, and Barbara Dautrich for her outstanding work on attention deficits. Finally we thank George Grosser for his insightful comments on the chemistry of learning.

In New Hampshire, we thank elementary teacher Nancy Frane for her invaluable, practical help with the sections on teacher effectiveness. Joe Onosko helped with the controversial frameworks concerning teaching for higher-order thinking. Phyllis Abell helped with multicultural education material. Judy Day and Gail Hahn made helpful suggestions of recent literature on the regular education initiatives. Joanna Wicklein was particularly helpful with the action research section. Also in New Hampshire, technical help with typing from Micki Canfield was very much appreciated. Editorial suggestions came from Anne Bryer and Rita Weathersby amidst words of friendly encouragement. While in Springfield, we thank the typists and word-processing experts Lynn Turner, Heidi Reese, Beth Jones, and Kathy Pollard.

In North Carolina, we take special note of the help from Robin Hughes, now a veteran of four editions. Her accuracy and speed have always been impressive. Most of all, however, her unflappable demeanor stands out. She has been and is always "there" for us.

The McGraw-Hill group is also noteworthy. This is Lane Aker's third revision. His ideas continue to be helpful particularly in pointing out new trends as well as ideas whose time has passed. We were particularly fortunate to again have Sheila Gillams as our senior editing supervisor. She has a most skillful manner of gently persuading us to write more clearly as well as ensuring continuity throughout the work; gentle insistence might best describe her help.

Closer to home, we do need to recognize both the professional and moral support from our spouses. Lois Thies-Sprinthall, an experienced teacher/educator, is really responsible for the heavy emphasis on theory to practice. Her work in "mentoring" provides a rich arena to test out our ideas in the real world of classrooms. Dianne Sprinthall's background in art and art education continues to inform us of the importance of the visual mode in communicating ideas and feelings. And Jon McMillan now knows what it is like for a spouse to work on a revision with tight deadlines and what seems like endless tasks. His support and understanding was important throughout the entire process.

Norman A. Sprinthall

Richard C. Sprinthall

Sharon N. Oja

1

INTRODUCTION AND HISTORY

At first sight it may seem that the process of teaching and learning is simple and straightforward, that all the educator has to do is arrange the material in a logical sequence, present it to the students, and then repeat the process across the curriculum. In fact William James, who originated psychology as a field of study on this continent, portrayed exactly such a circumstance by comparing teaching to warfare:

> In war, all you have to do is to work your enemy into a position in which the natural obstacles prevent him from escaping if he tries to; then to fall on him in numbers superior to his own. . . . Just so in teaching, you must simply work your pupil into such a state of interest—with every other object of attention banished from his mind; then reveal it to him so impressively that he will remember it to his dying day; and finally fill him with devouring curiosity to know what the next steps are (James, 1958, p. 25).

From the teacher's perspective nothing could be plainer or simpler. The science of general pedagogics could not be clearer. Then James mentioned the other side of the classroom equation, schooling from the pupil's point of view, by reminding teachers that

> The mind of your own enemy, the pupil, is working away from you as keenly and eagerly as is the mind of the commander on the other side from the scientific general. Just what the respective enemies want and think and what they know and do not know are as hard things for the teacher as for the general to find out (James, 1958, p. 25).

Thus, teaching like other forms of human interaction only seems easy. In fact, as we shall point out, teaching is among the most complex of activities that humans can attempt. In this chapter we shall outline these issues beginning with an inquiry into the nature of educational psychology: Is it mostly education or mostly psychology, or a hybrid, or some inadequate compromise? This inquiry will be followed by a discussion of the so-called two-culture problem of theory versus practice and the four-corner problem of teaching. To give you some historical perspective, we then will review the early beginnings of our discipline as a basis for the art and science of teaching.

The only projection we can make for sure is that teaching effectively will become even more complex as the twentieth century draws to a close. The increasing complexity is due partly to a growing national awareness of the need for an educated and literate population that will include all segments of our society. Structural changes in our society, such as the dramatic increase in the number of families where both parents work outside the home, the increase in single-parent families, the increase in the number of students from minority backgrounds, the recognition of the importance of early education, and the move toward greater mainstreamed education, to name a few of the most obvious, confront all of us with the need to reach more pupils, more effectively (Goodlad, 1990). A postindustrialized society such as ours needs workers with "thinking skills," but that's only part of the story. A democracy needs informed citizens to make intelligent decisions at both the local and national level. We certainly cannot afford an educational system which drops out one-third of our teenagers and undereducates a second third (Heyns, 1988; Kozol, 1992). Our third president, Thomas Jefferson said it best: "If a nation expects to be ignorant and free in a state of civilization, it expects what never was and never will be" (1816).

EDUCATIONAL PSYCHOLOGY: A BRIDGE STEPPED ON AT BOTH ENDS?

Educational psychology as a field of study has quite literally struggled throughout its history with an identity problem. Existing by definition somewhere between psychology and education, the discipline has experienced the crosscurrents and whirlpools often created when two great oceans meet. Psychology as the science of human behavior has as a major concern the discovery of laws. As such, it focuses on basic description and prediction to uncover gradually the nature of human beings. In this mode psychology is a science, a body of knowledge about ourselves. In the tradition of rigorous science, the questions it raises are generic. The rate of progress is slow. Human beings have been and will be more complex than psychological theories. Indeed, psychology as a science is forever limited by the size of the cerebral cortex of the investigators. Ultimately, we study ourselves. Even at best, progress in basic theory proceeds more at the speed of a glacier than at that of great oceans on the incoming tide.

Psychology's theorists are committed to a careful and comprehensive analysis of what it means to be human. This is a long-term enterprise. The payoff is future-oriented. As a professor of psychology and education puts it, "It's like investing in recreational land in Labrador. Don't expect an immediate return." At the same time theorists are quick to point out that without theory, practice has nothing to guide it. Thus, those who wish to act without an informed theoretical basis do so at their own hazard. The traditions of science require a conceptual framework for practice.

On the other side, we have the profession of education. A profession generally has exactly the opposite agenda to a science. Education—like law, medicine, and business—has practice as its foremost concern. The practical world is completely different from the scientific realm. To many in a profession, applied knowledge is the only kind that matters. Otherwise, they claim, "It's too theoretical" or "It will never work." "It's another case of excessive navel gazing," they might say, or, "Remember that according to theory the bumblebee can't fly." Such comments are quite understandable. Educators, like other professionals, confront the realities of practice every day. A teacher, counselor, or school principal cannot withdraw in the middle of a class, counseling session, or budget proposal and say (perhaps wistfully?), "Well, we need more basic research on that point so I'll stop now, close the school, and go back to the drawing board. Class dismissed for the next three years." Nor can a doctor in the middle of an operation stop suddenly, look up, and say, "We don't have an absolutely scientific basis for this surgery, so tell the patient (when he comes to) to take a number and we'll get back to him as soon as we can." We cannot imagine a lawyer's leaving, halfway through his or her summation for the defense, with the words, "We don't have a completely clear framework of precedents, so (members of the jury) put everything on hold. More research is needed."

THEORY AND PRACTICE: TWO CULTURES?

C. P. Snow (1963) in a famous volume denoted the problem of **theory versus practice** as a legitimate disparity between two cultures, the scientific and the humanistic. The same split can be seen in educational psychology. Neither tradition is better, although the status of the two cultures may be different. In fact, the status problem has only clouded the central difficulty. In this country, and certainly in nearly all modern technological societies, scientific achievement is

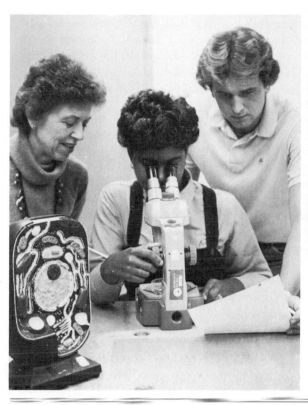

According to C. P. Snow, there is a disparity between scientific culture, which emphasizes objectivity, and humanistic culture, which is more subjective.

more highly regarded than professional activity. Science is more glamorous. Breakthroughs are announced in media blitzes. Money flows to basic research. However, the status difference is not really central to the problem. In our terms the difficulty is that the two traditions have different histories, different pressures, different procedures—indeed, fundamentally different ways of understanding what the problem is in the first place.

As you experience both scientific and professional courses, you will gain firsthand knowledge of the distinctions between these two different cultures. When C. P. Snow uses the term *cultures*, he means two different societies, or what the Germans call *Weltanschauung*—different world views. The behavioral scientist may interview literally hundreds of subjects to uncover possible systematic variations in cognitive processes. The teacher wants to know what to do at a given moment with a student. The movement here is from the general, the scientific, and the objective to the particular, the active, and the subjective. Both groups can become easily annoyed with each other. The scientist often answers the professional with a shrug followed by a long, complex, and seemingly evasive nonanswer. The professional may retort in a

situation, "Well, why don't you emulate the philosopher Bishop Berkeley. He isolated himself in a cave for a very long time, trying to get his mind together. We will keep things going here as best we can, in the meantime."

As you enter the field of education, then, do not accept at face value any of the simpleminded statements that are made about educational psychology. The idea that we synthesize two diverse traditions with the wave of a hand does not hold up. Realize that comments such as "It's a connector science" or "It's an applied science" or "It's the science of education applied to the art of teaching" are oversimplifications. Educational psychology as a bridge between two different traditions is still being built. Indeed, the progress in the last decade has been substantial, but the discipline is still stepped on regularly at both ends. It isn't quite scientific enough for psychology nor is it quite practical enough for the profession. However, the overall movement is positive. Just pick up some earlier reviews of teaching, for example. It was common to conclude in the past that educational psychologists didn't really know anything or have anything to contribute. Talk about a field in search of an accident about to happen! Researchers concluded after reviewing hundreds of studies on teacher effectiveness:

> Existing research has a long but disappointing history (Hyman, 1971).
>
> We do not know how to define, prepare for, or measure teacher competence. . . . Reviewers have concluded, with remarkable regularity, that few relationships between teacher variables and effectiveness criteria can be established (Shulman, 1978).
>
> Research has not identified consistent replicable features of human teaching (Gage, 1978).

We won't enumerate all of what we now know about teaching. That will have to wait for later chapters in this volume. We can say, though, that the current state of the art indicates a solid basis for both theory and practice.

Why Theory? Why Practice?

Let's look at another aspect of the two-culture question. In most cases science reserves the most important place for theory, while the profession takes the opposite position—that practice is the overriding concern. The purpose of theory, as any elementary text points out, is to provide a set of abstract, logically coherent explanations. Theory provides reasons and principles and is therefore descriptive. Practice provides a series of concrete behaviors activities to do—and is therefore prescriptive. The question, then, is whether we really need both. Well, let's imagine for a moment that we don't. Then the following scenario might unfold: A new theory has been proposed. Preliminary evidence shows that tall people may have a different learning style than short people. "So what?" you ask. "The new theory doesn't tell me anything about what I should do differently. I'm left with a general idea but no details. At best, all I can do is to speculate. Also, I just heard that another researcher claims that the only difference between tall and short people is in height, not learning style." So there you have it. The theory enables us perhaps to know something new about humans, yet the knowledge remains abstract.

Now, let's look at it the other way around. You are listening to some professionals. One says, "I decided to try something different in my class. I heard somewhere that another teacher had good luck in using the discovery method of teaching." That's it.

By word of mouth, a promising practice is suggested. You have some specific details as to how to set up the room, ask open-ended questions, and use maps without cities designated. In fact, the suggestions for practice are very clear and very detailed. It is just the opposite of theory. As an educator you may instinctively feel that the second approach is clearly superior. You have the directions but you don't have any explanation. You don't know why the method works. The danger is that all teachers will use the same method on all students. Without theory, you have no way of knowing when to use it and when *not* to use it. The practical advice doesn't allow systematic prediction of the outcome.

Another way to think about the issue is from the viewpoint of the performing artist, such as a violinist, a ballet dancer, or an opera singer. Such artists are clearly committed to practice, practice, practice. In fact they often avoid theory altogether. James Allen (1992) interviewed a gifted thirteen-year-old soloist with the question, "What goes through your mind when you play?" "Nothing," she replied (p. 8). The idea, of course, is that action and performance are the ultimate criteria. Anything else, such as reflection, discussion, or theory seems to fail the test. "But what is the use of that?" the performer asks rhetorically. Allen points out the mutual distrust and "reciprocal condescension" (p. 8) between the performer and the intellectual critic. The performer is viewed as an empty vessel (a robot) by the critic. The critic, on the other hand, is viewed as hopelessly abstract and removed from real life by a screen of words, words, words. This is probably best captured in a slightly different context when Eliza Doolittle (*My Fair Lady*), embittered about her treatment at the hands of her mentor, Professor Henry Higgins, complains, "Don't talk of words, show me!"

The debate between theory and practice has a long history. Educational professionals and humanists often like to decry "cold" theory. Goethe, a great German dramatist, put the case clearly and emotionally: "Theory is all grey and the golden tree of life is green." Sartre, a famous French philosopher, criticized scientists in this way: They build "great theoretical cathedrals, but actually live in a small outhouse next door." On the one hand, theory without practice, then, can be abstract speculation. Practice without guiding theory, on the other hand, may be random—or even worse, frenzied—activity without point or consequence. One commentator remarked that practice by itself quickly becomes a fad wandering around somewhere between the cosmic and the trivial, without knowing which is which. We have scientific reasoning divorced from reality, or folklore separated from logic. Basic research can become sanctimonious aimlessness. Practice can become just aimlessness. Clearly, we need both even though each tradition works against an overall integration.

One Theory or Many?

Still another related question, if you are convinced of the need for both theory and practice, is which theory should be selected as a basis for informed practice? As any study of psychology quickly shows, there are many contending theories. How can you know which is best? Where is the supertheory for educational practice? Naturally, there is no easy answer. Many dedicated psychologists have literally given their entire lives to the search. Promising theories emerge but then do not stand up and so are replaced. The scientific community attempts to evaluate theory on the basis of two principles, parsimony and reductionism. Sometimes this is as difficult as serving two masters.

The first term means just what you think; *parsimony* equals stinginess. Like a person who spends money very carefully, theory should be succinct and compact. A parsimonious person doesn't throw money around needlessly. A theory should not be more elaborate or more abstract than it needs to be to explain the facts. To give an example, one of the current and largely justified criticisms of Freud's classical psychoanalytic theory is that it is based on a long series of assumptions that could not be tested out—assumptions such as unconscious motivation, the suppression of libido drives, castration anxiety, penis envy, the Oedipus complex, homosexuality and paranoia, the Electra complex, and others. A theory is not parsimonious if we have to accept, on faith, such a number of suppositions. The theory becomes more a set of beliefs or an ideology than a scientific basis for prediction. In order to make the theory fit, we are forced to add a number of qualifications. The theory becomes interesting in a sense yet ends as pure speculation.

A medieval philosopher, **William of Occam,** revolted against the wild theorizing of his day. You may have heard about a religious controversy concerning how many angels could dance on the head of a pin. Highly speculative and elaborate theories evolved to resolve this controversy in Occam's time. He wrote

a scathing statement pointing out the need for parsimony. His work shook the scholastic world so severely that his thesis became known as Occam's razor, the tool to cut away needless elaboration and qualifications. Ideas had to be clear, concise, and to the point. Many a pseudotheory was slashed by Occam's razor (Sabine, 1937).

This is not the whole story. Other theorists, heeding (or fearing) Occam's razor, decided to go in a completely different direction from the woolyheaded theorists of Occam's day by paring theory to its bare bones. They eliminated as many assumptions, qualifications, and suppositions as possible. In psychological theory the best example was early behaviorism. All known human characteristics such as learning styles, temperament, feelings, stages of cognition, and so on were eliminated. In fact, everything in psychological theory was cut away except one principle, the law of effect. In attempting to protect against meaningless elaboration, the drive to parsimony sometimes goes too far. In such an instance parsimony is called *reductionism.* In seeking to streamline theoretical thought, too many ideas are dismissed. This is sometimes called "tossing out the baby with the bath water."

Effective theory can be judged somewhere at the midpoint of an unusual continuum. The English scholar William of Occam sits in the middle, honing his razor; angels dancing on the head of a pin at one end; a baby in a tub of dirty water at the other, waiting to be tossed. Naturally, as a new student to educational psychology you cannot realistically be expected to evaluate theories accurately on this continuum. However, you should realize that our current elaboration of theories for education does reflect our best estimates of the midpoint. The developmental approach provides a theory describing how students grow and change through a series of stages. This model for educational psychology does incorporate many of the best features of prior theories; in addition, it can and does change as new information is tested and found valid. We explain such a process in the succeeding chapters. The theories we will be examining have direct relevance to practice. You will find contributions from many theories joined together in the developmental framework. You will also find aspects of prior theories eliminated, ideas that were either too speculative or too narrow (Jackson, 1990).

One final point of theory: Do not expect a theory to tie together all loose ends. Our theories represent our best current understanding, not the final solution.

Wooly-headed Thinking   Parsimony   Reductionism

Human behavior is not a closed but an open system. As we learn more and test more ideas, our understanding changes. Theory is dynamic. In the process of moving forward, it leads to successive approximations as our knowledge of human development slowly evolves. Theory can never be complete because of the nature of human beings. There is always a lack of total understanding and of closure. However, each new generation of educational psychologists does stand on the shoulders (not the face) of previous generations. You will become accustomed to the idea that while certain actions or activities represent our best current understanding, they do not come with an absolute guarantee. We act on the basis of informed judgment. In the words of Harvard psychologist Gordon Allport, we are "wholehearted but half-sure."

EDUCATIONAL PSYCHOLOGY: FOUR PROBLEMS TO SOLVE SIMULTANEOUSLY

One cause of difficulty in understanding educational psychology is the hybrid nature of science and education. Both theoretical and practical concerns are intrinsic to the nature of each field. Now, to up the ante, we turn to the problems that educational psychology seeks to solve. What is the world on which we focus? The simple answer is the teaching-learning process. That has a nice clear ring to it—it couldn't be simpler. Yet, the moment we examine the question more closely, we immediately confront four interrelated concerns: the students, the teacher, the classroom strategies, and the content to be taught. We can refer

to this as the **four-way agenda of teaching** (see Table 1.1).

First we need to know what pupils are like. After all, we are not dealing with pieces of wood or rocks but with real, live, human beings. Each human is unique—and yet is like some other humans and like all other humans in some ways. This statement, you will find, is quite often made by both psychologists and educators. But when you listen carefully, you may find that they quickly ignore their own words. It is a concept honored only in the breach. In other words, while offering three different versions of human behavior—the idiographic, which focuses on the uniqueness of individuals; the nomothetic, which looks for characteristics that all humans share; and an idiographic-nomothetic middle ground—both educators and psychologists all too often settle on one version. But you need to know about individual differences, group similarities, and the combination. So one part of the agenda is the oftentimes bewildering variety of information on the nature of students, your classroom learners.

A second part of the agenda shifts the focus from the pupils to you as a teacher, your own attitudes and understandings about learning. What are the goals for your classroom? What do you expect from your pupils? What is your level of self-understanding as a person and as a professional? The teacher's really unspoken feelings about his or her role and the students are sometimes called the "hidden agenda" of the classroom. In fact, research has shown just how powerfully some of the unintentional behavior that results from this hidden agenda affects the pupils. So while you are learning about pupils in the classroom,

TABLE 1.1 THE FOUR-WAY AGENDA OF TEACHING

STUDENT CHARACTERISTICS	TEACHERS
1. Physical	1. Attitudes to learning
2. Physiological	2. Attitudes to students
3. Cognitive	3. Attitudes to self
4. Personal	4. Understanding research
5. Moral/Value	
6. Motivations	
7. Individual and group behavior	
8. Special needs	
9. Cultural and gender	

TEACHING STRATEGIES	SUBJECT MATTER
1. Learning theories in practice	1. Structure of the disciplines
2. Teaching methods and models	2. Basic concepts of material being taught
3. Individual methods	3. Sequencing of subject matter
4. Lesson planning	4. Priorities in content selected
5. Variations in structure	5. Degree of specialized content
6. Student discipline	
7. Questioning	
8. Use of tests	

they are most likely learning about you—"where you are coming from," as the saying goes.

A third part of the agenda is represented by the explicit set of teaching strategies, the actual classroom behaviors, you employ. Some years ago, during the so-called know-nothing period when researchers kept bemoaning how little we knew about teaching, the solution as to which teaching methods to use was breathtakingly simple. Since the experts didn't know, you could "just do your own thing." Be spontaneous and creative was the dictum. As you might suspect, that is easier said than done. Flying by the seat of one's pants has always had an attractive, romantic aura about it. But in the classroom it often led to disaster. There are a series of very important specific teacher "moves" that must be learned. However, they cannot simply be applied like ingredients you would add as you follow a cooking recipe. Certain specific skills must be mastered before you can achieve true flexibility as a teacher.

The fourth part of the agenda is represented by the content of your teaching—that is, language arts, math, science, social studies, and so on. Undoubtedly, it's hard to teach history if you don't know the field. Knowing the field as a teacher also means knowing how to divide up the content and sequence it in accordance with learning priorities. Clearly, content stands on a par with the other three parts of the agenda. All four are involved in the process of teaching.

In this book, you may be relieved to know, we are concentrating *only* on the first three parts: students, teachers, and strategies. That makes it just a three-ring circus, you may be thinking, as you review the enormous amount of material in those areas. This text will help you with three parts of the teaching-learning process. They are not the entire story, nor do they encompass all there is to know about teaching. Although we will not delve into the subject matter area, we do not see it as less important than the other three.

Students, teachers, subject matter, and strategy constitute the four-way agenda for teaching.

There are four problems, and they must be solved simultaneously. Such has not always been the case. We will now turn to the history of educational psychology in order to give you a taste of its somewhat checkered past.

EDUCATION YESTERDAY AND TODAY

Yesterday: Trivia in the Classroom

In the late nineteenth century, a visitor to the public schools concluded that most classroom activity consisted of a game of recitation. The pupils and the teacher followed a systematic question-and-answer exercise. The teacher would ask a series of short, factual questions with the rapidity of a machine gunner: "Now class, pay attention. . . . Tell me, who discovered America? What year? How many ships were there? What were their names? How long was the voyage?" Each question was followed by a brief pause, and then students with hands raised were called on, again with the speed of light, until one student gave the correct answer. At this point the teacher would fire the next question and skip around the class, calling on pupils whose hands were raised until the next right answer was called out. The observer in the nineteenth-century classroom noted that the interaction between teacher and pupil seemed excessively mechanical. The process seemed to emphasize rote learning, the repetition of memorized facts from the textbook or given by the teacher. Inquiry was unknown. "In several instances when a pupil stopped for a moment's reflection, the teacher remarked abruptly, 'Don't stop to think, but tell me what you know'" (Rice, 1893).

These impressions of what we might call **trivia in the classroom** were given further credence by other observers. An English educator in 1908 noted the "time-honoured" tradition in U.S. classrooms of question-and-answer recitation, in distinct contrast to the lecture method used on the continent of Europe. A study of classroom interaction further substantiated question-and-answer as the predominant approach to teaching in this country. Using stenographic notes

One researcher at the turn of the century found that over 80 percent of classroom talk consisted of asking and answering brief, factual questions.

of actual classroom discussions (this was in the days before tape recorders), a researcher in 1912 found that over 80 percent of all classroom talk consisted of asking and answering brief factual questions—questions that called for a good rote memory and an ability to phrase the answer in the same terms the teacher used. The teacher asked between one and four questions per minute, much as in today's TV quiz games in which contestants (pupils) are given a few seconds to come up with the right answer; if they don't have the answer at the tip of their tongue, they lose their turn, and the quiz master (teacher) moves on. The researcher noted:

> The fact that one history teacher attempts to realize his educational aims through the process of "hearing" the textbook, day after day, is unfortunate but pardonable; that history, science, mathematics, foreign language and English teachers, collectively are following in the same groove, is a matter for theorists and practitioners to reckon with (Stevens, 1912, p. 66).

William James, one of this country's first and perhaps greatest commentators on the problems of teaching and learning, provided the following example of the recitation quiz game in the classroom.

> A friend of mine, visiting a school, was asked to examine a young class in geography. Glancing at the book, she said, "Suppose you should dig a hole in the ground, hundreds of feet deep, how should you find it at the bottom—warmer or colder than on top?" None of the class replying, the teacher said: "I'm sure they know, but I think you don't ask the question quite rightly. Let me try." So, taking the book, she said: "In what condition is the interior of the globe?" and received the immediate answer from half the class at once: "The interior of the globe is in a condition of igneous fusion" (1958, p. 106).

Today: Still Trivia in the Classroom?

Nearly a century after the above observations were made, educational researchers studying classroom interactions between teachers and pupils made the following comments: (1) The teachers tend to do about 70 percent of all talking in the classroom. (2) Most of this talk consists of questions. (3) Between 80 and 88 percent of all these questions call for rote memory responses. (4) The teachers typically ask two questions per minute. (5) Pupil talk is almost exclusively a short response to the teacher's question. (6) Inquiries and suggestions from pupils are virtually nonexistent (Bellack, Kliebard, Hyman, and Smith, 1966).

Similarly, a 1974 study of 156 randomly selected classrooms across the country found the same pattern in all but 5 percent of the classes (Goodlad and Klein, 1974, p. 51). And, unfortunately a study ten years later (Goodlad, 1984) reached the same conclusion as did the Jeness study in 1990. In fact, Michael Cole provides an interesting historical perspective. He found that pupils some 6,000 years ago were just as likely to have lists of information to memorize as their modern-day counterparts. The content was different, for example, eighty-four different types of trees versus the fifty state capitals, but the process was the same (Cole, 1990, p. 96).

You may be struck by the remarkable similarity in the results of these studies—after so many years the same mode persists. The state of affairs raises two questions: Is the rapid-fire question-and-answer trivia quiz an effective educational method? If it isn't, then why does it persist?

Perhaps the best way to begin understanding the effect of rapid-fire question-and-answer procedures would be to ask you to remember such a situation in your own experience. You are in the third grade, sitting in a class of thirty children. The teacher towers over you physically, a difference exaggerated when she stands in front of the seated class. The class has been studying a unit on the American Indian. After a series of questions on Native American lore and myths, which you know about but don't get called on for (she had scolded you sternly, saying that you were to remain seated when you raised your hand), the teacher suddenly wheels around and looks directly at you: "What did the Navaho call their houses?" In the confusion (for you are still thinking about a previous question), you don't have the answer. The class falls silent. Twenty-nine children turn toward you. The teacher waits a few seconds that seem like years and then says, "Well?" "Tepee?" you say, hoping that it's right, but mostly wishing there were a place to hide. "Hogan," the teacher replies. "Hogan—oh, that what I meant to say," you add in a near-whisper. The moment does pass as the girl two seats away from you expertly fields the next question about how a hogan is constructed. A few minutes later recess mercifully arrives, and you manage to sneak out as unobtrusively as possible. So much for the question-and-answer quiz and the promotion of learning.

WILLIAM JAMES

William James, American psychology's founding father, was born in 1842 in New York City. During his early years he showed little evidence of the academic brilliance that was soon to follow. In fact, his early education was rather meandering and informal. He attended several private schools in this country and abroad. The only consistent educational experience he had was with his family at the dinner table. Conversation abounded there on every conceivable topic. All members had the opportunity to test their wits against the others. His multiple talents seemingly prevented him from settling on any one career. His brother, Henry James, became a famous novelist. It has often been said that William James was a psychologist who wrote like a novelist, and Henry James was a novelist who wrote like a psychologist. During his youthful years William studied art for a while in Newport, Rhode Island, before deciding to attend Harvard College and specialize in chemistry. However, he maintained his interest in art throughout his life.[a] After two years he switched his field again, transferring to comparative anatomy and physiology. At this point James wrote to a friend that the problem of career choice was limited to four alternatives, "Natural History, Medicine, Printing, and Beggary," and since he had sworn not ever to become a beggar, he settled on medicine. But once again he felt some discontent and decided to interrupt his studies, first to collect specimens from the Amazon River and later to spend time recuperating from illness by taking a trip to Europe. Finally, in 1869, he did complete his medical studies and was awarded the only academic degree he ever earned, an M.D. A scholar commented that it "seems a strange one for a man who was to make his mark as a psychologist and philosopher." But the real education of William James was not received in universities and did not lead to degrees. It had been in his home with his family.

When offered a position as instructor at Harvard at the age of thirty, James jumped at the chance to drop the sheer drudgery of medicine. He moved from the practice of medicine into the classroom. For James this was an important step; for psychology it turned out to be momentous. He thrived on academic life, worked hard at the craft of college teaching, and very early displayed a talent for both research and teaching. Once again, however, his enormous and restless talent stretched beyond the conventional and passed by the then-recognized academic disciplines. In 1876 he created and began teaching the first psychology course ever taught in this country. His originality and creativity burst forth, and he poured out lectures that increased in popularity. Essentially he was simultaneously creating a field of study, shaping the content, and outlining the sequence of topics. He wrote a monumental two-volume basic text for

A series of studies has shown, perhaps not as dramatically or as personally as the above incident, that the classroom trivia quiz does not promote learning unless we really think that the recitation of textbook facts is equivalent to learning. If we view the objectives of teaching and learning more broadly, then we can only conclude that a form of "Button, button, who has the button?" or "Hogan, hogan, what's a hogan?" does not help students learn except in a negative way. You do learn to play the game after a while; that is, you learn to say the right thing and to act out of reflex. You do remember the acceptable phrases and terms, whether they concern the kind of a house a Navaho lived in or the state of igneous fusion in the center of the earth. But is this the process of inquiry we consider desirable? Is this the goal of human thinking? Does this create the excitement of seeing new relationships among ideas? Is this the process through which we learn about ourselves?

EMERGENCE OF A THEORETICAL FRAMEWORK

Fundamentally, the problem faced by education and psychology has been to create a framework that is

these courses, simply titled *Principles of Psychology*, a text that is still referred to as the single-greatest work in American psychology. Here he outlined the basic tenets of psychology with such vision and clarity that his text even today has an incredibly modern flavor. Because of this book, James established himself not only as the premier American psychologist, but, in the minds of many, the founder of American psychology itself.[b] He started the first psychology laboratory in the United States and anticipated the theory of conditioning later demonstrated by Pavlov, as well as the importance of critical stages of learning and some of the principles of gestalt psychology. So substantial was his vision that his original book can still provide a modern reader with a relatively up-to-date version of psychology.

For the field of educational psychology James became both an educator and a philosopher. He saw the importance of tailoring educational material to fit the learner's true condition, not the condition that the teacher assumed the learner should be in. His pride in his own teaching meant that he could model effective instruction as well as tell others how to achieve it, a talent that few academic scholars can manage even today. In this way James was devoted to the idea of improving all teaching. Education, then as now, tended to be classed as slightly less respectable than certain other disciplines. James's independence of mind and his ability to go beyond the conventional once again were in evidence. As a Harvard professor, renowned scholar, and originator of the field of psychology, he devoted much effort and energy to improving the quality of classroom education. His famous lectures, *Talks to Teachers on Psychology*, are very briefly quoted in the text to give you some feel for his flair with concepts as well as the significance of his thinking. His major point was that the entire enterprise of education is determined by the actual classroom teacher.

In these days of national curriculum projects and technological prescriptions for the classroom, we need to recall the central Jamesian theme: "Psychology is a science—teaching is an art; and sciences never generate arts directly out of themselves. An intermediary inventive mind must make the application, by use of its originality." James was convinced that the future of education depended directly on the quality of the intermediary inventive minds of the teachers. It was they who would do the job in the classroom and they who needed to apply psychological principles humanely. James was convinced that teaching could be improved by understanding the nature of children and adolescents as behaving organisms.

An educational theorist, Paul Woodring, probably summed up James's significance to education most succinctly. He noted that if James had been read carefully by teachers and teacher-educators over the past fifty years, many of our educational difficulties might have been avoided.

James's long and productive life ended in 1910 after some thirty-five years of teaching. The world lost that rare combination of talents—those of teacher, scholar, leader, and philosopher able to go well beyond current thinking. James has even been called "the most gifted writer of expository prose this country ever had."[c] With all this, he had a personality so vivid that his sister described him as "born afresh every morning."

―――――――――――――

[a] Leary, D. E. (1992). William James and the art of human understanding. *American Psychologist, 47*, 152–160.

[b] Johnson, M. G., and Henley, T. B. (1990). *Reflections on the principles of psychology: William James after a century.* Hillsdale, N.J.: Erlbaum.

[c] Adelson, J. (1982). Still vital after all these years. *Psychology Today, 16*, 52–59.

broad enough to provide working solutions to the four-part agenda of concerns we mentioned earlier. William James, this country's first psychologist, was also the first to grapple directly with the problem. The scope and depth of his vision provided initial and brilliant insights. Unfortunately, the field did not follow his views until very recently. Because of his importance we will describe his work in detail as well as some of the reasons for the long eclipse of his thinking and his current relevance. After that, we will look at the contributions of some other theorists—E. L. Thorndike, John Dewey, and Maxine Greene.

William James: The Early Promise

William James exerted tremendous early influence on the whole field of psychology and was probably this country's most significant educational psychologist. In the nineteenth century, psychology was considered part of philosophy, not a separate discipline. It was William James at Harvard in the 1880s who began to give systematic attention to psychology as a discipline in its own right and, more importantly for us, began to consider most seriously the question of applying psychology to the problems of the real world rather than leaving it in the laboratory.

James was concerned that the so-called scientific tradition would capture psychology and turn it away from its important purpose of helping us understand more about the processes of teaching and learning. He delivered a series of famous lectures (*Talks to Teachers on Psychology*) that are as relevant today as when they were originally delivered. At that time, "scientific" experiments were thought to be able to give us all the answers, including all the laws that govern human behavior. James feared the dangers of such an exclusive dependence on science. He warned that laboratory scientists "would go off by themselves and use apparatus and consult sources in such a way as to grind out in the requisite number of months some little peppercorn of new truth worthy of being added to the store of extant information on the subject" (James, 1958, p. 38). Such efforts might produce a mount of peppercorns but not necessarily truth.

James wisely saw that psychology had to look to the natural environment for much of its information. Laboratory studies, especially animal studies, might not be such a great help when it came to teaching children. He therefore launched the effort to examine and understand the process of teaching and learning in the classroom. He observed classrooms (remember his igneous fusion anecdote) and also suggested positive alternatives to the state of affairs he observed. For example, he pointed to the central importance of starting lessons at a point just beyond the pupils' present comprehension. The famous dictum "Start where the learner is and proceed" was derived from this insight of William James.

> If the teacher is to explain the distance of the sun from the earth, let him ask ... "If anyone there in the sun fired off a cannon straight at you, what should you do?" "Get out of the way," would be the answer. "No need of that," the teacher might reply. "You may quietly go to sleep in your room, and get up again, you may wait until your confirmation-day, you may learn a trade, and grow as old as I am—then only will the cannon-ball be getting near, then you may jump to one side! See, so great as that is the sun's distance!" (James, 1968, p. 333).

James's most important effort was to try to convince educators that the observations, thoughts, and questions they brought out of their work with pupils would be a significant source of "scientific" feedback. He was particularly concerned to retain the human mind, or as he called it, "mental life," as a proper object for psychology; in fact, he deliberately defined

psychology as the "science of mental life." What goes on "inside" a person's head—thoughts, feelings, interests, values, sentiments—these were what James thought psychologists should study in order to shed light on human strivings and motivations.

James was the first to warn teachers and educators not to depend on psychology to provide all the answers and to warn psychology not to present itself as a mirror image of physical science. He saw psychology as a natural science filled with uncertainty, an "open system" of questions concerning that most complex of all "systems," the human being. That was the problem, but it was also the challenge.

The difficulties of James's view were many. For example, to say that teaching is a process that we can never fully understand is unsettling to those in search of the truth. To say that we will have to be content with a series of approximations of good ideas and practices rather than perfect ideas or perfect practices is likewise unsettling.

Obviously it was, and still is, extraordinarily difficult to consider educational problems in such a broad perspective. James wanted educational psychology to study teaching and learning in the classroom in order to view educational problems in their real, or natural, environment. James wanted to focus on both the objective and the subjective nature of educational problems.

In rejecting James's views as too unwieldy, educational psychology headed in a logical direction. It seemed sensible when confronted with complexity to narrow the focus, to examine the effect of one variable at a time. And to add strength to this tendency, there was, at the time, an almost passionate desire for psychology to pattern itself after the physical sciences and to search for the "molecules" of human behavior. This is sometimes referred to cynically as "physics envy." In fact the shift was so strong that Cahan and White (1992) found that the James view was considered as a "second psychology," a movement that became moribund with his death at the turn of the century. This meant that the emphasis shifted away from naturalistic studies of pupil and teacher behaviors in classrooms. There were too many uncontrolled variables operating in such settings; the open system of a classroom was not a scientifically researchable problem. The desire for precision in measurement and research design forced educational psychology into the laboratory. The era produced many useful pieces of information, especially about some aspects of learning. On balance, however, the focus was too narrow. Too much was left untouched. The class-room, as we noted at the beginning of this chapter, remained tragically similar to its early twentieth-century antecedent. To understand the impact of the new focus and its limitations, we will turn to the researcher whose name became synonymous with educational psychology, Edward L. Thorndike.

E. L. Thorndike: Scientific Education

The person most responsible for channeling education toward an emphasis on measurement was **E. L. Thorndike** (1913, 1932), a famous professor at Teachers College of Columbia University. Thorndike sought to eliminate speculation, opinion, and naturalistic investigation. In fact, he considered visiting a classroom an extraordinary waste of time. It was much more "scientific" to understand the learning process by experimenting on cats in a laboratory than by observing children in a classroom. And experiment he did. Thorndike studied the behavior of his famous cats in specially designed puzzle boxes. He was interested in discovering how long it took the cats to solve the puzzles (which usually involved getting out of the box) and in learning what rewards were the most effective in achieving the objective. (Will a hungry cat learn faster than a "fat" cat—or, in more scientific language, "an organism deprived of nutrition for forty-eight hours"—if food is the reward?) This procedure led to an almost endless number of empirical studies documenting how many trial-and-error sequences took place before the cat finally "learned" to stick a paw through the grating, lift up the latch to open the cage, and then stroll triumphantly over to the food. As you can see, Thorndike was focusing on one aspect of learning—that which takes place by trial and error. By putting a cat through this sequence often enough, a bond would be formed, a stimulus-response connection in the nervous system, so that the cat would "remember" what to do.

It has been said that Thorndike was so influential that all subsequent research in education was merely a footnote to his work. His critics noted humorously of his influence that if one of Thorndike's cats behaved unpredictably, it would affect the curriculum for an entire nation.

On the positive side it should be stressed that Thorndike was an important influence because he exploded many of the educational myths of the day. The classical curriculum of the secondary school (four years of Greek, four years of Latin, and so on) had

been justified on the grounds that such exercise would "train" the mind: Spending time and effort on Latin, for example, would make it easier to learn French, while Greek would improve English usage. Using precise measurement procedures, Thorndike was able to show that little, if any, disciplining of the mind could be transferred from one subject to another. In an almost-singular way, he could proclaim, "If you want to improve your English, study English, not Latin or Greek." Thorndike believed that transfer occurred only when elements in one situation were identical or at least similar to elements in a second situation. Many a subsequent generation had Thorndike and his empirical research to thank for disposing of the mythical justification for the study of Latin and Greek. So Thorndike's contribution cannot be dismissed. However, his importance and influence were so great that educational psychology became almost preoccupied by trial-and-error learning and measurement techniques. All other ideas, perspectives, and theories were practically abandoned. The field grew more narrowly scientific, objective, and empirical. We began to be able to measure educational problems more effectively, but the problems we were measuring were increasingly less significant. In a word, we developed more precise ways of measuring increasingly insignificant educational problems. The range of what we could know was limited to what we could measure.

The single most significant effect of this emphasis on empirical measurement was that it was more suited to showing what was wrong than what was right. This is not to say that educational psychology does not need rigorous measurement procedures and evaluation systems, but it cannot progress as a field if that is its only focus. The movement was more and more to the laboratory, for more and more replications and refinements of essentially the same studies. When William James warned of grinding out peppercorns, he was predicting the direction the field actually took. Literally thousands of studies have been produced that have had little influence on learning and the practice of teaching. Instead of a narrow focus, educational psychology needed to broaden its view to include again studies in the natural environment.

John Dewey and Human Interaction

One of this country's most important theorists, **John Dewey,** always used the phrase "some organism in

EDWARD L. THORNDIKE

Born in 1874 as the son of a Protestant minister and brought up in the mill towns of Massachusetts, E. L. Thorndike completed his undergraduate studies in classics at Wesleyan University. A somewhat singular and solitary person, he demonstrated early in his life a capacity for hard work, long hours, and precision. Almost a personification of the Protestant work ethic, Thorndike simply abhorred making even the slightest error and consequently was always striving for perfection in his work. He had enormous amounts of mental energy and virtually threw himself into the task of defining a scientific base for psychology.

At Columbia University's Teachers College he completed his doctorate in the department of philosophy, psychology, anthropology, and education in the late 1890s. At that time departmental specialization was not yet established. The field of educational psychology was amorphous and resisted a generic definition. Academic psychology and the so-called brass-instrument laboratories and physical measurements represented one stance. At the other end, William James at Harvard was lecturing on the art of teaching, separate from the science of psychology. In between there was a range of philosophers, educators, and psychologists all attempting to give definition and coherence to the field. This was educational psychology's moment of a "cultural revolution." A hundred flowers were blooming when the youthful but dedicated E. L. Thorndike appeared on the scene. Apparently he was not at all intimidated by the first-generation psychologists and educators. As a brand-new assistant professor at Teachers College in 1898, he took pleasure in attacking his elders. He referred to this period as his early assertive years. "It is fun to write all the stuff up and smite all the hoary scientists hip and thigh. . . . My thesis is a beauty. . . . I've got some theories which knock the old authorities into a grease spot." For such a fledgling—he was still in his twenties—to have the inner strength to attack the heroes of the day both in print and in association meetings was most unusual. Possibly within himself Thorndike transformed the Protestant ethic into a messianic vision not of religion but of scientific logical positivism. In other words, the dedication that a person might feel toward a religious mission was apparently shifted so that science became his religion.

some environment" (1916). This was his way of emphasizing that you could not study learning in the abstract and ignore the broader context—the environment in which that learning took place. Here is one of his sardonic comments on traditional education:

> The entire range of the universe is first subdivided into sections called studies; then each one of these studies is broken up into bits, and some one bit assigned to a certain year of the course. No order of development is recognized—it is enough that the earlier parts were made easier than the later. To use the pertinent illustration of Mr. W. S. Jackman in stating the absurdity of this sort of curriculum: "It must seem to geography teachers that Heaven smiled on them when it ordained but four or five continents, because starting in far enough along the course it was so easy, that it really seemed natural, to give one continent to each grade and then come out right in the eight years" (Dewey, 1956, p. 103).

Unfortunately, Dewey's important ideas were misinterpreted. He was thought to be advocating the so-called child-centered curriculum rather than the significant ecological concept of person-in-environment. Cafeteria-style education—in which a child was free to choose anything, even to play all day if he or she wanted—was supposedly the result of Dewey's work. However, these "progressive" views on education clearly missed Dewey's point. What he advocated was careful, guided experience for children, arranged according to their interests and capacities. The importance of these concepts for educational psychology should not be missed.

The central idea of Dewey's work was that the

For the entire forty-one years of his professional life, Thorndike remained at Columbia Teachers College. He defined educational psychology as essentially the psychology of laboratory experimentation. His life work was to create a base of scientific knowledge through careful experiments, changing one variable at a time and using precise measures. He insisted that the operational definition was the only definition for science. If you couldn't see, measure, and directly record the phenomenon under investigation, then it was not scientific or even worthwhile. Look, see, and collect data were his words of advice for investigators. In fact, he really viewed himself more as an investigator than a scholar. He once noted that he had probably spent over 10,000 hours in reading and studying scientific books and journals, but he devoted even more time to his own experiments and writing. His bibliography runs to a prodigious 500 items. Science, he would say, was to be built by research, not proclamation.

When Thorndike finished his classic work on measurement for educational psychology, he sent a copy to William James. The amusing dialogue that resulted went as follows:

Thorndike to James, with academic modesty: "I am sending you a dreadful book which I have written which is in no end scientific but devoid of any spark of human interest."

James's reply: "I opened your new book with full feelings of awe and admiration for your unexampled energy. It was just the thing I had hoped for when I was teaching psychology. . . . I am glad I have graduated from the necessity of using that kind of thing any longer. I shall stick to 'qualitative' work as more congruous with old age!"[a]

His work, as we have noted in the text, became almost an endless series of studies on trial-and-error learning. His famous cats in the puzzle box represented his observable data. He persuaded his university to create a psychology laboratory for him; and there he remained, building the wall of scientific knowledge brick by brick. Thorndike reached the pinnacle of his career in 1934, when he was elected president of the American Association for the Advancement of Science. No psychologist had ever been so honored. In fact, only one social scientist had ever been elected to head the professional organization that represented the entire scientific community.

For Thorndike, then, this was truly the moment of glory. The years of hard work, the struggle to create a scientifically respectable basis for educational psychology, had at last achieved the ultimate recognition. His biographer, Geraldine Jonçich, has noted that an editorial in *The New York Times* in January 1934 pleased him above all else when it said of him, "But first and last, he is a scientist."

---

[a] Jonçich, G. (1968). E. L. Thorndike: The psychologist as a professional man of science. *American Psychologist, 23*(6), 444.

child was not an empty vessel waiting patiently and quietly to be filled up with knowledge. In fact, Dewey's best writing took these traditional assumptions of education to task. For example, he tells of visiting a manufacturer of school furniture one day and having a difficult time finding what he wanted for his school. One dealer, apparently more intelligent than the rest, commented. "I am afraid we have not what you want. You want something at which the children may work; these are all for listening" (Dewey, 1956, p. 31).

In addition to the concept of active learning, Dewey also stressed the idea of stages of growth and development. In this he foreshadowed the now-classic work of Jean Piaget. Dewey noted that the child was often assumed to be a small version of an adult. "The boy was a little man and his mind was a little mind—in everything but size the same as that of the adult. . . . Now we believe in the mind as a growing affair, and hence as essentially changing, presenting distinctive phases of capacity and interest at different periods." (Dewey, 1956, p. 102).

Finally, Dewey's most significant assertion was that teaching and learning interacted, that the pupil was as much a part of the learning environment as the teacher. He constantly battled against what he saw as the artificial separation between learning and the pupil.

Dewey's central view, then, was to promote a balance between experiential learning and careful, rational examination. He did not want pupils simply to experience in a vacuum. Supposedly, a teacher, in seeking employment at Dewey's laboratory school, said that he had ten years of teaching experience.

JOHN DEWEY

Without question one of this country's major educational theorists, John Dewey had a long and significant influence on the actual practice of both psychology and education. Born in 1859, his life spanned almost a century, from 1859, just before the Civil War, to

1952. During that time, the education of American pupils went through a transformation that paralleled the historical changes occurring in the United States, in large part because of John Dewey's ideas and his practice.

In some ways Dewey was a true product of nineteenth-century America. Naturally intelligent and serious about his educational mission, he wanted most of all to develop an educational philosophy that could be put into practice. The concepts had to be tested in the real world of schools and in the classrooms. Many psychologists were content to theorize about education and write learned essays, but for Dewey, this was not enough. If the ideas were not translated into action and tested, then the practice of education would forever remain overly theoretical. An American pragmatist, he had little patience with glossy educational rhetoric. He clearly was a doer.

Born in New England, his early years as a Vermont Yankee fostered in him a great respect for natural

growth as well as for the critical relationship between person and environment. These themes recur throughout his educational writings. After graduating from the University of Vermont, he completed his Ph.D. at Johns Hopkins (under the tutelage of G. Stanley Hall) at the tender age of only twenty-five.

His first professorship was at the University of Minnesota, followed quickly by moves to the University of Michigan and then on to the University of Chicago in 1894, where he served as chairman of the department of philosophy and pedagogy. It was at Chicago that he established the first major educational laboratory school in the country. Here at last he had the natural learning environment he needed to test and revise his unique educational ideas. At that time the country's educators were convinced that children ought to sit quietly in a classroom and learn by rote a classical curriculum, an approach that has been labeled the "formal discipline theory." Instead of strengthening the mind, however, such a learning environment too

---

Dewey quickly retorted, "Was it really ten years or was it one year ten times!" In other words, what had the person learned from the experience? How much reflection, examination, and analysis of the experience had occurred? Thus, learning through experience includes what is commonly called "intellectual analysis." Dewey viewed this process as a means of promoting cognitive thought structures. In this area he essentially anticipated a second Piagetian concept of cognitive structures, or schema, as the framework for understanding how children come to know and think. The classroom should be a natural environment in which living and learning occur together. In this way Dewey pioneered today's emphasis on education as an interactive process.

Maxine Greene: The Teacher as Stranger

Perhaps the best way to close such a far-ranging chapter is to focus on the individual teacher. **Maxine Greene,** one of this country's leading educational philosophers, conceptualizes the role of teacher with a strikingly vivid metaphor, "the teacher as stranger." That concept may be somewhat unsettling at first sight. Teaching is intensely personal. How is it possible to think of a teacher as separated from students, as an alien or foreigner in a land of pupils? Greene would be the first to agree that teaching is an interpersonal process. It must involve the heart and soul as well as the mind. Teaching is not divisible. Yet, the teacher cannot be one of the pupils. Instead, there is

often placed students in an exceptionally passive role. Anticipating the ideas of Piaget and the open classroom, Dewey developed learning environments which ensured that children would actively engage in learning. His dictum of learning through doing became famous. Experience should precede or at least be concurrent with educational concepts and ideas. This was a revolutionary stance to the educators of the day, because it turned the educational process inside out. His objective was to create an experience-based curriculum to promote both more effective learning and greater competence in living.

By this time in his career he was easily the most widely known educational psychologist of his day. In 1886 he wrote an important textbook, titled *Psychology*, and in 1896 he published his famous paper on the nature of the reflex arc (which, although a strong statement of the Functionalist position, also foreshadowed some of Wertheimer's later ideas as to the importance of the "Gestalt."). He constantly argued for a focus on the study of the "*whole* child and its *adaptation* to the environment." Clearly Dewey became a psychological functionalist in the tradition of William James. In 1904 he moved to the center of educational thought on this continent, the famous Teachers College at Columbia University. While at Columbia he became an ardent supporter of women's rights, and even marched in parades supporting a woman's right to vote. During one of these parades he is said to have quickly picked up a placard without reading it, and apparently amused and puzzled the onlookers by carrying a sign that read "Men can vote. Why can't I?"[a]

He remained at Columbia until his formal retirement, twenty-six years later. During that time, he not only taught, but also authored many books and lectured throughout the United States. An innovator, he was one of those very rare educators who lived to see his ideas put into practice and become important educational doctrine.

Unfortunately, however, his most significant idea was also the most easily misunderstood. His concept of child-centered, progressive education was distorted in many instances into a laissez-faire curriculum, and in the late 1940s and early 1950s it became quite fashionable to criticize Dewey as soft-headed and to blame him for problems of classroom discipline. Fortunately for the country's children, the misunderstanding has since been cleared up. Learning by doing finds expression in today's schools in a variety of ways. Learning laboratories and centers, workshops, lesson units, and school programs devoted to all aspects of human growth are reflections of his views in action. Perhaps Dewey's most important idea, or indeed vision, was the democratic ideal that always remained his goal. By developing significant education for all children, the American dream of free people in a free country might be realized. In his ninety-third year John Dewey died, the vision intact and, hopefully, the country closer to the goal.

[a] Hergenhahn, B. R. (1992). *An introduction to the history of psychology* (2d ed.). Englewood Cliffs, N.J.: Prentice-Hall.

always a gulf, a separation. As a teacher you are the leader, the responsible adult. Our society grants a teacher special status. In fact, the pupils are not given the freedom of choice to attend school. Thus, there is fundamental asymmetry. Your purpose is clear—namely, to promote their growth. Their role is not to promote yours, even though it not only may but does occur. That is not, however, the primary agenda.

For the teacher the agenda is the pupils. Your role with the students is more that of a mentor than a colleague. You are constantly alert to individual differences, to signs of growth, to indicators of student interest, curiosity, or their need to know. This means you are with them, but part of you is separate. You can step back and review the process, ask yourself new questions, such as What strategy should I try with Carolyn? What's the best way to reach Douglas? How can I help Jane gain confidence as a learner? Somewhat ironically, your increasing reflective ability is the key element in becoming Maxine Greene's "stranger."

By reflecting, you increase the depth of your understanding of teaching and children. Rather than simplify, you come to appreciate your deepening wisdom. In the broadest sense Greene's teacher becomes a philosopher, but in a special way. We usually think of a philosopher as someone almost hopelessly lost in abstractions. That's not Greene's definition. She sees the crux of teaching in the actual art of doing philosophy. The teacher is not a mechanic but a seeker

Dewey developed learning environments that ensured children would actively engage in learning. His famous dictum of "learning by doing" became a byword.

of truth. Learning philosophy by doing teaching is her way of connecting art and science. As you grow in effectiveness through such a process, you will then experience what she means by the word *stranger*, namely, a person who, by being somewhat removed from the others, has a clearer vision of the goals as well as the ability to stay on course.

In her most recent work, *The Dialectic of Freedom* (1988), she stresses the importance of a broad definition of freedom that includes learning how to learn as well as social responsibility. Freedom is not rampant individualism, but rather helping each person become a self-reflective individual in full recognition of our common democratic goals of equality, an equality that includes sharing of the benefits as well as the burdens. Thus, she picks up the theme from Dewey that education is not only for intellectual development but also for human development. Freedom be-

comes, somewhat ironically, the exercise of human equality in interdependence. Greene puts the case more elegantly through metaphorical language. Read the lines below and see what images you experience. First, think of the times when you as a student truly experienced deeper teaching with a particular adult. Second, imagine yourself in the role of teacher surrounded by pupils, your charges:

> If the teacher is able to think and do while being vitally present as a person, then others may be aroused to act on their own freedom. Learning to learn, some of those persons may move beyond the sheltered places until they stand by their own choice in the high wind of thought.

She concludes, employing the metaphor of children as growing trees:

MAXINE GREENE

After completing her undergraduate program at Barnard College, in 1938, with a liberal arts degree and a Phi Beta Kappa key, Maxine Greene began to follow what was then a traditional path: marriage, children, and a role as a suburban homemaker. However, in the late 1940s she made a mistake that changed the course of her life. She began graduate work at New York University in English, also a traditional area of study for females. The mistake was to take some work in philosophy with George E. Axtelle, whom she later described as a truly memorable teacher. It was the perfect match of person and ideas, and it provided a focus for the career she was to follow.

Combining philosophy with her intellectual interest in literary analysis, derived from her English studies, she soon saw philosophy as the master discipline. These two elements were the necessary foundations, but not the whole story. In addition, she had two other enduring interests, art and action. It was probably her interest in art as an aesthetic experience that provided the bridge between ideas and action. The result has been the careful development of a framework for educational philosophy that seeks to set forth a series of principles and actions, ideas and experiences, thoughts and feelings. In fact, the major goal of her publication record, which is quite vast, is to synthesize thought and action as a basis for a living philosophy.

Such was, of course, not the tradition of the so-called analytic school of philosophy. In that view, the goal of philosophy is analysis, in-depth and logical—the philosopher as critic. The difficulty with such a conception as a goal for philosophy is that it can too quickly lead to criticism for criticism's sake and, indeed, render the obvious obscure.

In breaking through the traditional career roles for women, Greene has also broken through the traditional framework for educational philosophy. She approaches philosophical goals quite differently and with a refreshing vigor. Rather than delve into levels of increasingly arcane meta-analyses, she always holds up ideas and goals to the real world of practice and action. There is a vivid existential quality to her work, and it is not the negative existentialism of the "life is absurd" school of thought. Instead, she produces a positive existentialism in her continued insistence on philosophy as thought in action.

Her work began to enter the educational paradigm slowly at first. Analytic philosophy was, after all, the main school of thought, and it was not about to disappear overnight. But Greene's voluminous writings, coupled with her frequent, powerful conference presentations and keynote addresses, gradually created a major place for her ideas as a philosophy for education and educational psychology. In 1975 she was appointed to the endowed William F. Russell Professorship at Teachers College of Columbia University. A long series of honors and elections soon followed: Educator of the Year by Phi Delta Kappa, Best Educational Book of the Year from Kappa Delta Gamma, president of the American Educational Research Association, chairperson of the John Dewey Society, president of the Philosophy of Education Society, and election to the National Academy of Education.

For education the Greene philosophy becomes a set of guides to living the "good life" as a manager of child growth and development. As noted in the text, her idea of the teacher as stranger sets the role tasks clearly in the growth context. To act and reflect in the real world according to democratic ethical guides represent to her the means of living philosophy, of teaching as "doing philosophy." She sees the educator's role as not simply to teach subject matter or skills or to maintain discipline. Those are only intermediate objectives. Instead, the framework suggests a far greater purpose, even though the purpose itself may be a paradox. As she says, "How can one act on one's commitment and at once set others free to be?" Her own career stands as the best answer.

SPOTLIGHT ON TEACHING

The View from the Pupil's Desk

Reflective teachers ask questions that require reflective answers of their students.

As you consider your own goals for teaching, it is well to remember the William James comment about the students. Their views are important too, particularly as a basis for understanding where they are coming from. A simple yet revealing exercise is to ask them three questions for written responses.

Some sample answers from a middle school were as follows:

Question 1: Why should children (or adolescents) attend school?

"To get involved in education and learn to get along with others."

"To learn and understand about different things and about life."

"To get a good education, get ready for high school and have fun doing it."

"To get a good job and get along with others."

Obviously the academic and the interpersonal were both important goals.

Question 2: How do children learn best?

"By observing and by learning from friends."

"By studying and paying attention."

"By watching, observing, and doing. We do it over and over 'til we get it just right."

"Through the teacher. They teach us, and we do a lot of activities."

"We learn by having fun while we work."

"Children learn from teachers explaining how things work and what makes it work."

There are a variety of views from teacher-directed learning to learning through observation and by doing.

Question 3: What is the teacher's job?

"To help children learn . . . not all the time but be there when help is needed."

"To teach us so we can become something good in life."

"To help us get a good education without boring us."

"To give us challenging assignments but explain it so we can do it."

"To make us feel special while we try to be good students, to believe we can do it, so we can believe it ourselves."

As you can see from the students' view, the teacher's job is just about as complex as our theorists from William James, John Dewey, and Maxine Greene have said. Perhaps the students say it more personally.

Note: We thank Stella Farrow from Lee County, North Carolina, for supplying us with these student comments.

The teacher, too, must raise shadowy trees and let them ripen. Stranger and homecomer, questioner and goad to others, the teacher can become visible to one's own self by doing philosophy. There are countless lives to be changed, worlds to be remade (1978, p. 298).

THE ART AND SCIENCE OF TEACHING

We have clearly pointed out the complexities of managing the four-way agenda of the teaching-learning process. We have also pointed out how, until recently, the science of educational psychology and the profession of education were more like ships passing in the night than interacting disciplines. We have shown how the scientific basis for psychology led to the laboratory and the professional basis for education to the classroom. The traditions of both promoted separation. Then we noted the reasons for optimism, primarily a growing cumulative basis for theory and practice that forms the content of this book. In the end, of course, whether any of this makes a difference will depend on you, the teacher. For teaching as practice is fundamentally an art as is any human services profession, such as law, medicine, or business management. In each case there are established scientific principles or, as one leading educational psychologist puts it, "the scientific basis for the art of teaching" (Gage, 1978). This means what it says. Art represents the skill, the art of putting it together in the real world of the classroom. Your own professional identity becomes the agenda for educational psychology.

By now you realize that our goal is to bridge the discipline of psychology and the practice of profes-sional education. The solution is almost paradoxical: a theoretical practitioner, a practical theorist. To be successful in teaching requires both. There is the need for you to interact in the moment with students. There is also the need to reflect, to inquire, and to critique your own efforts.

In fact, if there is one common thread in all contemporary literature on teaching, it is the concept of a reflective practitioner. Virginia Richardson (1990) has commented that experience in teaching is only educative with careful and systematic reflection. This only increases the importance of both. And certainly given the enormous changes in store for schooling, particularly the increase in cultural diversity, teachers in all phases of their career will require greater sophistication in both cognition and action. Echoing John Dewey, Lampert and Clark (1990) noted that experience is not necessarily expertise. Although it is an overused concept, empowerment of teachers can be attained only through a balance or praxis of action and reflection.

One of the unique characteristics of teaching as a career is that you rarely practice in the company of other adults. The isolation comes with the territory. Supervision, collegiality, and the analysis of teaching with other adults are highly unlikely. This only increases the need to develop a reflective and a doing capacity. You cannot afford either as an exclusive mode. Acting and reflecting represent the key processes for professional growth, indeed, they serve as a kind of Rosetta stone for teacher effectiveness. So the struggle you embark on is highly significant and difficult, filled with frustration, apparent contradictions, and at times overwhelming complexity. The two goals of becoming both artist and scientist can be achieved, however.

SUMMARY

In introducing you to the field of educational psychology, this chapter has presented a series of major issues with which the field has struggled. As Snow noted in the metaphor of two separate cultures, the scientific and professional traditions more often than not go their own ways. The field of educational psychology attempts to bridge those traditions.

Both theory and practice are needed. Without theory, practice is aimless; without practice, theory is abstract speculation. Theory is nothing more than successive approximations that gradually increase our understanding. In arriving at theory, we must steer clear of the twin fallacies of wooly-headed thinking and reductionism. William of Occam expressed the ideal as one of parsimony: A theory should be neither more elaborate nor more abstract than it needs to be to explain the facts.

The teaching-learning process is a four-way agenda. That is, its four main concerns are pupils, teachers, teaching strategies, and subject matter.

These elements must be considered together to account for the complexity of the enterprise.

Educational psychology did not gain a foothold in the classroom until relatively recently. In the early part of the century, William James and others noted the presence of trivia in the classroom. To a certain extent, this emphasis on learning facts continues today. But there is a growing consensus on the need for theory and practice for effective teaching and learning. Thanks to the pioneering efforts of James, Thorndike, and Dewey, teachers now have a firm theoretical foundation on which to base their practice. The essence of good teaching, though, seems to be captured in Maxine Greene's metaphor of the "teacher as stranger"—the one who by reflective distancing learns to see the true needs of each student. That metaphor requires the teacher to become both scientist and artist.

KEY TERMS AND NAMES

John Dewey
four-way agenda of teaching
Maxine Greene
William James
C. P. Snow

theory versus practice
E. L. Thorndike
trivia in the classroom
William of Occam

THEORY INTO PRACTICE: YOUR PHILOSOPHY AND ASSUMPTIONS ABOUT TEACHING AND LEARNING

Even though you have covered only one chapter, it can be helpful at that initial point to decide in your own mind where you stand on a philosophical orientation. Certainly, reading about the views of humanists, empiricists, pragmatists, and existentialists gives you a flavor of just how different those basic orientations are from one another. As a first step, then, in the process of becoming a self-reflective educator, you can start by rating some of the following statements about teaching and learning.

	VERY IMPORTANT	MODERATELY IMPORTANT	UNIMPORTANT
The role of the teacher is:			
1. To impart knowledge and skills, to transmit the culture.	_____	_____	_____
2. To employ a process approach, particularly learning how to learn.	_____	_____	_____
3. To provide an atmosphere that allows each student to develop at his or her individualized pace.	_____	_____	_____
4. To understand the developmental needs of students and use an appropriate form of differentiated teaching.	_____	_____	_____
5. To focus on basic education for achieving literacy in the three R's as the building blocks for future learning.	_____	_____	_____
6. To view teaching and learning as a discovery activity.	_____	_____	_____
7. To be a resource person on call to meet the psychological and intellectual needs of students.	_____	_____	_____
8. To discern the developmental status of the students and select from my repertoire those teaching methods that best fit the students' needs.	_____	_____	_____

(continued)

	VERY IMPORTANT	MODERATELY IMPORTANT	UNIMPORTANT
9. To make sure that the students master the facts prior to any individualizing of instruction.	———	———	———
10. To help students understand the structure of the academic discipline under investigation.	———	———	———
11. To help students experience close interpersonal relationships in the classroom.	———	———	———
12. To combine doing and reflecting at different levels depending on the students' ability to draw meaning from the experience.	———	———	———

This will give you a picture of where you are now. Then we'd suggest you put it away and reexamine it near the end of the semester. Look for the similarities in attitudes as well as the areas about which you find you've changed your views. Reflect on the reasons for the areas of stability (the ideas and values in which you still believe) and the reasons why you have changed in other areas. This will also help you become aware of your own learning process. How much new theoretical and practical evidence does it take to confirm your "old" beliefs and how much does it take to convince you to give up some of your old beliefs in order to accept some new concepts? Ratings of Very Important for items 1, 5, and 9 indicate that you have a strong preference for direct instruction as a method and a basic approach to subject matter as content; for items 2, 6, and 10, that you value an inquiry-discovery teaching method and process goals; for items 3, 7, 11, that you strongly value pupil-centered teaching as both method and content; for items 4, 8, 12, that you value developmentally based instruction as a method for promoting concept formation.

Naturally, your answers probably did not all fall exclusively either in or out of one of the four clusters. Most likely, your philosophy at this point is a blend of the four. Yet, it will be interesting to see how the emphases within this blend may change as you proceed to develop an understanding of how you learn and then how you may teach others.

If after you've completed the exercise, there are some additional ideas you want to express, write them down here to preserve them for future reference.

The ratings indicate that my major initial educational beliefs are as follows:

_____

_____

_____

_____

REFERENCES

Allen, J. S. (1992). Educating performers. *The Key Reporter, 57*(3), 5–9.

Bellack, A., Kliebard, H., Hyman, R., and Smith, F. (1966). *Language of the classroom*, New York: Teachers College Press.

Cahan, E., and White, S. (1992). Proposals for a second psychology. *American Psychologist, 47*(2), 224–235.

Cole, M. (1990). Cognitive development and schooling. In L. Moll (Ed.), *Vygotsky and education* (pp. 89–110). Cambridge: Cambridge University Press.

Dewey, J. (1916). *Democracy and education.* New York: Macmillan.

Dewey, J. (1956). *The child and the curriculum: The school and society.* Chicago: University of Chicago Press.

Gage, N. (1978). *The scientific basis for the art of teaching.* New York: Teachers College Press.

Goodlad, J. I., and Klein, M. F. (1974). *Looking behind the classroom door.* Worthington, Ohio: Press.

Goodlad, J. I. (1984). *A place called school.* New York: McGraw-Hill.

Goodlad, J. I. (1990). *Teachers for our nation's schools.* San Francisco: Jossey-Bass.

Greene, M. (1978). *The teacher as stranger.* Belmont, Calif.: Wadsworth.

Greene, M. (1988). *The dialect of freedom.* New York: Teachers College Press.

Heyns, B. (1988). Educational defectors. *Educational Researcher, 17*(3), 24–32.

Hyman R. T. (1971). *Contemporary thoughts on teaching.* Englewood Cliffs, N.J.: Prentice-Hall.

Jackson, P. (1990). The functions of educational research. *Educational Researcher, 19*(7), 3–9.

James, W. (1958) *Talks to teachers on psychology and to students on some of life's ideals.* New York: Norton.

James, W. (1968). *Psychology.* New York: Macmillan.

Jefferson, T. J. (1816). Letter to Colonel Charles Yancey.

Jeness, D. (1990). Making sense of the social studies. New York: Macmillan.

Kozol, J. (1992). *Savage inequalities.* New York: Harper-Collins.

Lampert, M. and Clark, C. (1990). Expert knowledge and expert thinking in teaching: A response to Floden and Flinzing. *Educational Researcher, 19*(5), 21–23.

Rice J. M. (1893). *The public school system of the United States.* New York: Century.

Richardson, V. (1990). Significant and worthwhile change in teaching practice. *Educational Researcher, 19*(7), 10–18.

Sabine, G. (1937). *A history of political theory.* New York: Holt.

Shulman, L. (1978). *Review of research in teacher education,* Vol. 5. Itasca, Ill.: Peacock.

Snow, C. P. (1963). *The two cultures: And a second look.* New York: Mentor.

Stevens, R. (1912). *The question as a measure of efficiency in instruction.* Contributions to Education No. 48. New York: Columbia University.

Thorndike, E. L. (1913). *Educational psychology,* Vol. 2, New York: Teachers College Press.

Thorndike, E. L. (1932), *The fundamentals of learning.* New York: Teachers College Press.

CHILD AND ADOLESCENT GROWTH

2

FUNDAMENTALS OF GROWTH AND DEVELOPMENT

Of all the species that inhabit the earth, the one whose growth and development is the slowest is *Homo sapiens*. The human being spends many long years in a state of physical immaturity, depending on the care and protection of others in order to survive. During the months that are required for the child to learn to walk and run with consistent steadiness, to communicate fears, joys, and needs, other species grow to full maturity. A two-year-old rhesus monkey has already attained sexual maturity, and a two-year-old rat may already be senile. In muscular development and the ability to achieve any degree of mobility, the two-year-old child is about at the same level as a chimpanzee of two months, a rabbit of two weeks, a colt of two hours, or a bird of a few minutes.

Some years ago a study dramatically illustrated the difference in growth rates between species: A husband-and-wife psychology team raised their infant son, Donald, along with a baby chimpanzee named Gua. Donald and Gua were treated as much alike as possible. They wore the same clothes, were fed the same food in the same way, and in general were given the same tender, loving care. They were also taught in the same way and given the same amount of practice in such things as standing, walking, eating with a spoon, and even toilet training (Kellogg and Kellogg, 1963).

The whole situation must have been a competitive nightmare for poor little Donald, because Gua outstripped him at everything. When Donald was barely able to pull himself into an erect position, Gua was walking, running, and pirouetting with the grace of a ballet dancer. When Donald still had difficulty even picking up a spoon, Gua was using the spoon to feed herself easily and with little spilling. When Donald was propped up and strapped to the seat of a swing, where he hung limply and loosely, Gua was performing like a trapeze artist on another swing.

The enormous difference in heredity and rate of maturation obviously allowed Gua to reach her genetic potential far sooner than Donald. Eventually, when Donald was nine months old (and the study was ended), he was beginning to catch up to Gua in certain areas, such as following verbal instructions,

27

Although the human infant in this picture may be the same chronological age as the cat, the cat is already capable of independent living while the infant will be dependent on adult assistance for many years to come.

and to surpass Gua in others, such as speech development. But as for achieving physical mobility, Donald was still far behind.

In another attempt to find out whether environmental stimulation can compensate for heredity, another husband-and-wife team, with no children of their own, took a chimpanzee, Vicki, into their home and raised her as they would have raised a baby (Hayes and Hayes, 1951). Above all else they wanted to see whether they could teach Vicki to talk. Despite their efforts, and despite the fact that Vicki did learn to respond to verbal commands, the attempt to teach her to speak ultimately proved to be futile. After three years Vicki could occasionally utter words such as *cup, mama,* and *papa* in an appropriate context, but that was as far as her language skills ever developed. In contrast, by three years of age the typical human infant has a vocabulary of almost 900 words.

In the early 1970s, an attempt was made to train a chimpanzee named Sarah in the use of symbolic communication (Premack, 1971). Sarah attained a vocabulary of about 120 symbols, the symbols being plastic shapes of various colors used to represent words. Although by chimpanzee standards Sarah's ablity to communicate was fairly sophisticated, it was still a far cry from the language abilities demonstrated by even a two- to three-year-old human child. We have been warned to be extremely conservative in

estimating Sarah's "human language ability" (Limber, 1977). And even the linguistically sophisticated Nim Chimpsky, the seemingly brilliant chimp named after the linguist Noam Chomsky, didn't do much better than either Vicki or Sarah. Said Nim, "give orange me give orange me eat orange give me eat orange give me you"—hardly a mind-bending oration (Bickerton, 1990).

You may be wondering at this point why studies such as these were ever performed—they may seem as absurd as raising a human baby and an eagle together in a nest to see which one would be the first to fly. It may be obvious to you that different species mature at different rates and that chimpanzees achieve physical maturity more rapidly than humans. You may even wonder why anyone would bother trying to train chimps to talk, for if it were possible, it seems likely that someone, somewhere, would have observed chimps talking to one another (Gardner and Gardner, 1970).

The best way to appreciate why these studies were conducted is to know something about psychology's brief but often stormy history. Our purpose is not to take you on a guided tour of dusty museum oddities but to give you a general historical background against which the present state of our knowledge will be more meaningful and, we hope, better appreciated.

THE NATURE-NURTURE CONTROVERSY

Of all the great debates in the history of psychology—and there have been many—the one that has generated the most heat and caused the greatest division in the field is the controversy over nature and nurture. More words have been written and more voices have been raised in anger over this issue than over any other.

The warring camps made their positions clear. The hereditarians, who favored nature, stridently claimed that all psychological traits were transmitted directly through the genes from generation to generation. Environment was of little consequence. If your father was a horse thief, you would be a horse thief, and if your mother's IQ was only 90, then you shouldn't make plans to go to medical school.

On the other side, the environmentalists as rigidly and shrilly claimed that a person's whole being was shaped by how and in what circumstances one was raised or "nurtured." Genetic endowment was a romantic myth, used to keep kings on their thrones, but of no use to science. The environmentalists held that all people were born genetically equal and that later differences among them were only a result of different environmental opportunities. Any baby could be molded into any kind of adult, provided the appropriate stimulus conditions were present.

Goddard's 1912 study of the two branches of the Kallikak family—the "good strain, resulting from Martin Kallikak's marriage to a worthy Quakeress," and the "bad" strain, resulting from an amorous adventure with a feeble-minded tavern girl—served to support the hereditarians' position.

The Hereditarians Speak: Henry E. Goddard and the "Bad Seed"

In 1912, **Henry Goddard** published an account of the extremely damaging effects of an inferior genetic endowment, a "bad seed," on generation after generation of a family named **Kallikak** (Goddard, 1912). According to Goddard, who gleaned this material from books, newspapers, personal interviews, and other records, Martin Kallikak (a pseudonym chosen by Goddard to protect the family) was an American Revolutionary War soldier who was responsible for developing two completely different family strains. The "good" Kallikaks (and Goddard traced his strain through 496 descendants) resulted from Kallikak's marriage to a "worthy Quakeress." She bore him "seven upright, worthy children," and from these seven children came "hundreds of the highest types of human beings"—doctors, lawyers, business leaders, and even college presidents. Only two of the

nearly 500 "good" Kallikaks were of below average intelligence.

Goddard also traced the descendants of an amorous adventure that Martin Kallikak had with a feeble-minded tavern girl. The result of this affair was an illegitimate son, later known to his friends and neighbors as "Old Horror." Fortunately for Goddard's story, even Old Horror apparently wasn't considered horrible by everyone, for he went on to father ten children of his own. Goddard identified 480 of these descendants, the "bad" Kallikaks, and found nothing but the lowest forms of humanity—horse thieves, prostitutes, alcoholics, and so on. Also, of the bad Kallikaks, he found only forty-six who were of normal or near-normal intelligence. The rest, of course, were well below average.

Goddard wasted no time worrying about details, such as the dramatic environmental differences that existed between Kallikak's legitimate children and

JOHN BROADUS WATSON

One of American psychology's most vocal and most influential environmentalists, John B. Watson, was born near Greenville, South Carolina, in 1878. As a student in public school, the young John Watson's performance was something less than spectacular. He later attributed his lack of early school success to his own "laziness," a rather subjective explanation from the man who would later demand so much objectivity from others. He attended Furman University, where he studied such topics as mathematics, Greek, Latin, philosophy, and chemistry. In 1900 he went to the University of Chicago to study under the philosopher-psychologist John Dewey. He soon found that Dewey was "incomprehensible" to him, and so he changed majors and began studying with James R. Angell, a psychologist, and H. H. Donaldson, a biologist and neurologist. During his studies, he said his thinking was shaped by reading the works of the great British empiricists, David Hume and John Locke. Said Watson, "I got nothing out of Kant and least of all out of John Dewey."

In 1903 Watson received the first Ph.D. degree in psychology ever conferred at the University of Chicago. For the next five years he taught psychology at the University of Chicago and then in 1908 he left Chicago and went to Johns Hopkins University in Baltimore as a full professor. He immediately set up an animal laboratory, and in 1913 he shook the world of psychology with the publication of a paper entitled "Psychology as the Behaviorist Views It." In this paper Watson attacked virtually all forms of psychology up to that time, and he announced a new school of psychological thought—behaviorism. He said that the only valid data in psychology was the behavior of the organism. He saw no room in psychology for mentalistic concepts like "mind" or "consciousness," and said that psychology needed introspection about as much as did chemistry or physics—that is, not at all. The data of psychology should be the observable response, and the best approach, in order to rule out any mentalistic overtones, was to study only the responses of organisms. He later said, "Belief in the existence of consciousness goes back to the ancient days of superstition and magic."[a] To be scientifically respectable, psychology must be behavioristic, objective, deterministic, mechanistic, and materialistic.

Watson then acquired a powerful ally. He had read about I. P. Pavlov and the conditioned reflex, and Watson pounced on this concept and made it a central theme of his own behaviorism. Like Pavlov, he became more interested in the search for specific stimuli that would control particular responses than he was in studying the response itself.[b] In 1919, in collaboration with one of his students, Rosalie Rayner, Watson began his now-famous study on the conditioning of baby Albert B. To-

Old Horror. The explanation was simple: The difference was hereditary.

Goddard's evidence, which was seriously cited in many psychology texts as late as the 1960s, is considered truly fantastic by modern geneticists. Even if intelligence were as directly and simply related to genotype as eye color is (which it isn't), there would still have to be far greater numbers of intelligent members of the "bad" Kallikaks, and vice versa. After all, Martin Kallikak was himself half responsible for Old Horror. But Goddard was out to "prove" his point of view, and a cherished belief clouded any scientific vision. Charles Davenport, one of America's leading geneticists at the time (1911), even went so far as to argue that human behavioral characteristics had straight Mendelian explanations—laziness being inherited through dominant genes and ambition through recessive genes, for example. Thus, according to Davenport, the genes we inherit from our parents account not only for how intelligent we are but also for how motivated we are.

The Environmentalists Speak:
John B. Watson and "Give Me the Baby"

The strict environmentalists argued against the position of Goddard and the hereditarians. This group

gether they showed how an apparently normal, healthy baby could be conditioned to fear virtually anything in his or her observable environment.

In 1920 Watson's career at Johns Hopkins came to an abrupt halt. Amid great notoriety Watson was divorced by his wife and then asked by Johns Hopkins to resign his professorship. Later that year Watson married his research collaborator, Rosalie Rayner, and in 1921 he went to New York's Madison Avenue and spent the rest of his working life in the world of advertising. He soon became not only famous, but also rich and famous.

Despite leaving the academic world in 1920, Watson continued to write books and articles that advanced his views on child rearing and teaching. It was not until 1927 that Watson thundered forth his famous words, "Give me the baby." In 1928, he wrote his enormously popular book, *The Psychological Care of the Infant and Child,* a book that became an overnight best-seller (over 100,000 copies in just the first two months). He rather cynically dedicated the book to "the first mother who brings up a happy child." This was the book in which

he instructed the mothers of America to never hug or kiss their children, and never let them sit on their laps. "If you must, kiss them once on the forehead when they say good night. Shake hands with them in the morning." He also decried a mother's coddling remarks: "When I hear a mother say 'Bless its little heart' when it falls down, or stubs its toe, or suffers some other ill, I usually have to walk a block or two to let off steam," and he uttered dire warnings about maternal affection: "Remember when you are tempted to pet your child that mother love is a dangerous instrument, an instrument which may inflict a never healing wound which makes infancy unhappy, and adolescence a nightmare."[c]

Watson retired from the business world in 1946 and died in 1958, having exerted great influence on the fields of psychology and education. He made educational psychology more behavioristic, and he emphasized the importance of conditioning in the classroom and in child-rearing practices. It was Watson who set the stage for the work of B. F. Skinner and the proponents of behavior modification in the classroom.

His granddaughter, the actress

Mariette Hartley, said that the lack of physical closeness her mother had with Watson as a child filled her mother with a fear of getting too close to people. This fear was then passed on to Mariette. She feels that she has since worked out those repressed feelings (by turning to Freudian analysis for help) and now feels more comfortable with other people and even with the memory of her late grandfather, who within the family was known as "Big John" (Hartley, 1990). After recovering from her own father's suicide, Mariette took a sentimental journey back to her grandfather's exquisite stone house where she "could still smell the whiskey in the carpets, . . . and when I walked out back and remembered the picnics we had there I thought about [my grandfather] and of how much he had influenced my life."[d]

[a] Watson, J. B. (1925). *Behaviorism.* New York: Norton.

[b] McPherson, M. W. (1992). Is psychology the science of behavior? *American Psychologist, 47,* 329–335.

[c] Watson, J. B., and Watson, R. R. (1928). *The psychological care of the infant and child.* New York: Norton, pp. 81–87.

[d] Hartley, M. (1990). *Breaking the silence.* New York: G. P. Putnam's Sons

allied itself with philosopher John Locke (1691), who said that the mind was a blank slate upon which experience writes. As far as the environmentalist is concerned, the baby is nothing more than a lump of clay that can be molded and fashioned into any shape by the hands of that master artisan, the environment.

Perhaps the most eloquent advocate for the environmental position was the early behaviorist **John B. Watson.** It was Watson's belief that people are made, not born; that a baby can be shaped into any adult form—trapeze artist, musician, master criminal—through the judicious use of conditioning techniques. Watson began writing about the time (1913) that Pavlov's work in Russia on the conditioning of dogs was

beginning to be recognized in the United States. Watson reasoned that if a dog could be conditioned, so too could a baby. In a now classic study, Watson and his colleague, Rosalie Rayner, tested this theory by conditioning a nine-month-old baby named Albert to fear a whole variety of objects (stimuli). This was done by presenting Albert with a certain conditioned stimulus (CS), a white rat, and then banging loudly with a hammer on a steel bar a few inches behind Albert's head. Watson assumed that the conditioned stimulus, the white rat, was originally neutral in its fear-inducing properties. Watson knew, however, that the unconditioned stimulus (UCS), the loud sound, would automatically produce

© 1955 United Feature Syndicate, Inc.

a fear response in the baby. Because the CS was paired with the UCS, Albert formed an association between the two stimuli and reacted to the rat as he originally had responded to the loud sound. Albert had *learned* to associate the rat with the terrific din and, according to Watson, had thus learned to fear the rat. Later, Albert became afraid, through a process called stimulus generalization, of any stimulus that reminded him of the rat. By the time the study was completed, two months later, poor little Albert was intensely afraid of white rats, rabbits, dogs, fur coats, Santa Claus masks, cotton, wool, and anything else that remotely resembled animal fur. Watson also checked babies for other fear responses and found, for example, that if they were dropped they exhibited a fear response.

How much can children's cognitive development be shaped by the environmental stimuli presented them? Could Watson have made this child into an engineer by manipulating the toys available to him?

In order to "cure" Albert of these conditioned fears, Watson proposed, though never actually tried, presenting him with the fear-provoking object again, while "stimulating the erogenous zones (actual). . . . We should try first the lips, then the nipples and as a final resort the sex organs" (Watson and Rayner, 1920).

Not everyone has found Watson's evidence for emotional conditioning thoroughly convincing.

> It may be useful for modern learning theorists to see how the Albert study prompted subsequent research, but it seems time, finally, to place the Watson and Rayner data in the category of interesting but uninterpretable results (Harris, 1979).

Recent evidence is also beginning to cast some doubt on Watson's assumption that Albert's conditioning had taken place in a mechanical fashion, or that any stimulus Albert was able to detect could be linked to any response Albert could make. As we shall see later, it may be that Albert was more biologically prepared, or genetically sensitized, to learn to fear a live rat rather than, say, a picture of a rat (Bolles, 1980). The behaviorists have come under increasing attack because of their failure to incorporate those important variables that critics say didn't happen to fit their original hypotheses (Ahsen, 1990).

At the time, however, Watson believed that he had come upon ultimate truth in psychology—that, no matter what the genetic background, environmental stimulation in the form of conditioning could produce any behavior. Watson later said wryly:

> The Freudians twenty years from now, unless their hypotheses change, when they come to analyze Albert's fear of a seal skin coat . . . will probably tease from him the recital of a dream which upon their analysis will show that Albert at three years of age attempted to play with the pubic hair of the mother and was scolded violently for it (Watson and Rayner, p. 14).

A few years later, Watson thundered his now famous words, "Give me the baby," and this became the battle cry of environmentalists everywhere.

> Give me the baby and I'll make it climb and use its hands in construction of buildings of stone or wood. . . . I'll make it a thief, a gunman or a dope fiend. The possibilities of shaping it in any direction are almost endless. Even gross anatomical differences limit us far less than you may think. . . . Make him a deaf mute, and I will build you a Helen Keller. Men are built, not born (Watson, 1927 p. 233).

After reading about how Albert had been scared half to death by the sound of a steel bar being pounded behind his head and by being dropped, and how it was proposed to "cure" him by manipulating his genitals, the mothers of America did not line up to give Watson their babies.

Watson was striving to provide psychology with hard, scientific facts. His behaviorism was definitely not based on any humanistic view of human behavior or of society in general. Rather, he saw his mission as that of fact finder and cared little if his audience like or disliked the facts. His approach was clinically aseptic and coldly detached. Even Watson's prescription for raising children was laced with the objectivity and detachment of cool science. Watson told America's mothers to treat their toddler as though the children were young adults: "Let your behavior always

be objective and kindly but firm. Never hug and kiss them; never let them sit on your lap. If you must, kiss them once on the forehead when they say goodnight. Shake hands with them in the morning" (Watson and Watson, 1928).

Even today, behaviorists exhibit a similar disinterest. They often see their ultimate goal as far too cosmic to be constrained by any feelings of sympathy for a particular child. B. F. Skinner, today's leading exponent of behaviorism, was once criticized for having allegedly said that if given a choice he would rather burn his children than his books. Skinner's self-righteous answer was that he had not used the word *burn*.

> The word was *bury*. . . . Much as I admire my children and grandchildren and as dearly as I love them, I still believe that my contribution through my books will prove to be greater than that through my genes. How could a thorough-going environmentalist say otherwise? (Skinner, 1975, p. 2.)

EDUCATIONAL PSYCHOLOGY: THE BATTLEGROUND

Nowhere were the lines between hereditarians and environmentalists more sharply drawn than in the field of educational psychology. The reason for this was that the major influences on education from the field of psychology were the measurement practitioners (those in the testing tradition) and the learning theorists. The measurement practitioners (the IQ and achievement testers) were, by and large, hereditarians. The learning theorists, with very few exceptions, were behaviorists, and behaviorists were environmentalists. Thus it was inevitable that these two groups, both solidly entrenched in the field of educational psychology, and with diametrically opposed views in the nature-nurture debate, would be in constant conflict.

The IQ Testers

The testers had traditionally emphasized heredity, at least on the subject of intelligence. The history of the testing movement goes back to England and **Sir Francis Galton,** Darwin's cousin. During the later part of the nineteenth century, Galton created the first tests designed to measure intellectual potential. Galton believed that intellectual potential was a function of one's sensory equipment, one's power to discriminate among stimuli. He believed that sensory equipment was inherited. Parents who could detect slight differences among stimuli (could discriminate among subtle differences in tonal pitch, for example) were apt to have children with similarly keen powers. Furthermore, Galton believed, these sensory powers had survival value for the species. Cave dwellers who could detect the slight hiss of a rattlesnake were more likely to stay alive. **James McKeen Cattell,** who spent some time in Europe studying with Galton, brought this point of view back to the United States and, as Galton had done earlier, devised a series of sensorimotor tests (auditory range, visual range, reaction time, etc.) designed to measure a human's intellectual potential. Cattell was so enamored of this new area of study that he named his daughter, "Psyche." It was Cattell, in 1890, who first used the phrase *mental test.* Cattell was also the key figure in early studies of reading, despite the fact that his major interest was in testing and individual differences. "His work on letter and word recognition, legibility of letters and print types, and stimulus intensity formed the groundwork for most basic reading research of the next 30 years" (Venezby, 1977).

G. Stanley Hall, a distinguished psychologist and the first president of Clark University, had also studied in Europe, under Wundt, and had also concluded that intelligence was primarily inherited. Hall became enormously influential among psychologists in this country for a variety of reasons. His doctoral stu-

G. Stanley Hall was the foremost American advocate of intelligence as an inherited trait.

dents, such as Goddard, Terman, and Gessell, became indoctrinated with Hall's theoretical position and when they received their degrees they went out to spread the gospel. Also, as the *first president* of the American Psychological Association, as well as being the editor of the *American Journal of Psychology,* Hall had the power to influence psychology's agenda in very direct ways, for example, in deciding which articles would be published (Sokal, 1992).

The Stanford-Binet IQ test, which the testers used to obtain much of their data, was introduced into the United States by one of Hall's students, Lewis M. Terman. Starting with the original 1905 Binet scale, Terman created new norms based on U.S. standardizing groups and revised so many of the original items as to practically create a new test (1916). The data collected in his later studies of gifted children seemed to support a genetic explanation of intelligence.

The First World War gave tremendous impetus to the testing movement. Suddenly, millions of men were not only available to the psychologists, but the U.S. government was insisting that all these new recruits be given intelligence tests. For the testers, this became an unimagined opportunity, both to demonstrate their testing skills and also to gain public visibility. In the eyes of the testers, this opportunity was translated into an overwhelming triumph. James McKenn Cattell toasted the occasion when he chortled that the war had put psychology not only on the

Lewis Terman, Hall's student, revised Binet's original scale and introduced the Stanford-Binet tests in 1916.

map but also on the "front page." Thus, the testers, whose influence on psychology became increasingly powerful, used their front-page status to spread the genetic gospel they had originally "inherited" from Europe.

The Learning Theorists

The learning theorists, mostly Americans, were bound to be a strong influence on educational psychology. After all, what better contribution could psychology make to education than a more thorough understanding of the principles of learning? However, the major force among American learning theorists was behaviorism, and behaviorism was definitely an environmentalist position. Watson, the father of American behaviorism, sounded the clarion call when he wrote, "The data of psychology is behavior" (Watson, 1913, p. 160). And we have already seen ("Give me the baby") Watson's extreme environmental stance. The behaviorists—Watson, Thorndike, Guthrie, Hull, and Skinner—spread a kind of mechanical-person gospel. They spent little time studying the organism's growth and development. The emphasis was on how the organism learns, regardless of its inherited potential, regardless of its stage of physical or psychological development, and often re-

gardless of its species. In brief, they saw learning as a result of associations formed between stimuli and actions or impulses to act. These simple associations would accumulate and form larger groups of learned associations. Learning was seen largely as a result of conditioning, similar to Pavlov's dogs' learning to salivate at the sound of a certain tone. From his command post at Columbia Teachers College, E. L. Thorndike issued basic laws of learning that dominated the field of educational psychology, not to mention classroom practices, for over fifty years.

And this was true despite the efforts of those early psychologists to separate themselves as much as possible from the "lowly army of frontline teachers" (Powell, 1971). Many of these psychologists had an image of themselves as superscientists, their white lab coats symbolizing the purity of their endeavors. In fact, the goal of many of these early psychologists was to provide research that would substantiate their own previously authored educational systems.

Few American learning theorists ever studied children in the classroom or, in fact, ever studied any children at all. Thorndike and Guthrie worked primarily with cats, Hull with rats, and Skinner with rats and pigeons, but the principles of learning derived from these studies were generalized to human beings. Not that these generalizations were always invalid. They weren't! A child in a classroom can be conditioned to remain in his or her seat, just as a rat can be conditioned to press a lever. But it is the solid contention of this book that there is much more to human learning than mere conditioning.

The learning theorists certainly had their day, and from 1920 to well past the Second World War the learning theorists with their environmental bias were calling many of the shots in educational psychology in this country.

Why Was an Environmental Position So Attractive in the United States?

There are at least six ways to answer the question of why the environmental position appealed to U.S. educators:

1. American psychology was dominated by liberals and, almost without exception, they lined up on the side of environmentalism. To their way of thinking, heredity doomed humans to a tooth-and-claw world, a racist society in which social change was impossible. The nature-nurture ar-

gument was rephrased in more "democratic" language as "**instinct** versus learning," or even "beast versus man." An ideology, a cherished tradition, was getting between the psychologists and their data.

2. Even among some of those psychologists who recognized the importance of genetic influences, the feeling was that heredity was fixed at conception and that there was no point in studying something that couldn't be changed. Environmental influences, however, could be manipulated, and heredity became unimportant simply because of its inaccessibility.

3. Genetics as a discipline is a relatively new field, and some of the major breakthroughs have occurred only fairly recently. For example, it was only in 1962 that Watson and Crick won the Nobel prize for their pioneering work on genetic composition.

4. Very few psychologists were familiar with the information that was accumulating about genetics. Psychologists were more familiar with the related fields of sociology and cultural anthropology than they were with genetics. For example, Margaret Mead and Ruth Benedict were better known to students majoring in psychology than were Thomas Hunt Morgan or even Charles Davenport.

5. The special field of behavioral genetics is of very recent origin. Although foreshadowed by a study published in 1924 (Tolman, 1924), it was only in 1940 that Robert Choate Tryon of the University of California at Berkeley published a classic study that set the stage for the current work in this area (Tryon, 1940). Tryon had a large group of rats learn a maze, and then removed those animals that learned the maze quickly from those which learned slowly. By breeding the fast learners only with other fast learners, and the slow learners only with other slow learners, Tryon demonstrated that after seven generations he had created two significantly different groups of rats: maze-bright animals and maze-dull animals. Breeding experiments like this came *after* many of the behaviorists had already made their strong environmental statements.

6. The final reason for neglecting heredity was the long-term damage done by the instinct theorists at the turn of the century. Now thoroughly discredited, instinct theory attempted to explain behavior by describing it in other terms. Why do people fight? Obviously they have an aggressive instinct. Why do people get together in groups?

They have a gregarious instinct. And, of course, the reason people twiddle their thumbs is because they have a thumb-twiddling instinct. This kind of reasoning commits what is called the **nominal fallacy;** it confuses description with explanation. As B. F. Skinner has pointed out, this tactic is extremely dangerous: If we assume that a redescription is an explanation, we may feel we have answers when in fact we don't; and we may give up the search (Skinner, 1953).

Today, this insistence on the importance of environmental factors to the exclusion of genetic inputs (that for so long dominated American psychology) is giving way to a far more balanced view. The danger now might even be that the current swing away from environmentalism could go too far and set the stage for bringing back the tyranny of biological determinism (Plomin, 1989).

ETHOLOGY

Although it was easy for American psychologists to dismiss the naive views of instinct theorists as unworthy of serious consideration, they could not ignore the carefully detailed work of the European ethologists. **Ethology** is the study of behavior, especially animal behavior, in the natural setting (as opposed to a laboratory setting). Ethologists are primarily interested in discovering innate behavior patterns, or, as they are called in ethology, **innate releasing mechanisms** (IRMs)—patterns many American psychologists overlooked, partly because they insisted on studying animals in aseptic, artificial laboratory situations. Even worse, the psychologists insisted on using specially bred rats for most of their research studies, rats that had been bred for many generations to be exceptionally timid and nonaggressive (for the protection of the researchers).

The following story, possibly apocryphal, nevertheless makes the point. It seems that a graduate student in experimental psychology, unable to obtain a group of specially bred, gentle white Sprague-Dawley rats, undauntedly captured some wild rats from the local dump. To the dismay of the student, these rats, rather than learning the route through the complicated maze, simply ate their way through the wooden sides of the maze and quickly devoured the entire sack of food pellets. By the same token, it is highly unlikely that a Sprague-Dawley rat, its IRM reactions bred out of it hundreds of generations ago,

Do people have an inborn aggressiveness tendency that makes them fight? Yes claimed the instinct theorists, who confused description for explanation, a nominal fallacy.

could stay alive for five minutes at the city dump. One can only imagine a scene with this forlorn rat sitting passively, waiting to be presented with a lever to push.

During the early 1900s, a study was actually conducted that bears directly on this issue. One of J. B. Watson's professors, Henry Donaldson, wanted to find out whether a group of well-bred lab rats might learn to survive in a natural environment, in this case a small island in Long Island Sound. In order to give the lab rats a fighting chance, Donaldson exterminated the island's native rat population. Upon returning a year later, Donaldson could not find a single lab rat still alive. He did, however, find the chewed-up remains of some of them. They had been bitten to death by the few native rats that had somehow survived the attempted extermination (Carnegie Institute, 1911).

So, in effect, not only were the research situations artificial, but so too were the animals being studied. Ethologists, in contrast, were interested in nature's animals: in how they survived in nature's own settings and how they were affected by natural *releasers*,

the stimuli in an organism's environment that trigger unlearned behavior patterns. For example, if the male stickleback fish sees the color red, a rather violent attack response is released. During the breeding season all stickleback males develop bright red bellies, and if one red-bellied fish happens on another's nesting site, the intruder is roundly attacked and driven out of the nesting area.

CHERISHED BELIEFS AND SCIENTIFIC FACTS

As we have now seen, psychologists in general and educational psychologists in particular have battled for years over the question of the relative contribution of heredity and environment to behavior. Each side felt that it had the answer. As often happens when narrow or even single causes are sought to explain anything, the search for this single cause results more in the creation of controversy than in the accumulation of knowledge. Each side becomes rigid and dogmatic, and cherished beliefs begin to cloud scientific

SPOTLIGHT ON IMPRINTING

A Special Kind of Learning

Perhaps the ethologists' most important finding—important from the point of view of forcing American psychologists to reevaluate their position on instincts and the role of heredity in determining behavior—came as a result of the work of the great German ethologist, **Konrad Lorenz.** Although it was noted as far back as 1873 that newly hatched chicks seem to follow the first moving stimulus they see, it was not until 1935 that Lorenz revived the term **imprinting** to describe this special form of learning. He also discovered that this phenomenon could occur only during one critical time period in the chick's life. Lorenz noted that goslings would follow not only their mother but any other moving stimulus that presented itself within the first few hours of their lives. If Lorenz presented himself during this critical period, he found that the goslings would parade after him with a devotion usually reserved for their mother, and that this habit would continue throughout the bird's lifetime.[a]

Although imprinting was first noted in the organism's natural environment, it has also been demonstrated in the artificial world of the

Konrad Lorenz, the imprinted "mother" to these goslings, leads his charges on a morning stroll. Imprinted behavior depends on both inheritance and an environmental event in the life of the organism that has lasting effects.

laboratory, proving that psychology and ethology are not necessarily at cross-purposes.[b] In fact, under laboratory conditions it was possible to show the exact points in time when imprinting had the most impact. Imprinting in ducks, for example, can occur up to thirty-two hours after hatching, although the optimal time is between thirteen and sixteen hours of age.

Imprinting provided the perfect example of the careful blending of heredity, environment, and time in producing behavioral changes, and showed in dramatic form the interactive importance of these three variables.

---

[a] Lorenz, K. (1937). The companion in the bird's world. *Auk, 54,* 245–273.
[b] Hess, E. H. (1959). Imprinting. *Science, 130,* 133–141.

---

vision. If Watson had been less zealous in the cause of environmentalism, he could not possibly have overlooked the importance of heredity. Nor could Goddard have overlooked the obvious environmental difference between the "good" and "bad" Kallikaks had not his cherished opinion, his "pride of authorship," clouded his vision.

Nor was his clouded vision totally innocent. Stephen Jay Gould has recently discovered that in the original volume of Goddard's Kallikaks, three of the photographs allegedly depicting "bad" Kallikaks had been obviously retouched. The pictures "were phonied by inserting heavy dark lines to give eyes and mouths their diabolical appearance" (Gould, 1981). If the bad Kallikaks hadn't really looked stupid and depraved enough, it now appears that Goddard saw to it that they would.

This problem is not confined to psychology or to

KONRAD LORENZ

Konrad Lorenz was born in Vienna, Austria, in 1903. His father, Adolph, was a world-famous orthopedic surgeon and a professor at the University of Vienna. Even as a child, Lorenz had been observing, studying, and learning to understand the ways of wildlife. During these early years Lorenz learned to understand the signal code, or language, of various animal species and even learned to imitate this code in order to establish two-way communication. During Konrad's childhood, the family spent the summer months at a country home in Altenberg. It was there that Lorenz became fascinated by the natural wildlife of his native country. He explored the woods and ponds, and by age nine had set up his own microscope for studying the wonder world of the freshwater pond. He also raised a multitude of dogs, geese, and monkeys, as well as the fish, crustaceans, and insects that he brought home from his favorite pond. Said Lorenz, "For he who has once seen the intimate beauty of nature cannot tear himself away from

it again. He must become either a poet or a naturalist. . . . He may well become both," and Lorenz certainly did become both. His books and articles show his prose to have an almost-lyric quality. In 1928 he received his M.D. degree from the University of Vienna, but his love of animals continued and so did his studies. In 1933 he earned a Ph.D. degree in zoology, and for the next four years he continued his research on the behavior of animals in their natural habitats. In 1937 he began his teaching career as an instructor of comparative anatomy and animal psychology at his beloved University of Vienna. That same year he also published his now-famous article "The Companion in the Bird's World." In this article Lorenz described the intricate biological mechanism of imprinting. During their first few hours of life, certain organisms will become imprinted on the first moving stimulus object in their visual field and then follow this object—usually, of course, the mother—with slavish devotion and marching-band precision. This is how young organisms, especially birds, know which species they belong to, and it also accounts for their gregarious flocking behavior. Lorenz had revived the long-discredited instinct theory and made it scientifically respectable.

In 1940 he became a professor of psychology at the University of Königsberg in Germany. By this time World War II was raging through Europe, and Lorenz was called into the German army, eventually fighting against the Red Army on the eastern front. In 1944 he was cap-

tured by the Russians, and after a long and arduous ordeal was released, three years after the war had ended. He immediately went back to his beloved Austria and the University of Vienna, but in 1950 he went to Germany again, this time as the assistant director of the Max Planck Institute for Behavioral Physiology. Later he became director of the Institute for Behavioral Physiology, also in Germany. In October 1973 Lorenz won the Nobel Prize in medicine for his investigations of animal behavior in the wild. At the time of his death in 1989 he was survived by his wife, Margarethe, two daughters, Agnes and Dagmar, and a son, Thomas.

Among his numerous publications are *King Solomon's Ring* (1952), *Man Meets Dog* (1954), *Evolution and Modification of Behavior* (1965), *On Aggression* (1966), and *Studies in Animal and Human Behavior* (1970).

Lorenz has established ethology, the study of animal behavior in the natural setting, as a serious and respectable discipline. In large measure because of his careful work, ethology no longer suffers from the early damage done by the naive instinct theorists. The message from Lorenz is: If you want to understand animal behavior, study the animal in its own environment, not in the artificial confines of the laboratory. And perhaps in educational psychology this message translates to the following: If you want to understand schoolchildren, study them in the classroom, not just in the principal's or guidance counselor's office or in a college laboratory.

These two photos of Kallikak family members are doctored. Note what seems to be the obvious alteration in the mouths and eyes in order to dramatize an illusion of feeble-mindedness.

education. In our long quest to gain knowledge about our environment and ourselves, we have often been blinded by cherished beliefs. Advances in astronomy were thwarted for centuries by our egocentric view that the earth, our habitat, must be at the center of the universe. Only slowly and grudgingly did we give up this notion and then only on the understanding that if the earth is not at the center, surely the sun, at the center of our solar system, is at the core of a revolving universe. Ptolemy's heliocentric view of the universe went virtually unchallenged for over a thousand years. Even today it is still for some a sore point to realize that the earth is only a dust spot in this vast and expanding universe. And if we struggled to preserve our special place in the cosmos, it was only a dress rehearsal for the real drama of preserving our glorified role on earth.

Despite our reluctance, we finally accepted our place in the universe—in the sixteenth century. Ptolemy gave way to Copernicus, the earth was put in its proper place, and the ground was prepared for the later theories of Newton and Einstein.

In other areas, however, we were even more backward: Physiology as a discipline did not really come into its own until the nineteenth century (it seemed even more threatening to our ego to learn that our bodies were open to the objective scrutiny of science). But the "most unkindest cut of all" was the thrust of the newest scientific discipline, psychology; it insisted on probing our very inner being.

It is thus no accident that our search to understand ourselves has only recently come under scientific observation. In the evolution of scientific disciplines there has been a fairly orderly sequence based on the degree to which each science has threatened our self-esteem. As we have seen, and will continue to see, cherished beliefs are hard to give up; this is certainly true of educational psychology in the twentieth century.

NATURE-NURTURE: A MODERN SOLUTION TO AN OLD PROBLEM

It is now clear, in the last two decades of the twentieth century, that the old question of heredity versus environment is unanswerable because it is meaningless. Behavior is not the result of a single cause, but of multiple causes. It is the result of heredity interacting with environment interacting with time (see Figure

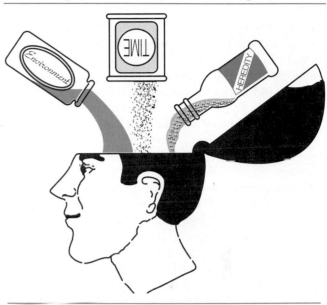

FIGURE 2.1 Behavior is the result of heredity interacting with environment interacting with time.

2.1). Our hereditary potential can be nourished or stifled depending on the type, amount, and quality of our environmental encounters and depending on when these encounters occur. (They can occur too early or too late to be of optimum benefit.)

Chapter 3 provides a cursory look at the biological basis of behavior. In the chapters that follow we outline some of the major considerations that have moved educational psychology beyond the nature-nurture controversy. Since human behavior is determined by the interaction of both (recall Dewey's phrase, "an organism in some environment"), we need to look at nature and nurture simultaneously. We can then begin to consider, not in a single- or narrow-minded way but within a broad context, how to educate children and adolescents. We need to know both how to strike and when the iron is hot. In Chapter 4 we present some of the central ideas about the significance and lasting effects of initial experience. In Chapters 5–7 we present the stages of cognitive and personal development to show, in our metaphor, just when the iron is hot. We can then shift our attention to arranging the environment for learning and teaching, which we discuss in later chapters.

SUMMARY

The causes of behavior are multiple and complex, and it is dangerous to build a psychology of human behavior on the basis of animal studies alone. Growth rates differ markedly among species, and the rate of growth and development among humans is comparatively slow. Those studies that compared the rates of maturation between humans and lower species found humans to lag behind. The nature-nurture controversy created a great division within the field of psychology. Henry Goddard's study of the Kallikak family attempted to "prove" that heredity was the most important factor in determining a person's psychological makeup. John B. Watson argued that environmental influences, through the process of conditioning, were paramount in determining psychological traits. In the field of educational psychology, the measurement practitioners (IQ testers) were typically strong believers in heredity, whereas the learning theorists were environmentalists. Also among the hereditarians were the instinct theorists—psychologists, especialy during the 1920s, who tried to explain all behavior on the basis of inherited instincts. By so doing, these psychologists made the fundamental error of confusing description for explanation (the nominal fallacy). By the 1930s, however, American psychologists as a group tended to believe that environmental influences were the most important.

Ethology, which is the study of animal behavior in the natural setting (as opposed to the laboratory), made the study of certain types of instinctive behavior more respectable. The ethologists concentrated on studying responses that were attached to innate releasing mechanisms (IRMs). The ethologists also demonstrated a special form of learning called imprinting, which occurs only during a short and critical time period in an organism's life.

Scientific objectivity has historically suffered as a result of the cherished beliefs and strong attitudes held by both the scientists themselves and by society in general. Psychology has perhaps been the most affected by this, for it is the discipline concerned with probing our inner beings and motivations. It is also the discipline for which many laypersons feel a certain familiarity and degree of expertise, even without professional training.

The modern solution to the age-old nature-nurture controversy is that neither heredity nor environment should be seen as the sole cause of behavior. Instead, behavior should be viewed as the result of heredity interacting with environment interacting with time. This final point is critical to an understanding of the rest of this text, and is considered today by most theorists to be one of psychology's most important principles.

KEY TERMS AND NAMES

James McKeen Cattell
ethology
Sir Francis Galton
Henry H. Goddard
imprinting
innate releasing mechanism (IRM)

instinct theory
Kallikak family
Konrad Lorenz
nature-nurture controversy
nominal fallacy
John B. Watson

THEORY INTO PRACTICE: ARE YOU A HEREDITARIAN OR AN ENVIRONMENTALIST AT HEART?

Although we pointed out quite clearly at the conclusion of the chapter that the issue of nature versus nurture cannot really be considered an either/or question, many human beings actually have a fundamental belief system that leans very heavily on one or the other side of the question. One way to find out how strongly these beliefs or attitudes are embedded in oneself is to answer the questions that are posed on the next page then figure out the score and interpret its meaning.

	STRONGLY AGREE	AGREE	DISAGREE	STRONGLY DISAGREE
1. At a family reunion it is most important to look for personality traits handed down from grandparents to parents to children.	___	___	___	___
2. In deciding upon a choice of major in college, a most important factor would be how the parents and/or relatives achieved in different areas.	___	___	___	___
3. In choosing between going to an opera or a football game, it would be wise to find out how earlier generations felt about opera versus football.	___	___	___	___
4. If a person is having a very difficult time learning mathematics, the first place to look for an explanation would be family history. Is there an uncle or aunt, father or mother who always had trouble with math?	___	___	___	___
5. To be really successful in life, the best path to follow would be in the family's footsteps. You can't make a silk purse out of a sow's ear.	___	___	___	___
6. The success or failure a person experiences is really "in the cards." After all, don't most juvenile delinquents come from delinquency-prone parents?	___	___	___	___
7. Anyone can succeed in any field with the right teaching and lots of motivation.	___	___	___	___
8. Show me a successful musician and I'll show you someone who's been positively reinforced every step of the way.	___	___	___	___
9. If you examine the background of any famous person, you will find somewhere a parent mentor or teacher who cultivated the achievement.	___	___	___	___
10. When a person fails, you can't really say he or she is to blame. Most likely you'll see a history of inadequate teaching or inadequate parenting. Don't blame the victim.	___	___	___	___
11. The problem with special education is not with the children at all. It is really the labels that are at fault. Since everyone believes that such a child is a slow learner, the child will act like one. It's a self-fulfilling prophecy.	___	___	___	___
12. Motivation and drive determine who excels. Aptitude makes very little contribution. After all, Thomas Edison said genius was 1 percent inspiration and 99 percent perspiration.	___	___	___	___
13. I find that it is important each day to check my horoscope, especially if I'm facing very important decisions.	___	___	___	___
14. Character traits such as introversion and extroversion are transmitted through a long evolutionary chain that is clearly fixed by the time of birth.	___	___	___	___
15. If you want to succeed, follow Horace Greeley's advice to go west; the climate is more conducive to achievement there.	___	___	___	___
16. People who spend all their time delving into the past, tracing family genealogy, looking for the Rosetta stone of their personalities are just wasting their time.	___	___	___	___

To figure out the score, code the responses on a scale of 4 to 1 points, beginning with 4 points for Strongly Agree. A hereditarian will strongly agree with items 1–6, 13, and 14; and an environmentalist will strongly agree with items 7–12, 15, and 16. The maximum score on each set of eight items is 32 points.

The problem, or difficulty, with either extreme position is simply that it leads to attributions or interpretations of behavior that can be quite misleading. Thus, the belief of hereditarians that a person's potential is fixed at birth might lead them to be against programs for young children, such as Head Start. In contrast, an environmentalist might favor a policy of educating a severe and profoundly retarded child in classes intended for the gifted and talented. To make a final check on these assumptions, go back and answer the questions in two modes. First answer the items as if you were J. B. Watson, then as if you were Henry Goddard.

REFERENCES

Ahsen, A. (1990). *Behaviorists' misconduct in science.* New York: Brandon House.

Bickerton, D. (1990). *Language and species.* Chicago: University of Chicago Press.

Bolles, R. C. (1980). Ethological learning theory. In R. A. Hinde and J. Stevenson-Hinde (Eds.), *Theories of learning.* Itasca, Ill.: Peacock.

Carnegie Institute of Washington (1911). *Yearbook, No. 10,* 83.

Gardner, B. T. and Gardner, R. A. (1970). Two-way communication with an infant chimpanzee. In A. Schrier and F. Stollnitz (Eds.), *Behavior of nonhuman primates.* New York: Academic Press. The authors believe that chimps do communicate with each other, not verbally, but through a kind of sign language. Some years ago, a chimpanzee was trained in the use of the American Sign Language of the deaf, and the chimp's performance compared favorably with that of a three-year-old child who was deaf from birth.

Goddard, H. (1912). *The Kallikak family.* New York: Macmillan.

Gould, S. J. (1981). *The mismeasure of man.* New York: Norton.

Harris, B. (1979). Whatever happened to Little Albert? *American Psychologist, 34*(2), 158.

Hartley, M. (1990). *Breaking the silence.* New York: G. P. Putnam's Sons.

Hayes, K. G., and Hayes, C. (1951). The intellectual development of a home-raised chimpanzee. *Proceedings: American Philosophical Society, 95,* 105–109.

Hess, E. H. (1959). Imprinting. *Science, 130,* 133–141.

Kellogg, W. N., and Kellogg, L. A. (1963). *The ape and the child.* New York: McGraw-Hill.

Limber, J. (1977). Language in child and chimp? *American Psychologist, 32*(6), 285.

Lorenz, K. (1937). The companion in the bird's world. *Auk, 54,* 245–273.

McPherson, M. W. (1992). Is psychology the science of behavior? *American Psychologist, 47,* 329–335.

Plomin, R. (1989). Environment and genes: Determinants of behavior. *American Psychologist, 44,* 105–111.

Powell, A. G. (1971). Speculation on the early impact of schools of education on educational psychology. *History of Education Quarterly, 11,* 406–412.

Premack, D. (1971). Language in chimpanzees? *Science, 172,* 808–872.

Skinner, B. F. (1953). *Science and human behavior.* New York: Macmillan.

Skinner, B. F. (1975). Bury not burn. *A.P.A. Monitor, 6* (November), 2.

Sokal, M. M. (1992). Origins and early years of the American Psychological Association. *American Psychologist, 47,* 111–122.

Tolman, E. C. (1924). The inheritance of maze learning ability in rats. *Journal of Comparative Psychology, 4,* 1–18.

Tyron, R. C. (1940). Genetic differences in maze-learning ability in rats. *Yearbook of the National Society for Studies in Education, 39,* 111–119.

Venezby, R. (1977). Research on reading processes. *American Psychologist, 32*(5), 339.

Watson, J. B. (1913). Psychology as the behaviorist views it. *Psychological Review, 20,* 158–177.

Watson, J. B. (1925). *Behaviorism.* New York: Norton.

Watson, J. B. (1927). The behaviorist looks at instincts. *Harper's Magazine* (July), 233.

Watson, J. B., and Rayner, R. (1920). Conditioned emotional reactions. *Journal of Experimental Psychology, 3,* 8.

Watson, J. B., and Watson, R. R. (1928). *The psychological care of the infant and child* (pp. 81–82). New York: Norton.

Weller, S. (1988) Mariette Hartley is clicking on her own. *McCall's* (November), 56–66.

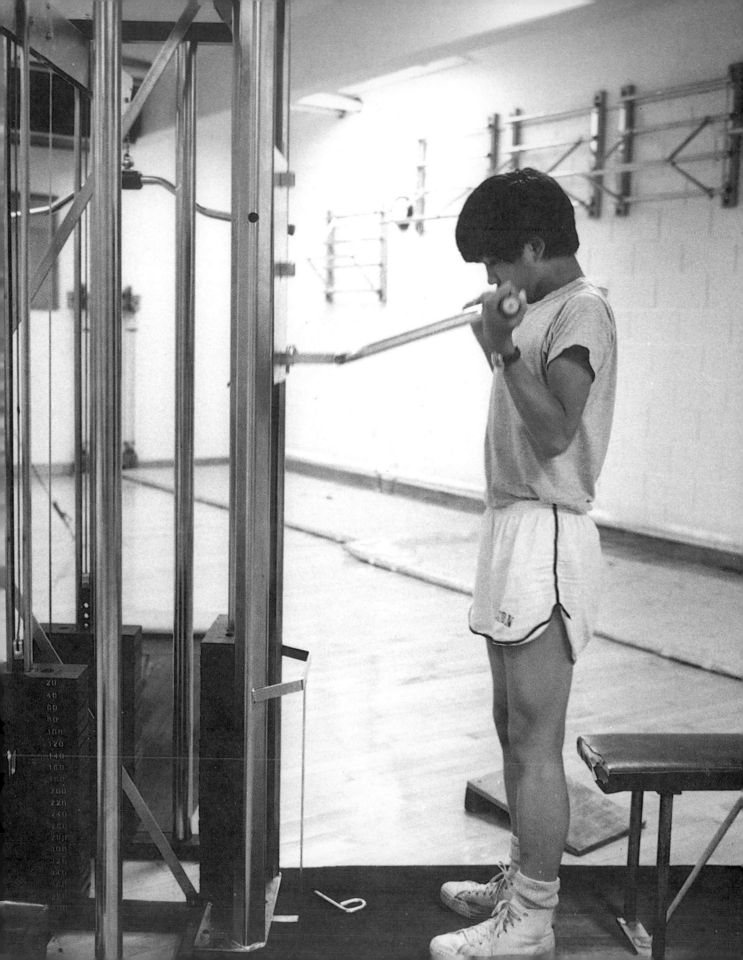

3

PHYSICAL GROWTH AND DEVELOPMENT

Each of us begins life as a tiny, watery speck smaller than the period at the end of this sentence. This speck, technically a **zygote**, contains the genetic background that will shape and direct our development for the rest of our lives. The zygote is formed at the moment of conception, when the sperm cell of the male fertilizes the egg cell of the female. Half of the genetic background contained in the zygote comes from the father, half from the mother, so that the baby will be like both parents, but not exactly like either one. Thus the zygote contains the hereditary component that will be constantly molded and modified through environmental interactions. And these interactions begin immediately. If the zygote were to be surgically removed from the uterus and placed in a foreign environment, like a glass of water, it would soon perish. If the zygote remains in the uterus and the uterine environment remains healthy, then growth and development continue, and some nine months later the baby is born.

It is important to recognize that all during the nine months environmental encounters are occurring. To be sure, the uterine environment is relatively constant, but not totally so. Toxic agents in the mother's uterus can modify, damage, or even halt the development of the zygote. Studies have shown, for example, that expectant mothers who have two or three drinks of alcohol a day may produce neonates who have lowered arousal levels and who in later childhood may even show higher-than-average incidences of learning disabilities. Also, women who smoke during pregnancy tend to place the fetus at risk. By age four, the children of mothers who smoked during pregnancy showed lower attention spans than did children who had not been so exposed (Streisguth et al., 1984). Another study even suggests that learning can occur in the uterus (Spelt, 1948). It has also been found that strong emotional arousal on the part of the expectant mother can be transmitted to the developing fetus (Lubchenco, 1976). Although there are no direct neural connections between mother and fetus, a mother's emotionality in the form of specifically released hormones can pass through the placenta and change the physiology of the yet-unborn child. In short, our basic axiom that behavior is a result of the interaction of heredity, environment, and time covers one's entire life from the moment of conception.

THE ABCs OF GENETICS

Our knowledge of genetics is of very recent origin. The science of **genetics** is based on the study of heredity, the biological transmittal of characteristics from parent to offspring. The nature-nurture argument was based in large part on the fact that not enough was known about nature, and what was known about heredity wasn't fully understood by many psychologists, especially in the United States.

The fundamental unit of analysis in genetics is the **gene.** Genes are tiny particles that carry the hereditary characteristics. (For a more complete coverage of the composition and function of the gene, see Nora

FIGURE 3.1   DNA and RNA.

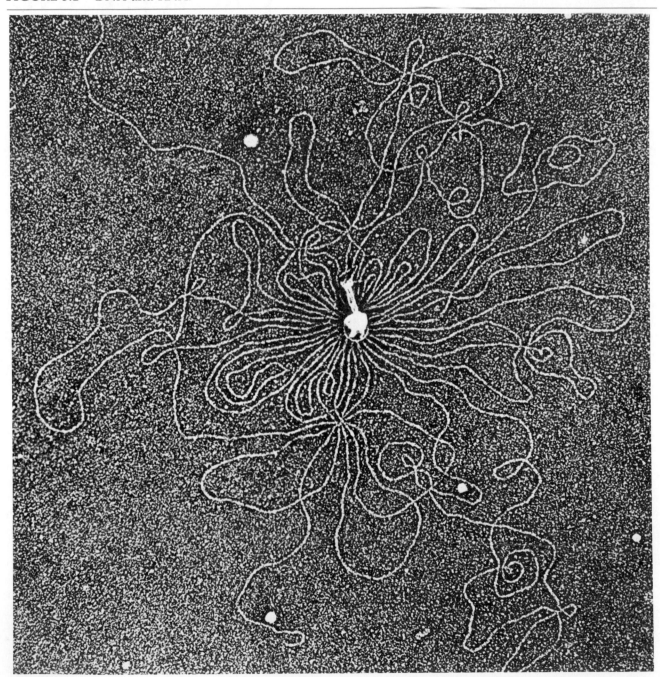

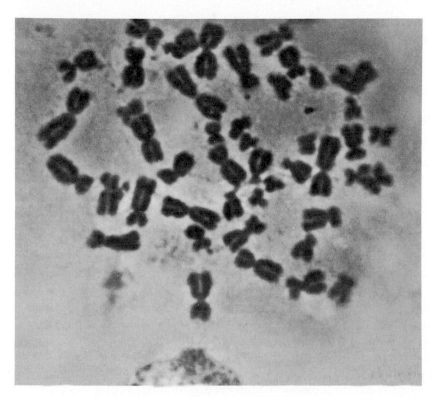

FIGURE 3.2 Human chromosomes.

and Fraser, 1989.) The genes are located in the nucleus of each of the body's cells, where they occur in pairs, one gene from each parent. Estimates of the total number of genes in any single human (the human genome) run anywhere from 5 million to 10 million. Since at conception each parent contributes to this vast number of genes, there is obviously room for great genetic variation in the resulting offspring. Except for identical twins, every individual is genetically unique. Because of this, scientists are now able to identify suspects in criminal investigations by the use of DNA "fingerprinting." The procedure involves the extraction of DNA from small bits of blood, hair, tissue, or semen found at the scene of a crime and then matching it to the DNA taken from the cells of a suspect.

Genes are composed of the rather large organic molecule: **DNA (deoxyribonucleic acid)** and **RNA (ribonucleic acid)** (see Figure 3.1). These nucleic acids (DNA and RNA) are located in the **chromosomes,** which lie in the nucleus of every cell in the body. A single strand of human DNA if stretched to its full length would measure more than three feet in length, the height of the average preschool child. But when it is crammed into its proper slot in the heart of the cell, it measures only about a millionth of an inch

across. The job of packing DNA into its tiny compartment is accomplished by the special proteins called *histones* that squeeze the DNA down to size. These histones also have the job of switching genes on and off along the DNA molecule in order to control its various functions.

Chromosomes are fairly long, threadlike bits of protein, and each of the cells in the human body contains twenty-three *pairs* of these chromosomes (see Figure 3.2). However, the germ cells (sperm cells in the male and egg cells in the female) carry only twenty-three individual chromosomes, or half the number (forty-six) that exist in the body cells. At conception, then, the zygote receives half of its chromosomes from each parent, twenty-three from each, and thus achieves its full complement of twenty-three pairs.

The chromosomes direct the development of all structures in the body, including the gender of the new person. One pair of chromosomes, the twenty-third pair, is responsible for this. If this pair is identical (both X chromosomes), the person will be female, and if the pair is different (one X and one Y chromosome), the result is a male. Since the female carries only X chromosomes, the sex of the offspring is determined by the father; that is, it depends on whether the fertilizing sperm happens to carry the X or Y chromosome. In the average ejaculation there are more sperm carrying the X chromosome than there are carrying the male-spawning Y. Yet every year, ironically, more boys than girls are born, about 110 male births for every 100 female births. This is because even though there are fewer Y chromosomes to begin with, they end up penetrating more than half of all the eggs (Bean, 1990). The Y chromosome, even though smaller than the X, seems to have more genetic muscle and is more able to barge in ahead of the X. Dr. Barry Bean sees this as indicating that there is a biological discrimination against women even before they are born. However, despite this initial male advantage, the difference is dramatically reversed as life progresses, to the point where there are far more older women alive than older men.

The DNA and RNA molecules are located within the nucleus of each cell, where the chromosomes are arranged. The DNA molecule contains chains of atoms and simpler molecules that code and store information about growth and development. Their arrangement allows the DNA molecule to reproduce itself exactly—that is, to achieve precise self-duplication. For this to occur, the chemical environment must be appropriate. DNA acts as a blueprint or, as it is called by the geneticists, a template, for the formation of certain enzymes that help guide the development of the organism. The coded information contained in the DNA molecule is transmitted to other parts of the cell by the RNA molecules. DNA may be thought of as the architect's blueprint, while the RNA would be the builder translating this blueprint into a finished home. It must be remembered, however, that these reactions do not occur in a vacuum. The chemical environment must be appropriate for the DNA "architect" and the RNA "builder" to work effectively. Thus, the developing organism is both biological and psychological, and its biological nature should be constantly viewed as it relates to the whole organism in all its splendid complexity (Dewsbury, 1991).

DOMINANTS AND RECESSIVES

One of the first discoveries in the field of genetics occurred over a hundred years ago when the Austrian monk **Gregor Mendel** (1822–1884) learned an important fact about inheritance. In his study of the flower color of garden peas, Mendel discovered that organisms contain both **dominant genes** and **reces-sive genes.** Mendel found that if he crossed a red-flowered pea with another red-flowered pea, the resulting plant would have red flowers. Similarly, if he crossed a white-flowered pea with another white-flowered pea, the resulting plant would have white flowers. But if he crossed a red-flowered pea with a white-flowered pea, the resulting plant would have red flowers. Thus, the genes that determine flower color can be dominant or recessive, and in this case, red is dominant over white—that is, the trait carried by the dominant gene shows up in the flower. Crossing a red with a red, or a white with a white, produces a pure offspring, whereas crossing a red with a white produces a hybrid. When a dominant gene is paired with a recessive gene, the resulting hybrid always exhibits the dominant trait.

Among the human traits that follow this rule, perhaps the best example is eye color. Brown eyes are dominant over blue eyes. Thus, if both parents have blue eyes, their children must have blue eyes. This is because, for individuals to have blue eyes, they must be carrying only the recessive genes for eye color. If they were to have a dominant brown-eyed gene and a recessive blue-eyed gene, their eyes would have to be brown. If, however, both parents are brown-eyed but both are carrying a recessive gene for blue eyes, their children still might have blue eyes. Chances are greater, however, that they will have brown eyes.

Two hybrid parents, each with brown eyes, have only a one-in-four chance of producing a blue-eyed child. The trait that shows up is the **phenotype,** whereas the one that remains hidden is the **genotype.** A person with a phenotype of brown eyes may have a genotype of two brown-eyed genes or a genotype of one brown-eyed and one blue-eyed gene.

A trait like eye color, in which a single pair of genes determines the phenotype, is a fairly rare case in genetics. Most behavioral traits, such as measured intelligence, result from the combination of large numbers of genes. This is called **polygenic inheritance** and again dramatizes the enormous potential for genetic differences among individuals.

We can see from even this simplified excursion into genetics that heredity has lawful relationships, and it is certain that future discoveries in this field will uncover many more definite patterns and laws that influence physical traits and behavior. Studies have already shown that, in addition to motor skills and intelligence, schizophrenia and manic depression have rather strong hereditary components. This is not to deny that environmental influences are important;

they are! But the genes do carry constitutional predispositions toward various behaviors that the environment may stifle or nourish.

DOWN SYNDROME

As stated, normally each human carries 46 chromosomes in 23 pairs. Scientists have numbered each of the 23 pairs, and if anomalies in this arrangement occur, severe problems may follow. For example, an extra chromosome at the point of chromosome pair 21 results in a form of mental retardation called Down syndrome, which occurs in 1 out of every 600 live births and is said to be the most common chromosome anomaly (Widerstrom et al., 1991). In over 95 percent of all cases of Down syndrome, the extra chromosome is contributed by the mother. Interestingly, chromosome 21 is also a strong suspect in Alzheimer disease, and it is known that people with Down syndrome who live until their forties have an above-chance likelihood of contracting Alzheimer disease (Cummings, 1985).

BEHAVIOR GENETICS

Psychologists are able to examine the possible effects of genetic endowment through both animal and human research. Though the results of animal studies cannot be directly generalized to humans, the animal data may be at least suggestive of hypotheses that might later be pursued when researchers attempt to understand the results of human studies. The studies in **behavior genetics,** both animal and human, have as their goal the discovery of lawful relationships between genetic endowment and observed behavior.

Animal Studies

The genetic studies of animals are typically of two types: inbreeding and selective breeding. Inbreeding studies usually involve the mating of brothers and sisters in order to obtain as much homozygosity in the population as possible. **Homozygosity** means that the gene pairs are identical. When animals are inbred, the like-sexed members come to have the same, or almost the same, genotype. Inbreeding experiments are commonly carried out on such organisms as mice and fruit flies (*Drosophila*).

In selective-breeding studies, animals of a given strain are tested for some behavioral criterion, such as ability to run a maze. Then the animals demonstrating extremes of this behavior are selectively mated for generation after generation—the animals with the best performance on the maze, for example, are mated with one another, as are the animals with the poorest

Many birth defects, such as the mental retardation indicated here, are the result of hereditary chromosome anomalies.

maze performance. In Chapter 2 it was pointed out that one study of this type, carried out by R. C. Tryon, established that after seven generations two significantly different groups of rats had been created: maze-bright animals and maze-dull animals (Tryon, 1940).

In another study white mice were separated according to the amount of aggressiveness they exhibited. The most and least aggressive mice were identified and then selectively bred. Again, after seven generations, dramatic differences in the aggressiveness displayed by the offspring became apparent (Lagerspetz, 1964).

Human Studies

Since social taboos would argue against breeding experiments at the human level (not that there would be a shortage of student volunteers), psychologists must rely on after-the-fact, or post hoc, data in studying human genetic endowment. In some studies lineage records are traced backward in an attempt to establish the possiblity of direct ancestry, a method used by Henry Goddard (Chapter 2) in his study of the Kallikaks. The problem with this kind of research is that genetic background and environmental influences are easily confounded: Martin Kallikak's "good seed" descendants were subjected to different environmental conditions than were the descendants of "Old Horror." Sir Francis Galton, the father of intelligence testing, was the first to use this lineage technique when he compared the achievements of successive generations of his own brilliant family with those of a less fortunate family.

In another type of human research in genetics, adopted or foster children are compared with both their biological and foster parents. If the children are behaviorally more similar to their biological parents (whose influence on the child's environment is presumed to be zero) than to their foster parents, the similarity is attributed to heredity.

Perhaps the most popular technique at the human level is to examine for behavioral similarities identical twins who have been reared apart. Since identical, or **monozygotic (MZ), twins** reared separately still have precisely the same genetic endowment, any remaining behavioral similarities are presumed to result from genetic causes. In one study, an attempt was made to discover whether or not there is a genetic component in schizophrenia (Gottesman and Shields,

1972). In this study, MZ-twin members (called the *probands*) who had been diagnosed as schizophrenic were located and their cotwins then searched out. The percentage of cotwins of probands who are also schizophrenic is called the **concordance rate.** When this concordance rate was compared with the concordance rate among fraternal, or **dizygotic (DZ) twins,** researchers found the MZ concordance rate to be substantially higher. Also, in the case of MZ twins reared apart, the concordance rate was roughly 60 percent, a figure that certainly lends some support to the author's genetic interpretation. The role of genetics in diseases other than schizophrenia is only beginning to be understood.

Other studies have shown that heredity plays a significant role in many other traits and conditions including aggressiveness, alcohol dependence, emotionality, hypertension, epilepsy, several forms of mental retardation, nervousness, and extraversion (Wimer and Wimer, 1985; Loehlin, 1989). Thus, it is suggested that a baby might even be born with a predisposition to neuroticism. Could it be that a day-old neonate might start yearning for the "good old days"?

PSYCHOLOGY'S FIRST PRINCIPLE

Psychology's first principle and most fundamental axiom is that the organism is a product of heredity interacting with environment and with time, as shown in the following formula:

$$O = H \leftrightarrow E \leftrightarrow T$$

It is meaningless to ask whether intelligence, introversion, or any other psychological trait is inherited or learned. It's like asking which is more important in running a car, the engine or the gasoline; or which is more important in determining the area of a rectangle, the height or the width.

Even something as seemingly directly inherited as physical height is profoundly influenced by environment and time. An individual with the inherited potential for tallness will still be short if the environment prevents physical exercise or proper vitamin intake, espeically if this deprivation occurs in early childhood (time).

Keep this first principle constantly in mind during the rest of this chapter. When we dicuss developmental stages, we will give various age norms. How-

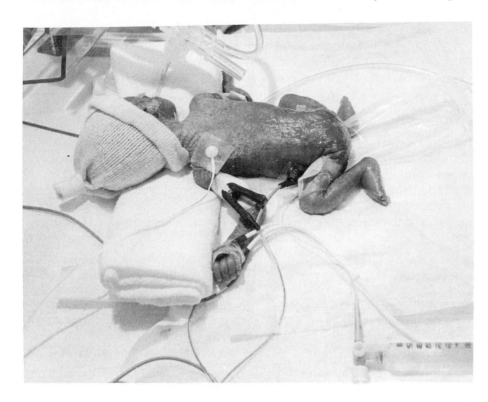

Some birth defects, such as the cocaine addiction in the baby shown here, are the result of environmental factors during prenatal development.

ever, it is crucial to remember that they are only averages, that there are large discrepancies between the averages and any individual case. For example, the averages show that children usually utter their first word at twelve months. But, in fact, some children say their first word at eight months, some at twenty-four months. A great deal depends on the amount and quality of environmental stimulation.

Duke University's Greg Kimble has recast psychology's first principle by saying that behavior is the product of relatively enduring underlying potentials (both genetic and learned) and relatively *temporary* instigations to action (Kimble, 1990). In this statement Kimble uses the term *potentials* to mean any psychologial outcomes that are possible for a person (a rather enduring capacity) and the term *instigation* to refer to all environmental conditions that provoke or prevent an action, where the timing may be both short and crucial.

Though the time factor is given great importance in the following discussion, it must be remembered that time is only one factor. Though it is a convenient factor to utilize in discussing physical development, it is only part of the total equation. The organism is a product of heredity, environment, and time in constant interaction (Vale, 1980).

LIFE BEFORE BIRTH

At birth the human baby is already about nine months old. As a matter of fact, during that first nine months, from conception to birth, more growth occurs than will ever occur again: That tiny speck, the zygote, has grown into a seven- or eight-pound baby by the time it emerges into what William James calls the "blooming, buzzing confusion" of the external environment.

The nine months of growth before birth can be conveniently divided into three periods.

The Zygote

The zygote, the cell formed by the union of two gametes, floats freely in the fluid inside the uterus. After about two weeks it attaches itself to the wall of the uterus and becomes a parasite, receiving all its oxygen and nourishment from the mother's body. By the time the zygote attaches itself to the wall of the uterus, it has already begun to differentiate into three parts: the outer layer, or ectoderm, which will form the brain; the middle layer, or mesoderm, which will form the heart; and the inner layer or endoderm, which will form the liver.

The Embryo

The second stage of prenatal development, the embryonic stage, begins two weeks after conception, at the time the zygote attaches itself to the uterus. At this point the developing organism is called an **embryo.** The embryonic stage lasts until about eight weeks after conception, and during this stage the organism increases its weight by 2 million percent. Also during this period the heart begins beating, sex organs are formed, hands and feet are formed and can be flexed, and all the internal organs are formed. By the end of the embryonic period, the organism is clearly identifiable as human.

The Fetus

From eight weeks after conception until birth the organism is called a **fetus**. Though the growth rate of the fetus is not as spectacular as the zygote's or embryo's, it is still extremely rapid by postnatal standards. The fetus is definitely a behaving organism, and its behavior can be studied.

Current medical techniques have established a fetal age of just over twenty weeks as the dividing line between whether or not the fetus can survive if prematurely born. At this age the fetus is capable of true breathing and can even vocalize a thin crying sound.

With increasingly sophisticated medical care, it is likely that the dividing line between fetal viability and nonviability will be reduced from the current age of somewhat over twenty weeks. This may be especially true for the female fetus, who seems less susceptible to problems of prematurity, anoxia (abnormally low levels of oxygen in the blood), and maternal infection.

Reactions to stimuli   It is known that the fetus can react to stimuli as early as eight weeks after conception. At this time it is sensitive to stimulation of the nose, lips, and chin. The area of sensitivity gradually increases, and by the fourteenth week, the whole body is sensitive, except for the top and back of the head. The top of the head doesn't respond to stimulation until after birth.

Changes in body proportions as a function of age. The figures are adjusted to the same height. Data from N. Bayley, "Individual Patterns of Development," *Child Development* (1956), 45–74.

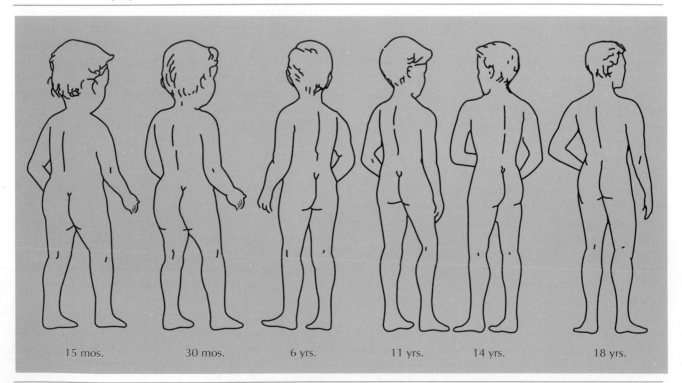

| 15 mos. | 30 mos. | 6 yrs. | 11 yrs. | 14 yrs. | 18 yrs. |

Spontaneous action   Along with the ability to react to stimuli, the fetus can also act spontaneously. Certainly after the fourth month the mother is aware of fetal activity. This activity is quite diffuse—that is, movements are slow and involve several parts of the body at once.

All the preceding stages, from conception to birth, are collectively called the *prenatal stage of development.* Prenatal development is characterized by its rapidity and by a maturation rate that enables the fetus to perform certain functions well before they are actually needed. For example, the fetus can make breathing movements by the fourth month, walking movements by the fifth month, and sucking movements by the sixth month. These activities are not needed until birth, yet they are already months ahead of time.

PHYSICAL DEVELOPMENT IN CHILDHOOD

The newborn baby, or neonate, is certainly not a miniature adult. Compared to other parts of the body, the baby's head and trunk are much larger, proportionally, than they will be at adulthood. For example, the head will only double in size from birth to adulthood, whereas the arms and legs may grow to five times their original length.

Although all normal babies follow the same overall patterns, the growth of girls seems to be more steady and constant than that of boys. Boys are more apt to show growth spurts, even though the general timetables are similar for both sexes. (Kagan, 1984).

The Nervous System

In one sense the nervous system is complete at birth—that is, the number of typical nerve cells never increases after birth—but the size of these cells does increase. Also, although the neonate comes equipped with a fully structured nervous system, it is many years before this system can function efficiently.

Each nerve cell, or neuron, has two basic parts: fibers and cell bodies. Think of the neuron as a fiber with branches at both ends and a bulge (cell body) in the middle. The function of the neuron is to transmit messages (neural impulses) to and from all parts of the body. The branches, or fibers, pick up the messages and send them on their way. The receiving end of a neuron is the dendrite, and the transmitting end

is the axon. In order not to short-circuit the electrically charged neural impulses, most of these fibers are insulated with a white sheath called *myelin.* The gray-colored cell body does not have this covering. Therefore the myelin-covered neural pathways are called *white matter* and the uncovered cell bodies are called *gray matter.* The myelinization of the nervous sytem is not complete at birth, so that a great deal of short-circuiting among the baby's neural impulses does indeed occur. This, in part, accounts for the mass activity that is characteristic of a baby's physical reactions. Touching a baby's foot doesn't result in just a foot response but is usually followed by gross movements of both feet, both arms, and even the trunk. It's as though you had no insulation on the wires leading to your electrical appliances, so that when you turned on the TV, the radio and stereo would go on, the alarm clock would buzz, the dishwasher would start, the coffee pot would begin percolating, and the doorbell would ring. Although the nervous system is structurally complete at birth, it is nowhere near functionally mature. The cerebral cortex, which is crucial for learning and complex behavior, doesn't become functionally mature until about age two, and some maturation continues until about age twelve or fifteen.

Sleep

Newborn babies spend most of their days asleep, averaging about sixteen hours a day. This time decreases rapidly until by age one they are sleeping only a little over ten hours a day.

Motor Development

One of the most dramatic features of infancy is the development of motor skills. Compared to the neonate, the two-year-old child is a study in grace and physical coordination. In one of psychology's truly classic studies, M. M. Shirley assembled a series of painstakingly detailed observations of the development of infants on a week-to-week basis. As can be seen from Table 3.1, Shirley's data suggest that there is a definite pattern to motor development: infants hold up their heads before they sit alone, sit before they crawl, and crawl before they walk. This pattern of development is almost exactly the same for every human baby, and each child passes through each of

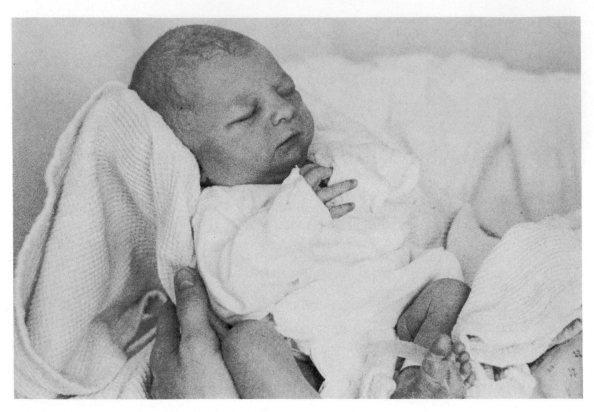

Newborn babies spend most of their days asleep, averaging about sixteen hours a day.

these physical stages at almost the same age (Shirley, 1931).

Since this study was done, many others have researched the age norms for infant motor development, and yet despite slightly different terminology and even slightly different age criteria, Shirley's data have certainly withstood the test of time.

Studies have also shown that motor development occurs according to at least three general rules.

1. *Cephalocaudal progression*—meaning that motor ability develops from the head on down to the toes. The neonate's head is closer to the eventual adult sizes than is the rest of the baby's body. Also, the infant has more motor control of the head than of the muscles lower down the body. The progression of motor control follows this pattern: first the head; then the shoulders, arms, and abdomen; and finally the legs and feet.

2. *Proximodistal progression*—meaning that growth and motor ability develop from the central axis of the body on outward. Trunk and shoulder movements occur earlier than separate arm movements. Control of the hands and fingers comes last.

3. *Mass- to specific-action progression*—indicating that the baby's first actions are global and undifferentiated. Slowly, the infant's ability to make specific responses emerges. Refined activity of the fingers and thumb usually doesn't occur until the baby is about a year old.

Motor development is thus heavily influenced by biological maturation, though practice is certainly necessary for the full development of this inherited potential. Studies have clearly shown that for such activities as walking, for example, early practice is a key ingredient in the action's maintenance and further development. It has even been suggested that since unaided walking is under the influence of several environmental factors, it may be that an infant's true developmental status might better be determined by the assessment of a higher-order skill, such as walking, than by the more traditional testing of simple reflexes (Zelazo and Barr, 1989).

TABLE 3.1 STAGES IN MOTOR DEVELOPMENT

The skills listed here illustrate the progressive development of control over different groups of muscles. This development proceeds in an orderly fashion from the head region down the body and out to the ends of the limbs.

DESCRIPTION OF STAGE	NUMBER OF CASES	AGE, WEEKS MEDIAN
First-order skills (control of the neck muscles)		
On stomach, chin up	22	3
On stomach, chest up	22	9
Held erect, stepping	19	13
On back, tense for lifting	19	15
Held erect, knees straight	18	15
Sit on lap, support at lower ribs and complete head control	22	19
Second-order skills (control of the trunk and upper-limb muscles)		
Sit alone momentarily	22	25
On stomach, knee push or swim	22	25
On back, rolling	19	29
Held erect, stand firmly with help	20	30
Sit alone one minute	20	31
Third-order skills (beginning of body-limb coordination in prone position)		
On stomach, some progress	17	37
On stomach, scoot backward	16	40
Fourth order skills (balance in upright position with support; locomotion in prone position)		
Stand holding to furniture	22	42
Creep	22	45
Walk when held	21	45
Pull to stand by furniture	17	47
Fifth-order skills (unsupported locomotion in upright position)		
Stand alone	21	62
Walk alone	21	64

Adapted from M. M. Shirley, *The first two years, postural and locomotor development*, Vol. I (Minneapolis: University of Minnesota Press, 1931), p. 99.

Sensory Development

Many studies have been done to determine what infants are able to receive through their sensory equipment. Since infants obviously cannot give verbal answers to questions, research in this area is much like animal research. If a researcher is trying to find out whether a rat can sense the difference between the colors red and green, the rat can be presented with a red light and some food in one goal box and a green light with no food in the other. After a number of trials, if the rat goes consistently to the red light, even when it is randomly switched to the goal box that has no food in it, the researcher would know that the rat can discriminate between red and green. (Studies have shown that rats, in fact, cannot make this discrimination between red and green colors when the amount of illumination is held constant.)

Newborn babies have been shown capable of discriminating between sweet and sour tastes, taste being the most highly developed of all the senses at birth. Responses to different smells have been observed within a few hours after birth.

Some babies respond to sound almost immediately after birth, whereas others may take a few days to gain this sense. This difference is a result of the time it may take for the amniotic fluid to drain out of the newborn's hearing mechanism. Once the fluid is drained, however, neonates not only show the ability to respond to sound, but can even discriminate

The sequence of motor development.

among certain sounds. Even neonates as young as three days old, for example, show a marked preference for the mother's voice over the voices of others (DeCasper and Fifer, 1980).

Vision develops more slowly than many of the other senses. Responses to light and darkness (the pupillary reflex) is functional within two days after birth, and by ten days infants can follow moving objects with their eyes. The newborn's visual acuity is understood to be rather poor, however, and has been estimated to be in the range of 20/600, versus 20/20 among older normal children (Banks and Salapatek, 1983). Since neonates can still focus down to a distance of about eight to ten inches, nursing newborns can certainly see the mother's face (Smolak, 1986). They are also capable of imitating the mother's facial expressions, a fact that indicates that they not only are perceiving these expressions but have enough motor control to reproduce them. It is believed that this extremely early visual-motor coordination helps prepare the neonate for later cognitive growth (Bjorklund, 1989). There is even some evidence that the neonate's brain contains "grandmother cells," cells in the visual cortex that are so specialized that they respond to a specific face (Galluscio, 1990).

The specialization of cells may also be a function of environmental interactions. Some migratory cells in the developing cortex become specialized on the basis of the first stimuli that they are exposed to (Walsh and Cepko, 1992). Thus, young neurons can wander around the cortex, and then become functional as a result of *environmental inputs.* When a cell becomes a visual neuron, it is because it roamed into the visual cortex and was exposed to signals from neighboring cells and from the optic nerve. If the same cell had happened to have been in the auditory cortex, it would have matured into a neuron involved in hearing. Thus, the environment can be seen as meshing with the genes to sculpt the brain. More and more, scientists are discovering the crucial importance of environmental stimulation on all parts of the developing organism.

By six months of age infants can discriminate between circles and triangles, and between the faces of parents and strangers. In fact, in one study it was found that infants as young as one month old could distinguish between familiar and unfamiliar faces (Maurer and Salapatek, 1976).

One classic study has demonstrated that infants at six months have the ability to perceive depth and thus avoid situations in which they might fall (Gibson and Walk, 1960). In this study the babies were placed on a plate of glass that extended from a tabletop across a three-foot drop. When the babies reached what they perceived as the edge of the table, they refused to crawl across the rest of the glass. This perceived dropoff is called the **visual cliff,** and it has been shown not only with infants but also with lower organisms such as cats and rats. The ability to perceive the visual cliff and act on that perception has obvious survival value for the species. Some researchers have even suggested an innate link between the visual and motor systems that tends to emerge at just about six months of age (Richards and Rader, 1981). By the time children reach first or second grade, they are typically learning to refine their basic visual-motor skills. After this they usually don't develop many new basic skills, but they do learn to improve the quality and complexity of those skills they already possess (Malina, 1982).

Emotional Development

Neonates, of course, do not have the capacity to experience or express the full range of human emotions, but this ability does begin to emerge very soon after birth. The earliest emotions seem to show only a general diffuse anxiousness or excitement, although even neonates have displayed a few very basic emotions. For example in one study the faces of neonates showed different expressions for surprise, disgust, and distress (Trotter, 1983). Such emotions as happiness and anger tend to develop somewhat later. Feelings of shame and guilt arise much later because they depend on an understanding of social situations and relationships, the most obvious example being the ability to grasp the significance of social approval and disapproval (Lazarus, 1991). Tests to determine how neonates experience emotions are difficult to conduct for two reasons. First, the researcher must try to resist the temptation to anthropomorphize, that is, to attribute adult feelings to the actions and expressions of the newborn. Second, as Lazarus has shown in numerous studies, the relationship between cognition and emotion is extremely intimate. Lazarus explains that all emotions begin with a diffuse and general arousal of the nervous system. Thus, the *situation* in which the child finds himself or herself when aroused may provide that child with direct clues as to how these diffuse feelings should be labeled. The developing baby has to learn the appropriate clues, usually from the caretaker, to use in order to identify which feelings are appropriate to which situation. Thus, the nature of emotional communication be-

Babies as young as six months can perceive depth.

SPOTLIGHT ON BONDING

A Mother-Child Connection

Some researchers believe that a process similar to imprinting among birds occurs among humans, specifically between mother and child. This is called maternal infant **bonding,** which is said to produce a strong emotional attachment between the mother and her baby. The bonding process requires direct physical contact between mother and child and apparently must take place within the baby's first three days of life. Part of the reason for this is that during those first three critical days, the neonate is more alert and more able to respond than will be the case for the several days that follow.[a] Thus, the existence of a sensitive period among humans—a specific time frame in which bonding may appear—has been hypothesized. Researchers in this area have cited the failure to form this crucial psychological bond as a possible reason for later episodes of child neglect and even child abuse.[b]

---

[a] Brazelton, T. B. (1981). Clinical issues of the Brazelton Neonatal Assessment Scale. In M. Coleman (Ed.), *Neonatal neurology.* Baltimore: University Park Press.

[b] Marano, H. E. (1985). Biology is one key to the bonding of mothers and babies. In H. E. Fitzgerald and M. G. Walraven (Eds.), *Human development* (pp. 85–86). Guilford, Conn.: Dushkin.

---

tween infant and adult may be far more organized than had previously been thought (Tronik, 1989).

Speech Development

At birth, speech is restricted to general, undifferentiated crying, yet by the second month the baby can communicate both discomfort and contentment through the use of loud crying or gentle cooing. Of all the developmental factors covered so far, speech is obviously the one most influenced by learning. Yet even speech is built on a biological foundation. Studies of the various sounds made by infants throughout the world have found that certain sounds occur at about the same time and in about the same order in all infants. By listening to the sounds of a baby lying contentedly nearby, one can hear the basic sounds of all languages throughout the world, from the German guttural *r* to the singsong intonation of Chinese.

Learning theorists, such as B. F. Skinner, believe that babies keep some of these sounds—those reinforced by their parents and slowly discard those that are not encouraged. By the ninth or tenth month they are able to imitate some of the sounds made by others around them.

Other theorists, such as Noam Chomsky, believe there is a heavy genetic component in language acquisition. Rather than learn language solely on the basis of reinforcement and imitation, Chomsky argues, children may acquire language as the result of an inborn "language acquisition device," which directs the infant's ability to learn (Chomsky, 1980). One researcher calls this inborn device a "bioprogram," which is a specific genetically driven grammatical model that each child amends, probably through trial and error, to match the peculiarities of the native tongue. This genetically based machinery guides language acquisition, especially during the critical period between ages two and four, when babies turn from babblers to novice talkers (Bickerton, 1990). Maratsos agrees that language acquisition is genetically based, believing that the neonate enters the world with a built-in language "bias" that undoubtedly serves an evolutionary purpose (Maratsos, 1983). Also, it is known that among adults language is processed in an area of the brain's left hemisphere (Geschwind, 1979) and that this left-hemisphere processing area is significantly larger than the comparable area of the right hemisphere. This cortical size difference is found not only among adults, but also among neonates *and even among fetuses* (Wada et al., 1975). These facts lend further credence to the hypothesis that there is probably a genetic basis for language receptivity and acquisition.

By about one year of age, babies can associate the sounds they make with specific objects and thus they begin to utter their first words, such as *dada, mama,* or *bye-bye.* The young mother is often depressed over the fact that she's been through an uncomfortable

SPOTLIGHT ON CHILDREN

A Time to Play

As the great psychologist Erik Erikson (see biography on p. 152) said many years ago, the early years, especially ages three to six, are years when playtime is extremely important in the developmental process. Play affords the child with a nonthreatening opportunity to try out reciprocal social roles and even to learn cooperative strategies. William Damon (more on him in Chapter 7) has pointed out that playtime also provides a safe opportunity for the child to express thoughts and feelings that might otherwise remain bottled up and distorted. For example, Damon cites the story of two preschool neighbors who were both presented with baby sisters at about the same time. Although both children seemed to be overtly kind and affectionate to their new siblings, they often played a game with each other called "bad baby," in which a certain doll was used as a scapegoat for their natural jealousies and hostilities. The doll, that is, the "bad baby," was scolded, rejected, and severely punished during this emotionally releasing game. In another more blatant example, a five-year-old names her "favorite" doll, Allison, after her one-year-old baby sister. About every two weeks or so, she would announce that she was going to play a game called "Let's Give Allison Away," and the doll would then disappear for a few hours or even days. On one occasion, the mother found the doll halfway down the toilet. Damon feels that this kind of play is developmentally healthy since it allows children to discharge pent-up emotions and come to grips with their true inner feelings.[a] David Elkind even argues that the young child who is not given enough playtime, who is pushed too hard and too soon to achieve, the "hurried child," is at a developmental disadvantage, not only for emotional growth but, ironically, for cognitive growth as well.[b]

---

[a] Damon, W. (1983). *Social and personality development: Infancy through adolescence.* New York: Norton.

[b] Elkind, D. (1981). *The hurried child: Growing up too fast, too soon.* Reading, Mass.: Addison-Wesley.

---

pregnancy and has spent sleepless nights in feeding, changing, and comforting the baby, only to hear the baby's first word— *dada*.

After the first word, the infant's vocabulary increases slowly for the next few months. This slowness may be due to the total attention the infant is devoting to learning the intricacies of walking. Once the child has mastered walking, usually at about eighteen months, language development speeds up. There is, of course, a definite lag between speech production and speech recognition. It has been estimated that by eighteen months of age babies can recognize up to six times as many words as they can produce (Benedict, 1979).

Between eighteen and twenty-four months of age there is typically a fairly dramatic vocabulary spurt. The baby at twelve months is able to produce approximately 30 to 50 words, and by eighteen months is typically producing at least 400 words (Brandstadter-Palmer, 1982).

These figures are, of course, only averages, and there are great individual differences from one child to the next. For example, children with high IQs begin talking, on the average, as much as four months earlier than the average child. Also, girls begin talking sooner than boys, use more words in each sentence, and master larger vocabularies. Moreover, as they get older, girls have fewer speech problems than boys. Boys are more prone to stuttering, more apt to have difficulty articulating the consonants *l* and *r*, and more likely to fill up their speech with hesitation sounds such as "uh" and "er." Later in life there are still some dramatic speech differences between the sexes. Among stroke victims, for example, it is far more common for men to lose their ability to speak than it is for women (Restak, 1979).

Speech and early experience Speech, like other developmental abilities, is a product of heredity, environment, and *time*. The sensitive-period hypothesis illustrates the importance of time. If environmental stimulation comes too late, normal language acquisition is prevented. Evidence supporting a sensitive-period explanation of language acquisition comes

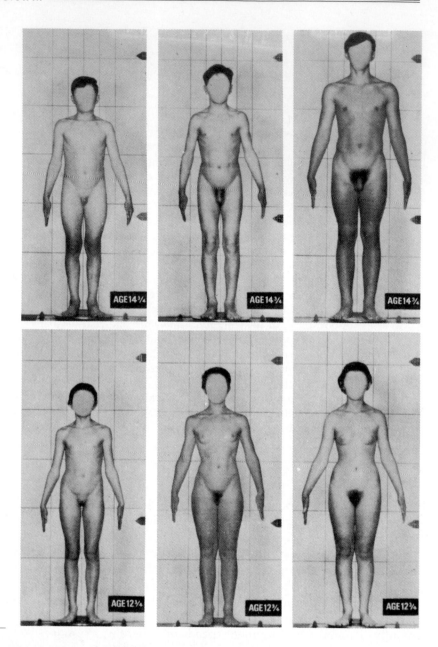

FIGURE 3.3 The adolescent growth spurt typically occurs earlier in girls than in boys.

from a true "horror story" about a young girl reared in unbelievably impoverished circumstances (Curtiss, 1977). The girl, Genie, was locked by her father in a bare room when she was only twenty months of age. During the day she was strapped naked to a potty chair, and at night she was tied into her crib. On those occasions when she was visited, either by her brother or her father, she never heard the sounds of human language. The father and brother would only bark or growl at her, in mock imitation of a dog. Any attempts by Genie to make any vocalization were severely punished by her father, who, as one author suggests, "lends renewed dignity to the notion of

insanity" (Maratsos, 1979). When Genie was finally released *twelve years later,* she was, of course, unable to talk, but since that time she made great progress—further testimony to human resilience. Genie acquired some ability to talk—"Want think about Mama riding bus"—but her speech patterns never came up to what could be called normal language ability. For example, she never used pronouns and had no verb tensing, nor did her voice carry any inflections. In short, the study of Genie seems to indicate that at age thirteen, it's too late to acquire normal language, that the critical period for language acquisition has long since passed.

PHYSICAL DEVELOPMENT IN ADOLESCENCE

Although physical growth proceeds in fits and starts from two years of age to adolescence, it is not until adolescence that another really dramatic growth spurt occurs, and it occurs earlier in girls than in boys (see Figure 3.3). Though boys are typically taller and heavier than girls at age ten, by age thirteen the girls are taller and heavier than the boys. By age sixteen, the situation returns to the way it had been before the onset of adolescence, with the boys again taller and heavier.

In girls, adolescence is signaled by the occurrence of the **menarche,** or the first menstruation. This happens concurrently with breast development, usually by age thirteen, though it is not uncommon for some girls to reach menarche as early as age ten or as late as age sixteen. The timing and variation in the onset of menarche are partly influenced by environmental factors such as nutrition and general health. Nutrition is especially important since menarche occurs at both a fairly consistent weight, approximately 106 plus or minus 3 pounds, as well as percentage of fat to body weight, about 17 percent. Anorectic girls, or girls who overtrain in athletics, may not reach the required body fat levels and therefore may retard the onset of menarche. Despite these environmental factors, the genetic age range for the onset of puberty is innately wired into the species (Scarr and Kidd, 1983).

Adolescence in boys does not have such clear-cut criteria. If we use such indices as the appearance of pubic hair, the first seminal ejaculation or increase in the size of the penis and testes, adolescence in boys usually begins between the ages of eleven and seventeen. Again, there is great variation in the age at which boys reach puberty.

Special Problems of Girls

Menarche can be a traumatic event in the life of a young girl who is psychologically unprepared. This is especially true for the early maturing (EM) girl. However, the girl who is secure in her sex identification and who has had adult support and guidance may regard her first menstruation with pride, as a sign that she is "grown up" and is no longer a child. The girl whose parents have prepared her for this new experience is less likely to be anxious about her menarche.

Breast development has special psychological overtones in western culture. The United States has been described as a breast-oriented nation, and certainly the popularity of the Playmate of the Month, the billboard ads for suntan lotion, the TV ads for "the slightly padded bra," and the direct stares of males of all ages do much to validate this description. During adolescence, then, breast development becomes a psychological symbol of approaching wom-

Maturation rates for girls may vary substantially during early adolescence.

SPOTLIGHT ON SEX DIFFERENCES

Learned or Genetic?

Aside from the obvious anatomical differences between males and females, there is a question of growing concern as to whether psychological differences between the sexes are learned or innate. The question is indeed of momentous importance, for if the differences are learned and if, as some suggest, they favor the male, then it is up to us, to society, to change the childrearing and educational practices that produce this lack of fairness. For example, if boys are trained and shaped at an early age to be better equipped to succeed in our competitive society, then it's time the rules and norms were amended so that the girls can be given an equal opportunity to achieve success. If, however, there are in fact physiological-psychological differences that are built into the species, then educational (and psychological testing) practices should be altered so that every member of each sex will be given full opportunity to make the most of his or her potential.

The differences that have been the most consistently noted over the years are the following:

1. During the first few months of life, boys are less sensitive to and less often startled by sounds and do not turn as often toward them.
2. Girls show superior development of fine-motor coordination, not just with their fingers, but even in the small muscles of the larynx and pharynx—hence, they even sing in tune at a younger age.
3. Girls learn to speak at a younger age, develop larger vocabularies, and generally retain a linguistic superiority throughout life. In school, they learn foreign languages more easily.
4. Boys suffer far more from speech difficulties, stuttering, stammering, and the use of "um" and "er" interjections, and so on.
5. Boys are more overtly aggressive than girls, as children and especially as adolescents. Boys are less able to sit still for long periods of time—thus, they are far more apt to be diagnosed as hyperactive when they reach school age.
6. Boys are superior in tests of spatial relations, such as indicating which of four rotated shapes is identical to an original model or mentally traversing a maze.
7. On IQ tests, females consistently outperform males on a number of verbal subtests, especially those concerning vocabulary, whereas males do better in other areas, notably in those concerning arithmetic. David Wechsler has even provided a formula for a "masculinity-femininity" score,[a] based on comparing a person's performance on subtests typically excelled in by males with those typically excelled in by females.

Environmentalists, on the one hand, explain all these differences as a result of the way our culture treats and differentially reinforces the sexes. No wonder little boys are more active and aggressive: They are told to be so by parents, teachers, and storybooks. Little girls are admonished not to run, jump, or be boisterous, because it simply isn't "ladylike." Through reinforcement, then, little girls condition themselves to sit more quietly and to develop their fine-motor coordination by drawing, learning to sew, or playing with dolls—all generally more passive pursuits. Boys are allowed to throw themselves into rough-and-tumble games, and because of their conditioning, they

anhood and sexuality. Typically, physical development of the breast from bud to full size occurs in about three years, from about eleven to about fourteen years of age. The bud stage almost always precedes menarche and the first signs of pubic hair.

Special Problems of Boys

Boys who begin puberty relatively late suffer psychological distress for a variety of reasons. Late-maturing (LM) boys are apt to be shorter and physically weaker than the early maturers and are thus less apt to become outstanding athletes. Because social reinforcements are fewer, the late-maturing boy more often turns psychologically inward, becoming introverted.

The size of the penis is also of great concern to the adolescent boy. In the shower room after gym classes the adolescent quickly glances from boy to boy, to see whether he "measures up." The boy with the small penis is often openly ridiculed and his masculinity challenged. He worries that he will be an unsuc-

are less able to sit passively and exercise and develop their fine-muscle coordination. With language development, the situation is similar. Girls, having been *conditioned* to be more passive, are much better able to listen to language, imitate new sounds, and sit still long enough to read a book. Therefore, it's no wonder that they will acquire larger vocabularies. As for speech problems, again culture is the culprit. Society demands more of little boys, and when a three-year-old male misspeaks, the parents make a major issue out of it. So much pressure is put on the male child to speak correctly that he becomes overanxious. After all, isn't he eventually going to have to be the competitive breadwinner of the family? Anxiety then builds on anxiety and a snowball effect is produced with speech pathology as the result. As for spatial relations, boys are encouraged more to be curious about the world of nuts and bolts and hammers and saws. Therefore, it's no surprise that they learn to manipulate spatial concepts. They get more rewards for it. In short, the differences are due to cultural stereotyping, and the sooner we as a society do away with our preconceived notions, the better we'll all be. Girls will then be more able to reach their full potential—

and boys will be, too, since they will be less wracked by pressures to perform.

The geneticists, on the other hand, insist that the cultural argument, though valid to some extent, has been generalized far beyond the physiological facts. For example, neurologist Richard Restak says that there are indeed fundamental differences, both chemical and morphological, between the male and female brains. The left hemisphere of the female brain is more heterogenous, more neurologically complex than the male's. (In right-handed persons, and even in 60 percent of left-handed persons, the left hemisphere contains the language centers.) Even among left-hemisphere stroke victims, far more women than men retain their ability to speak and to understand language.[b] Problems based on spatial relations, however, are controlled by the right hemisphere, and here the male brain is more complex. There are, say the geneticists, innate sex differences in brain organization and to ignore them is simply to escape into fantasyland.

Society's task is really to adjust for these differences, not to deny them. Since boys tend to excel in right-hemisphere tasks, "then tests such as the National Merit Scholar-

ship Examination should be radically redesigned to ensure that both sexes have an equal chance. As things now stand, the tests are heavily weighted with items (spatial relations and mathematics) that virtually guarantee superior male performance.[c] Also, elementary grades should be restructured to allow boys more freedom of action and thereby help reduce the stress that might trigger such problems as hyperactivity, speech problems, and learning disorders. Sociologist Carol Tavris warns us that we should never confuse the very real differences in male and female experiences with the way culture translates these differences. Society must strive for equality of acceptance, a goal not of denying or exaggerating differences but of eliminating the unequal consequences that too often flow from them.[d]

---

[a] Wechsler, D. (1958). *The measurement and appraisal of adult intelligence* (4th ed.). Baltimore: Williams and Wilkins, p. 150.
[b] Kimura, D. (1986). Male brain, female brain: The hidden difference. *Psychology Today* (November), 68–75.
[c] Restak, R. (1979). *The brain: The last frontier.* Garden City, N.Y.: Doubleday, p. 205.
[d] Tavris, C. (1992). *The mismeasure of women.* New York: Simon & Shuster.

cessful lover. The facts, however, as reported by William Masters and Virginia Johnson, are that the size of the penis is not highly correlated with the he-man physique or with great physical size. The largest penis they measured (without erection or stretching) was five and a half inches and belonged to a man only 5 feet 7 inches tall. The shortest penis, just over two and a third inches, was found on a man almost 6 feet tall (Masters and Johnson, 1966).

Further, Masters and Johnson found little evidence for the widely held myth that the larger the penis,

the greater the potential for giving sexual satisfaction. Because the vagina distends when excited in order to permit entry and then contracts around the penis in a snug grip, the size of the penis is of little importance.

Adolescent Sexuality

In his classic study on sexuality, Alfred Kinsey reached a series of conclusions concerning sexual behavior. Kinsey gathered his data in two major studies

Early maturity seems to be regarded more favorably in boys than in girls in our society. Thus, early maturing boys enjoy more self-esteem and higher social status than their female counterparts.

during the 1940s and 1950s. He reported the following:

1. Men reach their period of greatest sexual activity (defined as sexual arousals leading to orgasm) between sixteen and seventeen years of age.

2. Women tend to be less easily sexually aroused at any age, compared to men, and seem less preoccupied by sex than men.

3. Fifty percent of women and 85 percent of men had intercourse before marriage.

4. Forty percent of women and 95 percent of men masturbated to orgasm (Kinsey et al., 1953).

In another study of human sexuality, conducted by Masters and Johnson, the interviews of their subjects were combined with the actual observation of their subject's sexual activities (Masters and Johnson, 1966). (Subjects in these studies were all volunteers.) In general, the conclusions drawn from this study both supported and extended Kinsey's position. They found, for example, that masturbation is a common sexual practice and that it is not harmful. Fears of "going crazy," ruining your complexion, becoming impotent, weakening physical capacity, and so on are all myths. In addition, they found that women are capable of numerous climaxes in a relatively short time and that female orgasms occur in the clitoris and not in the vagina, as had been previously suggested.

Probably their most significant conclusions were that humans can remain sexually active throughout life and that at least half of married adults suffer from sexual inadequacy. Masters and Johnson point to the need for effective educational programs to help reduce feelings of sexual inadequacy and to eliminate some of the popular misconceptions about human sexuality.

There is no question that part of the so-called hidden agenda of education during the junior and senior high school years is a concern about human sexuality. Accurate information alone, of course, will not solve the complex issues of sexual inadequacy, but it can be an effective first step.

The Sissy-Boy Syndrome

That there may be growth trends in the development of adult male homosexuality has been suggested by the psychiatrist, Richard Green. Green asserts that he has identified a pattern of male development, called the *sissy-boy syndrome*, which seems to predict the later onset of homosexuality. Green's longitudinal study followed the lives of a large group of young boys, originally selected because they possessed some or all of the following behavioral traits: dressing in girls' or women's clothes, playing with dolls, pretending to be a mommy, playing games almost exclusively with girls, and completely avoiding rough-and-tumble play. When contacted fifteen years later, (in their early twenties), 75 percent of these males acknowledged that they were either homosexual or bisexual. Of Green's control group, made up of men

Adolescent boys are often concerned with penis size. According to researchers Masters and Johnson, the size of the penis is not highly correlated with physical size.

who had previously been found to have been typically masculine boys, only one had become bisexual (Green, 1987). Evidence obtained in another study, this one done on twins, points rather convincingly to the suggestion that there is a genetic basis for homosexuality (Bailey and Pillard, 1991). In this study it was found that 52 percent of identical twin brothers (MZ twins) of homosexual men also were homosexual, compared with 22 percent for fraternal (DZ) twins, and only 11 percent among genetically unrelated brothers (brothers by adoption). These researchers examined fifty-six identical twins, fifty-four fraternal twins, and fifty-seven adoptive brothers, and concluded that although they feel that the case for a genetic component has been strengthened by their data, it does not rule out all other factors, such as social conditioning. Finally, a study that examined a deep interior formation of the brain, called the hypothalamus, showed an anatomical difference between homosexual and heterosexual men. One specific node of the hypothalamus is nearly three times larger in heterosexual men than in homosexual men. In fact, the anatomical form of that node is remarkably similar in women and homosexual men, and substantially different in heterosexual men (Le Vay, 1991). Even this anatomical difference, however, may not be inborn, but may be a result of environmental treatment and stresses, or even the individual's own reaction to that treatment. For example, it has been found among males in lower species that cells in the hypothalamus may become larger *as a result of behavior.* When male fish fight to obtain social dominance, the winner undergoes a series of physical changes, beginning with an increase in the release of a hormone called gonadotropin, which triggers the enlargement of both the hypothalamus and the gonads. Conversely, within days the defeated male shows a reduction in the size of the hypothalamus, as well as a shrinkage of the testes and the concomitant reduction of sperm production (Bond et al., 1991).

None of the above studies should be interpreted as indicating that biology should be equated with destiny, but all do show significant genetic possibilities that cannot be ignored.

Early and Late Maturation

Much research has gone into discovering what differences exist between early-maturing and late-maturing adolescents, differences other than the rate of physical maturity. One must be careful, in interpreting these studies, not to leap to the conclusion that these other differences between EM and LM adolescents are due only to the adolescent's changing biology. Personality variables, for example, are especially influenced by the way others perceive and, accordingly, treat us. A boy of seventeen whose voice hasn't changed yet, whose body proportions are still as they were when he was twelve, is all too often treated by those around him as though he were, in fact, still only twelve years old. Similarly, the twelve-year-old boy who is speaking in a rich baritone, whose shoulders have broadened, and who shaves daily, is more apt to be treated with dignity and respect.

Social psychologists tell us that the way people respond often depends on how others treat them. People who are treated like children very often respond in childlike ways, and those who are treated like adults respond with more maturity. Early maturity can itself be a problem, however. If teachers and parents see early maturity as a negative characteristic, the adolescent can be adversely affected. However, studies that have been done over the years on early and late maturers (Jones, 1965; Wilson et al., 1969; Siegel, 1982; Simmons and Blyth, 1987) have been fairly consistent in revealing the following:

1. There are almost no differences in IQ, grade placement, or socioeconomic status between early-maturing (EM) and late-maturing (LM) adolescents. There is some evidence, however, that EM girls had somewhat lower grades in the fifth or sixth grades than did their LM counterparts, but this difference seems not to persist into high school (Simmons and Blyth, 1987). This grade difference is somewhat difficult to interpret, however, since more of the EM girls became high school dropouts, a fact that changed the makeup of the group at large. Perhaps the girls who dropped out were the very ones who had weighted down the average of the EM girls in the first place. It is also known that children with extremely high IQs tend to be early maturers.

2. EM boys were rated by their peers as being physically more attractive and better athletes, and they were more often elected to student office.

3. On personality tests, EM boys showed more self-control, more interest in girls, more extraversion, and higher levels of self-esteem.

4. EM girls were rated by adults as being below average on many social and personality traits, whereas LM girls were rated above average. By the time they reach high school, EM girls tend to be shorter, stockier, and less satisfied with their figures, whereas LM girls become taller, thinner, and more satisfied. Back in the fifth and sixth grades, however, the EM girl was significantly more satisfied with her body image. She was also aware that her new physical appearance was a source of much attention by the boys in her class as well as older boys. At the risk of stating the obvious, body image is an imporant source of concern during adolescence. In fact, when teenagers of both sexes are asked what they disliked most about themselves, fully one-half of the girls and one-third of the boys reported "physical appearance" more than anything else (Conger and Peterson, 1984). In another study it was found that among those subjects who overestimate their physical attractiveness, the vast majority are males (Gurman and Balban, 1990). Also, adolescents who are least satisfied with their body images tend to be more self-conscious and have lower levels of self-esteem (Adams and Gullota, 1983).

5. EM girls dated earlier and more frequently than the LM girls. They were also more likely to become sexually active, a pattern that extended into high school.

6. In comparing the peer ratings of EM boys and girls, EM boys were perceived in a more favorable way on a variety of personal and social traits than were the EM girls.

Thus, when it occurs, early maturity is more apt to be an advantage to the boy than to the girl in our society.

GROWTH PERIODS AND EDUCATIONAL PROBLEMS

At each age and stage of development, children and adolescents need continued assurance from adults in order to accommodate themselves to and assimilate the effects of constant change. During adolescence, diversity and change are at peak intensity and the differences between the sexes and within the sexes are at a maximum. The junior high school years, especially, represent diversity in such areas as physical

SPOTLIGHT ON ADOLESCENCE

The Workplace

A Department of Education Survey, conducted in 1990, showed that about half of all U.S. high school sophomores, two-thirds of all juniors, and three-fourths of all seniors held after-school jobs. At first glance, this may look like a very positive picture of American teenagers, showing them to be ambitious and ready to compete in the free-enterprise system. Aside from the monetary gain, it might seem that the teenager holding an after-school job would benefit in a variety of ways—building character, self-reliance, and good work habits. The evidence, however, is not nearly so positive. Says one study, "Contrary to popular belief that working during adolescence is beneficial to young people's development, the findings presented here indicate that the correlates of school year employment are generally negative."[a] In this survey it was found that compared to classmates who did not work at all, or who worked only a few hours a week, the working students received lower grades, spent less time on homework, cut classes more often, and were less involved in extracurricular activities. The workers also showed more somatic complaints, higher rates of drug and alcohol use, more delinquent behavior, greater freedom from parental control, and lower levels of self-esteem. These behaviors were especially pronounced among students who worked more than twenty hours a week, but were significantly less likely among students working fewer than ten hours a week. The issue, therefore, may not be simply a function of whether or not a student works, but how much *time* the student spends working. Finally, the authors cautioned that it is possible that the results of this study may not reflect a genuine causal relationship. It may be that the work force is especially attractive to youngsters who are already predisposed to some of those negative habits and who need extra money to pay for them.

[a] Steinberg, L., and Dornbusch, S. M. (1991). Negative correlates of part-time employment during adolescence: Replication and elaboration. *Developmental Psychology, 27,* 304–313.

growth, glandular-sexual changes, social changes, and cognitive shifts. Each individual student and each subgroup of students needs extra support during this critical period. For example, the late-maturing boy needs help in developing confidence and needs assurance that before long he too will reach full maturity. Similarly, the early-maturing girl needs special support to withstand some of the intense pressures she is under from both adults and peers. Handling this situation can be extremely delicate. Class discussions may often do more harm than good, especially when they focus attention on specific students in the class. A public discussion of a particular student's problem may be a humiliating and destructive experience for the individual on whom the spotlight falls. Teachers need to develop an extra awareness of and sensitivity to those aspects of this often-hidden classroom agenda. Careful listening to student concerns and some judicious reading between the lines will provide the teacher with more than a few cues as to possible reasons for a student's sudden, "unexplainable" upset, mood change, or rapid attention shift.

In physical education and health classes, posting pictures and charts showing growth curves during adolescence may indeed be a case in which a picture is worth a thousand words. It should also be helpful to present the students with some facts of sexual growth and maturation. A few facts in this area may remove the mystery and correct some of the blatant untruths that students often pass on to one another. Information of this sort may often be followed by an audible and collective sigh of relief from the class. This is not to suggest that the teacher should deluge the seventh-grader with graphic illustrations from Masters and Johnson, for the student may confuse sex education with sexual encouragement. If a teacher overreacts to this information deficit, the students can be overstimulated. The object is to present information in a style that will help the pupils become comfortable with their own and their peers' physical, emotional, and sexual growth and less preoccupied by it. The goal is anxiety reduction, not sexual trauma.

The AIDS scare has added new impetus to the drive for sex education in the schools. The logic is summarized in the argument that if youngsters are indeed going to be sexually active, then they had better know more about what they are doing. And the majority of today's teenagers are apparently sexually active. According to one survey, 60 percent of white males have had intercourse by age eighteen; 60 percent of white females by age nineteen; 60 percent of black males by age sixteen; and 60 percent of black females by age eighteen (Hofferth and Hages, 1987).

However, several studies have confirmed the nagging suspicion that sex education isn't automatically translated into any positive behavioral change. For example, in one study it was found that the use of condoms by teens actually declined after they had studied a sex education unit specifically designed to provide information on the risks of AIDS (Kegeles et al., 1988).

SUMMARY

An understanding of the biological basis of behavior is important to understanding developmental psychology. American psychology for too long ignored this important aspect of its own discipline. Little attention, for example, was paid to the emerging field of genetics. Genetics is a relatively new discipline. It is the study of how characteristics are biologically transmitted from parent to offspring.

The basic unit of analysis in genetics is the gene, a tiny particle of heredity located in the nucleus of each of the body's cells. Genes are composed of DNA and RNA molecules. The DNA acts as a blueprint—or template—and contains the coded genetic information within the nucleus of the cell. RNA transmits this information to other parts of the cell. One of biology's most spectacular recent achievements was the deciphering of this genetic code.

Since each offspring receives twenty-three genes from each parent, the new individual is genetically unique, except in the case of identical twins, who begin life as only one cell. Psychologists are able to examine the effects of genetic endowment through both animal and human research.

Psychology's basic principle is that behavior is the result of heredity interacting with environment interacting with time.

Before birth, the human organism goes through three basic stages of development: (1) zygote, (2) embryo, and (3) fetus. Tremendous changes occur during the prenatal period. The organism increases its size dramatically, from a tiny speck to a seven- or eight-pound baby, in a period of nine months.

Maturation both before and immediately after birth occurs on a time schedule that is fairly consistent for all members of a given species. The maturation of various organs occurs safely ahead of the time when they must be used.

Reflex and motor development, such as holding the head erect, sitting, crawling, and walking, is heavily influenced by biological maturation, though environmental encounters at the appropriate time are important for full development of the biological potential.

Sensory maturation shows functional development either at birth or within a few days of birth. Touch, smell, taste, and hearing develop slightly before vision.

Bonding is a process that requires direct physical contact between mother and child and occurs within the baby's first three days of life. It is said to produce a strong emotional attachment between the mother and child, and failure to form this bond may cause later episodes of child neglect or even child abuse.

Speech develops from the grunts and cries of the newborn to a recognizable word by the one-year-old. Once the child masters the intricate details of walking, the verbal repertoire increases dramatically.

Adolescence marks the beginning of another growth spurt, a spurt that occurs earlier in girls than in boys. The early-maturing girl and the late-maturing boy may have special problems in our culture. Adolescents need extra support and understanding during this critical period of development.

Sex education must be handled sensitively and with compassion. If a teacher spends too much time attempting to detail the intricacies of sex education, adolescents may feel overstimulated. They may confuse education with encouragement and thus their psychological problems may increase rather than decrease.

KEY TERMS AND NAMES

behavior genetics
bonding
chromosome
concordance rate
deoxyribonucleic acid (DNA)
dizygotic (DZ) twins
dominant gene
embryo
fetus
gene
genetics
genotype

homozygosity
menarche
Gregor Mendel
monozygotic (MZ) twins
$O = H \leftrightarrow E \leftrightarrow T$
phenotype
polygenic inheritance
recessive gene
ribonucleic acid (RNA)
visual cliff
zygote

THEORY INTO PRACTICE: OBSERVING CHANGES IN GROWTH

To help understand just how dramatic the process of physical growth and development is during the first few years of life we suggest that you focus on the process of motor development.

1. Use Table 3.1, Stages in Motor Development, as a reference point.

2. Set up a series of visits in order to observe young children at different ages.

    a. A newborn unit at a local hospital for infants up to two weeks in age.

    b. A day care or a home-care center for children ranging from six to eighteen months old.

    c. A preschool program for children three- to four-years-old.

Newborns: birth to two weeks   Start with the youngest group and see if any of the newborns can hold up their chin or their chest. Since you'll probably have to observe from behind a glass wall, it may be difficult to see very much movement. If so, then ask the nurse in charge what is the range of motoric activity that newborns demonstrate, for example, grasping fingers, moving legs, crying, and if there are noticeable individual differences in the amount of motor activity? Spend a few moments taking in the entire scene, observing the tiny tots, most of them sleeping quietly; the activities of the nurses and attendants; and the general layout.

Day care or home care: six–eighteen months   First, notice the dramatic differences in motor activity compared to the newborns. By the time the infant is six months old, you should be able to observe that they attained all of the first-order skills listed in Table 3.1. Also, by six months, many of the children should be demonstrating the second-order skills, such as sitting alone, rolling, and doing a kind of pushup.

Next, look for some one-year-olds. Notice how fast some can crawl and creep and especially how the coordination in getting the legs and arms working together has improved. If you happen to see a six-month-old lying stomach down, with arms and legs flailing but still not moving in any direction and nearby a one-year-old scooting along the floor with arms and legs coordinating, the differences will be readily apparent.

The final observations at this age concern eighteen-month-old children. Many will be in the process of mastering walking and running. You may have the opportunity of observing some children in transition from crawling to walking. Notice how uncoordinated the first steps are, accompanied by lots of "unnecessary" motion, such as the waving of arms or tilting of the body. Then, gradually, the coordination improves and the unnecessary movements drop away. The children begin to scoot about with deftness and grace.

A second point to notice during the transition from creeping to walking is regression. A child may take a few steps haltingly to obtain a desired toy across the room and then suddenly sit down and crawl rapidly. In Piaget's terms (Chapter 5) the child hasn't yet accommodated to the new skill of walking and so returns to an earlier method of problem solving that is only temporarily a better solution.

The last point to notice during the transition is the child's exclusive concentration on the new task of walking. During this phase, children often halt development in other areas. Thus, it is not uncommon for them to stop talking, or at least reduce the amount of talking, as they focus on mastery in locomotion. You may not be able to observe this directly in a single visit. You might ask the day-care workers for their observations on this point.

Preschool for three- to four-year-olds   The first thing that will strike you is just how sophisticated the motoric activity has become in such a relatively brief time period. Walking, running, jumping are now all performed without hesitation. Compare what you see in this age group to the motor activity of the newborns and then to that of the six- to eighteen-month-olds. There is a quantum leap forward in ability. The basic physical work of such motor activity has been accommodated and assimilated so that it is part of the natural repertoire of activity.

Also notice that as a result of these skills, the style of play and interaction has changed. There is more grouping. Children gather in clusters for joint play rather than play in parallel. The groups coalesce around something of common interest and then quickly disband and reform with different members around a new object. If the classroom has a water table, note how the children pour water from large containers to smaller ones (without spilling too much), watch one another do it, and then disband, moving to the puzzle corner of the room and a new set of activities.

What may appear as episodic or even perhaps aimless wandering is really an expression of the children's ability to explore freely and enjoy the sense of mastery that bipedal locomotion provides. They are obviously more efficient and more effective than either the six-month-olds who try to bump along on their bottoms or the twelve-month-olds who crawl from place to place.

A final note   Observation of young children can become an extremely important part of any one of a variety of professional roles: teacher, child-care worker, theorist, researcher. In fact, you will find out that some of our major theories of development actually started with the seemingly mundane process of child watching. This Theory to Practice unit is really only a beginning step toward sensitizing you to the process. Also, somewhat arbitrarily, we have focused on locomotion. The chapter notes other possibilities, such as sight, smell, language, and physical development itself. If you spend one day observing in any seventh-grade classroom, you would be struck by the enormous variability between girls and boys in size and physical coordination, for example, between the early maturers and the late maturers. Thus, developing a keen sense of observation may well be one of the key attributes for anyone who is interested in the process of child and adolescent development as teacher, theorist, and/or researcher.

REFERENCES

Adams, G. R., and Gullota, T. (1983). *Adolescent life experience.* Monterey, Calif.: Brooks-Cole.

Bailey, M. J., and Pillard, R. C. (1991). A genetic study of male sexual orientation. *Archives of General Psychiatry,* 48, 1089–1096.

Banks, M., and Salapatek, P. (1983). Infant visual perception. In P. Mussen (Ed.), *Handbook of child psychology,* Vol. 2, *Infancy and developmental psychology* (4th ed.). New York: Wiley.

Bean, B. (1990). Progenitive sex ratio among functioning sperm cells. *American Journal of Human Genetics, 47,* 351–353.

Benedict, H. (1979). Early lexical development: Comprehension and production. *Journal of Child Language, 6,* 183–200.

Bickerton, D. (1990). *Language and species.* Chicago: University of Chicago Press.

Bjorklund, D. F. (1989). *Children's thinking, developmental function and individual differences.* Pacific Grove, Calif.: Brooks-Cole.

Bond, C. T., Francis, R. C., Fernald, R. D., and Adelman, J. P. (1991). Characterization of complementary DNA encoding as the precursor for gonadotropin-releasing hormone and its associated peptide from a teleost fish. *Journal of Molecular Endocrinology, 5,* 931–937.

Brandstadter-Palmer, G. (1982). Ontogenetic growth chart. In C. Kopp and J. Krakow (Eds.), *The child.* Reading, Mass.: Addison-Wesley.

Brazelton, T. B. (1981). Clinical issues of the Brazelton Neonatal Assessment Scale. In M. Coleman (Ed.), *Neonatal neurology.* Baltimore: University Park Press.

Chomsky, N. (1980). The linguistic approach. In M. Piatelli-Palmieri (Ed.), *Language and learning.* Cambridge: Harvard University Press.

Conger, J. J., and Peterson, A. C. (1984). *Adolescence and youth* (3d ed.). New York: Harper & Row.

Cummings, J. L. (1985). *Clinical neuropsychiatry.* New York: Grune & Stratton.

Curtiss, S. (1977). *A psycholinguistic study of a modern-day wild child.* New York: Academic Press.

Damon, W. (1983). *Social and personality development: Infancy through adolescence.* New York: Norton.

DeCasper, A. J., and Fifer, W. P. (1980). Of human bonding: Newborns prefer their mother's voices. *Science, 208,* 1174–1176.

Dewsbury, D. A. (1991). Psychobiology. *American Psychologist, 46,* 198–205.

Elkind, D. (1981). *The hurried child: Growing up too fast, too soon.* Reading, Mass.: Addison-Wesley.

Galluscio, E. H. (1990). *Biological Psychology.* New York: Macmillan.

Geschwind, N. (1979). Specializations of the human brain. *Scientific American, 241,* 180–201.

Gibson, E. J., and Walk, R. D. (1960). The visual cliff. *Scientific American, 202,* 2–9.

Gottesman, L. I., and Shields, J. (1972). *Schizophrenia and genetics: A twin study vantage point.* New York: Academic Press.

Green, R. (1987). *The sissy boy syndrome and the development of homosexuality.* New Haven: Yale University Press.

Gurman, E. B., and Balban, M. (1990). Self-evaluation of physical attractiveness as a function of self-esteem and defensiveness. *Journal of Social Behavior and Personality, 5,* 575–580.

Hofferth, S. L., and Hayes, C. D. (Eds.) (1987). *Risking the future: Adolescent sexuality, pregnancy and childbearing,* Vol. 2. Washington: National Academy of Science.

Jones, M. C. (1965). Psychological correlates of somatic development. *Child Development, 36,* 899–911.

Kagan, J. (1984). *The nature of the child.* New York: Basic Books.

Kegeles, S. M., Adler, N. E., and Irvin, C. E. (1988). Sexually active adolescents and condoms: Changes over one year in knowledge, attitudes and use. *American Journal of Public Health, 78,* 460–461.

Kimble, G. A. (1990). Mother nature's bag of tricks is small. *Psychological Science, 1,* 36–41.

Kimura, D. (1986). Male brain, female brain: The hidden difference. *Psychology Today* (November), 68–75.

Kinsey, A. C., Pomeroy, W. B., Martin, C. E., and Gebhard, P. H. (1953). *Sexual behavior in the human female.* Philadelphia: Saunders.

Lagerspetz, K. (1964). *Studies on the aggressive behavior of mice.* Helsinki: Suomalainen Tiedeakatemia.

Lazarus, R. S. (1991). Cognition and motivation in emotion. *American Psychologist, 46,* 352–367.

LeVay, S. (1991). A difference in hypothalamic structures between heterosexual and homosexual men. *Science, 253,* 1034–1036.

Loehlin, J. C. (1989). Partitioning environmental and ge-netic contributions to behavioral development. *American Psychologist, 44,* 1285–1292.

Lubchenco, L. O. (1976). *The high risk infant.* Philadelphia: Saunders.

Malina, R. M. (1982). Motor development in the early years. In S. G. Moore and C. R. Cooper (Eds.), *The young child: Reviews of research, 3,* 211–230. Washington: National Association for the Education of Young Children.

Marano, H. E. (1985). Biology is one key to the bonding of mothers and babies. In H. E. Fitzgerald and M. G. Walraven (Eds.), *Human development* (pp. 85–86). Guilford, Conn.: Dushkin.

Maratsos, M. (1979). Is there language after puberty? *Contemporary Psychology, 24* (6), 456.

Maratsos, M. (1983). Some current issues in the study of the acquisition of grammar. In P. Mussen (Ed.), *Handbook of child psychology* (4th ed.), Vol. 4. New York: Wiley.

Masters, W. H., and Johnson, V. E. (1966). *Human sexual response.* Boston: Little, Brown.

Maurer, D., and Salapatek, P. (1976). Developmental changes in the scanning of faces by young infants. *Child Development, 47,* 523–527.

Nora, J. J., and Fraser, F. C. (1989). *Medical genetics: Principles and practice.* Philadelphia: Lea and Febiger.

Pillard, R., and Weinrich, J. (1987). Cited in *Psychology Today* (April), 66. Also in *Archives of General Psychiatry, 43,* 808–812.

Restak, R. (1979). *The brain: The last frontier* (p. 205). Garden City, N.Y.: Doubleday.

Richards, J., and Rader, N. (1981). Crawling-onset age predicts cliff avoidance in infants. *Journal of Experimental Psychology: Human Perception and Performance, 7,* 382–387.

Scarr, S., and Kidd, K. K. (1983). Developmental behavior genetics. In P. H. Mussen (Ed.), *Handbook of child psychology* (4th ed.). New York: Wiley.

Shirley, M. M. (1931). *The first two years: Postural and locomotor development,* Vol. I. Minneapolis: University of Minnesota Press.

Shirley, M. M. (1933). *The first two years,* Vol. III, *Personality manifestations.* Minneapolis: University of Minnesota Press.

Siegel, O. (1982). Personality development in adolescence. In B. B. Wolman (Ed.), *Handbook of developmental psychology.* Englewood Cliffs, N.J.: Prentice-Hall.

Simmons, R. G., and Blyth, D. A. (1987). *Moving into adolescence.* Hawthorne, N.Y.: Aldine.

Smolak, L. (1986). *Infancy.* Englewood Cliffs, N.J.: Prentice-Hall.

Spelt, D. K. (1948). The conditioning of the human fetus in utero. *Journal of Experimental Psychology, 38,* 338–346.

Steinberg, L., and Dornbusch, S. M. (1991). Negative correlates of part-time employment during adolescence: Replication and elaboration. *Developmental Psychology, 27,* 304–313.

Streisguth, A. P., Martin, D. C., Barr, H. M., and Sandman, B. M. (1984). Intrauterine alcohol and nicotine exposure:

Attention and reaction times in 4-year-old children. *Developmental Psychology, 20,* 533–541.

Tavris, C. (1992). *The mismeasure of women.* New York: Simon and Shuster.

Tronick, E. Z. (1989). Emotions and emotional communication in infants. *American Psychologist, 44,* 112–119.

Trotter, R. J. (1983). Baby face. *Psychology Today, 44* (August), 12–20.

Tryon, R. C. (1940). Genetic differences in maze-learning ability in rats. *Yearbook of the National Society for Studies in Education, 39,* 111–119.

Vale, J. R. (1980). *Genes, environment and behavior.* New York: Harper & Row.

Wada, J., Clarke, R., and Hamm, A. (1975). Cerebral hemispheric symmetry in humans. *Archives of Neurology, 32,* 239–246.

Walsh, C., and Cepko, C. L. (1992). Widespread dispersion of neuronal clones across functional regions of the cerebral cortex. *Science, 255,* 434–440.

Widerstrom, A. H., Mowder, B. A., and Sandall, S. R. (1991). *At risk and handicapped newborns and infants.* Englewood Cliffs, N.J.: Prentice-Hall.

Wilson, J. A. R., Robeck, M. C., and Michael, W. B. (1969). *Psychological foundations of learning and teaching* (pp. 188–189). New York: McGraw-Hill.

Wimer, R. E., and Wimer, C. C. (1985). Animal behavior genetics: A search for the biological foundations of behavior. *Annual Review of Psychology, 36,* 171–218.

Zelazo, P. R., and Barr, R. G. (1989). Do challenges to developmental paradigms compel changes in practice? An introduction. In P. R. Zelazo and R. Barr (Eds.), *Challenges to developmental paradigms: Implications for theory, assessment and treatment.* Hillsdale, N.J.: Erlbaum.

4

EARLY EXPERIENCE

"As the twig is bent, so grows the tree." "You can't teach an old dog new tricks." "Train them during their formative years." These statements and others like them attest to the fact that we have long recognized the significance of early experience for growth and development. Yet it is only within this century that we have come to appreciate how important **early experience** really is. It is also only recently that we have begun to recognize in how many ways our psychological and physical beings are affected by the amount and quality of our early experience.

It is true that psychologists have for some time recognized the importance of early experience for emotional growth. Freud, for example, wrote many papers at the turn of the century indicating that personality development is a product of one's childhood. Many educators agreed with this, and special schools were designed to enhance emotional and personal growth during those crucial years. In England, A. S. Neill established **Summerhill,** a boarding school at which the major emphasis was on encouraging healthy emotional adjustment (Neill, 1969). At Summerhill every student participates in school and curriculum decisions. No classes, books, or exams are required. Free expression of ideas and talent is encouraged, and only minimal restraints are placed on the children in all areas of their lives. There are many

schools like Summerhill throughout the world, and it is safe to say that most schools today, not just the Summerhills, have been influenced to some degree by this alternative to the traditional, more authoritarian approach to education.

The point is that as psychologists learn more about human development, educators do respond accordingly—and sometimes too zealously. An indiscriminate embracing of a new theory may produce a curriculum that emphasizes one particular area at the expense of other important areas. For example, it has been seriously argued that the Summerhills may be nurturing emotional growth at the expense of intellectual growth.

Despite the fact that for many years now early experience has been considered critical in shaping emotional development, it wasn't until much later that psychologists began to recognize the importance of these same early years on intellectual development.

EARLY EXPERIENCE: THE KEY TO THE NATURE-NURTURE PUZZLE

The nature-nurture question remained unresolved for many years because the issue was stated as an either/or proposition: The hereditarians emphasized heredity at the expense of environment, and the environmentalists emphasized environment at the expense of heredity. Neither side fully recognized the importance of the third dimension, time. Development is a result of heredity interacting with environment, but a key question remains: Is there a critical or best time for the interaction to take place?

With regard to imprinting, it must be remembered that goslings learn to follow the moving stimulus only if the stimulus is presented during a certain critical time of their lives: from about ten to thirty hours after hatching. Presenting the stimulus thirty-five or forty hours after hatching is no good—no learning occurs. It is obvious that this form of learning requires a hereditary potential as well as an environmental encounter. But which is more important? In fact, neither matters at all until we mix in the third ingredient, the time at which the encounter occurs. If it happens too soon, no learning or minimal learning occurs, and the same is true if the encounter is too late.

Two Studies of the Critical Time Hypothesis

A number of years ago, a forward-looking psychologist, Myrtle McGraw, did a comprehensive study of human development, using a pair of twin boys as subjects (McGraw, 1935). One of the twins, Johnny, was given a great amount of early training in a wide variety of activities. The other twin, Jimmy, was given no practice in these activities until months later.

McGraw found that special, early practice had little or no effect on some behaviors, such as creeping, hanging by the hands, grasping objects, or even walking. Though Johnny was given stepping practice almost from birth, both twins took their first halting steps alone at nine months and both learned to walk almost simultaneously at twelve months. McGraw called behaviors such as these *phylogenetic acitivities* and concluded that they are not influenced very much by the environment or by special practice. However, with regard to certain special skills that McGraw called *ontogenetic activities*, the trained twin, Johnny, learned faster than his brother. Johnny began learning to roller-skate when he was twelve months old, just when he was learning to walk, and by fourteen months he was both skating and walking with considerable grace. Jimmy did not begin skating lessons until he was twenty-two months old, and he did not profit nearly as much from this late training. McGraw found that delaying the training made it more diffi-

cult to learn this skill. The development of other motor skills, however, was actually damaged by early training. Johnny was given special training in tricycling when he was eleven months old and displayed little progress until he was about nineteen or twenty months old, when he suddenly improved rather dramatically. Jimmy began tricycling when he was twenty-two months old, learned the skill quickly and efficiently, and became superior to his pretrained brother. The twin with the early training formed poor habits and was unable to develop the skill as well as the twin whose training was delayed.

McGraw concluded that there are optimal time periods during development when special training will assure the full acquisition of various motor skills. Said McGraw, "There are critical periods when any given activity is most susceptible to modification through repetition of performance" (McGraw, 1939, p. 3).

McGraw's research was carried out many years ago, but her insights into human development placed

There are critical, optimal periods when children can most easily be taught certain motor skills. For example, it is best to teach a child to roller-skate at the same time he or she is learning to walk. However, development of some motor skills is actually retarded by early training.

The teachable moment and readiness are central to the problems of growth.

group of two-year-olds was given the training for only one week, the last week of the experiment. The children in the second group, older and presumably more mature when their training began, initially learned these tasks more quickly than did the other group, but they never fully caught up. The group with the early (and longer) training maintained superiority at the experiment's end (Hilgard, 1932). Josephine Hilgard, Josie to her friends, died in 1989, but as was recently written, "she will endure in the hearts and minds of those who were fortunate enough to have been touched by her life" (Bowers, 1990).

A great deal of research remains to be done in this important area. At this point there are few hard data to indicate precisely when the various critical periods occur. We do know, however, that critical periods generally coincide with the periods of most rapid growth. John P. Scott has defined the critical period as a "time when a large effect can be produced by a smaller change in conditions than in any later or earlier period in life." Scott further states that "there must be changes taking place within the animal which are correlated with time and hence account for the existence of critical periods" (Scott, 1968, p. 68). Thus, the concept of critical periods has profound importance in education. We must hope to catch the child at exactly that time when environmental encounters will most effectively allow his or her hereditary potential to flourish. Damage can be done, impairment can occur, if we are either too early or too late.

her far ahead of her time. She died in 1988, but her legacy lives on. It was said recently that her passion for truth and the truth-seeking process were the primary dedications in her life (Lipsitt, 1990). She was the first psychologist to speak of **critical periods** in human development, and although her views were not widely accepted during the heyday of American behaviorism, they now have a modern ring. In child-rearing she advocated a middle road between constantly urging the child to practice new activities and just sitting back, relaxing, and allowing nature to take its own sweet time. Forcing children into activities before the critical period, when their nerves and muscles are simply not ready, is not only useless but, more important, may even be damaging.

In another classic study, Josephine R. Hilgard provided a special twelve-week practice period for a group of two-year-old children on such motor tasks as stair climbing and cutting with scissors. Another

EARLY EXPERIENCE: OBSERVATIONS AND THEORIES

The Berkeley Growth Study

Nancy Bayley, another in the tradition of brilliant female psychologists specializing in growth and development, and her colleagues at the University of California, Berkeley, began a long-term project known as the *Studies in the Development of Young Children*. This was a longitudinal research study in that the same subjects were followed and continually tested over the years. Actually, data are still being collected on the original group of subjects, all of whom are now approximately in their midseventies (Bayley, 1940). Although the study has contributed vast amounts of new data and fresh insights on the flow of human development, we will focus on only four specific observations at this time.

NANCY BAYLEY

Nancy Bayley was the first woman ever to win the American Psychological Association's prestigious Distinguished Scientific Contribution award. Bayley received this recognition in 1966, and her citation included the following: "For the enterprise, pertinacity and insight with which she has studied human growth over long segments of the life cycle. . . . Her studies have enriched psychology with enduring contributions to the measurement and meaning of intelligence. . . . Her participation in a number of major programs of developmental research is a paradigm of the conjoint efforts which are essential in a field whose problems span the generations."[a]

Nancy Bayley was born in 1899 in a small town, called the Dallas, near the northern border of Oregon. She attended local schools there and went on to earn her B.S. and M.A. degrees from the University of Washington. She received her Ph.D. in psychology from Iowa State in 1926, just two years after completing her M.A. degree. For the next two years, she taught at the University of Wyoming, and in 1928 began teaching at the University of California at Berkeley. During the following year she began her famous longitudinal Berkeley Growth Study, starting with sixty-one healthy newborn infants. Testing and retesting this group over the years, both psychologically and physically, she produced many fresh and startling insights into the complex phenomenon of human growth.

In 1954 Bayley left Berkeley to become chief of the child development section at the National Institute of Mental Health in Bethesda, Maryland, but periodically returned to Berkeley to locate and test her sample subjects for the Berkeley Growth Study. In 1964 she returned to Berkeley to serve both as the administrator of the newly formed Harold E. Jones Child Study Center and as a research psychologist at the University of California. She retired in 1971.

In addition to being selected as the American Psychological Association's Distinguished Scientist, Nancy Bayley won the G. Stanley Hall award in 1971, a special award presented by the American Psychological Association's Division of Developmental Psychology. She has contributed nearly one-hundred scientific publications so far, and it is clear that as her 1929 sample continues to ripen and mature, it will continue to enrich psychology's book of knowledge.

[a] *American Psychologist*, 1966, p. 1191.

1. *IQs are not constant:* Bayley's results have challenged the belief cherished by some psychologists that one's IQ score is immutable. Bayley found considerable variation in measured intelligence over long periods of time; in other words, the IQ score is not indelibly carved in the brain at birth but is instead a human quality that ebbs and flows as a result of environmental circumstances (Jones et al., 1971).

2. *IQ variability is greatest during the first few years of life:* By comparing correlations between IQs measured at various ages, Bayley found that the older the child, the greater the IQ stability. This evidence foreshadowed the main thrust of Benjamin Bloom's hypothesis, to be discussed in the next section.

3. *Intellectual ability may continue to grow throughout life:* Bayley's data also indicate that intellectual ability does not top out in the late teens or early twenties but may continue to increase at least up to age fifty, when Bayley's subjects were last tested. Again, whether an adult's intellect grows or declines seems to be a function of environmental stimulation. The high school dropout who spends all his or her working life bagging groceries in a supermarket is less apt to experience intellectual growth than someone who works in areas requiring more strenuous mental exercise. More recent research has validated Bayley's ideas in this area. Older adults who remain intellectually curious and active typically maintain a high level of cognitive functioning (Datan, Rodeheaver, and Hughes, 1987).

SPOTLIGHT ON GROWTH

Identifying Trends with the Microgenetic Method

One problem with the research methods used in developmental studies, whether longitudinal or cross-sectional, is that although they can show—usually in broad brush strokes—the general age ranges for the growth of various physical and cognitive skills, they often miss the precise timing of these changes. As we have seen over and over again, development proceeds in fits and starts, not as a single straight line. To really catch those critical periods when, as J. P. Scott has emphasized, the smallest input produces the richest gains, new research strategies are coming on stream. One such recent approach, called the *microgenetic method*, homes in on a short period of time, often only several weeks, but then studies this period intensively to find out exactly when the developmental breakthroughs occur. Rather than taking a few static snapshots at various points in the child's life, the microgenetic approach takes many reels of film over a short time period.[a] For example, although it has generally been known that the acquisition of binocular depth perception occurs in infants sometime between the ages of twelve and twenty-four weeks, microgenetic methods have been able to establish that virtually all of that development occurs within a time span of only one or two weeks.[b]

[a] Siegler, R. S., and Crowley, K. (1991). The microgenetic method: A direct means for studying cognitive development. *American Psychologist, 46,* 606–820.
[b] Shimojo, S., Bauer, J., O'Connell, K. M., and Held, R. (1986). Prestereoscopic binocular vision in infants. *Vision Research, 26,* 501–510.

4. *The components of intellect change with age level:* Perhaps Nancy Bayley's most provocative contribution is her suggestion that intellectual development in childhood occurs in qualitatively different stages. In her view, the fact that a child's growth score gradually shifts in strength from area to area supports the notion that changes occur in the organization of intellectual factors from one age to another. This view is consistent with that of Jean Piaget, to be presented in the next chapter.

Bloom's Hypothesis

Benjamin Bloom (1964) in a classic book has analyzed, sorted, and sifted through virtually all the studies on intellectual growth. Bloom plots a **negatively accelerated growth curve** for intellectual development—that is, with increasing age, there is a decreasingly positive effect from a beneficial environment. Three-year-old children profit far more from enriching experiences than seven- or eight-year-old children. Bloom argues that beneficial early experience is absolutely essential for cognitive growth. Almost two-thirds of our ultimate cognitive ability is formed by the time we are six years old, the age, incidentally, when most children are just entering school. By the time formal education begins, the child's potential for further intellectual development is beginning to slow. Earlier intervention is required, especially among disadvantaged groups. Experience has its most profound effect very early in life, during the period of most rapid growth.

This finding is consistent with Scott's argument regarding critical periods. Scott feels that critical periods occur when rapid organization of some kind is going on within the individual. Those mental changes that take place during a period of rapid development often occur easily and accidentally and then become a fixed and fairly permanent feature of the newly stabilized organization. Scott also reasons that any time we form new relationships, especially social relationships, can be a critical period for that relationship. Since most new relationships occur in early childhood, this is when most critical periods should occur. However, major new relationships also take place in adolescence and in adulthood. One of the most important critical periods, in fact, often occurs during adolescence, when young people may form their first sexual relationships. The sexual problems an adult suffers are probably the result of events happening during adolescence. Another major critical period may take place during adulthood, when many women bear their first child; and this may be a critical period for both parents.

Bloom concludes that not only does lack of an enriched environment itself hinder a child's intellectual development, but the loss of precious time is especially harmful because there is no way to compensate for it later on. Just as in the case of Konrad Lorenz's goslings, there may be critical periods for intellectual development: Once the period is over, new stimuli have less and less effect.

Stimulus Variety: The Basic Ingredient

J. McV. Hunt reviewed the literature on early experience and reported that early stimulus deprivation is more likely to prevent normal motor development than early motor restriction (Hunt, 1969). For example, Hopi children who are reared on cradleboards, which almost completely inhibit their movements, walk as early as Hopi children reared with full use of their legs. Thus, as far as walking is concerned, early motor restriction does not seem seriously to affect later motor development. However, the effect of early stimulus restriction is, as Hunt points out, dramatically different.

Not only is early stimulus deprivation damaging to later intellectual development, but it also appears to impair later motor development. Wayne Dennis discovered an orphanage in Teheran where the children were kept in a condition of extreme isolation, each one living in a separate, almost soundproof, white cubicle (Dennis, 1960). The result of this severe sensory restriction was that virtually all the children were mentally retarded, despite the fact that they came almost exclusively from the literate population of Iran. This, of course, is further evidence that intellectual development is a function of both environment and heredity. But the most remarkable finding of the Dennis study is that those stimulus-deprived children who had complete motor freedom were also physically retarded. Sixty percent of the children were unable to sit up alone when they were two years old, and 85 percent could not walk when they were four years old. Compare this with the cradleboard-reared Hopi children. Hunt points out that "these Hopi children reared on cradleboards were often carried about on their mothers' backs. Thus, while their arms and legs might be restricted, their eyes and ears could feast upon a rich variety of input" (Hunt, 1969, p. 52).

As Hunt has been insisting for many years, the crucial ingredient in intellectual development is stimulus variety. The more the child hears, sees, and touches, the more the child will *want* to hear, see, and touch, and the more intellectual growth will occur. Motivation can therefore be generated from experience. However, Hunt is careful to advocate against suddenly overwhelming the child with stimulus variety. In what he calls the "problem of the match," Hunt points out that the variety of inputs must somehow be matched with the child's present level of growth. Too much stimulus heterogeneity, and the child withdraws in frustration; too little, and the child withdraws in boredom. Hunt tells us that there is a level of optimum variety of stimulus that children naturally seek; when this is reached, children display a joy, a spontaneous interest in learning, and continued cognitive growth. This is very similar to **Lev Vygotsky's** concept of the zone of proximal development, that some challenge is needed for maximizing intellectual development. The **zone of proximal development** is the distance between one's present developmental level and the level of potential future development (Vygotsky, 1978).

This growth can be seen in a variety of areas, including language acquisition. In studying the rate of a child's language development as a function of the amount and complexity of maternal speech, it has been found that those children who are the quickest in developing language skills have mothers who spend the most time speaking directly to them (Smolak, 1983). However, the complexity of maternal speech has to be moderated and matched to the child's language level. Although maternal speech should be complex enough to challenge the child, too much complexity can overwhelm the child, and may even delay language development (Gleitman et al., 1984).

It is important to emphasize that Hunt and others are not implying that intelligence is fixed, nor that stimulus variety must be matched with innate potential. Quite the contrary! Intellectual abilities grow and are nourished by stimulus variety. The match is between stimulus inputs and the child's present position on the growth continuum, a position that itself results in large measure from the child's own past experiences and environmental encounters. These encounters begin at birth. There is even evidence that some learning takes place before birth, while the fetus is still in the uterus (Spelt, 1948). In another fascinating study of this type, babies whose mothers had read a certain passage to them during the last six weeks of pregnancy, showed a decided preference

Bruner insists that a variety of stimuli and a changing environment are necessary for proper cognitive growth.

for those same word sounds when tested after they were born (DeCasper and Spence, 1986).

Bruner on Early Experience

Jerome Bruner, the great Harvard theorist, and one of the very first American psychologists to adopt a cognitive point of view, also stresses the importance of early experience. Bruner maintains that cognitive growth depends on a process of model formation: the creation of rules and strategies for coping with the environment. As children develop, they should learn various techniques that will enable them to make maximum use of the information their environments provide. Bruner insists, however, that for proper cognitive growth to occur, the young child must be exposed to a **variety of stimuli,** a shifting environment. Stimulus heterogeneity at an early age is the critical condition for continued cognitive growth (Bruner, 1969).

Piaget on Early Experience

Like Bruner, Piaget (See Chapter 5 and the biography on page 100) is also a strong supporter of the early-experience school of thought, and tells us that the developing child is analogous in many ways to a scientist performing experiments on the physical world and personally discovering the principles of mathematical and physical reasoning. That is, Piaget viewed the young child as *acting* on a rather *passive* environment. However, the more environmental encounters, especially during the first few years of life, the richer the cognitive stage becomes. Some more recent cognitive theories take a more social approach and view the child as similar to an apprentice, learning through participation in problem-solving tasks under the tutelage of more skilled members of society (Rogoff, 1990). And just as the skilled tutor can affect the development of the child, so too can the child's responses alter the behavior of the tutor. Thus, the focus is increasingly on the *interactive* nature of the social contexts and on the manner in which they might be changed by the growing child (Winegar, 1989).

THE BIOLOGICAL BASIS OF EARLY EXPERIENCE

Now that we have seen that psychologists such as Scott, Bloom, Hunt, and Bruner have all pointed to the importance of early experience in determining intellectual level, the questions that follow might logically be: What is the biological basis for this argument? Are there corresponding physiological changes taking place as a result of a beneficial early environment?

The eminent physiological psychologist **Donald O. Hebb** has outlined a theoretical model of the organization of neural activity in the brain (Hebb, 1949). Hebb contends that this organization depends on environmental stimulation, that proper development of the neural arrangements in the brain will not occur unless the developing organism has the opportunity to experience environmental changes.

The A/S Ratio

Hebb noted that there were significant differences among organisms in the proportion of association and sensory areas within the brain. Compared to the human, a lower organism such as a rat has fewer association areas and more sensory areas. Thus, the rat, that workhorse of American psychology, is more sensory-bound, more responsive to the stimuli in its environment than is the human. The human brain, with its greater number of association areas, is capable of far more and probably many different varieties of learning than the rat brain. Also, the relatively small sensory area makes the human less a creature of the moment, less apt to respond impulsively to every minute environmental change. It also means that as we go up the phylogenetic continuum, as the ratio of association areas to sensory areas **(A/S ratio)** increases, the developmental importance of pronounced stimulus heterogeneity also increases. Humans, after all, cannot perceive subtle changes in odor as well as some of the lower primates are able to.

Hebb emphasized the critical importance of early experience on later development, especially on cognitive development. Hebb saw the human brain as unorganized and capable of only relatively simple forms of learning during infancy and early childhood. As the child experiences more and more environmental stimulation, the brain slowly becomes organized. A group of neurons begins to work as a unit. Hebb called this organized pattern of brain cells a **cell assembly.** With the formation of a variety of cell assemblies, new learning takes place more quickly. As this process continues, as more cell assemblies are formed, a larger organization takes place: A series of cell assemblies, called *phase sequences*, are formed. Finally, as the phase sequences begin acting in concert, wide-spread organization of the brain results, and the child is now capable of extremely rapid learning. The difference between a young child in the cell-assembly stage slowly and painstakingly learning a simple task, and an older child, with a series of smooth-functioning, integrated phase sequences already formed, quickly learning complex relationships and concepts, is similar to the difference between a do-it-yourself carpenter and an experienced prefab team. The do-it-yourself carpenter, to borrow an analogy (Bugelski, 1964), could take months to construct a home that the professional crew could complete in days.

Based on Hebb's hypothesis of cell assemblies and phase sequences, researchers at McGill University compared the performance of animals of enriched early experience with animals of impoverished early experience. The McGill researchers wanted to determine whether organisms provided with stimulus variety during the early period of cell assemblies would reflect this early enrichment in their performance as adults. The researchers found what they were looking for.

Using the Hebb-Williams maze, a kind of animal IQ test, Hebb compared rats raised in the impoverished environment of laboratory cages with rats raised in the home as pets, and found the home-reared animals superior. Other investigators found an even greater difference when they performed the same experiment using dog littermates (Thompson and Heron, 1954). The results of this study also favored the home-reared pets, lending further support to the suggestion that as we go up the phylogenetic continuum (as we select species with higher A/S ratios), the beneficial effects of an enriched early environment increase.

Hebb is certain that the results are precisely the same at the human level. Children who are raised up to the age of six in impoverished slum environments never fully make up for this crucial intellectual deficit. The lack of stimulus variety early in a child's life cannot be adequately compensated for by later enrichment "because such damage is not reparable" (Hebb, 1978, p. 1143).

The Evidence from Krech

More direct and even more startling evidence supporting the early-experience position has been supplied by the exciting and innovative research of David Krech (1969). It had been shown that certain drugs, such as Metrazol, may increase an organism's ability to learn, and that other drugs, such as magnesium pemoline, may increase the organism's ability to retain what has been learned (Grosser et al., 1967). Krech reasoned, however, that the reverse might also be true—that is, if chemical agents could effect changes in the learning process, then environmental manipulation might bring about changes in the chemistry of the brain. By selecting twelve pairs of rat twins and randomly assigning them to two groups, Krech was able to control for possible genetic differences. One group of rats was raised in a stimulating environment, in a cage equipped with ladders, running wheels, and other rat toys. These animals were let out of their cages for thirty minutes each day and allowed to explore new territory. They were also trained to perform numerous learning tasks and in general received a rich and varied array of stimulus inputs. The other group of rats was raised in a condition of extreme stimulus homogeneity. These rats lived alone in dimly lit cages, were rarely handled, and were never allowed to explore areas outside the cage. All animals, however, received exactly the same diet.

After about three months all the animals were sacrificed and their brains analyzed morphologically and chemically. If Hebb's theory were valid, the brains of the stimulated animals—the animals that had been exposed to a wide variety of learning situations—would be anatomically different from the brains of the deprived animals. That is, if the act of learning does indeed form neural cell assemblies and phase sequences, there might be some physical evidence for this in the brains of the stimulated rats. In fact, Krech may have supplied the evidence. The brains of the enriched rats were chemically and structurally different from the brains of their siblings. The cortex (gray matter) was larger, deeper, and heavier in the stimulated rats. Three components have been identified as contributing to this increase in brain size: (1) an increased number of glia cells (possible repositories of memory traces), (2) increased size of the cell bodies and their nuclei, and (3) an increase in the diameter of the blood vessels supplying the cortex.

Chemically, the brains also differed. The brains of the enriched animals showed greater quantities of an important enzyme—acetylcholinesterase—an enzyme that readies the nerve cells for further neural transmissions. Krech has thus demonstrated that providing stimulus and response variety during the early life of these animals caused chemical and structural changes in their brains and increased their ability to

learn and to solve problems. In a very real sense he may have identified some of the physiological correlates of Hebb's constructs.

Environmental Stimulation for Physiological Development

It is now clear that for proper physiological development to occur, environmental stimulation is necessary; the nervous system and the perceptual apparatus do not mature automatically according to some preset internal clock.

Critics of the early-experience position often fall back on the neurological argument that since no new brain cells are added after birth, the central nervous system must remain unchanged, with or without environmental stimulation. They argue that the baby comes into the world with a full complement of typical brain cells and that, since no new cells are added, the baby must make do with the original equipment. However, as Krech has shown, the way this original equipment is organized and modified is definitely a function of environmental interactions. Krech proved that structural and chemical changes within the brain resulted from the type of early experience provided.

Further evidence comes from the exciting research of Joseph Altman (1967). Altman has challenged the traditional view that newborn children have all the brain cells they will ever get. Altman has found that tiny nerve cells (microneurons) do arise in the brains of young animals after birth. These newly discovered tiny neurons apparently provide interconnections for some of the larger, more typical brain cells.

Neurons send out branches—axons and dendrites—so that the neural impulse can travel from one neuron to the next (see Figure 4.1). The junction between the axon of one neuron and the dendrite of the next is called the *synapse*. The neuron sends a message out along one axon, and the dendrite of the next neuron picks up the message at the synapse. Often, the dendrite, the receiving branch, sends out a physical projection called a *dendritic spine*. This is something like adding another length to your TV antenna in order to get a better picture. Neurologists have found, however, that if these synapses are not used, the dendritic spines wither away and finally disappear. If a synapse is used frequently, new dendritic spines appear.

With increased practice the actual physical structures of the synaptic endings become altered, making them more likely to transmit their neural messages.

FIGURE 4.1 Neural impulses travel from one neuron to the next along the branches—the axons and dendrites—of the neuron.

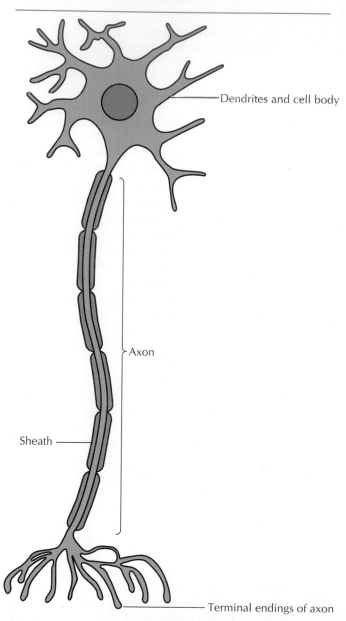

- Dendrites and cell body
- Axon
- Sheath
- Terminal endings of axon

(Sokolov, 1977). It's as though the size and complexity of the antenna were a function of how often the TV set was used. It has also been found that sensory apparatus must be stimulated by the environment in order to develop properly. Neurons on the retina of the eye may become damaged unless they are given visual stimulation.

And what is behaviorism's answer to this wave of evidence in support of enriched early experience?

Skinner's Air Crib— Healthful but Unstimulating

The late B. F. Skinner, still the world's most influential behaviorist, in an article entitled, "Skinner Agrees He Is the Most Important Influence in Psychology," urged parents to raise their children in his invention, the air crib. The *air crib* is an "air-conditioned, temperature-controlled, germ-free, sound-proof compartment in which the baby can sleep and play without blankets or clothing other than a diaper" (Rice, 1968, p. 27). While in this cubicle, the baby is less likely to catch cold or to suffer from heat rash. However, the air crib, or "Heir Conditioner" as Skinner also once called it, puts the baby in a constant environment and may not provide the enriching variety of stimulus inputs so important to intellectual development. By the time the baby outgrows the air crib, it may be too late to compensate for this early deprivation.

HEAD START'S SUCCESS: PERRY PRESCHOOL PROGRAM

You may be wondering what all these studies of children raised on cradleboards, rats raised in enriched environment, chimps raised in darkness, and so on have to do with the intellectual growth of children. What proof do we have that these theories and studies have any validity in the real world of the schoolchild? Hasn't the early-experience theory been tested, for example in the **Head Start** program, and been found wanting?

In fact, Head Start was deemed a failure almost from its inception. The Westinghouse Learning Corporation and Ohio University released a highly critical evaluation of Head Start as early as 1969, only four years after the first Head Start program was put into effect. Later, there was general agreement with such statements as H. M. Levin's (1977), that "good preschool programs are able to produce salutary increases in IQ for disadvantaged children, but these improvements *are not maintained* when the children enter the primary grades." New evidence suggests that the critics may have spoken too soon.

The Head Start Synthesis Project of 1983, an analysis of outcomes from virtually all Head Start programs up to that time, found that they were indeed effective, that Head Start could be isolated as a causal variable in improving intellectual performance (Hubbell, 1983). In fact, for Head Start the news gets even better. The report showed that Head Start programs

Skinner's daughter Debbie is shown here in the air crib he invented.

have produced improvements over the years, in terms both of the intellectual gains found when the children entered regular school and, more important, in the tendency of those gains to persist.

The **Perry Preschool Program** of Ypsilanti, Michigan, has reported the results of a longitudinal study of Head Start participants who have been followed over the years from ages three and four to age nineteen (Berrueta-Clement et al., 1984). This Head Start program was repeated each year for five successive groups of entering children. The evidence presented here is based on the first two entering groups, those that began in the early 1960s.

The main finding, in brief, is that Head Start has dramatic long-term effectiveness and that a quality preschool program can change the lives of low-income, educationally at-risk children and their families.

Design of the Study

The Perry Preschool Program was set up as a true experimental design, with random assignment of matched subjects to the experimental group (who received the preschool program) or to the control group (who received no preschool program). The subjects, 123 black youths from families of low socioeconomic status, all had normal to below-normal Stanford-Binet IQs, that is, from 60 to 90, and none showed signs of organic handicap.

The children in the experimental group participated in the program for two school years at ages three and four, and the children *in both groups*, experimental and control, received the same schedule of comparison tests and interviews (ruling out continuing evaluations as a confounding variable). Classes for the experimental group ran for two and a half hours each morning, Monday through Friday, from October to May. Teachers (there was one teacher for every five children) also visited the homes of all their students for one and a half hours weekly, meeting with both mother and child together. Each mother was, therefore, kept aware of her child's progress, and the resources of the mother were strengthened in the hope that the child's development would be aided by the mother during after-school hours.

The curriculum for the program was especially designed to provide a wide variety of stimulus inputs without overwhelming the child. Hunt's "problem of the match" was of vital concern to the framers of the curriculum, but, in their words, "program effectiveness is much more dependent upon the overall quality of program operations than on a specific curriculum" (Berrueta-Clement et al., 1984, p. 108).

Outcomes of the Study

Although the experimental and control groups were repeatedly measured over the years, the outcome data to follow are based on the most recent measures, taken when the participants had reached age nineteen.

Increased school success   Those subjects who had attended the preschool program showed a significant increase in overall school success, as measured by a number of key factors:

1. Better academic grades

2. Fewer failing marks

3. Fewer absences in elementary school

4. Fewer special-education placements

5. Higher scores on the Adult Performance Level (APL) Survey, a standardized test developed by the American College Testing Program for assessing the skills needed for educational and economic success in modern society

6. Greater likelihood of graduating from high school

7. Greater likelihood of continuing their education after high school

8. A more favorable attitude toward high school (a particularly important finding, since it points to the fact that early childhood education increases the efficiency of later schooling).

IQ differences   Although preschool participants in the Perry Program showed significantly higher Stanford-Binet IQs on entering first grade, the difference narrowed by the time the children reached fourth grade. It may very well be that ages three and four are too late to effect dramatic IQ improvement, but not too late to provide the enrichment for disadvantaged children to do better in school in the long run.

Socioeconomic success   Those who participated in the preschool program generally showed marked increases in socioeconomic success at age nineteen, as measured by two factors: (1) increased employment and (2) less reliance on welfare, food stamps, or other assistance programs.

Social responsibility   Another long-lasting consequence of the Perry Program was an increase in social responsibility. Those who participated in Head Start were found to have (1) fewer police arrests, both as juveniles and as adults; (2) fewer out-of-wedlock pregnancies; and (3) greater desire to undertake helping activities for family and friends, such as cooking meals, mowing lawns, making repairs around the house, and caring for children.

A Good Investment for Society

From these data the study's principal investigators build a strong case for the cost effectiveness of the preschool program. The cost of the Head Start program to the taxpayer is more than compensated for by the reduction in the later costs of special education, welfare, and, especially, the lower costs associated with crime, both to the state and to the potential victims. For a small upfront investment, society can reap enormous and recurring dividends in later years.

Finally, as Table 4.1 shows, in an analysis of seven separate longitudinal studies on the effects of preschool programs, Lawrence Schweinhart (1984) reports that the documented effects of early childhood education show the following outcomes:

TABLE 4.1   THE SEVEN STUDIES: PROGRAM INFORMATION

STUDY	BEGINNING AGE OF CHILD	PROGRAM DURATION IN YEARS	PROGRAM FOR CHILDREN	PROGRAM FOR PARENTS
Milwaukee	3–6 months	6	Full-time Year-round	Educational/ vocational
Perry Preschool	3 or 4 years	2 or 1	Part-time	Weekly Home visits
New York Pre-K	4 years	1	Part-time	Opportunities for classroom involvement
Rome Head Start	5 years	1	Part-time Jan–Aug	Opportunities for classroom involvement
Early Training	3 or 4 years	3 or 2	Part-time In summer	Weekly home visits during school year
Mother-Child Home	2 or 3 years	2	Twice-weekly Home visits	Twice-weekly Home visits
Harlem	2 or 3 years	1	Twice-weekly 1:1 sessions	No separate program

From J. R. Berrueta-Clement, L. J. Schweinhart, W. S. Barnett, A. S. Epstein, and D. P. Weikart. *Changed lives: The effects of the Perry Preschool Program on youths through age 19* (Ypsilanti, Mich.: High/Scope Press, 1984), p. 99. Used with permission.

Early childhood—improved IQ scores

Elementary school—better scholastic placement (fewer children in special education) and improved academic achievement

Adolescence—less delinquency, higher rates of high school graduation, and high rates of employment following high school (Schweinhart, 1984).

In another study of the effects of Head Start, conducted among black children in New Jersey and Oregon, it was found that although the immediate advantages in cognitive and analytic skills following exposure to the program were powerful, the effects tended to diminish over time. For example, follow-up tests conducted on the children showed that although the Head Start children maintained educationally substantive gains, the effects were not as large as those found immediately following the intervention (Lee et al., 1990). This lessening of the effect was interpreted as being due to the fact that the Head Start children, typically the poorest of the poor, usually go to the lowest socioeconomic public schools, and are likely to receive less favorable treatment in such

schools (resulting in reduced learning opportunities). And we cannot expect, as Zigler has said, to completely inoculate children in only one year against all the ravages of an early childhood of deprivation (Zigler, 1987).

The Milwaukee Project

The **Milwaukee Project** attempted to stimulate the cognitive growth of children by providing systematic and structured training to low-IQ slum children. This training began early, almost from the child's birth. Staff members began their interventions as soon as mother and child returned home from the hospital.

In 1981 the project directors reported that the significant IQ differences between the children involved in the program and a control group of children not enrolled was being sustained in favor of the preschool group, at least up to age ten (Garber and Heber, 1981).

It is now fairly certain that early experience is one of the key ingredients in cognitive growth. Had we known this years ago, the disparity between the "good" and "bad" Kallikaks might have been avoided.

SPOTLIGHT ON EARLY EXPERIENCE

The First Three Years

One of today's most influential members of the early-experience position is Harvard psychologist Burton White. White has long contended that intellectual and psychological competence are largely determined during a very brief time span in the individual's life, the first three years.[a] Even that may be too broad an age-range category, since White is convinced that the critical period for proper psychological growth may actually occur during the first eight to eighteen months of the baby's life. Growth during the first eight months seems to take care of itself, for early development is so heavily influenced by biological factors that, aside from normal care, there is little the mother can do either to arrest or facilitate this physiological process. From ages eight to eighteen months, however, environmental encounters become absolutely crucial, and here White focuses on the role of the mother, whose personal resources are so important to the infant's later cognitive and emotional growth.

Mothers of competent children are alert and responsive to their infant's needs without being overly intrusive. The competent mother provides reassurance, guidance, and attention whenever the child needs this kind of encouragement, but does not needlessly intervene just to prove to herself that she's a super mother. Although White suggests that the child be provided with suitable toys and materials in the home, he firmly believes that the real key to sound growth is based on the quality of the child's interpersonal exchanges, especially with the mother. Finally, White even instructs mothers to encourage their children to adopt a certain amount of competitiveness by exposing the child to competitive situations where there is no implication of punishment.

---

[a] White, B. L. (1975). *The first three years*. Englewood Cliffs, N.J.: Prentice-Hall.

The Critics Speak

Critics of the early-experience school of thought have not been quiet. **Richard Herrnstein** has argued that if we do provide a uniformly beneficial environment for a number of children, we will simply make intelligence more susceptible to hereditary influence than it would otherwise be (Herrnstein, 1971). Thus, according to Herrnstein, society should not expend either its funds or its energy in attempting to improve the lot of its poor or its black citizenry. As one incredulous reader of Herrnstein's account phrased it:

> It is this present, imperfect society that Herrnstein, in the end, urges upon his black fellow citizens. They should abandon their agitation for equality lest they win the self-defeating victory that would expose the poverty of their genetic endowment. In sum, they should stop reminding us of their accusing presence (Piel, 1975, p. 458).

Admittedly, individual differences could in no way be caused by a uniform environment; whatever individual differences do arise have to be due to heredity. It should be added, however, that a uniformly bad environment would do exactly the same, that is, make all the individual differences in intelligence the outcome of hereditary influences. But in the first instance, the IQs would fluctuate around a high average value, while in the second, the IQs would scatter around a low average value. Surely it would be more pleasant for the children themselves, and more beneficial to society in general, to let heredity decide differences among high IQs than among low ones (Grosser and Sprinthall, 1972).

A related theory argues that the "bottom half is always below average." Thus, or so the theory proclaims, if all intelligence quotients are raised by improved educational techniques, the lower class would still be at the bottom of the social order, and nobody's social status would be changed. This argument implies that society need not try to help the lower class by improving educational opportunities, for the result would only be to freeze present social arrangements. This requires comment.

A large factor in social status is occupation. Limitations of intelligence disqualify an individual from ever becoming a good engineer, physician, or attorney, for example. We might think of a threshold IQ for each occupation. With a very high intelligence one has all the intellectual requirements for being everything from a ditchdigger to an engineer. With a very low intelligence one cannot qualify for high- or middle-status occupations. Therefore, the higher the IQ, the more occupations the individual is qualified to fill. But here we arrive at an interesting point. When we consider IQ—the sheer ability to perform a given task—as an occupational requirement, it is the absolute level of intelligence that matters, not the relative level. If the whole IQ scale were lifted above the threshold for the job of power lineman, those jobs requiring less intelligence would all share the same low IQ status, but social-class standing might not seem as important. Many occupational differences would no longer be due to limitations of intelligence but to a difference of preference and interest, surely a more satisfying arrangement.

A WORD OF CAUTION

With all the recent evidence accumulating on the importance of early experience to cognitive growth, a word of caution to educators is in order. Although it now seems fairly conclusive that stimulus conditions can be provided that will allow for maximum intellectual development, the importance of providing conditions designed to promote emotional growth must not be overlooked.

A FINAL COMMENT

You may be wondering whether, if early experience is so significant in determining intellectual ability, there will be anything left for you to accomplish by the time the child reaches school age. Remember: The cognitive growth that takes place during those first critical six years simply provides the base for the intellectual structure the classroom teacher must build. The child should be allowed to begin formal schooling with the necessary background of cognitive skills so as to be able to take full advantage of the formal educational process. The goal of the early-experience theorists and practitioners is to prepare the child to profit fully from the educational experience. The job of the teacher, then, becomes more challenging, more stimulating, and less frustrating when the child enters school equipped with the necessary tools to learn. Educational experiences pick up where early experience leaves off, and studies have clearly shown that the quality of the educational experience influences both rate and maximum level of the cognitive growth achieved by an individual (Klausmeir, 1977).

SUMMARY

Though psychologists have for some time pointed to the importance of early experience for emotional growth, only recently has the same attention been paid to cognitive or intellectual growth. It was known, even as long ago as the 1930s, that early in a child's life certain activities could best be learned during certain critical periods. The work of McGraw on the twins Johnny and Jimmy made this point clear. Also, Bayley's Berkeley Growth Study was aimed at ferreting out some of the facts regarding changes that occur during the process of intellectual growth. A later attempt is the work of Bloom.

Bloom states that with increasing age there is less and less effect on intellectual growth from environmental influences. Children at age three, for example, profit more from enriching experiences than children at age nine or ten. Almost two-thirds of one's ultimate cognitive growth occurs by age six.

Hunt sees stimulus variety as the crucial ingredient in cognitive growth. In the "problem of the match," Hunt points to the importance of matching up the proper amount of stimulus variety with the child's present position on the cognitive-growth continuum. This is similar to Vygotsky's concept of the *zone of proximal development*, which is defined as the distance between a child's present development level and that child's level of potential future development. Vygotsky insists that some degree of cognitive challenge is needed for maximizing intellectual development.

Piaget and Bruner have developed explanatory systems of how and when cognitive growth occurs. Both indicate the importance of sensory inputs and environmental encounters during the child's early years.

Hebb stresses the internal, physiological changes that occur during cognitive growth and development. He cites the neural organization occurring within the brain as the child's ability to learn increases. At birth the brain cells are relatively unorganized, and the cellular organization occurs as a result of the child's own series of learning experiences.

The Krech study on rats shows that the structure and chemical composition of the brain results in part from the quality and quantity of an organism's early experience. Physiological development requires early environmental stimulation.

The long-term evidence from the Head Start programs is just now beginning to surface. In one study, the Perry Preschool Program, measures taken on nineteen-year-old youths who as children had been in the program were compared with a control group of youths who had not. In virtually every measurement category, the impact of the program had positive effects, ranging from an increase in academic ability and achievement to a decrease in criminal activity. Evidence from other studies, such as the Milwaukee Project, has raised cautious hopes that intellectual growth can be maximized through the use of innovative educational interventions during the early childhood years.

The early experience school of thought contends that by providing a more beneficial environment during a child's preschool years, higher levels of intellectual functioning can be expected, especially from culturally deprived youngsters. Though providing more uniform environments does make hereditary effects more pronounced, the early-experience position is that the intellectual differences among adults will still be lessened, and people will thus have more occupational choices available to them.

The job of the teacher is in no way minimized by the efforts of the early-experience specialists. It is hoped that children will be better able to reach their intellectual potentials and thus better able to profit from the educational experiences provided in the classroom. The teacher's job should, accordingly, be more challenging and less frustrating.

KEY TERMS AND NAMES

A/S ratio
Nancy Bayley
Benjamin Bloom
cell assembly
critical periods
early experience
Head Start: Perry Preschool Program
Donald O. Hebb

Richard Herrnstein
Milwaukee Project
negatively accelerated growth curve
stimulus variety
Summerhill School
Lev Vygotsky
zone of proximal development

THEORY INTO PRACTICE: EARLY EXPERIENCE— LEARNING THE CONCEPTS

Since the chapter has focused on background factors in the development of young children, we will orient this section toward helping you comprehend the basic concepts and theorists.

Part I   The first phase is to identify the chief theorists with their critically important ideas. For each name in the left-hand column, write the number of the matching concept chosen from the right-hand column.

NAME	CONCEPT
_____ Myrtle McGraw	1. A/S ratio
_____ Nancy Bayley	2. Roller-skating twins and critical periods
_____ David Krech	3. The air crib and controlling the environment
_____ Benjamin Bloom	4. IQ variability is greatest during the first few years
_____ J. McV. Hunt	5. The negatively accelerating growth curve
_____ D. O. Hebb	6. Stimulus variety and stimulus deprivation
_____ B. F. Skinner	7. Brain chemistry and environmental stimulation or deprivation

As you look down the list, probably the easiest and most vivid memory you'll recall is the picture of the child roller-skating (item 2 in the concept column) and the name of Myrtle McGraw. Next you'll probably think of the picture of the baby in the air crib (item 3) and imagine yourself as B. F. Skinner's daughter. For IQ variability, you will probably correctly choose Bayley if you associate her with the Berkeley Growth Study. If, instead, you selected Bloom for this item, you may also be correct, as long as your reasoning process has clearly demonstrated an overall *understanding* of the concepts involved. For example, if you remembered that Bloom's growth curve showed that the environmental stimulation of intellectual development is most influential during the early, formative years of life, then you may have correctly deduced that IQ variability must also be at its highest level during these critical early years. Of the four remaining choices, the problem now is to pick out three that you either know for sure, or at least feel the most confidence about. Let's say you just can't recall anything about Bloom, but you're quite sure of Hebb and the A/S (associative/sensory) ratio of brain cells. This may then also remind you of that other brain researcher, David Krech, and the chemical changes in the brain. So now you're down to two names (J. McV. Hunt and Bloom) and two choices (the negatively accelerating growth curve or stimulus variety). At this point, the associative part of your brain remembers something about Hunt and the Hopi Indian children and you choose stimulus variety. This leaves Bloom's curve for your final correct answer.

Part II   The second phase of comprehension is to move from identification to description. You've been able to pick out or identify the concept and relate it to the theorist. Now the question is: Can you describe the connection in your own words? To try this out, pair the names and the concepts, for example, McGraw–roller-skating twins and critical periods. Review the pairings and then think how you would describe each relationship and explain its significance. In other words, ideas may be interesting but that's not the point. Why would anyone who is interested in understanding children need to know about the findings?

Write one or two paragraphs on each of the pairs, using your own words. Then check your work with the descriptions in the glossary–study guide at the back of this book and/or with the material in the chapter itself. Note where you were on target and most importantly note where you may have missed. Analyzing your own mistakes is the quickest way to unlearn the wrong connections and replace them with the correct relationships. Also, you will be practicing a process of being able to elaborate on the concepts so that you'll have a larger knowledge base to draw upon. To prove this point, cover up your answers to the identifications and go back and review Part I. Check how fast and accurately you can now spot the answers.

Part III   This final part involves constructing an essay on the general topic of early experience. The question is usually phrased as follows:

> Discuss and critically analyze the major theorists and research findings that support the importance of early experience as a key to resolving the nature-nurture controversy. Outline implications for educational programming. (30 minutes)

After reading the question, you'll realize it has two parts. The first really calls for a presentation of the key concepts, theorists, and research findings. Hence, you would describe how experience in the first few years of life is the key to the nature-nurture puzzle by showing how "brain power" develops (Hebb, Bayley, Krech, Hunt) in a stimulating environment.

You can also point out the reverse, namely, the premature reduction of intellectual growth in environments that deprive a child of variety. Then you could mention Bloom's research, which demonstrated just how much brain power is developed before the first grade. You might add the critical-period concept (McGraw's roller skaters), which supports the idea that it is important to provide stimulation and growth opportunities that match the developmental sequence.

For the second part of the essay, you would want to point out the connection between theory and research as a basis for new educational practices. Stop for a moment and go back and review Table 4.1, which presents the findings of the Perry Preschool Program and other early-childhood educational programs. You'll quickly see how the first part of the essay relates to these programs. The theorists had all predicted that if a rich, stimulating environment with appropriate variety is provided, intellectual development would blossom (to say "Bloom" would bring groans). In fact, the Perry follow-up studies on eight outcomes proved the point.

With this in mind, you can then wind up the essay by generalizing on the importance of educational experience during childhood. To strike while the iron is hot is one appropriate metaphor or, to quote Napoleon (and change the metaphor), "the hand that rocks the cradle rules the world."

REFERENCES

Altman, J. (1967). Postnatal growth and differentiation of the mammalian brain. In G. C. Quarton, T. Melnechuk, and F. O. Schmitt (Eds.), *The neurosciences.* New York: Rockefeller University Press.

American Psychologist, 1966, 21, 1191.

Bayley, N. (1940). *Studies in the development of young children.* Berkeley: University of California Press.

Berrueta-Clement, J. R., Schweinhart, L. J., Barnett, W. S., Epstein, A. S. and Weikart, D P. (1984). *Changed lives: The effects of the Perry preschool program on youths through age 19.* Ypsilanti, Mich.: High/Scope Press.

Bloom, B. S. (1964). *Stability and change in human characteristics.* New York: Wiley.

Bowers, K. S. (1990). Josephine R. Hilgard, *American Psychologist, 45,* 1382.

Bruner, J. S. (1969). Cognitive consequences of early sensory deprivation. In R. C. Sprinthall and N. A. Sprinthall (Eds.), *Educational psychology: Selected readings* (pp. 34–36). New York: Van Nostrand-Reinhold.

Bugelski, R. (1964). *The psychology of learning applied to teaching.* Indianapolis, Ind.: Bobbs-Merrill.

Datan, N., Rodeheaver, D., and Hughes, F. (1987). Adult development and aging. *Annual Review of Psychology, 38,* 153–180.

DeCasper, A. J., and Spence, M. J. (1986). Prenatal maternal speech influences newborns' perception of speech sounds. *Infant Behavior and Development, 9,* 133–150.

Dennis, W. (1960). Causes of retardation among institutional children: Iran. *Journal of Genetic Psychology, 96,* 47–59.

Garber, H. L., and Heber, R. (1981). The efficacy of early intervention with family rehabilitation. In M. J. Begab, H. C. Haywood, and H. L. Garber (eds.), *Psychosocial influences in retarded performance*, Vol. II, *Strategies for improving competence* (pp. 71–88). Baltimore, Md.: University Park Press.

Gleitman, L., Newport, E., and Gleitman, H. (1984). The current status of the motherese hypothesis. *Journal of Child Language, 11,* 43–80.

Grosser, G. S., and Sprinthall, R. C. (1972). A rejoinder to Herrnstein. *The Atlantic Monthly* (February), 38–39.

Grosser, G. S., Sprinthall, R. C., and Sirois, L. (1967). Magnesium premoline: Activation of extinction responding after continuous reinforcement. *Psychological Reports, 21,* 11–14.

Hebb, D. O. (1949). *The organization of behavior.* New York: Wiley.

Hebb, D. O. (1978). Open letter: To a friend who thinks the IQ is a social evil. *American Psychologist, 33*(12), 1143.

Herrnstein, R. (1971). I.Q. *The Atlantic Monthly* (September), 43–64.

Hilgard, J. R. (1932). Learning and motivation in pre-school children. *Journal of Genetic Psychology, 41,* 36–56.

Hubbell, R. (1983). *Head Start evaluation, synthesis, and utilization project.* DHHS Publication OHDS 83-31184. Washington, D.C.: U.S. Government Printing Office.

Hunt, J. McV. (1969). Revisiting Montessori. In R. C. Sprinthall and N. A. Sprinthall (Eds.), *Educational psychology: Selected readings* (pp. 45–55). New York: Van Nostrand-Reinhold.

Jones, M. C., Bayley, N., MacFarlane, J. W., and Honzik, M. P. (Eds.). (1971). *The course of human development.* Waltham, Mass.: Xerox.

Klausmeir, H. J. (1977). Educational experience and cognitive development. *Educational Psychologist, 12*(2), 179–196.

Krech, D. (1969). The chemistry of learning. In R. C. Sprinthall and N. A. Sprinthall (Eds.), *Educational psychology: Selected readings* (pp. 152–156). New York: Van Nostrand-Reinhold.

Lee, V. E., Brooks-Gunn, J., Schnur, E., and Fong-Ruey, L. (1990). Are Head Start effects sustained? A longitudinal follow-up comparison of disadvantaged children attending Head Start, no preschool, and other preschool programs. *Child Development, 61,* 495–507.

Levin, H. M. (1977). A decade of policy developments in improving education and training for low-income populations. In R. H. Haveman (Ed.) *A decade of federal antipoverty programs: Achievements, failures and lessons* (pp. 521–570). New York: Academic Press.

Lipsitt, L. P. (1990). Myrtle McGraw. *American Psychologist, 45,* 977.

McGraw, M. B. (1935). *Growth: A study of Johnny and Jimmy.* New York: Appleton-Century.

McGraw, M. B. (1939). Later development of children specially trained during infancy. *Child Development, 10,* 1–19.

Neill, A. S. (1969). The idea of Summerhill. In R. C. Sprinthall and N. A. Sprinthall (Eds.), *Educational psychology: Selected readings* (pp. 194–198). New York: Van Nostrand-Reinhold.

Piel, G. (1975). The new hereditarians. *The Nation* (April), 458.

Rice, B. (1968). Skinner agrees he is the most important influence in psychology. *The New York Times Magazine,* 17 (March), 27 ff.

Rogoff, B. (1990). *Apprenticeship in thinking: Cognitive development in social context.* New York: Oxford University Press.

Schweinhart, L. J. (1984). Preschool's long-term impact: Summary of the evidence. In J. R. Berrueta-Clement et al., *Changed lives: The effects of the Perry preschool program on youths through age 19* (pp. 95–105). Ypsilanti, Mich.: High/Scope Press.

Scott, J. P. (1968). *Early experience and the organization of behavior* (p. 68). Belmont, Calif.: Wadsworth.

Shimojo, S., Bauer, J., O'Connell, K. M., and Held, R. (1986). Prestereoscopic binocular vision in infants. *Vision Research, 26,* 501–510.

Siegler, R. S., and Crowley, K. (1991). The microgenetic method: A direct means for studying cognitive development. *American Psychologist, 46,* 606–820.

Smolak, L., and Weinraub, M. (1983). Maternal speech: Strategy or response. *Journal of Child Language, 10,* 369–380.

Sokolov, E. N. (1977). Brain functions: Neuronal mechanisms of learning and memory. *Annual Review of Psychology, 28,* 85–112.

Spelt, D. K. (1948). The conditioning of the human fetus in utero. *Journal of Experimental Psychology, 38,* 338–346.

Thompson, W. R., and Heron, W. (1954). The effects of restricting early experience on the problem solving capacity of dogs. *Canadian Journal of Psychology, 8,* 17–31.

Vygotsky, Lev (1978). *Mind in society.* Cambridge: Harvard University Press.

White, B. L. (1975). *The first three years.* Englewood Cliffs, N.J.: Prentice-Hall.

Winegar, L. T. (1989). *Social interactions and the development of children's understanding.* Norwood, N.J.: Ablex.

Zigler, E. F., (1987). Formal schooling for four-year-olds? *American Psychologist, 42,* 254–260.

5

COGNITIVE GROWTH

As we pointed out in Chapter 1, it is very important to gain an understanding of how children actually think in learning situations. The pupil, one of the four concerns of the teaching-learning agenda, is the focus of this chapter. We will hold off other considerations such as teacher characteristics and teaching strategies in order to present a clear and detailed picture of the child as a learner. The framework we have selected comes from a long tradition of careful study of children through close observation. You will see just how the insights of this framework came to be and gain an understanding of the current state of our information base.

This chapter takes a special look at the kinds of cognitive steps or plateaus of development that occur during childhood and adolescence. Since cognitive development depends on interaction between the child and the learning environment, we will examine the problems of matching the child to the most appropriate learning tasks. This is another way of saying that we must have some informed basis for determining what we present to pupils and how we present it. Just as we know we cannot expect children to roller-skate before they can stand, we must also know when we can expect them to be ready to learn the various intellectual or cognitive tasks. If we understand how the cognitive systems develop, we can avoid both teaching children something before they are ready to learn it and missing a golden opportunity by waiting until they are well past the most sensitive moment. The major work of Jean Piaget will be featured throughout this chapter.

STAGES OF GROWTH AND DEVELOPMENT

Our understanding of the growth of brain power has changed so enormously in the past two decades that a veritable revolution in learning has taken place (Case, 1992). Previously, the general view was that intelligence was, for all practical purposes, determined prior to birth. This meant that there was nothing to do but accept those inborn differences as natural and provide different educational experiences depending on whether the child was a fast or a slow learner. In other words, the erroneous assumption of innate differences in intelligence produced an unfortunate educational assumption. We assumed that the differences in intelligence were largely differences in the speed of thinking. In fact "mentally retarded" was almost always translated as "slow learner." This meant that the differences in learning were seen as differences in degree, or more precisely, as quantita-

By understanding how and when cognitive systems develop, we can avoid, on the one hand, teaching children something before they are ready to learn it and, on the other hand, missing a golden opportunity by waiting to well past the most sensitive moment.

tive differences. Pupils could be rated—much as if they were on a track team—as slow, moderately fast, or superfast learners.

The most damaging effect of viewing learning differences as being fixed at birth and as being quantitative (slow to fast) was on educational programs. In general, the educational curriculum reflected this idea: The same material or the same curriculum was given to all students but at different paces, since the ''slower'' children would not be expected to learn as much or to go as far as the ''faster'' children. (The word *curriculum*, by the way, comes from a Latin word meaning ''a course to be run.'') Starting from a standard curriculum, we would water it down for the ''slow learners'' and enrich it for the ''accelerated learners.'' The ''slow'' children would cover, say, half the material that the ''fast'' children would cover in any given period. For example, the ''slow'' children would memorize only half as much poetry as the ''fast'' children, learn fewer spelling words, less arithmetic, or hand in shorter compositions in English. Since there was little or no recognition of major stages of cognitive growth, the differences between a first-grade pupil and a twelfth-grade pupil were largely

differences in how much they knew and how fast they learned it. In the same way, differences among first-graders (as among twelfth-graders) were also quantitative—how much material they learned and how fast they learned it. It has, unfortunately, taken us a long time to get away from these ideas.

Arnold Gesell (1940), who established the famous Institute of Child Development at Yale University during the 1930s, was the first to try to convince educators that growth and development occurred in an unvarying sequence. Many of his ideas and theories were later discarded because they were oversimplifications, but this one concept lasted. Growth stages are major periods of change. Each child goes through periods of major reorganization followed by periods of integration during which a new stage is reached and the changes are assimilated. Although Gesell made a significant contribution with his idea of developmental growth stages, he erred in the details of his stages. He made the mistake of overgeneralizing from studying only a few children, and he presented an overly detailed ''map'' of development. For example, he made hard-and-fast statements about all two-year olds, all two-and-a-half-year-olds, all three-year-olds, and so on. This created much confusion in the 1930s and 1940s. Parents were literally measuring their children every six months or so against Gesell's

''Actually, I'm a little too old to believe in you, but I don't want to take any chances.''

From The Wall Street Journal—permission, Cartoon Features Syndicate.

Arnold Gesell was one of the first to advocate that growth and development occur in an unvarying sequence.

developmental graphs. Cross generalizations resulted: "All twos are terrrible"; "The threes are terrific"; "At four and a half all children . . . ." For a time, parental demand for Gesell's truths outran his ability to produce books: *The First Years of Life* was followed by *The Child from Five to Ten*. One mother was heard to comment despairingly, "I don't know what to do with my children anymore. They are eleven and thirteen, and Gesell stopped at ten!" You are invited to read some of these now historical books. They may help you understand some of the influences on your grandparents as they raised your parents.

The idea of sequential levels of development was most important in all the work of Gesell's institute. He illustrated that growth took place in stages and that the stages themselves were like great leaps forward followed by periods of integration. Therefore, in order to understand cognitive development, you will have to understand more about the process of growth. At what ages do the major breakthroughs occur and when are the periods of consolidation?

JEAN PIAGET: THE LATE DISCOVERY OF HIS WORK

Throughout the period 1930–1960, while efforts to break away from the idea of fixed and quantitative

intelligence were singularly unsuccessful (with the exception of Gesell's general concept of growth), **Jean Piaget** was working quietly and almost unnoticed at the J.J. Rousseau Institute for Child Study in Geneva. Using direct, careful, and systematic observation of children (including his own, the now-famous Jacqueline, Laurent, and Lucienne), Piaget began to form a view that would revolutionize our understanding of intellectual growth.

Although in the United States there was some brief interest in his work in the 1930s, it did not become fully known and appreciated until after the 1960s. There are two main reasons for such a long period of neglect by American psychologists. First, his ideas ran very much counter to the mainstream of educational psychology. He proposed that we start by investigating the child rather than following the official Thorndike view that we research "laws" of learning in the abstract. What went on in the mind of a child, so to speak, was considered either too complex to understand or simply irrelevant. Thus, while Piaget was carefully observing and noting how children thought, most of the establishment in psychology considered his model inappropriate.

We cannot, however, place the blame just on this side of the Atlantic. Piaget himself made his own rather unique contribution. Steeped in the tradition

JEAN PIAGET

Jean Piaget was born in Neuchâtel, Switzerland, in 1896. Piaget was a curious, alert, studious, and extremely bright child. By age ten he had published his first scientific paper, a description of an albino sparrow he had observed in a local park. Between ages eleven and fifteen Piaget worked after school as a laboratory assistant to the director of a natural history museum and in the process became an expert on mollusks and other zoological topics. When he was fifteen, he was offered the job of curator of the mollusk section at a Geneva museum. He received his degree from the University of Neuchâtel at age eighteen and his Ph.D. in natural sciences three years later. Paiget had published more than twenty papers in the field of zoology before reaching his twenty-first birthday. In short, Piaget demonstrated a rare intellectual precocity during his childhood and adolescent years.

Despite his early interest in natural science, the young Piaget read widely in sociology, religion, and philosophy. While studying philosophy he became especially interested in epistemology, the study of how knowledge is obtained. With his background in zoology, Piaget be

of European scholarship, he seemed almost to enjoy writing his findings not only exclusively in French but in a brand of that language that almost guaranteed to obscure rather than enlighten. There is no way of knowing for sure, but enough stories have circulated to suggest that he enjoyed the independence of his views and held a kind of lofty indifference to the problem of clearly transmitting his ideas to the wider world of psychology. To be fair, of course, most innovators who single-handedly move a field to a new level of understanding exhibit many of these same tendencies. The result, however, is most important: During most of his adult life, his work was unknown here. Now it is just the opposite. He is among the first group of psychologists cited in academic references. John Flavell, one of this country's renowned experts on child development, summed up Piaget's work as follows: "Piaget's contributions to our knowledge of cognitive development have been nothing short of stupendous, both quantitatively and qualitatively" (1985, p. 4).

Indeed, by the late 1960s (in part due to Flavell's excellent translation of Piaget's writings), when Piaget made one of his rare visits to this country, the occasion was like an astronaut's reception. As described by Maya Pines:

It was a memorable occasion. With his fringe of long, straight white hair down the sides and back of his balding head, his high forehead, horn-rimmed glasses, gold watch chain and well-worn leather briefcase, he looked like a stock character—The Professor. On the platform, he commanded instant respect. Speaking in a booming voice, in French, he began by describing some of the key stages of children's intellectual development (Pines, 1970, p. 58).

came convinced that biological principles could be utilized in understanding epistemological problems. His search for a bridge between biology and epistemology brought him finally into the world of psychology.

After receiving his doctorate, Piaget sought training in psychology and so left Switzerland to study and gain experience at a number of European laboratories, clinics, and universities. During this time he worked for a while at Alfred BInet's laboratory school in Paris, where he did intelligence testing on French schoolchildren. He became fascinated, not by a child's correct answer to a test item, but by a child's incorrect response. He doggedly pursued the incorrect answers in the hope of learning more about the depth and extent of children's ideas and mental processes. His goal was to understand how children of various ages came upon their knowledge of the world around them. This became Piaget's lifework, to find out how children go about the business of obtaining knowledge.

Later Piaget took detailed, minute-by-minute notes of the mental growth of his own three children, Jacqueline, Lucienne, and Laurent.

In 1929 Piaget went to the University of Geneva, where he became the assistant director of the J. J. Rousseau Institute, and in 1940 he assumed the duties of director of the University of Geneva's psychology laboratory.

Piaget wrote a tremendous number of books and articles on cognitive growth in children. He believed that intellectual growth is a direct continuation of inborn biological growth. The child is born biologically equipped to make a variety of motor responses, which then provide the framework for the thought processes that follow. The biological givens impose on the developing a child an invariant direction to the development of cognitive processes. The ability to think springs from the physiological base. Clearly, Piaget kept his early training in natural science firmly in mind as he went on to develop his system of cognitive growth.

In his twilight years, Piaget ac-tively sought answers to some of psychology's most fundamental questions. According to his biographer, friend, and former student, David Elkind, Piaget rose early, about 4 A.M., and wrote at least four publishable pages before teaching his morning classes. His afternoons were devoted to taking long walks and thinking about his current studies and research, and his evenings were spent in reading. As soon as his classes were over for the summer, Piaget went to his mountain retreat in the Alps. As fall approached, the mountain air turned crisp, the leaves began to change color, and Piaget came down from the mountain, laden with new material for several articles and books. Piaget came down that mountain for over fifty autumns, and the volume of his writing was enormous. He died in Geneva in September 1980, in his eighty-fifth year.

Just as Freud's name has become synonymous with the study of emotional growth, Piaget has become known as psychology's foremost expert on cognitive growth.

The Concept of Cognitive Growth

Piaget's contribution to our understanding of mental growth as a process of interaction accounts for his significance. Through an intensive study of children over long periods of time—a painstaking process of almost endless observation—Piaget began to chart the unexplored territory of the human mind and to produce a map of the stages of cognitive growth. He proposed, first of all, that cognitive growth takes place in **developmental stages.** This means that the nature and makeup of intelligence change significantly over time. The differences are not of degree (slow learners and fast learners) but of kind (qualitative). The transformation of the human mind as it develops can be compared to the transformation of an egg into a caterpillar and then into a butterfly. The stages of growth are distinctively different from one another, and the content of each stage is a major system that determines the way we understand and make sense of our experiences (particularly the experience of learning from someone else). Obviously, if we wish to provide experiences that will nurture and facilitate growth, we must take into account the intellectual system the child is using at the time. Piaget's work provides us with the broad outlines of the different cognitive systems children use at different periods in their lives. Each new, evolving system is a major qualitative transformation.

Research through Repeated Observations

It is important to know something about the way Piaget worked, how he was able to propose a system explaining such a highly complex process as intellectual development. You might think, in these days of

"Keep an eye on the kids for awhile, will you, Jean?"

supertechnology, that he would have used a complicated computer-based program and enormous research teams. But you would be mistaken. As we have already mentioned, Piaget's work was based on careful and detailed observation of children in natural settings, such as homes and schools. From a research methodology point of view, he was using repeated naturalistic observations. Thus, in some way his method is most like the kind of research a teacher or school counselor might do.

Starting almost like that other great "clinical" scientist, Sigmund Freud, Piaget very carefully examined the functioning of intelligence in a few children. On the basis of these subjective impressions, he began to ask himself some questions. Why, for example, did children become confused over family relationships? A child could readily acknowledge "I have a brother" but would still not understand that the brother also had a brother (or sister). He also found that children at certain ages seemed to have great difficulty in understanding "simple" ideas.

It seems hard to imagine that children don't understand that when they pour beans from a short, fat glass to a tall, thin glass, the number of beans remains constant. In one of his classic experiments, Piaget found that if he took two piles of beans, had a child actually count both piles to be sure they had the same number, and then left one pile spread out on the table, and bunched the second pile together, that—

well, see if you can guess what the child would say. Remember, the child goes by what *seems* biggest. For example, if you ask children of four or five whether they would rather have a nickel or a dime, they are likely to name the nickel, "because it's bigger."

In yet another observation, Piaget asked preschool children to draw a picture of a glass half-filled with water. He then asked a child to draw the glass upside down. Figure 5.1 shows what one child drew.

At each point in each successive experiment, Piaget would carefully reexamine his own questions (hypotheses) and then develop some further ways of testing them. As a result, it has taken almost an entire lifetime to convince skeptical researchers of his scheme. At first his studies were dismissed out of hand because he would try problems out on a single child or on three or four children. Also, because his sample was so small, he often did without statistics. (In this way he joined hands with such theoretically disparate researchers as Freud and B. F. Skinner.) To make matters even worse, he didn't follow a standard interview format: He wouldn't necessarily ask the same questions of each child, and so no two interviews were exactly comparable. It was almost too easy to criticize and dismiss his work on the grounds that his research designs were not standard.

Thus, partly because Piaget did not follow a standard research model and partly because his ideas, if understood, would have necessitated a major revision in our theories of cognitive growth, his work remained largely confined to Geneva. However, his findings were eventually noticed and have been widely accepted in the past ten to twenty years. Scientific skeptics began to take notice of his work. Piaget continued to direct a series of studies, including some that used large samples. Essentially, however, it wasn't the sheer number of subjects that mattered but the emergence, over and over again, of the same principles of intellectual transformation. Through repetition, rather than the single critical experiment, Piaget accumulated sufficient evidence to become the major theoretician of intellectual development today.

The Meaning of Cognition: Piaget's Definition

Before we describe the stages of cognitive development, it is important to explain just what Piaget meant by the term *cognition*. Essentially cognition—thinking, or rational processing—is considered an active

FIGURE 5.1 Piaget's experiments with preschoolers: The first picture shows a child pouring beans from a short, fat glass into a tall, thin one. The second is a child's drawing of a half-filled glass of water—right side up and then upside down.

and interactive process. The mind in everyday language is not simply a blank sheet of paper on which the environment writes. But neither is it a totally separate apparatus that exists in splendid isolation. Flavell probably provides the clearest description when he says, "Thus the mind neither copies the world, passively accepting it as a ready-made given, nor does it ignore the world, autistically creating a private mental conception of it out of whole cloth" (1985, p. 5).

This means that cognition is the constant process of going back and forth between the person and the environment. Another way to describe it is a dialectical process, which means that cognition never takes place entirely "inside" the child nor is it entirely the result of outside stimulation. A third way to describe cognition is as the regulating mechanism that connects the person to the environment. The most important single point in all these different descriptions is that the cognitive process is active, not passive. A person affects the environment, and the environment affects the person at the same time. When we describe the specific implications of this definition, we will continually come back to this same basic point. The child is not an empty organism. Nor is learning passively filling up an empty vessel.

PIAGET'S STAGES OF COGNITIVE GROWTH

After examining the thinking patterns that children use from birth through adolescence, Piaget began to find consistent systems within certain broad age ranges. There are four major stages (see Table 5.1).

Since the four major stages are quite broad, each stage has subcategories. The important thing to remember, however, is that each major stage is a system of thinking that is qualitatively different from the preceding stage. Each stage is a major transformation in thought processes—compared to the preceding stage, a quantum leap forward, a breakthrough. It is also important to remember that the child must go

TABLE 5.1   STAGES OF COGNITIVE GROWTH

AGE	STAGE
0–2	Sensorimotor
2–7	Intuitive or preoperational
7–11	Concrete operations
11–16	Formal operations

through each stage in a regular sequence. It is impossible to skip or miss a stage or bypass it: The stages of cognitive growth are sequential and follow an invariant sequence. Children cannot overcome a developmental lag or speed up their movement from one stage to the next. They need to have sufficient experience in each stage and sufficient time to internalize that experience before they can move on.

Our main concern as educators is to understand the major substance of each stage. Only then can we begin to consider what to teach and how to teach. Although the major substance of each stage is the main structure or scheme for the age span specified, these stages never exist in a pure form. There will always be some elements of the preceding and future stages mixed in. In other words, although a major intellectual activity does define each stage, bits and pieces of other stages will also be present.

In fact, most recent research has established that it is only for the sensorimotor stage, from birth to two years, that universal agreement exists as to the starting point and the end. Sandra Scarr sums it up rather succinctly with the rhetorical question, Do you know anyone who did not make it through the sensorimotor stage? (1976, p. 185)

Beyond that point, however, the stage-to-stage differences are not as great nor are the changes as abrupt as originally described by Piaget. Recent research, for example, has demonstrated that some symbolic thought, usually associated with later stages of development, actually occurs during the first stage. Similarly, research has indicated that children in the second stage have a greater ability to classify numbers than was previously estimated by Piaget's research (Flavell, 1985; Gelman, 1982).

One of the continuing problems in this question is the time lag in publication of many of Piaget's observations just prior to his death in 1979. A recent publication in English by Piaget and Garcia (1991), for example, indicates that children at each stage often use cognitive fragments of higher stages. Piaget had shown that a fully functioning adult can employ sixteen methods of logical and formal thought. Young children use some of these methods, such as grouping, negation, correspondence, etc. These operations might be called "protologic," early but incomplete forms. Thus even though a child in the preoperational or concrete mode might make occasional use of higher-order thought, the child's primary method of problem solving would still be in those earlier modes. The adage "one swallow does not make a summer"

might describe this view. This also means that researchers who are trying to disprove Piaget by showing a few early indicators of higher functioning either haven't stayed current with his studies or—to stay in the adage format—are making mountains of rejection out of molehills of cognitive fragments.

The important point to remember as you read and learn about stage characteristics is that there are no pure types. You will not find any single child who will exhibit all the characteristics of a given stage, with the exception of the sensorimotor stage. Instead, you will see major trends and clusters of learning approaches that are truly consistent with the stage types. You will also see, as child development researchers are finding out, that some evidence exists of more-advanced-stage thinking at earlier stages. In other words, you can expect some overlap. Children during elementary school will exhibit very clear concrete thought, but there will be some foreshadowing of formal and abstract reasoning, though not much. The same foreshadowing of an advanced stage is true of the preschool child compared to the elementary school child. So keep in mind that these two ideas are not contradictory but rather deepen our understanding: Each stage has major characteristics of its own that describe in a consistent manner how a child processes experience; at the same time the child also will exhibit some signs of the next stage as well as prior stages.

Also in this regard Rolando Garcia (Piaget and Garcia, 1991) maintains that the stage and sequence of Piaget are neither static nor complete. This means that the path of cognitive development is an open system with no end point. Garcia notes that intuition of the type suggested by postformal operations or problem finding can never be truly formalized. In other words we don't really know how far beyond our present understanding of formal operations might be possible. Human cognitive systems are not finite but depend upon interaction. We do know, however, the inverse. Cognitive growth can be stopped. If we cut off exchanges with the environment, growth ceases. Garcia in rather strong words notes that for cognitions, "equilibrium is death" (p. 129). This means that each stage is a period of relative stability, of a preferred problem-solving strategy, not a static equilibrium.

Thus to sum up, recent research has shown that

1. The sequence of stage changes is in the order proposed by Piaget.

SPOTLIGHT ON PIAGET

What If Piaget Had Studied Animals?

Since so much of Piaget's work has been repeated with children from different backgrounds and different cultures, sooner or later the question had to be raised. What about animals? Do animals, especially those who are further along developmentally, such as a chimp (versus a slug), exhibit Piaget-like progressions in growth? The main experiments as the child reaches two years focus on the establishment of object permanence. The tests become quite sophisticated. The child may be shown a small toy cat. The examiner holds the cat in his or her hand, then moves the hand underneath three separate napkins. The cat is randomly deposited under one. The empty hand is opened in full view of the child. Usually the child smiles and then quite systematically looks under each napkin until the hidden cat is fully and triumphantly uncovered. This ability to track the events, so to speak, mentally indicates the end of the sensorimotor period and the onset of internal and symbolic thinking.

So far, research with animals, using similar tests of object permanence, indicates that cats progress partway through but stop short of full attainment. They can't track the shift from one hiding place to another. Monkeys, in contrast, can achieve the same level of functioning as a two-year-old human but then seem to top out. Chimps clearly reach this level as well as some measure of symbolic thinking at the next stage. In this sense, then, the research evidence does support the idea of intellectual development in humans and in animals. Careful observation of different species shows some of the same progressions during the sensorimotor period. Thus far, it appears that chimps and apes are the only species besides the human species that clearly make it all the way through the sensorimotor period.[a]

As we noted in Chapter 2, chimps can learn sign language and thus can communicate at a more human level than other animals. This development of language is the hallmark of the preoperational stage. In fact, for a while in the 1970s it was suggested that chimps could master some of the elementary rules of grammatical sentence structure, a clear parallel to human development during the preschool years. At present, however, there is no firm evidence that the chimps really display the ability to create original sentences. Instead they apparently imitate adult repetitions.[b] If this finding is borne out through additional research, then we can mark a point somewhere in the preoperational period at which chimps cease further cognitive-stage growth, leaving the field of further cognitive development exclusively in the province of the human species.

---

[a] Flavell, J. H. (1985). *Cognitive development* (p. 37). Englewood Cliffs, N.J.: Prentice-Hall.
[b] Kalat, J. W. (1988). *Biological psychology*. Belmont, Calif.: Wadsworth.

---

2. Cross-cultural studies reconfirm the sequence, though the amount of time within a particular stage may vary.

3. Transition periods between stages are broader and more flexible than predicted and therefore less abrupt.

4. Elements of earlier-stage cognitions and later cognitions are more apparent, though the modal characteristics of each particular stage remain as the dominant scheme.

Studies with Swiss, British, U.S., Canadian, Thai, and Malaysian children support the above generalizations (Ginsberg and Opper, 1988). The result of all this current work has led, in Robbie Case's words, to "a revival of the structural hypothesis" or, less loftily described, to "the return of Piaget" (1987, 1992).

Sensorimotor Experience (Birth to Two Years)

Cognitive activity during the **sensorimotor stage** is based primarily on immediate experience through the senses. The major intellectual activity of the stage is the interaction of the senses and the environment. Activity is practical. Without language to label experiences or to symbolize and hence remember events and ideas, children are dramatically bound to imme-

Piaget's equation: Activity promotes cognitive growth.

diate experience: They see what is happening and feel it, but they have no way of categorizing their experience. Responses are almost completely determined by the situation. For example, a hungry child will figuratively scream the house down for food. It does no good to "tell" a six-month-old, "Now just wait a minute; I'm warming your bottle." The child has no way to represent the idea that in one or two minutes a nice warm bottle of milk will appear, and obviously the baby doesn't know what a minute is or, for that matter, what any of those other words mean. It's like speaking in English to someone who understands only Armenian. The child cannot, so to speak, go to the mental equivalent of an instant replay and say, "Oh, when she says that, it means something good is coming, so I won't be hungry much longer, and my yelling isn't going to make it come faster."

Being tied to immediate experience during this stage also means that there is almost nothing between the child and the environment. The mental organization lives in the raw, so that the quality of experience is unusually significant. Thus, what and how the child learns will remain an immediate experience, as vivid as any first experience. It would be fair to say that learning in the sensorimotor stage is a continuous peak experience. It is something like going through each day as if it were the first day of school, the opening night of a play, your first final exam, your

first date, your first encounter with death, the first time you found yourself completely alone, and so on—all in the same day.

To give you some idea of how easily children at this age are bound by experience and can be victimized by it, we need only think of six-month-olds. This is the age at which children begin to be able to follow an object with their eyes (visual pursuit). Their eyes swing back and forth, following the path of a shiny object, fifty to a hundred times. They literally can't take their eyes off the moving object. Because this is the "first" time they have seen an object move from side to side, they will follow its visual path almost indefinitely unless we wisely choose to change the environment.

The development of visual pursuit (a sensorimotor behavior) is critical to mental development. Visual pursuit has to be learned before a very important concept called *object permanence* can be learned. As children begin to grow intellectually, they understand that when an object disappears from view, it still exists even though they can't see it. Whether it's a button hidden under a pillow, a person leaving the room, or a boy or girl hiding behind a door, children who have developed the concept of object permanence know the disappearance is only temporary and are thus liberated from endless visual pursuit.

The ability to notice and follow objects might be

likened to a first stage of recognition. The growth of object permanence is almost like the beginning of an elementary memory. Children can "hold" in their minds a picture of the missing object; no longer is out of sight out of mind. The experience of seeing things in the first few months of life and then of seeing those same things disappear and reappear plays an important role in mental development. Piaget has compared sighted babies with those born blind: "The inadequacy of the initial scheme [mental organization] leads to a lag in development of three to four years and more" (Piaget, 1970, p. 30). Lacking visual experience during the critical period of sensorimotor learning (birth to two years) prevents the growth of mental structures.

The adage "There's no substitute for experience," best summarizes the sensorimotor period of cognitive development. This is so true of children from birth to age two that it accounts for the recent trend of providing babies with interesting crib mobiles and is also responsible for bringing back the popularity of some of the old-fashioned baby toys like rattles to shake and suck and blankets to hug. Linus, from the Peanuts cartoon, learning with his blanket in tow, stands as the prototype of a child in the sensorimotor stages. A rich and responsive sensory environment is the best means of developing the young child's intelligence.* Note how this relates directly to some of the research findings mentioned in Chapter 4 concerning the development of "intelligent" animals by exposing them to "creative" toys and "interesting" cages. The quality of experience during this first stage prepares the child to move to the next stage.

One final point: Babies during this stage are primarily learning through their senses and are most strongly affected by their immediate environment. However, since object permanence develops in this stage, especially between year one and year two, we now know babies are capable of some representational thought much like that of the next stage. Young babies can store information, even though their ability to do so may seem quite crude. We will make a mistake if we assume that because their talk, gestures, and manipulations are so poor, there is no thought during the sensorimotor period. As Flavell so cleverly puts it, "They just *look* incompetent to the naked eye" (1985, p. 39).

* The implications for the recent growth of day-care centers in this regard are obvious. Failure to operate quality programs—rich and responsive sensory environments—will induce, at a critical juncture, serious developmental lags.

Intuitive or Preoperational Thought (Two to Seven Years)

During the **preoperational stage**, the quality of thinking is transformed. Children are no longer bound to their immediate sensory environment. They started to develop some mental images in the preceding stage (object permanence, for example), and in this stage they expand that ability by leaps and bounds. Their capacity to store images (words and the grammatical structures of language, for example) increases dramatically. Vocabulary development, including the ability to understand and use words, is especially noteworthy. The average two-year-old understands between 200 and 300 words, while the average five-year-old understands 2,000 words—a huge percentage increase.

During this stage, then, there is a major breakthrough in the use of language. Since this is the time when children are maximally ready to learn language, adults who talk a great deal to children, read to them, teach them songs and nursery rhymes—in other words, use language to communicate with them—have a significant effect on the children's language development.

The predominant learning mode at this stage is intuitive; preoperational children are not overly concerned with precision but delight in imitating sounds and trying out lots of different words. They are also unconcerned about the consequences of language. This is the time, for example, when preschoolers regard "bathroom" language as hysterically funny, taking great glee in using choice expressions such as "poop face."

Obviously, the richer the verbal environment at this time, the more likely it is that language will develop. This is not to suggest that we should force-feed language teaching. In fact, teaching is almost unnecessary. The advantage of the intuitive mode is that children are capable of free associations, fantasies, and unique illogical meanings. They can pretend that stuffed toys are real, they can have imaginary friends, tell wild stories about their parentage, have whole conversations with themselves as well as with inanimate objects—these are all ways children have of trying language out, of teaching themselves. Intuition frees them to be experimental regardless of reality.

From the adult's point of view, the spontaneous nature of a child's language may have its drawbacks. Since the child doesn't worry about logic or reality, if talking to a tree, a dog, or a stranger in the street

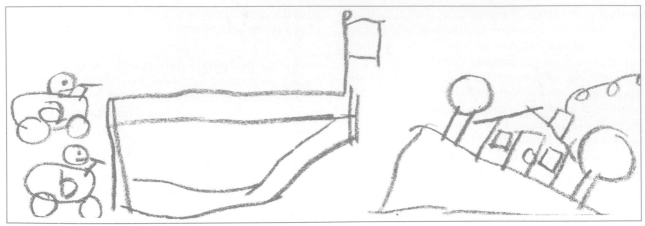

Intuitive preoperational reasoning. "If cars A and B get to the finish together, they go at the same speed" is one example of intuitive preoperational reasoning.

Preoperational child's drawing of a house on a hill.

"feels" OK, you can be sure the child will do it. How many stories have you heard about children who suddenly say something like, "Hey Daddy, look at that fat guy standing next to you." We have to remember that such comments are for the purpose of practice. In spite of embarrassing moments, the more extensive the practice, the greater the future verbal facility and competency. Studies have shown that children who are deprived of speech to any significant degree during this period suffer a developmental lag that may be irreversible.

Piaget, in studying the use of language during this period, found that children seem to talk at rather than with others. We have all had the experience of realizing that other people weren't really listening to us; that they were talking over, around, and through us, mostly to hear themselves talk, as the old saying goes. With three- to seven-year-old children this is the predominant mode. Piaget has called it *collective monologue*. If you ask a group of children to tell you a story, together, you will find as many different stories as there are children. Their speech patterns are egocentric; each child's remarks bear little relationship to what the others are saying. However, in terms of practice, the collective monologue is another means children have of trying out words without having to wait their turn.

The intuitive period is truly a golden opportunity

A child who is thinking at a preoperational level and is asked to draw an upright pencil falling usually cannot draw the sequence of steps shown here. Similarly, if asked to draw a picture of someone dropping a ball, the child will usually draw the beginning and the end, but not the ball in the process of falling, as pictured here.

Piaget's second stage involves intuitive, or preoperational, thought. Oral vocabulary development is especially significant during this stage.

for facilitating language development. But we should also make it clear that preoperational thought is a general mode during this time. This is why a child at this level would choose a tall, thin glass of water rather than a short, wide one. Intuitively, the tall glass seems to have more water in it because it's taller. "Let's not worry that it's thinner," the child might say, "because being taller is enough. It looks bigger to me!" You may think this is a cavalier disregard of the facts, and that's just the point—it is. And it will do absolutely no educational good to tell a child of this age the "real" reasons why the amount of water is the same in both glasses. All you would accomplish would be to get the child to parrot back what you say, without the slightest understanding. There are literally thousands of uproariously funny stories that illustrate how children understand abstract concepts. Ask a six-year-old to say, and then explain, the pledge of allegiance to the flag ("the republic of Richard Stands and one naked individual") or some biblical references ("Pontius the pilot on the flight to Egypt"; "The Father, Son, and Holy Smoke!"). These will remind us of another aphorism: "The child is not a midget-sized adult." A child's understanding is qualitatively different from an adult's.

Piaget has also shown that children at this age have difficulty realizing the reversible nature of relationships. He illustrates this fact with the following interview. A four-year-old girl is asked:

Have you got a sister?
Yes.
And has she got a sister?
No, she hasn't got a sister. I am my sister (1964, p. 85).

We can say, then, that the mental structures at the preoperational stage are largely intuitive, freewheeling, and highly imaginative. Do not assume, however, that because the process seems illogical it is necessarily inferior as a mode of thought. Indeed, much work in the area of creativity suggests that intuition and free association are an important aspect of creative or original problem solving. Intuition allows us to break out of the constraints imposed by reality. Inventors, artists, and other creative people commonly find that many of their ideas come to them intuitively or, as it is sometimes called, preconsciously. When we say, "From the mouths of babes, . . ." we are testifying to the importance of intuitive thinking.

Thus, we can say that the system of thinking that children typically employ during this period is creative and intuitive. Puff the Magic Dragon lives. Yet remember, there are some few signs during this time of an impending shift toward a greater recognition of reality. Recent research has shown a greater ability among preschoolers to distinguish between the real and the imaginary and to understand number sequences than was originally thought. This means children can learn to count better than "one, two, three, ten zillion" and can learn letters better than "1 and emma p." There is also evidence that children at this stage can show some signs of self-discipline (Mischel, 1981). The increase in language ability essentially means that children can talk to themselves about resisting temptation. Some instruction in a formal sense will not damage children. This does not mean, however, that a teacher should structure any substantial portion of a preschool day on learning letters and numbers. Remember, just as was the case with the sensorimotor period, some attributes of the next stage are evident. These new characteristics, however, are very fragile.

The major significance of the period is best summed up by Flavell, who notes that while sensorimotor learning is slow, step by step, concrete, and tied to immediate experience, preoperational learning is lightning fast and mobile. It is the beginning of symbolic thinking, with ideas replacing concrete experience. The child's ideation can range over the past, present, and future in a wink. The greatest single difference is, of course, the level of communication. Children can now share their cognitions socially. Sensorimotor experience is much more private and uncommunicative. "Each baby is imprisoned in her own separate cognitive world" (1985, p. 28).

Concrete Operations (Seven to Eleven Years)

Piaget's next stage represents another major reorganization of mental structure. In the preoperational stage children are dreamers, with magical thoughts and fantasies in abundance. Now, in the **concrete operations stage**, they are young logical positivists who understand functional relationships because they are specific, because they can test the problems out. For example, if we show children at this age the pile of beans or the water-glass experiment, they will tell us there is no change in volume. This time around they understand the specific, or concrete, aspects of the

"You said we could paint anything we wanted to!"

© 1967 NEA Journal.

problem. Now they can measure, weigh, and calculate the amount of water or number of beans so that an apparent difference won't "fool" them.

However, in their wholehearted abandonment of magical thinking, fantasies, and imaginary "friends," they become almost too literal-minded. Their ability to understand the world is now as "logical" as it once was "illogical." For example, they can easily distinguish between dreams and facts, but they cannot separate hypothesis from fact. Five-year-olds usually describe a dream as something that happens in their bedroom, that they watch like a movie, while nine-year-olds describe dreams as mental images inside their heads. Also, once a nine-year-old's mind is made up on a question, new information will not easily change that point of view. In one study, seven- to ten-year-old children were presented with a number of reasons for concluding that Stonehenge (a prehistoric site in England) was a fort rather than a religious center. See the box for the outcome.

In humor we also find evidence of the literal-mindedness of this stage. This is the time when children delight in using explicitness and literalness as a basis for their jokes. Slapstick and pie-throwing reach their zenith during this period. "When am I going to get my just desserts?" asks the fall-guy comedian plaintively. "Are you sure you want it now?" says the partner, holding a cream pie behind his back. You can fill in the balance of the dialogue and imagine the screams of delight from an elementary-age audience.

SPOTLIGHT ON STONEHENGE

A Fort or a Religious Temple?

David Elkind, a leading Piagetian scholar, teaches a discovery unit in elementary school social studies to illustrate the inability of concrete-thinking pupils to distinguish between facts and theories.[a] He shows a series of pictures of Stonehenge. He points out a large number of facts—the huge size of the stones, their placement in an open field, the circular trenches of outer and inner "defense" lines, and similar bits and pieces of information from which it is possible to conclude that Stonehenge was a prehistoric fort. He is careful to list a very large number of facts to back up the conclusion. He then presents just a few facts, such as the open field and the two stones (the heel and the altar) that line up perfectly with the sunrise on June twenty-first each year, thereby suggesting that the site was really a religious temple. This second conclusion has fewer facts behind it, yet it is essentially more logical. The children, however, will not change their minds. To them, the large number of concrete facts, a quantitative difference, is more important than the smaller number of facts that "prove" the religious nature of the site. Essentially, for children at this age, there is no difference between theories and facts. What is important is how many. This means that the basis for complex scientific and logical reasoning is not yet available to elementary-age children.

You can try similar activities with students at this age. Pile up many facts on one side of an argument versus a more abstract set of reasons on fewer facts. In history this could be the defeat of the British at Yorktown (the importance of strategic position and the flanking by the French fleet, versus sheer numbers of soldiers, cannons, rifles, supplies, etc.). In science it could be whether the earth or the sun is in the center of our system (the earth is more important with people, technology, civilization, etc., versus orbits). In any case, the idea is to clarify student opinion to understand the difference between concrete and abstract thought.

[a] Elkind, D. (1970). *Children and adolescents* (p. 54). New York: Oxford University Press.

If, during the previous stage, children play around with fantasies, during concrete operations they play around with literal-mindedness. One researcher illustrates this juvenile sophistry with the following story (again, a favorite at this age): An eight-year-old boy comes to the table with his hands dripping wet. When his mother asks him why he didn't dry his hands, he replies, "But you told me not to wipe my hands on the clean towels." His mother throws up her hands and replies, "I said not to wipe your *dirty* hands on the towels." Another reported the following as a most popular story, "A mother loses her child named Heine. She asks a policeman, 'Have you seen my Heine?'" (Wolfenstein, 1954). Usually by this time children are laughing so hard that we never hear the punch line. And we must admit, compared to the previous period where the simple phrase "poop face" was considered hilarious, concrete-stage humor is more sophisticated, if not more appealing, to adult tastes.

Schooling and concrete operations   In many ways schooling at the elementary age seems to fit the pupils' cognitive stage rather well. Where the school emphasizes skills and activities such as counting, sorting, building, and manipulating, cognitive growth will be nurtured. Field trips to historical sites or science through "kitchen physics" are additional examples. Activities can now have rules. In fact, you could almost say during this time that making the rules for a game or classroom activity is more significant than the activity itself. Whereas the preschool child will obey rules without understanding why we have them, the elementary school child understands rules because of their functional value. You cannot play real baseball without following the rules. However, we must also remember that they have a literal understanding of the concept of rules: Rules are given laws that cannot be changed. Adults understand that rules are a system of regulations that can be replaced by another system, but children see them as fixed, necessary, and arbitrary. The danger, then, is that we will exploit their literal-mindedness in order to maniplate rather than educate them.

Difficulties to avoid   Thus, although schooling at this age is generally successful when it emphasizes skills and concrete activities, certain other aspects are not useful. For example, there is increasing interest in teaching elementary-age children the structure of knowledge in the various disciplines—math, English, history, science—throughout the entire school sequence. Thus, we no longer teach history as facts or events but as a way of thinking. How does a historian think? What is the process whereby he or she knows (in our earlier example) that Stonehenge was a religious site? Given this broad objective of teaching structure, we then try to develop a spiraling curriculum. At each grade we present the concepts in a more sophisticated manner.

Where this process breaks down is precisely at the pupil's level of cognitive understanding. Since their mode of thinking is concrete and they don't have the mental equipment to grasp the cognitive abstractions, they translate the abstractions into concrete and highly specific terms. Boys and girls at this stage develop their own way of understanding the subjects in accord with specific everyday experience. They learn to add in the first grade, take away in the second grade, fractions in the fifth . . . and so on for each subject and each teacher. In the case of subjects in the new curriculum, the same situation prevails but the words have changed. For example, in the "new" math they learn set theory in the second grade, rational and irrational numbers in the fourth, and so on. In other words, the compartments the children use are a reflection of the concrete operations they learn to perform every day in school. All they have learned, in the meantime, is a new set of rote responses. Mary Alice White (1968), a renowned school psychologist, observed the same situation when it came to the question of what parts of the curriculum are considered most important by the children. You can guess by now that they chose the subjects having the most tests and the most homework. Obviously, from a concrete point of view, that is the way to judge the importance or value of a subject. Even though teachers may say that all the subjects are important, actions speak louder than words, especially during this stage.

In Piaget's third stage, concrete operations, activities now can have rules; schooling at this age should emphasize skills and concrete activity.

Parents of these children also get caught in the trap of the literal-minded thinker. Many parents report being upset and frustrated when they try to help their children with schoolwork. Children comment, "But that's not the way the teacher wants us to do it! She wants us to make the plus sign this way, not that way." "Teacher says we have to do spelling first, then arithmetic." "Fractions come from decimals." Usually neither the parent nor the teacher realizes that the difficulty lies in the child's cognitive level. Instead, parents frequently get mad at their children for not realizing, for example, that decimals and fractions are equivalent. And they get annoyed at the teacher for teaching in such simplistic black-and-white terms. At the same time, the teacher gets equally annoyed at reports of such literal-minded parents. The children are caught in the middle between two equally arbitrary systems, neither of which they understand.

During the prior stage of intuitive reasoning, children exhibit a small amount of ability to reason concretely. So too, during the concrete stage, children exhibit some fragile ability to reason abstractly, especially when the learning task is simplified. Thus, there is some foreshadowing of the next stage. This does not mean, however, that it is worthwhile to spend large amounts of academic learning time attempting to promote formal thinking during the elementary school years. When such attempts were made in the 1960s, the programs did not succeed. Elementary children could not develop the ability to think abstractly in learning concepts such as culture or society (Jones, 1968).

Some cognitive-developmental researchers attempt to find evidence of potential for abstract thought during the elementary years. By simplifying the task and then intensively training the children, it is possible to "prematurely" bring about some aspects of growth. However, as Eleanor Neimark points out, these same training or teaching methods have vastly different effects on adolescents as compared to elementary-age pupils. She notes that concepts such as "love, country, parent change their meaning with age" (1982, p. 494). Also, prompting elementary children to say (that is, memorize) such abstract definitions does *not* mean the children will generalize what they have learned. Thus, it is much better for teachers to wait for the onset of puberty and the start of formal operations to really begin instruction designed to promote abstract concept formation. Neimark concludes: "Practically all of the available research regardless of the task employed or the theoretical persuasion of the investigator shows a clear change in the quality and power of thought during the 11 to 15 years age ranges" (1982, p. 493).

Formal Operations (Eleven to Sixteen Years)

The shift to the **formal operations stage** is quite noticeable to the teacher because of the remarkable differences in the characteristics of thinking. Table 5.2 outlines the four main differences.

Possibilities and hypothesis testing   To an elementary-age child the difference between a possibility and a probability is not particularly strong. This point can be illustrated by the findings of studies in which students played what is sometimes referred to as "The Las Vegas Game." It involves an apparatus with three buttons—red, yellow, and blue. When the correct button (red) is pressed, a reward or prize drops into a small chute. The catch is that the machine is adjusted so that it pays off only 66 percent of the time. Thus, the most efficient strategy is to push the red button repeatedly. Both elementary children and adolescents have been tested on the game, and researchers have discovered marked differences from age to age in how the children approach the game.

In one study conducted with this game, elementary school children were puzzled by the fact that no matter which of the three buttons they pushed, the prize came out only part of the time. For example, Lisa,

TABLE 5.2   COMPARISON OF CHILDHOOD AND ADOLESCENT THOUGHT

CHILDHOOD	ADOLESCENCE
Thought limited to here and now	Thought extended to possibilities
Problem solving dictated by details of the problem	Problem solving governed by planned hypothesis testing
Thought limited to concrete objects and situations	Thought expanded to ideas as well as concrete reality
Thought focused on one's own perspective	Thought enlarged to perspective of others

In Piaget's fourth stage, formal operations, children can develop formal patterns of thinking and are able to attain logical, rational strategies.

age nine, concluded that the best strategy was shifting from button to button—for example, "If you win, you shift, and if you lose, you shift." Once she and other nine-year-olds had settled on a strategy, they stuck with it, even when it was apparent that their strategy did not always lead to success. As a result, they received many fewer prizes than they would have had they simply pushed the red button repeatedly. Fifteen-year-old Angie also entertained the idea that the strategy might be a complex one. But once Angie saw that the strategies she tried were not successful, she abandoned them and fairly quickly came to the conclusion that the most efficient way to play the game was to push the red button repeatedly. Her score was much higher than Lisa's.

Essentially, then, Lisa had decided that since there were three buttons, somehow all had to be pushed at one time or another. The teenager recognized the variety of possibilities and then logically focused on the sequence with the highest probable payoff. To put it another way, elementary-age children tend to think about what is; adolescents, about what might be (Sprinthall, Collins, and Edwall 1994).

Such testing of hypotheses is another characteristic difference. This means the teenager has a greater potential for examining logical evidence before reaching closure. A classic demonstration of this characteristic of thought involves the task of finding the combination of five colorless chemicals that will produce a solution of a particular color. Most adolescents know immediately that the right answer is one of the logi-

cally possible combinations of colorless chemicals. Most of them proceed to solve the problem by simply trying each possible combination in turn until the right color shows up. Younger children, however, are less likely to conceive the possible combinations of so many liquids, nor can they proceed systematically through the possible combinations in search of the correct ones (Inhelder and Piaget, 1958).

Expanded thought: Metathinking   Another extremely important shift is adolescents' ability to think about their own thinking and the thoughts of others. This is what is meant by the term *metacognition*. This kind of self-reflection allows for a wide-ranging stretch of the imagination. Ideas can be tried out in the mind. In addition, teenagers can become aware of *how* they know as well as what they know. Being conscious of a variety of learning strategies that might be used is another important characteristic of the teenager. This means the opportunity for self-correction in problem solving is much greater. Teenagers can talk to themselves, a process sometimes called an internal dialogue, and reach new insights without actually needing to test each solution in concrete reality.

Perspectivistic thought   Closely related to meta-thought is the new awareness that different people have different thoughts about the same idea or situation. In other words, a kind of relativism develops. There is no longer one single and correct point of view. Not everyone understands the same way. In fact, Piaget demonstrated repeatedly that young children tend to think everyone views situations as they do. He described these young children as egocentric because they were centered or focused on their own view. Adolescents, however, are more likely to recognize that others' viewpoints are different from their own. It is as though they understand that others have different interests, knowledge, and ways of thinking than they have.

This characteristic of formal operational thinking (and the other three as well) may have a direct connection to the process of reading development. How students actually process and derive meaning from the words they read may be significantly different, depending on children's level of formal operations. When the potential for abstract thought is developed, students are able to attain logical, rational, abstract strategies. Symbolic meanings, metaphors, and similes can now be understood. Stories with a moral can be generalized. Games and simulations can be presented so that the pupil understands their implications. For example, if we want to teach something about economic theories and principles, we can use a game like Monopoly, as long as we ask questions that point to the general principles. If we tried this at the elementary age, we would find that the children could understand the game only as a game; they could not generalize from it. Other powerful means of stimulating abstract thinking are viewing movies and film clips and participating in art activities, such as painting, drama, dance, and music. There are many sources of symbolic material besides those contained in the traditional school subjects. And the more active the symbolic process, the more it enhances cognitive growth. During this stage, writing poems is more effective than viewing them; taking part in an improvisational drama more effective than observing it. Probably the most creative and significant task confronting secondary school teachers is the challenge that this theory of growth presents in building new approaches to the development of curriculum materials.

EDUCATIONAL IMPLICATIONS OF PIAGET'S THEORY

Intelligence and Activity

A significant educational implication of cognitive development is that growth in any one stage depends on activity. In other words, the development of brain power is not fixed at birth but is a function of appropriate activity during any particular stage. Children must engage in appropriate activities to learn. This does not mean they should sit and listen to or observe others. In speaking of development in the first two years, Piaget has said: "Sensorimotor causality does not derive from perceptive causality; to the contrary, visual perceptive causality is based upon a tactico-kinesthetic causality that is itself dependent upon the activity proper" (1970, p. 34). This quote, while demonstrating how difficult it can be to understand a passage from Piaget, also indicates the significance of his equation: Intelligence = activity. Anthropological studies, especially studies of prehistoric humans, have indicated that our brain power increased after the invention of tools. The manipulation of tools, acting or "operating" with axes, knives and primitive shovels, induced the brain to grow. In a sense, primitive men and women, as they began to use tools, were almost challenged to come up with new uses for tools and to invent more efficient and effective tools. The effect of rising to the challenge posed by this activity, the manipulation of tools, itself increased our capacity to understand and become more sophisticated cognitively—the activity developed our mind. The critical point for us is the key phrase in all of Piaget's writings, that *activity produces cognitive growth*. Thus, over and over in his writings to educators, Piaget calls for the **active school**.

The American Question: Can We Speed Up Growth?

In a technologically oriented society such as ours, someone inevitably asks Piaget what is called **the American question**: How can we speed up development? "The first question which I am always asked in the United States is, 'Can one accelerate these stages?'" The answer obviously is no. Given all that Piaget has shown, we cannot speed up the process of intellectual growth.

Barnaby Barratt (1975), an English psychologist, has actually researched the question. He selected students aged twelve, thirteen, and fourteen from the top tracks in math and presented them with difficult reasoning tasks. Then he quite systematically instructed the students in how to solve similar problems. He taught them the steps to use and the reasons. The results indicated that the training "took" with the fourteen-year-olds but was ineffective with the thirteen-year-olds and even less effective with the twelve-year-olds. This means that the improvement was a result of two factors—the critical teaching *and* the stage of cognitive development. In everyday terms this means that the pupils had to be far enough along developmentally in order to grasp the reasoning process and generalize it to similar word problems.

The study also substantiated a second point. How did the "trained" fourteen-year-olds compare to their same-age cohorts? Might not other fourteen-year-olds in the top math tracks also show a similar ability to solve the new problems? It turned out that the same-aged controls did *not* show the same level of reasoning. This is sometimes called the "other side of the American question." If we can't speed up growth, can we simply let students mature at their own pace, a kind of gradual unfolding? Barratt's second set of results, then, indicates that if left alone adolescents will not necessarily develop to their potential in employing formal operations. In fact, a series of studies at the University of Oklahoma demonstrates quite convincingly that educational programs can be effective at all ages (Renner et al., 1976). For example, the researchers in those studies created materials to emphasize the concrete aspects of **conservation** during the early elementary school years. These years are a time when children are at the transition between preoperational and concrete patterns. It is difficult for them to hold their perceptions constant on tasks such as transfer of liquid or solid amount (for example, the spread-out versus bunched-up beans). The researchers systematically instructed such children by employing many hands-on experiences in six types of conservation: (1) numbers, (2) liquid amount, (3) solid amount, (4) weight, (5) length, and (6) area. In general, the results indicated that such careful teaching did improve the ability of children to conserve in problem solving in most of these aspects.

Thus, the answer to the American question is to nurture the process of growth at particular stages rather than simply attempt to accelerate constantly. Teachers do not need to carry the banner "Onward to Formal Operations." Rather, it is important to follow the suggestion of Piaget: "Present the subject to be taught in forms assimilable to children of different ages in accord with their mental structures" (1970, p. 153).

Patricia Arlin: Beyond Piaget

One of the criticisms of Piaget's theory is that the end point of cognitive development, formal operations, may be too limited. A focus on logical reasoning may exclude thought in other areas such as widsom and/or creativity. In fact, it is Robert Sternberg's opinion (1986) that traditional Piagetian theory is really not concerned with individuals of exceptionally high levels of cognitive talent. The reason for the lack of attention to additional stages of development may be that Piaget first concentrated heavily on the thought process of children and then on early adolescence. Recently, a researcher at the University of British Columbia, **Patricia Arlin**, has begun to explore the possibility of postformal operations as a new and more advanced stage (1986). According to Arlin, this stage is characterized by the ability to develop new solutions, devise programs based on broadened visions, and formulate the "productive questions" that enable individuals to expand the knowledge base and gain fresh insights.

Arlin specifies that this advanced stage represents an expansion—not a rejection—of Piaget's theory. Indeed, the ability to define concepts and reason abstractly is a platform upon which problem-finding ability may rest. Arlin notes, however, that most assessments of Piaget's formal-operational period involves asking a person to solve a problem. Finding a new problem, or discovering new questions, is simply not accounted for in the Piaget scheme.

Arlin's work in postformal operations has continued (1990). She has recently identified specific cognitive elements which represent the process of problem finding. These include:

1. Complementarity
2. Detecting asymmetry
3. Openness to change
4. Redefinition of limits
5. Intuition and taste for levels of significance
6. Preference for creativity/originality

Complementarity has a special meaning in that it is the ability to connect unrelated or even contradictory ideas in a new format. For example, Piaget himself brought two ideas together, assimilation and accommodation, to form a larger theory of how we learn. Before Piaget, the general view was that learning was either inductive or deductive. He joined two apparent contradictions and formed a new synthesis; each previous idea was an equal partner in contributing to the new idea. Here is another way to think of this process: Elements that are added together more than increase the total. The metaphor of 1 plus 1 equals three represents the complement. (Notice that this is not the same as a similar-sounding word having to do with a social *compliment*.)

In detecting asymmetry, the process is almost the opposite of complementarity. While most observers would accept an idea or problem solution as accurate, the problem finder would notice perhaps a subtle difference. It was, of course, Piaget himself who noticed differences in children's thinking. Before, many thought that children were simply miniadults in cognitions. Piaget spotted the asymmetry and launched his inquiry. Just think how many persons saw apples fall from trees before Isaac Newton, and yet did not detect gravity.

Openness to change means simply the ability to remain cognitively flexible. Knowledge development is seen as the process of successive approximations. The problem finder creates solutions yet does not close the patent office, so to speak, on new theory and practice. Erikson's revision of his theory of psychosocial development, described in Chapter 6, is an example. He saw the need to combine the bipolar milestones.

In pushing the limits, the problem finder is willing to change current theories. Behavioral scientists always operate from a particular model or paradigm. By testing out the cases or instances where the information doesn't fit, the finder may uncover weaknesses. For example some of the Piagetian critics actually found examples of children's thought more than one stage past their preferred mode. Such a challenge created the need for more research and theory change.

To some degree it is difficult to define the intuition involved in maintaining a bedrock view of what is fundamentally important. In everyday language we often speak of those who get so focused on the trees that the forest disappears. The problem finder can maintain a broad perspective even when it is necessary to focus on small and intricate details. For example, Kohlberg (see Chapter 7), while spending countless hours developing an exact coding scheme for his interview method, never lost sight of the larger philosophical issues of moral judgment.

The final element is a preference for particular conceptual modes involved in exploration and temporary closure. Perhaps the best example is that of famous but fictional detectives, such as Sherlock Holmes or Jane Marple. They use both quantitative and qualitative methods. In fact the hallmark in all their stories is the period of reflection. Sherlock is often staring off into the wilderness or playing the violin, cognitively rearranging the empirical facts. For Jane Marple, on the other hand, it would be her ability to review all the facts and then see a theoretical resemblance to characters from her own small village, St. Mary Mead, for the clues. She often undergoes such a process silently while knitting. In the process of sorting through ideas, the facts are often rearranged to reach novel solutions.

All six elements, then, are involved in the postformal operations stage in adulthood. Arlin's work also illustrates that elements or fragments of postformal cognitions will appear in adolescence and young adulthood, foreshadowing their more complete emergence later in the life cycle. The problem for the educator at this point is to enhance such abilities to prepare for the transition beyond formal operations. In fact, the key word here is to provide experiences in each of these elements as a means of promoting development. She quotes Pasteur, the famous French scientist, who noted that new discoveries don't just happen by chance but come to a "prepared mind" (Arlin, 1986). Arlin's research may help us understand the stage framework more clearly and create teaching strategies to enhance such growth. Her work, then, can be considered as a new map for the journey beyond our current understanding, itself perhaps the best of wisdom as the art and science of problem finding.

Accommodation and Assimilation

In broad outline the stages of cognitive growth—sensorimotor, intuitive or preoperational, concrete, formal, and possibly postformal—represent major transformations of mental organization. Each stage is qualitatively different from the one preceding and is a new means of dealing cognitively with the world. However, it is important for educators to understand how cognitive growth occurs. We have already noticed the critical importance of activity. Equally significant are Piaget's concepts of **accommodation** and **assimilation**. Children at particular stages are maximally able to assimilate particular kinds of experiences. This means, for example, that sensorimotor experiences can be most fully taken in from birth to two years, preoperational from two to seven, and so on. And it also means the opposite, that it is difficult to assimilate experiences beyond the level of mental development. Thus, as teachers, we can get children to say they know, or force them to memorize, but we should not be fooled into believing that they really understand. Piaget might say, "To know by heart is not to know."

SPOTLIGHT ON GENDER

Differences in Verbal Ability Are Disappearing Too

While such studies show the disappearance of differences in math by gender, Janet Hyde and Marcia Linn[a] found a parallel in verbal differences. For many years the existence of female superiority had been considered a virtual truth and was commonly cited in all basic psychology textbooks. So it came as a major surprise when Hyde and Linn, using the new techniques of meta-analysis, found those differences disappearing also. They examined 165 studies containing almost 1.5 million participants. On an overall basis the effect size by gender is almost zero. Also in terms of specific verbal abilities, for example, vocabulary, analogies, reading, writing, anagrams, and the SAT V, the results were close to zero. They even examined for differences in cognitive process, such as ability to retrieve, select, and analyze relevant information. Again no real differences. It is, of course, difficult to pinpoint the causal factors; why, for example, do so many current studies so clearly disprove the earlier view? The authors only speculate. Have boys been encouraged in classrooms to write and reflect more and girls less? Or were the differences partly caused by the researchers themselves? Hyde and Linn[a] found two interesting points: Male researchers more often than female researchers obtained gender differences, and journals seemed to favor publication of studies reporting differences. These two factors combined may have added significantly to the "validity" of the earlier view. In any case the current evidence is clear: Males and females are equivalent in verbal ability, no matter how it is measured.

[a] Hyde, J., and Linn, M. (1988). Gender differences in verbal ability: A meta-analysis. *Psychological Bulletin* 10(4), 53–69.

According to Piaget, the activity of assimilating certain experiences from the environment forces the child to accommodate, or internalize, them. Internalizing experiences is critical to cognitive growth and cannot take place if experiences are allowed, in effect, to go in one ear and out the other. Piaget suggests that the most complete development takes place when children assimilate experiences from their environment, since only then will they be able to accommodate, or internalize, those learnings. As we have indicated, this is the major new challenge facing educators—to develop an array of such experiences to provide maximal cognitive development.

Another way to think of the two processes is suggested by Piagetian scholar **Hans Furth** (1981). He notes that assimilation by itself means that the person simply takes all new experiences into his or her mind without worrying in the least whether they really do fit. Thinking as assimilation is more like daydreaming or imagining. We don't check out our views. We take in new experiences but our understanding does not change. Furth calls taking in experiences and ideas from the outside world without changing what they mean an *inside process*. Accommodation by itself is, of course, just the opposite. We may think about a new experience or idea, but we do not try to take it into our consciousness. We keep the new information at arm's length, so to speak. A student who dutifully memorizes a string of abstractions without any understanding is an example of a kind of pure accommodation. The words are said but the meaning isn't there. In fact, psychologists every once in a while run across a human being who exhibits monumental feats of memory such as reciting an entire Shakespearean play, reeling off the names of all the Roman emperors, or itemizing all Köchel numbers of all Mozart's work. When quizzed more closely, we realize that these people do not really comprehend the meaning of any of the material they spout forth. Some persons with this ability are called *idiot savants*, which means literally stupid-wise people. The learning may have been by rote or because of a photographic memory. The information remains separated from understanding, a kind of splendid isolation, not to be confused with genuine learning.

If assimilation and accommodation remain as separate, isolated experiences, then no real mental occurs. In a manner similar to the way two-year-olds play in parallel, the two processes don't interact. When they do interact, however, a most significant

FIGURE 5.2 Piaget's learning interaction. Equilibration is the process of balancing assimilation and accommodation.

Assimilation

Fitting experiences into our present stage of cognitive development. One of William James' children at approximately two years of age, on seeing an orange for the first time, insisted that it was a ball. When he saw a corkscrew for the first time, he called it "bad scissors."

Accommodation

Changing our present stage of cognitive processing to incorporate new experience. Any child after being sprayed by a black-and-white furry animal: "That kitty can't be a kitty!"

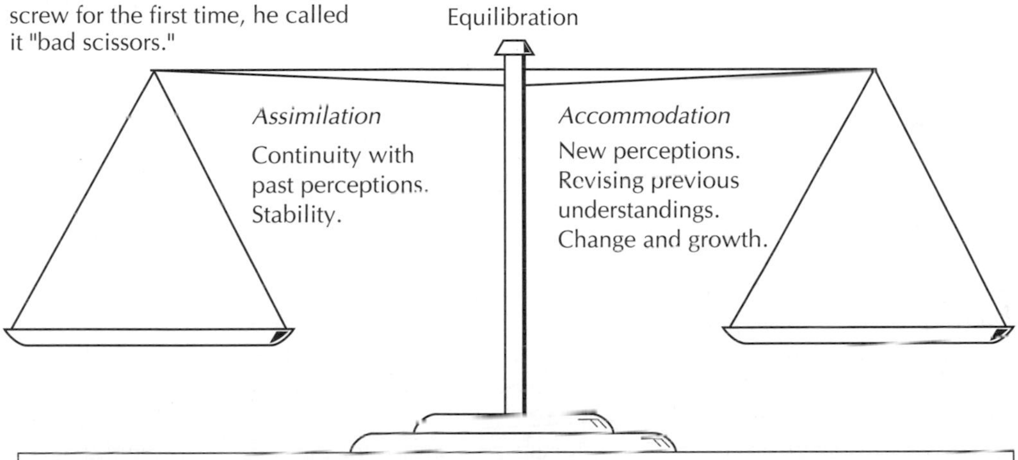

Equilibration

Assimilation

Continuity with past perceptions. Stability.

Accommodation

New perceptions. Revising previous understandings. Change and growth.

Equilibration is the balancing act between the "old" and the new—between perceptions and experiences. It is a dynamic process that attempts to reduce dissonance.

An eight-year-old "equilibrating" on the volume conservation task.
   "It sure looks like there is more water in the tall, thin glass, but when I pour it back into the short, fat glass, it's the same—I wonder. . ."
A secondary school pupil "equilibrating" during a rereading of *Moby Dick*:
   "When I read this as a kid I thought it was just a neat whaling story—how to harpoon, the dangers of the sea. Now it seems different. Why is the Captain so obsessed with this whale? Does it have some special meaning?"

learning activity takes place, the process of equilibration.

Equilibration, or Knowledge Disturbances

As illustrated in Figure 5.2, **equilibration** is the process of balancing what we already know (assimilation) and what we may be asked to learn that doesn't quite fit (accommodation). Furth calls this a process of *knowledge disturbances*. Remember that there is an important developmental assumption about the propensity to know, variously termed "curiosity drive," "competence motivation," "the intrinsic need to master the environment," or "personal efficacy." Studies have shown that monkeys will "work" for long hours on interesting puzzles. So too will human babies. In fact, Flavell has pointed to recent research that shows that babies will also "work" in order to get at interesting pictures, sounds, and puzzles. This means that there is an intrinsic (built-in) drive, motivation, or personality disposition to learn new things. Children are not simply empty, waiting passively for outside stimulation. Rather, Piaget's theory assumes just the opposite: Humans act on the environment. As we interact we become curious about any new event or unfamiliar idea. That is what Furth means by knowledge disturbances. Our natural bent doesn't allow us to be content just to exist; so when new things don't fit our past assimilations we ask why. Such is the basic learning motivation to master problematic situations. We learn by balancing the old information *and* the new—the process of equilibrating.

But how does the process work? Do we simply continually expose children to a wide variety of new experiences, a kind of force-feeding, to move the child to higher stages? Clearly not, because growth occurs slowly. New information and experiences are balanced (equilibrated) slowly so that the scales never dip too far. This is called "learning by exposure to a moderately discrepant environment." Another way to describe it is as a slight mismatch—new information not quite fitting with our old views. The end result of such experiences is the gradual development of more complex cognitive structures, or learning sets. First growth occurs within a particular stage as a result of small discrepancies and slow equilibration. Then there is movement to the next stage, followed again by a new set of mismatches and the slow incorporation for growth within the new stage. The slight imbalance on the accommodation side creates an adapting intelligence—not a fixed but an ongoing process. In this sense intellectual growth is the gradual development of more complex and more efficient rational problem-solving capacities that we can generalize to new problems.

Furth provides an interesting description of a seven-year-old German boy starting to accommodate new information. Furth's example illustrates that once the new information is taken in through equilibration, the boy thinks in a new way. The boy learns that churches have steeples. Then, during a bike ride, he overhears a number of adults entering a house say they are going to church. The boy muses. A regular house can't be a church. It doesn't have a steeple. It seems nearly impossible to consider a simple house as a real church. His father tells him not to bike near the house on Sundays because of the traffic. Soon he hears other people nearby talking of attending services there. He continues to deny the validity of the new insights. Gradually, however, the moderate discrepancy pushes him to reconsider his earlier impossibility. After talking, listening, seeing (and perhaps even peeking inside during a service), he comes to a new understanding of the idea of a church with or without special architecture. In Furth's description he very carefully points out that no one tried to argue with the boy, nor did the situation become stressful. In fact, he pointedly notes that the boy was "in a relaxed state of mind" when he began to think through the discrepancies (1981, p. 267).

It's clear you should not force accommodation. Equilibration takes place when there is a threshold of new awareness, or curiosity. There is some sense of uneasiness, an awareness that might be expressed as "Somehow my thinking doesn't quite handle the new information. Gradually I'll need to change my mind."

One final illustration: A small child in the first grade reported with a broad smile on arriving home each day, "I'm going to get a present for going to school!" After a few more days a parent asked, "Are you sure you're going to get a present?" "Oh, yes," came the answer brightly. "She said when she called our name you could say 'here' or 'present'." So in time we come to know when a house is a church and, as one of the authors of this book so vividly remembers, when a present isn't a present. When such an accommodation takes place, there is a qualitative shift in thinking. We cannot go back to our old way of thought once the change is really incorporated.

Under conditions of accommodation and equilibration, we sense that a new explanation is better, or we intuitively begin to feel that a new level of understanding is starting to dawn. We are not quite sure, and in fact may be a bit apprehensive, about exploring an unknown; part of us may be attracted to the change, while another part (our old, comfortable way of thinking) resists. The feelings gradually have to be worked through during equilibration. Some of the old must be relinquished to make room for the new, a process that can involve anxiety.

As a teacher introducing new concepts, slightly better problem-solving methods, or somewhat more comprehensive theories, remember that you are inducing some equilibration process in the pupils. They will need extra psychological and personal support during such transition periods.

In addition to giving extra personal support during new learning, also remember that there is little sense in teaching preoperational or early concrete thinkers to think abstractly. If for the sake of equilibration we present information that is over the heads of the pupils, new learning will not take place—there will be no reconciliation of new ideas. In fact, the only notable increases may be in pupil frustration, anxiety, and perhaps rote memorization.

To sum up the phases of the learning of new concepts (that is, how we accommodate and then assimilate knowledge disturbances), Table 5.3 outlines a seven-step process that includes both the thoughts and feelings that the learner experiences. Gradualness, curiosity, and relaxed reflection lead eventually to mastery of the new concept, self-confidence as a

TABLE 5.3   PHASES OF DEVELOPMENTAL LEARNING

EQUILIBRATING THE NEW AND THE OLD

1. Awareness of a moderate discrepancy arises in understanding the meaning of an event or idea.

2. A feeling of puzzlement ensues: curiosity, uneasiness, affective arousal.

3. More new information accumulates that doesn't fit the prior understanding.

4. During periods of relaxed reflection, one tries to fit the new pieces of information into the old scheme; talking to oneself.

5. A new balance is reached. The new information moves from accommodation to assimilation.

6. After sufficient time the new information becomes "old" information and can be generalized to similar situations.

7. A new moderate discrepancy arises and the process continues.

learner, and the ability to generalize the idea to other similar circumstances. This learning process is quite obviously different from rote memorization.

Lev Vygotsky: Teaching for Growth

As we have noted, Piaget, if not actively opposed to educational applications, was at least ambivalent. Almost simultaneously with Piaget's early work, a Russian researcher, **Lev Vygotsky**, was to validate and in some cases precede Piaget's original work on stages. More important, however, was Vygotsky's willingness to indeed demand that those insights needed to focus on application. In a sense that was an easy transition for him to make, as he was a teacher before becoming an educational psychologist. He also worked directly with another major Russian psychologist, Alfred Luria, soon after the Communist Revolution in the 1920s. Prior to that time huge segments of the Russian peasant population had been held in positions of illiteracy. The new government under Lenin found itself confronted with a major and fundamental educational challenge. Luria and Vygotsky worked to create educational methods to teach these populations not only how to read but more importantly how to comprehend what they were reading (Blanck, 1990). As a result of those experiences they

found four stages of cognitive growth which paralleled those of Piaget. For example, in Uzbekistan his subjects would answer the following question in accord with their stage of development.

> In Siberia all bears are white. My friend Ivan was in Siberia and saw a bear. What color was it?

At an abstract level the subject would immediately answer correctly. At the concrete level the answers were quite different; for example, "I've never been to Siberia so I don't know" or "Ivan is your friend, ask him."

These results convinced Vygotsky that learning to read without comprehension was fruitless. His experiences led to a series of extremely important instructional principles.

1. Effective teaching marches just ahead of the current developmental stage of the learner.

2. The child must be actively involved in learning, not a passive receptacle.

3. Education includes a major social interactive component with parents, teachers, and peers. Learning activity should include reflective discussion with others.

4. Stages of cognition are a series of radically transformed systems which undergo restructuring and reorganization.

5. Each stage is qualitative, and transitions involve disintegration prior to a new and more complex integration. Without appropriate interaction no growth occurs.

6. The cerebral cortex undergoes neurological reorganization (similar to Hebbs's cell-assembly concepts, see Chapter 4) during stage growth.

Thus there are similarities to Piaget on the basic structural components of cognitions and stages. For example, memorization was seen as a dead end. Vygotsky called that approach "fossilization" (1985). Also he saw the higher-order cognitive process as the essential building block for logical thought, comprehension, and generalization.*

---

* Actually it was probably this goal which caused him to fall from favor with the Stalinist regime. Vygotsky refused to tailor his research to Stalin's view, and his work was banned in the Soviet Union from the early 1930s until the late 1950s.

Shared Cognitions

Although Vygotsky's work bears many similarities to Piaget's, important differences are also apparent. Vygotsky did not view the learner as a kind of Robinson Crusoe (Davydov, 1990). The learner is not relegated to an isolation booth to build his or her own conceptual tools through an exclusive internal dialogue. Instead the learner's cognitions are shared. Reflective discussions with others provide perspectives for cognitive growth. The role of formal and information discussions provide the social interactions for improving cognitive problem solving. Opportunities to test one's reflections help broaden perspectives. In fact a recent researcher has found that by matching a concrete conserving peer with a nonconserver, growth occurs. Using Piaget's water glass transfer, the mismatched dyads were asked to do the experiment and discuss among themselves how to explain the difference in water level. There was a major difference between the experimental and control groups in ability to solve such conservation problems. From the mismatched pairs, 80 percent of the nonconservers reached conservation versus 50 percent for regular classroom instruction (Tudge, 1990).

The Zone of Proximal Growth

Vygotsky was also careful to distinguish between effective development instruction and traditional classroom learning. Remember his truism that teaching can tow development. "The only good kind of instruction is that which marches ahead of development and leads it: It must be aimed not so much at the ripe as at the riping" (1962, p. 104). He coined the phrase *zone of proximal growth* to denote this concept. Education should lead development but be only slightly ahead of the learners' current preferred mode.

From these insights then Vygotsky clearly has resolved the Piagetian ambivalence about instruction, or, as we have called it, "The American Question." Vygotsky does not call for acceleration but rather for a slow and careful sequencing of instruction. The teacher should not and cannot do the cognitive work on behalf of the child. Instead the teacher can present problems to be solved, and then must be willing to provide substantial time and place for the discussion process. The problems selected, of course, can be only slightly beyond the present competence while a new means of problem solving is demonstrated. This is both active teaching and active learning through meaningful activities. The students are not told what to say or asked to memorize lists of facts but rather to engage in problem-solving activities and then to try to draw out reflective meaning through discussion. Insights are not given by the adults but rather are created and tested out by the children. The bottomline in all this is Vygotsky's emphasis on comprehension. Learning without comprehension, which we point out throughout this volume, borders on the fraudu-

According to Vygotsky, meaningful learning occurs when the teacher is able to engage students in problem-solving activities that are just beyond their current level of functioning. He called this the "zone of proximal development."

SPOTLIGHT ON RICHARD LIGHT

Vygotsky-Piaget Groups at Harvard

Richard Light has been assessing the approaches to college teaching through a series of seminars at Harvard University. Although he did not set up a direct experiment on the developmental approach, his work clearly points in the direction of peer interaction. He selected one of the most terrifying subjects, statistics, for his work. Rather than follow the conventional lecture and demonstration method, he used peer-led small groups. On an intuitive basis he selected group leaders who were slightly ahead of their peers in background and leadership. He then met with the leaders on a regular basis to review the content and the demonstration proce-

dures. The leaders in turn met with small groups (five to eight students) for instruction. The atmospheres became more relaxed as the term progressed. The fear, anxiety, and mutism were replaced by increasing levels of interaction. The noise level went up as the participation increased. Thus all the elements of the Piaget-Vygotsky model were present. And, as you've most likely guessed, the outcome was also positive. The students did better in stastistics under the peer-led interaction than with conventional large-group instruction. In fact Light, who is a very dynamic and highly rated teacher himself, was so impressed by the findings that

he recommended this approach to the teaching of any subject from statistics to moral reasoning. Faculty guidance to be sure was important. Light termed it *mentored small groups.* The socially isolated students actually gained the most from the peer interaction.[a]

You can try the Light method by setting up small groups with a student teacher for each. The format looks like the diagram.

Don't forget to meet regularly with the leaders of the groups to supervise their techniques and keep the content valid.

---

[a]Light, R. J. (1990). *The Harvard Assessment Seminars.* Cambridge: Harvard University.

Traditional Section

Teaching Fellow

Mentored Cluster

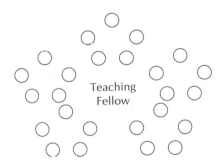

Teaching Fellow

- Group of twenty to twenty-five students meeting with teaching fellow each week.
- Group meets same time, same place each week.
- Discussion is led by teams of two or three students with teaching fellow present.

- Groups of five students meet without a teaching fellow each week.
- Teaching fellow acts as resource between section meetings.
- Teaching fellow meets with student discussion leader before and after each session.
- One student acts as discussion leader each week.

lent because it creates the myth that education has somehow taken place. Vygotsky was so committed to the dynamic process of cognitive problem solving that he even viewed standardized IQ tests as measuring merely static and fossilized knowledge. It is interesting to note in this regard that the current revisions in national tests such as the National Teacher Examination and perhaps even the Scholastic Aptitude Test are moving in the Vygotsky direction of presenting more problem-solving questions and less testing of memorized recognition of facts.*

Classroom Instruction: Peer Interaction and Relaxed Reflection

The problems and opportunities for instruction within the developmental framework then have particular relevance to the classroom. Learning has a major interpersonal component through peer discussion. The framework, however, is not that of a random or somewhat romantic view—pupils on their own achieving great leaps forward and new insights for the civilized world. The role of the teacher is critical in selecting problems and setting up the laboratory like conditions for guided exploration and development. Shared ignorance is not the goal. The process is slow and complex within a supportive class atmosphere.

Dimant and Bearison: A Community College Study

In addition to teacher-directed learning focused on the zone of proximal growth, there is the possibility of effective peer interaction under certain conditions. As noted earlier, Tudge (1990) reported success in promoting conservation among elementary-age pupils by setting up dyads of conservers and nonconservers in problem-solving situations. A similar study was conducted at the community college level by Dimant and Bearison (1991). They had observed that not all college sudents were actually functioning at the level of formal operations. In fact some estimates run as high as 50 percent that certain students are still functioning at a concrete level in some subject areas (Hudak and Anderson, 1990). As a result, Dimant and Bearison decided to set up dyads from a pool of forty-five college students. In one grouping

they had seven pairs of formal and concrete thinkers (the mismatched group). The second group was composed of eight pairs of concrete thinkers (the matched group). The third group consisted of fifteen students as a control, receiving standard didactic instruction. All groups studied the same problem-solving activities over a six-week period, figuring out how to combine liquids in a chemical mixture. The dyads were instructed to discuss the procedures and the solutions between themselves ("Talk out loud as you explore the problem") while attempting to answer the questions posed for each problem.

The dyad instruction, then, followed the Piagetian model. The learning was activity-based and inductive. The dyads engaged in the mixing tasks. Also there was substantial reflection through discussion as the pairs sought to figure out and agree on the reasons. The Vygotsky zone was also created for the mismatched pairs in which one member was slightly ahead of the other. The results were most interesting.

1. The mismatched pairs achieved the greatest gains in formal operations.

2. Both members of the dyad in the mismatched group gained.

3. The matched concrete pairs showed no gains and were similar to the controls.

The Dimant and Bearison study, then, confirms the approach used with elementary school children but also extends the implications. Their study indicated that the mismatched group used more planning strategies, reasoned out loud more, and interacted more frequently than the others. They were noisier, yet with a purpose. Perhaps most surprising was the second finding, namely that both sides of the dyad benefited. It is perhaps easier to see why the concrete thinker improved, but why would the formal thinker benefit? The program does not rob Patricia or Peter to pay Pauline or Paul. The answer probably lies in the interaction. The formal thinker would improve by the act of explaining and seeking consensus. This reminds us of the old truism that one who teaches, learns. It also reminds us of two other outcomes: Conventional instruction and peer interaction by themselves are not particularly effective.

Vygotsky and Affect

Vygotsky, along with Piaget and Furth, was also concerned about the cognitive and the affective. Sarcasm, hostile questioning, poking fun at student error and

---

* Some years ago a researcher with the Educational Testing Service found that such objective tests required memorization in over 70 percent of the items tested (Frederiksen, 1984).

the like are at least as destructive if not so more so in this model. Periods of relaxed reflection in group activity are important, with the teacher or a peer modeling respect for thoughtful pupil contributions. The zone of proximal growth in fact has a heavy affective component. Just think for a moment of the positive and excited feelings you've experienced when you have been just on the verge of new understanding. Such breakthroughs are the best examples of your self-concept as a learner. It is the feeling that comes from a realization that fragments of ideas and concepts are now being reorganized and restructured into a more meaningful whole. The glimpse is the first step in the zone as the positive feelings build. In education it is almost a truism to distinguish between extrinsic and intrinsic motivation. The extrinsic is learning in order to receive some kind of an external reward (money, a grade, a gold star). The intrinsic is vastly different, the enjoyment that comes from learning and problem solving itself. The zone creates the framework for such intrinsic motivation. On the other hand it does require careful observation and understanding by the teacher. If the teacher is too far ahead, then the experience is just as meaningless as when the level of teaching is too far behind. In fact one developmental scholar has commented somewhat ironically that often teachers get trapped in between stages: "Either we are too early and they can't learn it or we're too late and they already know it" (Duckworth, 1987, p. 31).

Vygotsky's Contribution

Tragically, Vygotsky died at the relatively young age of 37. Apparently he was aware of his failing health for a number of years, which may have accounted for the almost-frenzied pace of producing over 180 written contributions in a very short time. To put this in perspective, remember that much of his research was conducted in remote villages and that he was constantly forced to spend a good deal of time earning a living through teaching. Somehow he was able to integrate these many activities while turning out a huge number of scholarly papers. Today his work stands as a major contribution, especially for educational psychology. He was clearly interested in basic research, yet he was even more committed to the translation of these ideas to practice. In Chapter 1 we spoke about the four corners of teaching and learning; Vygotsky's concept of social interaction within the zone of proximal growth shed important light on the problem. His brief and meteoric career in the 1920s

and 1930s has very significant implications for educational practice.

BRAIN PHYSIOLOGY AND PIAGET'S STAGES

As our ability to assess brain functions from a technical standpoint has increased, particularly through the use of electroencephalograms (EEGs), a question arises. Is there any relation between changes in the brain and the stages of cognitive development? Piaget had made the claim without benefit of such advanced technology. Appropriate interactive experiences produce stage growth up to a point, and then transformation (a qualitative shift) occurs. The person employs a new and more sophisticated system of cognitive process. Recent EEG work by William Hudspeth at the University of Northern Colorado and Robert Thacher at the University of Maryland has shown changes that coincide with those assumed by Piaget (Denton, 1987). The process of brain maturation was found to be discontinuous rather than linear. This meant that there were growth spurts that lined up with the sensorimotor, preoperational, concrete, and formal stages. The only significant differences between these findings and Piaget's estimates were that the sensorimotor stage may extend from birth to three and a half years rather than two years. In addition, the EEGs revealed the possibility of a fifth stage. Formal operations matured between eleven and fifteen years. The EEGs of young adults suggest a postformal period much as Patricia Arlin's work has outlined. These studies are preliminary but may well represent major new findings. At this point, what is known about the physiology of changes in the brain does suggest a clear relationship in the organization of the brain between stagelike cognitive growth and structural change.

Basically, the physiological research points out that the brain at higher stages of growth is organized more efficiently. A person who can process experience at an abstract level is more competent. It is not the case that such higher-order thought means that the person has to work harder to comprehend or understand. Rather, the opposite is the case. Research by Richard Haier, at the University of California at Irvine, finds that abstract thinkers actually use *less* brain power (glucose metabolism) in problem solving than their concrete-thinking counterparts. Brain scans showed that the concrete thinkers "burned glucose like crazy" when confronted with complex problems (Hostetler, 1988). Thus, it is the quality of the cognitive process, abstract versus concrete, not the quantity of effort, that pays off in complex learning. The finding of changes in brain structure, nerve insulation, and myelinization supports the basic Piagetian position that cognitive growth is not just linear and quantitative.

Brain changes, however, do not occur automatically. Important differences take place according to interaction. Recent research has shown that a rich and stimulating environment for rats produces brains with a heavier cortex, larger neurons, more connectors, and more support cells. This is another reminder of the developmental truism of appropriate "hands-on" experience as the engine for growth. To prove the point, one study placed adult rats in a stimulating environment (a cage loaded with rat toys). Baby rats as well were placed in the same cage. Unfortunately, the adults dominated the scene. They played actively with all the toys. The babies watched on the sidelines. You may guess who benefited from the interactive experience. The baby rats did not develop. Robert Sylvester drew some apt parallels. How many times do adults organize activities for children that only play out adult fantasies (Little League baseball, ballet, piano for tots) and do not provide children with growth opportunities? A second parallel even closer to the classroom is the continued reliance on memorization, drill, and workbooks. Sylvester suggests such busywork provides an environment like that of rats in "culturally impoverished" cages with only one running wheel. He said those rats didn't develop either; "shades of continual drudgery with workbooks and long division problems" (1986, p. 93).

The research then makes two related points. Brain physiology exhibits changes in general accordance with Piaget stages. Appropriate hands-on active learning experiences are important to nurture such growth. Dull, passive experiences don't help. Adult experiences somewhat watered down also don't help.

At the same time, it is just as important to underscore what the recent brain research does not show. Some have suggested that brain changes called **periodizations** are directly relevant to teaching. In this view, periods of rapid growth may be followed by periods of no growth. Children may not be capable of learning much of anything when growth ceases (Epstein, 1978).

At this point we must remember that no evidence supports such a position. As Kurt Fischer and Lazerson summarize the findings, "They suggest that there is only a broad, nonspecific relation between brain development and Piagetian periods. They do not support the argument that children cannot learn new skills during times when their brains are growing slowly" (1985 p. 70). Thus, it is important to be alert to any suggestion that a child may be like a computer and be "down" and unable to learn just after the growth-spurt periods. Growth depends on appropriate interaction before, during, and after stage shifts.

PIAGETIAN THEORY: NEW DIRECTIONS

By far the most important research program in the post-Piaget era is the work of Professor **Robbie Case** and his colleagues first at the Ontario Institute for Studies in Education and most recently at Stanford University. Case has systematically set out to examine the Piaget model one step at a time through an impressive series of linked studies. In this manner he avoids the difficulties experienced by the first wave of anti-Piagetians who would conduct studies in a narrowly focused area of information processing, find exceptions to the stages and pronounce an end to the theory. Case found, for example, that some evidence of advanced thought in young children could be produced only under extreme testing conditions. A second problem was that such early competence was very task-specific and different from the tasks used to assess the same competence later on. A third problem was the inability of young children to generalize. For example, while some might show an indication of conservation prior to the age of 5 or 6, there was, in Case's words, "massive failure" to promote the general competence of conservation at an earlier age. The overall problem, then, is that the researchers critical of Piaget themselves overgeneralized from their findings. Those researchers, Case noted, "sacrificed too much of the original Piaget" (1992, p. 376).

In order to right the balance and not, following our metaphor in the first chapter, toss out the baby with the bath water, Case carried out a long series of research. Certainly one of the major weaknesses of the interpretation of Piaget's early work was an assumption that each stage was a generalized set of mental operations which was very broad across a wide variety of intellectual, interpersonal and value domains. Not to mix too many metaphors in the same paragraph, but the sense was that each stage was a comprehensive worldview, like the early rock song, "The Eggplant That Ate Chicago." In the language of technical research this is called the *question of synchronous versus asynchronous development*. Is the pro-

Robbie Case's research validated Piaget's earlier findings that cognitive growth occurs in stages and that, while individual differences occur within stages, the sequence of stages seems to remain intact for all humans.

gression across domains even or uneven? If it is uneven, referred to as a *décalage*, that is, a systematic gap in development, then do we eliminate the concept of qualitative stage? Also, it was clear that the research studies certainly supported the idea of uneven growth versus a single-stage model.

As a result, Case accepted the idea of different domains and then wanted to test out the question of stage growth *within* specific competencies. Usually he and his associates set up problem-solving activities for children in different groupings, generally four, six, eight, and ten years of age, and in some studies added groups of adolescents or even younger children. Also some of the studies were conducted cross-culturally.

The domains assessed included

1. Physics problems—some standard Piaget tests of the balance beam

2. Social tasks—sharing gifts and juice at a birthday party

3. Telling time and changing money—numerical concepts

4. Empathy—feelings of being happy, sad, angry, etc.

5. Story telling—completing stories for intentionality

6. Spatial concepts—relationships in children's drawings

7. Motor development—the use of utensils with yogurt, peas, carrots, etc.

The children represented a variety of intellectual levels. Most studies were conducted with normal-range IQs and then cross-validated with other groups such as high-IQ gifted or children with learning disabilities (LDs). Reading these studies as a whole, one cannot fail to be impressed with the care and patience of the researchers in questioning the children to determine their cognitive structure. The researchers didn't lead but rather clarified and supported the children as the answers were being disclosed. Imagine, for a moment, what was involved in studying the motor development, watching and tracking an eighteen-month-old attempt to scoop yogurt, keep peas on a spoon, mash a banana with a fork. The room must have been awash with food fragments, yet the researchers intrepidly continued. Or imagine the researcher who traveled to an extremely rural area in Africa's Upper Volta, translated the material into the local language (Ewe), and then negotiated particularly with the local chiefs for consent to travel from house to house (shades of Vygotsky and Luria in their treks to Uzbekistan).* Of course, at least as important as the process was the outcome of such investigations.

---

* Ironically and tragically, this particular researcher, Thomas Fiati, withstood all the rigors of rural Africa, only to be killed in an auto accident near home, just after submitting the final draft of his doctoral thesis.

With normal-range IQ children, the results supported the following conclusions:

1. Growth in each of the seven domains progressed in a stage sequence.

2. Individual differences were always within each stage and never exceeded two substages.

3. The different domains do not represent a single larger stage but rather are parallel and somewhat independent, e.g., a multilevel conception of domains.

4. Stage of complexity is more important than the information-processing working memory in solving problems.

This means that the amount of unevenness, asynchrony, or individual differences in information processing remains *within* each stage and does not span *across* the stages. As a result, then, individual differences in, say, working memory will vary within a group of six-year-olds but will not reach across the two-year age range to explain the problem-solving competency of the eight-year-olds in the various domains under investigation. Also this means that we cannot think of concrete operations as a single stage but rather as concrete operations in different domains. An earlier study by one of the authors had compared groups of eight-, nine-, and ten-year-olds across three domains—physics, interpersonal, and emotional. The results were similar. The age trend confirmed a developmental stage sequence, yet there was a very low intercorrelation (relationship) across the domains. The children were growing at different rates across the domains (Sprinthall and Burke, 1985).

Case and associates also conducted more severe tests of the individual differences versus the stage differences in the studies with the gifted. He used three groups of gifted: high verbal, high performance, and high on both measures. They examined performance on nine different measures and found very few differences when compared to same-age average-ability peers. This indicates that the stage of development was by far the most important variable. The one interesting exception was on learning tasks which involved providing cues and feedback. The high IQs were much more likely to employ the cues in modifying their solutions. This indicates that the high IQs do not differ significantly from normals in a wide variety of domains such as story telling, story complexity, art, counting, speed, etc. On the other hand, Case also compared the high-IQ youngsters to a group of older children with the same "mental" age. The results indicated that the high-IQ group scored lower than their same mental age peers on the same seven tests. From this, the conclusion appears to be that stage is more important than other factors and that development in those domains was equal for the most part. Giftedness seems more likely an indicator of rapid learning within a stage and not that the students are rapid stage developers.

Two additional studies provided more convergent validity to the neo-Piagetian model. The LD children did not show any major asymmetry across domains when compared to non-LD. Such children were slower in their processing rate but not more than one substage lower. In the cross-cultural study comparing schooled city children with nonschool rural youngsters from the Upper Volta river in Africa, the results also indicated the importance of the stage domain sequence. Assessments in four domains with three age groups indicated that there was only one exception to the stage progression. For the completely nonschooled rurals, numerical representation lagged behind the performance of their schooled urban peers, otherwise the sequence remained intact.

Case and associates have been able to cross-validate some of Piaget's basic concepts, change some aspects of the model, and provide a framework for incorporating information processing with the redesigned theory. As the work continues, further clarifications will emerge. For now, however, the conclusions and implications are significant. The concept of stagelike cognitive structures that are **qualitatively** different has been reconfirmed. There are variations of performance within each stage according to information-processing concepts of working memory and speed of learning, for example, **quantitative** differences. Rather than global stages, there are a series of different domains of stage and sequence in problem solving. This means that educators should continue to employ the stage and sequence model from Piaget along with modifications supplied by Professor Case and his associates at Stanford. This is not, however, the final word on needed modifications. Professor Sternberg, at Yale University, has also made some important discoveries for revising stage theory.

Cognitive Development: Too Narrow a Focus?

Psychologist **Robert Sternberg** (1986) at Yale, has cautioned that an exclusive focus on cognitive development may be misleading. His argument is that both lay people and professionals tend to equate cognition with logical reasoning, problem solving, and speed of learning. Also, he notes that most standard measures of intelligence (see Chapter 16) actually assess a very limited aspect of cognitive ability. As a result of his surveys, he now concludes that we are really missing the boat. Instead of one domain, intelligence, he suggests two additional areas of equal importance, wisdom and creativity. He defines *wisdom* as involving concepts such as judgment, fairness, sagacity (willingness to consider advice from others as well as interpersonal sensitivity), perceptiveness, and information seeking. Thus, he takes the position that intelligence and wisdom may overlap in some areas, yet the domains also have some distinct differences. In his discussion of the third domain, creativity, he partly covers previous theory in distinguishing between intelligence and creativity. Thus, *creativity* is seen as imaginative, unconventional, aesthetic, flexible, a novel integration of information, and similar processes. The major problem concerning creativity, however, is not so much with the concept but with the present state of measurement (see Chapter 15). In fact, he takes the position that current measures of creativity are trivial.

Sternberg's major point is that a three-factor model of brain power will provide us with a more accurate framework for understanding the process of cognitive growth. Also, at least implicitly, he is suggesting that the goals of schooling ought to be broadened. A focus on intelligence and achievement leaves the other aspects of development either to random forces or else to oblivion. He cites a longitudinal study of the famous "Quiz Kids," children of unusually high intelligence who performed in a radio program of that name in the 1940s: The study underscored their apparent lack of creativity as adults (Sternberg and Davidson, 1985). In fact, a careful and systematic study of superior academic achievers at Johns Hopkins University, reported by Paul Janos and Nancy Robinson, classified the Phi Beta Kappa graduates as "stable, stodgy, and unoriginal," intelligent but not creative (1985). It is also noteworthy that the recent study of talented youth by Benjamin Bloom (1985) could find no adequate definition of interpersonal competence, and so the area was dropped from further study. Sternberg, of course, would say that an extremely important aspect of wisdom was overlooked. Imagine for a moment the brilliance of the late Dag Hammarskjold in his leadership at the United Nations (1981). With diplomatic skill, a vision of inter-national justice, and an ability to deal with culturally diverse world leaders, he would stand as a prime example of wisdom. Such competence is quite different from our usual definition of intelligence.

It will be important, as Sternberg's work progresses, to follow this line of inquiry. His metaphor is that "three heads are better than one." A fully functioning person would ideally possess all three traits: intelligence, wisdom, and creativity. This means that Piaget's work is important but not all-inclusive.

CHILDREN ARE NOT LIKE ADULTS

Piaget makes it clear that cognitive growth is a continuation of inborn motor processes—that is, the child comes into the world genetically equipped to make certain motor responses, and these form the foundation on which later mental structures will be built. Thus, the biological givens inescapably direct cognitive growth. Further, Piaget considers the difference among his four major stages to be based on differences in the way the child interacts with his or her environment and on the child's own reality. Finally, though Piaget feels that in general the stages of development cannot be speeded up, he does concede that they may be retarded under conditions of low environmental stimulation. Thus, though the onset of the stages is, in a sense, predetermined, environmental stimulation is needed at the right time for the bud of each stage to come to full flower on schedule.

Piaget's theory of cognitive growth, in contrast to earlier views, shows how our thinking processes take dramatically different forms during different periods of growth. It also underlines the role of experience and active learning in generating growth and change. Above all, it stresses the importance of assessing the stage to which the pupil as a learner has developed, within the framework of developmental cognitive growth. It is extraordinarily easy to assume that children think almost like adults. For an educator, such a view is both simple-minded and somewhat dangerous.

Adults Are Not Like Adults Either

Before we conclude the discussion on cognitive development, a final point should be made: We cannot assume that all teenagers function at the formal level. Nor can we assume that all adults, including ourselves, function at the formal level in all domains.

TABLE 5.4   ADULT BEHAVIORS ILLUSTRATING PIAGET'S PREADULT STAGES

PIAGET STAGE	ADULT BEHAVIORS
Sensorimotor: Emphasis on immediacy of feelings, inability to attend to consequences. The "here and now" is all.	Getting high on booze just before an important task.
	Smoking "pot" just prior to an important exam because it feels good.
	Going parachuting for thrills instead of meeting commitments at work.
	Throwing a temper tantrum instead of attempting to resolve conflicts.
Preoperational: Belief in intuition, magical thinking; fantasies are real. Superstitions abound.	Believing, as some athletes do, that each baseball bat has a magical number of hits (or that one must wear "lucky" clothes).
	Making significant life decisions according to horoscopes.
	Believing in mind-reading activities—for example, bending spoons with one's mind, reading a paper through one's nose, communicating with the dead (dialogues with Julius Caesar).
	Believing, as some bridge players do, that sitting parallel to the water pipes in the bathroom influences the cards.
	Giving away one's life savings to a total stranger who has a secret map locating Spanish gold (the flimflam).
Concrete: Emphasizing facts, routines; only one way to do things. Never vary any routine in spite of changed circumstances.	Always making the same sales calls on customers at the same time and day of the week.
	Repeating the same funny stories in lengthy and exacting detail to those who have heard them many times over (the "Ancient Mariner" routine).
	Always using the same play in game situations. (The Pittsburgh Steelers for years started each game with the fullback up the middle for three yards.)

Thus, if we have not been exposed to a careful balance of experience and guided reflection in all areas of human activity, then it is highly likely that our own development may be incomplete. We may still operate at an intuitive or concrete level in certain areas. For example, it is often the case that graduate schools are filled with students who perform brilliant feats of theoretical syntheses in the areas of personality, abnormal psychology, history, and philosophy, and yet immediately revert to concrete or even preoperational thinking in their first required course in statistics. Similarly, we may be at the level of formal thought in literature yet preoperational in understanding simple principles of physics. Look at the number of college graduates well educated in the humanities who will pick out certain boxes of food in a grocery store because they seem larger than others. The bottle and box manufacturers of the country

intuitively know that most adults apparently don't understand volume conservation. We adults merrily wend our way through the aisles, picking out tall, narrow cereal boxes; tall, thin salad bottles; skinny soap-powder containers—all the while feeling that we're getting a bargain for our money. Actually, the list of such misconceptions is endless. In the aesthetic world, think how many of us really believe that taking photographs always involves carefully posing the subjects or that symphonies must always be performed in the same concrete manner. Table 5.4 gives a description of Piaget's stages and examples of common adult behaviors. After looking at these descriptions, see if you can add a few based on your own experience. The point of the exercise is not only to remind ourselves of the need for humility but also to help us remember that human development is most likely never completed. Formal operations represent a laudable goal, even though few humans actually reach that level of functioning in all domains.

Thus, we cannot assume that all elementary school children function at the concrete level all the time or that all adolescents are at the formal level all the time, or that we adults operate in all domains at the formal level. From an educational standpoint, however, this does not mean that as pupils or adults we are permanently relegated to less complex and complete systems of thought and action. Given the conditions of support and manageable new learning tasks, we can continue the process of growth. Accommodation and assimilation can proceed.

SUMMARY

According to the definition of cognitive developmental stages presented here, growth is qualitative rather than quantitative. It is characterized by great leaps forward, followed by periods of integration rather than linear, step-by-step changes in degree. Piaget came to this conclusion on the basis of repeated observations of children in natural settings.

Piaget's work created a new and significant theory regarding the process of cognitive-growth stages. The stages are defined by system of thinking employed and by modal age. In the sensorimotor stage, from birth to twenty-four months, learning is tied to immediate experience; object permanence is learned at this stage. When a child moves into the preoperational stage, from two to seven years of age, language development allows the child to free-associate and fantasize; creativity is a characteristic of this age. Children from seven to eleven years of age are usually in the concrete operations stage, when literal-mindedness reigns. Finally, children reach the stage of formal operations, from eleven to sixteen years, when thought enlarges to include possibilities, hypotheses, ideas, and the perspective of others. Although children usually operate at the stage appropriate to their age, they are sometimes capable of next-stage-up thinking, and teachers should encourage such development.

A basic Piagetian concept denotes activity as a central ingredient of intelligence at all stages. Active learning experiences tend to promote cognitive growth while passive and vicarious experiences tend to have minimal impact.

To the American question—Can we speed up growth?—Piaget's answer is that constant acceleration of learning is not possible because of the limitations of thought processes at various ages. But the process of growth can be nurtured.

To promote growth requires attention to accommodation and assimilation. When new information is presented that does not fit the learner's current understanding, a knowledge disturbance is created. Taking in such new information represents accommodation. The next phase involves making the new concept fit with previous knowledge, or assimilation. Equilibration involves a balancing of accommodation and assimilation.

Furth has pointed out not only how this process works but also the feelings of anxiety and worry that go along with the struggle between the old way of thinking and the changes needed to grasp the new concept. There is a relationship between the intellectual and the affective when the previous balance is upset. Probably the best example of application comes from the work of Vygotsky, who demonstrated how to promote growth within the zone of proximal development through carefully managed peer interaction.

A new addition to the model has been provided by Patricia Arlin. She has shown how the problem-finding stage is actually a prototypical fifth stage in the scheme. She outlined the elements in this stage, which may define higher-order cognition as wisdom. Robert Sternberg, like Arlin, found the Piaget model somewhat lacking in the domain of wisdom to the point of suggesting that the importance of creativity as separate from wisdom stands as a third part of his triad model. We also reviewed the most recent research of Robbie Case in a neo-Piagetian model. He found substantial evidence to cross-validate the theory. He pointed out, however, the need to view stages of growth according to different domains.

What should be clear to teachers, however, is that children are not adults and should not be treated like miniature adults in the classroom. Realizing that activity is often neglected as a major mode of learning, you may find an additional way to reach children and teenagers. The hands-on approach is highly recommended, whereas passive watching of plays, listening to orchestras, visiting museums, and so on are not viewed as having as much educational merit.

KEY TERMS AND NAMES

accommodation
active school
the American question
Patricia Arlin
assimilation
Robbie Case
conservation
developmental stage
equilibration
Hans Furth
Arnold Gesell

periodization
Jean Piaget
  concrete operations stage
  formal operations stage
  preoperational stage
  sensorimotor stage
Robert Sternberg
qualitative development
quantitative development
Lev Vygotsky

THEORY INTO PRACTICE: APPLYING PIAGET

In this section, we provide a series of Piagetian tests that you can use to assess some levels of cognitive development. The first set provides a means of measuring concrete operations. The second set assesses abstract reasoning (formal operations). The tests can be administered individually or to small groups of students. The students' answers, particularly their reasons and explanations, will provide insight into their present cognitive functioning. Remember, however, that a developmental stage, by definition, is completely different from a traditional IQ score or a special-education label, which are permanent classifications. A developmental stage is only a picture of current functioning, like a photograph of a rising

rocket. Do not make the mistake of assuming that current-stage functioning is fixed at any particular age.

Measuring Aspects of Concrete Operations*

The following tests are designed to assess children at the elementary school level on their ability to conserve and to classify.

---

*   The items in this section and item 3 in the next section were developed by Pisila Taufé Ulungaki, a specialist in tests and measurements from the University of Minnesota.

Instructions: (1) Read each item carefully. (2) Answer all the items. (3) Mark the correct answer. (4) Explain your answer.

Practice item: Before you begin, look at the practice item below. Study it carefully to see how you are to find the right answer.

Shown below are two sets of fruit.
Set A has oranges. Set B has apples.

Set A: ◯ ◯ ◯ ◯ ◯ ◯ ◯ ◯

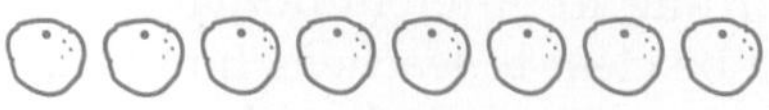

Set B: ◯ ◯ ◯ ◯ ◯
◯ ◯ ◯

A. Of the two sets, which set has the most fruit?

☐ a. Set A has the most fruit.
☐ b. Set B has the most fruit.
☑ c. They have the same number of fruit.
☐ d. None of the above answers is correct.

B. Explain your answer. *Set A has 8 oranges. Set B has 8 apples. Therefore, both sets have the same number of fruit. (or) Set A = 8. Set B = 8. Therefore, Set A = Set B.*

1. Shown below are two groups of marbles. Each circle represents a marble.

   Group A: ○ ○ ○ ○ ○ ○ ○ ○ ○
   Group B: ○○○○○○○○○

A. Of the two groups, which group has more marbles?

☐ a. Group A has more marbles.
☐ b. Group B has more marbles.
☐ c. Both groups have the same number of marbles.
☐ d. None of the above answers is correct.

B. Explain your answer. _____

_____

_____

_____

2. Shown below are nine wooden blocks.

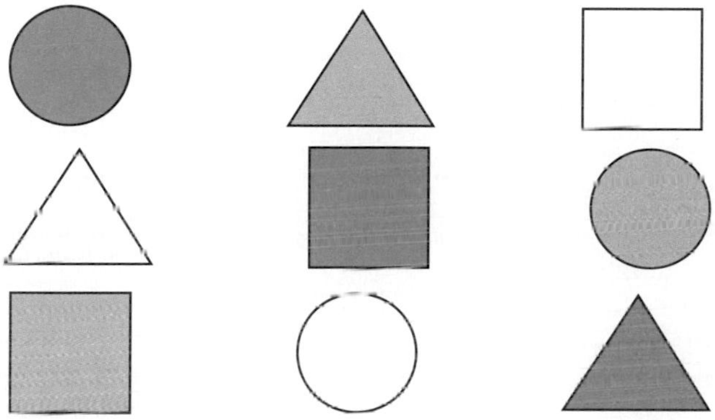

A. Two ways to sort the blocks into groups that are alike would be

☐ a. By color and by groups of two blocks.
☐ b. By shape and by groups of four blocks.
☐ c. By color and by shape.
☐ d. None of the above answers is correct.

B. Explain your answer. _____

_____

_____

_____

3, 4. Shown below in Picture A is a bottle half full of water.

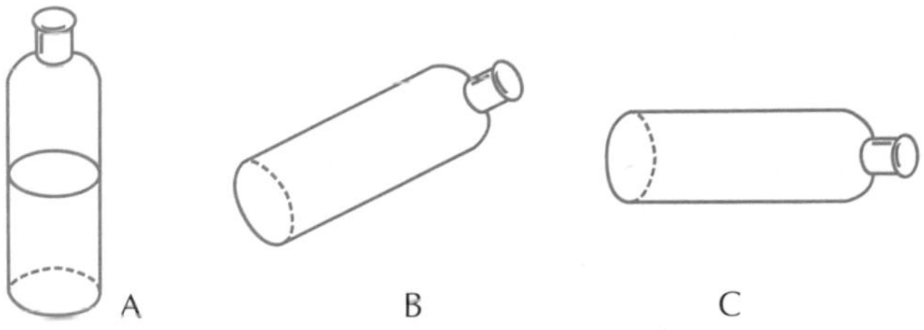

A. Suppose the bottle is tilted as shown in Picture B, and then placed flat as shown in Picture C. Draw the water levels on the bottles in Picture B and in Picture C.

B. Explain your answers. _____

_____

_____

_____

5. Shown below is a bowl half full of water. Beside it is an iron ball.

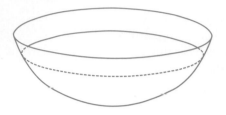

A. Suppose the iron ball is placed into the bowl of water. Will the water in the bowl go up or down, or will the water level remain the same?

☐ a. Remain the same.
☐ b. Go up.
☐ c. Go down.
☐ d. None of the above answers is correct.

B. Explain your answer. _____

_____

6. There are three girls named Jane, Mary, and Susan. Suppose Jane is taller than Mary and Mary is taller than Susan. Is Jane taller than Susan?

☐ a. Yes.
☐ b. No.
☐ c. Both are the same height.
☐ d. Not enough information is given.

Explain your answer. _____

_____

Answers: 1. c; 2. c; 3, 4. B   C   5. b; 6. a

Measuring Aspects of Formal Operations

The following methods represent different approaches to measuring formal operations. The ability to think at an abstract level is the major element that separates people at this level from those at the prior stage.

1. *The meaning of proverbs and aphorisms.* Ask students to describe the meaning of any sayings such as:

Still water runs deep.

A stitch in time saves nine.

A rolling stone gathers no moss.

Make hay while the sun shines.

Let no good deed go unpunished.

Penny wise and pound foolish.

The louder he proclaimed his honor, the faster we counted the silverware.

Don't look a gift horse in the mouth.

In my beginning is my end.

Concrete thinkers will give literal descriptions tied very closely to the content: "When the water is very still, it means it's very deep," as opposed to "A quiet person often observes and understands the complexities of life." Or, "A farmer should gather in the hay before it rains" versus "When a good opportunity is at hand, act."

2. *Logic problems: The bean, bird, fish, snail islands puzzle.** This puzzle is about four islands in the ocean. People have been traveling among these islands by boat for many years, but recently an airline started in business. Students must listen carefully to the clues given about possible plane trips. The trips may be direct or they may include stops on one of the islands. When a trip is possible, it can be made in both directions between the islands. Here is how the puzzle should be presented:

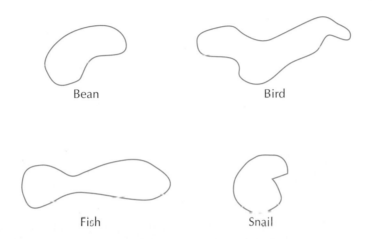

Bean   Bird

Fish   Snail

This is a map with the four islands, called Bean Island, Bird Island, Fish Island, and Snail Island. You may make notes or marks on your map to help you remember the clues. Raise your hand if you have questions about the clues.

First clue: People can go by plane between Bean and Fish Islands.

Second clue: People cannot go by plane between Bird and Snail Islands.

Use these two clues to answer Question 1.

QUESTION 1: Can people go by plane between Bean and Bird Islands?

☐ a. Yes
☐ b. No
☐ c. Can't tell from the two clues.

Explain in your answer. _____

_____

_____

Third clue: People can go by plane between Bean and Bird Islands.

Use all three clues to answer Questions 2 and 3. Don't change your answer to Question 1.

---

* This item is from *Research, Teaching and Learning wiht the Piaget Model*, by J. W. Renner, D. G. Stafford, A. E. Lawson, J. W. Mckinnon, F. E. Friot, and D. H. Kellogg. Copyright © 1976 by the University of Oklahoma Press.

QUESTION 2: Can people go by plane between Fish and Bird Islands?

☐ a. Yes
☐ b. No
☐ c. Can't tell from the two clues.

Explain in your answer. _____

_____

_____

QUESTION 3: Can people go by plane between Fish and Snail Islands?

☐ a. Yes
☐ b. No
☐ c. Can't tell from the two clues.

Explain in your answer. _____

_____

_____

Concrete thinkers will have difficulty remembering the combination of clues. Usually their explanations will indicate their inability to consider all the clues simultaneously.

Answers: 1. Can't tell; 2. Yes—take plane from Fish to Bean and Bean to Bird;
3. No—the second clue makes that impossible.

3. *Physical properties problems:* Ask students to answer the following physical science questions.

(a) The diagram below represents a scale. Beside it are several rings representing balls of different weights for balancing the bar of the scale.

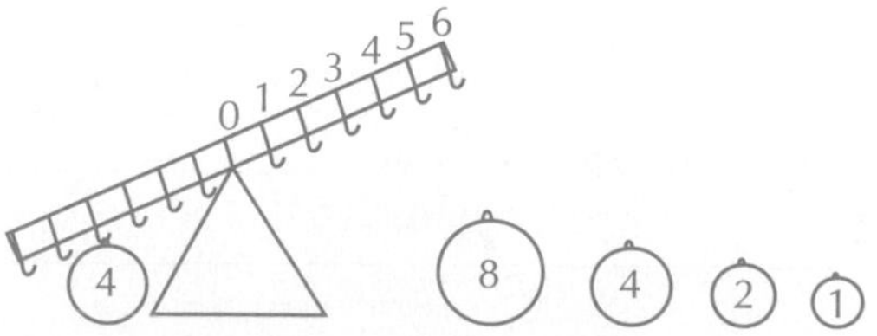

A. Suppose a four-ounce ring was placed on the scale as shown at point 4 in the diagram. By using one of the weights below, show how the bar could be balanced.

☐ a. Place the 8-ounce ring on 2.
☐ b. Place the 4-ounce ring on 5.
☐ c. Place the 2-ounce ring on 2.
☐ d. None of the above.

B. Explain your answer. _____

_____

_____

_____

(b) Shown below is a pendulum made in the form of an object hanging from a string. Also shown are pendulums with different string lengths and different weights.

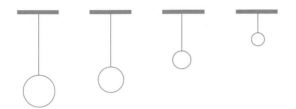

A. A science class made some trials to see if the pupils could find out what made the pendulum swing faster or slower. The following is a record of the class observations of swing.

Length	Weight	Rate	Comment
short	light	slow	false
short	heavy	fast	true
long	light	fast	false
long	light	slow	true
short	heavy	slow	false
short	light	fast	true
long	heavy	fast	false
long	heavy	slow	true

By studying the above table of observations, select the choice that seems best.

☐ a. It is the weight.
☐ b. It is the length.
☐ c. It is the combination of both.
☐ d. None of the above.

B. Explain your answer. _____

_____

_____

Answers: 3(a). a, 3(b). b

REFERENCES

Arlin, P. K. (1986). Problem finding and young adult cognition. In R. Mines and K. Kitchener (Eds.), *Adult cognitive development* (pp. 22–33). New York: Praeger.

Arlin, P. K. (1990) Wisdom: The art of problem finding. In R. J. Sternberg (Ed.), *Wisdom: Its nature, origins and development* (pp. 230–243). New York: Cambridge University Press.

Barratt, B. (1975). Training and transfer in combinational problem-solving: The development of formal reasoning during early adolescence. *Developmental Psychology, 11*(6), 700–704.

Blanck, G. (1990). Vygotsky: The man and his cause. In L. C. Moll (Ed.), *Vygotsky and education* (pp. 31–58). Cambridge: Cambridge University Press.

Bloom, B. (1985). *Developing talent in young people.* New York: Random House.

Case, R. (1987). The structure and process of intellectual development. *International Journal of Psychology, 22,* 571–607.

Case, R. (1992). *The mind's staircase.* Hillsdale, N.J.: Erlbaum.

Davydov, V. V. (1990). *Soviet studies in mathematics education: Vol. 2: Types of generalization in instruction.* Reston, Va.: National Council of Teachers of Mathematics.

Denton, L. (1987). EEG's bolster Piaget theory. *APA Monitor, 18*(8), 27.

Dimant, R., and Bearison, D. (1991). Development of formal reasoning during successive peer interactions. *Developmental Psychology, 27,* 277–284.

Duckworth, E. (1987). *'The having of wonderful ideas'.* New York: Teachers College.

Elkind, D. (1970). *Children and adolescent.* New York: Oxford University Press.

Epstein, H. (1978). Growth spurts during brain development: Implications for educational policy. In J. A. Chall and A. F. Mirsky (Eds.), *1978 Yearbook of the National Society for the Study of Education.* Chicago: University of Chicago Press.

Fischer, K., and Lazerson, A. (1985). Research: Brain spurts and Piagetian periods. *Educational Leadership, 41*(5), 70.

Flavell, J. H. (1985). *Cognitive development.* Englewood Cliffs, N.J.: Prentice-Hall.

Frederiksen, N. (1984). The real test bias: Influences of testing on teaching and learning. *American Psychologist, 39*, 193–202.

Furth, H. (1981). Piaget and knowledge (2d ed.). Chicago: University of Chicago Press.

Gelman, R. (1982). Basic numerical abilities. In R. J. Sternberg (Ed.), *Advances in the psychology of human intelligence,* Vol 1. Hillsdale, N.J.: Erlbaum.

Gesell, A. (1940). *The first five years of life.* New York: Harper & Row.

Ginsberg, H., and Opper, S. (1988). *Piaget's theory of intellectual development.* Engelwood Cliffs, N.J.: Prentice-Hall.

Hammarskjold, D. (1981). *Markings.* New York: Knopf.

Hostetler, A. (1988). "Smart" brains work better not harder. *APA Monitor, 19*(5), 15.

Hudak, M., and Anderson, D. (1990). Formal operations and learning style predict success in statistics and computer science courses. *Teaching Psychology, 17*, 231–234.

Inhelder, B., and Piaget, J. (1958). *The growth of logical thinking from childhood to adolescence.* New York: Basic Books.

Janos, P., and Robinson, N. (1985). Psychosocial development of intellectually gifted children. In F. D. Horowitz and M. D. O'Brien (Eds.), *The gifted and talented: Developmental perspectives* (pp. 149–196). Washington; American Psychological Association.

Jones, R. (1968). *Fantasy and feeling in education.* New York: Harper.

Light, R. J. (1990). *The Harvard Assessment Seminars.* Cambridge: Harvard University.

Mischel, W. (1981). Metacognition and the rules of delay. In J. H. Flavell and L. Ross (Eds.), *Social cognitive development.* New York: Cambridge University Press.

Moll, L. C. (1990). *Vygotsky and education.* Cambridge: Cambridge University Press.

Neimark, E. D. (1982). Adolescent thought: Transition to formal operations. In B. B. Wolman (Ed.), *Handbook of developmental psychology.* Englewood Cliffs, N.J.: Prentice-Hall.

Piaget, J. (1964). *Judgment and reasoning in the child.* Paterson, N.J.: Littlefield Adams.

Piaget, J. (1970). *Science of education and the psychology of the child.* New York: Viking.

Piaget, J., and Garcia, R. (1991). *Toward a logic of meanings.* Hillsdale, N.J.: Erlbaum.

Pines, M. (1970). *A revolution in learning.* New York: Harper & Row.

Renner, J., Stafford, D., Lawson, A., McKimmon, J., Friot, F., and Kellogg, D. (1976). *Research, teaching, and learning with the Piaget model.* Normal, Okla.: University of Oklahoma Press.

Scarr-Salapatek, S. (1976). An evolutionary perspective on infant intelligence: Species patterns and individual variations. In M. Lewis (Ed.), *The origins of intelligence: Infancy and early childhood.* New York: Plenum.

Sprinthall, N. A., and Burke, S. (1985). Intellectual, interpersonal, and emotional development during childhood. *Journal of Humanistic Education and Development, 24*, 50–58.

Sprinthall, N. A., Collins, W. A., and Edwall, G. (1994). *Adolescent psychology: A developmental view.* New York: McGraw-Hill.

Sternberg, R. J. (1986). Intelligence, wisdom and creativity: Three is better than one. *Educational Psychologist, 21*(3), 175–190.

Sternberg, R. J., and Davidson, J. E. (1985). Cognitive development in the gifted and talented. In F. D. Horowitz and M. D. O'Brien (Ed.), *The gifted and talented: Developmental perspectives* (pp. 37–74). Washington: American Psychological Association.

Sylvester, R. (1986). Synthesis of research on brain plasticity: The classroom environment and curriculum enrichment. *Educational Leadership, 44*(1), 90–93.

Tudge, J. (1990). Vygotsky, the zone of proximal development. In L. C. Moll (Ed.), *Vygotsky and education* (pp. 155–174). Cambridge: Cambridge University Press.

Vygotsky, L. (1962). *Thought and language.* Cambridge: MIT Press.

Vygotsky, L. (1985). Pensée et language. Paris: Editions Sociales.

White, M. A. (1968). The view from the pupil's desk. *Urban Review, 2*, 5–7.

Wolfenstein, M. (1954). *Children's humor.* Glencoe, Ill., Free Press.

6

PERSONAL GROWTH

Although this chapter concentrates on personal development during childhood and adolescence, it is important to remember that the various stages of growth are not separate from one another. We indicated earlier that the mind is not a discrete entity, any more than is the body. Mind and body function together and are intimately interconnected. In the same way, we cannot really separate personal development (the growth of personality) from cognitive development (the growth of intellectual skills). For example, a basic part of our personality resides in our self-concept; how we perceive and think about ourselves, especially in relation to other people, will certainly affect our personal development. Therefore, as you read this chapter, be careful not to assume that personal growth takes place in a vacuum.

To present ideas of growth and development in this very difficult area, we have based this chapter largely on Erik Erikson's elaboration of Sigmund Freud's original work. It was Erikson who transformed Freud's theories of emotional growth into a major development scheme as a means of understanding the process of healthy personal growth.

PERSONAL GROWTH: THE PRE-FREUDIAN VIEW OF MINDLESS CHILDREN

Before the earthshaking discoveries of Sigmund Freud, at the turn of this century, it was generally assumed that, until they reached the age of six or seven, children were mindless creatures, more like animals than humans. It was important, naturally, to meet their physical needs, but beyond that they were thought to be in a kind of incubation period, too young to know or feel anything. There was little reason to take the early years seriously as a time when anything significant could occur.

Interestingly enough, this view of young children is common to many cultures throughout the world. In both modern and primitive societies, many practices are based on the notion that children are unthinking creatures, with no minds of their own or emotions of any consequence. These cultures sharply demarcate the beginning of the juvenile period (about seven years of age) from the age of mindlessness (birth to six). English common law and Catholic canon law, for example, both assume that children do not know anything before their seventh year. In nonwestern cultures, a variety of initiation rites, performed between the ages of six and seven, are based on similar assumptions. In fact, one culture actually killed children who became seriously ill before the age of six, in the belief that they were not really children at all but snakes masquerading as humans (S. White, 1968).

In this country, one of the pioneers in establishing childhood as a significant era in human development was **Lawrence K. Frank.** A child psychologist of particular eminence, he devoted his entire professional life to pointing out those practices within and across cultures that were designed to meet adult needs and that ignored the needs of children. He documented the entire array of childrearing practices that assumed children were little more than pieces of clay to be molded into any shape by adult "master craftsmen." Molding and shaping had everything from physical to psychological manifestations. In some cultures heads are flattened, feet are bound, necks are stretched, skin is punctured or tattooed. In other cultures natural physiological functions, such as breathing, feeding, and sleeping patterns, are altered. The array of psychological practices is even greater, especially in the realm of what we could call character building. Using extreme forms of punishment, from beatings to severe scolding, adults have tried for centuries to defeat and deflect the process of personal growth. As Frank put it, "Civilized man has survived *despite*, not because of, these methods of child care." The methods were too often created to suite the adult, not the child, and were based on an almost absolute ignorance of the special nature of childhood. As a result, "In the area of conduct and belief there apparently are no limits to the grostesque, the cruel and brutal, the diabolical ingenuity of man in warping and twisting human nature" (Frank, 1969, p. 71).

The theoretical justification for all this beating, scolding, and molding is detailed by Rolf Muus (1988). The idea that a young child is a midget-sized adult is termed *preformationism*. In that view—also called the *homunculus view*—there are no qualitative or stage differences between or among children, adolescents, or adults; a baby is simply a preformed little adult and therefore should be treated like one. The preformationist approach to teaching is illustrated by the copybook of the youthful Timothy Orne, laboriously written in 1738.

With these prior assumptions clearly in mind, we can now have some understanding of the shock wave set off by the works of Sigmund Freud.

SIGMUND FREUD: THE DISCOVERY OF CHILDHOOD

In searching for the causes of adult emotional difficulties, **Sigmund Freud (1960)** began to create a revolutionary view of childhood that in no way resembled the prevailing view of childhood as a time of benign emptiness. Freud, using the methods of clinical research, hypnotized his clients or asked them to free-associate ("Tell me the first thing that comes to mind")

or to recount their recent dreams. He found, over and over again, that major aspects of his clients' personal development originated during the patients' first six years of life. In fact, Freud discovered that he could understand the adult personality only by examining the kind of experiences and personal relationships the adult had had in childhood (before entering school). To know an adult, Freud would say, know the child. Hence the famous phrase, "The child is father of the man." In early experience could be discovered the foundations of later personal development. Uncovering significant childhood experiences is the essence of **psychoanalytic theory.**

Freud, with a kind of possessed genius, had to withstand enormous vilification as his theories became known. He was literally hated and feared, almost like the messenger in ancient times who was executed for being the bearer of bad news. Freud's bad news was simple: Adults must stop treating children as if they were too young to know or experience anything. There could be no justification whatsoever for childrearing practices that mangle, distort, inhibit, and break the young spirit.

EMOTIONAL GROWTH DURING CHILDHOOD: FREUD'S NEW VIEW

Freud discovered that during their first years of life children go through a sequence of emotional stages, much as Piaget found them to go through a sequence of cognitive stages. In charting the course of emotional growth, Freud named three major stages of development from birth through seven years: the **oral stage** (birth to eighteen months), the **anal stage** (one and a half to three years), and the **phallic stage** (three to seven years).

According to Freud, this sequence of major emotional transformations leaves an indelible imprint on the adult personality. Also, as with cognitive growth, certain dimensions of personality are maximally affected at each of these stages. During the oral stage, for example, the quality of nurturing that children receive, especially as related to feeling, will maximally affect children's future feelings of dependence and trust in the world. During the anal stage (the name is derived from the universal requirement for bowel training), independence and control are at the forefront of development. In the phallic stage, sexual identity is the major aspect of personality formation.

Freud suggested that a period of latency (seven to twelve years) follows, in which the oral, anal, and

Training children as midget adults: Freud believed that children, far from being smaller images of adults, have a rich emotional life that can be divided into stages. In this sense, Freud "discovered" childhood.

Fingers firmly gripping the thin shaft of a quill pen, many a student in an early American school labored over his copy book, tracing the elaborate dips and swirls of the ABCs and struggling with the accompanying writing exercises.

Each page of the large, clothbound text contained examples of the exacting script of the teacher. On blank lines below the teacher's writing, the students meticulously sought to achieve the same effect, repeatedly tracing garnished letters of the alphabet and copying sentences of a relentlessly uplifting tone. Hour after hour they toiled, and some of the more gifted among them ultimately went on to achieve calligraphy so ornate as to be virtually unreadable.

The reward for this drudgery was the book itself, page upon page of the most elegant penmanship, often cherished for years by such scholars as Timothy Orne.

phallic dimensions are integrated and no new elements are added. However, during adolescence (the genital stage), the period of so-called *Sturm und Drang* (a German expression meaning a period of extreme stress and strain), all the previous elements—oral, anal, and especially phallic—are brought back into play. During adolescence the basic elements are reworked into an adult character. This is a time for recapitulation, for going back over the issues of dependence (oral period), independence (anal period), and identity (phallic period) to prepare for a fully functioning adulthood in which, according to Freud, we can live and work productively—a simple but profound human objective.

Freud established once and for all that extremely significant personal and emotional aspects of our development are determined during the first six years of our lives. It was no longer possible to assume that the young child had no mind or any significant emotions. Instead, Freud's theory provided valid information to buttress an old adage, "Just as the twig is bent, the tree's inclined." The adult personality is affected in major ways by the emotional experiences of childhood.

In other words, the interactions between the child and significant adults during the first six years determine whether or not the adult will be able to function efficiently. Inadequate or negative childrearing practices will result in a personality that is flawed. The person might function adequately but would show major deficiencies.

ERIK ERIKSON: THE SEQUENCE OF STAGES AND TASKS OF PERSONAL DEVELOPMENT

Erik Erikson, one of Freud's students, has done more than any other theorist to modernize Freudian theory and make it into a more complete theory of child and adolescent development. In a sense, one of the major difficulties with Freud's view was that it was too deterministic. According to Freud, by the time we are six or seven years old, personal growth is essen-

SIGMUND FREUD

If there is a single name in all psychology that is synonymous with personality theory, it is Sigmund Freud. Born in Freiberg, Moravia in 1856, he spent his early years as a member of a tightly knit family in Central Europe. Reportedly, his youth was marked by serious personality problems, including severe bouts with depression and anxiety states. These difficulties apparently started him on a journey of discov-

ery aimed at understanding the roots of personality and gaining insight into the relationship between personality structure and actual behavior. It was to be a long and productive professional journey, beginning with his graduation from medical school at the University of Vienna in 1881. His career extended all the way to the beginning of World War II in 1939.

After completing his medical studies, he became increasingly interested in diseases of the nervous system. Instead of continuing to look for physical and physiological reasons, he shifted his attention toward a new arena, the mind. If diseases such as hysteria, high-anxiety states, and deep personal depression were not connected to a physical cause, then the usual types of medical treatment, from actual operations on nerves to prescriptions for drugs, were bound to fail. Such activities were merely treating symptoms. Often, after these treatments, patients simply developed a new set of symptoms. As a result of these ideas, Freud decided to study with Josef Breuer, a physician famous for his treatment of hysteria through hypnosis. Freud found that inducing hypnotic trances was somewhat limited as a treatment of choice. Some patients could not be successfully

hypnotized and others simply shifted symptoms.

Freud began to experiment with unique treatment methods, primarily asking patients to free-associate and to report on their dreams. In some ways this appeared an outrageous procedure for a physician to use. Imagine Freud asking a patient to stretch out on his soon-to-be-famous couch, then suggesting that he or she say whatever came to mind. (The first rule of psychoanalysis was to speak out and not repress any hidden thoughts.) All the while Freud himself was sitting behind the couch, quietly jotting down notes, rarely speaking. Such a procedure seemed the work of a mad genius at best or of a charlatan at worst. Not only did Freud break with the traditions of his time completely, but he even went so far as to carry on psychoanalytically oriented treatment by mail: In the famous case of "Little Hans," he successfully treated a young boy by writing to the father and explaining, step by step, how to cure the patient of a severe case of horse phobia. Since horses provided most of the transportation in those days, Hans's malady can be compared to that of a child today who would run and hide at the sight of an automobile.

Always an innovator, Freud con-

tially all over. Our basic personality structures are already set. As shown in Table 6.1, Erikson (1982) expanded the ideas of stages of development into a broader framework—a life cycle—and outlined the positive and negative dimensions of each period. This helped clarify and balance Freudian theory as a means of understanding personal growth.

Whereas Freud had emphasized the negative and pathological aspects of emotional growth, Erikson directed the theory into a broader context. He saw development continuing throughout one's entire life and yet gave special significance to childhood (birth

to six years), the juvenile era (six to twelve years), and adolescence (twelve through the college years). Although he has suggested stages of development well into adulthood, we will concentrate on these three categories.

The Epigenetic Principle: The Engine for Growth

You may recall that Piaget discussed the importance of equilibration as the mechanism that promotes cog-

tinued to evolve creative treatment techniques throughout his life; however, his major contribution was his insight into the causes of behavior. Through hours of quiet listening to patients' free associations and descriptions of dreams, he began to construct a theory of personality. He heard the same themes repeated over and over again and in time created his theory of infant sexuality. Adult patients were helped to gradually recall early feelings, thoughts, and sexual fantasies from their childhood. To suggest to the world that innocent little children had such sexual feelings was almost too much for the Victorian age to accept. Nevertheless, despite the enormous criticism generated and the departure of some of his closest associates, Freud continued to expand on the importance of sexuality as a determinant of personality during the early years of life. His three-part typology of the mind—the id, the ego, and the superego—combined with his three layers of thought—conscious, preconscious, and unconscious—led to his famous dictum that all human behavior was overdetermined. His clinical approaches demonstrated that our present behavior is related to a whole series of "causes." The task of the psychologist is to uncover great amounts of psychic material

and then gradually help the patient understand how many of the factors from the past had been regulating his or her present behavior. In fact, Freud said that the psychologist is like an archaeologist—carefully and systematically digging through the past in order to slowly uncover the intrapsychic traumas of a person's early history. Here he found the structure of the past influencing present behavior; here was the repository of events, feelings, disconnected ideas, fantasies rooted in the unconscious.

The unconscious, according to Freud, is the key to human behavior. Even though individuals may try to suppress or repress inner thoughts and feelings and push them into the unconscious, the repressed material sneaks out in disguised form. Slips of the tongue, unfortunate "accidents," forgetting important events, getting names of familiar people mixed up, and similar unusual human behavior are not just incidental activities or randomly determined. He was able to show how such events are instead a direct expression of an individual's unconscious motivation. For example, a guilt-ridden criminal might "accidentally" leave a trail a mile wide from the scene of a crime in order to bring about his own punishment. Other examples

abound in everyday life.

The insights of Freud changed our level of understanding in dramatic ways. It has been said that the greatest contribution was to end, once and for all, the age of innocence. Also, some have remarked that it would have been impossible to understand the horrors of the twentieth century without his theories of why and how people react. These theories demonstrated the importance of both sexual and aggressive human drives. The adverse interpersonal relationships so common in this age are current reminders of this insight. The desolation created by two major world wars, the total annihilation of innocent populations, the use of ultimate weapons from A-bombs to gas chambers—these products of a so-called advanced civilization can be better understood through his views. It is to be hoped that his insights will teach the world the importance of recognizing and gradually developing control over these destructive human drives. Ironically, he spent many of his last years in Nazi Germany, as a captive of the most demonic human being of this century. His final year of life was spent in England in 1939. He watched the world he knew collapse once again in a paroxysm of hatred, tragic testimony to his deepest fears for humanity.

nitive development. There is a built-in drive to acquire more complex systems of thinking. In a parallel sense, Erikson says much the same for personal growth. His terms are different, but the assumptions are the same. Erikson refers to the **epigenetic principle.** Personality itself goes through structural elaborations in accord with a ground plan. Development is not random but proceeds according to the outline. Nor is development automatic; the ground plan is really a map of potential. If the child's interaction with the environment is healthy and the basic crisis of each stage of development is resolved, then the

child will be ready for the next stage. We do not have to force a child to grow as a personality. The epigenetic principle means the potential for growth already is a given.

Originally Erikson posed his framework in terms of stages of crises, with bipolar definitions of the crisis at each stage—for example, trust versus mistrust. More recently, he has suggested that each of these opposites can be combined. During the first years the child wrestles with the problem of how trustful or distrustful to become. Under appropriate conditions of nurture, these opposites are resolved into a new

TABLE 6.1   ERIKSON'S GROUND PLAN FOR PSYCHOLOGICAL GROWTH

AGE	BIPOLAR CRISES AT EACH STAGE (OUTLINED)				
Birth to twenty-four months	Basic trust vs. mistrust	Early autonomy, etc.	Early initiative	Early mastery	Early identity
Two to three years	Later forms of hope, etc.	Autonomy vs. shame	↓	↓	↓
Four to six years	↓	Later forms of will	Initiative vs. guilt	↓	↓
Six to twelve years	↓	↓	Later forms of purpose	Mastery vs. inferiority	↓
Thirteen to eighteen years	↓	↓	↓	Later forms of competence	Identity vs. diffusion
Eighteen years through college	↓	↓	↓	↓	Identity (moratorium and achievement) vs. continued diffusion
Resolution:	Hope	Will	Purpose	Competence	Fidelity

condition called "hope." Thus, as the first two years of life end, the child's personality disposition can be toward a basically positive outlook. Similarly, the resolution to the second stage, autonomy versus shame, is now termed "will." It is interesting to note that Erikson was quite uneasy denoting the resolutions in terms such as hope, will, purpose, competence, and fidelity. He apparently was worried that such "old-fashioned" terms might lead psychologists to dismiss his work as more philosophy than behavioral science. However, such terms actually clarify the goals of each stage as a meaningful synthesis, a new combination. For example, under the old system it was difficult to resolve the trust-versus-mistrust polarity as trust. Hope, however, represents more a resolution of two opposite tendencies than an either-or choice. The same is true of the other stages, as you will see in the following descriptions.

Childhood (Birth to Six Years)

Trust versus mistrust (birth to twenty-four months): Hope   Erikson subdivided the period of childhood into three categories that almost precisely duplicate Freud's. The first of these categories, from birth to

twenty-four months, he labeled the stage of trust versus mistrust. In Freudian terms, this is the oral period, in which there is great emphasis on feeding, sucking, biting, drooling. The quality of nurture—the quality of care and affection that go into feeding, cuddling, bathing, and dressing the child—will develop feelings of trust or mistrust. The extent to which a baby's first experience of the world is of a dependable, warm place will create a general outlook, ranging from positive and trusting to negative and mistrusting. We are not talking about the old controversy of breast feeding as opposed to bottle feeding (for a long time that seemed to be the single controversy), but rather about the need for affectionate physical contact and comfort during feeding and other childrearing activities. A cold, tense mother breast-feeding could be as lacking in good nurture as a bottle prop (a device that allows no human contact in feeding the baby).

Evidence for the importance of early experience has been provided by several researchers. Harry Harlow's research has supported the concept of the importance of early nurturing patterns. Harlow raised baby monkeys under different conditions of nurturing for numerous studies. Figure 6.1 depicts two types of substitute monkey "mothers": one, a warm, soft cloth and the other, a cold, harsh wire. Both are capa-

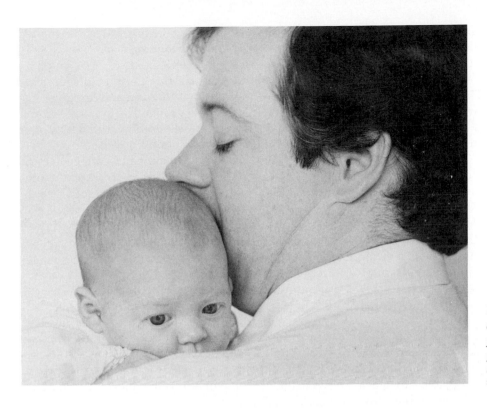

Erikson's periods of childhood almost duplicated Freud's. He labeled his first stage trust versus mistrust and felt that good nurturance would develop feelings of hope in the child.

FIGURE 6.1 Harlow gave baby monkeys two kinds of substitute "mothers": one was a warm cloth and the other was a cold wire. The wire mother's babies manifested bizarre behavior as adults—for example, they were unable to mate, and they exhibited characteristics similar to those of schizophrenia.

ble of providing milk, but as you might expect, the wire mother's babies manifested substantial bizarre behavior as adults. They were unable to mate, to relate to strange or novel objects, and in fact, showed many behaviors reminiscent of schizophrenia. the cloth mother's babies, however, were able to explore strange and terrifying situations and demonstrated an ability to master their environment (Harlow and Harlow, 1962).

Equally dramatic was a study conducted by Rene Spitz (1946). He studied the effects of orphanage experiences on very young children. Even though the children were given adequate physical care, washed, fed, and kept in warm, clean rooms, there was an almost complete lack of human warmth and contact. During an epidemic, the orphanage children were dramatically less able to withstand disease compared to children of nearby families. In fact, when the figures were published, they were very hard for people to accept—thirty-four of ninety-one orphanage children died, compared to almost none of the other children in the area.

Erikson notes that maternal warmth and care teach children through the senses (as Piaget might say) that they can depend on the world.* The mother is practically the entire world for very young children. Through her they learn that, although she disappears at times, she also always reappears. From the regularity as well as the quality of the experience, children develop their outlook on life and prepare to move to the second stage. As with the stages of cognitive growth, the stages of personal development are sequential. This means that if children's basic dependency needs are met during their first twenty-four months of life, they will be ready to move to the second stage of personal development. However, if these needs are not properly met, children may not be able to move on.

The dramatic studies of extreme cases of early deprivation of nurturance cited above indicate that the failure to develop could result in actual physical death (failure to thrive) or a kind of psychological death in the form of emotional withdrawal from the world (in so-called anaclitic depression). Children supposedly raised by wild animals, such as the wild boy of Averyon, who was called a *feral child*, exhibited similar irreversible disturbances.

There is apparently no adequate compensation for lack of nurturing during this period. In fact, for a while it was thought that the primary caregiver had to be the child's natural parents. The famous example in England during the 1940 bombing blitz was often cited as evidence. Young children were moved from the cities and placed in model child-care centers directed by experts, including Anna Freud and Dorothy Burlingham. In spite of the best efforts of these experts, the children separated from their natural parents showed definite developmental lags. The problem, of course, is with the interpretation of causes. Wartime separation from parents for extended periods (sometimes parents could visit only once a month due to travel restrictions) is not really a fair test of substitute parenting. In an atmosphere of high anxiety and extended separation, it may be more significant that the children didn't regress more markedly. The caregivers were responsible for the children's well-being twenty-four hours a day, week after week, and the ratio of adults to children was far from ideal.

More recent evidence—namely, a careful review of early-childhood programs—seems to indicate that although babies are extremely sensitive to experience, they are also resilient. In other words, the negative effects of early deprivation are not quite as longlasting or as indelible as originally thought. The idea of critical periods was borrowed too directly from studies of ducks and other animals. Human babies are more adaptable. They can overcome the negative effects of deprivation (Zigler and Berman, 1983). Certainly that is welcome news. At the same time, this evidence in no way negates the importance of providing young babies with positive environments. A rich and stimulating experience is still best. In addition, the primary caregiver does not have to be the natural mother. As long as the primary caregiver provides the child with a consistent, sensitive, and nurturant environment, the child will have a good chance to resolve the polar conflict between trust and mistrust as personal hope.

Autonomy versus shame (two to three years): Will During this second period of childhood, emotional and personal development move into what Erikson calls the stage of autonomy versus shame. This is when children emerge from their almost total dependence on a primary caregiver and begin, literally and

---

* Erikson consistently refers to the indispensable role of the mother. He does not consider the role of the father in nurturance, though some commentators suggest that his theory can be accommodated to nurturers of either sex. Recent research by Risman (1986) would support such a contemporary interpretation.

figuratively, to stand on their own two feet. The physical maturation that allows them to crawl, walk, run, and climb provides the means for a great leap into personal autonomy. This is a time of intense exploration, when they seem to be actively involved in almost everything. Physical maturation also frees them from dependence on the bottle or the breast and enables them to learn how to control their bowels and bladders. Thus, the positive aspect of this period is a fundamental sense of self-direction.

Erikson makes it clear however, that there can be negative emotional development, too. We noted that in the first stage children are particularly sensitive to the way in which their dependency needs are met. In this second stage they need to be independent, and the way in which that need is met will maximally affect their sense of personal autonomy. If children at this stage are punished excessively for exploring their house or neighborhood, if they receive particularly harsh and punitive bowel training, or if they are so overprotected that they are almost "smothered," then Erikson indicates that the major emotional lesson from this period will be personal shame. The growing sense of self-control ("I can do it myself!") can be impaired as easily as it can be nurtured during this second period of childhood.

It may be difficult for adults to learn not to interfere but rather to support the child's desire for freedom and autonomy. For example, if you watch a boy of three trying to tie his shoes, you may see him work with extraordinary motivation even though the loops aren't matched, and well over half the time as he tries for the final knot, he ends up with two separate laces, one in each hand. Then watch parents as they watch their children attempt a task like this. Too often the parent will step in and take over, tie the shoes the "right way" and defeat the child's growing attempt at self-mastery. The same goes for putting on boots, coats, and even playing with toys. It is exceedingly easy to fall into the trap of almost always responding negatively to a child at this age. Commonly, a parent might say no up to 200 times a day at this stage. Such nagging not only is aversive in the extreme, but also a constant reminder to the child of his or her lack of self-control.

This is also the time when language begins, and here again the child's sense of independence is clearly in the balance. Adults need to understand that their child's first attempts to speak will always be halting. All children stutter somewhat during this time, just as all tumble constantly as they learn to walk and run. Attempts to speak need encouragement and modeling: Adults should not baby-talk back to a child, nor should they overcorrect a child's use of language. The surest way to promote stuttering at this stage is to harp on the misuse of language. It will definitely promote a sense of personal shame if, when children first try to talk, they are criticized for not taking the "right way."

Burton "Bud" White (1987) formerly of Harvard, has shown that patterns of mothering and fathering at this stage are clearly related to the child's sense of personal mastery, independence, and self-control. Even at this early stage, certain patterns of interaction between parents and children can accurately predict competence and future mastery. The most successful patterns are found in homes where the parents do substantial indirect teaching. Effective parents talk clearly and do a great deal of "labeling" ("This is a dog," and then, gradually, "This is a big dog," and so on). Children in these homes are also allowed substantial initiative in selecting activities; there is a balance between activities initiated by a parent and activities initiated by the children. A mother or father may ask for children's ideas and ask questions to help them understand the activity (for example, "Now what do you suppose will happen if I put the piece in the puzzle this way?" or "if you pour all the water from the big glass into this little cup?" and "What will Little Red Riding Hood find when she goes into the bedroom?").

White has shown, then, that parents who provide an interesting, stimulating environment, talk frequently to their children, give them some initiative, and do a great deal of indirect teaching by asking questions and drawing out their perceptions and ideas have the most positive effect on their children's developing sense of competency. Their sense of being "doers" and being able to control and affect the environment receives a major boost during this time.

Quite recently, White's research has been applied in a special preschool project. His studies show that developmental delays in personal growth can be identified reliably as early as two years. He and other experts have concluded that effective programs to unlock growth can be started at the same time. In this way his research has two sets of implications, one for parents in general and one for school systems. There is strong support for the idea that school-based projects can teach principles of effective parenting, and the results of a current longitudinal study provide further support for the concept. Parents who

SPOTLIGHT ON EARLY EDUCATION

Is Day Care as Good as a Mother?

An issue of major importance is the question of the effects of day care on infants, especially in their first two years. On the one hand, both Freud's and more directly Erikson's theories strongly imply that there is no satisfactory substitute for a close bond between an infant and one primary caregiver. (It could be either parent or another adult.) In addition to theory, both experimental research (Harlow's monkeys) and clinical observations (the English children during World War II) support that view.

On the other hand, there have been major changes in child care both since World War II and since the experimental studies were completed. And from a sociological standpoint, the great majority of families in this country now have both parents working outside the home. Thus, the question of parenting takes on new theoretical and practical importance. As a result, Jerome Kagan and his colleagues at Harvard decided to test the effects of day care in a highly formal way.[a] They set up two matched groups of infants between three and six months

participated in the special preschool project were able to learn to encourage healthy personal development. From the point of view of this chapter, the most significant finding is that the project helped parents to work effectively during the autonomy-versus-shame stage to promote a resolution toward "will." Will is not willfulness in the usual sense. When we speak of a willful child, we usually mean one who is stubborn. However, what Erikson is referring to is really a stage of initial independence. Children learn to think for themselves as they shift from sensorimotor to symbolic thought at about this time. There is a similar

potential change in their understanding of themselves as individuals. *Will* really means "self-direction" and "individuality" and, in fact, is the beginning of a sense of identity. The tension between autonomy and shame can be resolved. As Erikson puts it, "In balancing these two tendencies, rudimentary willpower supports a maturation both of free choice and of self-restraint" (Erikson, 1959, p. 78).

As you work with older children you may find some who have not adequately resolved the dependence-independence polarity and who alternate between willfulness and excessive compliance. In such

old. During the two-year study, day care (from 8 A.M. to 5 P.M.) was provided for one sample, while the other sample was reared exclusively at home. The parents were largely from workingclass backgrounds.

A wide variety of measures of child development indicated no major or even minor differences between the two groups of children. In fact, some clinical evidence indicated that the day-care experience was somewhat better. The researchers noted a subtle difference. On the one hand, the natural mothers tended to be somewhat overly emotionally involved with their own child (all were either first- or second-born children). The carefully selected and trained day-care workers, on the other hand, seemed able to provide a less intrusive yet not overly detached experience. Before you conclude, however, that all previous research and theory was wrong, there are some important factors to consider.

In the first place, the program was truly ideal. The day-care workers were all carefully screened. Rather than rely on academic qualifications, the experts directly observed how sensitive the staff applicants were in handling real children. In addition, the workers were carefully trained in the latest techniques, and the program materials and physical space were state-of-the-art. All the staff members selected also had prior experience in raising their own children. Continuous supervision and staff development were also part of the program. Perhaps most important was the staff-to-baby ratio. Each worker was responsible for three babies for the first fifteen months. The ratio for toddlers was one to five. In a sense the most significant finding, then, was that there is no appreciable difference in development for babies between three and fifteen months as long as there is one effectively trained worker for every three babies. Any further generalization to either higher ratios or less than ideal conditions is not warranted during Erikson's trust-versus-mistrust stage. In fact, Kagan was mightily impressed by these workers. They were truly gifted in providing just the right amount of nurturance to each of their three charges. When feeling distressed, such babies would immediately pick out their own worker for comfort. When feeling pleased, they would do the same for contact.

Did such surrogate mothers actually replace the natural mothers? The results here also indicated no real differences between the two groups. The day-care children still viewed their mothers as the most "salient adult figure," and so the program did not interfere with that process. From this we can conclude, at least tentatively, that an ideal or model program can provide young babies with a trust-enhancing psychological experience. Working parents who place their children in such programs do not have to feel pangs of guilt that somehow their baby will miss out on the resolution of trust-mistrust as an outlook of hope.[b]

[a] Kagan, J., Kearsley, R., and Zelazo, P. (1980). *Infancy*. Cambridge: Harvard University Press.

[b] Naturally enough, such research doesn't really settle such an issue. Most recently, ignoring the Kagan results, Deborah Fallow has written extensively to prove the point that there is no effective substitute. See Fallow, D. (1985). *A mother's work*. Boston: Houghton-Mifflin.

cases it is very important to help the children develop appropriate self-control and direction. You may be sorely tried at times, but remember the epigenetic principle: The ground plan for growth is a given. We need to nurture each positive type of growth at each stage.

Initiative versus guilt (three to six years): Purpose
Personal development during the third stage of childhood takes place in the areas of initiative and guilt. This is the time when the child's identity as a boy or as a girl is maximally affected. In the preceding stage the child discovers that he or she can be a person with self-direction. Now the task is to discover what kind of a person he or she is, especially with regard to a sense of maleness or of femaleness. Children at this stage begin to identify with the appropriate adult and to model, or copy, aspects of the adult's behavior. This can be seen most readily in those families that allow children to express themselves without a lot of censoring. In such an atmosphere boys will directly express their growing maleness by becoming unusually interested in their mothers. They engage in what becomes almost a rivalry with their father for their

ERIK ERIKSON

Born at the turn of the century, Erik Erikson spent his early years in Europe. As a son of well-to-do parents, he received an education that was both formal and informal. Like other upper-class children, when he finished his regular school work, he traveled the European continent. He described this period as his *moratorium*—a term he used in his later theory of human develop-ment to describe a temporary life space that adolescents go through between the completion of general academic education and the choice of a life career. He noted that at the time of his own young adulthood, it was fashionable to travel through Europe, gaining a perspective on civilization and one's own possible place in it. He chose the avocation of portrait painting as an activity during this time. It permitted maxi-mum flexibility for travel and yielded some productive output as well. Obviously talented, he soon gained a reputation as a promising young artist, expecially for his por-traits of young children.

The turning point in his life came when he was invited to a villa in Austria to do a child's portrait. He entered the villa and was introduced to the child's father, Sigmund Freud. There began a series of informal dis-cussions as he completed his work. A few weeks later, he received a written invitation from Freud to join the Psychoanalytic Institute of Vi-enna and study child analysis. Erik-son has commented that at this point he confronted a momentous deci-sion: the choice between a continued moratorium with more traveling and painting, and a commitment to a life career. Fortunately for psychol-ogy and particularly for our even-tual understanding of children and adolescents, Erikson ended the mor-atorium.

After completing his training, he migrated to this country and served from 1936 to 1939 as a research asso-ciate in psychiatry at Yale, and he worked with Henry Murray of TAT fame (Thematic Apperception Test) at Harvard. From 1939 to 1951 he served as a professor at the Univer-sity of California and then moved to the Austen Riggs Clinic in Pitts-burgh. With each move, his reputa-tion grew in importance. His theo-retical framework was adopted in toto by the White House Conference on Children in 1950. The conference report, a national charter for child and adolescent development in the United States, was almost a literal repetition of his thoughts. In 1960 he was offered a university professor-ship at Harvard in recognition of his national and international stature in the field of human development. The career that started so informally that day at Freud's villa culminated in al-most unprecedented eminence in a professorship in one of the country's

mother's attention and affection. The same is true of girls who, in discovering their femaleness, become very attached to their fathers. Many families report the humorous comments their children make at this age. A boy may say how happy he feels when daddy isn't home, all the while glancing rather obviously toward his mother. Similarly, a girl may wish to go off with daddy in the car. There are often pointed remarks concerning marriage: "I'm not going to marry anyone," a five-year-old boy might declare, "I am going to stay home and take care of mommy when daddy gets too old!" These are not simply humorous comments but reflect questions of sexual identity that are surfacing for the first time.

Adults often have difficulty understanding the im-portance of such issues. It seems, on the face of it, rather absurd for a four- or five-year-old girl to pro-claim that she would like her mother to go away. But if adults punish such statements, the child is left with strong feelings of guilt concerning her identity. To punish her for expressing her natural desire to estab-lish herself as a female will have lasting negative effects. And ridicule or sarcasm will be just as damag-ing as physical punishment, for it will make her feel very small and insignificant, guilty at having ex-pressed some of her inner feelings about what kind of a person she hopes to become. As we have seen, particular aspects of personality are unusually af-fected during each stage. Between three and six years, it is the personal identity that is most affected. Thus

oldest and most prestigious institutions of higher education—all without the benefit of a single earned academic degree. Ironically, he was offered only associate status in the American Psychological Association as late as 1950. This oversight was partially removed in 1955, when he was elected as a fellow of the division of developmental psychology without ever having been a member.

His work, as we have noted in the text, has made a major contribution to our understanding of healthy psychological growth during all aspects of the life cycle. In addition to the high quality of his insight, Erikson possessed a genuine flair for linguistic expression, both spoken and written. In fact, one could almost compare his command of the English language with the benchmark established in this century by Winston Churchill. In many ways Erikson's scope was as broad and comprehensive as that of Churchill. Erikson's genius has been his ability to see the threefold relationship among the person, the immediate environment, and historical forces. Thus, each human is partially shaped by environmental and historical events, but each human, in turn, shapes the environment and can change the course of history. Erikson is equally at home describing the balance of individual strengths and problems for a single "average" child or teenager as in analyzing major historical figures such as Martin Luther and Mahatma Gandhi. He shows through personal history how events and reactions during childhood and adolescence prepare humans to be adults. Ralph Waldo Emerson said that there is no history, only biography. Erikson's work attests to this wisdom.

If there is a criticism of his overall framework, it would concern his differentiation between the sexes. As might be expected, he was conditioned and shaped by the major historical and psychological forces of his own time, following in the tradition of a predominantly male-oriented theory of psychology. This reminds us of the limits set by historical circumstances, which impinge on all humans. He was able to break with many of the limiting traditions of his time, particularly in moving the concept of development from an exclusive pathological focus to a view that emphasized the positive and productive aspects of growth. He was, however, not successful in breaking with the cultural stereotypes regarding female growth.

Now well into official retirement, Erikson continues as an active leader in the cause of healthy development for all humans. In 1983 he addressed the annual meeting of the American Psychiatric Association. As you might guess, he was concerned with a broad and compelling issue of our time, namely, survival in the nuclear age. He closed his speech with a call for civilization to turn back from the brink of a nuclear holocaust and "learn to use our technological genius for the development rather than the destruction of mankind." At the age of eighty-two, he received a standing ovation. His vision for humanity has not dulled nor become myopic; instead, his life even in retirement epitomizes the life cycle completed, the stage of wisdom.

In sum, Erikson has personified his own theory of development in achieving a sense of personal and professional integrity. He reaches the end of life with a certain ego integrity, "an acceptance of his own responsibility for what his life is and was and of its place in the flow of history." These factors include his limitations as well as his many successes.

it is especially important for children at this time to be reassured that they will become full-fledged adults and not to be made to feel guilty over these wishes. Erikson notes:

> Both the girl and the boy are now extraordinarily appreciative of any convincing promise of the fact that someday they will be as good as father or mother—perhaps better, and they are grateful for sexual enlightenment, a little at a time, and patiently repeated at intervals (1959, p. 78).

In school itself, especially in kindergarten and the first grade, many of these same issues are plainly visible. Boys often become so enamored of their teacher that they forget and sometimes call their own mother by their teacher's name. "Some kids really know how to hurt a mother," one mother remarked, half humorously, when this happened to her. Recently, a first-grade teacher invited her class to her wedding. This happens every so often, but this particular wedding was featured in a television news broadcast. And there, for all the world to see, was the class—little girls in crinkly party dresses, bubbling over with excitement as they focused all their attention on the groom; and the boys, in coats and bow ties, weeping as the beaming bride swept down the aisle. This makes the point, perhaps melodramatically, that emotions and feelings at this stage are genuine, legitimate, and need to be accepted.

Promoting initiative instead of guilt in children is a key task between 3 and 6 years.

time to develop a sense of humor, the beginning of an ability to laugh at oneself. "The play age, furthermore, 'occurs' before the limiting advent of the school age, with its defined work roles." What he seems to be saying quite directly is, Let's not move too far in the direction of early formal education for children during this stage. Extensive structured and basic education in reading, math, and writing may serve to inhibit the child, reduce a sense of healthy purpose, and constrain the growth of creativity. It is particularly unfortunate that some parents have been oversold on the idea of infant stimulation and have begun formal instruction at home well before even this stage. Armed with flash cards for numbers and letters, such parents seem to be drilling their children into premature socialization as midget-sized students. In a vain attempt to raise a child's IQ score through such artificial drill and practice, the parents may instead inhibit successful resolution of purpose by their children. As Erikson says:

> This long childhood exposes adults to the temptation of thoughtlessly and often cruelly exploiting the child's dependence by making him pay for the psychological debts owed to us by others, by making him victim of tensions which we will not or dare not correct in ourselves or in our surroundings. We have learned not to stunt a child's growing body with child labor; we must now learn not to break his growing spirit by making him victim of our anxieties (1959, p. 77).

Children's physical size, compared to adults, can also increase any anxieties they may have at this age. In a world of adult "giants," children may fear that they will never grow big enough to be adults. When Erikson used the phrase "perhaps better" in the previous quote, he was referring to children's need for reassurance that they will not only grow to become full-fledged adult men and women but that they will also surpass their parents. We can imagine nothing worse than growing up to be thirty- or forty-year-old "pseudoadults" who still live in the shadow of our parents. As in childrearing, so too in teaching—the ultimate test of how effectively we assist the formation of personal identity is the extent to which we help children outgrow their need for us. By deliberately reinforcing and nurturing children's male or female identities at this stage, we will help build a firm foundation for the next stage of emotional growth. And we will help them continue their general progress from dependence to independence.

Erikson is particularly concerned that at this stage of development children have ample time to play. In fact, in his most recent writing he called this time the *play age*. Remember that from a cognitive view, preoperational, free-wheeling fantasy thinking peaks at this age. He says that the child can well use this

Probably the most persuasive research on the importance of Erikson's theory at this age comes from the follow-up of the Brookline Early Education Program (BEEP) (Hauser-Cram, Pierson, Walker, and Trinan, 1991). They employed a Piaget type of active learning program for young children. The focus was on promoting initiative and competence motivation through a variety of large-group, small-group, and individualized experiences. Social, emotional, motoric, and cognitive activities were carefully planned. No one domain was dominant. Further, the approach in each area was on child-centered activity with minimal didactic instruction. On the other hand, the program was not simply unstructured "play." There was an educational purpose embedded in such activities. The teachers themselves (in concert with our definitions of effectiveness—see Chapter 13) varied the amount of structure and support in accord with the developmental needs of the children.

In addition to the school program, a parallel plan was to educate the parents. The researcher set up three levels of programs according to the observed competence of the parents. They were seeking to reduce possible dissonance between home and school and, for those parents who needed it, help in becoming more effective. The program was broad, with nearly 300 children, almost 40 percent from minority backgrounds including almost 20 percent from non-English-speaking homes.

The results were dramatic. The BEEP children over a one- and three-year follow-up outperformed controls in both academic and social development. The experimentals produced both ways, higher achievement and social development as well as fewer academic failures and referrals for behavior difficulties. The highest success rates were with the children initially "at risk." A careful analysis of the program indicated that it was the developmental nature of the activities that promoted such growth. In fact a comparison indicated that a preschool oriented toward academic achievement that employed behavior modification techniques actually harmed initiative and competence. A twelve-year follow-up of that study found higher rates of school behavior problems and delinquency (Schweinhart, Weikart, and Larner, 1986) just as Erikson would have predicted. This stage is not the time to force-feed an academic regimen to young children. Also and perhaps most obvious is the advantage which children experience regardless of socioeconomic status or minority background, when both home and school educate through a developmental framework.

The Juvenile Period (Six to Twelve Years)

Mastery versus inferiority: Competence   During the elementary school years, Erikson indicates that personal and emotional development turns outward. Children enter a new world—the classroom, the neighborhood, the gang. These become the arenas for growth. The home remains an important base of operations, but the other arenas have special significance. In sheer number of hours, children now spend much more time (excluding sleeping) away from home than ever before. As juveniles they can fully participate as members of a same-sex gang. We may recall from Piaget that not until they are six or seven years old can children genuinely listen to or talk with other children. Now that "collective monologues" have been replaced by genuine discussion, important new groups can be formed.

During this time neighborhood and classroom gangs become major socializing agents. As opposed to adolescent cliques, the juvenile gangs are almost always made up of boys only or girls only. Occasionally a boys' gang will allow a particularly talented tomboy to join, but in general the juvenile world is stable and neatly stereotyped. That world is divided into two camps on everything: boys versus girls, good guys in white hats versus bad guys in black hats; all infants are "babies"; all adults are always right (including all teachers). There is no room for relativity in anything. Again if you will recall Piaget, this is the stage of concrete thought. From the personal point of

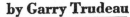

DOONESBURY   **by Garry Trudeau**

view, this factor provides for a period of considerable emotional stability. The juvenile usually stands in an unambiguous relationship at home. He or she may have considerable freedom to roam the neighborhood. Adults are not overly concerned about academic performance in school, although children at this age are, in fact, interested in learning many of the skills that are taught. At a concrete and functional level it is "fun" to decipher words, learn to write, add, and subtract, since each of these skills makes a whole new realm of experience available to them— reading for comic books, writing for notes to pass around, adding for figuring out how much a new bike will cost, and so on. There is no need to lecture children at this age about the importance of learning these skills.

In addition to the many school-oriented skills, children during this period also develop a general sense of personal mastery. The sheer number of new activities and games they learn at this age is enormous— swimming, riding, sailing, skiing, roller skating, camping, boating, baseball, basketball, football, hockey, kick-the-can, sewing, cooking, collecting things (look in any child's pockets at this age!)—the list is almost endless and is testimony to the raw amount of energy and **competence motivation** that exists at this age. The old saying that a child has 10,000 muscles that want to move and only one set

to sit still is most appropriate. At the same time, we should understand Erikson's major point: This tremendous amount of energy can be put to the service of personal competence motivation. If children are not encouraged to engage actively with the surrounding world, their sense of personal industry will give way to personal inferiority. In other words, this is the time when the child's need to function and actively acquire multiple skills will *maximally affect* his or her sense of personal industry.

Erikson's term *competence*, to reflect the resolution of that industry, is unusually appropriate. In fact, it's possible to guess that Erikson's choice came from his association with another Harvard psychologist, Robert W. White. White (1959) actually coined the phrase "competence motivation" to describe what he considered a universal attribute of humans and other species. White reviewed all the major theories and research evidence for personal development and concluded that there is an inborn "drive" to master the environment. This drive is in our very bones, so to speak. We humans—and other animal species as well—are not the empty organisms, or so-called black boxes, that classic stimulus-response theory would suggest, nor are we passive agents who merely react to but never act on the world, as classic psychoanalytic theory would say. White found, to the contrary, that humans and animals are naturally curious and

The period between ages six and twelve (Erikson's stage of mastery versus inferiority) presents a special challenge to both teachers and parents. During this period children have a natural desire to master new goals and control their environment. Robert White uses the phrase "competence motivation" to describe this attribute.

seek to master and control the world around them. Just watch a child in a supermarket for a while, and you will see a perfect example of the need to explore and master the environment.

The reason the idea of competence is so important for educators is perhaps obvious by now. Personal and emotional development from six to twelve years of age takes place largely in school. Children of this age spend more time in school than anywhere else. Thus, the classroom situation will be a major influence on their development at this stage. We too often overhear teachers making comments such as, "What can we do with a child who comes from a bad home environment?" The point is, we should not assume that we cannot have a positive effect on personal development and especially on the competence motivation of our pupils. In fact, elementary school teachers are in a particularly strategic position to emphasize activities that can both nurture and, in some cases, restore a sense of mastery. Our elementary schools are gradually shifting away from rote learning, passive listening, and neatness ("Always color inside the lines!"), and are moving toward the open, active classroom. The so-called open classroom emphasizes many different activities and individual projects and absorbs great amounts of energy. By stressing doing instead of listening, the active school will do much to promote the pupils' sense of personal mastery. Erikson says that children are maximally ready for active learning between the ages of six and twelve. Our task as educators is to respond to this natural tendency so as to facilitate rather than impair healthy personal growth. We shouldn't worry so much about creating quiet, orderly, neat, and polite pupils. That objective will work directly against the opportunity to affect personal industry and mastery.

One of the major challenges at this stage then is to continue the growth process. An important recent study has shown the adverse effects of substance abuse at this stage. Randall Jones (1992) studied over 500 children in grades 3 and 4. He found about 25 percent ($N = 131$) had been involved with drug abuse (cigarettes, smokeless tobacco, alcohol, glue, marijuana, and cocaine) over a five-month period. He then compared their scores on Erikson's stage to the nonabusing group. The differences revealed that the abusers had psychosocial scores lower on *trust* and *industry*, while the nonabusing group gained on all the measures of psychosocial stages. There were no gender differences. Jones speculated that the effects of drug abuse at this stage, then, may impair the process of healthy development. Lacking trust and industry, such students may not be prepared for the next stage of identity formation.

Adolescence (Thirteen through the College Years)

Identity versus diffusion: Fidelity   Adolescence, in which the major issue is identity versus diffusion, is perhaps the most famous of Erikson's stages. The changes that take place during adolescence bring about a major shift in personal development. We have already seen (Chapter 5) that cognitive development in this period gives the adolescent a completely new way to understand and think. We also have noted (Chapter 3) how the very substantial glandular changes at this time represent a major new system. Puberty obviously marks a major qualitative departure from the past. Changes of this magnitude in cognitive and physiological areas will by themselves create major psychological change. "How do I understand what is happening to me when so much is different?" someone in this stage might ask. It is no understatement to say that of all the stages of personal development, none is more radical than adolescence. Change is the name of the game during this period.

Early adolescence and self-concept   The changes in physiological, glandular, and psychological systems experienced during early adolescence constitute the most substantial shift a human being undergoes. The adolescent can now experience the world in a major new way. He or she begins to think in relativistic terms and can appreciate the difference between objective reality and subjective perception. In addition, the adolescent develops the important ability to perceive feelings and emotions both in self and others, as well as the ability to take the perspective of another person (figuratively to place oneself in another person's shoes). And finally, he or she is now able to understand as-if situations and distinguish between symbolic and literal meaning. In short, the thinking system that begins to develop during this period provides the adolescent with a new and sophisticated mechanism for making meaning from his or her own experience, particularly in reference to understanding one's own identity as a person. To summarize, as an adolescent begins to think about self and identity, he or she can perform the following operations:

Self-consciousness and social conformity often accompany the first stage of identify formation.

1. Differentiate feelings and emotions in self and others

2. Distinguish between objective and subjective reality

3. Adopt the perspective of another person

4. Understand symbolic meaning, and role-play as-if situations

In one sense, then, it seems that personal development during adolescence represents a great leap forward, since one can now be more complex, comprehensive, empathic, and abstract and can now maintain a broad perspective on self and others. However, as one distinguished psychologist, **David Elkind** (1978), points out, such is not the case. In fact, just the reverse takes place. The more complex thought system raises the adolescent to new heights of mental operations, yet lowers him or her to new depths. On first entering this new stage, the teenager tends to become excessively egocentric in thought.

The external world is no longer viewed as permanent and unchanging, but rather as relative, subjective, and phenomenological. Accordingly, the teenager may begin to perceive himself or herself as the center of the universe.

This egocentrism, unfortunately, is accompanied by excessive self-consciousness. The teenager is unusually vulnerable to pressures to go along with the crowd. The extent of social conformity in junior high was demonstrated in a well-designed study specifically employing a developmental-stage framework. The researchers predicted the level of conformity on the basis of stage of ego development. Their results indicated that eighth-grade pupils of both sexes had the highest scores on social conformity as well as on ego stage—the equivalent of Lawrence Kohlberg's Stage III (see Chapter 7). Both younger students with lower-stage scores and older students with higher-stage scores were less other-directed. The pupils with Stage III scores were the most strongly concerned with how others perceived them and with going along with the group (Hoppe and Loevinger, 1977).

The influence, then, of peers continues to be highly significant. A massive national survey by Schultz (1989) clearly demonstrated that during adolescence, peers replace others as the main source for discussions about important decisions. The rank order was (1) peers (2) parents (3) relatives (4) teachers/advisors. Peers were chosen almost as frequently as all other groups combined.

In another, less formal study, researchers interviewed junior high students on their personal perceptions of self and others. The results can be summed up in the words of one of the subjects. When asked, "What is the most real thing to you?" her unhesitating reply was, "Myself" (Kohlberg and Gilligan, 1971).

Elkind on adolescence   Elkind (1970) has noted that how an adolescent views his or her "self"—that is, the self-concept—can be described along two basic dimensions of egocentric thinking: (1) the personal fable and (2) the imaginary audience.

The personal fable is a deep-rooted belief in one's personal uniqueness—the notion that no one else in the world can possibly understand how "I" really feel. As Elkind notes, the complex beliefs create an aura—"only he can suffer with such agonized intensity or experience such exquisite rapture." To retain this image an adolescent may create a personal fable, "a story which he tells himself (and others) and which is not true" (1978, p. 130).

Possibly the best example of sexual fantasies and egocentrism can be found in the novel *Catcher in the Rye*, by J. D. Salinger (1964). Holden Caulfield, "everyperson as an adolescent," describes a classic dialogue with one of his near friends, "Old Ackley," in which the two are discussing sexual prowess. Holden narrates that he listened silently as Ackley described in monotonous detail how he "made it" with a girlfriend the previous summer. Holden is patient to a point, but he has heard Ackley's story at least a hundred times. The trouble is, each time the story is different. In Elkind's terms this is Ackley's personal fable—an untrue story repeated ad infinitum (and ad nauseum, one might add).

Essentially, the imaginary audience refers to the belief that everyone else in the world is preoccupied with the personal appearance and behavior of the adolescent—as if the entire world paused each morning to see how the teenager was dressed for school or waited with hushed anticipation for the adolescent to speak his or her lines. In front of such imaginary audiences adolescents can swing from excessive self-criticism (admiring one's own martyrdom) to the other extreme—self admiration to the point of boorishness. Elkind cites the famous passage from *Tom Sawyer* of Tom witnessing his own funeral as a universal fantasy of adolescents: "They will really miss me when I'm gone and be sorry too for all the mean things they said."

On an optimistic note, Elkind finds that adolescents can be helped to gradually distinguish between real and imaginary audiences, as well as to differentiate between themselves and others in both thoughts and feelings. Given the support of adult understanding, both the personal fable and the imagined audience are progressively modified and diminished. It is to be hoped that as adults, we can retain some of the positive aspects of this stage, namely, a healthy respect for our own individuality.

The crisis of personal identity Because adolescence represents such a major discontinuity in growth, Erikson has singled out one critical issue as the major task of this stage—resolving the crisis of personal identity. Our definition of self—how we see ourselves *and* how others see us—forms the foundation of our adult personality. If that foundation is firm and strong, a solid personal identity results; if not, the result is what Erikson calls a diffuse identity. Identity diffusion is something like suffering from amnesia or like perpetually wandering over a landscape, trying to "find" a selfhood. With no sense of past or future, the diffuse personality is like a stranger in his or her own land, with no roots, no history. The sense of personal alienation prevents the establishment of a stable core for the personality.

Western societies have made it extremely difficult for adolescents to come through this stage with a firm sense of personal identity. Industrialized societies have exaggerated the marginal status of adolescents by grossly overextending the period of dependency. This is justified by the amount of special learning and

Adolescents often hold the belief that everyone else in the world is preoccupied with the adolescents' personal appearance and behavior. In front of this "imaginary audience," teens may be excessively self-critical or self-admiring.

training that is needed to survive in our complex world. However, it is easy to forget the negative personal effects of keeping a twenty-one-year old, or even an eighteen-year old, in a position of dependency. To make matters worse, adults seem to be unable to decide just when it is that an adolescent becomes an adult. The age of legal adult responsibility is extremely inconsistent in this country: The legal age for marriage differs not only by sex (girls are permitted to marry without parental consent earlier than boys) but also according to state residency, with some states permitting legal marriage as early as fourteen years of age. And there are similar discrepancies in the legal age for going to work, driving a car, entering into a legal contract, voting in elections (for most of this nation's history adolescents were old enough to die for their country in war before they were old enough to vote in elections), drinking alcoholic beverages, and enlisting in the military services.

These few examples serve to highlight the problem of identity formation. Erikson notes that adolescents are caught between two major systems, both of which are in flux. They have to cope with internal, cognitive, and glandular changes at the same time that they are confronting a series of inconsistent and changing external regulations. And they go through all this while simultaneously discarding the identity they had in the previous stage, the age of mastery. Playing kick-the-can, riding a bike, participating in the Boy or Girl Scouts, enjoying the antics of the Three Stooges on TV, acting like a tomboy, and most important, viewing adults as almost always correct because they are older and bigger—these dimensions of personal development during the elementary age all have to be discarded. Adolescence is almost like entering a foreign country without knowing the language, the customs, or the culture; only it's worse because the "voyagers" don't even have a guidebook. It is truly a major shock during adolescence to find that adults are not always right and, in fact, are often working very hard to cover up their mistakes. The discovery of relativism, especially in the moral behavior of adults, further exaggerates the difficulties of personal development. On the one hand, adolescents learn that some police officers take bribes, some professors plagiarize, some teachers copy lesson plans, some major corporations "fix" prices, some elected officials solicit bribes, some professional athletes play under the influence of drugs, and so on. On the other hand, these same adults have a tendency to lecture adolescents on the subject of responsibility, the importance of obeying rules, and above all, of showing respect to adults. The resulting overreaction is well known. If you can't

rely on some adults, don't trust anyone over thirty! If some businesspeople are overly materialistic, all businesspeople are Babbitts! If some adults are unfaithful, all marriages are institutionalized hypocrisy! This list is endless, and serves as a poignant reminder of how difficult it is to understand the highly complicated problems of living and personal development in a modern society.

JAMES MARCIA: IDENTITY STATUS DURING COLLEGE

The major contribution of **James Marcia** (1966, 1976) has been to focus attention on the specific phases of identity formation during the college years and to chart the actual transitions.

In interviews Marcia asked questions in three areas of concern common to college students: (1) occupation, (2) religious ideology, and (3) worldview. The format allowed students to talk at length about their own thoughts. For example, he asked "How would you compare your own political ideas with those of your folks?" (political ideology). On religion, he asked, "Is there any time you've doubted any of your religious beliefs?" On occupation, he asked, "How have you become interested in—career?" Of course, whether such an approach yields informative data depends on the skill of the interviewer in not leading respondents to specific answers but in stimulating reflective thought. Fortunately, Marcia and his staff were highly skilled counselors who were comfortable with silences and could ask a wide variety of open-ended questions until they were convinced that they had a good sample of the students' worldview in a particular area.

On the basis of a series of studies with this technique, Marcia found that he could group the students' thought according to four distinct aspects of identity formation. Essentially, he uncovered two intermediate phases between the bipolar identity and diffusion extremes. He labeled and described the phases as follows:

Identity Diffusion

A state of suspension from life is a predominant mode in **diffusion.** There are few, if any, commitments to anyone or to any set of beliefs or principles. Instead, there is a major emphasis on relativity and living for the moment. No area of personal gratification is relinquished; all things are possible. There seems to be no core to the person; social roles are tried on

James Marcia found that identity formation among college age students moved from a very diffuse sense of identity, where social roles are tried and abandoned quickly, to a gradually more permanent sense of self, which often emerged following a period of intense experience gathering and self-reflection.

and abandoned quickly. The person seems egoless, directionless, and wandering.

Identify Foreclosure

The main theme in **foreclosure** is the avoidance of autonomous choice. The person is other-directed rather than inner-directed. There is very little questioning: The person largely accepts whatever role authority figures or influential friends prescribe. There seems to be little dissonance. The person accepts somewhat fatalistically what adults say about career, religion, and politics. The struggle to establish the self as an independent and autonomous person is avoided. It is as if the person were fearful of the responsibility that goes with personal freedom.

Identity Moratorium

A **moratorium** is often a result of a painful and deliberate decision to take time off from the current press, such as school, college, or a first job. The goal is to create some breathing space in order to explore more fully both one's own psychological self and objective reality. The surface difference between moratorium and diffusion may appear subtle; yet underneath, the difference is substantial. In moratorium there is a genuine search for alternatives, not simply a biding of one's time. There is a major need to test oneself in a variety of experiences to increase one's in-depth knowledge of self. Commitments are temporarily avoided for legitimate reasons: "I need more time and experience before I can commit myself to a career such as medicine." Or "I am not ready to go for a Ph.D. in history. There are too many unknowns I need to explore first." Thus a moratorium is not simply a cop-out so that the person can drift aimlessly. Instead, it is an active process of searching, with the major goal of preparing for commitment. Erikson's own life, as the biography points out, contained a very significant moratorium, as well as an even greater commitment. One flowed from the other, Erikson would say.

Identity Achievement

The final phase of identity formation results in identity **achievement.** Erikson's definition is the clearest: "the accrued confidence that one's ability to maintain inner sameness and continuity is matched by the sameness and continuity of one's meaning for others'" (1959, p. 89). The person gradually incorporates each successive childhood identification, yet goes beyond those earlier forms. A new personal entity is formed as a unique individual. The process, however, is reciprocal, as we noted earlier. The emergence of such individuality and self-direction on the part of the person (the core personality) is acknowledged by others. It is this aspect of identity formation that can be the most troubling and troublesome, since such recognition is neither automatic nor necessarily universal. In fact, now-recognized great persons often had a major crisis during which their emergent achieved identity was not immediately recognized by adult society in general. Erikson's biography of Martin Luther (*Young Man Luther*) contains the most complete account of this phenomenon, and similar episodes can be found in the personal histories of major figures such as Malcolm X, George Bernard Shaw, and Marie Curie.

Marcia found, most importantly, that identity achievement almost always contained elements of personal crisis, confrontation, and thoughtful decision making. The person was aware of the variety of tough choices life offers: The choice selected was accompanied by commitment, that is, a personal pledge that the psychological resources the individual possessed would be placed in the service of the goal.

ALAN WATERMAN: THE ORDER OF IDENTITY PHASES

With Marcia's finding, there was an assumption that the process of development during the college years was largely linear and sequential, starting with diffusion and proceeding to foreclosure, moratorium, and achievement. However, **Alan Waterman** and other researchers created a more complex model of the paths taken by college students toward the goal of identity formation and fidelity. The researchers identified four possible phases, each with a series of options (1985, 1992).

The theoretical model, diagrammed in Figure 6.2, illustrates the twists and turns in the developmental

FIGURE 6.2   The sequence of identity development. Waterman takes the position that a moratorium cannot be maintained indefinitely. He also suggests that one cannot regress from moratorium to foreclosure once the crisis stage has been reached during a moratorium.

Phase One (Starting at Diffusion)

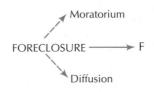

Phase Two (Starting at Foreclosure)

Phase Three (Starting at Moratorium)

Phase Four (Starting at Achievement)

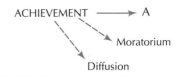

Adapted from A. Waterman (1985). Identity in adolescence: Processes and contents. *New Directions for Child Development*. San Francisco: Jossey-Bass, p. 18.

process during the college years. It also clearly illustrates that the progression from identity diffusion to achievement and fidelity does not necessarily proceed in a straight line—and that students have several possible options they may follow. For example, a student can remain in diffusion or move to foreclosure or moratorium. A student in foreclosure can remain there, slip back to diffusion, or move up to moratorium. Similar possibilities hold for students in the other phases, particularly for those in the achievement phase. Students who have reached achievement are not assured of the ultimate emergence of fidelity. They may instead shift to either moratorium or even diffusion. The diversity of college environments can aid in promoting growth, yet psychological growth is not automatic and it is not guaranteed. Further longitudinal research, including intensive case studies, may help clarify who chooses which path and under what conditions.

Recent Research on Identity Status

There has been a major increase in identity status research in the last decade, some of which cross-validates and some of which changes the original views. At the most general level, the status research consistently finds a clear relationship between the more advanced statuses, e.g., moratorium and achievement and a wide variety of measures of development. Identity achievement particularly is positively linked with the following:

> Ego development level (Loevinger), Formal operations (Piaget), Ethical reasoning (Kohlberg), Locus of control (Rotter), as well as psychological well-being, healthy psychological adjustment, coping, personal efficacy, and low status of anxiety (Waterman, 1992, p. 63).

In addition to positive relationships between achievement and general measures of maturity and self-direction, the opposite was also found. College students in foreclosure demonstrated highly stereotyped personal relationships and low levels of personal expressiveness, personal efficacy, and cognitive complexity. It is interesting to note, however, that students in foreclosure had high levels of self-esteem and goal directedness. In a sense this suggests that their self-esteem and career goals are tied directly to their unquestioned acceptance of their parents' wishes. This is also a reminder that a variable like positive self-esteem should not be considered as a goal of development unless we know the context. Otherwise we would be caught in a developmental contradiction: positive self-esteem as an outcome of sacrificing the drive toward self-direction and autonomy. Also the rigidity and authoritarianism that is associated with foreclosure may account for Randall Jones's finding (1992) that students in foreclosure were *twice* as likely to become substance abusers as were those in the comparison statuses. Even the moti-

vation for drug abuse was different: "bored" for the students in foreclosure versus "exploration" for the others.

As you can surely guess, the most troublesome status for college students was diffusion. Such students displayed low levels of personal expressiveness, goal-setting ability, and cognitive complexity but high levels of impulsivity: they were least effective in helping and had the greatest difficulty with intimacy. Certainly all these results confirm Erikson's original contentions on the positive nature of identity achievement and the psychological problems associated with either foreclosure or diffusion. Moratorium tends to be rated as similar to identity achievement in almost all domains except anxiety. The consistent difference between these two statuses is affective. The achievers are not anxious, whereas students in moratorium experience high levels of anxiety (Waterman, 1992). Active exploration apparently does exact some emotional toll during the process.

Identity Formation and Minority Status

As in so many other areas of psychological research, the question of minority status and identity has only recently emerged. This is so, in spite of W. E. B. Dubois's eloquent comment at the turn of the century that African Americans are faced with not one but two identity issues: How should one resolve "two warring idols in one dark body"? (1963, p. 17) The same holds true for other adolescents from devalued ethnic backgrounds. The first challenge, then, is the development of an achieved identity, which all adolescents face, but then this challenge is compounded by the issue of ethnic identity. Although teenagers, even from socially favored ethnic backgrounds, must resolve such issues, ethnicity is not a particularly salient problem since there is a substantial lack of racial prejudice directed toward them. In fact the opposite may be so, for they may even feel a sense of entitlement. For racially distinct minorities from devalued backgrounds, however, the story is completely different. During the elementary school years, the identity question is usually resolved in an awkward and nonfunctional manner. Such children often exhibit a very low ethnic awareness or a preference for the majority culture. In the now famous Supreme Court case of *Brown vs. The Board of Education*, young African-American children expressed exactly this view. Research by Phinney and Rosenthal (1992) has found similar examples during early adolescence: either a

SPOTLIGHT ON BLACK IDENTITY

Malcolm X and Self-Esteem

One of the ironic consequences of racism is often that the victim tries to identify with the groups who are the oppressors. Many years ago, Bruno Bettlehein, during his years in a Nazi concentration camp, described examples when a few of the Jewish prisoners tried to make over their garb to resemble the SS uniforms and played some of the same games as their guards such as punching each other as hard as they could. In a similar vein, Malcolm X, an African-American reformer who was later assassinated, described an incident during his adolescence when he became ashamed of his African traits, particularly his kinky hair.

To make himself over was no easy task. It involved what was called "conking" to straighten the curly Afro hair. The method was crude: Apply lye, the kind plumbers use to open clogged drains, to smooth out the curls. The result would be hair more similar to the majority white population and different from his natural look. He asked his friend "Shorty" to help him and describes how they mixed lye, thin-sliced potatoes, and eggs in a mason jar. He could feel the jar heat up. After applying a thick coat of petroleum jelly, Shorty administered the hot mixture to Malcolm's hair. Suddenly his head was afire, the lye dripping down his cheeks; his eyes watered and his nose ran as Shorty worked furiously to spray and rinse. "The first time's always worst. You get used to it better before long," said Shorty. "You got a good conk." Malcolm later observed, "How ridiculous I was! Stupid enough to stand there simply lost in admiration of my hair now looking 'white'."[a]

Recently, research by Jean Phinney and Linda Line Alipuria[b] validated the point. Ethnic identity was a most important component in self-esteem specifically for students from minority backgrounds. Such students showed a strong need during adolescence to find out about their ethnic backgrounds and make a commitment to that identification. Accepting and feeling proud about one's ethnic roots was central to self-respect and self-esteem. Such students would not need to drip burning lye down their faces to change their appearance.

---

[a] Malcolm X (1964). *The autobiography of Malcolm X*. New York: Grove Press.

[b] Phinney, J., and Alipuria, L. L. (1990). Ethnic identity in college students from four ethnic groups. *Journal of Adolescence, 13*, 171–183.

---

preference for the majority culture or an unexamined acceptance of an ethnic identity. Certainly the example of Malcolm X stands as a vivid example of just how far a teenager might go in attempting to identify with the majority culture. Other ethnic minorities have used other means to achieve similar goals, for example, changing family names or facial characteristics in an attempt to gain acceptance.* Such instances may recede as the majority culture becomes more mature in respecting cultural diversity and as the emerging minority groups continue to develop self-affirmation and pride. For example, the stigma formerly attached to being a Japanese American has abated to the extent that ethnicity is no longer as salient as for other Asian groups in identity (Phinney and Rosenthal, 1992, p. 163). Also for African-American females, the importance of skin color and adolescent identity has changed. No longer is being "whiter" desirable. A middle ground, not too white and not too black, has become the currently desired skin color (Robinson, in press). This rather precise middle ground is still a color designation, however, and indicates that there is still some psychological ambivalence over accepting one's ethnic background, but that issue is also common to many adolescents.

Thus, ethnic minorities face a more difficult process of identity formation. In general, they have fewer opportunities for open exploration when in fact they need more time and support to "sift through two sets of cultural values and identity options" (Markstrom-Adams, 1992, p. 177). The lack of such exploration will result in premature foreclosure, and this only

---

*   In a recent TV interview Mario Cuomo noted that some twenty-five years ago he was advised to change his name to Mark Conner when, after graduating number one in law school, he was turned down by every major law firm in New York City. He finally was hired by a small firm in Albany. He wryly commented that a name change wouldn't have worked anyway—"not with this face."

increases the risk of the teenager's joining one of the many cults, gangs, or other extremist groups.

If there is one issue which exemplifies the problem most clearly, it is the question of academic achievement in secondary school. The terms may vary—"acting white," "being an Anglo," "trying to pass," and so forth—but the message is the same: If you succeed in school, you will be rejecting your ethnic heritage. This creates a no-win situation. The choice seems to be to reject the majority culture and join a gang or to become raceless. Eric Watts, as a college student, writes of his experiences in secondary school as an African American. He was particularly discouraged when his peers denigrated his studying or his use of standard English with comments such as "Eric, stop talking like a white boy" (Watts, 1992, p. 48). One who strives for such academic achievement is regarded as a "square" or, even worse, as a "preppie." The alternatives, as John Ogbu (1988) points out, at least for inner-city youth, fall into three categories: (1) act *cool*—streetwise, (2) play *the jester*—prankish, or (3) be *the antagonist*—the fighter. None of these identity choices will serve the long-term interests of minority adolescents.

When ethnic minority adolescents are provided with the psychological and social support to resolve the dual-identity questions, the outcomes are unusually positive. Once they have learned to withstand the negative peer pressure and the negative influence of some community adults, minority teenagers and college students actually reach more advanced levels of psychological development than their majority-culture peers. In a study of college-age Mexican, Asian, and African Americans, those who had successfully resolved the identity-achievement question had significantly higher scores on four measures of psychological adjustment. The result was validated at the high school level (Pinney and Rosenthal, 1992). In a sense these results confirm the Eriksonian truism: The teenager has to coordinate his or her own emerging identity while interacting with an environment of peers and adults that has increasingly potent influence. Leaving the relative safety of elementary school, the adolescent from an ethnically devalued background has fewer resources and a greater task to resolve. School programs can help. Certainly the example of the Locke and Faubert research (1993) demonstrates what can be done by modifying the classroom environment. They have shown that minority youth can develop a positive ethnic identity and achieve academically as well through a school

that is developmentally oriented. Otherwise, as Courtland Lee (1990) points out, the ethnic adult community has to compensate for the lack of acknowledgment and affirmation by the school in particular or by the adult society in general.

Lee in a study of rural minority teenagers found multiple examples of discrimination and prejudice by school and community adults which may have been unintentional, and yet the effect was the same. The national *Quality Education for Minorities Project* (1990) indicated the same unfair treatment in schools across the country. Certainly minority youth deserve more positive help in resolving the identity question.

Identity Formation and Gender

As is the case with ethnicity, a substantial new research base is helping clarify and extend identity status to the gender issue. As we've noted, Erikson did exhibit a rather substantial blind spot on the gender question, suggesting that the biology of females' "inner space" predisposed them away from achievement and toward affiliation. This dichotomy of males as instrumental and of females as caring puts the same limitation on identity formation as we have shown in the domain of moral development. In fact some of the earlier research in identity had suggested that foreclosure was actually more adaptive for females than the movement to achievement, self-direction, and personal efficacy. It was felt that a foreclosed identity would protect women from conflicts over personal achievement—the syndrome denoted as "fear of success." During the 1970s a series of studies underscored the worries that achieving females experienced in college (Horner, 1972; Larkin, 1987). This research presents an eerie parallel to the discussion, in the preceding section, of peers and of society in general sending a message to minorities about "acting white." Here a similar message was sent to women about "acting male." The context of the message in the form of rigid societal expectations clearly created a major psychological conflict. If a female wanted to become an M.D., would she lose her chance to become an "M-r-s"? It wasn't feminine to hit the books or to grind it out in "hard" science. You would probably remove yourself from the marriage pool.

Also, as was the case for minorities, society in general may perpetuate the stereotypes. They send the social conformity, affiliative, "you can't succeed in 'male' domains" message to females. Eccles (1986) has shown that it was mothers who believed the myths of female incompetence in math and science, whereas Jones and Wheatley (1989) found it was female (and male) science teachers who sent the same negative message to female adolescents. Arnold (1987) found a major decline of female identity as an academic achiever in a sample of former high school valedictorians. Sigmund Freud, years earlier, had referred to such difficulties when he described persons who were "wrecked by success" (1957).

Given these findings, then, it is no wonder that a foreclosed identity appeared to be a safe means of avoiding conflict. The problem, of course, as for minorities, is that such a solution relegates over half the population in this case to a subservient role. Research in psychological development as we've pointed out so many times in this text demonstrates that females have the same potential for development as anyone else. It is clear, however, that neither *foreclosure* nor *diffusion* is adaptive in the long run. Foreclosure will obviously not work since the majority of women in this country will become the head of household and main breadwinners for the family as a result of divorce, abandonment, or death of a spouse. To carry out such responsibility competently without achieving a firm sense of an individual identity would be close to impossible. Similarly, to remain in *diffusion* would be maladaptive. Josselson (1987) has shown that adult women in diffusion have little sense of direction and cannot make commitments, that they are distant and estranged from their families, and that they cannot maintain firm and stable interpersonal relationships—hardly a psychological state conducive to mental health.

Sally Archer (1992a, 1992b) has taken the lead in revising the stereotyped views of identity formation for females. She does not suggest that we can simply transform the male model in toto into a female model. Identity formation at least in the foreseeable future contains the same levels of development for both males and females but will be more difficult and painful for females due to the external barriers to development. For example, Archer finds that sex differences are the exception now rather than the rule in identity status. There are no differences by gender and identity by vocation, religion, sex roles, values, and dating.

A recent study by Eva Skoe (1991) continues to confirm the lack of sex differences. In a college sample, she found no differences between males and females on *identity status, moral judgment,* and a spe-

cially constructed *care interview.* The higher stages, in general, correlated positively for both groups, cross-validating Waterman's summary already noted. For example, higher identity scores were related to higher moral judgment scores and in this case higher scores on the care interview, as well.

The major continuing difference is in the family-career priorities (Archer, 1992b). Males in grades 6, 8, 10, and 12 see almost no connection between career and family and do not make any mention of the problems of child care, the psychological or economic impact on children, or the need to facilitate the development of their spouse. Archer's sample of high school seniors responded as follows to the question, "How concerned are you about the issue of balancing career and family demands?"

	GREAT CONCERN	SOME CONCERN	NO CONCERN
Males	0%	25%	75%
Females	42	42	17

As a result, Archer points out that a most crucial issue, career and family, remains a singular struggle for females even though they have now entered the work force in huge proportions. Who, she asks rhetorically, will help them resolve this aspect of *identity achievement*? Must such women wait for the departure of children before they can pursue identity commitments of their own? In fact, some research indicates that it is only the women who maintain continuous employment who also follow the stepwise sequence. This, at least, indicates that context rather than Eriksonian biology is a critical factor in identity development (Patterson, Sochting, and Marcia, 1992).

In summarizing, Archer points out that the failure of society in general to support the process of identity formation creates an unfair burden. Females bear the costs of such invisibility. "There is a remarkable dearth of investment in the recognition of these identity concerns by parents, peers, school counselors or classroom instructors" (Archer, 1992b, p. 98). Thus, while there are no major differences by gender in most of the identity domains either in this country or cross-culturally (Costa and Campos, 1992), the area of career and family remains largely a female concern, with females left to their own singular resources for resolution. Unfortunately, Archer's interviews reveal a major naïveté in some of their current reflections.

The identity correlates of realism are low when a high school female brightly announces that she will complete college, get married, go to medical school, take a few years off to have children, and resume her career—all without help from anyone. Archer concludes that too often females are caught up with such "fairy tales." "Like all other toys, they must eventually be stored away; but in this case before they do irreparable damage" (Archer, 1992b, p. 99).

EDUCATIONAL IMPLICATIONS

As educators, we need to take special note of the challenge posed by the immensely complicated problem of adolescence. There are no easy solutions. But this does not mean that nothing can be done. For years it was fashionable to say that adolescence is a tough period, but everyone outgrows it eventually, so all you can do is grin and bear it. We now realize that such advice is mere rationalization and in no way excuses us from responsibility. The number of psychological casualties during adolescence is now too obvious to permit such an attitude. For example, we now realize that adolescent drug abuse is a symptom of the problem of personal identity formation or, in Erikson's terms, an attempt to solve the problem of identity diffusion. It is only an attempt because it is a nonsolution. The moment the drug wears off, the same problems are still there, waiting to be attended to.

As we noted, educators are by definition in a strategic position to help guide personal growth. Adolescents feel a need to pull away from their own parents, and so other adults can be of special significance. It is therefore our responsibility to develop effective ways to make this influence work. Erikson makes it obvious that to assist growth we need to provide adolescents with increasing amounts of independence and responsibility. We said that in the previous stage—mastery—activity was the key. In this stage our objectives as educators should be to provide real experience and genuine responsibility.

Thus, the variety of school programs, especially at the secondary level, involving peer and cross-age teaching, community internships, peer counseling, and teenage health "consultants" is important primarily because such role-taking can involve genuine responsibility. In these programs teenagers learn to teach, counsel, and care for younger classmates. Such responsibility stimulates their own leadership devel-

opment and psychological maturation. Thus, the potential for empathic understanding and human caring that is available for development during adolescence can be capitalized on in the service of healthy personal growth.

The problem, of course, is that to achieve developmental goals, the learning experiences need for the most part to be "real world" activity plus a careful balance of introspection, readings, and reflection. When done well, the results are impressive. For example, James Leming (1992) found that the most positive of all approaches to drug abuse prevention in high school was through the use of carefully trained peer counselors. Another study has shown that high school females trained as math tutors to aid fifth-grade females was successful on three counts: (1) the teenage tutors developed a greater level of psychological/identity growth toward independence, (2) the elementary school females improved in actual math achievement, and (3) the fifth-graders also learned to attribute their success to their own effort. It is equally important to note that in a control class of teenage teacher aides, without weekly readings and discussions, there was no change in development. Also, in the control class of fifth-graders there was no change in math achievement and (unfortunately) a decline in success attribution to self (Sprinthall and Scott, 1989).

A third recent study demonstrated the positive impact of a peer counseling program with high school students as group leaders of middle school pupils whose families were going through a divorce. The high-schoolers spent one semester in an elective course in peer counselor training and then led the "divorce" groups for a semester. The results again were threefold: (1) The leaders moved to higher levels of psychological/ego development, (2) the middle school students improved in their "locus of control" and ego development, and (3) the middle school students also indicated a greater ability to adjust/cope with the family disruption (Sprinthall, Hall, and Gerler, 1992). The controls showed no change. Similarly positive results have been found with college students as peer helpers (Zimmerman, 1989; Mann, 1992).

Thus, the peer influence can be channeled into important educational and developmental activity. It does require a comprehensive educational plan, namely weekly classes to discuss the issues involved and training in the use of teacher or counselor skills. Peer programs without the reflection review component either have no positive goals or in some cases move toward negative goals. A study by Paul Adams (1988) with college students involved in unguided small-group discussion indicated that students at higher stages of development actually lowered their level of reasoning to match that of a peer. This reminds us that social conformity in a developmental sense may peak in middle school but continues to exert substantial influence even in college. Adolescent peers do represent a potential resource for identity development, but not if left to themselves.

PSYCHOLOGICAL DEFENSES DURING ADOLESCENCE

Anna Freud has outlined the most common psychological defenses that adolescents employ (1958). She feels that much of the so-called pathology during this stage is in reality the normal upset that can be expected to accompany massive internal changes. In fact, she suggests that the only abnormality would be for adolescents to show no signs of psychological unrest. She points out that if we accept such turmoil as normal, we can avoid extreme overreactions. One parent typified these feelings when she said of adolescents, "We should bury them at twelve and dig them up again at twenty-one." Mark Twain allegedly commented on his own adolescence, "I thought my father was the dumbest person in the world, yet by the time I reached my twenties, he sure had learned a lot!"

Anna Freud lists the psychological systems in the following order:

Displacement: To transfer feelings and needs from one situation or person to another object. Commonly, adolescents may begin to feel attached to their parents, especially the parent of the opposite sex, and defend against this by becoming overly attached to other adults. Crushes on movie stars, rock singers, and attractive schoolteachers are well-known examples. Displacement also is often accompanied by substantial acting-up and heightened emotional expressiveness.

Reversal of affect: To turn needs and feelings inside out. This occurs when adolescents suddenly change the manifestation of feelings from one extreme to the other. Thus, instead of showing anger, an adolescent may display an exaggerated coolness. The desire for closeness may be demonstrated by withdrawal, alienation, and hiding out in one's room. Feelings and needs for excitement and curiosity may become inverted and appear as remarks such as, "but life is so boring."

Withdrawal: To psychologically hide out. This is a more extreme defense in the sense that the adolescent begins to more actively separate himself or herself from both adults and peers. There is a greater use of fantasies and a decline in reality testing. Adolescents who see themselves as the new Messiah, capable of superhuman feats or of reading others' minds, are examples.

Regression: To return to an earlier stage. This is quite simply the attempt to remain a child, to avoid growing up. Boys and girls, especially at the onset of obvious signs of puberty, may attempt to deny the changes and dress and play as if they were still in elementary school.

Asceticism: To deny pleasure. Some adolescents may attempt to deny the development of pleasurable feelings by becoming ascetics. The increase in the depth and range of emotions is checked by (metaphorically, at least) putting on a hair shirt and rejecting food, sleep, and normal comforts. Shaving heads and putting on monks' robes are other manifestations.

Uncompromising behavior: To rigidly adhere to a narrow, prescriptive ideology. This is by definition an attempt to avoid accepting the complexities of life, the shades of gray, including compromise and cooperation. All issues become dichotomized into right and wrong. Dogmatic positions abound.

Anna Freud also wisely points out that these syndromes are common yet difficult for an adolescent to understand. We all are blind to certain aspects of our own behavior and dynamics, and know that such psychological blind spots don't suddenly disappear when we are told about them. Thus, although it is important for teachers to recognize these **psychological defenses**, it is not necessarily wise to then confront the adolescent with an interpretation. Such confrontations often make adults more defensive—and what is true for adults is doubly true for this age group. Anna Freud suggests that educators understand these common defenses, realize when an adolescent is employing one, yet respond to the *person*, not the *defense*. Otherwise, we may find ourselves in long and unproductive arguments about whose interpretation is most accurate.

For example, probably the most common defense during adolescence is the displacement of sexual feelings toward a teacher. **Crushes** can develop in girls for attractive male teachers or in boys for particularly sensitive and understanding female teachers. It requires great tact by the adult in this situation to avoid either extreme of playing up to the fantasy or putting

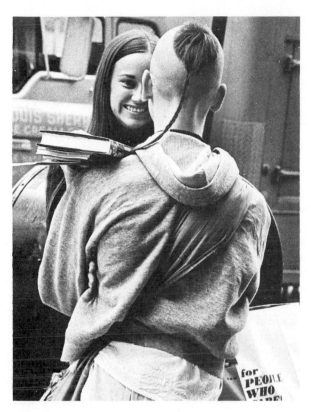

Some adolescents may attempt to deny the development of pleasurable feelings by becoming ascetic.

down the adolescent with sarcasm and ridicule. On the one hand, playing up to the fantasy is most inappropriate. Pupils at that age perceive sexual connotations in practically everything in the world anyway. If the teacher becomes coy and seductive in response to an adolescent's crush, then it's almost as if his or her wildest dreams may come true. The adolescent's nonverbal signs will be readily apparent, such as amorous looks, excessive volunteering of help, and putting down "immature" classmates. On the other hand, if the teacher chooses to ridicule these first stirrings of feelings of closeness and attraction, then the pupil may be genuinely shamed. Instead, as a teacher, you must be prepared to help the adolescent understand that it is quite normal and natural to have strong feelings of liking for a person just a "bit" older. This means that the adolescent is in the process of growing up. At the same time, however, you can also help him or her realize that it would be quite inappropriate for you as a teacher to play favorites and that eventually you are sure that someone closer in age will seem attractive. These times when adolescents develop their initial impulses for tenderness

and caring are very sensitive. Probably the least appropriate response by a teacher would be silence, since ambiguity actually increases projection and fantasy thinking. The so-called hidden agenda of sexual awareness by junior high pupils is an extremely volatile issue that needs careful attention as well as tact and diplomacy. Classroom atmospheres charged with rampant sexual fantasies certainly, at a minimum, impede intellectual concentration and motivation for learning.

One final point to remember: All of the psychological defenses are methods (some better than others) of coping with the environment as the adolescent struggles to become an adult. It really is difficult for someone in the identity stage to "get it all together," or, in Erikson's words, to achieve ego integration. Yet it is essential to develop a healthy personal identity. In ringing phrases Erikson says,

> Indeed in the social jungle of human existence there is no feeling of being alive without a sense of ego identity.... The danger of this stage is identity diffusion; ... Youth after youth, bewildered by some assumed role, a role forced on him by the inexorable standardization of American adolescence, runs away in one form or another, leaving schools and jobs, staying out all night, or withdrawing into bizarre and inaccessible moods (1959, pp. 90–91).

ERIKSON'S CONTRIBUTION

Each stage in personal development is characterized by certain aspects that can be maximally affected either positively or negatively. For too long, personal and emotional development was considered out of bounds for educators and as the exclusive province of child guidance clinics and of those specially trained to deal with pathological problems. Erikson's great contribution has been to bring the problems of personal growth out of the shadows of pathology and to integrate them into the overall process of healthy personality development. Erikson spells out the major personal issues for us so that we can understand much more about our pupils at each of the various stages. We hope that such insight will guide us to more effective ways of helping children and adolescents during important, indeed critical, times.

Erikson sums it up:

> Each successive step, then, is a potential crisis because of a radical *change in perspective*. There is, at the beginning of life, the most radical change of all: from intrauterine to extrauterine life. But in postnatal existence,

too, such radical adjustments of perspective as lying relaxed, sitting firmly, and running fast must all be accomplished in their own good time. With them, the interpersonal perspective, too, changes rapidly and often radically, as is testified by the proximity

in time of such opposites as "not letting a parent out of sight" and "wanting to be independent." Thus, *different capacities use different opportunities* to become full-grown components of the ever-new configuration that is the growing personality (1959, p. 55).

SUMMARY

Personal development should not be regarded as a process separate from other aspects of development. There is a common tendency to pay lip service to the idea that aspects of development are not really separate but then to talk about these domains as if they were compartmentalized.

Prior to Freud, the common assumption about children younger than six was that they were empty, literally mindless creatures. Accordingly, little was expected of them. Freud was a pioneer in emphasizing the importance of sensitive growth periods for personal development during childhood.

This chapter focused on Erikson's theory of a series of stages extending over the period of the life cycle. Each stage is marked by psychosocial crises that require the resolution of opposite, or bipolar, traits. How adequately a person resolves the crisis of each stage helps determine and promote strength for succeeding stages. The stages are linked together in an interdependent manner.

Trust versus mistrust, resolved as hope

Autonomy versus shame, resolved as will

Initiative versus guilt, resolved as purpose

Mastery versus inferiority, resolved as competence

Identity versus diffusion, resolved as fidelity

Evidence supports the importance of the specified major issue at each stage. For example, Harlow's work, Spitz's research, and Anna Freud's studies all suggest the critical importance of careful, warm, and consistent parenting in the first twenty-four months to establish hope in the infant.

White's studies detail the significance of patterns of parenting during preschool years as a means of building competence, autonomy, and initiative in young children. During the child's juvenile years, it is important for educators to encourage and facilitate personal competence.

Newer evidence on the process of identity formation during adolescence has been included based on the work of Marcia and Waterman. The phases of foreclosure, diffusion, moratorium, and achievement were outlined along with the transition pathways. A particular focus was the identity formation question vis-à-vis minority youth and females. The sequence appears the same for such groups as for males in general, yet it is more difficult—a result of particular societal barriers.

Educational programs designed to promote development were reviewed as indicators of the positive aspect of peer helping methods available to schools and colleges. The chapter closed with an outline of common psychological defenses employed by teenagers and appropriate responses.

KEY TERMS AND NAMES

Sally Archer
David Elkind
Erik Erikson
  competence motivation
  epigenetic principle
Lawrence K. Frank
Anna Freud
  crushes
  psychological defenses
Sigmund Freud

anal stage
oral stage
phallic stage
psychoanalytic theory
James Marcia
  achievement
  diffusion
  foreclosure
  moratorium
Alan Waterman

THEORY INTO PRACTICE: IDENTITY FORMATION PHASES— AN INTERVIEW GUIDE

To provide you with a sense of the Marcian phases of identity formation, we suggest one of two alternatives. Either ask yourself the following questions or interview a friend or colleague. We have provided some prototypical examples of answers that represent the different phases. The main point of such an interview is not so much to obtain any specific answer but rather to help the person elaborate on the reasons for any specific choice. Also, if you choose to interview someone, be sure to remain nonjudgmental concerning the reasons provided by the person. The process involves asking open-ended questions with no right or wrong answers; the interviewer must remain value-neutral during the questioning. Your goal is to find out how the person really thinks and feels about the questions without the influence of any evaluation by the interviewer.

Sample Questions in One Domain (Occupation)

How have you gone about choosing a career for yourself? Have you had this in mind for a long time?

What factors or persons have been most important in influencing you?

How sure are you about your choice?

What other fields have you considered?

How do you feel about your choice or choices?

Note: The point of questions such as the foregoing ones is to provide a great deal of scope to the person being interviewed so that you can listen for themes and reasons. Sometimes much information can be solicited simply by asking, "As you think about choosing a career, what stands out?"

The Marcian approach also asks similarly open-ended questions in the domains of religious orientation and worldview, or politics. Depending on how much time you have, you can switch to those areas for further elaboration after you complete the occupational questions.

A final point: As noted in Chapter 1, you may not find such pure types as in the sample answers, so be prepared to listen for shades of meaning. The probe questions should help to clarify the person's thinking, but do expect some overlap in responses.

Sample Responses to Occupation Questions

Foreclosure   "Well that's easy, I've always known from elementary school on that I wanted to be a civil engineer. My dad is one, and he always told me that engineering work is for me. Even when I had trouble in high school math and began to find an art course much more enjoyable, my dad hired a math tutor for me, and I made it through.

"So when it came to college, it was pretty clear where I'd go. Actually, I visited only one kind of college. Also, it turned out I had to take an extra year in prep school to get my SAT Q score up high enough for admission.

"The work itself is a real grind but my dad always said, 'College is like a bank account. You can't make withdrawals until you make deposits.' So I'll keep plugging along. I'm just below a graduation GPA but I'm getting tutored in two subjects, so I think I'll squeeze through. My family has all said how proud they'll be when I become an engineer. I'm sure I'll be proud, too. Everybody I know wants to see me succeed in engineering."

Diffusion   "I don't really think about it much. I mean, I know I'm supposed to be in college to become something, but if I'm honest, I'd have to say that the whole thing is a drag. I change my mind so often. Last week, I met this guy who is an audioengineer in charge in recording sessions for one of the top record companies. He's got it made—money, a great car, a wardrobe—the works. So I said, Yeah that's for me. But you know, just before that I got all charged up about being an anthropologist after watching a special on Jane Goodall. I guess what I'm going to do is just wait and see what develops. After all, college is a lot of fun, so why worry? Maybe something will come along and motivate me, but for now I'm really here just to have a good time. I'm sure sooner or later something will happen."

Moratorium   "You know, that's one of the most interesting questions you can ask. I used to think of the square peg in the square hole. There is one perfect job for me. Find it. Now what I've been realizing is that I keep discovering new interests and even new abilities here in college. I'm not the same as I was in high school. I'm taking a course in geology—you know, 'Rocks for jocks'—and its very interesting. The field trips. Even the reading. I'm doing extra work, even though some of my friends think I'm crazy to work that hard, but it is interesting and then the same is happening in a course in music—you know, 'Clapping for credit'—but I find all kinds of interesting information. I actually listen to music differently. I can analyze how the compositions are put together.

"I used to think college, the study part, would be a drag, but it's not. I'm learning, yet I'm [also] learning that I had better keep my choices open. It's too soon to choose. And you know I used to envy these people who could tell you from day one, "I want to be a flight surgeon' or something like that. Now I say that's maybe OK for them but not for me. I've got lots of things I want to explore first."

Achievement   "It has taken me a long time to figure out where I want to go now that I'm finishing college.

All through high school and in the first two years here, I must have changed my mind a hundred times. First, it was a teacher-coach in the tenth grade, then an English teacher in the eleventh, then a business executive, and so forth. Gradually, however, I found that more and more of my attention and interest was on foreign-policy questions. I joined two clubs, spent a summer in central America, and started taking all the electives I could in international relations. I even talked the poli. sci. department into creating an interdisciplinary major for me. Every time I turned around I found myself pointed in that direction. I mean, what could be more exciting than to become a diplomat, represent the country, and work toward international understanding? I know it will be frustrating. There are still lots of myopic people. But that's also a real challenge.

"So I'm off to graduate school in international relations after I finish a two-year stint with the Peace Corps. I figure some real experience is called for, not just striped pants and high tea."

REFERENCES

Adams, P. S. (1988). Peer influence and moral decision-making in undergraduate cliques. *Moral Education Forum, 13(3),* 9–15.

Archer, S. (1992a). A feminist's approach to identity research. In G. Adams, T. Gullotta, and R. Montemayor (Ed.), *Adolescent identity formation* (pp. 215–249). Newbury Park, Calif.: Sage.

Archer, S. (1992b). Females at risk: Identity issues for adolescents and divorced women. In C. Vandenplas and B. Campos (Eds.), *Interpersonal and identity development: New directions* (pp. 87–102). Porto, Portugal: University of Porto.

Arnold, K. (1987). Retaining high-achieving women in science and engineering, AAAS Symposium on Women and Girls in Science and Technology, University of Michigan, Ann Arbor, July 1987.

Costa, M. E., and Campos, B. (1992). Socio-educational context and beginning university students' identity development. In C. Vandenplas and B. Campos (Eds.), *Interpersonal and identity development: New directions* (pp. 79–86). Porto, Portugal: University of Porto.

Dubois, W. E. B. (1963). *An ABC of color.* Berlin: Seven Seas.

Eccles, J. (1986). Gender roles and women's achievement. *Educational Research, 15(6),* 15–19.

Elkind, D. (1970). *Children and adolescents.* New York: Oxford.

Elkind, D. (1978). Understanding the young adolescent. *Adolescence, 13,* 127–134.

Erikson, E. (1959). Identity and the life cycle. *Psychological Issues, I.* (Monograph I)

Erikson, E. (1982). *The life cycle completed.* New York: Norton.

Frank, L. K. (1969) quoted in R. C. Sprinthall, and N. A. Sprinthall *Educational Psychology: Selected Readings.* New York: Van Nostrand.

Freud, A. (1958). Adolescence. *Psychoanalytic study of the child, 13,* 225–276.

Freud, S. (1957). Some character types met with in psychoanalytic work: Those wrecked by success. In J. Strachey (Ed. and Trans.), *The standard edition of the complete psychological works of Sigmund Freud* (Vol. 14, pp. 316–331). London: Hogarth Press. (Original work published 1916.)

Freud, S. (1960). *A general introduction to psychoanalysis.* New York: Washington Square Press.

Harlow, H. F., and Harlow, M. K. (1962). Social deprivation in monkeys. *Scientific American, 207,* 136–146.

Hauser-Cram, P., Pierson, D., Walker, D., and Trinan, T. (1991). *Early education in public schools.* San Francisco: Jossey-Bass.

Hoppe, C., and Loevinger, J. (1977). Ego development and conformity. *Journal of Personality, 41,* 497–504.

Horner, M. (1972). Toward an understanding of achievement-related conflicts in women. *Journal of Social Issues, 28,* 157–175.

Jones, G., and Wheatley, J. (1989). Gender influences in classroom displays and student-teacher behaviors. *Science Education, 73(5),* 535–545.

Jones, R. M. (1992). Ego identity and adolescent problem behavior. In G. Adams, T. Gullotta, and R. Montemayor

(Eds.), *Adolescent identity formation* (pp. 216–233). Newbury Park, Calif.: Sage.

Josselson, R. (1987). *Finding herself: Pathways to identity development in women.* San Francisco: Jossey-Bass.

Kohlberg, L., and Gilligan, C. (1971). The adolescent as a philosopher. *Daedalus, 100(4),* 1051–1086.

Larkin, L. (1987). Identity and fear of success. *Journal of Counseling Psychology, 34,* 38–45.

Lee, C. (1990). Black male development: Counseling the "Native Son." In D. Moore and F. Leafgren (Eds.), *Problem solving strategies and intervention for men in conflict* (pp. 125–137). Washington: American Psychological Association.

Leming, J. (1992). The influence of contemporary issues curricula on school-aged youth. *Review of research in education, 18,* 111–161.

Locke, D., and Faubert, M. (1993). Getting on the right track: A program for African American high school students. *School Counselor* (in press).

Mann A. (1992). Tutoring in college: A cognitive developmental approach. Unpublished doctoral dissertation. North Carolina State University, Raleigh, N.C.

Marcia, J. (1966). Development and validation of ego identity status. *Journal of Personality and Social Psychology, 3,* 551–558.

Marcia, J. (1976). Identity six years after. *Journal of Youth and Adolescence, 5,* 145–160.

Markstrom-Adams, C. (1992). A consideration of factors in adolescent identity formation. In G. Adams, T. Gullotta, and R. Montenmayor (Eds.), *Adolescent identity formation* (pp. 173–192). Newbury Park, Calif.: Sage.

Muus R. (1988). *Theories of adolescence.* New York: Random House.

Ogbu, J. (1988). Cultural diversity and human development. In D. Slaughter (Ed.), *Black children and poverty* (pp. 11–28). San Francisco: Jossey-Bass.

Patterson, S. J., Sochting, D., and Marcia, J. (1992). In G. R. Adams, T. P. Gullotta, and R. Montemayor (Eds.), *Adolescent identity formation* (pp. 9–24). Newbury Park, Calif.: Sage.

Phinney, J. S., and Rosenthal, D. A. (1992). Ethnic identity in adolescence: Process, context and outcome. In G. Adams, T. Gullotta, and R. Montemayor (Eds.), *Adolescent identity formation* (pp. 145–172). Newbury Park, Calif.: Sage.

Quality Education for Minorities Project. (1990). Cambridge: Massachusetts Institute of Technology.

Risman, B. (1986). Can men "mother"? Life as a single father. *Family Relations, 35,* 95–102.

Robinson, T. (1993). African American adolescents and skin color. *Journal of adolescence* (in press).

Salinger, J. D. (1964) *The catcher in the rye.* New York: Bantam.

Schultz, J. B. (1989). AHEA's survey of American teens. *Journal of Home Economics, 81,* 27–28.

Schweinhart, L., Weikart, D., and Larner, M. (1986). Consequences of three preschool curriculum models through age 15. *Early Childhood Research Quarterly, 1,* 15–45.

Skoe, E. E. (1991). Identity, care-based and justice-based moral reasoning in women and men. Paper presented at the Association for Moral Education Annual Conference, November 1991, Athens, Georgia.

Spitz, R. A. (1946). Hospitalism: A follow-up report. *Psychoanalytic Study of the Child,* Vol 2. New York: International University Press.

Sprinthall, N. A., Hall, J. S., and Gerler, E. R. (1992). Peer counseling for middle school students experiencing family divorce. *Journal of Elementary School Counseling, 26(4),* 279–294.

Sprinthall, N. A., and Scott, J. (1989). Promoting psychological development, math achievement and success attribution of female students through deliberate psychological education. *Journal of Counseling Psychology, 36(4),* 440–446.

Waterman, A. (1985). Identity in adolescence: Processes and contents. *New directions for child development.* San Francisco: Jossey-Bass.

Waterman, A. (1992). Identity as an aspect of optimal psychological functioning. In G. Adams, T. Gullotta, and R. Montemayor (Eds.). *Adolescent identity formation* (pp. 50–72). Newbury Park, Calif.: Sage.

Watts, E. A. (1992). The color of success. *Brown Alumni Monthly, 92(7),* 47–48.

White, B. L. (1987). *Educating the infant and the toddler.* New York: Heath.

White, R. W. (1959). Motivation reconsidered: The concept of competence. *Psychological Review, 66,* 297–333.

White, S. (1968). Changes in learning processes in the late preschool years. Paper presented at American Educational Research Association Convention, Chicago.

Zigler, E., and Berman, W. (1983). Discerning the future of early childhood intervention. *American Psychologist, 38(8),* 894–906.

Zimmerman, N. (1989). Effects of a role-taking curriculum on the psychological maturity of college students. Unpublished doctoral dissertation. North Carolina State University.

7

VALUE DEVELOPMENT

It is perhaps quite ironic that in the area of value and moral development, there has been a major disagreement between professional educators and psychologists. On the one hand, from the very beginnings of the public or common school, educators have insisted that a pupil's character and values should be the proper object of teaching. Horace Mann, considered the architect of free public education, maintained stoutly in the early nineteenth century that veracity, probity, and rectitude were the significant goals of education. "Train up a child in the way he should go, and when he is old he will not depart from it" (Cremin, 1957. p. 100). Character and citizenship, then, were viewed as major objectives of schooling. Practically every public school had a printed curriculum objective extolling the virtues of character development. The Boston Public Schools' guide of a few years back was typical of many:

We are unfit for any trust till we can and do obey.

Honor thy father and mother.

True obedience is true liberty.

The first law ever God gave to man was a law of obedience.

On the other hand, psychologists have maintained, at least for the last fifty years, that attempting to inculcate traits and virtues was almost totally ineffectual. In other words, while educators were stoutly maintaining that schools mold character, psychologists were busily refuting all claims that values could be taught. In this chapter we shall review some of those classic character-trait studies and then turn to a relatively new framework for understanding the process of value development, with specific implications for curriculum strategies.

EXPLODING THE MYTH OF CHARACTER EDUCATION

In the 1920s two researchers, **Hugh Hartshorne and Mark May** at the University of Chicago, conducted a long series of studies, which they replicated again and again (1928–1930). Their results were a bombshell. In every study they arrived at the same conclusion: Formal character instruction had no positive effect. They studied regular school classes in character education, special Sunday-school classes, Boy Scout classes, and others. After studying over 10,000 children and adolescents, they concluded that there was no correlation at all (essentially an r of 0) between character-education-virtue training and actual behavior (such as cheating). They also found essentially no consistent moral behavior in the same person from one situation to another based on character education. This seemed to imply that people who cheat in one situation may or may not cheat in the next situation. (The sample honesty tests accompanying this discus-

The Hartshorne and May Technique

This is a *sample honesty test* as well as an eye-hand coordination and memory test. At the signal for each trial, place your pencil at point X. Study the circles, then *close your eyes* and write the number 1 in the first circle, the second circle, the third circle, and so on. For the second trial, open your eyes, place your pencil at point X, *close your eyes* and write the number 2 in the first circle, the second circle, and so on. For the third trial, follow the same procedure and write the number 3, and so on. Proceed for five trials.

After each trial, put a check mark in the score box for each time you hit the correct circle. Count the checks and enter the total in column T. After the last trial, add up column T. This is your total score. The maximum is 50.

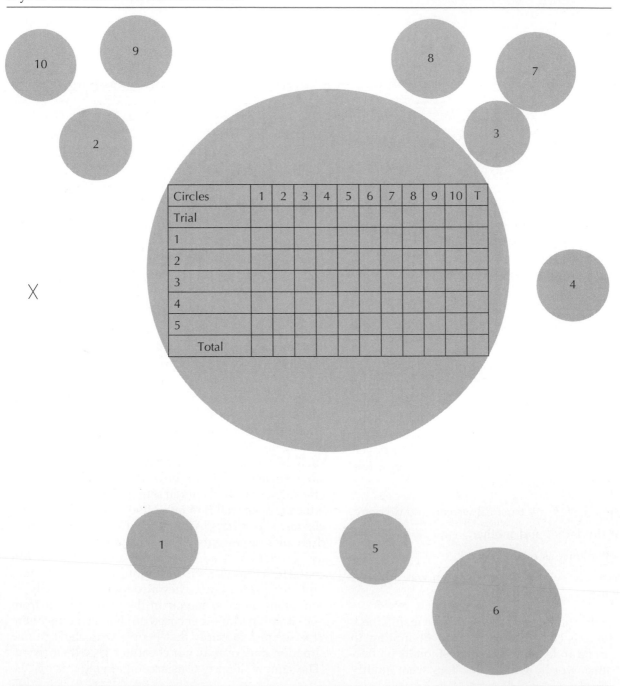

Circles	1	2	3	4	5	6	7	8	9	10	T
Trial											
1											
2											
3											
4											
5											
Total											

sion may help demonstrate such an assertion.) In general, moral behavior seemed unpredictable and moral character traits mythical. If ingrained character traits such as honesty or dishonesty did exist, then it would be possible to predict behavior accurately.

To make matters worse (Hartshorne and May were as dismayed as everyone else), the researchers also found no relationship between what people said about morality and the way these same people acted. People who expressed great disapproval of cheating or stealing actually stole and cheated as much as anyone else. Hartshorne and May concluded that the risk of detection was the single most important factor in deterring cheating. They also found that it was meaningless to divide people into simple categories and label them as either honest or dishonest. Like so many other aspects of human nature, cheating is normally distributed around a level of moderate cheating. (Results that have a *normal distribution* can be fitted to a bell-shaped curve. The distribution will look the same as that for measured intelligence, height, weight, or coin flipping for heads or tails. See Chapter 15 for further discussion on the meaning of normal distribution.) Hartshorne and May found that what was true for supposed pairs of traits such as honesty/dishonesty was also true for traits such as altruism/selfishness and self-control/impulsiveness. What this does, of course, is to call into the question the entire concept of character traits.

One of the criticisms of the Hartshorne and May research was that the situations set up in tests such as the eye-hand coordination and memory test did not really create a battle of conscience. In other words the stakes were low, so maybe the students didn't really care and merely opened their eyes out of curiosity or some other motive. If proved, that of course would be a fundamental flaw in the whole argument. In a quite ingenious study, a researcher built a special computerlike ray gun complete with video screen. The game was rigged to yield a score just below the level needed to win a special prize as a sharpshooter. In the first test, over 80 percent of the students cheated on their reported score, thus confirming the original research findings. In a second study, however, the critical findings were completely different. More gadgetry was added to increase the battle of conscience— or at least that was the intention of the researchers. With additional computer equipment, a new sequence was rigged. Now the students would reach the very brink of success. Then they would miss. Under these new conditions only 15 percent of the one-hundred children cheated. What happened? This was a total reversal of all previous findings—or was it? Interviews revealed that the students in the second study thought that the machine was indeed wired into a real computer that kept the actual score. There was no point in cheating. So with children, then, "even if we are successful in arousing stronger emotional conflicts . . . we still have to conclude that moral behavior is essentially defined by situational factors, including expediency" (Kohlberg and Candee, 1984, p. 502).

What is true for Hartshorne's and May's seemingly old-fashioned virtues is equally true for the virtues we may cherish today. This means that if we ridicule the idea of teaching children to be "thrifty, brave, clean, and reverent," a traditional bag of virtues, it is also meaningless to try to teach children to be "spontaneous, open, authentic, or genuine." A bag of virtues is a bag of virtues. None is particularly amendable to being taught. Merely changing the content of the virtues to be taught will not change the outcome. We may prefer the more modern traits, but this does not advance the educational problems of student growth and discipline. "Telling" is not teaching, and the same holds true for character development. Telling children and teenagers to adopt particular virtues or manipulating them until they say the right words will not produce significant personal or cognitive development.

KOHLBERG'S THEORY: A DEVELOPMENTAL VIEW

Lawrence Kohlberg (1968), working first at Chicago University and then at Harvard, revolutionized our understanding of moral development. He found that people cannot be grouped into neat compartments with simplistic labels, "This group is honest," or "This group cheats," or "This group is reverent." Instead, he found that moral character develops. And this idea, that moral growth occurs in a developmental sequence, has completely revised our basic assumptions.

After conducting a long series of studies with children and adults, Kohlberg found that **moral development** occurs in a specific sequence of stages regardless of culture or subculture, continent or country. This means that we can no longer think of moral character in either/or terms, or assume that character is something we do or do not have. Instead of existing as fixed traits, moral character occurs in a series of developmental stages. In other words, what Piaget identi-

Lawrence Kohlberg

fied as stages of congitive development, and what Erikson suggested to be stages of personal development, Kohlberg described as stages of moral development. You may recall from the chapter on cognitive growth (Chapter 5) that a developmental stages, by definition, has four components. Each stages has the following features:

1. It is qualitatively different from the preceding stage.

2. It represents a new and more comprehensive system of "mental" organization.

3. It occurs in an **invariant sequence.**

4. It is age-related within general groupings.

With this definition in mind, we can now examine some of the specific aspects of this view.

KOHLBERG'S SIX STAGES OF MORAL GROWTH

Kohlberg identified six stages of moral growth, each distinctly different. He derived the stages by studying the system of thinking people actually employ in dealing with moral questions. By asking people from different backgrounds and of different ages to respond to problems involving moral dilemmas, he found that their responses fell into six judgmental

systems, on which he based his six categories. The following two examples illustrate the type of problem he used:

1. Joe's father promised he could go to camp if he earned the $50 for it, and then changed his mind and asked Joe to give him the money he had earned. Joe lied and said he had earned only $10 and went to camp using the other $40 he had made. Before he went, he told his younger brother, Alex, about the money and about lying to their father. Should Alex tell their father?

2. In Europe, a woman was near death from a special kind of cancer. There was one drug that the doctors thought might save her. It was a form of radium that a druggist in the same town had recently discovered. The drug was expensive to make, but the druggist was charging ten times what the drug cost him to make. He paid $200 for the radium and charged $2,000 for a small dose of the drug. The sick woman's husband, Heinz, went to everyone he knew to borrow the money, but he could only get together about $1,000, which is half of what it cost. He told the druggist that his wife was dying and asked him to sell it cheaper or let him pay later. But the druggist said: "No, I discovered the drug and I'm going to make money from it." So Heinz got desperate and broke into the man's store to steal the drug for his wife. Should the husband have done that?

As you can see, the problems are complex; they have no single, correct answer. In fact, the least significant part of the response is the direct answer yes or no. Most significant are the reasons given for why the person should not behave in certain ways. In other words, the way in which suggested behavior is justified defines the respondent's level of moral development. Table 7.1 outlines the six stages of moral growth.

Preconventional Morality: Stages I and II

Stage I obedience and moral decisions are based on very simple physical and material power—"Big fish eat little fish"; "Might makes right"; "The survival of the fittest." Stage I behavior is based on the desire to avoid severe physical punishment by a superior power.

Stage II actions are based largely on satisfying one's own personal needs, or "looking out for number one."

The idea is to figure out ways to make trades and exchange favors—"You scratch my back and I'll scratch yours"—but trying to come out a little bit ahead on each trade. The orientation is materialistic in that moral discussions are expressed in instrumental and physical terms. If, for example, a person is caught stealing a car, punishment is determined by how much the car cost. This also means that it is perfectly permissible to use influence to fix any so-called wrongdoings. Fixing traffic tickets, bribing people, stealing from the boss, and similar misdemeanors are OK as long as you get away with it. If students alter their report cards, it's a Stage II response, provided they are successful. The clever con man or flim-flam artist is a further example. In philosophical terms this category of moral thinking is referred to as *instrumental hedonism*, characterized by little human regard for the other person ("Nice guys finish last"). Genuine empathy is lacking.

In spite of the obvious shortcomings as a system of moral thinking, Stage II—"Let's make a deal"—does represent an advance over Stage I. Gypping people financially, ignoring other's feelings, cheating at elections, and similar behaviors are not as bad as physical torture or death. Thus Stage II thinking represents a more adequate method of problem solving, but only when compared to Stage I, where right and wrong are determined by the fastest gun, the quickest fist, or the biggest bomb.

These first two stages are sometimes classified together as the preconventional stage of moral development. The reason for calling it "preconventional" will be obvious when we look at the next two levels, Stages III and IV.

Conventional Morality: Stages III and IV

These next two stages are classified as the conventional stage of moral development.

Stage III is characterized by social conformity. At this stage a person makes moral judgments in order to do what is nice and what pleases others. At the same time, Stage III thinking is more comprehensive and more complex than Stage II. At this level a person does begin to take into account how others genuinely view the dilemma situation. The egocentrism of Stage II is replaced by the ability to empathize, to feel what others may be feeling, or, as it's called, by an increase in social-role-taking perspective.

The problem with this stage, however, is that individuals may have great difficulty in resolving the conflicting feelings of all those involved in a dilemma situation. Thus, in the Heinz case mentioned above, a Stage III response would probably conclude that it was wrong to steal because almost all the people in the community say that stealing is wrong. "I will go along with the majority consensus, or social convention. I understand that most people hold that view and I would feel very uncomfortable going against the wishes of the majority." Thus, moral judgment is equated with following the leading crowd.

Stage III moral thinking depends on the existence of distinct stereotypes and sharp differences. Relativism and complexity are absent. In this sense, moral

Kohlberg's Stage II actions are based largely on satisfying one's own personal needs.

TABLE 7.1   KOHLBERG'S STAGES OF MORAL GROWTH

BASIS OF JUDGMENT	STAGES OF DEVELOPMENT
Preconventional moral values reside in external, quasi-physical happenings, in bad acts, or in quasi-physical needs rather than in persons and standards.	*Stage I:* Concern about self. Obedience to a powerful authority. Fear of punishment dominates motives. One sees oneself as being dominated by other forces. Actions are judged in terms of their *physical consequences*.

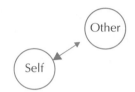

Stage II: One-way concern about another person (what he/she can do for me, how we can agree to act so *I* will benefit). The basic motive is to *satisfy my own needs*. I do not consider the needs of the other person, unless I think it will benefit me to do so.

| Conventional moral values reside in performing good or right roles, in maintaining the conventional order, and in meeting others' expectations. | *Stage III:* Concern about groups of people, and conformity to group norms. There is a two-way relationship (we are good to each other). Motive is to be a "nice guy/gal," to be accepted. Affection plays a strong role. |

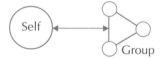

Stage IV: Concern for order in *society*. Honor and duty come from keeping the rules of the society. The focus is on *preserving the society* (not just obeying, as in Stage I).

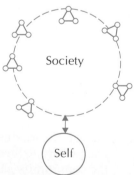

behavior is other-directed. Stage III behavior conforms strictly to the fixed conventions of the society in which we live. We don't look inward to the "self" and attempt to work through a decision independently. Kohlberg often illustrates Stage III behavior by referring to the comic-strip character Charlie

Brown. Charlie is usually caught in a hopeless predicament because of his trying to please everyone. His pleading with the iron-willed Lucy is both a comic and a poignant illustration of what it is like to try to live life always looking to other people for direction.

At *Stage IV*, the individual looks to rules, laws, or

BASIS OF JUDGMENT	*STAGES OF DEVELOPMENT*

Postconventional moral values are derived from principles which can be applied universally.

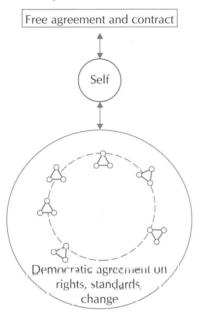

Stage V: Social contract, legalistic orientation. What is right is what the whole society decides. There are no legal absolutes. The society can *change standards* by everyone agreeing to the change. Changes in the law are usually made for reasons of the greatest good for the greatest number of people. Where law is not affected, what is right is a matter of personal opinion and agreement between persons. The U.S. Constitution is written in Stage V terms.

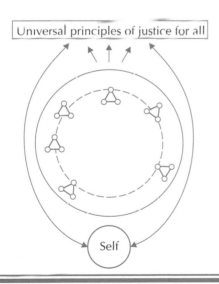

Stage VI: Universal ethical principles. What is right is a decision of one's conscience, based on ideas about rightness that apply to *everyone* (all nations, people, etc.). These are called *ethical principles*. An ethical principle is different from a rule. A rule is specific (Thou shalt not kill). An ethical principle is *general* (All persons are created equal). The most important ethical principles deal with justice, equality, and the dignity of all people. These principles are *higher* than any given law.

The pictorial diagrams were created by Philip Shaeffer, Ph.D., University of Minnesota.

codes for guidance in dilemma situations. In one sense, civil- and criminal-law codes in our society represent a more stable and comprehensive system of resolving moral dilemmas than attempting to solve such questions on the basis of social conventions, community popularity, and what the leading crowd decides is the "nice" thing to do. Laws and rules as codified wisdom can be viewed as a positive glue, providing a society with stability and cohesion by guarding against rampant fads, quickly changing social customs, and societal anarchy or mob rule. The laws or rules represent society's attempt to set the

LAWRENCE KOHLBERG

Born in 1927 from parents who were both eminently successful, Kohlberg's life started in a very conventional path of materialistic comfort and academic achievement in elite private schools. That, in fact, may have been about the only conventional activity of his life. Before entering college, he took a three-year moratorium in the Erikson sense, yet with a moral purpose. He served as a junior engineer on a ship smuggling Jewish refugees into Israel. Unlike the movie *The Exodus*, he was caught by the British and imprisoned, an early experience upon which he noted he could ponder serious questions of justice and fairness. After his release, he enrolled at the University of Chicago and completed his degree requirements in only two years.

Kohlberg clearly demonstrated a great capacity for academic scholarship, and it was natural for him to en-roll as a Ph.D. candidate at the same university. He completed his doctorate in 1958; after spending only two years for his undergraduate studies, it took him nine years for the Ph.D. He remarked wryly that it only proved you couldn't accurately predict human behavior in all cases.

His concern for the welfare of others, however, did not diminish while in graduate school. Assigned for clinical internship to a mental hospital, he soon noticed that the resident staff, including his own supervisor, were using electric shock therapy, not as a treatment but as a means of punishing uncooperative patients in a manner which foreshadowed the classic film *One Flew Over the Cuckoo's Nest*. All his colleagues looked the other way.

It was left to him, an intern with the lowest status on the medical hierarchy, to challenge his superiors. He did and was promptly dropped from the placement.

His research inquiry in graduate school was less volatile personally but turned out to be almost as provocative. Instead of accepting the then current notions of a psychoanalytic model for child development, he began to evolve an alternate set of ideas to explain the process of growth, and particularly the concept of moral reasoning.

What started as a traditional thesis on the relationship between the superego (the Freudian term for *conscience*) and moral behavior was transformed into a remarkably original framework for moral development in stages. It is rare for a young Ph.D. candidate to produce truly new insights into human behavior theory. It was uniquely creative for his thesis to force almost a complete revision of moral development theory as well.

In 1962, with the completion of the thesis and after nine years of work, he accepted an assistant professorship at the University of Chicago. Just six years later he was offered and accepted a full professorship at Harvard University and joined that faculty to form an innovative graduate program in human development. He was also awarded a special five-year Research Career Award by the National Institute of Mental Health to promote his longitudinal study on stages of moral development in adults as well as in children and adolescents.

His center at Harvard became the focal point for two decades of research and development. He attracted established national and international scholars as well as an extraordinary crop of eager young people. Yet he never lost sight of the importance of both theory and practice. Thus it was not surprising to find him working as hard at application as at developing new theory. He spent three years on a weekly basis working with female prisoners and their guards to create a humane and rehabilitative atmosphere on site. He spent even more time creating high schools based on his concepts in an urban ghetto, a blue-collar community, and a suburban district. Few researchers have been as willing as Kohlberg to subject their best work to the acid test of practice.

In 1987 Larry Kohlberg died after a long, debilitating illness. Perhaps the best tribute to his work is the huge number of scholars, whom he always regarded as genuine colleagues, who have continued the inquiry. Most importantly, this new crop of followers has provided a dynamic legacy to his work, as new ideas and practices continue to emerge.[a,b,c]

[a] Boyd, D. (1988). In honor of Lawrence Kohlberg: Some directions of current work. *Journal of Moral Education, 17*(3), 167–245.

[b] Kuhmerker, L. (1991). *The Kohlberg legacy.* Birmingham, Ala.: REP Books.

[c] Schrader, D. (1990). The legacy of Lawrence Kohlberg. *New Directions for Child Development, 47*, 1–16.

same standards of conduct for all its citizens. Moral judgments are made by individuals in accordance with those rules. A person thinking at this level, then, does not simply look out for number one (Stage II) or follow the leading crowd (Stage III), but rather makes decisions that square with the existing legal codes.

Difficulties arise, however, with this rigid, law-and-order orientation. What do we do when the laws conflict or are unclear? Lawyers have a saying that difficult and complex social problems make for "bad" laws. In the Heinz case, for example, the law protects the druggist against stealing, but what about an equal-rights law that gives the wife a right to life? It is always possible to come up with exceptional cases to any comprehensive fixed law. For example, there are a few cases each winter in which an electric or gas company has turned off the customer's power service for nonpayment. Contract law is clear: If a person doesn't pay the bill, then the provider of the service is not obligated to continue service. But what happens when the nonpayee dies of the cold? This may be an overly dramatic example, but such exceptional cases do occur. To handle such questions more comprehensively, we need recourse to a higher stage of reasoning.

Postconventional Morality: Stages V and VI

In the Kohlberg scheme, an individual at the stage of postconventional morality, the highest stage of moral development, behaves according to a social contract (Stage V) or according to a universal principle such as justice (Stage VI). Moral thinking and judgments are complex and comprehensive. Diverse points of view are considered. Each situation is examined carefully in order to derive general principles to guide behavior appropriate for all. There are never any easy solutions to complex human problems and moral dilemmas. Judgments and decisions are neither simply situational and conveniently relative, nor easy and fixed in their application of a rule. At this level, we have to account simultaneously for all the situational aspects, motivations, and general principles involved.

The system of thinking at this level, then, represents a more adequate method of problem solving. Laws are viewed as a system of governance: Each law can be judged in terms of the extent to which it squares with the principles of the system.

At *Stage V* the principles are usually written as a document of assumptions or a declaration of ideas.

For example, the U.S. Constitution sets forth a series of principled rights as the basis for judging the adequacy of each law. As you can readily see, the key issue is to resolve dilemmas and conflicting laws by interpreting the intent of these written principles—justice, freedom, liberty, and equality of opportunity, to name a few.

It is also important to realize that problem solving on moral questions, social justice, or squaring my freedom with your freedom is not necessarily simpler at Stage V. Commonly, there is confusion on this issue: People believe that higher-stage reasoning is better because it's easier. Such is not the case. Reasoning at this level requires the ability to think abstractly (to view laws as a system of governance), to weigh competing claims, to take into account both the logical and emotional domains, to take a stand and yet remain open to future, more adequate interpretations of social justice.

At *Stage VI* the principles of social justice are universal, yet not necessarily in written form. It is always difficult to explain the exact difference between Stage V and Stage VI because in some ways both systems are based on similar concepts. Also, analytical, philosphers themselves are unclear as to the distinctions. The "official" definition of Stage VI is that the principles are abstract, ethical, universal, and consistent. As Kohlberg notes, "At heart, these are universal principles of justice, of the reciprocity and equality of human rights, and of the respect for the dignity of human beings as individual persons" (1975, p. 671).

Comparing the Stages

One way to see the different levels of complexity involved in judgments at each stage is to examine and compare the different response patterns associated with the preconventional (Stages I and II), conventional (Stages III and IV), and postconventional (Stages V and VI) levels. Let's look at some typical responses, at different levels, to the Heinz case.

A Stage I or II response (preconventional) would say that it was OK for Heinz to steal the drug because the druggist was himself a robber, or simply because Heinz needed it. However, he should be smart enough not to get caught. A Stage III or IV response (conventional) would say that Heinz was wrong in breaking into the store. Either it isn't nice to steal ("What if everyone went around just taking things?"), or the law must always be obeyed regardless of circumstance ("What happens to a society if we all break laws according to our own whim?"). In either case, the social convention or the rule says unequivocally, "Thou shalt not steal." Heinz should be judged the same way an escaped convict would be judged. There is no difference between Heinz and Clyde Barrow of *Bonnie and Clyde* fame. A Stage V or VI response (postconventional) would weigh Heinz's behavior against universal principles. How does the value of life compare to the value of property? What general rights do all people have? What constitutional provisions are there for such behavior? Also, what are the provisions for changing laws? Since there may be bad laws, what avenues are available for seeking redress? Is the law that allows the druggist to make whatever profit he can such a bad law? If so, does this justify, or does it simply rationalize, Heinz's theft? These are essentially Stage V considerations. Moral decisions are based on a system of laws themselves judged on the basis of the common good and social utility. This means that at Stage V we don't view the problem in terms of a single law, but in terms of the entire system.

At Stage VI the consideration would be based not so much on a system of laws (such as a written constitution), but on unwritten, moral, and universal principles. A moral principle would be something like the Golden Rule ("Do unto others as you would have them do unto you"), or it would be an ethical principle like Immanuel Kant's categorical imperative ("Act only as you would be willing that everyone should act in the same situation"). Stage VI principles apply across all social classes and cultures and, in fact, can be considered genuine principles only if they can be applied universally.

The idea of universal application is really the other half of "Love thy neighbor as thyself." In this case, then, it is irrelevant whether the woman in the Heinz dilemma is his wife. At Stage VI the concept of justice means that no matter who she is, rich or poor, friend or stranger, the respect for human life requires action to save her. Such a requirement, the philosopher John Rawls (1971) argues, is based on the concept of justice as equity. This means that in a democratic society— where our creed calls for life, liberty, and the pursuit of happiness—each person has a responsibility to all others. We are not, at this level, individuals concerned only about ourselves or those whom we know well.

Thus, at Stage VI, decisions are made on the basis of a universal law or a "higher" law that may not be written or even codified. However, the principles are implicit: value for human life, equality, and dignity. These are distinguished from static virtues and character traits because the values and principles are universal and dynamic. This also distinguishes such principles as "justice" from narrow and prescribed rules, such as "Thou shalt not steal." Stage VI requires that we consider the circumstances and the situation, as well as the general principles and the reasons behind the rules.

Thus, in the Heinz case, a Stage VI response might consider Heinz to be justified in stealing the drug since the value of human life is greater than the value of property—a universal principle. At the same time, Heinz should also be willing to accept legal punishment for stealing. The key here is the reasoning that makes it clear that Heinz deliberately challenged the law that allowed the druggist to make large profits and that he committed an act of civil disobedience and was willing to accept society's punishment for stealing. Socrates's refusal to alter his principles even to save his own life is an example of a Stage VI response. This is an important distinction. A certain behavior in and of itself is not necessarily an indicator of high-moral-stage thinking.

There needs to be a logical relationship between a person's behavior and the reasoning behind it. On the one hand, to steal the drug to please my neighbor is clearly not principled reasoning. On the other hand, to say that life is more important than property and yet not steal is just as clearly not principled behavior.

The accompanying excerpt from Martin Luther King, Jr.'s "Letter from the Birmingham City Jail" is an example of Stage VI judgment:

> You express a great deal of anxiety over our willingness to break laws. This is certainly a legitimate concern. Since we do diligently urge people to obey the Supreme Court's decision of 1954 outlawing segregation in the public schools, at first glance it may seem rather paradoxical for us consciously to break laws. One may well ask: "How can you advocate breaking some laws and obeying others?" The answer lies in the fact that there are two types of laws: just and unjust. One has not only a legal but a moral responsibility to obey just laws. Conversely, one has a moral responsibility to disobey unjust laws. I would agree with Saint Augustine that "an unjust law is no law at all."
>
> Now what is the difference between the two? How does one determine when a law is just or unjust? A just law is a man-made code that squares with the moral law or the law of God. An unjust law is a code that is out of harmony with the moral law. To put it in the terms of Saint Thomas Aquinas: An unjust law is a human law that is not rooted in eternal law and

natural law. Any law that uplifts human personality is just. Any law that degrades human personality is unjust (1963, p. 85).

The Research Evidence

Figure 7.1 indicates the results of a series of cross-cultural studies conducted by Kohlberg in the 1960s. There are a number of important points to note. First, the trends are constant. Stage I and II behavior becomes less frequent as age increases, and Stage IV, V, and VI behavior increases during the same span. From this point of view we can say the sequence is developmental and invariant. The stages occur in order; that is, moral behavior develops from lower to higher stages, and no stages are skipped over. In this way, moral growth is similar to cognitive growth.

Since Kohlberg's original set of studies in the 1960s, there has been a substantial increase in the amount of research evidence in support of the stage and sequence framework. These will be detailed throughout the chapter in the appropriate sections discussing the new longitudinal results, the relation between moral behavior and stage, the cross-cultural evidence, and the question of sex differences.

STAGES OF MORAL DEVELOPMENT: CURRENT ISSUES

Age Trends

In 1979 all of the longitudinal data that formed the basis for the six-stage theory were rescored. This rescoring was necessary as part of a large-scale effort to improve both the reliability and validity of the scoring system. An extensive measurement manual is now available that permits a much more exact assignment of student responses. There are more detailed examples of interview answers and more systematic rules for assigning "mixed" responses—that is, answers that contain different stage levels. The critics of the earlier, more or less intuitive scoring system have now been answered by the new scoring manual. However, important as this new manual is for the researcher, even more significant is what the new results say to the educator. The new norms substantially change some of the basic program goals. Essentially, the single most important change is a revision downward as to when postconventional Stage V reasoning and Stage VI reasoning occur in general.

In fact it now appears that so few subjects ever reach Stage VI that the stage itself can be considered only as a theoretical possibility. None of the longitudinal studies in three countries provided empirical evidence for Stage VI (Kohlberg, 1984, p. 270). As a result, Kohlberg suspended his claim for the stage except through case studies such as King's letter from the Birmingham jail, as already noted, or from his longitudinal subjects. The only living example of such reasoning and behavior is described by Kohlberg as the "Case of Joan," a young female social worker who defends the rights of a delinquent teenager from the arbitrary rules of her case work manager and a judge's legal ruling. Both her reasoning and behavior represent the highest level of justice and respect for human personality (1984, p. 486).

Figure 7.2 presents the age trends based on the rescoring of the research subjects' "old" responses—that is, their answers at ten, thirteen, and sixteen years of age—plus their "new" answers during their early and late twenties. Remember that the key to a longitudinal study is that the researchers work with the same subjects over a long time span—in this case, over a period of twenty to twenty-five years. The change in the system of reasoning, then, is based on the answers that the same subjects gave to the Heinz dilemma and to similar stories after being tested every three or four years (Colby, Kohlberg, and Gibbs, 1979).

The age trends, in general, are similar to those in the earlier studies previously discussed; that is, the sequence remains the same. There is no skipping of stages. The lower stages always precede the higher. However, it is now clear that principled reasoning (Stage V) does not emerge in any substantial way during the secondary school years. Earlier estimates suggested that 30 to 35 percent of moral reasoning during the period from sixteen to eighteen years could be classified as principled, that is, based on a clear understanding of the universality of democratic principles such as freedom and justice for all, the right to due process, the necessity of free speech, majority will and minority rights, and equality before the law. It is now clear that such reasoning is more complex than the earlier scoring system was capable of detecting. In other words, when the researchers compared the earlier responses given by a subject at age sixteen and then the dilemma resolutions given by that same person at age thirty, they noted major structural differences in the thought processes. The responses scored "blind" indicated that much of the reasoning explained by the sixteen-year-old was

FIGURE 7.1   Early cross-cultural studies.

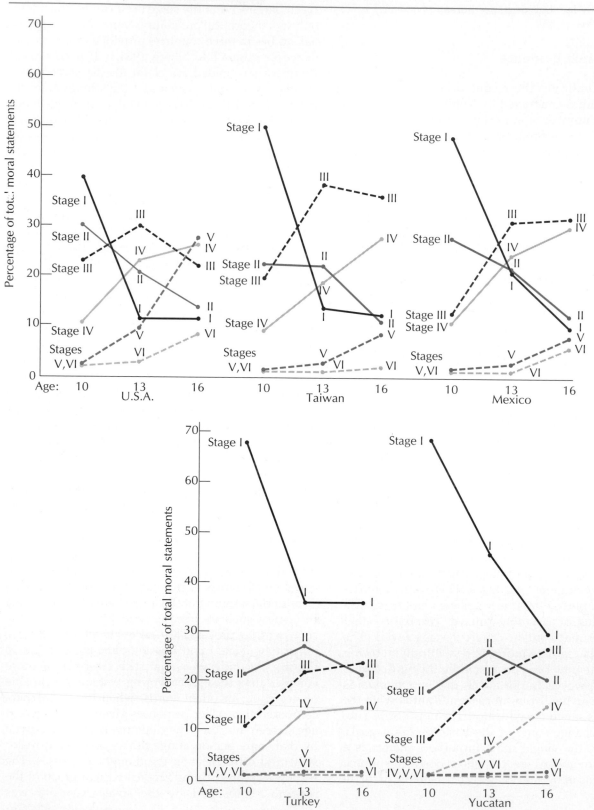

FIGURE 7.2 New norms: Percentage of moral reasoning at each stage.

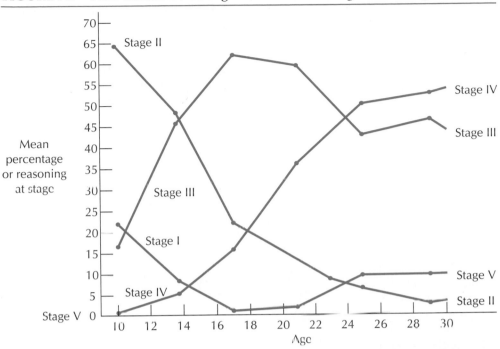

pseudoprincipled. The thinking was not generalizable at a principled level. In other words, the earlier scores were overestimates of the subjects' actual ability to process dilemmas.

The new norms indicate that at the junior high level, the two most common modes of reasoning are Stage II and Stage III—almost 45 percent each. The lower stage, Stage I, accounts for about 7 percent, and the higher stage, Stage IV, for about 4 percent. This means that pupils have moved substantially beyond Stage I (almost 25 percent at age ten). Also, it is apparent that Stage II thinking is declining rapidly, while Stage III thinking is increasing in a major shift. The junior high pupils are in the process of giving up an exclusive concern with their own materalistic rewards. Instead, more of the moral and value judgments are governed by a conformity to group norms. This finding indiciates, in a manner similar to personal development outlined in Chapter 6, that the value choices are increasingly other-directed during this time.

During senior high school, the shifts that are apparent at ages thirteen to fourteen continue. Stage II declines further, to less than 20 percent—almost equaling the rise in Stage IV to 15 percent. The major increase is clearly the emergence of Stage III. This form of moral reasoning now accounts for 60 percent

of judgments at ages sixteen to eighteen. That is the peak. The power of the peer group as well as of other reference groups is strongest at this time. It is important to remember the second part of this point. It is almost common folk wisdom to agree that the peer group during middle adolescence helps mold value orientations. James Coleman's classic *Adolescent Society* clearly indicates the extent to which the high school "leading crowd" determines the value content. Most teenagers follow the dictates of the group. However, Kohlberg's results indicate that such direction can come from sources other than the peer group. In other words, many teenagers are other-directed in general. The source of direction may be the leading crowd of the peer group or certain charismatic adults. The power of pseudoreligious cults, gurus, and other adult-directed extremist groups has enormous appeal during this stage. The weakness of Stage III reasoning is particularly apparent under these conditions. Although it may not be the most important event of a lifetime for a teenager to process moral judgment according to the leading crowd in high school, there is no assurance that the adolescent would not be equally vulnerable to the exhortations of a cult that demanded shaved heads, public begging, and participation in drug-induced, religiouslike rituals.

During the early twenties, the shifts noted at junior

and senior high continue. Stage I virtually disappears, and Stage II declines to less than 10 percent. Similarly, Stage III begins to turn down from its peak at sixteen to eighteen years. The most significant shift is the major increase in Stage IV judgment. By ages twenty-four to twenty-six, reasoning in accord with democratic laws becomes the major mode. Also, there is a small but highly significant development of principled reasoning to almost 10 percent at this time. In both cases, these two modes emerge much later than suggested by the earlier norms. The overall trends remain the same but the usage at the higher, more complex stages occurs much later than was previously reported. If anything, this indicates the need for more effective developmental programs to help stimulate the process of moral judgment. The new data on Piaget's norms indicated that secondary pupils were capable of but not using formal operations. The situation in moral reasoning is similar. Students are capable of Stage IV reasoning at the secondary level, yet most do not use that mode. Similarly, students at the college level are capable of Stage V reasoning, yet rarely employ it. The potential, however, is there. It appears that more effective developmental experiences are needed in order for children to become informed citizens, as required by a democratic society.

Modal Stage Plus One: A Preference for More Complex Reasoning

While the rescored norm results may be discouraging because the base rates are lower, there is a very important and optimistic point. Two of Kohlberg's graduate students (now professors), James Rest (1973b) and Eliot Turiel (1966), demonstrated that students who reason in a modal sense at one particular stage actually understand and value reasoning at the next level up on the scale—that is, modal stage **"plus one."** We will discuss at greater length at the end of the chapter what implications these findings have for teaching. At this point, however, the main idea is to note that students usually reason in their modal stage about 40 to 50 percent of the time. Part of their reasoning is at a lower stage but part is higher; no one is totally in one stage at any single time. The higher reasoning component exerts a kind of pull and can gradually draw the student to a more complex level. Thus, it is important to remember two things about stage reasoning: First, the modal level is simply the most common system and is employed about half the

Moral development—like both cognitive and personal development—appears to proceed in an invariant sequence of developmental stages. A child cannot skip stages in moral development but, interestingly, will prefer moral judgments one level beyond his or her own. This fact has significant implications for the classroom teacher.

time; there is variation. Second, there is a built-in preference for the next highest stage in the sequence. Table 7.2 summarizes both the modes and the plus-one stages.

An Invariant Sequence

There is an important point to remember about the concept of development. To qualify as a developmental change, as we may recall from Chapter 5, a change can take only one direction: up. A developmental change can occur only from a lower to a higher stage. As Figure 7.2 suggests, not all people end up at Stage VI with Gandhi, Martin Luther King, Mary McCloud Bethune, Jane Addams, Harriet Tubman, or Abraham Lincoln. However, there can be no reversals! With a few extreme exceptions (e.g., schizophrenics and other institutionalized patients), the researchers have found that major regressions in moral growth do not occur (Rest, 1973a, 1983).

The longitudinal results, in fact, showed a downward shift in scores only 8 percent of the time. Since the subjects had been tested a total of six times over

TABLE 7.2   VARIATION IN STAGE USAGE BY AGE GROUP (MODAL STAGE CIRCLED)

KOHLBERG STAGE	AGES			
	10	13–14	16–18	20–22
Stages I and II (Mix)	(47.6)	8.1	2.2	0
Stage II (Specific)	33.3	16.2	11.1	0
Stages II and III (Mix)	14.3	(56.8)	17.8	9.4
Stage III (Specific)	4.8	16.2	(44.4)	31.3
Stages III and IV (Mix)	0	2.7	24.4	(40.6)
Stage IV	0	0	0	18.8

a thirty-year period, the downward shifts noted fall within the acceptable error of measurement. The re-testing also indicated that every case of reversal at one age was more than made up at the next. These results provided firm evidence supporting the direction of growth as a graduated sequence from less to more complexity. The results also showed quite clearly that the growth was systematic—one stage at a time. While there were no genuine reversals, neither did any of the subjects bypass or skip a stage (Kohlberg, 1984).

Moral Judgments and Moral Action

A key element so far missing from this discussion is the connection between stages of moral growth and actual behavior in the "heat of battle," so to speak. This is an important issue, especially in this book, in which we have stressed that thinking about issues is no substitute for acting in real situations. The evidence for moral maturity and moral behavior comes from a series of studies. Naturally, if the theory of moral development has any meaning, we would predict significantly different behavior according to significantly different levels of moral judgment. For example, we would expect that almost all who responded to the Heinz dilemma at Stage I or II ("It's all right to steal, especially if you get away with it") would themselves cheat or steal if given any chance at all. And, at the opposite extreme, we would expect that almost no one who responded at Stage V or VI would cheat or steal.

To put this expectation to the test, a series of studies using "cheating" tests has been conducted. In these studies the situations were varied. Some were traditional classroom experiments on tests, similar to the Hartshorne and May (1928–1930) approach, such as taking a vocabulary test, an aptitude test, or coding a foreign language. Other situations were more unique, such as a problem of returning an important questionnaire or a whistle-blowing situation (e.g., willingness to report obvious cheating). The results are summarized in Table 7.3 and clearly show almost a linear (straight-line) relationship between stage and behavior. The higher the stage, the greater the ability to resist the temptation to cheat.

A further question remains. What might be the effect of intelligence and cheating behavior? Is it moral judgment or IQ which affects such behavior? Kohlberg and Candee (1984) actually found that the two groups most likely to cheat were those with the *highest IQ scores* and *the lowest moral judgment* ratings, on one hand, and those with the *lowest IQ scores* and *the lowest moral judgment*. Both sets of students cheated over 80 percent of the time in these situations. Thus, we can safely conclude that moral judgment level and IQ score are separate components. Do not assume that a person with a high IQ score will necessarily process moral dilemmas at an advanced level. Table 7.4 presents the distribution of moral judgment scores from a sample of high IQ/high achieving students to illustrate the range within an academically homogeneous group. Moral judgment is normally distributed across the full range of principled reasoning

TABLE 7.3   SUMMARY OF RESULTS: CHEATING STUDIES—PERCENT OF CHEATING AT EACH STAGE

1a. Vocabulary Test	
Stage V	17%
Stages I–IV	53%

(*N* = 35, college students)

1b. Coding a Foreign Language	
Stage IV	43%
Stage III	64%
Stage II	80%
Stage I	73%

(*N* = 302, adolescents)

1c. Krebs-Kohlberg Tests of Honesty	
Stage V	20%
Stage IV	55%
Stage III	78%
Stage II	64%
Stage I	81%

(*N* = 123, adolescents)

1d. Failing to Return an Important Questionnaire	
Stage V	0%
Stage IV	9%
Stage III	60%
Stage II	66%

(*N* = 31, college students)

2. A College Aptitude Test	
Stage V	5%
Stages III and IV	14%
Stages I and II	27%

(*N* = 154, college students)

3. Remaining Quiet in Whistle-Blowing Situation	
Stage V	12%
Stages I–IV	65%

(*N* = 25, college students)

Source: Section 1a–d: From L. Kohlberg and D. Candee, The relationship of moral judgment to moral action. In L. Kohlberg (Ed.), *Essays on moral development*, Vol. II. (New York: Harper & Row, 1984), pp. 498–581. Section 2: E. Lonky and J. Reihman, Self-regulation & moral reasoning as mediators of moral behavior. Paper presented at the annual convention of the American Psychological Association, New Orleans, La., August 1989. Section 3: M. Braebeck, Ethical characteristics of whistle blowers. *Journal of Research in Personality, 18* (1984): 41–53.

TABLE 7.4   RANGE OF MORAL DEVELOPMENT SCORES—ACADEMICALLY GIFTED ADOLESCENTS*

MORAL DEVELOPMENT STAGE	N = 235
Low (0–29)	58 (25%)
Moderate (30–49)	107 (44%)
High (50 and above)	70 (30%)

* All above 95th percentile on academic ability.

From M. Howard-Hamilton, The effects of a DPE program on the moral reasoning, identity formation and achievement motivation among gifted adolescents. Doctoral dissertation (Raleigh: North Carolina State University, 1991); P. F. Vincent, The teaching of ethics as a means to facilitate moral development in gifted adolescents. Doctoral dissertation (Raleigh: North Carolina State University, 1991).

even though all the students were above the 95th percentile on standardized measures of academic ability.

In another, more dramatic study of behavior the tests of moral judgment were administered to subjects who had participated in the famous experiments of **Stanley Milgram,** in order to rate their level of moral maturity. Briefly, in the Milgram experiments research subjects were told to "follow orders" exactly as specified by a scientific investigator. The subjects were told that they were going to administer a series of strong electric shocks to an innocent "victim" in the next room. The subjects could hear the "victim" pounding on the door, wincing, and screaming every time they pushed a button marked "high voltage." The experiment was set up to test how long subjects would follow orders and continue to administer increasing amounts of electricity to another human being. (In fact, of course, the supposed victim was part of the experiment and was not actually hooked up to the electric current.) The study itself caused a tremendous stir because the results revealed that, in general, fully 65 percent of all subjects, regardless of age, background, or educational level, were willing to obey orders, no matter what! In other words, in spite of the screaming, pounding, and pleading from the "victim" in the next room, almost two-thirds of the subjects were willing to follow the scientists' directions. Figure 7.3 shows various phases of this classic experiment.

The results of the moral judgment testing showed that only 13 percent of the subjects rated at Stages I to IV actually refused to obey the orders, while 75 percent of the subjects rated at Stages V and VI re-

FIGURE 7.3   Various phases of Milgram's classic experiment: (a) A shock generator. (b) A subject being strapped into place. (c) A subject refusing to obey orders. (d) An obedient subject being introduced to his unharmed "victim." Below is a chart relating Kohlberg's stages to the results of this experiment.

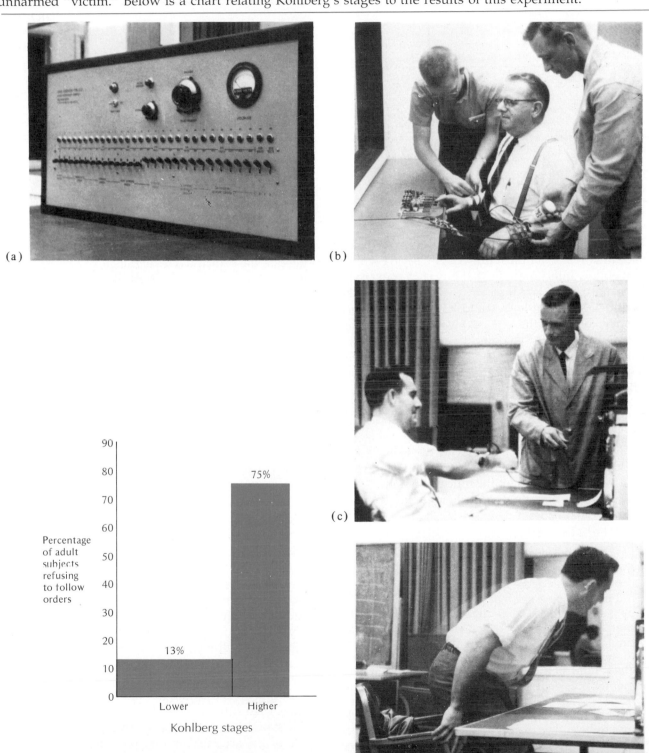

Photos: © 1965 by Stanley Milgram. From the film Obedience, *distributed by the New York University Film Library.*

TABLE 7.5   PERCENT OF COLLEGE STUDENTS HELPING A DRUGGED STUDENT ACCORDING TO MORAL STAGE SCORE (THE McNAMEE STUDY)

KOHLBERG STAGE SCORE	NUMBER	HELPED BY REFERRING VICTIM	THOUGHT THEY SHOULD HELP
II	11	9%	36%
III	29	27	77
IV	17	38	69
V	29	73	83

fused to obey. This, of course, very closely fits the concept of moral maturity at the postconventional level. Only at that level would we expect a person to refuse to follow the rules and say, in effect, "I really don't care what the experiment is all about or whether a scientist tells me I must do what he says. I will not deliberately inflict harm on that guy in the next room. He is more important than any experiment." In other words, only at that level could a person distinguish between obeying the law and valuing human life. We might recall at this point the number of times in history that humans have been willing to exterminate helpless victims on the grounds that they were "just following orders."

Another study of particular interest in detailing the relationship between moral thought and action was conducted by Shari McNamee (see Table 7.5). Sometimes referred to as a test of the Golden Rule and the parable of the Good Samaritan, her experiment was conducted with college students. They were to participate in a "psychology subject" program. She describes it as follows:

Undergraduates who agreed to be interviewed on the standard moral dilemmas were led to a testing room. As they were entering the room they were intercepted by a student presenting himself as the next subject for the experiment. The student stated that he had just taken drugs and was having a bad time. He had come to the experiment because he thought that the experimenter, being a psychologist, could help him. The response of the experimenter was that she was a research psychologist, not a therapist. The drug-user persisted in soliciting aid, hoping that the experimenter could refer him to help. The experimenter replied that she had no experience with drugs and did not know what facility could help him. She told him to reschedule his testing session. The drug-user slowly left the

room. The subject was faced with the choice of whether to remain an uninvolved bystander or whether to intervene (1977, p. 27).

Almost three-fourths of the students who were rated at the principled level (Stage V) offered to help the victim. There was a linear relationship between stage score and willingness to help, so that 38 percent of Stage IV, 27 percent of Stage III, and 9 percent of Stage II offered assistance. Thus, the relationship between stage score and actual behavior in a high-stress dilemma situation was clearly established. Two other points of interest: In McNamee's study the authoritative scientist was a female and in Milgram's experiment the scientist was a male, yet the outcomes were similar. Also, in both the McNamee and the Milgram studies, equal numbers of male and female subjects were used, and there were no sex differences in response by stage.

One final point on the McNamee study: In addition to observing actual helping behavior, McNamee also asked the subjects if they thought that they should help a distressed person. This is a kind of lip-service test to see if some of those who said they should help actually didn't. The results are most interesting. The greatest discrepancy occurs among those at Stage III. More than three-fourths of the subjects at that level said they ought to help, but just over one-fourth actually did. This is a 50-percent difference between lip-service and helping behavior. If you review the major characteristics of Stage III reasoning, you will see that the theory would predict exactly such an outcome. Since obedience to social conformity peaks at this stage, such subjects would agree to a socially acceptable statement yet be unable to resist the authoritative role of the scientist's social pressure. These results, then, further validate the Kohlberg theory.

A major review of over eighty studies of the relation of moral behavior to reasoning has been done by Gus Blasi (1980). He examined the research design results and the theoretical assumptions from each study. Although not all of the studies were well designed, Blasi concluded that on an overall basis the view that moral behavior and moral reasoning are definitely interrelated was strongly supported. Even more important was his conclusion that at higher levels of reasoning humans behave in a more consistent and altruistic manner than at lower levels of reasoning. The strongest finding of all was that at higher stages there was a much greater resistance to following the crowd or to going along in order to get along. The Milgram and McNamee results, plus other studies of the abilty to resist authoritarian commands, are summarized in Table 7.6.

From the meta-analysis and a specific look at individual studies, we do find convincing evidence of the stage-behavior relationship. You may have noticed, however, that the outcomes aren't perfect. For example, a few persons assessed at the principled level cheated on exams, wouldn't "blow the whistle," or refused to help the "victim." Also the opposite occurred. At least a few at lower stages behaved in a principled manner. In addition to the stage of moral reasoning, then, there must be other factors involved. One researcher, Blasi (1990), now suggests we need to focus on the question of moral motivation as an important factor. Rest (1986) suggests that the process includes at least four components:

1. Identification of the problem as a moral issue

2. Understanding the problem at an emotional level

3. The willingness to set aside personal nonmoral motives

4. The ego strength to act in spite of public opposition

The last component, which demonstrates that actions speak louder than words, may be the greatest challenge for anyone. Thus, if you find yourself in a dilemma, and later on you discover that your actions were not in concert with principled judgment, you can use the Rest model. By understanding the stage level and feelings of the participants, examining your own motives, and developing the strength to act (whether or not it pleases others), you will experience firsthand the problem of consistency, stage, and behavior. The whole question is among the most complex which behavioral scientists study.

TABLE 7.6   SUMMARY OF RESULTS: RESISTING AUTHORITARIAN COMMANDS (Percent Resisting at Each Stage)

1. Refusing to Administer "Electric Shocks"	
Stage V	75%
Stage I–IV	13%
(N = groups of 30, adults)	

2. Under Duress, Helping a Bystander	
Stage V	73%
Stage IV	38%
Stage III	27%
Stage II	9%
(N = 86, college students)	

3a. Arrested for Civil Protest	
Stage V	73%
Stage IV	44%
Stage III	31%
Stage II	10%
(N = 339, college students)	

3b. Follow-up Study: Arrested Protesters (15 years later)	
Stage V:	
Free Speech Leaders	69%
Student Leaders	43%
Random Comparison	17%
(N = 77, adults)	

Note: Studies 1 and 2 were laboratory studies of human behavior. Studies 3a and 3b were natural-setting investigations.

Source: Sections 1, 3a: From L. Kohlberg, The meaning of moral judgment. In L. Kohlberg (Ed.), *Essays on moral development* (New York: Harper & Row, 1984), vol. II, pp. 415–422. Section 2: From S. McNamee, Moral behavior, moral development and motivation. *Journal of Moral Education,* 7(1), 27. Reprinted by permission. Section 3b: From A. Nassi, Survivors of the sixties: Comparative psychological and political development of former student activists, *American Psychologist 36.* (1981), 753–761.

Sex Differences: Gilligan's Critique

When the Kohlberg theory was first validated, there were two studies, one in Canada (Sullivan, McCullough, and Stager, 1970) and one in the United States (Turiel, 1976) that specifically examined the relationship between gender and stage. Both studies indicated that there was no gender difference, and the topic was largely dropped as a matter of research interest. **Carol Gilligan,** however, challenged these findings and did so most dramatically. As a 1977 journal article that was soon expanded to book length, her *In a Different Voice,* published in 1982, created a major controversy. Relying mostly on historical evidence, case studies, and small-scale empirical research presented with a flair for the dramatic, she proclaimed that the Kohlberg theory was sex-biased. Not only did the scoring system penalize females, in her view, but his description of postconventional (Stages V and VI) reasoning systematically left out a concern for human caring. In other words, she claimed the Kohlberg theory defined principled reasoning as too objective and narrowly rational. Human compassion was absent from his system. Gilligan also was alert to point out that the original longitudinal sample was all male. Quoting from source material ranging from Portia in *The Merchant of Venice* and Nora in *A Doll's House* to characters from Mary McCarthy's novel *The Group,* she made a most persuasive case. She claimed that psychological theory was only one instance of pervasive sexism from a male-dominated society:

> As we have listened for centuries to the voices of men and the theories of development that their experience informs, so we have come more recently to notice not only the silence of women but the difficulty in hearing what they say when they speak. Yet in the different voice of women lies the truth of an ethic of care, the tie between relationship and responsibility, and the origins of aggression in the failure of connection (1982, p. 173).

Her views had an immediate impact not only on psychology but also on the larger community. In 1984 she was named Woman of the Year by a leading national feminist magazine. Soon many theorists and researchers began to review their prior studies. How could so many have missed such an obvious bias? Could it really be true that all of Kohlberg's work was valid for only one-half of the population?

One of the first comprehensive reviews was published by James Rest, a professor at the University of Minnesota, where the tradition of precise measurement is extremely strong (1986). In fact during the early days of Kohlberg's interview-rating approach, Rest had created an objective paper-and-pencil test of Kohlberg's theory. Researchers used his instrument with teenagers, college students, young adults, and professionals. The samples were large and represented both genders. Rests's quite startling finding was that there was no empirical evidence to support Gilligan's charge. By far the most frequent finding was that there was no difference between male scores and female scores, regardless of the sample. Further, he found that when sex differences were found in a few studies, the differences were in favor of the females, as shown in Table 7.7.

Although Rest's written-test method had been validated, the interview approach was still suspect. Gilligan had been especially critical of the interview method, claiming that whenever the raters came across comments suggesting the importance of love, caring, sympathy, and the like, those ideas were immediately classified as Stage III (social conformity).

Lawrence Walker (1984) published a major analysis of both approaches to judgment, the Rest objective method and the open-ended Kohlberg dilemma system. When his methodology was criticized (Baumrind, 1986), he redid his analysis and expanded the research base to include about 10,000 subjects. The results were exactly similar to those of James Rest, namely, no differences were recorded from either method according to gender (Walker, 1986). Mary Braebeck's reviews (1982, 1987) reached similar conclusions. All these studies, however, were cross-sectional in that none but the original Kohlberg sample followed the same subjects over time. It was still possible that Gilligan's claim was valid without findings from longitudinal research as well.

The major longitudinal study including both males and females was analyzed by Loren Lee and John Snarey (1988). In fact they reviewed not only life span changes in moral judgment but in the related domain of ego development as well and included over 400 females and 225 males from a variety of educational backgrounds. They found no differences by gender on an overall basis. On the other hand they did find that females tended to have slightly higher ego development scores than men. In either case, however, the results did not favor males. Of course, it is important to remember that in all these studies males and females were compared also on the basis of equal education and/or career opportunities. An earlier study by Constance Holstein (1976) has shown that males who had completed college and had begun working had higher moral judgment scores than their spouses who had less education and did not work outside the home. Behavioral scientists do not think that such differences as Holstein found can be attributed to either a gender difference or a biased scoring system

TABLE 7.7   GENDER EFFECTS: MORAL JUDGMENT LEVEL
(Principled Reasoning Score)

	MALE (N = 1401)	P SCORE	FEMALE (N = 1391)	P SCORE
Junior high school	(N = 528)	19.1	(N = 519)	19.7
High school	(N = 424)	28.7	(N = 436)	30.4
College	(N = 449)	44.1	(N = 436)	45.8

Note: The observed differences in scores are not considered theoretically significant.

From J. R. Rest, *Moral Development* (New York: Praeger, 1986), pp. 114–115.

since those differences disappear when education and job status are controlled (Kohlberg, 1984).

Furthermore a study by Rigby (1989) demonstrated that there was no gender difference in moral attitudes to authority by delinquent adolescents. In a cross-cultural review males and females were equally likely to resist. Thus the stereotype of females demonstrating greater compliance was not validated at least for those classed as delinquents.

Moral Dilemma Content: Are Females Changing?

Some years ago, Professor Nick Colangelo (1982) published a study of the types of dilemmas which teenagers formulated on their own. He found that males always wrote stories about a male confronting a personal dilemma whereas females were equally split in their choice of a male versus a female. Six years later Cynthia Baldwin (1988) replicated the study but with completely different results. In her study all the females wrote about a female as the main charater, the protagonist, and one-third of the males selected a female—almost exactly the opposite of the earlier finding. This could indicate that females are developing greater identity and differentiation and that they can imagine themselves as major persons struggling directly with important issues. Perhaps this also indicates that at least some males can also imagine a female caught on the horns of a dilemma. In the classic Frank Stockton story, "The Lady or the Tiger," the reader must guess which door the male will choose. As times change and women continue to move toward stage equality, such stories may be transformed: A woman may have to choose between "the man or the troglodyte."* However, since both

Colangelo and Baldwin assessed samples of gifted and talented teenagers, we cannot say whether such changes are representative of teenagers as a whole.

As to the content of the themes generated by the students themselves, Kathleen Galotti (1989) reported no differences by gender. Galotti asked a sample of college students to describe in their own words a situation in which values conflict. A content analysis revealed that both sexes generated similar themes. The number of themes classed as "*masculine*" (legal issues, religious teaching, rights justice, etc.) versus "*feminine*" (effects on self, what others would think, personal guilt, caring, etc.) were equal. Perhaps even more interesting, however, was that both males and females produced similar themes in proportion. Two-thirds of all the stories were classed as feminine. This could indicate that at least for adolescents (even those in college), the interpersonal is still more important than the larger issues of justice. In a parallel study by Skoe (1991) with a sample of college students (see Chapter 6), there were no gender differences across measures of moral judgment, identity status, and a "Care Interview" response.

Care, Gender, and Ethnicity

Perhaps the most trenchant criticism of the Gilligan dichotomy comes from a careful review of Gilligan's most recent work at the Emma Willard School—a private school for girls (Gilligan, Lyons, and Hammer, 1989). Diane Scott-Jones (1991), a leading expert in ethnic identity formation during childhood and adolescence, pointed out an extreme irony in the study. The Gilligan group had reported at length on the special, caring orientation of the small sample of predominantly white female teenagers raised in the elite private school atmosphere. Scott-Jones noted that the limitations of the care orientation was evident

---

* Some cynics may say that's no choice at all for many women.

when one considered the experience of black girls at the school (Scott-Jones 1991, p. 31). She reports that seven black students experienced continuous racial discrimination and exclusion and that they soon developed their own organization for mutual support. Apparently, the caring orientation of the white girls did not extend to those whose only difference was skin color. Scott-Jones concludes that "maximizing and romanticizing differences between males and females may be appealing . . . but it may have the long-term effect of maintaining a women's traditional subordinate status (1991, p. 32).

To a major degree, then, the charge of sex bias has not been proved. To an even greater degree, Gilligan's claims continue to be puzzling.* It is true that Kohlberg's sample was male, but there have been an enormous number of studies since that time (including cross-cultural replications) with both sexes. The results are highly consistent with the claim of a universal sequence for both sexes. This does not mean, however, that there is nothing of substance to Gilligan's view. She has served as a valuable reminder that issues of caring and compassionate concern for others are important components of moral judgment. She has also correctly pointed out that the content of many of the standard dilemmas themselves (Heinz, Joe and the camp, and the sergeant in Korea) routinely depict males as the key actors. As we move toward genuine sexual equality, fairness would require more females as the main figures.

Kohlberg himself was certainly sensitive to Gilligan's position and noted that the revised scoring manual avoids automatically classifying "caring" content as Stage III. Perhaps a less obvious but, in the long run, a more significant change is the definition of postconventional (Stages V and VI) reasoning. In his most recent writings, Kohlberg described the Golden Rule as have two elements: (1) Do unto others as you would have them do unto you, *and* (2) love thy neighbor as thyself. The first part has been routinely mentioned in all his earlier writings and linked to the philosophy of Immanuel Kant. The focus on the second clearly reflects an ethic of caring, which is really Gilligan's central point.

In Kohlberg's own words, "Our theory recognizes affect in appeals to respect for the dignity of persons as well as in appeals to caring and responsibility between persons" (1984, p. 291).

An eminent educational philosopher, Israel Scheffler, also views the Gilligan dichotomy as false. "The recent suggestion that an ethic of care is to be counterpoised as an alternative to an ethic of principles has never seemed to me persuasive since respect for persons is a high, perhaps the highest form of care, and care in any case needs to be apportioned, equitably" (1990, p. 100).

Universal Stages across Cultures

Kohlberg originally demonstrated, both across cultures (from Malaysian aborigines to white middle-class Americans) and within cultures (lower- to upper-class Americans), that the sequence is the same not only within country, class, and caste, but also within major religious categories. Kohlberg's stages, like Piaget's and Erikson's, represent a systematic, one-way sequence from preconventional levels (Stages I and II) to conventional levels (Stages III and IV) and culminating in postconventional levels (Stages V and VI).

This means that the formal sequence of understanding and developing moral judgment is limited by developmental age and stage. The content may vary, but not the structure of judgment. Thus, a ten-year-old Taiwanese village boy would say it was OK for Heinz to steal the drug: "Otherwise the wife would die and he'd have to pay for the funeral and they cost a lot"; a ten-year-old Malaysian boy would say it was OK to steal the drug: "Otherwise the wife dies and he needs her to cook for him"; and an American middle-class boy of the same age would say Heinz should steal the drug: "Especially if the wife could turn out to be an important person—or if she died then he would have to go to the trouble of finding a new wife." The logical structure in all three cases is the same. The wife is viewed exclusively as an instrument of the husband in concrete and operational terms.

The cross-cultural question could not be completely settled on the basis of these studies, however. Cultural anthropologists had long maintained, starting with Margaret Mead's important research, that each culture was really unique. This so-called snowflake theory essentially said each society, like each snowflake, was different from all others. Cross-cul-

---

* It is perhaps even more puzzling if some of her own earlier research is examined carefully. The Gilligan, Kohlberg, Lerner, and Belenky study of 1971 found no sex differences in moral judgment with a sample of teenagers. The Gilligan and Belenky 1980 study reported a positive correlation ($r = +.61$) between moral judgment on the Kohlberg scale and improved life circumstances with a sample of adult females. Thus, her own earlier research showed no bias in the Kohlberg theory.

TABLE 7.8 THREE VERSIONS OF THE CLASSIC "HEINZ AND THE DRUG" DILEMMA

ORIGINAL UNITED STATES VERSION*

In Europe, a woman was near death from a special kind of cancer. There was one drug that the doctors thought might save her. It was a form of radium that a druggist in the same town had recently discovered. The drug was expensive to make, but the druggist was charging 10 times what the drug cost him to make. He paid $200 for the radium and charged $2,000 for a small dose of the drug. The sick woman's husband, Heinz, went to everyone he knew to borrow the money, but he could only get together about $1,000, which is half of what it cost. He told the druggist that his wife was dying, and asked him to sell it cheaper or let him pay later. But the druggist said, "No, I discovered the drug and I'm going to make money from it." So Heinz got desperate and broke into the man's store to steal the drug for his wife.

Should Heinz have done that? Why or why not?

ADAPTED KENYAN VERSION†

In a rural area of Kenya, a woman was near death from a special kind of heart disease. There was one kind of medicine that the doctors at the government hospital thought might save her. It was a form of medicine that a chemist in Nairobi had recently invented. The drug was expensive to make, but the chemist was charging 10 times what the drug cost him to make. He paid 80 shillings for the drug, and then charged 800 shillings for a small dose of the drug. The sick woman's husband, Joseph, went to everyone he knew to borrow the money, but he could only get together 400 shillings, which was half of what it cost. He told the chemist that his wife was dying, and asked him to sell it cheaper or let him pay the rest later. But the chemist said, "No. I'm the one who invented this medicine, and I'm going to make money from it." So Joseph got desperate and broke into the store to steal the drug for his wife.

Should Joseph have done that, broken into the store to take the drug? Why or why not?

ADAPTED TURKISH VERSION‡

A man and wife have just migrated from the high mountains. They started to farm, but there was no rain and no crops grew. No one had enough food. The wife became sick from having little food and could only sleep. Finally, she was close to dying from having no food. The husband could not get any work and the wife could not move to another town. There was only one grocery store in the village, and the storekeeper charged a very high price for the food because there was no other store and people had no place else to go to buy food. The husband asked the storekeeper for some food for his wife, and said he would pay for it later. The storekeeper said, "No, I won't give you any food unless you pay first." The husband went to all the people in the village to ask for food, but no one had food to spare. So he got desperate and broke into the store to steal food for his wife.

Should the husband have done that? Why or why not?

* Originally appeared in Lawrence Kohlberg, *Global rating guide: Preliminary moral judgment scoring manual* (Cambridge, Mass.: Center for Moral Education, 1969).

† Originally appeared in C. Edwards, Doctoral dissertation, Harvard Graduate School of Education, Cambridge, Mass., 1974.

‡ Originally appeared in E. Turiel, C. Edwards, and L. Kohlberg, Moral development in Turkish children, adolescents, and young adults," *Journal of Cross-Cultural Counseling,* 9 (1978), 75–85.

From J. Snarey, Cross-cultural universality of social-moral development, *Psychological Bulletin,* 97(2) (1985): 214.

tural universality was a myth. In fact, one researcher claimed that the Kohlberg system itself was only an example of cultural bias. The researcher cited case studies in order to prove her point (Simpson, 1974).

As with the charge of sex bias, the charge of cultural bias was dealt with by going to the newer research literature. Since research like Kohlberg's had been conducted in over forty-five countries in the past fifteen years, surely there must be some hard evidence to confirm or deny the case-study position of cultural anthropology. **John Snarey,** of Emory University, in fact, did a careful, current, and exhaustive review (1985). One question of importance has to do with the content of the dilemmas. Snarey demonstrated how the stories were transposed to fit the

specific cultural traditions and mores. Table 7.8 demonstrates three versions of the Heinz story—the original and adaptations to Kenya and Turkey. The general issues remained the same, but the form was changed so the issues were not exclusive to a western culture such as ours.

The second issue Snarey checked out was the so-called invariant sequence problem. Do the original trends from the longitudinal study still hold? Employing both cross-sectional and longitudinal studies from different cultures, he found that all stages of development were represented. Also, there were no regressions in the major longitudinal studies, and none of the subjects skipped a stage. Thus, the major assumptions of the earlier studies were validated by current research. The subjects' level of moral reasoning shows the same sequence of development from the less complex to the more complex levels. The process proceeds one stage at a time with no skipping. Also there were no regressions beyond that from measurement error.

One final point: Was there evidence of principled reasoning, Stage V or higher, in other countries? Here the results were most interesting. In all urban western and in nearly all urban nonwestern cultures, some subjects were found who reasoned at the level of democratic, principled thought. In a review of eight tribal, rural, folk societies, Stage V or higher reasoning was completely absent. Thus, the main cross-cultural difference that now shows up is that which exists between urban versus tribal societies rather than western versus nonwestern. One such example of a tribal society is the Atayal culture in Malaysia. The elders arrange to prevent the development of abstract arrange to prevent the development of abstract reasoning in their adolescents through a process similar to brainwashing. The elders insist during the rites of passage that the young adults maintain their beliefs in black magic, the existence of demons, and other aspects of folklore (Kohlberg, 1984). Such aboriginal cultures are, of course, committed to maintaining myths in order to ensure the continuation of tribal cohesiveness; this is the opposite of our views on the importance of developing each person's individuality and human potential. The main point is that the cross-cultural research supports Kohlberg's developmental assumptions, with the exception of tribal cultures. This also proves another point. Development is not automatic but depends on interaction. If we do not provide humans with an appropriate learning environment, their development will not unfold, even in the area of value judgment.

The cultural question, however, remains a difficult and controversial aspect of value development. Diana Baumrind, for example, takes the position that there are no cultural universals. Thus, she avers that the principle that holds that life is more important than property represents a narrow western bias (1986). The difficulty is readily apparent. Customs and rituals are basically considered to be on the same level as a "universal" principle such as the sanctity of life. According to that view, there is no value-stage difference between beating a wife black and blue in the Hindu Brahmin culture and having a haircut after a parental death (Turiel and Killen, 1988). In fact, in that culture, having the haircut was considered a much graver moral transgression. Similarly, in rating the value of

life as less than that of property, such cultural relativism permits the burning of brides in order to force dowry payments.

The question, then, cannot be resolved without a far-reaching debate on the central point. Can unique cultural customs take precedence over such fundamental values as the right to life and human dignity? Folklore and cultural customs, while providing cohesion for a community, also carry with them the price of arbitrary and seemingly capricious injury to innocent victims. Is the greater good really served? Without belaboring the point, we do wish to point out that so-called advanced western cultures are not immune to the relativism of elevating custom to the status of universal principles. The slaughter of 12 million "undesirables" in Nazi Germany during the 1930s or the recent "cleansing" in the Balkans was based on a culture custom of purifying the race.

Of course, given the complexity of the issue, the cross-cultural questions have remained an important focus for continuing research. The number of studies now reaches over fifty different countries. Also there continues to be more longitudinal research in countries like Turkey, Taiwan, and Israel. These results were the same as for the U.S. samples, namely, there were no gender differences, no one skipped a stage, and the sequence was always from lower to higher. Further, there continues to be a difference not between western and nonwestern countries but between industrialized versus tribal communities. In the latter case, tribal communities organized around feudal concepts create a context in which principled morality (Stages V and VI) does not appear (Gielen and Lei, 1991). Finally, a very intriguing study conducted in India demonstrated that those who were rated at the principled level (Stages V and VI) actually employed two types of reasoning, one based on justice, noviolence, and individual dignity and the other based on connectedness and harmony both within the human and the natural world (Vasudeu and Hummel, 1987). These findings may help to broaden the basis for the claims of cross-cultural universality. Certainly Kohlberg had always maintained that historical figures from different cultures such as Socrates, various Jewish prophets, Siddharta Gautama, and Confucius represented principles of justice. Closer to the point, Gielen comments on some work noting that classical Chinese philosophy denotes virtue as *ren* (pronounced *jen*) with a meaning similar to the Golden Rule. Apparently in Gielen's view the challenge to western industrialized countries is to focus more attention on the need for harmony and the

Golden Rule versus a constricted world view that seems to emphasize autonomy and individualism (Gielen, 1991).

Peer Interaction

One of the key factors in moral development is the amount and quality of peer interaction. It is thought that peer relationship experience prepares the pathway to higher and more complex forms of moral judgment. It is perhaps ironic but it is often the case that peer interaction plays a larger role in development than interaction with adults. The reason is that there is an obvious imbalance of power and authority in relationships between children and adults. Within children's groups, however, there is greater equality, greater give and take, and a greater need for consensus in reaching decisions. Even the concept of kindness has a different meaning. With peers, it means to act socially—helping and caring for others. With adults, it means obeying adult authority without complaining. Rules are handed down by adults (Youniss, 1980).

William Damon (1990) has studied this process of peer interaction carefully and has shown how groups at elementary school age discuss concepts of fairness and justice when confronted with difficult group decisions. The interactions are based more or less on mutuality. This isn't to say that children will spontaneously follow democratic principles but there is a greater likelihood of the children's sharing and testing out a variety of positions.

A further reason for the importance of peer interaction at this age is that difficulties, spats and disagreements are brief. Arguments are relatively short-lived, differences easily repaired. Thus, the give and take occur in a relatively "safe" atmosphere. Perhaps because there is not the same depth of feelings as there is during adolescence and adulthood, the differences don't run the risk of escalating to the breaking point. There are hurt feelings, to be sure, but the friendships remain intact. As a result, the probability of continued interaction, discussion, and compromise is increased during this period, and the peer group becomes a training ground for later growth. Damon notes that by learning this direct reciprocity,

> The child learns respect for established rule and conventions; and, most importantly, learns respect for the social order from which all rules and social conventions arise. This, too, is a life long legacy, for it

will enable the child to become a full citizen in society, with all of a citizen's leadership prerogatives and fellowship responsibilities (1990).

Before you get carried away by the rhetoric and ideals of democratic society, it is well to remember that elementary school students learn to negotiate. This does not, however, ensure a social justice outcome. To keep out feet solidly placed in reality, Damon reports the following verbatim:

> Seven children, all wearing hockey uniforms, walked into the pizza parlor to order one large cheese pizza. The incident began when the waiter delivered the pizza.

> *Waiter:* OK kids, here's your pizza. [The children then each took one piece.]
> *Child 1:* Hey, there's eight pieces here. What about the extra piece?
> *Child 2:* The guy who's the oldest should get it. How old are you?
> *Child 1:* Nine.
> *Child 3:* I'm nine and a quarter.
> *Child 1:* My birthday's coming up this summer. I'm—I'll be ten in one, two months.
> *Child 2 (to Child 4):* How old are you?
> *Child 4:* Eleven, and I'll be twelve next month.
> *Child 2:* Well, I'm twelve, so I'll get the extra piece.
> *Child 1:* What about giving it to the one with the small piece?
> *Child 4:* Well, who's got the smallest piece?
> *Child 1:* I've got the smallest piece—look at it!
> *Child 2:* C'mon, let's cut it. The oldest kid will get one piece and the kid with the smallest piece will get one piece.
> *Child 3:* I bet I can name everybody's names here. You're Michael, you're Louie, you're Johnie.
> *Child 2:* You're Joey, you're Louie . . . [Names all the other children.]
> *Child 4:* [Names all the others' names faster than Child 2 or 3.]
> *Child 5:* Hey, can we get some water here? Who's gonna play hockey tomorrow?
> *Child 3:* I am, I am. [Jumps up and moves over to the pizza tray, which still has the extra piece on it. Begins picking cheese off the top. Child 1 and Child 2 gather around, each taking chunks of the extra piece, with Child 3 getting the lion's share.]
> *Child 6:* Who's the biggest eater here? Who's the piggiest?
> *Child 2:* I can eat seven pieces of pizza, but I gotta give one to my mother.
> *Child 6:* No, no, who's the biggest eater of us all?
> *Child 4:* Joey [Child 3] is.
> *Child 1:* Yeah, Joey is.

Child 3:   Yeah, I can eat two whole pizzas myself.
Child 1:   Two whole pizzas.
Child 6:   Yeah, you're the biggest pig all right (1990, pp. 44–45).

This reminds us of two points. Children learn about justice and fairness through sharing, yet the process is slow. Damon notes: "Nothing can substitute for the child's actual confrontations in real life peer engagements."

Family Influences and Moral Judgment

One rather large gap in the moral development literature has been the lack of interest in investigating the influence of the family on the growth of values. **Sally Powers** (1988) in fact found a real dearth of studies in this area. In part, of course, it is a most difficult research problem since it involves adults and children at different stages all interacting. Most prior research had been inconclusive. Such a daunting task, however, did not stop Powers. She created a category system to analyze family dialogue as the family attempted to resolve moral dilemmas. She found three negative codes and three positive ones associated with moral development during adolescence. Families which used the codes of *focus, challenge* (but not conflictual), and *sharing* promoted growth. On the other hand, families employing *distraction, distortion,* and *rejection* codes inhibited development. Powers also, and probably most importantly, found that the emotional atmosphere of the family was extremely crucial. Atmospheres of praise, encouragement, and noncompetitive humor promoted open participation. Sarcasm, hostility, threats, and devaluing contributions promoted tension and conflict and inhibited participation and development. It may seem obvious that if we want adolescents to increase in their ability to reason, participation, support, and clarifying discussion are central; yet too often Powers found the opposite atmosphere. Picture an early adolescent haltingly presenting a somewhat controversial defense of Heinz stealing the drug. Then the father, a practicing attorney, takes the argument apart piece by piece, sarcastically putting down lawbreakers as anarchists and ridiculing his child's attempt. The contest is so one-sided that the discussion ceases. The young teenager is chastised and quickly learns to keep such ideas out of the family dialogue.

In fact, Powers discerned that conflict and tension with the father actually was associated with lower

The research of Sally Powers into the effect of family atmosphere on children's moral development supports the commensense notion that an atmosphere of support and encouragement promotes moral development while an atmosphere of hostility and authority stunts such development.

levels of moral judgment. Mothers at high levels of moral judgment were more supportive and more able to tolerate clarifying differing opinions. They were less defensive and hostile to teenagers who initially took a different point of view. It seems almost as if the fathers wanted to hammer their children into compliance whereas the mothers could listen and extend the dialogue.

What Powers has not been able to discern is the

differential question: Is there an ideal environment for children and adolescents at different developmental stages? She does think that we cannot specify one best environment because the proportions of focus, challenge, and sharing in a supportive atmosphere probably will shift by age and stage. We do know that distraction, distortion, and rejection in a conflictual atmosphere inhibits growth. Those atmospheres are not as bad or as extreme as the violence in the Irish and Lebanese study noted later in the text; however, verbally humiliating a teenager in a dilemma discussion does have negative long-term consequences, an opportunity for development missed.

MORAL GROWTH: UNDERSTANDING AT YOUR OWN STAGE AND ONE STAGE UP

We have seen that children and adolescents generally understand moral judgments at their own stage and one stage above it. Generally, people operate out of one major stage (such as Stage III, the social-conformist orientation), but they also incorporate a few elements from the next higher stage (in this case, Stage IV, the law-and-order orientation). This enables them to understand judgments one stage up and also, because of the nature of development, to prefer it to their own mode. Each higher stage is more universal and less self-centered and so requires fewer rationalizations. At the same time, it is useless to present people with moral systems more than one stage beyond their own. Students, or adults for that matter, simply cannot comprehend that far in advance of their present level of understanding.

From an educational point of view, it is well to remember that we can get pupils or adults to make rote statements that sound like the very highest level of moral development. However, if they themselves are more than one stage down from the moral system embodied in such memorized statements, they will not internalize that system. Instead, we will succeed only in producing more lip service. Say, for example, that we wanted to coach the high school debating team to present their arguments at Stage VI. We could teach them to mouth the concepts of universal principles of justice to support their position. However, unless they were already close to that level themselves, we would find, much to our chagrin, that when it came time for the rebuttal, our game plan would fail miserably. Once on their own, our debaters

would immediately lapse back into their own level (probably Stages II, III, or IV), thereby undoing all our work. Instead of arguments based on principles such as justice, we would hear arguments in accord with the students' own natural levels. In the classroom, too, there is a need to match the level of discussion to the pupil's developmental stage. The research evidence on this point is supportive. All children were able to understand and represent correctly all stages below their own as well as those at their own level. Some children could spontaneously understand and represent thinking one stage up from their own level. Almost none were able to comprehend and translate thinking two or more stages above their level.

Moral Education in the Classroom

Recent evidence indicates that special classroom teaching techniques can affect the level of the pupil's moral maturity. It is also important to note the factors that make a difference. Because of the limits imposed by developmental stages, it makes little sense to start discussing moral dilemmas before students reach elementary school age. There is the possibility, however, of starting discussions then to promote the idea of choosing among alternatives in everyday situations. Also, it is possible for pupils in elementary school to gain a sense of the reasons behind actions. Such discussions would help students become aware of a series of reasons for rules and would help them compare these ideas.

Research evidence strongly supports the dilemma-discussion approach (Rest, 1986). A major review indicated that the discussion method was consistently effective; Table 7.9 presents the results. There were

TABLE 7.9 EFFECTS OF MORAL DILEMMA DISCUSSIONS
Correlation by Academic Class

	CLASSES	EFFECT SIZE
1. Moral dilemma discussions	23	+ .41
2. Control	17	+ .09
3. Academic	9	+ .09
4. Control	7	+ .16

* *Effect size* is a measure of the amount of positive change or level of moral judgment. Effects below .20 are considered insignificant.

From J. R. Rest, *Moral development* (New York: Praeger, 1986).

some important characteristics to bear in mind in separating the effective methods from the ineffective ones. First, time was generally an important variable. Twelve- to sixteen-week courses were effective; short-term workshops, two-week "units," or one-shot presentations were not. Second, the discussion method worked well with all age groups, from early adolescents to adults, and generally the older the students, the greater the positive change. Finally, the gains were modest. In other words, we should not expect students in any age grouping to demonstrate huge stage gains.

Since the process of moral reasoning is closely related to age, stage of cognitive development, level of experience, and the ability to reflect from different points of view, such a reasoning process cannot be changed overnight (Likona, 1991). One of the possible frustrations that teachers often experience in running such discussions is the slow growth rate. Students generally will maintain their own modal level, especially in dealing with difficult dilemmas. If you do decide to lead such discussions, it's important to remember that a slow pace is to be expected. You can, or course, interrupt at any point and teach them to say the "right answers" at a principled level. You will find, however, like the coach of the high school debating team, that once back on their own resources in discussing a different dilemma, their modal levels will reappear.

The Berkowitz Approach: Support and Challenge

A further refinement of the discussion method comes from the work of **Marvin Berkowitz,** of Marquette University (Berkowitz, 1984). He had the good idea of examining different methods of group leadership in the discussion format. What Berkowitz found out has direct relevance to the teaching question. First, he found that effective discussion requires flexibility and the use of indirect teaching strategies. (See Chapter 12 for a further discussion on indirect methods.) This meant quite simply that lecturing, telling, or reading to students *about* moral dilemmas has little impact. Just think of how many times lecture material "goes in one ear and out the other." Second, he found that the leader needs to balance the distribution of questions between supportive ones and challenging ones. This means that sometimes the leader restates, reflects back, and paraphrases what the student says. This helps the student think out loud, so to speak.

At other times, however, the leader needs to challenge the student's statement (and remember, you are challenging the idea and not the person). By asking the student to carry an illogical view to its logical conclusion, the weakness of the argument may be revealed to the student and others in the class. The student may be asked to refine and extend a view and even to defend the view against competitive or alternate points of view. The "Spotlight on Leading Moral Dilemma Discussions" in the box contains some examples of questioning designed to test and challenge the student's view as well as questions designed to paraphrase and clarify. The effective leader uses both techniques. The one thing the effective leader never does is "put down" a student. Sarcasm, belittling, or making fun of a student's view all serve to hamper discussion. Excessively critical teaching in general (see Chapter 13) has been shown to reduce both academic achievement and positive self-concepts. The same is true in moral-dilemma discussions. So remember that a ratio of supportive questions to challenging ones is essential for student growth. Challenge in this case is not license to cut off a child at the ankles, so to speak, with withering ridicule.

Discipline and moral development can become a direct part of a positive educational program. Discussions of moral dilemmas can be introduced to classes by use of headline stories from newspapers, everyday incidents, popular moral issues (e.g., capital punishment, civil disobedience, an "attractive" nuisance), or incidents from movies or readings. The teacher's job is to present the case material in a systematic and provocative way by asking questions. The idea is to promote a flow of ideas about what actions might be proposed. We have provided some examples at the end of the chapter for such practice.

Violence: How to Stop Moral Growth

Exposing children or adolescents to constant violence has always been known to induce psychological distress. In psychiatric terms such effects have been classified as posttraumatic stress disorder, which results from experiencing major and acute danger. For children growing up in areas of continuing violence such as Lebanon and Northern Ireland, there are also major effects on their level of moral growth. Research reported by Garabino, Kostelny, and Dubrow (1991) has shown that such chronic danger actually halts the growth process literally in its tracks. Instead of

SPOTLIGHT ON LEADING MORAL DILEMMA DISCUSSIONS

The Questioning Method

A. Starting

1. First, getting the facts straight:

   Be sure the content is accurate.
   Paraphrase what the issues are.
   Make sure all are tuned in.

2. To start the actual discussions, use open-ended questions:

   "What should Person X do? Why, or what are the main reasons?" Survey the group.
   If any of the reasons aren't too clear, then ask *clarifying questions.* For example:
   "Would you say a little more . . . ?"
   "Do you mean . . . ?"
   "Let me see if I can paraphrase . . . ?"

   OR

   Ask others in the group if they understand Person X's reasons.

Goal

Make sure everyone has the chance to make an opening statement. Use "wait time" if needed in questioning.

B. Continuing the discussion

To continue the discussion and help develop greater elaboration, the following techniques are helpful:

1. *Alternative consequences:* What might happen if the person did A, or B, or C?
2. *Role switch:* What would your reasons be if you were Person X, Y, or Z? Put yourself in the shoes of the other person.
3. *Feelings and emotions:* How do you suppose Person X is feeling? How might you feel in such a situation? What might be some consequences of those feelings?
4. *Personal experience:* Has anything like this ever happened to you? What were your thoughts, feelings, actions? Looking back, is there anything you would change?

5. *Change a key element:* "Let's say that the person in the situation is someone you didn't even know, rather than someone very close to you. How might that change things?"
6. *"Some people say":* "Some say there is never a good reason to break a law. How would you answer that view?"
7. *Have discussants talk back and forth to each other:* "Henry, how would you answer Amy?" "Jill and Troy seem to be on opposite sides . . ."

C. Reaching closure

1. *Issue-related questions:* "Now that we viewed it from so many different positions, what are the *key elements,* or most persuasive issues? Is there any particular element that would cause you to switch your view?"
2. *Justice-related questions:* "From a justice-and-fairness-to-all perspective, what solution would be best?"

---

moving from Stage I to Stages II and III during early adolescence, virtually none of the children in the Irish or Lebanese sample did. Basically such children had learned that a vendetta mentality was appropriate and acted to encourage the next generation of terrorist recruits. Unfortunately, moderate leaders in such communities who attempted to promote dialogue and higher levels of moral reasoning were soon silenced by extremist groups of adults.

When children are exposed to continuing violence, such abnormal environments truncate moral growth. Extremist ideology does provide the children with support. Garabino et al. note, that the children however, need to "find ways to help them make sense of their experience and to find the paths in their difficult journey that will increase morale and resilience without spawning fanaticism and intransigence (1991, p. 382).

SUMMARY

The theoretical breakthrough provided by Kohlberg revolutionized our understanding of moral development. His work parallels Piaget and Erikson in that it includes specific, age-related stages of growth. Each stage represents a system of thinking defined by how we process moral-ethical and value questions. Each stage is also part of an invariant sequence and represents a qualitatively more comprehensive system of understanding than the previous one.

Kohlberg's framework "emerged" from interviews with his research subjects. By presenting moral dilemmas to people from different backgrounds, he was able to sample the system of reasoning, thinking, and judging—the reasons behind their decision. In analyzing these reasons, Kohlberg formed the six-stage category system. Then he set out to cross-validate the system both cross-sectionally and now longitudinally. Recent research has not supported Gilligan's critique of the system as sex-biased.

The stages are defined by the major set of assumptions a person uses to think through, reason, and rationalize, or justify, an important ethical decision. Each stage is "better" than its preceding one; higher stages take into account an increasingly broader perspective, represent more complex and abstract thought, contain more personal empathy, and "solve" social problems more on the basis of principles. Thus, the direction of the system is highly congruent with the principles of a democratic society—values and ethics based on principles of justice.

The cross-cultural question is very complicated yet the research both from the interview method and the objective test method supports the universality of Stages I through IV. In tribal cultures, however, there appears to be an absence of emphasis on individual rights as denoted by Stages V and VI.

In behavioral terms, there is not an exact one-to-one relationship between moral stage and actual behavior. However, the trends in practically all studies are almost always consistent with the theory—whether it be performance on "cheating" tests or behavior in the Milgram and McNamee studies.

In relating the Kohlberg system to the classroom, the teacher's job is to present or to encourage statements and reasons that are slightly ahead of those of the majority of the class. This means that the teacher must do a great deal of probing—asking clarifying questions and seeking elaboration of the pupils' thought processes. It also means the teacher has to withhold his or her own judgments and not get overly angry or lecture the pupils. Exhortation, though tempting, is not teaching for moral development.

The teaching for moral development needs to be understood as a slow and complex process. On the one hand, we cannot really accelerate moral development beyond the limits set by the stage concepts. On the other hand, we cannot just sit by and beg the value question. We also know from recent research how exposure to violence can prevent the development of more complex moral judgment.

Undoubtedly the most important aspect of the entire chapter is that it confronts educational psychology with questions of character education in the form of stages of moral maturity. For almost half a century such questions of moral education and general education have been avoided or not considered a legitimate area for inquiry. Kohlberg has changed all that. We now must think through the value questions as part of a developmental sequence.

KEY TERMS AND NAMES

Marvin Berkowitz
William Damon
Carol Gilligan
Hugh Hartshorne and Mark May
invariant sequence
Lawrence Kohlberg

Stanley Milgram
moral development
"plus one"
Sally Powers
John Snarey

THEORY INTO PRACTICE: LEADING A DILEMMA DISCUSSION

Without doubt, the best way to understand the dilemma approach is to practice leading a small group of friends or students in discussing an actual dilemma. The content can vary according to the composition of the group. For example, if you were working with a group of junior-high or middle school students, you might try the following dilemma:

Middle School and Caught in the Middle

You've just moved to a new school. You hated to leave your old school. You had many close friends, and even many of the teachers were all right. Your father has just started a new job with lots of pressure, and he travels more now, too. Your mother has decided to work since your two older brothers are now in college and the expenses are increasing. You're not exactly miserable, but you are not happy at all. You don't know anybody at school. It's a lot bigger, and the kids don't seem very friendly. You've told your parents how awful things are, but they are busy and say you will outgrow it anyway. What's worse is that it's the middle of the year, and your courses are all different, and you're behind in all your subjects.

One day as you walk home from school, alone as usual, four kids who are really the "in crowd" (you know because you've seen them practically running the school) stop you and ask if you would like to join them. You say, "Why not?" to look cool and try not to show how much you want to be in with somebody. All of you stop at one of the homes. Both parents are working there, too. After a while you are really starting to enjoy it. It's a really neat house, and the kid has all the latest rock videos, and there's a lot of good-natured kidding around. It reminds you just how bad things have been. These kids are really cool, and they accept you.

After some cokes and pizza from the microwave, one of the kids pulls out a funny-looking hand-rolled cigarette. After lighting it, the kids take turns, and everybody seems to be having more and more fun. Suddenly, it's your turn. All your new friends are saying, "Listen, this won't hurt you," and "Look at adults; they're always drinking and smoking, and this stuff doesn't even give you a hangover. Besides, we all do it and it hasn't hurt us." You don't know what to do. Would you go along?

Instructions   We suggest very strongly that you tape-record the discussion. Then, after the session, replay the tape and make a tally mark for each time you followed one of the Berkowitz elements.

CHECKLIST

1. Getting the facts straight by asking the students to state the dilemma
   - _____ a. Checking for understanding by paraphrasing
   - _____ b. Use of open-ended questions
2. Elaborating and clarifying
   - _____ a. Alternatives and consequences
   - _____ b. Role-switches
   - _____ c. Feelings
   - _____ d. Personalizing
   - _____ e. Key element changes
   - _____ f. "Some people say . . ."
   - _____ g. Student-to-student talk
3. Closure
   - _____ a. Review key issues
   - _____ b. Raise the issue of justice for all questions

As you review the findings, regard them as a picture of your own currently preferred mode of discussion leading. If you find very few, or no, marks in certain areas, then consider running a second discussion with that (those) element(s) in mind. In all probability, you may be responding inadequately in the area of feelings and emotions. Often teacher education, unfortunately, does not acknowledge the importance of emotions in learning. In fact, one researcher found that, on the average, teachers clarified students' feelings once out of every thousand interactions. In dilemma discussion, almost by definition, there should be strong feelings on the issues. Examining and exploring emotions is central to the growth process. Some continual practice may be necessary.

The second activity is to listen for the structural content of the positions the pupils take. What types of reason do they give on their own? What follows is a list of reasons students may offer in trying to figure out a solution. Alongside each statement is the Kohlberg level for the reason.

STAGE	REASON
I	What are the chances of being caught?
III	How important are the new friends?
II	Will you lose a lot of privileges at home if you are found out?
IV	You might be arrested and charged in juvenile court.
III	Even though its risky, you will be "in" with the group.
III	You are being tested by the new group to prove you would fit into their life style. You need to go along to get along.
III	What will happen to your reputation if you say no, and they spread it around? Will you be isolated as a "goody two shoes"?
IV	How Important is it to stand up for yourself and obey the law?
VI	You understand the issue of societal values for mental and physical well-being for yourself.
V	You think about yourself, your new friends, and responsibility for the good of everybody.
II	Your parents had just promised you your own video and an increased allowance for tapes if you don't experiment with drugs.

After you have tried out a dilemma discussion with school students, you might consider someone closer to home. If you are about to do student teaching, gather a small group of colleagues, turn on the tape, and try the following:

A Student Teacher: Caught in the Middle

You and your cooperating teacher have been working hard this term to help one of your students, the principal's child. He has been marginal, and his grade will determine whether he graduates. Without being overbearing, the principal has sent a clear signal that you will receive an extra strong recommendation if all goes well.

The cooperating teacher has noted that the student is really working well for a change; assignments are on time and quality is up to a C−. You are pleased with his progress.

The student's final term paper is handed in. The cooperating teacher grades it as a C+, enters the grade, and with a sigh of relief says, "Well, we both deserve credit. He made it. Take a look at the paper. It's not great, but it is solid. Meanwhile I'll report the grade and tell the principal."

That night you glance at the work. You are halfway through the paper when you suddenly realize that much of the work has been lifted from a just-published anthology.

DISCUSS IN SEQUENCE

	RESPONSE
1. What are the issues? What are the feelings?	
2. What are possible actions? (Brainstorm; don't judge.)	
3. Outline the possible consequences.	
4. What would the best solution be in fairness to all involved? Is that what you would do?	

Instructions   At the end, replay the tape and do an analysis of discussion leading. Examine your checklist as a guide for your own further development. Also, consider rating the reasons by Kohlberg level.

Additional resources   See K. A. Strike and J. F. Soltis (1985), *The ethics of teaching* (New York: Teachers College Press). This work has an excellent discussion of the philosophical issues, basically the conflict between Stage V consequentialism and Stage VI reciprocity, that is, with the Golden Rule as a framework. Then the authors present a series of very challenging ethical dilemmas that teachers often face. We would suggest employing these case studies for teacher education, particularly with a small-group discussion method in the Berkowitz mode.

REFERENCES

Baldwin, C. (1988). Sex differences in moral dilemmas written by gifted adolescents. *Counseling & Values, 33,* 65–68.

Baumrind, D. (1986). Sex differences in moral reasoning: Response to Walker's (1984) conclusion that there are none. *Child Development, 57,* 511–521.

Berkowitz, M. (1984). Process analysis and the future of moral education. Paper presented at the annual meeting of American Educational, Research Association, New Orleans, April 23. See also Berkowitz, M., and Gibbs, J. (1983). Measuring the developmental features of moral discussion. *Merrill-Palmer Quarterly, 2*(4), 399–410.

Blasi, A. (1980). Bridging moral cognition and moral action. *Psychological Bulletin, 88*(1), 1–45.

Blasi, A. (1990). Kohlberg's theory and moral motivation. *New Directions for Child Development, 47,* 51–57.

Braebeck, M. (1982). Moral judgment: Theory and research on differences between males and females. *Developmental Review, 3,* 274–291.

Braebeck, M. (1987). Editorial, Special Issue: Feminist perspectives on moral education and development. *Journal of Moral Education, 16*(3), p. 163.

Colangelo, N. (1982). Characteristics of moral problems formulated by gifted adolescents. *Journal of Moral Education, 11,* 219–232.

Colby, A., Kohlberg, L., and Gibbs, J. (1979). The measurement of stages of moral judgment. *Final report to the National Institute of Mental Health.* Cambridge, Mass.: Center for Moral Development and Education.

Cremin, L. A. (1957). *The republic and the school.* New York: Teachers College Press.

Damon, W. (1990). *The moral child.* New York: Free Press.

Galotti, K. (1989). Gender differences in self-reported moral reasoning: A review and new evidence. *Journal of Youth and Adolescence, 18,* 475–488.

Garabino, J., Kostelny, K., and Dubrow, N. (1991). What children can tell us about living in danger. *American Psychologist, 46*(3), 376–383.

Gielen, U. (1991). Research on moral reasoning. In L. Kuhmerker (Ed.), *The Kohlberg legacy* (pp. 18–38). Birmingham, Ala.: REP.

Gielen, U., and Lei, T. (1991). The measurement of moral reasoning. In L. Kuhmerker (Ed.), *The Kohlberg legacy* (pp. 61–84). Birmingham, Ala.: REP.

Gilligan, C. (1982). *In a different voice.* Cambridge: Harvard University Press.

Gilligan, C., and Belenky, M. (1980). A naturalistic study of abortion decisions. In R. Selman and R. Yando (Eds.), *Clinical-developmental psychology: New directions for child development,* Vol. 7. San Francisco: Jossey-Bass.

Gilligan, C., Kohlberg, L., Lerner, M., and Belenky, M. (1971). *Moral reasoning about sexual dilemmas: Technical report of the U.S. Commission on Obscenity and Pornography.* Washington: U.S. Government Printing Office.

Gilligan, C., Lyons, N., and Hammer, T. (1989). *Making connections: The relational worlds of adolescent girls at Emma Williard School.* Troy, N.Y.: Emma Willard School.

Hartshorne, H., and May, M. (1928–1930). *Studies in the nature of character,* Vols. 1, 2, 3. New York: Macmillan.

Holstein, C. B. (1976). Irreversible, stepwise sequence in the development of moral judgment: A longitudinal study of males and females. *Child Development, 47,* 51–61.

King, M. L. (1963). Letter from Birmingham jail. In *Why we can't wait* (pp. 84–85). New York: Harper & Row. Copyright 1963 by Martin Luther King, Jr. Reprinted by permission of Harper & Row, Publishers, Inc.

Kohlberg, L. (1968). The child as a moral philosopher. *Psychology Today, 7,* 25–30.

Kohlberg, L. (1975). The cognitive-developmental approach to moral development. *Phi Delta Kappan, 56*(10), 671.

Kohlberg, L. (1984). The meaning and measurement of moral judgment. In L. Kohlberg (Ed.), *Essays on moral development,* Vol. II (pp. 415–422). New York: Harper & Row.

Kohlberg, L., and Candee, D. (1984). The relationship of moral judgment to moral action. In L. Kohlberg (Ed.), *Essays on moral development,* Vol. II (pp. 498–581). New York: Harper & Row.

Kuhmerker, L. (1991). *The Kohlberg legacy.* Birmingham, Ala.: REP.

Lee, L., and Snarey, J. (1988). The relationship between ego and moral development: A theoretical review and empirical analysis. In D. Lapsley and C. Power (Eds.), *Self, ego, and identity: Integrative approaches* (pp. 151–178). New York: Springer-Verlag.

Likona, T. (1991) *Education for character.* New York: Bantam.

McNamee, S. (1977). Moral behavior, moral development and motivation. *Journal of Moral Education, 7*(1), 27. Reprinted by permission.

Powers, S. I. (1988). Moral judgment development within the family. *Journal of Moral Education, 17,* 209–219.

Rawls, J. (1971). *A theory of justice.* Cambridge, Mass.: Belknap Press.

Rest, J. R. (1973a). Patterns of preference and comprehension in moral judgement. *Journal of Personality, 41,* 86–109.

Rest, J. R. (1973b). The hierarchical nature of moral judgment. *Journal of Personality, 41,* 86–109.

Rest, J. R. (1983). Morality. In P. Mussen (Ed.), *Handbook of Child Psychology* (4th ed., pp. 556–629). New York: Wiley.

Rest, J. R. (1986). *Moral Development.* New York: Praeger.

Rigby, K. (1989). Gender, orientation to authority and delinquency among adolescents: A cross-cultural perspective. *Journal of Moral Education, 18*(2), 112–117.

Scheffler, I. (1990) Moral education beyond moral reasoning. In D. Schrader (Ed.), *The legacy of Lawrence Kohlberg* (pp. 99–102). *New Directions for Child Development, 4,* San Francisco: Jossey-Bass.

Scott-Jones, D. (1991). From 'voice' to 'fugue' in females' development. *Educational Research,* 31–32.

Simpson, E. (1974). Moral development research: A case study of scientific cultural bias. *Human Development, 17,* 81–106.

Skoe, E. E. (1991). Identity, care-based and justice-based moral reasoning in women and men. Paper presented at the Association for Moral Education Conference, Athens, Ga.

Snarey, J. (1985). Cross-cultural universality of social-moral development. *Psychological Bulletin, 97*(2), 202–232.

Sullivan, E., McCullough, G., and Stager, M. (1970). A developmental study of the relationship between conceptual, ego, and moral development. *Child Development, 41,* 399–411.

Turiel, E. (1966). An experimental test of the sequentiality of developmental stages in the child's moral judgment. *Journal of Personality and Social Psychology, 3,* 611–618.

Turiel, E. (1976). A comparative analysis of moral knowledge and moral judgment in males and females. *Journal of Personality, 44,* 195–208. Actually, in this study the females scored higher than the males at the outset; the differences disappeared by midadolescence.

Turiel, E., and Killen, M. (1988). Morality: Its structure, functions and vagaries. In Kagan and S. Bloom (Eds.), Press.

Vasudeu, J. and Hummel, R. C., (1987). Moral stage sequence and principled reasoning in an Indian sample. *Human Development, 30,* 105–118.

Walker, L. K. (1984). Sex differences in the development of moral reasoning: A critical review. *Child Development, 55,* 677–691.

Walker, L. K. (1986). Sex differences in the development of moral reasoning: A rejoinder to Baumrind. *Child Development, 57,* 522–526.

Youniss, J. (1980). *Parents and peers in child development.* Chicago: University of Chicago Press. In addition, Nancy Eisenberg found the same outcome; not once did children explain their own prosocial acts as being a result of adult authority; Eisenberg, N. (1982). *The development of a result behavior,* New York: Wiley.

LEARNING THEORY

8

LEARNING BACKGROUNDS

The study of **learning** has been at the very heart of psychology, especially American psychology, since its origin about a hundred years ago. During the 1890s the great Harvard psychologist William James contrasted the importance of learning with habit, which he called that "enormous fly-wheel of society, its most precious conservative agent. . . . It keeps the fisherman and deckhand at sea through winter; it holds the miner in his darkness. . . . It keeps different social strata from mixing" (James, 1890, p. 79). James felt that learning, especially during childhood, shapes and directs our later lives against habit's negative effects: "Could the young but realize how soon they will become mere walking bundles of habits, they would give more heed to their conduct while in the plastic state" (James, 1890, p. 83). We might paraphrase James by saying that if society realized how soon its children would become walking bundles of habits, that society would give more heed to the importance of its early childhood education programs.

Though the study of learning has been the core area of American psychology, the pursuit of this study has been anything but serene. Great debates, full of sound and fury, over the nature and process of learning all but shattered the foundation of the fledgling discipline. Some psychologists, rigid behaviorists like John B. Watson, felt that learning involved

the patterning of overt responses. Knowledge, to these psychologists, resides in muscular reactions, not in cerebral exercise. As you drive to your favorite ice cream store, it would be your arms and legs that would "know" the route, not your head. These psychologists were correct—to some extent. Certain kinds of learning do occur as a result of response patterning. For example, try explaining to a youngster how to tie a necktie. It is almost impossible to transmit this knowledge through words alone, for it doesn't exist completely at the conceptual level. You will probably find that you have to demonstrate and, even then, you will stand behind the child, since your responses are so restricted and rigid that you can't tie a necktie while facing it. In playing the piano, knowledge of certain intricate passages seems to reside in your fingers. You may have forgotten a certain tune, but after fiddling around on the keys for a few minutes, your fingers suddenly "remember." Or in sports like skiing and golf, despite hours of verbal instruction, you ultimately have to learn a certain "feel," a certain muscular patterning.

In fact, many psychologists now believe that we have at least two separate modes of learning and memory, one called declarative and the other called procedural (Alper, 1986). *Declarative learning* stores information about names, dates, past events, episodes in one's life, and facts, whereas *procedural learning* is made up of motoric patterning and conditioning. This theory is used to explain why Alzheimer victims may still recall motoric patterns, such as tying shoes, riding a bicycle, or hitting a golf ball, but are not able to activate such declarative memories as the names of their children. More will be said on this important issue in Chapter 11.

Other psychologists, cognitive theorists like Max Wertheimer, Wolfgang Kohler, and Kurt Lewin, felt that learning required thinking and insight. As you drive to your favorite ice cream store, to return to a previous example, your arms and legs wouldn't be any help without a more general cognitive map, probably located in your brain. To the cognitive theorists, teaching children by drill or rote is like training a bunch of parrots. Children really learn only when they discover solutions for themselves, only when they "understand."

ASSOCIATION LEARNING AND COGNITIVE LEARNING

Now that the dust has settled on some of the great theoretical debates of the past, two main schools of thought on learning have emerged, though many variations still exist. These two main schools of thought are **association learning** and **cognitive learning.**

Association theorists, on the one hand, see learning as the result of connections (associations) between stimuli (sense impressions) and responses. Dogs salivating when they hear the can opener opening their food, babies waving "bye-bye" on cue from their mothers, or fifth-graders saying "seventy-two" to the stimulus "nine times eight" are all examples of association learning. A bond has been formed between two elements, a stimulus and a response.

Cognitive theorists, on the other hand, view learning as a reorganization of a number of perceptions. This reorganization allows the learner to perceive new relationships, solve new problems, and gain a basic understanding of a subject area. A fifth-grader suddenly realizing that multiplication is successive addition; an ape suddenly understanding that by putting two short sticks together, a banana that was out of reach is now obtainable; or an eighth grader discovering a way to calculate the area of a parallelogram—these are all examples of cognitive learning.

These two views of learning parallel the two sides

of another controversy that has historically split the field of psychology: behaviorism versus gestalt psychology. The behaviorists have typically been associationists, whereas the gestaltists have been cognitive theorists.

THE ORIGINS OF LEARNING THEORY: WILLIAM JAMES AND WILHELM WUNDT

It must be remembered that psychology as a separate discipline was a product of the late nineteenth century. Its origins are philosophy and physiology. For example, many philosophical overtones are apparent in the work of the first major American psychologist, William James. In fact, James had great difficulty deciding whether to cast his lot with philosophy or with psychology, being first in one department and then in the other at Harvard. And this vacillation occurred in spite of the fact that he created Harvard's psychology department.

Wilhelm Wundt, who set up the first experimental psychology laboratory in Europe around 1879, was also strongly influenced by philosophy. However, he was influenced by physiology as well, having begun his career as a physician and having later become a physiologist.

In a sense, then, psychology as a separate discipline resulted from a marriage between philosophy and physiology, with Wundt performing the ceremony. Like the philosophers who preceded him, Wundt was interested in studying conscious experience, and he sought to do this by analyzing consciousness into its smallest components. He was looking for the basic elements of psychology, the smallest parts of analyzable consciousness. This was analogous to the physicists having, at roughly the same time in history, constructed the atomic table. As physics had its elements, so, too, thought Wundt, would psychology. Wundt felt that by analyzing consciousness into these tiny elements, or "atoms," he could make psychology as respectable a science as physics.

The main thesis of Wundt's work was that these basic elements of the mind are connected through association; that is, the mind is composed of individual elements, or atoms of experience, linked by associations. The problem was to ferret out these elements for study. To accomplish this, Wundt used the technique of **introspection.** He trained subjects to look within themselves and report all their most fleeting and minute feelings and sensations (Wundt, 1910). Both behaviorism and gestalt psychology began in reaction to Wundt; he set the stage for the great controversy to come.

The Gestaltists Attack Wundt

A group of psychologists, led by Max Wertheimer, got together around 1910 at the University of Frankfurt and began the school of psychology known as **gestalt psychology.*** The gestaltists felt that Wundt had led psychology down the primrose path—that in order to produce his neat atomic chart of psychology, Wundt had lost sight of the reality of human experience. They felt that by analyzing experience into its smallest parts, Wundt had, in effect, destroyed the total experience. He was like a musician analyzing each note separately and never hearing the melody. "The whole is more than the sum of its parts," thundered Wertheimer. You must study the whole, the totality, the entire configuration, or, to use the German word, the *Gestalt.* The gestaltists felt that the study of the associations formed between tiny elements, whether they are elements of consciousness or stimuli-response connections, is misleading. It is misleading because elements often act and look differently when they are taken out of context. For example, Wertheimer would say that if you were to study each frame in a motion picture, you would never see movement, which is what a motion picture is all about.

The Behaviorists Attack Wundt

The school of **behaviorism** was born under the impetus of John B. Watson at Johns Hopkins University. The behaviorists attacked Wundt because of his use of introspection as a scientific tool. The behaviorists believed in elements, all right, but they didn't like the way Wundt went about finding them. In the now-classic paper, "Psychology as the Behaviorist Views It," Watson proclaimed that behavior constitutes the real data of psychology (Watson, 1913). According to Watson, introspection is as useless to psychology as it would be to chemistry or physics. The only thing that is really observable and therefore the only thing

that really allows for the use of the scientific method is the subject's overt behavior. Watson also announced to the world what would and what would not be proper areas for psychologists to study. If consciousness can be studied only through introspection, and if it has no behavioral correlates, then throw it out of psychology. As we have seen, Watson was not one to equivocate.

Behaviorists and Gestaltists Attack Each Other

Although these two powerful schools of psychology began by fighting independent battles with Wundt, the scene of battle soon shifted and they began fighting each other. Watson fell in with a powerful ally, Ivan Pavlov, the Russian whose work on the conditioned reflex was being recognized at about the same time Watson was preparing for combat. Watson found just what he needed when he needed it—the conditioned reflex, something observable to replace Wundt's nonobservable elements. Watson soon felt that all learning could be explained on the basis of **conditioning,** that is, the association of stimuli with responses. A new unit of analysis had been found that was both observable and consistent with the principle of association. Watson was ready to take over American psychology, and through his direct influence and through the indirect influence of those who followed—Edwin Guthrie, Clark Hull, E. L. Thorndike, and B. F. Skinner—Watson certainly did manage to shape and direct the course American psychology was to take. Learning was a matter of accumulating a series of stimulus-response associations. There is no need to study insight, or even thinking in the traditional sense, for conditioning pretty much explains it all.

The gestaltists did not agree. Wertheimer, and later Kohler and Lewin, felt that learning could not be dissected into little stimulus-response associations and still be consistent with what they saw as reality. Children could be conditioned ad nauseam, trained to recite the multiplication tables, the state capitals, the major agricultural products of each country—but without insight or real understanding, the information would be virtually useless. According to the gestaltists, if you want children to learn nonsense, go ahead and condition them; but if you want them to learn meaningful relationships, then a different approach is needed—a cognitive approach.

---

* Schools of psychology refer to schools of thought, not specific colleges and universities.

SPOTLIGHT ON
THE EXPERIMENTAL STUDY OF LEARNING

Ebbinghaus the Pioneer

Ebbinghaus hoped to lay the basis for a scientific study of learning by memorizing long lists of nonsense syllables and then measuring his retention capacity. His pioneering research on learning earned him the title of "father of learning psychology."

The experimental study of learning had quiet beginnings. In Germany during the 1880s, **Hermann Ebbinghaus** carried out the first of these studies, and produced pioneering work that eventually earned him the title "father of learning psychology." Because he wanted to study learning in its pure form, he chose to control for the influence of meaningfulness. In order to do this, Ebbinghaus used long lists of nonsense syllables (*cav, lek, pum,* etc.), which he felt allowed him to control for original difficulty. Since so many words have past associations or inherent interest, they might be easier for some people to learn than for others, whereas all lists of nonsense syllables should be of comparable difficulty and would have to be learned from scratch. At first, Ebbinghaus was his own subject, and he spent many long and lonely hours learning these meaningless words. His work led him to draw two major conclusions:

1. Once something is learned, it is not forgotten at an even rate. Most of what is forgotten is lost very quickly, and the rest is lost at a slow and fairly stable rate.
2. In order to learn new material, it is more efficient to space the

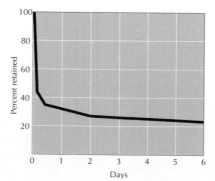

Ebbinghaus's retention curve. Most of the learned material is lost very rapidly and the rest more and more slowly.

practice sessions than to mass them. For example, if you had one hour to learn something, you would retain more by taking four fifteen-minute practice sessions spread over a few days, than by spending one full hour working without a break.[a]

The results of these studies, although interesting to the learning theorist, seemed to have limited practical use in the classroom. Laws governing the learning of meaningless information may not always be directly generalized to the learning of meaningful material. Material learned in the classroom should, of course, be meaningful, although unfortunately students are still made to memorize vocabulary, long passages from poems, and arcane grammatical rules—material that at the time may be no more meaningful to them than were the nonsense syllables to Ebbinghaus.

More recent studies, however, have added considerable strength to Ebbinghaus's contention that several practice sessions well spaced is a more efficient learning strategy, especially when studying vocabulary lists, than is one long massed session.[b]

[a] H. Ebbinghaus, *Memory: A Contribution to Experimental Psychology,* translated by H. A. Rogers and C. E. Bussenius (New York: Teachers College, 1913; originally 1885).
[b] F. N. Dempster, Effects of variable encoding and spaced presentation on vocabulary learning. *Journal of Educational Psychology* (1987), 22, 1–21.

The Associationists versus the Gestaltists

We now turn to a discussion of how the association learning and cognitive learning positions were formed and eventually translated into action. We begin with those theories that dominated the first half of the twentieth century, spotlighting the early associationists Thorndike, Pavlov, and Guthrie, in that order. Watson, though not singled out for independent coverage in this section, is intermittently mentioned in the discussions of the other three. Watson's influence on the early behaviorist-associationist movement was very significant.

The discussion of the early cognitive theorists focuses on Wertheimer and Kohler, two gestaltists who made important contributions to our current knowledge of cognitive learning. In Chapter 9 we examine in some detail the two most influential spokespersons for each position: B. F. Skinner and Jerome Bruner. The present chapter provides a background for appreciating the significance of Skinner and Bruner in education today.

THE EARLY ASSOCIATION THEORISTS

E. L. Thorndike

In 1899 **Edward Lee Thorndike** published a paper entitled "Animal Intelligence" and thereby was catapulted to the forefront of the emerging field of learning psychology. From his headquarters at Columbia Teachers College, Thorndike issued his concepts and laws of learning for many years thereafter. For most of the first half of the twentieth century, he was truly Mr. Educational Psychology in the United States. His studies of cats learning to escape from puzzle boxes are now legendary.

Thorndike viewed learning as a series of stimulus-response (S-R) connections, or bonds. His theory of learning described the ways in which these S-R connections could be strengthened or weakened. He felt that learning was basically a trial-and-error enterprise, and he paid little attention to the possibility of concept formation or thinking (Thorndike, 1898).

The three major laws Thorndike postulated three major laws of learning:

1. **The law of readiness:** When an organism is in a state in which the conduction units (S-R connections) are ready to conduct, then the conduction is satisfying. If the conduction unit is not ready to conduct, then conduction is annoying. Thorndike was speaking here of a brief, neurological readiness, not the kind of maturational readiness that, as we saw in Chapter 4, was of concern to Myrtle McGraw. Thorndike was referring to a more momentary phenomenon, a kind of neurologically teachable moment.

2. **The law of exercise:** This law, also called the law of use and disuse, states that the more an S-R connection is used, the stronger it will become; the less it is used, the weaker it will become. This law is obviously based on the old maxim about practice making perfect. Thorndike, especially in his later writings, made it clear that practice led to improvement only when it was followed by positive feedback or reward. Blind practice, with no knowledge of the consequences of the act, had no effect on learning.

3. **The law of effect:** This was by far Thorndike's most important law. It states that an S-R connection followed by satisfaction (reward) is strengthened. Also, a connection followed by annoyance (punishment) is weakened. In later years Thorndike played down the importance of the second part of the law. In fact, he changed his mind about the significance of punishment as a means of weakening learned associations. He came to feel that reward strengthened learning far more than punishment weakened it. His evidence for changing his position on this issue was, to say the least, rather flimsy. It was based on a study of symbolic reward and punishment, where the reward consisted of saying "Right" to the student and the punishment consisted of saying "Wrong." The results might have been quite different if the reward had been a candy bar and the punishment a mild electric shock.

There is no doubt that Thorndike had a dehumanizing effect on American education. His first work involved the study of how cats solve problems. He saw little basic difference between animal and human learning—never mind the qualitative differences in learning that Piaget insists occur at different periods during human development. Thorndike spread a kind of mechanical-person gospel that viewed animals and children as akin to robots.

His contribution to education, however, cannot be minimized. He was, through his law of effect, the first

Thorndike first stressed the importance of motivation in learning, an aspect overlooked by Ebbinghaus.

psychologist to stress the importance of motivation in learning. When an individual is rewarded for learning, then learning is far more apt to occur. This aspect of learning seems to have been overlooked by Ebbinghaus. Since he was so close to his experiments (he was, after all, his own subject), Ebbinghaus could hardly take note of his own fantastically high motivation. If you have any doubts about the strength of Ebbinghaus's motivation, try spending a few months doing virtually nothing but learning lists of nonsense syllables.

In addition to stressing the importance of motivation in learning, Thorndike also made much of another crucial concept, that of transfer. His law of identical elements specified that the learner is better able to confront new problems if these new problems con-

tain elements similar to those the learner has already mastered. This, after all, is largely what schooling is all about. If we learned how to use an encyclopedia while we were in school, we are more likely now to be able to diagnose what is wrong with our car by looking it up in our owner's manual, or to prepare a gourmet meal from the directions in a cookbook, or to plan an advertising campaign by making use of appropriate library resources. Transfer will be discussed in greater depth in the next chapter.

Ivan Pavlov

The laboratory work of the Russian physiologist **Ivan Pavlov** was of great importance to the study of learning. Though most modern physiological psychologists consider his theory of the neurological process of learning a historical curio, his laboratory techniques and findings are still of great significance. In 1904 Pavlov won the Nobel Prize in medicine for his work on the digestive activity of dogs. His lasting fame, however, resulted from what at the time were incidental and chance observations regarding digestion in his dogs. Pavlov noted that the dogs salivated not only when meal powder was placed directly in their mouths, but also well before that (for example, when they heard the trainer's footsteps coming down the stairs). Pavlov later coined the term "conditioned reflex" to describe his phenomenon (Pavlov, 1927).

A reflex must have an identifiable stimulus that automatically elicits the response, even though no learning has occurred. For example, when a bright light shines directly into a person's eyes, the pupils automatically contract. No learning or training is required for this to occur. Similarly, when food is placed in a dog's mouth, salivation automatically occurs. Reflexes are therefore directly caused by an unconditioned stimulus, much as pulling the trigger of a loaded gun automatically causes the gun to fire.

Pavlov also noted that if a neutral stimulus—one that does not elicit a certain response—is repeatedly paired with an unconditioned stimulus—one that does automatically elicit a certain response—the neutral stimulus will eventually take on the power to elicit the response. This is now called **classical conditioning,** and an example will illustrate. When meat powder is placed directly in a dog's mouth, the dog automatically salivates. This is a reflex action and does not have to be learned. However, if a 2,000-cycle tone is presented immediately before the meat powder is given, the tone soon comes to evoke the salivation. Through association with the meat powder, the tone begins to act as a signal that meat powder will follow, and the dog eventually learns to respond to the signal the same way it used to respond only to the meat powder. Technically, the meat powder is called the **unconditioned stimulus** (UCS), since responding to it does not depend on prior experience or learning. The tone or signal is called the **conditioned stimulus** (CS), since the response to it must be learned. For the same reasons, salivation to the meat powder is called the **unconditioned response** (UCR), and salivating to the tone is called the **conditioned response** (CR).

When John B. Watson studied the acquisition of fear in baby Albert, this was the technique he used (see Chapter 2). When Watson first presented Albert with a white rat, Albert showed no sign of fear. Then Watson struck a steel bar right beside Albert's head, and this loud sound (unconditioned stimulus) automatically made Albert cry (unconditioned response). After repeated pairings of the white rat and the loud sound, Albert began crying as soon as the rat came in view, even when he heard no loud sound. The rat (conditioned stimulus) took on the power to elicit the crying (conditioned response). Note that the conditioned and unconditioned responses are the same: salivation in the case of Pavlov's dogs and crying in the case of Watson's baby. The difference is what brings them about. The conditioned response is one that is elicited by a stimulus that has to be learned through association.

One reason educators must know about conditioning is that a great number of autonomic reflexes can be conditioned while the child is still in school. Just as Albert was conditioned to fear a rat, so the schoolchild may be conditioned to fear math, science, spelling, or any other school subject. Autonomic responses, such as sweating, rapid heartbeat, or general feelings of anxiety, may be conditioned by certain cues that come to be associated with various aspects of the school setting. Children who have been conditioned to such an extent that they are literally paralyzed by fear at the mere sight of a math problem are unlikely to be able to learn much math. They might sincerely try to learn the subject, but because of a great and crippling discomfort, they are not able to.

This is not to say that teachers deliberately create these fears, but they can unwittingly set the stage for such conditioning. For example, a math problem is presented, followed by some other action of the teacher that may already be associated in the child's past experience with feelings of tension, and now the math problem itself triggers autonomic reactions of anxiety on the part of the child. After a few associations of this kind, the mere presentation of the math problem (CS) begins to elicit anxiety (CR). Sometimes this process occurs because teachers themselves have a conditioned fear of math and unwittingly transmit it to their students in the form of scolding, bullying, or a generally "uptight" approach to learning the subject.

Stimulus generalization   Pavlov found that reflex conditioning had some extremely important by-products. For example, once a dog was conditioned to salivate to a 2,000-cycle tone, it would also salivate to a 1,300- or 2,700-cycle tone, even though these new stimuli were never used in training. In other words, once a given conditioned stimulus is associated with a reflex, other similar stimuli also take on the power to elicit the response. This is called **stimulus generalization.** The original conditioned stimulus becomes generalized, and the organism begins responding to other stimuli that are in some way similar to the original one. Once Watson's young subject, Albert, was conditioned to fear the rat, he was also afraid of a Santa Claus mask, a sealskin coat, human hair, a dog, a rabbit, and cotton wool. The point is, reflex conditioning has wide-ranging effects. A child who is conditioned to fear math problems may generalize this fear to many other school subjects, perhaps even the entire school situation. Phobic reactions can be understood in this way. Suppose an unruly child is punished by being locked in a closet. The conditioned stimulus might be generalized so that the child becomes fearful of any enclosed area. The result, claustrophobia, could carry over into adulthood, and the person so afflicted might live a severely restricted life.

Pavlov found that the only way to break the association between a conditioned stimulus and a conditioned response was through a process called **extinction.** Extinction is achieved when the CS loses its power to evoke the CR; it is accomplished by repeatedly presenting the CS without following it with the UCS. If the 2,000-cycle tone is consistently presented without the meat powder, the dog eventually stops salivating when he hears it. It is important to note that for extinction to occur, the conditioned stimulus must be repeatedly presented by itself. Unfortunately, when the conditioned reflex is fear, the afflicted individual naturally avoids the conditioned stimulus, and extinction is never allowed to occur. Joseph Wolpe, a famous psychotherapist, uses techniques of classical conditioning and extinction in treating phobias.

Edwin Guthrie

The last of the early associationists we will cover here is **Edwin Guthrie.** Guthrie was the behaviorist-associationist par excellence. Following directly in Watson's footsteps, he rejected any psychological concepts that might have "mentalistic" overtones. He postulated one law of learning: learning by association or, as he called it, *contiguity.* According to Guthrie, if a certain stimulus (or pattern of stimuli) is followed by a response, then the next time that stimulus appears, the same response will follow.

That's all there is to it—stimuli and responses in sequence. There is no need to call on reward, reinforcement, or "effect" in order to explain how learning occurs. He also believed that learning occurs the first time the stimulus and response become associated (Guthrie, 1935). To create conditions that will promote learning, Guthrie believed that the teacher should provide the stimulus and the student should respond. For example, the teacher might point to a map and the students would then reply with the name of the city. The important thing was for the appropriate stimulus to be presented before the desired response occurred.

A frenzied mother once brought her child to Guthrie. The child had been in the habit, on coming home from school, of opening the door of his home, taking off his coat, and throwing it on the floor. The mother told Guthrie that no matter how many times she told her child to pick up the coat and hang it in the closet, the child continued this behavior. Guthrie did not reach for any deep psychological explanation, like finding out what throwing the coat on the floor symbolized, what it "meant" to the child. He simply told the mother to rearrange the stimulus-response sequence. When the child throws his coat on the floor, he should not be told to hang it up. He should instead be told to put the coat on, go back outside, come through the door and, only then, hang up the coat. Thus hanging up the coat could become a response to the stimulus of entering the house rather than to the stimulus of the mother's command, "Take your coat off the floor and hang it up."

The advice apparently worked, for from then on the child hung up his coat correctly. Fortunately for Guthrie, and especially for the child, a longer sequence of S-R associations did not form. That is, according to Guthrie's system, the child might have forever learned to come home, open the door, throw the coat on the floor, pick it up, put it on, go back outside, come back in, then hang up the coat!

THE EARLY COGNITIVE THEORISTS

Max Wertheimer

Max Wertheimer, as noted earlier, founded the school of psychology called gestaltism, or configurationism. Wertheimer insisted that it was useless to study small parts of psychological concepts, like perception or learning. Studying parts in isolation was unjustified, because changing any single part necessarily changes the whole. Similarly, the whole may remain, even when all the parts have changed. For example, if we play a tune in two different keys, even though the individual notes are different each time, the tune retains its integrity.

Wertheimer was concerned with the way children learn, particularly in school. He was against the use of rote memorization, especially when it so often seemed to be an end in itself. Above all else, he wanted children to achieve understanding, to have insight into the nature of the problem.

Wertheimer explained that there are two kinds of solutions to problems, type A and type B. Type A solutions are those which use originality and insight, whereas type B solutions are those which make use of past associations in a rigid, inappropriate way. Wertherimer used the example of teaching a child how to find the area of a parallelogram (see Figure 8.1).

The child is first taught how to find the area of a rectangle, not by memorizing the formula but by understanding why the formula works. The rectangle is divided into smaller squares, and the child sees that the total area is composed of the number of squares in a row times the number of rows. Wertheimer then cut a parallelogram out of paper and asked the child to determine its area. Some children persisted in multiplying the length times the height, a type B solution. Others used type A solutions, like cutting off one of the triangular ends and fitting it against the other end. At this point, the child had created a rectangle and could correctly utilize the previously learned formula. Another type A solution involved bending the parallelogram into a loop with the two angular ends abutting each other, then making one vertical cut which would also create a rectangle. The children using type A solutions had obviously discovered a real geometric relationship (Wertheimer, 1945).

FIGURE 8.1 Wertheimer's parallelogram problem. Part A shows Wertheimer's way of explaining why the area of a rectangle equals the product of length times width, in this case 16 by 5. Part B shows the parallelogram for which he asked subjects to find the area. Part C shows one person's solution to the problem—cutting off one end, moving it to the other end, and thus converting the parallelogram into a rectangle.

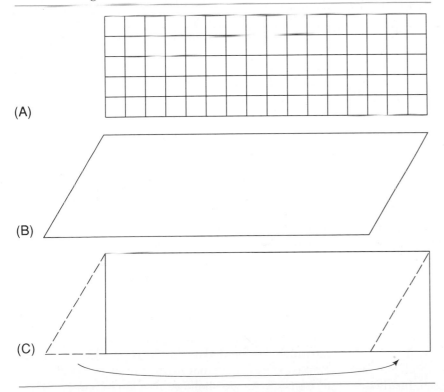

MAX WERTHEIMER

Max Wertheimer was born in Prague in 1880, the son of a schoolteacher. As a student, young Wertheimer's interests were far-ranging. He studied law for a while, then switched to philosophy, and finally began to study psychology. After at-

tending a number of schools and universities, Wertheimer received his Ph.D. degree at Wurzburg in 1904. For the next six years he continued his work in psychology at Prague, Vienna, and Berlin.

Wertheimer had been schooled in the structuralist psychological tradition, which held that all psychological phenomena could be broken down and analyzed into their smallest parts, or elements. In 1910, while traveling by train from Vienna to a Rhineland vacation resort, Wertheimer was suddenly struck by an idea. He began to ponder this structuralistic viewpoint, and the more he pondered, the more he doubted. Suddenly he decided to forget his planned vacation and left the train at Frankfurt. He rushed to the nearest toy store and purchased a child's stroboscope. This was in the days before motion pictures, and a stroboscope was a device that, when turned at a constant speed, exposed

a series of still pictures that appeared to move. In his hotel room Wertheimer examined his new purchase. He spun the stroboscope, fascinated by the apparent movement that the device produced, and in one of the history of psychology's great examples of insight, thought, "Aha, Wundt and the structuralists must be wrong." Here was a psychological perception, apparent movement, which simply could not be explained or understood by analyzing the individual still pictures. When the elements of this perception were studied individually, the total phenomenon of perceived movement was lost. The whole must be more than just the sum of its parts. In order to understand this perception of movement, one had to study all the parts together in their particular *Gestalt,* a German word that means "whole," or "totality," or "configuration."

Wertheimer went to the Univer-

Wolfgang Kohler

Wolfgang Kohler, like Koffka, had also worked with Wertheimer at Frankfurt. Later, however, during World War I, he spent several years on the island of Tenerife, off the coast of Africa. There he performed gestalt psychology's most famous animal studies. Kohler arranged an ape's cage so that there were bananas hanging from the top and a couple of boxes on the floor. In order to reach the bananas, the ape had to stack one box on top of another and then climb to the top. The ape's solution to the problem appeared to Kohler not to be one of blind trial and error. Instead, the ape seemed to size up the situation and then, almost in a flash, it understood the problem and "saw" the solution. The ape displayed what Kohler called **insight,** and Kohler felt that this was more typical of learning, especially human learning, than Thorndike's concept of blind trial and error.

In another experiment, Kohler put food outside the cage, beyond even an ape's long reach. Inside the

cage, however, there were some sticks. At first the apes would throw the sticks at the banana. Then they "realized" that by using the stick as a kind of tool they could reach out and rake the banana in. One especially intelligent ape, named Sultan, was even able to join two short sticks together to rake the food in.

Kohler's explanation was that the apes were able to see the problem as a unified whole. In the box-stacking problem, the ape did not see the boxes and bananas as separate elements but came to realize that they belonged together as part of a whole. Similarly, the sticks and bananas were perceived as belonging together, and it was only after this reorganization of perceptions that insight into the solution to the problem occurred.

Insight has been called the "a-ha" phenomenon. Kohler made much of the concept of insight, perhaps too much. He felt that insight learning did not depend on past experience, that it was not just a special case of transfer. As we shall see in a later chapter, Harry

sity of Frankfurt and began a series of controlled experiments. His first subject was Wolfgang Kohler, who was later joined by Kurt Koffka. Early in 1912 Wertheimer explained to Kohler and Koffka the results and meaning of his studies. Gestalt psychology had been born. Both Kohler and Koffka became zealous advocates of this new school of thought, and both went on to produce many experiments, articles, and books in support of it. Both became famous gestalt psychologists in their own right.

In 1912 Wertheimer published his now famous article, "Experimental Studies of the Perception of Movement." As a result of this single revolutionary article, a tremendous new movement in psychology was under way, and thousands of articles and books were written and are still being written on this important subject.

In 1916 Wertheimer joined the faculty at the University of Berlin, where he worked with another soon-to-be-famous gestalt psychologist, Kurt Lewin. In 1933 Wertheimer came to the United States, where he taught at the New School for Social Research in New York City. He remained at the New School until his death in 1943.

Wertheimer was a man with a cause, but he was not arrogant or authoritarian. He was a gentle, warm, deep-thinking man. He had a close personal relationship with Albert Einstein, and he was deeply concerned with the social and ethical issues of his times.

Wertheimer was also interested in education and the techniques of good teaching. He pointed out the importance of gestalt principles as they apply to learning in the classroom. He criticized the use of repetition and rote memorization, explaining that such procedures lead only to blind, nonproductive learning on the part of students. He insisted that educators should teach for understanding and that understanding is made possible when the teacher arranges the material so that the student can see the "whole," or the *Gestalt*, and not just a series of seemingly unrelated parts. In his book *Productive Thinking*, Wertheimer stressed the importance of gestalt theory in the practical problem of educating children.

Whereas Watson and Guthrie were concerned with overt responses, stressing always what the student *did*, Wertheimer placed his emphasis on the child's process of mental organization, stressing instead what the student *understood*.

Today the Wertheimer tradition lives on. His son Michael, also a distinguished psychologist, has served as president of four different APA divisions, is currently teaching at the University of Colorado, and in 1991 was presented with the APA's prestigious award for "distinguished education and training contributions."

Harlow's studies on learning sets have since cast some doubt on the validity of Kohler's interpretation.

Recently, not only has Kohler's interpretation been challenged, but also his motivation. An American psychology professor, Ronald Ley, visited the island of Tenerife in hopes of finding the ape research station where Kohler first conducted his classic experiments during World War I. He uncovered instead the long-kept secret that while doing his learning studies on apes, Kohler may have also been engaged in a far more dangerous activity—that of wartime spying for Germany, using his laboratory as a cover for espionage activity (Ley, 1990).

NEW DIRECTIONS IN PSYCHOLOGY AND EDUCATION

You may now be wondering why nobody tried to bridge the gap between the two learning theory traditions, for both positions evidently have some merit.

The behaviorists did have a strong case for insisting that overt responses are the appropriate data for psychology. If you were trying to judge people's attitudes toward some issue, you would, in all probability, be more influenced by what they did than by what they said. For example, if your boss constantly bragged of being an equal opportunity employer and yet never hired black applicants, you might rightly feel that "actions speak louder than words."

Yet you probably feel equally sure that the gestaltists also had a good case; learning, understanding, discovering new relationships must be more than just the mere conditioning of certain responses. Some reorganization of perceptions, something going on within the organism, must account for understanding and discovery.

In fact, some psychologists did attempt to bridge the gap. **E. C. Tolman,** for example, produced a theory called *purposive behaviorism*. It was called purposive because Tolman insisted that, far from being random and chaotic, learning was goal-directed. The

SPOTLIGHT ON KURT KOFFKA

Gestalt's Foreshadowing of Modern Cognitive Psychology

Kurt Koffka, who had worked under Wertheimer at the University of Frankfurt, extended many of his mentor's ideas and produced a theory that in this age of the cognitive revolution has an extraordinarily modern ring. He talked about learning as resulting from what he called the *memory process,* which is the brain activity that accompanies incoming stimulation. Thus, an environmental experience produces a memory trace that can be permanently etched in the mind of the learner.[a] As Koffka saw it, the brain could carry an internal representation of the stimulus information, a phenomenon that is today called *encoding.* (See Chapter 11.) The various traces, resulting from the myriad of similar experiences that occur over time, form interrelated aggregates, or internal gestalts, that come to govern both our perceptions and our continued learning. These interrelated traces, called by Koffka *trace systems,* allow the child to become an increasingly more efficient problem solver. For example, the child may develop trace systems that correspond to a class of objects or events, such as books, cars, games, boys, girls, and so on. As learning expert B. R. Hergenhahn says of Koffka,

These trace systems will be a kind of neurological summation of all our experiences with objects in a certain class, such as cows, or clowns. . . . If we look at an individual elephant, the process aroused by that elephant will be influenced by the trace system that resulted from all our other experiences with elephants. The resulting experience will be a combination of the two influences, with the trace system being the most important. Our memory of that event, then, will be one of "elephantness" that has little to do with any particular elephant but has more to do with what they have in common."[b]

As we shall see in Chapter 11, this is virtually identical with what the current cognitive psychologists are calling *concept formation,* or the *schema.* The point of all this is that the gestaltists viewed the learner as not just a repository of discrete stimulus-response associations, but as the beneficiary of abstractions and learning strategies that allow for the development of higher levels of reasoning and learning.

(For a more complete discussion of the Koffka system, see Hergenhahn's *An Introduction to Theories of Learning,* 1988).

---

[a] K. Koffka, *Principles of Gestalt Psychology* (New York: Harcourt Brace, 1935).

[b] B. R. Hergenhahn, *An Introduction to Theories of Learning* (Englewood Cliffs, N.J.: Prentice-Hall, 1988), p. 267.

---

learning organism is a striving organism, striving to give meaning to behavior. Yet Tolman's theory was also behavioristic because he believed that scientific validity could be achieved only by observing objective behavior.

Tolman stated that both rats and humans learn by forming cognitive maps of their environment (Tolman, 1948). This explains how organisms get from place to place. They form hypotheses, see relationships, and then select out appropriate responses on the basis of their cognitive maps. Although Tolman did not emphasize stimulus-response connections as the basic units of analysis, he was still an associationist because he saw learning as a result of bonds formed among a number of stimuli. The learner forms an association between some new stimulus, or sign, and a previously encountered and therefore meaningful stimulus, or "significate." Tolman's behaviorism is therefore an S-S (sign-significate) psychology, rather than a Watsonian S-R psychology.

Tolman was more responsive to the work of the developmental psychologists than were most of the behaviorists. He postulated his famous H-A-T-E variables (heredity, age, training, endocrine) as of crucial importance in understanding and predicting behavior. Heredity sets certain limits on what environmental manipulation can accomplish. Age determines how much impact training can have. Training is, of course, vital, since learning cannot occur in a static environment. Endocrine, or internal physiological, factors also play an important role in learning. Thus Tolman, perhaps more than any other learning theorist, understood the importance of individual differences. Recent studies, such as those reported by Mark

SPOTLIGHT ON THE STUDY OF LEARNING

The All-Time "Greats"

The importance that psychologists have attached to the study of learning can be seen in the results of a poll recently conducted among psychology's historians to name the all-time greats in their field.[a] The results were as follows:

Rank	Individual
1	Wundt
2	James
3	Freud
4	Watson
5	Pavlov
6	Ebbinghaus
7	Piaget
8	Skinner
9	Binet
10	Fechner

Notice that among the elite top ten, six of the psychologists—James, Watson, Pavlov, Ebbinghaus, Piaget, and Skinner—that were selected by the experts are primarily identified with the study of learning. Even the remaining four—Wundt, Freud, Binet, and Fechner—all spent some time addressing the issue of learning.

[a] J. H. Korn, R. Davis, and S. F. Davis, Historians' and chairpersons' judgments of eminence among psychologists. *American Psychologist* (1991), 46, 789–792.

Rosenzweig, have shown how strong the relationship is between environmental and training variables and the internal physiology of the organism (Rosenzweig, 1984). And in many ways the ensuing years have been kind to Tolman's position. It is now known that rats and other animals have far more flexibility in making choices and solving problems than could be explained by the orthodox Watsonian and Pavlovian models of straight S-R conditioning (Domjan, 1987).

With all its sophistication and thoroughness, Tolman's system never really caught on in education. Tolman never exerted the influence on teachers that Thorndike or Watson did. Though he may be rediscovered in the next decade, and in the long run may have more influence than Thorndike, that is not yet the case.

Why was Tolman so ignored by the field of education during his lifetime? There are a number of reasons, but it is primarily because he never translated theory into practice. The teacher might learn from Tolman that a rat at a choice point in a maze hypothesizes a solution before acting, but this hardly helps the teacher in the classroom. The teacher wants answers to specific questions regarding learning and discipline in the classroom, not sophisticated and elegant theorizing. Further, Tolman failed to develop his theory to its fullest potential. He didn't do enough experiments to make his cognitive position firm enough to generate precise predictions. As Winfred Hill, a modern expert in the field of learning, has said of Tolman, "His system is more a road sign or a pious hope than it is an accomplished fact" (Hill, 1971).

And so educational psychology turned away from the old-line theorists and turned toward psychology's "new breed" theorists, psychologists who talked to teachers, who told teachers what to do in given situations, who told teachers how to produce desired behavior changes or set up conditions that aid discovery. Educational psychology turned to B. F. Skinner and Jerome Bruner.

SUMMARY

The study of learning has been of utmost importance in psychology for over a century. Though psychologists agreed on the importance of learning as an object of study, they disagreed on the mechanics of how the learning process occurred.

The major schools of thought were

1. *Behaviorist-associationists:* Those who viewed learning as resulting from the forming of connections between stimuli and observable responses.
2. *Cognitive-gestaltists:* Those who believed that learning resulted from the reorganization of perceptions and the forming of new relationships.

Both the behaviorists and the gestaltists began their schools of thought as reactions to Wundt's associationist-introspectionist brand of psychology. The gestaltists, led by Wertheimer, challenged Wundt's associationist position, while the behaviorists, led by Watson, attacked Wundt's use of introspection.

Wertheimer and the gestaltists argued that psychological phenomena could not be understood by studying simple associations among tiny elements but must be viewed as a total configuration or, to use the German word, as a *Gestalt*. Wertheimer argued that the whole is more than just the sum of a group of separate parts. Learning was seen as the understanding of a total, meaningful relationship, and the only acceptable approach to the study of learning was a cognitive one. Watson and the behaviorists, although not objecting to the study of separate parts, did denounce Wundt's use of introspection. Watson argued that the only true scientific data in the field of psychology were observable responses. Thus, if a concept such as consciousness could not be seen, touched, or observed in any way, it should be thrown out of psychology. Watson believed that learning could be thoroughly understood on the basis of Pavlov's principles of classical conditioning.

The first experimental studies of learning were conducted by Ebbinghaus during the late nineteenth century. In order to control for past associations, Ebbinghaus studied the learning of nonsense syllables. He discovered that the forgetting of learned material does not occur at an even rate, that most of what is forgotten occurs very quickly, and that the rate of forgetting eventually slows down to a fairly even pace.

Thorndike, an early associationist, posited three major laws of learning: (1) the law of readiness, showing the importance of neurological anticipation; (2) the law of exercise, showing the importance of practice; and (3) the law of effect, indicating the importance of motivation.

Pavlov, a Russian psychologist, discovered some lawful relationships between stimuli and responses. He showed how learning could take place through conditioning, a trained association among stimuli and a certain response. Pavlov's system is now called classical conditioning and applies only to reflex activity. Pavlov also introduced such concepts as extinction, stimulus generalization, and discrimination learning.

Guthrie, a psychologist in the behaviorist-associationist tradition, felt that all learning was a result of stimuli and responses in sequence. Guthrie saw no need to use concepts such as motivation or reinforcement to explain learning.

Wertheimer, the first of the cognitive-gestalt psychologists, was concerned with how the learner achieved understanding and insight when confronted with a problem. He felt that rote memorization did not lead to real understanding.

Kohler, also of the cognitive-gestalt school, performed several important animal studies. Kohler's studies on apes led him to conclude that learning was a result of a series of insightful solutions, not blind trial and error.

Tolman attempted to bridge the gap between behaviorists and gestaltists by creating a type of psychology called purposive behaviorism. Tolman thought that striving toward a goal gave meaning to the resulting behavior. Learning occurs when a new stimulus (or sign) is associated with a previously encountered and therefore meaningful stimulus (significate).

The two basic positions, behaviorist-associationist and cognitive-gestaltist, have their contemporary proponents in B. F. Skinner and Jerome Bruner. Skinner (the behaviorist) and Bruner (the cognitive theorist) are especially important in educational psychology today, for each devotes a great deal of time to talking directly to the classroom teacher.

KEY TERMS AND NAMES

behaviorism
Hermann Ebbinghaus
gestalt psychology
Edwin Guthrie
Kurt Koffka
Wolfgang Kohler
  insight

learning
  association learning
  cognitive learning
  stimulus-response learning
Ivan Pavlov
  classical conditioning
  conditioned response

KEY TERMS AND NAMES (Cont.)

conditioned stimulus
conditioning
extinction
stimulus generalization
unconditioned response
unconditioned stimulus
Edward L. Thorndike

law of effect
law of exercise
law of readiness
E. C. Tolman
Max Wertheimer
Wilhelm Wundt
  introspection

THEORY INTO PRACTICE: LEARNING BACKGROUNDS—FOCUSING YOUR THINKING

Exercise A

A more complete understanding of the historical roots of current views of the learning process can be facilitated by adopting a more focused approach to these background issues. As we pointed out in the chapter, the two major precursors of today's positions are the behaviorist-associationist and the cognitive-gestaltist theories. Both carry other theoretical positions with them, and these may help illuminate the differences between the two contemporary viewpoints. For example, as was stated back in Chapter 2, the behaviorist-associationists tended to ally themselves with the blank-slate position of John Locke, whereas the cognitive-gestaltists felt strongly that the neonate came into the world equipped with some biological givens.

Using the foregoing distinctions, indicate whether the following psychologists would tend more toward explaining behavior on the basis of nature or of nurture:

1. Wertheimer

2. Watson

3. Kohler

4. Guthrie

5. Tolman

Exercise B

Thorndike insisted that learning occurred as a result of the formation of stimulus-response connections in one direction. If, for example, you were studying a foreign language by first being presented with the

foreign word (stimulus) to which you were then to respond with the English word, the learned association would go largely in that direction, that is, you would then find it difficult to reverse the association and respond with the foreign word when the English word was given as the stimulus. For example, try learning the following paired associates by looking first at the German word and then repeating the English word:

GERMAN	ENGLISH
1. Sagenhaft	Mythical
2. Ruckzug	Retreat
3. Klug	Clever
4. Jux	Fun
5. Heikel	Tricky
6. Funken	Radio
7. Fremd	Strange
8. Adler	Eagle
9. Antwort	Answer
10. Ubel	Nasty

Once you feel you know the words well enough to go through the list with few if any errors, try reversing the process. While covering the column of German words, read the English word and attempt to respond by giving the German word. You will find, as Thorndike suggested, that this is not an easy task. Hence, Thorndike felt that he had explained why children who have learned the alphabet from A to Z find it virtually impossible to repeat it backward. If you don't believe him, try it yourself! Or try repeating the Pledge of Allegiance backward.

The cognitive gestaltists, however, believe that we

learn not just on the basis of an S-R sequence, but, instead, as a result of forming a new whole that has an underlying coherence and meaning. That is, Wertheimer believed that rather than learn unidirectional relationships between items, we actually learn on the basis of whole units.

How might Wertheimer explain why we are apparently able to learn the German-English sequence in only one direction at a time, or why we have great difficulty repeating the alphabet backward?

Exercise C

As we have seen, Wertheimer argued that a child who knows how to find the area of a rectangle by multiplying its base by its altitude may have great trouble trying to apply that type B solution when a parallelogram is substituted for the rectangle. Wertheimer felt that the child who used a type A solution, however, could easily solve the problem by creatively snipping off the triangular ends of the parallelogram and then attaching these leftovers in such a way as to recreate the rectangle (see page 219).

How might Thorndike show that his theory of learning is still needed in explaining how a child might attain the numerical solution to the parallelogram problem? How might Wertheimer reply?

Exercise D

Ebbinghaus, the father of the experimental study of learning, produced evidence that indicated how quickly we forget what we've just learned (see page 214). To some, the Ebbinghaus data have been used to suggest that learned material is extremely fragile, so fragile, in fact, that much of what a child learns in school will have largely disappeared soon after it has been learned.

Let's use the Ebbinghaus approach and by so doing gain, we hope, a more focused view of this seeming dilemma.

Take the following list of nonsense syllables and try to commit them to memory: *MUM, WEN, SED, HOM, DOD, HUR, WUZ, FON, CAM, TEL, SIK, PAM, UND*. Once you feel you have it, wait about an hour (without using the time to rehearse) and then see how many of the thirteen syllables you can recall. Write the number down. If you're like most people, your recall even after as short a time interval as one hour will be severely limited.

Now let's rearrange the list of syllables and present them as follows: *PAM, CAM, HOM, WEN, HUR, MUM, TEL, FON, UND, SED, DOD, WUZ, SIK*. Next, read the following sentence: Pam came home when her mom telephoned and said dad was sick. Rehearse the sentence for a few minutes and try again to list all thirteen syllables. You should discover that your recall has dramatically increased. Wait an hour, and try again. Write down the number of syllables you correctly remembered, and compare this with the number you had previously written down.

Why has the rearrangement of the syllables and the accompanying sentence aided you in preserving the content of the list?

Model Answers

Exercise A   (1) Nature, (2) nurture, (3) nature, (4) nurture, (5) both nature and nurture.

Notice in this section that in order to answer the items correctly you needed an underlying understanding of the differences between the behaviorist-associationists and the cognitive-gestaltists. However, you also needed a background of facts in order to determine which psychologist represented which view. In this case, as in most learning situations, the background of facts and the deeper understanding form a reciprocal relationship. You need some facts to reach understanding, and with understanding the facts themselves become more organized and easier to recall.

Exercise B   Wertheimer as well as other cognitive-gestaltists might suggest that these tasks were rigged in order to validate answers that the behaviorist-associationist had already deduced. For example, it is of course easier to produce the English word as a response to the German word. The English word is already an integral part of your working response repertoire. It is always easier to produce a verbal response you already possess than one that is not in your vocabulary. Also, the alphabet has no coherent unity to begin with. There is no opportunity in such a task to utilize the principles of understanding or insight. The alphabet has no more internal coherence than would be found in a list of digits drawn from a random number table.

Exercise C   Thorndike might argue that no matter how creatively you cut up the parallelogram, if you didn't possess the ability to multiply, learned largely through associative conditioning, you would have great difficulty applying the creative solution in such a way as to correctly calculate the area. Wertheimer would then add that even if learning to multiply was originally based on type B conditioning, the number facts inherent in multiplication will become far more meaningful, and thus easier to recall, when they are used in producing type A solutions.

Exercise D The rearrangement of the list in such a way as to conform to the sequence of words in the sentence increased your ability *both* to commit the syllables to memory and to retain them for future use. Thus, although the Ebbinghaus forgetting curve may be valid for nonsense syllables that remain non-

sensical, once the syllables are given even the slightest hint of meaning, the learning becomes far more long-lasting. As a teacher you should remember this lesson well. Presenting facts (names, dates, mathematical operations, etc.) in the absence of any underlying schema or theme forces the pupil to operate at the level of Ebbinghaus and his nonsense syllables. The pupils may seem to learn the material, but sometime in the near future—the next hour, the next day—the learning will be gone. It will be like the Ebbinghaus forgetting curve, a figurative case of in one ear and out the other. If, however, you can weave these facts into an overall unified structure, a structure that allows the pupil to reach some degree of understanding (the more the better), the material may become truly consolidated into a coherent whole that could possibly last a lifetime.

REFERENCES

Alper, J. (1986). Our dual memory. *Science 86* (July–August), 44–49.

Dempster, F. N. (1987). Effects of variable encoding and spaced presentation on vocabulary learning. *Journal of Educational Psychology, 22,* 1–21.

Domjan, M. (1987). Animal learning comes of age. *American Psychologist, 42,* 556–564.

Ebbinghaus, H. (1913, originally 1885). *Memory: A contribution to experimental psychology,* trans. by H. A. Ruger and C. E. Bussenius. New York: Teachers College.

Guthrie, E. R. (1935). *The psychology of learning.* New York: Harper.

Hergenhahn, B. R. (1988). *An introduction to theories of learning.* Englewood Cliffs, N.J.: Prentice-Hall.

Hill, W. F. (1971). *Learning: A survey of psychological interpretations* (p. 129). Scranton, Pa.: Chandler.

James, W. (1890). *The principles of psychology* (pp. 79, 83). New York: Henry Holt.

Koffka, K. (1935). *Principles of gestalt psychology.* New York: Harcourt-Brace.

Korn, J. H., Davis, R., and Davis, S. F. (1991). Historians' and chairpersons' judgments of eminence among psychologists. *American Psychologist, 46,* 789–792.

Ley, R. (1990). *A whisper of espionage.* Garden City Park, N.Y.: Avery.

Pavlov, I. P. (1927). *Conditioned reflexes.* London: Oxford University Press.

Rosenzweig, M. R. (1984). Experience, memory and the brain. *American Psychologist, 39,* 365–376.

Thorndike, E. L. (1898). Animal intelligence. *Psychological Review, Monograph Supplement, 2,* No. 8.

Tolman, E. C. (1948). Cognitive maps in rats and men. *Psychological Review, 55,* 1–4.

Watson, J. B. (1913). Psychology as the behaviorist views it. *Psychological Review, 20,* 158–177.

Wertheimer, M. (1945). *Productive thinking.* New York: Harper.

Wundt, W. (1910). *Physiological psychology* (5th ed.). New York: Macmillan.

9

LEARNING
THEORY
TODAY

Now that we have had a look at some of the positions learning theorists have taken over the years, you may be questioning whether there is anything in all these theories for you, the future classroom teacher. If the study of learning is so complicated as to have generated so many different and often conflicting explanations, how can the prospective teacher begin to understand the learning process, let alone stand up in front of a roomful of children and help them learn? Is the study of learning really as complicated as the controversies that we have outlined seem to indicate?

Part of the reason that there are so many theoretical positions is that learning means so many different things to so many different people: a child memorizing a poem, a rat finding its way through a maze, a baby trying to imitate an adult saying bye-bye, a consumer choosing one brand of toothpaste over another, a teenage boy fearing and thus avoiding all contact sports, a young geometry student suddenly seeing the solution to a difficult problem, and on and on. Almost all our thoughts and behavior have been learned. Learning may be adaptive or maladaptive, conscious or unconscious, overt or covert. Feelings and attitudes are learned just as certainly as facts and skills. Learning means so many different things that

controversies sometimes result merely because different theorists are studying different aspects of learning. Like the blind men feeling the elephant, each theorist describes only that part with which he or she happens to come in contact. And yet, our present knowledge of learning is neither so incomplete nor so complicated that the classroom teacher can't profit from it. There are scientific principles of learning that can be translated into classroom use in order to make learning more efficient and productive.

In this chapter the spotlight falls on two important theorists, B. F. Skinner and Jerome Bruner. Each has a dramatically different philosophical lineage: Skinner, until his death in 1990, was still the most important behaviorist-associationist, and Bruner has been considered the most influential cognitive-gestaltist. In fact, it was Bruner's foresight, back in 1960 when he set up the Center for Cognitive Studies, that set the stage for the important new work in learning called *information processing*. Also, both Skinner and Bruner have had a great deal to say to the practicing classroom teacher.

Part of the problem in the past was that some learning theorists were of virtually no help to the educator. It may have been glorious to contemplate

BURRHUS FREDERICK SKINNER

B. F. Skinner was born in Pennsylvania, in 1904; his father was a lawyer. Young Skinner attended the local schools, graduating from high school in 1922. He was a quiet child, and was known for not having much to say. He then went to Hamilton College in New York, where he majored in English, not psychology. During his senior year in college, Skinner had written some poetry, which he sent to Robert Frost for comment and evaluation. Frost's response was so flattering that, following college graduation, Skinner took time out to do what he felt would be some serious writing. He was not pleased with the result. Said Skinner of this experience, "I discovered the unhappy fact that I had nothing to say, and so I went on to do graduate study in psychology, hoping to remedy that shortcoming." And remedy it he apparently did, for Skinner was not at a loss for something to say for the rest of his life.

The young Skinner showed an early interest in utopian societies. He had been born only a short distance from where Joseph Smith had written the *Book of Mormon,* and as a young man he had read *Walden Pond*—Thoreau's classic gem about getting away from the world as it is and creating a world of one's own.

In 1928 Skinner entered Harvard, where he found himself attracted to the ideas of John B. Watson. Watson, though not at Harvard himself, was very influential in American psychology at that time. Skinner pursued a degree in experimental psychology and received his Ph.D. in 1931. He remained at Harvard under various research fellowships until the fall of 1936. At this time he joined the faculty at the University of Minnesota, where he stayed until after World War II. During the war Skinner participated in an extremely provocative government research project, the results of which were not made public until 1959. He had been conditioning pigeons to pilot missiles and torpedoes. The pigeons were so highly trained that he said they could guide a missile right down into the smokestack of a naval destroyer.

In 1945 Skinner went to the University of Indiana as chairman of the psychology department, a job he held until 1948. During this time he developed the now-famous "air crib," a soundproof, air-conditioned, germ-free, glass-enclosed box for raising children in a scientifically controlled environment. One of his daughters, Deborah, spent much of her first two years of life in an air crib. Skinner later attempted to market the box as the "Heir Conditioner," but the device was not widely acclaimed by the mothers of America. Skinner's grandiose plans for mass-producing the box were quietly dropped. Deborah was also toilet trained by another of Skinner's contraptions—a music box that was placed inside the toilet and played the "Blue Danube" whenever it got wet.

In 1948 Skinner was appointed to the faculty at Harvard, and from his command post in Cambridge he influenced a whole generation of students in the experimental study of learning. In order to study learning among rats and pigeons, he developed the experimental chamber, or as it is now affectionately called, the "Skinner box." This device has enabled American psychologists to study animal responses with a precision and ease never before possible. While the animal is in the chamber, its every movement can be recorded and made ready for analysis by automated equipment.

the elegance of Clark Hull's "oscillation of reaction potential" or Kenneth Spence's paper on the transposition controversy, but neither gave much comfort to the teacher trying to find out why Johnny couldn't read.

This chapter focuses on the theories of Skinner and Bruner. Another important theoretical model of learning, information processing, will be covered in Chapter 11.

B. F. SKINNER AND RESPONSE ANALYSIS

No psychologist ever dominated American behaviorism to the extent that **B. F. Skinner** still does today. John B. Watson commented that behavior is the data of psychology and thought that responses, not conscious experience, should be studied and analyzed. Skinner wholeheartedly agreed, and in 1938 with the

After visiting his daughter's arithmetic class in elementary school, Skinner became extremely interested in educational psychology. He says of that visit that he had been witness to "minds being destroyed." He felt that human beings should be trained in much the same fashion as the rats and pigeons that he had conditioned in his lab. Children, too, could be conditioned, step by step, each correct response followed by reinforcement, until they acquired complex forms of behavior. He developed and tested his first "teaching machine" in the 1950s and as a result has been credited with creating a revolution in the technology of education. Many teachers saw the teaching machine, or programmed instruction, as a threat to their jobs. Skinner took great pains to assure teachers that programmed instruction is a learning aid, not a substitute teacher. He has also assured educators that the children trained with this device will not become mechanized little robots but instead will be more likely to reach their intellectual potential.

Skinner's division of the learning process into operant responses and reinforcing stimuli also led to the development of behavior modification techniques in the classroom. Under this system, teachers are trained to wait for their students to emit appropriate responses and then to reinforce these responses speedily and consistently. Behavior modification is the second revolution in teaching technology attributed to Skinner.

Skinner was a most prolific researcher and writer. His books and papers are far too numerous to summarize here, but his best-known works are *The Behavior of Organisms* (1938); *Walden Two*, a novel about a utopian society where everyone's behavior is shaped according to conditioning principles (1948); *Science and Human Behavior* (1953); *Verbal Behavior* (1957); *Schedules of Reinforcement* (1957); *The Technology of Teaching* (1968); and *Beyond Freedom and Dignity* (1971). Skinner also wrote a lively autobiography, *Particulars of My Life* (1976), in which he discusses many of the intimate details of his life history. This was followed (1979) by a second autobiographical account, *The Shaping of a Behaviorist*.

Skinner, of course, will be remembered as an avowed behaviorist in the tradition of J. B. Watson, and is now recognized as having been America's most important and honored behaviorist psychologist. Skinner died in August 1990, only days after having addressed the APA's national convention in Boston. He may have been a quiet child, coming in like the proverbial lamb, but at age 86 he went out like a lion. During this final address, he soared to new heights of scornful derision as he castigated psychology's new emphasis on cognitive psychology. Said Skinner:

So far as I am concerned, cognitive science is the *creationism of psychology*. It is an effort to reinstate that inner initiating-originating-creative self or mind which, in a scientific analysis, simply does not exist. I think this association [here referring to the APA] has been through a recent trial just because of this difference. It has, as you know, suffered a secession by cognitive psychologists who are unhappy when they associate with so many practitioners. And I would regard it not as a secession, *but as an improvement*. I think it is time for psychology as a profession and as a science to realize that the science which will be most helpful is not cognitive science searching for the inner mind or self, but selection by consequences represented by behavioral analysis.[a]

On August 10, 1990, in a final tribute, the American Psychological Association, presented Skinner with a citation for his outstanding lifetime contribution to psychology. And shortly after Skinner's death, the president of the APA called Skinner "the greatest contemporary psychologist . . . whose contributions helped shape modern psychology and who continued decade after decade to refine and develop his powerful concepts."[b]

---

[a] *A.P.A. Monitor* (1990), 21, 6.
[b] R. D. Fowler, In memoriam, *American Psychologist* (1990), 45, 1203.

publication of his *Behavior of Organisms*, he outlined a system of response analysis that was far more thorough and detailed than anything ever seen before. Although behaviorists were already preoccupied with response analysis up through the mid-1930s, Skinner's arrival changed this preoccupation to a near obsession. To the Skinnerians, every little squiggle on the cumulative recorder may be fraught with profound significance.

Skinner's work is not concerned with what goes on inside the organism, the organism's motivational or emotional state, or even its neurology. Skinner's psychology is an "empty organism" psychology, a psychology of environmental conditions (stimuli) associating with and affecting the organism's response repertoire.

To Skinner, the mind (or, in fact, any internal factor) is irrelevant to an understanding of why people behave as they do. Skinner's line of descent, back through Watson, Thorndike, and the other early associationists, is clear and direct. He views *learning* as an association between stimuli (S) and responses (R), although not always in that order. He emphasizes R-S associations as much as S-R associations; that is, he has found that conditioning takes place when a response is followed by a reinforcing stimulus.

Skinnerian psychology is based on a totally environmental view of behavior. Since the consequences of a response influence further action and since these consequences occur in the outer environment, it is the environment that causes changes in behavior. All that a person does, or even can do in the future, is a direct result of that person's own unique history of reinforcements and punishments. This is essentially Skinner's "theme song."

Throughout our discussion of Skinner's system, we focus on the conditioning of rats and pigeons. Although his data were derived primarily from work with these animals, Skinner's findings are, nonetheless, relevant to education. Many of his results have also been found valid when classroom children became the experimental subjects. A fairly thorough knowledge of Skinner is essential to the classroom teacher, for as we shall see later, Skinner believes that his techniques do work in the classroom just as surely as in the aseptic confines of the Skinner box.

Reinforcement

Skinner picked up the behaviorist-associationist tradition about where Thorndike left off. You may recall that one of Thorndike's three major laws of learning was the law of effect, which stated that learning is an association between a stimulus and a response as a result of the *consequences* of an act. If the S-R sequence is followed by a satisfying state of affairs, the association is strengthened; that is, learning takes place.

Skinner borrowed the law of effect, streamlined it somewhat, and called it **reinforcement.** Thorndike had spent considerable time defending his law of effect against the charge that it was subjective and mentalistic (a charge leveled by behaviorists who were even more tough-minded than Thorndike). Skinner's concept of reinforcement needs no such defense. He totally stripped his concept of any subjective or mentalistic overtones. Reinforcement neither offers a reward nor creates a feeling of satisfaction in the learner. Reinforcement, like all of Skinner's

concepts, is defined strictly in operational terms, that is, in terms of the way it is observed or measured. Thus, a **positive reinforcement** is any stimulus that, when added to the situation, increases the likelihood that the response will occur. Similarly, a **negative reinforcement** is any stimulus that, when removed from the situation, increases the probability that the response will occur. That is all there is to it. There is no mention of subjective feelings, only a description of the observed events. If a pellet of food is a positive reinforcer to a hungry rat, it is only because the rat pressed a lever to get another pellet. Reinforcement is defined as something that is observed to increase the likelihood of a response's recurring. Skinner is no hedonist basing his concepts on the search for pleasure but an objectivist defining his concepts in operational terms.

Please notice that Skinner insists that reinforcement *always* strengthens learning, whether the reinforcement is positive or negative. The response rate always increases following a reinforcing stimulus, otherwise it is simply not considered a reinforcer. Think of positive reinforcement in terms of a plus sign (+), that is, a stimulus which is "added" to the situation, like adding a pellet of food when the lever is pressed. Think of a negative reinforcer in terms of a minus sign (−), that is, a stimulus that is "subtracted" from the situation, like turning off (subtracting) an electric shock when the lever is pressed.

Responses: Two Types

Skinner, like the earlier behaviorists, based his system on the observation of overt responses. He divided all responses into two categories: respondents and operants. Respondents are those responses which can be automatically triggered by a specific unlearned or unconditioned stimulus; Pavlov called them *reflexes.* Pavlov, and later Watson, based a whole system of learning on the fact that reflexes can be conditioned. Skinner accepted the fact that **respondents** (his name for reflexes) can be conditioned in precisely the manner Pavlov described, but he didn't consider respondent conditioning to be nearly as important as Pavlov and Watson had. The reason is that many living organisms have very few respondents. To generalize the laws of classical conditioning to the whole range of human behavior is to carelessly overwork a fairly restricted formula. As Skinner pointed out, a human being is far more than a mere jack-in-the-box with a list of tricks to be elicited by pressing the correct buttons. The bulk of an individual's response repertoire takes another form.

Operants   All those responses that cannot be classified as respondents are known as **operants.** An operant is a response that occurs spontaneously, without having to be triggered by an unconditioned stimulus. For example, when you stretch your legs, raise your hand, or shift in your seat, there are no known unconditioned stimuli that automatically force those responses.

An operant is therefore a response for which the original stimulus is either unidentified or nonexistent; it may be loosely thought of as voluntary behavior. The consequences of operant behavior, however, can be observed, even though the stimulus is not known. In operant conditioning, reinforcement is contingent on the operant's first being emitted. Thus, the organism must "operate" on the environment in order for the reinforcement to follow. Before Skinner came along, psychologists called operant responding "instrumental responding." Skinner strongly believed that most human behavior is of the operant type.

Some responses we first think are respondents turn out not to be when they are subjected to further analysis. For example, putting your foot on the brake pedal to the stimulus of a red traffic light is not a reflex. You had to learn the significance of a red traffic light. You didn't come into the world already equipped to press your foot down automatically at the sight of a red light. This response is an example of a conditioned operant.

Operant Conditioning

The best way to understand **operant conditioning** is to examine the experimental situation Skinner has used over the years. Figure 9.1 is an illustration of the experimental chamber or, as it is so often called, the *Skinner box.* It is a small box, the sides and top of which are made of clear plastic. A lever protrudes from one side, and there is a tube that empties into the food cup next to the lever. The experimenter decides which operant to condition; in this case it will be pressing the lever. The experimenter then simply waits while the rat explores the cage. Since there aren't that many things to do in a Skinner box, the rat eventually presses the lever. A pellet of food (a reinforcing stimulus) immediately drops down the tube into the food cup. The rat pounces on the food, and conditioning has begun. It is important to note that when the rat, after wandering around the cage for a while, chances to press the food-producing lever, the response is not a reflex action triggered by a particular unconditioned stimulus. Skinner said that operants are emitted by the organism, whereas reflexes or respondents are elicited by unconditioned stimuli.

FIGURE 9.1   The experimental chamber, often called the *Skinner box.*

Thus, the sequence of events for operant conditioning is as follows.

1. The emitting of the free operant (the rat chancing to press the lever);
   followed by

2. The presentation of a reinforcing stimulus (the rat is given a pellet of food);
   followed by

3. An increase in the probability that the response will occur again

The response is now becoming controlled, or predictable. Note that the events must follow in the order specified above. The food must come after the response is emitted. How long after? The sooner the better. For optimum conditioning, the reinforcement should immediately follow the response. This is an important Skinnerian principle. Skinner believed that in the classroom the student should be reinforced as soon as the appropriate response is emitted.

Note that, unlike the case of reflex or **respondent conditioning,** the experimenter cannot force the response to occur. The experimenter may have to wait a while until the rat chances on the lever and emits the appropriate operant. Pavlov had no such wait, for he could automatically trigger the desired response (salivation) by simply presenting the unconditioned stimulus (meat powder).

In operant conditioning, although the experimenter might have to wait as long as fifteen or twenty minutes before the rat presses the lever for the first time, after a few reinforced responses the rat begins pressing ever more frequently. It is not unusual to see a conditioned animal pressing the lever 300 to 400 times in the space of one hour. With a highly conditioned rat, the sound of lever-pressing emanating from the Skinner box is reminiscent of the sound of a high-speed typist.

The law of operant conditioning   We may now state Skinner's general principle: If the occurrence of the operant is followed by a reinforcing stimulus, the rate of responding, for that particular operant, will increase.

Remember that the free operant originally had no connection with a stimulus. In operant conditioning, the response produces the reinforcing stimulus, or in Skinner's terms, the reinforcement is contingent upon the occurrence of the response. In this case, then, a response-stimulus connection is formed, not a stimulus-response connection.

We have said a number of times that as conditioning proceeds, the rate of responding increases. Increases over what? The rate increases over what is known as the **operant level,** or the frequency with which the response typically occurs in the untrained animal. For conditioning to take place, a response must occur before it can be reinforced. The experimenter must therefore select a response that the animal is apt to make on its own, such as rising on its hind legs, stretching its neck, or more commonly, pressing a lever. When first placed in the experimental chamber, the naive rat may happen to press the lever three or four times during the course of an hour, even though the lever is not producing any food. That is, the animal will occasionally press the lever even without positive reinforcement. The operant level is, therefore, the rate at which the free operant is typically emitted prior to conditioning.

Extinction

Extinction may be loosely thought of as a kind of forgetting process. For example, as has been seen, an animal may be conditioned to the point at which it is pressing the lever 400 times per hour. Similarly, the response may be extinguished, or the animal *deconditioned* to the point at which it will press the lever only three or four times per hour. The technique is simple. Allow the conditioned response to occur, but do not reinforce it. With the Skinner box, this means that pressing the bar no longer produces a food pellet. After enough nonreinforced lever presses, the animal "gives up," and the rate of response returns to its preconditioned, or operant, level. Note that extinction does not cause the animal to stop pressing the lever completely, but does cause the response frequency to return to the operant level.

It is important to remember that extinction requires that the animal emit the response and that the response not be reinforced. If the animal were somehow prevented from making the response, extinction would not occur. For example, if a conditioned animal were removed from the Skinner box and returned to its home cage, where there was no lever to press, the animal would retain the conditioning. If the animal were returned to the Skinner box, even a year later, lever-pressing would be resumed.

The first time a conditioned animal's response is extinguished, **spontaneous recovery** of the response will occur. This requires time, though sometimes as little as an hour. If the animal whose behavior has been extinguished is taken out of the Skinner box for an hour or so and then returned to it, lever-pressing will resume, even though no new training has taken place. These spontaneously recovered responses will extinguish more quickly, however, than did the original extinction. Several extinction-spontaneous recovery sequences may be necessary before extinction is complete to the point at which the animal remains at the operant level with no further evidence of spontaneous recovery.

Discrimination

Although in its original state the free operant is not attached to a stimulus, it may become so through training. This technique is called **discrimination training,** and the operant that has become associated with the stimulus is called a *discriminated operant.* Discrimination training is accomplished in the following manner: We introduce a new stimulus to an animal that has been conditioned to press the lever, such as a light that we turn off and on in a random time sequence. We now reinforce the animal only for pressing the lever when the light is on. Since any lever-pressing that takes place when the light is off is not reinforced, the response is extinguished as far as periods of no light are concerned. The animal emits the response only when the light is on; that is, the operant has become attached to the stimulus "light on." At this point the operant is no longer free, but is firmly controlled by the stimulus.

Technically, the stimulus for which responding is reinforced is called the *discriminated stimulus,* or the S^D—in this case "light on." The stimulus for which responding is extinguished is called the *stimulus delta,* or the S$^\Delta$—in this case "light off." A response to the discriminated stimulus (pressing the lever) is followed by reinforcement (food pellets). The following sequence of events is crucial to the development of discrimination: (1) stimulus, (2) response, and (3) reinforcement.

The same techniques used to teach the rat to differentially respond to the S^D and S$^\Delta$ can also be applied to humans in a variety of situations, including remediation programs. For example, in one study of severely dyslexic male children, all of whom had been (among other problems) confusing *d*'s with *b*'s and *p*'s with *q*'s, Stan Deno, was able to eliminate all the children's identification errors by using a combina-

tion of reinforcement and extinction procedures (Deno and Chiang, 1979).

Teachers who decide to use discrimination techniques, however, must be aware that the children should not be reinforced only for the correct response, since children also have to know when and *why* their responses are incorrect. The most effective feedback strategy involves not only praising the child for the right answer, but also providing information to the child when the answer is wrong (Getsie, 1985). Also, more important than the amount of reinforcement is the way the reinforcers are delivered. The use of praise in the classroom is most effective when it is (1) contingent on the behavior to be strengthened, (2) specific to behaviors the child can understand and, (3) believable to the child (Nafpaktitis et al., 1985). It's hardly believable, for example, if the verbal praise is being contradicted by the teacher's tone or general body language.

Stimulus Generalization

Once discrimination training has been completed— that is, once the animal has attached an operant to a certain stimulus—the stimulus may become generalized. **Stimulus generalization** means that other stimuli similar to the one used in training may take on the power to produce the response. If the animal has been trained to respond to a bright light, through generalization it may also respond to a dim light, even though the dim light was never used in training. Or perhaps a buzzer was used as the stimulus; through generalization, the animal may also be found to respond to a clicking sound or even a bell.

When generalization is noted, further discrimination training may be used to train the animal to respond only to a fairly specific stimulus magnitude. For example, if the original discrimination training used "light on" as the S^D and "light off" as the S$^\Delta$, the animal will eventually respond only when the light is on. However, because of generalization, responses will occur at many different light intensities. Perhaps the original S^D was a fairly bright light, but because of generalization the animal also responds to a dim light. We may now "correct" for this generalization by a new discrimination series in which the bright light is the S^D and the dim light is the S$^\Delta$. That is, we continue reinforcing responses to the bright light, while extinguishing responses to the dim light. This procedure allows the experimenter to determine the animal's capacity for distinguishing between rather subtle stimulus differences. For example, we can probe such questions as how small a difference in light intensity the animal is capable of identifying. Experiments have even been carried out in which the S^Δ was a card printed with the words "Don't Press," and the S^D a card with the word "Press." The experimental animal, in this case a pigeon, then displays the seemingly uncanny ability to "read" by rushing over to the lever and pecking whenever the "Press" card is shown. The pigeon reacts on cue, much in the way that a studio audience on a TV show frantically claps when the "Applause" sign is presented. As one TV narrator said in describing such an experiment, "It gives new meaning to the term *birdbrain*." And if training birds to discriminate between written letters seems amazing, listen to this. At Reed College, Dr. Allen Neuringer, noting that pigeons have extremely sharp acuity for sounds, trained them to differentiate between musical selections from Bach and Stravinski. The birds accomplished this with ease. Then the pigeons were exposed to music by five other composers which they had to classify as sounding like either Bach or Stravinski. Neuringer says that of the five composers used, the birds correctly categorized all but one. They incorrectly grouped Vivaldi with Stra-

vinski (*The New York Times*, 1991). On further reflection, maybe the birds had that one right too.

Conditioned Reinforcement

A stimulus that is not originally reinforcing may take on reinforcing power through repeated presentation with one that is. For example, if lever pressing produces both a light and a food pellet, the light, by association with the food, will take on the power of reinforcement. The sequence of events for establishing **conditioned reinforcement** is (1) response; (2) neutral stimulus, such as a light or buzzer; followed by (3) the primary or unconditioned reinforcement. It is important that this order of events be followed, for if the neutral stimulus is presented before rather than after the response, discrimination, and not conditioned reinforcement, will result. If a light is presented before the response has been emitted, the light will become an S^D, whereas if it follows the response, it becomes a conditioned reinforcer. In a sense, discrimination training teaches the rat to respond *to* the light, whereas conditioned reinforcement teaches the rat to respond *for*, or in order to get, the light.

Although the teacher may sometimes use primary reinforcers such as candy, conditioned reinforcers such as good grades, promotions, prizes, and teacher approval are usually more appropriate.

Schedules of reinforcement   The way in which the reinforcers are arranged determines in large measure the strength of the resulting conditioning. Responses that are reinforced periodically, rather than each time they are emitted, tend to be conditioned more strongly and are thus more difficult to extinguish. Though there are many variations on the major themes, Skinner has identified five major **schedules of reinforcement:**

1. *Continuous reinforcement (Crf):*   As the name implies, the Crf schedule provides for reinforcement each time the operant is emitted. For example, a rat in a Skinner box will receive a pellet of food every time the lever is pressed.

2. *Fixed ratio (F.R.):*   Under the F.R. schedule the reinforcement occurs only after a fixed number of operants have been emitted. For example, on an F.R. schedule of 3:1, the rat in a Skinner box must press the lever three times in order to get one pellet of food. Skinner has demonstrated that the ratio can go as high as 196:1 and still maintain the conditioning.

3. *Fixed interval (F.I.):*   Rather than based on the number of responses being emitted, the F.I. schedule is keyed to a fixed *time* interval. That is, a given period of time must elapse, regardless of what the organism is doing, before the reinforcement is presented. For example, on an F.I. schedule of thirty seconds, this thirty-second time period must be allowed to elapse before the organism's next response will be reinforced.

4. *Variable ratio (V.R.):*   Like the F.R., the V.R. schedule is also based on the number of responses being emitted. Under the V.R. schedule, however, the ratio is constantly being varied so that the organism never knows which response will be reinforced. The rat might be reinforced after five responses, then after fifteen responses, then after the very next response, and so on.

5. *Variable interval (V.I.):*   On this schedule the time periods, rather than the number of responses, are varied. The rat may have to wait thirty seconds, then five seconds, then fifty seconds, and so on before the pressing of the lever will deliver the reinforcement.

Analysis of the reinforcement schedules   Each of the reinforcement schedules creates differences in the way the resulting conditioning is exhibited. The Crf schedule, though extremely useful for the acquiring of new behavior, does not result in a great deal of perseverance. Extinction can occur rather rapidly when a response has been conditioned on the continuous schedule. Parents in the United States may be guilty of using too much reinforcement in bringing up their children, and consequently nurture such qualities as a lack of perseverance, low frustration tolerance, impulsiveness, impatience, and a generally low level of ego strength.

Children at home, or rats in the Skinner box, tend to give up easily (have a low resistance to extinction) when the reinforcers are continuous. This is especially true in a highly industrialized nation in which continuous reinforcement is built into the society.

> The conveniences provided by technological gadgets work in concert with parental indulgence by providing immediate gratification with great consistency while requiring little effort. Coke machines, television sets, automobiles, and many other devices yield rewards quickly and consistently with a minimum of sweat. Indulgent parents, who readily provide their children the means for making life easy and convenient, should not be surprised to find that their children lack some of the old-fashioned traits that the parents were taught to admire in their early lives (Carpenter, 1974, p. 28).

The other schedules, F.R., F.I., V.R., and V.I., are all of the intermittent type: They require that the organism learn to wait out the hard times. Responses conditioned in this way become highly resistant to extinction. Intermittent reinforcement does condition perseverance and perhaps hope.

Life outside the Skinner box creates many conditions that are analogous to the various intermittent schedules. For example, factory workers or farm laborers who are paid on a piecework basis are being conditioned on an F.R. schedule. In piecework one's pay is based on a set number of items produced or apples, or other produce, picked. Workers who are paid by the hour or by the week illustrate the F.I. schedule. An example of the V.R. schedule might be a door-to-door encyclopedia salesperson who is paid on a commission basis. The salesperson knows that he or she must emit a number of responses but never knows which response is going to lead to a payoff. Slot machines and other forms of gambling are set up on a V.R. basis. Because the V.R. schedule creates responses that are highly resistant to extinction, people can often become addicted to gambling. This helps explain why the gambler can persevere through long, dry spells and still go back to the game. The V.I.

Even though Skinner's data came primarily from working with rats and pigeons, he thought the results could be applied to humans.

schedule also creates strongly conditioned responses that are maintained at a rapid rate and are highly resistant to extinction.

In one clever example of the V.I. schedule, a person fishing watches a bobber float on the water. At varying time intervals, however, the bobber disappears below the surface, sometimes, alas, just because of the pull of tide or current, but, happily, at other times because a fish has grabbed the hook. The person fishing remains encouraged and hopeful by this variable payoff (McMahon and McMahon, 1986).

The variable schedules are typical of most social situations. Human interaction is characterized by inconsistent reinforcement, and the result is a repertoire of responses that may become almost extinction-proof. Habit, as William James has told us, that great flywheel of society, keeps people doing the same things over and over again, even when the habits are self-destructive.

THE ENGINEERING OF SOCIETY

Skinner suggests that through the judicious use of reinforcement schedules, a society free of war, crime, poverty, and pollution could be behaviorally engineered. The individuals in the society could be shaped to reflect the best of human traits: honesty, altruism, ambition, and so on. It is Skinner's conviction that this not only could be but should be done. A culture should be designed in which the behavior of the individuals is systematically controlled. As Skinner has said, "A refusal to use the knowledge we have could mean the difference between the survival and the destruction of our civilization or even the species" (Skinner, 1978, p. 32).

Skinner feels that a democratic society cannot provide true justice because it must ignore minority opinion. A society should be planned and managed by someone (presumably Skinner) who is interested in the good of all. Skinner does not seem overly concerned about who will decide which behaviors are to be reinforced and which are to be extinguished.

> The relation between the controller and the controlled is reciprocal. The scientist in the laboratory, studying the behavior of a pigeon, designs contingencies and observes their effects. His apparatus exerts a conspicuous control on the pigeon, but we must not overlook the control exerted by the pigeon. The behavior of the pigeon has determined the design of the apparatus and the procedures in which it is used (Skinner, 1971, p. 169).

Thus, just as the scientist in the laboratory is to some extent under the control of the pigeon, so too

SPOTLIGHT ON THE ENVIRONMENT

The Master Controller

The heart of Skinner's message is that we are all at the mercy of environmental controls. What we do, who we are, what we become, all result from the particular set of environmental stimuli that have impinged on us and that will impinge on us. We humans are yoked to our environments just as rigidly as animals are to theirs. Environment—and only environment—controls behavior, and whoever controls the environment, controls the people. People are directed not by cherished ideals, strong emotions, or the forced will of profound ideas, but by the environment. Humans and animals dif-

fer not because of varying complexities of perception or ideation, but only because of varying environmental complexities. Skinner spent his professional lifetime insisting that the environment and the reinforcement schedules provided by the environment are the true and only prime movers.

For Skinner, then, the one who controls the reinforcers is the one who ultimately controls behavior, and this may not be as bad as it first sounds. The Skinnerian argument is essentially that our behavior is constantly being shaped by reinforcers, regardless of whether we are aware of that fact. As Her-

genhahn has said, it is not a "question of whether behavior is going to be controlled, but who or what is going to control it."[a] Parents may wish to guide their child's emerging personality by reinforcing certain behaviors they deem appropriate, or they can step aside and let society rear their children by leaving the reinforcers in the hands of peers, baby sitters, and the TV set.

[a] B. R. Hergenhahn, *An introduction to theories of learning*, 2d ed. (Englewood Cliffs, N.J.: Prentice-Hall, 1988), p. 84.

will the controller of a society be influenced by the members of that society. Despite Skinner's view on the apparent equality between the controller and controllee, some of you may feel you'd prefer the role of experimenter to that of pigeon.

Verbal Behavior

Skinner uses his system to explain all animal and human learning. For example, Skinner believes that learning to talk follows the principles of operant conditioning. Picture for a moment a one-and-a-half-year-old baby contentedly lying in a crib. The baby is cooing, gurgling, uttering a whole series of disconnected sounds. Suddenly, from out of the babble, and surely by accident, the baby chances on the sound *da-da*. The parents, who have been listening intently, are beside themselves with joy. They heap praise on the baby and, sure enough, the baby soon says "da-da" again.

In technical Skinnerian terms, from the entire repertoire of possible verbal operants, the baby has emitted the operant da-da. This is immediately followed by positive reinforcement, increasing the probability that the operant will be repeated. After more da-da

responses are followed by more reinforcements, the baby will emit the operant at a fairly frequent rate. Conditioning of the operant has occurred. Now, however, the parents' expectations are raised so that reinforcement no longer follows each and every utterance of the magic word. The parents begin teaching the baby to discriminate, so that only when the father himself is presented as the stimulus does baby get reinforced. When the baby says "da-da" to the mother's presence, no reinforcement follows, and the response to that stimulus is extinguished. In this case the father is the S^D, the stimulus for which responding will be reinforced, and the mother is the S^Δ, the stimulus for which responding will be extinguished.

This discrimination will occur quickly, but because of stimulus generalization, the family may be in for an embarrassing moment. A few days later the postman stops in with his delivery. The baby, seeing the male figure, proudly calls out "da-da." Obviously, further discrimination training is in order. When the baby says "da-da" to other male figures, reinforcement is withheld. Finally, the father is perceived as the only appropriate S^D for that operant, and the family perhaps breathes a sigh of relief.

Attaching a verbal response to an S^D in this manner

is called, by Skinner, *tacting*. Skinner believes that language is acquired in this general fashion, and he has added other terms, such as *mands* for verbal responses that specify their own reinforcers, *echoics* for verbal responses that parrot the speech of others, and *autoclitics* for verbal responses that provide grammatical framework. In short, during language acquisition, what are learned are the verbal responses, not the thoughts lurking behind them. An operant is conditioned so that it occurs regularly, and then, through discrimination training, it is attached to its appropriate stimulus. Perhaps the child later generalizes the word *car* to include all wheeled vehicles. Through discrimination training, the child then learns the appropriate responses that will correct for this stimulus generalization.

Skinner's contention that verbal behavior is learned strictly through operant conditioning has not gone unchallenged. Specialists in the field of psycholinguistics believe that language acquisition is not a mere matter of conditioning.

Noam Chomsky, for example, sees the child as genetically prewired, born with biological givens that direct the course of language development. In this way Chomsky feels he can explain how children learn sentence structure and the complex grammatical sequencing of words—both of which he says children learn far more easily and *quickly* than the principles of operant conditioning can explain. Evidence in support of Chomsky's notion has been provided in a number of studies. One researcher has found that motor and language development occur hand in hand (or is it foot in mouth?), and this development is independent of culture (Gentile, 1978).

Operant Conditioning in the Classroom

Only Skinner's general approach to the problem of classroom teaching will be treated in this section. Specific techniques, such as teaching machines and the arrangement of reinforcements to promote student control, will be covered in the next chapter.

Education is the learning of certain responses that will be useful later in life. How can this best be accomplished? The teacher, says Skinner, should use the techniques that produce meaningful behavioral changes. Though the teacher may sometimes use primary reinforcers such as M&M candy, conditioned reinforcers such as good grades, promotions, prizes, and the generalized social reinforcement of approval are usually more appropriate. One of the real prob-

Skinner is against aversion techniques since punishment in school always leads to attempts to escape the classroom situation.

lems with the use of conditioned reinforcers, however, is that they are often too distant. As we have seen, operant conditioning is most effective when reinforcement is immediate. This is one of the reasons why Skinner strongly favors the use of the teaching machine. It can provide immediate reinforcement and help bridge the gap between student behavior and the most distant conditioned reinforcers such as promotion or grades. Skinner is against the use of punishment in the classroom, not because it won't control behavior—it will—but because it may produce a host of negative emotional reactions. Negative emotional reactions, conditioned through the use of punishment, may prevent further learning and even further school attendance. Punishment always leads to attempts to escape, and when children do escape from the classroom situation, formal learning in the classroom is obviously impossible.

Just what is the goal of education according to Skinner? Skinner believes that education should maximize knowledge. This is done through operant conditioning, through building up a student's repertoire of responses. Understanding a subject, such as history, is simply the result of having learned a verbal repertoire. Skinner insists that when students can answer questions in a given area, and speak and write fluently about the area, then, by definition, they understand that area. A verbal repertoire is not a sign of knowledge—it *is* the knowledge. In order to teach a knowledge of biology, one must teach the specific behavior from which the knowledge is inferred. That is, in order to say that students know something, we must observe certain responses: how they speak, the diagrams they draw, the equations they can solve, and so on. These, then, are the very responses that should be trained into the students who don't display this knowledge.

Good teaching is thus the ability to arrange the proper sequence of reinforcements and to make sure that these reinforcements are contingent upon students emitting the appropriate responses.

BEHAVIORISM TODAY: THE FUNCTIONAL VIEW

Traditional behaviorism generally adhered to three underlying principles:

1. Organisms enter the world, come into any new situation, as virtual blank slates. Under the leadership of Watson, behaviorists as a group were extremely strong environmentalists. They clung to the cherished belief, previously espoused by English philosopher John Locke, that the mind was a "blank slate upon which experience writes," or "nothing in the intellect not first in the senses." And in a way they clung to this belief in a manner that probably would have made John Locke blush, since Watson most certainly would have considered Locke a mentalist for having used such terms as *mind* and *intellect*. Behaviorists paid little attention to internal cognitive structures and even less, of course, to genetic predispositions.

2. There are few important differences in learning and/or conditioning styles across species. An understanding of rat and pigeon behavior could be easily extrapolated to the human condition.

3. Any response an organism is capable of producing could be linked through training with any stimulus the organism could be made aware of. Learning was seen as occurring in an automatic fashion, and the learner was typically seen as a recipient of environmental stimuli, not a selector of stimuli.

Given these premises, it is little wonder that behaviorism had to adhere to a robot model of learning and that the twin concepts of growth and development had to play, at most, a secondary role. In large measure the behaviorists painted themselves into a corner. Because of their almost slavish insistence on these three fundamental principles, they had to overlook, or attempt to explain away, empirical data that ran counter to their position. Anomalies began to appear, and traditional behaviorism went into what Thomas Kuhn would call a "crisis" stage (Kuhn, 1970). Attempts to stem the flow soon gave way in the face of a virtual torrent of new evidence.

The Challenge Today

More recent work in conditioning is offering a strong challenge to the traditional behaviorist position. Martin Seligman, for example, has shown that responses to some stimuli are much easier to condition than responses to others. Seligman's position is that each organism comes into the world biologically prepared to be conditioned more quickly to certain environmental stimuli than to others and that this preparedness differs from species to species. Birds, for example, are conditioned easily to visual stimuli, whereas human infants are conditioned more quickly to verbal stimuli. Seligman says that the organism carries within itself "certain equipment and predispositions [which are] more or less appropriate to that situation" (Seligman, 1970).

Seligman believes, therefore, that since organisms have evolved a variety of adaptive behavior sequences over millions of years, it is unlikely that today's conditioning procedures can countermand these built-in predispositions. For example, was Watson's conditioning of little Albert really as automatic as it appeared, or was Albert already biologically prepared to learn to fear the white rat? In one study, usually overlooked by the behaviorists, Elsie Bregman at Columbia Teacher's College, attempted to replicate this experiment of Watson's. Her finding—an obvious anomaly for orthodox behaviorism—was that fear in a child could indeed be conditioned if the CS was a live animal, but conditioning did not take place if the CS was an inanimate object (Bregman, 1934). It is therefore highly likely that humans are born biologically prepared to suspect that live animals might do them harm and, because of that tendency, learn quickly to fear and avoid them. Seligman also believes that common phobias, such as the fear of snakes, enclosed places, or speaking in public, undoubtedly have biological roots in an evolutionary survival system (Seligman, 1972). Although few of us have ever actually been bitten by a snake, locked in a closet, or pelted with stones by an angry crowd, these extremely common phobias are too easily acquired to be explained on the basis of the traditional principles of conditioning.

Keller and Marian Breland have also discovered serious anomalies in the behaviorists's paradigm (Breland and Breland, 1961). Using operant conditioning techniques, the Brelands trained raccoons to pick up coins and deposit them in a slot in order to receive a food reinforcer. Although the raccoons dutifully learned this routine rather easily, the conditioning soon decayed and literally drifted into a different behavioral sequence. The raccoons, despite continued reinforcement, soon began rubbing the coins together as part of an instinctive washing ritual (as though preparing to eat them). This action broke up the conditioning sequence. The Brelands called this phenomenon *instinctive drift* and stated that many of the artificial conditioning routines produced so easily in the laboratory will soon drift back toward the organism's natural behavioral repertoire.

Could it be that the behaviorists have consistently been lucky in arranging their studies in such a way that the conditioning environment just happened to meet the organism's preparedness? As we have seen, Watson was certainly lucky in choosing a live rat as a CS, since Albert would not have been conditioned nearly as easily, if at all, to a stuffed rat or a picture of a rat. Were Thorndike and Skinner also as lucky? Certainly a rat can be conditioned quickly to press a lever for food. But what if one of Thorndike's cats were substituted for one of Skinner's rats? Cats, although they can learn that pressing a lever delivers food, soon stop pressing and simply sit and wait—and the hungrier they get, the more they crouch down and wait. The difference is in the types of food-gathering techniques utilized by the two species. Rats actively seek out food in their environment, whereas cats are great ambushers that normally crouch patiently while awaiting their prey. Also, note that the lever in a Skinner box is always made of metal, not plastic or wood; nonmetallic levers would probably simply be eaten by the rats rather than pressed.

With pigeons, the typical Skinnerian arrangement is to substitute a small, lighted key *to be pecked*, rather than a lever to be pressed. High-speed photographs of this pecking response show clearly that the pigeons are, in fact, not simply pecking the key but trying to eat it (Moore, 1973). In a summary statement of the pigeon studies, R. C. Bolles said:

> The picture that emerges from this work is that key pecking in pigeons, which surely must be the most studied and most characteristic of all operant responses in the Skinnerian tradition, is not an operant after all, and is not even learned because of reinforcement. It is simply another instance of the misbehavior phenomenon; the pigeon pecks the key because, when the discriminated stimulus is on (the light), the key is evaluated as food (Bolles, 1980).

A Message to Educators

What should we, as educators, derive from this evidence? Traditional behaviorism should no longer be accepted at face value. What seemed like an almost noninteractive model of conditioning should now, most assuredly, be viewed as extremely interactive. The environmental manipulations that produce conditioning interact decidedly with the particular organism's innate predispositions. Again, we see behavior as resulting from the interplay of heredity and environment. Conditioning should not be seen as completely automatic in its nature, nor as permanent in its result, as the behaviorists have led us to believe. Instinctive drift can override and even countermand conditioning sequences that attempt to compete with innate predispositions. Just as with the raccoons, children who have been conditioned to act in a particular way through the use of tokens or whatever may quickly "drift" out of that conditioned behavior, *especially if the situation changes.*

Conversely, we should not glibly use the instinctive drift argument to give up on changing behavior we can't seem to control. It becomes all too easy to say "This kid was born to be bad" when his or her disruptive behavior continues despite efforts to change it. We must keep in mind that whatever the genetic basis might be for a particular set of responses, the innate predisposition is still being expressed *in learned ways.*

Perhaps the most provocative of the new research is the work relating learning and conditioning to what we now know of age-related changes in capacity. No longer can we afford to smugly set forth universal laws of associative learning; we must, instead, attempt to identify the adaptive importance of particular instances of learning found at particular stages of development. The human organism is, after all, biological as well as psychological.

JEROME BRUNER AND THE PROCESS OF THOUGHT

Whereas Skinner has presented a behaviorist-associationist account of learning, borrowing heavily from Watson and Thorndike, the position of **Jerome Bruner** is more consistent with the cognitive-gestaltist position. For example, Bruner insists that the final goal of teaching is to promote the "general understanding of the structure of a subject matter" (Bruner, 1962). When the student understands the structure of a subject, he or she sees it as a related whole. "Grasping the structure of a subject is understanding it in a way that permits many other things to be related to it meaningfully" (Bruner, 1962, p. 28). He sees children as "makers of meaning in the ordinary conduct" of their lives; that is, they shape and are shaped by their home culture (Bruner, 1990, p. 19). These are hardly the words of a behaviorist-associationist. Bruner stresses the importance in learning of forming global concepts, of building coherent generalizations, of creating cognitive *Gestalts*. Bruner tells the teacher—and he constantly aims his message at the working classroom teacher—to help promote conditions in which the student can perceive the structure of a given subject. When learning is based on a structure, it is more long-lasting and less easily forgotten. The student who once studied biology, for example, may forget many of the details over the years, but these details can be more easily and quickly reconstructed if the general structure is still there.

Bruner calls his position a theory of instruction, not a learning theory. He feels that a learning theory is *descriptive;* that is, it describes what happens after the fact. A theory of instruction, on the other hand, is *prescriptive:* it prescribes in advance how a given subject can best be taught. If a learning theory tells us that children at age six are not yet ready to understand the concept of reversibility, a theory of instruction would prescribe how best to lead the child toward this concept when he or she is old enough to understand it.

Bruner's theory has four major principles: motivation, structure, sequence, and reinforcement.

Bruner's First Principle: Motivation

Bruner's first principle, **motivation,** specifies the conditions that predispose an individual to learn. What are the critical variables, especially during the preschool years, that help motivate and enable the child to learn? Implicit in Bruner's principles is the belief that almost all children have a built-in "will to learn." However, Bruner has not discarded the notion of reinforcement. He believes that reinforcement, or external reward, may be important for initiating certain actions or for making sure they are repeated. He insists, however, that it is only through intrinsic motivation that the will to learn is sustained. Bruner is far more concerned with intrinsic motivation than with what he believes to be the more transitory effects of external motivation.

Perhaps the best example of intrinsic motivation is curiosity. Bruner believes that we come into the world equipped with a curiosity drive. He feels this drive is biologically relevant, that curiosity is necessary to the survival of the species. Bruner suggests that young children are often too curious; they are unable to "stick with" any one activity. Their curiosity leads them to turn from one activity to another in rapid succession, and the curiosity must therefore be channeled into a more powerful intellectual pursuit. Games like twenty questions help develop a sense of disciplined curiosity in the child.

Another motivation we bring into the world with us is the drive to achieve competence. Children become interested in what they are good at, and it is virtually impossible to motivate them to engage in activities in which they have no degree of competence.

Finally, Bruner lists reciprocity as a motivation that is built into the species. Reciprocity involves a need to work with others cooperatively, and Bruner feels that society itself developed as a result of this most basic motivation.

Bruner has been using a variant of the transactional model to describe language acquisition, which he feels depends strongly on the myriad of small but continuing interactions between mother and child. Through these interactions, the child not only learns the words but also what language is used for. A child may learn to utter a request perhaps up to a year before the request can be properly phrased as a sentence. Because of these mother-child transactions, the child who is learning language is also learning the

JEROME BRUNER

Jerome Bruner was born into a successful upper-middle-class family that fully expected him to become a lawyer. Bruner, however, had other ideas. He graduated from Duke University in 1937 and then went to Harvard, where in 1941 he earned his Ph.D. degree in psychology. When Bruner first arrived at Harvard, his interest was focused on the investigation of perception in animals. Harvard had only recently (1933) created an independent department of psychology, and under its chairman, the brilliant E. G. Boring, the research emphasis was directed toward animal learning and perception. Bruner chose to study under the great Harvard researcher and physiological psychologist, Karl S. Lashley. With the outbreak of World War II, Bruner's interests shifted to social psychology, and he wrote his doctoral dissertation on the techniques of Nazi propagandists. During the war, Bruner joined the Army and worked on psychological warfare at General Eisenhower's headquarters in Europe. After the war he returned to Harvard and in 1947 published a significant paper on the great influence of needs on perception. In this study he showed that poor children are more likely to overestimate the size of coins than are well-to-do children. From this study he concluded that values and needs strongly affect human perceptions and also that people create meaning out of their perceptions by making them consistent with their past experiences. People are thus able to reduce the possibility of mental strain by viewing the world in such a way as to minimize environmental surprises. These findings led to what became known as the "new look" in perception theory and also laid the groundwork for an American school of cognitive psychology. Cognitive psychology deals with the human being's ability to obtain

cultural conventions that are so important to the process of socialization (Bruner, 1983).

According to Bruner, the intrinsic motivations are rewarding in themselves and are therefore self-sustaining. How can the teacher take advantage of this in the classroom situation? Bruner's answer is that teachers must facilitate and regulate their students' exploration of alternatives. Since learning and problem solving demand the exploration of alternatives, this is at the very core of the issue and is critical in creating a predisposition to the long-term pursuit of learning.

The exploration of alternatives has three phases: activation, maintenance, and direction.

Activation   In order to activate exploration, in order to get it started, children must experience a certain level of uncertainty. If the task is too easy, they will be too bored to explore alternatives, and yet if it is too difficult, they will be too confused to explore alternatives. This is similar to J. McV. Hunt's problem of the match or Vygotsky's zone of proximal development, already discussed in Chapter 4. The teacher must provide students with problems that are just difficult enough for the children's intrinsic curiosity motivation to itself activate exploration.

Maintenance   Once activated, exploration must be maintained. This involves assuring children that exploration is not going to be a dangerous or painful experience. Children must view exploration under the guiding hand of the teacher as less risky, less dangerous than exploration on their own. The advantages of exploration must be made greater than the risks.

Direction   Meaningful exploration must have direction. The direction of exploration is a function of

knowledge and develop intellectually. Although the field of cognitive psychology had been important in Europe, America, under the heavy influence of the behaviorist tradition, had turned a deaf ear to anything as subjective and "unscientific" as the study of thinking. Bruner changed all that. In 1960 he established Harvard University's Center for Cognitive Studies, and although he didn't invent cognitive psychology, he certainly went a long way toward making it a respected scientific discipline. Bruner was the "Minuteman" who fired the first shot in what is now called the "cognitive revolution."

Always the empiricist, Bruner kept science's basic rule clearly in mind: Begin by observing the data from which the conclusions are to be drawn. Once, when several academic psychologists were debating the possible impact a certain film might have on children, Bruner was

brought in as a consultant. After listening to this group of armchair speculators for a while, Bruner suddenly interrupted them and said, "Why not get a child, show him the film, and then we'll ask him what he thought of it."

This is also Bruner's approach to the problems of educational psychology. If you want to know how children go about the business of learning in the school situation, then study children in the classroom rather than rats and pigeons in cages.

In 1962 Bruner published an extremely important book, *The Process of Education*. As *Harper's* magazine said, "To people starved for reasonable comments on education in intelligible English, Bruner's writings are above reproach." In this book Bruner developed three important points. First, schools should strive to teach the general nature, or structure, of a subject rather than all the details and

facts of a subject. Second, any subject can be taught effectively in some intellectually honest form to any child at any stage of development. And finally, Bruner stressed the importance of intuition in learning. Intuition is a problem-solving technique whereby a child relies on insight or immediate apprehensions rather than the planned steps of formal analysis.

Bruner's work has not gone unnoticed by his colleagues. In 1963 the American Psychological Association awarded him the Distinguished Scientific Award, and in 1965 Bruner was elected president of the American Psychological Association.

Jerome Bruner has made things happen in educational psychology. Says *Harper's*, "He is the first person to come along in years—perhaps the first since John Dewey—who can speak intelligently about education to his fellow scholars as well as to educators."

two factors: knowledge of the goal and knowledge that the exploration of alternatives is relevant to the achievement of that goal. Children must know what the goal is and how close they are to achieving it.

Thus, Bruner's first principle indicates that children have a built-in will to learn. Teachers must manage and enhance this motivation so that children will see that guided exploration is more meaningful and satisfying than the spontaneous learning they can achieve on their own. In short, Bruner's first principle is a justification for formal schooling.

Bruner's Second Principle: Structure

Bruner's second principle, **structure,** states that any given subject area, any body of knowledge, can be organized in some optimal fashion so that it can be transmitted to and understood by almost any student. If appropriately structured, "any idea or problem or

body of knowledge can be presented in a form simple enough so that any particular learner can understand it in a recognizable form" (Bruner, 1966). This is not to say that all of the nuances of Einstein's theory of relativity can be fully mastered by a six-year-old child. It does mean, however, that if properly structured, Einstein's general position could be understood by the child, and that under questioning the child could convey to a physicist a recognizable account of the theory.

According to Bruner, the structure of any body of knowledge can be characterized in three ways: mode of presentation, economy, and power.

Mode of presentation   Mode of presentation refers to the technique, the method, whereby information is communicated. One of the reasons teachers fail to convey some fundamental point to a seemingly uncomprehending child is that the teacher's mode of

Teenagers playing in a high school orchestra exemplify two motivating factors: a drive to achieve competence and a need to work with others cooperatively.

presentation simply does not fit with the child's level of experience. The child will remain uncomprehending as long as the message is incomprehensible. Bruner believes that a person has three means of achieving understanding: enactive, iconic, and symbolic representation.

Enactive representation is needed for very young children, who can understand things best in terms of actions. For example, children can demonstrate their understanding of the principles of a balance beam by referring to their experiences on a seesaw. If the child on the other end is heavier, you compensate by sliding farther back on your own end; if the other child is lighter, you push yourself farther forward. Young children also define words in terms of the actions that are associated with them: A chair is to sit on, a spoon is to eat with, and so on. When children are in the enactive stage of thinking, it is important that

the teacher's messages somehow make contact with their muscles. Even adults may revert to enactive representation when learning something new, especially a new motor skill. Teaching an adult to ski is best accomplished wordlessly. A skilled ski instructor doesn't just tell students to "edge into the hill" but will instead ask them to imitate her own stance. In short, when young children are in the enactive stage of thinking, the best, the most comprehensible messages are wordless ones.

Iconic representation may be used with somewhat older children. They learn to think at the iconic level when objects become conceivable without action. Children can now draw a picture of a spoon without acting out the eating process. They may even be able, at this stage, to draw a diagram of a balance beam, for they now possess an image of it that no longer depends on action. This is a significant breakthrough in the development of intellect, for the use of pictures or diagrams allows children at this stage to be tutored in simpler ways.

Symbolic representation can be used at the stage at which children can translate experience into language. The balance beam can be explained through the use of words rather than pictures. Symbolic representation allows children to begin making logical derivations and to think more compactly. Bruner says that through symbolic representation "powerful representations of the world of possible experiences are constructed and used as search models in problem solving" (Bruner, 1966, p. 14).

Which of these modes should the teacher choose in order to facilitate the learning process? It depends on the learner's age and background and on the subject matter itself. For example, Bruner believes that teaching a problem in law demands symbolic representation, whereas geography is well suited to the iconic. New motor skills are often best communicated by enactive representation, especially at first. Mathematics can be represented, and often should be, by all three modes.

Economy of presentation   Economy in communicating a body of knowledge depends on the amount of information the learner must keep in mind in order to continue learning. The fewer bits of information, the fewer facts the learner must bear in mind, the greater the economy. The best way to provide economy in teaching is to give the learner concise summaries. For example, Bruner feels that it is more economical to "summarize the American Civil War as a battle over slavery than as a struggle between an expanding industrial region and one built upon a class society for control of federal economic power" (Bruner, 1966, p. 46).

Power of presentation   Bruner believes that nature is simple; hence, to be powerful, a presentation of some aspect of nature should reflect nature's simplicity. Teachers often make difficult what is inherently easy. A powerful presentation is a simple presentation, one that is easily understood. It allows the learner to see new relationships, to find connections between facts that may at first seem quite separate. Bruner feels that a powerful presentation is especially important in the field of mathematics.

Bruner's Third Principle: Sequence

The extent to which a student finds it difficult to master a given subject depends largely on the sequence in which the material is presented—Bruner's third principle. Teaching involves leading the learner through a certain sequence of the various aspects of the subject. Since Bruner believes that intellectual development is innately sequential, moving from enactive through iconic to symbolic representation, he feels it is highly probable that this is also the best sequence for any subject to take. Thus, the teacher should begin teaching any new subject with wordless messages, speaking mainly to the learner's muscular responses. Then the student should be encouraged to explore the use of diagrams and various pictorial representations. Finally, the message should be communicated symbolically, through the use of words.

Bruner's Fourth Principle: Reinforcement

Bruner's fourth principle is that learning requires reinforcement. In order to achieve mastery of a problem, we must receive feedback as to how we are doing. The timing of the reinforcement is crucial to success in learning. The results must be learned at the very time a student is evaluating his or her own performance. If the results are known too soon, the learner will become confused and his or her explorations will be stifled. If they are known too late, the learner may have gone beyond the point at which the knowledge would have been helpful, and by this time the child may have incorporated false information. The teacher's role is indeed sensitive. If the learner has gone on to incorporate false information, this must now be unlearned in order for the learner to get back on the right track.

Discovery Learning

Though it is possible to memorize a poem, the multiplication tables, or the state capitals, meaningful learning often requires actual discovery. The facts and relationships children discover through their own explorations are more usable and tend to be better retained than material they have merely committed to memory. Teachers can provide the conditions in which **discovery learning** is nourished and will grow. One way they can do this is to guess at

During the symbolic stage the child can translate experience into language.

SPOTLIGHT ON THE LEARNER

Challenging through Impasses

Some theorists believe that for children to discover and learn new concepts, they must first confront an impasse, or a more difficult problem that just can't be solved in the usual way.[a] That is, this view purports that if you don't constantly supply the child with new and difficult challenges, discovery learning and cognitive growth will be impeded. As we saw in Chapter 4, this is essentially the position taken by Hunt and Vygotsky. Both researchers felt that cognitive growth depends on the child's always reaching for somewhat more difficult levels of thinking and being challenged by ever-increasing stimulus complexity. On the other side is the more moderate view that although impasse learning may account for many childhood discoveries, it doesn't cover them all.[b] For example, Siegler has shown that in Piaget's number conservation, young children solve problems by counting and comparing the number of objects in the two rows. Even though this approach produces consistently correct answers, older children shift away from it and base their answers on the reasoning that the act of merely spreading out or contracting a row could not possibly change the number of objects.[c] Similarly, in language acquisition, children shift from the incorrect use of verbs ("I falled down") to the correct use ("I fell down") without confronting any apparent impasse and often without any external pressure at all.[d]

[a] K. Van Lehn, Towards a theory of impasse driven learning. In H. Mandl and A. Lesgold (Eds.), *Learning issues for intelligent tutoring systems* (New York: Springer-Verlag, 1988), pp. 19–41.

[b] A. Newell, *Unified theories of cognition: The William James lectures* (Cambridge: Harvard University Press, 1990).

[c] R. S. Siegler and E. Jenkins, *How children discover new strategies* (Hillsdale, N.J.: Erlbaum, 1989).

[d] M. Bowerman, Commentary. In B. MacWhinney (Ed.), *Mechanisms of language acquisition* (Hillsdale, N.J.: Erlbaum, 1987), pp. 443–466.

answers and let the class know they are guessing. The students can then analyze the teacher's answer. This helps prove to them that exploration can be both rewarding and safe, and it is thus a valuable technique for building lifelong discovery habits in the students.

Bruner is not saying that discovery learning is the only form of learning. Nor is he saying that students must discover for themselves the solutions to every problem in a given field. That would be extremely wasteful, if it were even possible, for it would mean that each generation would have to rediscover the ideas and technology of its culture. Beginning physics students, for example, shouldn't have to discover the technology of radio transmission, as Marconi once did. Students can, however, through insightful questioning and prompting by the teacher, discover for themselves some of the basic principles that account for radio transmission. Learning through such discoveries enables the student to reach a level of understanding that far surpasses the rote memorization of a radio chapter in an electronics book.

Discovery learning is more conceptual, and studies have repeatedly shown that conceptual learning has longer-lasting consequences than nonconceptual activities. Also, conceptual retention promotes greater feelings of self-esteem on the part of the learner (Deci et al., 1980).

The process of learning the strategies of discovery is also important in nourishing creative thinking, a mode of thinking Bruner finds crucial to the well-developed mind. Creative thinking supplies the poet, the storyteller, the innovator (who lurk within all of us) with the potential to break away from the formal rules of logic. Thinking, after all, is not just an exercise in formal logic. Thinking is nested in a person's total sphere of awareness, including beliefs, desires, expectations, emotions, and intentions. In fact, Bruner rails against some of the cognitive psychologists of the 1980s, especially those who rely solely on the computer model to explain thinking. These psychologists, Bruner tells us, actually impoverish psychology, since they emphasize only the logical mode of thinking (Bruner, 1987).

Teaching for discovery is obviously not easy. The teacher must be bright and flexible and must really know the subject matter. In order to communicate knowledge, the teacher must have mastery of that knowledge. Finally, the good teacher is a patient teacher, for discovery teaching cannot be hurried. It is often frustratingly slow, but the goal of real student understanding is well worth the wait.

A FINAL COMPARISON

At times it may seem that Skinner and Bruner are from two different worlds, that they discuss entirely different concepts. In part, this is true. Skinner's data came primarily from his work with rats and pigeons; Bruner's, from his observations of children in learning situations. Skinner is an associationist; Bruner, a cognitive theorist. Skinner is an avowed behaviorist; Bruner speculates on events occurring within the child's mind. Yet both are discussing learning, and both are talking to working teachers. Skinner speaks of the laws of conditioning, and Bruner, acknowledging that the teacher is a potent reinforcer, insists that the teacher should know these laws.

Piaget has stated that there are really two kinds of learning, P learning and LM learning. **P learning** is physical learning, learning that takes place when physical things act on us. **LM learning** is logico-mathematical learning, learning that results from our actions on things (Piaget, 1959).

That distinction of Piaget's is similar to the distinction between associative and cognitive learning. P learning is, in effect, conditioning, and it's the kind of learning that has been so thoroughly analyzed by Watson, Thorndike, and Skinner. P learning is externally motivated; it is made up of the properties of the physical objects that act on us (the sweetness of candy or the aversive properties of a slap on the hand) that have a potential reinforcing effect. This, of course, is precisely the way the behaviorists have described motivation in learning; and indeed this is exactly the way they should have described it, since they have been describing P learning almost exclusively. When Skinner, on the one hand, tells us that learning is the result of a given response followed by a reinforcing stimulus, he is in effect defining P learning—a physical event acting on the learner. LM learning, on the other hand, has been more the province of the cognitive-gestaltist theorists. LM learning is the result of our continuous experience of organizing and reorganizing our actions as we proceed toward the goal of understanding. Piaget says that LM learning is intrinsically motivated, that is, the discovery of a new relationship is self-rewarding. When children experience new LM relationships that they have discovered through their own actions, they feel pleasure, a joy that swells up from within.

After examining the positions of Skinner and Bruner, can we now say which one is right—which theory says it all? The answer, of course, is that both are right, though neither one is likely to have the supertheory. Skinner's laws of conditioning are certainly valid. The evidence with regard to operant conditioning overwhelmingly supports his position. Skinner has much to teach us about how to teach. He has simplified and made more efficient the learning of the informational background children need in order to think creatively. It must be remembered that P learning, though perhaps not as glamorous as LM, is crucial to intellectual growth. Skinner has given us invaluable aids for transmitting this P-learning base.

Bruner, too, has made an extremely important contribution, but at a different level. In his theory of instruction he has pointed out ways of carrying children beyond mere conditioning, or P learning. Bruner's interest is more in the area of cognitive organization, understanding, LM learning. To some extent, Bruner's theory may be more speculative than Skinner's, but exciting advances in science have often in the past been foreshadowed by sophisticated spec-

ulation. This isn't to imply that Bruner's position is not perched on an empirical base. After all, Bruner has spent long hours watching children going about the business of learning.

Now, in the 1990s, there seems finally to have occurred some elements of real compromise between the behaviorists and the more cognitively oriented theorists. In fact, an approach called *cognitive-behavior modification* has recently been gaining more and more adherents. These theorists accept much of what Skinner expounded over the years, but they utilize the Skinnerian methods within a context of cognitive reorganization. For example, instead of just having the child reinforced for emitting the appropriate operants, the child is also taught to mentally repeat phrases over and over, such as "I know I can be quiet and stay in my seat while the teacher is talking" (Meichenbaum et al., 1989). In this way, there is a stronger possibility of the external reinforcers being linked to the child's internal cognitions.

It is certainly true that all the answers are not yet in on this complex phenomenon called learning, but it is also true that Skinner and Bruner have pointed us in the direction of knowing more about what the questions are.

SUMMARY

Two major theorists in educational psychology are spotlighted in this chapter; Skinner, representing the behaviorist-associationist tradition, and Bruner, representing the cognitive-gestalt tradition. Both Skinner and Bruner discuss issues in learning that are of practical importance to the classroom teacher.

Skinner based his view of learning on the data gathered from his experimental laboratories, with little in the way of any theory building or deductive interpretations. Operant conditioning occurs when a response is followed by a reinforcing stimulus. The rate of responding then increases. Skinner distinguishes between operants (responses that need no stimuli to set them off) and respondents (responses that do need unconditioned stimuli to be activated). Skinner uses the term *respondent* to describe the same kind of behavior that Pavlov had previously described during his conditioning studies on dogs—that is, Skinner's *respondent* is synonymous with Pavlov's *reflex*.

The operant conditioning system also includes such other concepts and techniques as extinction, spontaneous recovery, discrimination, stimulus generalization, and conditioned reinforcement.

Skinner has also conducted research into the schedules of reinforcement--that is, the methods by which reinforcers are arranged. Responses that are reinforced periodically, either on the basis of time or the number of responses emitted, are conditioned more strongly and are thus more difficult to extinguish.

Skinner indicates that language is learned via the principles of operant conditioning. Also, such cognitive-sounding concepts as understanding and knowledge are really examples of operant conditioning. In order to gain knowledge, one must be equipped with the specific set of responses from which that knowledge may be inferred.

Good teaching, according to Skinner, is the ability to arrange the proper sequences of reinforcements for the student and then to be certain that the presentation of these reinforcers is contingent on the student's emitting the correct response.

Behaviorism today faces two important challenges, one due to internal, experimental anomalies (experimental results that are not consistent with the theory), and the other due to the rise of a more ethological and functional interpretation of behaviorism's known facts. Any theory faces a severe test when another theory can predict outcomes with more accuracy and entails fewer assumptions.

Bruner's position regarding learning is in the cognitive-gestalt tradition. His goal is to create a theory of instruction that will allow a teacher to prescribe how a given subject can best be taught.

Bruner's theory has four major principles: (1) motivation, (2) structure, (3) sequence, and (4) reinforcement. These four principles are aimed at producing a learning based on understanding and meaning, rather than on the conditioning of facts and details.

Bruner insists that meaningful learning requires the child to search actively for solutions. Such discovery learning is far more long-lasting and useful than learning based on memorization and conditioning. Good teaching demands that the student be encouraged to explore alternatives and discover new relationships. Bruner also insists that when presented appropriately, any subject matter can be understood by almost any child.

The theories of Skinner and Bruner, though seemingly diametrically opposed, share a common framework when viewed from the position of Jean Piaget. Piaget distinguishes between P learning, learning that takes place when physical things act on us, and LM learning, learning that results from our actions on things. Skinner's position seems consistent with Piaget's P learning, while Bruner may be discussing Piaget's LM learning.

KEY TERMS AND NAMES

Jerome Bruner
    discovery learning
    enactive representation
    iconic representation
    LM (logico-mathematical) learning
    motivation
    P (physical) learning
    structure
    symbolic representation
Noam Chomsky
B. F. Skinner
    conditioned reinforcement
    discrimination training

extinction
negative reinforcement
operant conditioning
operant level
operants
positive reinforcement
reinforcement
respondent conditioning
respondents
schedules of reinforcement
spontaneous recovery
stimulus generalization

THEORY INTO PRACTICE: LEARNING THROUGH UNDERSTANDING*

The behaviorist-associationists, Skinner, Thorndike, and Guthrie, all insist that learning results from the associations that are developed through the combining of stimuli with responses. The cognitive-gestalt view, however, stresses that learning should be based not on blind trial and error but instead on an overall understanding at a conceptual level. Because of this,

some cognitive theorists have perhaps gone too far in downgrading the learning of facts and rote memorization. Such expressions as "mere facts," which appear frequently in the cognitive literature, attest to the disdain the cognitivists feel for this type of learning. Jerome Bruner, however, although certainly a cognitive theorist, still acknowledges that the memorization of facts may still provide important components to the learning process. Some facts and specifics are essential in the development of meaningful understanding. For example, it would be difficult to solve

---

* We are indebted to Jerome Bruner and J. Richard Hayes for the idea behind the example we use in this Theory into Practice exercise.

an inertia problem in the physics lab, regardless of how much "understanding" is involved, if the student doesn't yet know how to multiply fractions. Bruner calls these facts the *stuff* of learning. Without some data to process, discovery learning and concept formation are difficult indeed. However, Bruner insists that one must go beyond just the facts (names, dates, events) for a cognitive reorganization to occur. In this exercise, we will attempt to put some of Bruner's notions to the test. The focus will be on both the development of concepts and the use of the iconic mode of representation.

If possible, select some younger children. (If that's not possible, ask your roommate or friends to help.) Present them with the following example:

Assume that plane flights in the south are limited to serving just five cities: (1) Charlotte, North Carolina; (2) Atlanta, Georgia; (3) Daytona, Florida; (4) El Paso, Texas; and (5) Birmingham, Alabama. Further assume that the flights occur in such a way that one can fly only from

Birmingham to Charlotte

Daytona to Charlotte

Atlanta to Birmingham

Atlanta to El Paso

Charlotte to Daytona

Charlotte to El Paso

Birmingham to Atlanta

Charlotte to Atlanta

Allow the subjects to study the list and, if they wish, even to memorize it. When they feel comfortable with the background of factual information, ask them to tell you the shortest way, or the most efficient route, to take in order to make a round-trip between Atlanta and Daytona. Now despite having memorized the information, the subjects will soon see that it is virtually impossible to come to a solution just by trying to process all that information in their heads.

Next, provide some conceptual help by introducing a more efficient method of holding the information in storage. Rewrite the list so that the five cities are now presented in alphabetical order: A—Atlanta, B—Birmingham, C—Charlotte, D—Daytona, and E—El Paso. Tell your subjects to categorize this information as follows:

Atlanta to Birmingham (A to B)

Atlanta to El Paso (A to E)

Birmingham to Charlotte (B to C)

Birmingham to Atlanta (B to A)

Charlotte to Atlanta (C to A)

Charlotte to Daytona (C to D)

Charlotte to El Paso (C to E)

Daytona to Charlotte (D to C)

Although the solution now becomes somewhat easier to imagine, it is still extremely difficult to keep all those sequences in mind and to move them around into a coherent model.

Finally, ask your subjects to diagram the various route combinations by using arrows to indicate the possible directions. Such as

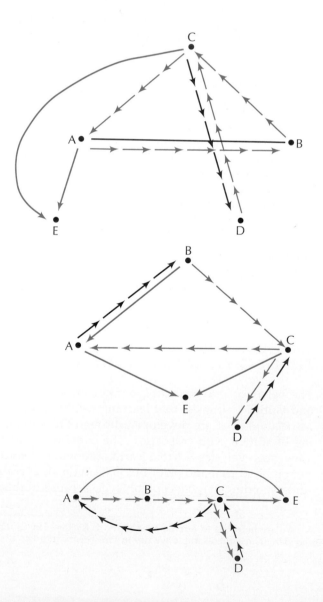

Notice the various diagrams which result. Some, such as the one at the bottom, produce a picture of the problem that represents the information in an extremely powerful form. The diagram at the top, although consistent with the parameters of the problem, does not show the same economy of thought. At this point, the problem begins to solve itself, and it becomes readily apparent that there is only one way to make a round-trip between Atlanta and Daytona: from Atlanta to Birmingham, from Birmingham to Charlotte, from Charlotte to Daytona, from Daytona back to Charlotte, and finally, from Charlotte

back to Atlanta. It then becomes apparent that El Paso is just a trap.

The diagram has provided a cognitive map of the entire problem, and through the use of this symbolic representation the subject was able to process the information more economically. As shown, the subject did need some facts to work with, but the facts alone, without a cognitive reorganization, were not sufficient to produce a valid solution. The symbolic representation provided the driving force for the final understanding.

REFERENCES

A.P.A. Monitor (1990). *21*, 6.

Bolles, R. C. (1980). Ethological learning theory. In G. M. Gazda and J. Corsini (Eds.), *Theories of learning* (p. 199). Itsaca, Ill.: Peacock.

Bowerman, M. (1987). Commentary. In B. MacWhinney (Ed.), *Mechanisms of language acquisition* (pp. 443–466). Hillsdale, N.J.: Erlbaum.

Bregman, E. O. (1934). An attempt to modify the emotional attitudes of infants by the conditioning response technique. *Journal of Genetic Psychology, 45*, 169–178.

Breland, K., and Breland, M. (1961). The misbehavior of organisms. *American Psychologist, 16*, 681–684.

Bruner, J. S. (1962). *The process of education.* Cambridge: Harvard University Press.

Bruner, J. S. (1966). *Toward a theory of instruction.* Cambridge: Harvard University Press.

Bruner, J. S. (1983). *Child's talk.* New York: Norton.

Bruner, J. S. (1987). *Actual minds, possible worlds.* Cambridge: Harvard University Press.

Bruner, J. (1990). *Acts of meaning.* Cambridge: Harvard University Press.

Carpenter, F. (1974). *The Skinner primer* (pp. 8–9). New York: Free Press.

Deci, E. L., Scheinman, L., Wheeler, L., and Hart, R. (1980). Rewards, motivation and self-esteem. *Educational Forum, 44*, 429–433.

Deno, S. L., and Chiang, B. (1979). An experimental analysis of the nature of reversals errors in children with severe learning disabilities. *Learning Disabilities Quarterly, 2*, 40–45.

Fowler, R. D. (1990). In memoriam. *American Psychologist, 45*, 1203.

Gentile, J. R. (1978). A cross-cultural, multidisciplinary proof of the newly discovered developmental linguistic law of concordance of speech and motor development in children. *American Psychologist, 33*(8), 761.

Getsie, R. L. (1985). Meta-analysis of the effects of type and combination of feedback on children's discrimination learning. *Review of Education Research, 55*, 9–22.

Hergenhahn, B. R. (1988). *An introduction to theories of learning* (2d ed., p. 84). Englewood Cliffs, N.J.: Prentice Hall.

Kuhn, T. S. (1970). *The structure of scientific revolutions* (2d ed.). Chicago: University of Chicago Press.

McMahon, F. B., and McMahon, J. W. (1986). *Psychology: The hybrid science* (5th ed., p. 223). Chicago: Dorsey.

Meichenbaum, D., Price, R., Phares, E. J., McCormick, N., and Hyde, J. (1989). *Exploring choices: The psychology of adjustment.* Glenview, Ill: Scott, Foresman.

Moore, B. R. (1973). The role of directed Pavlovian reaction in simple instrumental learning in the pigeon. In R. A. Hinde and J. Stevenson-Hinde (Eds.), *Constraints on learning.* New York: Academic Press.

Nafpaktitis, M., Mayer, G. R., and Butterworth, T. (1985). Natural rates of teacher approval and disapproval and their relations to student behavior in intermediate school classrooms. *Journal of Educational Psychology, 77*, 362–367.

Newell, A. (1990). *Unified theories of cognition: The William James lectures.* Cambridge: Harvard University Press.

The New York Times, April 9, 1991, p. C9.

Piaget, J. (1959). Apprentissage et connaissance (première partie) (pp. 21–67). In P. Greco and J. Piaget (Eds.), *Etudes d'épistémologie génétique*, Vol. 7. Paris: Presses Universitaires de France.

Seligman, M. E. P. (1970). On the generality of the laws of learning. *Psychological Review, 77*, 410.

Seligman, M. E. P. (1972). Phobias and preparedness. In M. E. P. Seligman and J. L. Hager (Eds.), *Biological boundaries of learning.* New York: Appleton-Century-Crofts.

Siegler, R. S., and Jenkins, E. (1989). *How children discover new strategies.* Hillsdale, N.J.: Erlbaum.

Skinner, B. F. (1971). *Beyond freedom and dignity* (p. 169). New York: Knopf.

Skinner, B. F. (1978). Why don't we use the behavioral sciences? *Human Nature, 1*(1), 32.

Skinner, B. F. (1988). What ever happened to psychology as the science of behavior? *Counselling Psychology Quarterly, 1*, 111–122.

VanLehn, K. (1988). Towards a theory of impasse driven learning. In H. Mandl and A. Lesgold (Eds.), *Learning issues for intelligent tutoring systems* (pp. 19–41). New York: Springer-Verlag.

10

LEARNING IN THE CLASSROOM

"In an American school, if you ask for the salt in good French, you get an A. In France you get the salt." This statement by B. F. Skinner illustrates perhaps the major feature of the educational process (Skinner, 1953). The concepts, skills, and techniques we teach are not only useful in the present, but more important, will also be useful at some later time. One of the major goals of education is to equip us to transfer what we learn in the classroom to future situations. Learning to add, subtract, and spell results in the immediate advantage of good grades, a gold star, a promotion to the next grade, or perhaps a teacher's or parent's general approval. Eventually, however, the advantages become more compelling. In later life we learn that our ability to spell or multiply or derive square roots has enormous practical consequences, for example, in helping us earn a living. Some of us learn this too late. "If only I had paid more attention in school," we moan. And, we might add, we might have paid more attention if our classroom experience had been structured differently.

TRANSFER

Transfer is the key to classroom learning. **Transfer** takes place when learning task A influences learning task B. Transfer may be positive or negative. When learning A facilitates learning B, **positive transfer** is said to have taken place; conversely, when learning A inhibits learning B, **negative transfer** has occurred. Here are a few examples of positive transfer: Learning to ride a motorcycle is easier if you already know how to ride a bike; learning Italian is easier if you already know Latin; writing a letter to Santa Claus is easy if you have learned your second-grade spelling. Here are some examples of negative transfer: Learning to lean forward while snow-skiing may cause you to fall on your face when you learn to water-ski; learning to keep your elbows away from your body to hit a baseball may cause a disastrous slice when you learn to hit a golf ball; studying a French assignment until the wee hours may wreak havoc with the Spanish exam you take the next morning.

There is also a special case of negative transfer in which the influence works in reverse. You successfully learn A and then learn B; when you try to recall A, you draw a complete blank. This is called *retroactive inhibition*, and it happens when the second task works retroactively to inhibit recall of the first task. More will be said on this important topic when we discuss information processing in Chapter 11.

Formal Discipline

Current theories of transfer can be traced back to the early Greek notion of formal discipline. According to this view, the role of the school is to discipline the students' minds. It was thought that the mind, like an athlete's muscles, must be systematically exercised until it becomes so strong it can learn and understand virtually any new material. The theory of formal discipline remained in vogue until the early twentieth century. Subjects such as logic, Latin, and Greek were taught not for their practical value, but because they were thought to strengthen the student's mind to the point at which all later problem solving would be easy.

The challenges to formal discipline   The theory of formal discipline was challenged around the turn of the century by three important psychologists. The first, William James, put the theory to the test (James, 1890). He spent 132 minutes, over an eight-day period, memorizing a long segment of poetry (Victor Hugo's *Satyr*). He reasoned that if the theory of formal discipline was correct, exercising the mind by memorizing another poem would make further memorization easier. He therefore spent the next thirty-eight days memorizing Book I of Milton's *Paradise Lost.* Finally, he tried to memorize another segment of the *Satyr,* equal in length to the first segment he had memorized, only to find that it took him even longer than it had previously. The results of this rather informal test led James to suspect the validity of the theory of formal discipline.

The second challenger, E. L. Thorndike, had subjects practice estimating the length of lines one-half to one-and-one-half inches long (Thorndike and Woodworth, 1901). When the subjects achieved a certain degree of accuracy in the task, Thorndike introduced a different, though similar task: estimating the length of lines six to twelve inches long. Thorndike found that there was little, if any, improvement on the second task as a result of the practice gained from the first task. Although he believed that he had thoroughly refuted the theory of formal discipline, Thorndike still maintained that transfer could occur. Thorndike based his explanation of transfer on the existence of certain elements in the second task that were identical to those in the first task.

The third challenger, Charles Judd, took on both the theory of formal discipline and Thorndike's "identical elements." In a classic experiment, Judd trained two groups of boys to hit a target submerged in twelve inches of water (Judd, 1908). One group of boys, the experimental group, was instructed in the general principles of refraction; the control group was not. Although both groups did equally well while the target was at the twelve-inch depth, when the target was later raised to a depth of four inches, the boys in the experimental group performed significantly better. The boys in the control group, who had not been given any of the principles of refraction, responded to the new task as though it were a completely new problem. On the basis of this experiment, Judd postulated the theory of transfer by generalization, which stated that transfer is far more efficient when the theory or the generalization behind the task is learned. The boys who had simply learned to hit a target submerged in twelve inches of water transferred this skill only to other targets also submerged twelve inches deep. When the target depth was changed, no transfer took place.

Judd thus insisted that classroom students should be taught abstractions and generalizations as well as the details of a subject. Students should still learn certain facts and possess certain information, but their ability to transfer depended equally on a basic understanding of the theoretical generalizations that allow those facts to be interpreted.

The Learning Curve

Many studies of the learning process have shown that the acquisition of new information or of a new skill proceeds in a predictable fashion. When first confronting a new subject, we begin learning slowly and then pick up speed rather dramatically. Finally, our pace slows down and begins to level off.

Figure 10.1 shows a typical **learning curve.** It is

FIGURE 10.1   A typical learning curve

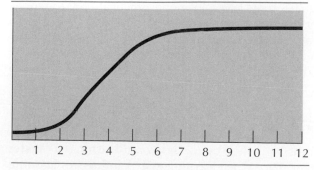

said to be negatively accelerated because as the number of trials increases, there is less and less increase in the amount learned. After the first few trials, in which the learner is "catching on" to the basic procedures, rather huge gulps of new learning are quickly assimilated. As time goes on, however, improvement becomes less and less pronounced and finally levels off. This leveling off is called a *plateau*. Novice golfers may score 150 their first few times around the course, but after their fourth or fifth round they may be down to around 120. At this point they may feel that it's easy to excel at golf and that, if they can continue lopping 30 strokes off their score, they will soon be ready for "the tour." They soon learn, however, that lowering their score from 100 to 90 is far more difficult than lowering it from 120 to 110.

Students learning a new skill may reach a whole series of plateaus. Typing students, for example, may proceed fairly rapidly at first and then level off. Perhaps they were learning the keyboard letter by letter. Suddenly, they notice another increase in performance, for now they have learned certain letter sequences like *ing*, or *tion*, or *the*, which can be rattled off as though they were single letters. This is actually an example of positive transfer, in which the previous learning finally builds up to the point at which a sharp increase in new learning has become possible.

Learning Sets

Harry Harlow has done some important research in learning, using monkeys as subjects. Harlow coined the phrase **learning set** to describe the phenomenon of learning how to learn. He found that with practice his monkeys became increasingly skilled at solving discrimination problems. They improved not only on the previously learned problems but on novel problems as well. The fact that the monkeys developed these learning sets freed "them from the restrictions of the slow, trial-and-error process of the original attempts" (Harlow et al., 1971, p. 301).

Using straightforward reinforcement techniques, Harlow trained monkeys to respond to an odd item among a set of three items. For example, the monkey would be presented with three geometric shapes, two circles and an "odd" item, in this case a triangle. Once the monkey learned to respond to the triangle, a different three-item set was presented, say two knives and a fork. With enough previous training, the monkeys would show the ability to select the fork, the new odd item. In short, the monkeys had learned a

rule or a relationship rather than a simple discriminated response to the triangle.

Harlow feels that his concept of learning sets has explained what the gestalt psychologists had labeled as insight. He sees the sudden spurt in learning, the so-called a-ha phenomenon, as just another extension of the theoretical concept of transfer.

Students can also be trained in learning how to learn. Through instruction, students have demonstrated an increased ability to learn relationships, which aided them in the retention of both classroom and textbook materials (Brown et al., 1981).

Massed versus Distributed Learning

If you had four hours to parcel out any way you wished, how could you make the most of this time to learn a new skill? In learning new motor skills, the evidence is fairly clear—distributed practice of, say, sixteen fifteen-minute segments is more efficient than a **massed learning** dose of four straight hours. When learning to skate, ride a bike, or perform a new skill in a physical education class, this distributed practice prescription is indeed sound advice. Not only are the shorter sessions less fatiguing but by their very nature, motor skills are best learned a step at a time.

The Spacing Effect

The value of spaced learning over massed learning is now called the **spacing effect,** and documentation of this phenomenon goes back more than a hundred years. In 1885, Hermann Ebbinghaus stated that "with any considerable number of repetitions a suitable distribution of them over a space of time is decidedly more advantageous than the massing of them at a single time" (Ebbinghaus, 1885). A few years later, in 1901, the great Harvard psychologist, William James, in his talks to teachers and students, advised that it is better to learn new material over many different days than "again and again on just a few days" (James, 1901).

Since those early days of Ebbinghaus and James, the literature in educational psychology has been filled with studies in support of the facilitative nature of the spacing effect. (For an impressive summary of these studies, see Dempster (Dempster, 1988). And these studies continue to pile up. For example, it has been found that students exposed to a short course in statistics learned more when the material was spread out over several sessions than when the same material was covered in a single long session (Smith and Rothkopf, 1984). Also, in learning and understanding the main points of a certain text, it was found that well-spaced presentations were significantly more effective than was a single, longer presentation (Reder and Anderson, 1982). Finally, in a study concerned with the learning of word definitions, acquisition was shown to be definitely enhanced by the spaced presentations, a finding that held up whether the words were presented with or without sentence context (Dempster, 1987).

On the strength of such a long and solid record of careful documentation, teachers should make more of an effort to include the spacing effect in their presentations and curriculum plans. One fairly straightforward approach could be based on increasing the amount of class time spent on review, with a special emphasis on spacing these review sessions. Also, the teacher might encourage students to space their study times, and also warn students of the deleterious effects of cramming for exams.

Whole versus part learning   The question of whether the material to be learned should be carved up and doled out in small units or whether it should be presented as an integrated whole, if only sketchily, is of great concern to educators. Is it more efficient for you, the reader, to try to master the material in this chapter by reading three pages a day or by reading through the whole chapter first and then going back and attempting to iron out the details? The message from Jerome Bruner is clear—the more meaningful the material, the easier it is to learn. Therefore, breaking it down into parts is a risky venture, unless the material to be learned is something like Ebbinghaus's nonsense syllables. To learn a simple problem or a short passage of poetry, working on it as a whole is probably best, since breaking that kind of material down into tiny units makes it less meaningful and, perhaps, could even destroy its meaning completely. Bruner has stressed the importance of keeping a subject internally coherent and meaningful when setting up efficient learning conditions. When longer material must be learned, a compromise can be worked out; the material can be divided into meaningful units and then learned as separate wholes.

The trouble with learning material in parts is that the parts eventually have to be pieced back together, and that can be extremely time-consuming. In many learning situations the best approach is to work first on the whole and then go back to the various parts. When presenting a new unit in, say, social studies, the teacher should spend some time discussing the general point of view of the whole unit before introducing the details. Giving the student an overview of the whole unit makes even the use of a teaching machine more effective.

SOCIAL LEARNING OR MODELING

Albert Bandura, an important contemporary psychologist, has suggested that a significant part of what a person learns occurs through imitation or modeling. Bandura has been called a social learning theorist in that he is concerned with the learning that takes place in the context of the social situation. During social interactions an individual may learn to modify his or her behavior as a result of how others in the group are responding.

Bandura's **social learning theory** is truly an all-inclusive psychology, borrowing as much from behaviorists as from cognitive theorists. Bandura sees behavior, internal cognitive structures, and the environment as interacting so that each acts as an interlocking determinant of the other (Bandura, 1978). People are to some extent products of their environments, but they also choose and shape their environments. It's not simply a one-way street.

Modeling versus Operant Conditioning

Though recognizing the importance of Skinner's operant conditioning, Bandura insists that not all learning takes place as a result of the direct reinforcement of responses. People also learn by imitating the behavior of other people, or models, and this learning takes place even though these imitative responses are not themselves being directly reinforced. For example, young children may stand up when the "Star-Spangled Banner" is played because they see their parents stand. A child's response in this instance is not immediately followed by an M&M candy or any other primary reinforcer. The child simply imitates the response made by the parents.

Learning new responses   In the previous example, the child's ability to stand up was, of course, already a part of his behavioral repertoire. Bandura further says that people can also learn *new* responses simply by observing the behavior of others. A child learns to ski or an adult learns a tennis stroke simply by imitating the behavior of the instructor. The language-lab method of teaching a foreign language is based on the premise that people can efficiently learn to imitate the electronically reproduced sentences and phrases the lab user listens to. The list of new forms of behavior that can be learned through **modeling** is virtually endless, and though the previous examples stress positive forms of learning, modeling may also create undesirable responses. A child may learn to become overly aggressive or deceitful and dishonest through the modeling mechanism.

In a now-classic study, Bandura subjected a group of young children (ages three to six) to the improbable spectacle of watching adult models punch, kick, and yell at a large, inflated Bobo doll (Bandura et al., 1963). When later allowed to play with Bobo themselves, these children displayed twice as many aggressive responses as a control group of children who had not witnessed this performance. The form of imitation in this study was indeed direct. The children even yelled the same phrases the adults had used: "Kick him," "Sock him in the nose," and so on. One might speculate that had the adults danced with Bobo rather than punching it, the children, too, would have behaved in this gentler fashion.

Reinforcement and modeling   Though, as has been shown, learning through modeling does not require direct and immediate reinforcement, Bandura has suggested that reinforcement may still be involved. In the first place, many of the significant models in the child's world, parents and teachers, are also in charge of the child's reinforcement schedule. The parent may not only provide the modeling stimulus but may also reinforce the child when the behavior is imitated. Second, Bandura has demonstrated that a child is more apt to imitate an adult model's response when the adult is being reinforced for that response (Bandura and McDonald, 1963). In other words, the child who observes an adult being praised for a certain action is more likely to respond in the same way than a child who views the action but not the subsequent reinforcement. Bandura calls this *vicarious learning*, since the learner in this instance is not being reinforced but is merely witnessing the reinforcement.

Thus, reinforcement and modeling can together create very potent conditions for behavior change. Many of our most persistent habits and attitudes are a result of this combination of powerful forces.

Modeling and retention   Reproducing the behavior of the model when the model is no longer present is facilitated when the learner uses verbal coding to symbolically store the behavior sequence in memory. That is, modeled behavior is retained longer if the learner can describe the behavior in words. This allows for internal rehearsal and organization. Although the learner can still model on the basis of visual imagery, verbal coding encompasses a far wider range of the kinds of activities usually found in schools (Bandura, 1982).

Modeling as a therapy technique   Bandura has also shown that the modeling process can be used as a technique in psychotherapy. Just as persons can learn certain fears through modeling, so too can these fears become unlearned. A child, for example, may learn to fear snakes by observing his father recoil in horror at the sight of a snake. In one study, Bandura attempted to cure a group of individuals who had severe snake phobias (Bandura et al., 1969). The subjects in one group watched, in various stages of agitation, while the experimenter or model handled and played with a king snake. The experimenter then urged the subjects to imitate his behavior, asking them first to touch the snake while wearing gloves, and later with their bare hands. After ten sessions, the cure rate was a phenomenal 100 percent. All the subjects in the group were able to pass the criterion test, that is, sit quietly for thirty seconds while a large snake was allowed to crawl all over them.

Significance in the Classroom

Other than the parents, the classroom teacher may be the most important model in the child's environment. Many children have been known to model their teacher's behavior so closely that they in a sense "become" the teacher when interacting with younger brothers and sisters at home. In some cases, these children demand that the younger siblings call them by their teacher's name—"I'm not Debbie, I'm Mrs. D." The teacher's likes and dislikes regarding subject matter may become obvious to the students and result in imitative attitudes. The teacher who loves music but hates math may, through vicarious learning, transmit these feelings to the class. So-called math blocks may be created in this way, and the student can be permanently affected.

Other types of negative teacher behavior may also

Bandura exposed a group of young children to adults who punched, kicked, and yelled at an inflated "Bobo" doll. Later, in playing with the doll, these children displayed twice as many aggressive responses as children who had not seen the aggressive behavior.

be imitated by the students. A first-grade teacher was having a very difficult time maintaining what she considered to be proper discipline in her classroom. She began spending more and more time screaming at the children. The parents of one of the children found that each day, after school, the child would shut herself up in her room and scream at her dolls (even using the same words the teacher had used). A teacher's attitude toward minority-group students can also have a significant effect, both on how the minority student learns to perceive himself or herself and on how the student is perceived by the other members of the class. In short, teachers provide conditions for learning in the classroom not only by what they say, but also what they do.

OPERANT CONDITIONING IN THE CLASSROOM

As we saw in the previous chapter, Skinner's principles of operant conditioning can be translated into specific classroom techniques. The Skinnerians feel that colleges have failed to equip prospective teachers for the actual day-to-day job of educating children. The new teacher, no matter how knowledgeable in educational theory, is usually at a complete loss when it comes to putting theory into practice. The teacher may understand the importance of recognizing individual differences, and may know full well that learning requires motivation and that students' interest must be captured, but then what? What happens when, in order to motivate students, the new teacher proudly displays the best student's written work on the bulletin board, only to find the next day that the essay is on the floor and the thumbtacks have been stolen? What happens when the new teacher, steeped in the philosophy of fairness, leaves the room and asks the students to cover their eyes so that the one guilty child can come discreetly forward and return a dime that has been stolen from another child? Not only is the dime not returned, but one young philanthropist, missing the teacher's point entirely, loudly offers to contribute a dime to the aggrieved child so that the class can go on to important matters. What happens when the new teacher demands that an unruly child sit down and be quiet, only to have the child stare back coolly and say, "Make me!"? What happens when . . . and on and on.

The current popularity of operant conditioning techniques is due in large measure to the fact that operant conditioning offers the teacher a precise prescription for handling specific classroom situations. The Skinnerians do not resort to such clichés as "seizing the teachable moment" or being an "educational provocateur." The Skinnerians are specific, and they urge the teacher to be just as specific.

The Case for Behavior Modification

Some of the essentials of this thing we now call behavior modification have probably been with us since time immemorial. As soon as people "discovered" that their behavior could be affected by environmental conditions, some aspects of behavior modification came into being. Many of today's college students, on hearing their first lecture on behavior modification, respond with a smug yawn and ask, "So what else is new?"

The fact is, however, that despite its apparently long history and despite its obvious overtones of "mere common sense," **behavior modification** as it is technically understood and used today is of fairly recent origin. It is a powerful technique that has been derived from both learning theory, especially as suggested by B. F. Skinner, and also from the accumulated results of numerous learning studies provided to us from the laboratories of experimental psychologists. The prospective teacher should be aware that the American Psychological Association is adamant in demanding that behavior modification techniques be used only in the pursuit of positive goals, that is, to reduce human suffering and increase human functioning (Stolz et al., 1975).

As we survey the behavior modification literature, it is also important to remember that a particular problem child does not exist in a vacuum. The child is not just a member of your class but also a member of various outside peer and social groups and, especially, a member of a family. Positive intervention is far more successful when accomplished through teamwork, with members of the child's family as part of the team. "Parent and family priorities and needs, as well as their values and beliefs, will continually influence the content and style of intervention" (Widerstrom et al., 1991).

Finally, it should be pointed out that behavior modification, unlike Freud's theory of psychoanalysis, assumes that the most important forces affecting any individual are the current life experiences, not the memories of childhood events and traumas.

Defining objectives   Every teacher has a general idea of educational goals for the class as a whole or for individual students. It is crucial that these goals be specifically stated in objective, behavioral terms, so that both the teacher and the students know what the goals are and when they have been reached. Furthermore, goals should be specified not just for the term but for each day of the term.

Behavioral terminology avoids words such as *understanding*—that is, words that do not describe a demonstrable behavior. A behaviorally formulated objective is one that describes the behavior that will result when the objective is attained. For example, students can be said to have learned multiplication when they can recite the multiplication table with no errors. In terms of daily goals they may be expected to make no more than five errors the first day, no more than two the second day, and none at all the third day. Each time a goal, or **terminal behavior,** is reached, a new goal is set so that the first goal is just a step in a continuing process toward an overall goal.

Say the goal, or the terminal behavior, for a certain child is to develop better study habits in the classroom. This must then be defined in behavioral terms. Perhaps the teacher wants the child to not gaze into space, to talk and fidget less, and to read and write more. When the goal is objectified in this way, the teacher can accurately judge whether or not the terminal behavior is achieved, and if it is, exactly when.

Reading skills can be objectified as the ability to recognize correct definitions for a hundred selected words. Music appreciation can be objectified as the ability to identify the composers of twenty musical compositions. The proponents of behavior modification argue that anything that can be taught can be objectified, and that all educational goals can be stated in behavioral terms. Critics may argue that being able to recognize twenty composers "isn't what we mean by musical appreciation" or that recognizing definitions of a hundred selected words "isn't what we mean by reading skills." If so, the Skinnerians would say that it is up to the critics to state clearly what they do mean in order that these goals can be knowingly reached:

> Mathematical behavior is usually regarded, not as a repertoire of responses involving numbers and numerical operations, but as evidences of mathematical ability or the exercise of the power of reason. It is true that the techniques which are emerging from the experimental study of learning are not designed to "develop the mind" or to further some vague "under-standing" of mathematical relationships. They are designed, on the contrary, to establish the very behaviors which are taken to be evidences of such mental states or processes (Skinner, 1954, p. 86).

Establishing the operant level   Once the goal has been defined (and nobody says this is easy, but then, good teaching is not easy), the teacher must observe the student and establish the operant level, or the rate at which the behavior occurs naturally in the classroom. Since student responses are so often specific to the stimulus situation, it is important that the operant level be established by observing the classroom. Many children who are disruptive in class are as good as gold in the counselor's or principal's office. If unruly students are sent to the psychologist's office, they are not as likely to display their disruptive behavior, since the releasers for this behavior remain back in the classroom.

Let's visit a fifth-grade classroom and observe the behavior of an eleven-year-old boy, Walter S. An art lesson is in progress. As the teacher begins giving the directions for today's project, Walter stands on top of his desk and calls out his own name, "Wally, Wally, Wally," and makes strange, grunting sounds for two minutes. After the teacher's tenth request, Walter sits down and remains silent for just over one minute. The students then file toward the front of the room to pick up their supplies. Walter spends the next two minutes running back and forth, occasionally sliding, as though going into home plate. The teacher brings Walter's supplies to his desk, where Walter remains seated quietly for almost three minutes. Among the art supplies are some elastic bands which he suddenly discovers can be put to use in an aggressive way. He flicks them at the other students for the next thirty seconds, or until he runs out. One girl receives a direct hit and calls loudly to the teacher, who is three rows away helping another student. Walter laughs at the girl's discomfort but immediately takes his seat when the teacher comes over to investigate the uproar. Walter finally gets down to work and remains quietly at his seat for almost ten minutes. Suddenly, he discovers that a certain piece of cardboard, which he had previously cut, doesn't quite fit where he had planned to glue it. He leaps back on top of his desk, makes loud noises, and contorts his face. The class seems to enjoy his performance, and despite the teacher's pleas, he remains on top of his desk for almost three minutes.

Out of twenty-two minutes of class time, Walter

has now spent just over seven minutes engaging in disruptive behavior. His operant level for disruptive behavior is, thus, a little over 34 percent.

What should be done with Walter? Behavior modification experts, such as Charles and Clifford Madsen, say that the teacher has the responsibility to help Walter. He is obviously a problem child. In testing Walter, the school psychologist discovers that Walter's home life is extremely bad: He has no father, his older siblings engage in delinquent behavior, there is no supervision in the home at all, and so on. Walter's test scores show him to be "precariously adjusted." Perhaps the teacher now feels a sense of compassion toward Walter and even some guilt for having disliked him so. Walter is probably headed for real trouble and may someday spend a great deal of time in a more structured institution than a school. Should the teacher give up on trying to interact meaningfully with Walter? The proponents of behavior modification say no.

In discussing the problem child, in this case the proverbial "Johnny," Madsen and Madsen say:

> The truly pathetic situation is that no one will teach Johnny. The one place where there is some hope for Johnny is the school. Yet, many teachers quickly abdicate responsibility once his history is known. Johnny can discriminate. He can be taught new responses to deal with that world outside the home. He can learn to read, write, spell; he can learn new rules of social interaction and thereby break the cycle of the past. If cooperation (with the home) is impossible, he can even learn these responses in spite of a bad home. It is not easy to deal with the Johnnies [or the Walters]. They take time, energy and a disciplined teacher. All the Johnnies do not survive; yet for these children the school is their only hope. Who has the responsibility of discipline?—The teacher (Madsen and Madsen, 1970, p. 14).

The modification of behavior   Once the educational goals have been defined behaviorally and the operant level assessed, one can begin the job of modifying behavior. The techniques used are those outlined in Chapter 9. In order to change responses, in order to modify behavior, we must allow the operant to occur and then provide an appropriate stimulus situation. For example, if we wish to strengthen a certain response (i.e., increase the rate of a given operant), the response must be allowed to occur and then be followed by positive or negative reinforcement. Recall that a positive reinforcement is a stimulus that, following a given response, increases the rate of that response. A negative reinforcement is a stimulus that, when removed, increases the response rate. Both positive and negative reinforcement increase rather than decrease the strength of a given response. Punishment, however, is an aversive stimulus that reduces the rate of the response. We will discuss punishment in detail later in the chapter, but it is important to note now that punishment and negative reinforcement are very different kinds of stimulus situations that have exactly opposite effects on response rates.

The Use of Reinforcement

Positive reinforcement   In the classroom, positive reinforcement may be provided by a primary reinforcer, such as milk, cereal, or candy, or it may be a conditioned reinforcer, such as gold stars, high grades, social approval, or, in the case of younger pupils, physical contact.

> A certain student, John D., would not remain attentive or even attempt to do his numerical reason problems. The teacher set the behavioral goal of nineteen correct solutions out of twenty problems. Observation of the student indicated that his operant level was zero; he simply would not do the work. After a conference with his parents, the boy was sent to school each morning without any breakfast. The teacher used milk and cereal as the positive reinforcers for correct math solutions. The student reached the desired goal on the fourth day.

> Tommy L., a third-grade student, was boisterous and noisy in class and prevented other students from concentrating on their own work. The first behavioral goal was set at thirty minutes of complete silence. Tommy was presented with an M&M candy each time he remained quiet for forty-five seconds. On the eighth day the goal was reached. At this point a new goal was set for sixty minutes of silence. Also the reinforcement schedule was altered so that Tommy had to remain silent for two minutes in order to receive the M&M reinforcement. The new goal was reached in only three days.

Such primary reinforcers as food for the child who has had no breakfast or candy for the child who loves sweets are obviously of a positive nature. When it comes to conditioned reinforcers, however, the teacher must observe the situation closely, for, as the proverb states, "One man's meat may be another man's poison." What the teacher may consider a positive reinforcer will not necessarily be such for each and every student. If we think of a particular child as having the goal of teacher attention (just as the rat in the Skinner box has the goal of obtaining the food), then the actual conditioning is based on learning that a specific behavior leads to the attainment of a specific goal (Rescorla, 1987). Usually, however, the teacher can select from conditioned reinforcers. Madsen and Madsen suggest the following:

1. Words—spoken and written
2. Expressions—facial and bodily
3. Closeness—nearness and touching
4. Activities and privileges
5. Things—materials, awards, toys (Madsen and Madsen, 1970).

Negative reinforcement   Negative reinforcement —the removal of an aversive stimulus in order to increase response rate—has been used in a variety of school settings. One fairly common use of this is the so-called time-out procedure, a technique, incidentally, that is commonly used by parents in the home (Sears et al., 1957). In a study conducted at the University of Kansas on preschool children with poor cognitive, language, and social skills, the time-out procedure has produced some dramatic results. A child who exhibits low self-control is placed for brief periods of time in a small room next to the classroom. When the child's behavior becomes more positive and less hyperactive, he or she is allowed to return (aversive stimulus is removed) to the regular classroom. This technique is especially potent when it is later combined with the use of various positive reinforcers, which can then be used to build up a repertoire of desirable responses. In fact, one of the reasons the time-out procedure has proved to be so effective is that while the child is in isolation there are few if any positive reinforcers for maintaining the child's undesirable behavior (Brantner and Doherty, 1983).

Negative reinforcement has proved successful in shaping a variety of desired responses. In one instance a student who had not done his homework assignment was placed in a time-out room and told to complete the work. Only when the assignment was finally completed was the student allowed back into the classroom. In this case, the removal of the aversive stimulus (escape from the isolation room) acted to strengthen the behavior (doing the assignment).

Negative reinforcement should be used only with great caution. An example cited by Madsen and Madsen involved a second-grade boy whose teacher made him wear a girl's ribbon in his hair until he began acting in a more controlled fashion. Whenever his behavior improved, the hair ribbon was removed. Madsen and Madsen question the advisability of this particular technique on the grounds that it might affect the child's perception of his sex identification.

A teacher should examine carefully the possible disturbing consequences whenever considering the use of negative reinforcement. There is a real difference between placing children in a time-out room, where they have the opportunity to finish their work, and shoving them into an unlighted closet with the door closed. It is obviously very easy for the teacher's intended negative reinforcement to become simple punishment. When that occurs, as Skinner has pointed out, the whole purpose of reinforcement is defeated (Skinner, 1969). Control by aversive means may provoke a counterattack; day-dreaming, dropping out, vandalism, refusal to learn assignments are all common indications of an attempt to avoid aversive control.

Consistency   Perhaps the major premise underlying the technique of behavior modification is that consistency should be observed at all times. Once a child is placed on a reinforcement program, the teacher must not waver. As Skinner's research on animals has shown, behavior that is intermittently reinforced is the most difficult to extinguish. If children are told that every time they act in a certain way they will be sent to the principal's office, they must be sent to the office every time they act that way. There can be no exceptions. Inconsistency teaches just that—inconsistency. As Madsen and Madsen point out,

> The child does not remember the 1,321 times he went to bed at 8 P.M., he remembers the two times he got to stay up. The third grader does not really believe that the teacher will send him to the time-out room (isolation) for ten minutes. This is already the sixth time the teacher has threatened and nothing has happened yet. The ninth grader cheated before and didn't get caught; why should he get caught this time? The college student has turned in late papers before; why should this professor be such a hard nose? (Madsen and Madsen, 1970, p. 34).

Consistency is a key ingredient in the success of any behavior modification program. The cute little student who pleads, "Can't you make an exception just this once?" may be hard for the teacher to resist, but resist the teacher must. Once the teacher breaks the rules, the children learn only too well that the rules are there for the breaking.

> A ninth-grade creative writing class was slowly but surely getting out of control; assignments were not being turned in, the students were becoming increasingly boisterous and rude both to the teacher and to each other. The teacher, Miss W., pleaded with the students to be fair and meet her half way, but this had no effect. It was suggested to Miss W. that reinforcement principles might be applied. She thereupon informed the class that if they behaved well for two successive days, they would go on a trip downtown to see the movie *Hamlet*. The next two days found the class no different, just as rowdy, just as out of control. Virtually every five minutes Miss W. shouted (to those who could hear her) that if they didn't behave, the trip would be canceled. In fact, she actually canceled the trip three times, but on the third day, the class pleaded with her and she relented. They saw the movie, and the next day the classroom situation deteriorated even more. Miss W. was beside herself. "I've tried everything, even behavior modification, and nothing works." She went back to class and pleaded with the students to be fair.

In her discussion of discipline in the classroom, one educator has suggested two basic rules:

1. Be consistent.
2. Know your subject matter.

From personal experience, that educator discovered those rules as she went through her first year of teaching. She found that initially children will not give back kindness for kindness; they must be shown rules, and these rules *must never be relaxed*. Nor can a threat of punishment be made unless it will be carried out—every time. As she notes,

> That second year of teaching, I began the first classes with a quiet statement of the rules: no one could leave his or her seat without permission; no one could communicate with a fellow student without permission; no one could call out an answer without first being recognized. The penalty for the smallest infringement of the rules was to remain after school in my room from three until five o'clock. No exceptions would be permitted. Invariably, some inoffensive student would open his mouth by mistake. He would be given a note on his desk, unobtrusively, to report at three. The next morning, after a dull session of gazing at me or resting his head on the desk, the

student "got the word around." "She's tough, be careful." Two or three students slipped—and suffered utter, long boredom. The result was a quiet room, not of surly students, but of careful, somewhat surprised young people (Spettel, 1983).

Thus, the teacher in the classroom, like a first-rate sports referee, must be an absolutely consistent enforcer of the rules. When a referee calls a foul, the player can't stop the game to negotiate a better deal, or beg for an exception just this once, or promise not to do it again. Once the rules have been explained, the teacher should not be put off by the child who constantly asks why. "Why" isn't always a question; it can also, as every parent knows, be a subterfuge, a stall, or an opening salvo in a new barrage of negotiations.

The timing of reinforcement   To modify behavior effectively, the reinforcement must be timed to occur after the desired response has occurred. The teacher should never, never deliver the reinforcement on the promise that the behavior will occur later. For example, a teacher asks the students in his class to turn in their assignments at the beginning of each class period. At the start of the next class period no assignments are handed in. The teacher then tells them that if they promise to begin turning in their assignments the following Monday, they can have a record party for the last half hour of today's class period. The class quickly promises, has the record party, and the teacher is still waiting for the homework.

A seven-year-old boy enters his house muttering an innocuous swear word. His mother becomes upset and urges the boy never to say that word again. In exchange for his promise to obey her, the mother gives him a quarter. An hour later he returns demanding a dollar, saying, "If you think that word was bad, wait 'til you hear this!"

Reinforcement must follow actual behavior. We learn by doing, not by talking about doing or by promising to do. As the behavior modifiers argue, the reinforcement must be made contingent on the appropriate response.

Punishment

The use of **punishment** to control behavior has been a controversial issue among both learning theorists and educators. Thorndike, for example, changed his position on the question of punishment. His original law of effect stated that reward and punishment had equal but opposite effects, reward strengthening and punishment weakening a learned stimulus-response connection. Later in his career, Thorndike revised this law drastically, saying that reward was far more effective in reinforcing learning than punishment was in weakening it. Later still, the Skinnerians demonstrated that if a rat was reinforced, say, a hundred times for pressing a lever and thus had a rather large buildup of responses waiting to be emitted, punishment would temporarily slow down the response rate but would not reduce the number of responses that would be emitted once the punishment was removed.

The typical experiment used a rat in an experimental chamber. The rat was reinforced with a food pellet for each lever press, until lever-pressing became highly resistant to extinction. (The rat's lever-pressing response was strengthened until the animal would emit, say, 200 responses without being further reinforced.) The lever was then electrified so that the rat now received a punishing shock every time it pressed the lever. The rat learned very quickly to stay away from the lever. However, once the shock was removed, the animal went determinedly back to the lever and all 200 responses were finally emitted. Punishment had merely held the responses in abeyance, suppressing them temporarily until the aversive stimulus was removed.

Because of Thorndike's changed position, the rat data from the Skinnerians, and other studies and theoretical positions, many psychologists and educators assumed that punishment had no real effect on learning. This scientific news was greeted with some skepticism, especially by older teachers who recalled the effect of the hickory stick on class control. Many parents and grandparents also found it difficult to mesh this "scientific breakthrough" with their own experiences in raising children.

More recent psychological studies, especially those carried out in the past ten years, have shown that punishment is indeed an effective technique for controlling behavior. The problem with the previously mentioned rat study was that it was an extremely artificial situation. In the first place, the rats were exceptionally highly motivated to press the lever—the lever was the route to life-sustaining food for these poor starving creatures. In the second place, no alternative response would produce the reinforcement. If a rat is given another response option during the time the punishment is in force, the original lever-pressing response does indeed weaken very rapidly. Punishment may not be a humane conditioning technique, and it may create some serious side effects, but it does control behavior. Even the most humanitarian parent seems to know this in moments of crisis. A child who is playing on a busy highway is quickly punished and then shown another area where he can play safely. A baby is not "reasoned with" when she is found poking her fingers into a light socket.

Punishment in the classroom usually takes the form of disapproval or of withholding a positive reinforcer. Severe disapproval by the teacher may often be an effective form of controlling behavior, but it does not instill a love of learning. Withholding a positive reinforcer, if the rule of consistency is religiously followed, is also an extremely effective behavior modifier. This method of aversive control takes such forms as the loss of privileges, objects, or pastimes the students value. The purist should note that withholding a positive reinforcer when used as punishment is not the same as extinction.

> In extinction, consequences that ordinarily follow the behavior are simply discontinued; in punishment, behavior results in the application of aversive consequences through forfeiture of positive reinforcers. Thus in extinguishing aggression sustained by peer attention, the behavior is consistently ignored; under the punishment contingency, however, the rewards of peer attention are pitted against the negative effects of confinement to one's room, loss of television privileges, or some other type of negative outcome (Bandura et al., 1969, p. 338).

Proponents of behavior modification have made extensive use of punishment in psychotherapy. For example, male homosexuals have been treated by showing them slides of nude men and women. While viewing the slides of male nudes, the patient receives an unpleasant shock through electrodes attached to his leg. While viewing the female nudes, no such punishment is administered. The proponents claim this technique has been successful in changing the sexual orientation of a number of subjects.

Children who suffer from stuttering have also been treated by the administration of electric shock whenever they begin stammering. Fairly dramatic recovery rates, within two weeks or less, have been attributed to the use of this technique. (It is important to point out here that successful treatment of stuttering has also been claimed for techniques using positive reinforcement.) (Craig and Cleary, 1982).

Punishment has even proved effective with severely disturbed children, children who unless restrained bang their heads against hard objects, tear and bite off pieces of their own flesh, pummel their own faces, and so on. Despite the fact that these children might be assumed to enjoy being hurt, they apparently don't enjoy being hurt by others. Research in this area indicates that the use of shock, administered whenever self-injurious behavior is observed, can drastically reduce and even eliminate self-destructive responses.

There is, however, growing concern that the use of electric shock on people may be ethically wrong and an infringement on the individual's civil liberties (Davison and Stuart, 1975). No doubt, there are moral issues and even problems of possible physical harm to be considered. One report describes treatment of a psychotic child for self-injurious behavior by administering painful electric shocks with a cattle-prod device. This technique resulted in the total elimination of such behavior after *167 days of treatment* (Tate and Baroff, 1966). American companies are even advertising radio-controlled "Remote Shockers" that can "deliver a painful shock from up to 300 feet away." These devices have been displayed at psychology conventions. A plea has been advanced that if a person who may not have the capacity to give full and informed consent is to be subjected to such aversive conditioning procedures, then an outside, objective advocate should be called in to determine the person's best interests (Koocher, 1976). Thus, retarded or psychotic children and adults will be protected from the possible abuses arising from the indiscriminate use of a painful shock as an aversive stimulus.

Does punishment cause emotional disturbance? The question of whether the use of punishment causes any long-term emotional damage is one that has as yet not been fully answered. The traditional, almost legendary view is that punishment is very much involved in the origin of behavioral disorders. One theorist has outlined a long series of punishment-provoked problems, including rigidity, social deviance, poor adjustment, and regression (Maurer, 1974). However, other psychologists are not so sure. One expert in the field of punishment argues that many punishment procedures produce no long-term emotional outcomes. The real question to be argued is not whether some forms of aberrant behavior can be produced by certain punishment procedures but whether these reactions are typical results of punishment. "The answer to this question is clearly 'no,' although specific circumstances can be contrived to

produce such effects" (Walters and Grusec, 1977, p. 158).

Many of the experts in behavior modification now lean toward the view that most of the alleged negative side effects of punishment can be eliminated or at least minimized if the punishment is administered correctly and if alternative behaviors are available and encouraged. Teachers and parents, however, should never rely on punishment as the behavior modifier of choice. The overuse of punishment can produce in children the feeling that they are always doing something wrong. Eventually, the child may even begin to desire punishment in order to alleviate these feelings of guilt (Newsom et al., 1983).

Aversive Stimuli in the Classroom

The use of aversive stimuli in the classroom, whether as negative reinforcement or as punishment, should be viewed with extreme caution. Although certainly an effective means of controlling behavior, it rarely instills in the student a joyful attitude toward learning. Aversive stimuli can also act to classically condition emotional responses that can cause "blocks" to future learning (see Chapter 9). Punishment's effect on behavior, although possibly very depressing in the presence of the aversive stimulus, may not generalize at all beyond that stimulus. As has been stated elsewhere, punishing a student for a certain behavior does not necessarily mean that the student stops engaging in the behavior. "Rather, the student may simply learn not to engage in that behavior in the presence of the teacher. The behavioral pattern may remain with the student in all other environments" (Hurt et al., 1978, p. 32).

If punishment is to be used, it should be used sparingly and only in conjunction with a positive reinforcement of some alternative response. That is, while the punishment is suppressing an undesirable response, positive reinforcement should be used to strengthen a socially approved alternative response. Punishment has only a short-lived effect on people who have few response options. This is why it is so often ineffective in the case of criminals—they have few, if any, socially approved means of achieving the material things our society values. In short, behavior modification brought about through positive reinforcement is more likely to be lasting and, eventually, self-perpetuating than that brought about through the use of aversive controls.

Psychologist Bruno Bettelheim has long been an opponent of the use of punishment as a method for changing behavior. Taking a humanistic position, he argues that punishment may traumatize the child and/or make the child become more devious. The best way to discipline a child, Bettelheim asserts, is to tell the child that "we are sure that had he known he was doing wrong he wouldn't have done so" or that "we disapprove of what he has done but are convinced that his intentions were good" (Bettelheim, 1985). Treating children in this manner, Bettelheim believes, can promote a healthy sense of moral discipline within the child, rather than destruction of self-esteem.

Extinction

A basic principle in learning is that behavior that is not reinforced will slowly be extinguished. A rat that has learned to press a lever 400 times per hour will eventually press it only four or five times per hour if his lever-pressing response ceases to be reinforced. Learned responses are abandoned when they no longer result in a payoff.

Studies of extinction in rats and humans have uncovered an interesting phenomenon. During extinction the rate of responding initially increases before it begins to peter out. The teacher who discovers that her display of anger toward a certain student somehow positively reinforces his undesirable behavior decides that she will simply ignore the student in order to extinguish his behavior. To her dismay, the teacher notes that the student's behavior increases rather than decreases. At this point consistency may be difficult, but it must be maintained if the extinction technique is to be successful. The student who is suddenly denied reinforcement for his undesired behavior tries even harder before finally realizing that the situation has really changed.

Extinction techniques will work only if the teacher can

1. Identify what is reinforcing the student's behavior
2. Eliminate that reinforcer
3. Remain faithful to the program

Shaping

Shaping is the technique of reinforcement by **successive approximation** until the desired response is emitted. For example, a rat newly introduced into an experimental chamber doesn't immediately rush over to the lever and start pressing it in order to receive the reinforcer. If left completely on its own, the rat may take an hour or even longer to stumble upon the lever. In order to speed up the conditioning process, the experimenter will shape the rat's behavior by reinforcing it first for simply facing the lever; then, each time the rat makes a new response that results in a further approach to the lever, the behavior is immediately reinforced. The point is to get the animal winning as quickly as possible even if the ultimate behavioral goal has not been exhibited.

In the classroom, this shaping technique is an important aspect of behavior modification. It is important, especially in the younger grades, that children attain success *quickly and often*. Later, the number of reinforcements may be stretched over longer periods of time and thereby reduced. With young children, the use of food is extremely effective. Again, as time goes by, the food may be paired with social stimuli such as smiling, nodding, praising, so that later on conditioned reinforcers may replace the primary reinforcers.

Madsen and Madsen provide an excellent example of shaping in which M&M candy is used to reinforce the responses of young children on the first day of school.

> The teacher may start the very first class with an M&M party. While the children are eating, the teacher says, "We will have another M&M party if everyone is quiet while I count to ten." The teacher counts aloud quickly, making sure they win. After giving the candy the teacher says, "If everyone is quiet for five minutes we will have another party, but if someone talks we will not get to have one." Now the teacher sits back and waits; in all probability someone will talk, whereupon the teacher says, "Oh, I'm very sorry. Mary talked before our time was up; now we will not get to have a party. Maybe tomorrow we may have one if everyone is quiet." Some children will think this is not fair. Because the teacher does not get angry at Mary, Mary cannot give her problem to the teacher (Madsen and Madsen, 1970, p. 26).

The Token System

Another behavior modification technique that is being used more and more is the **token system,** or the token economy. In this system, individuals receive various tokens for emitting desired responses, and

SPOTLIGHT ON SELF-DIRECTED LEARNING

Behavior Modification in Action

Virtually all the behavior modification techniques described so far can in fact be used by individuals wishing to change their own behavior.[a] In effect, you can act in the dual role of both subject and experimenter. You choose the responses you want to reinforce, and you choose the reinforcers and even the scheduling of the reinforcement. You must select your own behavioral goals, and as your own controller, you must discipline yourself so that you will not violate the law of consistency—no matter what the distractions might be. For example, suppose you decide that you want to lose ten pounds. Next, decide what the reinforcer should be, and in this you must be totally honest with yourself and choose something that you really do want. Let's say that you are an ardent fan of your school's basketball team. Next, set up a schedule that is realistic, such as two pounds per week. Don't try for the whole ten pounds all at once. Remember, there are such things as successive approximations and shaping. Now comes the hard part: *Don't allow yourself to go to next week's home game unless the two pounds have been lost!* Continue this procedure each week until the shaping has changed your shape. Actually this is just one example in a general area called *self-regulated learning* (see Chapter 19). Behaviorists, as in the above example, focus on tangible goals,[b] whereas cognitive psychologists prefer to talk about less tangible outcomes, such as self-actualization or reduced cognitive dissonance.[c]

---

[a] D. L. Watson and R. G. Tharp, *Self-directed Behavior*, 4th ed. (New York: Norton, 1985).
[b] F. C. Mace, P. J. Belfiore, and M. C. Shea, Operant theory and research on self-regulation. In B. J. Zimmerman and D. H. Schunk (Eds.), *Self-regulated learning and academic achievement: Theory, research and practice* (New York: Springer-Verlag, 1989), pp. 27–50.
[c] B. J. Zimmerman, Self-regulated learning and academic achievement: An overview. *American Psychologist* (1970), 25, 3–17.

---

these tokens are later exchanged for prizes or privileges (just like the use of money). The token system is simply another method for employing a work-payment incentive program. Rather than keep a large refrigerator stocked with tasty food and drink beside the desk, the classroom teacher can set up a token economy.

Tokens, or conditioned reinforcers, can be virtually anything the teacher has available: pieces of colored cardboard, colored wool, gold stars, or poker chips, for example. The tokens are assigned point values and may eventually be turned in for some treasured prize, privilege, or desired activity. Tokens are awarded for desirable student behavior: accurate spelling, a certain number of correctly solved math problems, learning a specified number of lines of poetry, participating in class discussions, whatever. The colored pieces of cardboard may be set so that a red piece is worth, say, five points, a blue piece three points, and a white piece one point. Point values are assigned to the prizes so that a child can accumulate enough points in one day to earn a moderately valued prize, but may have to spend an entire week working toward a particularly desirable prize. This system has two advantages: It maintains a high daily rate of desirable responses, and it teaches delayed gratification or an ability to think in long-range terms.

One example of the use of the token system involved a group of retarded children. One of the girls, who had been labeled "trainable retardate," especially enjoyed listening to records. Every time she earned twenty points for various academic accomplishments she was allowed ten minutes at the record player.

Under this reinforcement system she was learning to read, write, and do arithmetic, skills that were thought impossible for her. Needless to say, she now had a teacher who didn't believe in limiting children by categories, but who started with what the student could do and tried to take her further. This teacher's only complaint was that he had to spend so much time developing new materials as his "trainables" learned the old (Meacham and Wiesen, 1969, p. 50).

Some psychologists have questioned the use of the token system for two reasons. First, since the token system relies for its effect on extrinsic reinforcement,

The game of Monopoly, in the context of play, can teach children the value of token money.

it may in the long run decrease a student's intrinsic motivation to learn. Second, it may be that once the tokens are withdrawn (and a student cannot be kept on a token system forever), the resulting behavior changes may be extinguished.

Perhaps token systems in school settings are best employed when they are viewed from the outset as temporary arrangements. Token systems in the classroom should only be started, says one educator, "when teachers know how and plan to remove the system. Books and things learned from exciting teachers maintain interest, not the tokens" (Stephens and Cooper, 1980).

The Premack Principle

The **Premack principle** states that behavior that occurs at a naturally high rate of frequency may be used to reinforce behavior that occurs at a naturally low rate of frequency (Premack, 1965). For example, if left to their own devices, many children will spend far more time watching TV than reading. According to

Premack, when such children have finished a given amount of reading, allow them to watch TV for a while. The teacher should carefully observe the children during free-choice periods and note the behaviors that naturally occur most frequently. These behaviors can then be used as positive reinforcers for low-probability responses. Teachers usually find that academic behavior has a low natural frequency, meaning that, when given a choice, most children prefer not to do schoolwork.

BEHAVIORAL TECHNOLOGY AND THE THREE R's

Since the publication of such critiques of American education as the Coleman report (1966), the Jencks report (1972), and more recently, *A Nation at Risk* (1983), concerned citizens are loudly wondering what is wrong with our educational system and even whether schools really do make a difference.

The answer from the behaviorists is that, yes, schools *can* make a difference, *if only professional educa-*

tors would utilize the technology that is now available to them. In fact, this behavioral technology has been around for several decades—at least since the publication of Skinner's seminal work, "The Science of Learning and the Art of Teaching." So why aren't the educationists taking advantage of these tried-and-true techniques? Wayne Piersal, in a provocative article, has suggested that our reluctance to implement behavior modification programs is rooted in our culture's insistence on blindly clinging to tradition. He cites evidence to indicate that this has always been true, at least in western cultures. In fact, the discovery that lemon or lime juice could cure scurvy occurred in 1601, but it took another 180 years before the British navy acted on this knowledge and began employing lime juice on a regular basis (Piersal, 1987).

As evidence that behavior programs are effective in solving many of the substantive problems of the classroom, data on learning spelling, handwriting, oral reading, and mathematics have been offered (Piersal, 1987).

Spelling

A number of studies, dating back at least to the 1960s, indicate that strict adherence to a specific reinforcement approach can have a facilitative effect on spelling ability. To cite just one study, a group of fourth-grade children, all of whom had had spelling difficulties, was put on a reinforcement plan that set a success criterion of 100 percent. The reinforcements were all based on preferred activities (Premack effect), such as listening to records. Within a short period of time, 64 percent of the children attained the criterion measure (Axelrod, 1982).

Handwriting

Regarding handwriting, the evidence produced over the years also seems to be clearly indicative of a positive effect for behavior programs. In one example, a program of self-instruction and self-correction led to an increased level of performance in both copying paragraphs and writing lists of words (Kosiewicz et al., 1982).

Oral Reading

Studies in the area of oral reading also suggest the efficacy of behavior programs. Teachers used positive reinforcers, including candy, to train a group of moderately retarded girls in oral reading by (1) pronouncing aloud a word the student missed, (2) instructing the student to point to the given word and repeat it aloud a number of times, and then (3) asking the student to read the entire sentence all over again. The results showed that this procedure produced a marked increase in each student's oral reading ability (Singh et al., 1984).

Mathematics

Finally, in the area of mathematics, especially number facts, behavior programs have a long history of positive results. Setting up a program in this area is relatively easy, since the correct response is self-evident. In just one example, reinforcement in the form of praise produced a solid increase in arithmetic performance (Schunk, 1981). In this study, incidentally, reinforcement that followed modeling (a demonstration by the teacher of how to solve division problems) was even more effective than reinforcement that followed didactic instruction alone.

In examining this rather impressive list of solid results, we must again be reminded that the implementation of these programs was always energized by a live, human hand. It takes a caring teacher to breathe warm life into the cool technology of behavior modification.

PROGRAMMED INSTRUCTION

The general concept of **programmed instruction** is probably as old as formal schooling itself. Each grade level has a certain small portion of our accumulated knowledge allotted to it, and each child is expected to master that segment before being allowed to proceed to the next grade. Children who don't keep up with the rest of the class are held back and repeat the year. Children who are not challenged by the content in their grade are skipped ahead to a level more consistent with their ability. The proponents of behavior modification agree with this practice in general (except in cases in which the pressure of the social promotion pushes all the children ahead, regardless of achievement), but they argue that the practice is too general and not tailored to the needs of the individual child. The individual child, they urge, needs a system of precision teaching, an educational prescription written just for him or her.

SPOTLIGHT ON TECHNOLOGY

Computers in the Classroom

As of 1991, there were roughly 2.7 million computers in the nation's 100,000 schools, or about 1 for every 16 students. And along with the various add-ons and peripherals, such as modems, disk drives, printers etc., the estimated cost to the schools has been running somewhat above $4 billion a year. With all that time and money spent on this powerful educational technology, why are our schoolchildren still performing at lower levels than was promised by the advent of the computer as a teaching device? Why are we continuing to show rising rates of illiteracy, declining math scores, and lower levels of reading comprehension?

This question is especially ironic since most studies of computer-assisted instruction (CAI) show that the new systems can work. Computer-driven drill and practice seem to make children better spellers, and the integrated learning systems, which deliver entire curricula to students sitting at computers, virtually guarantee that grade averages will go up. But one of the real problems is that despite having the new technology available to them, teachers have not always been prepared sufficiently to take full advantage of this electronic opportunity. Even though teachers are allegedly being instructed in the most effective use of CAI, this preparation is too often cursory, incomplete, and frustrating. Too many teachers have had to go through the painful and personally expensive process of self-education. One result is that there are now dramatic differences among teachers in their computer expertise as well as in their ability to communicate this knowledge to the students. This is especially critical, because, after all, good teachers will always be the heart and soul of good education. All of this has led to six important rules for gaining the most benefit from the new technology:

1. Give computers to teachers before placing them in the classroom.
2. Move the machines out of the computer labs and into the classrooms.
3. Provide at least one computer for every three students.
4. Give teachers the time and free-dom to restructure their curriculum around the technology. It has been shown that although CAI has the potential to radically transform how teaching and learning occur in the public schools, preservice teacher preparation plays an important role in whether this transformation will actually occur.[a]
5. Give teachers instruction in the basics of computer networking. This is especially useful for the teacher who is at all research-oriented. The tools of research are no longer just based on library card catalogs. A computer network allows the user to electronically browse through and retrieve articles and documents essential for the research process.[b]
6. Don't expect overnight miracles. It may take up to a few years before seeing any significant gains.

[a] E. A. Ashburn and D. M. Cilley, Teaching and learning to teach through technology. *IBM Higher Education* (a supplement to the *T.H.E. Journal*), March 1992, 32–36.
[b] J. H. Hoh, Creation of an information infrastructure. *The AAHE Bulletin* (1992), *8*, 2–4.

Programming is the arrangement of the material to be learned in a sequence of steps designed to lead the students to the final goal. The steps are usually quite close together, ensuring a gradual increase in difficulty. The material being presented is broken down into small units called *frames*, which can be presented to students by mechanical means (the **teaching machine**). The entire program may have hundreds of frames, and the frames are written in such a way as to maximize the possibility of success. They may sometimes seem repetitious, but this is the result of a deliberate attempt to prevent any misconceptions from forming in the student's mind. A good program is one in which the students make very few errors, no more than 5 percent. This means, of course, that the students are constantly experiencing success or that they are on what is close to a continuous reinforcement schedule. Teachers can add their own reinforcers (such as prizes or desired activities) for the completion of, say, every twenty-five items. This puts the students on an intermittent schedule of reinforcement (fixed ratio) for the external reinforcers while they remain on a continuous reinforcement schedule for the intrinsic success reinforcer.

A good academic program may employ various techniques in the construction of frames. Certain frames may consist basically of words which serve as prompts through familiarity and experience. Other frames may merely introduce new material and ask easy questions about it. Logical order is another criterion used to determine the next frame to be presented, and degree of difficulty is still another consideration. At various times in the program a word might be requested which requires a synthesis of earlier concepts. From time to time frames may review previous material or require that it be used in new contexts. Programing, then, is not a sterile, mechanized technique, but offers a wide range of possible responses (Meacham and Wiesen, 1969, p. 100).

Almost anyone with some degree of literacy can go through a program. Students will not all proceed at the same rate, but that, after all, is the story of individual differences. The first frame is always very easy, and the students are led by small steps into more complicated frames until the unit is completed or until the students have achieved the desired *terminal behavior*.

Programs may be written in book form, with the questions on one page and the answers on the facing page. The students cover the answers, respond, and then uncover the answers as a self-check. Programs may also be placed in machines that are set so as not to move from one frame to the next until each one in turn has been successfully completed. Some machines are even equipped with a buzzer or bell that sounds when a correct response has been given. The buzzers and bells act as further conditioned reinforcers for correct responses.

Programmed instruction has several key advantages.

1. The student must pay attention, for if the program is to continue, responses must be given. The student is, therefore, an active participant in the learning process, not a mere passive observer.

2. Each student proceeds at his or her own rate. One student may finish in one hour a program that takes another student five hours to complete.

3. Reinforcement, to use Skinner's term, or feedback, to use Bruner's, is immediate. There are no delays between the response and knowledge of results.

4. Learning that takes place in a programmed setting is always by positive reinforcement. Aversive techniques are never used. Machines don't shout, or hit, or "tell parents."

5. Machines can be set automatically to keep track of errors. These can be discussed later with the student, and in this important student-teacher dialogue, any misconceptions about the subject matter can be allayed.

Probably the main disadvantage to programmed instruction is that many students report finding it boring. "If that same question is asked one more time, I'll scream," said one student facing the seventeenth successive frame making the same point. In their zeal to increase frame difficulty ever so slowly, certain programmers have simply not increased the frame difficulty at all for long periods in the program. This is often resented by the alert student.

Computer-Assisted Instruction

Even the teaching machine is being phased out and replaced by what is called **computer-assisted instruction (CAI)**. With the advent of the microcomputer, CAI has taken a great leap forward. In past years CAI was restricted to fairly wealthy school districts. It consisted of using a computer (usually just one) together with TV screens and typewriters to allow groups of students to try their hands at programming in BASIC or to go through fairly stilted preprogrammed lessons. These earlier computers were expensive and had very limited internal memory. During the 1980s this somewhat cumbersome technique almost completely disappeared, being gradually replaced by the inexpensive yet powerful microcomputer.

The increase in capacity and the decrease in cost of the computer has been dramatic. Only a few years ago, one of the major mainframe manufacturers was selling a computer called the Century 200. It sold for what at the time was hailed as a breakthrough price of only $250,000. Of course, there were a few necessary extras, such as a $95,000 "clean room," a special, dust-free environment with built-in monitors for constant temperature, pressure, and humidity control. The machine's internal memory was 64K (kilobytes), or about the same memory capacity as today's $100 microcomputer. It has recently been estimated that had automobile technology advanced at the rate of computer technology over the past thirty-five years, a Rolls-Royce would now cost $2.50 and would get 2 million miles per gallon of gas (Rochester and Gantz, 1983).

The microcomputer, the small, stand-alone, desktop computer with its own central processor, has now

Microcomputers now make computer-assisted instruction (CAI) a possibility for all students.

found its way into virtually every school system in the country. To be sure, some microcomputers are still being used to promote computer literacy and programming skills (see the box on computer literacy), but many have become supplemental teaching tools in such traditional subjects as math, geography, history, and English grammar. Thus the microcomputer has taken on the role of personal tutor, aiding students in sharpening their skills and increasing their understanding of basic curriculum mainstays. And, as with any personal instructor, the student can proceed at his or her own pace.

The earliest software programs were designed to promote drill and practice; that is, they were much like flashcards on a screen. Then came the software tutorial, a program for taking a student through a discrete lesson unit. The latest software has as the final goal the mastery of global concepts. The student makes many choices throughout the running of the program and, in effect, is prodded into discovering a concept for himself or herself. A student's error automatically triggers a program review of the material not fully comprehended. Thus CAI is constantly interactive, forcing the student to respond, to make choices, to participate. Unlike TV instruction, CAI does not allow the student to become a passive recipient of information.

When teachers have been properly prepared, the research findings on CAI have been largely positive. Children are learning more and liking it better. In an

analysis (meta-analysis) of over fifty different studies, James Kulik has shown the striking effectiveness of CAI in grades six through twelve (Kulik et al., 1983). Computer-based teaching, Kulik found, raised final exam scores from the fiftieth to the sixty-third percentile, and these gains were maintained in follow-up examinations given several months after the completion of instruction. CAI was also found to be more efficient than traditional instruction in that it significantly reduced the amount of time the students needed for learning. In addition, CAI was shown to be more effective at the secondary level than it had proved to be among college students. Because of this, Kulik wondered if CAI might be even more effective with elementary school children than with older students.

A study performed by the Educational Testing Service (ETS) appears to lend substance to Kulik's suspicion. Using a sample of several thousand elementary school children divided into CAI (experimental) and non-CAI (control) groups, the ETS found that at the end of the first year CAI students scored at the sixty-fourth percentile while the control groups scored at the fiftieth percentile on a standardized math test. At the end of the second year, the CAI students had jumped to the seventy-first percentile, and after the third year to seventy-sixth. "In other words, the increase in their test scores was steady over several years" (Ragosta, 1983, p. 108).

It may very well be that learning through computer

interaction has both developmental and cumulative effects. The earlier the child begins, the better the learning strategies being incorporated; hence CAI may have a snowball effect as training continues. CAI has also been shown to be especially beneficial to homebound students—students who, for a variety of reasons, cannot attend school in the normal fashion. In one report, from Maryland, homebound students, from K through 12, were provided with home computers and the skills to use them (by teachers who had been thoroughly trained in a National Science Foundation summer-long workshop). These students demonstrated not only that they could keep up with their in-school peers, but that in many cases they could surpass the schoolchildren (Copper, 1991). Finally, aside from the achievement outcomes, CAI has proved to have produced other important effects.

Affective-motivational outcomes   Gerald Bracey reported that from kindergarten through grade twelve students consistently display positive attitudes toward computers (Bracey, 1982). Students almost unanimously report that they enjoy working at their own pace and appreciate the elimination of public embarrassment over making mistakes. Students are more willing to try, to take chances in the secure knowledge that a wrong guess is never going to expose them to public scorn. In Jerome Bruner's analysis of learning, for true discovery learning to occur, the student must be willing to take chances and explore new areas. This can only take place when the student knows that exploration is both rewarding and safe (Bruner, 1966).

Because students feel more in control of their educational destinies when CAI is involved, they are less likely to explain away poor performance as just a matter of bad luck. They gain a feeling of mastery, which may be at least as important an outcome as academic achievement itself (if indeed the two can be separated).

Social outcomes   The dire warnings that CAI will dehumanize the classroom, usually issued by an educational philosopher who has never seen students busily working *together* on a personal computer, are beginning to appear groundless. Bracey reported that CAI often fosters a cooperative group atmosphere. When two or three students are working together on a single computer, there is more "collaboration, or cooperative problem solving, than there is anywhere else in the school" (Bracey, 1982, p. 54). The students

are typically immersed in trying to get the program to run and are not blatantly competing to be the first person with a hand in the air, signaling the teacher that "I won."

The prevailing consensus is that CAI is an asset in the classroom. It tends to promote achievement, motivation, and a spirit of cooperation—an extremely powerful academic mix. Also, as a teaching aid CAI can provide simulations of activities the student otherwise might never experience. This is probably most pertinent in science courses, where laboratory supplies might be scarce or where running a particular experiment could be too dangerous, expensive, or time-consuming. Perhaps CAI simulations can reverse the trend, reported by the National Science Foundation, of students' dropping out of science and science-related courses (Lepper, 1985).

A note of concern has recently been sounded by Cole and Griffin, who found that CAI may not always be used on a fair and equitable basis. They say that more computers are being placed in the hands of America's affluent children than of its poor children, and even when the poor children do get computers, the equipment is used almost exclusively for rote drill instead of cognitive enrichment (Cole and Griffin, 1987).

Obviously, a great deal more research is needed in this important area. As M. R. Lepper points out, the influence of this new technology "is likely to have more important effects on the lives and the social and psychological functioning of children than any other technological advance in the past century" (Lepper, 1985, p. 18).

The Teacher's Role

Although computers have proved effective in transmitting facts and, to some extent, even concepts, the teacher is needed to tie these facts and subconcepts into more global abstractions. The teacher can use current examples of certain principles, thus helping to make the computer lesson seem more alive and thus more effective. Bruner has said that the student must have a background of facts, the "stuff of learning," before discovery learning can take place. A computer can obviously supply that "stuff." Knowing a few names and dates does allow for a certain level of understanding, which will aid a student in further exploration and discovery. A student who thinks that John Dewey and Aristotle were classmates together at Columbia, for example, may find it difficult to appreciate the significance of the historical succession

SPOTLIGHT ON COMPUTER LITERACY

How Much Is Enough?

Without a doubt, the computer revolution is upon us. Computers and their "magic" chips do everything from making out the payroll and scanning income tax returns to running cars, watches, and cameras. It's little wonder that educators have begun insisting that every educated person should become "computer literate" and that no self-respecting classroom should be without at least a couple of these electronic miracles.

Even first-grade children are being introduced to the computer and are being taught some elementary programming skills. They are also learning what not to do, such as never removing the floppy disk while the little red drive light is still on. Thrilled parents bask in the reflected glory of their children's computer accomplishments and secretly dream of the day when their children will be winning a Nobel prize for having achieved some new and exotic technological breakthrough. In short, "computer literacy" has become the catchword phrase of the 1990s and a given in our various curricula. To argue against computers is viewed as akin to seeing the first automobile roll down the road and saying, "I'd rather have a horse" or "The only accelerator I'll ever need is a buggy whip."

What has made the computer revolution even more compellingly dramatic has been the advent of the microcomputer, that incredible little desktop machine. The micro is a stand-alone computer with its own input device (the keyboard), internal memory (RAM), central processor, memory storage system (usually a floppy disk), and output

display (the screen). The memory capability of even the least expensive of today's micros exceeds that of many of the mainframes of just a few years ago.

But the question is not whether today's computers are extraordinary marvels of electronic wizardry—they are. It is whether every child should become computer-literate and, if so, how literate.

Computer literacy seems to have several definitions, but most are some variation of the following:

> By computer awareness and literacy is [sic] meant a general understanding of computers, their uses and applications to everyday living. Knowing what a computer can and cannot do, how they [sic] are used in today's world, and how they may affect our lives are central themes which run throughout a program in computer awareness and literacy.[a]

Problems begin, however, as soon as we begin to operationalize the generalities in this definition. For example, to some experts, knowing what computers can and cannot do demands expertise in programming.

> To tell a computer what you want it to do, you must be able to communicate with it. To do that, you will need to learn a language for writing your ideas down. . . . If you can tell a computer how to do the things you want it to do, you are computer literate.[b]

To others, learning to program the computer is not essential:

Computer literacy is a familiarity with a device that enhances one's ability to live in and cope with the modern world. This does not mean, however, that students must acquire the ability to program, but rather the ability to manipulate computer technology.[c]

The issue of whether or not to include programming in the definition of computer literacy is, therefore, one that divides the experts. Some experts, mercifully of the minority, claim that computer literacy is virtually synonymous with achieving a degree in computer science. The student should have courses in everything from machine language to FORTRAN, from computer architecture to advanced Pascal, and much much more. Admittedly, some students should probably follow this rigorous path, but all students?

A more modest goal of those advocating programming is that each student learn at least one programming language, usually either BASIC or LOGO. Their argument is not that learning to program is an end in itself but that it teaches the student how to think. Learning to create logical algorithms and translate them into a programming language is alleged to produce, in a sense, a strong and disciplined mind. Even those holding this view, however, issue this warning:

> A certain amount of elementary programming—in LOGO or BASIC—might also be introduced in the early grades. However, there is danger in carrying this too far. Without competent, informed computer teachers, students often pick up very bad

programing habits that must be broken later. This is a well-documented fact. It may be better, therefore, to postpone the bulk of programing instruction until students reach a junior high class taught by the specialist.[d]

Advocates of programming also urge that students be taught the binary numbering system. Since computers can respond only to on-off commands, to understand what a computer goes through, one must learn to convert base 10 to base 2, and at least be able to add and subtract in base 2. A thorough knowledge of the binary system, it is felt, is essential for understanding the rudiments of any programming technique.

Others feel that programming skills are not necessary, that computer literacy is like automobile literacy: You only have to learn how to make it go, not the physics involved. Those who hold this view define computer literacy as being able to turn on the machine, insert a disk, and follow a "user friendly," menu-driven program. And since the use of a computer demands entering data of some sort, they argue that the student is far better off taking a course in typing than one in base 2 math. A parallel argument is that taking courses in BASIC is like taking a course or two in French. It might be fun to then go to a French restaurant and order your meal directly from the menu, but if you need a highly accurate translation of more difficult material, you'd better hire an expert. Besides, in programming, a little learning can be dangerous: If you start breaking into a prepackaged

program in order to change a line or two, you can ruin the whole program. This position also sees the learning of base 2 as a waste of time. The machine may have to "think" in on-off terms, but the student doesn't.

A final antiprogramming argument is that in a few years BASIC and LOGO will be dead languages, important historically but of little relevance to students entering the twenty-first-century job market. The computers of tomorrow will still be programmable, "but nobody except the experts will do the programming. . . . The final custom-fitting of all commercial programs will be done by the user, but in English, not in BASIC."[e]

What can we expect of students in the 1990s in the way of computer literacy? The consensus among those holding the middle-ground view is that minimal computer literacy should include:

1. Knowing a little about the history of computers, the sequence from giant, vacuum-tubed mainframes of yesterday to the miniaturized microcomputers of today.
2. Knowing the basic parts of the computer, from input to output.
3. Knowing how to handle format and copy disks as well as how to protect them from damage.
4. Knowing at least one word-processing program and one math program. (Research strongly suggests that the use of at least these two types of programs enhances a student's writing and math skills.)[f]
5. Knowing how to handle the computer safely and intelli-

gently, and, as much as possible, learning the basic damage-prevention techniques.

Obviously, some students should be provided with more than just these minimal competencies. The choice of what to include should also take into account each student's own special aptitudes and interests. Students interested in science, for example, should be exposed to laboratory simulations on the computer, whereas those preparing for an office career should be trained in data-base and spreadsheet techniques.

In short, the ultimate goal of computer literacy should be to provide students with skills they can use in all their traditional courses in order that they may be better students today and better citizens tomorrow. In the words of one expert, "The schools, relying primarily on computers and teachers for instruction, will play a central role in the moral and intellectual development of U.S. youngsters."[g]

[a] N. Watts, A dozen uses for the computer in education, *Educational Technology*, April 1981, 20.

[b] A. Luehrmann, Computer literacy: What it is; why it's important, *Electronic Learning*, May/June 1982, 162.

[c] R. Scher, The computer backlash, *Electronic Learning*, January 1984.

[d] A. Luehrmann, The best way to teach computer literacy, *Electronic Learning*, April 1984, 39.

[e] F. D'Ignazio, Beyond computer literacy, *Compute*, September 1983, 41.

[f] G. Bracey, Computers in education: What the research shows, *Electronic Learning*, November/December 1982.

[g] P. Wagschal, A last chance for computers in the schools, *Phi Delta Kappan*, December 1984.

of philosophical ideas. There are, however, some areas that simply can't be fully taught by the computer. History and literature would be reduced to a pile of bits and pieces (or perhaps even bits and bytes) without the teacher to integrate the material into a living picture.

School systems should not be misguided into spending large portions of their budgets buying ever more sophisticated computers in the fond belief that CAI alone will turn our schoolchildren into budding rocket scientists. This is especially true when the computer purchase comes at the expense of teacher salaries. One of the most glaring problems facing American education today is the failure to pay teachers a decent wage. "We will not attract the brightest and best people into the teaching field until we treat this profession as the priority we believe it to be" (De Concini, 1988, p. 117).

As we saw at the beginning of this chapter during the discussion of whole versus part learning, when material is learned in discrete units, the parts must be put back together. No programmer can ever anticipate all the ways in which children may misinterpret how the separate parts should be glued back together into a meaningful whole. The teacher must be there, on the spot, guiding, motivating, doing the real job of teaching in its true sense.

SUMMARY

Learning in the classroom involves the concept of transfer. What is learned in class is thought to transfer into later-life situations, so as to enable the learner to earn a living and enjoy a fuller life.

Theories of transfer date back to the early Greek notion of formal discipline, in which the mind, considered comparable to an athlete's muscles, was thought to require systematic exercise if it was to grow. Even as late as the early twentieth century, proponents of this position created academic curricula that stressed such subjects as logic, Greek, and Latin not because these subjects had any practical value, but because they "strengthened" the mind.

Formal discipline theory was seriously challenged by a number of psychologists, including William James, E. L. Thorndike, and Charles Judd. All of their studies pointed to the fact that "training the mind" had little if any lasting benefits.

Educators today are no longer concerned with the theory of mental discipline, but they are concerned with promoting positive transfer between learning in the classroom and living effectively in later life.

The learning curve, a plotting out of one's learning speed, typically shows negative acceleration, which means that when confronted with a new subject, students learn a great deal of the material in a relatively short time and then, with increased practice, add less and less new learning.

Harlow coined the phrase learning sets to explain what gestalt psychologists had previously labeled as insight.

Massed versus distributed practice involves the question of how the learner should allocate his or her time for maximum efficiency. In learning a new physical skill, distributed practice (an hour a day for a week) is more efficient than massed practice (seven straight hours in one day). On intellectual tasks, however, distributed practice may destroy the meaning of the material. In this case it is best to divide the material into meaningful units and then work on each unit in a massed-learning session.

The efficiency of spaced learning over massed learning is now called the spacing effect, and its documentation as a valid phenomenon goes back at least as far as the seminal work of Hermann Ebbinghaus in the first decade of this century.

Whole versus part learning involves the question of whether learning is most efficient when the material is broken down into small, discrete units or left in a total, organized whole. The best method seems to be to work first on the whole in order to gain a general overview of the material and then go back and work on the various parts.

Albert Bandura has suggested that a large part of what a person learns occurs through imitation, or modeling. This is called social learning theory, since it is concerned with learning that takes place within a social situation. Bandura has shown that learning that occurs through modeling need not be based on direct reinforcement of the response. Other than the parents, the teacher may be the most important model in the child's environment. Conditions for learning are thus established not only by what the teacher says but by what he or she does.

The current popularity of operant conditioning in the classroom is due in large part to the fact that the teacher is presented with a very precise prescription for handling specific classroom problems. Changing a student's behavior through the use of conditioning techniques is called behavior modification.

To use behavior modification techniques, the teacher must first define the educational objectives in behavioral terms, that is, determine exactly *what* the student should learn and *how* the student is to show that the learning has taken place. The teacher can infer that learning or understanding has taken place only by observing the *behavior* of the student.

Once the objectives have been defined, the teacher observes the student's initial rate of response, or operant level, for the activity in question. The operant level, or base rate, for the given activity should be observed in the classroom situation.

After the behavioral goal is set and the student's operant level is established, the teacher can use reinforcement to strengthen (condition) some student behavior and withhold reinforcement of (extinguish) other student behavior. Reinforcement always increases response rate. Positive reinforcement occurs when the response rate increases by adding the reinforcer (giving the student M&M candies, gold stars, or high grades), and negative reinforcement occurs when the response rate increases by taking away the reinforcer (removing an aversive stimulus when the desired behavior is emitted). Aversive stimuli should be used as negative reinforcement or punishment *only* with great caution since they can result in the student's acquiring not only the goal behavior the teacher intended but also other, potentially damaging responses.

The key to the successful use of behavior modification techniques is *consistency*. The teacher must follow through on the established reinforcement schedule without exception.

Reinforcement must *follow*, not precede, the student's response. Usually, the sooner the reinforcement follows the response, the more impact it will have in changing behavior.

Behavior modification proponents also make use of the token system, a system based on the use of conditioned reinforcers, or tokens. The token system has two main advantages: (1) It maintains a high daily rate of desirable responses, and (2) it teaches delayed gratification.

The Premack principle states that behavior that naturally occurs at a high rate can be used to reinforce behavior that occurs at a naturally low rate. Thus, one set of responses may be used to reinforce another set of responses. If a student has a higher rate of TV-viewing responses than reading responses, then viewing TV can be used as reinforcement for a certain amount of reading. Success in using behavioral modification techniques has been shown in the following basic-skills areas: spelling, handwriting, oral reading, and mathematics.

In programmed instruction the material to be learned is arranged in an orderly sequence of steps designed to reach a certain goal. A good program is one in which the level of difficulty increases very slowly, so that students make very few errors (less than 5 percent). The material to be learned is broken down into small units, or frames, and can be presented to students by mechanical means (the teaching machine). The basic advantage of programmed instruction is that each student can proceed at his or her own rate. However, some students, especially the brighter ones, become bored with the long succession of similar items. Also, when material is learned in bits and pieces, it is often hard for the student to integrate the discrete parts into a meaningful whole.

Even now, teaching machines are in the process of being phased out in favor of computer-assisted instruction. With the advent of the microcomputer and the recent upgrading of instructional software, CAI has proved to be an important teaching adjunct. Research findings indicate that CAI has been effective in increasing academic achievement. It appears also that CAI has other personal benefits, especially in the affective-motivational and social areas.

Despite its apparent success as a "private tutor," CAI can never replace the teacher. He or she must remain as the major component in the total educational enterprise. The teacher's role becomes even more critical during this technological age of bits, bytes, and chips. Without the teacher to explain relationships and integrate concepts, CAI's long-term success may turn out to be shallow. Critics suggest that CAI may be in danger of producing a generation of child robots whose knowledge base, though admittedly large, will be superficial and perhaps even random.

KEY TERMS AND NAMES

Albert Bandura
   modeling
   social learning theory
behavior modification
computer-assisted instruction (CAI)
learning curve
learning sets
massed learning
Premack principle
programmed instruction

punishment
shaping (successive approximation)
spacing effect
teaching machine
terminal behavior
token system
transfer
   negative transfer
   positive transfer

THEORY INTO PRACTICE: OPERANT CONDITIONING

Since an operant is any response an organism can emit without the presentation of an identifiable stimulus, operant conditioning can be easily demonstrated in a variety of situations. You don't need rats or pigeons or fancy automated equipment in order to show how a freely emitted operant can be conditioned. The operant will condition as long as it is consistently followed by a reinforcer. For demonstration purposes, we will focus on the freely emitted eye blink (not an eye blink response that is elicited by the presentation of a puff of air). It is important to remember that the same response may be both an operant and a respondent, depending on what produces it. For example, a tap on the patellar tendon will act as an unconditioned stimulus in producing a knee jerk. However, if you happen to kick up your leg in the absence of any known stimulus, that same response would have been emitted and therefore classified as an operant. Similarly, the blink of an eye as a response to a puff of air would be a respondent, whereas that same blink in the absence of any stimulus would be an operant.

First, prepare two tally sheets. On each sheet write the numbers 1 to 150 in neat, straight columns. Next, select someone from your class, give him/her one of the tally sheets and instruct the subject to make a check mark next to a number, beginning with the number 1, every time a tap of the pencil is heard. You must then carefully watch your subject's eyes, and each time you observe an eye blink, lightly tap your pencil on the desk. Thus, the tap will be *contingent on the blinking response* and will, therefore, act as

a reinforcer. In short, each time your subject blinks, you tap. The subject's column of check marks will become a running tally of the number of blinks he/she emitted. Continue this procedure for two minutes. *Be sure not to let the subject know that his/her blinking behavior is influencing your taps.* Then take a one-minute break. After the break, provide the subject with the second tally sheet and continue the same procedure for another two minutes. At the end of this time period, count the number of check marks that the subject has made on each tally sheet. Compare the results. If conditioning has occurred, there will be a significant increase in the number of check marks on the second sheet. This will indicate that the rate of operant responding has increased as a result of the operant's having been paired to a reinforcing stimulus. The reinforcer, of course, is the tap.

Why is the tap reinforcing? The fact that the tap acts as a reinforcer actually needs no further explanation as long as the operant rate showed an increase during the second time period. After all, Skinner insists that no internal inferences need be made. If the stimulus that follows a response results in an increased response rate, the stimulus is, by definition, a reinforcer. If you must speculate further, however, you might question your subject. It could be that when someone is told to respond (make a check mark) only after hearing a certain signal, then that person may begin to want to hear the signal (since not hearing it could be frustrating).

It must be pointed out again that the response being conditioned here is the eye blink, not the inscription of the check mark. The reinforcing stimulus, the tap, is presented *after each eye blink.* If you want further proof, you might set up a third trial in which you never tap your pencil, no matter how often the subject blinks. Thus, you would be running your subject through an extinction period, during which the rate of blinking should decrease. Of course, as with any conditioned operant, we cannot expect to cause blinking to cease completely. But we can expect, even-

tually, that the response rate will return to its operant level (that is, its preconditioned rate).

If possible, you might try this procedure with children in a classroom. Remember to send the chosen subject out of the room while you explain the real purpose of the study to the child who will do the tapping. Also, explain to the other children in the room the importance of not divulging the actual purpose of the demonstration to the subject.

REFERENCES

Ashburn, E. A., and Cilley, D. M. (1992). Teaching and learning to teach through technology. *IBM Higher Education* (a supplement to *T.H.E. Journal*) (March), 32–36.

Axelrod, S. (1982). *Behavior modification for the classroom teacher* (2d ed.). New York: McGraw-Hill.

Bandura, A. (1978). The self system in reciprocal determinism. *American Psychologist, 33,* 344–358.

Bandura, A. (1982). Self-efficacy mechanism in human agency. *American Psychologist, 37, 344–358.* See also Bandura, A. (1980). Self-referent thought: The development of self-efficacy In J. Flavell and L. D. Ross (Eds.), *Cognitive social development: Frontiers and possible futures.* New York: Cambridge University Press.

Bandura, A., Blanchard, E. B., and Ritter, B. (1969). Relative efficacy of desensitization and modeling approaches for inducing behavioral affective and attitudinal changes. *Journal of Personality and Social Psychology, 13,* 173–199.

Bandura, A., and McDonald, F. J. (1963). Influence of social reinforcement and the behavior of models in shaping children's moral judgments. *Journal of Abnormal and Social Psychology, 67,* 274–281.

Bandura, A., Ross, D., and Ross, S. A. (1963). Imitation of film-mediated aggressive models. *Journal of Abnormal and Social Psychology, 66,* 3–11.

Bettelheim, B. (1985). Punishment versus discipline. *The Atlantic* (November), 51–59.

Bracey, G. (1982). Computers in education: What the research shows. *Electronic Learning* (November/December).

Brantner, J. P., and Doherty, M. A. (1983). A review of timeout: A conceptual and methodological analysis. In S. Axelrod and J. Apsche (Eds.), *The effects of punishment on human behavior.* Orlando, Fla.: Academic Press.

Brown, A., Campione, J., and Day, J. (1981). Learning to learn: On training students to learn from texts. *Educational Researcher, 16,* 14–21. See also Novak, J. (1980). *Handbook for the learning how to learn program.* Ithaca: New York State College of Agriculture and Life Sciences.

Bruner, J. S. (1966). *Toward a theory of instruction.* Cambridge: Harvard University Press.

Cole, M., and Griffin, P. (1987). *Contextual factors in education.* Madison: Wisconsin Center for Education Research.

Coleman, J. S. (1966). *Equality of educational opportunity.* Washington: U.S. Department of Health, Education, and Welfare, Office of Education.

Copper, L. R. (1991). CAI with home-bound students proves successful in model program. *T.H.E. Journal, 18,* 68–69.

Craig, A. R., and Cleary, P. J. (1982). Reduction of stuttering by young male stutterers using EMG feedback. *Biofeedback and Self-Regulation, 7,* 241–255.

Davison, G. C., and Stuart, R. B. (1975). Behavior therapy and civil liberties. *American Psychologist, 30,* 755–763.

De Concini, D. (1988). America's little red school house: Is it holding up today? *American Psychologist, 42,* 115–117.

Dempster, F. N. (1987). Effects of variable encoding and spaced presentation on vocabulary learning. *Journal of Educational Psychology, 22,* 1–21.

Dempster, F. N. (1988). The spacing effect: A case study in the failure to apply the results of psychological research. *American Psychologist, 43,* 627–634.

D'Ignazio, F. (1983). Beyond computer literacy. *Compute* (September), 35–43.

Ebbinghaus, H. (1913, originally 1885). *Memory: A contribution to experimental psychology* (p. 89), trans. by H. A. Ruger and C. E. Bussenius. New York: Teachers College.

Harlow, H. F., McGaugh, J. L., and Thompson, R. F. (1971). *Psychology* (p. 301). San Francisco: Albion.

Hoh, J. H. (1992). Creation of an information infrastructure. *The AAHE Bulletin, 8,* 2–4.

Hurt, H. T., Scott, M. D., and McCroskey, J. C. (1978). *Communication in the classroom* (p. 32). Reading, Mass.: Addison-Wesley.

James, W. (1890). *The principles of psychology.* New York: Henry Holt.

James, W. (1901). *Talks to teachers on psychology and to students on some of life's ideals.* New York: Holt.

Jencks, C., Smith, M., Acland, H., Cohen, D., Gintis, H., Heyns, B., and Michelson, S. (1972). *Inequality: A reas-*

sessment of the effects of family and schooling in America. New York: Basic Books.

Judd, C. H. (1908). The relation of special training to general intelligence. *Educational Review, 36,* 28–42.

Koocher, G. P. (1976). Civil liberties and aversive conditioning for children. *American Psychologist, 31,* 94–95.

Kosiewicz, M. M., Hallahan, D. P., Lloyd, J., and Graves, A. W. (1982). Effects of self-instruction and self-correction procedures on handwriting performance. *Learning Disabilities Quarterly, 5,* 71–78.

Kulik, J. A., Bangert, R. L., and Williams, G. W. (1983). Effects of computer-based teaching on secondary school students. *Journal of Educational Psychology, 75,* 19–26.

Lepper, M. R. (1985). Microcomputers in education: Motivational and social issues. *American Psychologist, 40*(1), 18.

Luehrmann, A. (1982). Computer literacy: What it is; why it's important. *Electronic Learning* (May/June), 162.

Luehrmann, A. (1984). The best way to teach computer literacy. *Electronic Learning* (April), p. 39.

Mace, F. C., Belfiore, P. J., and Shea, M. C. (1989). Operant theory and research on self-regulation. In B. J. Zimmerman and D. H. Schunk (Eds.), *Self-regulated learning and academic achievement: Theory, research and practice* (pp. 27–50). New York: Springer-Verlag.

Madsen, C. H., and Madsen, C. K. (1970). *Teaching-discipline* (p. 14). Boston: Allyn & Bacon. This quote and the ones on pp. 264 and 268 are reprinted by permission.

Martin, G., and Pear, J. (1983). *Behavior modification.* Englewood Cliffs, N.J.: Prentice-Hall.

Maurer, A. (1974). Corporal punishment. *American Psychologist, 29,* 614–626.

Meacham, M. F., and Wiesen, A. E. (1969). *Changing classroom behavior* (2d ed.; p. 50). This quote and the one on p. 269: Copyright © 1969, 1974 by Harper & Row, Publishers, Inc. Reprinted by permission of Harper & Row, Publishers, Inc.

National Commission of Excellence in Education (1983). *A nation at risk: The imperative for educational reform.* Washington: U.S. Department of Education.

Newsom, C., Favell, J. E., and Rincover, A. (1983). The side effects of punishment. In S. Axelrod and J. Apsche (Eds.), *The effects of punishment on human behavior.* Orlando, Fla.: Academic Press.

Piersal, W. C. (1987). Basic skills education. In C. A. Maher and S. G. Forman (Eds.), *A behavioral approach to education of children and youth.* Hillsdale, N.J.: Erlbaum.

Premack, D. (1965). Reinforcement theory. In D. Levine, *Nebraska symposium on motivation* (pp. 123–180). Lincoln: University of Nebraska Press.

Ragosta, M. (1983). Computer assisted instruction and compensatory education: A longitudinal analysis. *Machine Mediated Learning, 1*(1), 108.

Reder, L. M., and Anderson, J. R. (1982). Effects of spacing and embellishment on memory for the main points of a text. *Memory and Cognition, 10,* 97–102.

Rescorla, R. A. (1987). A Pavlovian analysis of goal-directed behavior. *American Psychologist, 42,* 119–125.

Rochester, J. B., and Gantz, J. (1983). *The naked computer* (p. 15). New York: Morrow.

Scher, R. (1984). The computer backlash. *Electronic Learning* (January).

Schunk, D. H. (1981). Modeling and attributional effects on children's achievement: A self-efficacy analysis. *Journal of Educational Psychology, 73,* 93–105.

Science & engineering education for the 1980's and beyond (1980). National Science Foundation Report. Washington: National Science Foundation of the Department of Education.

Sears, R. R., Maccoby, E., and Levin, H. (1957). *Patterns of child rearing.* Evanston, Ill.: Row, Peterson.

Singh, N. N., Singh, J. S., and Winton, A. S. (1984). Positive practice overcorrection of oral reading errors. *Behavior Modification, 8,* 23–37.

Skinner, B. F. (1969; originally 1965). Why teachers fail. In R. C. Sprinthall and N. A. Sprinthall (Eds.), *Educational psychology: Selected readings* (pp. 164–172). New York: Van Nostrand-Reinhold.

Skinner, B. F. (1953). *Science and human behavior* (p. 402). New York: Macmillan.

Skinner, B. F. (1954). The science of learning and the art of teaching. *Harvard Educational Review, 24,* 86–97.

Smith, S. M., and Rothkopf, E. Z. (1984). Contextual enrichment and distribution of practice in the classroom. *Cognition and Instruction, 1,* 341–358.

Spettel, G. B. (1983). Classroom discipline—now. *The Clearing House* (February), 267. Reprinted with permission of the Helen Dwight Reid Educational Foundation. Published by Heldref Publications, 4000 Albemarle St., N.W., Washington, D.C. 20016. Copyright © 1983.

Stephens, T. M., and Cooper, J. O. (1980). *The educational forum* (November), 112.

Stolz, S. B., Wienckowski, L. A., and Brown, B. S. (1975). Behavior modification: A perspective on critical issues. *American Psychologist, 30*(11), 1027–1048.

Tate, B. G., and Baroff, A. S. (1966). Aversive control of self-injurious behavior in a psychotic boy. *Behavior Research and Therapy, 4,* 281–287.

Thorndike, E. L., and Woodworth, R. S. (1901). The influence of improvement in one mental function upon the efficiency of other functions. *Psychological Review, 8,* 247–261, 384–395, 553–564.

Travers, J. F. (1972). *Learning: Analysis and application* (p. 166). New York: McKay.

Wagschal, P. (1984). A last chance for computers in the schools. *Phi Delta Kappan* (December).

Walters, G., and Grusec, J. (1977). *Punishment* (p. 158). San Francisco: Freeman.

Watson, D. L., and Tharp, R. G. (1985). *Self-directed behavior* (4th ed.). New York: Norton.

Watts, N. (1981). A dozen uses for the computer in education. *Educational Technology* (April), 20.

Widerstrom, A. H., Mowder, B. A., and Sandall, S. R. (1991). *At risk and handicapped newborns and infants: Development, assessment and intervention.* Englewood Cliffs, N.J.: Prentice-Hall.

Zimmerman, B. J. (1990). Self-regulated learning and academic achievement: An overview. *Educational Psychologist, 25,* 3–17.

11

INFORMATION PROCESSING

The cognitive theorists, using the computer as their basic model and E. C. Tolman as their ancestral hero, have provided another important theory of learning and memory called **information processing.** Tolman, as we have already seen, was essentially a behaviorist, but a behaviorist with a decided difference. He held that maze learning could not be explained as a mere collection of tiny S-R connections but must instead be based on the organism's internalization of a cognitive map of its environment. Even a rat could therefore incorporate a picture of its surroundings and find its way through the maze on the basis of that picture. The cognitive map, then, was viewed as an internal representation of environmental *information.* Information regarding the organism's expectancies (or the anticipation of what leads to what) were then incorporated into the organism's cognitive map. Therefore, for Tolman, learning was based more on information that was stored by the organism rather than that just fed from muscle twitches. These are clearly not the thoughts of a Watsonian behaviorist.

Although at first glance the information processing model may seem like a step backward into the era of Wilhelm Wundt, who attempted to analyze consciousness into its various components, it is in reality far more empirically based. Wundt presumed to be using empirical techniques when he instructed his subjects to look within themselves at the elements of their own conscious awareness. Wundt called this technique *experimental introspection,* but from the viewpoint of science it was far too subjective and unreliable. Introspective reports varied from subject to subject and, worse, from laboratory to laboratory. The data were too inconsistent to provide psychology with anything resembling a firm foundation. The information processing theorists, in contrast, analyze mental events in terms of their behavioral effects—effects that can be reliably observed and measured. Such overt measures as reaction times (chronometric measures) and verbal recognition of various stimuli can be and are used to verify inferred mental constructs.

Although the information processing theorists take a behavioral stance with respect to measurement, they have traditionally leaned toward the gestalt orientation when it comes to theory. They have been addressing such issues as the organization of thinking, the role of meaning in learning, cognitive strategies in problem solving, the structure of human awareness—in short, most of the same areas that had earlier been studied by such gestaltists as Max Wertheimer, Wolfgang Kohler, and Kurt Koffka. This is not to say that this "new look" at learning and memory in any way denies the evidence from the behavioral studies of classical and operant conditioning. Skinner's functional relationships between stimuli and responses are accepted as established facts. But the information processing theorist wants to know not just that an organism can be conditioned, but *how* the pigeon learns to discriminate among stimuli, *how* the rat learns its way through the maze, and *how* the child learns to recognize words on the printed page. What learning *rules* underlie these regular relationships? Because of its cognitive-gestaltist orientation, however, some psychologists, especially the behaviorists, have not looked kindly on this new approach. For example, Skinner has said:

> The cognitive revolution is a search inside the mind for something that is not there. You can't see yourself process information; information processing is an inference from behavior and a bad one at that. If you look carefully at what people mean when they talk about the mind, you find it just refers to how they behave (Skinner, 1987).

In a speech to the American Psychological Association's annual meeting in 1990, delivered just days before his death, Skinner heaped even more criticism on cognitive science by calling it, not a science but the "creationism of psychology . . . an effort to reinstate that inner initiating-originating-creative self or mind which, in a scientific analysis, simply does not exist. And to those cognitive scientists feeling oppressed by the APA and threatening to leave the meeting, Skinner bade them good riddance and said that he would regard their departure "not as a secession, but as an improvement" (Skinner, 1990). Skinner asked the question "Can psychology be a science of the mind?" and then answered his own query with a resounding no. Instead, he insisted, psychology is and always will be the *study of behavior* (Skinner, 1990).

Despite Skinner's critiques, the torrent of new studies and fresh insights currently streaming from the cognitive laboratories make the information processing model too important to be overlooked by the educational psychologist of the late 1990s.

LEARNING AS INFORMATION PROCESSING

Information processing theory is loosely modeled on the way in which computers process information. The assumption is that in order for information to be remembered, it must move through several stages and that these stages proceed sequentially. The goal is to understand the "architecture with which the child is innately equipped and explain how this architecture interacts with environmental stimulation to yield changing mental representations" (McShane, 1991, p. 13).

Just as data to be entered into a computer must be encoded in a form that the computer can store and process, information that flows through the sensory receptors and is attended to must also be encoded before it can be stored and processed. At the psychological level, **encoding** involves the creation of memory traces, which are abstractions based on the salient features of the incoming information. It is also thought that at the physiological level the nervous system adopts an internal code that represents the external stimulus. In this way, the encoded representation of the external object or event becomes internal information and is thus readied for storage.

Although there are several variations in the specifics of how the information processing model of learning appears to work, the consensus view is that learning and remembering are based on the flow of information that passes *within* the organism. The sense organs respond to and pass along incoming information, which is encoded in the memory and nervous system. The encoded information is then stored and processed in a manner that allows it to be retrieved and acted on. Thus, as with the computer, the information processing model consists of input of encoded information, storage and processing, and finally output, or retrieval.

Cognitive theorists have suggested that there are at least two modes of information processing, one that operates automatically, incidentally, and without any real voluntary control, and another that is deliberate, intentional, and under a person's full, volitional control. One of the implications of this theory is that the automatic processing of information occurs at the preconscious or even at the unconscious level, whereas the intentional mode is at the conscious level (Kihlstrom, 1987). The model to be presented in this chapter will focus on the intentional mode, that is, on intentional learning, which fits more closely with the major mission of the schools.

Storage refers to internal memory, or the persistence of information over time. In one form, it is analogous to the computer's use of disks or tape to save information for future use. Unless damaged, of course, a computer's disk stores information that does not change over time, whereas there is considerable debate over whether human memory possesses that type of etched-in-stone immutability.

The first phase of information processing is encoding, which involves the formation of memory traces that may entail physiological changes.

Retrieval is the output end of the memory process. It refers to the utilization of the stored information, loosely comparable to accessing the computer's data base. To be retrieved, stored information must be not only available but also accessible to the individual. That is, although stored information may be theoretically available, it may not always be easily located and utilized (Murdock, 1974).

With this brief analogy in mind, we will now turn to how learning is acquired in the view of information processing theorists. Figure 11.1 shows in diagram form the main features of the information processing model of learning.

The Sensory Register

When information from the environment first impinges on a receptor (sense organ), there is an extremely brief moment—half a second to perhaps as many as four seconds—when it is held in sensory memory. This memory, also known as the **sensory register,** is called *iconic memory* for visual items and *echoic memory* (or sometimes acoustic memory) for auditory items. The visual representation is called an *icon* because of its pictorial quality, and a stored auditory item is called an *echo*, because of its sound quality. Echoic memory endures long enough to enable us to piece together a series of sounds, as when listening to music or to someone speaking, whereas iconic memory seems to fade in as short a time span as a few milliseconds. Regardless of how long they last, the icon and the echo play the important role of holding information in the sensory register until (or if) further processing is to occur. There is some evidence to suggest that this is where the beginning of the pattern recognition process takes place (Daehler and Bukatko, 1985).

Because the sensory memory holds only raw, unprocessed sensory information, it is sometimes seen as a sensory buffer, or way station, situated between the external environment and internal memory (Rozenzweig and Leiman, 1982). Although both iconic

FIGURE 11.1   The information processing model of intentional learning.

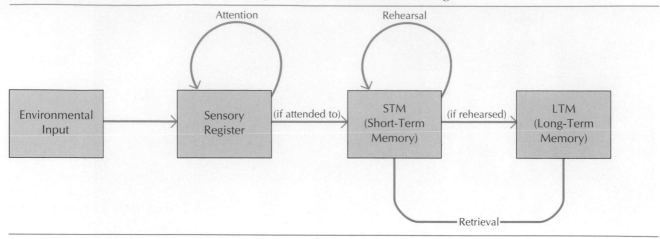

and echoic memory are based on neural traces (electrochemical changes in neurons) in the receptors and the nerves leading from the receptors to the brain, it seems that the traces are held for a slightly longer period in echoic memory than in iconic memory (Kolers, 1983). Other sensory memories may also exist, such as touch, taste, and smell, but the evidence regarding sight and sound is now more direct. Regardless of the sensory mode involved, the activation produced by incoming information may create a recognition pattern, or an internal connection between the external stimulation and previously encoded information. The brief and volatile sensory memory trace disappears almost immediately unless it is attended to, recalling to us the old adage "in one ear and out the other."

It should be pointed out that there is currently some debate among the information processing theorists regarding the status of sensory memory. Since the sensory register is based on the activation of the sense organs and sensory neurons leading to the brain, and therefore not in the brain itself, it may not be a true memory process. Also, even if there is a sensory register that momentarily holds information about the physical environment, it may have little relevance to the information storage process over longer periods of time (Haber, 1983).

If the individual is paying attention to the incoming stimulation, the information is encoded and moved along from the sensory memory register into storage. A critical component here is attention, for if the information is not attended to immediately, it most likely will be lost. For example, if you are intro-

duced to someone at a party and don't really pay attention to the introduction, moments later you may not even recall the person's name.

Some theorists do suggest, however, that under certain conditions it is possible to activate a kind of incidental-acquisition process whereby some information from the environment may be automatically encoded in the sensory register without either attention or intention (Hasher and Zacks, 1979).

Short-Term Memory

The first of the two main systems for storing the information encoded in sensory memory is **short-term memory (STM)**—sometimes called *working* or *active* memory (Wickelgren, 1981). It appears that short-term memory can encode only about seven separate items (plus or minus two) and can hold them for only a limited time (Miller, 1956). Estimates of how long information may be retained in STM vary from about a few seconds to almost a minute (Broadbent, 1984). Since seven is the typical number of separate items in a telephone number, STM is often referred to as *telephone number memory*. Thus, if you were verbally given a phone number, you could most probably hold it in STM long enough to pick up the phone and dial the number. However, if the other party didn't answer the ring or there was a busy signal, you probably couldn't recall the number long enough to dial a second time.

Even though STM is restricted to about seven items, the items may be grouped together, or *chunked*. In this way, several items may be packaged

Sight and sound are the most direct routes for sensory input.

together and processed as a single element. For example, you might be asked to repeat a series of nine digits, a number that is pushing the limit of the "magical" value of seven plus or minus two. By chunking the digits into groups of three, however, you then have to hold only three separate items in mind, not a difficult task. The same is true for letters. Whereas a random set of seventeen letters pushes STM far beyond its limit, by chunking the letters, retention can be made easy. Take the letters OPECIBMSONAR-RADAR, which is a total of seventeen letters. If you chunk them into OPEC, IBM, SONAR, and RADAR, the task of remembering them falls far short of STM capacity (Drenowski, 1980). Radio and TV commercials make use of this strategy, especially when giving telephone numbers. They tell you that telephone operators are standing by to receive your call. Rather than present you with eleven separate numbers to dial in order to get your volume of *Art Treasures of the World,* you are told to dial 1-800 ART INFO, which is at most only three separate units. The toll-free 1-800 part has probably already been chunked and encoded by the listener, leaving only ART and INFO

to be retrieved when getting to the phone. It has also been shown that chunking, especially around gestalt laws of perception, can aid in the recall of visual as well as auditory stimuli.

The magic 7 ± 2 value that has been placed on STM could easily create a bottleneck problem in the transfer of information from sensory storage, on through STM, and finally to LTM. Immediate memory is, therefore, like the narrow end of a funnel, opening into the vastness of LTM. That is, tremendous amounts of information can be stored in LTM, but the corridor leading in can get quickly jammed up. The bottleneck would be a severe constraint if all information were processed serially, that is, in the form of a series of processes occurring one at a time with no overlaps. Today, however, cognitive theorists talk of parallel processing, where two or more processes occur simultaneously. During parallel processing, LTM, STM, and even sensory storage interact and work together in concert. It is clear, however, that STM is easily disrupted by distractions.

Long-Term Memory

The information from STM can be passed along to be processed and consolidated into **long-term memory (LTM).** Encoding into LTM can typically take up to about twenty minutes, but this time interval can be dramatically shortened in certain situations, such as in "flashbulb" storage (Squire, 1987). LTM has the potential for holding encoded information for a lifetime. However, not all information from STM enters LTM. The key to LTM storage is in being motivated enough to engage in rehearsal of the items from your STM.

This is yet another example of one of E. L. Thorndike's major laws of learning, the law of exercise, or the idea that under the right conditions practice helps make perfect. A story is told about a visitor to New York City who asked a cab driver if he could tell her how to get to Carnegie Hall, and the cabbie replied, "Practice, madam, practice." If at a party, you were introduced to an extremely attractive person, your level of motivation might automatically be high enough to prod you into saying over and over again to yourself, or aloud, not only the person's name but also the vital phone number (if you were lucky enough to get it). Also, when being introduced to someone new, force yourself to think only of that person and his or her name. Don't divide your attention by concentrating on yourself and the kind of impression you're making. Make every effort to use that person's name during the conversation—"I like your tie, Jim" or "That's a nice dress, Lisa."

When listening in class, you should *always* take notes. Not only do you have the notes to refer to later, but the act of note taking itself is a rehearsal strategy. Persons remember more after taking notes, even if they lose the notes, than do those who simply sit and listen (probably because the act of writing also engages procedural memory).

Rehearsal: Two Types—Maintenance and Elaborative

Maintenance rehearsal is the rote repetition of the information in STM, like repeating the above-mentioned phone number a few dozen times. **Elaborative rehearsal,** on the other hand, is not based on mere repetition but occurs when the information is expanded, embellished on, and related to other items or concepts already in LTM. Most theorists now believe that elaborative rehearsal plays the more important role in the transfer of information from STM to LTM and leads to greater depth of processing (Ashcraft, 1990).

Two Long-Term Memory Systems?

Researchers in the areas of both cognitive and brain science are now suggesting that we may have at least two long-term memory systems, one for declarative memory and the other for procedural memory (Alper, 1986).

1. **Declarative memory** represents the brain's storehouse of names, dates, facts, places, faces, and past experiences. It is called "declarative" because it can be brought to mind and stated or declared in the sense of a fact, proposition, or image. Most theorists today are convinced that there are two types of declarative memories, episodic (sometimes called *autobiographical* memory) and semantic memory (Tulving 1985).
   a. **Episodic declarative memory,** as its name implies, consists of one's memory for past episodes in one's life. It is made up mostly of images from personal experiences organized on the basis of when and where they occurred. It's as though our lifetime experiences were on a long reel of movie film, and we rewind the reel to go back and look at the images on a few frames. Your ability to recall what you

did last night or last week (or even years ago) is based on your retrieval of episodic memory. Try to remember your childhood home, its color and shape, your bedroom, its wallpaper or paint and whether you got out of bed to the right or left and where your parents slept. Or can you recall your first-grade school, the classroom you were in, the area you played in at recess, your first fight with a neighborhood bully? According to the Atkinson-Shiffrin model, first proposed back in 1968, these memories are stored as images and are related to one another by space and time, and so if you shut your eyes and relax, you can probably imagine many of those childhood scenes.
   b. **Semantic declarative memory** contains our storehouse of words and the meaning of words, facts, general information, concepts, and rules and strategies for learning—most of the things that we were supposed to learn in school. Since words are stored in semantic memory, some children with reading problems, for example dyslexics, are thought to be less efficient in retrieving verbal labels from their memory cores due to semantic memory deficits. This is not always the case, however, since in one study it was found that dyslexics with rather severe retrieval problems for words did demonstrate deficits in their abilities to *process* verbal material, but had no accompanying semantic memory problems (Murphy et al., 1988). Nor is semantic memory just a matter of school-facts material. Many of the principles and rules that we learn on the playground or in social situations, so-called street smarts, are also stored in semantic memory. The organization of this memory is grounded, not on an ordered-time basis, but on networks of interconnected relationships and ideas called *schemata,* as a plural, or **schema** in the singular. For example, you might have a schema which covers virtually everything you know about football: that there are referees, that there are eleven players on each side, that players may get injured, that a touchdown counts for six points, and so on. That is, any body of information related to a central core concept represents a schema. The organization of a schema can be rather complex, but this very complexity may later be of enormous help during retrieval. It allows you to try several retrieval routes to your goal. As you associate around the fact or principle you're searching for, first trying one network then another, you continue to increase the likelihood of finding the target.

Learning to dance involves procedural memory, which is directly related to physical practice in this case. Procedural memory may or may not be accompanied by an ability to verbally describe one's performance (declarative memory).

This is because as you activate one thought or concept, a number of other related concepts will be activated through what is called the *spread of activation*. For example, a student was trying to remember the name of Alexander the Great's horse (only Heaven knows why), and he dug diligently into his Alexander-the-Great schema. He kept searching, much of the time out loud, talking about Alexander—that he was from Macedonia, that his father was named Philip, that Aristotle was his tutor, and so on. Then all of a sudden, as though out of the blue, he triumphantly shouted "Bucephalus." The spread of activation is similar to a fishing net being pulled in: By first pulling a single strand, all the other strands are eventu-

ally drawn up behind until the entire net is clearly exposed. Cognitive theorists believe that the idea of the spread of activation is fundamental to an understanding of recall from long-term memory.

2. **Procedural memory** contains traces of motor skills, typically learned through repetitive practice and/or conditioning. Procedural memory can be displayed, as when an expert skier gracefully descends a mountain, but this kind of knowledge is difficult to declare, or put into words. You can generally describe to someone how to ski, but actually learning to ski requires doing it, feeling it, and then practicing it. A person relies on procedural memory when tying shoes, playing scales

on the piano, riding a bicycle, hitting a golf ball and so on. Anyone who doubts that procedural memory is a valid phenomenon should try asking typists where certain letters are on the keyboard. Watch as their fingers flex out the answer. That this memory system is separate from declarative memory is evidenced by a series of reports on individuals who have undergone brain surgery and apparently, on occasion, lost one type of memory but not the other. Also, patients with Alzheimer disease often show no impairment of their procedural memory, but can't recall the names of their children. In one case, a golfer who was suffering from the disease retained his perfect golf swing, but only seconds after hitting the ball, he couldn't remember where the ball had landed.

According to the popular **dual-code theory** some information in LTM may be coded twice, both as a visual image and as a verbal representation. Thus, certain concrete words, as opposed to abstract words, can be doubly encoded, once as a verbal symbol and then also as an image-based symbol. This has been shown to increase one's recall ability (Paivo, 1971). Even though they may not have been in your consciousness for years, you can still probably recall the visual picture of your childhood home and perhaps the sounds you heard while playing in your backyard.

Because verbal representations play such an important role in our LTM, some theorists believe that we can retain few, if any, memories of events that occurred prior to our acquisition of language. This view is not universally held, however, as there is a growing body of research which seems to show that children have much more understanding of their environment, and its implicit social rules, than had previously been thought. This cognitive skill appears to begin early, even before there has been any language development and certainly before children can verbalize any memory of their understanding (Lazarus, 1991). Either way, with or without language, we all have long-term memories that seem to be permanently stored.

Permastore   Psychologists are using the term **permastore** to describe these permanently etched long-term memories, since the durability of these memories is analogous to permafrost, or "the unchanging nature of the permanently frozen state of the soil a few feet beneath the ground in Arctic regions" (Baddeley, 1990, p. 239). In one study, it was found that some aspects of a foreign language, Spanish, are retained in some cases for up to 50 years, despite not being rehearsed or even used at all (Bahrick, 1991).

It has even been suggested that every experience a person has, especially when emotions are involved, leaves a permanent memory trace on the brain and therefore that our freedom to act or think might be forever compromised if at one time we happened to participate in or even witness a particularly dreadful scene (Johnson, 1990). Such memories remain indelibly inscribed in the permastore and continue to influence our lives.

Retrieval from long-term memory   Once information has been stored in LTM, it is available but, as was mentioned earlier, it is not always easily located and utilized. John P. Houston, an expert in the area of learning theory, gives the example of the student who knows (has stored) the names of all the states of the Union, but at any given moment in time, he may not be able to retrieve all of them (Houston, 1991). Therefore, even though the information is in storage and available, it may not always be accessible. The student may know the names of all the states abutting, say, Indiana, but explains forlornly that he just doesn't seem to have them handy or that they have momentarily escaped him or, in more recent vernacular, that he can't locate the exact track on the hard disk of his memory. Theorists have drawn a distinction between availability and accessibility (Tulving, 1983):

1. A memory may not be accessible because it was never fully stored in the first place or because it was stored but has long since faded away. Such a memory is simply no longer available.

2. There are memories that are not accessible at the present time, but are still being retained, and if these memories are given the right set of circumstances or a changed situation, they may come tumbling forth. Memories such as these are retrievable but not accessible under prevailing conditions.

3. Certain memories are both retrievable and accessible. Prompting, by providing cues, aids the student in his or her storage search and eventual retrieval. This is why, when meeting a long-ago acquaintance, you may find it so much easier to remember the person's face than his or her name.

Some people feel they are unique in that they have "a good memory for faces but not for names." That, of course, is true of all of us. Remembering the face

SPOTLIGHT ON THE TOT

The Tip-of-the-Tongue Phenomenon

All of us at one time or another have been stuck in midsentence for a word or name, and chances are it has even happened to you today. We know how this can lead to some socially embarrassing moments. Our words have somehow become stuck on the tip of our . . . um . . . oh . . . like, you know, our whatchamacallits? Memory researchers say that this occurs as a result of a temporary retrieval failure in our long-term semantic memory systems, and they have even given a technical-sounding name to this problem, calling it the *tip-of-the-tongue phenomenon*, or TOT. Psychologists have found, not surprisingly, that TOTs increase with age, but it is also clear that each and every one of us, including elementary school children, are subject to their occasional annoyance. Psychologist Alan Brown has found that young adults report having a TOT experience at least once a week, whereas older adults acknowledge having them about two to four times as often. Brown believes that these self-reports, however, may be underestimating the real frequency of the problem, since many TOTs may seem so trivial that they are simply not important enough to

be tracked down or, more likely, to be publicly announced to the researchers. People say that their TOTs occur most often when they are trying to remember names of friends, acquaintances, or famous persons. Brown suggests, however, that perhaps we are more apt to remember the TOTs that involve friends, because they can often produce the most embarrassment. Brown says that if you were at a family gathering and suddenly couldn't remember the name of one of your relatives, it might just prove a tad more unsettling than if you couldn't think of the name of some actor in a movie you just saw. You could always change the subject and talk about a different movie, but you can't very well come up with a synonym for your dear aunt's name—or at least not one that you'd want to use out loud.

The TOT phenomenon is certainly largely a retrieval problem, but it may also be a function of how the information was stored in the first place. Why is stored information momentarily not usable? Brown feels that the answer to that question may someday uncover some of the answers to questions involving the entire memory pro-

cess—how information is stored in general and how the retrieval process works in particular, that is, how information is accessed from LTM. Brown believes that by having psychologists look at that very moment when the gears of memory are out of mesh, the study of TOTs may make it easier to get a good look at the entire memory system.[a] Sometimes, after an extremely frustrating TOT, you might simply give up and seem to forget about it. Then later, and suddenly in the midst of doing or thinking about something else, the word or name seems to pop right up out of your head. Perhaps the retrieval process is not always at the fully conscious level. One hint when this tormenting syndrome occurs is to do a little free associating, no matter how far-fetched the associations may seem. Think of everything you can that is in some way associated with the lost word or thought. By massaging the engram in this way, the word you're looking for is more likely to come bubbling to the surface.

---

[a] A. Brown, A review of the tip-of-the-tongue experience. *Psychological Bulletin* (1991), *109*, 204–223.

is a recognition task (the face is right there in front of you), but the name is strictly a matter of recall. Also, it's been shown that recognizing a face is even easier if it is in some way unusual (Bartlett et al., 1984). The dual-code theory would predict this, since both visual and verbal encoding are involved simultaneously during the initial storage. Perhaps when meeting the person, you had said to yourself, "He has the thickest eyebrows I've ever seen" or "That certainly is a bad case of acne."

Recognition is also the reason why multiple choice and true-false tests are easier than exams that require unaided recall. For example, compare the following items:

1. Who was president of the United States immediately after Franklin D. Roosevelt?

2. True or False: Harry S Truman was president of the United States immediately after Franklin D. Roosevelt.

Item 2 should be easier because you are being offered more ways to search your memory. Item 1, the recall item, demands that you access your memory of Franklin Roosevelt and then search for Truman. But for item 2, the recognition item, you could search from Truman to Roosevelt, even if you could not access it the other way around, from Roosevelt to Truman.

Finally, according to Wyer and Srull, three stages of long-term memory retrieval have been identified (Wyer and Srull, 1989). First, the individual must identify the correct storage bin in memory and then search for the appropriate schema (and then the item within that schema). Second, those schemata that have been most recently used will be at or near the top of the storage bin and will therefore be easier to find and use again. Third, when a person has an integrated and coherent schema, the recall of odd or "expectancy inconsistent" information will precede the recall of more consistent items.

Concept formation   Information processing is more than just the shuffling of stimulus inputs from sensory memory to short-term memory to long-term memory and then retrieving the bits of information. Information is also processed into conceptual form and becomes part of our semantic memory in a process known as **concept formation.** It is based on identifying the typical characteristics of stimuli, often called the *prototypes,* and then on organizing them in such a way as to provide encoded meaning (Ashcraft, 1989). Since memory for the meaning of events lasts longer than memory for specific, physical details, once information is processed into concepts, it is not only more easily stored in LTM but, perhaps more important, more easily accessed for retrieval. According to David Ausubel, concepts can be formed with or without verbal representations. In fact, Ausubel suggests that concepts are learned in two stages. First, the child learns the representative image of the concept and then later learns the verbal representation (Ausubel and Robinson, 1969).

This view portrays language as adding additional meaning to an already acquired concept. Because of its focus on both images and language, Ausubel's position on concept formation is consistent with the dual-code theory of information processing. Ausubel clearly recognizes that the two stages, imaging and verbalizing, may occur simultaneously, especially in older children, though it need not. Harry Harlow's study of learning sets (see p. 257) showed dramati-

cally that chimps could learn to form concepts and that these concepts were based strictly on image (considering the chimps' rather restricted vocabulary).

As children learn to increase their verbal-conceptual bases, their ability to comprehend written material also increases. One expert in the area of reading, Joanne Carlisle, has found that children can be trained in the use of strategies designed to increase reading comprehension (Carlisle, 1983). Carlisle's technique is based on a "learning how to learn" approach, in which children are provided with numerous examples and lots of practice in forming abstractions, looking for relationships, and then retrieving the concepts. In short, the children are deliberately provided with learning sets.

It seems clear that individuals who have formed learning sets will acquire and be able to use new information more efficiently than those who haven't, a fact that partially explains the difference in acquisition speed between the novice and the expert in a given cognitive area.

Another, although related, difference between the novice and the expert is in their backgrounds of chunked material (Walberg, 1988). Chunked material, as we have seen, is the representation of linked groups of items, even abstract groups, as clusters that can be processed as a single ensemble. This background of chunked items is stored in LTM and can be called upon when new material is entering STM to dramatically increase STM's storage capacity. Thus, as stated earlier, rather than information flowing in a stage-by-stage, or serial, manner (100 percent of processing occurring in each stage before the next stage can kick in), STM may be interacting with LTM early on with incoming stimulation. The processing may therefore be parallel, rather than linear and/or serial. This allows the expert to size up a situation with a "practiced eye," such as when a master chess player can look for a few seconds at a complicated board arrangement of twenty pieces or more and then later reproduce it perfectly. Interestingly, when chess pieces are laid out in random fashion, the expert doesn't do much better at remembering them than does the beginner. But when game situations are involved, the expert far surpasses the beginner. The expert has already encoded thousands of possible chess arrangements, some say as many as 50,000, and so the encoding process involved in memorizing the new arrangement can be done in only two or three parallel chunks (Baddeley, 1990). Says Herbert Walberg, "Such chunks may underlie mental processes

SPOTLIGHT ON LONG-TERM MEMORY

Episodic versus Autobiographical Memory

Researchers on long-term memory have typically taken two views on the manner in which studies should be conducted. The term *episodic* memory[a] has usually been used by researchers who prefer to conduct their studies under the controlled conditions of the university laboratory, where, hopefully, all extraneous variables are ruled out. Usually, the experimental task is low in the amount of meaning provided to the subject, and the to-be-remembered words are deliberately made difficult to associate with past experience. Just as was true with the Ebbinghaus studies, this is done to ensure that each subject starts out on a level playing field. Researchers who use the term *autobiographical* memory, however, base their work on the study

of past events that are laden with meaning to the subject, and no attempt is made to either restrict meaning or the subject's past experience.[b] For example, in one study of autobiographical memory, college graduates were selected from the classes of 1979, 1969, 1959, 1949, and 1939 and sent a twenty-item questionnaire. As a partial test of the "flashbulb" memory theory, the twenty items were designed such that ten were concerned with emotionally charged events, while the other ten were judged to be neutral. For example, one of the "emotional" items was "your first significant male/female relationship," whereas one of the "neutral" items was "the subjects you took as a college freshman." The respondent was asked to

check on a scale of 1 to 10 how well the event was remembered. Statistical analysis showed that the emotional items were recalled significantly more than were the neutral items. It may be that what college graduates remember best about their first year of college is not, alas, classroom assignments, but the onset and ending of affairs of the heart.[c]

[a] E. Tulving, Elements of episodic memory (New York: Oxford University Press, 1983).
[b] M. A. Conway, In defense of everyday memory. *American Psychologist* (1991), 46, 19–26.
[c] R. C. Sprinthall and P. Burns, Flashbulb memory among college graduates. *A.I.C. Alumni News* (1991), 24, 9.

ranging from childhood stages of cognitive development as identified by Jean Piaget, to new scientific discoveries" (Walberg, 1988, p. 77).

Emotions and Memory

Emotions are known to play an important role in memory, sometimes inhibiting memory and sometimes enhancing it. Many of us have probably been in situations in which our emotions were so strong that we barely remembered our own names. Students have even been known to panic during exams, and then complain that although much time had been spent studying, at the moment when the blue books were passed out, so did they. "My mind drew a blank" is the often-heard plea to the wary instructor. Two things are important in this connection. First, the better the material is learned, perhaps even over-learned, the less anxiety will be generated. People are less nervous doing things they do well. Second, self-

conscious efforts at relaxation (especially deep muscle relaxation) may often reduce the amount of felt anxiety, thus mitigating its crippling effects.

There is also, however, a phenomenon called **flashbulb memory,** which is an extremely vivid recollection of an event or situation that was etched into memory because the individual was then in a highly charged emotional state (Brown and Kulik, 1977). For example, we may have almost total recall of the moment we heard the news of some close relative's death or, for those old enough, the moment we heard that President Kennedy had been assassinated, or the moment we learned of the *Challenger* space shuttle disaster. Flashbulb memories seem to be most enduring when they involve death, accidents, or sex (Rubin and Kozin, 1984). At the physiological level, the strong emotional content apparently releases a group of hormones (epinephrine, ACTH, vasopressin, and opioid peptides) all of which appear to be involved in flashbulb memory (McGaugh, 1983, 1990).

SPOTLIGHT ON HOW WE THINK

Is Computer Thinking Like Human Thinking?

The difference between human and artificial intelligence can be summarized this way: Humans think; computers compute.

Since the information processing theorists have typically used the computer as their model, it is little wonder that research has been generated in the area of **artificial intelligence.** Artificial intelligence is predicated on the belief that human thinking can be simulated by computer programs, *if we understand how human beings think.* Typically, a theory on thinking is first devised, and then a computer program is written that simulates the theory. Allen Newell and Herbert Simon wrote a program called The Logic Theorist, which attempted to simulate a series of rules for solving problems in formal logic.[a] The program worked well enough to solve most of the complicated problems that had been advanced by the logicians Alfred Nash and Bertrand Russell in their 1925 masterpiece, *Principia Mathematica.*

The question at issue really shouldn't be whether computers can think but rather whether computers can be programmed to parallel, even roughly, the human thought process. So far, the answer is a decided no. Despite more than twenty years of research, no program yet written approaches the human ability to display intelligent behavior. To some extent this is due to the obvious fact that even the most technologically sophisticated computer is hopelessly naive when compared to the intricacies of the human mind. It is also due, alas, to the fact that psychology has still not gained a full understanding of how human intelligence is organized.[b]

Even though some theorists, such as Herbert Simon, feel that computer programs have actually been shown to think, and even, on occasion, to show flashes of insight,[c] others take a decidedly different view. For example, Michael Wertheimer says:

All of the requisite thinking, insight and understanding go into the writing of the program; once the program is running, neither the computer nor the program nor the combination of hardware and software thinks: all the thinking has been done beforehand, and was used in constructing the program.[d]

In short, our human ability to extract meaningful information from the environment and form abstractions and high-order cognitive structures has so far been only roughly approximated by the computer. Although computers have

THE INFORMATION PROCESSING THEORY OF FORGETTING

Forgetting, to the cognitively oriented information theorist, is defined as the inability to retrieve information. The two major reasons for forgetting, according to these theorists, are decay and interference.

Decay

Decay is the passive loss of the memory trace due to inactivity or lack of rehearsal. Actually, this is not a new idea. Thorndike, an early S-R theorist, postulated as one of his three major laws of learning the law of exercise. In this law, Thorndike stated that the more

long been likened to the human brain, they are in fact far different. A computer has a central processor acting on meticulously programmed instructions. It breaks a task into tiny components and acts on them very rapidly, but always in a preset sequence. The brain has billions of neurons, each of which is connected to thousands of other neurons, and they operate as a group. Thus, the power of the brain comes not just from its sheer numbers of neurons, but from the multiple interconnections among these neurons.

Top chess masters can still (as of this writing) beat the computerized chess programs, even though chess is one of the better programs to have been developed.[e] But despite the elegance of computer chess programs, they still cannot incorporate information and abstractions of the environment as well as the average three-year-old child. Also, as one mathematician has said, human thinking is not the same as the action of some very complicated computer, since the computer lacks consciousness, emotions, and motivations. The computer cannot "perceive poetry or the beauty of an evening sky or the magic of sounds; it cannot hope or love or despair."[f] One computer-driven device did, how-

ever, seemingly demonstrate motivation. Called the "tortoise," the little robot would scurry around the floor until its batteries ran low, at which point it would rush over to the nearest power socket, plug itself in, and recharge its own batteries. When thoroughly charged (satisfied?), it would then detach itself from the socket and go off on its way across the floor.[g] Another group of programmers, however, tried to teach a computer a motivational sequence as well as what to do when hungry. The computer was instructed to react in a variety of ways to hunger instructions, and finally when asked what it would do when it wanted a mid-afternoon snack, the computer replied that it would go to the nearest pizza stand. When asked what it would do when it got there, the computer responded that it would "eat the pizza stand." Another group of programmers prepared a Pentagon computer to answer questions to be posed by a visiting four-star general. When the general arrived, he typed in "Will it be peace or war?" and the computer answered "Yes." "Yes what?" asked the general. "Yes, *sir,*" answered the dutiful computer.[h]

Thus, a critical difference between artificial intelligence and hu-

man intelligence is that although computers can obviously compute better than humans, they are much worse than humans at matching. The computer can match incoming words against those stored in its memory only if those words are exact counterparts. As Morton Hunt says, "Any two-year-old child could do better."[i] Can the computer ever be expected to account for the complex patterning and economy of the human mind?

[a] A. Newell and H. A. Simon, *Human problem solving* (Englewood Cliffs, N.J.: Prentice-Hall, 1972).

[b] J. R. Anderson, *Cognitive psychology and its implications* (San Francisco: Freeman, 1980).

[c] H. A. Simon, The information processing explanation of gestalt phenomena. *Computers in Human Behavior* (1986), *2*, 241–254.

[d] M. Wertheimer, A gestalt perspective on computer simulations of cognitive processes. *Computers in Human Behavior* (1985), *1*, 20.

[e] J. B. Best, *Cognitive psychology* (2d ed.). (St. Paul: West, 1989).

[f] R. Penrose, *The emperor's new mind: Concerning computers, minds, and the laws of physics* (New York: Oxford University Press, 1989), p. 447.

[g] Ibid.

[h] K. Jennings, *The devouring fungus: tales of the computer age* (New York: Norton, 1990).

[i] M. Hunt, *The universe within* (New York: Simon & Schuster, 1982).

an S-R connection is used, the stronger it becomes; conversely, the less it is used, the weaker it becomes. Hence, through inactivity, the S-R connection simply rusts away, or passively decays over time.

The information processing theorists accept decay as an important influence on forgetting, especially at the input stage of the processing sequence. Sensory

memory, you will recall, decays in a matter of less than a few seconds, and information in STM, if not rehearsed, is lost in less than about a minute. But what about LTM? Here the evidence is not totally clear. Some theorists claim that once information is brought into LTM, it is stored quite permanently. For example, Wilder Penfield feels that the brain is like a recording tape and that all its memories are *permanently* stored (Penfield, 1969). While performing brain surgery, Penfield stimulated, with a slight electric current, various areas of a patient's cerebral cortex. (The patient was conscious.) As long as it persisted, each stimulation produced in the patient extremely vivid memories of long-past events. When the stimulation ceased, so too did the memory. The images and memories reported by the patient were so dramatically distinct that the patient felt as though they were being relived. The patient also believed that these memories had been completely forgotten. Thus, Penfield argued that the memories had remained organically intact and would remain so for life but that under normal circumstances the patient simply couldn't retrieve them.

This experiment, provocative though it may be, doesn't absolutely close the book on the case for permanent LTM. Critics suggest that Penfield's patient may not have been recalling actual events but instead was experiencing new sensations that only resembled past events (Houston, 1991).

Other theorists believe that decay does take place in LTM, but *at a much slower rate* than in STM. Estimates of the decay rate in LTM vary somewhat, but most theorists concede that once in LTM, information will probably remain relatively intact for many years. Memories such as these are said to reside in *perma-store*. (See page 292.)

Interference

Forgetting also occurs because of interference, which takes place when the recall of one event is inhibited by the incursion of another event. Again, this is not a brand-new explanation. For example, S-R theorist Edwin Guthrie, in his 1930s learning theory, put forth interference as the sole reason for forgetting. Interference is viewed as being of two types: proactive inhibition and retroactive inhibition.

Proactive inhibition   When you learn A, then later learn B, only to discover that your previous learning of A has in some way disrupted your recall of B, that is called **proactive inhibition (PI).** The previously learned, older material (A) has worked forward in time to hamper your efforts to retrieve that newer material (B). You might take a French course one semester and a Spanish course the next. On the Spanish final, your recall might well be disturbed by the interference effects produced by having previously taken the French course.

Retroactive inhibition   When the learning of new material (B) works backward and prevents the recall of older material (A), that is called **retroactive inhibition (RI).** To use the foreign language example again, after finishing the Spanish course you might now find your recall of French disrupted. You might very well confuse your *estars* with your *êtres*. Your knowledge of French would have remained more solidly intact had you not spent the intervening semester working on Spanish. Some students cram for a final until they drop off to sleep in the early morning hours in a state of exhausted confusion. On awakening, just before the exam, the material suddenly seems less confusing and more understandable. Some students attribute this to the fact that they have continued learning in some mysterious fashion while asleep. Though this theory is admittedly seductive, a simpler explanation is that sleeping helped to prevent retroactive inhibition. Going to sleep, rather than adding to the store of knowledge, may simply prevent a large degree of interference.

There is even some evidence that the brain may continue to process information during periods of sleep. Since virtually no new stimulations are being added, the brain tends to rework the information it already contains (Evans and Evans, 1983). Also, dreaming itself may be involved in the memory process. Francis Crick (of DNA fame) is now suggesting that a sleeper's dreams are part of a natural housecleaning system, ridding the mind of unwanted, false, or nonsensical memories, and thereby clearing the way for new information (Crick and Mitchison, 1983). Also, on awakening, the student is obviously less tired and more alert for the retrieval process. In general, the best way to take a break while studying for an exam is to do something as different as possible from the exam material. For example, if you are studying for an educational psychology exam, it's better to take a fifteen-minute Ping-Pong break than to read over your sociology notes.

Houston has prepared an exercise that should give you a quick, firsthand impression of how retroactive inhibition works (Houston, 1991). Cover the three telephone numbers on the right side of Table 11.1, and concentrate on the number to the left. Spend about thirty seconds looking at and rehearsing that number. When you're satisfied that you know it, cover the entire table and wait for about forty-five

TABLE 11.1   TESTING RETROACTIVE INHIBITION

NUMBER TO BE LEARNED FIRST	NUMBERS TO BE LEARNED SECOND
562-7201	617-5317
	413-2096
	783-0301

seconds. During this waiting period, *do not rehearse the number.* Think of other things, such as how many different brands of soft drinks you can name. After the forty-five seconds have elapsed, try to recall the phone number. You will probably be able to repeat it correctly. Now prepare yourself for the demonstration of retroactive inhibition by covering the left-side number that you just learned. Concentrate on memorizing the three numbers on the right side. When you think you have them down pat (it should take about a minute), try to recall the left-side number. Unless you encode and process information at a level far beyond the ability of the average person, that first number is now virtually impossible to retrieve.

Offsetting the effects of interference   The process of storing information (learning), then, can disrupt both past and future learning. Says Houston, "The very act of learning itself constitutes an ironic source of forgetting" (Houston, 1991, p. 226). Don't make too much of this accurate, though somewhat restricted, statement, however. You needn't assume that you'd better not learn too much now or it will make it that much more difficult to learn new material later. Nor should you be wary of tackling new material for fear of forgetting what you've already learned. As we shall soon see, the facilitative action of positive transfer may more than compensate for the inhibitory effects of interference. In fact, it has been shown that a background of information, especially when that information is *organized,* can offset the effects of interference (Reder and Ross, 1983).

Even the so-called memory experts must work to keep their information intact. In one celebrated case, Stephen Pawelson memorized all twenty-four books of Homer's Iliad, an absolutely monumental task. To appreciate how amazing this feat really is, remember that the Iliad consists of almost 16,000 lines, and none of these lines is really very easy. For example, the first line is, "The wrath do thou sing, O goddess of Peleus's son, Achilles," and reciting the entire epic

takes all day long, from "rosy fingered dawn to dark-browed night." Pawelson, a former accountant, said that each time he'd memorize a new book his recall of the previous book would start to fade, a classic example, incidentally, of retroactive inhibition. To overcome this loss, he'd have to go back and reweave his memory of the material that was unraveling. He said that this was like filling a leaking bucket, since only by constantly going back over the previous books could he plug all those leaking memory holes (Galvin, 1988).

Aids to Retrieving Learned Material

Processed information is of little use unless it can be retrieved. What, therefore, can be done to increase a student's ability to recall and utilize processed information and to compensate for interference?

Overlearning   Studies show that retention is longer and retrieval easier when material is over-

Retention is easier when material is overlearned.

learned—that is, learned to a point beyond which it appears to be mastered (Keppel, 1968). Teachers should encourage students to keep at it, even though the students feel the material has been fully learned. Overlearning is especially valuable with those areas that students find difficult. The alert teacher will spend extra time going over such material. It has even been suggested, perhaps tongue in cheek, that the best way to remember is to forget, for example, forgetting your sweetheart's birthday—just once.

Understanding   Teachers should stress the understanding of concepts rather than concentrate only on the repetition of facts. When provided with categories of understanding, students are more likely to learn new information quickly and efficiently. When equipped with a conceptual framework, students are more apt to be able to deduce solutions to new problem areas. Also, abstractions are easier to develop when an underlying understanding of a concept has been incorporated. Conceptual learning becomes self-perpetuating, since each new concept provides an anchorage that makes the acquisition of new information and new concepts more efficient. It's as though entering new information into a computer literally expands the computer's internal memory. Learning then requires less effort and becomes more enjoyably efficient. Also, as a myriad of studies have shown, the more meaningful the material is, the greater the likelihood of both its acquisition and retrieval. It is virtually impossible to teach for understanding if the material seems random and meaningless. For example, suppose you were given the following sequence of numbers to memorize: 100816449362516941. Since this series is far beyond the STM limit of seven, as a random sequence it is virtually impossible to recall. With understanding, however, it becomes a relatively simple task, since it is composed of the squares of the numbers from 10 to 1 in that order.

Building an organized knowledge base   The acquisition and retrieval of new information can be made easier when it builds on previously incorporated information. The evidence from studies on positive transfer as well as Harry Harlow's data on learning sets show that acquisition improves when it is built on an existing knowledge base. Just as new motor skills are improved by positive transfer (learning to ride a bike aids in learning to ride a motorcycle), so too are more cognitively based skills. Concepts build on facts, and *concepts build on concepts*. Knowing

how to add, subtract, multiply, and divide is obviously helpful to the student taking a course in algebra. Having taken algebra, in turn, makes a course in physics more understandable. The ability to access and utilize information is a direct function of the number of previously incorporated categories available to a student. Recalling that Truman succeeded Roosevelt is facilitated by stored information about Truman, Roosevelt, and any other facts relating to the United States at the end of World War II. These encoded facts also increase the likelihood of a student's acquiring a schema, or the organized concepts relating to that historical time period. It is clear from the research that the more organized associations one has, the deeper the processing. These concepts, in turn, help ensure a more complete understanding of such concepts as the restructuring of the postwar economy or of the sociopolitical justifications for the establishment of the United Nations. Thus, as students acquire more different *organized* categories into which information may be processed, the information becomes ever more accessible to retrieval and use.

The main message here is that the better we organize information and relate it to what we already remember, the better we can recall it. An expert chess player remembers the pieces on the board better than the beginner not because of a better inherent memory, but because the expert understands the entire situation as an organized and coherent whole. The beginner, in contrast, is trying to remember the individual pieces as separate units, a much more difficult task.

Relating new material to the existing knowledge base   The teacher should always strive to interweave new material with relevant existing learning. When new material is tied into the student's existing knowledge base, teaching effectiveness is increased (White and Gagne, 1976). Part of the reason for this is that information is then stored in several categories, and each of the associations then serves as a cue to a source of retrieval. Thus, the more categories under which new information is indexed, the more readily it can be retrieved. The student should constantly be reminded of these related categories as new information is presented.

Using cue associations   When attempting retrieval, the student should be taught to work on actively producing as many cue associations as possible. Since retrieval of stored information is often cue-dependent, an *active* search of all relevant cues often brings the information back into working memory. For example, in trying to retrieve the name of Abraham Lincoln's assassin, the student should think of as many things as possible about Lincoln, perhaps the fact that he was assassinated at a play, the name of the theater, or even the quotation "*Sic semper tyrannis.*" The more associations the better, since eventually one of them might cue the name, John Wilkes Booth. This technique is often called *associative searching*, since it usually makes use of less commonly employed pathways among the various concepts and facts related to the information being retrieved. Its opposite is *active searching*, in which information is accessed along more practiced pathways (Klatsky, 1984). Obviously, the student should be encouraged to utilize the associative search only if a direct search comes up empty.

Mnemonics

Mnemonic devices (Mnemosyne was the Greek goddess of memory) are techniques for aiding both the acquisition and retrieval of learned material. An example of a mnemonic would be the simple rhyming scheme, "Thirty days hath September, April, June, and November." Mnemonic devices may be either visual or verbal. Suppose, for example, you wanted to remember to pick up some ice cream, bread, and milk. As an aid to memory, you might attempt to produce a vivid visual image of your grocery list, perhaps by imagining a gigantic ice cream cone soaking in milk and surrounded by slices of bread. With that bizarre picture fixed firmly in mind (in fact, the more outlandish the image, the better), your grocery list should be secure.

The reason for using bizarre associations is that in creating them, and perhaps even visualizing them, you force yourself to pay attention, and anything that focuses attention becomes an extremely potent factor in both the encoding and retrieval of learned material. Furthermore, anytime you force yourself to focus your attention, the physical arousal activates certain brain chemicals which can then help to promote learning. With adolescents or adults, such stimulants as the caffeine in coffee can artificially produce an increased arousal level which then aids memory (Blum, 1984).

Or, instead, you might choose a verbal mediator and simply think of the letters IBM—ice cream, bread, and milk. Just don't make the mistake of forgetting what the letters stand for and inadvertently bring home instant coffee, bananas, and margarine.

The ancient Greek and Roman orators used to employ imagery to help them memorize the key points in their speeches. The orator would imagine himself strolling down some well-known path and then tie the image of a passing landmark to each successive rhetorical point. This is now known as the *method of loci*, and as many after-dinner speakers will attest, it still works today as well as it did in early Greek days. You might even use it on your way to take an educational psychology exam. Suppose, for example, you need to do some last-minute cramming on Thorndike's three major laws of learning. As you leave the dorm, the flagpole is on your left, and on top of the pole you picture a gymnast going through an "exercise" routine. Next, as you pass the library, you visualize a large cat at the main entrance poised to pounce on a mouse; the cat appears to be coiled in "readiness." Finally, before entering the classroom building where the test is to be given, you walk by the campus snack bar and remember the "effect" the cold french fries had on you the last time you were there. As you mentally rewalk the route during the test, you recall the laws.

Verbal mediators are also used as mnemonics. Fifth-graders, for example, may learn the acronym HOMES in order to remember the names of the five Great Lakes: Huron, Ontario, Michigan, Erie, and Superior. Such acronyms are called *first-letter mnemonics*, since the peg word, HOMES, contains the first letters of all the items to be recalled. Research in this area has shown rather convincingly that if the peg word itself is not too complicated, the use of the first-letter mnemonic definitely aids recall (Nelson and Archer, 1972). The novice handling a boat might learn to use the mnemonic "red, right, returning" in order to recall that the red buoys should be kept to the right when returning to the harbor. Many so-called memory experts utilize long and intricate mnemonic devices when performing their amazing feats of recall (Lorayne and Lucas, 1974).

Mnemonic devices, however, may be so complex that recalling the original stimuli is even more difficult than it might otherwise have been. One college student had learned a long poem that was designed to ensure the memorization of all the U.S. presidents in order. The first letter in each word of the poem corresponded to the first letter in the last name of the president. Sometimes, however, the student would forget a word or line from the poem, and at other times he would forget the name the letter had designated. For example, once when asked who the thirteenth president was, he paused, repeated the poem to himself, and then proudly answered, "Franklin." (This is not to suggest, of course, that he also believed that Fillmore was the name of a stove.)

Another use of the peg word mnemonic combines the verbal mediator with a visual image. The following example, one of the simplest peg systems, uses rhymes for numbers (Kantowitz and Roediger, 1980). First, rehearse and put into memory storage the following words:

1 Gun   6 Sick
2 Shoe   7 Heaven
3 Tree   8 Gate
4 Floor   9 Wine
5 Hive   10 Hen

Now have some other person give you a verbal list of ten items, slowly and in order, such as

1 Book   6 Orange
2 Football   7 Track meet
3 Bathtub   8 Rose Bowl
4 Coke   9 Professor
5 Candle   10 Dice

As each item is announced, create a mental picture associating the item with the peg word. Here's an example, although you can probably do this far more creatively yourself.

1. Gun—a *book* that has been hollowed out and contains a gun
2. Shoe—a large shoe kicking a *football*
3. Tree—a *bathtub* perched high in the limbs of a large tree

4. Floor—a bottle of *Coke* spilled all over a kitchen floor
5. Hive—a beehive with flaming *candles* inserted in it
6. Sick—eating an *orange* and becoming violently sick from it
7. Heaven—a *track meet* in heaven, with angels competing in each event
8. Gate—a large gate at the entrance to the *Rose Bowl*, festooned with admission tickets
9. Wine—your *professor* drinking too much wine and acting in a foolish fashion
10. Hen—a large hen laying a dozen *dice* instead of eggs

Once you've stored these images, the other person can either give you a number, say four, and you'll respond with "Coke"; or an item, say track meet, and you can respond with the number "seven." It's not hard to do, and you'll definitely impress your friends and relatives with your "amazing" powers of memory. Students have even been known to wager against such feats.

The pros and cons of mnemonics in the classroom
Mnemonic devices are unquestionably effective in aiding the recall of specific information. They may be troublesome at the start of a learning sequence, since they take time to initiate, but once in place they allow information to remain systematically stored—like an office filing system.

Yodai mnemonics, first introduced in Japan, literally means "essence of structure" and makes use of virtually all the mnemonic techniques mentioned so far, such as vivid imagery, poems, and even songs. In one study, using the Yodai technique, it was found that third-graders in the United States learned to manipulate fractions in a few hours—a feat that typically takes two to three years. According to the study, once these manipulative math procedures are acquired, understanding naturally follows (Higbee and Kunihira, 1985). The use of songs as memory enhancers, such as having first-graders sing "ABCDEFG," has long been a part of most elementary school curricula in the United States. After all, what child can't sing all the words to the latest soft-drink commercial or the most current Michael Jackson hit? In the teaching of reading, great success has also been claimed for the "Hooked on Phonics" method, where audiotapes are used to teach children how to associate letter sounds with musical tones (Gateway, 1988). However, even though the phonics approach can be of great benefit to the beginning reader, sooner or later the child must begin to sight-read, rather than forever continue the slow and sometimes painful process of sounding out each word.

This seemingly bright picture has another side, however. Too much reliance on mnemonics may actually prevent understanding and especially creativity. Advocates of this view believe that mnemonic devices are merely tools for rote memorization, better used for training parrots than children. Material learned in this fashion is difficult to relate to larger concepts. As one critic notes, "Mnemonics may help children learn arbitrary associations but are likely to be less helpful when the material to be learned has conceptual links not expressed by the mnemonic cover story (Kilpatrick, 1985).

IQ AND INFORMATION PROCESSING

Studies dating back to the 1920s have consistently shown that IQ and the acquisition and retention of new material are highly correlated. A child with an IQ of 130 will typically learn and retain more information than a child whose IQ is only 100. But what about forgetting? In a series of studies, first reported in 1959 by Herbert Klausmeir and John Feldhausen, children with high, average, and low IQs were shown to retain about the same *proportion* of what they had learned (Klausmeir et al., 1959). That is, although in absolute terms the high-IQ children learned and retained the most, the percentage of what was retained over time remained the same for all three IQ groups. Thus, the proportion of information retained seems to be a constant across a wide range of IQ values (Gentile et al., 1982).

Yale psychologist Robert Sternberg has also studied intelligence as it relates to information processing (Sternberg, 1982). Sternberg has found that people who score highest on IQ tests are not necessarily the ones who are the fastest responders at all stages of the information processing sequence. In fact, the highest IQs are registered by people who spend *more time* encoding the relevant cues in a given problem and then *less time* in strategically processing the information during the solution phase. The greater time spent during the early encoding stage is, thus, compensated for by a lessening of the time spent later in the sequence and in an increased likelihood of finding the correct solution.

DEVELOPMENTAL ASPECTS OF INFORMATION PROCESSING

There are, of course, obvious differences between the infant's and the adult's ability to process information. And once again, we find the nature-nurture controversy arising. At the two extremes, one view states that cognitive development is a straight function of genetic unwinding (nature); the other view is that it is based solely on experience. The position that we will take falls between these two poles—that is, that the human information processor develops increasingly sophisticated strategies as a result of the overall interaction of heredity, environment, and time. Cognitive maturity thus depends on a genetic predisposition interacting with environmental encounters occurring within a range of specific age levels. The developing child acts on and reacts to his or her environment, and, as a result, the quality of the child's information processing system is transformed.

On average, older children obviously have better memories than younger children. Much of this has to do with language. As language acquisition progresses, the older child has more categories of verbal representations to use to encode and retrieve information. Also, as we have seen in our discussion of Jean Piaget, qualitative differences in the child's cognitive style and level develop over time. As the child's cognitive base broadens and matures, higher and more abstract levels of thought processing typically become the rule. In fact, the latest studies have even pointed to the fact that the child goes through critical periods in the development of processing capacities (Kail, 1984). Each passing day brings fresh evidence demonstrating the linkage between the information processing model and the currently accepted parameters of cognitive growth. Let's now examine some of the developmentally related components of the information processing model.

Differences in Processing Input

Earlier studies had suggested that younger children were less able to take as much information into their sensory registers (or hold it as long) as older children and adults could. But doubt is now being expressed about this finding. More recent studies have indicated that five-year-old children do not differ from adults in the amount of information they perceive or the time they hold it in the sensory register. What the earlier studies had interpreted as a sensory difference now appears to be a difference in how much information can be encoded into STM before it simply decays in the sensory register. It is at this stage of the process that older children show superiority. Nor can this advantage be explained solely on the basis of language differences (Solso, 1979). The mature learner's apparent superiority in the amount of information recorded in sensory memory may actually be due to a more refined strategy of sensory rehearsal. In fact, the literal sensory image (icon) is believed to persist even longer in the young child than in the adult. Thus, at least with regard to visual memory, the infant is simply *processing* the information more slowly, even though the actual duration of the icon may remain intact somewhat longer (Lasky and Spiro, 1980).

Processing speed Again, although earlier studies seemed to have found that processing speed was a direct function of age, the current view is more cautious. In the earlier studies investigators had typically presented the subjects with a simple stimulus, then measured the time it took for recognition to occur. But what had at first appeared to be a difference in processing speed may instead have been an artifact of the experimental methodology. Perhaps older children were more willing to take a guess at what the stimulus might be and, because of their broader knowledge base, were more accurate when they did guess.

Thus, the evidence on processing speed is still unclear. Its importance from a developmental point of view, however, should not be minimized. As Robert Solso states, "If children indeed process individual stimuli more slowly, the cumulative effect of this deficit across large numbers of stimuli could be substantial" (Solso, 1979, p. 362).

Attentional processes Since the ability to attend to or focus on relevant stimuli is a key element in the transfer of information from the sensory register to STM, the study of the growth of attentional processes is of major significance to developmental psychologists. Researchers are especially interested in two forms of the attentional process—actually two sides of the same coin—selective attention and divided attention.

Selective attention is shown when the child is able to home in on one source of incoming information, while ignoring other possible distractors. Can the child continue to listen to the teacher while simultaneously tuning out a peer conversation in the back of the classroom? Can the child pick out the salient features in a workbook problem without getting lost in the extraneous details? In one study of the way first-grade children solve arithmetic word problems, it was found that performance increased when the stimuli, in this case *pictures* of the objects to be quantified, were different rather than the same. For example, the children were better able to add 5 stegosaurs plus 1 brontosaur than when presented with 5 stegosaurs plus 1 stegosaur. The use of different objects to represent these quantities provided a more interesting and novel visual array and thus increased the child's ability to attend selectively to the important information in each question (Sprinthall and Nolan, 1991). Also, for dyslexics (children with severe reading problems), selective attention may be difficult to sustain because they are receiving too many incoming stimuli. The distribution of visual receptors on the dyslexic's retina has been shown to differ from that of the nondyslexic (Grosser and Spafford, 1990). Dyslexic children have significantly more receptors for detailed vision (called *cones*) in the peripheral region of the retina, and as a result they are receiving stimuli from a wider-than-normal visual field. This may be an asset in certain athletic endeavors, but it presents problems to the child trying to attend selectively to a word or words on a printed page. For most children, however, the ability to attend selectively tends to increase naturally with age (Higgins and Turnure, 1984). For example, many teenagers seem able to study, and comprehend, despite the distraction of loud music blaring from a nearby radio.

The other side of the coin is called **divided attention,** and is shown when the child can listen to the teacher *and also* pick up the peer conversation in the back of the room or when the teenager is studying a history lesson with the radio on, and is able to attend to both sources of incoming information. This ability is also developmentally based, with adolescents being much better at this than are younger children (Shiff and Knopf, 1985). This isn't to say that adolescents should be encouraged to study while the television or radio is on. It's just that they are better able than younger children to perform that kind of information balancing act.

Thus, the evidence in this area is fairly straightforward. The research clearly shows that older children are indeed better able to focus and control their attentional processes than are younger children. A child's potential ability to attend to relevant cues and ignore the irrelevant seems to be a direct function of growth and development.

Encoding The ability to internally encode incoming information also seems to have a substantial developmental component. Whereas young children typically incorporate only a small number of stimulus dimensions, sometimes only one or two, older children engage in what is called **multiple encoding** (Solso, 1979, p. 363). In the processing of complex stimuli, which have a large number of encoding alternatives, multiple encoding becomes especially important. A stimulus may be encoded on the basis of its size, distance, density, color, shape, texture, name, and so forth. In short, older children tend to encode by using many of these alternatives; younger children focus on only a few.

Differences in Storing Information

Rehearsal strategies Age-related differences have also been found in rehearsal strategies (Ornstein et al., 1975). This is an obviously important factor, since rehearsal allows STM codes to be processed into LTM. The major findings in this area indicate that as children get older, they develop more organized rehearsal strategies, which, because of their cumulative effects, allow significantly more information to be consolidated into LTM. Younger children, although still attempting to rehearse, do so in a less systematic fashion than older children.

Chunking techniques Closely related to rehearsal strategies are **chunking** techniques, since both depend on organizational skills and the ability to form abstractions. A list of words—such as *airplane, train, bus, couch, table, chair, piano, guitar, trumpet*—are easy to remember when chunked into the three categories of modes of transportation, furniture, and musical instruments. If the list is encoded as nine separate and seemingly random items, retrieval becomes far more difficult. Younger children, even when prompted as to the obvious chunking categories, have difficulty memorizing this type of list. Up to about third grade, children seem not to do any better on easily categorized items than they do on unrelated items.

Retrieval skills Retrieval skills have also been found to be based on age-related strategies. As children mature, they develop what appears to be an almost spontaneous increase in the use of retrieval strategies. This, after all, should not be surprising. Since the developing child is encoding and organizing information in an increasingly sophisticated manner, it is little wonder that he or she can access the processed information more efficiently. The older child utilizes more categories, more information storage bins, and because of this is better able to use retrieval cues to facilitate the search. It has also been suggested that older children possess more knowledge about their own memory skills and thus are better equipped to know when certain retrieval skills are appropriate. This concept of having internal knowledge about memory has been called *metacognition,* or *metamemory,* by John Flavell and others (Flavell, 1985). Thus, young children may not use as many retrieval aids as older children, either because the younger children don't yet have the aids or, if they do, don't know that they have the aids—or even that the aids might be helpful in retrieval. The difference between cognition and metacognition is in the students' self-awareness and control. Cognitive processes often grow over time, with little awareness or effort on the part of learners. Metacognition involves definite awareness, and even conscious monitoring and control. Elizabeth Bondy puts it this way: "A student who summarizes the chapter he/she has just read exercises cognitive skills. When the student constructs a summary as a means of obtaining feedback on his/her understanding of the material, the student engages in metacognition" (Bondy, 1984, p. 236).

Metacognition is thus defined as thinking about thinking, and Bondy believes that these metacognitive strategies can be taught, that classroom teachers can promote the development and use of metacognitive abilities. Among other strategies she suggests are

1. Providing opportunities for feedback

2. Having students keep a daily learning log

3. Providing instruction in self-questioning techniques

4. Teaching students to rate their own abilities to comprehend

SPOTLIGHT ON A LEARNING PROBLEM

Attention Deficits

One extremely perplexing problem, common among learning-disabled children*, is a condition known as the **attention deficit–hyperactivity disorder,** or **ADHD.**[a] The child who suffers from this syndrome is simply unable to concentrate for a sustained period of time or even to pay much attention to incoming information, such as when trying to listen to the teacher in class. This is, of course, extremely troublesome to the learner, since the information cannot get processed at all if it never enters STM in the first place. Children who suffer from this condition are said to show impulsive rather than reflective thinking.[b] Among preschoolers, and even among some older children, some of the symptoms associated with this condition are fairly common and should not be viewed as especially dangerous. At very young ages they may signal only a temporary developmental lag. But by grades four and up, this syndrome can become an extremely incapacitating condition for the developing learner and may indicate that the child is learning-disabled. ADHD children have great difficulty attending to instructions, even in game situations, especially games like "Simon Says." To be diagnosed as having ADHD, the child must exhibit a large number of specific criteria. The criteria listed (in descending order of discriminating power) by the American Psychiatric Association for ADHD are as follows:

But he was here a second ago.

Portrait of a typical ADHD child.

1. Fidgets with hands or feet or squirms in seat
2. Has difficulty remaining seated when asked to do so
3. Is easily distracted
4. Has difficulty awaiting turn in games
5. Blurts out answers to questions before they are completed
6. Has difficulty following through on instructions
7. Has difficulty sustaining attention in tasks or play

8. Shifts from one incomplete activity to another
9. Has difficulty playing quietly
10. Talks excessively
11. Interrupts or intrudes on others
12. Has difficulty listening to what is being said
13. Often loses things needed for activities at school or at home
14. Often engages in dangerous activities without considering the consequences, such as running out into the street without looking[c]

Now, since it is the rare child indeed who hasn't shown many, or even all, of these behaviors at one time or another, the American Psychiatric Association carefully points out that to be given a valid diagnosis of ADHD, the child must display at least eight of the fourteen listed criteria, must show the onset before age 7, and must exhibit these symptoms for a period of six months or longer. When this condition is suspected, the teacher should notify the school psychologist.[d] Although many ADHD children seem to grow out of this condition by the time they reach midadolescence, by that time much of the damage is done. Early learning that should have taken place may not be compensated for by later effort.

The alert teacher should also be made aware of the fact that attention deficits are not always accompanied by great bursts of hyperactive energy. The condition called *at-tention deficit disorder*, or *ADD*, without hyperactivity can be even more insidious, especially because ADD children are less apt to advertise their struggles.[e] The ADD child does not display the overt and dramatic symptoms of ADHD and is thus more difficult to identify, at least at first. In fact sometimes a teacher may even welcome such a nondisruptive child. The careful observer, however, might notice a faraway look in the child's eyes as though the child had "spaced out." The ADD child simply cannot *maintain* a well-organized thought pattern or maintain a focus on incoming information. The ADD child may be able to do the first few word problems correctly, but then starts making errors on the next few problems even though they are not any more difficult.[f]

However, the child who daydreams or who displays indifferent, seclusive, and withdrawing behavior is showing symptoms that may be warning signs of a more serious problem than ADD. The withdrawn child who begins not acknowledging other people, who displays rigid thinking patterns, and who uses a private language (often muttering meaningless phrases) may be drifting off on to the lonely road to unreality. Detecting these prepsychotic signs can often be done by the caring teacher. This does not mean that all teachers must train to be professional psychologists, but, like it or not, we all do psychologize when-ever we make inferences about how or why people behave as they do. Also the teacher is in an especially advantageous position in this regard, for outside of the parents, perhaps nobody else has the unique opportunity of being able to observe the child for so many hours and in such a variety of situations.

* The term *learning disability* is used in relation to a child who has normal or near-normal intelligence but also displays a baffling variety of learning and behavior problems, such as an IQ-achievement discrepancy, the possibility of central nervous system dysfunction, information processing difficulties, learning problems not due to an impoverished environment, and even some emotional problems (as defined in Hallahan and Kauffman 1991; see note b).

[a] B. Henker and C. K. Whalen, Hyperactivity and attention deficits. *American Psychologist* (1989), 44, 216–230.
[b] D. P. Hallahan and J. M. Kauffman, *Exceptional children: Introduction to special education*, 5th ed. (Englewood Cliffs, N.J.: Prentice-Hall, 1991).
[c] American Psychiatric Association, *Diagnostic and statistical manual of mental disorders (DSM III-R)*, 3d ed., rev. (Washington: American Psychiatric Association, 1987).
[d] J. D. McKinney and D. L. Speece, Academic consequences and longitudinal stability of behavioral subtypes of learning disabled children. *Journal of Educational Psychology* (1986), 78, 365–372.
[e] D. R. Jordan, *Attention deficit disorder*, 2d ed. (Austin, Tex.: Pro-Ed, 1992).
[f] D. R. Jordan, Whatever happened to ADD without hyperactivity? *Ch. A.D.D. ER* (1991), 4, 4.

SPOTLIGHT ON READING FOR COMPREHENSION AND UNDERSTANDING

Metacognition in Action

It's one thing to learn to read, but it's just as important to learn how to understand what is being read. Comprehension difficulties are often related to the reader's failure to participate actively in the reading process. We have all been told many times that teaching students to become more strategic when reading not only increases the student's understanding of important textual information but also the student's motivation. Too often, however, we as teachers are told to teach these strategies without any specific information as to how that might be done. The Nolan technique, described here, has been used many times in different teaching environments and has proved to be invaluable, especially with children who are below average in comprehension ability.

The Nolan technique is based on combining *two* cognitive strategies, self-questioning and prediction. Previous research on the use of strategy and reading comprehension has typically focused on the effects of a single technique. However, relatively little has been done with the combination of two cognitive strategies in a single intervention.

Outline of Training Steps for Nolan Technique

Children using the combined metacognitive strategies are given a series of short passages to read, and then, while reading, are taught to utilize the following steps, called self-questioning with prediction, or SQWP.

1. Identify the main idea.
2. Write down the main idea.
3. Think of a question based on main idea and write it down.
4. Answer your question.
5. Predict what will happen next.

Results show that after as few as a half-dozen sessions, students who used self-questioning with prediction scored significantly higher on measures of reading comprehension than those who used only self-questioning or a more traditional vocabulary development intervention. Combining two cognitive strategies in a single intervention encourages students to actively monitor their states of reading. Self-questioning directs the student's attention to critical aspects of the text, thereby increasing understanding of important textual elements. The prediction component stimulates a purpose for reading because the student is forced to anticipate coming events in the passage. Motivation is increased by the anticipation of discovering whether one's guess will be confirmed. Importantly, the combined metacognitive strategies benefited both those students whose reading comprehension was

slightly below grade level as well as those whose comprehension was severely below grade level.

Further, in follow-up studies students have reported that they continued to use the combined metacognitive strategies months after the training period has ended:

"Using a strategy helps me in social studies to find important facts in the paragraph."

"I'm more in charge of what I'm doing when I use a strategy during reading."

"I feel good when I use a reading strategy since it helps me in my classes to answer questions about what I read."

Finally, because metacognitive strategies facilitate reading comprehension, they may be applicable not only across content areas but also across skill areas, such as creative writing and artistic endeavors.[a]

[a] T. E. Nolan, Self-questioning and prediction: Combining metacognitive strategies. *Journal of Reading* (1991), 35(2), 132–138.

Studies aimed at the direct instruction of children on the use of these metacognitive strategies have consistently reported increases both in their usage as thinking tools *and in memory performance* (Lodico et al., 1983).

Finally, retrieval sometimes takes a rather concerted effort on the part of the learner, and younger children may not be as willing to exert themselves in the search for cues. Also, retrieval takes more effort when the incoming information is relatively new and unorganized. The younger child probably has to exert *more* effort in retrieving information simply because it is not as easily accessed.

In summary, then, the evidence emerging from the information processing studies has confirmed the developmental aspects of this important theory.

THE PHYSICAL LOCUS OF MEMORY

In Search of the Engram

Before closing this chapter, we should take a brief look at the physical side of the learning organism. As prospective teachers, your appreciation of the overall information processing model in general and the learning child in particular should be enhanced by developing some awareness of recent research into the biological correlates of learning and memory. How does a memory form in the physical sense? And if we can find out how it is formed, can we also discover its physical location? Finally, are there any physiochemical procedures available for enhancing one's memory capabilities?

Even though psychologists have spent over one hundred years on memory research, most of the studies have focused on how the memory system works, not on what the functions of memory are or what the memory system does for us—questions that William

James certainly would have asked. Rather than concentrate solely on analogies from physics and computer science, some of today's theorists want to remind us of the Jamesian message of functionalism and nudge us more into the area of biology, where a clearer picture of these matters of *function* may emerge. These researchers insist that biology, as opposed to physics, is better able to apply population thinking and therefore to help us recognize the importance of individual differences and variation (Bruce, 1991).

Implicit in all discussions of the memory process is the ghost of the "black box," or the thought that explanations which are based on physical or physiological analogies are merely hocus-pocus illusions and are therefore really no explanations at all. Even today, behaviorists often charge physiological and cognitive psychologists with "stuffing" the black box, or creating internal, neural explanations to cover their own ignorance. But even the most ardent behaviorist cannot allay the gnawing thought that when learning is identified at the behavioral level, even as a new squiggle on a Skinnerian cumulative record, somewhere, someplace, somehow changes are taking place within the organism's nervous system. The actual, physical location of the memory trace has been called the **engram**.

During the height of behaviorism, in the 1940s and 1950s, those researchers who dared give voice to these

Students can be helped to develop their metacognition, or their ability to think about thinking.

nagging thoughts, such as the great Harvard physio-logical psychologist, Karl Lashley, usually spoke of electrical reverberating circuits and saw the brain as a direct analog of the electronic computer. But when these researchers tried to find the precise location within the nervous system of these reverberating circuits and failed, Karl Lashley uttered his plaintive, though tongue-in-cheek comment, "Learning is just not possible" (Lashley, 1950, p. 480).

Beginning in the mid-1950s, however, a different approach was taken, one based on a biochemical model. Theorists began to focus on chemical changes. The Swedish biochemist Holger Hyden was one of the first, in 1959, to put forth the **RNA theory** (Hyden, 1959). In order to support a biochemical account, it seemed essential to find molecules large enough and complex enough to store the millions of memories that an individual might accumulate over the years. Logic seemed to dictate, therefore, that the enormously large, life-controlling nucleic acids, RNA and DNA, might possibly be the storage sites. Hyden suggested that since we are born with roughly 10 billion brain cells, and that within each of these cells there are millions of RNA molecules, then the RNA theory could logically account for trillions of images and memories. Hyden then did an experiment and found that changes in the RNA within nerve cells occurred *as a direct result of environmental stimulation.* Although this, of course, did not prove that memories are encoded in RNA molecules, it certainly suggested that RNA might play a role.

About the same time as Hyden's early work, James V. McConnell began reporting some rather astonishing findings, so astonishing in fact as to create some skepticism among many of his colleagues (McConnell et al., 1959). McConnell, working with flatworms, or *Planaria,* had first succeeded in training these tiny organisms to respond to a conditioned stimulus. He then cut the worms in half, allowing the heads to regenerate new tails and the tails to regenerate new heads. Both sets of "new" planaria retained the conditioned response, indicating that perhaps memory could be chemical in nature. If this were the case, McConnell reasoned, then it might be possible, in effect, to transplant a memory from one organism to another if the right chemicals from the trained worm could be injected into an untrained worm. This approach simply did not work. McConnell then recalled that under certain conditions flatworms will eat one another, and since they have only a rudimentary digestive tract, it might even be possible that tissue from one worm could pass into the body of the cannibal worm in a relatively unchanged state. The new experiment was a success: After grinding up trained worms and feeding them to untrained worms, McConnell found that the untrained worms responded to the conditioned stimulus. He felt sure that memory had been chemically transferred from one organism to another.

Also working from a biochemical model, William Corning and E. Roy John trained a group of planaria, cut them in half, and allowed the halves to regenerate, some in normal pond water and some in a solution of ribonuclease, an enzyme that is known to break up RNA. Under both conditions, pond water and ribonuclease, the heads that regenerated new tails retained the conditioning. However, only the pond-water tails that regenerated new heads retained the learning. The tails that had regenerated heads in the ribonuclease failed to show evidence of conditioning (Corning and John, 1961).

This was a fairly significant finding in that it showed a direct link between RNA and learning. Since the heads of planaria contain about 75 percent of their nervous systems, the fact that the RNA inhibitor did not affect them is not surprising, since most of the coded RNA was simply retained in the head. However, the tails, which had to regenerate the bulk of their nervous systems, were affected by the ribonuclease. The ribonuclease apparently prevented the coded RNA from being duplicated in the new head cells. Again, it must be underscored that although this is not definite proof that memory resides in the RNA molecule, it does point a tantalizing finger in the direction of RNA's being at least involved in the memory process. John further believes that memory is not localized to one section of the brain but is more probably spread throughout the brain (John, 1976).

The Two-Stage Memory Process Revisited

During the late 1950s and early 1960s, it became increasingly evident that memory could not be explained on the basis of a single process and that the engram was not a single unit, like a computer's silicon chip or a bank's safe-deposit vault. Some researchers today are even avoiding the term *engram* completely because of its localized connotation (Allison, 1992). Even Lashley's own studies (as imprecise as they may seem by today's standards) seemed to indicate that memories were not just localized into neat little pockets, but were probably spread throughout the brain. But Lashley's concept of the reverberating electrical circuits was itself especially vulnerable as an explanation of long-term memory, yet it was clear from our knowledge of the neural impulse that its electrical properties were somehow involved.

The **two-stage memory process** system was originally foreshadowed by the work of William James. (What, in modern psychology, was not?) James had said that consciousness occurred in two stages, transitive and substantive. James hypothesized that all ideas first enter consciousness in a transitive state, that is, as fleeting will-o'-the-wisps of only marginal existence. The idea then *may* or *may not* proceed into substantive form. If it does, the idea gains stability because of its transformation into a physical substance (James, 1890). Then much later, in 1949, D. O. Hebb set forth his famous dual-trace memory theory. As Hebb stated it:

> The conception of a transient, unstable reverberatory trace is therefore useful, if it is possible to suppose also that some more permanent structural change reinforces it. There is no reason to think that a choice must be made between the two conceptions; there may be traces of both kinds and memories which are dependent on both (Hebb, 1949).

As we have seen, current theories imply that memory is governed by at least two stages, short-term and long-term, and perhaps, as James and Hebb had suggested earlier, these stages are qualitatively different. Short-term memory is probably largely electrical, whereas long-term memory may be largely chemical. STM may be fleeting because no permanent change takes place within the organism. The short-lived electrochemical process decays rapidly. But sometimes, before the short-term trace disappears, a second series of events occurs in the brain that may involve the production, as Hyden has suggested, of new proteins. Thus, although STM is accompanied by transient electrical changes in the brain, LTM may be accompanied by the physical production of new, permanent brain proteins. Thus, permanent learning may exist in the form of a protein molecule (Lynch, 1984).

Interestingly enough, this theory is not inconsistent with the previously mentioned RNA theory, in that the RNA is needed for **protein synthesis.** Further, even the prime mover of the RNA theory back in the late 1950s, Holgar Hyden, has since suggested that the retrieval of stored information depends on, among other things, the presence of unique *proteins* in the neuron (Hyden, 1970).

Some familiar phenomena seem to support this

position. People who suffer head injuries with loss of consciousness usually sustain a loss of memory for events just preceding the trauma. This is called **retrograde amnesia** and indicates that when the brain is jolted, a long-term memory may somehow be prevented from consolidating (Crovitz et al., 1983). Some experimental evidence has been supplied by Murray Jarvik and his associate (Jarvik and Kopp, 1967). In a series of studies, they demonstrated that if organisms are given a jolt of electric current to the brain, a current just strong enough to scramble the brain's electrical circuitry, the organisms are unable to recall the training that preceded the shock. There have, however, been some questions raised concerning the interpretation of these data. For example, is the memory permanently gone, or is it simply currently irretrievable due to emotionally induced interference factors? It has been found, for example, that human amnesia patients may sometimes have their seemingly lost memories restored under conditions of sedation. Using a different approach, Bernard Agranoff, another advocate of the two-stage memory theory, has worked with the antibiotic puromycin, which inhibits the formation of new proteins (Agranoff, 1965). When puromycin was injected into the brains of trained organisms just prior to learning, they showed no memory impairment at first. However, when tested a few hours later, they evidenced far less retention of the task than did a control group that had not received puromycin. The action of the puromycin, it appears, prevents the short-term memory from consolidating into the more permanent long-term memory. Other researchers have validated this finding, and the general phenomenon is now called the *puromycin effect* (Flexner and Flexner, 1970).

Because so many studies have demonstrated that protein inhibitors can block the formation of memory, it's becoming increasingly apparent that the synthesis of new proteins is clearly involved in the consolidation of at least some memories (Davis and Squires, 1984). In addition, just as some chemical agents have been shown to inhibit memory, others (such as Metrazol and magnesium pemoline) have been shown to facilitate the consolidation process (Grosser et al., 1967).

And the search goes on. In 1983 James V. McConnell reported on a study conducted by Ewen Cameron in which elderly senile patients were found to have significantly higher levels of ribonuclease in their bloodstreams than did the nonsenile elderly. Since ribonuclease is an enzyme that, as we have seen, breaks up and destroys RNA, an attempt was then made to lower the ribonuclease levels in the senile patients by injecting them with yeast RNA. It was hoped that the ribonuclease would then destroy the yeast RNA rather than the RNA produced in the brain. Also, in order to enhance RNA production in the brain, other patients were given the drug magnesium pemoline. The results in both cases proved promising. Some of the patients given yeast RNA did recover memory, though not all. The patients who had been injected with magnesium pemoline also showed improved memory, but as soon as they were taken off the drug, memory deterioration again set in (McConnell, 1990).

In an animal study conducted by Michael Warren, two groups of "elderly" mice were kept in dramatically differing environments. One group was constantly stimulated, trained, and handled, whereas the other group was confined to sensory isolation chambers. The stimulated mice proved to be better problem solvers and also had *more RNA in their brains.* Warren, extrapolating this finding to the human level, suggested that older people who continue to lead an active and challenging life have less chance of developing intellectual impairments than do those who sit around in gloomy silence (Warren et al., 1982).

MEMORY AND PHYSIOLOGY— FROM PROTEINS TO CALPAIN

Neuroscientist Gary Lynch believes that the two long-term memory systems, declarative and procedural (outlined earlier), are based on qualitatively different physiological principles. Lynch says that these two forms of memory reside in different structures of the brain and are even under different biochemical controls. Lynch sees the protein model as best fitting the data on procedural knowledge and, as we have seen, the studies mentioned above, by McConnell, Corning and John, and Jarvik, were all based on learning through conditioning. Regarding declarative memory, Lynch is offering a somewhat different mechanism. When a neural impulse travels from one neuron to the next, it must cross a small gap called a *synapse.* At this point, the impulse releases tiny amounts of certain chemicals called *neurotransmitters.* When these neurotransmitters bind to the next neuron (to its dendritic spines) permanent changes take place in the responsiveness of the synapse and in the shape of the postsynaptic neuron. The key to this permanent change is an enzyme called *calpain,* which is activated in the postsynaptic neuron as a result of the release

of the neurotransmitters from the presynaptic neuron. The calpain increases when nerve cells are stimulated and consequently exposes more receptors. This sequence promotes new synapses on the nerve cell which, in turn, facilitates new learning. It is also known that this mechanism functions most efficiently in those areas of the brain involved in declarative memory. Thus, there are major differences in the biochemistry of the two long-term memory systems, declarative and procedural, and there are also differences in their physical locations. Procedural memory, although primarily dependent on activity of the cerebellum, seems to be more widespread in the brain (including even the brain stem), whereas declarative memory is, at least originally, more focused. The current position is that declarative memory is first stored in the hippocampal region (an area located near the base of the brain), and then later becomes integrated into regions of the cortex where the higher levels of brain functioning take place. For example, visual information is stored mostly in the occipital lobe, while auditory and verbal memories tend to be in the parietal and temporal lobes. Thus, human memory is probably not a broad power of the mind, but is made of separate abilities, carried out in different brain locations with the hippocampus as the command center linking the various brain sites. When a hippocampal nerve cell is electrically stimulated, new synaptic nerve connections are formed in seconds (Lynch, 1986). Also, when the hippocampus is damaged or removed, only the memory for facts and events (declarative memory) become lost. The memory for physical skills, that is procedural memory, remains untouched (Squire and Zola-Morgan, 1991).

To summarize, the old electrical model of learning and retention, which was most vulnerable in attempts to explain long-term memories, has been revived to explain short-term memories in a way that fits the empirical data. Permanent, possibly lifelong memories, however, are better explained via the biochemical model, and this too fits with the experimental data.

Friendly Rivals

As we have now seen, students of memory seem to have formed two distinct groups. On one side, there are the cognitive psychologists (which includes the information processing theorists and artificial intelligence experts) who have built complex systems modeled after the general field of computer science. On the other side are the neuroscientists, the brain experts, who are looking for the physiological correlates of human behavior. For the past decade, these two groups, cognitivists and neuroscientists, have to some extent been friendly rivals. Neuroscientists have criticized the cognitivists for relying too heavily on computer analogies while ignoring the most important clues to the workings of the mind: the actual functioning of the brain (Ambros et al., 1990). Cognitivists, on the other hand, have felt that the neuroscientists have ignored the thinking process, and have become hopelessly mired in the billions of connections among the neurons. The neuroscientists have even begun using the term *wetware*, presumably because the brain is moist as it sits in the cranium, as opposed to the software and hardware analogies used by the cognitive scientists. In fact at a 1991 artificial intelligence meeting of the Cognitive Science Society, Gary Lynch said that he felt out of place at the conference, since he was a student of "wetware among a software and hardware crowd of computer hackers" (Safire, 1991). The two groups, however, are beginning to join theoretical forces and even in some cases to collaborate on studies in memory and learning. Several cognitive theorists, including Howard Gardner, have asked us to use the term *cognitive neuroscience* to define this new hybrid (Gardner, 1991; Granger et al., 1989).

SERENITY IN THE COGNITIVE PATCH?

It must be pointed out, however, that all is not total serenity in the cognitive patch. For example, one researcher has complained that the concept of the memory trace, so near and dear to the hearts of information processing theorists, is merely a metaphor, a figure of speech rather than an empirical fact. Because the memory trace has therefore been *reified* (the fallacy of treating an abstraction as though it were real), it is alleged that cognitive scientists have been confusing psychology with physiology and, worse yet, that this has resulted in attempts to integrate cognitive psychology with neuroscience and even artificial intelligence. We are warned that this may produce even greater confusion in the near future (Watkins, 1990).

However, despite this warning, the merger of educational psychology, cognitive psychology, and neuroscience has come of age in the 1990s and has made the Krech prophecy of a few years ago now even more compelling.

As David Krech predicted:

> Both the biochemist and the teacher of the future will combine their skills and insights for the educational and intellectual development of the child. Tommy needs a bit more of an immediate memory stimulator;

Researchers have suggested that there is a qualitative difference between short-term memory, which we may use to remember a phone number just recited to us, and long-term memory, which we may use to recall an experience from the past as we glance at a photo. Short-term memory probably involves fleeting electrical changes in the brain, whereas long-term memory involves more permanent chemical changes.

Jack could do with a chemical attention-span stretcher; Rachel needs an anticholinesterase to slow down her mental processes; Joan, some puromycin— she remembers too many details and gets lost (Krech, 1969).

The story of the physical side of memory is just now unfolding. Despite the evidence being supplied by physiological psychologists, our knowledge in this exciting and provocative area is still extremely limited. The point is, however, that researchers are now looking for answers within the organism, and the old admonition to avoid "stuffing the black box" is today as anachronistic as a portrait of George Washington seated happily in front of a computer terminal.

SUMMARY

The information processing model of learning and memory has a cognitive-gestalt orientation and is based on a computer analogy. The theory attempts to correlate the psychologist's understanding of thought processes with what is known of computer technology. Learning and remembering are seen as resulting from the flow of information that passes through various stages within the organism.

The model presented in this chapter is focused on intentional learning. Incoming information is encoded within the organism both at the psychological level (in the form of a conceptual representation) and at the physiological level (in the form of the neural memory trace). The stimulus information first enters the sensory register, where it is held for only a few brief seconds. If the learner is paying attention to these stimuli, they enter the first of the two main storage compartments, short-term memory, or STM. STM has only a limited capacity, about seven (plus or minus two) items, and only a limited duration, less than a minute. If the learner is motivated enough to rehearse the contents of STM, the information may then be passed along into the second storage bin, called long-term memory, or LTM. LTM has the potential for holding information for up to a lifetime. Rehearsal can take two forms: maintenance, where the learner uses rote repetition, and elaborative, where the learner relates the new information to other concepts and therefore expands his or her conceptual base. LTM provides for two different systems, declarative and procedural. Declarative memory represents the brain's storehouse of names, dates, and past experiences, whereas procedural memory contains traces of motor skills, typically learned through repetitive practice. Further, declarative memory has two components, episodic, which consists of memory for past episodes in one's life, and semantic, which involves the memory of words and the meaning of words.

Semantic memory also contains what researchers call schema (schemata, in the plural). A schema is any body of information that is related to a central concept. Because LTM can be so long-lasting, the term permastore has been used to describe permanently etched long-term memories. On the output side, information becomes available for retrieval when it can be located and accessed. A variety of retrieval strategies are available to aid in the storage search, but in general, the greater the number of organized categories into which information has been placed and the more meaningful these categorizations, the more accessible the information becomes. Memory for the general meaning of information is both longer-lasting and more easily accessed than is memory for specific and unrelated details.

Emotions can play a role in the memory process. Strong feelings of fear or anxiety may act to hinder memory, whereas the impact of an emotional event, such as hearing the news of the death of a loved one, may be permanently etched in what is called a flashbulb memory.

Forgetting occurs as a result of both decay and interference. Decay is thought to occur passively over time. Two important interference factors are proactive inhibition (PI), in which past learning interferes with the processing and recall of new information, and retroactive inhibition (RI), in which new learning interferes with the recall of past learning.

Studies have shown that retrieval can be facilitated by the following: (1) overlearning, (2) understanding new information, (3) building an organized knowledge base, (4) relating new material to an existing knowledge base, (5) using cue associations, and (6) using mnemonics. Mnemonic devices, such as visual imagery, peg words, and rhyming, can be used as memory aids both for learning new information and retrieving already processed information. But some critics warn that mnemonic devices should not be overused, since material learned in this way may not be easily related to other concepts in a meaningful way.

Studies of the relation of IQ to information processing show, not surprisingly, that those with higher IQs learn and retain more information than those with lower IQs, though the percentage of what is retained over time remains about the same. Also, those with high IQs spend more time encoding and less time processing information than those with lower IQs.

The sequencing of information processing has extremely important developmental aspects, and researchers are now proposing a number of age-related correlates of the processing model. The developing child is seen as both acting on and reacting to his or her environment, and as a result, the quality of the child's information processing system is transformed. The processing system is also enhanced as the child incorporates metacognitive skills, or the ability to understand one's own memory and learning strategies.

Since the entire processing model is based on incoming information getting through STM and into LTM, and since this step requires the _attention_ of the learner, a great deal of research has gone into the problem of attention deficits. The most dramatic example of an attention deficit problem is illustrated by the child suffering from ADHD, attention deficit–hyperactivity disorder. Theorists describe two forms of the attentional process—selective attention and divided attention. Selective attention is shown when the child is able to focus on one source of incoming information while ignoring other possible distractors. Divided attention occurs when the child can tune in on more than one source of incoming information, such as reading a book and listening to the radio. Studies show that this ability seems to be developmentally based, with teenagers much more adept at this than are younger children.

The material presented up to this point comes from the theories and research of the cognitive psychologists. Another group of researchers, called neuroscientists or brain scientists, are also working on unraveling the mysteries of learning and memory. These scientists are examining the physiological components of the learning model. The search for the biological underpinnings of memory has led researchers to believe that the production of cortical ribonucleic acid (RNA) and the synthesis of new brain proteins are important links in the internal chain of neurologically grounded memory events.

Most neuroscientists now believe that the two long-term memory systems, procedural and declarative knowledge, involve different physiological processes. The protein theory seems more consistent with the data involving procedural memory, whereas permanently induced changes in both the synapse and postsynaptic neuron fit best with the facts obtained for declarative knowledge. These researchers now suggest that chemical agents may soon be used to enhance the information processing abilities of both children and adults.

KEY TERMS AND NAMES

artificial intelligence
attention—selective and divided
attention deficit–hyperactivity disorder (ADHD)
chunking
concept formation
declarative memory—episodic and semantic
dual-code theory
encoding
engram
flashbulb memory
information processing
intentional learning
long-term memory (LTM)
mnemonic devices
multiple encoding

permastore
proactive inhibition (PI)
procedural memory
protein synthesis
rehearsal—maintenance and elaborative
retrieval
retroactive inhibition (RI)
retrograde amnesia
RNA theory of memory
schema
sensory register
short-term memory (STM)
storage
two-stage memory process

THEORY INTO PRACTICE:
IMPROVING YOUR MEMORY

Now that you've been exposed to the major theories of memory and information processing, it's time to put some of these ideas into the well-lit arena of practicality. Let's focus on some of the topics in the area of memory, and see if you can both improve your own processing skills and also, perhaps, discover some fresh insights of your own.

1. Mnemonics

First, we'll look again at those encoding devices known as mnemonics. Several mathematicians, who also happen to be memory experts, have demonstrated what seem to be amazing feats with regard to their skills at retrieving enormously long strings of digits. Some are able to recall the value of pi out to thousands of decimal places. In fact, the current (1992) pi champion is Hideaki Tamoyori of Japan, who proved that he could remember pi out to, believe it or not, 40,000 places. Imagine the thrilling excitement when listening to that recitation! Part of the fascination with memorizing pi seems to be its transcendental quality: the virtually random sequence of digits following the decimal point seems to be infinite. To find out how it is done, let's try to memorize pi as far as ten decimal places, which equals 3.1415926536.

Now, although it's clearly possible to chunk these digits and then memorize them as numbers, an easier technique (and also the one the memory experts use) is to learn a simple series of sentences—the more meaningful, the better. Then, we count each letter of each word in the sentence and retrieve the digits on the basis of the number of letters per word. An example for pi might be

How I want a drink. Yesterday my thirst would not quench.

Breaking it down, we have HOW (three letters), I (one letter), WANT (four letters), A (one letter), DRINK (five letters), and so on. Within a matter of a few minutes, you'll have it—the astonishing ability to rattle off pi to ten places. For 20 places, try

How I wish I could enumerate pi easily, since all these [censored] mnemonics prevent recalling any of pi's sequence more simply.

To prove the efficiency of this method, select a few pupils or friends and ask some to memorize the sequence as simply a series of random digits. For a second group, ask others to memorize the sequence by chunking the digits, that is, to learn

314, 159, 265, and 36.

For a third group, teach them the sentences shown above. Time the individuals in each group on the basis of how long it takes to repeat the sequence three times with no errors. A day later, check them a second time.

2. Meaning

As you have read, the more meaningful any information is, the easier it is to encode and retrieve. One way to increase the meaningfulness of information (as cited in the text), is to categorize it on the basis of an organized knowledge base. Let's say you want to memorize the following list of a dozen items: trombone, bicycle, footstool, piano, chair, car, skateboard, tuba, couch, clarinet, bus, and end table.

First, organize the items into categories that are already known to you, that is:

Musical Instruments	Furniture	Modes of Transportation
clarinet	couch	car
trombone	end table	bus
piano	chair	skateboard
tuba	footstool	bicycle

Then, within each category, reorganize on the basis of the size of each item, from say, largest to smallest.

Musical Instruments	Furniture	Modes of Transportation
piano	couch	bus
tuba	chair	car
trombone	end table	bicycle
clarinet	footstool	skateboard

Now, see how many items on the list you can repeat. Try this list with a group of students or friends, as a random list for some, as organized by category for others, and as organized by size and category to a third group. This time, let each person hear the items just once, and then the next day, find out the number of items each person can correctly recall.

Finally, take the following sentences (which were read aloud at an AERA meeting in California by Professor David Rumelhart.)

Mary heard the ice cream truck coming. She remembered her birthday money and ran into the house.

Read the sentence to a friend, and then a few hours later ask the friend to repeat what you had said. This should provide you with a dramatic example of how memory is shaped by past associations. This is what you can expect to hear:

> A little girl, I think her name was Mary, ran home to get her birthday money, or was it her allowance, to buy some ice cream. She bought the ice cream and was happy.

In looking at the original sentences, nowhere are we told that Mary is a young girl or even that she wanted to get her money to buy ice cream. We simply assume these extra facts on the basis of inferences we made that were shaped by our past associations. Mary may have been a college student, who heard the ice cream truck all right but who at that moment was merely going into the house to get money for a textbook. Or, as Professor Rumelhart suggests, read the sentence again, changing only a couple of words, *ice cream truck* to *bus*, or *birthday money* to *gun*. With these not-so-subtle changes, you may find incredible differences in interpretations.

REFERENCES

Agranoff, B. W. (1965). Molecules and memories. *Perspectives in Biological Medicine, 9*, 13–22.

Allison, M. (1992). New research in the neurobiology of learning. *Headlines, 3*, 2–11.

Alper, J. (1986). Our dual memory. *Science, 86*, 44–49.

Ambros, I. J., Granger, R., and Lynch, G. (1990). Simulation of paleocortex perform hierarchical clustering. *Science, 247*, 1344–1348.

American Psychiatric Association. (1987). *Diagnostic and statistical manual of mental disorders* (DSM III-R), (3d ed., rev.). Washington: American Psychiatric Association.

Anderson, J. R. (1980). *Cognitive psychology and its implications*. San Francisco: Freeman.

Arai, A., Larson, J., and Lynch, G. (1990). Anoxia reveals a vulnerable period of the development of long-term potentiation. *Brain Research, 511*, 353–357.

Ashcraft, M. H. (1989). *Human memory and cognition*. Glenville, Ill.: Scott, Foresman.

Atkinson, R. C., and Shiffrin, R. M. (1968). Human memory: A proposed system and its component processes. In K. Spence and J. Spence (Eds.), *The psychology of learning and motivation*. New York: Academic Press.

Ausubel, D. P., and Robinson, F. G. (1969). *School learning: An introduction to educational psychology* (p. 62). New York: Holt, Rinehart & Winston.

Baddeley, A. (1991). *Human memory: Theory and practice*. Needham Heights, Mass.: Allyn & Bacon.

Bahrick, H. P. (1991). A speedy recovery from bankruptcy for ecological memory research. *American Psychologist, 46*, 76–77.

Bartlett, J. C., Hurry, S., and Thorley, W. (1984). Typicality and familiarity of faces. *Memory and Cognition, 12*, 219–228.

Best, J. B. (1989). *Cognitive psychology* (2d ed.). St. Paul: West.

Blum, K. (1984). *Handbook of abusable drugs*. New York: Gardner.

Bondy, E. (1984). Thinking about thinking. *Childhood Education* (March/April), 234–238.

Broadbent, D. E. (1984). The maltese cross: A new simplistic model for memory. *Brain Behavior Science, 7*, 55–94.

Brown, R., and Kulik, J. (1977). Flashbulb memories. *Cognition, 5*, 73–99.

Brown, A. (1991). A review of the tip-of-the-tongue experience. *Psychological Bulletin, 109*, 204–223.

Bruce, D. (1991). Mechanistic and functional explanations of memory. *American Psychologist, 46*, 46–48.

Carlisle, J. F. (1983). Training in reading comprehension. *Annals of Dyslexia, 33*, 187–202.

Conway, M. A. (1991). In defense of everyday memory. *American Psychologist, 46*, 19–26.

Corning, W. C., and John, E. R. (1961). Effect of ribonuclease on retention of conditioned response in regenerated planaria. *Science, 134*, 1363–1365.

Crick, F., and Mitchison, G. (1983). The function of dream sleep. *Nature* (July), 14.

Crovitz, H. F., Horn, R. W., and Daniel, W. F. (1983). Interrelationships among retrograde amnesia, post-traumatic amnesia, and time since head injury: A retrospective study. *Cortex, 19*, 407–412.

Daehler, M. W., and Bukatko, D. (1985). *Cognitive development*. New York: Knopf.

Davis, H. R., and Squires, L. R. (1984). Protein synthesis and memory: A review. *Psychological Bulletin, 96*, 518–559.

Drenowski, A. (1980). Attributes and priorities in short-term recall: A new model of memory span. *Journal of Experimental Psychology: General, 109*, 208–250.

Evans, C., and Evans, P. (1983). *Landscapes of the night*. New York: Viking.

Flavell, J. H. (1985). *Cognitive development*. Englewood Cliffs, N.J.: Prentice-Hall.

Flexner, J. B., and Flexner, L. B. (1970). Further observations on restoration of memory after treatment with puromycin. *Yale Journal of Biology and Medicine, 42*, 235–240.

Galvin, R. M. (1988). Stephen Pawelson's amazing memory. *Harvard Magazine* (January–February), 113–116.

Gardner, H. (1991). Mind explorers merge their maps. *The New York Times* (Friday, February 8) C30.

Gateway Educational Products. (1988). *Hooked on phonics.* Orange, Calif.: Gateway Press.

Gentile, J. R., Monaco, N., Iheozor-Ehofor, I. E., Ndu, M., and Ogbonaya, P. K. (1982). Retention by fast and slow learners. *Intelligence, 6,* 125–138.

Granger, R., Ambros, I. J., and Lynch, G. (1989). Derivation of encoding characteristics of layer II cerebral cortex. *Journal of Cognitive Neuroscience, 1,* 61–87.

Grosser, G. S., and Spafford, C. S. (1990). Light sensitivity in peripheral retinal fields of dyslexic and proficient readers. *Perceptual and Motor Skills, 71,* 467–477.

Grosser, G. S., Sprinthall, R. C., and Sirois, L. (1967). Magnesium pemoline: Activation of extinction responding after continuous reinforcement. *Psych. Rep. 21,* 11–14.

Haber, R. N. (1983). The impending demise of the icon: A critique of the concept of iconic storage in visual information processing. *Behavioral and Brain Sciences, 6,* 1–11.

Hallahan, D. P., and Kauffman, J. M. (1991). *Exceptional children: Introduction to special education* (5th ed.). Englewood Cliffs, N.J.: Prentice-Hall.

Hasher, L., and Zacks, R. T. (1979). Automatic and effortful processes in memory. *Journal of Experimental Psychology, 108,* 365–388.

Hebb, D. O. (1949). *The organization of behavior.* New York: Wiley.

Henker, B., and Whalen, C. K. (1989). Hyperactivity and attention deficits. *American Psychologist, 44,* 216–230.

Higbee, K. L., and Kunihira, S. (1985). Cross-cultural application of Yodai mnemonics in education. *Educational Psychologist, 20,* 57–64.

Higgins, A. T., and Turnure, J. E. (1984). Distractibility and concentration of attention in children's development. *Child Development, 44,* 1799–1810.

Houston, J. P. (1991). *Fundamentals of learning and memory* (4th ed.). San Diego: Harcourt Brace Jovanovich.

Hunt, M. (1982). *The universe within.* New York: Simon & Schuster.

Hyden, H. (1959). Biochemical changes in glial cells and nerve cells at varying activity. In O. Hoffman-Ostenhoff (Ed.), *Biochemistry of the central nervous system.* London: Pergamon.

Hyden, H. (1970). The question of a molecular basis for the memory trace. In K. H. Pribram (Ed.), *Biology of memory.* New York: Academic Press.

James, W. A. (1890). *The principles of psychology.* New York: Holt.

Jarvik, M. E., and Kopp, R. (1967). An improved one trial passive avoidance learning situation. *Psychological Reports, 2,* 221–224.

Jennings, K. (1990). *The devouring fungus: Tales of the computer age.* New York: Norton.

John, E. R. (1976). How the brain works. *Psychology Today, 9,* 48–52.

Johnson, G. (1990). *How we build the world inside our heads.* New York: Knopf.

Jordan, D. R. (1991). Whatever happened to ADD without hyperactivity? *CH. A.D.D. ER, 4,* 4.

Jordan, D. R. (1992). *Attention deficit disorder* (2d ed.). Austin, Tex.: Pro-Ed.

Kail, R. (1984). *The development of memory in children* (2d ed.). New York: Freeman.

Kantowitz, B. H., and Roediger, H. L. (1980). Memory and information processing. In G. M. Gazda and R. J. Corsini (Eds.), *Theories of learning: A comparative approach.* Itasca, Ill.: Peacock.

Keppel, G. (1968). Retroactive and proactive inhibition. In T. R. Dixon and D. L. Norton (Eds.), *Verbal behavior and general behavior theory* (pp. 172–213). Englewood Cliffs, N.J.: Prentice-Hall.

Kihlstrom, J. F. (1987). The cognitive unconscious. *Science, 237,* 1445–1452.

Kilpatrick, J. (1985). Doing mathematics without understanding it: A commentary on Higbee and Kunihira. *Educational Psychologist, 20,* 65.

Klatzsky, R. (1984). *Memory and awareness: An information-processing perspective.* New York: Freeman.

Klausmeir, H. J., Feldhausen, J., and Check, J. (1959). *An analysis of learning efficiency in arithmetic of mentally retarded children in comparison with children of average and high intelligence.* U.S. Office of Education, Research Project 153. Madison: University of Wisconsin.

Kolers, P. A. (1983). Perception and representation. *Annual Review of Psychology, 34,* 129–166.

Krech, D. (1969). The chemistry of learning (p. 156). In R. C. Sprinthall and N. A. Sprinthall (Eds.), *Educational psychology: Selected readings.* New York: Van Nostrand-Reinhold.

Lashley, K. S. (1950). In search of the engram (pp. 454–482). *Society of Experimental Biology Symposium,* No. 4, Cambridge University Press.

Lasky, R. E., and Spiro, D. (1980). The processing of tachistoscopically presented visual stimuli by five-month-old infants. *Child Development, 51,* 214–225.

Lazarus, R. S. (1991). Cognition and motivation in emotion. *American Psychologist, 46,* 352–367.

Lodico, M. G., Ghatala, E. S., Levin, J. R., Pressley, M., and Bell, J. A. (1983). The effects of strategy-monitoring training on children's selection of effective memory strategies. *Journal of Experimental Child Psychology, 35,* 203–277. See also Paris, S. G., Lorayne, H., and Lucas, J. (1974). *The memory book.* New York: Stein & Day.

Lodico, M. G., Ghatala, E. S., Levin, J. R., Pressley, M., and Bell, J. A. (1983). The effects of strategy-monitoring training on children's selection of effective memory strategies. *Journal of Experimental Child Psychology, 35,* 203–277. See also Paris, S. G., Newman, R. S., and McVey, K. A. (1982). Learning the functional significance of mnemonic actions: A microgenetic study of strategy acquisition. *Journal of Experimental Child Psychology, 34,* 490–509.

Lynch, G. (1984). A magical memory tour. *Psych. Today, 18.*

Lynch, G. (1986). *Synapses, circuits and the beginnings of memory.* Cambridge: MIT Press (A Bradford Book).

McConnell, J. V. (1990). *Understanding human behavior* (5th ed.). New York: Holt, Rinehart & Winston.

McConnell, J. V., Jacobson, A. L., and Kimble, D. P. (1959). The effects of regeneration upon retention of a conditioned response in the planaria. *Journal of Comparative and Physiological Psychology, 52,* 1–5.

McGaugh, J. L. (1983). Hormonal influences on memory. *Annual Review of Psychology, 34,* 297–324.

McGaugh, J. L. (1990). Significance and remembrance: The role of neuromodulatory systems. *Psychological Science, 1,* 15–25.

McKinney, J. D., and Speece, D. L. (1986). Academic consequences and longitudinal stability of behavioral subtypes of learning disabled children. *Journal of Educational Psychology, 78,* 365–372.

McShane, J. (1991). *Cognitive development: An information processing approach.* Oxford: Blackwell.

Miller, G. A. (1956). The magical number seven plus or minus two: Some limits on our capacity for processing information. *Psychological Review, 63,* 81–97.

Murdock, B. B. (1974). *Human memory: Theory and data.* New York: Wiley.

Murphy, L. A., Pollatsek, A., and Well, A. D. (1988). Developmental dyslexia and word retrieval deficits. *Brain and Language, 35,* 1–23.

Nelson, D. L., and Archer, C. S. (1972). The first letter mnemonic. *Journal of Educational Psychology, 63*(5), 482–486.

Newell, A., and Simon, H. A. (1972). *Human problem solving.* Englewood Cliffs, N.J.: Prentice-Hall.

Newman, R. S., and McVey, K. A. (1982). Learning the functional significance of mnemonic actions: A microgenetic study of strategy acquisition. *Journal of Experimental Child Psychology, 34,* 490–509.

Nolan, T. E. (1991). Self-questioning and prediction: Combining metacognitive strategies. *Journal of Reading, 35*(2), 132–138.

Ornstein, P. A., Naus, M. J., and Liberty, C. (1975). Rehearsal and organizational processes in children's memory. *Child Development, 45,* 818–830.

Paivo, A. (1971). *Imagery and verbal processes.* New York: Holt, Rinehart & Winston.

Penfield, W. (1969). Consciousness, memory and man's conditioned reflexes. In K. Pribram (Ed.), *On the biology of learning.* New York: Harcourt Brace Jovanovich.

Penrose, R. (1989). *The emperor's new mind: Concerning computers, minds and the laws of physics* (p. 447). New York: Oxford University Press.

Reder, L. M., and Ross, B. H. (1983). Integrated knowledge in different tasks: The role of retrieval strategy on fan effects. *Journal of Experimental Psychology, 9,* 55–72.

Rozenzweig, M. R., and Leiman, A. L. (1982). *Physiological psychology.* Lexington, Mass.: Heath.

Rubin, D. C., and Kozin, M. (1984). Vivid memories. *Cognition, 16,* 81–95.

Safire, W. (1991). There's no wearware. *The New York Times* (Sunday, July 7, magazine section), 6.

Shaywitz, S. E., and Shaywitz, B. A. (1987). *Attention deficit disorder: Current perspectives.* Paper presented at the National Conference on Learning Disabilities. Bethesda, Md.: National Institutes of Child Health and Human Development (NIH).

Shiff, A. R., and Knopf, I. J. (1985). The effects of task demand on attention allocation in children of different ages. *Child Development, 56,* 621–630.

Simon, H. A. (1986). The information processing explanation of gestalt phenomena. *Computers in Human Behavior, 2,* 241–254.

Skinner, B. F. (1987). As quoted in *The New York Times* (August 25).

Skinner, B. F. (1990). Can psychology be a science of mind? *American Psychologist, 45,* 1206–1210.

Solso, R. L. (1979). *Cognitive psychology.* New York: Harcourt Brace Jovanovich.

Sperling, G. (1960). The information available in brief visual presentations. *Psychological Monographs, 74* (Whole No. 498).

Sprinthall, R. C., and Burns, P. (1991). Flashbulb memory among college graduates. *A.I.C. Alumni News, 24,* 9.

Sprinthall, R. C., and Nolan, T. E. (1991). Efficacy of representing quantities with different pictures in solving arithmetic word problems. *Perceptual and Motor Skills, 72,* 274–276.

Squire, L. R. (1987). *Memory and brain.* New York: Oxford University Press.

Squire, L. R., and Zola-Morgan, S. (1991). The medial temporal lobe memory system. *Science, 253,* 1380–1386.

Sternberg, R. J. (1982). Who's intelligent? *Psychology Today, 16,* 30–39.

Sternberg, R. J. (1985). *Beyond IQ: A triarchic theory of human intelligence.* New York: Cambridge University Press.

Tulving, E. (1983). *Elements of episodic memory.* New York: Oxford University Press.

Tulving, E. (1985). How many memory systems are there? *American Psychologist, 40,* 385–398.

Walberg, H. J. (1988). Synthesis of research on time and learning. *Educational Leadership, 45,* 76–85.

Warren, J. M., Zerweck, C., and Anthony, A. (1982). The effects of environmental stimulation on old mice. *Developmental Psychobiology, 15,* 13–18.

Watkins, M. J. (1990). Mediationism and the obfuscation of memory. *American Psychologist, 45,* 328–335.

Wertheimer, M. (1985). A gestalt perspective on computer simulations of cognitive processes. *Computers in Human Behavior, 1,* 20.

White, R. T., and Gagne, R. M. (1976). Retention of related and unrelated sentences. *Journal of Educational Psychology, 68,* 843–852.

Wickelgren, W. A. (1981). Human learning and memory. *Annual Review of Psychology, 32,* 21–52.

Wyer, R. S., and Srull, T. K. (1989). *Memory and cognition in its social context.* Hillsdale, N.J.: Erlbaum.

TEACHING EFFECTIVENESS

METHODS AND MODELS OF TEACHING

As we noted in Chapter 1, a research basis for understanding the process of teaching effectiveness has expanded rapidly in the last decade. In this chapter we will review and generalize the research suggestions. We will also show how these results, single pieces of research evidence, can be incorporated into a broad framework to guide your practice. A model of teaching basically represents a specific cluster of teaching strategies designed to reach a particular type of learning outcome with pupils. However, no single model represents the best way to teach. Instead, overall effectiveness will depend on your ability, first, to master specific techniques and, second, to combine them within a particular model. Finally, you must develop the ability to use a variety of models. When you have reached that point, you will be on your way to mastery of a repertoire of teaching models.

In Chapter 13 we will switch focus from the teacher to the students, addressing the question of how to apply the different models according to your goals as well as the needs of the students. For now, however, we will concentrate first on discrete teacher skills and then move from specific skills to models. We start with a review of elements of teaching effectiveness and then look at the use of a system of analyzing teaching as a bridge to the more general models.

ELEMENTS OF TEACHING EFFECTIVENESS

The most comprehensive review of elements of teaching effectiveness has been completed by **Herbert Walberg** from the University of Illinois. Using the techniques of statistical meta-analysis, he compiled more than 3,000 studies, then carefully analyzed them to determine just how important each particular element was in student learning (Walberg, 1986). More recently, he was part of an Australian-U.S. team which assessed 134 reviews of 7,827 field studies and several large-scale U.S. and international surveys of learning (Fraser, Walberg, Welch, and Hattie, 1987). From his results, he compiled a list of weighted factors. In Table 12.1, we have selected from his overall list the elements that are most closely related to teacher behavior in the classroom—in other words, the kind of procedures a teacher may actually employ. Each of the selected teaching processes listed in Table 12.1 will be discussed here in turn: engaged academic learning time, use of positive reinforcement, cues and feedback, cooperative learning activities, classroom atmosphere morale, higher-order questioning, and use of advance organizers. In this chapter and the two which follow we will also focus

HERBERT J. WALBERG

If you were to ask any educational psychologist to list the ten most productive and influential scholars in the field, you would be sure to find Herbert Walberg's name in that select group.

Walberg is an eminent scholar and a prolific writer. His manner is quiet and unassuming. His particular genius has been his policy research and his mastery of educational psychology's three components of theory, research, and practice. Thus, his work speaks to all educational psychologists. The theorists see in his work a synthesizing of ideas, a means of combining previously separate conceptual frameworks into a more cohesive cluster of directing concepts. The researchers follow very carefully his new system of meta-analysis as a means of combining empirical results from a wide variety of studies. No longer are educational studies dependent on one or a dozen or even a hundred studies. Walberg has shown the field how to review 2,000 to 3,000 studies and end up with meaningful conclusions. In the pre-Walberg era, many reviews of the research literature would suggest that there was little in the way of substantial knowledge and (often with a whimper) conclude that "more research is needed." A few years later, another review would be published with similar results and end up with the same call.

To some degree the most important aspect of his work may be its implications for practice. His recent summarization of the research on teaching effectiveness is a clear example of just how practical research can be in the hands of such a brilliant man. He avoids any allegiance to a particular school of thought and instead reviews all studies on the basis of parsimony both theoretically and empirically. One of the continuing complaints about educational psychologists in general is that if you know the theoretical framework of the researchers, you can safely predict their conclusions without even looking at the data. Walberg, however, stands apart from any specific tradition and lets the actual analysis of the findings determine what elements really make a difference in distinguishing effective from ineffective teaching.

Shortly after completing his Ph.D. at the University of Chicago in 1964, he joined an outstanding team of researchers at the Harvard Graduate School of Education in Harvard Project Physics. Over a three-year period the group developed and evaluated an innovative approach to teaching physics in secondary schools. While at Harvard he authored or coauthored thirty-four journal articles, and thirteen were immediately reprinted by other authors. He was much sought after as a speaker, consultant, and editor. Since he was a midwesterner at heart, it was not surprising that he quickly accepted a professorship at the University of Illinois, Chicago Circle. He had learned a great deal on the East Coast, among other things how much he missed Lake Michigan and the proper midwest English. Soon after his return to Chicago, he was named, in rapid succession, associate professor, professor, and then research professor. In fact, one of the difficulties in reporting on his progress is how quickly any comment is outdated. As we go to press, he has written or edited fifty-two books and over three-hundred-fifty articles, chapters, and monographs. In a recent conversation, he shared with us two current endeavors from which he derives a great deal of satisfaction. First, he is a member of the National School Board of the National Assessment Governing Board which is responsible for examining the educational progress of United States students with respect to major school subjects through the use of national assessments. Second, for five years he has chaired the Scientific Advisory Group for the Education Indicators Project of the Organization for Economic and Cooperative Development whose international offices are in Paris. This group is comparing students' achievement to other educational characteristics of modern countries. We look forward to the results forthcoming from these important national and international studies. We surmise that with Herbert Walberg involved, the results will encompass and synthesize both prior and current research.

TABLE 12.1   THE EFFECTS OF SELECTED TEACHING TECHNIQUES AND PROCESSES

TECHNIQUE OR PROCESS	SIZE OF EFFECT ON ACADEMIC ACHIEVEMENT*
Engaged academic learning time	+.38
Use of positive reinforcement	+1.17
Cues and feedback	+.97
Cooperative learning activities	+.76
Classroom atmosphere morale	+.60
Higher-order questioning	+.34
Use of advance organizers	+.23

* The size represents units of standard deviations; for example, in the case of "cues and feedback," teachers employing this mode had students whose achievement scores averaged almost one standard deviation higher than those in control classes.

Data from H. Walberg (1986). Synthesis of research on teaching. In M. C. Wittrock. (Ed.), *Handbook of research on teaching.* New York: Macmillan, pp. 214–229.

on related teacher behaviors and classroom interaction patterns which contribute to and differentially affect the learning of students of different ethnicity, economic status, and gender.

Academic Learning Time

Although it may seem too obvious to note, academic learning time in the classroom has emerged as an important variable. Studies have shown that the amount of on-task behavior can vary as much as 40 percent from one classroom to the next (Walberg, 1988). Even how quickly a teacher calls the class to order can vary all the way from one to ten minutes. Thus, how efficiently you plan your lessons, how long you take to get started, how you handle digressions, off-task behavior, and discipline, and how you handle transitions will have an effect on student learning.

Important as academic learning time is, there is not an exact relationship between time on task and learning outcome. Moreover, it is difficult, if not impossible, to measure what is going on in a student's mind at a specific moment. In fact, one study showed that students who appeared to be paying attention (engaged in academic learning time) were actually thinking about nonacademic issues (Peterson and

Swing, 1982). Students soon learn the importance of putting on a good face in order to protect their privacy. As a result of these and other factors, time is an important necessary condition but far from the whole story. In measurement terms the efficient use of instructional time has an impact equal to 38 percent of one standard deviation. Basically, academic achievement was moderately affected by the efficient use of time (Dempter, 1987).

Some teachers structure academic learning time differently for different groups of students based on the students' perceived level of academic achievement or their race, gender, ethnicity, and class. We discuss the research on these issues and the effects of teachers' expectations in Chapter 14.

Use of Reinforcement

By far the single, most significant discrete instructional variable in Table 12.1 was the use of positive reinforcement. The careful and consistent use of Skinnerian reinforcement techniques, both verbal and nonverbal, had an effect greater than one standard deviation. This means that if one class, for example, scored an average of 80 points on a hundred-item test and the standard deviation was 10 points, then a similar class without positive reinforcement would score one standard deviation below, or an average of 70 points. The reinforced class on the average would be at a B level, versus a C level for the other class.

Does this mean, then, that the teacher should apply principles of positive reinforcement to all students all the time? As was the case with academic learning time, it's not quite that simple. The relationship between positive reinforcement and achievement is nonlinear. You must be selective; indiscriminate praise doesn't work. The effect will wear out if the students hear you praise all activities and products, even those of marginal competence.

Table 12.2 gives some important guidelines for the effective use of praise. Jere Brophy has carefully outlined and compared different methods (Brophy, 1981). To add to the complexity, it turns out that the effect of praise, even when properly applied, varies according to student characteristics. Students from middle-class backgrounds are not as susceptible to praise as are students from lower- or working-class backgrounds. The method still works but not as powerfully. Lower- and working-class parents tend *not* to use positive reinforcement as frequently as do mid-

TABLE 12.2   GUIDELINES FOR EFFECTIVE PRAISE

EFFECTIVE PRAISE	INEFFECTIVE PRAISE
1. Is delivered contingently	1. Is delivered randomly or unsystematically
2. Specifies the particulars of the accomplishment	2. Is restricted to global positive reactions
3. Shows spontaneity, variety, and other signs of credibility; suggests clear attention to the student's accomplishment	3. Shows s bland uniformity, which suggests a conditional response made with minimal attention
4. Rewards attainment of specified performance criteria (which can include effort criteria, however)	4. Rewards mere participation, without consideration of performance processes or outcomes
5. Provides information to students about their competence or the value of their accomplishments	5. Provides no information at all or gives students information about their status
6. Orients students toward better appreciation of their own task-related behavior and thinking about problem solving	6. Orients students toward comparing themselves with others and thinking about competing
7. Uses students' own prior accomplishments as the context for describing present accomplishments	7. Uses the accomplishments of peers as the context for describing students' present accomplishments
8. Is given in recognition of noteworthy effort or success at difficult (for *this* student) tasks	8. Is given without regard to the effort expended or the meaning of the accomplishments (for *this* student)
9. Attributes successes to effort and ability, implying that similar successes can be expected in the future	9. Attributes success to ability alone or to external factors such as luck or easy task
10. Fosters endogenous attributions (students believe that they expend effort on the task because they enjoy the task and/or want to develop task-relevant skills)	10. Fosters exogenous attributions (students believe that they expend effort on the task for external reasons to please the teacher, win a competition or reward, etc.)
11. Focuses students' attention on their own task-relevant behavior.	11. Focuses students' attention on the teacher as an external authority figure who is manipulating them
12. Fosters appreciation of and desirable attributions about task-relevant behavior after the process is completed	12. Intrudes into the ongoing process, distracting attention from task-relevant behavior

From J. Brophy (1981), Teacher praise: A functional analysis. *Review of Educational Research, 51,* p. 26. Copyright © 1981 by American Educational Research Association, Washington, D. C. Reprinted by permission.

dle-class parents. As a result, such children are more affected when praise is used. Praise by itself, then, has to be used carefully in order to produce the desired effects.

In addition, the quantity and quality of reinforcement given to students seem to vary according to student characteristics. For example, girls receive significantly less attention from classroom teachers than do boys, and African-American girls have fewer interactions with teachers than do white girls, despite evidence that they attempt to initiate interaction more frequently (AAUW Report, 1992). Another example of differential reinforcement according to gender was found by Myra and David Sadker and Susan Klein who reported that when boys called out, teachers listened, but when girls called out, they were told to

raise their hands if they wished to speak (Sadker et al., 1991). Boys also get more precise teacher comments about both their scholarship and conduct.

Reinforcement is important in helping determine to what students attribute their successes and failures. Teachers need to consider what they are reinforcing—ability, effort, conformity, risk taking, the right answer, neatness, cooperation, and so on. It is imporant to examine whether the amount and type of reinforcement vary according to gender, race, and class.

Cues and Feedback

To some extent the use of cues and feedback is related to the process of questioning. Through cueing, the teacher provides some help to students in answering

DOONESBURY by Garry Trudeau

DOONESBURY by Garry Trudeau

questions. In the so-called good old days, many a famous university professor would earn a reputation for tearing students apart in the process of questioning. In the now-classic movie *The Paper Chase*, Professor Kingsfield was shown again and again carefully dissecting a quivering student. Intimidation and sarcasm were the stock-in-trade. Current research in teaching effectiveness shows the opposite. Good teachers cue the students. They help a student develop an answer. Such a teacher will pick up part of an answer and then ask for clarification or elaboration—for example, "Yes, Columbus did lead the expedition in 1492, and do you remember who sponsored the voyage?" Such prompting can reduce the anxiety of the classroom trivia methods (Chapter 1) and expand the students' thinking. Another important point to remember is that teachers are more likely to prompt and encourage boys than girls, even when the boys do not volunteer to give an answer or opinion (AAUW,

1992); so you will want to try to use prompts equitably among all your students.

A second component of effective cueing is sometimes called wait time, which gives the student some time to think about the question. By providing time and then helping a student elaborate an answer, the teacher will increase academic achievement and decrease anxiety.

Providing constructive (also called corrective) feedback is the other part of this strategy. Ever since the famous Ellis Page study, it has been shown conclusively that feedback improves academic achievement. Page demonstrated this by systematically providing brief written comments on assignments (Page, 1958). When teachers merely collect assignments and then either say nothing or simply make a check mark, then an opportunity for growth has been missed. The same is true for homework. In fact, Walberg found that graded homework with comments was 50 percent more effective than homework by itself. Constructive feedback obviously provides the student with information on which to build learning. Walberg (1990) summarizes: "the effects of cues, engagement, reinforcement, and corrective feedback are enormous."

Cooperative Learning

There are many ways of organizing classrooms of students, and it is important when doing so to use a range of organizational configurations (one-on-one with the teacher and individual seatwork, small groups, group projects, whole class) because individual differences and learning styles among children, as well as cultural and family backgrounds, may influence how comfortably and effectively children participate. To address the diversity of styles, you must provide a variety of organizational formats. One strategy that is thought to be more comfortable for some individuals and members of cultural groups is **cooperative learning**.

Research about the factors associated with women's success in mathematics classrooms, for instance, is quite consistent in showing that girls may learn more effectively in cooperative rather than competitive situations (Buerk, 1985; Isaacson, 1990; Barnes and Coupland, 1990, Fennema and Leder, 1990). "Girl-friendly" classrooms are described as having "low levels of competition, high levels of cooperative learning or individualistic learning structure, high levels of teacher communication . . . [about] the intrinsic value of math and the link between math and various interesting occupations" (Eccles, 1987, p. 158). Char Morrow (1991) and James Morrow (Morrow and Morrow, 1992) describe the highly successful SummerMath program for girls and teachers which uses a cooperative learning community approach to teaching and learning mathematics. Strategies for establishing connection are key SummerMath teaching objectives achieved through cooperative learning; these include confirmation of self in the learning community, learning in the believing mode of communication and questioning, taking on challenges *with* support, the development of voice, and becoming a constructor of knowledge.

Hilda Hernandez (1989) summarizes research in Native-American communities which strongly suggests the importance of cooperative learning strategies.

Especially critical in the Native-American communities observed by researchers were instructional demands that students respond competitively and individualistically. These appeared to violate the norms within the culture emphasizing cooperative and group effort. Hence, sensitivity to the culture of Odawan students demands recognition of less obvious aspects of "interactional etiquette," such as avoiding direct commands and refraining from placing students in the "spotlight" (Mohatt and Erickson, 1981). On the Warm Spring Indian Reservation, Philips (1983) found that one-on-one contact between students and teachers or aides and the use of group projects and cooperative learning activities were most compatible with the interational patterns of the students' culture (p. 50).

The effectiveness of cooperative learning (refer to Table 12.1) is a most interesting new finding. We will provide a substantial discussion on this approach in Chapter 20. The main point here is the importance in the classroom of employing small-group techniques with cooperative objectives. Such a procedure encourages student participation and also results in improved academic performance. Basically, such an approach requires a blend of techniques, and hence it is not really a single technique.

Classroom Morale

This is another process that, like cooperative learning, is not strictly a teaching strategy. Still, it is important not to lose sight of the fact that classroom atmosphere obviously has a significant impact on learning. Walberg's research found that the old-school view of strict discipline and tight control is not effective nor is the casual, "laid-back" approach. Instead, feelings of cohesiveness, satisfaction, goal direction, and student perceptions of a friendly atmosphere make a positive difference in learning. These findings were cross-validated by Thomas Good's research (Good, 1983). He found that one main element of effective teaching is the need to create a relatively relaxed learning environment within a task-oriented focus. We will have more to say on this when we move to models of teaching that illustrate the relation between class morale and methods. At this point it is clear that positive class morale cuts across specific techniques as a general factor producing student achievement.

Essential to conducting an equitable and effective classroom environment for all students is the stated, discussed, practiced, and reinforced value of acceptance and appreciation for similarities and differences among members of the classroom (and school) community. Differences in ethnicity, race, class, religion, gender, primary language, sexual orientation, learning style, ability and disability, family configuration, and lifestyle must all be respected and acknowledged for classroom morale to be positive for all. We can identify the elements of classroom morale that are important to each of the diverse groups of students in order to achieve an optimum learning atmosphere. For example, the *Women's Ways of Knowing* researchers Mary Belenky, Blythe Clinchy, Nancy Goldberger, and Jill Tarule (1986) identified specific elements of classroom atmosphere that had great impact on female students—what they and Carol Gilligan have labeled "connected" as opposed to "separate" education. (See Spotlight On Connected Teaching.) **Connected teaching** and knowing are a part of what's being studied by researchers trying to understand different learning needs. These issues will be discussed further in Chapter 13.

Higher-Order Questions

Since teacher questioning has an unusually long history, examining its use as a strategy is clearly important (Redfield and Rousseau, 1981). Generally, as we illustrated in the opening chapter, the common questioning approach is more like a game of Trivial Pursuit than education. But asking rapid-fire questions calling for rote, almost robotlike answers does not increase achievement. How the questions are posed obviously makes a difference. A higher-order question is basically a query that requires the student to analyze and produce a reasoned response, not a mimic of the teacher's words. In other words, there is not an already prescribed factual answer to the question. Asking a student to name the year of the Columbus expedition is clearly a low-order question. Asking the student to explain why Columbus was able to convince the monarchy of a country different from his own to support his voyage calls for greater intellectual work, and thus it qualfies as a higher-order question.

Recently there has been a remarkable upsurge in the "teaching of thinking." Such a process, which involves logical analysis and argumentation principles, is most encouraged by higher-order questioning. Thus, an idea that has lost favor in the 1970s—namely,

to distinguish between the lower- and higher-order questions—has returned as a result of newer research evidence and a general interest in formal instruction designed to promote "thinking." This will be discussed in detail in the next chapter.

One of the continuing problems in the research on classroom questioning, however, is the problem of wait-time. Perhaps the effectiveness of higher-order questions in particular is determined not so much by their actual frequency but how much time is provided for them. Students obviously need reflection time to process a complex question. The research of Mary Budd Rowe (1986) has shown that simply increasing wait-time by a few seconds both after the question is posed and after the student has responded has a very positive effect upon student learning. She says to the teacher, "Slow down to speed up."

In a similar view, Kenneth Tobin (1986) has shown the positive effect of wait-time. In this case, the teachers in an experimental sample waited an average of three to five seconds in teaching math concepts. The results were dramatic. On all twelve measures of outcome, the results favored the experimental group of teachers. Teacher "talk" declined, and student achievement increased. The most interesting finding was that the student answers changed. Instead of mimicking the teacher or mindlessly repeating a memorized phrase, the student gave longer, more thoughtful answers. Also, there was an increase in their comprehension. In short, the expanded wait-time helped the students think more deeply about the concepts being taught. Tobin concluded that for subjects such as mathematics and language arts, in which higher-order cognitive outcomes are desired, the wait method is highly recommended. Of course, from the standpoint of this book, we would not limit such goals exclusively to those two disciplines. Certainly, higher-order questions and thinking are appropriate for all adolescents and all school subjects. Wait-time, however, is not a straight-line variable. This means that if three to five seconds is good, then ten to fifteen is not better, and on and on. Excessively long periods of wait-time can be almost as bad as too brief a period. Too much dead air in the classroom is to be avoided just as much as the rapid-fire trivia approach.

Advance Organizers

The final skill involves the use of the deductive approach. The student is told in advance what the main

SPOTLIGHT ON CONNECTED TEACHING

1. *Incorporating personal individual experience:* Connected learning is based on personal individual experience while acknowledging existing uncertainties. It is strongly influenced by the Deweyan notion of significant experience followed by self-reflection and discussion. Connected teaching accords respect to and allows time for the understanding that emerges from firsthand experience.

2. *Nurturing each other's thoughts to maturity:* The connected classroom provides a culture for growth—a "yogurt" kind of class. It is something like the actors' studios where dialogue and plot are created as a scene progresses; it is not like a movie theater where people are mere spectators. The connected teacher tries to create groups in which members can nurture one another's thoughts to maturity. Sometimes this is in the form of triads or working small groups. In a connected class no one apologizes for uncertainty. It is assumed that evolving thought will be tentative.

3. *Constructing truth through consensus not conflict:* The connected class constructs truth not through conflict but through consensus, defined as a feeling or sensing together.

4. *Bridging private and shared experience:* Consensus in the previous statement implies not agreement, necessarily, but a crossing of the barrier between one and another, which can also be described as bridging private and shared experience.

5. *Respecting each other's unique perspectives:* Connected teachers welcome diversity of opinion in class discussion. Teachers and students collaborate in constructing a new interpretation. In a connected class, like a community, people get to know one another. They do not act as representatives of positions or as occupants of roles but as individuals with particular styles of thinking.

6. *Basing teacher's authority on cooperation, not subordination:* Connected teachers are careful not to abandon themselves to their students' perspectives. A connected teacher is not just another student; the role carries special responsibilities. It does not entail power over the students; however, it does carry authority, an authority based not on subordination but on cooperation.

7. *Using participant observation methodologies:* A form of connected knowing used in investigations is called *participant observation*. Teachers participate with students in order to undergo experiences similar to those of the students. In this way teachers use their own reactions to formulate hypotheses about the students' reactions. A teacher trusts each student's experience, although as a person or a critic, the teacher might not agree with it. To trust means not just to tolerate a variety of viewpoints, acting as an impartial referee. To trust means to try to connect, to enter into each student's perspective.

8. *Emphasizing belief over doubt:* Connected teachers are believers; they trust their student's thinking and encourage them to expand it. Yet an adversarial doubting model predominates much of education. Only a handful of the women interviewed described a powerful and positive learning experience in which a teacher aggressively challenged or doubted their notions. On the whole, women found the experience of being doubted debilitating rather than energizing.

9. *Midwife education versus banker concept of education:* Connected teachers educate through a problem-posing model. The connected teacher helps students articulate and expand their latent knowledge; more like a midwife teacher. Midwife teachers are the opposite of banker teachers. It seems that the banker concept of education is dominant today. While the bankers deposit knowledge in the learner's head, the midwives draw it out. Connected teachers assist the students in giving birth to their own ideas, in making their tacit knowledge explicit and elaborating it. They encourage students to use their knowledge in everyday life. Connected teachers use their own knowledge to put the students into conversations with other voices, past and present.

Note: Connected teaching outlines an educational context which women constructed as examples of teaching practices that fostered their own learning. Presented here are some of the key phrases which identify the characteristics of connected versus separate teaching. These are the themes which recurred over and over in the interviews with the 135 women in the study when they described important learning experiences. Mary Field Belenky, Blythe McVicker Clinchy, Nancy Rule Goldberger, and Jill Mattuck Tarule, *Women's Ways of Knowing* (New York: Basic Books, 1986), chap. 10.

SPOTLIGHT ON PROCEDURES

Teaching Tip

As a teacher, you can alleviate some of the artificiality of classroom discussions by acknowledging right off that classrooms have their own rules which are unlike real exchanges or dinner-table talk. Students must be assured that silence is not only okay, but valued. Preface your questions with a statement such as, "This will require a bit of thinking time. Raise your hands when you have a response. After 10 hands are up, I will call on someone to share." Or ask students to respond to questions by first talking to their seat mates. This way they can work out the kinks in their emerging ideas in a less threatening forum. Say, for example, "Take one minute to reflect on this question with the person sitting next to you." Or ask students to write out their responses, then invite several to read aloud what they have written.

Wait at least three seconds after asking a question before you take any responses at all. Research shows that when wait time is increased to three seconds or more, the amount of elaboration and the chance of being correct are greater. Finally, ask students to come to class with three questions that they have prepared in advance. After all, if one can pose a question, one is on the edge of understanding it.

One classroom study shows that teachers average 200 questions per class whereas students do not average one question each. Teachers pose 11 questions for every student inquiry. Remind yourself that *you* do not need to display your knowledge, for it is the students, not teachers, who need opportunities to practice the skills of posing and answering questions. Do not apologize for the silence in your classroom if you judge it as educational silence.[a]

---

[a] Ruie Jane Pritchard, North Carolina State University, College of Education and Psychology. In *Emphasis: Teaching and learning*, I(II), January 1992. A publication of NCSU

---

point or the main concepts to be covered will be. On the one hand, such advance organizers have been shown to help students focus attention on the key points. On the other hand, the effect is positive but not particularly strong, representing about a 25 percent improvement in the standard deviation. In all probability, then, an advance organizer is a good method to get a class clued in. Since some learners need a clear road map of the main points in a lesson in advance, the method should not be ignored (Gage, 1985).

In fact, some recent research by William Doyle has suggested that a more careful application of advance organizers can improve the impact on student learning. He has shown that in some of the earlier research studies, a major problem was created. Often, it could be shown that the teacher never clearly established the advance organizer. Thus, if the first step in the system was not always in place, it is small wonder that some of the studies showed no positive effects. In his own study, he assessed the effect or the outcome after he had determined that the organizer was in place (Doyle, 1986). When the students understood the organizer then there was significant transfer of learning over a seven-day period. Naturally, this one study does not prove the point. It certainly suggests, however, that the use of organizers is positive. More to the point, however, is the need to pay attention to how well the students can grasp the concept. Taking a developmental perspective, Doyle notes that intellectually complex advance organizers that assume the students are already using formal abstract reasoning may fail if such concepts are not closely matched to the appropriate level of cognitive development. We will say more about this problem of matching and mismatching concepts and developmental level in the next chapter. For now, in using organizers, it is important to remember the need to attend to comprehension by the students. If the point of the advance organizer is a mystery to the students, confusion and ambiguity will follow.

TEACHING EFFECTIVENESS: DIRECT INSTRUCTION EXCLUSIVELY?

As a result of meta-analysis of teaching, there was a growing tendency to view effective instruction as synonymous with direct instruction. The Center at the Institute for Research on Teaching at Michigan State, in particular, generated large numbers of studies supporting the contention that gains in academic achievement are often associated with this method. Essentially, direct instruction in highly structured. The teacher presents the material in small steps, uses advance organizers, checks for understanding, has students answer turn by turn in an ordered fashion, and provides immediate feedback on their answers. Furthermore, the teacher accomplishes all this at a brisk and businesslike pace (Rosenshine, 1987). By implication, the teacher would spend very little time, if any, on other methods, such as inductive or discovery teaching. The research seemed to support the idea that effective teaching is a sequence of carefully and constantly monitored actions. In fact, the claim was that the direct method was appropriate for all subjects at all grade levels. In the words of one of the major researchers in this area, Jere Brophy (1988),

> Thus, if we take into account both (a) knowledge and skills taught because they are considered important in their own right and (b) knowledge and skills taught because they are prerequisite to accomplishment of higher level objectives, we can say the principles derived from process-outcome research will apply to most of what is taught in school.

Finally, the claim was that not only will academic achievement improve across the board but also affective and personal development will be promoted.

In assessing the validity of these conclusions, it is important to understand the many limitations. The main research base has been elementary school classrooms rather than secondary schools. Further, the research has been limited to a few specific subject areas at an introductory level, and there was no attempt to involve a true cross-section of school types, for example, urban, rural, high and low socioeconomic status, majority and minority. Thus, doubt can be cast upon the claim of generalization. Finally, the greatest problem is that effective teaching cannot ever simply reach the point of prescribing a single set of teacher behaviors good for all pupils, for all subjects, and for all time.

As a result, we take the position that the direct method represents only a partial picture of the teaching process, and we caution against some of the current generalizations. Certainly, we agree with both Larry Cuban's (1988) critique and Lee Schulman's (1986, 1987) much more moderate views calling for

a broader conception. The research tried to focus on one variable at a time as if it were possible to freeze teaching frame by frame. Teaching is too interactive and involves a synthesis of many variables rather than success with just a single variable. Also, follow-up showed that not all of the trained behaviors continued to correlate with achievement gains, that some of the experimental teachers did not always use the prescribed pattern, and that not all the prescribed behaviors were necessary for improved achievement. In other words, a fine-grained analysis of the claims could not support the contentions of the direct school of teaching. The final, most telling point was the complete absence of theory to explain the findings. Without theory, as we noted in Chapter 1, there is little to guide practice and there is no systematic way to explain the inconsistencies in the behavioral observations. A fair conclusion is that direct or active teaching does provide some but not all the answers to the complex problems of teacher effectiveness.

In Chapter 13 we present an alternative to direct teaching called *comprehension teaching*, or teaching for higher-level understanding. This model adds to our understanding of the complex problems of teacher effectiveness.

THE FLANDERS SYSTEM: BRIDGING TO MODELS

One weakness of such a massive meta-analysis as Walberg's is that the result cannot depict actual patterns of teaching. A robot could be programmed to use certain elements in a sequence, but student learning wouldn't necessarily be affected. Classroom interaction between teacher and students would be frozen while the machine cranked through its program. To understand how the elements fit together more clearly, we turn to the work of **Ned Flanders** (1970). He and his associates did extensive classroom observations of teachers at different levels and across different content areas. He found that teacher talking behavior could be clustered into seven categories (and student talk into three), as shown in Table 12.3. In Table 12.4 you can also see how much of his system, developed in the 1950s and 1960s, still relates to current research on teaching behaviors.

The seven categories represent the most commonly observed teaching behaviors, which brings us to the next question. What is the relation between these behaviors and student achievement? Actually, a major analysis of the Flanders studies was done by **Na-**

NED FLANDERS

knowledge of subject matter to effective performance in the classroom. These so-called characteristic studies produced very little valuable information; instead, the results were inconclusive and often contradictory. One study might find a small but statistically significant correlation between a trait such as friendliness and teaching effectiveness; the next study was just as likely to show no relationship.

When Flanders began to develop the concept of direct versus indirect teaching, he also started a series of field studies to test the possible relationships. As we have noted in the text, his central findings remained consistent through a long series of studies. With various subject matters, at different grade levels, and in different school settings, teachers employing indirect teaching styles were producing higher levels of academic learning in their pupils than were those using direct methods.

As we move toward educational accountability, with the general public demanding increasing documentation of teaching effectiveness, the Flanders system gives evidence of becoming a major index of effective teaching. In 1962 Flanders moved from Minnesota to the University of Michigan, where he continued his work. He has published *Teaching with Groups* and *Analyzing Teaching Behavior*, as well as numerous articles reporting his research on teacher interaction analysis. In 1970 Flanders returned to California, where he was with Far West Laboratory for research in teaching. Now enjoying retirement atop one of San Francisco's most beautiful hills, he has maintained an active professional interest in teacher behavior.

Born in 1918 and raised on the West Coast, Ned Flanders gradually migrated eastward. He completed an A.B. degree at the University of California in 1940 and received a B.S. from Oregon State College in 1944. He then left the Coast and completely changed his field of academic interest. From his undergraduate work in chemistry and a B.S. in electrical engineering, he shifted to educational psychology, completing both a master's degree and a Ph.D. at the University of Chicago. He remained at Chicago for a brief period and then, from 1949 to 1962, served as an assistant and then associate professor of educational psychology at the University of Minnesota.

It was during his period at Minnesota that his research focus matured. He began to successfully crack one of the most difficult problems in education—creation of a theoretical and practical model to define teaching effectiveness. Prior to his work, hundreds of research studies had been conducted in this area, almost always yielding insignificant results. Researchers had tried to correlate personality characteristics, temperamental traits, personal interests, cultural backgrounds, social and economic status, marital state, birth order, and similar variables to effective teaching performance. Attempts had also been made to relate measures of a teacher's "warmth" or

TABLE 12.3 CATEGORIES FOR FLANDERS INTERACTION ANALYSIS

TEACHER TALK	**INDIRECT INFLUENCE**	**1. Accepts feelings:** Accepts and clarifies the tone of feelings of the students in an unthreatening manner. Feelings may be positive or negative. Predicting or recalling feelings are included. **2. Praises or encourages:** Praises or encourages student action or behavior. Jokes that release tension, but not at the expense of another individual; nodding head and saying "um hm?" or "go on" are included. **3. Accepts or uses ideas of students:** Clarifies, builds, or develops ideas suggested by a student. As teacher brings more of his or her own ideas into play, shift to # 5. **4. Asks questions:** Asks a question about content or procedure with the intent that the student answer.
	DIRECT INFLUENCE	**5. Lecturing:** Gives facts or opinions about content or procedure; expresses his or her own ideas, asking rhetorical questions. **6. Giving directions:** Directions, commands, or orders that students are expected to comply with. **7. Criticizing or justifying authority:** Statements intended to change student behavior from unacceptable to acceptable pattern; bawling someone out; stating why the teacher is doing what he or she is doing; extreme self-reference.
STUDENT TALK		**8. Student talk—response:** Talk by students in response to teacher. Teacher initiates the contact or solicits student statement. **9. Student talk—initiation:** Talk initiated by students. If "calling on" student is only to indicate who may talk next, observer must decide whether student wanted to talk. **10. Silence or confusion:** Pauses, short periods of silence, and periods of confusion in which communication cannot be understood by the observer.

From N. A. Flanders, *Analyzing teaching behavior* (Reading, Mass.: Addison-Wesley, 1970), p. 34. Reprinted with permission.

thaniel Gage (1978) in his book *The Scientific Basis for the Art of Teaching*. Rather than examine one element at a time, however, Gage grouped the system into two broad categories: indirect teaching—types 1, 2, 3, and 4; and direct teaching—types 5, 6, and 7. You can see that the main difference between the two modes is basically whether teaching is viewed as asking questions or giving directions and lecturing.

In comparing the modes Gage also wanted to examine possible differences according to grade level, elementary versus secondary. He found very clear evidence that teachers who employed the indirect mode at the secondary level produced greater academic gains on the part of their pupils than teachers who used the direct mode. This means that the academic performance of teenage students will be enhanced through the effective use of questioning and open inquiry. The finding held true across subject matter. However—and this is most important to remember—this research does not mean that the secondary teacher must stay exclusively in the indirect

mode. The evidence is based on ratios of time expended in one mode versus the other. At the high school level effectiveness is increased if the teacher uses the indirect mode more than half the time. Obviously, there will be times for giving careful directions, lecturing, and criticizing students for misbehavior, yet for the most part, employing questioning, reinforcing, cueing, and responding to feelings will produce academic gains to a greater degree.

To further buttress this approach to teaching and learning, researchers conducted a series of independent studies at the college level. Although the actual Flanders system was not used, the overall results were quite similar. The college researchers found that professors who provide time for student questions, allow students to question one another, and encourage students to make statements in class fostered cognitive growth and greater complexity of thinking on the part of their students (Chickering and McCormick, 1973). So, results from both high school and college students indicate the advantage of the indirect

TABLE 12.4   A COMPARISON OF TEACHER EFFECTIVENESS: FLANDERS AND WALBERG

FLANDERS' TYPE	WALBERG'S ELEMENTS OF TEACHING EFFECTIVENESS
(6) Gives clear directions	Academic learning time
(2) Praises or encourages	Use of positive reinforcement
(3) Accepts and builds on student ideas	Use of cues and feedback
A combination of indirect modes plus (6), gives clear directions	Cooperative learning
(1) Accepts feelings	Classroom morale
(2) Praises	
(3) Accepts ideas	
(4) Asks questions	Higher-order questions
(3) Accepts and builds on student ideas	
(6) Gives clear directions	Advance organizers
(5) Lectures	
(4) Asks questions	

mode with older students. Certainly if you think about Piaget's work, you will remember that during adolescence students can develop greater capabilities for abstract reasoning and greater independence in thinking than earlier in their development. This is probably a main factor favoring the indirect mode. We will have more to say about the interaction between teaching method and pupil development in the next chapter.

At the elementary level, Gage's review yielded somewhat different results. He found less of a relation between the indirect modes and pupil learning. There were some positive outcomes in the indirect mode but also many in the direct mode. In fact, more recent research especially at the elementary level seems to indicate that the more directive approach to teaching can be quite significant in producing student achievement (Gage, 1985). For example, in elementary school instruction in both reading and mathematics, the teacher-directed approach yielded stronger gains. Actually it took reading teachers and researchers a very long time to finally understand that young nonreaders need to be taught to "break the code" and learn the letter symbols (instead of learning through the ask-and-guess technique). Similarly, direct methods in math are necessary to teach the rudiments of the number system. Again it is important to underscore the point of these findings. The results indicate that a ratio is desirable—spending more time on direct methods, but not focusing exclusively on them. To use direct methods exclusively would miss the point.

The effective elementary teacher needs to ask questions, praise, build on ideas, and respond to feelings. However, the elementary teacher may well use the more direct methods more than half the time. The careful use of advance organizers and a low level of ambiguity provides younger students with helpful guidance for learning.

With this background we can now move to the next level of generality in regard to teaching, namely, comprehensive models of teaching. A model is a cluster of strategies that is logically consistent with a certain set of assumptions about how students best learn. Another way to view it is as a "school of thought" regarding how best to manage the development of the pupil. So now to models.

MODEL ONE: THE TRANSMITTER OF KNOWLEDGE

Probably the most common teaching model, and certainly the one with the longest tradition, is that which views teaching as the transmission of knowledge. This view assumes that there exists a well-known and finite body of knowledge from which the teacher selects certain facts and concepts to pass on to pupils. In a metaphorical sense, the teacher looks over all the knowledge "stored" in the Library of Congress, pores through books and pamphlets, reads and digests everything, and takes some of it to school, where it will be disseminated.

Teaching is interactive, and the teacher's job is to manage and direct the instructional process, not the telling process.

This model emphasizes the need to give pupils basic facts and information before they can be expected to think for themselves. They must learn what is already known before they can come up with any new ideas that might fit in with the existing knowledge.

The assumptions are clear. Learning new information is essentially a linear step-by-step sequence. The teacher's expertise is needed to arrange both the content material to be mastered and the method of presentation. Probably the most obvious distinguishing characteristic of this model is the high degree of structure employed.

In Model One, the teacher uses advance organizers (Ausubel and Sullivan, 1970). At the outset of a lesson the teacher presents the pupils with the general rule, the generalization, or the main "point" of the activity. For example, a social studies unit might start with, "Today we are going to study about the origins or beginnings of civilization—the early settlements on the banks of two rivers in the Middle East." Thus, at the outset, the goal of the lesson is described at a generalizable, conceptual level—learning about the origins of civilization. This technique helps the students tune in immediately to the overall objective. It creates, at least theoretically, a set of expectations that is clear and explicit. The pupils are ready.

Immediately following the presentation of the generalized idea, the teacher then changes the level of abstraction to concrete examples. The rule or principle stated at the outset creates a readiness in the pupils. Their cognitive attention is focused. The concrete examples help them understand the connections between the facts and the general point. Thus, in the social studies example, the teacher would now present a series of concrete facts and examples: "For many thousands of years tribes would wander from place to place; food was gathered as it grew naturally; as the seasons changed, the tribes would pick up and move on, seeking less hostile climates." These examples would set the stage for the understanding of the generalized idea. The teacher would proceed to a presentation of a long series of facts: "Gradually, as groups of tribes were settling temporarily all over the globe, the group that settled in Mesopotamia happened to hit upon a most fortuitous set of circumstances—a benign climate and incredibly rich soil. These circumstances, together with a series of other factors, led to the permanent establishment of cities and government, to economic specialization, to the beginning of architecture, even to the establishment of schools—in short, to all the elements of what we call civilization."

The presentation of examples, finally, is followed by the restatement of the generalized principle. In this sense, the transmission-of-knowledge model is often called *guided discovery*. Through various examples, all pupils are led to the same generalization.

Ambiguity is low. It is clear from the outset what the goal is; concrete examples are carefully selected to support the point; and at the end, the pupils are reminded what rule or generalization they have learned.

Probably the strongest example of this model of transmitting information is the lecture format. Although it can be used with other teaching strategies, this model is most effectively used as a format for lectures, or for minilectures. If you recall your own experience as a pupil, you will readily remember instances of hopelessly disorganized lectures that did not follow this model. Look back at your own notes, or the lack of them, from these lectures. You may find a few random comments in your own writing, lots of questions and false starts, perhaps even a scribbled memo to yourself: "But what's the point of today's lecture? He can't seem to make up his mind. Where is it all going? He must have eighteen hands—on the one hand this, on the other hand that—I hope the period ends soon!"

Thus the transmission-of-knowledge model, through the use of advance organizers, can provide a clear and systematic approach to teaching. One of the disadvantages of the model is that so much of the work of learning is controlled and directed by the teacher.

This is why, as we noted in the previous section, the effective use of advance organizers and teacher-led instruction also requires much attention to maintaining pupil activity. If teachers aren't careful, then pupil passivity can increase markedly for some students, particularly the low achievers. One study found that low achievers did not understand the directions, spent most of their time watching their peers speed through the assignment, turned in incomplete work, and were frequently criticized. Such a cycle was repeated, often to the distress of both the students and the teacher (Good, 1983; Berliner, 1984). Also, it is clear that some students will do better under learning conditions that are less teacher-directed and controlled.

MODEL TWO: INDUCTIVE INQUIRY

Another common teaching model that came into vogue in the 1960s suggests that the teacher's role is to reveal or unveil the fundamental structure of a discipline. The idea here is to teach concepts or the process of inquiry, not facts. In some ways this is like teaching for problem solving, whereby we learn to solve problems by understanding the framework or the structure of the concepts. For example, pupils used to learn to cross-multiply fractions to solve a division problem. In Model Two, the teacher focuses on the concepts of fractions and divisions so that the pupils understand that cross-multiplying is really dividing both sides of an equation by a common number. Similarly, in a social studies class, or what used to be called geography, pupils are no longer asked to memorize the principal cities and products of a state. Rather, they might be given a blank map showing topographical features such as hills, mountains, valleys, rivers, and lakes, and then they might be asked to figure out where cities might be located. In other words, they go through an inquiry process that helps them understand why big cities grow in certain locations. The Model Two teacher produces minischolars in the various disciplines.

According to this model, the sheer intellectual excitement of discovering the reasons behind events—for example, the logic a historian or a mathematician actually uses—motivates the pupils to further activity and exploration. Teaching and learning resemble an archaeologist's uncovering of one fragment after another of some mysterious object. The archeologist's curiosity about the fragments naturally makes him or her want to make sense of the puzzle; this curiosity produces both activity and excitement. The discovery method of teaching is based on this model. The teacher, by analyzing material and asking questions but not giving answers, spurs the pupils to learn by helping them discover the answer. The experience and the insight resulting from having put the puzzle together nurture the entire educational process.

There are a variety of specific methods that enhance discovery learning, such as the inductive-thinking strategy of Hilda Taba, the inquiry-training method of Richard Suchman, and the scientific-inquiry technique of Joseph Schwab (see review in Joyce, 1978). These methods are related to John Dewey's original project method, which emphasized the process of inquiry rather than content acquisition as central to learning. In each case, the teacher arranges material that is open-ended in order to stimulate the processes of asking questions and exploration by the pupils.

It is, of course, possible to overemphasize learning by discovery. It can be exasperating to never have any of your questions answered. It isn't necessary to discover everything for yourself in order to learn. Most important, however, it is difficult to know, espe-

SPOTLIGHT ON OPEN EDUCATION

Fall and Rebirth

During the 1960s teacher education began to deemphasize the traditional teacher-directed, self-contained classroom and to stress open education. Classrooms and indeed entire buildings were rebuilt to accommodate the new approach. Learning centers, reading corners, and science (kitchen physics) areas were installed. Children moved freely through a sequence of activities individually and in small groups. The lockstep approach of twenty-five or so pupils all learning the same material at the same time was abandoned. Excitement was high. It seemed as if the old mold for education was at last about to break. Optimism was further increased by some early research findings that suggested positive outcomes in academic achievement. Equally if not more important was the suggestion of gains in pupil autonomy and responsibility. It seemed as if open education was able to fulfill two simultaneous objectives: achievement and growth in self-concept.

Then the bomb fell. In 1976 Neville Bennett, a British psychologist, published the results of a single study that concluded open education was a failure.[a] Since England itself had been a prime mover in the innovation, it seemed as if the home ground was now fatally shaken. One of our country's most prestigious newspapers, *The New York Times,* did a feature giving the claim even greater exposure and, indirectly at least, validity. In addition, Nathaniel Gage, one of our country's most respected educational psychologists, published a summary in 1978 that also concluded open education was a failure.[b]

Of course, these three events by themselves could not account for the shift away from open education. The country as a whole was moving toward a more conservative viewpoint. Both conservative politicians and conservative educators happily seized upon these findings. We should return to the basics in education—no more "frills," no more experimentation, no more "liberal" philosophy. Open education became almost a lightning rod, a convenient target for those in both arenas who wanted to keep schools as they were in the "good old days." The results of their efforts were all too successful. In the public's mind open education was just another failed innovation.

Although the public and conservative politicians may still adhere to that view, educational psychologists don't. A careful reanalysis of Bennett's original findings uncovered basic statistical errors.[c] Then Gage himself undertook a more complete and careful review. He also noted his earlier errors: "I reviewed a small and regrettably haphazard set of some seven of those studies and concluded that they showed that students learned less."[d] His more complete review of 150 studies came to the opposite conclusion. He found that there were no real differences in academic achievement. The students did not learn less. Also the open-education students demonstrated greater creativity, more independence as problem solvers, and had more positive attitudes toward school and teachers.

---

cially at the elementary level and in junior high, exactly how much the pupils genuinely understand about the structure of a discipline taught in this way. The idea of a structure is itself abstract and therefore beyond the comprehension of the concrete stage of thinking in which most of these children are. To understand such concepts and such processes, substantial cognitive sophistication is necessary. For example, to learn how a historian "thinks," we must understand concepts such as fact, an opinion, a value, cultural relativism, subjectivity, and objectivity—to name a few.

A major debate has been going on between those who advocate this approach and those who hold other views. Jerome Bruner, formerly a professor at the Harvard Center for Cognitive Studies, is a leading advocate for teaching for the structure of knowledge. One of his most provocative statements promotes this view: "Any subject can be taught effectively in some intellectually honest form to any child at any stage of development" (Bruner, 1966, p. 44). Thus, according to Bruner, the six-year-old minischolar can learn to think like a historian or a mathematician.

We have already mentioned (Chapter 5) some of the problems inherent in the so-called spiraling curriculum, a system that teaches children the same concepts, with increasing sophistication, throughout their entire schooling. The difficulties, especially at the elementary level, are enormous. The cognitve structure of elementary-age children makes it difficult

Whether the general public will again accept and support open education remains to be seen. Fortunately, the integrity of educational psychologists shows through clearly in this case. Errors in analysis can be corrected and policy issues reevaluated.

Herbert Walberg[e] recently reviewed the synthesis of 153 studies done by Rose Giaconia and Larry Hedges,[f] and he writes as follows:

These studies showed that open education had worthwhile effects on creativity, independence, cooperation, attitudes toward teachers and schools, mental ability, psychological adjustment, and curiosity. Students in open programs had less motivation for grade grubbing, but they differed little from other students in actual achievement, self-concept, and anxiety.

However, Giaconia and Hedges also found that the open programs that were more effective in producing the positive outcomes with regard to attitudes, creativity, and self-concept sacrificed some academic achievement on standardized tests. These [open education] programs emphasized the role of the child in learning and the use of individualized instruction, manipulative materials, and diagnostic rather than norm-referenced evaluation. However, they did not include three other components thought by some to be essential to open programs: multiage grouping, open space, and team teaching.

Giaconia and Hedges speculated that children in the most extreme open programs may do somewhat less well on conventional achievement tests because they have little experience with them. At any rate, it appears that open classrooms enhance several nonstandard outcomes without detracting from academic achievement unless they are radically extreme.

If open education becomes emphasized again because of the many positive outcomes listed above, we wonder if current efforts toward standardized authentic testing and performance-based testing for academic achievement in place of standardized multiple-choice assessments will put to rest even further the old claims that open education detracts from academic achievement.

---

[a]S. N. Bennett, *Teaching styles and pupil progress.* (London: Open Books, 1976).

[b]N. Gage, *Hard gains in the soft sciences.* Bloomington, Ind.: Phi Delta Kappan (1984).

[c]M. Aitkin, S. N. Bennett, and J. Hesketh, Teaching styles and pupil progress: A re-analysis. *British Journal of Educational Psychology* (1984), 51, 37–41.

[d]Gage, *Hard gains* (p. 17).

[e]H. J. Walberg, Productive teaching and instruction: Assessing the knowledge base. *Phi Delta Kappan* (1990), 470–478.

[f]R. M. Giaconia and L. V. Hedges, Identifying features of effective open education. *Review of Educational Research* (1982), 52, 579–602.

---

for them to understand abstract concepts, and therefore they tend to translate the abstractions into concrete terms and miss the connections altogether. Jean Piaget has said that Bruner's statement "has always filled me with the deepest wonderment." Imagine, for a moment, trying to teach a three- or four-year-old the structure of algebra or the idea that historical knowledge is relative and biased.

Nor is the educational problem strictly limited to the elementary ages. Much secondary school material is based on the assumption that all teenagers are already well into formal operations, which we know is not the case. Model Two teaching, though it has a laudable objective, rests on a doubtful assumption. There is a difference between assuming the ability to think abstractly and carefully creating a series of experiences that will nurture and promote the development of this ability. Teaching to reveal the abstract structure of the disciplines may often result in a mismatch between the curriculum on the one hand and the pupils on the other.

Thus, an important component of the inductive method is to work at developing the student's potential to reason more openly and independently. This means, in addition to substantial cueing in questioning, that use of structure and advance organizers may also be necessary, especially at the outset. We should also point out that the inquiry or discovery method can be modified for the elementary level. Certainly, the revised research findings concerning

CARL R. ROGERS

Born at the turn of the century in a Chicago suburb, Carl Rogers spent his early years deciding how to focus his career. In 1919 his first interest at the University of Wisconsin was in scientific farming. Simultaneously, he was extremely active in church work, including attendance at a Christian youth conference in Peking, China. Upon his return to this country he shifted his undergraduate major to history. He felt that such a change was more in line with his emerging desire to go into evangelical work. He received an A.B. in history in 1924 from Wisconsin. Ironically, in view of his subsequent eminence in the field, he had

but a single academic course in psychology as an undergraduate, and that by correspondence.

To prepare for the ministry, Rogers attended Union Theological Seminary in New York. There he began to change his emphasis once again, in this case from the dogma of religion to more general questions concerning the nature of the helping relationship. His interest in the healthy personal and psychological development of each person as an individual became more important than the formal, organized practice of religion. It was here that one of his key concepts took shape, the unique and special nature of "personhood." Much later, this idea was actualized with the establishment of his famous Center for Studies of the Person. With this shift in focus, it was not surprising for Rogers to transfer from Union to Columbia Teachers College. He received his Ph.D. in 1931, having spent much of his time doing fieldwork in Rochester, New York, with the city's child study department for the prevention of cruelty to children.

His interest in preventive treatment for mental health problems, another lifelong theme of his professional career, had its roots in this

early work. One of the major difficulties that proponents of psychological treatment as a concept have grappled with almost from its inception has been this matter of preventive treatment. To provide help after a person becomes emotionally upset—that is, treatment after the fact—had been a major model of psychotherapy. It was really borrowed from the practice of medicine. Psychological help, then, in this view, takes the form of diagnosis, prognosis, treatment, and cure. People with problems would be classed into categories of mental illness, become patients, and, if the psychotherapy was successful, would be cured. Rogers felt almost from the beginning that this approach had severe limitations. Diagnostic categories easily became negative labels. Focusing on mental disturbance could cause therapists to overlook the positive forces for growth inside each person. Treatments designed to help people often encouraged dependency or became a purchase of friendship. Rogers waged a long battle with the traditional psychological and psychiatric establishment on these issues. In his view, it was most important to prevent personal problems from being treated as long-term

open education (see the Spotlight, p. 338) indicate that elementary school children can benefit from some experiences with the inductive discovery model.

MODEL THREE: INTERPERSONAL LEARNING

While the first and most common teaching model emphasizes learning the facts and the second stresses the discovery of concepts, the third and most recent model, interpersonal learning, stresses the development of warm human relationships between teacher and pupil. If the teacher can convey a genuine af-

fection and empathy, a warm, facilitative classroom climate will be created, and the pupils will take it from there. The quality of the human interaction, especially the degree to which the teacher treats the pupils with sincerity and honesty, is the key to creating the best environment for learning.

A leading exponent of this third model was **Carl Rogers**. Rogers has said that teaching as deliberate instruction is a vastly overrated function. The educator should, instead, concentrate much more attention on creating the conditions that will promote experiential learning. Rogers emphasizes experience and feeling rather than thinking or reading as the proper pathway to knowledge—an odd thought, no doubt,

mental illness. An ounce of prevention is always worth more than a pound of cure. In this vein, he tried to develop counseling techniques that would encourage the positive growth forces within each person. To grow psychologically strong people was his answer to the treatment question.

Essentially, the entire career of Carl Rogers has been a pilgrim's progress toward the goal of personhood for all. After spending almost a decade at the Rochester Clinic, he moved into the university setting, first at Ohio State from 1940 to 1945 and then at the University of Chicago. At Chicago he created a now-famous client-centered counseling agency for the university. With this as a laboratory, he began to provide not only a significant new approach to college counseling but also a research base to document his work. He was the first counselor therapist to record his sessions on tape. By analyzing the actual transcripts of the counseling interactions, he was able to dispel many of the myths surrounding psychological treatment. He was not well received by the more orthodox establishment. His openness in providing a public record of counseling challenged therapists to examine their own work and attest to its effectiveness. Up to that time, treatment failures were almost always blamed on the patient. If patients didn't get well, there were three possible explanations: They might be too disturbed, they might be untreatable, or they might have a chronically weak ego. Rogers was able to show that many treatment problems were actually derived from the therapists.

Research on the counseling process began to show that particular conditions were absolutely essential if the person was to be helped. In a series of significant research studies started first in Chicago and then moved to Madison, Wisconsin, Rogers concluded that three conditions represented the core of the therapeutic relationship: unconditional positive regard, empathy, and congruence. (These are explained in the text.) The famous Rogerian triad became the central ingredient in the helping process. What was true for psychotherapy, he felt, applied equally to counseling and teaching.

Throughout his career, he has stressed the importance of the quality of interpersonal relationships, that how we relate to each other as human beings is central to the development of the person. Too often, he would say, we neglect this fundamental truism. Just as John Dewey can be thought of as the major proponent of education as a democratic ideal, so Carl Rogers can be viewed as a lifelong fighter for the democratization of counseling and psychotherapy. He saw the need to develop equal and genuine relationships between people. The ability to help and care, according to Rogers, is an important resource within each human being, and we all have a responsibility to use it, as part of our mutual human interdependence. His work was always focused on that goal.

In his invited address to the American Psychological Association in 1972, he once again challenged psychologists to move out of a narrow scientific and even narrower professional stance and teach the principles of healthy growth to all people. "If we did away with 'the expert,' the 'certified professional,' the 'licensed psychologist,' we might open our profession to a breeze of fresh air, to a surge of creativity, such as it has not known for years."

In 1987, after completing an exciting but demanding visit to Russia, Carl Rogers died during an operation for a broken hip at the age of 85. His goal of world peace seems closer now due to his efforts.

as you sit reading a textbook! Rogers is convinced that traditional learning is so impersonal, cold, and aloof that it really goes in one ear and out the other. According to him, we learn only what is really important and relevant to us as people. In his classic work *Freedom to Learn*, Rogers (1969) presents three necessary and sufficient conditions for the promotion of learning: empathy; unconditional positive regard; and congruence, or genuineness. **Empathy** allows us to communicate to our pupils that we really understand the emotions they are experiencing and permits us to accurately "read" their feelings. **Unconditional positive regard** allows us to accept our students for what they are without passing judgment. This acceptance is unconditional and involves none of the usual bargaining. ("If you do this for me, then I will like you.") Rogers repeatedly says that teachers must place no conditions on these relationships and must accept students without reservation. **Congruence**, or genuineness, means being "real," honest. Going through the motions and pretending we like children or listening to their feelings and emotions half-heartedly is not enough.

If teachers provide these conditions, then, according to Rogers, the children will be free to learn. The natural makeup of children and teenagers is such that if we remove the inhibitions imposed by outside direction, then self-directed learning will follow.

Model Three teaching is not as concerned as Model One is with disseminating appropriate information, nor does it worry too much about understanding concepts or discovering the structures of a discipline. Model Three teaching is primarily concerned with human interaction. This may also be its major drawback.

We realize that classroom atmospheres are important; clearly, pupils have difficulty learning anything if the anxiety level is high. Under such conditions our perception, how much we can "see," becomes narrow. Studies have shown that nonsupportive, critical, and negative classroom "climates" have adverse physiological and psychological effects on the pupils: heartbeats increase, the galvanic skin response (GSR is a scientific term for sweaty palms, etc.) goes up, the resistance level (measured in ohms) increases. In the psychological domain the pupil's self-concept as a learner decreases, and self-direction in learning declines. Also, as one might expect, negative attitudes toward the teacher increase. Finally, and perhaps most important, the academic achievement of the pupils declines under the stressful directive-critical teaching atmosphere. Even pupils' voices—both the content of what they say and how they say it—reveal differences clearly in favor of supportive classroom atmospheres. Thus, the quality of the interpersonal relationship between the teacher and pupils does have an impact on many facets of classroom interaction and on how the pupil actually learns (Flanders and Morine, 1973).

Greta Morine-Dershimer (1985) described further the elements of the complex interpersonal communication environment in the classroom: between teachers and students, among peers; construction of contexts and meanings; student participation levels; and student ability assessments. In one study in a multi-ethnic community, she found that students with higher academic status participated more frequently and were listened to by their peers more carefully. Ethnic minority students in these classes had lower academic status and received significantly less attention than the other students. One thing to keep in mind is Morine-Dershimer's finding that the use of nonstandard English in classroom communication among students has not been found to be a causal factor in school achievement, whereas negative teacher expectations and perceptions based upon students' usage of the language may influence how much a student learns. We will be discussing further the topics of ethnicity and status of pupils in relation to achievement and teacher expectations in Chapter 14.

We cannot necessarily conclude that teaching and learning can be explained exclusively by the three Rogerian conditions. We can all think of examples from our own experience in which ideas, directions, and other types of academic content were important, and a skeptic might be quick to conclude that love alone is not enough. We are not suggesting either extreme. Obviously, unconditional positive regard is not sufficient; but just as obviously, such facilitating conditions are important and necessary.

One final point: Recall that Walberg's massive summary of pupil achievement outcomes denoted classroom morale as a key factor in learning. In this sense, the atmosphere or climate can enhance morale or do just the opposite. If pupils feel prized as persons instead of feeling unworthy, then the learning outcome is positive. There are always exceptions, of course. Someone is bound to say, "I really felt put down all the time in that class, but I learned the material." Individuality is such that a few can learn even under the worst possible conditions. Remember, these are exceptions, not the rule.

SYNTHESIZING TEACHING

From a developmental view, each of the three general models of teaching we have discussed has assets as well as liabilities. It would be a great mistake to settle exclusively on any one of these methods. There is something to be said in favor of each one, as well as something to be said against each one. Certainly, from the point of view of the pupil, the deficits are clear. **Bruce Joyce**, one of the country's leading researchers in the teaching-learning process, has commented that the actual teaching styles of most teachers are extremely limited. As a result, it is most important to "add and blend" a repertoire of models—that is, synthesize teaching—in order to enhance effectiveness. In other words, the old advice that advocated finding your own model, learning it, and sticking with it no longer holds. Joyce notes a series of personal experiences to underscore the need for variety. His account, which follows, illustrates how a teacher may so overuse one approach that the student soon becomes sick of the subject matter.

When I was in high school, I was one of the poorest members of a good swimming team. The coach used drill-and-practice methods to teach us the strokes and how to increase our speed. He was tremendously encouraging to all of us, including those who really were not doing the team that much good. We loved him, enjoyed each other, and felt good about ourselves. As my body matured in college, I showed some promise as a long-distance swimmer and was taken under the wing of a fairly genial but hard-driving coach who emphasized practice rather than instruction. Given the academic demands of college, our little group had keys to the pool and were asked to swim for four to six hours sometime during each evening or night. It was, of course, not his fault that he couldn't be there to provide variety, but one of the side-effects of that experience is that I have not swum five consecutive laps since I was 20 years old. I love to play in the water, but I have an incredible aversion to anything remotely resembling swimming practice (Joyce, 1978, p. 18).

Avoiding Rigidity

Having learned to use the various Flanders categories outlined in Table 12.3, you will be able to combine clusters that will most naturally fit the major teaching models presented at the outset. Employing advance organizers in the transmission-of-knowledge model (Model One) means that category 5 (lecturing) would be the most common technique used. Similarly, the inductive modes associated with Model Two would rely heavily on category 4 (asking open-ended questions) plus categories 2 and 3. The interpersonal model (Model Three) would include a strong emphasis on category 1 (accepting feelings) as well as on categories 2 and 3. The goal, then, is to learn to apply these models with skill in order to increase the variety of learning experiences for the pupils (Joyce, Showers, and Rolheiser-Bennett, 1987). Joyce warns that it is very important to avoid a heavy-handed or singular reliance on any one model day in and day out. Recent research has shown that the effective use of a blend of models does yield consistent increases in student achievement.

> When I am working with my classes, there are certain days when I simply have a terrific urge to get things clarified or when I want to express myself and the way I think about material. On those days, I am very likely to lecture with the use of advance organizers. There are other days when I would be bored silly by that same approach, and use another to stay lively and help the students stay with me. Pretending that we are not people would be a serious error in teaching, and our intuition about what feels right on any given day should be listened to, even though we select models on an analytic basis much of the time (Joyce, 1978, pp. 18–19).

Enhancing Flexibility among Models

Good teachers work at avoiding rigidity and enhancing their flexible use of different models of teaching. Kathy Carter (1990) summarized the research on teachers' knowledge and learning to teach. In her review are helpful examples of teachers who attempt to be flexible within their preferred primary models of teaching. She presented the following two examples, drawn from case studies of four teachers by Tom Russell and Phyllis Johnston (1988). In exploring teachers' professional knowledge, Russell and Johnston (1988) and their colleagues Hugh Munby and Charlotte Spafford (Russell, Munby, Spafford, and Johnston, 1988) focused their analysis on the extent to which teachers can interpret the events of their practice and act on their new understandings in subsequent teaching events. In addition, they examined how these teachers' images of teaching helped or hindered their ability to learn from their experiences, increase their flexibility in using the different models of teaching, and synthesize or construct their own genuine teaching style appropriate to the students' needs.

> For example, the teacher who appeared to be constrained the most by her image of teaching and learned the least from her experience was Wendy, a high school science teacher who saw herself as a transmitter of knowledge. During her first 2 years of teaching, she came to explore methods of helping students participate more fully in classroom work, but she was not able to reframe her experience in ways that resulted in notable changes in her teaching actions. She did modify and improve a number of her teaching techniques, but her teaching stayed largely consistent with the transmitter view, despite her expressed wish to change. Russell and Johnston argue that Wendy appeared to view teaching through a "conduit" metaphor, a metaphor that describes her prevailing view of teaching as carrying students through the curriculum.
>
> In contrast, Roger, a fifth-year science teacher of seventh and eighth grades, came to teaching with a strongly held belief in the inquiry approach, but he learned from watching his students that, although they enjoyed working with science in this fashion, their *learning* of the content and concepts of science was sometimes questionable. Roger began to read criticisms of the inquiry approach to teaching that he had supported, but he initially greeted these criticisms with anger and resentment. Later he experimented by using his own blend of inquiry and content knowledge in science, and, seeing that his students

All three models—the transmittal of knowledge, inductive inquiry, and interpersonal learning—are important to the classroom teacher, and effective teaching demands a combination of the three. Certainly it would be a mistake to depend exclusively on any one.

were constructing much-improved meaning about the subject of science, he altered his original view of teaching and continued to construct his own interpretation of teaching from his classroom experiences and from his reading of theory about how children learn. Russell and Johnston illustrate how Roger's metaphors for teaching revolved around students and their understandings of science and conveyed a view of teaching that was focused on attending to how students learn from the activities that he enacted with them in classrooms (Carter, 1990, p. 301).

Development toward greater flexbility in teaching starts when teachers become aware of the teaching strategies with which they are most comfortable, and act on refining these strategies. Teachers attempt to look at their practice from different perspectives and increase their flexibility among the models of teaching. They initially maintain a coherent framework for their teaching and often ignore feedback from students which doesn't fit into this framework. (In a Piagetian sense of new learning, we could call this part of the pattern *assimilation,* as we discussed in

Chapter 5). At the next level of awareness, teachers become more attentive to students' reactions and feedback. The teachers then reflect on puzzling situations, and do start to reframe their teaching practices to accommodate the new, disequilibrating information. Russell and Johnston refer to this step in the pattern of change as reflection-in-action. As their practices change, teachers may become more able to express their views of teaching analytically.

NONVERBAL BEHAVIOR

In addition to the need for blending in Joyce's sense, there is yet another important component of teaching effectiveness. To an ironic degree the nonverbal aspect of being human is so obvious that we often overlook it. In fact, until the work of theorists such as **Charles Galloway** (1977), of Ohio State University, and a few others, the area of body language, or nonverbal communication, was largely ignored in teaching and teacher education. This happened in spite of earlier and pioneering research work that indicated most clearly just how significant the phenomenon was.

It's hard to imagine, but from 75 to 90 percent of a message's impact is tranmitted nonverbally. The actual verbal content turns out to be far less important than tone of voice, facial expression, and posture. In the classroom, how you stand or sit, move, gesture, and raise and lower your voice, for example, will convey what you really mean to your students. But unfortunately, as Galloway points out, too often we are almost totally unaware of our own nonverbal modes. We rarely see ourselves in interaction and hence do not really understand what impact we may be having on others.

Perhaps even more important is the extent to which we convey how we really feel about others without words. Studies have shown that teachers who have positive attitudes toward the world actually employ an important set of facilitating nonverbal cues to encourage student participation and involvement. Those with negative attitudes display **nonverbal behavior** designed to discourage and inhibit student involvement (Smith, 1981). Researchers could predict what type of nonverbal behavior a teacher would use if they knew the teacher's attitude set. Moreover, it was obvious that the children understood the meaning of the different body language systems.

As a result Galloway and his colleagues developed a nonverbal version of the Flanders system. Instead of coding verbal messages, however, they rated the body language of the teachers. Table 12.5 outlines

TABLE 12.5   NONVERBAL BEHAVIORS: THE GALLOWAY SYSTEM

		CONGRUENT	INCONGRUENT
DIRECT INFLUENCE	1, 2	Nonverbal behavior is consistent with words. No "mixed messages" are given. Body language demonstrates an appropriate range of feelings.	Behavior contradicts words; for example, smiles when annoyed. Body language is overcontrolled. Feelings are rarely if ever shown.
	3	*IMPLEMENT* As teacher uses ideas of pupils, nonverbals are consistently encouraging; for example, leans toward, smiles.	*PERFUNCTORY* Nonverbal behavior indicates no genuine interest in student ideas; for example, bored posture or facial expression.
	4	*PERSONAL* Teacher maintains face-to-face eye contact, is "connected" with the class, maintains a comfortable "psychological" distance.	*IMPERSONAL* Teacher avoids eye contact; for example, talks to the floor or ceiling or maintains excessive distance.
INDIRECT INFLUENCE	5	*RESPONSIVE* Tone, pace of talk are designed to keep student interest.	*UNRESPONSIVE* Teacher drones on and on, with little variation in tone, and screens out student cues.
	6	*INVOLVE* Nonverbal behavior encourages student participation in clarifying directions and rules.	*DISMISS* Nonverbal behavior cues students to avoid participation.
	7	*FIRM* Nonverbal behavior is consistent with firm language in controlling misbehavior.	*HARSH* Nonverbal behavior is severe, aggressive, genuinely intimidating.

SPOTLIGHT ON TEACHER ENTHUSIASM

Regular Education and Special-Education Classrooms

Whenever we think of teaching effectiveness, a question frequently asked is: What about enthusiasm? Doesn't it make a difference if the teacher is genuinely interested in and eager to convey the subject matter? Certainly Thomas Good's concept of active teaching seems to indicate the need for well-paced instruction.[a] Obviously, a teacher who labors over each point in a slow, pedantic manner must have a negative effect. Such a teacher, humorless, plodding, and somewhat out of touch with reality, represents almost a Hollywood version of an ineffective educator.

It was Jacob Kounin who first formalized a framework to help understand the concept of **teacher enthusiasm**.[b] How alert, wide awake, or "with it" a teacher is does make a major difference, particularly in handling discipline and in moving from one subject to the next. In other words, one of the keys to a good learning environment is the avoidance of "down time," when nothing seems to be happening in the classroom. Thus, managing a group involves a pace or tempo.

From a logical viewpoint, then, teacher energy is clearly important. What does the research say?

The first series of studies was done by Barak Rosenshine through careful observation of actual classroom instruction. Through such naturalistic study, Kounin's ideas were validated. The enthusiastic, "with it" teachers outperformed their cohorts. The pupils gained in academic achievement. The positive correlations to achievement ranged between .30 and .60.[c] But since such findings weren't particularly surprising, they received only modest notice in the educational psychology literature. It remained for a new group of researchers to put the concept at the forefront through a series of provocative and somewhat controversial studies, the "Dr. Fox studies."

Every once in a while, a group of behavioral scientists will come up with a startling new approach to a phenomenon. D. H. Naftulin, J. E. Ware, and F. A. Donnelly decided to push the study of enthusiasm to the limit.[d] At a professional conference they hired an actor to give a lecture. Introduced with all the appropriate (though "fake") expert credentials, the actor used charisma, enthusiasm, and style in delivering a basically meaningless talk. At times, it even verged on double-talk. Of course, by now you may have guessed the outcome. The audience solemnly proclaimed through evaluations that the talk was well-organized, clearly presented, and "stimulated thinking." The redoubtable Dr. Fox had indeed outfoxed his audience. National newspapers and the media quickly picked up the study.

Naturally, there is and has been much debate about what such a study actually proves. It does not suggest that in a real classroom over the course of an entire school year students will learn meaningful content from meaningless lectures. After all, you can't fool all the people all the time. Further studies have shown that when real content is included, the "expressiveness" of the teacher continues to have a significant effect not only on student ratings but on achievement as well. So what is now be-

the main elements of the patterns of communication divided into two main areas: nonverbal behavior that (1) facilitates students' development or (2) constricts their growth. He has also organized the nonverbal categories according to indirect methods and direct approaches.

The results of Galloway's research have two major implications. First, there is a clear connection between a teacher's nonverbal behavior and the classroom atmosphere. We noted both in the teaching model focused on interpersonal relationships and from the meta-analysis on the importance of classroom morale that such elements have an important effect on learning. Essentially, your nonverbal behavior will set the tone in the classroom.

Second, teachers need to make a deliberate attempt to become more aware of their own basic repertoire of nonverbal behavior. This doesn't mean you need to enroll in a method acting school. It does mean you should recognize and improve areas in which your nonverbal behavior may be inhibiting student growth. Obviously, the use of videotapes of classroom performance is one major way of gaining awareness and seeing the effect of a new behavior. Another is to ask a good friend to observe and write down examples of how your behavior fits into the Galloway system.

The most difficult problem is that there can be no exact prescription of how to behave. You need to find a comfortable middle ground between a cold, aloof,

ing referred to as "an extended visit with Dr. Fox in the classroom" essentially agrees with Kounin's original contention and Rosenshine's first series of naturalistic studies.[e] The experimental studies help to cross-validate the original findings.[f] Enthusiasm makes a difference.

A recent study by Frederick Brigham, Thomas Scruggs, and Margo Mastropieri[g] focused on teacher enthusiasm in learning disabilities classrooms. Students with learning disabilities in two junior high-school special-education classrooms were given instruction in science over a two-week period with levels of teacher enthusiasm manipulated in a crossover design. Results suggested that more enthusiastic presentations resulted in significantly higher academic achievement as well as lower levels of off-task behavior. The authors cite two possible theories to explain why enthusiasm produces such positive changes in students. The first theory was based on Rosenshine's earlier work which suggested that enthusiastic "with-

it" teachers with their varying positions, voice tones, and gestures attract high levels of attention from students and consequently excellent cognitive engagement and achievement. These authors suggest a second possible explanation: Students consciously or unconsciously model the enthusiastic attitude that the teacher exhibits toward the content, and consequently concentrate more, think more about the subject, and achieve more than they would have with a less enthusiastic teacher. Further research could lend support to one or more of these ideas to explain why enthusiasm continues to make a difference.

[a] T. L. Good, Recent classroom research: Implications for teacher education. In D. C. Smith (Ed.), *Essential knowledge for beginning educators* (Washington: American Association of Colleges of Teacher Education, 1983), pp. 55–64.

[b] J. Kounin, *Discipline and group management in the classroom* (New York: Holt, Rinehart & Winston, 1970).

[c] B. Rosenshine, Enthusiastic teaching: A research review. *School Review* (1970), *78*, 499–514.

[d] D. H. Naftulin, J. E. Ware, Jr., and F. A. Donnelly, The Dr. Fox lecture: A paradigm for educational seduction. *Journal of Medical Education* (1973), *48*, 630–635.

[e] R. G. Williams and J. E. Ware, Jr., An extended visit with Dr. Fox: Validity of student satisfaction with instruction after repeated exposure to a lecturer. *American Educational Research Journal* (1977), 14(4), 449–458.

[f] See A. G. Larkins, C. W. McKinney, S. Oldham-Bass, and A. C. Gilmore, Teacher enthusiasm: A critical review. In H. S. Williams (Ed.), *Educational and psychological research*. (Hattiesburg: University of Southern Mississippi, 1985). This is an excellent, comprehensive review of the concept of enthusiasm, including a detailed examination of the research design employed.

[g] F. J. Brigham, T. E. Scruggs, and M. A. Mastropieri. Teacher enthusiasm in learning disabilities classrooms: Effects on learning and behavior. *Learning Disabilities Research and Practice* (1992), 7, 68–73. A summary of research on teacher enthusiasm in regular education and special-education classrooms is included in their article.

restricted set of behaviors and their opposite—a rushing, gushing, overpowering, and hectic nonverbal repertoire. If you are naturally inclined to be quiet and to limit your nonverbal behavior, then you will want to work on adding to your repertoire. If, however, your nonverbal behavior seems to indicate that you are running the class as if you were conducting a fire drill, then you'll want to relax more and express less of yourself nonverbally. Incidentally, this also holds even in the area of discipline. The old truism used to be "Don't smile 'til Christmas" if you were a new teacher (Ryan, 1970). The idea was to keep the students in line right from the start through stern composure. We now know that's wrong. Effective teachers are skillful not only in stating their expecta-

tions but also in demonstrating a genuine interest in listening to and working with the student, thus conveying an atmosphere of mutually shared expectations. They can even smile before Thanksgiving.

Communicating Expectations

Teachers communicate expectations to students verbally and nonverbally. It is important to be aware of the way you communicate expectations nonverbally because students' performance is often influenced by a teacher's subtle, as well as not-so-subtle and blatant approaches. What personal convictions or opinions a teacher communicates about a student's competence has a powerful effect on student performance, and sometimes teachers have "reference group" expectations about an entire category of people that can have an impact on all members of that group. We can add school, societal, and family expectations to our discussion of communicating expectations (see Chapter 14).

A recent study of nonverbal behavior of teachers yielded some interesting as well as distressing results. The researchers studied three groups of experienced teachers—preschool, remedial, and elementary—by viewing video clips of the teachers' classroom behavior. The ratings yielded two general patterns of nonverbal behavior: pattern 1 behavior was flexible, democratic, and warm; pattern 2 was hostile, condescending, and dogmatic (Babad, Bernieri, and Rosenthal, 1987). There were, however, very few differences in other aspects of teacher behavior, particularly at the verbal level. At the nonverbal level, it was a different story. First, there was a major difference associated with teaching area. Pattern 1—flexible, democratic, and warm—was highest for the preschool group, second for the remedial teachers, and lowest for the elementary teachers. Thus, there is major variation in nonverbal behavior. The second finding of importance was that the main nonverbal channel for conveying the negative feelings of hostility, condescension, and dogmatism was through facial expressions. The face more than body posture, voice tone, or other elements of nonverbal behavior was the main channel. It is also interesting to note that those who rated the video clips—the research judges—showed the greatest reliability in rating the facial dogmatism messages. If this study is replicated, it may well provide us with a very significant clue about the question of classroom atmosphere, morale, and affective states as they relate to pupils' feelings. The most important point here is to remember that it is your facial expression which transmits the affective message. This may explain why actors in training spend so much time practicing their routines in front of a mirror.

The final issue here is expressed as a question. If the teacher's nonverbal behavior influences students, does the converse also hold true? As you've probably guessed, it does work both ways. Teachers can be clearly influenced by a student's physical appearance, posture, and tone of voice (Woolfolk and Brooks, 1983). As a result some students receive frequent approval while others not only receive less approval but also less eye contact, fewer smiles, and more disapproval. We'll comment more on this when we dis-

cuss the personal aspects of teaching (Chapter 14), since it relates very much to the basic attitudes a teacher may have toward pupils and the self-fulfilling prophecies that result.

Cross-Cultural Differences

If you think about it, you will quickly realize that body language varies considerably according to a person's cultural background. Some nonverbal behavior may have a very different meaning in different cultures. As a result, when the cultural background of the child and the teacher vary widely, nonverbal messages may be misinterpreted. Two examples illustrate the point. Some Native American children are taught not to maintain steady eye contact with an adult. In some tribes an adult who looks straight into another person's eyes is seen as untrustworthy. This does not mean that you can't look at Native American children; however, if you force the child to look directly into your eyes, you may be sending a very mixed message. Similarly, the amount of physical space that is psychologically comfortable varies considerably among cultures. A newly arrived student from Great Britain may require more "personal space" than a student from Mexico. At the same time, however, it is most important not to overgeneralize. Many English children and Mexican children would welcome either closer or more distant contact. What they are accustomed to may also depend on how Americanized their family has become.

In dealing with children from culturally different backgrounds, it is wise to watch for signs of incongruity. When the children's behavior is incongruent, it may indicate that whatever you are attempting to communicate nonverbally is being misunderstood. In other words, they may be decoding your nonverbal message in a way you didn't intend. Because of the enormous complexity of cross-cultural differences, it may be impossible for research to develop a definitive list of them. As a teacher, you should be sensitive to their existence and observe the nonverbal responses to your own behaviors as an index of effective communication. In addition, you should actively seek to find out more about these differences by asking other school personnel, parents, and community members, and by further reading and attending cultural events. Cross-cultural differences can be discussed in class (or privately) with students; it is an important area of study and understanding.

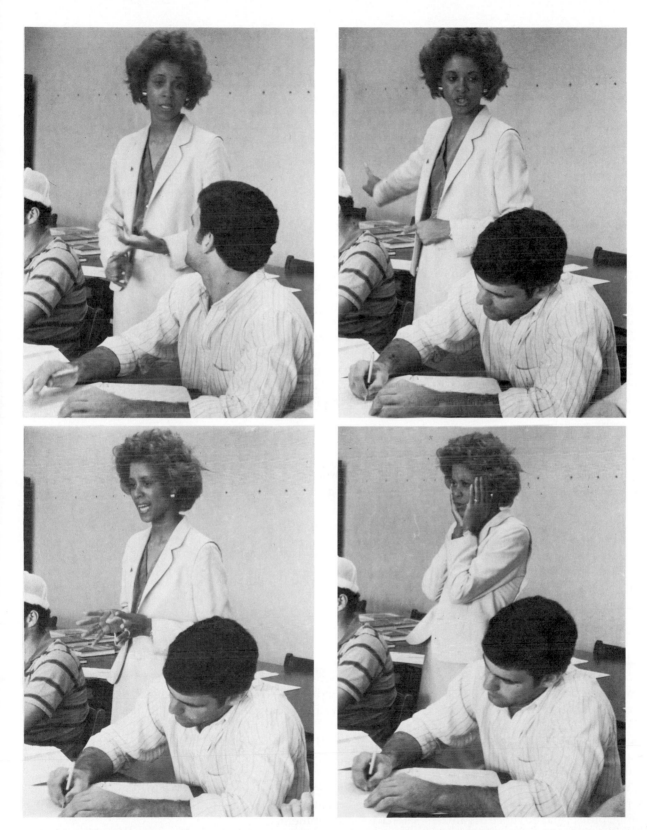

As Galloway's research on nonverbal behavior points out, actions speak louder than words in the classroom.

SUMMARY

Recent research on teaching effectiveness based on large-scale meta-analyses conducted by Walberg indicates that the following factors are key elements: engaged academic learning time, positive reinforcement, cues and feedback, cooperative learning, positive class atmosphere, higher-order questioning, and advance organizers. The system of instruction developed by Flanders shows how these elements fit together in actual classroom interaction.

Teaching elements can also be grouped into general models of teaching. In Model One the emphasis is on the transmission of knowledge. Use of advance organizers and direct teaching methods are the main features. Model Two involves inquiry or discovery-based teaching. It emphasizes the indirect methods of open-ended questioning and of building on student ideas. The focus of Model Three is the quality of interpersonal relations. A positive classroom atmosphere is a central component of the model. Elements of connected teaching enhance the learning atmosphere for some students, particularly women.

Joyce emphasizes the need for a variety of teaching models. Instead of relying exclusively on any single model, he suggests synthesizing methods. Teachers thus need to practice the different skills involved with each method in order to achieve teaching effectiveness.

One of the main criticisms of the teaching models has been the absence of any emphasis on teacher nonverbal behavior. Based on Galloway's system, a new method of analyzing teacher nonverbal behavior has been developed that parallels Flanders's framework. Galloway's work underscores the importance of teacher awareness of how actions often do speak louder than words in the classroom. In the area of cross-cultural differences, there are few, if any, consistent nonverbal differences. It is important, however, for teachers to become aware of possible incongruities between pupil words and body language. Thus, teachers need to learn about not only their own nonverbal channels of communication but those of their pupils as well.

KEY TERMS AND NAMES

connected teaching
   cooperative learning
Ned Flanders
Nathaniel Gage
Charles Galloway
   nonverbal behavior
   teacher enthusiasm

Bruce Joyce
Carl Rogers
   congruence
   empathy
   unconditional positive regard
Herbert Walberg

THEORY INTO PRACTICE: VERBAL AND NONVERBAL BEHAVIOR

In developing your own awareness of your verbal and nonverbal teaching behavior, you will need to practice single elements at first. The method has been called *microteaching*, which means to divide the complex process of instruction into smaller-sized components and then practice each skill separately. Basically, this is the format we have followed in the chapter. We presented some very concrete elements, such as positive reinforcement, cues and feedback, questioning, praise, and advance organizers. Then we showed how these elements can be blended into a

more general system (Flanders) and finally into models. So to practice, we suggest going back to the Walberg components or the Flanders outline. Do not start with the models.

The second aspect of the method emphasizes relatively short practice on one skill. The practice is then followed as soon as possible by a review playback as a check. This way you will reduce the likelihood of maintaining any ineffective teaching skill under development.

For Verbal Behavior

1. Select one microskill from either the Flanders or Walberg list.

2. Prepare a brief unit or lesson plan to teach to a small group of students (peers or volunteers).

3. Set up an audiotape recorder so that it is relatively unobtrusive.

4. Teach the unit for ten to fifteen minutes or so. Specifically try to use the designated microskill.

   For example, if you want to practice positive reinforcement, use a unit that will allow you to pose a number of questions. Then, when students respond, you'll have the opportunity to reinforce. The same holds true for areas such as cues or responding to feelings.

5. When you've finished the unit, turn off the tape. Before starting the playback, make a chart such as the one below, to organize your analysis. To reduce defensiveness, plan to do this kind of review and playback *by yourself* at least for the first few times. It can be disconcerting, especially at the outset, to hear the difference between what you intended to do and what actually happened. Also, you'll need time to become less self conscious. Keep it to yourself at a start.

MICROTEACHING CHART— VERBAL
Focus Area: Use of Positive Reinforcement
AUDIO PLAYBACK

1. How many questions were asked? _____

2. How many questions were answered correctly? _____

3. How many times did I offer a positive reinforcer to correctly answered questions? _____

4. List examples of the words and phrases used as positive reinforcers.

5. Review the ratio between correct answers (item 2) and positive reinforcers (item 3).
   a. Are you satisfied with the number of times you followed the correct answer with a reinforcer?

   b. If not, then recycle the unit (or another one) and try again.

6. Review the content of your verbal reinforcers as listed in item 4.
   a. Are you satisfied that you have enough variety in your responses or are you relying on one or two "pet" expressions?

   b. If not, then repeat the exercise after writing down some additional phrases in your own words that you could use.

For Nonverbal Behavior

1. Select one microskill, such as eye contact, voice tone, or body stance.

2. Prepare a brief unit or lesson plan to last ten to fifteen minutes.

3. Set up a video camera. Since this can be somewhat complex the first time, allow yourself some extra time to become familiar with the equipment. Set the camera in a corner with the wide-angle lens focused on the place where the small group will be sitting. Check the recording level to be sure the sound is being picked up. Then turn on the equipment.

4. Teach the unit to the group and consciously try to emphasize the particular nonverbal behavior you selected for practice.

5. When done, turn off the equipment and rewind the tape. Before playback, prepare a chart, in the same manner as before, for use in analyzing what you observe on the tape. See page 352.

   After reviewing all of the above, you may decide to recycle. It is important, however, to recycle by continuing to concentrate on one specific skill. Do not fall into the trap of trying all the components at once. That will overload your learning circuits, so to speak.

Summary   Only after you have mastered a number of these individual teaching skills should you consider evaluating yourself on the entire Flanders scale. That would be the next step toward synthesis.

For further information on this approach, see S. Rogers (1987), "If I Can See Myself, I Can Change," *Educational Leadership*, 45(2), 64–67.

MICRO TEACHING CHART— NONVERBAL
Focus Area: Eye Contact
VIDEO PLAYBACK

1. How many times did I look up at the students as a group? _____

2. How many times did I maintain eye contact of at least two seconds with a specific pupil during the unit? _____

3. Review the ratio of times you looked up (item 1) to times you maintained contact (item 2).

a. Are you satisfied with the number of general glances at the class compared with individual contacts?

b. In reviewing the tape, how would you characterize the quality of the eye contact? Was it friendly or staring? How did the students react? Review their body posture and compare their attention during times when you glanced at them in a general way versus times of specific contact.

c. Did you feel uncomfortable throughout the unit or did you find yourself becoming less self-conscious by the end of the session?

REFERENCES

American Association of University Women (1992). *How schools shortchange girls*. Washington: AAUW Educational Foundation.

Ausubel, D. P., and Sullivan, E. V. (1970). *Theory and problems of child development* (2d ed.). New York: Grune & Stratton.

Badad, E., Bernieri, F., and Rosenthal, R. (1987). Nonverbal and verbal behavior of preschool, remedial, and elementary school teachers. *American Educational Research Journal, 24*(3), 405–415.

Barnes, M., and Coupland, M. (1990). Humanizing calculus: A case study in curriculum development. In L. Burton (Ed.), *Gender and mathematics* (pp. 72–80). London: Cassell.

Belenky, M. F., Clinchy, B. M., Goldberger, N. R., and Tarule, J. M. (1986). *Women's ways of knowing: The development of self, voice, and mind*. New York: Basic Books.

Berliner, D. C. (1984). The half-full glass: A review of research on teaching. In P. L. Hosford (Ed.), *Using what we know about teaching* (pp. 51–77). Alexandria, Va.: Association for Supervision and Curriculum Development (ASCD).

Brophy, J. (1981). Teacher praise: A functional analysis. *Review of Educational Research, 51,* 5–32.

Brophy, J. (1988). Research linking teacher behavior to student achievement: Potential implications for instruction of Chapter 1 students. *Educational Psychologist, 23*(3), 275–276.

Bruner, J. (1966). *Toward a theory of instruction*. Cambridge, Mass.: Belknap Press, Harvard University.

Buerk, D. (1985). The voices of women making meaning in mathematics. *Journal of Education, 167,* 59–70.

Carter, K. (1990). Teachers' knowledge and learning to teach. In W. R. Houston (Ed.), *Handbook of research on teacher education* (pp. 291–310). New York: Macmillan.

Chickering, A., and McCormick, J. (1973). Personality development and the college experience. *Research in Higher Education, 1,* 43–70.

Cuban, L. (1988). Researchers advising policymakers: A word to the wise. *Educational Psychologist, 23*(3), 287–293.

Dempter, F. (1987). Time and the production of classroom learning. *Educational Psychologist, 22*(1), 1–22.

Doyle, W. H. (1986). Using an advance organizer to establish a subsuming function concept for facilitating achievement in remedial college mathematics. *American Educational Research Journal, 23*(3), 507–516.

Eccles, J. (1987). Gender roles and women's achievement—Related decisions. *Psychology of Women Quarterly, 11*(2), 135–171.

Fennema, E., and Leder, G. (Eds.). (1990). *Mathematics and gender*. New York: Teachers College Press.

Flanders, N. A. (1970). *Analyzing teacher behavior*. Reading, Mass.: Addison-Wesley.

Flanders, N. A., and Morine, G. (1973). The assessment of proper control and suitable learning environment. In N. L. Gage (Ed.), *Mandated evaluation of educators*. Stanford: California Center for Research and Development in Teaching.

Fraser, B. J., Walberg, H. J., Welch, W. W., and Hattie, J. A. (1987). Synthesis of educational productivity research. *International Journal of Educational Research, 11,* 73–145.

Gage, N. L. (1978). *The scientific basis for the art of teaching*. New York: Teachers College Press.

Gage, N. L. (1985). *Hard gains in the soft sciences*. Bloomington, Ind.: Phi Delta Kappan.

Galloway, C. (1977). Nonverbal. *Theory into practice, 16*(3).

Good, T. L. (1983). Recent classroom research: Implications for teacher education. In D. C. Smith (Ed.), *Essential knowledge for beginning educators* (pp. 55–65). Washington: American Association of Colleges of Teacher Education.

Hernandez, H. (1989). *Multicultural education*. Columbus, Ohio: Merrill.

Isaacson, Z. (1990). They look at you in absolute horror: Women writing and talking about mathematics. In L.

Burton (Ed.), *Gender and mathematics* (pp. 20–28). London: Cassell.

Joyce, B. R. (1978). *Selecting learning experiences: Linking theory to practice*. Washington: ASCD.

Joyce, B., Showers, B., and Rolheiser-Bennett, C. (1987). Staff development and student learning: A synthesis of research on models of teaching. *Educational Leadership, 45*(2), 11–23.

Mohatt, G., and Erickson, F. (1981). Cultural differences in teaching styles in an Odawa school: A sociolinguistic approach. In H. T. Trueba, G. P. Guthrie, and K. Hu-Pei Au (Eds.), *Culture and the bilingual classroom* (pp. 105–119). Rowley, Mass.: Newbury House.

Morine-Dershimer, G. (1985). *Talking, listening, and learning in elementary classrooms*. New York: Longman.

Morrow, C. (1991). *A description of SummerMath, a process oriented mathematics learning community, and resulting student attitudes toward mathematics*. Paper presented to the National Council of Teachers of Mathematics, New Orleans.

Morrow, C., and Morrow, J. (1991). *The SummerMath program for minority girls and teachers*. Annual Report to the National Aeronautics and Space Administration Project. South Hadley, Mass.: Mount Holyoke College.

Page, F. B. (1958). Teacher comments and student performance. *Journal of Educational Psychology, 49*, 173–181.

Peterson, P., and Swing, S. (1982). Beyond time on task: Students' reports of their thought processes during classroom instruction. *Elementary School Journal, 82*, 481–491.

Phillips, S. U. (1983). *The invisible culture*. Research on Teaching Monograph Series. New York: Longman.

Redfield, D. L., and Rousseau, E. W. (1981). Meta-analysis of experimental research on teacher questioning behavior. *Review of Educational Research, 51*(2), 237–246.

Rogers, C. R. (1969). *Freedom to learn*. Columbus, Ohio: Merrill.

Rosenshine, B. (1987). Explicit teaching and teacher training. *Journal of Teacher Education, 38*(3), 34–36.

Rowe, M. B. (1986). Wait time: Slowing down may be a way of speeding up! *Journal of Teacher Education, 37*(1), 43–50.

Russell, T., and Johnston, P. (1988). *Teachers' learning from experiences of teaching: Analysis based on metaphor and reflection*. Paper presented at the annual meeting of the American Educational Research Association, San Francisco.

Russell, T., Munby, H., Spafford, C., and Johnston, P. (1990). Learning the professional knowledge of teaching: Metaphors, puzzles, and the theory-practice relationship. In P. P. Grimmett and G. L. Erickson (Eds.). *Reflection in teacher education* (pp. 67–90). New York: Teachers College Press.

Ryan, K. (1970). *Don't smile until Christmas*. Chicago: University of Chicago Press.

Sadker, M., Sadker, D., and Klein, S. (1991). The issue of gender in elementary and secondary education. In G. Grant (Ed.), *Review of research in education* (pp. 269–334). Washington: American Educational Research Association.

Shulman, L. E. (1986). Paradigms and research programs in the study of teaching. In M. C. Wittrock (Ed.), *Handbook of research on teaching* (p. 12). New York: Macmillan.

Shulman, L. E. (1987). Knowledge and teaching: Foundations of the new reform. *Harvard Educational Review, 57*(1), 1–22.

Smith, H. (1981). Nonverbal communication in teaching. *Review of Educational Research, 49*(4), 631–672.

Tobin, K. (1986). Effects of teacher wait time on discourse characteristics in mathematics and language arts classes. *American Educational Research Journal, 23*(2), 191–200.

Walberg, H. J. (1986). Synthesis of research on teaching. In M. C. Wittrock (Ed.), *Handbook of research on teaching* (pp. 214–229). New York: Macmillan.

Walberg, H. J. (1988). Synthesis of research on time and learning. *Educational Leadership, 45*(6), 76–81.

Walberg, H. J. (1990). Productive teaching and instruction: Assessing the knowledge base. *Phi Delta Kappan*, 470–478.

Woolfolk, A. H., and Brooks, D. M. (1983). Nonverbal communication in teaching. *Review of Research in Education, 10*, 103–150.

13

TEACHING OBJECTIVES

Sooner or later all those involved in the educational enterprise confront the question of teaching objectives. What is the point and purpose of the curriculum content? Is it content mastery, or academic skills acquisition? Is it personal growth? Or are process goals the ultimate purpose? Essentially, the basic problem involves examining the question, education for what? And, as you may have guessed, there are as many proposed purposes as there are questions. In this chapter, we shall discuss the problem in a global sense, and then outline a framework that provides significant guidance for the choices that teachers face.

We will also present information on the general principles involved in lesson planning. Such planning can become an important vehicle for attaining specified objectives.

OBJECTIVES: THE PROBLEM OF WHAT TO TEACH

What objectives do we want to achieve in teaching anybody anything? A few years ago this very question was given perhaps its best portrayal in *The Saber Tooth Curriculum*, a book written under the pen name of J. Abner Peddiwell. It was a spoof, but it made its point most dramatically and effectively. In Paleolithic times a tribe developed an educational curriculum based on survival needs. The young were taught how to scare away saber-tooth tigers with firebrands, how

to club woolly horses for clothing, and how to fish with their hands. However, as time passed and the Ice Age began, the survival needs changed: The tigers caught cold and died, the woolly horses ran away, and the fish disappeared in muddy water. In their places came big, ferocious bears that weren't scared by firebrands, a herd of antelope that could run like the wind (the woolly horses had been slow-footed and clumsy), and new fish that hid in the muddy water. It soon occurred to the tribe that their educational curriculum was, in today's parlance, not relevant. Scaring tigers, clubbing horses, and catching fish by hand were relics of the old days. The tribe now needed to learn how to trap bears, snare antelopes, and make fishnets. However, the "educational establishment" of the tribe declared in august tones:

> Don't be foolish. . . . We don't teach fish-grabbing to grab fish; we teach it to develop a generalized agility which can never be developed by mere training (in net-making). We don't teach horse-clubbing to club horses; we teach it to develop a generalized strength in the learner which he can never get from so prosaic and specialized a thing as antelope-snare setting. We don't teach tiger-scaring to scare tigers; we teach it for the purpose of giving that noble courage. . . . (Peddiwell, 1939).

The debate on educational objectives has a long history. The controversy usually covers the same terrain; namely, advocates of teaching skills for survival are in opposition to those who would teach for intrinsic and general education. Each side has some merit. We certainly do need to learn survival skills, but if that is all we learn, it is obvious that our skills are destined to become obsolete. Critics compare this approach to training a generation of dinosaurs—animals that, because of their inability to adapt to changing times, were unable to survive.

In addition to the time-limited nature of specific skill training, a second aspect of education as content acquisition is almost always raised by critics of that approach. Memorizing facts and mastering information generally have almost no long-term effects. In a series of classic studies conducted in the 1930s, Ralph Tyler demonstrated quite clearly that pupils unlearn almost as fast as they learn. He studied the amount of content retained. The pupils "forgot" almost 50 percent of the content taught after one year. The figure shot up to 80 percent after two years. As an aside, he ironically noted that most pupils in this country in the 1930s thought that all banks paid 6 percent compound interest since that was the figure commonly used in arithmetic word problems (Tyler, 1933). So much for the argument that the goals of education should be to inculcate specific skills and content! When Jean Piaget said that "to know by heart is not really to know," he neatly summarized the fundamental flaw in this educational goal.

However, proponents of learning for its own sake claim that a "classical education" will train the mind for disciplined thought. Mind training could never become obsolete, because skills we have developed can be brought to bear on any problem we meet in life. However, as you may recall from Chapter 1, E. L. Thorndike conducted a series of studies showing that the theory of mind training through the study of Greek and Latin was false. Such learning could not be generalized. Such a classical general education for the disciplining of the mind seemed as nebulous a goal as memorizing specific concrete skills.

EDUCATIONAL GOALS: BLOOM'S TAXONOMY

Education has always been unable to decide between those who advocate a curriculum of relevance and those who desire a program of general education. In the mid-1950s, a team led by Benjamin S. Bloom of the University of Chicago bravely decided to settle the matter once and for all, and developed the now famous taxonomy, or classification, of educational objectives (Bloom, 1956).

Bloom felt that one of the major difficulties confronting anyone interested in education was the definition of goals, that is, what we want to strive for as teachers, counselors, or educational administrators. If you ask any of your friends to define their goals as teachers, you are likely to receive either an impossibly abstract statement ("I want to help students realize their full potential as individuals—to become self-actualizing") or some very explicit and narrow statement ("My job is to teach the multiplication tables").

Bloom examined this problem of considering educational objectives from either an impossible cosmic or hopelessly trivial point of view. He came up with a scheme that classifies educational objectives and relates each objective to specific classroom procedures. Bloom's approach has a very healthy effect in that it forces teachers to specify their goals and the means of getting there; it fits procedures and materials to instructional strategies. Bloom's system also specifies a sequence of six stages or levels of objectives that are matched to a sequence of assessment strategies. We will describe each level of his system by defining its content and briefly discussing its associated assessment procedures.

Level One: Basic Knowledge

Definition   Students are responsible for information, ideas, material, or phenomena. They have to know specific facts, terms, and methods.

Assessment   Direct questions and multiple-choice tests are applicable. The object is to test the students' ability to recall the facts, to identify and repeat the information provided. The teacher doesn't ask the students to form new judgments or to analyze ideas; he or she simply tries to find out how much material they can recall.

Level Two: Comprehension

Definition   Students must show they understand the material, ideas, facts, and theories.

Assessment   A variety of procedures are applicable. Students can restate the material in their own words, reorder or extrapolate ideas, predict or estimate. In other words, at this level students are as-

BENJAMIN S. BLOOM

The eminent psychologist and scholar Benjamin Bloom was born in 1913. After completing his undergraduate work and master's degree at Penn State, Benjamin Bloom moved to the University of Chicago. He was named instructor of educational psychology in 1940, completed his Ph.D. in 1942, and remained there for over thirty years. He rose through the ranks to a full professorship, all the while building a reputation for careful and significant scholarship. His insistence on precision in educational thought soon led to the now-famous taxonomy for educational objectives in both the cognitive and affective domains, scholarship that literally revolutionized the process of lesson planning for classroom teaching. His system of classification soon became the standard for describing objectives and the process of achieving them. Not content to rest on these laurels, Bloom next stepped into the raging controversy concerning the nature of intelligence. His scholarship and care were once more tested. He published the classic *Stability and Change in Human Characteristics*, in which he attempted to resolve the nature-nurture controversy. His work clearly indicated the significance of early experience and the critical nature of early learning as factors that promote intellectual growth. He has also created a new approach to teaching, mastery learning, in search of methods as effective as individual tutoring. His most recent study is on the process of gifted and talented performance. A lifetime of significant scholarship for educational psychology perhaps best sums up his valuable contributions to the field.

sessed on the basis of their capacity to act upon, or process, information. Assessment at this level requires more activity from the pupil than assessment at level one. Objective or multiple-choice questions can still be used, but they would be of a different order, since they must provide evidence that the pupils have some understanding or comprehension of what they are saying.

Level Three: Application

Students must be able to apply their knowledge to real situations. At level two we are satisfied if they understand the ideas. At level three we want them to demonstrate that they can actually apply their ideas correctly.

This particular level has been one of the stumbling blocks of educational psychology itself. In Chapter 1 we raised the question of why, after fifty years, the mode of classroom teaching has changed so little. We also cited the research showing the predominance of what we called trivia in the classroom. Educational psychology, as a field, contains much basic knowledge (level one) and understands much of it (level two) but has been unable to apply the ideas to real situations (level three). The application of knowledge is critical because it means putting knowledge into action, rather than merely talking about what might be done.

Assessment   We have to go well beyond the usual procedures in order to assess how well students apply what they learn. If, for example, we are teaching them to play volleyball, the test would be obvious: Put them on either side of a net and evaluate their performance. It is easy to see whether children can apply their knowledge of addition or subtraction: Just give them some money, have them "buy" things in a mock store, and see if they end up with the correct change. In geometry, have them construct a right-angled triangle out of wood and then measure the length of each side. In physics, children can wire a bell and see whether or not it will ring. However, the one drawback to tests of this sort is the possibility that pupils may learn by rote how to apply the information. The teacher needs to be aware of this possibility and to vary application tests to ensure that pupils can genuinely put their knowledge into practice.

Level Four: Analysis:

Definition Analysis is essentially a more advanced aspect of level two (comprehension). Analysis requires that pupils classify or break material down into its components, understand the relationship between the components, and recognize the principle that organizes the structure or the system. (As you can see, it becomes increasingly difficult to describe the levels as we move from the simple and the concrete to the complex and abstract.)

Assessment The ability to analyze material can be assessed in a number of ways. For example, we might see whether students can identify the assumptions behind an argument or a debate. Thus, an advocate of the use of preventive nuclear war might argue that "in times of extreme danger, with national survival at stake, a country has to defend itself by striking at and destroying the enemy before the enemy attacks it." Students would be asked to identify the assumption from which this person's argument is constructed. In order to analyze the statement, students would have to ask some of the following questions: How extreme is the danger? Does the end (survival) justify the means (a nuclear war)? In everyday language, this kind of analysis is called *critical thinking*. Critical thinking allows us to separate fact from opinion and to compare theories so that we can take a position based on logic. Piaget's stage of formal operations involves just this kind of logical thinking.

Level Five: Objective Synthesis

Definition The educational objective at level five is to learn to synthesize material. This means making something new, bringing ideas together to form a new theory, going beyond what is now known, providing new insights. This is a "tall order" since it means guiding pupils beyond our own level of understanding—to help them create new ideas for themselves, and perhaps outgrow ours!

Assessment Assessment should be designed to produce new ideas, methods, or procedures. Some obvious examples might be writing an original short story, play, or poem; painting a picture; composing music. In other areas, term papers or essays might be vehicles for synthesis. Unfortunately, it is often difficult to judge whether an essay or term paper is a genuine synthesis, one that is indeed a novel or

creative approach to a topic. Creativity itself is a highly subjective matter and very difficult to measure. You might just see whether or not you find yourself saying, "Now, why didn't I think of that?" One of the major rewards of teaching comes when we realize that one of our pupils is breaking new ground, advancing our knowledge.

Level Six: Objective Evaluation

Definition Level six, the learning of value judgments, involves all the previous levels to some degree. Pupils are developing the ability to create standards of judgment, to weigh, to examine, to analyze, and most of all, to avoid hasty judgment. Evaluation requires a lengthy process of scholarly care, of minute examination.

Assessment Although it may sound circular, it is possible to evaluate evaluation—there are standards for judging the way others pass judgments. For example, we can judge the performance of an umpire at a baseball game (the fans, managers, and players do so all the time). In the same way we can judge the performance of a trial judge or a labor arbitrator or a newspaper editor. It is possible, but it is also difficult.

The basic principle of assessment at level six, then, consists of developing critical evaluation skills. Essay exams, especially at the college level, often ask for a critique of a particular theory, literary work, or historical interpretation. To do this successfully students need a comprehensive, logical framework as a basis for judgement. In writing such an essay they provide a sequence of reasons extensively spelled out so that the reader can follow a train of thought each step of the way to the conclusion. Thus, the judgment cannot remain intuitive. To say that a painting by a master such as Picasso is great because it makes you feel more deeply is not an adequate enough basis for your conclusion. In a critique you must consciously describe the standards you use for such a judgment call.

Table 13.1 summarizes the different Bloom levels and provides examples of questions that best reflect each level.

Taxonomy and Developmental Stages

Although Bloom and his associates did not directly connect their objectives to developmental and Piagetian cognitive stages, there is an implicit relationship. Bloom's levels one, two, and three–basic knowledge

TABLE 13.1   BLOOM'S TAXONOMY: KEYING QUESTIONS TO LEVELS

BLOOM LEVEL	QUESTIONS
Level One—Factual knowledge: Questions require factual recall of material.	How much is . . . Who is . . . What is . . . When was . . . How did . . .
Level Two—Comprehension: Questions require the student to think more broadly, to show more in-depth understanding, to explain using his/her own words.	Demonstrate the meaning of . . . Paraphrase, in your own words, . . . Give an example . . . How are these ideas similar to . . . Explain the meaning of (the story, a graph, etc.).
Level Three—Application: Questions ask the student to apply learning to a new situation or to develop a product.	What would happen if . . . Apply the formula to the following problem . . . Teach your friend the meaning of . . . Using your knowledge of angles, build a toothpick tower . . . Using the story as a basis, write . . .
Level Four—Analysis: Questions are designed to ask students to take the material apart and examine the pieces.	How are _____ the same, and how are they different? List the basic assumptions . . . Describe the variety of motives . . . Distinguish between theory and facts . . . Separate the major and minor themes . . .
Level Five—Synthesis: Questions attempt to get the student to go beyond our present knowledge	Describe the three major theories, and show how they may be combined . . . Write an essay proposing a new solution to the problem of . . . Write a play (paint a picture, do a musical score, construct a formula, etc.) which best illustrates a new way to understand . . .
Level Six—Evaluation: Questions are designed to require the student to evaluate ideas according to an explicit and detailed set of reasons. The system of judgment employed must be clearly explained.	Write a careful critique of _____ theory. Detail the strengths and weaknesses. Justify your conclusion. Evaluate the recent decisions by _____ , according to democratic versus expedient principles. Compare and contrast the approaches to _____ according to the following ethical principles . . . Detail the logical inconsistencies in theory X as an example of an inadequate scientific paradigm.

and facts, comprehension, and application—are all clearly within the grasp of elementary-age concrete thinkers. When we reach levels four, five, and six, we are moving toward the need for symbolic and logical thinking in Piaget's formal-operations sense. As you read the descriptions of the style of thinking required at these levels, you realize the importance of a careful instructional sequence to promote the growth of abstract thinking. We cannot assume that adolescents are automatically able to use formal operations at Bloom's level four to six without deliberate teaching that is aimed at this objective.

EDUCATIONAL OBJECTIVES AND DEVELOPMENTAL STAGES

David Hunt: Conceptual Stages

The work of **David Hunt** represents a more direct connection between educational objectives and developmental stages. Hunt has been able to specify the interaction between the conceptual level of the pupils and the expectations, learning atmospheres, and conceptual level of the teachers. We have stressed throughout this text that a developmental approach to education means that we have to look both ways, so to speak: at the pupils and their levels of development, and at the teachers. Hunt suggests that if it is important to assess the levels of the pupils, it is equally important to assess the levels of the teachers (and, as we will note later, the level of the curriculum material itself). Thus, Hunt (1974) presents a three-stage framework for educational objectives and instructional strategies.

Conceptual level proceeds through three general stages, characterized as follows:

Stage A—low conceptual level: Generally, thinking is concrete and stereotyped. There is a single "right" way to learn. Rules are fixed and unchangeable. Obedience to authority is unquestioned. Problem solving tends to be rigid. Social desirability and pleasing others are strong. Students are anxious for closure and seek highly structured learning activities.

Stage B—moderate conceptual level: Students exhibit some evidence of toleration for uncertainty and ambiguity and awareness of alternatives. There is some openness to new ideas, increased independence in thinking (inner-directedness), awareness of emotions, and increased inductive inquiry.

Stage C—high conceptual level: Students exhibit evidence of integration and synthesis in complex intellectual and interpersonal arenas. They weigh and balance alternatives and can simultaneously process their own view and that of others. Closure is temporary. Students employ successive approximation and principles in decision making, and they will not compromise those. They accept full responsibility for the consequences of their own behavior.

Young children tend to think very concretely (stage A) and need careful and explicit directions. Pupil "growth" proceeds in a developmental sequence from concrete to abstract, from simple to complex; and from being dependent on others toward self-

Young children tend to think concretely.

direction. Most important, Hunt shows that such developmental growth *does* depend on how the teacher structures the learning experiences. To facilitate the pupils' achieving increased levels of intellectual complexity, teachers need to match the learning tasks with the actual developmental functioning of the pupils. Thus, for stage A pupils, teachers need to provide high structure, explicit assignments, frequent feedback, and consistent and concrete rewards. For stage C pupils, of course, a significantly different environment, characterized by low structure, substantial freedom for pupils to develop their own assignments, less frequent feedback, and more abstract and intrinsic rewards, would be required.

Attribute-Treatment Interaction

The idea of matching teaching goals and methods to pupils' level of development is called the **attribute-** (or aptitude-) **treatment interaction (ATI)** model. The current system of thinking (a pupil's attribute) interacts with the teaching method (the treatment). The outcome of the experience, then, does not result from one or the other by itself. In a sense, what this means is that no generic teaching methods can be applied across the board. Some pupils learn more material and develop positive attitudes with one particular method while other pupils do better with a different method. In this model, teaching is not a one-way transaction nor is learning. This also explains why a teacher-proof or pupil-proof curriculum is impossible. The experiments with specified national curricula content and method in the 1960s showed the inadequacy of the single-mode approach. However, where attribute and treatment meet and match, the interaction determines the end result.

To illustrate the different effects of a learning environment and pupils' conceptual level (CL), Hunt demonstrated some aspects of variation. Figures 13.1 and 13.2 indicate that learning outcomes vary, especially for the low-CL pupils. Both figures show that stage A pupils understand learning material in significantly greater amounts when teachers employ advance organizers and the rule-example-rule sequence. The stage C pupils, in contrast, learn best under methods using low structure (examples only) and discovery. They also comprehend under high structure, but composite concept learning declines under the rule-example-rule sequence. Also, and this doesn't show in either of the figures, the stage C

FIGURE 13.1 Comprehension of academic content.

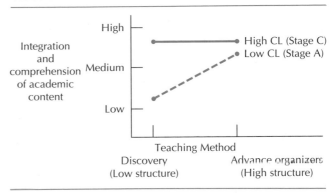

pupils are less motivated under either condition of high structure. Thus, according to Hunt, the teacher employs variable structure in order to achieve significant educational objectives. He uses the phrase *accessibility channels* to denote the meaning of developmental stages. The teacher tunes up the material and method in accordance with the different channels the pupils prefer to use.

Some students need a great deal of structure, concrete directions, immediate feedback, and so on; others don't (Hunt, 1981). Table 13.2 summarizes some of the main differences according to the stage of development of the pupil. With pupils at the concrete level of cognitive functioning (low conceptual level), a systematic sequence carefully directed by the teacher is appropriate. With pupils at a less concrete and more abstract level, a more interdependent approach is appropriate.

In fact, when ATI was first proposed by Hunt, the research base was thin (Cronbach and Snow, 1977).

FIGURE 13.2 Composite concept learning.

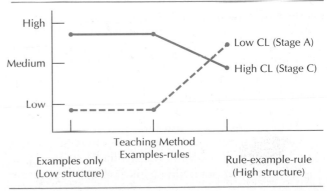

TABLE 13.2   *DIFFERENTIATION OF STRUCTURE*

FACTORS	HIGH STRUCTURE	LOW STRUCTURE
Concepts	Concrete	Abstract
Time span	Short	Long
Time on task	Multiple practice	Single practice
Advance organizers	Multiple use of organizers	Few if any advance organizers
Complexity of learning tasks	Learning tasks divided into small steps and recycled	Learning tasks clustered into "wholes"
Theory	Concretely matched with experiential examples	Generalized, including collaborative classroom research
Instructor support	Consistent and frequent	Occasional

However, more recent research, especially that of **Penelope Peterson** and her associates at the University of Wisconsin, has provided a solid basis for Hunt's earlier view. What Peterson found in a number of classroom investigations was a definite trend of interaction between pupil characteristics (such as different levels of ability, levels of anxiety, and attitude) and teaching method (Peterson, Janicki, and Swing, 1980; Levin and Peterson, 1984). She also found an interaction between pupil attributes and the kind of examination employed.

Thus, the whole approach to teaching effectiveness and educational goals needs to include the concept of ATI. A single approach to teaching is obviously not justified. For pupils of high ability, low anxiety, and positive attitudes, an approach more consistent with small-group instruction, open-ended questioning, and greater student initiative is called for. The opposite is true for those of lower ability, greater anxiety, and less positive attitudes. Such pupils much prefer a more highly structured and teacher-directed method. Peterson's research (1988) does support the general ATI model. The work, however, did not explicitly employ Hunt's conceptual-stage assessment of pupils' attributes or characteristics.

The most comprehensive review specifically of the Hunt model was conducted by **Alan Miller** (1981). He examined, as did Peterson, different teaching methods, particularly variation in levels of structure, as the "treatment." His measure of aptitude, however, was a direct assessment of the students' stage of conceptual development; thus, his summary provides

more direct support for the ATI theory. Basically, his conclusions are similar to Peterson's. Pupils who process information and experience at a more advanced conceptual level prefer greater involvement in learning, more exploratory "indirect" teaching, and participation in discussions; they can resist premature closure (or coming to a conclusion) in problem solving. However, such an open-ended or low-structured approach does not foster learning with pupils who are at a less advanced conceptual level.

At the college level the importance of varying the structure according to the cognitive-developmental level of the student was demonstrated by Widick and Simpson (1978). Concrete "dualist" college students required all the elements outlined in column 2 of Table 13.2. Students operating on a more abstract level benefited from open-ended inquiry. (More support for varying the structure according to the cognitive-development stages of the student is found in Chickering, 1981.)

More recently, David Lohman's work has supported both the Hunt position and the work of Penelope Peterson. In synthesizing all of the current work, he concludes that, "more able, older, and less anxious students may better profit from less externally structured activities such as discussion groups and guided discovery learning episodes (Lohman, 1986). These findings have been supported by the work of Mayer (1988) who found that **thinking skills** need to be closely related to specific subject matter. He also found that high-ability students do not benefit from the high-structure approach employed in the study.

The low-ability students, however, not only improved their comprehension but also could transfer the new learning strategies to other situations.

Matching or Mismatching:
The Art of Teaching

As we indicated in the opening chapter, the goals of education almost always include a reference to enhancing human development. Indeed, a developmental view clearly suggests growth as an outcome. If we view the ATI model from this perspective, then an immediate question arises. Suppose we match teaching methods to the pupils' conceptual level and the short-term outcome is improved academic achievement and positive attitudes. Does this **matching** aid the process of growth? Or does such a match keep a pupil in place, so to speak? Particularly for students who enter your class with low CL styles, wouldn't the continued use of a high-structured approach rob them of initiative? Wouldn't there also be times when even students with high CLs would need a more directive approach? In answering such questions, there are two important points to keep in mind: how CL is defined and how growth can be encouraged.

The initial preferred style In the first place CL refers to the **current preferred style of learning;** it is not a permanent classification. In Chapter 5 we indicated that Piaget described learning as a process of equilibrium, balancing the old (assimilation) and the new (accommodation). At any stage of development, we use a relatively coherent system to maintain consistency, or a steady state of equilibrium. Even when "knowledge disturbances" occur (recall the boy who was trying to reconcile his idea of church with a building that looked like a house), we try to maintain our present system. This is what we mean by a preferred method. We are used to thinking and problem solving in particular modes. These modes work best when matched with appropriate learning environments. To match the pupil's preferred style of learning, then, is another way to say, Start where the learner is. This also means starting with and accepting the pupils' current methods of problem solving— starting with how they think, not what they think. Hence, the first rule from ATI is to match, or start teaching in concert with, the pupils' level of development.

Graduated mismatching The second principle is **mismatching**—the process of shifting to a slightly more complex level of teaching in order to help the student develop. Recall that students have a potential or an intrinsic drive to learn, as Robert W. White and others have shown us. However, they will not shift quickly or suddenly to higher levels of conceptual development. Remember how long it took the boy to accommodate to the new concept of church, and that was a relatively simple "new" learning. You need to be prepared to present and review new material in a recycled manner, listening carefully to your students' questions. In this way you will understand who is "getting it" (accommodating to the new material and methods) and who needs further experience at his or her present level.

Another way to view the problem of matching and then mismatching is to recall information from Chapter 7: Kohlberg's research on modal stage plus one. In moral-dilemma discussions, leaders found that under relaxed conditions (a nonpunitive atmosphere) pupils would gradually understand and support reasoning just slightly ahead of their current preferred mode. The slightly higher level of complexity creates a kind of knowledge disturbance, or dissonance. In resolving the dissonance, the pupils end up with a more complex level of thinking; in other words, they experience developmental growth. So we can answer the first part of the earlier question: In dealing with pupils whose current conceptual levels and styles are low, the teaching strategy is to match the low level with high structure and very gradually shift. What about other students, those further along? Do we just stick with the low-structure approach? Not quite—and we'll describe why.

Two qualifications Certainly, the general rule with students who function at more complex levels would be to use less structure, more participation, more discovery, and so on. However, there are two important qualifications. First, development varies according to domain. A particular student may be an advanced thinker-reasoner in one area, yet not in another. When we discussed Piaget's stages of cognitive growth, we cited examples of adults not always thinking like adults. An advanced thinker in history or agronomy may be at a more concrete level in statistics, art, and music. Variations also exist within any subject matter. In psychology some students may quickly understand a variety of theories of personal-

SPOTLIGHT ON GIFTED DEVELOPMENT

What's the Price?

One of the continuing unanswered questions in education concerns gifted development: How far do we push and at what cost? Throughout history we have all read biographies featuring prodigious achievement, often at a very early age. Every four years the entire nation watches our Olympic athletes excel. We gasp in awe when we learn of some of their ages. We often hear in the interviews male teenage voices still in the process of maturing, and in some cases, especially in female gymnasts, see female bodies at the developmental level of junior high school. So too in other domains, we read about a teenage chess "phenom" who can match the masters or a teenage math whiz who discovers testing errors committed by a national assessment service. We then wonder about the process of development on the one hand and the process of education on the other. Are these "special" people who would have achieved no matter what, or are they ordinary people who have been "specially" educated? Once again, we face the nature-nurture question but in a slightly different form.

To discover answers, Benjamin Bloom, as he has done before in so many other areas, assembled a research team and did an intensive investigation of over a hundred subjects in a way to ensure the inclusion of enormously talented young persons from a wide variety of fields such as music, art, science, athletics, and research. All subjects had achieved national and/or international eminence prior to age thirty-five. The subjects were selected to represent outstanding performances in one of three areas: psychomotor, aesthetic, or cognitive. The researchers originally proposed a fourth area, interpersonal relations, but dropped it because of the difficulty of defining objective criteria.

The major findings indicate that a series of coordinated factors were quite similar across the domains. At the outset, as the child exhibited some unique achievements, parents provided careful and consistent encouragement. Some early chance factors also pointed the child toward a specific area—the team needed an extra swimmer, a local violin teacher was available at low cost, the child

had an unusually gifted elementary school teacher. After the initial period, chance factors faded almost completely. From then on, the secret of Olympic performance on the field, the stage, or the classroom was the same. In the words of a TV commercial, "They made it the old-fashioned way. They earned it." In fact, the case reports are all similar: long hours of practice with a carefully selected mentor. Local coaches and/or teachers were no longer involved. Some families moved to new areas to provide their child with special teachers. Others willingly purchased expensive special equipment. Although the training was a cooperative effort of the child and the mentor, often the entire family and in some cases neighborhoods were involved as positive supporting elements. At this point the third crucial element appeared, the evaluation by the mentor.

Bloom's group found that eminent performance could not be predicted up through early adolescence. The early and middle years are certainly important, but it was the later years (adolescence and early adulthood) that made the dif-

---

ity at an abstract level yet have problems understanding, say, physiological or experimental psychology. So even with so-called more advanced students, you may have to deviate from the general rule of low structure in your teaching because of systematic gaps in students' understanding of different subjects as well as different topics within one subject. When you discover such gaps, it's a sign to shift the teaching to higher structure and more direct instruction.

The second qualification has to do with pupil anxiety. Under stress, many students will lower their preferred style of solving problems. This is certainly un-

derstandable when we realize that when stress is too high, humans tend to narrow their perceptual field; that is, they screen out more and more information and experience. An extreme example is the story of a victim being quizzed by detectives immediately following an armed robbery. "All I saw was the barrel of the gun pointed at my face," he said when asked to describe the assailant. Of course, a classroom should never be quite that stressful. Yet in introducing new material and/or new learning strategies, pupils can be quite anxious. In specific cases, such as students who face excessive parental pressure for achieve-

ference. During those years the individual's life became almost totally consumed with the special activity and the relationship with the mentor. The mentors were in many cases products of a similar upbringing. This meant they evaluated harshly. They would not continue working with a person unless they were convinced that he or she really had both talent and commitment. Their standards were indeed Olympian and their work requirements Herculean. If the person did not show signs of international giftedness, he or she was dropped. Those who did show such talent were worked even harder. Such is the picture of *Developing Talent in Young People.*[a]

This study, of course, raises a number of interesting questions. First, it is clear that so intensive an approach is appropriate for only a tiny fraction of the nation's youth. In fact, Bloom's general rule was one special child in each family. Genes have an influence, but even within a single family there would be only one with world-class potential. Also, given the amount of family time and effort, there might not be sufficient "nurture" for a sec-

ond or third prodigy. Thus, it is clear this approach isn't a model for general development. Parents and educators must be careful not to generalize. These young people are by definition extremely rare. Most of us will never encounter such children. A second issue, however, is even more provocative: What happens to those who don't quite make it?

No study can answer all questions, and Bloom's group did not have a second and/or control group consisting of those who went through parallel experiences yet didn't quite measure up, or who momentarily made it, then burned out or flamed out. Thus, we can't assess the potential psychological costs of such intensive education. Basically, we can only talk to the winners, the medalists, the summas. Did they survive while others, almost as good, fell into despair and felt a major sense of time wasted, other opportunities missed, or other roads not taken? We simply can't say. We read media accounts of such fallen idols or near-misses that raise questions as to the psychological expense of intensive education. In fact, just re-

cently an international tennis association was considering the effects of tennis burnout on teenage stars. Both Tracy Austin and Andrea Jaeger were cited as examples of the negative physical consequences of intensive training during the growth years. The potential for psychological scars is at least as great; they just don't show from the outside.

The overall question, then, is not with training and/or development but with goals and objectives. The paradox is the eternal one of benefits versus costs. Any nation needs gifted humans. We need the new knowledge, the new techniques, the new performances that are unique to such special children. Until we understand the other side more fully, however, we must be careful not to promote a new fad, a shift from excessive "infant stimulation" to excessive "adolescent stretching."

[a] Bloom, B. S. (1985). *Developing talent in young people.* New York: Random House.

ment, the anxiety level may be even higher. Under such conditions it is highly appropriate to shift modes and provide more advance organizers, more explicit directions, and quicker feedback.

One final point on anxiety: Remember that during specific developmental transitions, anxiety also can be quite high. In other words, changes taking place within the pupil can be as anxiety producing as any changes you make in the teaching material and problem-solving work. In discussing Erik Erikson's work (Chapter 6), we noted particular psychological-personal milestones of development. During each of

these transition stages of personal growth, anxiety tends to be higher than usual. The most obvious example is puberty, accompanied by egocentrism, the personal fable, and the magical audience. Yet starting the first grade, leaving home, and shifting to the stage of mastery is also an important transition with its own anxieties, the "little worries" common to children. Certainly the same is true for entrance to high school and to college. Resorting to a more structured approach to teaching at such times is simply another way to start where the learner is. You will soon be able to move to a more open-ended approach, especially with secondary students, as the anxiety from the personal transition subsides and the teenager becomes accommodated more adequately to the new level of psychological maturity.

To summarize, then, the general rule of using an open-ended approach with abstract thinkers has some important qualifications: (1) There is variation across and within academic subject matter; pupils may not excel in all areas. (2) Pupils may experience high levels of anxiety when confronted with new material and/or when going through transitions in personal growth. In any of these situations, switching to higher structure in teaching will not impede pupil growth. You need not worry that you are robbing students of their chance for initiative by more adequately matching your method to a lowered ability. Instead, you are more likely to find that students experience a sense of relief. They can get back on the learning track and then resume their growth toward a more complex mode.

In an overall sense, then, the ATI model, by suggesting flexibility in teaching mode, helps you avoid two kinds of educational failure. First, you avoid the prospect of boring the students with a single "tried and true" teaching method. Second, you avoid the problem of either overmatching or undermatching. Overmatching, on the one hand, is teaching at a level well beyond the pupils' current preferred mode, such as expecting fourth-grade children to understand the symbolic meaning of Ahab and the white whale in *Moby Dick* or succumbing to the current fad of infant stimulation with flash cards for six-month-old babies. Undermatching, on the other hand, presents not "plus one" but "minus one" material to students: ideas and problems they already know and techniques that require "old" learning methods. Asking adolescents to memorize long lists of material when they should be learning to draw inferences is an example of undermatching. With either overmatching or undermatching, growth is not an outcome. Effective teaching from an ATI perspective requires a quite different approach, one that is more responsive to pupil needs and is more likely to nurture their growth and achieve the general educational goals of Bloom's taxonomy.

Mary Belenky, Blythe Clinchy, Nancy Goldberger, and Jill Tarule: Ways of Knowing

A teacher's plans to match and constructively mismatch in an ATI framework curriculum content and teaching to the needs of students should consider areas of students' development. Students' epistemology, that is, their ways of understanding and making meaning from their educational experiences, is also important to help determine the best match of instruction in the classroom.

Mary Field Belenky, Blythe McVicker Clinchy, Nancy Goldberger, and Jill Mattuck Tarule decided to use an intensive case study interview method to focus on possible differences as well as similarities in the cognitive processes and epistemologies of men and women. These researchers chose to study women's experience because the traditional research in ways of organizing thinking had most often focused on men (see, for example, William Perry's original study, 1970). Our attention has been drawn to these researchers and their study *Women's Ways of Knowing* (1986) because it helped us make sense of another aspect of intellectual development, the development of self and "voice" through connection. Using the metaphor of voice, a perspective of connection in knowing helps us understand our women students' growing ability to speak up and speak out, to be heard, and to say what they want to say. The study showed that in women's experience the sense of being involved and active in the learning process emerges as central. The data in the *Women's Ways of Knowing* study attests to the importance of connecting learning to personal experience. Blythe McVicker Clinchy, professor of psychology at Wellesley College, reported with other colleagues that the women from ages 16 to 60 from varied educational settings

> were not opposed to abstraction. They find concepts useful as ways of making meaning of their experiences. But they balk when the abstractions proceed the experiences or push them out entirely. Even the women who were extraordinarily adept at abstract reasoning preferred to start from personal experience (Clinchy et al. 1985, p. 34).

The four **Women's Ways of Knowing (WWK) researchers** were knowledgeable and well versed in the research to date on cognitive processes and intellectual development and also in the emerging work in psychology of women epitomized by people like Carol Gilligan, Nona Lyons, and Nancy Chodorow. The WWK researchers arranged for extended interviews with 135 women, a diverse sample from women in all socioeconomic levels and from a variety of educational institutions.

In their analysis, Belenky, Clinchy, Goldberger, and Tarule documented a progression of five different perspectives or stages that the women used to view reality, organize their thinking, and draw conclusions. These five epistemic perspectives are titled: silence, received knowing, subjective knowing, procedural knowing, and constructed knowing. They are ways of knowing that women have learned to cultivate and value, ways which are powerful but have been neglected by the more traditional intellectual development theories. *Voice* is used as a metaphor which applies to all aspects of women's experiences; it represents the intertwined development of a sense of voice, mind, and self.

Silence   Some individuals live in silence with "extreme denial of self and . . . dependence on external authority for direction" (p. 24). The individual who lives in silence is unaware of herself as a knower and feels subservient to authority and powerless. Silence connotes not being able to speak. Words are heard as weapons by others to divide and diminish the self. From this first perspective it is not possible for the individual to use words to express thoughts or feelings about the self. Both Mary Belenky and Nancy Goldberger are currently focusing on the characteristics of this position of silence. Belenky is founder of the Listening Partners Program, Marshfield, Vermont. This program focuses on how poor, marginalized women can be empowered to gain a public voice without abandoning the standpoint, language, and values of women engaged in mothering. Goldberger is on the faculty of psychology at the Fielding Institute. She is focusing on gender, race, class, and power; she is also investigating silence as an imposed burden—the process of "being silenced" as contrasted with a person's "choosing of silence" in specific situations, even though one had developed a public voice earlier. We discuss more of Goldberger's current work in Chapter 14 in the section on stages of racial identity.

Received knowledge   In this second perspective words now become central to knowing. Knowing comes from listening to others who are the authorities. All knowledge comes from outside the self; it is a view of the world and education that is concrete and dualistic. Everything is either right or wrong, black or white; facts are to be memorized and regurgitated. The received knower believes it is beyond one's capacity to develop or to create one's own knowledge. Individuals at this position are good followers and obedient workers. Feelings of low self-esteem and lack of originality prevail. The individual at this posi-

Recent research indicates that for most women meaningful learning of abstract concepts is enhanced if the concepts to be learned are somehow connected to their own personal experiences.

tion accumulates facts, and the words of others become one's own.

Subjective knowledge   At the third perspective a major change in knowing occurs, from power being outside the self to power coming from within the self. The source of knowing now comes from one's own personal experience. The subjective knower begins to listen to her inner voice, and as it comes alive, this individual becomes her own authority and her gut feelings are infallible. The awareness of other people's experiences rests with the right of others to have an opinion, as the experience of and focus on the self dominate. The trust in an outside authority is lost. This individual must begin to listen not only to herself, but to others as well; in time she will develop a public voice.

Procedural knowledge   The fourth perspective marks another shift in the metaphor of voice. Here the self actively listens and carefully speaks after observing and evaluating various perspectives. The voice of reason permeates through one's attitudes about authority, the world and oneself. Reason coupled with intuition and feeling predominate. Two categories evolve at this position, separate and connected knowing. The separate way of knowing functions under standard rules and conventions of rational thought, and the separate procedural knower is more concerned with principles and critical thinking procedures. In the connected way of knowing, knowledge and reason are gained through personal experience and relationships; the connected procedural knower is additionally concerned with caring, empathy, and patience.

Constructed knowledge   At the fifth perspective speaking and listening are used equally in active dialogue with others, and knowledge is constructed by persons who experience each other as equals. Here one "finds a place for reason and intuition and the expertise of others" (p. 133). The individual is aware that truth is based on the context in which it is embedded; thus one's frame of reference is important and directs one's knowledge and understanding. Constructed knowers are able to weave together reason and emotion, the objective and the subjective.

There are some similarities to Perry's earlier model, especially in the initial dualistic positions, but there are clear differences in women's experiences of "separation" and "connection," particularly as evidenced in the position of procedural knowledge. In this study women have said some important things about their learning. In traditional separate education, the student tries to look at the material through the teacher's eyes. In contrast, the data on teaching from women's experience describes the connected teacher who "receives and accepts the student's feelings toward the subject matter, looking at the subject matter and listening to it through the student's eyes and ears (Noddings, 1984, p. 177). In connected education the student is treated from the start not as a subordinate or as an object but as an "independent." Throughout the interviews from *Women's Way of Knowing* the importance of "connected education" is demonstrated. We've already described the different teaching practices that these women gave as examples which fostered connected knowing (see the classroom morale section of Chapter 12). Here we repeat the key phrases which identify the characteristics of connected education. *Connected education* describes an educational environment in which individuals value personal individual experience; nurture each other's thoughts to maturity; construct truth through consensus, not conflict; bridge private and shared experience; accord respect for each other's unique perspec-

tives; and base authority on cooperation, not subordination.

The *Women's Ways* authors suggest that connected knowing and separate knowing are gender-related, but not gender-specific. Connected knowing comes from personal experience and is grounded in the concrete and particular; the purpose of this kind of knowing is to understand. Separate knowing refers to rational, abstract thinking in which there is distance between the knower and the object; the purpose of separate knowing is to acquire knowledge and think critically. It can be argued, of course, that students need models of impeccable reasoning and that it is through imitating such models that students learn to reason. But none of the women interviewed named this sort of learning as a powerful experience in their own lives. Instead, students need models which show thinking as a human, imperfect, but attainable activity.

The dominant pedagogy in education is based on separate knowing; however, many teachers do use teaching practices that foster connected knowing. Also, some research methodologies are more attuned to connected knowing than others, for example, collaborative action research, which will be discussed further in Chapter 14. Jill Mattuck Tarule, Dean of Education at the University of Vermont, is currently focusing on collaborative learning and its relationship to connecting knowing and the characteristics of the position of "constructed knowledge."

The identification of the concepts of connected knowing enables us to examine with a new perspective teaching strategies which better match in an ATI framework the intellectual development needs of all students, and particularly women students. This kind of teaching provides for the inclusion of life experiences as well as the formal, more abstract, removed experiences which characterize much of traditional education. If as teachers we add the perspective of connected teaching to our strategies, we are addressing another dimension which may be part of all students' intellectual development. With the inclusion of connected teaching strategies, learning becomes more engaging. Blythe McVicker Clinchy is currently investigating the extent to which both men and women recognize and use their abilities for connecting knowing when this epistemological perspective is explored in interviews. See, for example, Clinchy (1989). We think that good teaching entails being able to teach in at least these two modes, the connected mode and the separate mode. The connected mode includes a number of the indirect teaching categories from Flanders, the characteristics of inquiry (Model Two), and interpersonal teaching (Model Three). The more traditional separate mode has more characteristics of direct teaching and Model One.

LESSON PLANNING: THE VEHICLE FOR EDUCATIONAL GOALS

So far in this chapter we have been stressing the need for a careful analysis of pupils' conceptual level as a basis for selecting particular modes or models of teaching. We have focused on the interaction between teaching as a process and the students' effort at drawing meaning from the teacher's strategies. There is,

Careful lesson planning involves, among other things, starting with developmentally appropriate objectives.

in addition to this ATI, another important part of teaching—namely, lesson planning. Sometimes it is best to think of planning lessons as similar to drawing a road map. The purpose of the plan is to provide you with a sequence of routes or steps to follow as you teach the material. Naturally, there is no single best way to organize a lesson or unit in a plan. Research and practice have shown, however, that some basic steps are effective. These fundamental components of a good plan are based on the work of **Madeline Hunter** (1984).

Step one: Anticipatory set   The first step is to increase the students' interest in and motivation to learn the material. It's an attempt to get the students to "lean toward" you with an orienting question. For example, in a high school unit on social studies, the teacher might say, "Today's topic will focus on the question of what the Native Americans experienced during the period of manifest destiny. Why do many Indians regard Thanksgiving as a national day of shame?" Hunter suggests a relatively brief yet somewhat provocative beginning to gain attention.

Step two: Objective and purpose   The initial rhetorical question sets the stage. The teacher now moves to tell students what the point of the unit is and why it's important. This is particularly necessary for concrete thinkers, those at low to moderate conceptual levels. Surprising as it may seem, discussions with pupils at the end of a class often reveal rather poignantly that they completely missed the point of the lesson. Presenting the objective is no guarantee of comprehension. Hunter says, however, that you will increase the probability by being quite explicit in spelling out the goals. Thus, the teacher who raised the Native American question might then explain, "The goal is to help you understand how differently a group of people in a country may interpret the meaning of a historical event. Most of us have been brought up to understand that Thanksgiving is a national holiday celebrating. . ." Hunter says you can reduce the ambiguity by describing the goals.

Step three: Input   Essentially, this is where you select and apply your specific teaching strategy. It could be a lecture (Model One), a small-group discovery (Model Two), an interpersonal discussion (Model Three), or a blend of direct and indirect methods. Teachers have often misinterpreted Hunter on this point and felt that they must use a direct model. Such is not the case. In fact, you need to decide (your best guess) which of a variety of models best suits the particular day, the material, and other available resources, including student presentations of information, filmstrips, video material, overheads, and even the blackboard. The idea is to select an input method that is keyed to the outcomes noted in step two. Thus, if your goal is to help students understand historical events from the Native Americans point of view, you would not have them memorize long lists of tribes.

Once again it may seem obvious, but Hunter did find that one of the most common errors in teaching was the failure to link input with teaching objectives.

Step four: Modeling   Think of modeling as a demonstration accompanied by verbal description of what you want the students to do. Sometimes, for example, if the students are to work in small groups, you set a small group up in a "fish bowl" for a brief demonstration. If you want students to look up Latin roots in a dictionary, you might put a dictionary entry on an overhead and talk the class through the process. The point of modeling is to ensure that the students employ the process in a manner that facilitates their understanding of the input.

Step five: Checking for understanding   Hunter makes it clear that effective planning of lessons is interactive. Thus, some time should be set aside for questions to check student understanding. Every once in a while a teacher is absolutely floored when the questions reveal how far off task a particular student is. Most students will not ask what may appear to be a "dumb" question. Your role is to maintain a class atmosphere supportive enough to encourage students who aren't sure to ask for help. You can increase the likelihood of students' feeling free to say that they do not know and to ask questions by using the strategies for connected teaching described in Chapter 12.

Step six: Guided practice   By this Hunter means that the students do the activity under your direct supervision. Guided practice precedes the last step, independent practice. Before you move to independent practice, either in class or as homework assignments, you should have the students perform some part of the task and show you their products. Suppose, for example, you are teaching a grammar unit

on the period (the punctuation mark). Have the students practice writing a paragraph and then compare their work to an overhead with correct punctuation. The idea is simply to prevent too many errors from occuring before you set them free to work on their own. It is clearly easier to correct errors early than to allow a student to do an entire assignment incorrectly. Unlearning bad habits is always more difficult than learning the correct procedure at the outset.

Step seven: Independent practice   The final step, either as seatwork or homework, occurs when students work on the material alone or in small groups without your direct supervision. This is basically a test of the first six steps. If the process has been successful, then you will see evidence in the student products that they have learned the material. Remember that the outcome of this independent practice can be keyed to any level on the taxonomy from basic knowledge to synthesis and/or evaluation. You start by keying the outcomes of independent practice to students' current level of functioning, and then gradually increase the level of complexity. Such building on success encourages and motivates students each step of the way.

The criticisms of the Hunter approach   While there is general acceptance of the Hunter approach, there is continuing controversy about some aspects of step two (objective and purpose) and step four (modeling). The problem with step two arises from a concern about how much structure is appropriate. Do all students need to be told the point of the lesson in advance? We have seen in the ATI section that such explicit identification can reduce the possibility of inquiry-discovery. Students, especially the more complex thinkers, may find that such statements of objectives at the outset reduce their motivation as well as the excitement that goes with not quite knowing what to expect. After all, how engrossing would a Sherlock Holmes mystery be if we knew in advance . . . ?

The problem with step four is similar in kind. By modeling the steps involved in the learning activity, there is the possibility of reducing some student initiative in problem solving. Remember that Lohman (1986) found that, on the one hand, the advanced thinkers in math actually learned less when taught through a concrete sequence. On the other hand, the careful stepwise sequence was helpful to the concrete thinkers. This means your modeling needs to be presented in a relativistic manner. You might say, "Many students have found this sequence helpful in solving the problem"; then present the model. Afterward, you can add, "You may decide to use all of these steps or you may use your own system." In either case, the test of effectiveness will come during the final phase of independent practice. The critical point, of course, is that a prescriptive model fits the needs of some learners but not all. For a more extensive discussion, criticism, and response to the Hunter method, see Gibboney (1987) followed by Hunter's response and Gibboney's reaction.

In Hunter's defense, we should add that at least part of the problem results from literal interpretations of her model. Her stepwise approach should never be applied every day, across the board. In her original article, she said it was a teaching decision whether to include or exclude each element. Variations were not only permitted but encouraged. The point was to examine the learning outcomes and use them as a guide for choosing an approach.

NEW EDUCATIONAL GOALS FOR ALL: TEACHING FOR HIGHER-ORDER UNDERSTANDING

Partly as a result of the discouraging findings reported by national assessments of educational progress and partly as a result of the new demands for a highly literate work force presented by a postindustrial society, there has been an upsurge of interest in teaching for critical inquiry (Ravitch and Finn, 1988). Ironically, the national tests have shown that basic skills in elementary school are improving but that comprehension and critical thinking in secondary school have not improved at all—in fact, if anything, such higher-order skills have declined. Coming at a time when the national leaders have designated educational development as a priority for the 1990s, the decline has caused major rethinking of educational goals. Thus, in the past few years, there have been multiple calls for a thinking skill curriculum. The work of Arthur Costa (see Costa, 1985; Costa and Margano, 1987) represents a very popular video-based staff development program for teachers, published by the Association for Supervision and Curriculum Development.

Costa takes the position that teachers must concentrate greater attention on the process of instruction.

Rather than focusing on standard classroom procedures, he encourages teachers to use a different vocabulary to promote critical reasoning by the students. It is pointless to continue to remind the students to think. That's too broad, too vague, and too overused. Instead, he suggests the use of careful questioning phrases such as:

Let's compare [not "look at"] these two pictures.

What do you predict [not "think"] will happen when. . . ?

How can you classify [not "group"] these materials . . . ?

What evidence do you have to support. . . ? [not "How do you know it's true that. . . . ?"]

If you return briefly to Bloom's taxonomy in this chapter, you will quickly realize that much of the current rhetoric on thinking skills can be considered as an updated version of the higher levels of objectives in the cognitive domain. Compare, for example, Costa's list above with questions of comprehension (level two), analysis (level four), synthesis (level five), and evaluation (level six).

Keeping the relationship of thinking skills and Bloom's taxonomy in mind, we turn your attention to a variety of conceptions of thinking in the seventies, eighties, and nineties. Then we focus on some current approaches to teaching for higher-level thinking.

Conceptions of Thinking in the Seventies, Eighties, and Nineties

In the seventies and eighties, researchers investigated generic teacher skills and behaviors like use of praise and wait-time (see the discussion in Chapter 12) to increase student learning. The emphasis was on student acquisition and retention of knowledge, focusing on academic achievement in a traditional sense, with a dependence on standardized achievement test scores as the measure of success in student learning. In the nineties, however, less investigation is being done in the format of process-product research on knowledge, retention, or generic teacher behaviors (like wait-time and praise), and more research is focusing on case studies of the relationship between teaching and learning in specific subjects. Two major researchers from the direct teaching "effectiveness" research suggest (see Brophy, 1992; Shulman, 1992) that the process-product research of the seventies and eighties established a good knowledge base for the case studies now being conducted. The current research has moved (1) from simplistic knowledge acquisition, simple concepts and ideas, to complex forms of understanding of theories and generalizations; (2) from studies of generic teaching and learning to indepth studies of teaching and learning in specific subject areas; and (3) from individualist models of learning to the social context in which learning takes place.

Perhaps future generations will judge that the decade of the nineties was a time when we Americans really looked carefully at the education of *all* children in our schools, not just the elite. Lauren Resnick (as quoted in Nickerson, 1988, p. 7) focused on the historic distinction between mass education and elite education as she also looked to the research of the nineties.

> "Mass education was, from its inception, concerned with inculcating routine abilities: simple computation, reading predictable texts, reciting religious or civic codes. It did not take as goals for its students the ability to interpret unfamiliar texts, create material others would want and need to read, construct convincing arguments, develop original solutions to technical or social problems" (Resnick, 1987, p. 5). What is new about the current growing interest in the teaching of higher-order cognitive skills in the

public schools, Resnick suggests, is not the inclusion of thinking, problem-solving, and reasoning in *some-one's* school curriculum but the idea that these things should be included in *everyone's* curriculum. "It is a new challenge to develop educational programs that assume that all individuals, not just an elite, can become competent thinkers" (p. 7).

Current research on teaching and learning indicates that more teachers see students as active participants in their own learning. Teachers recognize the need for more detailed knowledge of what students bring to the learning tasks in which they are engaged. In discussing what research on learning has to say about teaching, Gaea Leinhardt (1992) points to three elements which, she says, are fundamental to new approaches to the research on learning: (1) multiple forms of knowledge, (2) the role of prior knowledge, and (3) the social nature of knowledge and its acquisition. The student's job is to connect strategic action knowledge (explaining, interpreting, posing problems or solutions) with specific content knowledge of a field like history or mathematics (i.e., content topics such as the number system or eliminating slavery). Her point is that understanding depends on the learner's ability to process various types of knowledge specific to the domain or topic or subject. Leinhardt suggests that we think of prior knowledge as an issue of "access," "interconnectedness," and

Current views of learning and teaching focus on how students actively process new information based on the prior knowledge they bring to the learning task. Teachers are seen as change agents who help students actively modify their existing knowledge.

"depth." Newer research described in Jere Confrey's (1990) review of the research on student conceptions in mathematics, science, and programming shows how prior knowledge can help or hinder new learning.

In addressing the assets and limitations of prior knowledge, teachers can assist students in recognizing their own beliefs and in assessing and revising these beliefs as new learning occurs. Classroom discussion (with ground rules to counteract possible negative personal verbal attacks) can use the children's energy and creativity to pose ideas and refute misconceptions. Madeline Lampert (1986) describes classroom ground rules for a positive classroom social dialogue to promote learning using student's prior knowledge. Shared knowledge or socially constructed knowledge is as important as one's individual knowledge. This concept is built upon modern assumptions about learning: "(a) learning is an active process of knowledge construction and sense-making by the student; (b) knowledge is a cultural artifact of human beings: we produce it, share it, and transform it as individuals and as groups; and (c) knowledge is distributed among members of a group, and this distributed knowledge is greater than the knowledge possessed by any single member" (Leinhardt, 1992, p. 23). This seems basically to be an extension of the Piagetian notion of the importance of social interaction in new learning (see Chapter 5). Teachers that understand the social nature of knowledge provide time in class for talk, public reasoning, shared problem solving, and shared projects.

Approaches to Teaching Higher-Order Thinking and Understanding

Higher-order thinking can be related to Piaget's formal operational thought, Kohlberg's and Gilligan's postconventional thought, Bloom's categories of analysis, synthesis, and evaluation, and Belenky, Clinchy, Goldberger, and Tarule's concepts of connected knowing and the stages of procedural and constructed knowledge. There are a number of current approaches to fostering students' higher-level thinking and understanding. All include some balance of focus on the following components: (1) in-depth knowledge of a subject or topic (Glaser, 1984; Prawat, 1991), (2) critical thinking skills (Beyer, 1987; Perkins and Salomon, 1988), and (3) dispositions of thoughtfulness (Sizer, 1992; Perkins, Jay, and Tishman, 1992).

Although most researchers agree that these components are all needed, there is disagreement on the degree of emphasis to be given each of these three components when developing good thinkers.

Fred Newmann, director of the National Center on Effective Secondary Schools, describes the differences among in-depth skills in a subject, critical thinking skills, and intellectual dispositions. In-depth knowledge of a subject area includes knowing domain-specific skills such as solving quadratic equations in mathematics or using laboratory equipment in science or jurisprudential reasoning in social studies. Intellectual skills include the ability to identify and pose problems, interpret information and find new sources of information, offer evidence and detect bias, construct alternative solutions and generalize from data. The dispositions perspective goes beyond mastery of subject matter knowledge and skills, to a broader conception of thoughtfulness. **Dispositions of thoughtfulness** include curiosity and confidence to explore new questions, a tendency to be reflective and think things through for oneself, a willingness and flexibility to take risks to entertain alternative and original solutions to problems. (See, for example, Newmann, 1991.)

Richard Prawat (1991), chair of the Department of Counseling, Educational Psychology, and Special Education at Michigan State University, reviews four kinds of approaches or methods to teaching for higher-order thinking: (1) teach skills directly; (2) embed skills in the subject matter; (3) focus on concepts and ideas, and the skills will naturally follow; and (4) teach dispositions directly. In the first method, the *stand-alone* approach, thinking skills like comparing, ordering, classifying, and making inferences are taught separately from the subject matter. In the second method, an alternative called the *embedded* approach, thinking skills are embedded into the subject matter, and teachers focus on both the thinking skills and the subject content, trying to keep a balance between the two. In the third, more recent *immersion* approach, teachers assign the highest priority to the subject matter content of students' thoughts, and the subject matter ideas become the central factor in promoting higher-level thought. Although at this time no articulated program exists to teach *dispositions* directly, we wonder if concepts of connected teaching might enhance this fourth approach and encourage thoughtfulness in all students.

Principles and practices of good subject matter teaching that are common elements of experimental

TABLE 13.3   TEACHING FOR UNDERSTANDING AND HIGHER-ORDER APPLICATIONS

1. The curriculum is designed to equip students with knowledge, skills, values, and dispositions useful both inside and outside of school.

2. Instructional goals underscore developing student expertise within an application context and with emphasis on conceptual understanding and self-regulated use of skills.

3. The curriculum balances breadth with depth by addressing limited content but developing this content sufficiently to foster understanding.

4. The content is organized around a limited set of powerful ideas (key understandings and principles).

5. The teacher's role is not just to present information but also to scaffold and respond to students' learning.

6. The students' role is not just to absorb or copy but to actively make sense and construct meaning.

7. Activities and assignments feature authentic tasks that call for problem solving or critical thinking, not just memorization or reproduction.

8. Higher-order thinking skills are not taught as a separate skills curriculum. Instead they are developed in the process of teaching subject matter knowledge within application contexts that call for students to relate what they are learning to their lives outside of school by thinking critically or creatively about it or by using it to solve problems or make decisions.

9. The teacher creates a social environment in the classroom that could be described as a learning community where dialogue promotes understanding.

10. The teacher maintains sustained examination of a few topics rather than superficial coverage of many.

11. The lesson displays substantive coherence and continuity.

12. Students are given an appropriate amount of time to prepare responses to questions.

13. The teacher asks challenging questions and/or structures challenging tasks.

14. The teacher is a model of thoughtfulness.

15. Students offer explanations and reasons for their conclusions.

Note: Items 1 through 9 are from Brophy (1992), and items 10 through 15 are from Onosko (1992a). The items complement one another; Brophy's work derives mostly from the elementary level and Onosko's work from the secondary level. The entire issue of *Educational Leadership, 49*(7), April 1992, is entitled Beyond Effective Teaching, and describes the developing practices and goals that stretch beyond direct teaching and toward more indirect teaching strategies to foster higher-order thinking and understanding.

From Brophy, J. (1992), Probing the subtleties of subject-matter teaching. *Educational Leadership, 49*(7), 4–8; and Onosko, J. J. (1992), Exploring the thinking of thoughtful teachers. *Educational Leadership, 49*(7), 40–43.

programs designed to teach elementary and secondary school subjects for the goals of understanding, higher-order applications, and classroom thoughtfulness are summarized in Table 13.3. In writing about the elementary school level, Jere Brophy asserts that teachers will need to go beyond presenting information and modeling skills. They also will need to "structure a great deal of thoughtful discourse by using questions to stimulate students to process and reflect on the content, recognize relationships among and implications of its key ideas, think critically about it, and use it in problem-solving or decision-making applications" (Brophy, 1992, p. 6). Brophy summarizes the beginning of research from the Center for the Learning and Teaching of Elementary School Sub-

jects at the Institute for Research on Teaching at Michigan State University. This research focuses on instruction in reading, writing, mathematics, science, and social studies aimed at challenging students to engage in higher-order thinking. See Lampert (1991) for descriptions of additional programs at the elementary level.

Barak Rosenshine and Carla Meister (1992) suggest the use of instructional processes called *scaffolds* to teach cognitive strategies at the elementary level: "Scaffolds are forms of support provided by the teacher (or another student) to help students bridge the gap between their current abilities and the intended goal. Scaffolds may be tools, such as cue cards, or techniques, such as teacher modeling" (p. 26). Ro-

SPOTLIGHT ON SCAFFOLDS

How to Teach Higher-Order Cognitive Strategies

1. Present the new cognitive strategies.
   (a) Introduce the concrete prompt.
   (b) Model the skill.
   (c) Think aloud as choices are made.
2. Regulate difficulty during guided practice.
   (a) Start with simplified material and gradually increase the complexity of the task.
   (b) Complete part of the task for the student.
   (c) Provide cue cards.
   (d) Present the material in small steps.
   (e) Anticipate student errors and difficult areas.

3. Provide varying contexts for student practice.
   (a) Provide teacher-led practice.
   (b) Engage in reciprocal teaching.
   (c) Have students work in small groups.
4. Provide feedback.
   (a) Offer teacher-led feedback.
   (b) Provide checklists.
   (c) Provide models of expert work.
5. Increase student responsibility.
   (a) Diminish prompts and models.
   (b) Gradually increase complexity and difficulty of the material.
   (c) Diminish student support.

   (d) Practice putting all the steps together (consolidation).
   (e) Check for student mastery.
6. Provide independent practice.
   (a) Provide extensive practice.
   (b) Facilitate application to new examples

From B. Rosenshine and C. Meister, The use of scaffolds for teaching higher-level cognitive strategies, *Educational Leadership (1992), 49(7)*, 26. Copyright 1992 by the Association for Supervision and Curriculum Development. Reprinted by permission.

senshine and Meister claim that "although scaffolds can be applied to the teaching of all skills, they are particularly useful, and often indispensable, for teaching higher-level cognitive strategies, where many of the steps or procedures necessary to carry out these cannot be specified. Instead of providing explicit steps, one supports, or scaffolds, the students as they learn the skill" (p. 26). (See Spotlight on How to Teach Higher-Order Cognitive Strategies.)

How do secondary teachers of higher-order thinking think about their work? Joe Onosko, social studies professor and supervisor of practicing teachers in the University of New Hampshire Five-Year Teacher Preparation Program, worked on the Higher Order Thinking in the Humanities Project with Fred Newmann and colleagues. The study included numerous observations and interviews with forty-eight teachers from sixteen secondary schools across the United States. From the total sample, Onosko (1992a) compared ten social studies teachers that were identified as outstanding with ten less than outstanding teachers on the following six criteria: (1) there is sustained examination of a few topics rather than superficial coverage of many; (2) the lesson displays substantive coherence and continuity; (3) students are given an

appropriate amount of time to prepare responses to questions; (4) the teacher asks challenging questions and/or structures challenging tasks; (5) the teacher is a model of thoughtfulness; and (6) students offer explanations and reasons for their conclusions.

When these ten outstanding high school teachers were compared with their less successful colleagues, Onosko found a correlation between teachers' goals and perspectives and the climate of thoughtfulness perceived in their classrooms. Analyzing data from in-depth interviews, Onosko reported that outstanding teachers unanimously listed the development of students' thinking as a fundamental goal of their instruction. The outstanding teachers were willing to reduce content coverage to pursue the goal of understanding because they believed that stressing content coverage impedes students' thinking. They acknowledged the difficulty of getting students to higher-order thinking, yet they did not become frustrated with students. Outstanding teachers were also able to describe lengthier, more elaborate, and more precise perspectives on what thinking skills entail. For example: the student understands the relevance of data to a central theme, interprets information, determines points of view and identifies their effects, formulates

SPOTLIGHT ON
DESIGNING THOUGHTFUL UNITS

An Inquiry Approach

E. B. Wood

INTRODUCTION

This unit was developed to introduce students to the history of the Native Americans in the United States. I facilitated this unit after the students had studied Jacksonian America and the Civil War in order that they be familiar with the backdrop of both the Removal Act of 1830 and the Indian Wars of the 1870s and 1880s. The unit follows a chronological organization, but is focused solely on the experience of the Native Americans from the early 1800s to present day. The unit is broken down into seven distinct lessons, with the intention that each lesson encompasses more than one class period. The entire learning sequence can fill up two weeks of class time, depending on the depth of study. The focus of the unit is to encourage students to complete an in-depth study of the interaction of the Native and Euro-Americans through American History and to make personal judgments about the justness of the situation. In the course of the unit, students will design and evaluate alternative solutions to the persistent issue of how to accommodate inherent differences between minority and dominant cultures. By looking at the current conditions of the Cherokee Nation, students will understand the current manifestation of past governmental policies and will gain insight to the relevance of historical knowledge. . . .

LESSON FOUR

Lesson Focus: Indian Removal: A National Security Measure?

For students to begin thinking about alternative solutions to the "Indian problem" of the 1830s;

For students to understand that there are usually many factors that one must consider when developing public policy;

For students to gain an appreciation of Andrew Jackson's personal beliefs about Native Americans;

For students to understand the importance of re-assessing ideas in light of new information.

Procedure: Review lesson three in small groups. Review the previous discussion of the cultural differences leading to the Native American/Euro-American conflict over land. If possible, keep list of values and definitions on blackboard overnight.

Divide class into new small groups, creating equal numbers of *Little Tree* experts and Lockean experts in each group. Allow the groups approximately 15 minutes to discuss ways that both sets of values could co-exist mutually. Encourage groups to be creative with solutions to the land conflict by reminding them that the United States was only fifty years old at the time of the Removal and that restructuring its political or social frameworks would not be out of the question. Ask all students in the group to keep notes on ideas and possible solutions.

Give brief overview of President Andrew Jackson. Reconvene class for short lecture (approx. 10 minutes). Provide students with a biographical sketch of Andrew Jackson (remind them of what they learned in previous units), focusing on his interaction with Native Americans; give background information about the expansion of the United States and the "need" for border protection; utilize maps.

Whole-group discussion: Based upon assigned readings, small group discussions and the mini lecture, discuss the following questions:

1. According to Jackson's letter, what were the President's rea-

---

hypotheses and subjects some to criticism. The outstanding teachers, as opposed to the less outstanding teachers, identified a greater number of intellectual dispositions associated with thinking, like curiosity, confidence, a thirst for reasons, willingness to take risks.

The social studies teachers at Aragon High School, San Mateo, California, developed a successful design for teaching thoughtful units that they have used for a number of years with their students. The components of the unit plan include (1) a problem-based central question, (2) an "introductory grabber" to draw students into the content and thinking skills, (3) rich detail coming from students' in-depth exploration and research of the material, and (4) a culminating activity wherein students share their findings,

sons for removing the Native Americans?

2. Do you think this was the only reason for Jackson's actions? What other ideas influenced his policy decisions?

3. Should national security influence whether the US government honors its treaties?

4. Discuss this question in terms of "might makes right." Why was the Euro-Americans' security more important than the Native Americans' security?

Re-assessing alternative solutions: Have students return to their small groups and ask them to re-evaluate their earlier solutions in light of the problem of national security. Do your initial solutions increase or decrease national security for Euro-Americans? Should they be amended in light of the new concern of security? Can you come up with any new solutions?

Conclusion/Assignment: Conclude the lesson by sharing with students the overview of the next day's activities and assigning for homework a second reading from *The Education of Little Tree* (second excerpt, pp. 38–46).

LESSON FIVE

Lesson Focus: Indian Removal of the 1830s—The Best Option?

For students to gain an appreciation of the power that the United States' federal government had over the Native Americans in the 1830s;

For students to understand why many opposed the removal of the Native Americans;

For students to create and assess alternatives to the removal of the Native Americans beyond the Mississippi.

Procedure: Review earlier lessons. Prior to class, write basic provisions of the Indian Removal Act of 1830 on the blackboard. Once class assembles, open discussion and ask students for their "expert" opinions on whether the legislation was the best way for the U.S. government to "solve" the conflicts between Native Americans and Euro-Americans.

Small-groups brainstorm alternatives. Allow small groups to reconvene for 5–10 minutes to review their proposed solutions from Lesson Three. Ask them to decide on the best alternative to the Removal Act. If they agree that the Act was actually the best solution, ask them to come up with a defense.

Redirect attention to the central blackboard and ask each group to present their solution; record proposals on the board. Through class discussion, record support and objections on the board for each solution.

Assessment/Culminating Activity: Give students time to work individually on their final assignment, a letter to President Jackson either supporting or rejecting the 1830 legislation. If the student decides to support the Act, s/he must give reasons why s/he rejected the other options; if s/he rejects the Act, s/he must explain why s/he supports an alternative proposal.

Conclusion/Assignment: Conclude the lesson by discussing the length and scope of the final paper (minimum of a 5-paragraph essay, in a formal-letter format) and setting the due date (2–3 days later). Homework for the next day will be a reading on the attempted flight of the Nez Perce and Chief Joseph.

The introduction and Lessons Four and Five are excerpted from the entire lesson plan in E. B. Wood (1992), The treatment of Native Americans: Could the U.S. have done better? *Horizons, 14*(1), 42–50.

---

debate ideas, exhibit their accomplished learnings, and demonstrate their understandings focused about the central question (see description in Onosko, 1992b). Elizabeth Wood (1992), a student teaching intern, used this plan to design and teach a unit titled "The Treatment of Native Americans: Could the U.S. Have Done Better?" In the Spotlight On Designing Thoughtful Units: An Inquiry Approach, we include her unit plan introduction and two of the seven lesson plans for the unit (4 and 5) as an example of an inquiry approach to designing thoughtful units aimed at developing students' higher-levels of cognitive understanding.

One of the questions some teachers and administrators ask about the extensive focus on an inquiry approach to learning is: How do we measure the development of understanding or the ability to perform complex cognitive tasks that require the active management of different types of knowledge? Some researchers claim that the difficulty of assessment is a barrier to the more prevalent use of indirect teaching techniques and inquiry approaches to teaching and learning (Onosko, 1991). However, we think that the beginning emphasis on designing better measures for assessment of learning beyond standardized achievement tests holds hope for the future. Recently, an entire issue of *Educational Leadership* (49 (8), May 1992) focused on using performance assessment. Topics covered included what research tells us about good assessment, what we've learned about assessing hands-on science, how to create tests worth taking, what the differences are between authentic and performance assessments, how to evaluate problem solving in mathematics, and how to use portfolios for assessment in writing, literacy, mathematics, and computing.

You will realize that there is a substantial overlap with the higher levels of Piaget's stages of formal reasoning (Chapter 5). In a sense, the new emphasis on thinking represents a major opportunity to reintroduce cognitive-developmental goals into the school curriculum, particularly at the junior high and high school levels.

Not only is there an obvious theoretical linkage to Bloom, Piaget, and Vygotsky, and the WWK researchers, but also to the instructional strategies in the work

on attribute-treatment interaction. We had shown that older, able, nonanxious learners benefit from the inductive, low-structured approach. For the process to succeed, however, the teacher needs to understand that ATI means how he or she must consider the learning stage of the pupil and the particular lesson goal before launching an all-out drive for critical thinking. For example, in teaching for higher-order thinking skills in mathematics, students whom we would term concrete thinkers achieved better under conditions that provided careful step-by-step modeling. The directions were clear and to the point. Ambiguity was deliberately reduced. However, such concrete teaching actually impaired the performance of students who were at the abstract, self-directed stage. This second group of students whose inner direction was high, learned better with open-ended inductive and discovery-type questions (Lohman, 1986). Thus, the problem of any single approach to teaching, which ignores the developmental characteristics of learners, carries the danger of helping some and harming others. The warning, then, to the new calls for teaching for higher-order cognitive skills and understanding (from kindergarten to graduate school) is that teachers need to vary the questioning method and then gradually mismatch.

The success of the lesson will be determined by the amount of structure and the development of the questions asked.

SUMMARY

Objectives remain a topic of interest to educational psychologists. The spoof *The Saber-Tooth Curriculum* continues the debate about general education versus skill-based education that has been with us for centuries. Focusing on Bloom's taxonomy, we attempted to show how this classification system could be most useful in the selection of educational goals at different levels.

Hunt's scheme illustrates the different levels and modes of thinking that school students typically employ. Through his framework of ATI, Hunt tries to bridge the gap between teaching strategies you may use and the preferred learning strategies (CL stages) that the pupils employ. By attributes Hunt means the characteristic learning style of the pupil. By treatment he means the instructional method. Whether learning really takes place will depend on the interaction be-

tween the two. He further specifies that such interaction can follow a mode of matching (a strategy that fits the learner's current mode) followed by graduated mismatching (teaching at a level just beyond the current mode). There are some important qualifications, however, for using a highly structured strategy, even for students who generally function at higher conceptual levels.

Besides paying attention to the interaction between teaching style and student modes of learning, teachers must learn how to effectively organize their material through lesson planning. Hunter has suggested a system for lesson planning that can and should be keyed to learning outcomes. By following the steps she outlines, teachers can reduce the likelihood that students will misunderstand either the point of the unit or the learning activities expected of them. By preventing students from going down the wrong road, teachers can thus increase the amount of academic or on-task learning time.

Belenky, Clinchy, Goldberger, and Tarule's study has added information about the ways in which women understand and make meaning from their educational experiences. Particularly important at the procedural position are two modes of learning, connected and separate. A teacher's plans to match and constructively mismatch instruction to all students needs should consider these five positions, or ways of knowing. When teaching for higher-order thinking and understanding, teachers can use approaches which include in-depth knowledge in the subject, critical thinking skills, and dispositions of thoughtfulness.

KEY TERMS AND NAMES

David Hunt
   attribute-treatment interaction (ATI)
   conceptual level
Madeline Hunter
matching and mismatching
dispositions of thoughtfulness

Alan Miller
   teaching thinking skills
Penelope Peterson
preferred style of learning
saber-tooth curriculum
Women's Ways of Knowing researchers

THEORY INTO PRACTICE: A DETECTIVE APPROACH TO LESSON PLANNING

Since we have outlined the Hunter method in some detail, we will present an example of the inquiry approach to lesson planning. In this method, sometimes called the *detective approach*, you do not reveal the main point of the lesson content at the outset. You provide information in the form of a scenario of a problem to solve, but you do not solve the problem. Instead, your role is to continue to ask clarifying questions to promote greater inquiry.

Step one—explain your own role For example, say to the class, "I'm going to present a problem along with a series of facts. Your task will be to figure out which of the variety of explanations seems most logical and reasonable.

"Even though I have a good idea as to what the most logical answer might be, I'm not going to reveal it. I will give you the pieces of the puzzle, but you'll need to put them together yourselves."

Step two—the discrepant event: The lost colony Present the facts of a puzzling situation, for example, the famous case of North Carolina's lost colony. The facts are these:

1. There had been two previous attempts to establish a colony on Roanoke Island. In 1585, a group of a hundred, led by Ralph Lane, had stayed for one year. Discouraged by a lack of food and deteriorating relations with the local Native Americans, Lane and his group attacked and killed the local chief and others before evacuating the colony and returning to England. Shortly afterward, another English expedition landed. A small party of men was left to hold the island until a larger number of colonists could be brought over.

2. In 1587, the second group of over a hundred colonists arrived, but found no trace of the small group. The colonists, however, worked hard to build their homes in the new world while warding off attacks from the Native Americans. Also, the colonists themselves mistakenly attacked a group of friendly Native Americans. The situation remained tense.

3. Food was scarce. After a few weeks, the colonists implored Governor White to return to England for supplies. He left in August 1587.

4. As a result of the activities of the Spanish Armada (1588), it was three years before White returned. There was no trace of the colony except for the word "CROATOAN" carved in a tree. By a prearrangement, a cross was to have been carved as a distress sign. No cross was carved. The fort, in fact, was relatively intact.

5. A search of nearby Croatoan Island a few years later revealed no sign that the colonists had reached the island or indeed that they had even attempted to head in that direction. In fact, no trace was found at all. There was very little food on the island.

Step three—review and verify the basic information
Make sure the students understand the facts. Often, the best way to do this is to ask the students to state the facts and the problem in their own words, that is, check for understanding. This is similar to questioning at Bloom's levels one and two.

Step four—explore and identify relevant pieces of information   In this case, there are a number of excellent accounts, including some of the original documents. (See the reference to Parramore and Parramore, at the conclusion of this practice unit.)

1. There was no evidence of a massacre.

2. The distress sign was not used.

3. There had been Indian attacks and counterattacks prior to Governor White's return to England.

4. The colonists' fort was well built.

5. There was a history of tribal warfare among different groups of nearby Native Americans.

6. Food was scarce on Croatoan Island.

7. A Spanish ship in 1588 reported no sign of the colonists in the area.

8. There was no evidence of severe hurricanes in the area.

9. There were rumors later on of a small number of English living at the other end of Pamlico Sound, yet this could not be confirmed.

Step five—trial explanations   Be sure not to move too quickly to the theorizing. Remember that students may be uncomfortable with such an open-ended problem and seek to push for one right answer quickly. Your role here is crucial. You'll need to prevent early closure by paraphrasing, refocusing, and challenging. "What's the evidence for that position?" "How does the view that the colonists were all killed compare with the view that they moved to another part of the country and intermarried?" Or, "What about the possibility that another European power, Spain, attacked the colony and decided to keep the attack secret?" "Could the colonists have tried to return to England?" Or, "If the colonists settled with an Indian tribe, why was there no record or signs, or could they have been killed along with their friendly Native Americans by a hostile tribe?"

This is sometimes called synthesizing at Bloom's level five, or putting the facts together for the most logical and defensible explanations.

Step six—temporary closure   After a thorough discussion of the different theories, you move to what appears to be the best solution. One way of helping students understand the temporary nature of the conclusion, for example, what a successive approximation means, is to evaluate the competing theories, marshal the evidence, and conclude with what appears to be the best enlightened guess.

You end, however, by noting, "What new evidence which could come to light in the future might cause us to change our best theory today?"

An archaeological dig in shallow water reveals the remains of colonists and Indians, canoes and rafts, all apparently drowned, caught by a rogue wave.

Some Spanish records unearthed near St. Augustine in Florida indicate the intention to drive the British out of North Carolina.

A scuba diver fifty miles down the coast finds artifacts of a colony buried in shallow water, and evidence of a plague.

A stone is uncovered in Chowan County with the name "Virginia Dare" and the inscription "Gone to Heaven 1591." She was the first child born in the colony.

In this manner, you will help the students to begin to think like historians, to make logical interpretations after examining all sides of the issue, and to reach a conclusion while remaining open to further evidence.

Finally, of course, the goal is to turn student inquiry away from you as the teacher with the right answer to you as a person who models a process approach for promoting critical inquiry.

For a more detailed account of the lost colony, including examples of the actual reports and maps of the area see T. Parramore and B. Parramore (1984), *Looking for the "Lost Colony"* (Raleigh, N.C.: Tanglewood Press). For copies write to Tanglewood Press, 5012 Tanglewood Drive, Raleigh, NC 27612. This is an excellent example of how information can be structured to promote inquiry and concept attainment through discovery.

An additional example can be found in M. Weil and B. Joyce (1978), *Information Processing Models of Teaching* (Englewood Cliffs, N.J.: Prentice-Hall), pp. 156–173. It contains an actual classroom transcript of students' trying to solve the puzzle of a now-deserted island's culture. The elements are in a suggested sequence that is to be employed flexibly. Quite unfortunately, some school districts have adopted the Hunter model and rigorously enforced its use: if even a single step is skipped, the teacher is marked down. It is important to recall that Hunter has called for a flexible interpretation.

Our view is that learning outcomes and educational objectives can be achieved through the use of a modifiable sequence of lesson-planning steps. Since the overall goal is to increase the student's independence as a learner, lesson planning is a means of achieving the goal of helping students learn to think for themselves. Such planning, then, helps to liberate pupils rather than feeding their dependence.

REFERENCES

Belenky, M. F., Clinchy, B. M., Goldberger, N., and Tarule, J. (1986). *Women's ways of knowing: The development of self, voice, and mind*. New York: Basic Books.

Beyer, B. K. (1987). *Practical strategies for the teaching of thinking*. Boston: Allyn & Bacon.

Bloom, B. (Ed.) (1956). *Taxonomy of educational objectives, Handbook 1: Cognitive domain*. New York: McKay.

Brophy, J. (1992). Probing the subtleties of subject-matter teaching. *Educational Leadership, 49*(7), 4–8.

Chickering, A. W. (Ed.). (1981). *The modern American college*. San Francisco: Jossey Bass.

Clinchy, B. M. (1989). The development of thoughtfulness in college women: Integrating reason and care. *American Behavioral Scientist, 32*(6), 647–657.

Clinchy, B. M., et al. (1985). Connected education for women. *Journal of Education, 167*(3), 28–45.

Confrey, J. (1990). A review of the research on student conceptions in mathematics, science, and programming. In C. Cazden (Ed.), *Review of Research in Education, 16*, 3–56. Washington: American Educational Research Association.

Costa, A. L. (1985). Toward a model of human intellectual functioning. In A. L. Costa (Ed.), *Developing minds: A resource for teaching thinking*. Alexandria, Va.: Association for Supervision and Curriculum Development.

Costa, A. L., and Margano, R. (1987). Teaching the language of thinking. *Educational Leadership, 45*(2), 29–33.

Cronbach, L., and Snow, R. (1977). *Aptitudes and instructional methods*. New York: Irvington Press.

Cross, W. E., Jr. (1991). *Shades of black: Diversity in African-American identity*. Philadelphia: Temple University Press.

Gardner, H. (1985). *Art, mind and brain: A cognitive approach to creativity*. New York: Basic Books.

Gibboney, R. A. (1987). A critique of Madeline Hunter's teaching model from Dewey's perspective. *Educational Leadership, 44*(5), followed by Hunter's response, 51–53, and Gibboney's answer, 54–55.

Glaser, R. (1984). The role of knowledge. *American Psychologist, 38*, 93–104.

Hunt, D. E. (1974). *Matching models in education*. Toronto: Ontario Institute for Studies in Education.

Hunt, D. E. (1981). Teachers' adaptation: Reading and flexing to students. In B. Joyce, C. Brown, and L. Peck (Eds.), *Flexibility in teaching* (pp. 59–71). New York: Longman.

Hunter, M. (1984). Knowing, teaching and supervising. In P. L. Hosford (Ed.), *Using what we know about teaching* (p. 175). Alexandria, Va.: Association for Supervision and Curriculum Development.

Lampert, M. (1991). Looking at restructuring from within a restructured role. *Phi Delta Kappan, 72*(9), 670–674.

Lampert, M. (1986). Knowing, doing, and teaching multiplication. *Cognition and Instruction, 3*(4), 303–342.

Leinhardt, G. (1992). What research on learning tells us about teaching. *Educational Leadership, 49*(7), 20–25.

Levin, J., and Peterson, P. (1984). Classroom aptitude by treatment interactions: An alternate analysis strategy. *Educational Psychologist, 19*(1), 43–47.

Lohman, D. F. (1986). Predicting mathematic effects in the teaching of higher-order thinking skills. *Educational Psychologist, 21*(3), 191–208.

Lyons, N. (1988). Two perspectives: On self-relationship and morality. *Harvard Educational Review, 3*(2), 125–145.

Mayer, R. E. (1988). Teaching for thinking: Research on the teachability of thinking skills. Paper presented at American Psychological Association Convention, Atlanta, Georgia.

Miller, A. (1981). Conceptual matching models and interactional research in education. *Review of Educational Research, 51*(1), 33–85.

Newmann, F. M. (1991). Promoting higher order thinking in social studies: Overview of a study of sixteen high school departments. *Theory and Research in Social Education, 19*(4), 323–339.

Nickerson, R. L. (1988). On improving thinking through instruction. In E. Z. Rothkopf (Ed.), *Review of research in education*. Washington: American Educational Research Association.

Noddings, N. (1984). *Caring: A feminine approach to ethics and moral education*. Berkeley, Calif.: University of California Press.

Onosko, J. (1991). Barriers to the promotion of higher-order thinking. *Theory and Research in Social Education, 19*(4), 341–366.

Onosko, J. (1992a). Exploring the thinking of thoughtful teachers. *Educational Leadership, 49*(7), 40–43.

Onosko, J. (1992b). An approach to designing thoughtful units. *The Social Studies, 83* (5), 193–196.

Peddiwell, J. A. (1939). *The saber-tooth curriculum*. New York: McGraw-Hill.

Perkins, D. N., and Salomon, G. (1988). Teaching for transfer. *Educational Leadership, 46*(1), 22–32.

Perkins, D., Jay, E., and Tishman, S. (in press). Beyond abilities: A dispositional theory of thinking. *The Merrill-Palmer Quarterly*.

Perry, W. (1970). *Forms of intellectual and ethical development in the college years*. New York: Holt, Rinehart and Winston.

Peterson, P. (1988). Selecting students and services for compensatory education: Lessons from aptitude-treatment interaction research. *Educational Psychologist, 23*(4), 313–352.

Peterson, P., Janicki, T., and Swing, S. (1980). Aptitude-treatment interaction effects of three social studies teaching approaches. *American Educational Research Journal, 17*(3), 339–360.

Prawat, R. S. (1991). The value of ideas: The immersion approach to the development of thinking. *Educational Researcher, 20*(2), 3–10, 30.

Ravitch, D., and Finn, C. (1988). *What do our 17 year olds know?* New York: Harper & Row.

Resnick, L. (1987). *Education and learning to think*. Washington: National Academy Press.

Rosenshine, B., and Meister, C. (1992). The use of scaffolds for teaching higher-level cognitive strategies. *Educational Leadership, 49*(7), 26–33.

Shulman, L. (1992). In R. Brandt, On research teaching: A conversation with Lee Shulman. *Educational Leadership, 49*(7), 14–19.

Sizer, T. (1992). *Horace's school: Redesigning the American high school*. Boston: Houghton Mifflin Co.

Tyler, R. (1933). Permanence of learning. *Journal of higher Education, 4*, 203–204.

Widick, C., and Simpson, D. (1978). Developmental concepts in college instruction. In C. Parker (Ed.), *Encouraging development in college students*. Minneapolis: University of Minnesota Press.

Wood, E. B. (1992). The treatment of Native Americans: Could the U.S. have done better? *Horizons, 14*(1), 42–50. Available from The New Hampshire Council for the Social Studies, P.O. Box 475, Concord, NH, 03302.

14

TEACHING: THE PERSONAL DIMENSION

Thus far in our discussion of teaching effectiveness, we have focused on teaching from the standpoint of strategies, objectives, student characteristics, and planning. We now shift to the teacher as a person. How do you as an individual understand yourself in the teaching role? That is the basic question—a quite broad one, encompassing your attitudes toward yourself, the subject matter you are teaching, and finally your students. These three dimensions of knowing yourself make up the core material in this chapter. Without question, the person of the teacher exerts a telling influence on the classroom. You set the limits, you establish the tone, you model acceptable behavior, you make the rules, you translate the material, you organize the schedules—in short, you orchestrate the class.

How you think and feel about teaching, the material, and the pupils set an atmosphere or climate. Since your attitudes and perceptions do exert considerable influence, even though it may be subtle, it is important to examine them. The early Greek philosophers knew the significance of self-knowledge. To know oneself as a teacher, then, represents a key sensitivity and necessary awareness.

THE TEACHER AS A PERSON: THE ELUSIVE QUESTION

One of the most elusive questions in education is what human qualities make an effective teacher. One long-standing myth is that teachers should manifest all the noble virtues and have no human frailties. The problem is that no human can possibly live up to the myth. Even worse, teachers soon realize the impossibility of such a goal but have to keep busy preventing other people from finding out. A more realistic perception of the teacher would dispense with both the myth of human virtues (all teachers love all children all of the time) and the assumption that teachers are not responsible for the failure of children to learn.

What Is Teaching Really Like?

If done well, teaching is really hard, and it can't be done single-handedly. Good teachers consistently reflect on their practice, study their impact on students, and reevaluate their goals and methods, as they try to improve their expertise and their interactions with parents and co-workers, broaden their knowledge

SPOTLIGHT ON TEACHING

Be Everything at Once

JOB OPENING

Looking for a SELF-starting, SELF-propelled, SELF-confident, SELF-supporting, SELF-sufficient, SELF-promoting, SELF-cleaning, SELF-less individual.

MINIMUM wage guaranteed. Hours: 7:30 A.M.–4:00 P.M., plus evenings and weekends.

Average 60 stimulating hours per week—no over-time pay. Summers off (unless you have a mortgage or need a degree.)

Must be able to work independently in a chaotic, cooperative/competitive environment.

Applicant must have skills and knowledge in the following areas:

Diplomacy	Crowd control	Social work
Risk taking	Family therapy	Systems management
Communications	Time management	Motivational techniques
AV operation and repair	First aid	Bulletin board design
Community building	Interior decorating	Clerical procedures
Cooking	Plumbing	Administration
Aerobics	Legal affairs	Acrobatics
Acting	Pest control	Accounting
Carpentry	Current affairs	Psychology
Geography	Computer literacy	Writing
History	Math (new and old)	Foreign languages
Science	Literature	Art appreciation
Health	Music	Behavioral management

Some light housekeeping required. Sense of humor, compassion, and caring mandatory. Diplomatic, paramedic, and military experience helpful.

Prior seminars in stress reduction useful. Flexibility and courage a must! Interested applicants should apply to:

Your Local Public School

From Frances Morse, Nancy Frane, and Esther Kattef, teachers at Edward Devotion School, Brookline, Mass., who compiled these ideas from a faculty meeting where sixty staff members discussed the topic "Teaching as a Profession." Previously published in the *Boston Globe* (1991) and in *The Teachers' Network News* (Cambridge: Harvard Graduate School of Education, 1990).

base, meet students' individual needs, and examine their own assumptions about children, families, and education. (See Spotlight on Teaching: Be Everything at Once.)

What teachers need to do to become better teachers can be physically, intellectually, and emotionally exhausting. In order to continue this rigorous work, teachers need opportunities to solve problems collaboratively with colleagues, share frustrations and satisfactions, consult with other resources, engage in peer supervision, and take a day occasionally to observe in other schools.

A number of popular accounts have presented both the humorous and the tragic aspects of what it is really like to teach. Bel Kaufman's *Up the Down Staircase* (1964), Jonathan Kozol's *Death at an Early Age* (1967), Kevin Ryan's *Don't Smile 'til Christmas* (1970), and *Biting the Apple* (Ryan et al, 1979) are first-person accounts that reveal the disparity between the myth and the reality of school, depicting harried teachers trying to live up to some idealized version of patience, love, and total responsiveness, all of the time, every day. Sometimes teachers are like over-permissive parents who try to fulfill the perfect

The teacher: A model of perfection or a human being?

The Hidden Agenda

One of the most important—and discouraging—findings from recent research is the extent to which teachers' true feelings about children (as opposed to their idealized version) affect their ability to be effective educators.

We need to realize that our attitudes are not always clearly known to us. Because we develop our attitudes slowly over a long period of time, we are often not conscious of what they are or of how our attitudes and expectations influence our behavior. This is why we can say one thing and do another. We may pay lip service to one set of goals, yet a careful examination of how we act may reveal a completely different set. This discrepancy has been called the **hidden agenda** or the implicit curriculum of teaching.

The hidden agenda has special significance for the teacher. We have to be honest with ourselves in determining how much we act without consciousness. Our own attitudes toward learning will determine the conditions we create for learning in the classroom. We may not be aware of our own attitudes, but as teachers we have an obligation to become more fully aware because of how powerfully these attitudes affect what we convey to students. It has been shown that adults are poor at identifying the non-verbal messages they convey, and so you must have someone else help you identify the assumptions you may be transmitting.

For example, if we feel that learning requires that there be no ambiguity, that the "right" answers be presented, and that the pupils know exactly what to say, you can imagine what sort of classroom environment we would provide. Our attitude would affect the way the desks would be arranged, the choice of books and readings we would use, and the way we would manage the discussion time. And this environment would have a very definite influence on the pupils' learning "set." In other words, we affect the attitudes the pupils themselves develop toward learning. There is truth to the old saying "Actions speak louder than words"; our attitudes, motives, and perceptions influence the way we act, and they are transmitted to our pupils through our actions, thereby affecting their attitudinal development.

The Medium and the Message

Marshall McLuhan (1964) has suggested one of the ways our attitudes influence our communications.

mother or father ideal by withholding all genuine feelings ("Don't smile 'til Christmas!") and finally "boil over," screaming out and hitting their children. Teachers are no better than parents at holding in their genuine feelings. Some incident inevitably opens the floodgate, and all the pent-up anger and personal disappointment break loose. The class learns just what it had suspected all along and may, in fact, have been testing: The teacher was putting on an act of always being "nice."

Unfortunately, the teacher usually feels guilty about having lost control and therefore never realizes the true nature of the problem: It is the impossibility of living up to the myth that sets the entire process in motion. Instead of developing more realistic perceptions of teaching and learning, teachers who have tried and failed often adopt a set of attitudes that justify and rationalize their failures.

"Oh, my teacher and I communicate, all right . . . she looks at me in a certain way and I understand what I'd better do!"

McLuhan's famous phrase, "the medium is the message," expresses the idea that the verbal content of a message is interpreted, or given its true meaning, by the way it is delivered.

Our view is less extreme: Content is important, yet we do wish to emphasize the importance of the way messages are transmitted. We have all had the experience of being put down by someone. It isn't so much what that other person says but the *way* it is said (the medium). The real message lies in the person's tone, inflection, facial expression, demeanor. It is the nonverbal visual and auditory cues that deliver the real message. A poor attitude in the classroom is reflected in a bad medium, which in turn creates an atmosphere in which learning and growth cannot take place.

Teachers' attitudes can be grouped into three related categories: attitudes toward teaching and learning, attitudes toward pupils, and attitudes toward self.

ATTITUDES TOWARD TEACHING AND LEARNING

We have often mentioned that the way teachers perceive teaching and learning is crucial. Is "knowledge" a finite list of facts for students to memorize? Do we tend to encourage "correct answers" and focus on outcome, or do we consider the process of learning important? Do we consider teaching to be more like training, so that we "tell" pupils what to do? There are widely divergent assumptions about teaching and learning, and our own attitudes and the way we actually behave in class are molded by those assumptions.

If we had to single out one major attitude that pervades schools, it would be the cherished belief that knowledge equals truth. Teachers and pupils tend to believe that there is an answer for every question, that the truth is known, and that the teacher's voice is like the voice of God. In Chapter 1 we discussed classroom trivia, a form of rapid-fire question-and-answer interaction. Obviously, this kind of teaching reinforces the concept of knowledge as truth and puts the teacher in charge of deciding whether the pupil is "right." The teacher is the center of the classroom, the decision maker. "That's absolutely correct" means a bull's-eye. "That's almost right" means a near-miss. A scowl ("teachers' dirty looks") means the student was completely and absolutely wrong.

This view of knowledge as truth also has unfortunate consequences from a developmental standpoint. During elementary school, children move into Jean Piaget's stage of concrete operations (see Chapter 5) and are extremely literal-minded. They also, at this age, tend to divide the world into two camps, the "good guys" and the "bad guys" (see Chapter 7). In other words, children already have a built-in personal and cognitive bias in favor of "truth." If we then consider the special influence of initial learning experiences—recall how strongly we are affected the first time we experience something (see Chapter 4)—we begin to realize how easy it is for the pupils to accept the notion that there is only one answer. The main problem for teachers is the temptation to exploit this situation. It's very easy for them to become the fountainhead of all knowledge, the expert who knows the truth and then decides how close or far away the pupils' answers come. In fact, pupils actually encourage such behavior by the teacher. And teachers may enjoy their presumed omniscience.

In this way the teacher's authority can easily become authoritarian. The confusion of authority and authoritarianism is perhaps the basic dilemma teachers face. This is partly our own fault, especially if we are guilty of confirming the pupils' view of knowledge as fixed and unchanging. Many poignant exam-

The teacher should avoid the "knowledge as truth" syndrome and should discourage black-and-white thinking.

ples come to mind. Think of the number of times students of all ages ask questions like "What are you going to cover on the next exam?" "How much will this count toward the final grade?" Do we have to read all the assigned pages?" If you listen closely, you will hear exactly what such students have learned: To please the teacher, you only have to mouth the "right answer."

These attitudes have been learned for the most part in school. Don't blame the students if they are expert apple polishers. That is the behavior that has received the most positive reinforcement throughout their school life.

Conceptual Levels of Teachers

We pointed out in Chapter 13 that how a student understands knowledge is related to his or her conceptual level. The research and theory of David Hunt detailed how pupils at lower levels of conceptual development would prefer concrete to abstract concepts, high rather than low structure, immediate and concrete rather than delayed and intrinsic feedback and rewards. We discussed this as the ATI approach.

Now if that was true for students as persons, what are the implications for teachers as persons and their attitudes toward learning? David Hunt has examined just that. He has applied his research method to teachers themselves. Through the use of a test that assesses an individual's conceptual level (CL), he has found that teachers, like students, also have different conceptual systems in regard to teaching and learning. We've asked you to look and listen carefully to your students in order to understand how they understand the process. Hunt's work also suggests that with regard to yourself you look and listen just as carefully.

Hunt's research has indicated that teacher attitudes toward teaching and learning can be clustered into one of three stages. Joyce, Brown, and Peck (1981) provide an extended discussion and detailed examples of Hunt's research. Table 14.1 outlines the three stages.

As an example, a study examined the natural, uncoached teaching style of student teachers according to their stage of development on conceptual level. Using the Flanders index of direct versus indirect teaching modes, researchers found a significant difference between the high-CL and low-CL student

TABLE 14.1   TEACHER ATTITUDES TOWARD LEARNING AND TEACHING
(Based on Hunt's Conceptual Level Model)

STAGE A

Shows strong evidence of concrete thinking
Sees knowledge as fixed
Employs a single "tried and true" method
Exhibits compliance as a learner and expects the same from pupils
Is low on self-direction and initiative; needs detailed instructions
Doesn't distinguish between theory and facts
Relies almost exclusively on advance organizers
Believes teaching is "filling the students up" with facts
Stays at Bloom's level one and two regardless of student level
Enjoys highly structured activities for self and for pupils
Is very uncomfortable with ambiguous assignments
Does not question authority
Follows a curriculum guide as if it were "carved in stone"
Verbalizes feelings at a limited level; has difficulty recognizing feelings in pupils
Is reluctant to talk about own inadequacies; blames pupils exclusively

STAGE B

Shows growing awareness of difference between concrete versus abstract thinking
Separates facts, opinions, and theories about teaching and learning
Employs some different teaching models in accord with student differences
Gives evidence of teaching for generalization as well as skills
Shows some evidence of systematic "matching and mismatching"; can vary structure
Is open to innovations and can make some appropriate adaptations
Shows sensitivity to pupils' emotional needs
Enjoys some level of autonomy and self-directed learning as a goal for self and for the pupils
Employs Bloom's levels one through four when appropriate
Uses evaluations that are appropriate to assignments

STAGE C

Understands knowledge as a process of successive approximations
Recognizes that today's theories may be tomorrow's anachronisms
Shows evidence of originality in adapting innovations to the classroom
Is comfortable in applying all appropriate teaching models
Is most articulate in analyzing his or her own teaching in both content and feeling
Has high tolerance for ambiguity and frustration; can stay on task in spite of major distractions
Does not automatically comply with directions—asks examiner's reasons
Fosters an intensive questioning approach with students
Can use all six of Bloom's levels when appropriate
Responds appropriately to the emotional needs of all pupils
Can "match and mismatch" with expert flexibility
Exhibits careful evaluations based on objective criteria according to level of assignment

teachers, even though no difference showed up in grade-point achievement.

As Table 14.2 shows, the high-CL student teachers used all seven teacher strategies with a ratio of direct to indirect modes of close to 50 percent. The low CLs, in contrast, were much less flexible and used the indirect categories much less frequently, less than 33 percent of the time. This study is highly similar in outcome to numerous other contemporaneous investigations. The higher-stage teacher is less dependent, more flexible, and essentially more competent as a teacher.

TABLE 14.2 CONCEPTUAL LEVEL OF STUDENT TEACHERS AND CLASSROOM INTERACTION

	FLANDERS RATIO 1, 2, 3, 4
	1–7
High CL (N = 16) GPA = 3.1	45% indirect modes
Low CL (N = 13) GPA = 3.0	31% indirect modes

Based on over 6,000 teacher-pupil interactions.
N – number of student teachers.
GPA = grade-point average.

Data from L. Thies-Sprinthall, Supervision: An educative or miseducative process? *Journal of Teacher Education, 31*(2) (1980): 17–30.

Does Conceptual Level Make a Difference?

Naturally, a most important question is the empirical one: What is the relation between the teacher's conceptual level and actual teaching behavior? Is this just another case of an interesting and perhaps elegant set of ideas that doesn't translate to the real world of the classroom? In fact, a definite relationship has been found between the CL stage and teacher behavior. This research has been summarized by Miller (1981). At stage C teachers do the following:

Allow constructive student expression

Allow students to raise questions

Allow students to hypothesize

View the student as a participant in learning

View knowledge as an open-ended process

Vary the structure and pace according to learner need

Use a variety of teaching models

Exhibit empathy toward nearly all students

"Read and flex" with the students

In other words the stage C teachers can manage group instruction and respond to individual and small-group differences. The results indicated that academic performance in such classrooms was higher than in the other classrooms. The key seems to be

the concept of "reading and flexing." By that, Hunt means the ability of the teacher to be affected by the pupils and adjust the lesson accordingly. Some students need high structure, others less. The stage C teacher modifies the approach to meet the students' needs. Such flexibility in teaching is not random. Instead the teacher systematically selects different approaches in the best sense of matching and mismatching as described in the previous chapter.

The stage A teachers, on the other hand, hold quite strongly to the view that there is only one correct way to teach. Their concept of subject matter is just as singular. All material has to be boiled down to a group of facts that the students memorize. Stage A teachers give out large amounts of information almost exclusively in a directive fashion. The students are not allowed to raise questions. Rather they are asked a succession of precise factual questions, resembling our metaphor of classroom trivia. Such teachers also draw nearly all the conclusions for the students, regardless of the students' levels of development (Miller, 1981). In other words, everyone "gets" the same method whether they need it or not. In contrast, the stage C teachers also use a highly managed approach with some, but they use an interdependent approach with students who are ready to exercise more self-direction and autonomy in learning.

In philosophical terms Hunt's framework reminds us of the importance of understanding our own assumptions and beliefs about the purpose of teaching. At one level of complexity, students are grouped together as basically the same, as passive receptors of knowledge. The teaching methods are few, largely "tried and true." The outcomes indicate that students don't learn much, except that teaching and learning involve mostly passive memorization. In contrast, teachers who understand the process of teaching and learning at a more complex level, who essentially can apply all levels of Benjamin Bloom's taxonomy *to their own teaching*, are more likely to have a positive impact on a much broader cross-section of pupils.

ATTITUDES TOWARD PUPILS

Teachers' attitudes toward the pupil are also important in determining classroom atmosphere. Learning climates are subjective, and we were all adept as children in determining whether a teacher "likes kids." The feeling is readily apparent. Does the teacher feel we are competent? Does she or he expect us to do well? Do we feel that the teacher really wants us to be successful?

Teacher Expectations

The importance of **teacher expectations,** attitudes, and feelings about children has been demonstrated dramatically in a series of studies by Robert Rosenthal, a social psychologist (Rosenthal and Jacobson, 1968). He has shown that the teacher's expectations determine to a considerable extent how much pupils, or for that matter almost any animal, will learn. His studies have demonstrated, for example, that if experimental psychologists are told that the rats in their study are especially bred for intelligence, those rats will learn the mazes more quickly than the "control" rats, even though no such special breeding was carried out. In other words, Rosenthal has shown that when experimenters expect their rats to do well, those rats outperform their rivals. If the experimenters expect a good performance, they encourage the rats, handle them more carefully, pat them frequently, root for them—in short, treat them with concern and great care because they are expected to do well. If that is so for rats, what about pupils?

In the now-famous Oak-Hall School experiment, Rosenthal and coworker Lenore Jacobson told a group of schoolteachers at the beginning of the school year that particular pupils would have a "growth spurt" during the coming term. In order to lend credence to this prophecy, the researchers said that a special test, "The Harvard Test of Inflicted Acquisition," had been administered to all of the children in the elementary school. The results of the test became the basis for their alleged prediction. They identified some pupils as "growth spurters" even though the selections had been random: the identified pupils as a group were not any "smarter" than the remaining pupils.

At the end of the school term, the results showed that the pupils originally identified as in the growth-spurt group did much better on a series of tests than the other pupils. Their academic performances had improved and, especially in the early grades, their measured IQs were significantly higher than the other pupils'. Also, all the designated children received glowing comments from their teachers. Thus, a major research study has substantiated the effect of the self-fulfilling prophecy. When teachers expected some pupils to experience a growth spurt, the pupils improved in academic performance and intelligence.

A second major finding of this study—and one that is rarely reported—concerns the teachers' attitudes toward the other children. Rosenthal selected a subgroup of pupils in his control group, pupils who showed intellectual gains during the term but who hadn't been identified ahead of time to the teachers. He found that the teachers regarded these children as less well-adjusted, less interesting, and less affectionate than the others. In other words, the pupils who made it on their own, who gained intellectually in spite of the prediction, were perceived negatively by the teacher.

Thus, the **Rosenthal effect** is threefold: (1) Pupils who are expected to do well tend to show gains; (2) pupils who are not expected to do well tend to do less well than the first group; and (3) pupils who make gains despite expectations to the contrary are regarded negatively by the teacher. What the effect of those negative expectations may be on such pupils the next time around has not been determined. We can guess, however, what negative expectations in general will produce. Rosenthal quotes Eliza Doolittle from George Bernard Shaw's famous play *Pygmalion*:

> You see, really and truly, . . . the difference between a lady and a flower girl is not how she behaves, but how she's treated. I shall always be a flower girl to Professor Higgins, because he . . . treats me as a flower girl, . . . but I know I can be a lady to you, because you always treat me as a lady, and always will (Rosenthal and Jacobson, 1968, p. 183).

At the time of the original study, serious objections were raised concerning technical aspects of the research design. Very rarely can a researcher design a single study that is fail-safe. Rosenthal's response to the criticisms has been instructive. Rather than engage in an endless debate on details, he has instead sponsored a large number of continuing studies. In fact, by 1978, some ten years after the Oak-Hall School experiment, he had reviewed some additional 345 studies on the topic. He was able to show the cumulative significance of how our expectations unintentionally affect the outcomes of our studies (Rosenthal and Rubin, 1978).

The self-fulfilling prophecy of teachers' expectations has also been criticized on the grounds that it fails to take into account such factors as students' background experiences, malnutrition, and parental involvement. Wineburg (1987) and Rosenthal (1987) replied to these criticisms with the validity of the original research and subsequent evaluations of simi-

ROBERT ROSENTHAL

Born in 1933, Robert Rosenthal dashed over the academic hurdles in record time. He received his B.A. at twenty years of age and his Ph.D. by the time he was twenty-three, both at the University of California at Los Angeles. He then spent brief periods teaching at UCLA, Ohio State, and the University of North Dakota. His work attracted increasing notice throughout the professional world. The idea of the self-fulfilling prophecy was not new to psychology. What was new, however, was Rosenthal's ability to demonstrate how often this phenomenon was affecting the work of the psychologists themselves. His findings were almost immediately controversial. And, as if to create more controversy among psychologists, since his early work had not then been replicated, the department of social relations at Harvard University reached halfway across the country to North Dakota and offered Rosenthal a Harvard professorship, all by the time he was twenty-nine years old.

With the move to the East and more time for research, Rosenthal shifted into high gear. He not only replicated his original findings but began to produce studies on his important concept in a wide variety of areas. As noted in the text, each time one of his studies is criticized, he has been able to answer the critics not with rhetoric but rather with more research data to validate his position. The controversy itself, of course, continues. The major outcome has been to produce more evidence, more sophisticated research designs, and thus more comprehensive information for educational psychology. In addition, he has now established the importance of nonverbal channels as the means of communicating expectations to others.

lar research studies which show the striking effect of low expectations. It is important to underscore the unintentional nature of the influence. The adult (teacher, researcher, professor) does not consciously seek to affect the outcome, yet nonetheless our attitudes and perceptions shape how we interact.

Evaluations of the Rosenthal effect   Perhaps the best summary of the current state of the art with regard to the validity of teacher expectations comes from an independent source. In their evaluation, **Jere Brophy and Thomas Good** (1974) avoided too close an identification with either the original Rosenthal work or with the host of critics. Their somewhat dispassionate summary concludes:

> Regardless of where one stands concerning the original data, work by a large number of investigators using a variety of methods over the past several years has established unequivocally that teachers' expectations can and do function as self-fulfilling prophecies (p. 32).

In fact, Good and Brophy (1991) are careful to separate two different strands of research on the question. The earlier Rosenthal studies focused on experimental studies. He attempted to produce the effect by telling teachers that subgroups of children in their classes had different levels of learning potential. The teachers were misled by an experimental manipulation of their knowledge. There is, however, a quite different second strand of research. Observers either directly or with video evaluate natural teacher behavior in the classroom. No faked information is given to the teachers. Instead, teachers are simply watched. Then, if the observed and recorded teacher behavior reveals differences among the children, the characteristics of the children are analyzed. The second method may not be as experimentally pure from a research design perspective, but it is less fraught with interpretative problems. If, for example, a series of observational studies demonstrates that a large number of teachers treat high achievers positively and low achievers negatively, then we don't have to worry about whether the teachers understood or misunderstood the meaning of any of the research procedures in an experimental study. The differences in teacher behavior toward high and low achievers can be taken as an index of the normal repertoire of instructional differences. Also, we don't have to be concerned about the validity of the specific measure of academic outcome. Thus, the two biggest threats to research validity are removed. A series of replicated observational studies outlines a pattern of differences. No false information is provided. Most important, as we shall outline in the next section, the pattern of teacher behavior toward some pupils is exactly the opposite of the Walberg meta-analysis list of effective behaviors. Classroom observations reveal major differences in the use of these behaviors according to the status of the pupil.

Perhaps we should recall that the whole question of the self-fulfilling prophecy first came to light some seventy years ago. A horse in Germany who came to be known as "Clever Hans" gained notoriety for his ability to add, substract, multiply, and divide by tapping his foot. A psychologist named Pfungst, after long study, finally figured out that the questioners were unintentionally cueing the horse by lifting their heads up just before the horse reached the correct number of taps. He found that most humans who questioned Hans gave some cue without meaning to—raising their heads, lifting an eyebrow, or even dilating their nostrils. Pfungst concluded that he had spent far too much time "looking for, in the horse, what should have been sought in the man."

How expectancy messages are transmitted   Since teacher expectations are not for the most part conscious intentions, how are the messages conveyed? So far it seems as if the nonverbal communication channels are a main mode of transmission. Charles Galloway's work, cited in Chapter 12, pointed out the importance of nonverbal behavior. Rosenthal (1979), following this lead, has provided a creative series of studies detailing just how the expectations are communicated. He masks the verbal content of a statement so that those tested can't quite make out the words. Then he asks them to guess the meaning of the statement. The test, call **Profile of Nonverbal Sensitivity (PONS),** assesses the ability to read between the lines, so to speak, and understand quite accurately what the person really means, even with the exact content obscured.

In a recent study Rosenthal and colleagues (Babad, Bernieri, and Rosenthal, 1991) involved students as judges of teachers' verbal and nonverbal behavior. The judges in this study included students of differing ages as well as teachers differing in experience. These judges were shown very brief videotaped examples of unfamiliar teachers who were talking about or talking to pupils for which (unbeknownst to the judges) the teachers held high or low expectations. The judges did not see or hear the pupils on the videotape clips. The results showed that when teachers were involved with the pupils for which they held high expectations, the raters judged the unseen pupil more positively than when teachers were involved with the pupil for which they held low expectations. This study is interesting because it demonstrated that students can serve as observers and judges of unfamiliar teachers and that accurate detection of these teachers' expectancy levels can be made on the basis of brief videotaped exposure to these teachers. There has been relatively little research focused on students' perceptions except for that of Weinstein and her colleagues whose research studies established the fact that children are indeed highly sensitive to their own teachers' differential behaviors (see descriptions and results of these studies in Weinstein, 1989).

The work on teacher expectations clearly indicates that people can't really hide their true attitudes. Perhaps highly skilled actors, after disciplined practice, can successfully mask their real feelings, but most teachers, like everyone else, cannot do so: most students can read their teachers almost like a book. Yet "most teachers believed that their students would *not* know at all about the existence (and identity) of their pets and favorites" (see Babad et al., 1991, p. 230). Tone of voice, facial expression, body stance, eye contact, and similar aspects of body language act as channels, sounding clear messages about our real expectations. From research findings we know, first, that our expectations represent a self-fulfilling prophecy, and second, that our body language sends the message, either in a positive or negative mode. Thus, the findings help us understand how the process works. One highly surprising finding, however, is most important to note. Especially in Rosenthal's U.S. samples, adults were highly inaccurate in judging their own nonverbal behavior. The correlations were close to zero on the self-ratings. This should remind us of Robert Burns' famous line about our lack of power "to see ourselves as [others] see us." The research lends further credence to the notion that our expectations as well as the way they are communicated are unintentional. Rosenthal's findings suggest that we ask *not* ourselves how well we are doing but rather those with whom we are working.

Cultural Differences and Student Characteristics

The next question concerning teacher expectations shifts the focus to cultural differences and student characteristics. Is there any pattern or cluster of student characteristics that may be associated with positive or negative expectations? Rosenthal, remember, looked only at one variable in his original study, namely, student ability in terms of "readiness for a growth spurt." But, as it turns out, other student characteristics do have an impact on teacher expectations. And, in turn, student characteristics affect how students understand and interpret teachers' verbal and nonverbal expectations. For example, Lisa Delpit (1988) reminds us that "members of any culture transmit information implicitly to comembers. However, when implicit codes are attempted across cultures, communication frequently breaks down" (p. 283). Teacher expectations that are communicated implicitly may not be understood (or adhered to) by students of differing backgrounds. In her discussion, Delpit describes Shirley Brice Heath's (1983) examples of veiled teacher commands that are misinter-

preted by students of diverse backgrounds and different linguistic traditions. For example, while the statement "Is this where the scissors belong?" may be understood by some students as a direct command to put away the scissors, other students may regard it as a real question and not as a direct command.

> But those veiled commands are commands nonetheless, representing true power, and with true consequences for disobedience. If veiled commands are ignored, the child will be labeled a behavior problem and possibly officially classified as behavior disordered. In other words, the attempt by the teacher to reduce an exhibition of power by expressing herself in indirect terms may remove the very explicitness that the child needs to understand the rules of the new classroom culture (Delpit, 1988, p. 382).

The clearest way to insure that all students understand the rules, expectations, and codes of the school culture is to make these things absolutely explicit. For example, "Put those scissors on that shelf."

In Table 14.3 Hilda Hernandez (1989) summarizes four different perspectives that are evidenced in the assumptions and expectations of teachers. Each of these four perspectives attributes blame differently for the academic achievement outcomes that are different among cultural groups. Each of the four per-

Students from different cultural backgrounds may interpret the same teacher behavior quite differently. For example, would the female, Native American student in this picture be likely to interpret the teacher's corrections in the same way as a male student from the dominant culture?

TABLE 14.3   PERSPECTIVES ON DIFFERENTIAL ACADEMIC ACHIEVEMENT AMONG CULTURAL GROUPS

PERSPECTIVE	ATTRIBUTION OF BLAME	PRIMARY SOLUTIONS
Genetic inferiority: minorities fail to do well because they are genetically inferior	The groups themselves, not society	No solutions are possible because little can be done to change heredity
Cultural deficit: minorities fail to do well because their culture is viewed as deficient	The groups themselves, as well as social prejudice and discrimination	Train minorities to be less deficient and eliminate prejudice and discrimination
Cultural mismatch: minorities fail to achieve because their cultural traits are incompatible with those in the U.S. mainstream	No one; cultures just happen to be different	Change groups so that they can participate in the mainstream, but also change schools in order to better accommodate and ameliorate the mismatch
Contextual interaction: minorities fail to achieve because of unfortunate interaction of many factors	No one factor, group, or institution; outcomes produced through the interaction of many factors such as circumstances, cultural values, etc.	Change one or more of the factors or the context to alter interactions and thereby change the outcomes

Reprinted with the permission of Merrill, an imprint of Macmillan Publishing Co. From *Multicultural Education:* A Teacher's Guide to Content and Process by Hilda Hernandez, p. 37. Copyright 1989 by Merrill Publishing Co.

spectives also suggests different solutions for change to equalize academic achievement outcomes for different cultural groups. According to Hernandez, the fourth perspective of "contextual interaction" is the perspective with the most opportunity to make positive change possible in a way that doesn't devalue any culture or exalt any culture. The focus on contextual interaction provides, she says, a more "holistic, comprehensive, and dynamic view" (p. 38) of differential academic achievement than the other three perspectives. You may wonder what the research has shown about these different perspectives on cultural differences and school learning.

Shortly after the process of desegregating the public schools began in 1954, with "deliberate speed" akin to that of a glacier, a few minority children began appearing in the classrooms of previously segregated white schools. Often the transition was marked by riots, federal marshals, bomb threats, stonings, and the use of electric cattle prods. These were the outward and visible signs of massive resistance. With a few exceptions, that era has ended. The public schools became integrated. However, lack of integration between city and suburb, and increasing segregation of inner-city schools is an ensuing problem.

The resistance to cultural pluralism, however, did

not officially end with the removal of the last police dog, the breakup of the final gathering of white supremacists at the curbstone of the school, or the mapping out of new bus routes. The legal guarantees ended physical resistance. As the reality changed and increasing numbers of African Americans, Native Americans, and Latinos actually sat at the desks, a new set of barriers was erected. As we shall see in the chapter on intelligence, a new series of studies attempted to show just how inferior black children were because of an inadequate pool of inherited genes. (Shades of the "good" and "bad" Kallikaks!) The implication was direct: Desegregation would fill the schools with inferior humans of limited potential. Teaching procedures would have to be adjusted—downward.

Because the inferior gene pool theory could not be supported scientifically, a second theory was proposed: The problem was not poor genes; it was that most minority children came from psychologically deprived environments, for example, "the Negro family." The result was still the same, but the cause was different. Minority children entering school were still viewed as significantly less competent. As was the case with the genetic theory, careful reexamination of the so-called family deficit theory has shown that such a conclusion was a dangerous oversimplification. Certainly, some minority children do experience an inadequate home environment and come from economically weak families with parents who are incompetent and/or violent. Such families, however, are the exception, not the rule. Malnutrition, crowding, excessive noise, premature autonomy, and similar environmental problems will impair any student from any background. Yet to claim that all or nearly all minority children live in such disorganized families creates an unwarranted stereotype. Rather than attribute the difficulty to the minority status of the parents, it would be far more accurate to link such environments to economic poverty rather than ethnicity.

Thus, we have evidence that indicates that minority children do not inherit from an inferior gene pool, nor are minority families deficient as home environments. What about learning styles such as impulsiveness or concrete versus abstract thinking? A recent massive review of such learning style differences concluded in no uncertain language: "As the research evidence indicates, cognitive styles vary as much within ethnic, racial, socioeconomic status and language groups as they do between groups (Shipman and Shipman, 1985)."

Two major factors, however, do distinguish minority and nonminority children in a school situation. The differences are not explained by genes, by home environments, or by learning styles, but rather by psychological variables—attitudes. As noted in the text, minority children are systematically treated differently—namely, as less competent, with lowered achievement goals—and receive less adequate teaching strategies. Thus, one major factor is the difference in educational treatment, not in the children themselves. Minority children tend to receive less. While as a group they may enter the first grade slightly behind majority students, the longer they remain in school, the further behind they fall. In other words the school experience itself does not produce growth.

A second factor, which is even broader, has to do with the general social and economic goals available to all students. Putting it harshly, minority students ask, "What's the use of studying in school?" Not only is the daily experience more often negative than positive, but in the long run there may also be few opportunities for advancement. **John Ogbu,** a cultural anthropologist, has done a careful study of the origins of human competence in different countries (Ogbu, 1978). Each country had easily identified minority members regarded as "outcasts." These outcasts for a number of generations, indeed centuries, were systematically denied full participation in society. They were taught, often through violent means (beatings and murder), to remain in their "place." After so many years of harsh repression, such outcast minorities did learn their lesson. No matter how hard they worked in school, their future opportunity was extremely limited. Each new generation had ample evidence as to what happened to the previous generation.

A good example is the famous Supreme Court case *Griggs v. Duke Power.* Blacks working as laborers in a coal mine were barred from becoming miners unless they made a certain score on an IQ test. Those new rules virtually prevented promotion of any black laborers. Since the test score had no relationship to actual job performance, the Court ruled against Duke Power. The selection procedure was systemic discrimination in the words of the Court, "Built-in headwinds for minority groups." The system ensured that a disproportionate number of minorities would be excluded.

Ogbu's point is that the apparent "failure" of African-American, Latino, and other minority students to complete their schooling (e.g., the high school dropout rate for Native Americans is over 90 percent) has been a functional adaptation to reality. Until recently, the virtual exclusion of African-American, Latino, and Native American workers from any high-status and highly paid employment that required a formal education sent a strong message: If you want to get ahead in this society, don't waste your time studying. There has been, in Ogbu's words, a "job ceiling." Most of the adults whom minority youth knew were in low-wage, low-skill jobs for which a high school diploma was hardly a ticket to upward mobility. This has resulted in a situation that might be called a combination of fantasy and reality. A minority youth may say on one hand, "Yes I'd like to be a doctor or a lawyer," then turn around and take whatever low-paying job he or she can get.

What this means is that any differences between minority students and majority students in school performance are most likely *not* due to specific (or inborn) cultural differences. Characteristics that minority students are supposed to possess, such as short attention span, hyperactivity, verbal deficits, and so on, are simply stereotypes. There is no major evidence that identifies a unique cultural trait that either promotes or prevents learning. Instead, the differences you may observe are most likely a result of social conditions such as direct prior experience in negative schooling or a deep-seated feeling rooted in history that school achievement is not a pathway to a better life. Of course, since the enactment of civil rights legislation and the slow integration of schools, the atmosphere is changing. It may be years, however, before the majority culture can honestly and genuinely convince previously oppressed minorities of a real change in educational opportunity. Each time a teacher, even unintentionally, negatively reinforces a minority student, employs less eye contact, praises majority students more frequently, or uses different cues, that teacher reconfirms the suspicion in the minority student's mind and heart of unequal and unfair treatment. Each time the society as a whole uses what is called *systemic discrimination* to prevent access to better-paying occupations, higher education, and to professions, the job ceiling effect is reawakened.

The only meaningful difference, then, between minority and majority students in school situations is in motivational patterns. The motivation to learn has been redirected for many minority students. In the past such children received a strong message in the school itself as well as from the larger society. Their "place" was not with books and learning and upward economic mobility. Instead their place was with physically demanding, backbreaking, low-wage, and low-status roles. Educationally related career achievement was the road to nowhere.

The publicity concerning a successful New York businessman, Eugene Lange, seems to prove Ogbu's point quite dramatically. In 1980 he visited his old elementary school (P.S. 121). Instead of giving the usual Horatio Alger sermon to the ghetto sixth-graders, he promised the sixty-one students free college tuition. With the help of a concerned counselor, Johnnie Rivera, and the financial incentives, forty-eight of the original sixty-one graduated from high school. Rather than the anticipated 40 to 50 percent dropout rate, almost 80 percent completed. Even more encouraging were the twenty-five students who enrolled in college. As a case study, then, Lange's money and Rivera's guidance dramatically raised Ogbu's ceiling.

These findings have two implications. If you are from a majority background, as a teacher you will need to become particularly sensitive to the motivation issue. In fact you may have to go "the extra mile," at least in the beginning, to convince minority students that you will treat them in the same respectful manner and with the same effective methods as

the other children. Remember that such children and adolescents have every right to be suspicious and guarded. Too many prior generations have suffered at the hands of so-called white benefactors. Do not expect immediate acceptance, and do not push too hard. Gushing over a student's first halfhearted product will be viewed as a phony performance. Also, do not attempt to "buddy up" by quickly adopting any form of minority verbal expressions or vernacular. That too will be seen as false. Expect a period of legitimate testing to clear the air. Minority students, like all others, are fair and generous interpersonally, after you show them fairness and generosity in concrete ways. It's the actions they will look for, not the words.

How about the case of the minority member as teacher? If you are in that category, should you expect instant rapport? Yes and no. Obviously, it will be easier for you to understand the legitimate emotional and motivational needs of minority students. Most likely such issues are close to you personally. This doesn't mean, however, that you will have an automatic acceptance level with those minority students whose background may be different from your own. Thus, you will need to exercise some care if you begin to notice some mistrust. Also, and especially with adolescents, you may notice some hints or subtle feelings that your own educational attainment is only a case of "tokenism" and that you "sold out" to the white establishment. Such doubt on their part, while genuine, is apt to disappear quite rapidly as your humanity and care become more evident. So, on the one hand, you will start with minority students in a far stronger position than teachers from majority backgrounds. That's a real plus. But on the other, you will have another set of very difficult problems. Quite unfortunately, as the expectancy research shows, almost half of all teachers (your colleagues) do not accept their pupils on an equal basis. These are some of the teachers who believe the stereotype that any difficulty in classroom learning is caused by the skin color of the child. Failure is laid at the doorstep of the student. This can be a highly distressing situation for you. Such teachers, thoughtlessly, may start a practice of asking you to give those students "a good talking to," or they may make a series of increasingly disparaging comments in front of you about some of their minority students. In pointing a finger at such students, they are often unaware that they may be pointing the remaining three fingers at themselves. In any case, there are certainly no quick solutions to the problems of prejudice and racism. You can remind such teachers that their attitude can become a self-fulfilling prophecy and that no relationship exists between ability and ethnicity. It will also serve as yet another reminder of just how far we still have to go on the road to equity and full participation for all students.

Student Characteristics That Affect Teacher Expectations

Social class   **Howard Becker**, a sociologist, demonstrated the primary importance of the social class of the pupil a number of years ago in a now-classic study. He found that most teachers in the large urban school system he examined could be grouped as lower middle class on a socioeconomic scale (Becker, 1969). In general, these teachers valued conformity, obedience, neatness, cleanliness, punctuality, hard work—highly conventional values. He then interviewed over sixty such teachers to find out how they perceived their pupils. He found three sets of perceptions that closely followed class lines. The teachers perceived children from their own class (lower middle class and blue-collar working class) as the "best" pupils. They were neat, orderly, clean, and followed directions.

Teachers felt that pupils from lower-class backgrounds (essentially poor blacks) were, in general, morally unacceptable: The teachers reported being shocked by the "awful" language and upset because "they" (the lower-class students) were perceived as not really valuing education or wishing to improve themselves. It is not difficult to imagine how such attitudes affected the teachers' expectations regarding the pupils they described in those terms.

Finally, the teachers had a third set of attitudes toward children from upper-class, well-to-do homes. They found these children to be very fine students, bright, clever, quick—but very difficult to teach: "They are too unruly—have no manners—interrupt me—are quick to correct my mistakes," noted one teacher. Another said, "They all have maids and servants at home. They won't pick things up that they drop. One student said to me 'If I picked that up, there wouldn't be any work for the janitor to do.' "

The teachers also tended to be fearful of reprisal from the parents of the third group. Although the children from the ghetto could be dealt with severely if necessary (including being subjected to corporal punishment), the children from well-to-do back-

grounds were immune from direct punishment. The teachers were obviously worried about "influential" parents calling the school board or going directly to the superintendent with complaints about the teachers' actions toward their children.

More recent and psychologically oriented research has validated Becker's work on the importance of social class. Where the social class of the teacher and the pupils differ, especially if the pupils come from a lower socioeconomic class than the teacher, then there is a real possibility that the teacher systematically expects less from and does less effective teaching with such children (Good, 1983). For example, studies have shown that "middle- and upper-middle class students tend to be placed in higher [reading level] groups . . . [and] working class, poor, and minority students are overrepresented in lower-ability groups" (Farber, Wilson, and Holm, 1989, p. 47). The current discontinuity between teacher and student diversity is shown in the Spotlight On Demographics.

Ethnic background—Race   The first major study detailing the achievement outcomes of students whose racial or ethnic background was different from the teacher's was done by Eleanor Leacock and her associates (1969) at the Bank Street School in New York. Leacock's researchers, unlike Rosenthal or Becker, actually went into the classroom. They observed the teacher's behavior and checked student achievement. As a result, they found a fairly systematic pattern of negative attitudes and expectations toward most lower-class ghetto blacks. Teachers universally expected less of those pupils, even in the very first years of elementary school, than of other children. In addition, teacher expectations declined the longer the pupils were in school. Fifth-graders were seen as less capable and less competent than second-graders in the same school. Leacock found that the schools in this study in the areas where poor blacks lived were neither in continual rebellion nor were they a "blackboard jungle." Rather, the schools were populated by overworked, ineffective, and frustrated teachers and bored, uninterested and withdrawn children. There were one or two "troublemakers" in each class, but the majority of pupils were quiet and listless. Leacock also compared teacher-pupil interaction in the lower-class black schools with that in middle-class schools (with both black and white children) and found less than half as much interaction in the lower-class schools. This low rate of interaction meant that the "poor" children were

Discontinuity between Teacher and Student Diversity

C. A. Grant and W. G. Secada

The current demographic makeup of our student and teaching populations, as well as of the projections for the future, shows a striking discontinuity between teacher and student diversity. In 1976, 24 percent of the total student enrollment in U.S. schools was nonwhite; by 1984, the figure had risen to 29 percent. In the 20 largest school districts, the respective figures were 60 percent and 70 percent (Center for Education Statistics [CES], 1987a, p. 64). By the year 2000, between 30 and 40 percent of the total school enrollment will be of color (Hodgkinson, 1985). One in four students is poor (Kennedy, Jung, & Orland, 1986, p. 71); one in five students lives in a single-parent home (CES, 1987b, p. 21); and one in seven students is at risk of dropping out of school (Hodgkinson, 1985).

The intercorrelation among these various demographic characteristics has been well documented. For example, poverty and race are correlated. Of white children who were between one and 3 years old in 1968, 25 percent experienced some period of poverty over the next 15 years. For black children, the same statistic was 78 percent. The experience of poverty is more intense for black children. Of white children experiencing poverty, 20 percent lived in poverty for more than 4 years of their childhood; among black children similarly situated, the comparable statistic was 59 percent (Kennedy et al, 1986, p. 45).

Increasing numbers of children from minority language backgrounds are entering school with little or no competence in the English language (O'Malley, 1981). Though Spanish is the predominant first language for most of these children, and is likely to remain so into the next century, increasing numbers of children are entering school with non-Spanish language backgrounds including Arabic, Chinese, Hmong, Khmer, Lao, Thai, and Vietnamese (Oxford-Carpenter, Pol, Gendell, & Peng, 1984).

In contrast with an increasingly diverse student population, this nation's teaching force is homogeneous, and it is projected to become increasingly more so into the next century. Though the current school population is 29 percent nonwhite, only 12 to 14 percent of the current teaching force is nonwhite; and it is 67 percent to 68 percent female (CES, 1987a, p. 54; 1987b, p. 60). The median age for teachers steadily rose from 33 to 37 to 39 years in 1976, 1981, and 1983 (CES, 1987b, p. 60). Sixty-eight percent of all teachers have had 10 or more years of experience (CES, 1987a, p. 54).

These teachers will be replaced by an increasingly female and white cohort. In 1983, 67 percent of public school teachers in the United States were women, yet in 1980–1981, 1982–1983 and 1983–1984, 75 percent, 76 percent, and 76 percent respectively, of bachelor's degrees in education were awarded to women (CES, 1987b, pp. 60, 195, 183, 175). In Illinois, during the 1985–1986 school year, 70 percent of all teachers were women; however, 79 percent of those completing and 77 percent of those entering degree-granting teacher-training programs during the 1984–1985 school year were women (Illinois State Board of Education [ISBE], 1987, p. 19). In Illinois 15 percent of all public school teachers were nonwhite in 1985–1986. Yet only 10 percent of those completing and 10 percent of those entering teacher education programs during the 1984–1985 school year were from minority groups (ISBE, 1987, p. 19). Moreover, the use of tests for teacher certification is expected to reduce the certification rate for teachers of color even more (Cole, 1986; Darling-Hammond, 1988; Garcia, 1986; Gifford, 1986).

Not only is minority group representation in the teaching force dropping, but also its composition seems to be changing. Though 13.1 percent of all Illinois schoolteachers during the 1985–1986 school year were black, only 7.4 percent of those completing and 7.3 percent of those entering teacher education programs in 1984–1985 were black. In contrast, though 1.5 percent of public school teachers were Hispanic, 2.2 percent of those completing and 2.1 percent of those entering were Hispanic (ISBE, 1987, p. 19).

For the foreseeable future the teaching force will be predominantly white and female. Schools of education, themselves predominantly white and male, will be required to prepare this increasingly homogeneous teaching force to teach a student population that is becoming increasingly diverse in terms of race, class, language, and sex-role socialization patterns. The multiple discontinuities—between student population and teaching force demographics and between teaching force and teacher educator demographics—should elicit a broad range of responses among researchers, policymakers, members of the teaching profession, and others who are concerned about the education of our children.

---

being ignored, that most of the time they spent in class was passed in quiet boredom, and that their teachers displayed a genuine lack of interest. Also, the interaction that did take place tended to be twice as negative as that in the middle-class schools; teachers tended to undermine the children, were very derogatory toward the children's work, and were supercritical of their attempts to read, do math problems, and do blackboard work.

Another classroom observation study by Brophy and Good (1974) gave a detailed account of the different teacher behaviors according to the ethnic background of the children. They watched for teacher eye contact and the frequency of goal-setting behavior by teachers and pupils. The results are summarized in Table 14.4.

Brophy and Good examined public schools. Unfortunately, the recent research at other levels of education is also negative. A study of higher education using the same Brophy and Good observational instruments revealed patterns of professional behavior that differed according to the ethnic status of the students. Professors took more time to answer questions asked by nonminority students, asked less complex questions of minority students, and provided fewer cues and feedback to the latter. The results were the same in undergraduate and graduate classes. There was no difference in the general participation rates between nonminority and minority status (Trujillo, 1986).

The message is clear for inner-city children from lower-class backgrounds: They are either ignored, criticized, or undermined in their attempts to learn. This suggests that teachers in ghetto schools are teaching their children not to learn. Sometimes this behavior is deliberate, most often it is inadvertent, due to unconsciously held assumptions about the abilities of inner-city children. It therefore comes as no surprise to find that pupil achievement in such schools is significantly lower than in ethnically similar nonghetto schools. The teachers' unfortunate attitudes toward their pupils pervade some schools and doom those children to failure. Other research has indicated that such children end up not only with lowered academic achievement but also with a negative concept of themselves as learners. They have lower self-confidence in problem-solving situations. For such children, "formal" education in school may be worse than no education at all.

Family composition   A third factor that affects teacher expectations and also is beyond the control of the individual pupil is family background. Whether the pupil comes from a two-parent or a single-parent home makes a significant difference in teacher predictions. Diane Scott-Jones (1984) completed a most extensive review of the literature. Studies indicated that even when teachers viewed videotapes of children demonstrating precisely the same behaviors, their predictions differed. For children denoted as from one-parent homes, the teachers expected *both* lower academic performance and greater psychological problems. When children were said to be from intact homes, the attitude changed markedly despite the behavioral similarity. Further (almost to prove Rosenthal's point), another study indicated that both single and dual parents were accurate in their predictions of the different teacher expectations. In other words, the message did get through that teacher expectations differed just on the basis of family makeup.

Scott-Jones also noted that when social class is controlled as a variable, research studies indicated no difference in either intelligence or academic achievement between children from single-parent and intact homes. Since the number of single-parent homes has grown dramatically in the last decade, she was concerned about this teacher bias, with good cause. According to some estimates, as many as 60 percent of all children may at one time or another live in a single-parent family. Such estimates do vary with both ethnic background and family income. Unfortunately,

TABLE 14.4   TEACHER RESPONSES ACCORDING TO PUPILS' ETHNIC BACKGROUND

EYE CONTACT	TEACHER RESPONSE RATE
Initiated by white pupils	57% (14 to 8)
Initiated by black pupils	11% (35 to 4)

TEACHER GOAL SETTING WITH PUPILS*	
White middle-class school A	43 (12.3 instances/hour)
White middle-class school B	46 (15.3 instances/hour)
White lower-class school	18 (6 instances/hour)
Black lower-class school	15 (5 instances/hour)

* Based on three-hour-long observations.

the likelihood of living in a single-parent home is much greater among economically poor and ethnically different children; such children may be doubly impaired as learners because of negative expectancies. Teacher expectations are also affected by other nontraditional family arrangements involving adopted families, foster families, blended families, gay male families, lesbian families, as well as neighbors or relatives.

Student temperament   The fourth area of significance is represented by the students' basic personality temperament: At the broadest level, research has shown that teachers can be affected by the general social skills of children. Pupils with "easy" temperaments (that is, likable personalities) who were quick to adapt to the teacher's requests and were pleasant to be around were consistently overrated as to their actual abilities. "Slow to warm up" children, who were less likable, moodier, less quick to adapt, and more "emotional," were rated lower on the same estimates. In fact, one study suggested that such temperamental differences were more significant than IQ or socioeconomic status as factors influencing teacher expectations. There is insufficient evidence to back up such a claim. In any case pupil temperament does have an influence (Woolfolk and Brooks, 1983). Teachers are unintentionally more positive to likable children and less positive to the "slow to warm up" ones. As in the case of Brophy and Good's research, the teacher expectations were assessed at a nonverbal level. Their tone of voice was different and they maintained less eye contact with those they considered difficult to teach.

Gender differences   The influence of gender is a fifth area of concern. People may assume that a lot has improved in equitable treatment of students based on gender because there have been some political changes in the area of gender equity (most notably Title IX)! The recent AAUW report (1992) shows that there are still many subtle and not-so-subtle factors operating in classrooms to the educational detriment of females. Years ago, the standard view was that gender differences, particularly in elementary school, favored girls. Boys tended to be more hyperactive, noisier, shorter on attention span, and less "academic" than girls. As a result, it seemed natural to conclude that the teachers favored girls as more docile, easier to teach, and quicker to learn how to behave

like good pupils (Meyer and Thompson, 1969). Today, a case can be made for the converse. In the 1970s, for example, based on careful classroom observations in preschool, it appeared that teachers were responding to the sexes differently and to the disadvantage of girls (Maccoby and Jacklin, 1974). Teachers encouraged assertiveness, autonomous problem solving, and independence on the part of boys. They were more likely to devalue the very same behavior in girls. The girls were getting a different message—to show less activity and more docility in learning.

Evidence in the 1980s has confirmed those findings. Jeanne H. Block has shown that a large array of different expectations almost always favors boys. Teachers interact more favorably with boys and give them more positive feedback while directing more criticism at girls. In fact, in one particular study, Block (1984) reported, "Girls in the high achievement condition received the lowest level of supportive, ego-enhancing feedback; they also received significantly fewer laudatory attributional statements and significantly more disparaging attributional statements." She also noted that such negative expectancies can be found at all levels from nursery school to college. In preschool, boys receive more attention. In college, female intellectual aspirations are taken less seriously by professors. These expectations and the discouragement and denigration of female academic effort may well have, in Block's words, "pernicious effects."

Elizabeth Fennema and colleagues, in studies of math teaching at both elementary and secondary levels in the United States and around the world, indicate similar differences (See Fennema and Leder, 1990; Burton, 1990). Boys were encouraged and girls discouraged even though no major differences in ability were evident. Thus, there seems to be reasonable evidence that the gradual decline in mathematical achievement by females, which doesn't start until adolescence, is in part brought on by lowered teacher expectations (Hyde, Fennema, and Lamon, 1990).

Some teachers may not have accommodated their expectations to today's greater emphasis on educational equity, which stresses factors such as independence and self-direction as opposed to conformity and docility. The main point is that gender can result in different expectations (Sadker, Sadker, and Klein, 1991).

There are many checklists and activities which allow teachers to investigate and monitor their treatment of female and male students. Some can be used in the privacy of one's own classroom with audio- or videotape. Others can be used and discussed with colleagues. Teachers don't intentionally set out to treat students differently based on characteristics such as gender. Differential treatment occurs because we are unaware of how our biases and assumptions are acted out in the classroom. Any remedy for inequitable treatment of students must include developing awareness of and reflection on our biases and teaching behavior.

It is important to remember that gender *combines* with other factors that influence teachers' expectations of students. As we have mentioned previously, ethnicity and racial background are predictive of the level of classroom interaction.

> Majority males are more likely to interact with the teacher than minority males, and majority females are more likely to interact than minority females. In analyzing the imbalance in teacher-student interaction, it is useful to keep in mind that many males are not the recipients of significant teacher interaction and that there is significant inequity within gender groups as well as between them (Sadker, Sadker and Klein, 1991, p. 299).

Effects of Student Difference in Academic Achievement on Teachers' Behavioral Responses

Teachers' behavior in class differs according to their perception of students as low achievers or as high achievers. The most recent summary by Good and Brophy (1991) identifies eighteen differences. For low achievers, teachers provide

1. Less wait-time
2. Fewer cues or rephrased questions
3. Inappropriate reinforcement
4. Greater criticism
5. Less praise for correct responses
6. Less public feedback
7. Less interaction in instruction
8. Fewer opportunities to answer questions
9. Seating further away from the teacher
10. Less demanding experiences
11. Interaction in private

12. Less benefit of the doubt in grading
13. Less friendly interaction
14. Briefer feedback
15. Less eye contact and less generally responsive nonverbal behavior
16. Less use of effective, but time-consuming instructional methods
17. Less acceptance of ideas
18. More emphasis on repetition, facts, and drill and practice

It is both interesting and professionally depressing to realize that when Good and Brophy began their research on teacher expectations and academic achievement, they reported only four main differences— essentially the first four in the new list. Obviously, more focused and extensive research since that time has uncovered a much greater list of differences, and this is only in respect to academic achievement. What might be the outcome of more intensive research on teacher expectations with respect to social class, ethnicity, family background, and gender differences? On the one hand, would the list of differences continue to multiply in a fashion similar to the list for academic achievement? On the other hand, could teacher training programs focus more directly on the problem of expectations? Recent studies may point the way.

For example, Ross and Smith's (1992) case study of preservice teachers' perspectives on diversity describes a Research in Elementary Education course in which preservice students in their first field experiences are helped to identify and examine perspectives about the problems that confront diverse students in classrooms, their commitment to teaching diverse learners, and their beliefs about the causes of failure for diverse learners. The course emphasizes ethical issues related to educational equity.

Another interesting study was conducted to test procedures designed to change teacher expectations about physically or mentally challenged children. Teachers viewed a series of videotapes consisting of three 10-minute segments. The third segment demonstrated a highly interactive teaching method with two children who had moderate to severe mental handicaps. The results indicated quite clearly that teacher attitudes changed very significantly after the interactive teaching (Delcos, Burns, and Kulewicz, 1987). As opposed to the teachers in the control group, those

Learning Shame

Dick Gregory

I never learned hate at home, or shame, I had to go to school for that. I was about seven years old when I got my first big lesson. I was in love with a little girl named Helen Tucker, a light-complected little girl with pigtails and nice manners. She was always clean and she was smart in school. I think I went to school mostly to look at her. I brushed my hair and even got me a little old handkerchief. It was a lady's handkerchief, but I didn't want Helen to see me wipe my nose on my hand. The pipes were frozen again, there was no water in the house, but I washed my socks and shirt every night. I'd get a pot, and go over to Mister Ben's grocery store, and stick my pot down into his soda machine. Scoop out some chopped ice. By evening the ice melted to water for washing. I got sick a lot that winter because the fire would go out at night before the clothes were dry. In the morning I'd put them on, wet or dry, because they were the only clothes I had.

It was on a Thursday, I was sitting in the back of the room, in a seat with a chalk circle drawn around it. The idiot's seat, the troublemaker's seat.

The teacher thought I was stupid. Couldn't spell, couldn't read, couldn't do arithmetic. Just stupid. Teachers were never interested in finding out that you couldn't concentrate because you were so hungry, because you hadn't had any breakfast. All you could think about was noontime, would it ever come? Maybe you could sneak into the cloakroom and steal a bit of some kid's lunch out of a coat pocket. A bite of something. Paste. You can't really make a meal of paste, or put it on bread for a sandwich, but sometimes I'd scoop a few spoonfuls out of the paste jar in the back of the room. Pregnant people get strange tastes. I was pregnant with poverty. Pregnant with dirt and pregnant with smells that made people turn away, pregnant with cold and pregnant with shoes that were never bought for me, pregnant with five other people in my bed and no Daddy in the next room, and pregnant with hunger. Paste doesn't taste too bad when you're hungry.

The teacher thought I was a troublemaker. All she saw from the front of the room was a little black boy who squirmed in his idiot's seat and made noises and poked the kids around him. I guess she couldn't see a kid who made noises because he wanted someone to know he was there.

It was on a Thursday, the day before the Negro payday. The eagle always flew on Friday. The teacher was asking each student how much his father would give to the Community Chest. On Friday night, each kid would get the money from his father, and on Monday he would bring it to the school. I decided I was going to buy me a Daddy right then. I had money in my pocket from shining shoes and selling papers, and whatever Helen Tucker pledged for her Daddy I was going to top it. And I'd hand the money right in. I wasn't going to wait until Monday to buy me a Daddy.

I was shaking, scared to death. The teacher opened her book and started calling out names alphabetically.

"Helen Tucker?"

"My Daddy said he'd give two dollars and fifty cents."

"That's very nice, Helen. Very, very nice indeed."

That made me feel pretty good. It wouldn't take too much to top that. I had almost three dollars in dimes and quarters in my pocket and held onto the money, waiting for her to call my name. But the teacher closed her book after she called everybody else in the class.

I stood up and raised my hand.

"What is it now?"

"You forgot me."

She turned toward the blackboard. "I don't have time to be playing with you, Richard."

"What is it now?"

"My Daddy said he's . . ."

"Sit down, Richard, you're disturbing the class."

"My Daddy said he'd give . . . fifteen dollars."

She turned around and looked mad. "We are collecting this money for you and your kind, Richard Gregory. If your Daddy can give fifteen dollars you have no business being on relief."

"I got it right now, I got it right now, my Daddy gave it to me to turn in today, my Daddy said . . ."

"And furthermore," she said, looking right at me, her nostrils getting big and her lips getting thin and her eyes opening wide, "we know you don't have a Daddy."

Helen Tucker turned around, her eyes full of tears. She felt sorry for me. Then I couldn't see her too well because I was crying too.

"Sit down, Richard."

And I always thought the teacher kind of liked me.

From Dick Gregory (with Robert Lipsyte), *Nigger: An autobiography* (Copyright © 1964 by Dick Gregory Enterprises, Inc., E. P. Dutton, a division of New American Library).

who viewed the dynamic approach gave the two children much more positive ratings both in learning potential and in learning the specific task. Actually seeing how an expert teacher works interactively with such "different" children had a positive effect upon the novice teachers' attitudes. This should remind us that expectations are not immutable. Modeling more effective approaches in teaching groups of children who have traditionally been on the short end of positive expectations can be a positive step.

How Widespread Are Negative Expectations?

Having established the importance of teacher expectations, how they are communicated, and the different forms they take, we come to the final point. How broad is the phenomenon? Does it happen only infrequently and then only to a small proportion of pupils? Naturally, it is difficult to derive a firm index. One group of researchers estimates that as many as 33 percent of all teachers show highly differentiated teaching behaviors toward children perceived differently according to academic potential. This is a highly conservative estimate for two reasons. First, only teachers who were clearly (indeed almost blatantly) highly different were included. Second, the expectations were based on only *one* student characteristic, learning potential. If we add in the other findings indicating a bias due to social class, race, ethnicity, family configuration, temperament, and gender, we would have to conclude that negative expectations are probably operating in over half of all the classrooms in the country.

It is clear that for all who plan to teach, systematic awareness of expectations represents a crucial learning. The ability to relate in a positive and constructive manner to all children is not easily achieved; however, it can be developed. It is critical. How many of those factors known to bias teachers are within the student's current power to change—ability, social class, race, temperament, family, prior academic achievement? Should such unchangeable elements influence over half of those currently in teaching? As you review this material, try not to see it as just a litany of complaints about teachers. Instead, consider it an important agenda for change so that pupils may have a better chance to learn.

A fine example of a teacher's progress in learning to deal more openly with her own assumptions and behavior about racial and social differences among her students can be found in *White Teacher* by Vivian

Gussin Paley (1989). In their foreword to the book, James P. Comer and Alvin F. Poussant write:

> Paley is effective in helping people appreciate themselves because she respects human differences but is always mindful of human similarities. It was a relief, and a basis for hope, to discover that she didn't start out that way; that she grew to be comfortable with differences through a personal commitment to fairness and a determined effort to understand herself and culturally different people . . . the fact that she was able to grow and change is what is most significant (p. ix).

The lesson here is that we need to raise expectations and standards for all students. We can no longer conduct business as usual. We can achieve high standards in a great variety of ways and through a multitude of materials by finding and using culturally, multiculturally, and linguistically relevant materials in developing students' basic skills. We can also use a variety of approaches, from peer tutoring to dramatizations, in instruction. "Raising standards and expectations does not mean homogenizing instruction but creating new and different opportunities for learning for all students" (Nieto, 1992, p. 262). Nieto also reminds us that "good intentions are not enough" (Spotlight On Multicultural Education in Practice).

Denny Taylor and Catherine Dorsey-Gaines (1988) provide a dramatic example from their case study of poor, inner-city, black families with academically successful students. They found that these children consistently did their homework, made the honor roll, and had positive attitudes about school. Their parents motivated them to learn and study, communicated high hopes for their education, spoke optimistically about the future, and in fact considered literacy an integral part of their lives. These high parental and home expectations were prevalent in spite of such devastating conditions as family deaths; lack of food, heat, and hot water; and a host of other hostile situations. These researchers concluded that the fragmentation that takes place as these successful children move from the hopes of their families through an education system that "disconnects their lives" is overwhelming. When these children are successful, it is often in spite of, rather than because of the school system. Beverly Daniel Tatum (1992a) examined the experiences of black families in white communities from the viewpoint of the families themselves. Based on interviews with black families who are living, working, and raising children in the midst of a predominantly white community, Tatum highlights not

SPOTLIGHT ON MULTICULTURAL EDUCATION IN PRACTICE

Good Intentions Are Not Enough

Students' achievement is based on subtle and not-so-subtle ways in which teachers expect. The research (Rosenthal self-fulfilling) had mixed receptions from educators—some supporters, some not. But teachers' expectations were finally taken seriously. Prior to that, students' failure in school could be attributed wholly to individual or family circumstances. The continuing research also adds the effects of teacher attitudes and behaviors and school expectations. The significant factor is the manner in which teachers, schools, communities, and society often interact to produce failure. **Sonia Nieto** writes:

Expectations are bound up with the biases we have learned to internalize. If we expect children who come from economically poor communities to be poor readers, we may reflect it in modifications we make in the way we teach them. Similarly, if we expect girls to be passive and submissive, we may teach them as if they were. Although our teaching approaches are either frequently unconscious or developed with the best of in-

tentions, the results can be disastrous. We have seen many vivid examples throughout this book. Thus, having good intentions or even caring deeply about students is not enough. We need to consider our biases, which even the most enlightened teachers carry with them, every day that we step foot into the classroom. We are sometimes shocked when others point out to us, for instance, that we call on the girls in our class less often than the boys or that we accept slovenly work from some students and not from others. African American and Latino students have often stated that teachers were happy with a C from them in math, say, whereas they expected higher grades from other students in the class. We cannot mandate, of course, that teachers develop high expectations for all students or that schools become antiracist, antisexist institutions overnight, but we can suggest changes in the educational environment that help promote these processes.[a]

Sonia Nieto suggests a number of specific changes teachers can

make in each of the following areas:

I. Countering racism, sexism, and low expectations
   • Promoting and actively working toward creating a diverse staff
   • Making difference and similarities an explicit part of the curriculum
   • Making racism and discrimination an explicit part of the curriculum
II. Changing schools: Restructure and renewal
   • Investigating the effects of school organizational structures like tracking, testing, and disciplinary policies; the curriculum and pedagogy, as well as the physical structure of the school
   • Increasing the role of students, teachers, parental, and community involvement
III. Respecting and affirming cultural differences
IV. Perceiving linguistic diversity as a resource.[b]

[a] S. Nieto, *Affirming diversity: The sociopolitical context of multicultural education* (New York: Longman, 1992), p. 286.
[b] S. Nieto, pp. 284–301.

only the struggles these families face but the strategies they used to overcome the obstacles they encountered. These researchers concluded that the family context was strong. Why wasn't that family strength being represented in the school experience of these children? If educators were better able to recognize strengths of all kinds in their students, then negative expectations might change, thus positively affecting achievement of all students.

There are positive examples of children from the most economically disadvantaged families who have reached unparalleled levels of success in school in

spite of the tremendous odds against them. Ronald Edmond's (1986) research on effective schools found a substantial number of schools in which poor children demonstrated academic achievement as high as their peers in middle-class schools. The Success for All program reported by Robert Slavin, et al. (1990), is a comprehensive inner-city program designed to bring all children to grade level by third grade. It provides another positive example. The results from the first year of the program showed substantially enhanced language and reading skills compared to children who were involved in other programs. A number of

One of the characteristics associated with both successful schools and successful teachers is the ability to project high expectations for all their students. In such an environment, minority and lower-class children have demonstrated much higher academic success rates.

additional positive examples and suggestions can be found in the December/January 1992 issue of *Educational Leadership*, Volume 49, Number 4, entitled "Whose Culture?"

ATTITUDES TOWARD SELF

We humans have known about the importance of self-knowledge for a long time. Socrates said that the unexamined life was not worth living. It is obvious that the way teachers perceive and feel about themselves is a major determinant of classroom atmosphere and student performance. Self-confidence, poise, self-control, an eagerness to lead a class of children will obviously set the tone for cooperation and learning in the class. Similarly, a superanxious, trembling, insecure teacher will set the opposite tone.

As David Powlett-Jones makes clear in his discussion of the first day of teaching (see Spotlight On Teacher Attitudes toward Self), a teacher with an insecure self-concept can invite trouble in the classroom. How we see ourselves is a most important component in determinining classroom atmosphere.

A Concerns-Based Approach

Frances Fuller, of the University of Texas, pioneered an approach to the personal aspects of teaching effec-

tiveness (1969). She found that almost all student teachers and beginning teachers experience a similar sequence of phases of personal growth. She was able to chart the phases and called her approach the CBAM method (concerns-based adoption model). Table 14.5 outlines the central components of the scheme.

The phases can be grouped into three general categories: (1) self-concerns, (2) management, and (3) impact (Borich, 1988). In the first group of phases teachers are worried about whether the students really like them, how they are being evaluated, how they feel as teachers, and how they fit with the more experienced teachers in the building. Fuller has shown that such a concentration on self is a normal expectation. During the first phases then, a heightened selfconsciousness is the mode. After all, the situation is new. As a beginner, you are an outsider. The process is strange and the role unfamiliar. In Piaget's terms, the need to accommodate, to learn a new role, to adjust to an unfamiliar environment creates a classic disequilibrium. Recall, from Chapter 5, the outline of the process of knowledge disturbances (perturbations) that occur in pupils when new learning is required. Basically, Fuller was saying that this same process applies to you as a beginning teacher. During such a period of disequilibrium then, you can expect some preoccupation with yourself, your appearance, and relationships. This will have the effect of narrowing your

SPOTLIGHT ON TEACHER ATTITUDES TOWARD SELF

A Shaky Start That Came Close to Disaster

In R. F. Delderfield's award-winning novel *To Serve Them All My Days*,[a] David Powlett-Jones, the hero, has just returned to civilian life after a series of injuries at the close of World War I. He finds himself in front of his first classroom, a group of unruly fifteen-year-olds in an English prep school. He's had no real teaching experience and felt subtly pressured into accepting the position as a result of a very persuasive and charismatic headmaster. In addition, his physical recovery from his injuries has been quite slow, leaving him with an obvious case of tremors both in his hands and voice. In fact, he had originally looked forward to attending a major university but in his current condition that seems impossible, almost as unlikely as teaching school. He muses, "What headmaster in his senses would engage a wreck like me, who jumps a foot in the air every time a door bangs?"

The boys, of course, are quick to sense the whole picture. A partially shell-shocked veteran, unsure about his role, inexperienced, shaky, and desiring to retreat to the hills of his native Wales—the invitation to mischief is unmistakable. Quietly the boys go to work. Eyes dart. Hand signals are passed. The air is electric. The staged melodrama is ready. On cue one of the boys goes into a paroxysm. His distress looks real. He writhes on the floor. His companions run about—one to the window, one to the door, another to Mr. Powlett-Jones. "Don't worry, sir! Only one of Boyer's fits, sir!" The class waits in anticipation. Surely the teacher is on the verge of falling for the whole stunt. What a laugh the boys will have afterward. To defeat the newcomer on the first day will go down in the annals of Bamfylde. Little do they really care about this shaking, nervous teacher in front of them.

It is not to be. In spite of his inner feelings, Powlett-Jones is able to draw on his dwindling inner resources. Something about Boyer gives him a clue. The game is overplayed just enough to cast some doubt. Just on instinct he takes a chance. He steps back and, using his best military voice, calls, "Silence! Places!" The well-rehearsed trick has been uncovered. Boyer's face is now drained of color for real. The confederates are marched up in front of the class while the teacher now calmly dresses them down. "Quite a performance! But it needs working on Boyer! You're not bad, but your partner is a terrible ham."

He quickly reestablishes order, having gained an entirely different attitude toward himself. He is a teacher after all.

---

[a] R. F. Delderfield, *To serve them all my days* (New York: Simon & Schuster, 1972).

A shaky start.

---

perceptions at the outset. Given a reasonable amount of support and time, you will find yourself moving to the second group of Fuller phases.

In the management phase, the beginner is focused on teaching behaviors and strategies. The self-consciousness of the first phases gradually gives way to concerns about method. This means you will find yourself asking questions such as, Are the assignments on target? Are my instructions clear? Where can I find more planning time to revise some units?

Am I using positive reinforcement or am I reinforcing inappropriate behavior? In a sense, the focus is still on self but it is also on teaching behavior. Learning how to manage the class, to operate smoothly, handle the transitions, maintain order, and do it all with enthusiasm is obviously a major concern during this phase.

The impact category includes consequences, collaboration, and refocusing. It is notable that beginners actually proceed from self to management *before* they

TABLE 14.5   PHASES OF CONCERN: TYPICAL EXPRESSIONS

PHASE	EXPRESSION	FEELINGS
6. Refocusing	I've started to modify some of the standard techniques to promote inquiry and it works.	Competent, excited
5. Collaboration	I tried out a new unit on creativity that I'll share with a colleague. My colleague has been helpful to me.	Successful, confident
4. Consequence, impact	Are all my students learning enough? How can I match and mismatch? Are my expectations fair to all?	Positive, puzzled, occasionally apprehensive
3. Management	How can I control the class? Which management techniques work best?	Frustrated, discouraged, occasionally pleased
2. Personal	How do I look to the students? How am I in coming across to them? Do they like and respect me?	Anxious, self-conscious, scared
1. Information	There are an awful lot of ideas and teaching methods I need to find out about.	Curious but somewhat apprehensive
0. Awareness	I'm not really concerned even though I don't know how to teach	Apathetic

can become greatly concerned over impact. After you feel comfortable with the students in a reasonably controlled environment, you will be able to concentrate on teaching outcomes. At that point, you will be able to set aside the earlier concerns almost entirely and attend to what happens to the pupils. In our terms, you may begin to recognize individual differences, modify teaching methods, flex with and "read" the pupils, and vary the structure to meet student needs. In short, you will be on your way to becoming a complete teacher. You will be able to analyze and change your practice. Careful reflection will occur as a natural part of your work.

Unfortunately, Fuller's work has shown that student teachers and beginning teachers generally do not reach the level of impact. Instead, some remain at the personal level, while the majority reach management. The problem, however, is not the beginner's fault. It has been shown that novice teachers all too often do not receive adequate professional support and supervision (Griffin, 1985). It is not unusual for the newest teacher to receive the toughest assignment, the most difficult-to-reach children, the worst room, and an inadequate orientation. As noted at the beginning of the chapter, it is hardly surprising that under these conditions a novice has difficulty moving beyond survival (self). Somewhat ironically, a major review noted that the problems have been more than adequately identified, yet we are short on solutions (Veenman, 1984).

Quite recently, the question of more adequate support and guidance for beginners has received new attention. Although we cannot provide all the details, many states are now taking the question of beginning teacher induction seriously. One major example has been set up in North Carolina to provide special training in supervision (Thies-Sprinthall and Sprinthall, 1987). Such mentor programs result in providing the novice with on-site help on a continuous basis. Research has shown that novice teachers in these programs do proceed more quickly through the Frances Fuller phases of concern. This means that the beginner can attend more quickly and more competently to the needs of the students. We noted in Chapter 1 that classroom teaching involved four "corners": self, pupils, strategies, and content. Student teaching as traditionally organized and beginning to teach without adequate mentoring do not provide the conditions for professional growth. However, with recognition of the legitimate needs for guided assistance, both student teachers and novice teachers can reach competent levels of practice.

A Reflective Inquiry Approach

There are many ways for teachers to develop and maintain an awareness of their unconscious biases and differential behavior toward students.

1. Videotape a teaching session and rate your behavior as observed in the tape.

2. Have a colleague, student teacher, or even a student keep track of certain behaviors for a desig-

nated period of time. Design a checklist to keep track of who goes out of the room for special services, whose art work you hang up, which parents you invite to come into the classroom.

3. Write narratives about your teaching experiences.

4. Focus on one issue, such as how you plan groups for instruction, and then research it further with a group of interested colleagues.

5. Take classes or seminars in cultural and gender awareness. Investigate your own stages of racial identity and the racial identity development of other cultures.

Let us focus on an in-depth discussion of the last three items for teacher reflection.

Teacher narratives   The creation of and contemplation on teachers' stories contribute to professional growth. Teachers' stories represent attempts by teachers to reflect upon incidents in their lives and classrooms. Mary Renck Jalongo (1992) suggests that teachers' stories invite reflection and are, in themselves, a metaphor for change. She lists a dozen ideas which can be the starting point for teachers' stories (Jalongo, 1992, p. 69). You may want to try one of these to develop your own narrative.

1. Reflections on Improvement

2. A Metaphor for Myself

3. At Least

4. Joyful Moments

5. Imaginary Dialogue

6. Unrevealed Kindnesses

7. Remembrances

8. Low Points

9. Heights and Depths

10. Memorable Teachers

11. Packing Decisions

12. Looking Back

Nancy Frane wrote this short beginning of a narrative as one of her experiences in teaching first grade.

I remember teaching first grade the year that Nate was in my class. I clipped a little microphone onto my shirt and hooked the transmitter box onto my belt. Nate put the receiver around his neck, hooked the box to his belt, and switched one of his hearing

aids to a different setting. "Testing, testing, are we on?" I would say. If Nate grinned and shook his head, I would generally groan, and change any variable I could think of to make it work. After a while, the other children would help. "Nate, are you sure you are on Channel A?" "Did you remember to turn it ON, Ms. Frane?" they would ask. When we triumphed, we could all talk and hear about why some of the marigolds died, and why eleven is an odd number. When the darned thing would not work, there was an undercurrent of tension in the room, as I strained my voice and pantomimed everything I could. The other children waited patiently (and not so patiently) for me to repeat everything, and Nate strained to follow the discussion. In the middle of a heated conversation about whether or not 53 is a "five number" (a multiple of five) because, "after all, it has a five in it," Nate announced that we were "off." In fact, his whole hearing aid was off. Never minding about the five numbers, I flipped the old battery out of the hearing aid and passed it around. Under a pile of file cards and erasers in my desk, I found a new battery and passed that around. Nate passed his hearing aids around. I showed the transmitter box, and all the children took turns wearing the microphone. We talked about batteries, microphones, and ears of all kinds. After that, I noticed how easily the other children wore the microphone to talk with Nate during show and tell. At group time, the children on either side of Nate leaned in toward him, sometimes resting a head on his shoulder, to hear the sounds through his transmitter, and Nate would generously turn up the volume so that the others could hear the transmitter more clearly. (Frane, 1992, unpublished)

Another example of a short narrative is Vivian Gussin Paley's own experience with a student teacher.

Janet, my student teacher, was more sensitive to the feelings of children than the most experienced teachers I know. She instinctively understood the nature of objectivity and involvement. Her involvement did not encourage dependency and her objectivity could never be interpreted as indifference.

She liked every single child. This is a great comfort to children, having a teacher who likes everyone and knows how to show it. When you have a teacher who likes some and not others, you must keep maneuvering for her approval. This interferes with the more important business of learning to relate to your own peers.

Stuart was in our class that year, and he had a bad stutter. Stuttering, like skin color, is a characteristic most teachers prefer to ignore. Even after I could comfortably discuss color, I could not easily refer to a child's stuttering. I would look intently at the child and not let anyone interrupt, even in the natural way children always interrupt each other. I felt as though I was holding my breath.

Janet, by her example, showed me that I was afraid of the stuttering. My behavior revealed an inability to accept this stuttering child. After she had been in our class a few days, Janet was reading a story about a boy going to the Central Park Zoo in New York. Stuart excitedly tried to say that he had been there, but got stuck on the word "my" and could not extricate himself. Janet said, "Stuart, I see you have trouble with certain words, like 'my.' Some people call that stuttering. When you get older you'll figure out what to do about those words. But we don't mind waiting for you to say them. Not a bit. Take your time."

Larry was in the group listening to the story. "No, we don't mind. Not a bit," he repeated. Susan picked it up. "Sure. Just take your time." I realized what was going on. Janet had shown everyone it was all right to talk to Stuart about his stuttering. The message they had got from me was that it was not all right. And to Stuart, she was saying, in effect, "You don't have to try to keep this problem a secret."

Janet was interested in Stuart's problem, for one of her own children stuttered. She would say things like, "Stuart, you're having trouble with 'give' right now. Try saying, 'Let me have it' or 'I need it' instead of 'give it to me.'" She was showing him that the stuttering did not have to control him. He could manipulate a little, change a few words, make a game out of it. She was not acting like a speech therapist. She was just putting herself in his shoes and figuring out what *she* would do if she stuttered. He knew that and he felt good about it. (Paley, 1989, pp. 40–41)

Nona Lyons' (1990) work analyzes teacher narratives and reveals how teachers' perspectives toward knowledge and their views of themselves and their students as knowers enter into their teaching and can at times be part of their continuing personal development. Carol Witherell and Nel Noddings (1991) in their book *Stories Lives Tell: Narrative and Dialogue in Education* present teacher narratives that focus on themes of connection and separation in teachers' lives and the paradoxical struggle to become autonomous within the context of relationships at school. In these writings teachers share their individual inquiry and reflection on issues in their classroom.

Collaborative action research   This is a research process in which teams of teachers and university researchers study some aspect of their work in an effort to promote improved practice, develop staff, and contribute to theory in their field. It is based on the premise that those who are involved in the process of discovering the need and direction for change will be able to successfully carry it out. Action research was developed in the 1940s and 1950s (see Corey, 1953) as a means of applying the scientific method to social science and improving school practices. In the 1970s and 1980s, it was instrumental in effecting educational reform in England and Australia (Elliot, 1991; Kemmis and McTaggart, 1988) and has gained respect and usage in the United States (Holly, 1991). This brief overview compares collaborative action research with traditional research, and explains how the successful use of collaborative action research contributes to teacher development.

Traditional research is often conducted outside of the real-life educational context of the schools. Researchers who are not in close contact with the educational community may develop theories that are not in line with the concerns of the teachers and test them in ways that do not replicate the typical learning environment. In addition, there are few direct routes for the dissemination of research findings. Accessible resources are sometimes confusing due to technical language or difficult to apply in the classroom. Collaborative action research, on the other hand, is grounded in practice. The specific focus of the research grows out of issues that are immediately relevant to the teachers on a research team. The research is conducted within the school context and revised, when warranted, to meet the needs of the situation or the students or the teachers. For example, suppose that, in the course of collecting data on peer teaching, it is discovered that the chosen peer teaching format is too unwieldy for the number of students in a classroom. Rather than waiting to discover whether an unrealistic teaching strategy will yield good results the researcher can revise the format of the new peer teaching strategy immediately and resume the research. Consequently, the findings can be easily applied to the real-life setting. The gap between researcher and teacher is eliminated.

Teachers and university faculty working collaboratively can provide a good complement for this work. By sharing research skills and theoretical knowledge teachers, principals, counselors, and other school personnel may increase their access to broader technical and academic resources. In some projects teachers may direct the process while the university personnel act as consultants and offer technical support. In others, the university faculty can facilitate the overall collaborative action process while the teachers determine the specifics of the study. Leadership and involvement will shift naturally depending on what skills and expertise are necessary at various points in the project; yet the process should always remain democratic. Best results occur when communication between participants is open and frequent, and the school practitioners are integrally involved in every aspect of the research process.

The exact procedure for a collaborative action research study will vary depending on the nature of the group and the research question. However, the following provides a rough model:

1. *Choose a research focus.* This may come about when a group of educators identify a problem to be solved or a situation to be understood better. Alternatively, university teachers may provide an umbrella focus (e.g., the development of higher-order thinking skills) under which educators choose a specific research question or questions (e.g., What percentage of the teacher questioning currently stimulates higher-order responses? or, Will peer teaching produce greater results in accurate formation of concepts?). At this point, the team may choose to gather some baseline or current status data for later comparison or for more insight into the current situation by identifying specific ideas and questions to focus on.

2. *Review information related to research focus or question.* This can stimulate the development of specific research questions or provide in-depth understanding of already chosen questions. It can also serve to familiarize the group with possible approaches to conduct the study.

3. *Develop a plan to answer the specific research question.* This includes determining the kinds of data to be collected, from whom or what will be collected, research methods to be employed, and project length. It may also involve implementing an experimental practice for comparison or evaluation. Precisely defined research questions will be easiest to work with.

4. *Conduct the research.* Plans are modified and revised as needed.

5. *Analyze the data and apply the findings.* Findings may create impetus for action or warrant further study. Solid findings are generally applicable beyond individual classrooms, and a plan for their dissemination (discussion, school meeting, reports) may be formed. In this way the team members guide their own practice and contribute theory to the broader education community.

6. The above five steps are repeated in a process or cycle of continued planning, action, observing, reflecting, and replanning to investigate a classroom or school problem in a systematic way.

The process of collaboration and the opportunity to reflect on an experiment with practice are vehicles for both professional and personal growth. Collaboration offers opportunities to exchange ideas and consider other perspectives; it requires creating and acting upon group decisions. Through these, educators can become more flexible in thinking, increase their repertoire of action research and problem solving skills, further develop communication skills, and strengthen bonds of collegiality. Time for reflection enables teachers to evaluate practice. You may become clearer in your own educational philosophy and its connection to your actions in the school and classroom. Creating a context in which experimentation is the norm frees you to consider and test ideas without fear of criticism.

The identification of personal development during the course of these experiences is significant to teaching. Levels of adult development have been positively associated with the ability to facilitate learning. Teachers at higher stages of adult development are more able to "read" the needs of students and are more adaptive and flexible in their teaching styles. Thus they are better prepared to *provide* for the variety of learners and learning situations that are present in every classroom. It is evident that the *process* of collaborative action research may be as important as the individual practices researched (Oja and Smulyan, 1989).

When teachers work together in collaborative action research, they gain in their capacity to reflect on their values, assumptions, and attitudes and improve their teaching practices. Reflection then becomes self-initiated within a safety net of collaboration among colleagues. Teachers gain in their cognitive flexibility to meet students' learning needs and in their ability to understand the complexities of teaching. Teachers who advance in postconventional stages of development prefer the collaborative action research team for solving school and classroom problems because it is nonhierarchical and self-managed, it has norms of experimentation, it involves shared decision making, and it provides a context in which teachers can develop their own tasks, roles, and responsibilities in the process.

Additionally, teachers who work with their students in collaborative action research describe their classes as more alive. The teacher models inquiry methods and reflective practice, and the students become an increasing part of the classroom evaluation procedures. A spirit of inquiry permeates the classroom and school. Classrooms become restructured so that students' roles change. Students become less passive and more involved in planning, evaluating, and introspecting. Pride is developed in the classroom, and trust between teachers and students increases.

People who have participated in and studied the collaborative action research process have suggested various criteria for successful projects.

1. Choosing a question for inquiry that is important enough to warrant the time spent studying it

2. A willingness to examine one's own practice and an openness to the perspective of others

3. Effective group collaboration, including shared commitment to the process and project, opportunity for all voices to be heard, and good facilitation

4. Support of the school administration in terms of time and encouragement

The climate of the 1990s is increasingly conducive for teachers to become action researchers on school and classroom problems. Efforts by the districts to improve the schools are changing the administrative policies to allow teachers to be more active in the school. As a result collaborative action research is seen as an advantage and not as a threat to administrative decision making. Although time is a concern, school improvement programs encourage administrators to structure the day to provide more time for teachers to solve problems together. Successful collaborative action research requires a climate of trust. As collaboration among teachers grows, the traditional barriers and closed-door policies among teachers will change.

Racial identity stages   Racism is an unfortunate fact of life in society that profoundly affects people's aspirations and experiences. We think that the following models can be helpful for teachers to learn more about their own unconscious assumptions and beliefs about race. Talking about race, learning about racism, and using the racial identity development models may help make you more conscious of your own expectations about race and culture and help you teach *all* students in your schools more effectively.

Not only is it important to be conscious of your own biases and assumptions, but it is also important to be able to evaluate your students' developmental positions along the continuums of racial, cultural, and gender-based identity stages in order to better match and appropriately mismatch instructional strategies to students' developmental needs in the classroom. Like all the stage theories written about in this textbook, your place on these **racial identity stages** affects your ability to teach effectively, especially across racial and ethnic "barriers."

Educators who are attempting to match their instruction to their students' levels of development in an ATI framework need to consider the impact of race. It is important for teachers to understand their own assumptions about race and to deal seriously with issues of racism as experienced by students.

Beverly Daniel Tatum (1992b) compares the stages of white racial identity development by Janet Helms (1990) with William Cross's (1991) model of black racial identity development. She uses these two models because they are among the most frequently cited on black racial identity development and on white racial identity development. The two models of racial identity development are outlined briefly here.

Janet Helms (1990) describes the evolution of a positive white racial identity development as involving both abandonment of racism and the development of a nonracist white identity. She identified six stages in a model of white racial identity development. The first stage is the *contact* stage; one is unaware of cultural and institutional racism, and of one's own white privilege. There is often naive curiosity about or fear of people of color, based on stereotypes from media, family, or friends. Stage two is called the *disintegration* stage because the bliss of ignorance at stage one is replaced by the shame, guilt, and sometimes anger at the recognition of one's own advantage because of being white and the role of whites in the maintenance of a racist system. Stage three, *reintegration*, and the person's desire to be accepted by one's own racial group, may lead to a reshaping of the person's belief system to be more congruent with an acceptance of racism; the guilt and anxiety of the previous stage may be redirected in the form of fear and anger toward people of color (particularly black people), who are now blamed as the source of discomfort. At stage four, the *pseudoindependent* stage, one abandons beliefs in white superiority, but may still behave in ways that unintentionally perpetuate the system. At the fifth stage, *immersion/emersion*, one is uncomfortable with his or her own "whiteness," yet unable to be truly anything else, and the white individual begins a search to replace racially related myths and stereotypes with accurate information about what it means and has meant to be white in U.S. society. At the final stage, *autonomy*, a newly defined sense of oneself as white is internalized and the person is energized to confront racism and oppression in daily life.

Cross describes five stages in the development of black identity. In the first stage of *pre-encounter*, the African American has absorbed many of the beliefs and values of the dominant white culture. The individual seeks to assimilate and be accepted by whites and actively or passively keeps a distance from other black people. Movement into the *encounter* stage begins by an event(s) that forces the individual to acknowledge the impact of racism in one's life. Faced with the reality that he or she cannot truly be white, one is forced to focus on his or her identity as a member of a group targeted by racism. In the third stage of *immersion/emersion*, there are simultaneous desires to surround oneself with visible symbols of one's racial identity and to actively avoid symbols of whiteness. The fourth stage of internalization begins when one feels secure in one's own *sense of racial identity*. The individual at this stage is willing to establish meaningful relationships with white people who acknowledge and are respectful of his or her self-definition. *Internalization-commitment* is the final stage in which people have found ways to translate their personal, internalization of blackness into a plan of action for a sense of commitment to the concerns of African Americans as a group, and sustain this commitment over time. Movement through the five stages may be described as a spiral motion (as Perry and the *Women's Ways* authors describe in their stages of intellectual development). In new situations or as a result of new encounters, the person may go back to an earlier stage, to recycle through the stages, and deal with the new experience which may be different from the original experience. Each time a person reaches the next stage, she or he can look back and see the earlier position.

As a result of Tatum's study (1987) and review of the literature in the stages of racial identity (1992b), she suggests that for other students (Asian, Latin, Native American), the process of racial identity development may be similar to that described for African Americans (see, for example, Phinney, 1990).

Values and Teaching

One very common approach to the dilemma of values and teaching has been to say that teaching is like indoctrination. "Face it, teaching is a form of brainwashing," or so this view proclaims. Since adults know more than kids, it is right and just for the adults to induct each new generation of children into the ways of the adult world. There is no need to be upset by this indoctrination; it's simply the way things are—a natural law. This is something like saying, "Well, so what's wrong with teaching middle-class values; after all, that's the majority view. And most everybody would like to be middle class anyway!" The fact that such rhetoric makes the shabby rationalizations seem palatable to some raises more questions than it answers.

Another, more elegant, solution to the value dilemma has been to suggest that teaching should be value-free—that is, teachers really should express no genuine personal values. They should present all sides of any question fairly and impartially. Like anthropologists studying another culture, teachers would be trained for neutrality. Their only values would be plurality and relativism: All views would have merit and receive equal treatment. Not only would there be freedom for all views, but teachers would also be expected to pursue and embody all views with equal vigor.

Asa G. Hilliard III (1992) calls us to "awaken to the fact that no academic content is neutral nor is the specific cultural content of any group universal in and of itself" (p. 13). Perhaps the most adequate means of conveying the impossibility of value neutrality in teaching is to offer a brief example. A social studies teacher who was supervising a group of teacher trainees had become embroiled in this very controversy. His trainees insisted that the pupils were to be "free." They, as future teachers, had no right to impose their views on the children. The social studies master teacher at this point gave up on the dialogue and invited the teachers-in-training to observe his next class. To make his point as dramatically as he knew how, he decided to teach his pupils about the disadvantages and advantages of the concentration camps of World War II. After listing the obvious disadvantages, he proceeded "objectively" to list the advantages—the creation of jobs (guards, dog trainers, searchlight makers), the uncrowding of cities, the increase in availability of housing, and even the production of certain goods almost too grisly to mention.

The horrified practice teachers immediately protested that the master teacher was being unfair. How was it possible to even consider a concentration camp as an advantage to anyone? The master teacher had reduced the idea of value-free teaching to an absurdity. To say that he was merely presenting evidence from a "different point of view" was simply a means of begging the question of values.*

TEACHING GOALS AND STRATEGIES: A DEVELOPMENTAL MODEL

It is apparent that teaching can hardly be considered as brainwashing and that relativism just as obviously leads in a circle. We need to return to the ideas from prior chapters on strategies and goals as a framework for our role concepts. The attitudes we hold toward the role of the teacher bear a direct relationship to the strategies we employ and the goals we seek to achieve. If we examine the question from the student's point of view as well as in terms of the goals of a democratic society, we can begin to formulate an answer.

We have shown, especially in the first sections of this book, that all children enter school with potential for development. Such development takes place in the cognitive, personal, and value domains. By viewing students developmentally, we gain a picture of how pupils presently function *and* their potential for developing increasingly more complex systems of thinking, self-development, and value judgment. Whether or not such growth takes place depends on an appropriate match between where the learner is and what level he or she is moving toward. The teacher's role is to arrange the learning environment in all subject areas to stimulate the natural process of development. Each child brings to us a natural desire to learn, an innate urge to grow. Of course, as a result of past experience, this desire may not be as obvious with some pupils as it is with other, more openly eager learners. Yet all have the potential. We've called this the process of accommodation, the need to learn more about the world and find better ways to solve problems.

On one side of the teacher, then, we have a group of youngsters whose developmental needs are ready to be met in the service of their own growth. But consider a different perspective—the teacher as an agent for the democratic goals of the adult society. Without going into the deep philosophical questions, it is clear that the goals of a democracy absolutely demand effective education for its young people. The purpose of education in its broadest sense is to teach them how to think, especially about democratic principles. For adults to function successfully as citizens they must know not only how to work and contribute to the general welfare but also how to weigh questions, vote intelligently, understand equity and the generic meaning of democratic freedom and responsibility, and appreciate differences among people. For that to happen, for such broad societal goals to be achieved, the schools' role is critical. An informed public is the keystone to anyone's definition of democracy. Without development, our children will remain in prejudice, ignorance, and self-centeredness. Thomas Jefferson stated the issue most succinctly: "If a nation expects to be ignorant and free, in a state of civilization, it expects what never was and never will be."

The daily activity of the classroom can be a vehicle to accomplish this admittedly lofty goal. Mouthing great phrases and calling on eternal virtues will not do it. In fact, we have shown through Lawrence Kohlberg's research that talk and moral behavior do not go hand in hand. Thus the day-to-day process of gradual development in the classroom is very significant. We can't hurry the process; acceleration too often leads to low-level memorization. Thus, the goals and strategies of teaching aim to promote the developing potential of each child through a sequence from less complex to higher-order, more complex thinking, self-development, and value judgment.

Since this chapter has focused on the person of the teacher, where does that person come into this picture? Learning more intensively about children outlines their potentials for growth. Learning more about your own attitudes and stages outlines your potential. So we can hold up the same mirror. Your own growth as a professional teacher is a central consideration. As the orchestrator of the classroom, you determine much of what transpires. We have shown how negative teacher expectancies adversely affect student growth. We have also shown how a limited range of strategies has similarly negative outcomes. Only the teacher who gradually develops to higher levels of complexity as an individual can also increasingly master the art of teaching. Matching and

---

* This case example was provided by Bernard Seiderman, formerly of the Great Neck, Long Island, school system.

SPOTLIGHT ON PERSONAL GROWTH

Bill Perry's Wise Father

So far in this volume we have been stressing a set of assumptions that represents a system of values, attitudes, and perceptions we prize. We feel, for example, that the idea of stages of growth and development allows us to view the problems of education from the point of view of our children's needs. When L. K. Frank (see Chapter 6) spoke of the fundamental psychological needs of children as opposed to those of adults, he provided us with a basic framework for examining our values as educators. If children grow and develop at different rates and proceed through different stages, we as educators have the opportunity to facilitate and nurture that growth. We noted that certain sensitive periods provide us with an opportunity to nurture particular kinds of growth. We also outlined in greater detail the stages of cognitive, personal, and moral development. Equipped with this understanding, the teacher can draw up a self-definition as an educator that can include the objectives of promoting maximal growth and development within each stage and across all stages. Then we stressed the problems of intervention, both from a theoretical and from a practical point of view. These chapters should allow you to put theory to practice.

When we noted the problems confronting educational psychology in Chapter 1, we emphasized the troublesome dichotomy between thinking about educational problems and doing something about them. The teacher's self-image is clearly a key element in resolving this separation. If the self-image is that of someone who arranges practice and creates the conditions for maximal learning matched to the pupils' developmental stages, then the dichotomy disappears. By valuing the growth and development of each child and by knowing what the effective teaching techniques are, the educator comes close to the original definition of an educator. To educate, in its root sense, means to draw out, to elicit, to develop. We need to clear away the psychological blind spots imposed by social-class distinction, our own stereotyped perceptions, and the narrow and confining sets of attitudes we have toward knowledge, children, and ourselves. By putting on a new set of personal "lenses," we may come to see both ourselves and children in significantly different ways.

In closing this section, one final, very significant point should be made. Developmentally oriented teachers and professors are generally so convinced of the basic value of growth and development that they at times become overly zealous and ideological. If we are convinced that it is important for children and teenagers to learn to think more logically, systematically, divergently, and convergently, as well as to develop empathy, compassion, and their own humanness, then it is all too easy to become a single-minded "pusher" of our own pet goals. If we are convinced that growth is good, we may find ourselves constantly pulling, exhorting, cajoling, shoving, engendering perpetual dissonance, always "jamming," always saying to pupils in so many words, "Well, that's O.K., but not quite good enough. Let's move on!"

This creates a double bind for the pupil. If new growth requires constant agitation, we will soon opt out. We all get sick of being constantly prodded, nagged, or exhorted to excel. Thus, the educator needs a special blend of competence to create a learning atmosphere that helps pupils grow *and* affirms the acceptability of their current status.

Robert White has used the metaphor of the horticulturist as a way to sum up the paradox of human teaching and human learning:

> The nurturing of growth requires the patience of the gardener rather than the hasty intervention of the mechanic. It requires waiting for impulse to declare itself, for interest to appear, for initiative to come forth.[a]

William Perry presents the process and the paradox in more personal terms. He recently described an incident in his own life as an illustration. He was introducing his wife, Mary, to his aging father; only later did he learn his father was terminally ill at the time and this was to be the last meeting of Bill, his wife, and his father. At one point in the conversation, the father looked carefully at Mary and asked her if she was progressing. When she nodded in the affirmative, he then went on: "Well that's just fine, Mary, I'm glad that you're progressing. It's always important to grow, to improve yourself, to move ahead." At this point there was a moment of silence. Then the aging man leaned forward and, looking very directly at Mary, said: "But, remember, it's also important to be okay where you are right now!"

---

[a] R. W. White, *Lives in progress,* 2d ed. (New York: Holt, Rinehart & Winston, 1966), pp. 509–510.

mismatching requires a substantial ability to engage in *reflective teaching*. Teaching cannot be reduced to a series of robot moves. Reflective teaching means the ability to analyze the process of what you are doing and have an impact on children simultaneously. Sometimes this is called on-the-spot decision making.

Research has shown that even experienced teachers are not particularly adept at considering alternatives while teaching (Shavelson and Stern, 1981). Instead, the norm seems to be quick closure even though the research also indicates that such a limited ability to choose and select reduces student learning. The reason we point this out is that a strong tendency exists in all of us when we become aware of the developmental approach to expect that we can quickly go through a "growth spurt." In other words, we can accept the idea of gradual development, of slow but sure growth in others, but not in ourselves. We can take the "fast track" and get on with the process. The developmental method is for others. Bill Perry's wise father makes the point in the Spotlight on the opposite page: It is all right to "be" where you are right now, yet still understand that you can grow slowly.

Research has demonstrated that teachers who try out their current methods, master those, and systematically increase their repertoire of strategies show definite evidence of developmental growth (Thies-Sprinthall, 1984). An important component is cognitive reflection, that is, the ability to analyze your own teaching (Glassberg and Sprinthall, 1980). The two go hand in hand. You try a new approach and then review and analyze the results, make changes, and try again. To act without reflection leads to unguided fads, but reflection by itself leads to excessive introspection and inaction.

Fritz Oser (1986), a Swiss educator, has commented that teachers who actively engage in the process of *metareflection* will develop a discourse perspective. This means a growth in complexity of thought and an increase in confidence to express views or, in other words, to engage in discussions (discourse) with colleagues concerning the teaching-learning process.

SUMMARY

The personal side of teaching involves teacher attitudes in three general areas: (1) attitudes about teaching and learning, (2) attitudes toward pupils, and (3) attitudes toward self.

Teachers' attitudes toward learning sometimes harden into the belief that knowledge is truth; with this belief teachers expect pupils to look for the single correct answer to the problems posed in the classroom. Hunt has found that teachers' conceptual level influences how they teach. Teachers at a low conceptual level tend to be more authoritarian than teachers at higher levels and the former use a single method of teaching with all students.

Teacher attitudes toward students also influence teaching style. The early and now classic study of the importance of a self-fulfilling prophecy by Rosenthal and Jacobson illustrates the importance of such attitudes. A review of recent research documents the wide variety of student characteristics that "cause" teachers to treat some pupils negatively, reducing the possibility of academic achievement. Student social class, race, family background, temperament, gender, and academic achievement are among the important factors that influence teacher attitudes.

The attitudes toward self of teachers are also important. Frances Fuller (1969) catalogued seven phases of concern that teachers pass through in their personal growth in teaching. A continued reflective approach to teaching encourages teachers to think about attitudes toward self and the impact on practice. Methods for continued reflection on teaching include teacher narratives, collaborative action research, and investigation of racial identity stages. Teachers cannot be value-free in their interactions with students. They must strive to incorporate in their teaching a genuine developmental model designed to promote pupil growth both in subject matter competency and in the values needed for future citizenship in a democratic community which affirms diversity. By nurturing their own capacity for reflective teaching, teachers can play a major role in pupil growth.

KEY TERMS AND NAMES

Howard Becker
Jere Brophy and Thomas Good
developmental model
Elizabeth Fennema
Frances Fuller
hidden agenda

Sonia Nieto
John Ogbu
Profile of Nonverbal Sensitivity (PONS)
Rosenthal effect
racial identity stages
teacher expectations

THEORY INTO PRACTICE

The Process of Learning Self-Reflection

The most important dimension of the personal aspects of teaching concerns your ability to reflect upon experience. There is an old saying, "Ten years of experience or one year ten times," meaning, did the person learn anything new from experience? Reflection, however, is not an automatic process. Like nearly everything in education, reflection requires development. One way to begin the self-reflection process is to record your teaching experiences in a journal. The general guidelines for your journal are as follows:

1. The journal is to contain a focused account of your ideas and feelings before, during and after a series of teaching experiences.

2. The experience can be an individual tutorial, a small-group activity, or the teaching of an entire class. In other words, the experience itself must be real rather than a simulation or role-play.

3. Generally, it is best to regard the journal as your own private and confidential account* so that there will be a greater tendency for you to be honest with yourself. The result should be an uncensored account of your ideas and feelings.

---

* If, however, you have a professional supervisor or mentor whose role it is to facilitate your development, then you will find it helpful to share your journal with that person in order to obtain continuing feedback and suggestions to deepen your understanding.

4. You'll need to keep the journal over a reasonable time period, during student teaching, for example. Such a record will be meaningless, however, if you use it either sporadically or just at the beginning and the end. Continuity is crucial.

5. A journal is not a diary in the sense of recording running commentary or stream of consciousness. Instead, you need to keep the writing focused on the issues at hand in teaching. Also, it is not simply a content description of your activities (the so-called laundry list approach).

6. The goal of the journal is to provide you with an increasingly complex account of your cognitions and emotions. Such reflections under appropriate conditions can become a rich source of private information for self-development as a teacher.

7. At the outset, expect some personal dissonance unless you have done this activity once or twice before. Do not, however, become too critical of your initial accounts. Description without analysis is the approach most people use.

8. Often, beginning teachers find it helpful to use a checklist for their initial journalizing experiences. Others find that such structure is helpful for getting started and they then branch off into their own approach.

The checklist includes a series of directive questions such as:

---

1. List at least five feelings I experienced during the teaching episode:

2. List the teaching strategies I employed:

3. The main learnings I got from teaching this episode were:

4. Questions I have after reviewing my feelings, strategies, and learnings are:

5. Describe and analyze any notable student actions or reactions during the episode:

6. What concerns me most at the moment:

7. I rate my experiences in this episode as: Inadequate _____ Marginal _____ Excellent _____

The rule of thumb is that the journal entry needs to be longer than one page but less than four. Too brief an account will not give you enough feedback, while writing very extensively may become so burdensome that after an initial week or two you'll start skipping.

After you've made three or four entries, you might wish to check on your level of analysis. If so, go back to the section on Bloom's levels (Chapter 13) and review the characteristics. See if you are becoming more analytic in your commentary.

How are the feelings changing? How are they the same and how different?

How are the strategies changing? Are you more aware of differences in effectiveness with some content, or with some pupils?

Are you beginning to understand how the basic assumptions relate to different strategies?

A final note: Remember that these questions are only to serve as a means to focus your reflections on the personal experience of teaching. You may find the checklist approach too confining. If so, follow your own method. The point is to promote a regular and systematic approach to the subjective side of teaching. In so doing you will be making the first steps toward becoming a reflective practitioner. Hopefully your expectations of yourself and of individual pupils will become more complex.

Assessing Phases of Concern

In addition to learning how to reflect in general through journalizing, you can reanalyze the content of your journal by applying Fuller's phases. After you've made a series of entries, examine what you've noted as the major questions and what you've written down as your major feelings.

To practice identifying phases and feeling, see if you can classify the following statements, using the codes (phase numbers) that follow this table.

EXPRESSION	PHASE	FEELINGS
1. I don't have enough time to organize my class activities.	___	___
2. The students don't seem to think that I'm "with-it."	___	___
3. I feel absolutely drained after every class.	___	___
4. My planning period was interrupted again. I had a hard time trying to get all materials.	___	___
5. I keep hearing about how important clothes are in sending different messages—power colors—but I'm more comfortable in jeans.	___	___
6. A friend told me about a new curriculum guide in the library about teaching for thinking.	___	___
7. I noticed during the cooperative learning groups that I can see the different levels of student questions much more clearly.	___	___
8. I just came out of the teachers' room. Nobody paid any attention to me. They all seem so confident.	___	___
9. I just heard that I'm to be evaluated through a "surprise" visit.	___	___
10. At parents' night, I found out that three of my pupils who are doing very well in class were originally classified as mildly retarded and hated school.	___	___
11. Somebody said the assistant principal was spooking around. I don't know who that person is, and what's more I don't care.	___	___
12. We are trying a new approach. It's called team planning and teaching. I've learned a lot and many of my own ideas were received very positively by the other members of the team.		

CODE	PHASE	FEELINGS*
3	Management	Frustrated
2	Personal	Self-conscious
2	Personal	Anxious, exhausted
3	Management	Annnoyed
2	Personal	Confused, worried
1	Information	Curious
4	Consequence	Pleased, gratified
2	Personal	Scared, isolated
2	Personal	Apprehensive
4	Consequence	Proud, competent
1	No awareness	Apathy
5	Collaboration	Confident and accepted

* These should be considered as only a sample of feelings that may be generated and is in no way the complete range.

REFERENCES

American Association of University Women. (1992). *How schools shortchange girls.* Washington, DC: AAUW Educational Foundation.

Badad, E., Bernieri, F., and Rosenthal, R. (1991). Students as judges of teachers' verbal and non-verbal behavior. *American Educational Research Journal, 28*(1), 211–234.

Becker, H. (1969). Social class variation in the teacher-pupil relationship. In R.C. Sprinthall and N.A. Sprinthall (Eds.), Educational psychology: Selected readings. New York: Van Nostrand-Reinhold, pp. 300–308.

Block, J. H. (1984). *Sex role identity and ego development.* San Francisco: Jossey-Bass.

Borich, G. D. (1988). *Effective teaching methods.* Columbus, Ohio: Merrill.

Brophy, J. E., and Good, T. L. (1974). *Teacher-student relationships: Causes and consequences.* New York: Holt, Rinehart and Winston.

Burton, L.(Ed.). (1990). *Gender and mathematics: An international perspective.* Exeter, England: Cassell Educational Limited.

Corey, S. (1953). *Action research to improve school practices.* New York: Teachers College Press.

Cross, W. E., Jr. (1991). *Shades of black: Diversity in African-American identity.* Philadelphia: Temple University Press.

Delcos, V., Burns, M. S., and Kulewicz, S. (1987). Effects of dynamic assessment on teachers' expectations of handicapped children. *American Educational Research Journal, 24*(3), 325–336.

Delpit, L. D. (1988). The silenced dialogue: Power and pedagogy in educating other people's children. *Harvard Educational Review, 58*(3), 280–298.

Edmonds, R. (1986). Characteristics of effective schools. In U. Neisser (Ed.), *The school achievement of minority children: New perspectives.* Hillsdale, N.Y.: Erlbaum.

Elliot, J. (1991). *Action research for educational change.* Philadelphia: Open University Press.

Farber, P., Wilson, P., and Holm, G. (1989). From innocence to inquiry: A social reproduction framework. *Journal of Teacher Education, 40*(1), 45–50.

Fennema, E., and Leder, G. C. (Eds.) (1990). *Mathematics and Gender.* New York: Teachers College Press.

Fuller, F. (1969). Concerns of teachers: A developmental conceptualization. *American Educational Research Journal, 6,* 207–226.

Glassberg, S., and Sprinthall, N. A. (1980). Student teaching: A developmental approach. *Journal of Teacher Education, 31,* 31–38.

Good, T. (1983). Recent classroom research: Implications for teacher education. In D. C. Smith (Ed.), *Essential knowledge for beginning educators.* Washington: American Association of Colleges of Teacher Education.

Good, T. L., and Brophy, J. E. (1991). *Looking in classrooms.* New York: HarperCollins.

Griffin, G. (1985). Teacher induction: Research issues. *Journal of Teacher Education, 36*(1), 42–46.

Heath, S. B. (1983). *Ways with words.* Cambridge, Mass.: University Press.

Helms, J. E. (Ed.). (1990). *Black and white racial identity: Theory, research, and practice.* Westport, Conn.: Greenwood Press.

Hernandez, H. (1989). *Multicultural education: A teacher's guide to content and process.* Columbus, Ohio: Merrill.

Hilliard, A. G. (1992). Why we must pluralize the curriculum. *Educational Leadership, 49*(4), 12–16.

Holly, P. (1991). Action research: The missing link in the creation of schools as centers of inquiry. In A. Lieberman and L. Miller (Eds.), *Staff development for education in the 90's: New demands, new realities, new perspectives* (pp. 133–157). New York: Teachers College Press.

Hyde, J. S., Fennema, E., and Lamon, S. J. (1990). Gender differences in mathematics performance: A meta-analysis. *Psychological Bulletin, 107*(2), 139–155.

Jalongo, M. R. (1992). Teachers' stories: Our ways of knowing. *Educational Leadership, 49*(7), 68–73.

Joyce, B., Brown, C., and Peck, L. (1981). *Flexibility in teaching.* New York: Longman.

Kaufman, B. (1964). *Up the down staircase.* Englewood Cliffs, N.J.: Prentice-Hall.

Kemmis, S., and McTaggart, R. (1988). *The action research planner.* Victoria, Australia: Deakin University Press.

Kozol, J. (1967). *Death at an early age.* Boston: Houghton Mifflin.

Leacock, E. (1969). *Teaching and learning in city schools.* New York: Basic Books.

Lyons, N. (1990). Dilemmas of knowing: Ethical and epistemological dimensions of teachers' work and development. *Harvard Educational Review, 60*(2), 159–180.

Maccoby, E., and Jacklin, C. (1974). *The psychology of sex differences.* Stanford, Calif.: Stanford University Press.

McLuhan, M. H. (1964). *Understanding media.* New York: McGraw-Hill.

Meyer, W. J., and Thompson, G. C. (1969). Sex differences in the distribution of teacher approval and disapproval among sixth grade children. In R. C. Sprinthall and N.A. Sprinthall (Eds.), Educational psychology: Selected readings. New York: Van Nostrand-Reinhold, pp. 308–314.

Miller, A. (1981). Conceptual matching models and interactional research in education. *Review of Educational Research, 51*(11), 33–85.

Nieto, S. (1992). *Affirming diversity: The sociopolitical context of multicultural education.* New York: Longman Publishing Group.

Oja, S., and Smulyan, L. (1989). *Collaborative action research: A developmental approach.* London: Falmer Press.

Ogbu, J. (1978). *Minority education and caste: The American system in cross-cultural perspective.* New York: Academic Press.

Oser, F. (1986). Moral education and values education: The discourse perspective. In M. C. Wittrock (Ed.), *Handbook of research on teaching* (3d ed.). New York: MacMillan, pp. 917–941.

Paley, V. G. (1989). *White teacher.* Cambridge: Harvard University Press.

Phinney, J. (1990) Ethnic identity in adolescents and adults: Review of research. *Psychological Bulletin, 108*(30), 499–514.

Rosenthal, R. (1979). *Sensitivity to nonverbal communication: The PONS test.* Baltimore: Johns Hopkins Press.

Rosenthal, R. (1987). Pygmalion effects: Existence, magnitude, and social importance. *Educational Researcher, 16*(9), 37–44.

Rosenthal, R., and Jacobson, L. (1968). *Pygmalion in the classroom.* New York: Holt, Rinehart, & Winston.

Rosenthal, R., and Rubin, D. (1978). Interpersonal expectancy effects: The first 345 studies. *The Behavioral and Brain Sciences, 3,* 377–415.

Ross, D. D., and Smith, W. (1992). Understanding preservice teachers' perspectives on diversity. *Journal of Teacher Education, 43*(2), 94–103.

Ryan, K. (1970). *Don't smile until Christmas.* Chicago: University of Chicago Press.

Ryan, K., Newman, G., Mager, J., Applegate, J., Lasley, T., Flora, R., and Johnson, J. (1979). *Biting the apple: Accounts of first year teachers.* New York: Longman.

Sadker, M. P., and Sadker, D. M. (1988). *Teachers, schools, and society.* New York: Random House.

Sadker, M., Sadker, D., and Klein, S. (1991). The issue of gender in elementary and secondary education. In G. Grant (Ed.), *Review of Research in Education* (pp. 269–334). Washington: American Educational Research Association.

Scott-Jones, D. (1984). Family influences on cognitive developmental and school achievement. In E. W. Gordon (Ed.), *Review of research in education* (pp. 259–306). Washington: American Educational Research Association.

Shavelson, R. J., and Stern, P. (1981). Research on teachers' pedagogical thoughts, judgments, decisions, and behavior. *Review of Educational Research, 51*(4), 455–498.

Shipman, S., and Shipman, V. (1985). Cognitive styles: Some conceptual, methodological, and applied issues. In E. W. Gordon (Ed.), *Review of Educational Research,*

Vol. 12. Washington: American Educational Research Association.

Slavin, R. E., Madden, N. A., Karweit, N. L., Livermon, B. J., and Dolan, L. (1990, Summer). Success for all: First-year outcomes of a comprehensive plan for reforming urban education. *American Educational Research Journal, 27*(2), 255–278.

Tatum, B. D. (1992a). *Assimilation blues: Black families in a white community.* Northampton, Mass.: Hazel-Maxwell. First published in 1987 by Greenwood Press.

Tatum, B. D. (1992b). Talking about race, learning about racism: The application of racial identity development theory in the classroom. *Harvard Educational Review, 62*(1), 1–24.

Taylor, D., and Dorsey-Gaines, C. (1988). *Growing up literate: Learning from inner-city families.* Portsmouth, N.H.: Heinemann.

Thies-Sprinthall, L. (1984). Promoting the developmental growth of supervising teachers: Theory, research, programs, and implications. *Journal of Teacher Education, 35*(3), 53–60.

Thies-Sprinthall, L., and Sprinthall, N. (1987). Experienced teachers: Agents for revitalization and renewal as mentors and teacher educators. *Journal of Teacher Education, 169*(1), 65–75.

Trujillo, C. M. (1986). A comparative examination of classroom interactions between professors and minority and nonminority college students. *American Educational Research Journal, 23*(4), 629–642.

Veenman, S. (1984). Perceived problems of beginning teachers. *Review of Educational Research, 54*(2), 143–178.

Weinstein, R. S. (1989). Perceptions of classroom processes and student motivation: Children's views of self-fulfilling prophecies. In R. Ames and C. Ames (Eds.), *Research on motivation in education,* Vol. 3: *Goals and cognitions* (pp. 187–221). New York: Academic Press.

Wineburg, S. S. (1987). The self-fulfillment of the self-fulfilling prophecy: A critical appraisal. *Educational Researcher, 16*(9), 28–37.

Witherell, C., and Noddings, N. (1991). *Stories lives tell: Narrative and dialogue in education.* New York: Teachers College Press.

Woolfolk, A. E., and Brooks, D. M. (1983). Nonverbal communication in teaching. *Review of Research in Education, 10,* 103–150.

INDIVIDUAL DIFFERENCES: MEASUREMENT AND RESEARCH

15

MEASUREMENT AND INDIVIDUAL DIFFERENCES

The material presented in this chapter is aimed at giving you a general introduction to some of the techniques employed by statisticians and educational researchers. Though as a working teacher you may never have to compute the reliability or the validity of a measuring instrument, your understanding of these vital concepts will be greatly enhanced if you roll up your sleeves and "dirty your hands with the data." If you can calculate the standard deviation and Pearson r, you will not necessarily be a master statistician, but you will be better able to evaluate the statistical analyses of researchers in the field. In this chapter you will see how researchers use some of these techniques to achieve a better understanding of the facts and theories of educational psychology.

As a prospective teacher you will be expected to read and understand the literature in your own field. If you wish to further your studies and someday become an educational psychologist, you will have to spend considerable time honing your assessment skills. It has recently been stated that "the expanded role forecast for the educational psychologist in the twenty-first century is based on new approaches to assessment, clearly focusing on the purpose of assessment, and the validation of assessments in the context of use" (Tittle, 1991, p. 163). In any event, a basic introduction to statistical and research procedures

will enhance your ability to understand workshop and conference presentations as well as the research articles that you will be expected to read.

MEASUREMENT

As you look within yourself and at the people around you, you realize that you are a very special and unique being. Nobody else in the world is quite like you. Nobody else in the world has the same physiological equipment, the same genetic endowment (unless, of course, you are an identical twin), or has experienced the same sequence of life situations. Nobody else uses the identical blend of defense mechanisms that you use when encountering stress, and nobody else is guided by the exact mixture of motives, attitudes, and feelings. Thus, one of the basic themes of psychology is that of **individual differences:** No one is exactly like anyone else.

It is, however, impossible to avoid drawing comparisons as you look at the people around you. Perhaps you notice many similarities. You have a friend who seems to enjoy the same things you do. You play chess with someone who beats you just about as often as you beat her. You and your best friend spend about the same amount of time studying for an exam, and you make similar grades on that exam. Perhaps you have been pleasantly surprised to discover, during a conversation with someone you have just met, how similar your abilities, goals, tastes, and feelings really are. In many ways you are surprisingly like many other people. In some ways you are just like all other people, that is, you eat, drink, breathe, sleep, exercise, and have the same physiological needs. Therefore, it can be said that in some ways all people are exactly alike.

In order to assess how much you resemble and how much you differ from other people, you must in some way be measured. Meaningful comparisons cannot be made without meaningful measurements. **Measurement** is the assignment of a number to an object or event according to rules. This may represent something physical, as when you step on the scales and note, with dismay or pleasure, the number that indicates your weight. Or it may be more subtle, as when you take a vocational aptitude test and receive your score in mechanical aptitude. You have, in fact, been measured hundreds of times in hundreds of areas. In order to buy new clothes you must know your size. When you visit a physician, your temperature and blood pressure are taken. Before entering college, you probably took an aptitude test. Hundreds of numbers have been assigned to you, from shoe size to that first quiz grade you received in elementary school.

The importance of understanding testing techniques and the analysis of the measures they afford cannot be overemphasized to anyone contemplating a teaching career in the 1990s. Whether one agrees or disagrees with the recent proliferation of educational testing, it has become an obvious fact of American life. In 1988 almost 60 million primary and high school students took more than 100 million standardized tests, and even this number doesn't factor in the countless teacher-made tests to which America's schoolchildren are exposed (Fiske, 1988).

Reliability and Validity

In order to draw meaningful comparisons, measurements must be meaningful. In order to have meaning,

Measurement of progress is important in the classroom.

all measurements must satisfy two basic criteria: They must be reliable and they must be valid.

Reliability   **Reliability** is an indication of the consistency of a measurement; that is, if we measure something that is not itself changing dramatically, we should assign roughly the same number to it over repeated measurements. If you stepped on the scales and read 140 pounds one day, 240 pounds the next day, and 40 pounds the day after that, your faith in the precision of the scale would be severely shaken. The numbers would be meaningless. The same is true of psychological tests. If you took an IQ test one day and received a score of 140, and then you took the same test the next day and received a score of 50, you would undoubtedly feel bewildered. In order to have any meaning, our measurements must, on the one hand, be consistent over repeated measurements—that is, reliable.

On the other hand, a test cannot be so consistent as to be rigid and misleading. It was mentioned that a good test yields roughly the same scores over repeated measurements as long as that which is being measured does not change dramatically. Suppose, however, you went on a crash diet, and every day your friends commented on how much weight you had lost, and after a few weeks you found your clothes no longer fit. If, in this instance, you still found the scales were reading the same weight, it would be obvious that the measurements were too consistent to be an adequate reflection of reality.

Validity   Measurements must also be valid. **Validity** is an indication of the extent to which a test measures what it is supposed to measure. When you step on the scales you want to know your weight, not your IQ or mechanical aptitude or some unknown quality. One way to assess validity, called *predictive* validity, is to compare a set of test scores against some separate or independent observation of the thing being measured. For example, if we were trying to establish whether or not a certain test of flying ability is valid, we might give the test to a large group of student pilots and then compare their test scores with the flight instructor's ratings of each person's actual ability to fly a plane. If those with the highest test scores also turn out to be the best pilots, the test is considered valid. The validity of such a test is important, because it allows us to predict on the basis of a person's test score whether or not that person

will profit from flying lessons. Similarly, a valid test of college aptitude would predict whether an individual will be able to profit from the college experience. Thus, measurements must be an accurate reflection of what they are intended to measure—that is, they must be valid.

When using a test for a particular educational objective, it is up to the test publisher to supply the school with information regarding the way the test was validated and its level of validation. However, it is the responsibility of the user of the test, in this case the teacher, to become familiar with this information and to make the final determination regarding whether or not the test is appropriate for the job at hand (Geisinger, 1992).

Correlation   In order to give precise statements about reliability and validity, a statistical technique called correlation may be utilized. Although correlation does not allow for direct cause-and-effect statements, it does allow the scientist to make predictions.

Correlation is a statement about the strength of the association between two (or possibly more) variables. If the correlation between two variables is high, the variables will tend to vary together; that is, wherever one of the traits is found, chances are good that the other trait will also be found. If we observed that people with blond hair usually have blue eyes, then we would say that there is a correlation between the variables hair color and eye color. This is not to say that having blond hair causes one to have blue eyes, but it does allow us to predict, whenever we know that certain individuals have blond hair, that they are also likely to have blue eyes.

Correlation is one way to assess reliability. If a certain test is given to a large group of subjects on two separate occasions, and if those individuals who score high on the test the first time also score high the second time and those who score low the first time also score low the second time, the two sets of measurements are said to correlate and the test is considered reliable. A high correlation between the two sets of scores indicates reliability because it demonstrates that the test is yielding consistent scores. The two variables, that is, the scores on the first administration of the test and the scores on the second, are in fact occurring together, or correlating.

Correlation can also establish validity. To establish validity we would give a test measuring some ability or trait to a group of individuals and then correlate

SPOTLIGHT ON CULTURE-FAIR TESTING

A Question of Validity

Intelligence tests, to be useful, must predict something—academic performance, success in life, something. For white middle- and upper-class Americans, intelligence tests have had a fairly good record, with higher-validity coefficients than for any other type of psychological testing. But what about minority children? There are biases built into most of the well-known individual and group measures of intelligence. Minority populations have pointed out that many tests are not culture-fair and are therefore discriminatory against those minorities. The issue is not a new one in this country. During the early 1900s, immigrants arriving at New York's Ellis Island were tested by means of the methods available at the time. Henry Goddard, of Kallikak fame, used his own version of the Binet-Simon test, in pantomime, for the assessment of the non-English-speaking groups. His published results proclaimed that many immigrants from southern and eastern Europe were profoundly and innately retarded—79 percent of the Italians, 80 percent of the Austro-Hungarians, and 87 percent of the Russians.

Similarly, during World War I, the first group intelligence tests, the Army Alpha and Beta, were administered to large groups of non-English-speaking inductees. The groups were classified into four categories, A through D. The D category indicated feeblemindedness. The results also proclaimed that well over half the inductees from Poland, Italy, and Russia were retarded, while (astonishingly) those from England, Scotland, Holland, and Denmark had very low rates of retardation. Similar conclusions were later reached for native minority groups. In the words of Lewis Terman, the results using the Stanford-Binet indicated that mental retardation "is very, very common among Spanish-Indian and Mexican families of the Southwest and also among Negroes. Their dullness seems to be racial, or at least inherent in the family stocks from which they come."[a]

Apparently, it was never clear to some of the early giants of testing in this country (especially Goddard) that the intelligence tests they employed could not assess innate ability. If a youthful Albert Einstein, tested on the Army Alpha, did not know what the Brooklyn Nationals were called or what company in this country made revolvers, he might have been on his way to a grade D designation as a feebleminded immigrant. If a Native American on a reservation had difficulty with such Stanford-Binet questions as the meaning of a birthday cake and candles or identifying an umbrella or knowing how a ship and auto are the same or different, then such a person would also be on the way to the retarded class.

Thus, the critics of IQ testing point out that such tests are first, culturally biased, and second, inadmissible as evidence of genetic racial differences. In fact, as Leon Kamin points out, Alfred Binet never believed that a test such as his could be used as an indicator of innate ability. The problem with those early tests, then, was not in the people being tested but in the method of assessment. The techniques stacked the deck, so to speak, against anyone not from the standard American middle-class background.

Following the same logic, Jane Mercer, a sociologist, finds that current minority populations such as African Americans, Puerto Ricans, Spanish-Americans, Native Americans, and rural children in general are unfairly classified, since the IQ tests are not valid for these children. The current intelligence measures do not adequately sample the abilities of groups like these. For example, in one study it was shown that a black urban child was sixteen times more likely than a white urban child to be assessed as retarded, even though further assessment indicated the actual rates were not that disparate.

their scores with actual performances by these same individuals on the ability or trait being measured. For example, we might compare scores on a sales aptitude test with actual performance in selling a certain product. If, in fact, there is a correlation between the two variables (the test scores and the number of sales achieved), the test has been shown to be valid—it is indeed measuring what it is intended to measure.

Reliability and validity are only two ways to apply this extremely useful technique. Later in this chapter we will cite other applications of correlation in educational psychology, and we will present a simple mathematical procedure for computing correlation.

To readjust our assessment procedures, particularly the heavy reliance on IQ tests, Mercer suggests a method to broaden the behavior sample.[b] Mercer indicates that scores should be "adjusted" upward for minority children. And instead of using only an individual IQ test, she tests in four additional areas: (1) the family, (2) the neighborhood, (3) the school, and (4) the community. Her questions are designed to tap the child's behavior in performing a variety of roles in these domains. How much independence and self-direction does the child exhibit in these areas? How much activity must be monitored and supervised? How complex are the tasks that the child performs? These three themes form the basis for assessment —self-direction, internal control, and complexity.

She then proposes that educators use this information systematically to change the IQ test score. Each minority child in her system would receive an "adjusted intelligence quotient." Essentially, this means that the test score is changed on the basis of additional ratings of the child's competence. If, for example, a seven-year-old Spanish child from the Los Angeles barrios tested out at 80 on the Wechsler scales, the score would be adjusted upward if further study showed that she could find

her way around the neighborhood, shop in stores, responsibly take care of younger siblings, or take on similar kinds of social roles. The system of multicultural pluralistic assessment (SOMPA) method provides a calibrated system of adjusting IQ scores on the basis of such additional behavioral information on each child.

The controversy over testing, however, is not stilled by Mercer's work. In fact, one could almost say that critics on either side of the issue agree on only one thing, namely, that SOMPA may be a bad compromise. The conservative test constructionists are quick to point out some new gaps in both reliability and validity. How reliable are the questions of social competence? Don't questions like these become highly subjective? The ability to roam the neighborhood can be viewed positively or negatively. Also, the validity question arises: How do social skills relate to school performance? Just because a child may possess advanced interpersonal "cleverness" is no guarantee of a quick, inquiring mind. Thus, the more empirically bound test makers find much to criticize on the items, the norms, and the predictive power of the "adjusted" IQ.

On the other side, the critics of the "old" standardized tests are not really much happier with the

new version. Making a small adjustment with a "bad system" does not solve anything, according to this view. If IQ tests are not culture-fair, then toss out the tests. There is only one thing to do about such testing: Stop it! Raising a child's score a few points doesn't really change the injustice of subjecting that child to an entire battery of biased and prejudiced items. SOMPA may be only the newest version of the old white-liberal game—the appearance of sensitivity to the needs of minority children but "business as usual" underneath the façade. Why develop an IQ test whose norms are based primarily on white American children and then propose some adjustments for minority children only?

The answers are hard. The questions are easy. Do we adopt one standard or many? Do we choose cultural universalism or cultural relativity? Do we continue possibly to misclassify children on intelligence tests or do we continue to grope for more adequate measures? Is SOMPA a step forward or a step sideways? Has SOMPA increased the validity or simply dodged the question?

[a] L. J. Kamin, *The science and politics of IQ* (Potomac, Md.: Erlbaum, 1974).
[b] J. Mercer and J. Lewis, *System at multicultural pluralistic assessment* (New York: Psychological Corporation, 1978).

Distributions: Tables and Graphs

Since a picture can often be well worth the proverbial "thousand words," data can be described very effectively through the use of graphs and tables. In creating one type of table, the first step is to form a **distribution,** an arrangement of any set of scores in order

of magnitude. Table 15.1 presents a set of IQ scores. Arranging these scores into a distribution means listing them sequentially from high to low. Table 15.2 is a distribution of the IQ scores from Table 15.1.

A distribution allows the observer to see general trends more readily than the unordered set of raw scores does. To further simplify our inspection of the

TABLE 15.1
UNORDERED IQ
SCORES

75
100
105
95
120
130
95
90
115
85
115
100
110
100
110

TABLE 15.2
DISTRIBUTION
OF IQ SCORES

130
120
115
115
110
110
105
100
100
100
95
95
90
85
75

TABLE 15.4   BREAKDOWN VALUES

	GROUP A (COACHED)	GROUP B (NOT COACHED)
Number of students	425	434
Average SAT score	490.05	470.86
Range of scores	522	510

sample groups, A and B, with respect to performance on the verbal section of the Scholastic Aptitude Test, group A having been coached, the tabled values might look like those shown in Table 15.4. The table immediately informs us that the coached group did perform at a somewhat higher level than the uncoached group and, further, that both groups are displaying similar amounts of variability, and were of similar size.

In addition to presenting frequency distributions in tabular form, statisticians often present their data in graphic form. It is customary to indicate the raw scores, or actual values of the variable, on the horizontal, X axis, called the *abscissa*. The frequency of occurrence is presented on the vertical, or Y axis, called the *ordinate*.

When graphing data, two of the most popular approaches involve setting up the data in the form of either a frequency histogram or a frequency polygon. Before using either of these, however, you must first set up a frequency distribution. Assume that we had a set of scores from a group of first-graders being evaluated on the arithmetic subtest of the WISC-III. The scores range from a high of 15 to a low of 5. Using the procedure described previously, the frequency distribution should look like that shown in Table 15.5.

data, they can be presented as a frequency distribution. A frequency distribution is a listing of each score achieved, together with the number of individuals receiving that score. Table 15.3 is a frequency distribution of our IQ scores.

The X at the top of the first column stands for raw scores (in this case, IQ) and the f over the second column stands for frequency of occurrence. As can be seen, of the fifteen people taking the test, two received scores of 115, two received 110, three scored 100, two scored 95, and everyone else made a unique score.

Tables can also be set up as summary statements and often provide a rich, visual recap of what the data are showing. For example, in comparing two

TABLE 15.3   IQ SCORES PRESENTED AS A FREQUENCY DISTRIBUTION

X (RAW SCORE)	f (FREQUENCY OF OCCURRENCE)
130	1
120	1
115	2
110	2
105	1
100	3
95	2
90	1
85	1
75	1

TABLE 15.5

SCORE, X	FREQUENCY OF X, f
15	1
14	0
13	4
12	11
11	16
10	20
9	15
8	12
7	5
6	1
5	1

Total: $N = 86$ students

FIGURE 15.1

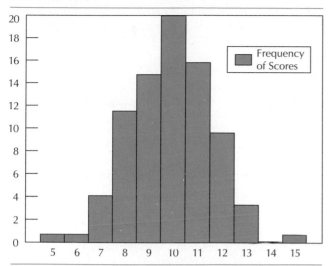

FIGURE 15.3   Frequency polygon of WISC III Subtest scores.

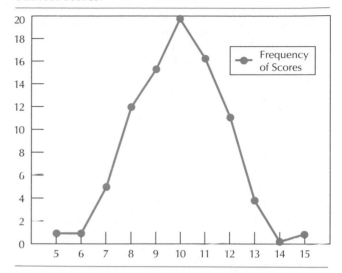

Now, to create the **histogram,** place all the scores on the X, or horizontal, axis (abscissa) at equal intervals and run the scores from the lowest on the left to the highest on the right. Then, indicate all the frequencies on the Y, or vertical, axis (ordinate), again using equal intervals and beginning with zero, and place a rectangular bar over each score up to the point where the score intersects the frequency. (See Figure 15.1.)

Another method for displaying histograms which has become increasingly popular, especially among statistical computer programs, is to express the frequencies horizontally rather than vertically, with each asterisk representing an individual score (Sprinthall, 1990). (See Figure 15.2.)

We can also use the same data to illustrate another commonly used graphic form, called the frequency

polygon. For the *frequency polygon,* place a dot over each score, again at the point where the score intersects the frequency. Then, connect all the dots with a series of straight lines (see Figure 15.3).

Stem-and-Leaf Display

Finally, a very economical way of graphing data, called the **stem-and-leaf display,** presents only the first digit in the stem column, while in the leaf column we find the trailing digits. For example, if we were to graph the scores on a certain reading test, where the values range from a low score of 60 to a high score of 100, the stem column would present the digits 6 through 10, with the 6 representing scores in the sixties, the 7 representing scores in the seventies, and so on. The leaf column would then include the trailing digit, so that a 0 next to the 6 would indicate a score of 60, the 3 a score of 63, and the 5 a score of 65. (See Figure 15.4.)

Note that in this example, most of the scores were

FIGURE 15.2

SCORE	FREQUENCY
15	*
14	
13	****
12	**********
11	****************
10	*********************
9	*****************
8	************
7	*****
6	*
5	*

FIGURE 15.4

STEM	LEAF
6	035
7	13578
8	04455569
9	00145
10	0

in the eighties, and were specifically 80, 84, 84, 85, 85, 85, 86, and 89. Also, notice that there was only one score of 100.

In both the histogram and the frequency polygon, it is essential that the base of the ordinate represent a frequency of zero—if not, the graph may tell a very misleading story. For example, suppose we are graphing data from a learning study that shows how increasing the number of learning trials increases the amount learned.

Let us plot the number of trials on the abscissa and the frequency of correct responses on the ordinate (Figure 15.5). Our graph shows that by trial four the subject made eight correct responses and that by trial ten the subject made twelve correct choices. These data are typical of the results obtained in learning studies; that is, a great deal of learning usually occurs during the first few trials, but, as the number of trials increases, further increase in learning lessens.

Suppose, however, the statistician wished to give a false interpretation of the data. He or she could simply focus on one small area of the graph (see Figure 15.6). Now the same data tell a very different story about how learning takes place. It looks as if no learning took place before trial four and that the great bulk of learning took place between trials four and ten. We know from the previous graph that this is incorrect. In fact, most of the learning took place during the first four or five trials, and between trials

FIGURE 15.6   Here, the base of the ordinate is not set at zero. Be wary of such graphs, since they can easily lead to a false interpretation of data.

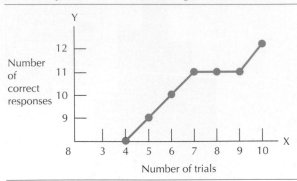

four and ten, the learning was actually beginning to top out or level off. This is one instance of how statistics can be used to distort data—if the audience is naive about statistical techniques. Whenever a graph is presented in which the base of the ordinate is not set at zero, be on the alert. The stage has been set for a possible sleight-of-hand trick.

Measures of Central Tendency

To help us understand how individuals differ and how they are alike, we have some useful techniques for finding the *average,* or typical score, in a distribution. Knowing the average IQ for a certain class may help us plan the curriculum, decide how extensively certain topics should be covered in class, or choose books for the library. Information about the typical score in a distribution allows us to interpret more meaningfully all the scores in the distribution.

Statisticians have three methods for obtaining the average, and each is designed, when used appropriately, to give us the most accurate picture possible of the distribution. The averages are called **measures of central tendency,** because they describe the typical, middle, or central score in a distribution; they tell us about our average or typical person's score. Choosing the appropriate method can be tricky because the interpretation of the data may vary widely, depending on how the average has been obtained.

The mean   If you were given a set of IQ scores and asked to find the average score, you would most likely compute the mean. That is, you would add all the IQ scores together and divide by the total number of scores. The **mean** is thus the arithmetic average; it is

FIGURE 15.5   Data that are correctly plotted.

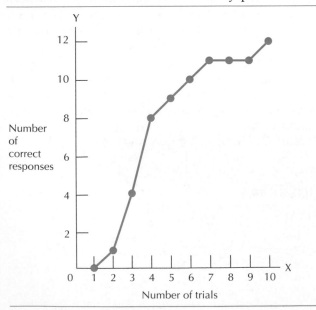

certainly the most commonly used measure of central tendency.

Statisticians have traditionally used the symbol $\bar{X}$ to denote the mean, although lately the symbol M has been increasingly popular, especially in journal articles.

$$\bar{X}, \text{ or } M = \frac{\Sigma X}{N}$$

The Greek letter Σ (sigma) is a symbol that tells us to add; it is read as "summation of." N stands for the number of cases. Thus, the equation tells us that the mean ($\bar{X}$) is equal to the summation (Σ) of the raw scores (X) divided by the number of cases (N). The mean of our distribution of IQ scores would be computed as in Table 15.6.

As it happens, the mean is an appropriate measure of central tendency in the preceding example because the distribution is fairly well balanced; that is, there are no extreme scores in any one direction. Since the mean is computed by adding together all the scores in the distribution, it is not easily influenced by extreme scores unless the extreme scores are all in one direction. The mean is typically a stable measure of central tendency.

Interpreting the mean can sometimes be very deceptive, especially in groups in which the population itself or the size of the population changes. For example, the mean IQ of the typical freshman class in a

TABLE 15.6   *CALCULATION OF THE MEAN FROM A DISTRIBUTION OF RAW SCORES*

X	CALCULATION
130	
120	
115	
115	
110	
110	
105	
100	
100	
100	
95	
95	
90	
85	$\bar{X}, \text{ or } M = \dfrac{\Sigma X}{N} = \dfrac{1545}{15}$
75	
1,545	$\bar{X}, \text{ or } M = 103$

TABLE 15.7   *DISTRIBUTION OF INCOME SCORES SKEWED TO THE RIGHT*

$10,000,000	
40,000	
40,000	
29,600	
29,500	
29,500	
29,400	(Median)
29,300	
29,000	
28,500	
28,000	
28,000	
27,600	
$10,368,400	

The mean or $\bar{X}$ = \$797,569.20

college is usually about five points lower than the mean of the same class when the students later become seniors. Does this indicate that students increase their IQs as they proceed through college? No, because since the size of the senior class is almost always smaller than the size of the freshman class, the two populations are no longer the same. Those with the lowest IQs in the freshman class are apt to leave college and never become seniors.

The median   In some situations, however, the use of the mean can lead to an extremely distorted picture of the "average" in a distribution. For example, look at the distribution of annual incomes in Table 15.7. One of the income scores (\$10,000,000.00) is so extremely far above the others that to use the mean income as a reflection of the average income would give a misleading picture of high prosperity for this distribution. A distribution that is unbalanced due to a few extreme scores in one direction is said to be *skewed*.

A much more accurate representation of central tendency for a skewed distribution is the **median,** or middlemost point in a distribution. Whereas the mean income in Table 15.7 was found to be \$797,569.20, the median would be only \$29,400.00, a far more accurate reflection of the typical income for that particular distribution. Since income distributions are usually skewed, you should be on the alert for an inflated figure whenever the mean income is reported. The median is generally a more appropriate

TABLE 15.8   CALCULATION OF THE MEDIAN WITH AN EVEN NUMBER OF SCORES

120
118
115
114 —114.5   (Median)
114
112
693
$\overline{X}$ = 115.50   (Mean)

value when reporting incomes. To calculate the median, be sure the scores are in distribution form, that is, arranged in order of magnitude. Then count down through one-half of the scores. For example, in Table 15.7 there are thirteen income scores in the distribution. We therefore count down six scores, and the seventh score coincides with the median. (There will be the same number of scores above the seventh score as there are below it.) If there are an even number of scores in a distribution (see Table 15.8), the median is found by determining the point that lies halfway between the two middle scores or, in this case, 114.5. Unlike the mean, the median is not affected by an extreme score in one direction. In Table 15.8, for example, the median would still be 114.5 even if the low score were 6 instead of 112, whereas the mean would be an unrepresentative 97.83 (see Table 15.9).

Figure 15.7 shows what skewed distributions look like in graphic form. In the positively skewed distribution, most of the scores are found at the low end of the distribution, whereas in the negatively skewed distribution, most of the scores are at the high end. We label this according to the direction of the tail. When the tail goes to the right, we call the curve positively skewed; when it goes to the left, it is negatively skewed.

TABLE 15.9   CALCULATION OF THE MEDIAN WITH AN EVEN NUMBER OF SCORES AND A SKEWED DISTRIBUTION

120
118
115
114 —114.5   (Median)
114
6
587
$\overline{X}$ = 97.83   (Mean)

FIGURE 15.7   A graphic presentation of skewed distributions: (a) negatively skewed; (b) positively skewed.

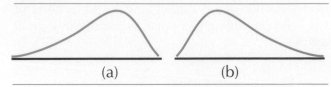

(a)   (b)

The mode   The third measure of central tendency is called the mode. The **mode** is the score that occurs most frequently in a distribution. In a frequency polygon the mode is located where the curve is at its highest point; in a histogram it is located at the tallest bar. Some distributions, called *bimodal*, have two modes (see Figure 15.8). Distributions of this type occur if scores are clustered in two separate places, or if the group being measured probably breaks down into two subgroups.

Assume that the distribution in Figure 15.8 represents the running speed (in seconds) in the seventy-yard dash for a large group of seventh-graders. There are two modes: one at thirteen seconds and the other at eighteen seconds. Since there are two scores sharing the same high frequency, it is probable that two subgroups are being portrayed. For example, the running speeds for boys may be clustering around one mode while the speeds for girls are clustering around the other.

VARIABILITY: THE NAME OF THE GAME IN EDUCATIONAL PSYCHOLOGY

Just as the measures of central tendency give us information about the similarity among measurements, **measures of variability** give us information about how scores differ or vary. Measures of variability are crucial in education since they give us vital information about one of psychology's basic themes—individual differences.

FIGURE 15.8   A bimodal distribution.

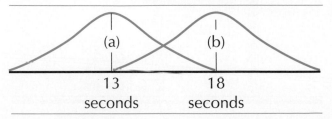

(a)   (b)
13   18
seconds   seconds

The Range

One way to describe variability in any distribution of scores is to compute the **range (R)**. The range is the difference between the highest and lowest scores, and it is a measure of the width of the total distribution. The range is given as a single value. For example, if the highest score in an IQ distribution is 140 and the lowest score is 60, then R would equal 80.

The Standard Deviation

The standard deviation is the absolute heart and soul of the variability concept. Although the range is important in giving some meaning to a set of scores, it does have one fairly significant limitation: It is based on only two scores, the highest and the lowest. The standard deviation, in contrast, takes into account *every single* score in the entire distribution. The **standard deviation (SD)**, therefore, is a measure of variability that indicates how far *all* the scores in a distribution deviate from the *mean*. The higher the numerical value of the SD, the more the scores vary around the mean, or the more the scores spread out around the mean. The smaller the value of the SD, the less the scores spread out from the mean—in fact, the more tightly they cluster around it. A distribution with a small standard deviation tells us that the group being measured is homogeneous, whereas a distribution with a large standard deviation describes a heterogeneous group of scores. This standard or typical deviation is always expressed as a single value.

To calculate the SD, follow the steps given with Table 15.10. After arriving at an answer for the standard deviation, always check its value for statistical logic. First, the standard deviation may never be negative, since you can never have less than no deviation. The smallest possible value for the standard deviation is zero, and this will occur only if every score in the distribution is the same. Second, the value of the standard deviation can never be greater than one-half the value of the range. In the example in Table 15.10, in which the range is equal to 15 − 2, or 13, the standard deviation cannot be greater than 13/2, or 6.50. Suppose you had forgotten to take the square root of 12.50 and mistakenly assumed that to be the standard deviation. By knowing that 12.50 is too high (greater than 6.50), you would have found the error because you would undoubtedly have checked your work. It is a wise idea to always check your standard deviation values even if you're using a computer.

TABLE 15.10   CALCULATION OF THE STANDARD DEVIATION FROM A DISTRIBUTION OF RAW SCORES

X	X_2	CALCULATIONS
15	225	$\overline{X} = \dfrac{\Sigma X}{N} = \dfrac{72}{8} = 9.00$
12	144	
10	100	
9	81	$SD = \sqrt{\dfrac{\Sigma X^2}{N} - \overline{X}_2} = \sqrt{\dfrac{748}{8} - 9.00^2}$
9	81	
8	64	
7	49	$= \sqrt{93.50 - 81.00} = \sqrt{12.50}$
2	4	$SD = 3.535 = 3.54$
72	748	

1. Add the X's to obtain ΣX.
2. Divide by N to obtain $\overline{X}$.
3. Square each X to obtain X^2.
4. Add these squares to obtain ΣX^2.
5. Divide the ΣX^2 value by N and subtract the squared mean, $\overline{X}^2$.
6. Take the square root to obtain the SD.

After all, even the most powerful computer programs have been known to have bugs in them.

In Figure 15.9 we see a representation of two IQ distributions, both of which have the same range (60) and the same mean (100). The distributions are different because they have different standard deviations. Distribution *b* has a relatively large standard deviation, indicating that the scores deviate widely from the mean. Distribution *a* has a smaller standard deviation, indicating that the variability is much less, that is, most of the scores are clustering rather tightly around the mean.

The Normal Curve

Many behavioral measures in educational psychology conform to what statisticians call the **normal**

FIGURE 15.9   Two IQ distributions with different standard deviations.

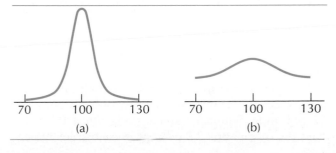

(a)   (b)

FIGURE 15.10   The normal curve is a frequency-distribution curve with scores plotted on the X axis and frequency of occurrence on the Y axis.

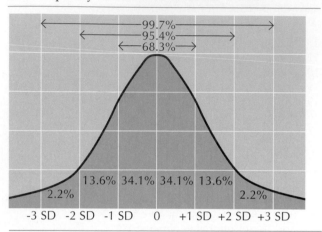

cent, or virtually all the cases, fall between ±3 SD units. Less than 1 percent of the scores lie beyond ±3 SD units.

These facts relating percentage of cases to units of the standard deviation are constants; that is, the facts are true regardless of the size of the standard deviation. These constants hold as long as the curve is normal.

If the distribution of scores is normal, then the standard deviation will take on a value that is equal to approximately one-sixth of the range. Thus, in a normal distribution of IQ scores, in which the range is equal to 90, the standard deviation will be equal to approximately 15. If when calculating the standard deviation on a large group of scores, you find that its value is less then one-sixth of the range, you can assume that there is less than the normal amount of variability among the scores and that the group being measured is rather homogeneous. If, however, the standard deviation turns out to be greater than one-sixth of the range, you may surmise that the group is heterogeneous.

curve (see Figure 15.10). The normal curve is actually a theoretical distribution, but so many measurements come so close to this ideal that it is of utmost importance. The normal curve is a frequency-distribution curve with scores plotted on the X axis and frequency of occurrence on the Y axis. However, it has a number of interesting features that set it apart from other frequency-distribution curves. First, in a normal curve most of the scores cluster around the center of the distribution, and as we move away from the center in either direction, there are fewer and fewer scores. Second, it is symmetrical, that is, the two halves of the curve are identical. It is in perfect balance. Third, the mean, median, and mode all fall at the same point, the midpoint of the distribution. Finally, the normal curve has some constant characteristics with regard to the standard deviation.

The mean divides the normal curve into two equal halves, with 50 percent of the scores falling above the mean and 50 percent falling below it. The area between the mean and a point one standard deviation above the mean includes 34 percent of the scores. Since the normal curve is symmetrical, 34 percent of the cases also fall between the mean and a point one standard deviation below the mean. Thus, between the two points that are one standard deviation away from the mean, that is, ±1 SD, there are 68 percent (just twice 34 percent) of all the cases. As we go away from the mean another full standard deviation, 13.5 percent of the distribution is added to each side. Thus, approximately 95 percent of the cases fall between ±2 SD units. Similarly, since going out a third SD from the mean adds 2.5 percent in each side, 99 per-

Standard Scores (z Scores)

It is difficult to compare scores on different tests without knowing the mean and standard deviation for each test. For example, if you were to get a score of 72 on a certain math test and 64 on an English test, you wouldn't know on which test your performance was higher. The mean on the math test might have been 85, and the mean on the English test might have been 50, in which case you scored higher on the English test even though your raw score was lower. The point is that information about the distribution of scores must be obtained in order that raw scores can be interpreted. For this reason, we use **z scores,** or **standard scores,** which take the distribution into account. This allows us to understand an individual's test performance relative to others taking the same test. The z score is equal to the difference between the raw score and the mean, divided by the standard deviation.

$$z = \frac{X - \bar{X}}{\text{SD}}$$

The z score indicates, in units of standard deviation, how far above or below the mean a certain score lies. If the mean of the math distribution (85) were subtracted from your math score (72) and divided by the SD (10), your z score would be −1.3.

$$z = \frac{72 - 85}{10} = \frac{-13}{10} = -1.3$$

Thus, on the math test you fell 1.3 SD units below the mean. A negative z score always indicates that the score is below the mean, while a positive z score shows that the score is above the mean. A score of 64 on the English test minus the mean of 50 and divided by the standard deviation, again of 10, yields a z score of 1.4

$$z = \frac{64 - 50}{10} = \frac{14}{10} = 1.4$$

Since the sign in this case is positive, your score on the English test falls 1.4 SD units above the mean. Though your raw score on the English test is lower than your raw score on the math test, your actual performance on the English test, compared to all other performances on the same test, is considerably higher. Thus, by converting raw scores into z scores, comparisons can be made between an individual's performance on various distributions that have different means and standard deviations.

Percentiles (Deciles and Quarteles)

A raw score can be described very precisely by converting it into a percentile. A **percentile** is that point in a distribution at or below which a given percentage of scores fall. For example, a score at the ninety-fifth percentile means that 95 percent of the scores in the distribution are at or below that point, whereas a score at the fifth percentile means that only 5 percent of the scores fall at or below that point. Knowing the percentage of cases falling between various SD units on the normal curve, allows you to calculate the percentile. In the distribution for the normal curve (Figure 15.10), for example, 34 percent of the cases fall between the mean and −1 SD Since 50 percent of the cases fall below the mean, and since 34 percent of these cases fall between the mean and −1 SD, we can see that 16 percent of the cases must fall below −1 SD A z score of −1, meaning a raw score one full SD below the mean, would yield a percentile score of 16. Or, a z score of +1, indicating a raw

score of one full SD above the mean, would mean a percentile score of 84 (the 34 percent falling between the mean and 1 SD plus the 50 percent falling below the mean).

Statisticians can determine the percentile for any z score, not just those for whole numbers. For example, a z score of 1.52 shows that about 44 percent of the cases fall between the mean and 1.52 SD units above the mean. Thus, the percentile for that z score would be 94 (the 44 percent falling between the z score and the mean plus the 50 percent lying below the mean). Statistical tables are available that indicate the exact percentage of cases lying between the mean and any z score (Sprinthall et al., 1990).

Assume that we are working with an IQ distribution whose mean is 100 and whose SD is 15. A student with an IQ of 122 would have a z score of 122 − 100, divided by the SD of 15, or 1.47. The student with an IQ of 122 would fall 1.47 SD units above the mean. A z-score table indicates that 43 percent of the cases fall between a z of 1.47 and the mean. Adding that to the 50 percent below the mean, we now know that the student with an IQ of 122 is at the 93rd percentile.

Other variations on the percentile theme include (1) deciles, each worth 10 percentile units, and (2) quartiles, each worth 25 percentile units. The table below illustrates the comparison, where D_1 = the 1st decile and Q_1 = the 1st quartile. Notice that the 50th percentile is equal to the 5th decile as well as the 2d quartile.

T Scores

T scores are also based on the normal curve and can easily be converted from z scores by simply setting the mean at 50 and the standard deviation at 10. This ensures that all T scores have positive values (unlike z scores, which are negative whenever they are below the mean). To calculate a T score, simply multiply the z score by 10 and add 50. Like the z score, the T score can be used as a measure of an individual's performance relative to the mean, and, of course, to the rest of the distribution. When raw scores are converted into T scores, they give us a measure of how far the raw score is from the mean of 50 in standard

Percentiles	0	10	15	20	25	30	35	40	45	50	55	60	65	70	75	80	85	90	95	100
Deciles		D1		D2		D3		D4		D5		D6		D7		D8		D9		
Quartiles					Q1					Q2					Q3					

deviation units of 10. Thus, a *T* score of 60 is one full standard deviation above the mean, and a *T* score of 40 is one standard deviation unit below the mean. *T* scores run from a low value of 20 (3 standard deviations below the mean) to a high of 80 (3 standard deviations above the mean). Thus, *T*-score values range from 20 to 80, which gives us a range value (*R*) of 60.

Normal Curve Equivalents (NCE)

Another increasingly popular standardized score is called the **Normal Curve Equivalent (NCE) score.** Like the *T* score, the NCE is again based on the normal curve, and is calculated by setting the mean at 50 and the standard deviation at approximately 21. Because of its larger standard deviation, the range of NCE scores is wider than for *T* scores, and approximates 0 to 100.

Stanines

Stanines, like *z, T,* and NCE scores, are also based on the normal curve, but unlike the others, stanines divide the distribution into units of nine intervals (whereas *z,* for example, divided the distribution into six intervals). The mean of the stanine distribution must equal 5 and the standard deviation must equal approximately 2. By examining Table 15.11, one can see that stanine 5 (the middlemost interval) contains 20 percent of the cases, stanines 4 and 6 contain 17 percent, stanines 3 and 7 contain 12 percent, stanines 2 and 8 contain 7 percent and, finally, stanines 1 and 9 contain the remaining 4 percent. A child who scored

in the 6th stanine, for example, would have performed better than 60 percent of those taking the same test. Many standardized tests in the field of educational psychology report scores on the basis of stanines.

Norm-Referenced and Criterion-Referenced Testing

The various tests used in psychology and education use either norm-referenced or criterion-referenced scoring systems. The difference is fundamental. In a **norm-referenced test** an individual's performance is *compared* to the average performance of the entire test-taking population. For example, for an IQ test, an individual's score is not reported in terms of the absolute number of correct answers given but instead on the basis of a comparison between the individual's absolute performance and the average performance of all the individuals of the same age who have taken the test. This procedure, in fact, was precisely the same as that used way back at the turn of the century by that giant in the field of intelligence testing, Alfred Binet. Binet used the term *mental age* to describe his scoring technique, and this early system is an example of norm-referenced scoring. In order to establish a student's mental age, Binet would give his intelligence test to large numbers of children of various ages. The average performance for a given age became the benchmark for evaluating a given student's performance. For example, he discovered how many items the average eight-year-old (having tested thousands of eight-year-olds) could answer correctly, and then a child *of any age* who answered the same number of items was assigned a mental age of eight. The

SPOTLIGHT ON TESTING

Comparing Scores

To help you convert scores from one form to another, a table, shown on the next two pages, has been prepared for allowing quick transitions among several popular scales. It includes raw score equivalents for the Scholastic Aptitude Test (SAT), Normal Curve Equivalent (NCE) scores, and the Wechsler IQ (WIQ) tests, which include the WAIS, WISC, and WPPSI). All conversions are based on the formula

$$Score = (z)(SD) + mean$$

TABLE 15.11

PERCENTILE	z	T	STANINE	SAT	NCE	WIQ	
1	−2.41	25.90	0.18	259	1.0	63.85	
2	−2.05	29.50	0.90	295	6.7	69.25	
3	−1.88	31.20	1.24	312	10.4	71.80	
4	−1.75	32.50	1.50	325	13.1	73.75	(1st Stanine)
5	−1.65	33.50	1.70	335	15.4	75.25	
6	−1.56	34.40	1.88	344	17.3	76.60	
7	−1.48	35.20	2.04	352	18.9	77.80	
8	−1.41	35.90	2.18	359	20.4	78.85	
9	−1.34	36.60	2.32	366	21.8	79.90	
10	−1.28	37.20	2.44	372	23.0	80.80	(1st Decile)
11	−1.23	37.70	2.54	377	24.2	81.55	(2d Stanine)
12	−1.18	38.20	2.64	382	25.3	82.30	
13	−1.13	38.70	2.74	387	26.3	83.05	
14	−1.08	39.20	2.84	392	27.2	83.80	
15	−1.04	39.60	2.92	396	28.2	84.40	
16	−1.00	40.00	3.00	400	29.1	85.00	
17	−0.95	40.50	3.10	405	29.9	85.75	
18	−0.92	40.80	3.16	408	30.7	86.20	
19	−0.88	41.20	3.24	412	31.5	86.80	
20	−0.84	41.60	3.32	416	32.3	87.40	(2d Decile)
21	−0.81	41.90	3.38	419	33.0	87.85	
22	−0.77	42.30	3.46	423	33.7	88.45	
23	−0.74	42.60	3.52	426	34.4	88.90	(3d Stanine)
24	−0.71	42.90	3.58	429	35.1	89.35	
25	−0.67	43.30	3.66	433	35.8	89.95	(1st Quartile)
26	−0.64	43.60	3.72	436	36.5	90.40	
27	−0.61	43.90	3.78	439	37.1	90.85	
28	−0.58	44.20	3.84	442	37.7	91.30	
29	−0.55	44.50	3.90	445	38.3	91.75	
30	−0.52	44.80	3.96	448	39.0	92.20	(3d Decile)
31	−0.50	45.00	4.00	450	39.6	92.50	
32	−0.47	45.30	4.06	453	40.1	92.95	
33	−0.44	45.60	4.12	456	40.7	93.40	
34	−0.41	45.90	4.18	459	41.3	93.85	
35	−0.39	46.10	4.22	461	41.9	94.15	
36	−0.36	46.40	4.28	464	42.5	94.60	
37	−0.33	46.70	4.34	467	43.0	95.05	
38	−0.31	46.90	4.38	469	43.6	95.35	
39	−0.28	47.20	4.44	472	44.1	95.80	
40	−0.25	47.50	4.50	475	44.7	96.25	(4th Decile and Stanine)
41	−0.23	47.70	4.54	477	45.2	96.55	
42	−0.20	48.00	4.60	480	45.8	97.00	
43	−0.18	48.20	4.64	482	46.3	97.30	
44	−0.15	48.50	4.70	485	46.8	97.75	
45	−0.13	48.70	4.74	487	47.4	98.05	
46	−0.10	49.00	4.80	490	47.9	98.50	
47	−0.08	49.20	4.84	492	48.4	98.80	
48	−0.05	49.50	4.90	495	48.9	99.25	
49	−0.03	49.70	4.94	497	49.5	99.55	
50	0.00	50.00	5.00	500	50.0	100.00	[Median (5th Decile)]
51	0.03	50.30	5.06	503	50.5	100.45	
52	0.05	50.50	5.10	505	51.1	100.75	

TABLE 15.11 (continued)

PERCENTILE	z	T	STANINE	SAT	NCE	WIQ	
53	0.08	50.80	5.16	508	51.6	101.20	
54	0.10	51.00	5.20	510	52.1	101.50	
55	0.13	51.30	5.26	513	52.6	101.95	
56	0.15	51.50	5.30	515	53.2	102.25	
57	0.18	51.80	5.36	518	53.7	102.70	
58	0.20	52.00	5.40	520	54.2	103.00	
59	0.23	52.30	5.46	523	54.8	103.45	
60	0.25	52.50	5.50	525	55.3	103.75	(6th Decile and Stanine)
61	0.28	52.80	5.56	528	55.9	104.20	
62	0.31	53.10	5.62	531	56.4	104.65	
63	0.33	53.30	5.66	533	57.0	104.95	
64	0.36	53.60	5.72	536	57.5	105.40	
65	0.39	53.90	5.78	539	58.1	105.85	
66	0.41	54.10	5.82	541	58.7	106.15	
67	0.44	54.40	5.88	544	59.3	106.60	
68	0.47	54.70	5.94	547	59.9	107.05	
69	0.50	55.00	6.00	550	60.4	107.50	
70	0.52	55.20	6.04	552	61.0	107.80	(7th Decile)
71	0.55	55.50	6.10	555	61.7	108.25	
72	0.58	55.80	6.16	558	62.3	108.70	
73	0.61	56.10	6.22	561	62.9	109.15	
74	0.64	56.40	6.28	564	63.5	109.60	
75	0.67	56.70	6.34	567	64.2	110.05	(3rd Quartile)
76	0.71	57.10	6.42	571	64.9	110.65	
77	0.74	57.40	6.48	574	65.6	110.10	(7th Stanine)
78	0.77	57.70	6.54	577	66.3	111.55	
79	0.81	58.10	6.62	581	67.0	112.15	
80	0.84	58.40	6.68	584	67.7	112.60	(8th Decile)
81	0.88	58.80	6.76	588	68.5	113.20	
82	0.92	59.20	6.84	592	69.3	113.80	
83	0.95	59.50	6.90	595	70.1	114.25	
84	1.00	60.00	7.00	600	70.9	115.00	
85	1.04	60.40	7.08	604	71.6	115.60	
86	1.08	60.80	7.16	608	72.8	116.20	
87	1.13	61.30	7.26	613	73.7	116.95	
88	1.18	61.80	7.36	618	74.7	117.70	
89	1.23	62.30	7.46	623	75.8	118.45	(8th Stanine)
90	1.28	62.80	7.56	628	77.0	119.20	(9th Decile)
91	1.34	63.40	7.68	634	78.2	120.10	
92	1.41	64.10	7.82	641	79.6	121.15	
93	1.48	64.80	7.96	648	81.1	122.20	
94	1.56	65.60	8.12	656	82.7	123.40	
95	1.65	66.50	8.30	665	84.6	124.75	
96	1.75	67.50	8.50	675	85.9	126.25	(9th Stanine)
97	1.88	68.80	8.76	688	89.6	128.20	
98	2.05	70.50	9.10	705	93.3	130.75	
99	2.41	74.10	9.82	741	99.0	136.15	
100	3.00	80.00	11.00	800	100	145.00	

mental-age technique, as with all norm-referenced scoring systems, thus provides information regarding a person's relative standing. Most of the mass-produced tests used in psychology and education today are of this type. Intelligence tests, achievement tests, aptitude tests, and so on are accompanied by national norms with which an individual's performance can be compared.

The **criterion-referenced test,** however, is not based on relative performance but on absolute performance. For this reason, it is also called a *mastery test,* since the focus is on what absolute fraction of the material covered on the test the student has conquered. For example, the Federal Aviation Administration gives a test to each prospective pilot before that pilot is allowed to solo. The applicant must get at least 70 percent of the questions correct before taking to the air without the instructor. Thus, the FAA demands that the pilot know the vast majority of the material on the test, regardless of how others have performed. The FAA reasons that it's not enough to have a high relative standing on the test, since it's possible that the majority of those taking the test are so ignorant of flying techniques and procedures that they would probably all kill themselves.

In point of fact, most teacher-made tests (and these, after all, account for most of the educational tests given each day throughout the country) are criterion-referenced. The teacher makes up a history test and scores it on the basis of the absolute percentage of a student's correct answers, not on the basis of what percentage of the class did worse than that student. The algebra teacher who wants to know how a given student is doing with reference to *instructional objectives* in a particular classroom is going to use a criterion-referenced test. It is even possible for the same test to be both norm- and criterion-referenced (Lyman, 1991).

Test specialist Arthur Bertrand and Joseph Cebula have identified three crucial components of good criterion-referenced testing.

1. Learning behaviors to be demonstrated by students must be clearly stated prior to the learning experience (e.g., the child will be able to punctuate a four-sentence paragraph).

2. Acceptable levels of success must be stated explicitly (e.g., punctuation must be done with 80 percent accuracy).

3. Test situations or conditions must be made available in order that the students can demonstrate

whether or not they have met the criteria (Bertrand and Cebula, 1980).

According to Lorrie Shephard, norm-referenced tests should be used for monitoring pupil (and program) progress over the long run, from fall to spring or from year to year. Criterion-referenced tests, however, are preferred for day-to-day testing in the classroom. These tests are more easily keyed to current instructional objectives (Shephard, 1979).

Also, and perhaps more importantly, studies indicate that students show higher levels of academic achievement in classes where teachers use tests, and use them often, than in those that rarely test or don't test at all. Frequent testing is even more effective when the students are of only modest ability (Bangert-Downs et al., 1986). Testing can now be accomplished in a very systematic fashion with the use of computer programs. No longer do professional, and often expensive, national testing firms have to be called on for the laborious job of scoring the tests and summarizing the results. Ready-to-run computer programs, which can be used on inexpensive personal computers, are now available for schools and/or school districts to do in-house standardizing. In this age of accountability, in-house testing has become increasingly popular, since it gives schools an economical way of determining the areas in which their students need extra help. It has been shown that when teachers are given clear and understandable data on student progress, student achievement levels increase (McKinnon, 1987).

Teachers typically prefer not to use standardized, norm-referenced tests, usually saying that their particular instructional activities should not be narrowed to those areas sampled by the norm-referenced tests. In fact, research shows that teachers usually don't use the results of norm-referenced tests in their academic decision making (Salmon-Cox, 1981).

Some critics allege that standardized testing creates an aura of classroom artificiality, since it forces teachers to "teach to the test." But in fact, goes the counterargument, teachers have always taught to their own tests, and should. It's really an issue of whose test is being taught to. To test students on material they haven't yet been exposed to seems to be an exercise in folly.

Ethnic bias can creep into standardized tests. Several years ago the word *regatta* was used in one of the College Board tests. This resulted in a storm of protest since that is not a word that is often bandied

Research indicates that frequent testing closely tied to classroom instruction not only increases student achievement levels, but provides teachers with valuable data on which to plan their instruction.

about in minority neighborhoods. Since that time, the Educational Testing Service has been careful to review each word for any such signs of cultural bias. But as ETS insists, "test results cannot be judged in isolation from the unequal outcomes produced by our educational, economic and social systems" (Educational Testing Service, 1991, p. 3). In other words, a fair and accurate test will in fact reflect the quality of academic preparation, and if it doesn't, it will not be a true indicator of educational accomplishments for any test taker, no matter what the student's educational or economic background might be. The concerns of minorities have also been addressed through the use of what is called *race norming,* where test scores within minority groups are compared only

with those from the same minority population rather than across the board.

Multiple-Choice Tests or Essays?

What about multiple-choice tests or, as many poorly prepared students like to call them, "multiple-guess tests"? One of the criticisms of the multiple-choice test is that it rewards rote memorization rather than true understanding. This can certainly happen if the test is poorly designed, but when thoroughly researched and carefully prepared, the multiple-choice test can assess a person's ability to apply concepts to problem-solving situations. Rather than break up the unity of knowledge and isolating the pieces, as the

SPOTLIGHT ON EVALUATION

The Portfolio Approach

Another testing technique, currently gaining in popularity, is called the **portfolio approach**. Just as an aspiring artist or model carries a portfolio of past work to a prospective employer, so too does the student who selects examples of his or her best work over a term or even an entire year of study. It is said that the portfolio approach places more emphasis on a student's overall accomplishments than on the ability merely to score well on a single battery of tests. As one reviewer stated it, "Asking students to select and reflect on examples of their own work provides rich products for assessments.[a] Typical portfolios include original poetry, plays, short stories, essays, and art projects. Even in math, a student might produce a series of fractions, showing their relationships to decimals, or an arrangement of dice to illustrate probabilities, or even present an essay on the life of Blaise Pascal. At the end of the year, the student hands over the portfolio to the teacher for evaluation. The development of a uniform scoring system for the portfolios, however, has so far been extremely difficult to accomplish. Teachers preparing for the twenty-first century should be made aware of this approach and should be given workshop preparation in learning to better calibrate the scoring procedures.

The portfolio method is also now being used to evaluate teachers, students, and the curriculum itself. A portfolio that includes, for example, "samples of student work, teacher developed plans and materials, videotaped teaching episodes, and the teacher's reflections on his or her own teaching can provide direct evidence of what a teacher knows and can do."[b]

Whether the portfolio approach proves to be as valuable as it promises is still in question, but there is no doubt that new testing methods will be employed as educational psychology approaches the twenty-first century. New testing procedures are on the horizon, procedures intended to bridge the gap between cognitive psychology and psychometric methods. As has recently been stated, new-item formats will appear, "along with a renewed interest in performance testing, to permit assessment of higher-order cognitive skills and important performance tasks such as writing, oral communications and problem solving."[c]

---

[a] C. K. Tittle, Changing models of student and teacher assessment. *Educational Psychologist* (1991), 26(2), 157–165.

[b] K. Wolf, The schoolteacher's portfolio: Issues in design, implementation and evaluation. *Phi Delta Kappan*, October 1991, 129–136.

[c] R. K. Hambleton, Meeting the measurement challenge of the 1990s: New psychometric models, methods and tests. *The Score* (1991), 14, 9.

SPOTLIGHT ON COMPUTER-ASSISTED TESTING

Assessment in the Nineties

The computer age has led to a high tech form of testing called **computer-assisted testing (CAT)**. Here the individual sits at a computer keyboard, and the questions are presented on the screen. The testing becomes personalized since the testing is interactive with the computer, in effect, custom designing the test to each student's skill level. For example, the questions may get progressively more difficult until a level is reached. When a student begins to get the questions wrong, an easier set of questions suddenly appears. This branching of easier and harder questions called going "up the ladder" or "down the chute," continues until the student's true level of competence is reached. The Educational Testing Service is currently putting both the SAT and the Graduate Record Exam (GRE) on a computer format. Supporters of this approach claim that CAT is viable, cost-effective, and a big improvement over paper-and-pencil testing (Vale, 1990).

SPOTLIGHT ON GRADE-EQUIVALENT SCORES

A Note of Caution

Grade-equivalent scores are based on relating a given student's score on a test to the average scores found for other students in a particular grade, at the same time of year, and of roughly the same age. For example, assume that in September a large, representative sample of third-graders (called the *norming group*), produced an average score of 30 on a certain arithmetic test. If a given student is then tested and receives a score of 30, that child would be assigned a grade-equivalent score of 3.0. If the child did somewhat better than that and had a score of, say, 3.4, it would indicate a performance equal to a third-grade student in the fourth month (December) of the school year. Grade-equivalent scores are typically reported in tenths of a year, so that a score of 5.9 refers to the ninth month (June) of the fifth grade, and a score of 0.0 to the first day of kindergarten. Thus, the scores range from 0.0 (or sometimes K.O.) through 12.9, representing the thirteen years of school from kindergarten through grade 12. The first of September is given on the scale as 0, whereas the end of September as 0.1, the end of October as 0.2, and on until the end of June, as 0.9. Grade-equivalent tables are provided for the major nationally standardized tests, and although they are quick and easy to figure (simply look up the raw score in the test publisher's table), they must be interpreted with some caution. First, as we have seen over and over again, children do not all grow and develop at the same yearly rate, never mind the same monthly rate, so don't be overly concerned when a seemingly bright child suddenly underperforms the norms by a few months. That same child may quickly catch up and even outperform the norms several months later. Second, don't be too quick to use a precocious child's high score in some area as a reason to have that child skip a grade or two.[a] A third-grader might even get a grade equivalent of 7.0 on a given test. This doesn't mean that the child is now ready for a fast promotion to junior high. What it does mean is that the third-grader has certainly conquered third-grade material, and, in fact, has done as well as a seventh-grader when measured on a *third-grade* test. However, there are undoubtedly many things the seventh-grader has learned and is expected to know which are simply not even part of a third-grader's consciousness and which, of course, don't appear on a third-grade test.

[a] L. R. Aiken, *Psychological testing and assessment,* 6th ed. (Boston: Allyn and Bacon, 1988).

---

critics typically charge, *a well-designed* multiple-choice test, such as the SAT, demands that the student be able to understand concepts and bring facts together. This is especially true of the SAT's reading comprehension section. Research evidence clearly shows that the SAT verbal score shares much in common with IQ, the correlation between them being an extremely high + .80 (Flynn, 1987). What about essay questions? There is the fear that standardized tests based only on essay questions and writing samples may have an adverse effect on cultural bias (Science Agenda, 1990). Verbally adept but uninformed students may bluff their way through an essay exam (Aiken, 1988), and this tactic is used less often by minorities. Although essay exams can often illuminate the student's thought process in more detailed form, the teacher with a large class of widely varying abilities, interests, and needs may have to rely on the multiple-choice test. It not only ensures reliability of testing, but more importantly it permits more free time to work with individual students and parents. It is often all too easy to blame standardized multiple-choice testing for deteriorating academic skills and overlook the more immediate culprits, overcrowded classrooms and underpaid teachers.

Curriculum Testing

Virtually any curriculum that is more that five years old requires a thorough evaluation. This is most obvious in fields such as science, but probably should be done in all areas. Although it has been traditional to use pupil achievement scores as a means for assessing the quality of the curriculum, student scores are only useful insofar as the tested curriculum matches both the planned and taught curriculum. Curriculum expert Jurg Jenzer points out that curriculum evaluation can be a positive tool for evaluating students, teachers and, of course, the school. This type of testing should answer the following:

1. To what degree have the curriculum's goals been reached?

2. Has the overall mission of the curriculum project been reached?

3. Is the curriculum content appropriate in view of the mission objectives?

4. Has the instruction been truly based on the curriculum?

5. Have the assessment procedures measured the taught curriculum *and* the planned curriculum? (For a complete examination of these important testing issues, the interested student is encouraged to see Jenzer, 1992).

CORRELATION: A USEFUL TOOL FOR MAKING PREDICTIONS

Although correlation does not imply causation, it is a useful tool for making predictions. A *correlation* is a statement about the relationship between two variables; it tells us the extent to which the two variables are associated, or the extent to which they occur together. There is, for example, a correlation between College Board scores and college grades. This means that the two variables, College Board scores and college grades, tend to occur together: People with high College Board scores tend to have higher college grade-point averages than do people with low College Board scores.

The Sign of the Correlation

Correlations come in three general forms: positive, negative, and zero. Positive correlations are produced when individuals who score high on the first variable also score high on the second, and those who score low on the first variable also score low on the second. For example, a positive correlation between height and weight means that those individuals who are above average in height are also above average in weight, and those who are below average in height are correspondingly below average in weight. Negative correlations are produced when individuals who score high on the first variable tend to score low on

the second, and those who score low on the first, score high on the second. A negative correlation between college grades and number of absences means that those who are above average in college grades tend to have fewer absences, whereas those who are below average in college grades tend to have more than the average number of absences. Finally, zero correlations are produced when individuals who score high on the first variable are as likely to score high on the second variable as they are to score low; or, when individuals who score low on the first variable are as likely to score low on the second variable as they are to score high.

Correlation Values and Their Interpretation

In order to express the degree to which two variables are associated, or correlated, a single number is used. This number may vary from $+1$ through zero to -1. A value of $+1$ indicates a maximum positive correlation. A maximum relationship is obtained when two measures of a group of individuals, for example, height and weight, associate perfectly. There can be no exceptions when the correlation is $+1$. Thus, every single individual in the group who is higher than another in height is also higher in weight. A value of zero indicates no relationship at all, or a zero correlation. A value of -1 indicates a maximum negative correlation. A correlation of -1 between college grades and number of absences would mean that every single individual in the group who is higher than another in college grades is also lower than that other in number of absences. Most correlations found in the literature fall somewhere between these perfect correlations of $+1$ and -1. The closer the correlation is to ±1, however, the more accurate the resulting prediction; and prediction, after all, is the major goal of correlation research. For example, if the correlation between height and weight is $+.65$, we can more accurately predict a given individual's weight, knowing the person's height, than if the correlation is only $+.25$.

Scatterplot Diagrams

In order to get a visual representation of how two variables might correlate, statisticians use a graphic device known as a scatterplot diagram. A scatterplot diagram is a correlation graph in which each dot represents a pair of scores: one for the distribution

SPOTLIGHT ON CORRELATION AND CAUSATION

The Chicken and Egg Riddle

Suppose a researcher found a correlation between the amount of exercise a person indulged in and the amount of money that person had in the bank. The correlation would probably be negative; that is, people who are involved in heavy exercise programs might tend to have smaller bank accounts. This would not necessarily mean that persons who exercise regularly don't have enough time left over to earn and save money, since it may well be that another variable, age, is being overlooked. Elderly persons who have had a lifetime in which to acquire money are probably less apt to jog five miles a day than a high school student who is still on a family allowance. Other studies of this type have found a strong, positive correlation between the amount of time teachers spend smiling and the achievement level of their students; that is, the more the teachers smiled, the higher the students' grades. One cannot conclude that smiling teachers cause students to achieve more, since, for one thing, we don't know which came first—the smiles or the achievement. Perhaps the teachers are smiling as a result of the high level of student achievement, apparently basking in reflected glory. Or it might be that a *third* variable is influencing both the smiling and the achievement. Perhaps some smiling teachers are happy optimists who see only the best in their students and therefore are more apt to award higher grades.

The important message here is that we should never leap to a cause-and-effect conclusion on the basis of the correlation alone! It is especially easy to look at a two-variable correlation and mistakenly assume that the variable that came first (preceded) somehow caused a change in the variable that followed. That type of conclusion commits what the scientists call the *post hoc fallacy*, which is written in Latin as *post hoc, ergo propter hoc* (translated as "because it came after this, therefore, it was caused by this"). Many examples of this fallacy come readily to mind. We have all heard someone complain that it always rains right after the car is washed, as though washing the car caused it to rain. Or the traffic is always especially heavy when you have an important exam to take, as though all the other drivers know when the exam has been planned and gang up in a contrived conspiracy to force you to be late. Or perhaps while watching a sporting event on television, you have to leave your TV set for a few minutes. When you return, you discover that your favorite team has finally scored. You angrily hypothesize that the team deliberately held back until you weren't there so you would not be able to enjoy the thrill of victory. Some correlation conclusions have been very similar to these rather blatant examples.

Of what use, then, is correlational research? Prediction! Even though causal factors may be diffi- cult to isolate, correlational studies do allow the researcher and/or teacher to make better-than-chance predictions. As for the correlation mentioned above between wealth and exercise, regardless of the reason, the negative correlation between exercise and bank account still allows for a better-than-chance prediction of the bank account value on the basis of exercise patterns—the more the exercise, the smaller the bank account. If, in a two-newspaper city, there is a dependable relationship between which newspaper a person buys (liberal or conservative), and the political voting habits of that person, then one might predict the outcome of certain elections on the basis of the newspapers' circulation figures. We can make the prediction without ever getting into the issue of what causes what. That is, did the liberal stance of the newspaper cause the reader to cast a liberal vote, or did the liberal attitudes of the reader cause the selection of that particular newspaper? We don't know, nor do we even have to speculate on causation in order to make the prediction. In short, accurate predictions of behavior do not depend on the isolation of a causal factor. One need not settle the chicken-egg riddle in order to predict that a certain individual might choose an omelet over a dish of cacciatore. But in making that prediction we must not allege that a cause-and-effect relationship has been established.

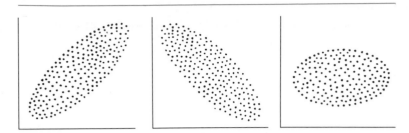

FIGURE 15.11 Scatterplot diagrams showing three kinds of relationships between two variables.

of one set of scores and the other for the distribution of the other set of scores. Figure 15.11 shows the three kinds of relationships that can exist between two variables. The scatterplot diagram on the left portrays a positive correlation: The array of dots goes from lower left to upper right, telling us that as one variable increases, so too does the other. The scatterplot diagram in the middle portrays a negative correlation: The array of dots goes from upper left to lower right, telling us that as one variable increases, the other decreases. Finally, the scatterplot diagram on the right portrays a zero correlation, or no relationship at all: As one variable changes, there is no related change in the other.

The Pearson *r*

One of the most frequently used correlation coefficients is the **Pearson product moment correlation** or, more simply, the **Pearson *r*.** This measure was developed by Karl Pearson, a student of Sir Francis Galton.

$$r = \frac{\Sigma XY/N - \bar{X} \times \bar{Y}}{(\text{SD}_X)(\text{SD}_Y)}$$

If you have learned to calculate a standard deviation, computing a Pearson *r* will be fairly easy. Assume that we are interested in testing the hypothesis that there is some relationship or correlation between math ability and spelling ability among fifth-grade students. We administer a twelve-item math quiz and a twelve-item spelling quiz to a group of fifth-graders. Let the math scores be represented on the *X* distribution and the spelling scores on the *Y* distribution. Then the Pearson *r* is calculated as follows:

1. Calculate the mean for each distribution. In Table 15.12, ΣX (or 65) divided by *N* (or 10) equals 6.5. Similarly, ΣY (or 70) divided by 10 equals 7.

2. Compute the standard deviation for each distribution. Square each score and add the squares. Thus, for the *X* distribution, the first score, 4, when squared equals 16. Next, the score of 12 is squared, yielding 144, and so on. These squared scores are then added, yielding 527 for the *X* distribution. The *Y* distribution is treated in exactly the same way: Square the first score, 6, and get 36. Add all the squares and get 576. Each of these values is used to obtain the standard deviation for each distribution. For *X*, divide ΣX^2

Karl Pearson, a student of Sir Francis Galton, devised the Pearson product moment correlation, the Pearson r, which indicates the strength of the possible association between two variables.

TABLE 15.12   CALCULATION OF THE PEARSON r

Student No.	MATH SCORE			SPELLING SCORE		
	X	X²		Y	Y²	XY
1	4	16		6	36	24
2	12	144		10	100	120
3	2	4		3	9	6
4	5	25		4	16	20
5	9	81		5	25	45
6	6	36		10	100	60
7	2	4		3	9	6
8	10	100		10	100	100
9	6	36		9	81	54
10	9	81		10	100	90
	10)65	527		10)70	576	525

$\overline{X} = 6.50$

$$SD_x = \sqrt{\frac{\Sigma X^2}{N} - \overline{X}^2}$$

$$= \sqrt{\frac{527}{10} - 6.50^2} = \sqrt{52.70 - 42.25}$$

$$= \sqrt{10.45}$$

$$SD_x = 3.23$$

$\overline{Y} = 7.00$

$$SD_y = \sqrt{\frac{\Sigma Y^2}{N} - \overline{Y}^2}$$

$$= \sqrt{\frac{576}{10} - 7.00^2} = \sqrt{57.60 - 49.00}$$

$$= \sqrt{8.60}$$

$$SD_y = 2.93$$

$$r = \frac{\Sigma XY/N - (\overline{X})(\overline{Y})}{SD_x SD_y} = \frac{525/10 - 6.5 \times 7}{3.23 \times 2.93} = \frac{52.50 - 45.50}{9.46}$$

$$r = \frac{7}{9.46}$$

$r = .739$, which is rounded to

$r = .74$

(527) by N (10) and get 52.70. From that, subtract the square of the mean (52.70 − 42.25). For the resulting value, 10.45, extract the square root, 3.23, which is the standard deviation. For the Y distribution, divide 576 by 10, which equals 57.60. Subtract the square of the mean (57.60 − 49.00) and get 8.60. Extract the square root, 2.93, to obtain the standard deviation.

3. Multiply each raw score in the X distribution by its corresponding score in the Y distribution. Thus 4 times 6 equals 24; 12 times 10 equals 120; 2 times 3 equals 6, and so on. These XY values are then added, yielding a total ΣXY of 525.

4. Divide ΣXY by N, and then subtract the product of the means. Thus 525/10 minus the product of 6.50 times 7 equals 7.

5. This value is then divided by the product of the

standard deviations of X and Y. Thus 3.23 times 2.93 equals 9.46. Dividing 7 by 9.46 gives us a Pearson r of .739, which can be rounded to .74.

Interpretation of r   Since the highest possible correlation is 1.00, which is a perfect positive correlation, the Pearson r of .74 indicates a fairly strong association between the two variables, math scores and spelling scores. Thus, our sample of fifth-graders provides data that tell us that students who perform well on the math quiz are also likely to perform well on the spelling quiz. Since the correlation is not 1.00, we cannot say that every student who is high in math ability is also high in spelling ability. Our correlation of .74 indicates that there will be some exceptions but that in general the relationship will be dependable. Thus, knowing a student's math score allows us to

ANNE ANASTASI

Anne Anastasi was brought up in New York City. She attended Public School 33, where she was awarded a gold medal for general excellence. She then entered public high school, but after two frustrating months she dropped out. Although she had found her stay at P.S. 33 to be happy and productive, she found high school to be a total waste of time. Her high school was overcrowded, and she resented both the fifteen-minute trolley-car ride and also the fact that her teachers were remote and impersonal.

During her dropout phase, there were many family discussions about her academic future. Finally, a friend suggested that she should simply skip high school completely and go to college. Thus in 1924, at the precocious age of 15, Anne Anastasi became a freshman math major at Barnard College. As a freshman, she took an introductory psychology course, and although she found the course interesting, it was not until her sophomore year, when she took a course in developmental psychol-

ogy, that she decided psychology was to be her lifework. Psychology gave her the opportunity to have the best of two worlds. She could satisfy her interest in mathematics through the study of psychological statistics and also her emerging interest in human development and behavior.

She graduated from Barnard at nineteen and immediately entered the Ph.D. program in psychology at Columbia University. She received her doctorate two years later. The high point of her short tenure as a graduate student came during the summer of 1929. She began that memorable summer as research assistant to the famous American geneticist Charles B. Davenport. Next she took a six-week course with the illustrious learning theorist Clark Hull. Finally, as the summer ended, she enjoyed the "heady privilege" of attending the International Congress of Psychology at Yale University. There she saw and heard great psychologists from all over the world, including Ivan Pavlov, Charles Spearman, and William McDougall.

In 1930 Anastasi joined the faculty at Barnard College, where she remained until 1939. She then went to Queens College in New York as chairman of the psychology department, and in 1947 she joined the faculty at Fordham University.

Anastasi considers herself to be a "generalist" in the field of psychology. Her interests range widely, and she has published in such diverse areas as the psychology of art, memory, personality, intelligence, emotion, statistics, language development, test construction, cultural differences, creativity, male and female differences, and the nature-nurture controversy. The bibliography of Anastasi's papers and books reads like a compendium of

the whole field of psychology. There are few areas in psychology to which this talented woman has not devoted some of her time and energy.

In 1971 Anastasi was honored by her professional colleagues by being chosen as the president of the American Psychological Association, a group at that time of over 31,000 members.

Anastasi is a firm believer in the influence of early experience on intellectual growth and development. She urges a program of concentrated effort on improving environmental conditions at early life stages, especially for disadvantaged groups. She feels that early in life the cumulative effects of an impoverished environment can be minimized. She is also a firm believer in intelligence testing, when the tests are administered properly and evaluated fairly. She feels that IQ tests should not be discontinued just because some children receive lower scores than others. This would be like asking a physician to throw away his thermometer just because children who are ill register an undesirable deviation from the norm. Measuring instruments don't produce social discrimination; only people do.

In 1958, in her paper "Heredity, Environment and The Question 'How?'" Anastasi argued that people should stop asking the question about which component, heredity or environment, is more important in determining individual differences. A better question is *how* heredity and environment interact in the development of behavioral differences. The focus should be on the mechanism of the interaction, because behavior is the result of the interaction. Anne Anastasi, the generalist, specifically recommends here that we take a new look at one of psychology's oldest and most often debated problems.

predict his or her spelling score, and because the correlation is fairly strong, we will be right in our predictions far more often than we will be wrong. Although correlation does not imply causation, it does allow for accurate predictions. We can't say that an individual is a good speller because he or she has high math ability, but we can say that, given information about the pupil's math ability we can predict fairly accurately how well he or she will spell.

SAMPLING: GENERALIZING FROM THE FEW TO THE MANY

Perhaps you have been told never to generalize, never to leap to conclusions on the basis of a few observations. An old proverb states that one swallow does not make a summer. Statisticians say, "Never generalize from an *N* of one." Someone once said that no generalization is absolutely true, even that one.

This is certainly all good advice. It prevents us from committing the **inductive fallacy**—that is, automatically assuming that all members of a class have a certain characteristic because one member of that class has it. It would be fallacious to say, "I once met a Mongolian who was a liar; therefore, all Mongolians are liars."

However, under certain prescribed conditions— that is, using certain strategies or rules of the game— it may be appropriate to generalize on the basis of a limited number of observations. Certain statistical techniques exist that allow us to generalize to a whole group after observing some part of that group. The key to these techniques is that the small groups must be representative of the entire group: they must reflect the traits and characteristics of the entire group. If we want to predict political attitudes of Americans in general, we cannot interview just men, or just women, or just Democrats, or just people who are receiving social security. We must interview a group that represents all these traits and many more.

The entire group, or the total number of people, things, or events having at least one trait in common is called a *population*. Any group selected from the population is called a *sample*. In order to ensure that the sample is representative of the population, statisticians usually use the technique of random sampling. **Random sampling** gives every single member of the entire population an equal chance of being selected for the sample. If you wanted to select a random sample of the population of students at your college, you could not do it by selecting every third person in the college cafeteria. Perhaps some students never eat in the cafeteria, and they would not be represented in the sample. Nor could you choose a random sample by selecting every *n*th person who enters the library. Again, some students avoid the library and would not be represented in the sample. To be sure to have a random sample, to be sure that every student in the college has an equal chance of being chosen, you would take the names of every student enrolled in the college, drop the names in a barrel, and, blindfolded, pick out, say, fifty or a hundred names. In this way the group selected would be truly random, and because the group was selected on a chance basis, it would likely be representative of the entire population. Random sampling allows the statistician to legitimately generalize to the population.

SUMMARY

Measurement is the assigning of a number to an observation (object or event) according to certain rules. To give meaning to these numbers, all measurements must satisfy two basic criteria: They must be reliable and they must be valid. Reliability indicates the consistency of a measurement, while validity is the extent to which a test measures what it is intended (and purports) to measure.

To make meaning out of the chaos of raw data from any study, the researcher typically arranges the raw scores in order of magnitude, called a distribution of scores. When the scores are presented beside another column, listing the frequency of occurrence for each score, a frequency distribution is created. Educational psychologists also use graphs to present data in a more meaningful form. The actual scores are indicated on the horizontal axis, or abscissa, and the frequency of occurrence is presented on the vertical axis, or ordinate. Another method of portraying frequency distribution data is called the stem-and-leaf display in which only the first digit(s) is (are) shown in the stem column and the trailing digits are shown in the leaf column.

In order to aid in our understanding of both the

ways in which individuals differ and also the ways in which they are alike, methods are employed for finding the average or typical score in a distribution. These techniques are called measures of central tendency, and include the mean, which is the arithmetic average; the median, which is the middlemost point in an ordered distribution; and the mode, which is the most frequently occurring score in a distribution.

Just as the measures of central tendency give us information with regard to similarity among measurements, measures of variability provide information regarding how scores differ or vary. Two important measures of variability are the range, which is the difference between the highest and lowest scores in a distribution, and the standard deviation (SD), which is a measure of how much each score generally varies or deviates from the mean. In addition, many behavioral measures in psychology conform to what is called the normal curve, a theoretical distribution that, in brief, shows the majority of scores as falling around the center of the distribution and that shows, as we move away from this center, in either direction, fewer and fewer scores. A standard score, or z score, is a translation of a raw score into units of standard deviation. The z distribution has a mean of zero and a standard deviation of 1.0. Similarly, a T score, also based on the normal curve, is derived by setting the mean at 50 and the standard deviation at 10. T scores range in value from 20 (3 standard deviations below the mean) to 80 (3 standard deviations above the mean). NCE scores, normal-curve-equivalents, are also standardized on the normal curve and are based on a mean of 50 and

a standard deviation of approximately 21. Finally, stanines are also translated from the normal curve and divide the curve into units of nine intervals. The stanine distribution has a mean of 5 and a standard deviation of approximately 2. A percentile is that point in the distribution at or below which a given percentage of cases fall. Variations on the percentile theme include (1) the decile, every ten percentile units and (2) the quartile, every 25 percentile units.

Tests can be scored by being (1) criterion-referenced and/or (2) norm-referenced. Criterion-referenced tests are those which evaluate an individual's performance on the basis of a comparison with some arbitrarily fixed standard. Norm-referenced tests judge the individual's performance on the basis of a comparison with the average performance of all the individuals who took that same test.

The correlation coefficient, first developed by Karl Pearson, is a numerical statement describing the strength of the association between two (or possibly more) variables. Though correlational statements should not, in and of themselves, be used to imply causation, they can be used to make better-than-chance predictions.

By using scientific sampling techniques, such as random sampling, the researcher can legitimately generalize the results of a few measurements taken on a small group to a much larger group. Thus, the educational psychologist may measure only a sample and yet is able to accurately generalize these measures to an entire population. The key issue in these sampling procedures is that the sample must be representative of the population to which the results are to be extrapolated.

KEY TERMS AND NAMES

Anne Anastasi
computer-assisted testing (CAT)
correlation
criterion-referenced test
distribution
grade-equivalent scores
histogram
individual differences
inductive fallacy
measurement
measures of central tendency
    mean
    median
    mode
normal curve

Normal Curve Equivalent (NCE) score
norm-referenced test
Pearson *r* (product moment correlation)
percentile
portfolio approach
random sampling
reliability
stanine
stem-and-leaf display
T scores
validity
variability measures
    range (*R*)
    standard deviation (SD)
z score (standard score)

THEORY INTO PRACTICE: STATISTICAL EVALUATION

1. You have been assigned to work with a classroom teacher to help in the interpretation of test grades. The teacher has prepared a 50-item multiple-choice test to be used on a group of thirty students after they complete a social studies unit on the causes of the Civil War. The test was timed and scored on the basis of the number of items a student correctly answered. The scores were as follows:

    31, 20, 23, 29, 30, 31, 34, 35, 44, 31, 31, 32, 21, 45, 39, 21, 37, 22, 31, 31, 35, 25, 36, 29, 29, 30, 29, 35, 34, 30

    Calculate the following measures of central tendency:
    a. The mean
    b. The median
    c. The mode
        Next, calculate the following two measures of variability:
    d. The range
    e. The standard deviation

    On the basis of your calculations, indicate whether the test has produced any indication of centrality among the scores. Also, write a statement regarding your views on whether the test showed the group to be homogenous or heterogeneous.

2. The teacher you have been assigned to also decided to use the same exam with another class, also following the presentation of the Civil War unit. This class was also composed of thirty students, and their scores were as follows:

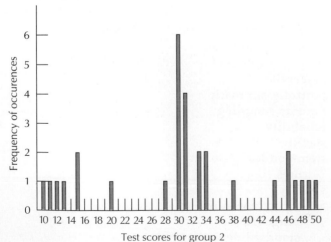

Test scores for group 2

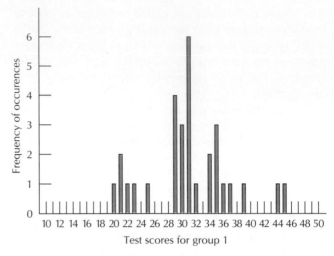

Test scores for group 1

15, 33, 46, 31, 10, 12, 50, 31, 31, 13, 11, 20, 30, 30, 44, 48, 49, 15, 30, 47, 30, 46, 30, 38, 30, 34, 34, 33, 31, 28

As before, calculate
a. The mean
b. The median
c. The mode
d. The range
e. The standard deviation.

Is there any noticeable difference between the performances of the two groups? Compare both the centrality and variability of the scores in the two distributions. Do the groups show the same degree of homogeneity or heterogeneity? Or are the two distributions about even in the amount of variability shown?

   Is there anything you might tell the teacher regarding your overall evaluation of the two groups?

3. Draw two histograms, one for each set of scores. Indicate the raw scores on the horizontal axis (abscissa), and the frequency of occurrence on the vertical axis (ordinate). As shown in the text, use a series of rectangles over each score in order to indicate frequency.

4. You have been given a large amount of student information from a local school district. Among the data, you find some measures that were obtained from a random sample of children selected from the kindergarten-grade–12 population (ages five to eighteen). The measures were as follows:

STUDENT'S NUMBER	SHOE SIZE (IN INCHES)	READING ACHIEVEMENT SCORES
1	5	10
2	8	12
3	11	21
4	13	22
5	13	20
6	10	20
7	11	18
8	10	20
9	9	19
10	7	16
11	9	23
12	10	16
13	7	13
14	11	21
15	12	30

A friend suggests to you that from a quick inspection of the data it looks as if there is a rather strong correlation between the variables, that is, the high scores on the reading test seem to be associated with larger foot sizes and the lower reading scores seem to be associated with smaller sizes. To find out if there is that association, you are asked to calculate a Pearson *r* correlation coefficient between the two variables.

a. What is the correlation?
b. What does this tell us about the relationship between these two variables?
c. Does the analysis prove that forcing children to wear larger shoes might cause an increase in reading ability? If so, why, and if not, why not?

Answers

1. (a) The mean equals 31.00. (b) The median equals 31. (c) The mode equals 31. (d) The range equals 25. (e) The standard deviation equals 5.99.
The scores seem to indicate that the group is relatively homogeneous and that there are definitely indications of strong centrality since the mean, median, and mode all occur at the same point.

2. (a) The mean equals 31.00. (b) The median equals 31. (c) The mode equals 30. (d) The range equals 40. (e) The standard deviation equals 11.69.
In this group, although the measures of centrality have virtually the same values as those in the first group, the variability is significantly larger, that is, in this group the scores are more heterogeneous and are thus producing higher values for both the range and standard deviation. The teacher should be aware, and probably already is, that the job of teaching the second group will be more difficult. Material that is understandable for the lower-achieving student may at the same time seem overly easy for the higher-level students (who might then become bored). Similarly, setting the level to accommodate the higher-level students may totally frustrate and confuse the lower-level students. The extremes of ability levels shown in this group will probably make the teacher's job more demanding in terms of teaching skills as well as social sensitivity and personal understanding.

3. The histograms should look something like those on the opposite page.

4. (a) The Pearson *r* correlation is +.85.
(b) The size of the correlation shows that there is a dependable relationship between foot size and reading ability among the pupils in the chosen sample, that is, children with larger feet tend to read at a higher level than children with smaller feet.
(c) As was pointed out in the chapter, correlation should not be used in an attempt to prove a cause-and-effect relationship. In this example, an extremely important third factor was left out of the two-variable analysis, and that was the age variable. Obviously, older children will tend to have bigger feet and should also, because of experience and maturation, be better readers. The problem of the "third factor" is one that haunts much of correlational research. Despite this limitation, the correlation could still be used for predictive purposes. In this case, for example, knowing a given child's shoe size should allow the researcher to make a better-than-chance prediction regarding the same child's score on a test of reading ability.

REFERENCES

Aiken, L. R. (1988). *Psychological testing and assessment* (6th ed.). Boston: Allyn and Bacon.
Bangert-Downs, R. L., Kulik, J. A., and Kulik, C. L. (1986).

Effects of frequent classroom testing. Paper presentation, *American Educational Research Association*, San Francisco.
Bertrand, A., and Cebula, J. (1980). *Tests, measurement and*

evaluation: A developmental process. Reading, Mass.: Addison-Wesley.

Educational Testing Service (1991). *Sex, race, ethnicity and performance on the GRE general test.* Princeton, N.J.: Educational Testing Service.

Fiske, E. B. (1988). America's test mania. *The New York Times* (November 13).

Flynn, J. R. (1987). The ontogeny of intelligence. In J. Forge (Ed.), *Measurement, realism and objectivity: Essays on measurement in the social and physical sciences.* Boston: D. Reidel.

Geisinger, K. F. (1992). Metamorphosis in test validation. *Educational Psychologist, 27,* 197–222.

Hambleton, R. K. (1991). Meeting the measurement challenge of the 1990s: New psychometric models, methods and tests. *The Score, 14,* 9.

Jenzer, J. (1992). Curriculum process and design. In *Mathematics curriculum resource handbook.* Millwood, N.Y.: Krauss International.

Kamin, L. J. (1974). *The science and politics of IQ.* Potomac, Md.: Erlbaum.

Lyman, H. B. (1991). *Test scores and what they mean* (5th ed.). Englewood Cliffs, N.J.: Prentice-Hall.

McKinnon, G. (1987). In-house standardized test scoring has numerous benefits. *Electronic Learning, 7,* 46.

Mercer, J., and Lewis, J. (1978). *System of multicultural pluralistic assessment.* New York: Psychological Corporation.

Salmon-Cox, L. (1981). Teachers and standardized achievement tests. *Phi Delta Kappan* (May), 631–634.

Science Agenda. (1990). New directions in educational testing. *Science Agenda* (August–September), 14.

Shephard, L. (1979). Norm-referenced vs. criterion-referenced tests. *Educational Horizons, 68* (1), 26–35.

Sprinthall, R. C. (1990). *Basic statistical analysis* (3rd ed.). Englewood Cliffs, N.J.: Prentice-Hall.

Sprinthall, R. C., Schmutte, G. T., and Sirois, L. (1990). *Understanding educational research.* Englewood Cliffs, N.J.: Prentice-Hall.

Tittle, C. K. (1991). Changing models of student and teacher assessment. *Educational Psychologist, 26*(2), 157–165.

Vale, C. D. (1990). The future of computerized testing: Technology, economics and marketability. *The Score, 13,* 6–7.

Wolf, K. (1991). The schoolteacher's portfolio: Issues in design, implementation and evaluation. *Phi Delta Kappan* (October), 129–136.

16

INTELLIGENCE: CONCEPTS AND MEASURES

Among the lay public, the term **intelligence** is probably the most widely used psychological concept of all. The media constantly bombard us with stories of new theories and studies, often anecdotal, on the topic of intelligence. Historians estimate the IQs of important persons from the past. People talk about whether they or others are intelligent enough for this job or that college or to marry this or that person. Politicians have even legislated immigration quotas on the basis of their versions of intelligence. Hardly a day goes by without your hearing the term mentioned at least once, but what does it mean? What is intelligence? Does it even exist, and if it does, is it displayed differently among different people engaged in different tasks?

WHAT IS INTELLIGENCE?

If you could step back in time and observe those first humans living among large and ferocious beasts, you probably wouldn't have given those weak, skinny, hairless creatures much chance for survival, never mind even an outside chance of taking over the planet. In an eagle-and-claw world, the human being would not have appeared as "fit" enough to survive. But we humans did survive and did take charge of our world. Why? Undoubtedly because of our wits.

We had no claws, no fangs, no protective shells. Our only armament was our intelligence. Our ability to size up new situations, learn from past mistakes, and create new patterns of thought all contributed heavily to our overall capacity to *adapt to new situations* and then *transmit our learning to new generations.* Intelligence had and continues to have survival value. Sandra Scarr has said that from the point of view of biology, intelligence has evolved as a primary adaptive mechanism and as such shows typical patterns of individual variability (Scarr, 1981).

Toward the end of the nineteenth century, the eminent psychologist Sir Francis Galton assumed from his research that intelligence was a unitary trait or an absolute, like height or weight. Since Galton's time, however, few psychologists have seriously considered such a simplistic notion. For example, just after the turn of the century, **Charles Spearman** theorized that intelligence was made up of several factors, an underlying *general factor* (*g*), and a series of very *specific factors* (*s*'s). According to Spearman's **factor approach,** the *g* factor acted as a driving force that would power a set of special skills unique to specific situations, such as verbal ability, mathematical ability, and even musical ability. The *g* factor, however, provided the main thrust for activating the *s* factors. According to Spearman's model, *g* was a form of dynamic brain energy that would set in motion the "specific engines" of ability. Spearman also believed that *g* was largely inherited. Recently, there has been renewed interest in Spearman's *g*. On the basis of an extensive survey of the evidence to date, some researchers now argue that Spearman may have been right all along, that there does exist a general *g* factor which, in varying degrees, dominates many of the specific types of cognitive skills that have lately been claimed (Carroll, 1989).

L. L. Thurstone, from the 1920s through the 1940s, worked diligently on an attempt to refine Spearman's factors but could find no substantive evidence to support the *g* concept. Thurstone suggested, instead, that intelligence was always a composite of special factors, each peculiar to a specific task. He identified seven different "vectors of the mind," or major components of intelligence: verbal comprehension, word fluency, numerical ability, spatial visualization, associative memory, perceptual speed, and reasoning. Since then, **J. P. Guilford's** factor approach has pointed to the possibility of intelligence being composed of up to 120 separately identifiable traits (Guilford, 1967).

More recently, psychologists such as Howard Gardner and Robert Sternberg have created new theories of intelligence that seem to share an almost humanistic perspective. As one reviewer has said, the creators of these new theories, "mindful of the pitfalls of IQ, borrow from cognitive psychology and neuroscience to define smartness as a complex web of abilities" (McKean, 1986). Gardner has identified seven kinds of intelligence: (1) linguistic, (2) logicomathematical, (3) spatial, (4) musical, (5) bodily-kinesthetic, (6) interpersonal (knowing how to deal with others), and (7) intrapersonal (knowledge of one's self). The problem, according to Gardner, is that traditional tests of intelligence measure only the first two. Gardner says that intelligence must entail "a set of skills of problem solving—enabling the individual to resolve genuine problems or difficulties that he or she encounters and, when appropriate, to create an effective product—and must also entail the potential for finding or creating problems—thereby laying the groundwork for the acquisition of new knowledge" (Gardner, 1985a). Gardner has even gone so far as to suggest getting rid of traditional IQ tests, even though he admits they are good predictors of school success. His argument is that despite their predictive accuracy, IQ tests have too often had destructive social consequences (Gardner, 1985b).

In a famous statement, first set forth in the 1960s, the noted psychologist P. E. Vernon, suggested three basic meanings for the concept of intelligence.

1. *Intelligence as a genetic capacity:*   This part of intelligence is due to the "luck of the genes," and is based on that understructure that is part of one's inherited equipment. D. O. Hebb once referred to this as intelligence A, the genotypic form of intelligence (see Chapter 4).

2. *Intelligence as observed behavior:*   This second meaning, referred to by Hebb as intelligence B, is based on observations of what the individual does. This is the phenotypic form of intelligence and is a result of the interaction of genes and the environment. In this sense intelligence becomes an adverb, and we define it on the basis of whether or not the individual acts *intelligently*.

3. *Intelligence as a test score:*   The third meaning of intelligence, intelligence C, is based on a strict operational definition of the concept. Intelligence is what the intelligence test measures. Though this seems to be a straightforward, no-frills definition, it creates a meaning of intelligence that can differ from what the majority of individuals would regard as intelligent behavior (Vernon, 1969).

Above all else, however, we must be reminded that intelligence does not act in a vacuum; it must always be seen in contextual terms. As has recently been said, intelligence is the "ability to master the skills and information necessary to succeed within a given culture, that is, to succeed at a given point in time within a defined context" (Locurto, 1991, p. 165).

Despite the numerous versions of intelligence, and even despite the controversies that have arisen over the use of IQ scores, few psychologists today would argue for the complete abandonment of intelligence testing. Since intelligence is ultimately based on observed behavior, a good IQ test is one way through which one's behavior can be objectively observed in a controlled situation. A test such as the **Wechsler Intelligence Scale for Children (WISC-III),** in the hands of a skilled examiner, samples a large variety of behaviors all of which are assumed to be indicators of various kinds of intelligence. Without question, IQ correlates more highly with virtually every measure of social and occupational success than does any other available assessment technique. As Charles Locurto says, "If we were limited to making one measurement of a seven-year-old child to predict that child's even-

SPOTLIGHT ON INTELLIGENCE

The Sternberg View

In his triarchic theory of intelligence, Robert Sternberg (who, as we saw in Chapter 11, views intelligence from an information processing perspective) has described intelligence as being of three major types: componential, experiential, and contextual.[a]

1. *Componential intelligence* is based on a person's ability to learn how to do new things, acquire new information, absorb the explicit knowledge taught in schools, store and retrieve that information, and carry out tasks speedily and effectively. In fact, Sternberg argues that most IQ tests typically focus only on componential intelligence.

2. *Experiential intelligence* is based on a person's ability to solve new problems, to act creatively, and to use insight. This form of intelligence also allows the person to process past information quickly, freeing the mind for the more important work of seeking creative solutions to new problems.

3. *Contextual intelligence* is based on a person's ability to use practical knowledge and common sense. Individuals high in contextual intelligence are typically called "street smart," are able to get along with other people, and usually able to stay out of trouble. Such individuals have the ability to adapt to their environments and even *reshape their environments to accommodate their strengths and minimize their weaknesses*. Sternberg calls this practical aspect of knowledge (out of which contextual intelligence is formed) *tacit knowledge*. He sees tacit knowledge in general as made up of all the important things you aren't formally taught in school. He is even convinced that success in life depends as much on tacit knowledge as the explicit knowledge you might obtain from more academic pursuits. The difference between tacit knowledge and explicit knowledge (and also, perhaps, different stages of moral development) may be illustrated by the following story:

Two young men are out hiking, one a graduate student in higher mathematics, the other a high-school dropout who is known for his "street smarts." The two enter an abandoned tunnel, and when about halfway through, they suddenly see a large and ferocious bear entering the tunnel behind them. The graduate student whips out his calculator, estimates such values as the distances involved and the speeds at which the bear and they might run, and then does some quick calculations. All this while, the dropout is taking off his hiking boots and lacing on his sneakers. "It's no use," says the graduate student, "my equations make it clear that we can't outrun that bear." And the dropout replies, "That may be, but the way I figure it, we don't have to outrun that bear. All I've got to do is outrun you."

---

[a] R. J. Sternberg, *Beyond IQ: A triarchic theory of human intelligence* (New York: Cambridge University Press, 1985).

---

tual success, . . . the one best measure would be that child's IQ" (Locurto, 1991, p. 160). Most psychologists agree that intelligence tests, even with their limitations, have made valuable contributions to the decision-making process in schools, clinics, and industry. Despite the empirical evidence, however, some psychologists still urge that IQ tests be abandoned. At least one researcher has even suggested that perhaps the use of intelligence tests may not be ethical since the tests are artificial procedures that measure everyone with the same yardstick, even though children are different (Messick, 1980). But then again, if children weren't different, there would be no need for the yardstick in the first place. As has been suggested, it is somewhat ironic to be talking about outlawing tests for the very reason for which they were designed— "to prevent subjective judgments and prejudice from being the basis for assigning students to special classes or denying them certain privileges" (Weinberg, 1991, p. 101).

ANTHROPOMETRIC
LABORATORY

For the measurement in various ways of Human Form and Faculty.

Entered from the Science Collection of the S. Kensington Museum.

This laboratory is established by Mr. Francis Galton for the following purposes:—

1. For the use of those who desire to be accurately measured in many ways, either to obtain timely warning of remediable faults in development, or to learn their powers.

2. For keeping a methodical register of the principal measurements of each person, of which he may at any future time obtain a copy under reasonable restrictions.   His initials and date of birth will be entered in the register, but not his name.   The names are indexed in a separate book.

3. For supplying information on the methods, practice, and uses of human measurement.

4. For anthropometric experiment and research, and for obtaining data for statistical discussion.

Charges for making the principal measurements:
THREEPENCE each, to those who are already on the Register.
FOURPENCE each, to those who are not:— one page of the Register will thenceforward be assigned to them, and a few extra measurements will be made, chiefly for future identification.

The Superintendent is charged with the control of the laboratory and with determining in each case, which, if any, of the extra measurements may be made, and under what conditions.

H & W. Brown, Printers, 20 Fulham Road, S.W.

SIR FRANCIS GALTON

In 1822 Francis Galton was born into a wealthy and highly educated English family. Among his relatives were many of England's most intelligent, accomplished, and gifted citizens, including Charles Darwin, who introduced the modern theory of evolution, and Arthur Hallam, the subject of Tennyson's "In Memoriam." Galton even published a list of his wife's "connections," citing that her father had been headmaster of Harrow and a brilliant educator.

In 1838 Galton began his studies in medicine, but two years later he shifted his career plans and majored in mathematics. Following college, Galton traveled several times to Africa, trekking into areas of that continent that had not been explored before. In 1854, Galton received the Royal Geographical Society's gold medal for his adventurous forays into Africa.

After his marriage in 1853, Galton turned to writing. His first book, *The Art of Travel,* was a practical guide for the explorer, and his second book, on meteorology, was one of the first attempts to set forth precise techniques for predicting the weather.

During the 1860s Galton became impressed with his cousin Charles Darwin's book, *On the Origin of Species.* He was fascinated with Darwin's notion of the survival of the fittest through adaptation, and he attempted to apply this concept to human beings, thus founding the field of *eugenics,* or the study of how the principles of heredity could be used to improve the human race.

In 1869 Galton published his first major work, *Hereditary Genius,* in which he postulated the enormous importance of heredity in determining intellectual eminence. He felt that "genius" ran in certain families, and he was eager to point to his own brilliant family as "exhibit A." He also became impressed with the wide range of individual differences that he found for virtually all human traits, physical as well as psychological. Assuming that intelligence was a function of the quality of a person's sensory apparatus, he devised a series of tests of reaction time and sensory acuity to measure intellectual ability. As a result, he is considered to be the "father of intelligence testing." Although Galton's tests seem naive by modern standards, his emphasis on the relationship between sensory ability and intellect foreshadows much of today's research on the importance of sensory stimulation in determining cognitive growth. Galton also invented what he termed the *index of co-relation* in order to analyze the test data that he was collecting. It was left to one of his students, Karl Pearson, however, to work out the mathematical equation for this index, which is now known as the Pearson r, or product-moment correlation.

Following the publication of *Hereditary Genius,* Galton wrote other major works, including *English Men of Science, Natural Inheritance,* and *Inquiries into Human Faculty.* His range of interests in psychology was extremely wide, embracing such topics as imagery, free and controlled associations, personality testing, and, of course, the assessment of intellect. Certainly Galton takes his place in history as an hereditarian, but he did not overlook environmental influences completely. To gain understanding of the possible interaction between heredity and environment, Galton performed psychology's first research studies on twins.

In 1909, just two years before his death, Galton was knighted. Galton's place in the history of psychology is ensured. More than any other person, he set psychology on the road to quantifying its data, and, of course, the whole testing movement in educational psychology owes a major debt to Galton's early work.

IN THE BEGINNING: THE HISTORY OF IQ TESTING

Over a century ago, Sir Francis Galton, the English psychologist mentioned earlier in the chapter, began speculating on a subject that has very recently become one of the most explosive in all of educational psychology. Galton, who was Charles Darwin's younger cousin, attempted to relate Darwin's theory of evolution to human intellect. Believing that intelligence was a result of one's sensory equipment and that one's sensory equipment was a result of heredity (since keen sensory powers would seem to have survival value), Galton tried to measure these sensory powers, and thus, intelligence. In 1882 he set up a testing booth in a London museum and charged people a fee to have their hearing, vision, reaction time, and other sensorimotor equipment measured. It is certainly an indication of Galton's own genius that he could devise a way to turn a profit while collecting his data. Perhaps the most significant fact to emerge from his data was the concept of individual differences: Galton found that people varied widely in their abilities to perform on simple sensorimotor tests. Despite their seeming simplicity, one thing is certain about Galton's tests—they were definitely not culturally biased.

Galton firmly believed that intelligence was inherited. He may have felt this way partly because he had some extremely bright relatives, including Charles Darwin. But he also felt he had objective evidence. He collected data on assumed intellectual relationships between pairs of twins. As we will see, virtually all later studies of intelligence are based on Galton's idea of studying relationships in the context of individual differences. As we saw in the last chapter, one of Galton's students, a mathematician named Karl Pearson, actually worked out the basic equation for the correlation coefficient, and thus furnished the statistical groundwork for the data analysis that has proved so useful in the study of intelligence.

Individual Differences and Correlation

Galton and Pearson were impressed by the fact that individuals varied so greatly in such characteristics as height, weight, and intellect. Because of this variety, the measurements of these characteristics would be more useful if they reflected the frequency with which the characteristics could be expected to occur in the population on the basis of chance, rather than their own absolute units of measurement, such as feet or pounds. The idea of relative standing is of great importance in psychology. It is more important to know that a man's height places him in the relative position of exceeding 50 percent of the adult male population than to know that he stands five feet, nine inches tall.

The concept of individual differences also makes it possible to find a common ground of comparison between different kinds of measurements. Even though height and weight cannot be compared directly because different units of measurement are

used, they can be compared in terms of how much each varies from its own average. In effect, this means that apples and oranges can be compared on the basis of whether, say, a given orange and a given apple are both larger or smaller, or juicier or riper, than the average orange and apple. Thus, the relationships between two measurements can be expressed in quantitative terms, and this value is called the *correlation coefficient*. As we saw in Chapter 15, correlations range in value from $+1$ through zero to -1. The stronger the relationship, the greater the deviation from zero.

Alfred Binet and Mental Age

In 1904, the minister of public instruction in Paris, France, appointed **Alfred Binet** to a special commission that was to study the problem of educating mentally retarded children. The commission concluded that separate schools should be established to educate those children who could not profit from the regular classroom situation. Binet and his colleague, Theodore Simon, developed the first real intelligence test for the express purpose of identifying these children. Binet discarded Galton's notion of measuring intelligence through the use of sensorimotor tasks and assembled instead a series of intellectual tasks. It was Binet's belief that intelligence was the ability to make sound judgments. The various tasks were arranged in order of difficulty and presented to a group of French children. Binet later used the concept of **mental age** to score the test. He discovered, for example, how many of the tasks the average six-year-old could pass, and then any other children who passed the same number of tests were assigned a mental age of six years. Thus, Binet defined mental age in terms of the age at which a given number of test items are passed by an average child. This means that from the very beginning the measurement of intelligence has been a relative measure of mental growth. Binet's intelligence scores were not absolute, for they were based on how well a given child does compared to the average child of the same age. As we saw in Chapter 15, this is a clear example of a norm-referenced system. Binet's scores were assigned relative to the performance shown by children of the *same age*, taking the *same test*.

Binet tried to define intelligence in terms of an individual's ability to make sound judgments. "To judge well, to comprehend well, to reason well, these are the essentials of intelligence. A person may be a

ALFRED BINET

Alfred Binet was born in Nice, France, in 1857. He later went to school in Paris and received a law degree in 1878. Practicing law did not appeal to Binet, and he soon decided to go back to school. In 1890 he received a degree in the natural sciences, and in 1894 he earned his Ph.D. in science, with a dissertation which focused on the nervous system of insects. During the time he was working on his doctorate, Binet became deeply interested in suggestibility, and in 1886 he published a book on hypnosis that showed the effect of different suggestions on subjects in both the hypnotic and waking states. He published another book in 1886 on the general topic of reasoning and intelligence. Later he would devote all his time to the pursuit of knowledge in this field.

In 1903 Binet wrote a book titled, *The Experimental Study of Intelligence*, using as his basic data the thinking processes displayed by his two daughters. He would give a logic problem to his daughters and analyze the steps they took to reach a solution. Though he found that they

attacked and solved some problems in the same way, he noted marked differences in their approach to other problems. In his own immediate family, Binet thus observed the pervasiveness and importance of individual differences, as well as various cognitive growth patterns.

When in 1904 the French minister of public instruction announced his wish to identify and place in special schools those children who were mentally retarded, it was no wonder that Binet took on the challenge. This was a situation made to order for a student of individual differences. He asked for and was granted an appointment to the special committee being set up for this purpose. If children who could not seem to profit from regular schooling were to be placed in special classes, a device or technique had to be developed to identify these children. Binet argued that the diagnostic technique should be intellectual, not medical. It had been the practice in France to use physicians to diagnose mental retardation, since retardation was believed to be a physical condition. Binet pointed to the errors and inconsistencies that occurred in these medical diagnoses. If a child was seen by three different physicians on three successive days, three completely different medical diagnoses could result from these examinations.

Thus, in 1905 Binet, with a collaborator named Theodore Simon, published the first real intelligence scale. For their test, Binet and Simon assembled a series of intellectual tasks, rather than the sensorimotor tasks that Galton had used. Binet believed that intelligence was displayed in one's ability to make sound judgments rather than in one's ability to

react quickly to a physical stimulus. Thus Binet took intelligence out of the medical-physiological realm and placed it squarely in the intellectual-psychological area. He wanted to test complex higher-order thinking processes that tend to vary with age.

In 1908 Binet revised his original test, retaining the best items from the 1905 scale and adding a number of new tasks. In scoring this 1908 test, Binet utilized a new phrase, *mental age*. The test would not be scored simply on the basis of the number of items a child passed but rather with reference to age standards. Binet's scoring technique thus defined intelligence as a *developmental* rather than as a static concept.

In 1911, shortly before Binet's untimely passing, a second and final revision of the Binet-Simon test was published. This test was a further refinement of the original scale, again substituting new items for previous items that had shown low validity.

Binet's death in 1911 shortened a career just reaching full bloom. It is certain that many of the controversies that erupted in the field of intelligence would have been lessened had Binet lived long enough to complete his work. For example, Binet believed that intelligence was not just a fixed, immutable individual trait, but rather a developing, trainable, dynamic cluster of abilities that could be nourished or stifled as a result of environmental inputs.

Binet's contribution to educational psychology was enormous. If a person's work can be measured on the basis of the amount of research the work has generated, Binet must stand near the top of his field.

moron or an imbecile if he lacks judgment, but with good judgments he could not be either" (Binet and Simon, 1905). But, unlike many of the theoreticians who followed, Binet spent little time fretting over the intricacies and possible embellishments of his definition. Binet's goal was to measure intelligence, not merely to talk about it. He understood intelligence by what it enabled children to do, in much the same way an electrician understands electricity. The point is, Binet's test worked. With it, he could predict reasonably well which children would do well in school and which ones would have difficulties. Of course, there were exceptions, but these were fewer and fewer as the test improved. Sometimes a bright but disobedient child would do worse in school than his intelligence test score would predict, and sometimes a dull but docile child would do better. This, however, may have been due as much to faulty teacher evaluation as to inaccurate test scores. Binet's test was an individual test of intelligence; that is, the test was given to one child at a time and administered by a trained examiner.

The Early Stanford-Binet

Binet continued working on his 1905 scale, creating new items to improve the test. He revised the whole test twice, in 1908 and in 1911. In 1916, an American psychologist, **Lewis M. Terman,** of Stanford University, published an American revision of the Binet test. Terman's test was standardized on American children and introduced so many new items that it was virtually a new test. He called it the **Stanford-Binet test,** and this test soon became immensely popular in this country. In scoring the test, Terman introduced to America the concept of the **intelligence quotient, or IQ.*** IQ was determined by dividing mental age (MA) by chronological age (CA) and multiplying by 100 to get rid of the decimals. Thus,

$$IQ = \frac{MA}{CA} \times 100$$

A six-year-old scoring a mental age of nine years would have an IQ of $9/6 \times 100$, or 1.5×100, or 150; a six-year-old scoring a mental age of five years would

have an IQ of $5/6 \times 100$, or $.833 \times 100$, or 83. Since the test was standardized in such a way that the mental age was determined by how well the average child in a given age group did on the test, the average IQ for each age group had to be 100. That is, a six-year-old child scoring a mental age of six years (as the average six-year-old had done), would have an IQ of $6/6 \times 100$, or 100. Since the IQ expresses a child's rate of mental growth, the child whose IQ is 100 is progressing at an average rate.

IQ TESTS TODAY

The Current Stanford-Binet

The Stanford-Binet test was revised in 1937, 1960, and again in 1985. The 1960 revision used a different method of computing IQ, a method previously used by **David Wechsler** and called the **deviation IQ.** The problem with the original method of calculating IQ was that by about age thirteen, the ratio began to break down. The mental age of teenagers no longer continued to increase as it did when they were younger. Nor do adults add to their mental age from year to year. Thus, the ratio of mental-to-chronological age could be used only with fairly young children unless statistical corrections were added in. The deviation IQ avoids this problem by using the percentage of cases in each age-group achieving a given score. Thus, a seventeen-year-old scoring at the 84th percentile for that age group (that is, equaling or exceeding 84 percent of all seventeen-year-olds taking the test) would have a Stanford-Binet IQ of 116. This is because the Stanford-Binet has a standard deviation of 16 IQ points. Statistical tables are used to find what percentages of cases fall below the various standard deviation unit points.

In 1972 the Stanford-Binet test was restandardized on a representative sample of 2,100 children. The new norms again produced a mean IQ of 100 and a standard deviation of 16. The 1972 standardizing group, unlike the one used in 1960, did include some black children and other nonwhites with Spanish surnames. The latest revision in 1985 was standardized on 5,000 persons ranging in age from 2 to 23 years. The sample was 75 percent white, 14 percent black, and 6 percent Hispanic. The rest of the sample was made up of Asians, Pacific Islanders, and "others" (Thorndike et al., 1985).

---

*   Terman borrowed the term IQ from a German psychologist, William Stern, who published a paper describing its use in 1913.

Binet defined mental age in terms of the age at which a given number of test items are passed by an average child. In 1916 Lewis Terman of Stanford University introduced the Stanford-Binet test. The latest version of the test, last revised in 1985, uses a different method of computing IQ. The method is particularly important in measuring the IQs of individuals.

DAVID WECHSLER

David Wechsler was born in Lespedi, Romania, in 1896, one of seven children. His family moved to New York City when he was six years old. He attended the New York public schools and in 1916 graduated from the College of the City of New York. Following college, he immediately enrolled in the graduate psychology program at Columbia, completing his master's thesis under R. S. Woodworth in 1917. With America's entry into World War I, Wechsler was drafted into the Army. While awaiting his induction, he joined the great Harvard psychologist E. G. Boring at Camp Yaphank on Long Island and helped administer and score the recently developed Army Alpha intelligence test. Because of his training in psychology, and especially because of his work with Boring on the Alpha test, he was assigned to Fort Logan, Texas, where his duties included testing thousands of recruits on the Army Individual Performance Scales, the Yerkes Point Scale, and the Stanford-Binet IQ test.

During this time, Wechsler became increasingly impressed by the disparity often shown between a man's tested intelligence and the quality of his previous work record. Often a man would test at a very low level on the various assessment devices, yet his past history indicated that he had been quite successful in his civilian job. The same man often proved later to be extremely competent in performing his military duties. Wechsler began to question the validity of some of these tests, especially the Stanford-Binet with its high verbal content. Perhaps the test did predict success or failure in school, but it was apparently less effective in predicting performance in the military. Wechsler concluded that perhaps by emphasizing the intellectual component, the Stanford-Binet was missing other aspects of a person's intellect that may contribute to overall intelligent behavior. It wasn't until 1939, however, with the publication of Wechsler's own intelligence test, that he was able to put these ideas into practice.

In 1919 the Army sent Wechsler to Europe, where, at the University of London, he had the rare opportunity of working with both Spearman and Pearson. From Spearman, Wechsler learned of the two-factor theory of intelligence, g and s, and from Pearson he was schooled in statistical techniques, especially the techniques of correlation.

After Wechsler was discharged from the Army in August 1919, he won a fellowship for study at the University of Paris and at the Laboratory of Psychology at the Sorbonne. During this time he met both Theodore Simon and Pierre Janet.

In 1922 Wechsler returned to the United States, where he became both a part-time graduate student in psychology at Columbia and a staff psychologist at the Bureau of Child Guidance. In 1925 he received his Ph.D. from Columbia.

From 1925 to 1932 Wechsler worked in private practice as a psychologist. During this period he also worked part-time for the Psychological Corporation, the company that was later to publish the tests that bear his name.

In 1932 he became chief psychologist at New York's Bellevue Psychiatric Hospital, and in 1933 he also joined the faculty of New York University's College of Medicine. From this point on, Wechsler devoted much of his energy to the creation of a new intelligence test, a test that would be suitable for adults and that would tap a wide variety of intellectual and performance abilities. After trying out many items from previous tests and adding new items of his own, Wechsler produced, in 1939, the now famous Wechsler-Bellevue Intelligence Scale. Concurrently, he published *The Measurement of Adult Intelligence,* a book which brought together all his ideas on the question of intelligence and the manner in which it should be measured. He defined intelligence as the global capacity of an individual to act purposefully, to think rationally, and to deal effectively with his environment. He saw intelligence, thus, not as a narrow ability or single factor but as a global capacity that includes many components. Wechsler did not separate intelligence from other personality factors.

Wechsler's name has become synonymous with intelligence testing in America. He is truly one of the great psychologists of our time, and up to the year of his death, 1981, he continued his contributions to our understanding of intelligence and its measurement.

 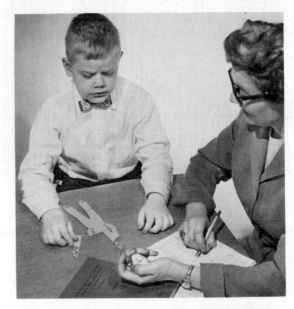

The Wechsler tests—those for both children and adults—measure IQ as a function of verbal as well as performance abilities. Wechsler's tests also perform another valuable function, that of personality evaluation.

The Wechsler Tests

David Wechsler has produced a number of individual intelligence tests. Like the Stanford-Binet, these tests are administered individually by trained examiners and take about an hour. Wechsler introduced his first test, then called the Wechsler-Bellevue, in 1939. This was an adult test, standardized on an adult sample group. In 1955 he revised his adult test, calling it the Wechsler Adult Intelligence Scale (**WAIS**). The adult test has since been revised yet again, in 1981, and is now called the **WAIS-R** (the R for "revised").

In 1949 Wechsler published the Wechsler Intelligence Scale for Children (WISC). In 1963 he published the Wechsler Preschool and Primary Scale of Intelligence (WPPSI), which was designed for children from four through six-and-one-half years of age. Since 1949, the WISC has been revised twice, in 1974 as the WISC-R and in 1992 as the WISC III.

The Wechsler tests mark a rather significant departure from the tradition of the Binet tests. Wechsler believed that the Binet tests were too heavily loaded with verbal items. According to Wechsler, "Intelligence . . . is the aggregate or global capacity of the individual to act purposefully, to think rationally, and to deal effectively with his environment" (Wechsler, 1944). Thus, not only is the poet with high verbal

facility able to score well on the WAIS-R, but so too is the garage mechanic who can expertly reassemble a four-barrel carburetor, but cannot quote long passages from Shakespeare. The Wechsler tests, which use a deviation IQ, produce three IQ scores: a verbal IQ, a **performance IQ,** and a full-scale IQ score. Thus, the garage mechanic may receive a verbal IQ of only 105, but with a performance IQ of 126 he would achieve a full-scale IQ of 115, which is at the 84th percentile.

The verbal subtests On the WISC-III, the verbal IQ is calculated on the basis of the following subtests:

1. *Information:* A series of orally presented items that test the child's general storehouse of information about the world.

2. *Similarities:* A series of orally presented pairs of words for which the child attempts to discover how the two things are alike. This test appears to measure a child's ability to think in abstract terms.

3. *Arithmetic:* A set of arithmetic problems that the child solves mentally. This test was designed to test the child's powers of mathematical reasoning.

4. *Vocabulary:* A set of orally presented words, which can be used to predict the size of the child's vocabulary.

SPOTLIGHT ON IQ TESTING

The WISC-III

The most recent version of the Wechsler Intelligence Scale for Children (WISC), called the WISC-III, was introduced in 1991. It was an attempt to improve the original rather than to redesign the instrument completely. Like its predecessors, the mean IQ on the WISC III is still 100, and the standard deviation is 15. Those trained to administer the WISC-R will find the transition easy and straightforward. In fact, some of the scoring rules have been simplified and the testing materials modified to make them more user-friendly. The WISC III has introduced a new subtest, called Symbol Search, that was designed to tap a child's cognitive processing speed. In fact, the subtests for the WISC III can be categorized on the basis of four key intellectual factors.[a]

The standardizing group for this update was composed of 2,200 children, ages 6 to 16, who were 70 percent white, 15 percent black, 11 percent Hispanic, and the rest "other." These percentages are virtually identical to those shown for the population at large according to the 1988 U.S. Census.

[a] D. Wechsler, *Wechsler Intelligence Scale for Children manual*, 3d ed. (New York: The Psychological Corporation, Harcourt Brace Jovanovich, 1991).

FACTOR I: VERBAL COMPREHENSION	FACTOR II: PERCEPTUAL ORGANIZATION	FACTOR III: FREEDOM FROM DISTRACTIBILITY	FACTOR IV: PROCESSING SPEED
Information	Picture completion	Arithmetic	Coding
Similarities	Picture arrangement	Digit span	Symbol search
Vocabulary	Block design		
Comprehension	Object assembly		

5. *Comprehension:*   A series of orally presented situations that evaluate the child's level of practical information, general ability to utilize past experience, and understanding of social rules and concepts.

6. *Digit span* (optional):   A test of short-term memory in which the examiner reads a series of digits and asks the subject to repeat them, some verbatim and some in reverse order.

The performance subtests   The performance IQ is computed on the basis of the following:

1. *Picture completion:*   The child is shown a set of colorful incomplete pictures and is asked to name the missing part. This is a test of visual recognition.

2. *Coding:*   The child must associate certain symbols with specific numbers, or shapes. The child draws the symbol (or shape) in squares containing the associated number. This is a test of speed of movement, processing speed, and memory.

3. *Picture arrangement:*   A set of pictures that, when arranged properly, tell a logical story. This is an attempt to measure the child's ability to size up and understand a total situation.

4. *Block design:*   The child is presented with a number of small blocks that must be put together to match a number of prearranged patterns. This is a test of perceptual analysis, as well as visual-motor coordination.

5. *Object assembly:*   The child must arrange various puzzle parts to form a certain object. This is a test of manual dexterity and powers of recognition. There are also two optional performance subtests, Symbol Search and Mazes.

As can be seen from the outline of the various subtests, all have been selected to tap many different abilities. The Wechsler tests were not designed to establish IQ as a unitary factor but, consistent with current thinking, as a general series of abilities made up of many factors. Some of the subtests home-in on a person's memory, some tap perceptual and motor skills, some call for the child to be able to reason abstractly, and so on.

In addition to being important instruments for measuring intelligence, the Wechsler tests have useful diagnostic capabilities that enable a skilled examiner to evaluate such personality characteristics as defense mechanisms, the ability to cope with stress, and the general mode of handling life's situations. Such well-documented procedures as the Personality Assessment System (PAS) have shown truly remarkable results in ferreting out important personality factors from Wechsler profiles (Couchon, 1983). Thus, a Wechsler test gives a three-dimensional picture of the subject, and can often tell us not only that a given child lacks motivation, but also why.

Group Tests of Intelligence

Though the Stanford-Binet and Wechsler tests have made an extremely important contribution to the field of intelligence testing, the fact that they are individual tests means that they are time-consuming and therefore rather expensive to administer. During World War I there was suddenly an urgent need to test huge groups of men quickly, and a new approach to testing was introduced. Two **group tests of intelligence** were devised in 1917, the Army Alpha test, for the men who could read, and the Army Beta test, a nonverbal test for illiterates. Though the nonverbal Beta test proved to be less effective than the Alpha, the success of the Alpha led to the development of a great number of group tests. These are also referred to as paper-and-pencil tests, and they usually consist of a series of multiple-choice items. They must be administered and timed precisely as stated in the directions. D. O. Hebb has even suggested that those giving IQ tests should be rigorously trained and strictly licensed, just as physicians are. IQ tests placed in the wrong hands can have tragic consequences (Hebb, 1978).

WHAT DO IQ TESTS PREDICT?

Academic Achievement

During our earlier discussion of Alfred Binet and the first intelligence test, we said that Binet's test was effective in predicting which children would do well in school. The evidence gained since then is generally consistent with Binet's early results. Over eighty years and hundreds of studies later, it is now clear that IQ tests do predict scholastic success. The correlation between IQ and grades in school runs better than +.50. Since the highest possible correlation is 1.00, IQ scores are not infallible predictors in every case. There are children whose IQ scores are lower than other children's but whose grades are higher, because a number of nonintellectual factors also influence scholastic success. Physical illness, emotional upset, and lack of motivation, for example, can interfere with success. Research suggests that lack of ego strength is another related factor. Academic achievement has been shown to be largely a result of a student's reality orientation, or ego strength. That is, successful students possess strong egos, are willing to postpone pleasure, are not so easily distracted, and are generally more able to pursue tasks in an organized fashion. Underachievers, in contrast, have low ego strength, are less able to control their impulses, and are especially unable to postpone gratification (Hummel and Sprinthall, 1965).

Success in Life

Although it is true that IQ tests do predict academic achievement with some degree of accuracy, this fact in and of itself may not seem all that important. After all, IQ is measured by means of tests, and grades are determined exactly the same way, by performances on tests. Perhaps all that this proves is that children who do well on one test also do well on other tests. How well does an IQ score predict success or failure in other areas of one's life? Do children with high IQs and high school grades also succeed in later life, financially and emotionally?

To help answer these questions, Terman in the 1920s began a monumental study of hundreds of California schoolchildren (Terman, 1925). All the children had performed exceptionally well on IQ tests (i.e., they all had tested IQs of 140 or more). Terman followed the lives of these subjects for the next twenty-five years in order to find out whether there were any significant adult correlates of a high IQ in childhood. Many of Terman's original subjects are still being studied today as part of a gerontology project (Cravens, 1992). It is interesting to note that whereas Terman's focus was on the gifted child, Binet had been aiding school administrators in identifying those chil-

they are likely to end up in classrooms with children who are larger because they are older.

On tests of emotional adjustment the gifted children were found to be better adjusted than the average child. They were also more socially adaptable and more likely to be leaders among their peers.

As adults, Terman's group continued to be successful. They earned more money, had more managerial jobs, and made far more literary and scientific contributions than the average adult. When checked in 1959, the group had published over 2,000 scientific papers and 33 novels and had taken out 230 patents. A great number of them were listed in *Who's Who* and in *American Men and Women of Science*.

Finally, they had fewer divorces than the average adult, and criminal convictions and alcoholism were rare. Even the death rate was about 33 percent lower than that for the general population.

In another study it was found that IQ has a significant correlation with income. As a matter of fact, IQ predicted a person's income better than such other measures as parents' education or parents' income (Duncan et al., 1972).

It is obvious that the IQ test predicts more than just elementary school grades. It must be pointed out, though, that not all of Terman's subjects attained that great success of the majority. It is also true that many highly successful people in this world do not have IQs of 140 or more. High IQs are associated with a wide range of achievement in a wide variety of areas, but high IQs do not tell the whole story. Personality variables such as ego strength and motivation, and physical variables such as health or accidents, also play a vital role in determining one's ability to live effectively and achieve success.

HEREDITY, ENVIRONMENT, AND TIME

In earlier chapters of this book, especially in Chapter 3, we pointed out that all human behavior, including intelligent behavior, is a product of heredity interacting with environment interacting with time. This is one of psychology's basic axioms, and nowhere is the validity of this axiom more compelling than in the area of intelligence.

Hereditary Factors

Heredity limits the extent to which intelligence can be influenced by environment and time. It is now

IQ scores are not infallible predictors of school achievement. Among other factors influencing academic success is ego strength, that is, how a student perceives himself or herself. Successful students possess strong egos.

dren who were "unintelligent" (von Mayrhauser, 1992).

First, Terman dispelled the myth that very bright children are physically fragile and undersized. Terman's subjects were above average on many physical characteristics, including height, weight, physical development, and general health. Also, the gifted children tended to be heavier at birth, cut their first tooth two months earlier than average, walked and talked two months earlier than average, and reached adolescence earlier than the average child.

While in school, the gifted children received significantly higher marks than their classmates and were more likely to be skipped ahead to a higher grade. In fact, by the end of elementary school, Terman's entire group of 1,500 children had averaged a skip of one full grade. Perhaps this is how the myth of the undersized and puny genius originated. Since children with high IQs do tend to skip frequently,

Terman's study of gifted children suggested that high-IQ children are healthier and stronger than average children, are better adjusted emotionally, and tend to be leaders among their peers.

fairly certain that intelligence has a genetic component. The genetic component sets the limits to how any given trait will respond to environmental stimulation. This genetically constrained range is the *reaction range* (Gottesman, 1974) and can be most clearly shown in the case of human height. Despite the fact that one's height, a polygenic trait, can be greatly influenced by environmental factors such as nutrition, there are some pygmy groups in Africa whose height could never approach that of the average American, regardless of environmental influences (Freedman, 1979).

As long ago as 1937, it was demonstrated that the closer two people are related genetically, the more similar are their IQs (Newman, Freeman, and Holzinger, 1937). This study was one of the first to show

that identical twins reared apart still had similar IQs. A review of the major IQ studies revealed the correlations shown in Table 16.1 (Locurto, 1991; Erlenmeyer-Kimling and Jarvik, 1963).

These data make it clear that genetic factors are indeed involved in determining IQ. The closer the genetic relationship, the higher the reported IQ correlations.

A study conducted at the University of Minnesota in 1980 showed that identical twins reared apart displayed marked similarities on such measures as intelligence, achievement, and a number of personality factors. Even the brain-wave tracings of these monozygotic (MZ) twins showed an extremely high degree of resemblance. The genetic prewiring for MZ twins appears to be significantly more similar than could be

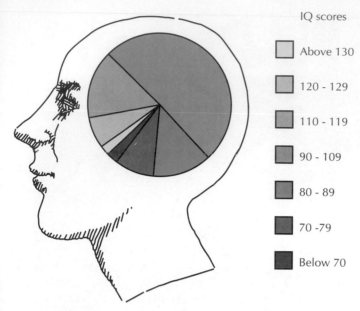

IQ scores

- Above 130
- 120 - 129
- 110 - 119
- 90 - 109
- 80 - 89
- 70 -79
- Below 70

According to the Wechsler Adult Intelligence Scale, 2.2 percent of Americans have an IQ over 130, and a corresponding 2.2 percent are mentally retarded. Of course, the majority are in the middle range, with IQs between 90 and 109.

accounted for on the basis of a straight environmental explanation (Holden, 1980).

Genetic inputs can be clearly seen in the early stages of language development. For example, in comparing twelve-month-old adopted children with both their natural and adoptive mothers, it has been found that infant language development correlated higher with the natural mother's cognitive skills than with those of the adoptive mother (Hardy-Brown et al., 1981). Genetic inheritance also plays a part in the development of nonintellectual traits. In a study on

TABLE 16.1   AVERAGE IQ CORRELATIONS

RELATIONSHIP	r
Monozygotic twins raised together	.85
Monozygotic twins raised apart	.76
Dizygotic twins	.56
Siblings raised together	.55
Siblings raised apart	.47
Parents and children	.40
Adopted siblings (youngsters)	.37
Grandparent and grandchild	.27
Adopted siblings (adolescents)	.00

infant shyness, it was found that among twenty-four-month-old adopted children, the less sociable the adoptive mother was, the shyer was the child; but when both the adoptive *and* natural mothers scored low in sociability, the child was even shyer (Daniels and Plomin, 1985).

Environmental Factors

The IQ correlation chart also shows the importance of environmental factors. For example, when identical twins are reared together in the same environment, their IQs are more similar than when they are raised apart. Note, too, that when unrelated children are reared together, there is a significant correlation between their IQs. In this instance, where there is no genetic linkage at all, similar IQs result from the similar environment.

In another very important study, a correlation of +.43 was obtained between the quality of the home environment and the child's IQ (Garber and Ware, 1970). In this study the homes of 133 children (mostly white and mostly of low socioeconomic status) were visited and scored on an instrument called the Home Environment Review. The significant correlation obtained indicates that the higher the quality of the

This child is a victim of protein malnutrition. Nutrition deficiencies occurring in early childhood can result in pronounced damage to intelligence.

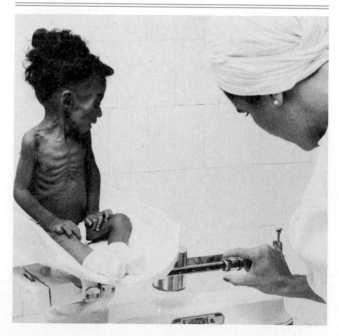

Environmental effects on intelligence are most pronounced during a child's first few years of life. By four years of age, a child has already achieved 50 percent of his or her adult intelligence.

home environment, the higher the IQ of the children. The most important of the home factors were the following:

1. The number of books and other learning materials in the home

2. The amount of reward and recognition the children receive from their parents for academic achievement

3. The parents' expectations regarding their children's academic achievement

It's not enough to talk in generalities about environmental influences. Just what are some of the specific environmental inputs that appear to affect intelligence?

Gross nutritional deficiencies can adversely affect IQs and even produce mental retardation. Kwashiorkor, an illness resulting from a protein-deficient diet, has been found to be extremely damaging to intellectual development (Eikenwald and Fry, 1969). If nutritional deficiencies occur in early childhood, the damage to intelligence can be pronounced, even if the protein deficit is less than that needed to produce kwashiorkor. The exact physiological link between nutritional deficiencies and mental retardation is still unknown. However, other studies have led to some speculation that inadequate protein intake prevents full development of the brain, especially those areas involved in memory storage (Harlow et al., 1971).

Further, as we pointed out in Chapter 3, Bonnie Kaplan's lively review of the relationship between inadequate dietary intake and mental deficiency presents rather convincing evidence that mental retardation can result from malnutrition. This is especially true if the malnutrition occurs during the nine months of gestation and the first two or three years of the baby's life (Kaplan, 1972).

A second important environmental factor in intelligence is stimulus variety, especially in early childhood. As we saw in Chapter 4, important figures in the field of psychology, such as J. McVicker Hunt, Jerome Bruner, Benjamin S. Bloom, and David Krech, feel that stimulus variety is perhaps the most important ingredient in intellectual development. Hunt states that the more we see, hear, and touch in early childhood, the more we will want to see, hear, and touch later on. The key to cognitive growth, according to Hunt, is matching the child's present intellectual ability with just the right amount of stimulus variety to bring out the natural desire to continue learning.

As was mentioned in Chapter 4, Vygotsky insists that cognitive growth is directly related to the challenge inherent in new experiences. Vygotsky speaks of the zone of proximal development, or the distance between one's present developmental level and one's potential level, which he believes can best be accomplished by what he calls *scaffolding,* such as adult guidance or working with advanced peers (Vygotsky, 1978). In order to reach higher stages of intellectual development, students should work within this zone. Therefore, since they don't go a bit beyond a child's present ability, many homework assignments that simply review well-practiced activities may even act as deterrents to cognitive growth (Clifford, 1991). Also, Bruner tells us that infants must be exposed to a wide variety of stimulus inputs and a shifting environment if normal intellectual growth is to be maintained. Bloom says that an abundant early environment is the key to full development of intelligence. And Krech has shown, at least in animals, that without stimulus heterogeneity, animals are less able to learn, and their brains never develop fully.

Past experience in learning situations is another crucial environmental ingredient in intellectual development. Children who learn to master one problem are able to transfer this knowledge to other problems they may encounter later. The knowledge gained from past experience may begin to snowball and provide the child with a solid base for future understanding. Harry Harlow has shown how this works with monkeys. Monkeys that were trained to solve a certain problem (the oddity problem) were far better at solving complex discrimination problems presented to them at a later time than monkeys that were not so trained. Through training, the monkeys had developed what Harlow called a *learning set.* They had, in effect, learned how to learn. As Harlow says, "Learning to learn is no doubt an essential feature of the intellectual development of monkeys, apes, and children growing up in their natural environments" (Harlow et al., 1971, p. 353).

Finally, Bloom lists three environmental variables that he feels are important in developing a child's intellectual abilities.

1. The amount of stimulation children receive for verbal development

2. The amount of affection and reward children receive for verbal-reasoning accomplishments

3. The amount of encouragement children receive for "active interaction with problems, exploration of the environment and the learning of new skills" (Bloom, 1964, p. 190).

Again we see that despite the genetic input, environmental factors, especially the timing of these factors in either stimulating or retarding development, play a key role in determining how the genetic blueprint will be expressed (Farber, 1981).

Time

We have seen the importance of hereditary and environmental interactions for intellectual development. It is also vital to understand the nature of this interaction from the point of view of time. Chapter 4 was devoted entirely to the importance of early experience on psychological development. Let us now look at some of the highlights.

Most psychologists today are convinced of the profound importance of early experience for proper cognitive growth. Bloom states the case forcefully in saying that environmental effects on intelligence are most pronounced during a child's first few years of life.

The heavy line in Figure 16.1 shows Bloom's famous negatively accelerating curve for intellectual growth. Notice that as age increases, intellectual development increases less and less. By four years of age we have already achieved 50 percent of our adult intelligence, and by eight years of age we have achieved 80 percent. The shaded area surrounding the main curve indicates the potential for changes in intelligence. You will notice that as age increases, there is also less and less potential for changes in intelligence. Therefore, during the first few years, a beneficial environment is most effective in increasing intellectual development, but as time goes on this beneficial environment comes to have less effect. Similarly, a stultifying environment is most damaging during those early, critical years. Bloom feels that the difference between a beneficial and a stultifying environment during these early childhood years can produce IQ differences of twenty points or more. Bloom may be too conservative, however.

Wayne Dennis's study of a Teheran orphanage in which the children were kept in a condition of extreme sensory deprivation also showed that stimulus variety at an early age is critical for cognitive growth (see Chapter 4). Almost all of those sensory-deprived children were intellectually retarded (Dennis, 1960). In another study, Dennis described a Lebanese orphanage where environmental conditions were so dismal that mental retardation was the rule (Dennis, 1969). The average IQ of the 133 children tested was

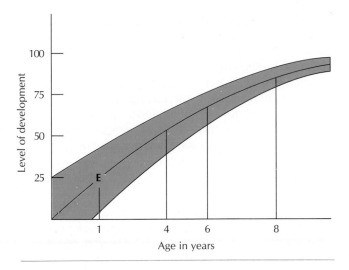

FIGURE 16.1 Bloom's negatively accelerating curve for intellectual growth.

only 53. This is probably the lowest average IQ ever reported for a group of children who were otherwise considered normal. Some of these children were later adopted by middle-class families and in every case dramatically increased their IQ. The more stimulating home environments provided an average gain of twenty-eight IQ points. Despite the improvement, the mean IQ of the adopted children was still only 81, again showing that improved environmental conditions at a later age cannot compensate fully for a deprived environment during the first few years of life. As Hebb says, "There are fundamental aspects of a baby's learning that must occur at the proper time if they are to have their full value as the basis of later learning" (Hebb, 1978, p. 1143). Thus Hebb is fully endorsing the early-experience position regarding mental growth. In fact, he says that you cannot take even a six-year-old out of the slums and expect to undo the damage already inflicted by that environment. "In a word, the child from a seriously deficient environment is an intellectual *cripple*," and this damage is no longer reparable (Hebb, 1978, p. 1144).

The Mix

It cannot be overstressed that the results of the various studies of intelligence should be interpreted on the basis of all three of the components of intelligence, namely, heredity, environment, and time. The interplay among these factors, although certainly complex, is of crucial importance in understanding the overall parameters of human behavior. As Sandra Scarr

keeps reminding us, even a person's genetic predispositions are involved in shaping the person's environment, and the environment, in turn, may nourish or stifle the unfolding biological messages. Highly active children, for example, tend to seek out activities and friends that may be more stimulating than (or at least different from) those selected by a low-activity child (Scarr and McCartney, 1983). Thus, heredity, environment, and time do not act out their roles in independent vacuums. Highly intelligent children may actively surround themselves with the kinds of environmental influences that tend to maintain and strengthen the children's maturing intellectual abilities.

INFANT INTELLIGENCE

Attempts to measure the intellectual potential of infants dates at least as far back as the work of Nancy Bayley (see biography, p. 80). Recently, **Marc Bornstein** has been conducting studies with an **infant intelligence test** in which six-month-old babies were measured on the basis of how long it would take them to process information concerning moving stimuli (Bornstein, 1985). Bornstein hypothesized that the more intelligent the baby, the sooner he or she would lose interest in the stimuli, since the more intelligent infant would process the information about the stimulus more quickly in the form of an internal stimulus representation. Later, when the child was four years old, he or she was given the Wechsler Preschool and Primary Scale of Intelligence (WPPSI) IQ test.

Bornstein found significant correlations ($r = .54$) between how well the subjects scored as babies and how they later scored as four-year-old children. This correlation of .54 is especially noteworthy, given the fact that both measures, the pretest and the posttest, were taken only on the child, and were independent of other predictors, such as parental education or the socioeconomic status of the family. The latter two measures have typically produced correlations as high as .60 (Zelazo, 1989). Also, it has been shown that when the baby began losing interest in the stimuli, it was a true test of processing speed, and not just a reflection of neuronal fatigue (Zelazo, Weiss, and Tarquinio, 1991). Bornstein also found a correlation between the child's IQ and the quality of the interactions between mother and child, assessed when the child was one year old. To be sure, the amount and quality of mother-baby interactions can vary with either party in the relationship. Do intelligent and responsive babies induce more parental responses, or are highly responsive parents responsible for the response levels of their offspring? The best guess is that the most important factor is the interaction itself, with both mother and baby playing critical roles in the quality of the interplay.

THE TRANSACTIONAL MODEL

The interplay between mother and child, in which each, in effect, shapes the other's environment, has given rise to a view of general development called the **transactional model** (Sameroff, 1975). These reciprocal influences affect not only the child's cognitive growth, but also the formation of the child's temperament. In a study of the development of temperament among infant males, Eleanor Maccoby discovered that if a mother perceived her son as having a difficult temperament, she may become so influenced by this perception that she begins withdrawing her efforts at socialization. The child, in turn, begins showing less and less self-control, and the frequency of temperamental outbursts increases (Maccoby and Martin, 1983). This may, of course, lead to the development of an emotional set that could make the child virtually uncontrollable by the time he reaches kindergarten (Smolak, 1986).

SEX DIFFERENCES IN IQ

The full-scale IQs of males and females of a given age are almost identical. This is partly due to the

averaging out of differences that do occur among various subtest scores. In the past, a number of studies seemed to suggest that males typically scored higher on spatial, mechanical, and numerical tests, whereas females scored higher on verbal tests and tests involving quick, manual movements and attention to detail. More recently, however, evidence is piling up that demonstrates a definite decline in these cognitive-gender differences. The only exception to this now appears to be the gap (still favoring males) that exists in numerical abilities, especially high school mathematics (Feingold, 1988).

The development of IQ also reveals certain sex differences. The mean IQ of males increases slightly after age six, while the female mean tends to go down (Haan, 1963). This difference may have a cultural explanation. If society demands more achievement from males than females (and this apparently is the case), and if achievement motivation and IQ correlate at all, then perhaps society's emphasis on inculcating the achievement motive more in males than females accounts for this difference. As social psychologists continually remind us, people tend to behave as others around them expect them to behave.

ARE THERE GENETIC DIFFERENCES IN INTELLIGENCE BETWEEN RACIAL GROUPS?

It has long been known that on standard IQ tests (standardized primarily on white sample groups) the average IQ of white children and the average IQ of black children generally differ. It is also known that the difference favors the white children. The two IQ distributions do overlap, so that despite the difference between the averages, there are still many black children whose IQs are higher than those of many white children. Studies on racial differences consistently show that there is much more variation within groups designated as races than between such groups (Zuckerman, 1990). Also, a trend has been identified, indicating that the black-white gap on intelligence and academic achievement tests has begun to narrow (Jones, 1984). Despite some concern over which students are more apt to identify themselves by ethnic backgrounds, data taken from the SATs clearly show a narrowing of the gap between white and black test takers, even though both groups have recently increased their scores. For example, the mean verbal SAT score for whites went from 442 in 1980 to 449 in 1985, for a gain of seven points. During that same time span, the mean verbal score for blacks went from 330 to 346, for a gain of sixteen points. Similarly, on the math section of the SATs, the white students' mean went from 482 in 1980 to 490 in 1985 (a gain of eight points), whereas the mean score for black students went from 360 to 376 (a gain of sixteen points) (Wainer, 1986).

A study of World War I Army Alpha IQ scores found that although the average IQ of black soldiers was lower than that of white soldiers, there were some fairly interesting reversals. For example, the average IQ of black soldiers from several northern states was higher than the average IQ of white soldiers from certain southern states (Yerkes, 1921). It has also been found that the more money a state spends on education, the higher the IQs of its schoolchildren, black and white (Spuhler and Lindzey, 1967). The correlation between the amount of money a state spends on education and the IQs of the state's children is +.70.

Arthur R. Jensen of the University of California at Berkeley, has interpreted the difference between the tested IQs of blacks and whites as implying that white children are genetically superior to black children. This argument claims that IQ has an extremely high genetic factor (about 80 percent) and that there must therefore be racial differences in intelligence (Jensen, 1969). Jensen says that differences in intelligence are "predominantly attributable to genetic differences, with environmental factors contributing a minor portion of the variance among individuals in IQ" (Jensen, 1969, p. 4).

This claim must be closely examined. The rules of science demand that in order to establish a cause-and-effect relationship, all the possible input variables must be controlled. If, for example, you wished to determine whether increased noise in a classroom had a depressing effect on reading speed, you wouldn't put all the fast readers in the low-noise group and all the slow readers in the high-noise group. Nor would you have different conditions of illumination in the two groups. Nor would you test one group at 9:00 A.M. and the other at 3:00 A.M. Instead, you would want the two groups to be as equivalent as possible: same age, same average reading speed, same conditions of illumination, same time of testing. If, after controlling for all the variables, the group tested under high-noise conditions reads significantly more slowly than the group tested under low-noise conditions, you could say that noise does, indeed, lower reading speed. This is the cautious way

science proceeds before assigning causal factors to observed differences. Perhaps Jensen is correct when he says that the assumption of a genetic difference in intelligence between the races is not an unreasonable hypothesis. But the point is, and this is an important point for the prospective teacher to remember, Jensen's hypothesis has not been proved, nor may it ever be a testable conclusion (Mackenzie, 1984).

As we have seen, intelligence has three crucial inputs: heredity, environment, and time. In order to determine the extent to which any one of these variables affects intelligence, the other two must be controlled. Large numbers of children, black and white, would have to be raised in identical (or, at the very least, reliably measured) environments. Also, because of the time variable, stimulus variety would have to be increased at precisely the same developmental stage for each child. The enormity and complexity of such a study make it appear improbable that Jensen's hypothesis could ever be adequately tested. All of Jensen's reported twin studies (which were all done on white children, incidentally) and all of his correlations (regardless of whether they're "corrected for unreliability") cannot alter the fact that the average black child is not raised under the same, or under even remotely similar, environmental conditions as the average white child. Does anyone seriously believe that if white children were raised in black homes in Harlem they would achieve the same scores on an IQ test as if they had been raised in Scarsdale.

IQ comparisons between the races are made even more difficult to evaluate because of the possibility that IQ scores may reflect the race of the examiner. A number of studies have suggested that the IQ scores of black children are underestimated by white examiners, or perhaps overestimated by black examiners. In one experiment a single group of black children was tested by both black and white examiners. By the use of different forms, L and M of the Stanford-Binet, the children were tested in a counterbalanced design, first by an examiner of one race and then by one of the other. The mean IQ score of these black children when tested by the black examiner was 105.7 but it dropped to a mean of 101.9 when tested by a white. This difference was statistically significant (Forrester and Klaus, 1964). Since both black and white examiners were equally trained and equally competent, the difference in IQ scores probably results from either differing expectations on the part of the examiner or differing motivational sets on the part of the children.

SANDRA SCARR

After graduating with high honors from Vassar, Sandra Scarr worked first as a case aide in a family clinic and then as a research assistant at the National Institutes of Health. It soon became obvious to her that, on the one hand, her career pattern could continue on in the same direction—serving as a helper and facilitator for other people's work. On the other hand, given her inquiring mind, it also became obvious that alternatives were possible. Youthful women honors graduates of liberal arts colleges did not necessarily have to be content to perform minor, ancillary roles as helpers and assistants. Such persons, as well as anyone, could aspire to leadership roles. There were very few women of eminence who had chosen to enter the competitive and heretofore male-dominated area of research psychology. With this in mind, she entered Harvard University, completed her M.A. degree in 1963, and entered the Ph.D. program in social relations.

Under the somewhat quaint Harvard tradition, Scarr was assigned to a sponsor, John Whiting, a world-renowned anthropologist, and to a thesis adviser, Irving Gottesman, an equally renowned genetic psychologist. She clearly thrived in the atmosphere of the Harvard program in social relations, with its diverse faculty which read like a list of "who's who" in psychology: Gordon Allport, Jerome Bruner, Robert White, B. F. Skinner, Roger Brown, Thomas Pettigrew, David McClelland, Jerome Kagan, and Eric Erikson. She quickly mastered the fundamentals of such a broadly gauged psychology, and she completed her Ph.D. in just two years with a research thesis titled "Genetics and Human Motivation."

Graduation was followed by a series of academic and administrative appointments at Bryn Mawr, the University of Maryland, the Carter Foundation for Child Development (as acting director), and the University of Pennsylvania. Her talent was obvious and her scholarship promising. Promotions were rapid. She moved to Minnesota in 1972 as an associate professor in the School Psychology Training Program. Just two years later, she was offered and accepted a full professorship at the university's Institute of Child Development. She was elected a Fellow of the American Psychological Association and a fellow of the American Association for the Advancement of Science, and she was also received into numerous other scientific and professional organizations.

She left Minnesota in 1977 and became the first woman ever to be named to a full professorship in the department of psychology at Yale University. In 1983 she was selected as the Commonwealth Professor of Psychology at the University of Virginia, where her students refer to her affectionately as "Sandra Scarr Super Star." She also served as the editor of the American Psychological Association's journal *Developmental Psychology* and as President of the Society for Research in Child Development. She is at present the editor of the The American Psychological Society's new journal *Current Directions in Psychological Science.*

It is important to note that the high correlation obtained between the IQs of parents and children overemphasizes the genetic explanation. An impoverished home environment has an adverse effect not only on the intellectual development of the children raised in it but also on the way those children eventually raise their own children. The childhood experiences of the second generation are a function of the childhood experiences of the previous generation:

Such handicaps combine to sustain the very conditions from which they are derived, so the vicious circle tends to be repeated for generation after generation. Clearly the correlations between IQs of parents and children are bound to be high, and give a superficial impression of genetic determination (Rose and Weinberg, 1976, p. 731).

One way to eliminate the possibility of a genetic interpretation of the similarity between the IQs of parents and children is to study the mental development of black children who are reared by socially advantaged white parents. Sandra Scarr conducted just such a study (Scarr and Weinberg, 1976). She analyzed 101 white, middle-class families who had adopted 176 children, 130 of whom were black and the rest of whom were Asian and American Indian. The mean IQ of these adopted black children was 106, which is twenty-one points higher than the national mean for blacks. More important, however, was the fact that the mean IQ for the black children who had been adopted as infants was 110. This latter group, of course, was in the advantaged cultural environment all through the early, critical periods of intellectual growth (Scarr and Weinberg, 1978a).

Heritability

Jensen based his argument on the concept of heritability. **Heritability** (*H*) is the proportion of the total variability in a population that is due to genetic, as opposed to environmental, factors. Thus, if all the variation in IQ scores in a given population is due to genetic factors, the heritability of IQ would be 1.00. If all the variability is due to environmental factors, then the heritability of IQ would be zero. Since, as we have seen over and over again, IQ is the result of heredity, environment, and time, the heritability value for IQ lies somewhere between 0 and 1.00. Jensen argues that the actual value is around .80. Even if Jensen were correct in saying that the heritability of intelligence is .80, this does not mean that 80 percent of an individual's IQ is due to the genes. Actually Sir Francis Galton made this point clear back in the 1860s when he did his genetic studies on the correlation between the height of fathers and sons. Even though the heritability of adult height approaches 90 percent, it does not mean that an individual who is 72 inches tall can attribute 61 of those inches to heredity and the other 11 inches to both the environment and the interaction between heredity and environment. Instead it means that 90 percent of the variation in height within a specified group of people can be attributed to heredity. Behavior geneticist Jerry Hirsch has said that heritability explains variation only "in some particular population at a single generation under one set of conditions" (Hirsch, 1971, p. 244). Thus, since heritability applies only to a specific environment, it really matters very little what the estimate of the actual heritability value is in the discussion of a given black child's IQ. "High or low heritability tells us absolutely nothing about how a given individual might have developed under conditions different from those in which he actually did develop" (Hirsch, 1971, p. 244).

Jensen appears to accept this definition when he says that heritability is a population statistic that has "no sensible meaning with reference to a measurement or characteristic of an individual. . . . Estimates of *H* are specific to the population sampled, the point in time, the manner in which the measurements were made, and the particular test used to obtain the measurements" (Jensen, 1969, p. 42). Despite the clarity and precision of this definition, Jensen then presents a case that goes far beyond the bounds of his own careful restriction. Jensen's estimated *H* value of .80 is generated by a review of identical-twin studies done exclusively on white American and English children, and yet he applies this value to both black and white children alike—hardly identical populations. As a matter of fact, in a study conducted by Scarr of over 1,000 twins of differing economic and racial backgrounds, it was found that the heritability of IQ is always higher among economically advantaged than among lower-class children (Scarr, 1971). Thus, it is not an unreasonable hypothesis that the value of *H* increases as a function of an increase in the socioeconomic backgrounds of the populations being studied. As one reviewer stated it: "In other words, 'native talent' may manifest itself conspicuously in people who grow up in favorable environments and remain suppressed in adverse environments" (Piel, 1975, p. 457). In fact Scarr argues that this is precisely how the nature-nurture interaction works. "When the environment is good, heredity exerts a strong influence on IQ," stronger than when the environment is impoverished (Scarr and Weinberg, 1978b, p. 33).

Jensen also argues that compensatory education has been tried and has failed. He makes two main points on this subject. First, he feels that experiments with early education (such as Head Start) have not lived up to expectations; that, although the Head Start program does produce some short-term IQ gains, these gains are not sustained over the years. Second, he implies that since the IQ disadvantage of blacks is mostly inherited, it is useless to spend money for early-education programs that obviously cannot affect the genes.

With regard to the first point, although Head Start did not at first live up to the hopes of many educators, newer studies suggest that Head Start's death knell may have been tolled too soon. Even though by the time children were enrolled in Head Start programs they may have already passed through many critical learning periods, recent evidence, such as that supplied by the Perry Program (see Chapter 4), shows that remarkable gains are still achievable. However, just as there are cumulative positive effects on intellectual growth as a result of an improved environment, so, too, there are cumulative negative effects from an impoverished environment. A study of white children from the "hollows" of rural Virginia found the average IQ of six- to eight-year-olds to be only 84, and the average for ten- to twelve-year-olds to be only 53 (Sherman and Key, 1932). The point is that with children from impoverished environments, early-education intervention would be a marked success if all it accomplished was the prevention of IQ decline.

The Cumulative Deficit in IQ

Studies such as the one on the children from the hollows of rural Virginia show that environmental deprivation tends to accumulate as the child grows older. That is, a child from an impoverished background who is one year below grade level by age six may fall back to two full years below grade level by age twelve. Just as the intellectually rich get richer, so too do the intellectually poor get poorer. Such studies lend dramatic support to the mounting evidence regarding the environment's power in affecting mental growth.

Ironically, the evidence from one of Jensen's more recent studies (Jensen, 1977) goes a long way toward providing perhaps the most damaging evidence yet obtained against the purely genetic interpretation. Jensen studied large groups of children, both black and white, from an area in the rural South. Jensen states that the blacks in this locality are "as severely disadvantaged, educationally and economically, as can be found anywhere in the United States today" (Jensen, 1977, p. 185). Yet what Jensen found was that for black children there was a progressive *decline* in IQ scores. And what caused the decline? The cumulative effects of an impoverished environment.

> It was found that blacks (but not whites) showed significant and substantial decrements in both verbal and nonverbal IQs as a linear function of age . . . from about 5 to 16 years of age (Jensen, 1977, p. 184).

Studies of this type, although not refuting the importance of heredity on intelligence, make it clear that time and environment are extremely important in determining later levels of intellectual functioning. "To overstress the genetic factor is inevitably to assert that the blame belongs on the shoulders of the victim. This whole method of diagnosis and treatment takes us into the theatre of the absurd" (Daniels and Houghton, 1972, p. 75). Jensen's comment that compensatory education has been tried and has failed may be like that of an observer who, after watching Orville Wright's first flight at Kitty Hawk, said that air travel has been tried and has failed.

Sir Cyril Burt and the Taint of Scandal

Some of Jensen's correlational evidence supporting the .80 heritability argument came from the work of the English psychometrician Sir Cyril Burt. Burt had allegedly conducted a large number of studies in which the IQs of monozygotic twins reared apart were compared with the IQs of monozygotic twins reared together. However, in 1977, three years after Burt's death, Leon Kamin published his now famous *The Science and Politics of IQ,* in which he demonstrated that much of Burt's data were not only flawed but fraudulent (Kamin, 1977). At least some of the raw IQ data that Burt had used to support his hereditarian view could not be found among his papers. The suspicion grew that Burt had simply created correlations out of nonexistent data (Eysenck and Kamin, 1981). Even Jensen has now acknowledged that Burt must have perpetrated deliberate fraud. Excluding the Burt data, Jensen now estimates the total heritability of IQ to equal .70. Finally, Jensen feels that even if newer studies indicate the true heritability value to be only .50, that would still show the effect of heredity as greater than any environmental variables (Jensen, 1981).

In a very reasoned and objective work on the history and current status of the IQ controversy, Raymond Fancher concludes that both the hereditarians and the environmentalists are right, though neither are as right as they would pretend. Says Fancher:

> It seems fair for a neutral observer of the IQ controversy to conclude that IQ heritability in our time and society is certainly less than .70, and probably less than .50. This still leaves room, of course, for a substantial genetic factor in intelligence. . . . Thus, there is no doubt that environment plays a large role in determining both average levels and individual differences in intelligence within our society. Its influence tends to be exerted gradually and cumulatively, however, through the pervasive effects of home and culture acting over years and decades (Fancher, 1985, p. 235).

Robert Carkhuff, an expert in the fields of counseling and human relations, makes the point that although the mean IQ of black children is about 86 when they enter first grade, it drops even lower by the time the children reach fifth grade. Carkhuff attributes this drop to environmental forces working on the black child in the school setting. Since teachers and counselors often treat black children as if they were devoid of intellectual resources, the children begin to fulfill this expectation by achieving less and less as the school years go by. Says Carkhuff, "The teachers and counselors respond to black children as if Jensen and Garrett were correct" (Carkhuff, 1971, p. 125).

To compound the felony, Carkhuff argues, the least competent teachers are assigned to ghetto and predominantly black schools. It can be no wonder, then, that black children often do not achieve beyond the eighth- or ninth-grade level, since it may be that the level of their teacher's own competence does not extend beyond this point. One study found that two-thirds of the teachers tested scored lower than junior high school level on tests of proficiency in the teacher's own specialty area (Brenton, 1970). Says Carkhuff of these teachers, "They could not pass their own exams" (Carkhuff, 1971, p. 264). In fact, the recent movement in this country to force teachers to take standardized competency tests in order to enter into, or remain in, the teaching profession has met with considerable resistance from the teachers. Teachers have suddenly been placed in the ironic position of seeming to say that testing is not a good way to judge people.

THE CONFLUENCE MODEL: THE FAMILY ENVIRONMENT

Robert B. Zajonc (rhymes with "science") has proposed a provocative theory of intellectual development that views the family unit as being the key ingredient in the formation of eventual IQ growth. Although Zajonc interprets his data on the basis of the family's influence as an environmental variable, there may again be a hint, as some critics suggest, of an interaction effect between the family's gene pool and its ability to produce a stimulating intellectual environment. Zajonc has interpreted the relationship between family size and intelligence as a product of general environmental stimulation. The data are as follows:

1. Firstborn children tend to have higher IQs than their younger siblings.

2. The more children there are in a family, the lower the IQs of all the children.

3. Twins have lower IQs than nontwins.

4. Children in one-parent homes have lower IQs than children from homes where both parents are present. (The younger the child at the time of parental loss, the more severe the resulting IQ deficit.)

5. The only child has a lower IQ than does the firstborn in a two- or three-child family (Zajonc, 1976).

In his interpretation of these facts, Zajonc uses what he calls the **confluence model,** a model that predicts that the intellectual growth of each child is a function of the intellectual levels of all the other family members. A given child's intellectual environment is based on the average of the intellectual levels of all the family members, and since children contribute less than their parents to the absolute level of the family's intellectual environment, the more children there are, the lower the absolute level. However, the more spacing between children, the less the damage to the family's intellectual environment. The data on only children do reveal a discontinuity in this prediction, and Zajonc suggests that a child in some way benefits from having younger siblings. The only child has less opportunity to be a "teacher," to show a younger brother or sister how to hold a pencil, grip a baseball bat, or tie shoes.

Zajonc has provided an interesting and provocative explanation, also based on his confluence model, of the steady decline in Scholastic Aptitude Test (SAT) scores that occurred during the 1970s. The decline was simply a reflection of the fact that, following World War II, American parents decided to have large families and to have these children close together. Further, since the size of American families began decreasing in the early 1960s, Zajonc predicted an upswing in SAT scores for the 1980s. To some extent this prediction proved accurate. For example, from 1980 to 1986 the average verbal SAT score went from 428 to 437, and the average math score from 491 to 501. The uptrend has recently reversed, however, with the 1991 verbal average at 426 and the math average at 497. It must also be pointed out that during 1991 more students, well over a million, took the SAT than ever before, and it has been shown, by Zajonc and others, that the larger the population of

SPOTLIGHT ON NATURE AND NURTURE

And the Beat Goes On

As we have seen in earlier chapters, the nature-nurture debate has been with us at least as far back as Socrates, Plato, and Aristotle. The inspired argumentation of the medieval scholastics pales beside the debates academicians have waged on this issue over the years. And the shouting matches are not over. Although during the 1970s and 1980s the IQ controversy had typically focused on intellectual differences between black and white children, researchers in the 1990s are becoming increasingly interested in the high educational achievements shown by Asian Americans. It has been found that Asians have higher IQs than do whites both in the United States as well as in Europe.[a] On the math portion of the SAT, and on high school grade-point averages, Asian Americans also score significantly higher than other American students.[b] In one dramatic study, it was found that of those precocious children who scored 700 or higher on the SAT in math *before the age of 13,* 43 percent were Asian, whereas less than 3 percent of the population at large were Asian. Even among the Southeast Asian boat people, those poverty-stricken refugees who finally arrived in the United States with nothing more than the clothes they were wearing, the children still tend to excel in school. In one study it was found that the children of these refugees had higher grade-point averages, especially in math and science, than were the

norms for their schools and that they also scored above the median on a standardized achievement test, the California Achievement Test.[c] These children, it must be remembered, had limited exposure to Western culture and knew virtually no English when they arrived. Because of their low economic status, virtually all these children were attending slum-area U.S. schools. Although they did less well in liberal arts courses, where more extensive language skills were required, their combined GPA was 2.64. To explain these data, the two long-standing rival positions, heredity versus environment, have again surfaced for renewed combat. On the side of heredity, Richard Lynn suggests that the most parsimonious explanation of these Asian advantages must be based on the genetic argument, especially since even cross-adoption studies (abandoned Korean babies reared in the homes of white Americans) show significantly higher IQs than those of even the adopting family. Lynn has suggested that Asians might have a genetic predisposition toward hard work—a motivational variable. On the other side, environmentalists, such as Stanley Sue and Sumie Okazaki, maintain that the difference is due to the Asian's reaction to U.S. discrimination. Because they encounter prejudice, both in school and in the workplace, Asian Americans tend to compensate by working and studying much

harder in order to obtain educational credentials for entry into the job market, especially the professions.[d] Also, because of the language barrier encountered by newly arriving Asians, these children tend to concentrate especially in the areas of math and science, where quantitative rather than verbal and cultural skills are emphasized.[e] Finally, it has also been noted that most of these transported Asian family units are extremely close and have an especially strong commitment to accomplishment and education. It seems safe to say that this nature-nurture argument, heard even in the days of Socrates and Plato, will continue well into the twenty-first century, perhaps with other racial groups and probably even in other parts of the world. 'Twas ever thus.

---

[a] R. Lynn, Educational achievements of Asian Americans. *American Psychologist* (1991), *46,* 875–876.

[b] S. Sue and S. Okazaki, Asian-American educational achievements: A phenomenon in search of an explanation. *American Psychologist* (1990), *45,* 913–920.

[c] N. Caplan, M. H. Choy, and J. K. Whitmore, Indochinese refugee families and academic achievement. *Scientific American* (1992), *266,* 36–42.

[d] S. Sue and S. Okazaki (1990), op. cit.

[e] S. Sue and S. Okazaki, Explanations for Asian-American achievements: A reply. *American Psychologist* (1991), *46,* 878–880.

---

test takers, the lower the average scores. For example, in South Carolina where almost 60 percent of the seniors took the test, the average SATs were the lowest in the nation, with a verbal score of only 395 and a math score of 437. In Iowa, on the other hand, where

only 5 percent of the seniors took the test, the average scores were the highest in the nation, verbal = 515, and math = 578.

There has also been an alternate explanation for the rise in SAT scores that occurred in the 1980s.

Since the population of students taking the test is self-selected, average SAT scores may be a function of the overall strength of the nation's economy. When economic times are good, more students are in a financial position to elect to go to college and therefore take the test. According to this explanation, during the 1981–1983 recession, the rise in SAT scores may have been due to the fact that fewer students were taking the test, and the very ones who opted not to take the test were most likely to be at the economic margin. Financially disadvantaged students as a group have traditionally not done well on the SAT. According to this theory, then, as the economy improves, SAT scores go down, and as the economy weakens, SAT scores go up (Wainer, 1986).

Regardless of whether Zajonc's model is correct or incorrect with respect to SAT scores, Zajonc believes it can be used to explain another phenomenon: racial IQ differences. Since black families generally have more children (and have them closer together) than do average white families, that fact alone could explain the difference in average IQ scores between the two groups. Add to this the further fact that more black than white families are one-parent families.

Zajonc's conclusions are based on studies conducted on well over 1 million subjects from four different countries: the United States, France, the Netherlands, and Scotland. And, more important, his predictions have held up regardless of nationality, race, social status, or income level.

Critics suggest that since the confluence model has been analyzed using correlational techniques, perhaps Zajonc has overinterpreted the direction of the relationship. Although it may be that Zajonc is correct and that large numbers of children in a family do tend to lower overall average IQ levels (an environmental argument), the reverse might also be true: that parents with lower IQs tend to have more children in the first place (a genetic argument).

SUMMARY

Psychologists have generally given three meanings to the concept of intelligence: intelligence as a genetic capacity, intelligence as observed behavior, and intelligence as a test score.

The history of intelligence testing begins with Sir Francis Galton. Galton believed that intelligence was largely an inherited characteristic and attempted to measure intelligence through the use of simple sensorimotor tests. Galton's test results led him to emphasize what later became the theme of all measurement practitioners—individual differences. Galton's student and colleague, Karl Pearson, analyzed the testing data and, in order to make some meaningful comparisons, introduced a new statistical technique, the correlation coefficient.

Binet discarded Galton's idea of measuring intelligence through the use of sensorimotor tasks and adopted instead the approach of using intellectual tasks. Binet used the concept of mental age in order to assign a numerical value to performance on his test.

In 1916 an American psychologist, Lewis M. Terman, published an American revision of the Binet test. The scoring of this test, the Stanford-Binet test, was based on the concept of the intelligence quotient, or IQ.

In 1939 David Wechsler introduced the first of a series of new individual IQ tests. Wechsler felt that the Stanford-Binet test was too heavily laden with verbal items, and so he created a series of performance tasks to be presented along with the more traditional verbal tests.

During World War I, group tests of intelligence were introduced, allowing for the testing of large numbers of people in one sitting. Because of their ease of administration and lack of expense, group tests of intelligence quickly became popular throughout most school systems.

What do tests of intelligence tell us that we couldn't determine before? Studies have shown that IQ tests do predict how well a child will perform in school. Studies also indicate that high IQ scores correlate with success in later life as measured by such factors as physical health, emotional adjustment, financial income, and literary and scientific contributions.

Intelligence, like all human behavior, is a product of heredity interacting with environment interacting with time.

1. *Heredity:* Studies show that the closer the genetic similarity between people, the higher the resulting IQ correlation.

2. *Environment:* Similar environments also produce similar IQs. The specific environmental parameters studied include home factors (such as number of books in the home and parental attitudes toward schooling), nutrition, stimulus variety, past experience, and parental encouragement.

3. *Time:* The Bloom curve indicates that environmental influences on intelligence are most pronounced during a child's first few years of life.

The transactional model of development states that the interplay between parent and child not only impacts upon the intellect and personality of the growing child, but also influences the ongoing behavior of the parent, which, in turn, further shapes the child.

Bornstein has provided evidence indicating that fairly reliable measures of infant intelligence can be achieved and that these measures correlate both with later IQ measures and with the quality of the interaction displayed between mother and child.

The question of racial differences in intelligence was raised by Jensen. The evidence thus far fails to substantiate any claims of racial superiority or inferiority based on intelligence. Though the average IQs of black and white children do differ, there is no reason to assume that this difference is due more to genetic than environmental factors.

Zajonc's theory, called the confluence model, predicts that the more children there are in a family, especially if the children are close together in age, the lower the IQs of all the children will be. Birth order is also important, since firstborns have the highest IQs, unless there is a wide age spacing between the children. Zajonc's findings have held up regardless of nationality, race, income level, or social status.

KEY TERMS AND NAMES

Alfred Binet
Bornstein's infant intelligence test
confluence model
deviation IQ
factor approach
group tests of intelligence
J. P. Guilford
heritability
intelligence
intelligence quotient (IQ)
Arthur R. Jensen

mental age
performance IQ
Charles Spearman
Stanford-Binet test
Lewis M. Terman
L. L. Thurstone
transactional model
WAIS (WAIS-R)
David Wechsler
WISC-III

THEORY INTO PRACTICE: TESTING FOR INTELLIGENCE-LEARNING

The concept of intelligence, as we have seen in the chapter, can be one of the most confusing in all of educational psychology. Just listen to almost anyone discussing issues of IQ, scholastic aptitude, or academic achievement and you'll undoubtedly hear just what we mean. People will say intelligence when they might really mean scholastic aptitude, or achievement when they mean intelligence, and on and on. It gets even worse if we were to add in a discussion about creativity and its influence on intelligence. And you're not alone when it comes to confusions about this abstraction called intelligence. Even the experts have not yet arrived at a consensus as to what behaviors should be labeled as intelligent (Snyderman & Rothman, 1987). The basic problem is that all too often discussions of intelligence become discussions of qualitatively different things (Sternberg, 1990). It is beyond the scope of this chapter to discuss all these issues in full detail. We can say, however, that the central focus has been on the concept of intelligence, the goals as well as the measurement procedures. To help you keep these goals and procedures clearly in mind, we have created a simulation of an intelligence test for children.

On one side of the page we will list examples similar to the ones found on the most widely used of the individually administered child IQ tests, the WISC-III (the Wechsler Intelligence Scale for Children.) On the other side of the page you are to ask a question, as on the TV game show, as to which subtest of the WISC is being identified. Then, unlike the game show, we ask you to list the reasons for your selection along with a brief comment on the subtest. Coming up with a valid reason for your choice will force you to think over the concepts involved and prevent you from simply trying to rely on rote memory.

Before starting this exercise, reread the section on the Wechsler tests found on pages 467 to 469.

Here's an example of our *Jeopardy* test quiz:

ITEM	YOUR ANSWER
How is a car like a bus?	What is a test of Similarities?

Reasons and explanation   This would be a test of Similarities, since to answer this item, the child would have to begin thinking in abstract terms. Notice, too, that different levels of abstraction can be demonstrated here. For example, the child who says "They both have wheels" is operating at a lower conceptual level than the child who says "They are both modes of transportation."

Another example:

ITEM	YOUR ANSWER
Repeat after me the following numbers: 1, 7, 3, 2, 8.	What is a test of Digit Span?

Reasons and explanation   This would be a test of Digit Span, since the ability to immediately echo a series of random digits taps the child's short-term memory bank. To get a more precise measure here, we could start with, say, three random digits—2, 5, 3—and then increase the length of the series until it results in failure.

Remember that an IQ test has the goal of assessing each person's capacity to think rationally, act purposefully, and deal effectively with the environment. Intelligence is thus seen as a general or global capacity. To measure the traits that make up intelligent thinking, Wechsler designed his test to assess cognitive functioning in a variety of areas. This was, in fact, Wechsler's rationale for including a whole series of subtests, since no single subtest by itself could be sufficient as an overall measure of intellectual capacity.

For this exercise, we will focus only on the following subtests (which are common to both the WISC and the WAIS): Information, Arithmetic, Comprehension, Vocabulary, Picture Completion, Object Assembly, and Similarities.

Now, on to the Jeopardy test quiz. . .

ITEM	YOUR ANSWER	REASONS AND EXPLANATION
1. What does the word *stalagmite* mean?	What is a test of _____?	
2. If a minivan holds eight people, how many vans do you need to carry 48 people?	What is a test of _____?	
3. How is a mouse like an elephant?	What is a test of _____?	
4. What should you do if you noticed large amounts of smoke in the back of the school auditorium during an assembly?	What is a test of _____?	

ITEM	YOUR ANSWER	REASONS AND EXPLANATION

5. Look at the picture and tell what important part is missing.

What is a test of _____?

6. What does the word *nail* mean?

What is a test of _____?

7. What does this saying mean? "A rolling stone gathers no moss."

What is a test of _____?

8. What should you do if you found another student's homework assignment lying on the floor of the school's hallway?

What is a test of _____?

9. How many states are there in the United States?

What is a test of _____?

10. Here are some pieces, as in a jigsaw puzzle. As quickly as possible, put them together to make something.

What is a test of _____?

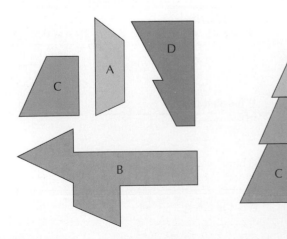

Discussion of the Reasons

1. Vocabulary   Discovering whether a child knows the correct definition of a sample of words aids in predicting the size of the child's total vocabulary. A definition of *stalagmite,* such as "a cylindrical deposit projecting upward from the floor of a cave" is perfect. But even here, in this relatively objective area, there can still be shades of gray. For example, the child who says that "the stalagmite projects downward from the roof of a cave" has a better idea of the meaning than someone who says it is "a German prison camp." A list can easily be drawn up that begins by requiring relatively easy definitions, such as, What is a banana? and goes on to words so difficult as to tax the limits of any child's vocabulary.

2. Arithmetic   Math items can be easily ordered as to difficulty. Also, an item such as the one shown requires an understanding of mathematical principles, not just the ability to recite the multiplication table or divide in one's head. Having a general concept of how to apply number facts is crucial to arriving at the correct answer of six vans.

3. Similarities   Here the ability to abstract is critical and indicative of the child's ability to organize facts into a meaningful and coherent structure. For example, saying that both the mouse and the elephant have tails is a lower-order answer than that they are both living creatures, or both animals or mammals. However, any of the above answers would be better than saying that they both squeak, except for the elephant.

4. Comprehension   A question such as this, although aimed at a child's overall level of comprehension, may also produce an indication of the child's level of social understanding. Notice that the children are not asked what they *would* do, but what they *should* do. Do they at least know what the right thing to do *should* be? The child who says he'd sneak out the side door, although certainly indicating a strong sense of self-preservation, is not showing the same degree of overall comprehension as the child who says she would quietly tell the teacher. The interaction between intellectual and personality factors can be seen in many of the answers to this question. For example, the child who says she would go up on the stage and order the band to play the "Star-Spangled Banner" and would then direct rows A through J to leave by exit 1 and rows K through Z by exit 2, could be illustrating a self-aggrandizing approach that typifies her general personality structure. Also, the child who answers by repeatedly insisting that he would not yell fire may be wrestling with an underlying problem of impulse control.

5. Picture completion   In this test, attention to detail and listening carefully to the instructions play key roles in the child's ability to succeed. For example, the question asks, "What is missing in the picture?" *not* "What is wrong with the picture?" The child who does not pay attention to the question is likely to jump in quickly and say that the steering wheel is on the wrong side rather than that one of the headlights is missing or even that the license plate is missing.

6. Vocabulary   The child who shows an understanding that a nail is a metal object used for holding pieces of wood together is giving us some indication of the extent of his or her vocabulary. This subtest is unusually rich in its ability to pull out overtones of personality. The trained examiner learns to use this subtest to ferret out personality as well as intellectual factors. The child who defines a nail as "something on the finger that can be polished, manicured, and made to look pretty" may be demonstrating needs that transcend any straight, cognitive interpretation.

7. Comprehension   The child who realizes that this saying is allegorical, not literal, shows a high degree of comprehension and developmental maturity. For example, an answer such as "People who are always on the move, who are overly restless, never stay in one place long enough to accumulate wealth or put down any lasting roots," is one that certainly shows an abstract understanding of the phrase. Even an answer such as "Busy people get their jobs done quickly, and are not bogged down by side issues and excuses," is qualitatively better than an overly literal answer such as "A stone that keeps rolling down a hill has all of its moss worn away and doesn't have any of its own moss left."

8. Comprehension   The child who says she would find the student who lost it and quietly hand it over is showing a marked degree of comprehension and social awareness. This is certainly a better answer than "I'd look at the homework, and if it's better done than mine, then I'd write my name on the top and pass it in." Even the child who answers by saying he'd make an appointment with the principal and then go down to the office and, perhaps even waiting for a fanfare, personally present the homework to the principal, is probably showing a higher need for recognition than the situation demands. Is this the same child who went up on stage after detecting smoke at the back of the school auditorium?

9. Information   Knowing the correct answer—fifty states—indicates an alertness to one's surroundings and the existence of an informational base that may have been effortlessly and almost automatically created by an inquiring and absorbent young mind. Again, even factual and informational questions can indicate degrees of knowledge and understanding. An answer such as five or 450 shows a lack of any conceptual base, whereas answers such as forty-eight or fifty-two, while not hitting the bull's-eye directly, are at least somewhere close to the target.

10. Object assembly   A test such as this one, which measures not just eye-hand coordination or motoric

speed, is especially valuable in determining the strength of the child's powers of recognition. Responses to this test may also be used to infer something of the child's mode of perception, the degree to which the trial-and-error approach is used, and even frustration tolerance in reaction to mistakes. The child who is easily upset, even to the point of not being willing to complete the problem, shows a different level of frustration tolerance than the child who, despite making some mistakes, stoically continues trying. Also, cognitive approaches to this problem can vary dramatically. For example, one child may blindly rush in and randomly flip the pieces around without the vaguest notion of what the parts represent. This approach may work, but it would certainly be a case of success by accident. Another child may spend a brief time looking over the parts, using this time to internally reorganize his or her perceptions, and only then begin to accurately and quickly put the pieces together. In many cases, you may even hear the child verbally announce the moment of insight with a phrase such as "Oh, I get it."

REFERENCES

Binet, A., and Simon, H. (1905). Application des méthodes nouvelles au diagnostic du niveau intellectuel chez des enfants normaux et anormaux d'hospice et d'école primaire. *L'Année Psychologique, 11,* 245–266.

Bloom, B. S. (1964). *Stability and change in human characteristics.* New York: Wiley.

Bornstein, M. (1985). How infant and mother jointly contribute to developing cognitive competence in the child. *Proceedings of the National Academy of Science, 82,* 7470–7473.

Brenton, M. (1970). *What's happened to teachers?* New York: Coward.

Caplan, N., Choy, M. H., and Whitmore, J. K. (1992). Indochinese refugee families and academic achievement. *Scientific American, 266*(2), 36–42.

Carkhuff, R. R. (1971). *The development of human resources.* New York: Holt, Rinehart & Winston.

Carroll, J. B. (1989). Factor analysis since Spearman: Where do we stand? What do we know? In R. Kanfer, P. L. Ackerman, and R. Cudeck (Eds.). *Abilities, motivation and methodology* (pp. 43–67). Hillsdale, N.J.: Erlbaum.

Clifford, M. M. (1991). Risk taking: Theoretical, empirical, and educational considerations. *Educational Psychologist, 26*(3, 4), 263—297.

Couchon, A. R. (1983). Approaches to the normal level. *Personality Assessment System Journal, 2,* 2–13.

Cravens, H. (1992). A scientific project locked in time: The Terman genetic studies of genius. *American Psychologist, 47,* 183–189.

Daniels, D., and Houghton, V. (1972). Jensen, Eysenck and the eclipse of the Galton paradigm. In K. Richardson and D. Spears (Eds.), *Race and intelligence.* Baltimore: Penguin.

Daniels, D., and Plomin, R. (1985). Origins of individual differences in infant shyness. *Developmental Psychology, 21,* 118–121.

Dennis, W. (1960). The mental growth of certain institutional children: Iran. *Journal of Genetic Psychology, 96,* 47–59.

Dennis, W. (1969). The mental growth of certain foundlings before and after adoption. Paper delivered at American University, Beirut, Lebanon.

Duncan, O. D., Featherman, D. L., and Duncan, B. (1972). *Socioeconomic background and achievement.* New York: Seminar Press.

Eickenwald, H. F., and Fry, P. C. (1969). Nutrition and learning. *Science, 163,* 644–648.

Erlenmeyr-Kimling, L., and Jarvik, L. F. (1963). Genetics and intelligence: A review. *Science, 142,* 1479–1488.

Eysenck, H. J., and Kamin, L. (1981). *The intelligence controversy.* New York: Wiley.

Fancher, R. E. (1985). *The intelligence men: Makers of the IQ controversy.* New York: Norton.

Farber, S. L. (1981). *Identical twins reared apart.* New York: Basic Books.

Feingold, A. (1988). Cognitive gender differences are disappearing. *American Psychologist, 43,* 95–103.

Forrester, B. J., and Klaus, R. A. (1964). The effect of race of the examiner on intelligence test scores of Negro kindergarten children. *Peabody Papers in Human Development,* 2(7), 1–7.

Freedman, D. G. (1979). Ethnic differences in babies. *Human nature,* 2(1), 40.

Garber, M., and Ware, W. B. (1970). Relationships between measures of home environment and intelligence scores. *American Psychological Association Proceedings,* 5, 647–648.

Gardner, H. (1985a). *Frames of mind: The theory of multiple intelligences.* New York: Basic Books.

Gardner, H. (1985b). Human intelligence isn't what we think it is. In F. Linder and J. H. McMillan (Eds.), *Annual editions: Educational psychology.* Guilford, Conn.: Dushkin.

Gottesman, I. I. (1974). Development genetics and ontogenetic psychology. *Minnesota Symposia on Child Psychology,* 8, 54–78.

Guilford, J. P. (1967). *The nature of human intelligence.* New York: McGraw-Hill.

Haan, N. (1963). Proposed model of ego functioning: Coping and defense mechanisms in relation to IQ change. *Psychological Monographs,* 11.

Hardy-Brown, K., Plomin, R., and Defries, J. (1981). Genetic and environmental influences on the rate of communicative development in the first year of life. *Developmental Psychology,* 17, 704–717.

Harlow, H. F., McGaugh, J. L., and Thompson, R. F. (1971). *Psychology.* San Francisco: Albion. See also Krech, D. (1968). The chemistry of learning. *Saturday Review* (January), 48–50.

Hebb, D. O. (1978). Open letter to a friend who thinks the IQ is a social evil. *American Psychologist,* 33, 1143.

Hirsch, J. (1971). Race, intelligence and IQ: A debate. In N. Chalmer, R. Crawley, and S. P. R. Rose (Eds.), *The biological bases of behavior* (pp. 244–245). London: Open University Press, Harper & Row.

Holden, C. (1980). Identical twins reared apart. *Science,* 207, 1323–1328.

Hummel, R., and Sprinthall, N. A. (1965). Under-achievement related to interests, attitudes, and values. *Personnel and Guidance Journal,* 44, 388–395.

Jensen, A. R. (1969). How much can we boost IQ and scholastic achievement? *Harvard Educational Review,* 39, 1–123.

Jensen, A. R. (1977). Cumulative deficit in IQ of blacks in the rural south. *Developmental Psychology,* 13, 184–191.

Jensen, A. R. (1981). *Straight talk about mental tests.* New York: Free Press.

Jones, L. V. (1984). White-black achievement differences. *American Psychologist,* 39, 1207–1213.

Kamin, L. (1977). *The science and politics of IQ.* Harmondsworth, England: Penguin.

Kaplan, B. J. (1972). Malnutrition and mental deficiency. *Psychology Bulletin,* 78, 321–334.

Locurto, C. (1991). *Sense and nonsense about IQ: The case for uniqueness.* New York: Praeger.

Lynn, R. (1991). Educational achievements of Asian Americans. *American Psychologist,* 46, 875–876.

Maccoby, E. E., and Martin, J. (1983). Socialization in the context of the family: Parent-child interactions. In P. Mussen (Ed.), *Handbook of child psychology* (4th ed.). New York: Basic Books.

Mackenzie, B. (1984). Explaining race differences in IQ. *American Psychologist,* 39, 1214–1233.

McKean, K. (1986). Intelligence: New ways to measure the wisdom of man. *Current* (January), 15–23.

Messick, S. (1980). Test validity and the ethics of assessment. *American Psychologist,* 35, 1012–1027.

Newman, H. H., Freeman, F. N., and Holzinger, K. J. (1937). *Twins: A study of heredity and environment.* Chicago: University of Chicago Press.

Piel, G. (1975). The new hereditarians. *The Nation,* 19, 457.

Rose, S., and Weinberg, R. (1976). IQ test performance of black children adopted by white families. *American Psychologist,* 31, 731.

Sameroff, A. (1975). Early influences on development: Fact or fancy? *Merrill-Palmer Quarterly,* 21, 267–294.

Scarr, S. (1971). Race, social class and IQ. *Science,* 174, 1285–1295.

Scarr, S. (1981). *Race, social class and individual differences in IQ.* Hillsdale, N.J.: Erlbaum.

Scarr, S., and McCartney, K. (1983). How people make their own environments: A theory of genotype-environment effects. *Child Development,* 54, 424–435.

Scarr, S., and Weinberg, R. (1976). IQ test performance of black children adopted by white families. *American Psychologist,* 31, 726–739.

Scarr, S., and Weinberg, R. (1978a). The rights and responsibilities of the social scientist. *American Psychologist,* 33, 955–957.

Scarr, S., and Weinberg, R. (1978b). Attitudes, interests and IQ. *Human Nature,* 1, 33.

Sherman, M., and Key, C. B. (1932). The intelligence of isolated mountain children. *Child Development,* 3, 279–290.

Smolak, L. (1986). *Infancy.* Englewood Cliffs, N.J.: Prentice-Hall.

Snyderman, M., and Rothman, S. (1987). Survey of expert opinions on intelligence and aptitude testing. *American Psychologist,* 42, 137–144.

Spuhler, J. N., and Lindzey, G. (1967). Racial differences in behavior. In J. Hirsch (Ed.), *Behavior-genetic analysis.* New York: McGraw-Hill.

Sternberg, R. J. (1985). *Beyond IQ: A triarchic theory of human intelligence.* New York: Cambridge University Press.

Sternberg, R. J. (1990). *Metaphors of mind: Conceptions of the nature of intelligence.* Cambridge, England: Cambridge University Press.

Sue, S., and Okazaki, S. (1990). Asian-American educational achievements: A phenomenon in search of an explanation. *American Psychologist,* 45, 913–920.

Sue, S., and Okazaki, S. (1991). Explanations for Asian-American achievements: A reply. *American Psychologist, 46,* 878–880.

Terman, L. M. (1925; revised 1926, 1930, 1947, 1959). *Genetic studies of genius.* Stanford, Calif.: Stanford University Press.

Thorndike, R. L., Hagan, E. P., and Sattler, J. M. (1985). *Stanford-Binet* (4th ed.). Chicago: Riverside.

Vernon, P. E. (1969). *Intelligence and cultural environment.* London: Methuen.

Vygotsky, L. (1978). *Mind in society.* Cambridge: Harvard University Press.

von Mayrhauser, R. T. (1992). The mental testing community and validity. *American Psychologist, 47,* 244–253.

Wainer, H. (1986). Minority advances in test performance: A response to Jones. *American Psychologist, 41,* 103.

Wechsler, D. (1944). *The measurement of adult intelligence.* Baltimore: Williams & Wilkins.

Wechsler, D. (1991). *Wechsler Intelligence Scale for Children manual* (3d ed.). New York: The Psychological Corporation, Harcourt Brace Jovanovich.

Weinberg, R. A. (1991). Intelligence and IQ: Landmark issues and great debates. *American Psychologist, 44,* 98–104.

Yerkes, R. M. (1921). Psychological examining in the U.S. army. *Memoirs of the National Academy of Sciences,* No. 15.

Zajonc, R. B. (1976). Family configuration and intelligence. *Science, 192,* 227–236.

Zelazo, P. R. (1989). Infant toddler information processing and the development of expressive ability. In P. R. Zelazo and R. Barr (Eds.). *Challenges to developmental paradigms: Implications for theory, assessment and treatment.* Hillsdale, N.J.: Erlbaum.

Zelazo, P. R., Weiss, M. J., and Tarquinio, N. (1991). Habituation and recovery of neonatal orienting to auditory stimuli. In M. J. Weiss and P. R. Zelazo (Eds.). *Newborn attention: Biological constraints and the influence of experience.* Norwood, N.J.: Ablex.

Zuckerman, M. (1990). Some dubious premises in research and theory on racial differences. *American Psychologist, 45,* 1297–1303.

MANAGING STUDENTS IN GROUPS

17

THE CLASS
AS A SOCIAL UNIT

Every classroom is a distinct social unit with its own set of norms, its own psychological atmosphere, its own set of role relationships, its own special blend of behavioral expectancies. Every classroom has a social climate unlike that of any other classroom. An observer walking from room to room in a typical elementary school finds one room charged with excitement and enthusiasm; another, tense, with submissive pupils going through the motions; and still another, bordering on anarchy.

The psychology of the classroom does not operate in a vacuum, for every classroom is part of the larger social unit, the school itself. Again, the observer traveling from school to school can sense differences in social climate among the various schools. The differences among schools may not be as blatant as the differences among classrooms, but the differences are there, and do have an effect.

What causes these differences among rooms, among schools, among any different number of groups? The quick and easy answer is the personality of the teacher or principal. This, however, is only part of the answer. Just as the principal's behavior helps shape the teacher's, so the teacher's behavior shapes the principal's actions. And just as the teacher's behavior influences the pupil's behavior, so the pupils' behavior has a profound effect on the teacher. Teach-

ers may firmly believe that their classrooms have the same social climate year in and year out, despite the shifting student population, but these same teachers will stare in shocked disbelief at a videotape showing one of their classes two or three years ago, or even last year. The shifting student population creates a shifting social climate. Sometimes the shift is subtle, but often it is dramatic. Many teachers freely confess that with one particular class they barely weathered the year, or the opposite: "For the first time in my life my class this year was an absolute dream." This chapter takes a look at some of the findings of social psychology, which, we hope, will increase your understanding of the classroom as a social unit.

SOCIAL PSYCHOLOGY DEFINED

Social psychology attempts to understand human behavior in the context of the social situation. Social psychologists study the ways people affect and are affected by other people. As a subfield of psychology, social psychology still uses the behavior of the individual as its unit of analysis—the individual's behavior in the social context. The social psychologist would probably not be interested in the lonely figure of Hermann Ebbinghaus going about the business

Different schools have different social climates.

of memorizing long lists of nonsense syllables, but would be very much interested in how Ebbinghaus's performance might have been affected by the presence of other people. The very first studies in the field of social psychology were concerned with the effect of a group situation on a person's behavior.

SOCIAL FACILITATION

Even before the turn of the century, studies indicated that on certain tasks a person's performance would improve when others were around (Triplett, 1897). This phenomenon later became known as **social facilitation.** It was also found that this was not a universal phenomenon. Social facilitation was most pronounced in the case of fairly simple mechanical tasks. The more difficult and the more intellectual the task, the less the effect of social facilitation. Later studies have revealed the operation of **social inhibition;** that is, on some tasks, a person's performance suffers when there are others around. In one study students were given a word-learning task to perform either alone or in the company of other students. Some of the tasks were designed to be easy; others were much

more difficult. On the easy tasks the students did better when in the presence of others (social facilitation), but on the difficult tasks they did much worse when in the presence of others (social inhibition) (Cottrell et al., 1967).

The effect of performing in front of others is also a function of one's ability level. A child who is an excellent speller, and knows it, often does even better when performing in front of an audience, whereas for a child of only modest ability the effect of the group becomes inhibiting. In one study, the skills of groups of above-average and below-average pool players were rated with and without a group of spectators looking on. The below-average players lost in accuracy in the group setting (social inhibition), whereas the better players actually gained in accuracy (Michaels et al., 1982).

Still other studies have shown that when a person is first attempting to learn something new, the presence of other people is detrimental. Thus, in preparing for a final exam, when the material has already been learned well, reviewing the course in a small-group situation would probably be facilitative. When the material is new, however, spending the night before the exam in absolute solitude would be more productive.

The Risky Shift

When people get together in group situations, one effect that has been demonstrated in several experiments is the **risky shift** (Pruitt, 1971). The group situation apparently produces an environment in which individuals become far less cautious than they would be if they were alone; consequently, an attitudinal shift in the direction of "throwing caution to the wind" occurs. Individuals are suddenly willing to take greater risks regarding their **attitudes** and behavior. They become less conservative and more willing to gamble. One explanation of this phenomenon is that individuals who are basically risk takers to begin with also happen to be more persuasive and better able to have their opinions prevail in the group setting. These high-risk people become opinion leaders when interacting in the group. Another explanation is that in our culture the daredevil is more revered than is the individual who prudently and

cautiously weighs all the outcomes before acting. We are more apt to honor an Evel Knievel than a stodgy, trust-department banker. Thus, many individuals would prefer to have the group see them as risk takers. They prefer the public image of being a "gutsy gambler" and therefore shift in the culturally approved risky direction when in a group situation.

Whatever the explanation, the risky shift is an empirical fact. The teacher who is aware of this is less apt to be overconcerned when some budding daredevil disrupts the class with an image-building display of bravado. Perhaps a short session alone with the student will be sufficient to restore the equilibrium and integrity of the classroom.

Brainstorming

The concept of social facilitation has also been used to promote a technique called **brainstorming,** in which individuals get together in an attempt to solve problems in new and creative ways. The idea is that because of the mutual stimulation of a brainstorming session, each participant will individually produce

Cooperative learning may lead to group cohesion.

more creative solutions than when in isolation. Individuals in a brainstorming session are urged to interact freely, to call out any ideas no matter how bizarre, and to hold nothing back. The technique is used in many businesses, especially in areas in which creativity is crucial, as in an advertising agency mapping out a new campaign.

The techniques involved in brainstorming can be taught, even to persons not considered to be overly creative. In one study, the presentation of a short course in innovative problem solving (IPS) demonstrated that individuals could be trained to improve their brainstorming skills. However, whether the improvement in brainstorming techniques actually translates into an increase in problem-solving ability is still somewhat at issue (Rice, 1984).

In fact, in the most famous of the brainstorming studies, it was found that in some areas people might be better problem solvers working alone than working in a group setting. In that study, subjects were assigned to work either in a five-person group or in an isolated situation (Taylor et al., 1958). In both situations, the subjects were given five problems to work on and a time limit of twelve minutes. One problem, for example, asked the subjects to suggest methods for increasing the number of European tourists visiting the United States. Subjects were told that they should come up with as many ideas as possible and that they should be as creative as possible. They were also told the following:

1. Criticism is ruled out. Adverse judgment of ideas must be withheld until later.

2. Freewheeling is welcomed. The wilder an idea, the better. It is easier to tame down than to perk up.

3. Quantity is wanted. The more ideas there are, the more winners there are likely to be.

4. Combination and improvement are sought. In addition to contributing ideas of your own, you should suggest how others' ideas can be improved or how two or more ideas can be put together into an even better one (Freedman et al., 1970).

The results of this study startled many social psychologists. Subjects who were isolated produced almost twice as many different ideas as the subjects who were working in groups. Also, the subjects working alone produced twice as many ideas judged to be unique and creative.

Differential Effects on Behavior

Research in the area of social facilitation thus suggests that people do behave differently when in a group. The seemingly contradictory results of the studies (groups sometimes enhance performance and sometimes inhibit it) show that the group has differential effects on behavior.

Working in a group has two main effects: It increases feelings of competition and motivation, on the one hand, and it increases feelings of anxiety and provides distractions, on the other. The presence of other people explicitly or implicitly creates a competitive situation. However, the research studies in this area may be slightly artificial, for it has been found that in these studies the subjects tend to become somewhat self-conscious. The subjects assume that the researcher may be making comparisons among them and/or they hope to impress other members of the group.

Cohesiveness

When individuals interact in a group situation, one possible by-product is the spread of a group phenomenon that social psychologists call **cohesiveness.** When cohesiveness develops, group members tend to stick together more and have more of a sense of "we-ness" than "I-ness." Some teachers have been known to feel threatened by this turn of events.

Cohesiveness is one of the few truly group concepts in social psychology. It is the cement that binds the group together, or the attraction of the group for its members. Groups can range from collections of unrelated individuals (strangers waiting together at a bus station) to highly cohesive groups, in which norms are shared and status and role relationships are highly structured. When students and teachers meet in the classroom for the first time in September, they resemble a collection of individuals more than they do a cohesive group. As the weeks go by, however, the social situation may change dramatically as the loosely knit collection of individuals becomes more cohesive. Cohesiveness may be enhanced by the following:

1. *Friendly interaction:* Interaction per se is not the crucial ingredient; a husband and wife fighting it out in divorce court are interacting. The interaction must be on friendly terms.

2. *Cooperation:* The more the group works together to achieve superordinate goals, the more cohesiveness is allowed to develop.

3. *Group status:* High-status groups tend to be more cohesive than low-status groups. If a classroom is broken down into various reading groups, for example, and if it is obvious to every child that the groups have been rank-ordered on the basis of ability, the top group will feel more cohesive than the bottom group. A teacher may also increase the status of the entire classroom by pointing out that it is in some way a special group and will have special privileges.

4. *An outside threat:* A group's cohesiveness may be dramatically increased by the presence of an outside threat. This is true of large and small groups. In wartime, when a country's very existence is threatened by an outside force, the country's morale and cohesiveness are often at their highest level. In a classroom this same kind of situation may inadvertently occur when a coercive teacher is perceived by the class as overly threatening. The class may band together and form a highly cohesive group—a group, incidentally, that does not include the teacher.

5. *Style of leadership:* We will look at this phenomenon in more detail in a later section.

Suffice it to say here that groups in which the leadership is based on democratic factors are usually more likely to be cohesive than are groups in which more authoritarian leadership techniques are employed.

Cohesiveness and productivity   Research indicates that there is no simple one-to-one relationship between cohesiveness and productivity. A cohesive group is one in which the members stick together, but this doesn't necessarily mean that the group is more productive. For example, a highly cohesive labor union is more likely to be able to call a strike (during which production on the job goes down to zero) than is a union whose members are not so attracted to one another. Highly cohesive groups may be more productive than less cohesive groups when the motivation of the members is positive, yet when the motivation is negative, the more cohesive group will be even less productive than the less cohesive group (Schachter, 1951).

Cohesiveness and conformity   Any group brings a certain amount of pressure to bear on its members to conform to the group's standards and norms. In a highly cohesive group the pressure to conform is greater than in a less cohesive group. This helps explain the previously mentioned relationship between cohesiveness and productivity. When the group norm is for high productivity, the highly cohesive group conforms to that norm; likewise, when the group norm is for low productivity, the highly cohesive group conforms to that norm, especially in matters of consequence to the group (working conditions and salary, for example).

Conformity

One of the most striking facts about life on this planet is that human beings form groups and live out their lives in group situations. Equally striking is the fact that while in the group situation, people tend to behave in a uniform way. **Conformity** is a fact of life. Wherever we look we find groups of people, and within each group almost everyone is behaving alike. The behavior of an individual may change from group to group, and the norms of any particular group may shift from time to time, yet the phenomenon of conformity remains. We may like to feel as if we can act with some degree of independence, and yet in truth our freedom of action is severely limited by group pressure.

In a structured situation such as a church service, conformity may be most obvious. People stand, sit, and kneel with the precision of a marching band. The pressure to conform, however, can be just as compelling in less structured situations. If, during the give and take of a dormitory "rap" session, someone suddenly stood up and started singing "Onward Christian Soldiers," that person might be referred to the counseling center.

The message from the group is always the same: Be like us! The pressure to conform is virtually irresistible and may come in a variety of forms. It may be physical force, as in the case of a bouncer's throwing a rowdy customer out of the local tavern—a customer who has exercised too much individuality. Or, it may be more subtle, as when the hostess at a formal dinner party raises her eyebrow when one of the guests chooses the wrong fork for the salad. Regardless of the form it takes, the pressure on the individual to conform makes itself known. Conformity has been demonstrated experimentally in many studies. The two most famous, however, are the classic studies by Muzafer Sherif and Solomon Asch.

Within a group, great pressure exists for conformity, and group pressure to conform is highest when the group is highly cohesive.

Sherif and the autokinetic effect   A stationary, pinpoint source of light in an otherwise darkened room will appear to move. You may have noticed this phenomenon yourself. You may have been looking up at a certain star, and out of the corner of your eye it appears that another star has suddenly moved. Or you may have been driving on a turnpike when the rear light of the car in front of you suddenly starts to dance crazily before your eyes. Some plane crashes have even been caused by this autokinetic effect. The stationary runway lights suddenly appear to move just before the pilot lands the plane. The effect is even more dramatic if the subject doesn't know how far away the light really is.

Sherif utilized this **autokinetic effect** to demonstrate conformity (Sherif, 1936). He put his subjects in a darkened room in groups of three, presented them with the pinpoint source of light, and asked them to call aloud their estimates of how far the light moved. The first subject might estimate that the light moved sixteen inches; the second subject, three inches; and the third subject, twenty-four inches. After a few trials, however, all three subjects reported essentially the same distance—a group norm emerged. Repeating this procedure with other groups, Sherif found that conformity occurred in ev-

ery case. The groups formed different norms, to be sure, but they all created some standard to which every member conformed.

Another interesting result of Sherif's study was that when he later tested many of the subjects individually, they still perceived the light on the basis of the norms created in the group situation. A member of a "seven-inch" group, for example, when later tested alone, would continue to conform to the seven-inch standard. A member of a "twenty-two inch" group would continue to see the light moving that distance, even when tested individually.

Sherif's study shows us that in a relatively unstructured situation, group norms will be created and individuals will follow these norms not only when they are in the group, but even when they are alone.

Asch and group pressure   Sherif had shown that conformity occurs in a fairly unstructured situation (remember that, in fact, the light didn't move at all), and Asch wondered whether the same result would be obtained in a more structured setting (Asch, 1952). Asch presented his subjects with cards showing four lines: three comparison lines and a standard (see Figure 17.1). The subject was asked to indicate which of the three comparison lines was closest in length to

FIGURE 17.1   Asch used a card such as this to study group pressures to conform.

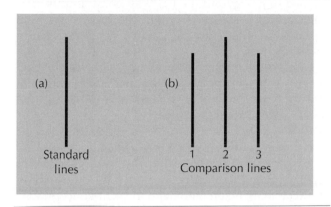

Standard
lines

(a)   (b)

1   2   3
Comparison lines

the standard line on the left of the card. As you look at the illustration, you may feel that the task is too easy, that the solution to the problem is too obvious. Yet, when Asch conducted this study, his subjects were in error one out of three times. The difference is that as you look at the lines, you are not being exposed to group pressure, whereas Asch's subjects most certainly were. Asch's subjects sat in a room with what appeared to be eight other subjects. In fact, these other "subjects" were really stooges, told beforehand just what to say and how to respond. Each group contained one naive subject and eight previously rehearsed bogus subjects. The subject was thus in a situation in which his eyes told him one thing, while all the other people in the room made a

unanimous judgment that contradicted his own. The stooges were set up in advance so that every once in a while they would all agree on a certain line, even though that line could not possibly be the correct one. It was in this setting that the subjects were incorrect one-third of the time; that is, 33 percent of their judgments were errors in the direction of the majority. As we have already said, group pressure is tremendous in its insistence on conformity.

As a matter of fact, the majority does not have to be so large. Asch's later studies revealed that a majority of three to one has just as much effect as a larger majority; that is, the naive subject made as many errors with three stooges as with eight. A two-to-one majority caused errors to drop only to about 12 percent, while the influence of only one stooge was negligible.

When the situation was reversed, when there was a naive majority of sixteen against one lone stooge, the errors of the stooge were met with uncontrolled laughter from the rest of the group.

Sherif and Asch thus demonstrated experimentally the compelling power the group exerts on the individual to conform. Sherif was able to produce norms in the laboratory and show how they govern individual behavior, and Asch, though artificially creating the norms, showed us the force of the group's influence in a relatively structured situation.

Can group pressure be liberating?   So far, conformity and group pressure have been shown to be repressive and limiting, generally robbing people of their individuality. Sherif showed us how a group of

"Well, heck! If all you smart cookies agree, who am I to dissent?"

Drawing by J. B. Handelsman; © 1972
The New Yorker Magazine, Inc.

people can come to believe that a stationary light is moving a certain distance; Asch showed that our need to conform to group standards will cause us to distort our perceptions and judgment. In fact, virtually all of the studies done in the area of conformity follow this theme: The noble individual is robbed of human integrity by the insidious pressure of the group.

The experiment by Stanley Milgram that was discussed in Chapter 7 shows the reverse side of the coin (Milgram, 1965). Milgram, in a somewhat frightening experiment, shows us that group pressure can also have a liberating effect. We say "frightening" experiment because Milgram's study also points up the destructive potential of human beings and shows what a thin veneer of socialization we have.

To establish a base line for our potential for hostility, Milgram asked subjects to deliver increasing amounts of electric shock to another person. Despite the "victim's" anguished cries and pleas for mercy, the experimenter urged the subject to keep increasing the voltage all the way up to 450 volts. The dial in front of the subject contained 30 voltage levels from 15 to 450 volts and was printed with such warnings as "Danger" and "Severe Shock." The subject had witnessed the "victim" being strapped into the electric chair and could clearly hear the "victim's" cries.

Milgram established his base line. Fully 65 percent of his subjects were willing to administer the maximum 450 volts; that is, almost two-thirds of the subjects were willing to risk killing a fellow subject.

Who were these subjects? Where and when was this experiment conducted? Were these Gestapo agents being trained in some sadistic Nazi laboratory during the 1930s? In fact, these subjects were ordinary American citizens, from twenty to fifty years of age, from all walks of life, and living in New Haven, Connecticut. The study was done at Yale University during the 1960s. The subjects were, of course, unaware that the "victim" did not really get shocked: The wires connecting the control panel to the electric chair did not really carry any electricity, and the victim was really an ally of the experimenter. Presumably, the subjects thought the shocks were effective and were nevertheless willing to deliver the shocks as the experimenter instructed.

The second phase of Milgram's study was to see what would happen in a group situation. How would subjects react if they were placed in the same situation with two other subjects who refused to follow the experimenter's commands? The results were dramatic. Under the condition of group pressure, only 10 percent of the subjects still pushed the lever all the way to 450 volts. The majority of the subjects refused to go beyond the halfway point. In this case, then, group pressure liberated the individual from the experimenter's authoritarian control and had a positive effect.

Conformity and group pressure may often be beneficial to the individual. Milgram's study suggests that they may help a person act in a more humane and less destructive manner.

Locus of control   Despite the insistent demands of group pressure, people differ on how readily they yield to the seductive lure of conformity. Studies have shown that a person who has a low self-concept, who is unsure of his or her private beliefs, and who is fearful of being perceived as different is the very person who is most likely to conform (Santee and Maslach, 1982).

Psychologists have categorized people on the basis of whether their **locus of control** is internal or external. Persons who have been identified as having an *internal* locus of control typically view themselves as being personally in control of their actions and in charge of their own destinies. Persons measured as having an *external* locus of control, however feel that they are largely at the mercy of environmental circumstances (Kobasa, 1982). It follows, then, that the individual who is externally controlled is more easily swayed by group pressures, whereas the internally controlled person is more apt to stand up to the group's demands and be more *flexible under conditions of stress* (Parkes, 1984).

Persons are more apt to develop an internal locus of control in areas in which they excel. Thus, locus of control and achievement typically go hand in hand, and the locus of control may change as a function of the general area of activity in which the child is involved (Weiner, 1980). The outstanding athlete may have a strong internal locus of control on the football field and exhibit poise and confidence while there but, because of past academic problems, develop an external locus of control in the classroom and appear to be timid and insecure. Sometimes a person reacts in a particular manner in one type of situation, and then when observed in another context, this same person seems like a different person with a different personality. Typically, the child who develops a strong sense of internal control has greater ego strength, greater feelings of personal competence, and is less likely to go along with the crowd.

(a)

(b)

(c)

(d)

(e)

Asch found, in studying conformity, that some subjects are able to maintain independent judgment throughout. Most, however, are unable to do so and yield to group pressure on at least one trial. (a) The experimenter gives instructions. (b) The critical subject, seated in the middle, listens to the instructions. (c) He makes his first judgment that disagrees with the consensus. (d) He leans forward as the next set of lines appears. (e) He feels conflict as he listens to new, incorrect peer judgments.

As we have seen, conformity pressures are pervasive in our society, and even the internally controlled person is not totally immune. In fact, the power of the group is enhanced even further when that group is composed of persons we tend to like (Marks and Miller, 1985).

SOCIALIZATION

Conformity is a key issue in social psychology because it is a driving power of socialization. **Socialization** is the process of learning society's rules and customs and is accomplished through pressures to conform. The newborn infant—at best an innocent little hedonist and at worst a savage bundle of Freudian instincts—is slowly transformed into a conforming member of society. The individual slowly but surely gives up personal independence as socialization continues, learning how and when to eat, where and when to urinate and defecate, how to interact with other people, and so on. Finally, the mature adult emerges who has learned these lessons so well that he or she conforms with the instinctive precision of a homing pigeon.

Socialization is the process of learning society's rules and customs. True nonconformists are rare.

Are there any nonconformists? There are only a few, and most of them are either in prison or in a psychiatric hospital. For example, you might think that members of a nudist colony are nonconformists, and yet they are all conforming to their own group norm. The only nonconformist in a nudist camp would be the person who is fully dressed. Or, you might assume that members of a commune are nonconformists, and yet they are conforming as rigidly to their norms as middle-aged Rotarians are to theirs. Each group is marching in unison, but to different drummers.

Who is the drummer in the classroom? Who sets the beat for the in-unison march of classroom members? To a large extent, it is the norms of society at large. After all, most students and teachers have been socialized in a common culture. The way they dress, the ideas they consider important, the way they interact, the way they express feelings are all determined by the core culture. The fact that most students feel a sense of competition is in large part culturally determined and already part of their characters before they ever set foot in the classroom. The fact that they are in the classroom at all, pursuing an educational goal, is a cultural dictate. But this doesn't explain it all, for each classroom has its own distinct set of norms that exists within the larger context of society's norms. The teacher contributes much of the tone, but so does

every single member of the class. The crucial ingredient in the formation of a norm, and thus conformity, is interaction among group members. Interactions produce group norms, which then set the limits within which further interactions can take place. Status and role relationships begin to emerge, and further demands and expectancies are set for each individual's behavior. Who sets the beat? The classroom, within the context of the larger social situation, sets its own beat, and every single member of the class participates in the process.

Cognitive Dissonance

Another aspect of socialization has been described by Leon Festinger. According to Festinger, people strive to achieve a state of equilibrium among their various attitudes (or learned predispositions to persons, situations, or things) and behaviors (Festinger, 1957). This is because we prefer consistency, or consonance, to inconsistency, or dissonance. Therefore, whenever we have a thought that is not consistent with our behavior, we experience **cognitive dissonance** and are motivated to restore the equilibrium. To avoid self contradiction, we can either change our thinking so that it conforms to our behavior or change our behavior so that it conforms to our thinking. For example, someone who enjoys smoking and who hears that smoking is a health hazard can either conclude that the evidence linking smoking with disease is flimsy or stop smoking. One smoker, it has been said, became so nervous after reading the evidence linking smoking with cancer that he gave up reading.

The point is that whenever our thoughts and deeds conflict, we are driven to reduce the anxiety-provoking dissonance. Teachers should be alerted to the possible consequences of cognitive dissonance when it occurs in the classroom. The desire for consonance operates within the individual and within the group. The chances against finding a classroom in which all thirty pupils and the teacher have totally compatible interests, attitudes, and values are so great that it is safe to say that dissonance is inevitable. The important thing is the way that dissonance is resolved. If the teacher decides to always "fight and never switch," if the pupils have to do all the changing, then the reduction of dissonance in the classroom will be more apparent than real. We will see in Chapter 19 that the way in which a teacher handles pupil discipline will help define the educational atmosphere of the class. The imposition of too strict a set of sanctions may reduce dissonance, but the resulting compliance is likely to be begrudging at best. Pupil discipline is just one instance of the general problem of the incongruity between the individual and the group.

Attribution Theory

Many years ago, the social psychologist Fritz Heider introduced the term **attribution** to refer to the explanations people give for their own or another person's actions or beliefs (Heider, 1958). When the attribution is based on an internal factor it is called a *dispositional* attribution, and when it is based on external factors it is called a *situational* attribution. For example, if a teacher attributes a child's poor performance on a test to basic laziness or general stupidity, that would be a dispositional attribution. If, however, the teacher views the poor performance as resulting from the child's temporarily feeling ill or having had a fistfight on the way to school, that would be a situational attribution. According to attribution theorists, when people attempt to explain another person's actions, they tend to overestimate dispositional factors and underestimate situational factors (Reeder, 1982). This is called the *fundamental attribution error*. Notice that this occurs mainly when someone is explaining an-

other person's behavior. For example, a teacher who has an unruly child in class may explain the behavior on the basis of the child's basic aggressiveness. When explaining our own behavior, however, we are far more likely to use a situational attribution. Thus, we are more likely to interpret another person's actions on the basis of the latter's inherent personal traits, whereas we see our own actions as logically fitting the reality demands of the situation. During a pupil–teacher conference, for example, the teacher might patiently listen to the pupil's list of situational reasons for failing the math quiz, but may privately view them as alibis for the pupil's inherent laziness. It has even been found that some members of minority groups make an effort to protect self-esteem by always attributing negative feedback to prejudice or discrimination, when in fact the negative consequences may at times be deserved (Vivian and Berkowitz, 1992).

Research also suggests that students who really begin to believe that their academic failures are due to dispositional factors are apt to lose motivation and stop trying altogether. If, however, the students become convinced that their failures are due more to transitory situational factors, academic motivation may increase (Wilson and Linville, 1982).

The fundamental attribution error is more likely to occur when the behavior in question is perceived as negative, such as rudeness, disruptiveness, or academic failure. When a student performs brilliantly, say on a standardized test, then the teacher is more willing to attribute this victory to a situational factor—in this case the teacher's own elegant instructional style.

Children who rarely experience success in the classroom, for example the learning-disabled, often attribute their failures to dispositional factors and eventually can be heard making statements like "I am too dumb to learn" (Bryan and Bryan, 1986). Such children need to be taught coping strategies for dealing with their failures.

Finally, in assigning reasons for another's behavior, two other variables must be included—how well liked the other individual is and how personally attractive. Thus, for example, when you dislike someone, your list of dispositional attributes will be extremely negative, and may include terms such as *manipulative, greedy, stupid, hostile*. When you're in love with the individual, your list will overflow with terms expressing noble and saintly qualities (Harvey and Weary, 1984).

SPOTLIGHT ON LEARNING DISABILITIES

Beyond the School Day and the Social Dilemma of Nonconformity

Learning-disabled (LD) children, as we saw back in Chapter 11, may experience deficits in a broad range of measurable skills, such as attention span, memory, motor control, perception, emotional control, and, especially, social skills. A teacher may report that a child who has perceptual deficits has difficulty copying from the board, organizing written work, and/or writing neatly, especially on or between the lines. However, these perceptual deficits also reveal themselves in areas far beyond the academic setting alone. The child who has deficits in depth perception, for example, is the child who in all innocence hugs everyone just a bit too tightly, or is just a little too rough when playing with the baby, or seems to tip over the milk at virtually every meal. If a child cannot judge the distance between himself and the person he is talking to, he will tend to get too close to another child's face and then, to make matters worse, talk too loudly. It is not long before the other children begin to avoid this child because they lose patience with his or her clumsiness or intrusive style. Because of these inappropriate social skills, learning-disabled children are frequently labeled "nerds" or "jerks" by their peers and siblings and thus become rejected by their peer groups. As the LD child becomes ever

more isolated from meaningful interactions with age-mates, the child soon has fewer chances to practice social skills, and the cycle of isolation becomes increasingly difficult to break.

If a learning-disabled child has a short attention span, which is certainly common, teachers will report that the child is not attending to instructions and parents complain that their child never listens to directions. Other children will say that the child with the short attention span is no fun to play with because he or she always leaves the game before it's finished. These LD children can in fact be very poor listeners; they tend to become restless and walk away when people are talking to them, often in midsentence. Playmates are simply not tolerant of the child who leaves games or conversations before they are finished. The LD child becomes an *unwitting nonconformist* and eventually is excluded from the peer group and is no longer asked to play games at all.

If the child also has a language-based learning disability, there will almost certainly be an academic difficulty in reading and writing. But the problem doesn't stop there. A language-based learning disability also affects the learning-disabled child *socially* because such a child does not always understand the language and jargon of the peer group. These are the children who

just never "get" the jokes or puns and as a result are perceived as being humorless or even stupid. The youngster who appears to be "not much fun to play with" is pressured by peers to leave the group, which means that the rejected child is no longer exposed to age-appropriate humor, futher delaying the development of both language and social skills.

Parents of learning-disabled children are particularly and painfully aware of their child's social difficulties. Parenting the learning-disabled child presents challenges not even dreamed of by other parents. To further compound the problem, the difficulties experienced by the learning-disabled child come to weigh heavily upon *all* the family members. Parents consistently report feeling frustrated, anxious, and sometimes even helpless in dealing with their LD child. And brothers and sisters also report suffering from and becoming embarrassed by the social blunders of their LD sibling. Thus, learning disabilities extend far beyond the school day and involve the LD child's whole life. Tragically, the untreated learning disability may then become a life disability.

This Spotlight was especially prepared for this volume by Dr. Nancy Hayes, Educational Psychologist and School Consultant, Longmeadow, Massachusetts.

AGGRESSION

Social psychologists have long been interested in the phenomenon of aggression. Human society is obviously fraught with violence. The United States has

the dubious distinction of leading the world in rates of homicide, rape, assault, and robbery. In fact, in 1991, there were over 25,000 homicides in the United States, twenty-two of them in one day in the little town of Killeen, Texas. Also in 1991, 10,000 Americans were killed with handguns, as opposed to only two in all of Great Britain. Over 3,000 children are murdered by their parents or caretakers every year in the United States, and even more common are the tiny broken bodies resulting from the *battered child syndrome*. As every football, hockey, and boxing fan knows, violence also has crowd appeal. And "hit 'em again harder" apparently is not reserved for the sports arena. On September 23, 1967, at a large southwestern university, when a depressed student crawled to the edge of a dormitory roof and threatened suicide, thousands of students stood below and chanted in unison, "Jump! Jump! Jump!" As for major conflicts, the world has rarely seen a day since the beginning of recorded history when there wasn't a full-scale war going on somewhere on the globe. These facts seem to argue that aggression is an inevitable by-product of people getting together in groups (Wrightsman, 1972).

Theories of Aggression

Psychology has generated four basic positions regarding the issue of aggression:

The Freudian According to Sigmund Freud, aggression is built into the organism and is as basic to human behavior as sexuality. The urge to violence is a result of pressure from our innate and irrational id instinct. The trouble with the Freudian hypothesis is that, by explaining so much, it may in fact not explain anything. To say that people are aggressive because they have a built-in aggressive instinct smacks of circular reasoning. This was referred to in Chapter 2 as the nominal fallacy.

The ethological Konrad Lorenz and other ethologists view aggression as a constant potential in virtually all organisms. If the proper releaser occurs, the potential for aggression will quickly be translated into action. For example, the male stickleback fish attacks whenever stimulated by the color red. Other ethologists have even found that among fish the attacking behavior itself has a profound effect on the physiology of the fish, especially its brain. In aggressive males, brain cells in the hypothalamus that control mating behavior have been found to be six to eight times larger than among more passive male fish. Further, these brain cells will change in size as a result of environmental clashes. For example, when an aggressive male is defeated in battle, these neurons

in the hypothalamus begin to shrink, followed by a similar shrinking of the testes, and eventually the loss of any desire to either mate or fight (Bond et al., 1991).

As for humans, Lorenz feels that aggression actually has survival value for the species. Since population density often outruns available food supplies, aggression acts both to reduce the size of the population and to spread the remaining population over a larger area (Lorenz, 1966). Another ethologist, Robert Ardrey, suggests that aggression results from a fundamental territorial need. Ardrey says that all organisms have an innate drive to own, defend, and gain territorial areas (Ardrey, 1966). The ethological explanation runs the risk of possibly having ventured beyond the actual observed data. Since Lorenz has based his theory on observations of lower organisms, more research is needed before extrapolation to the human level can become convincing.

Frustration-aggression Led by Neil Miller and John Dollard, a group of Yale psychologists in the late 1930s introduced the now famous **frustration-aggression hypothesis** (Dollard et al., 1939). Aggression was explained as the result of being frustrated, or of having one's goals blocked. Said Miller, "The occurrence of aggression always presupposes frustration" (Miller, 1941). In many instances the Miller-Dollard hypothesis is obviously valid. We have all seen people become angry, sometimes to the point of irrationality, over having a goal blocked: An individual already late for an important appointment becomes furious when the car won't start; a teenage boy gets into a fistfight on the way home from school after having been dropped from the varsity basketball team.

One psychologist has identified five important sources of frustration in modern life, frustrations that in some cases can become persistent sources of irritation (Morris, 1990).

1. *Delay*—As in the case mentioned above of the person made late for a meeting because the car wouldn't start

2. *Failure*—As in the case of the young man cut from the basketball team or a high school student being rejected for admission to a preferred college

3. *Lack of resources*—As when a lack of finances prevents the purchase of some dearly sought item

4. *Losses*—As when a close friend moves to a far-off city or an affair of the heart is abruptly ended

5. *Discrimination*—As when a society prevents some of its citizens from full participation in its resources because of race or sex

The frustration-aggression hypothesis, however, does have some major drawbacks as an explanatory model. Some people react to frustration not with overt aggression but merely by sitting quietly and seething inwardly. Another person may respond to goal blockage by regressing, that is, acting in a less mature fashion. Also, there are countless examples of aggressive behaviors that are not triggered by frustration. Being annoyed or attacked by another person often results in aggression aimed at the source of the annoyance. A student was playing poker in the dorm when, without provocation, another student moved quietly behind his chair and playfully poured beer on his head. Five seconds and two punches later the "playful pourer" was on his back and nursing a bruised eye and jaw.

For these and other reasons, the original frustration-aggression hypothesis has been revised, most recently by Leonard Berkowitz. Berkowitz says that frustration may produce a range of emotions from disappointment and depression to anger. Although anger may lead to aggression, other emotions generated by frustration usually do not. Also, how someone responds to frustration is in large measure a direct function of how the person handled frustration in the past.

In summary, Berkowitz says, "I therefore revised the [frustration-aggression] hypothesis to state that anger is only one of the possible emotional responses to frustration, and aggression is one of the possible behavioral responses (Berkowitz, 1983).

Social learning or modeling

As we noted in Chapter 10, Albert Bandura's social learning theory has been used to explain aggressive behavior. Children who watched an adult model punch and kick a large Bobo doll themselves punched and kicked the doll when they later got the chance. In this instance, the children were imitating the adult's aggressive behavior. The children had not been provoked, annoyed, or frustrated, and yet because of modeling they exhibited aggressive responses. It has also been shown that if children watch a film of an aggressive adult model, they, too, will imitate the aggressive behavior (Bandura et al., 1963).

That social learning is at least one of the factors involved in the development of aggressive behavior

"This will teach you not to hit people."
Copyright © 1951, reprinted by permission of *Saturday Review* and Stanley Stamaty.

seems now to be in little doubt. Many studies have reported that children who exhibit high levels of overt aggressive behavior typically have parents who use physical punishment. In fact, the parents of aggressive children are more apt to use punishment than reward when attempting to shape their children's general behavior. That this tends to be a potent influence is shown by the fact that the level of a boy's aggressiveness is usually formed by about the age of eight (even before the onset of puberty) (Eron, 1982).

It seems clear that children can and do learn aggressive responses by watching the aggressive behavior of parents and other adults. It is also true that children may learn to modify their aggressive responses by observing the consequences others have earned for their aggression (Slife and Ryschlak, 1982). For example, children are not so quick to imitate adult aggression when they also witness the adult being punished for that behavior.

Aggression and the Mass Media

One question that has recently become of great concern to social psychologists is whether the portrayal of violence in movies and on TV encourages aggressive acts on the part of the viewer. This question is especially important with regard to TV since most children are avid television viewers. One survey report indicates that the average sixteen-year-old has spent more hours of his or her young life in front of the TV than in class. Some of the studies done in this area have shown a relationship, especially among boys, between watching violence on television and the acting out of aggression. In the typical study a group of boys are asked to indicate which TV shows they watch, and these results are then correlated with the peer group's evaluation of each boy's overt aggressiveness. Significant relationships have been discovered. That is, boys who report watching the most TV violence are also the ones rated most aggressive by their peers (Eron, 1982). As we pointed out in Chapter 15, studies such as these are difficult to evaluate in terms of the direction of the possible cause-and-effect relationship. Does the violence on TV cause the boys to be aggressive, or does aggressiveness in boys cause them to select violent TV shows? Or are some boys aggressive by nature, and because of this do they act out their aggression more and do they also choose to watch more aggressive TV shows? With correlational research studies such as these, the direction of the relationship is virtually impossible to interpret.

Milgram attempted an experimental evaluation of this problem by using a large portion of the United States as his laboratory. Milgram talked CBS into creating two versions of a popular TV program, one version having far more aggressive cues than the other. Milgram was unable to detect any difference in the rates of violence among the cities on the basis of whether they received the aggressive or the nonaggressive programs, even though the cities were equated for prior levels of violent crimes (Milgram and Shotland, 1973).

Finally, in an attempt to subject this problem to a controlled, experimental analysis, a study was conducted in which the TV fare was actually manipulated (as an independent variable) by the experimenter (Feshback and Singer, 1970). The subjects, again all boys, were enrolled in private boarding schools or state residential schools. By random assignment, the boys were required to watch either violent or nonviolent shows. Both before and after six weeks of this controlled-viewing regimen, the boys were measured for both overt and covert aggressiveness. Overt aggressiveness was determined by a supervisor's daily tally of each boy's aggressive incidents. Covert aggressiveness was measured by projective personality testing.

The results showed that the boys who watched the violent TV shows expressed more covert or fantasy aggression as measured by the Thematic Apperception Test. The boys who watched the nonviolent shows, however, exhibited twice as many fist fights and far more overt, verbal aggression. The results suggest that TV violence has a possibly cathartic effect on boys, rechanneling their hostility so as to inhibit overt aggression. The authors of the study caution, however, that watching real-life violence on newscasts may increase rather than decrease the expression of aggressive responses on the part of the viewer. They say that "violence presented in the form of fiction is much less likely to reinforce, stimulate, or elicit aggressive responses than violence in the form of a news event (Feshback, 1969). Thus, whereas TV's coverage of a violent news story may increase viewer aggression, fictitious violence may possibly even inhibit overt viewer aggression. This is obviously a very difficult area to research. As we have seen, the results, and more important, the interpretations of the results in this area, seem to flip-flop.

Certainly, the amount of televised aggression has not diminished over the years. In one study, in which an index of TV violence was calculated, it was found that although the percentage of programs containing violence had not increased between the years 1967 and 1984, the number of violent acts per program had (Pearl, 1984).

Over a ten-year period, the National Institute of Mental Health (NIMH) has evaluated hundreds of studies on the issue of television and aggression. Their report suggests the following:

1. More violence is being portrayed in children's weekend cartoon programs than in adult, prime-time shows.

2. Heavy viewing of violence on TV is clearly associated with aggression, especially among young children (Pearl et al., 1982).

It is, of course, not clear from any of these studies whether the TV violence causes the behavioral aggression or whether children who are more overtly aggressive choose to watch the more violent TV programs. It is interesting to note that in this same report from NIMH it was pointed out that young boys watch more of the violent TV programs than do young girls.

It is also known that young boys are more overtly aggressive than young girls.

One cannot casually dismiss the possibly profound effects that television has on viewer behavior. The advertisers obviously believe that television affects behavior, and they back up their belief not just with a heartfelt wish but by spending millions of dollars for commercials.

Nature or Nurture?

Like the great intelligence debate, the question of whether aggression is primarily innate or learned has also stirred controversy among psychologists. The nature theorists see humans as instinctively violent, destined by their genes to be aggressive. The nurture position is that humans, being a product of environmental stimulation, can be shaped into peaceful and loving beings. Indeed, the four positions on aggression just outlined can be categorized according to this issue. Both the Freudian and ethological positions rest on the assumption that aggression is largely inherited. Both the frustration-aggression and social learning explanations, however, view aggression as basically a product of the environment.

The genetic argument   As pointed out in Chapter 3, white mice have been selectively bred for aggressiveness. In one study, a large group of mice was separated on the basis of the amount of aggressiveness displayed. The most aggressive and least aggressive mice were then selectively bred, and after seven generations two nonoverlapping groups were identified. That is, the least aggressive of the aggressive strain were more aggressive than the most aggressive of the nonaggressive strain (Lagerspetz, 1964).

At the human level, a number of studies have compared monozygotic (MZ), or identical, twins with dizygotic (DZ), or fraternal, twins on the criterion of aggression. Regarding crimes of violence, it has been found that the concordance rate (the percentage of cotwins having the trait) was significantly higher for MZ than for DZ twins (Rosenthal, 1970). Since MZ twins result from a single fertilized egg, they have identical genetic endowments. DZ twins derive from separate eggs fertilized at the same time and are thus no more alike genetically than other siblings.

The environmental argument   Psychologists holding the environmental view see aggression as resulting from the way society reinforces and punishes its members' attitudes and behavior. The environmentalists state that the attitudes of the majority of people in each society determine whether or not violence will be tolerated. Cultures are cited in which aggression is apparently almost nonexistent, and other cultures have been found in which hostility is a major characteristic. In short, the environmentalists argue that aggression is determined by group norms and the frustrations of day-to-day living.

Is there an answer?   As is the case with so many areas in psychology, all the answers are not yet in on the issue of human aggression. It is known, however, that behavior is caused by many factors, and perhaps the safest prediction is that aggression will be found to result from heredity interacting with environment interacting with time. The fact that there is a genetic component in aggression seems to be fairly well established. Also, the built-in aggressive tendencies emerge at different times through maturation, depending on individual differences, sex, and species. Just as certainly, since aggression can be expressed in so many ways and in so many different situations, there is obviously a very large learning component to it. Harry Harlow comments:

> There is little disagreement among comparative psychologists that aggression is part of the biological heritage of primates. However, some social psychologists who limit their studies to the human animal still believe that aggression is basically a learned behavior, and that the differences which occur between the sexes or among individuals within their sex group are accountable solely on the basis of experience. No doubt the late appearance of aggression in the developmental sequence has led some observers to underestimate its biological basis (Harlow et al., 1971, p. 114).

STATUS AND ROLE

If you met someone for the first time and she suddenly put her hand into your mouth, you might be pretty startled. Or, suppose a perfect stranger told you to take off all your clothes. Your reaction might be hard to predict. Yet all of us have been in situations like these and have hardly blinked. When the individual putting her hand into your mouth is a dentist, or the stranger telling you to undress is a physician, the situation has a context in which the behavior is expected.

Social psychologists use the term's **status** and **role** to describe expected behavior of this type. Status is the position we occupy in society's prestige hierarchy. Role is the behavior that is expected of us because of the particular status we have. Conformity is essential to status and role because status gives us an obligation to behave (act out the role) in the way society expects us to behave (conform to society's expectations). For example, our society expects far different behavior from a used-car salesman than from a college president. People might smile if the used-car salesman created a drunken scene in public, but they would be severely disapproving if the college president did the very same thing. Our behavior is expected to conform to society's norms for our position in life. If it does not conform to these expectations, society has ways of exerting great pressure to bring us back into line.

Because of the complicated nature of our society today, most people find themselves occupying different status positions at the same time. A man may have a job as a clerk in a shop and spend each day quietly taking orders, while at night he issues directives with an authoritative flourish in his capacity as Boy Scout executive. In each case his role conforms to his status. A given status often has multiple roles. A woman may have a number of status positions and roles, as mother, clubwoman, wife, and corporate executive. The variety of roles may create conflict and a feeling of frustration and despair if she feels that she cannot carry out all her roles—that, for example, she can't continue to work and also fulfill the role of a good mother. Yet if she doesn't work, she may feel frustrated and perhaps even guilty over the fact that she isn't living up to her full potential as a woman.

It is crucial to understand role behavior in order to understand human behavior. People tend to behave in the way society (as embodied by the people around them) treats them. One of the contributing factors in adolescent rebellion is the lack of consistency with which society treats this nonchild-nonadult. When adolescents are treated like children, they will tend to respond like children, no matter how many speeches they hear about their failure to assume responsibility or act maturely. The parents' words are often drowned out by the volume of their own contradictory behavior.

The Influence of Expectations

Expectations and older siblings   Just as a teacher's expectations and consequent treatment of a pupil may be in part a function of the child's looks, that is, in overrewarding the good-looking child and underrewarding the unattractive child (See Spotlight On Expectations and "Looks" on page 510), so too may teacher expectations be influenced by the past performances of a pupil's older sibling. Although teacher remarks such as "I never had this kind of trouble with your sister" tend to frustrate and burden a child, they can, in fact, work to the child's advantage. One study found that a child received higher grades from teachers who knew and admired an older sibling than from teachers who had no such previous knowledge (Seaver, 1973). This is simply one more example of the Rosenthal effect in the classroom—teacher's judgments are clearly affected by expectations.

A summary of the research on the relationship between teacher expectations and student achievement again demonstrates the power of this important phenomenon (Good, 1981). Because of its power, efforts have been made to train teachers to guard against this source of bias. The Teacher Expectations and Student Achievement (TESA) program was designed to sensitize teachers to their own, often subtle, negative treatment of those perceived as low-achieving children. The TESA technique appears to have had a positive impact when used as part of the Connecticut School Improvement Program (Proctor, 1984).

Expectations and personality   Even the developing child's basic personality structure is largely shaped by social expectations, especially those of the parents. Much of what a child begins to expect of himself or herself develops from the child's attempts to gain parental approval and to live up to parental expectations. As personality theorists Joseph Perez and Alvin Cohen say, "For the developing self, 'Mom and Dad are me' " (Perez and Cohen, 1969).

Expectations and teacher behavior   Just as the teacher's evaluation of a student is often clouded by certain preconceived expectations, so students' ratings of their teachers are influenced in the same manner. If a student has been told that her new teacher "really knows her stuff" or "has her act together," or that "she's a hard marker but you're really going to learn something," then the student will almost certainly perceive that teacher in a positive manner. As the weeks go by, however, the teacher must really earn the positive image that the student brought into

SPOTLIGHT ON EXPECTATIONS AND "LOOKS"

Never Judge a Book by Its Cover

It has long been assumed that some individuals tend to get by on their looks. That is, the individual's appearance, his or her own physical stimulus value, seems to influence the kinds of expectations and treatment provided by other people. Much research evidence suggests that this is indeed the case. In one study, now a classic, attractive individuals were judged to possess more positive personality traits, to hold more prestigious occupations, and to have more potential for future success than were unattractive people.[a] This stereotype about physical attractiveness apparently begins early in life, at least by the time the child reaches kindergarten.[b] By the time children are five years old they can differentiate between handsome and homely classmates. Attractive first-graders are thought by their peers to be more independent and better-liked. Asked who they would pick as someone who "scares you" or as someone who's "afraid of lots of things," children generally select unattractive peers. Studies have also shown that during the elementary and adolescent years, perceptions of physical appearance and social acceptance correlate strongly with a child's feeling of self-worth.[c]

But this type of bias is not just a childish, schoolroom phenomenon. Studies have consistently shown that employers pay unattractive people less money, bar or restaurant patrons offer smaller tips to unattractive waiters, jurors tend to find unattractive witnesses less believable, and voters tend to think that unattractive candidates for public office are less worthy of being elected.[d] In a study of sexual harassment cases, it was found that guilty verdicts are significantly more likely if the defendant (in this study the male) is unattractive and the female plaintiff is highly attractive.[e] "Even in the anti-glamor, egalitarian feminist movement, leader Betty Freidan says that her rival, Gloria Steinem, jumped ahead of her because of her looks."[f] Gloria Steinem, however, had underestimated her physical attractiveness and remained seemingly unaware of her good looks; for years she felt that she was really an ugly duckling. It wasn't until she increased her own inner feelings of self-esteem that she finally realized that she was also a beautiful woman on the outside.[g] This relationship between self-esteem and attractiveness can be reciprocal, since the research shows that when people overestimate their physical attractiveness (as opposed to underestimating it as Steinem had), they also tend to hold higher levels of self-esteem.[h]

Although we've all been warned not to judge a book by its cover, it is all too easy to ignore that sage advice. What this means to the teacher should be obvious: The attractive and docile child should not be overrewarded with high grades and praise—"looks" should not be confused with achievement.

---

[a] K. Dion, E. Berscheid, and E. Walster, What is beautiful is good? *Journal of Personality* (1972), 24, 285–290.

[b] E. Berscheid and E. Walster, Beauty and the best. *Psychology Today* (1972), 5(10), 42–46.

[c] A. Wigfield and M. Karpathian, Who am I and what can I do? Children's self-concepts and motivation in achievement situations. *Educational Psychologist* (1991), 26(3,4), 223–261.

[d] D. Umberson and M. Hughes, The impact of physical attractiveness on achievement and psychological well being. *Social Psychology Quarterly* (1987), 50, 227–236.

[e] W. A. Castellow, K. L. Wuensch, and C. H. Moore, Effects of physical attractiveness of the plaintiff and defendant in sexual harassment judgments. *Journal of Social Behavior and Personality* (1990), 5, 547–562.

[f] F. Grieve, For ugly people a hard cold world. *Boston Globe*, February 19, 1987, 67–68.

[g] G. Steinem, *Revolution from within: A book of self-esteem* (New York: Little, Brown, 1992).

[h] E. B. Gurman and M. Balban, Self-evaluation of physical attractiveness as a function of self-esteem and defensiveness. *Journal of Social Behavior and Personality* (1990), 5, 575–580.

the class. Some teachers have the ability to generate positive feelings in students from the very first day, even if the students have not received any information about the teacher's reputation. Research has shown that the teacher's physical appearance is the most important single source of initial student expectations (Hurt et al., 1978). The teacher who "looks good" is immediately perceived as a person who *is* good—at teaching, counseling, whatever. But again, as the term wears on, the students begin using more substantive measures of effectiveness. A teacher can get by on looks and style for only a limited time. Even firstgraders are soon able to spot the phony, the teacher who is really not doing the job. Style without substance is like a book with a pretty cover but filled with blank pages.

Sex Roles in Society and in the School

Right from the day the child is born, parents tend to perceive and then treat differently their male and female children. Even in the absence of objective differences, parents are apt to rate newborn girls as softer and smaller than newborn boys, whereas newborn boys are rated as bigger, stronger, and hardier than newborn girls. These differential perceptions tend to persist and strengthen as the child develops. Parents play different types of games with their male and female children, the boys virtually always being involved in more rough-and-tumble games (especially when playing with the father) (Huston, 1983). When all this is added to the fact that the bedrooms of boys and girls are decorated differently, that the toys they are given are different, that the activities planned for them are different, and that the *expectational demands* on them differ dramatically, it is little wonder that intellectual and temperamental gender differences eventually emerge (Snow, Jacklin, and Maccoby, 1983). Eleanor Maccoby, however, reminds us again that personality is not just a function of environment, that children are not just passive recipients of cultural pressures. We should remember psychology's important axiom concerning the interaction of environment, heredity, and time in the formation of personal traits and behaviors. Although society treats boys and girls differently, some elements of those differences are contributed by the children themselves. The influence between adult and child is a two-way street, and some of the treatment differences between the sexes reflect differences in the ways boys and girls react to these treatments (Maccoby, 1991).

Yet even in this seemingly enlightened age, the message of sexism can be stark. In the winter of 1989, one of the authors of this text witnessed the following scene at a Vermont ski area: The mother of a small boy reprimanded him for being, as she thought, overly cautious in his skiing. To dramatize her point, she suddenly pointed to a girl who was gliding effortlessly down the slope (a girl who was, incidentally, at least two years older than her son) and further admonished the boy by loudly proclaiming, "Look how brave she is, *and she's only a girl.*"

Just as the school often acts to transmit the traditional values of the larger culture in general, it also transmits society's version of the sex role. Boys are encouraged to be more "masculine" and girls to be "ladylike." One recent analysis indicated that this transmittal is done, often inadvertently, in three ways:

1. Schools encourage sex typing by separating male and female activities and interest areas. Young boys are more apt to be sent to the "block corner," whereas girls are placed in the "housekeeping" and art areas.

2. Teachers project sex-typed expectations—exactly the kind of situation that role theory would predict. If teachers expect little boys to be less manageable than little girls, the boys pick up these cues and don't let the teachers down.

3. Schools have typically created an ideal "pupil role." The ideal pupil is conforming, docile, dependent, and manageable—that is, the pupil exhibits the very traits that have traditionally defined the female role. By more easily adopting this role, girls learn to be more receptive than active. Boys, in contrast, have more difficulty in conforming to this ideal-pupil image and thus often find school to be a stressful and alienating experience (Lee and Gropper, 1975).

Role and Personality

Although the pressure of group expectancies is a powerful influence on our behavior, our basic personality will determine the way in which our role in the group is interpreted and carried out. The fact that individual behavior is consistent across different roles in different groups shows that we each bring an integrated and coherent behavioral unity to our groups. The way in which role and personality interrelate is reciprocal. The role we play in a group also has a definite impact on our personality. For example, an actor who for years plays the "tough guy" in the movies may slowly incorporate this image into his personality and may begin to believe and act as if he *is* that tough guy.

The therapy technique called *psychodrama* is based on this notion. Neurotic patients are put on the stage and given roles that they typically find uncomfortable to act out. With encouragement, and in the context of a nonthreatening situation, they learn the behavior required for certain roles and experience a concomitant personality change. The relationship between role and personality also works the other way. We will consciously or unconsciously select roles that are consistent with our underlying personality. Extroverted personalities usually assume roles that allow them to stay in the limelight, while introverts adopt roles that keep them away from stage front.

Studies have shown that the majority of college seniors majoring in education prefer to work with people rather than things and describe themselves as "conventional in opinions and values" (Davis, 1964). Teachers also tend to score above average in such personality areas as friendliness, sociability, and personal relations. A summary of the research on teacher personality profiles as determined by the Minnesota Multiphasic Personality Inventory (MMPI) describes teachers as the following:

1. Responsible, conscientious, conforming, and friendly

2. Likely to emphasize control of self and adaptation to the needs and demands of others (Johnson, 1970).

Evidence indicates that the personalities of teachers are fairly consistent with the role demands of their job. However, the research in this area is correlational, meaning that the interpretations can go either way. In other words, teachers may have a personality style that causes them to select the role of teacher, or the role demands of the teaching position may shape the personalities of those involved in the teaching profession. The best guess is that both selection and shaping are involved.

LEADERSHIP

The highest position in the status hierarchy of any group is that of leader. The leader has the most influence in shaping the group's norms and expectations. Before relating styles of leadership with group functioning, we must first get some understanding of the concept of leadership itself.

Is leadership something we either have or don't have? Are there people who, regardless of the group, the social setting, the cultural norm, will always rise to the top? Or is leadership strictly a function of the group norms, the task being performed, or the social context? In other words, is leadership a quality of the individual or a quality of the group?

Theories of Leadership

The great-leader theory   The great-leader theory sees leadership as a quality of the individual. In its boldest form the theory states that certain individuals possess just the right blend of looks, personality traits, and intelligence to be almost automatically thrust into leadership positions. These individuals—who are said to have **charisma**—will always become leaders in any situation or in any group. Charisma is a kind of personal magnetism and hypnotic appeal. When a charismatic person walks into a room, the room is suddenly charged with excitement, and the others in it become submissive and willing to follow the individual anywhere. As one theorist explains it, "charisma is a compulsive, inexplicable emotional tie linking a group of followers together in adulation of their leader" (Lindholm, 1990, p. 6). Some of history's charismatic leaders include Mahatma Gandhi, Joan of Arc, Winston Churchill, Cleopatra, John F. Kennedy, Martin Luther King, Jesse Jackson, and Pope John Paul II. Charisma also has its dark side in the form of Adolph Hitler and his Third Reich, Charles Manson and his "family," and Jim Jones and the "People's Temple." Each had a personal appeal that is spellbinding, almost mystical. People such as these, says this theory, have to become leaders regardless of the times in which they live.

The group theory   According to the group theory, almost anyone who fulfills some basic need of the group can be a leader. And, since the needs of the group shift, so too does leadership. For example, a group on a camping trip would see leadership constantly changing according to the dictates of the situation. If the group became lost, the individual with the compass would become the leader. If someone became injured, the person with first-aid knowledge and supplies would become the leader.

Even history's great leaders are explained on this basis. Winston Churchill became a leader late in his career, when the times called for someone with his special talents. Hitler would have found no followers and would have probably had to spend his entire life painting portraits in Austria had Germany not been rocked by runaway inflation and crushing depression. The group theory suggests that the unfolding of history is like the opening of a combination lock—only when a certain sequence of events occurs will a certain individual be called upon to lead.

A blending of the theories   The actual evidence regarding leadership now suggests that the best explanation lies somewhere between these two theories. Both theories are needed to account for the data. Certain individual qualities do seem to be more common in leaders than in other group members. For example, leaders tend to be taller but not too much taller, and more intelligent but not too much more intelligent, than other members of the group. Leaders also seem to possess more social skills than followers. For example, leaders are apt to give more information, ask for more information, and make more interpretations about a situation (Cartwright and Zander, 1953). Among other personal traits that appear to enhance a leader's effectiveness are:

1. Self-confidence
2. Ability to manipulate others
3. Ability to satisfy the needs of others
4. Great personal persistence
5. Strong motivation to attain a group goal (Barker et al., 1983).

But it has also become increasingly evident that the demands of the situation are crucial in determining the group's choice of a leader. One study of schoolchildren found that the boy who could spit the farthest was the leader in the first grade. By fourth grade it was the child who "sassed" the teacher the most. In high school the girl who had always stayed in the background in grade school suddenly blossomed into leadership because of her "dating power" (Cunningham, 1984). Also, the former major league pitching star and philosopher extraordinaire, Bill Lee, said that he never did think much of leadership as a unitary trait. "As far as I was concerned the best leadership is provided by a grand slam home run that overcomes a three-run lead, or by a shutout that stops a losing streak" (Lee, 1985, p. 98). Even the mystique of charisma, has by some, been partially defined in situational terms. In this sense, the leader is imbued with charisma by his or her followers when the number and intensity of the leader's behaviors are perceived as compellingly relevant to the current situation (Conger, 1989). Thus, the demands and values of the group are just as important in determining leadership as are many of the personal qualities listed above. Leadership results when the individual's qualities match the group's demands.

Leadership and Gender

Of all the personal traits usually assumed to correlate with effective leadership, perhaps the most pervasive is simply that of being a male. This is undoubtedly the result of conscious or unconscious bias, and, of course, sex stereotyping. The facts, however, tend to dispel this leadership myth. When men and women *of equal leadership experience* are compared on the basis of their actual influence on a group in getting the job done, there are usually no significant differences between them (Hollander and Yoder, 1980). Of course, differences in leadership skills do exist between experienced men and inexperienced women. However, despite the equal effectiveness of men and women, groups still tend to evaluate autocratic female leaders more negatively than autocratic male leaders (Jago and Vroom, 1982). This again points to a certain degree of bias against women leaders, perhaps in this case due in part to the fact that people in general have had less experience dealing with autocratic women in leadership positions.

Styles of Leadership

Most of you have been members of many different groups—scout troops, athletic teams, school clubs, whatever. You have thus been exposed to various styles of leadership, and you may have noticed that the efficiency of the group's performance and the satisfaction of the group's members were due in large measure to the style of the group's leadership. You may recall a coach who was so lenient that the team failed to perform according to expectations. Or perhaps you remember a scout leader who was so rigid and domineering that most of the members quit and the troop had to fold.

Many years ago Kurt Lewin, who had once been a student of Max Wertheimer, conducted an experiment to assess the ways in which groups respond to different kinds of leadership (Lewin et al., 1939). One aspect of the study was to compare the effects of **authoritarian** and **democratic styles of leadership** on group activity. The subjects were young boys who were placed in "club" groups under the direction of adult leaders. The authoritarian leader was domineering, never asking for suggestions about group activities and controlling every aspect of the group situation. The democratic leader, in contrast, guided the group gently, constantly asking for suggestions

SPOTLIGHT ON SOCIAL SKILLS

Training in the Classroom

There is a great deal of clinical and descriptive literature regarding the social behavior of many learning-disabled youngsters. This research has generated a growing recognition that most LD children experience significant social difficulties. Accumulated evidence supports the hypothesis that adequate peer social skills do play an important role in child development and academic success, as well as in the long-term adjustment of individuals. In fact, in terms of total-life functioning, social ineptitude tends to be more disabling than academic difficulties.[a]

The questions raised are: Can social skills be taught in the classroom? and Are teachers equipped to teach these skills? The answer to both questions is quite simply yes! In fact, the same methods used to teach academic skills can be used to teach social skills. The emphasis on increasing prosocial behaviors should be of benefit to all students in the classroom, not just the learning-disabled. Social skills interventions can be readily incorporated into the general management of the classroom so that no time be needlessly taken from academic lessons.[b] In addition, evidence suggests that social skills training is directly translated into improved academic performance by increasing the child's self-esteem, attending behavior, on-task behavior, and ability to follow directions and complete tasks.

Intervention strategies should target behaviors that are valued in the child's environment, for example, improving conversation skills or learning how to express feelings more appropriately. However, determining what is considered appropriate for a given child demands an understanding of the child and the child's background. Appropriate behavior may vary according to age, sex, socioeconomic level, race and, of course, the situation itself. Contextual variables must always be considered. Effective interventions include the following:

1. *Positive reinforcement*—which should be given whenever behavior is appropriate
2. *Cooperative learning strategies*—which help create an environment that increases the probability of positive social interactions
3. *Modeling appropriate behavior*—both in a natural setting or by observing a videotaped model
4. *Direct coaching*—which involves verbal instruction concerning the appropriate behavior
5. *Rehearsal*—which provides the opportunity for the child to practice the modeled behavior
6. *Constant feedback*—to help the child monitor improved behaviors
7. *Self-talk*—which helps the child develop strategies for retrieving the newly learned social skill and *maintain* a focus on the use of that skill

Research evidence clearly shows that the most important aspect in the teaching of social skills is to teach the *specific skills directly* rather than spend time sermonizing about general rules of conduct.[c]

This Spotlight was especially prepared for this volume by Dr. Antoinette Spinelli-Nannen, Director, School Psychology Program, American International College.

[a] A. Spinelli-Nannen, An investigation of the personality assessment system as a discriminator of socially misperceptive tendencies in elementary students. Unpublished doctoral dissertation (Springfield, Mass.: American International College, 1987).

[b] F. M. Gresham, Best practices in social skills assessment. In A. Thomas and J. Grines (Eds.), *Best practices in school psychology* (Washington: National School Psychology Association, 1990).

[c] S. N. Elliot, Acceptability of behavioral treatments in educational settings. In J. C. Witt, S. N. Elliot, and F. M. Gresham (Eds.), *Handbook of behavior therapy in education* (New York: Plenum Press, 1988), pp. 121–150.

and allowing the group to make decisions. The results of the study indicated that completely different atmospheres were generated in the two groups. The democratic group's members were more satisfied, more cooperative, less hostile, and better able to carry on group activities when the leader was not present. Though the authoritarian group did have a higher rate of production (building model planes), the work of the democratic group was of a higher quality.

Leadership style has been shown in study after study to affect the behavior, perceptions, and feelings of group members. Clearly, group members perceive democratic leaders more favorably than authoritarian leaders. Leaders who use the participatory leadership style are liked better by the group members than are those using the autocratic style. In one study, college students were placed in groups led either by a participatory (democratic) leader or an autocratic leader. The leaders who utilized the participatory style received more positive evaluations than did those using the autocratic style (Jago and Vroom, 1982).

Classroom Leadership

Although the teacher is handed the main leadership role in the classroom, other leaders are also present. In large measure, the broad base of influence from which the teacher operates shapes the social climate in the classroom. The degree to which the teacher is authoritarian or submissive or coercive or democratic sets the tone for norm formation in the classroom. But, once school has been in session for a few weeks, student leaders begin to emerge. Again, it is the teacher who, to a large extent, may determine which students attain leadership positions. The teacher may encourage and reinforce leadership behavior of one child and withhold reinforcement when the same behavior is exhibited by another child. Yet the teacher can also succumb to reinforcement. One prominent sociologist has said that "influence over others is purchased at the price of allowing one's self to be influenced by others" (Homans, 1961, p. 116). This sociologist feels that an influential leader must have the esteem of everyone in the group. This means that students can exert considerable pressure on a teacher by giving or withholding their esteem and that they can, by this means, shape their teacher's behavior. It also explains why a given teacher might be a successful leader with one group of students and not so successful with a different group.

Social psychology assumes that leadership ability is a set of behavioral skills that most people can learn. One psychologist says that effective leadership depends on the following.

1. Flexible behavior
2. The ability to know what behaviors are needed at a particular time in order for the group to function most efficiently
3. The ability to behave as required or to get other members of the group to do so

An effective leader must learn to spot what the group needs in a given situation and then be flexible enough "to provide diverse types of behaviors that are required under different conditions" (Johnson, 1970, p. 128). The effective leader must also get the cooperation of various members of the group so that they will help perform the necessary group functions.

GROUP DYNAMICS IN THE CLASSROOM

The classroom is a collection of interdependent individuals. The dynamics of their interrelationships depend on the roles that have been established through interaction. Whenever there is a change in the expected behavior of any group member, the dynamic interrelationships of the entire group—that is, the **group dynamics**—must necessarily change. The pressure on role behavior is so great that if a group has certain expectations about an individual's behavior, that individual usually responds in a way consistent with those expectations. The group's expectations become a self-fulfilling prophecy.

In a two-person group, or dyad, the expectations of the superordinate member clearly determine the behavior of the subordinate member. Suppose a mother is convinced that red hair causes a child to have a quick temper. She will then tolerate the temper tantrums of her red-haired child, while at the same time extinguishing these same responses in her blond or brunette children. Or, suppose a high school student complains that his mother treats him as if he were a child; an objective analysis of the student's behavior may reveal that he indeed doesn't let his mother down—he acts like a child. Or, imagine a husband who complains that his wife is domineering. During the conversation he mentions that he recently dropped one of his wife's plant pots and was thereupon banished to the cellar, where his son later brought him his supper. In each case, the dynamic relationship between the people involved could exist only if both members played their expected roles. If the student who was being treated like a child stopped acting like a child, his mother would have to change her expectations and thus her behavior toward him. The man with the domineering wife must have played the role of a dominated husband to the hilt. Why else would he meekly allow himself to be served dinner in the cellar? In the words of a once-popular song, "It takes two to tango." There can be no tango, or any other consistent form of interaction, unless both partners play their expected roles.

KENNETH B. CLARK

Kenneth B. Clark, noted educator and psychologist, was born in the Panama Canal Zone in 1914. Clark's father, Arthur B. Clark, was a passenger agent for the United Fruit Company in Panama. When young Clark was five years old, his mother left Panama for the United States, bringing her children with her. To support the children, Mrs. Clark worked as a seamstress in a New York garment factory, where she also helped organize a union. Clark says his first contact with social issues was listening to his mother tell of her problems in trying to organize the union in her shop.

Clark graduated from Howard University in 1935, and received his M.A. in 1936. For the next two years Clark taught psychology at Howard, but the following year he enrolled as a Ph.D. candidate in experimental psychology at Columbia University. He was awarded his degree in 1940, and during the academic year 1940–1941 he became an assistant professor of psychology at the Hampton Institute in Virginia. The following year, Clark worked as a social science analyst for the Office of War Information, traveling throughout the country studying morale problems in black population centers. In 1942 he joined the psychology department of the College of the City of New York; he became a full professor in 1960.

In 1946 Clark and his wife, Dr. Mamie Clark, established the nonprofit Northside Center for Child Development in New York City. The center is devoted to treating children with emotional problems. In 1950 Clark worked on a report that showed that segregation in the schools is detrimental to the growth and development of white as well as black children. The U.S. Supreme Court relied on Clark's study when, in 1954, it made its important decision that segregation in public schools is unconstitutional.

Clark has devoted his life to improving school conditions for all children. He has found racial prejudice to be a two-edged sword that harms both the prejudiced as well as the objects of the prejudice. In 1970 Clark received his colleagues' highest honor when he was named president of the American Psychological Association. During his presidency, he established the Board of Social and Ethical Responsibility for Psychology. His many articles and books include *Desegregation: An Appraisal of the Evidence* (1953), *Prejudice and Your Child* (1955), *Dark Ghetto* (1965), *A Relevant War against Poverty* (1968), and *Pathos of Power* (1974).

Clark is now president of Kenneth B. Clark & Associates, Inc., a consulting firm involved in personnel and race relations and affirmative action programs. In 1978 Clark was selected by the American Psychological Association to receive its Distinguished Contribution to Psychology in the Public Interest Award.

As an educator and psychologist, Clark ranks at the top of his profession. Although a brilliant theorist, he has not sought refuge in an ivory tower but prefers to remain on the front lines, working, doing, and making things happen. He is without question psychology's most prominent spokesperson for social justice.

Changing the role of one individual in the group may change the whole group, since the classroom is a collection of interdependent individuals and the dynamics of their interrelationship depend on roles established through interaction.

In a classic case reported by learning theorist Edwin R. Guthrie, a group of male college students decided to make an all-out effort to cater extravagantly to a shy, socially inept coed. They made sure she was invited to all the social functions, constantly flattered her with gifts and attention, and in general saw that she was the "belle of the ball." By the end of the college year she had developed an easy, confident manner and had become a popular campus favorite even among those not aware of the original plot. Says Guthrie, "What her college career would have been if the experiment had not been made is impossible to say, but it is fairly certain that she would have resigned all social ambitions and would have found interests compatible with her social ineptitude" (Guthrie, 1938, p. 158).

The influence of group expectations on individual behavior can also be seen in the area of racial prejudice. Though prejudice is primarily learned in the home, teachers may also implant prejudice, especially during the first few grades. They may not directly teach hatred, but the message still comes through loud and clear. The teacher's differential treatment of minority races and religions sets the stage for dif-

ferential student responses. Black children, for example, can hardly be expected to act maturely in the classroom when they are not treated with dignity and respect. The mass media have also helped to communicate this social distortion. Until the last few years movies typically cast blacks in subservient roles, as maids and servants. The movies also played up stereotypes, often characterizing a black as a wide-eyed, frightened fool. This sort of thing could hardly lend dignity to the black race.

Group expectations can be so powerful that the minority group members may learn to hold the prejudices and stereotyped attitudes toward their own group that the majority group holds. This can be very destructive to the minority group member's self-image (Sprinthall et al., 1971).

The classroom teacher is obviously a potent reinforcer, and through the judicious use of social approval he or she can shape the behavior of the entire class. The teacher must realize, however, that the classroom is a social unit with a dynamically balanced set of role relationships. Any shift in the role of one student necessarily results in a change in the social balance of the entire group. If the teacher clamps

SPOTLIGHT ON BILINGUAL EDUCATION

A Social, Psychological, and Educational Concern

Approximately 10 percent of the school-age population in the United States speaks a native language other than English. These second-language learners, or bilinguals, present special problems to educators. Until the early 1960s, such children were typically placed in the traditional English language curriculum alongside their native English-speaking counterparts in the belief that all ethnic groups should forced to blend into a single "all-American" cultural group. During the sixties, however, public schools suddenly experienced an influx of several thousand Cuban children who had immigrated to the United States with their families. These non-English-speaking children were dropping out of school at what soon became alarmingly high rates. The educational establishment was confronted with several major issues.

Because schools had experienced great difficulty in obtaining valid evaluations of the academic ability of these bilingual children, many children were being incorrectly placed in classes for the mentally retarded. This rather widespread, and certainly unfortunate, practice led in part to the 1974 Supreme Court decision (*Lau v. Nichols*) which set careful guidelines and regulations designed to reverse this trend. School districts were required by the Department of Health, Education and Welfare (DHEW) to develop bilingual educational programs whenever they had twenty or more students from a single language background. Then, in 1984, federal legislation reauthorized school systems to amend these programs to include placing bilingual children in regular school programs with the proviso that instructional aides be available to assist the classroom teacher.

There has been a lively debate among educators over which method is best for educating these children. Two very different approaches are currently in use. One method, the *native language approach*, sometimes called the *indirect method*, provides reading instruction in the child's native language. Proponents of this approach claim that disadvantaged children learn to read and understand concepts best by having their own native language structures reinforced. This allows the bilingual child to perceive the native language as worthwhile and also promotes the child's personal sense of self-esteem.

The second approach, the *direct method*, totally immerses the bilingual children in the language of their new culture. Its proponents believe this will more fully prepare the children for the language demands inherent in their eventual careers and life responsibilities. Advocates of this approach are not concerned with the development of reading skills in the children's first language. Because the numbers of bilingual students are increasing, the prevailing federal and local philosophy appears to be in line with this "direct" approach.

Some educational psychologists argue for a more integrative approach to close the gap between these two methods. This compromise approach is based on the belief that bilingual education methods should focus on assisting children to move as quickly as possible into English-based classes. Two key elements are apparently critical to the success of this approach: (1) that the integration of first-language goals into the curriculum helps develop in children an understanding of the basic components of reading and writing[a] and

down on the class joker, for example, the social climate could shift in a negative direction. The joker may be fulfilling the important role of relieving group tensions in moments of social stress. Removing that function could lead to a far more anxious social climate in which the conditions for learning could deteriorate. By the same token, shutting off the antics of a loudmouth who is motivated more by compulsive attention-seeking than by reducing class tensions could produce better learning conditions for the rest of the class. Some tinkering and adjusting can be attempted, but remember that changing the role of any individual in the group produces changes in the whole group.

All of the variables that have been mentioned in this chapter will be operative at one time or another in almost any classroom. The question is: What kind of a group will the classroom become? The teacher as leader can clearly exert a major influence on the definition of the group. We have noted that classes

(2) that the fostering of classroom conditions which allow students to utilize life experiences in their native language helps build self-confidence and self-esteem—necessary tools for optimal learning (see Chapter 18 on motivation in the classroom). Sarah Hudelson cites an extensive 1987 U.S. General Accounting Office report in which ten experts were asked to review bilingual education research. The conclusion drawn was that *quality* bilingual education is beneficial for English language acquisition.

Experts in the field would agree that not enough evidence is available to show us which is the better method. There are problems inherent in both models currently in use, and integrative methods—though seemingly viable—are still unsubstantiated alternatives. The direct method, for example, is not always being implemented effectively, especially among Spanish-speaking children. In addition, there appears to be a growing interest in the maintenance of ethnic languages, identities, and cultures to sustain a pluralistic society in this country. Our schools have begun to recognize what Catherine R. Stimpson of Rutgers University has called *cultural democracy*, or an understanding that we must listen to a "diversity of voices" in order to be knowledgeable about our culture, past and present.[b]

For these and other reasons, some educators seem to lean toward the native language approach. However, because of certain methodological problems, including the lack of adequate control groups and the possibility of confounding variables, studies have failed to fully support the superiority of that approach.

Part of the difficulty inherent in resolving the bilingual issue is that more research is needed in learning and information processing to shed light on double-language learning in early childhood. As we have seen, the problems produced by proactive and retroactive inhibition are significant under the best of circumstances and may be especially acute for the young child faced with having to learn two languages at the same time. However, we have learned that bilingualism does not necessarily have to impede cognitive development and that cognitive skills acquisition is transferable across cultures and languages.[c]

Currently no definitive answer exists to the question of how best to teach bilingual children. We are a long way from having enough evidence to show us the most effective method. And so the controversy continues, particularly in regions where the concentration of immigrant families is especially high. It would be important to keep in mind that "the fact that we live in a culturally and ethnically diverse society can present problems; but . . . this diversity can be turned into a positive experience for all of us."[d]

This Spotlight was especially prepared for this volume by Carol S. Spafford, American International College.

[a] S. Hudelson, The role of native language literacy in the education of language for minority children. *Language Arts* (1987), 64, 827–841.

[b] D. Ravitch, Multiculturalism. In J. Epstein (Ed.), *The American Scholar* (Washington: Phi Beta Kappa, 1990).

[c] C. J. Ovando, Bilingual/bicultural education: Its legacy and its future. *Phi Beta Kappan* (1983), 64, 538–539.

[d] R. F. Hessong and T. H. Weeks, *Introduction to the Foundations of Education* (New York: Macmillan, 1991).

can run the entire gamut from a collection of egocentric individuals "doing their own thing" to a smoothly functioning machine in which each individual may be defined only as a group member. If the teacher does not know about the social variables or chooses not to exert definitional leadership, the students will impose their own definition. This is likely to create a very awkward situation: The teacher's role will be totally defined by the group. The opposite extreme, in which the teacher sets the classroom atmosphere and educational objectives solely in terms of his or her own needs and values, is equally undesirable. Thus, the way in which a teacher uses concepts such as social facilitation, conformity, competitiveness, cohesiveness, and group pressure is part of the teaching problem. A question of equal significance involves the whole area of social goals and objectives. A knowledge of social psychology can truly help the teacher promote human development through education.

SUMMARY

Social psychology is the study of human behavior in the context of the group situation. Each classroom is a social unit with its own unique set of norms, role relationships, and behavioral expectations. Though the social atmosphere of the classroom is in large part shaped by the teacher, it is also a function of each student's behavior.

Sometimes the influence of the group acts to increase an individual's performance (social facilitation), and sometimes the group's influence decreases an individual's performance (social inhibition). Working in a group situation can increase feelings of competition and anxiety. A student's performance will be facilitated by the group's influence when (1) the student's motivational level is on the low side and (2) the task is neither overly difficult nor overly intellectual.

The risky-shift phenomenon occurs in group situations and seems to promote more risk-taking behavior among the group members than they would otherwise display were they alone. The group situation has also been used to foster the growth of creative ideas through a process called brainstorming, in which individuals are encouraged to call out any ideas they might have on a given subject, no matter how seemingly bizarre.

Cohesiveness is defined as the amount of attraction the group has for its members. Cohesiveness can be increased in a group as a result of (1) an increase in the amount of friendly interaction, (2) an increase in the amount of cooperation, (3) an increase in the group's feeling of status, (4) an outside threat, or (5) a change in the style of leadership.

One result of group life is the overwhelming desire of individuals to conform to the norms of their group. Two major studies indicate the compelling nature of conformity: Sherif's research on the autokinetic effect and Asch's study of group pressure. In each case, the behavior of individuals conformed to the group norm. Though most conformity studies tend to show the power of the group as being repressive to the individual, a study by Milgram showed that the influence of the group may actually allow an individual to act in a more humane and less aggressive fashion.

Despite the pressure to conform exerted by the group, some individuals are less likely to yield than others. Individuals whose locus of control is internal (i.e., who see themselves as being personally in control of their actions and in charge of their destinies) are less likely to conform than individuals whose locus of control is external.

The process of socialization is essentially produced by pressures to conform, whereby the child is literally forced into adopting society's standards. Socialization is necessary to society but produces some loss of personal independence.

Another aspect of socialization is dissonance. When a person feels a lack of consistency between attitudes and deeds, he or she undergoes cognitive dissonance, an uncomfortable feeling of disequilibrium. To reduce the anxiety, the individual attempts to restore consistency by changing actions to conform with attitudes or attitudes to conform with deeds.

Attribution refers to the explanations people give for their own or another person's actions or beliefs. When the attribution is based on internal factors it is called a dispositional attribution, and when based on external factors it is called a situational attribution. The fundamental attribution error occurs when we assign dispositional factors to the actions of others and situational factors to our own actions.

Social psychologists are also concerned with aggression. The Freudian and the ethological positions assume that a major portion of aggressiveness is innately determined; the frustration-aggression hypothesis and social learning theory view aggression as a product of the environment. Studies of the effect of violence in the mass media on aggression have had equivocal results: some indicate that violence on TV has increased aggressive behavior in viewers, while other studies suggest that it may have a cathartic effect.

The behavior of the individual also conforms to the expectations society forms on the basis of one's status and role. Status is one's position or niche in society's prestige hierarchy, and role is the behavior expected of a person having a particular status.

Society assigns roles by sex, and schools typically encourage these sex roles. Although society influences behavior by the role playing it encourages, the personality of each individual determines how a role is interpreted and carried out.

Leaders seem to be chosen on the basis of both personal characteristics and the demands of the group. In a study comparing styles of leadership, democratic versus authoritarian, it was shown that democratic leaders (those who gently guided the group, asked for suggestions, allowed for group decisions, etc.) were apt to have groups in which the members were more satisfied, more cooperative, less hostile, and better able to follow through on group projects even when the leader was absent.

Because of the present status and role requirements of the classroom, the teacher automatically holds the leadership position. He or she is not the only leader, however, for student leaders inevitably arise and can influence the behavior of both the teacher and the other students.

The group dynamics of the classroom, or of any group situation, are based on interdependent status and role relationships. When a group has a certain expectation regarding an individual's behavior, the individual usually responds in a way consistent with that expectation. This can be especially damaging to the minority group child when the group's expectation is based on prejudice and stereotyping.

KEY TERMS AND NAMES

attitudes
attribution theory
authoritarian leadership
autokinetic effect
brainstorming
charisma
Kenneth B. Clark
cognitive dissonance
cohesiveness
conformity
democratic leadership
frustration-aggression hypothesis

great-leader theory
group dynamics
locus of control
risky shift
role
social facilitation
social inhibition
social psychology
socialization
status
Wechsler Intelligence Scale for Children

THEORY INTO PRACTICE: IMPACT OF STATUS AND ROLE ON BEHAVIOR

In this chapter, we have seen, among other things, the impact of status and role on behavior. The influence of a group's expectations on the behaviors of group members can be truly enormous. As has been pointed out, a child who is treated as a baby will soon begin responding in less mature ways, and a child who is treated as an outcast will play the role of the object of the group's scorn. Perhaps even worse, the child who is perceived and treated as though he were stupid after a while begins to believe it and act in ways which confirm the expectations of those who are applying this label. For a fairly dramatic illustration of this phenomenon, try the following:

From your class select two students at random and ask them to leave the room for a few moments and wait outside in the corridor. During their absence, assign roles to each of them. Give one student a high-status position, such as that of a world-famous cultural anthropologist who is visiting your college as part of your institution's faculty development program. Assign a low-status role to the other student,

say, as a college "flunk out" who is still in the process of trying to find a job. When they are brought back into the classroom do not tell the returning students that these roles have been assigned. The class, or perhaps five or six students selected from the class, should engage in a round-table discussion on a certain topic, for example, an issue such as how the alumni of your college might be persuaded to make donations to a special fund designed to increase faculty salaries. During this discussion, the students must keep firmly in mind the roles that have been assigned to the two naive subjects. Treat the high-status student with dignity and respect, and the low-status student with derision and inattention.

This technique has been tried many times in the classroom of one of the authors, and it typically results in rapid and sometimes severe behavioral changes on the part of the role players. Within fifteen or twenty minutes the group's expectations usually begin affecting the subject's behaviors. The high-status student will probably try to dominate the discussion, perhaps even pontificating grandly for minutes at a time. The low-status subject will at first probably make repeated attempts to become involved, but as time passes these attempts will probably become increasingly less frequent. You may even observe the low-status person showing signs of regression. If a male, even the pitch of his voice may rise until it borders on an adolescent squeak. Or you may witness the low-status person slowly withdrawing from the scene to the point of even sitting stiffly in tight-lipped silence.

After completing the role play, question the subjects as to their feelings. Usually the high-status subject will admit to having had a great time, and will probably volunteer to take part in other class demon-

strations. The low-status subject may admit to feelings of frustration and perhaps even anger. Personality differences will naturally have some effect on how each of the subjects reacts. However, the group's pressure, if strong enough, should still impact on the subjects enough to produce predictable behavioral results, despite any original personality differences.

The lesson to be drawn from this demonstration is an important one that you as a prospective teacher should never forget. If just a few minutes of artificial group pressure can change the behavior of fairly mature college students, imagine the impact that real and long-term pressure might have on the lives of youngsters in the lower grades.

REFERENCES

Ardrey, R. (1966). *The territorial imperative.* New York: Atheneum.

Asch, S. E. (1952). *Social psychology.* Englewood Cliffs, N.J.: Prentice-Hall.

Bandura, A., Ross, D., and Ross, S. (1963). Imitation of film-mediated aggressive models. *Journal of Abnormal and Social Psychology, 66,* 3–11.

Barker, L. L., Wahlers, K. J., Cegala, D. J., and Kibler, R. J. (1983). *Groups in process* (2d ed.). Englewood Cliffs, N.J.: Prentice-Hall.

Berscheid, E., and Walster, E. (1972). Beauty and the best. *Psychology Today, 5*(10), 42–46.

Berkowitz, L. (1983). Aversively stimulated aggression. *American Psychologist, 38,* 1140.

Bond, C. T., Francis, R. C., Fernald, R. D., and Adelman, J. P. (1991). Characterization of complementary DNA encoding as the precursor for gonadotropin-releasing hormone and its associated peptide from a teleost fish. *Journal of Molecular Endocrinology, 5,* 931–937.

Bryan, T. H., and Bryan, J. H. (1986). *Understanding learning disabilities.* Palo Alto, Calif.: Mayfield.

Cartwright, D., and Zander, A. (1953). *Group dynamics* (p. 536). Evanston, Ill.: Row, Peterson.

Castellow, W. A., Wuensch, K. L., and Moore, C. H. (1990). Effects of physical attractiveness of the plaintiff and defendant in sexual harassment judgments. *Journal of Social Behavior and Personality, 5,* 547–562.

Conger, J. A. (1989). *The charismatic leader: Behind the mystique of exceptional leadership.* San Francisco: Jossey-Bass.

Cottrell, N. B., Rittle, R. H., and Wack, D. L. (1967). Presence of an audience and list type as joint determinants of performance in paired-associates learning. *Journal of Personality, 35,* 217–226.

Cunningham, R. (1984). Leadership and the group. *Group dynamics and education.* Washington: National Education Association Division of Adult Education.

Davis, J. A. (1964). *Great aspirations.* London: Aldine.

Dion, K., Berscheid, E., and Walster, E. (1972). What is beautiful is good? *Journal of Personality and Social Psychology, 24,* 285–290.

Dollard, J. M., Doob, L. W., Miller, N. E., Mourer, O. H., and Sears, R. R. (1939). *Frustration and aggression.* New Haven: Yale University Press.

Elliot, S. N. (1988). Acceptability of behavioral treatments in educational settings. In J. C. Witt, S. N. Elliot, and F. M. Gresham (Eds.), *Handbook of behavior therapy in education* (pp. 121–150). New York: Plenum Press.

Eron, L. D. (1982). Parent-child interactions, television, violence and aggression of children. *American Psychologist, 37,* 197–211.

Feshback, S. (1969). Film violence and its effect on children: Some comments on the implications of research for public policy (p. 5). American Psychological Association address, Washington.

Feshback, S., and Singer, R. D. (1970). *Television and aggression.* San Francisco: Jossey-Bass.

Festinger, L. (1957). *A theory of cognitive dissonance.* Stanford, Calif.: Stanford University Press.

Freedman, J. L., Carlsmith, J. M., and Sears, D. O. (1970). *Social psychology* (p. 188). Englewood Cliffs, N.J.: Prentice-Hall.

Good, T. (1981). Teacher expectations and student perceptions: A decade of research. *Educational Leadership, 38,* 415–421.

Gresham, F. M. (1990). Best practices in social skills assessment. In A. Thomas and J. Grines (Eds.). *Best practices in school psychology.* Washington: National School Psychology Association.

Grieve, F. (1987). For ugly people a hard cold world. *Boston Globe* (February 19), 67–68.

Gurman, E. B., and Balban, M. (1990). Self-evaluation of physical attractiveness as a function of self-esteem and defensiveness. *Journal of Social Behavior and Personality*, 5, 575–580.

Guthrie, E. R. (1938). *The psychology of human conflict* (p. 158). New York: Harper & Row.

Harlow, H. F., McGaugh, J. L., and Thompson, R. F. (1971). *Psychology* (p. 114). San Francisco: Albion.

Harvey, J. H., and Weary, G. (1984). Current issues in attribution theory and research. *Annual Review of Psychology*, 35, 427–459.

Heider, F. (1958). *The psychology of interpersonal relations.* New York: Wiley.

Hessong, R. F., and Weeks, T. H. (1991). *Introduction to the foundations of education.* New York: Macmillan.

Hollander, E. P., and Yoder, J. (1980). Some issues in comparing women and men as leaders. *Basic and Applied Social Psychology*, 1, 267–280.

Hudelson, S. (1987). The role of native language literacy in the education of language for minority children. *Language Arts*, 64, 827–841.

Homans, G. C. (1961). *Social behavior: Its elementary forms.* New York: Harcourt, Brace & World.

Hurt, H. T., Scott, M., and McCroskey, J. C. (1978). *Communication in the classroom.* Reading, Mass.: Addison-Wesley.

Huston, A. (1983). Sex-typing. In P. Mussen (Ed.), *Handbook of child psychology* (4th ed.). New York: Basic Books.

Jago, A. G., and Vroom, V. H. (1982). Sex differences in the incidence and evaluation of participative leader behavior. *Journal of Applied Social Psychology*, 67, 776–783.

Johnson, D. W. (1970). *The social psychology of education* (p. 57). New York: Holt, Rinehart & Winston.

Kobasa, S. C. (1982). Commitment and coping in stress resistance among lawyers. *Journal of Personality and Social Psychology*, 42, 707–717.

Lagerspetz, K. (1964). *Studies on the aggressive behavior of mice.* Helsinki: Soumalainen Tiedeakatemia.

Lee, B. (1985). *The wrong stuff.* New York: Penguin Books.

Lee, P. C., and Gropper, N. B. (1975). A cultural analysis of sex role in the school. *Journal of Teacher Education*, 26(4), 335–339.

Lewin, K., Lippitt, R., and White, R. K. (1939). Patterns of aggressive behavior in experimentally created social climates. *Journal of Social Psychology*, 10, 271–299.

Lindholm, C. (1990). *Charisma.* Oxford, England: Blackwell.

Lorenz, K. (1966). *On aggression.* New York: Harcourt, Brace & World.

Maccoby, E. E. (1991). Gender and relationships: A reprise. *American Psychologist*, 46, 538–539.

Marks, G., and Miller, N. (1985). The effects of certainty on consensus judgments. *Personality and Social Psychology Bulletin*, 11, 165–177.

Michaels, J. W., Blommel, J. M., Brocato, R. M., Linkous, R. A., and Rowe, J. S. (1982). Social facilitation and inhibition in a natural setting. *Replications in Social Psychology*, 2, 21–24.

Milgram, S. (1965). Liberating effect of group pressures. *Journal of Personality and Social Psychology*, 1, 127–134.

Milgram, S., and Shotland, R. L. (1973). *Television and antisocial behavior.* New York: Academic Press.

Miller, N. E. (1941). The frustration-aggression hypothesis. *Psychology Review*, 48, 338.

Morris, C. (1990). *Contemporary psychology and effective behavior* (7th ed.). Glenview, Ill.: Scott-Foresman.

Ovando, C. J. (1983). Bilingual/bicultural education: Its legacy and its future. *Phi Delta Kappan*, 64, 564–568.

Parkes, K. R. (1984). Locus of control, cognitive appraisal, and coping in stressful episodes. *Journal of Personality and Social Psychology*, 16, 19–84.

Pearl, D. (1984). Violence and aggression. *Society*, 21, 17–22.

Pearl, D., Bouthilet, L., and Lazar, J. (Eds.). (1982). *Television and behavior: Ten years of scientific progress and implications for the eighties*, Vols. 1 and 2. Washington: U.S. Government Printing Office.

Perez, J. F., and Cohen, A. I. (1969). *Mom and dad are me* (p. 7). Monterey, Calif.: Brooks-Cole.

Proctor, C. P. (1984). Teacher expectations: A model for school improvement. *Elementary School Journal* (March), 469–481.

Pruitt, D. G. (1971). Choice shift in group discussion: An introductory review. *Journal of Personality and Social Psychology*, 20, 339–360.

Ravitch, D. (1990). Multiculturalism. In J. Epstein (Ed.), *The American Scholar.* Washington: Phi Beta Kappa.

Reeder, G. D. (1982). Let's give the fundamental attribution error another chance. *Journal of Personality and Social Psychology*, 43, 341–344.

Rice, B. (1984). Imagination to go. *Psychology Today* (May) describes the IPS exercise and its results. On the relationship between brainstorming skills and problem-solving ability, see Mayer, R. E. (1983). *Thinking, problem solving, cognition.* New York: W. H. Freeman.

Rosenthal, D. (1970). *Genetic theory and abnormal behavior.* New York: McGraw-Hill.

Santee, R. T., and Maslach, C. (1982). To agree or not to agree: Personal dissent amid social pressure to conform. *Journal of Personality and Social Psychology*, 42, 690–700.

Schachter, S., Ellertson, N., McBride, D., and Gregory, D. (1951). An experimental study of cohesiveness and productivity. *Human Relations*, 4, 229–238.

Seaver, W. B. (1973). Effects of naturally induced teacher expectancies. *Journal of Personality and Social Psychology*, 28, 333–342.

Sherif, M. (1936). *The psychology of group norms.* New York: Harper & Row.

Slife, B. D., and Ryschlak, J. F. (1982). Role of affective assessment in modeling aggressive behavior. *Journal of Personality and Social Psychology*, 43, 861–868.

Snow, M., Jacklin, C., and Maccoby, E. E. (1983). Sex-of-child differences in father-child interactions at one year of age. *Child Development*, 54, 227–232.

Spinelli-Nannen, A. (1987). An investigation of the personality assessment system as a discriminator of socially misperceptive tendencies in elementary students. Unpublished doctoral dissertation, American International College, Springfield, Mass.

Sprinthall, R. C., Lambert, M., and Sturm, M. (1971). Anti-Semitism: Some perceptual correlates among Jews and non-Jews. *Journal of Social Psychology, 84,* 57–63.

Steinem, G. (1992). *Revolution from within: A book of self-esteem.* New York: Little, Brown.

Taylor, D. S., Berry, P. C., and Block, C. H. (1958). Does group participation when using brainstorming facilitate or inhibit creative thinking? *Administrative Science Quarterly, 2,* 23–47.

Triplett, N. (1897). The dynamogenic factors in pacemaking and competition. *American Journal of Psychology, 9,* 507–533.

Umberson, D., and Hughes, M. (1987). The impact of physical attractiveness on achievement and psychological well being. *Social Psychology Quarterly, 50,* 227–236.

Vivian, J. E., and Berkowitz, N. H. (1992). Anticipated bias from an outgroup: An attributional analysis. *European Journal of Social Psychology, 22,* 220–230.

Weiner, B. (1980). *Human motivation.* New York: Holt, Rinehart and Winston.

Wigfield, A., and Karpathian, M. (1991). Who am I and what can I do? Children's self-concepts and motivation in achievement situations. *Educational Psychologist, 26*(3,4), 233–261.

Wilson, T. D., and Linville, P. W. (1982). Improving academic performance of college freshmen: Attribution theory revisited. *Journal of Personality and Social Psychology, 42,* 367–376.

Wrightsman, L. S. (1972). *Social psychology in the seventies* (pp. 157–180). Monterey, Calif.: Brooks-Cole.

MOTIVATION IN THE CLASSROOM

But practice without zeal—with equal comfort at success and failure—does not make perfect, and the nervous system grows away from the modes in which it is exercised with resulting discomfort. When the law of effect is omitted—when habit formation is reduced to the supposed effect of mere repetition—two results are almost certain. By the resulting theory, little in human behavior can be explained by the law of habit; and by the resulting practice, unproductive or extremely wasteful forms of drill are encouraged.

E. L. Thorndike (1913)

MOTIVATION AND THE LAW OF EFFECT

If you were told that people learn more when they try harder, you would probably stifle a yawn and ask wryly, "So what else is new?" The fact that motivation is a crucial component in learning is so taken for granted that such a thought now seems like a statement of the obvious. Yet it wasn't always so. When Hermann Ebbinghaus spent those dismally boring months in learning long lists of nonsense syllables, his motivation level must have been unbelievably high, and yet he didn't mention it. Perhaps he didn't even notice it. Perhaps his motivation, like the air

around him, was so all-pervasive that it was virtually impossible for him to sense it.

It wasn't until early in the twentieth century that anyone experimentally validated the link between learning and motivation. E. L. Thorndike accomplished this task in his famous law of effect. Learning, Thorndike stated, is strengthened when it is followed by a *satisfying state of affairs*—satisfying, of course, to the learner. There it is—the obvious—but what a Pandora's box Thorndike opened with that innocent-sounding truism! Not that there wasn't ever anyone before Thorndike who had articulated such a notion. Several had. But it was Thorndike who provided both the experimental evidence and (because of his own personal prestige) the sounding board for getting the message heard.

Educators throughout the country listened when Thorndike spoke. Other psychologists also listened, but they didn't like what they heard. Thorndike was immediately challenged, first, on the grounds that the law of effect was circular in its logic, and second, on the basis that it was totally illogical to assume that an event (satisfactory state of affairs) can work backward in time to influence a previous event (pairing of stimulus and response).

In answer to the first criticism, Thorndike correctly

maintained that the law of effect was *not* circular (see *nominal fallacy* in the glossary) since he had given an independent, operational definition of the satisfying state of affairs. Said Thorndike, "By a satisfying state of affairs is meant one which the animal does nothing to avoid, often doing things which maintain or renew it" (Thorndike, 1913). In answer to the second objection, Thorndike argued that the intricacies of deductive logic cannot be used to refute an observable, experimentally validated fact. It would be like using a deductive proof to indicate that the moon is in a gaseous state despite the fact that Neil Armstrong brought back rock-hard evidence to the contrary. Though there remained a few diehards like Edwin Guthrie who said that motivation need not be directly involved in learning, Thorndike's answers were powerful enough to silence most of the critics, and by 1920 motivation was a firmly established concept in education and psychology.

A Current Appraisal

Today, virtually all psychologists acknowledge the impact of motivational variables on human behavior. It is little wonder that past students of educational psychology could never fully appreciate the concepts of growth, development, learning, and achievement without taking into account motivation. Teachers have long recognized that these motivational, or non-intellectual, factors are critical in determining the achievement of their students. Even if we were to develop an absolutely reliable, valid, and culture-fair measure of intelligence, no totally accurate prediction of academic achievement could be made without consideration of the motivational variables.

Implicit in the entire literature on underachievement and overachievement is the assumption that motivational and emotional variables play a crucial, if not *the* crucial, role in academic success. We have probably all known individuals loaded with IQ points and able to learn with seemingly little or no effort who nevertheless pathetically flunk more courses than they pass. It is more than just a glib cliché that some students seem to be desperately (though probably unwittingly) trying *not* to achieve academically. The student's veiled smile when the parents are presented with a report card filled with low grades is obvious evidence of a tragically self-defeating yet concerted effort at "striking back." "Show this around the country club" is the hidden message to many a coercive parent.

Although we have stressed throughout this book the extreme importance of early experience on the developing child, we should point out here that the environmental impact does not, of course, cease abruptly at age five or six. From the very first day the child—especially the middle-class child—enters school, society exerts enormous pressure to succeed academically. The young child often comes to see the entire adult world as though joined in an enormous conspiracy to urge, cajole, or threaten him or her into believing that scholastic success is the single most important thing in the world. First-grade teachers, and certainly parents of first-graders, have been known to admonish a child who might be having some difficulty in following the plot of a "see-Puff-jump" epic with the awesome threat, "You'll never get into college!"

The pressures often increase geometrically as the child progresses into high school. Some high school guidance counselors seem to believe that their very existence depends not on guiding the student toward opportunities for taking advantage of his or her greatest potential and aptitudes, but on what percentage of the senior class is accepted for college. One counselor proudly boasted that all but three of her graduating seniors had been placed in college, and two of those three would have gone on to college but because of emotional problems they had to be institutionalized. "But as soon as they get out, I'll get them into college," she proclaimed.

Motivation Never Acts in a Vacuum

Although the spotlight in this chapter will be clearly focused on motivation, it must be understood that motivation never acts apart from either learning or perception. Psychology's "big three"—learning, perception, and motivation—are in a constant state of interaction, each affecting and being affected by the other two. Not only does motivation affect learning, but learning also affects motivation. As we shall see, most human motives are learned or acquired. Nobody is born with a built-in motive for acquiring three-and-a-half by six-inch slips of green paper with a picture of George Washington printed on one side and the words In God We Trust on the other. Yet dollar bills have certainly been known to motivate people. The entire advertising industry is devoted to training and shaping our motives and, indeed, to supplying us with new ones. We are constantly bombarded by ads warning us that it is somehow unhealthy, immoral, or un-American not to *want* certain breakfast cereals, deodorants, cars, laxatives—the list is endless.

Motives also affect perception. We often "see" what we want to see and even fail to see what displeases us. We have probably all had the experience of waiting to meet someone at an airport, train, or bus terminal and then prematurely "seeing" that person—only to find out on closer inspection that we were in error. We "saw" the person we were hoping and wanting to see. The extent of our momentary embarrassment is a direct function of the volume of our greeting and of how dramatically we waved our hand.

Many years ago, a psychologist performed an experiment in which he showed people an extremely ambiguous picture, simply a blob of different colors daubed across a piece of cardboard. Interestingly enough, when persons who were hungry looked at this picture they reported seeing steak dinners, french fries, loaves of bread, and so on. The study clearly demonstrated that people tend to see the world from the point of view of their own motivational states (Sanford, 1936). As Shakespeare said in *A Midsummer Night's Dream:*

Or in the night, imagining some fear
How easy is a bush supposed a bear!

Another important psychological concept is that of perceptual defense. A number of studies have noted that people tend not to see those things in their environment or in themselves that for some reason they find distasteful (Postman et al., 1948). A student with a strong distaste for math may literally not see the next day's assignment, even though the teacher clearly inscribed it at the top of the chalkboard. That same student, however, might have eyes like a Mount Palomar telescope if the announcement on the chalkboard had read, "Half day of school tomorrow."

Thus, perception depends on motivation, motivation depends on perception, and both depend and are dependent on learning.

THE MOTIVE AND ITS COMPONENTS

Psychologists who have analyzed motivation have found that a **motive** has two identifiable components—a need and a drive. **Needs,** on the one hand, are based on some deficit within the person. The deficit may be physiological or psychological, but in either case the deficit must lie *within* the person. Physiological needs are often obvious, such as needs for water, food, sex, sleep, warmth—and all are based on a physical deficit within the body. Psychological needs, though potentially just as powerful, are often more subtle and less easily identified, such as needs for approval, affection, power, prestige, and so on. **Drives,** on the other hand, though certainly based on needs, have the added feature of an observable change in behavior. Drives imply motion of some sort. The person is not considered to be in a drive state until the need has goaded that person into action. The term **motive** refers to a drive (an activated need) that is directed toward or away from some sort of goal. Technically, then, the inner deficit (need) pushes the person into action (drive) toward or away from some particular goal (motive). Finally, the individual's ultimate behavior may rest on a series of goals, separately or in combination, and is therefore more often than not multimotivated. Human beings are complex creatures, seldom acting on the basis of a single motive. Real life is not like a Skinner box, in which the whole thrust of the rat's existence depends on whether or not the lever is pressed.

PHYSIOLOGICAL MOTIVES

As we said, motives may be physiological or psychological. The satisfaction of physiological motives is typically beyond the role of the teacher (although an obviously hungry or improperly clothed child should be reported). However, we should take a brief look at the physiological motives in order to make the whole topic more understandable.

Biological deficits are, of course, regulated within the organism. For example, it is known that the hypothalamus (a part of the brain) plays an important role in regulating the body's need for fat (Bennett and Gurin, 1982). **Physiological motives** are therefore based on physiological needs, or tissue deficits, within the body. At that level the motive, governed to some extent by the brain, will be aimed at reducing this deficit and returning the body to its natural state.

Physiologists use the term *homeostasis* to describe that process. Homeostasis is the tendency of the body to maintain a "steady state," or balance, among its various physiological components, like the internal organs, the blood, the hormones, and so on. The body does this more or less automatically, but often some overt, motivated behavior is also needed. For example, if one's body becomes too hot, sweating occurs and the automatic evaporation of the skin's moisture helps cool the skin area. However, the person also may *act* in ways designed to cool off the immediate environment, such as removing some clothing, opening windows, or turning on the air conditioner. Similarly, under conditions of extreme cold, the body shivers, and this reaction increases the metabolic rate. Thus, by burning the body's fuels faster, extra heat is generated. However, the individual also adds clothing, goes indoors, and generally seeks conditions that will reduce the discomfort. (Interestingly, the brain mechanisms involved in homeostasis may at times be misled by contrary cognitive information. For example, in one study, when subjects were told that the room temperature was higher than it really was, they all reported being just as comfortable as when the temperature was actually set at that higher level.) (Rohles, 1980).

Therefore, physiological needs can be adjusted to some extent by the internal mechanisms of homeostasis, but goal-directed action may also be involved. Deficits of water and food cannot be compensated for internally, and the individual *must* seek out replacements from the external environment. Complicating matters is the fact that the individual will probably be faced with a host of alternative goals in the environment. If a person is hungry, for example, the choice of which food to select is overlaid with all sorts of learned, or *acquired,* habits and tastes. In an extremely interesting study, Clara Davis took a group of six- to twelve-month-old infants and allowed them to select their own diets from a menu of natural, unprocessed, and unpurified foods (Davis, 1967). She found that these infants, not yet brainwashed by adults and various commercials, could be trusted to select a balanced diet if given a series of free choices among wholesome foods. Contrast this with adolescent and adult eating habits, such as taking in too many sweets, eating too little at breakfast, or snacking too much at bedtime. Not only human infants but also young and adult mammals generally have this ability, called *specific hunger.* Only human adults seem to lose it, through learning.

ACQUIRED MOTIVES

Earlier, we stated that motivation and learning are in constant interaction in the determination of behavior. We also pointed out that even physiological motives can have a heavy learning component, for example,

in choosing *how* to satisfy such basic needs as those for food, warmth, and sex. It seems, however, that there are some motives that are acquired—that is, they are entirely learned; they seem not to be continuously dependent on biological needs.

Functional Autonomy

The famous Harvard personality theorist, Gordon Allport, has proposed a theory of motivation called **functional autonomy** (Allport, 1967). In this theory Allport attempts to account for the myriad human motives for which no biological needs seem present. Allport tells us that many human motives arise when a *means to an end becomes an end in itself.* That is, the route chosen to search out a goal for satisfying a more primitive need may itself become a goal. We have all read newspaper accounts of some miserly recluse living in squalor, existing on fifty-cent cans of dog food, yet owning stocks and bonds and innumerable bankbooks worth hundreds of thousands of dollars. The original reason for saving the money—perhaps to satisfy the biological needs of food and warm shelter—was eventually taken over by the need for money itself and this began to override the original intent. The means (saving money) to the end (food and shelter) became an end (saving money) in itself. Thus the motive of saving money began to function autonomously, or independently. The motive came to have a life of its own and was no longer historically connected to its origin.

Suppose a young boy will practice on his violin only if his mother gives him an ice cream cone. Playing the violin is thus dependent on the primary reinforcer of ice cream. Then, one fine day the boy begins to play not for the ice cream but for the sheer joy of creating beautiful music. The motive for playing the violin comes to function autonomously and is no longer dependent on any earlier goal, or on any *external* goal. Someday perhaps that boy will play his violin on stage at Lincoln Center, and it is certainly fondly hoped that he won't have to go off into the wings between concertos and munch on a Dairy Queen special.

Emotions and Motivation

The types and levels of various emotions also have a strong impact on motivation. A child who is fearful reacts very differently to a situation than a child who feels confident and is self-assured; a teacher who, for one reason or another is feeling temporarily depressed will respond to the class in ways the pupils may find to be literally baffling. A child who is happily walking home from school carrying a report card filled with grades of A may not respond as aggressively to a classmate's taunts as a child whose report card is laden with grades of F.

Psychologists have even found that the physiological arousal associated with certain emotions can transfer from one motivational area to another. For example, people who were emotionally aroused by watching a violent hockey or football game later found themselves more easily aroused sexually than those who had not seen the game. Also, young males who have just finished working out (doing calisthenics and lifting weights) tend to respond far more aggressively to a problem situation than if they had previously been involved in some more sedentary activity (Riesenzein, 1983).

Finally, conquering the feelings associated with what one perceives to be a negative emotion may itself be extremely motivating. Some young daredevils even appear to be "addicted to their own adrenaline." Jumping from high places, or climbing the tallest trees, may at first fill the youngster with feelings of terror. But after a few attempts, although the initial fear is reduced, the emotional arousal may still be present and the child looks for even taller trees in order to re-create the excitement. Not climbing the tree has now itself become an aversion. Psychologists explain this phenomenon on the basis of what they call the **opponent process theory** of acquired motivation. It can sometimes put children in the ironic position of needing to show off their bravado by recklessly talking back to the teacher in front of the entire class. Not doing so has now become aversive (Solomon, 1980).

Intrinsic versus Extrinsic Motivation

Intrinsic motives are those which are satisfied by internal reinforcers. Behavior that is intrinsically motivated is engaged in for its own sake, for the sheer joy and satisfaction derived from the performance itself. **Extrinsic motives,** on the other hand, depend instead on needs that must be satisfied by external reinforcers. Extrinsically motivated behaviors are performed not out of interest in the behavior itself but because they are seen as instrumental to some separate goal (Deci et al., 1991).

Intrinsic motivation: learning for its own sake.

As we discovered in Chapter 9, Jerome Bruner, the great cognitive psychologist, is convinced that learning will be far more long-lasting when it is sustained by intrinsic motivation than when it is driven by the more transitory push of external reinforcers. Bruner does admit, however, that extrinsic motivation may be necessary to get the learner to initiate certain actions or to get the learning process started and off dead center. But once on its way, the sometimes fragile process of learning is better nourished and sustained by intrinsic motives. Bruner's position is similar in many ways to Allport's. Intrinsic motivation may require an external reinforcement to get it under way, but once it comes to function autonomously—that is, independently of the external reward—real learning can become a solid, lifetime pursuit.

Psychologists have been able to demonstrate which types of behaviors are more commonly influenced by intrinsic compared with extrinsic motivations (Callero and Piliavin, 1983). We must be careful, however, to remember that the same behavior may be internally motivated for some people and externally motivated for others. Intrinsic motivation, when it is present, usually builds on itself, thus producing an increased sense of motivation to continue the activity.

People who are intrinsically motivated in a certain area make a special effort to seek out even more challenging situations (Deci and Ryan, 1980). Those children who are willing to seek the challenge, to literally rise to the occasion, are also said to be high in self-efficacy (Schunk, 1991). It has also been found that the use of computers in the classroom increases intrinsic motivation (Lepper, 1985).

One educator has provided parents and teachers with a list of five principles for fostering intrinsic motivation in young children:

1. Provide a novel and varied home environment.

2. Provide experiences in which children may have an effect on their environments.

3. Provide environments that are responsive to a child's actions.

4. Respond positively to children's questions while still encouraging children to seek their own solutions.

5. Reward children often with praise, which gives them a feeling of competence (Gottfried, 1983).

Self-Regulated Learning

Psychologists have long been aware that there are certain "self-starting" learners who are extremely self-disciplined, able to postpone gratification, and virtually able to teach themselves with little supervision. These individuals don't even seem to need any external reinforcers because their own internal feelings of success and accomplishment provide motivation enough. These are the self-regulated learners, those high achievers whose own inner resources, intrinsic motivation, and self-reliance produce an almost irresistible formula for success. In fact, in one study, it was found that a student's scholastic achievement could be predicted with 93 percent accuracy on the basis of that student's measured self-regulation (Zimmerman, 1991). One of the key components in **self-regulated learning** is, of course, motivation. In fact, it is understood that self-regulated learning and motivation are interdependent processes. A learner's perception of personal academic self-worth is both a cause (motive) of learning as well as an effect (outcome) of learning. Consider the following: self-regulated learners don't just react to their learning environments, but they deliberately seek out further opportunities to learn (Zimmerman, 1989). They initiate activities designed to promote

self-awareness of their learning styles (Zimmerman and Martinez-Pons, 1990), and their increased motivation prods them into setting increasingly higher learning goals, a trait that Bandura calls "self-regulation" (Bandura, 1989).

Self-regulated learning and development   Research on self-regulation and development is fairly clear on this point: the ability to self-regulate and the age of the child go hand in hand. Young children (below age 7) may be motivated, but too often they lack awareness of their metacognitive strategies and seem overly naive about their ability to learn, in some cases regardless of outcome. As children approach adolescence, however, their capacity for self-regulation and cognitive self-awareness grows with the passing years (Zimmerman, 1991).

Maslow's Need Hierarchy

Abraham Maslow, an important psychologist in the area of motivation theory, has suggested that there is a definite order in which individuals attempt to satisfy their needs. When a person is in a situation in which several needs are operating simultaneously, the person strives to accommodate the need that is of the highest order of importance at that particular time. Maslow sees this order of importance as universal among human beings. Furthermore, he maintains that a person will remain at a given need level until those needs are satisfied, and then move on to the next level.

At the most basic level are physiological needs. Maslow contends that until these needs are at least partially satisfied, the individual will not be concerned with the needs of the next level, those of safety and security.

The Maslow **need hierarchy** is as follows:

1. *Physiological needs:* food, drink, sex, and shelter

2. *Safety needs:* security, order, protection, and family stability

3. *Love needs:* affection, group affiliation, and personal acceptance

4. *Esteem needs:* self-respect, prestige, reputation, and social status

5. *Self-actualization needs:* self-fulfillment and achievement of personal goals, ambitions, and talent

SPOTLIGHT ON SELF-REGULATION AND TEACHING

A Cognitive Approach

You may be wondering at this point why so much time and effort has gone into studying these self-regulated superstars of the classroom. They obviously do not need a whole lot of help from either teachers or researchers. The point is that if we can understand more about these self-regulated children, the strategies they use, the reasons for their motivation, and the developmental nature of these abilities, maybe we can teach other less motivated children how to increase their levels of academic achievement. Our focus here is on how the child may learn to transfer control from being overly "other-regulated" to becoming more self-regulated. Several teaching strategies have been identified as promoting self-regulated learning.[a]

1. Children can be taught to use inner speech to enhance personal motivation. For example, the child can learn to repeat phrases such as "I'll do better next time" or "I know I can succeed."

2. Children can be taught to change their implicit cognitive theories. This has been called the "top-down" approach. Since many children have faulty beliefs about the best methods to employ in the learning situation, they can benefit from the direct teaching of certain tactics. Teaching children to use more efficient learning strategies, however, should not be done in an arbitrary or domineering fashion, but in such a way that the children come to appreciate the value of these strategies. The child who simply and obediently follows a set of seemingly arbitrary cognitive rules will not retain the strategy nearly as well as the child who understands the reasons for, and makes a personal commitment to, the new approach. Some children seem to discover these better techniques on their own, simply through practice. When the child comes to realize that these tactics lead to better learning and more positive beliefs about learning (especially learning that can be transferred to other situations), this "bottom-up" approach may often spontaneously lead to the self-controlled use of increasingly sophisticated strategies.

3. Children can be taught to make their thinking public. Open class discussions allow thinking to be observed by the teacher as well as shared among classmates. In fact, some theorists believe that free-wheeling and open-ended discussions are at the heart of metacognitive training.[b] There is a double benefit to this approach, since it allows the teacher to hear and "see" the way the students are thinking, and thus diagnose processing difficulties, while evaluating how well the children are understanding the curriculum content.

4. Children can be taught strategies involving active participation and collaboration. Getting children to become active participants in the learning process promotes both increased motivation as well as more effective learning techniques. For example, peer tutoring owes much of its success to the fact that a child can't simply be a passive bystander, but must actively collaborate in the learning process. Reciprocal teaching demands that the students swap roles, from tutor to student, and it forces them to pay attention and monitor the other's thinking. As Paris and Newman have stated, "When students act as teachers, they are also given another opportunity to relearn what they may only have thought they knew. As students teach others, they develop a personal commitment to the strategies they are teaching."[c] And as these strategies are found to be successful, motivation also increases.

5. Children can be taught to ask themselves questions as they read and to summarize paragraphs. Studies have shown that this metacognitive strategy can have dramatically positive effects on comprehension.[d]

[a] S. G. Paris and R. S. Newman, Developmental aspects of self-regulated learning. *Educational Psychologist* (1990), 25, 87–102.
[b] S. G. Paris, D. R. Cross, M. Y. Lipson, Informed strategies for learning: A program to improve children's reading awareness and comprehension. *Journal of Educational Psychology* (1984), 76, 1239–1252.
[c] Paris and Newman (1990), p. 98.
[d] P. H. Bornstein, Self-instructional training: A commentary and state of the art. *Journal of Applied Behavior Analysis*, (1985), 18, 69–72; T. Nolan, Self-questioning and prediction: Combining metacognitive strategies. *Journal of Reading* (1991), 35(2), 132–138.

Maslow does not mean to imply that every human being achieves full success in satisfying all those needs. For example, not everyone gets to enjoy prestige and social status, let alone the ultimate goal of self-actualization. What he does mean, however, is that we must be alert to the fact that persons cannot even consider some of their more social needs when their basic needs are left unfulfilled. The hungry child, or the child riddled with anxiety due to a traumatic family situation, may not wholeheartedly pursue goals of prestige and self-actualization (Maslow, 1954).

Acquired Motives and Social Forces

Acquired motives, such as competition, power, status, approval, even achievement, are dictated by social rules and pressures—either in origin or in the form in which they are expressed. The cultural anthropologists, who have swarmed over every remote nook and cranny on earth, have been unanimous in telling us of the great variation in human motivation and in *how these motives are expressed*. Before the days of the great field treks by such anthropologists as Margaret Mead and Ruth Benedict, many early Western psychologists took the parochial view that what they observed in their own culture was true the world over. Because it was assumed that all these motives were present among all people everywhere, the term *instinct* was used.

William McDougall, who in 1908 wrote the first book to carry the title *Social Psychology,* felt that group life was an inherent part of our basic nature (McDougall, 1908). Therefore, to McDougall, all social life was a result of our inherited instincts. For example, McDougall stated that people get together in groups because of their gregarious instincts. Furthermore, he said that these instincts carried an emotional quality that made their fulfillment irresistible. McDougall's psychology was bleak indeed, for it meant that people were destined to play out the preprogrammed instincts that were built into their biological natures.

Because of the logical problems of the instinct approach (see *nominal fallacy* in the glossary), McDougall's version of social motivation finally became discredited and an object of real scorn. To declare that students achieved academically because of an achievement instinct meant that those students who were not so blessed were doomed to a school life of academic frustration and that *nothing could be done to change it*. By the mid-1920s psychology in general had

dismissed instinct theory as unscientific and ludicrous. And ludicrous it was. By 1924 it was found that McDougall and other instinct theorists had compiled lists of over 6,000 instincts to explain behavior. Virtually any conceivable bit of behavior that a person was capable of had been "explained" by the simple expedient of calling it instinctive. Everything from twiddling one's thumbs to "inserting the fingers in crannies to dislodge small animals hidden there" was seriously cited as a legitimate instinctive behavior. It is now clear that social motives differ widely among peoples throughout the world because social motives are in fact learned, or acquired.

Need for Approval

In retrospect, it is easy to see how instinct theory got started. Though social motives are learned, people tend to learn these lessons so well that they begin to behave with almost the kind of automatic precision of a homing pigeon. One of the best learned social motives is the **motive for social approval.** An infant soon learns to associate the sound of mother's voice with his or her own satisfactions. Since the mother is usually the one to provide food and warmth for the infant, her voice, and the various intonations of her voice, come to matter a great deal. The infant eventually learns that the sounds of approval follow some responses and the sounds of disapproval (and then perhaps punishment) follow other responses. As words are learned, the mother's voice becomes even more potent, and the child usually attempts to modify behavior in accordance with her verbal reactions.

Usually during the second year, the child also begins to learn that many of the things he or she really wants to do, like eating candy before meals or drawing on the wall, are constantly followed by disapproval. That is, the child begins to associate personal satisfaction with the sounds of disapproval. This reaction on the part of the child helps to explain the negativism of the "terrible twos," a dilemma for both parent and child. To make matters worse, the child is also faced with many situations in which the sounds of approval follow behaviors the child does *not* want to do, like helping to rake leaves, washing dishes, or going to bed. It is little wonder that most children are caught in an approval-disapproval conflict situation, the overtones of which can last for a lifetime.

Teachers must be alert to this conflict. Since approval, in the form of good grades, gold stars, a friendly "well done," is the teacher's most powerful ally, it is to the definite advantage of both teacher and student that this motive not be stifled. A teacher may unwittingly reduce the intensity of the child's approval motive by using approval too liberally in situations that the child finds distasteful. Too much self-sacrifice on the part of the child in order to receive approval may create a boomerang effect—even to the point at which approval is no longer sought. This may be one facet of the underachievement syndrome. The student has learned that approval can be gained only at a terrible price. Therefore, seeking it no longer seems worthwhile.

Although the approval motive obviously originated in the infant's need for physiological satisfaction, it is one of those many acquired motives that eventually seem to have lives of their own. The approval motive comes to function autonomously—even to the extent of overriding more primitive motives. People have been known to go hungry rather than give up the opportunity to hear the sounds of applause.

Peer approval   Though the teacher is in an especially powerful position, as are the parents, to shape a child's behavior through the vehicle of approval, adults are not the only source of this potent reinforcement. Students often play to the applause of their peers—a situation that can be extremely disruptive when the students and teacher have widely different goals. When peer approval becomes more important than the approval of the teacher, the classroom situation may clearly get out of hand. In order to avert too many open confrontations, it is sometimes wise for a teacher to ignore a certain amount of student horseplay. This approach must be handled carefully and judiciously because the teacher should not be perceived as a doddering fool in whose classroom anything goes. The students will most certainly test the limits of the teacher's permissiveness.

It is known that aggressive children tend to be less accepted by their peers, but the direction of this relationship is still not clear. Do the children become aggressive because they are not popular, or is their lack of popularity a result of their aggressive behavior? The importance of this issue is underscored by the fact that these unpopular children, who do not make friends easily and who are not accepted by their peers, are more at risk when it comes to personal adjustment in later life. As adults, they are more apt to engage in antisocial activities and show more signs

of psychopathology than those who enjoyed higher levels of peer acceptance (Parker and Asher, 1987).

Peer approval is closely linked to the need for affiliation. People differ regarding their desire to be with other people. Some children feel compelled to constantly seek out the company of others, while other children need more time to be alone. Students who can't stand being alone often find homework, a lonely activity at best, especially burdensome. Typically, people feel stronger needs to affiliate under conditions of stress. This seems to be especially true when the others with whom we might affiliate appear to be competent and strong (Rofe, 1984).

The ripple effect   Sooner or later, usually sooner, every teacher confronts the situation in which a student seeking peer approval acts out in some inappropriate way. Perhaps it begins with a student's surreptitiously making animal sounds, groaning, or throwing a paper airplane. Soon another student joins in, then another, and quickly bedlam ensues. This phenomenon, in which one disruptive student triggers disruption by the entire class, is known as the ripple effect (Kounin, 1970). Studies have shown that the ripple effect is far more prevalent in classes in which the motivation to learn is low. However, these same studies indicate that in highly motivated classes, the teacher's immediate attempt to restore order is greeted by student approval. In the studies, students in the highly motivated classes seemed to want an environment conducive to learning, and they stated that the teacher's efforts to scold the instigator made them even more willing to do their work. In the classes with low levels of motivation, students took every student-teacher confrontation as a fresh opportunity for more catcalls and general disruption. The general ability of the teacher to prevent such a ripple effect has been called *with-itness* by one psychologist (Kounin, 1970) and *keenness* by another (Cronbach, 1977). The teacher who is with-it creates the impression that "firm hands are on the wheel," that the situation is under control. On the one hand, the with-it teacher doesn't always jump in as soon as a child acts out. However, when the with-it teacher does move into the fray, she confronts the instigator one on one. In contrast, the not-with-it teacher usually lets the situation run on for too long, thereby allowing the ripples to become tidal waves. Then, when she does finally step in, she compounds the felony either by reprimanding *the class as a whole* or by punishing the last child she spots acting up.

Achievement

Perhaps no other acquired motive has been the object of as much discussion and research among educational psychologists as **achievement motivation.** Although it most probably originates in the service of physiological needs, or at least in association with the need for approval, the achievement motive may itself become autonomous. When it does, the student is in the happy position of possessing an intrinsic motive to achieve, that is, to achieve for the sake of the achievement itself.

The achievement motive is usually aimed at emphasizing a high level of ability and avoiding any display of low ability (Nicholls, 1984). One study that appears to support the back-to-basics movement found that children show higher levels of overall achievement when teachers spend larger amounts of time in the *direct* teaching of reading, math, science, and social studies than in music, art, or social awareness (Rosenshine, 1980).

The now-famous Coleman report found that a student's personal feeling of self-directed competence was the most important factor in determining academic achievement. This factor was discovered to be more important than a whole host of seemingly crucial variables, including social-class differences, race, pupil-teacher ratios, the number of books in the library, and even the educational background of the teachers. Academic achievement depended most heavily on the student's personal conviction of being in charge of his or her own fate. The high achievers did not ascribe their fate to luck or to the vagaries of chance but rather to their own personal decisions and efforts. Society's "losers" are far more apt to see their lot determined by impersonal, fatalistic forces than are the "winners" (Coleman, 1966).

Underachievers   Society's "losers," however, need constant study, evaluation, and help, for unless their condition can be reversed, society itself will be the real loser. The problem of the underachieving child is one of the more tragic dilemmas in education. When the student has the ability to learn and profit from the educational experience, it is indeed frustrating to witness, as every teacher has, the wasted talent of the underachiever. It is like an Indianapolis racing car with a high horsepower engine going no more than twenty miles per hour because of a mechanical failure that prevents the driver from depressing the accelerator.

The problem of the underachiever illustrates par

excellence the importance of the motivational variables in academic success. In one study the researchers, holding intelligence constant, found that academic achievement was a function of the student's ego strength or reality orientation (Hummel and Sprinthall, 1965). The study demonstrated that the underachiever possessed a weak ego and was unwilling to postpone pleasure. Underachievers were more easily distracted and less able to set about tasks in an organized manner. In short, these students were less able to control their own basic impulses and, therefore, their destinies.

Another study, in which achievement motivation was related to whether or not women went on to college, found that achieving women were more in tune with the norms of their peer group or reference group than were nonachieving women. The achieving women were better able to predict how members of their peer group would react in various situations (Sprinthall and Bennett, 1978).

Based on a long series of studies, **D. C. McClelland** and Alschuler have concluded that successful decision makers share certain characteristics: They compete with a standard of excellence in mind, they moderate risks, and make good use of concrete feedback. These three characteristics form what the authors term the *achievement syndrome.* People who excel in a variety of fields demonstrate these motivational characteristics. The most interesting aspect of McClelland and Alschuler's work, however, is not that their research has uncovered a group of psychological traits that lead to general achievement, but that a system of intervention has evolved from their research. In other words, they can teach pupils (or, for that matter, business executives, teachers, salespersons, or anyone at all) to become successful achievers. They can shape motivational patterns through a series of games and produce the achievement syndrome.

These techniques can put students more in control of their environment by helping them abandon excessive caution or excessive risk taking. These experiences help children learn that success is not just a matter of "fate" but that it is well within their own reach (McClelland, 1965). Thus, achievement motivation has implications that transcend achievement itself. The variables involved address the issue of personality development as well (Maehr and Kleiber, 1981). It's clear that achievement motivation and success are highly correlated, but, as is so often the case, it is sometimes difficult to determine the direction of this relationship. Was Sally's high achievement motivation in basketball a result of her superior ath-

SPOTLIGHT ON LEARNED HELPLESSNESS

Where Has All the Motivation Gone?

Just as higher levels of motivation can be learned, so too we can learn lowered levels. Some children (as well as adults) seem to lose their sense of motivation and become apathetic, extremely passive, and even emotionally depressed. This defeatist attitude appears to be learned through a series of frustrating situations in which the child has been treated in inconsistent and unpredictable ways. The result is that children feel they have no control over the consequences of their actions, that whatever they do results in failure—so why try?[a] This condition should in most cases be brought to the attention of the school psychologist, especially if it occurs during adolescence. Among teenagers, learned helplessness, and the possibility of concomitant depression, can become incapacitating and should be taken seriously. Depression during adolescence has been found to be a powerful predictor of depression in adulthood.[b] Although this condition often requires the assistance of a professional psychologist, the teacher can also be an important source of help. Such pupils should be provided with opportunities for frequent, little successes, given in small steps, and then followed by immediate feedback. Computer-assisted instruction (CAI) could also be tried, since with CAI the small steps and immediate feedback can be built right into the program. Above all, however, the teacher's expectations and rewards should remain as consistent and predictable as humanly possible.

Children who rarely experience success in the classroom and perceive themselves as academic failures (as in the case of the learning-disabled) often develop a syndrome that includes a variety of self-defeating motives. For example: (1) such children are far more apt to develop an external locus of control, (2) they are more easily influenced by extrinsic reinforcements, (3) they are low in self-regulated learning strategies, (4) they have low levels of self-efficacy, and (4) they are more apt to develop feelings of learned helplessness, showing little in the way of competence motivation.[c] Obviously, such children can be extremely difficult for the classroom teacher to handle, and they need the special help of the school psychologist in learning coping strategies for dealing with failure.

[a] D. L. Rosehan and M. E. P. Seligman, *Abnormal psychology,* 2d ed. (New York: Norton, 1989).
[b] J. Garber, M. R. Kriss, M. Koch, L. Lindholm, Recurrent depression in adolescents: A follow-up study, *Journal of the American Academy of Child and Adolescent Psychiatry* (1988), 27, 49–54.
[c] D. P. Hallahan and J. M. Kauffman, *Exceptional children* (Englewood Cliffs, N.J.: Prentice-Hall, 1988).

letic skills or was it the other way around? Was Billy's low achievement motivation in reading a result of or a cause of his poor comprehension skills? The evidence suggests that the two are reciprocal, each being sustained by and sustaining the other (Gottfried, 1985). One way of taking advantage of this reciprocity is through the use of peer tutoring. Giving help to another student, especially when it involves explanation and elaboration, produces higher learning and increased motivation on the part of the *helper* (Webb, 1983; Goodenow, 1992). In other words, tutoring increases both the skill level *and* the motivation of the tutor.

Achievement and sex differences   Academically, females definitely outperform males, especially in the earlier school grades. By the time they get to high school and college, however, the males catch up, and in the posteducational world the males move ahead of the females in virtually every area— arts, professions, sciences, corporate life, and so on (Maccoby and Jacklinn, 1974). Without doubt, this phenomenon is cultural and not genetic. Men are expected to achieve more; they are given more opportunities to achieve and are rewarded more for their achievements. Young men are constantly reminded that they are going to be the breadwinners in the family and that even the social status of their wives and children depends on their efforts. By the time he reaches high school and college, the average male in our society definitely hears this cultural message and begins to work harder, knowing that not only his own fate but that of his future family rests with his ability to achieve.

"Oh, Helen—I saw the counselor today, and he told me to start paying more attention to you."

From The Wall Street Journal, by permission, Cartoon Features Syndicate.

Sexism in society   The message of sexism is often subtle, but it seems ever present. One theorist has suggested that men and women converse in ways that are in some ways so different as to be likened to cross-cultural communication. According to this view, women are more apt to communicate in a language of connection and intimacy, whereas men converse in a language of status, independence, and power. As children, little girls use talk as a way of maintaining intimacy, and when playing in groups they tend to make more suggestions and give fewer orders than do little boys. For boys, talk is used more as a method of negotiating status. High-status boys give orders and push (or even bully) the low-status boys around (Tannen, 1990). Males have also been found to use conversational ploys to gain the upper hand in interactions with females (Parlee, 1979). These verbal power ploys were dubbed *conversational politics,* in which the men tended to ignore topics that the women raised and the women usually picked up on the subjects raised by men. The men were also more apt to interrupt women, even in midsentence— in the same way that parents interrupt children. In general, cultural pressures are so strong that both

males *and females* accept conversational power ploys like these as normal.

In an interesting attempt to discover whether the women's movement has made any impact on sexism, a number of couples went to various restaurants in order to discover whether the man or woman would get the check. Almost always, the check went to the man. Even when a female executive was taking a male friend to dinner and was clearly in charge— asking for the table, ordering for both, answering all questions—she still received the check only five out of thirty-six times. And waitresses, it turned out, were even less apt to give the woman the check than were waiters (Laner, 1979).

Sexism in schools   Although it appears that women rarely get the check in restaurants, they certainly often get the "shaft" in most American school systems. One survey showed that 90 percent of the nation's elementary school teachers are women, whereas only 18 percent of elementary school principals are women—fewer in fact, than there were ten years ago (Hechinger, 1979). It's apparently considered all right for women to teach our children but often not all right if they concern themselves with administering the educational enterprise.

Fear of success   **Matina S. Horner** has noted that an important factor in creating lower levels of achievement (and sustaining sexism) is the **fear of success** (Horner, 1968). She has also noted that females, because of their cultural brainwashing, are more prone to this condition than males. Many females assume that achievement brings with it many extremely unpleasant side effects, not the least of which is a "loss of femininity." Women also tend to perceive that competing for success is somehow too aggressive an act to be consistent with their stereotyped self-image of "being a lady."

Horner asked college women and men to complete a series of stories that began like this one: After first-term grades are out, Joan (John for the males) finds herself (himself) at the top of her class. The vast majority of women wrote stories clearly showing the fear-of-success theme, whereas the men typically wrote stories that implied a positive outlook toward success. The women's fear-of-success stories were of three general types: First, and most common, were stories indicating fears of being socially rejected, unmarriageable, unpopular, lonely, and isolated; second

MATINA S. HORNER

Born in 1939, Matina Horner has had a career little short of meteoric. After receiving her B.A. degree in 1961 from Bryn Mawr, Horner received her M.A. in 1963 and her Ph.D. in 1968 from the University of Michigan. With honors in psychology and an election to Phi Beta Kappa, she demonstrated substantial early promise. She was appointed a lecturer and then assistant professor at Harvard for the school year 1968–1969 in the department of social relations.

Her research focus gained almost immediate attention, not because of the topical nature of her investigation but because of the careful examination she performed and the significance of the findings themselves. Her work provided a breakthrough in understanding the paradox and the dilemma of female development. For educators, of course, the implications of her work are most far-reaching. Her theory, which indicates how societal expectations shape and mold the motivational systems for females, forces educators to revise practically all their assumptions concerning male and female differences. She has been able to show that such differences in motivational patterns are a result of social conditioning or social inventions. This means that educators need to revise their ideas, practices, and policies concerning young women in schools and colleges. The need is to promote full development for all, regardless of gender. Horner's work forms the important basis for these needed changes.

As if to indicate her own versatility and willingness to meet today's major educational challenges, Dr. Horner moved in 1972 from an assistant professorship at Harvard to the presidency of Radcliffe College—at the age of thirty-four. A model of achievement motivation, scholarship, and administrative talent, she sets a high standard for others to follow.

were stories that showed doubts about femininity and normality; and third were stories that flatly denied that such success was possible ("It was later discovered that there had been a mistake in the registrar's office, and Joan was really not first") (Horner, 1969).

More recently, a group of junior high school girls was tested, and although the majority did show evidence of a fear of success, there was an interesting and important sidelight. The girls whose stories predicted a more positive outlook (admittedly a minority) actually performed better by a margin of six to one on an intellectual task than did the girls whose stories reflected a fear-of-success theme (Harvey, 1975).

Finally, the seventeen-year-old daughter of one of the authors wrote the following. It perhaps indicates that the situation may be improving.

Joan realizes that she had to work very hard to get where she is, but having done so well, she decides she must keep it up. Joan faces a lot of pressure from her friends, who tell her she should put away the books and go to more parties—that she has already proven herself, so why keep pushing? Though Joan is tempted by her friends, she realizes that she wouldn't really be happy unless she was working up to her potential. One night, while in bed, Joan said to herself, "I want to do my best these next two years because this is the only life I have, and I want to make it a successful one."

Although there is obviously an element of conflict in the story, achievement does win out in the end.

Fear of failure   Fear of failure has also haunted some schoolchildren to the point where they won't take any problem-solving risks. To be judged as having failed is seen as so terrifyingly traumatic that an almost trancelike state sets in, causing the child to cling so tenaciously to "safe" knowledge that curiosity, discovery, creativity, and even cognitive growth itself may become stunted. To prevent this, "schools without failure," such as Summerhill, have been introduced. The theory is that the threat of failure does not motivate students but instead acts as a detriment to a secure and efficient learning environment. For these and other reasons, social promotions, whereby children are kept with their age-mates regardless of academic performance, have become increasingly common.

This view has not gone unchallenged. Robert Ebel believes that the removal of the threat of failures has, in fact, removed an important academic incentive (Ebel, 1980).

Competence

Robert White, a personality theorist, has suggested that one of the most fundamental human motives is based on a strong, personal desire to master one's environment. White calls this *competence motivation* (White, 1959). Competence motivation is without question an intrinsic motive and one that may even have survival value for the species. To become competent—to achieve a degree of mastery over one's environment—allows the individual to take charge of his or her own life, in fact, to be the author of his or her own fate. There is a real question as to whether the human race could have survived so long on this harsh planet without that strong desire for mastery. If we were, instead, simply passive blobs of protoplasm being buffeted about by an impersonal and seemingly cruel environment, perhaps our species would have died out thousands of years ago.

Competence motivation need not depend on culturally acquired achievement motivations but may itself have deep biological roots. Even at nineteen months of age, infants may display smiles of satisfaction on completing a job (a simple job, but nevertheless a job well done). Jerome Kagan calls these *mastery smiles* and presumes that they are indicative of an inner feeling of pride at having completed the task (Kagan, 1984).

A teacher can certainly take advantage of the competency motive in the classroom. Students are always going to be more interested in what they are good at, and in contrast it is nearly impossible to motivate them in areas in which they have no competence. In a sense, it's like J. McV. Hunt's problem of the match (see Chapter 4) or Piaget's *only* motivational concept, that of equilibration (see Chapter 5). The teacher must attempt to match up the new stimulus inputs with the student's level of competence. The most effective technique is to keep the new material a shade or two above the level at which the student is currently operating, always a little out of reach. Some degree of challenge helps initiate and maintain a student's competence motive.

Curiosity

Closely linked to the competence motive is **curiosity motivation.** Indeed, the two may be inseparable. There is much recent speculation that the curiosity motive is *not* an acquired motive at all but is, in fact, based on the physiological functioning of the nervous system. There seems to be mounting evidence that the curiosity motive functions autonomously right from birth, that it never depends on food or drink or on any other biological predecessor. **Harry F. Harlow** tells us, for example, that monkeys have been observed taking apart and reassembling a metal lock arrangement. Just like the child who takes a clock apart to see what makes it tick, monkeys will manipulate mechanical puzzles for no reinforcement other than the sheer joy of manipulation. One monkey continued taking a complicated metal lock apart for ten straight hours. "At this point the experiment was terminated because of experimenter fatigue; the monkey was still going strong" (Harlow et al., 1971).

In another study, a monkey was trained to push a certain panel inside the cage, with food as the positive reinforcer. In order to observe the monkey during the learning trials, the experimenter made a small peephole in the screen that separated him from the monkey. The peephole, however, immediately became an object of great fascination for the monkey, and when the experimenter tried to peer through the hole, all he could see was the eye of the monkey peering back.

Monkeys have also been found to be seemingly fascinated by watching the playback of color videotapes of the activities of other monkeys, a demonstration that is especially dramatic when male monkeys are allowed to observe tapes of female monkeys

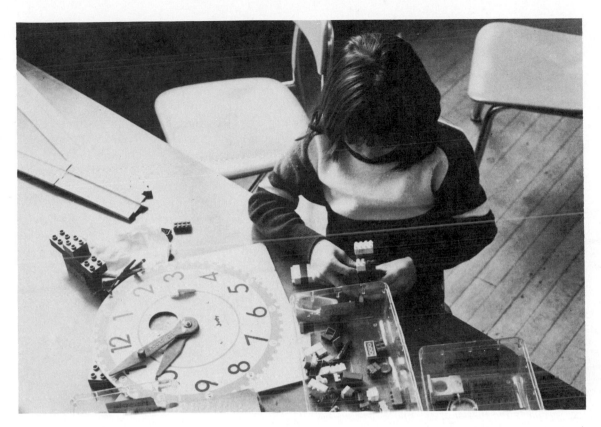

Curiosity may be inborn.

(Swartz and Rosenblum, 1980). Monkeys have actually been conditioned to discriminate between stimuli (a blue card and a yellow card) with the only reinforcer being the opportunity to open a small door in the training box and look out. Thus, the drive to manipulate objects and to explore the world visually "is fundamental and primary in monkeys and man" (Harlow et al., 1971, p. 272).

D. E. Berlyne has suggested that when a person (or animal) is in a situation in which conflicting responses are possible, a curiosity drive is generated and the person (or animal) is motivated to seek further information just to satisfy the drive. That could mean that discovery learning, as Bruner has suggested, is indeed self-reinforcing. Berlyne believes that there is an optimum level of arousal that is physiologically based. He sees arousal level as a function of brain excitation: If the arousal level is too low, the child may attempt to increase it by taking in new stimuli; if the arousal level is too high, however, the child will attempt to lower it by reducing the stimulus inputs (Berlyne, 1960).

Cooperation and Competition

Two other acquired motives that have importance for the teacher are those of cooperation and competition. First, let's dispel the myth that competition is built into the human species as some kind of biologically determined instinct. There is simply no evidence to support such a notion. Actually, anthropologists have found groups of people, for example, the Zuni Indians, in which competition is nonexistent. For the Zunis, the act of winning at anything is so frowned on that it brings disgrace and social ostracism. One young teacher who got a job working with Zuni children attempted to invoke a competitive spirit in order to increase their motivation. She had them all at their desks doing arithmetic problems, and she then asked that the first one to finish proudly stand. Instead, the Zuni children patiently waited for the last one to finish, and then, in unison, *they all stood.* Imagine being an official at a Zuni track meet!

The evidence, therefore, suggests that competition is an acquired motive, that our culture chooses to

Harlow's evidence supports the theory of an innate curiosity drive. One monkey continued to take apart a complicated metal lock for ten straight hours.

tem in evaluating students. This is certainly a major reason why the competitive motive is so strongly ingrained among Americans. That schools reflect the cultural norms of the society as a whole should come as no surprise. Actually, one study shows that the longer a person remains in school, the more competitive he or she becomes (Nelson and Kagan, 1972). Social psychologists have been concerned, however, that competitive grading may in fact have several harmful side effects. For example, negative attitudes, both toward the teacher and school in general, may result from too high a competitive level. Competition also engenders a general hostility, which causes many students to be highly critical of one another (perhaps in hope of building their own images). An important social psychologist, **Morton Deutch,** found that in comparing students in competitive versus cooperative classrooms, the competitive group atmosphere tended to create the following:

1. Students with higher levels of anxiety

2. Students who think less of themselves and their work

3. Students with less favorable attitudes toward their classmates

4. Students with a lowered feeling of responsibility toward others (Deutch, 1979)

Deutch has been studying these factors for over thirty-five years (Deutch, 1949), and his message to teachers is clear: The more cooperative the group tasks students can be involved in, the more positive will be the general classroom atmosphere. He urges that when possible, grades be assigned to group efforts—efforts in which the individual's goal can be achieved only if all the individuals in the entire group reach their goals. The focus should be on interdependence among members of the class and not simply on dog-eat-dog competition.

In another example of cooperative learning, Slavin had students work in mixed-ability groups of four members each. The individual members of each group were forced to cooperate in order to reach their academic goals, since the group was rewarded on the basis of how much *all the group members learned.* The students were, thus, motivated to help one another, and as a result the cooperative group effort produced an increase in student achievement. Slavin's cooperative learning methods have also been used effectively to reduce student prejudices in racially mixed classes and classes where special-education students have

reinforce competitive behavior, often at the expense of cooperation. Actually, Bruner has suggested that a case can be made for cooperativeness as the more fundamental of the two motives. Even biologists have long fretted over this seeming irony. After all, it would seem that the urge to survive is fundamentally selfish, and yet in species after species, from bacteria to humans, cooperative behavior can be observed. Certain bacteria cells hunt their prey in cooperative groups, cornering their targets just like a pride of lions homing in on a wounded gazelle or a group of vampire bats sharing food with unrelated but needy bats. Even fish will take on high-risk forays on behalf of their schools by scouting the surrounding waters for potential enemies. Therefore, Bruner says that reciprocity, which is a motive for working with others cooperatively, may in fact be built into human species and that society itself developed as a result of this most basic motive (Bruner, 1966).

Cooperation in the classroom   American schools have traditionally utilized a competitive grading sys-

SPOTLIGHT ON COOPERATION IN THE CLASSROOM

The Jigsaw Approach

One interesting attempt to utilize both competitive and cooperative motivation is called the *jigsaw approach*, which was first introduced in the late 1970s.[a] Since that time, this technique has been applied successfully many times in a broad range of educational and even business settings. Recognizing the importance of both sets of motives, cooperative and competitive, adherents of this approach set up classrooms or skill groups that combine an *individual reinforcement structure*, in which grades are assigned on the basis of individual performance, and a *cooperative structure*, in which groups of students must share their work in order to carry out assignments. In the latter case interdependence and the cooperation needed to attain a superordinate goal are vital for success. The group effort literally becomes a jigsaw puzzle in which each member receives a part, but only through interaction can the parts be formed into a whole. For example, a textbook chapter may be cut up into paragraphs, and each group member will receive only one paragraph. Using the jigsaw technique for at least part of every day helps reduce some of the destructive elements inherent in the competitive structure and can increase a student's feeling of interdependence and cooperation.[b]

[a] E. Aronson, N. Blaney, C. Stephan, J. Sikes, and M. Snapp, *The jigsaw classroom* (Beverly Hills, Calif.: Sage, 1978).

[b] E. Aronson, Teaching students things they think they know all about. Paper presented at the meeting of the American Psychological Association. Washington: August 1986

been recently mainstreamed (Slavin, 1983). Studies also seem to indicate that cooperative learning approaches lead to higher levels of *intrinsic* motivation, especially among less able children (Knight, 1982).

Deutch has even been using cooperative learning techniques to successfully combat the dropout problem among inner-city adolescents (Deutch, 1988). Says Deutch, "The probability of reward is positively linked so that as one's personal situation improves or worsens so do those of the others . . . To the extent I win, you win, and to the extent I lose, you lose" (Deutch, 1979, p. 398).

However, there are problems inherent in group-grading practices—a fact that Deutch freely admits. These include

development of vested interests in one's specialized role in the cooperative system, the growth of in-group favoritism that may lead to discrimination against out-group members, and the evolution of excessive conformity and reluctance to question the majority opinion (Deutch, 1979, p. 400).

Also, some students simply don't have the needed motivation to cooperate with a real sense of responsibility.

Group effects   Groups by their very nature change behavior. Working in a group situation has two main effects: It may increase feelings of competition and motivation on the one hand, and it may increase feelings of anxiety and provide distractions on the other. The presence of other people explicitly or implicitly may create a competitive situation. In research studies the subjects seem to assume that the researcher will be making comparisons and/or they hope to impress other members of the group. If the subject's motivation is high to begin with, increasing it may have a damaging effect. However, if the subject's motivation is low, the competitive atmosphere of the group situation may enhance performance.

The nature of the task is also of great importance. When an individual in a group situation begins feeling simultaneously more competitive and more anxious, his or her performance on simple, nonintellectual tasks is enhanced. As the task becomes more difficult and more intellectual, the effect of working in a group becomes increasingly detrimental to performance. Before using any of the group techniques in a learning situation, the teacher should carefully take into account both the level of the students' motivation and the nature of the task.

The classroom by its very nature is always going

Does competitive activity produce harmful side effects?

to promote some competitive feelings. Students, like the subjects in the previously mentioned research studies, assume that performance comparisons will be made. They will also try to gain the attention of their teacher and peers by various methods of "trying to impress." Despite these facts, the teacher can choose to emphasize competition in certain areas and to deemphasize it in others. Highly motivated students who are working on difficult math problems would probably be better off if left alone at their desks. Less motivated students who are working on simpler rote tasks might do better if the work were

done openly, for example, by using flash cards to drill the whole class in multiplication tables.

Competition can probably never be completely ruled out of an American classroom situation. Social psychologists have shown over and over again that even in situations where cooperation is the most efficient route to success, competition continues to dominate. Studies have shown that even when subjects fully realize that the rewards will be greater for cooperative group interaction, they still prefer to compete with one another (Minas et al., 1960).

Despite this powerful competitive tendency of

American students, the teacher can still set up conditions that reduce it. Preparing group projects for which a single grade is assigned helps promote cooperation. Any situation in which the students are working toward a superordinate goal—a goal none of them can attain independently—will help to reduce competitive responses.

Cooperation and cognitive development Cognitive psychologists like Jerome Bruner and Jean Piaget, although suggesting that motives toward cooperation and reciprocity may have strong biological underpinnings, warn that the strength of these motives may vary with the age of the child. For example, Piaget tells us that young children are limited in their ability to cooperate because of *egocentricity*—the inability to take another person's point of view (Piaget, 1932). As the child grows older, however, and acquires more sophisticated levels of thought, cooperative behavior becomes more possible. Moral principles like "mutual respect" can be acted on only when the child's level of cognitive growth allows for their full incorporation (Krebs, 1979). A great deal of research in this area is obviously needed—research that compares in general the effects of competitive versus cooperative structuring and that also makes particular comparisons at various age levels (Nelson and Dweck, 1977). The young child who firmly believes that obedience to adults is more important than loyalty to peers will have great difficulty appreciating the group spirit inherent in cooperative structuring.

UNCONSCIOUS MOTIVATION

Sigmund Freud stated that roughly two-thirds of all human motivation lies below the threshold of conscious awareness. That is, Freud estimated that most human behavior is motivated by reasons of which we are totally unaware and which are therefore largely irrational. It was Freud's contention that the human motivational system was much like a floating iceberg, with only a small fraction of its bulk above the surface. To Freud, and also to many modern psychologists, any effort to understand why people behave as they do must take into account **unconscious motivation**—that is, the irrational needs that lurk beneath the level of conscious awareness.

Although these motives may be unconscious to the person having them, a trained observer can often make sense out of this apparent irrationality. For example, a second-grade student is totally unaware of the reasons for his or her sudden change in behavior—using baby talk, wetting the bed at night, and not concentrating in class. The school psychologist might ascribe these responses to a general motive to regress—perhaps the young student has recently been presented with a baby brother. Similarly, a ten-year-old student suddenly develops symptoms of a full-blown school phobia: The child becomes a truant, getting to school only when brought in kicking and screaming. Again, the school psychologist might find that the youngster's home situation presents great conflict—perhaps the parents are getting a divorce. The teacher certainly should be alert to any dramatic behavior change on the part of a student and should at least be ready, if it continues, to make the proper referral.

Repression

One form of unconscious motivation that may be particularly perplexing to the teacher is repression, as when a child does something—perhaps in full view of the teacher and class—and then later denies any personal memory of the event.

> Fourth-grade student Kenny D. comes from a home where parental standards are exacting and nonpermissive. Kenny is typically quiet and conforming. He is what has been called an "overly steered" child. One day in class, Kenny uncharacteristically has a verbal confrontation with John H., a youngster suffering from cerebral palsy. Suddenly, Kenny knocks away John's crutches, pushes him to the ground, and begins to pummel the handicapped child. Both the teacher and the other students quickly pull Kenny away and accuse him of being evil. Later, in the principal's office, Kenny flatly denies that the event has ever taken place. He cries and says he is being falsely accused and even asks to take a lie-detector test.

In this instance, Freud might say that Kenny has repressed any memory of the guilt-provoking situation. Repression is the exclusion from consciousness of anxiety-producing memories, thoughts, or impulses. Repression differs from ordinary forgetting in two ways: First, with repression the memory loss is total, and second, repression is always triggered by anxiety.

Less dramatic cases of repression abound in the classroom—a student with a distaste for math constantly "forgetting" to do his assignment; a student with a fear of being in front of the class "forgetting" to prepare her oral report (and being genuinely surprised when called on); a student, traumatized by the thought of the physical contact involved in athletics, "forgetting" to bring his sneakers to gym class.

Some of these situations, of course, require the professional intervention of the school psychologist, but in many cases an understanding and compassionate teacher can provide the student with enough insight to minimize the trauma that caused the repression. A caring, nonjudgmental, and accepting teacher can often defuse the student's underlying anxieties.

The Zeigarnik Effect

The other side of the repression coin is a phenomenon called the **Zeigarnik effect.** In some learning situations, the thought of an unfinished assignment motivates the student in such a way that the memory is actually *enhanced*. Students are better able to recall unfinished assignments than those which have been completed (Zeigarnik, 1927).

Think of the time that you yourself had a term paper to write and tried mightily to put it off and out of your mind. Perhaps you went to a movie but couldn't enjoy it because the nagging thought of the unfinished paper haunted your every waking moment. That's the Zeigarnik effect! To alleviate the tension of the memory, you finally had to "bite the bullet" and start the paper.

To a large extent, therefore, the Zeigarnik effect plays into the hands of the teacher, since memory *enhancement* is obviously more positive than memory destruction or repression. It may at first seem as if the Zeigarnik effect and repression are self-contradictory. It may seem that the thought of an unfinished term paper must itself be so anxiety-provoking that the whole idea of it would be repressed. To some extent this is true. More recent studies have shown that if the unfinished task is so threatening that the individual's entire feeling of self-esteem is at stake, it is possible for the Zeigarnik effect to boomerang. In this situation, the finished tasks will be remembered more than the unfinished ones.

Thus, the teacher who attaches too many dire consequences to an assignment may find the Zeigarnik effect being reversed. When this happens, the assignment is no longer self-motivating through memory enhancement, and it may become repressed into the never-never land of "out of sight, out of mind."

MOTIVATION AND CONFLICT

Human behavior does not result from the simple action of a single motive. People constantly seek a number of goals, often simultaneously. One of these goals may act antagonistically to another, thus creating **motivational conflicts.**

Sources of Motivational Conflicts

Dependence and independence   Every child is faced with the conflict of dependence versus independence—a conflict that seems to reach a roaring crescendo during adolescence. The conflict arises on the one hand from the need to remain dependent, to have somebody else make one's decisions, to have a shoulder to cry on, and on the other hand from the equally strong drive to be free, to make one's own decisions, and to become self-reliant. Leaving the cocoon of womb and family can be a highly stressful stage of life. From birth on, the child is engaged in the long and sometimes painful process of slowly giving up dependence in order to attain independence; and even as an adult, there is compromise and balance between these two competing needs.

Sex   Another source of motivational conflict occurs in the area of sex. As children advance through puberty, they are confronted with the dilemma of becoming aware of their own sexual needs together with society's demand that these needs not be satisfied. Our society does not yet fully condone any form of premarital sexual release. The conflict is further heightened in today's society, for with advancing technology and the need for more and more education and training to compete successfully, marriage and its privilege of socially sanctioned sexual expression are further delayed.

Aggression   Aggression is still another source of motivational conflict. When persons occasionally have hostile tendencies (and who doesn't?), society allows very few opportunities for this hostility to be overtly expressed (see Chapter 17). Although overt aggression is acceptable in certain prescribed situations such as contact sports and warfare, it typically results in very serious legal consequences when practiced in day-to-day interactions.

Achievement and altruism   The child also faces the cultural paradox of competitive achievement versus the Judeo-Christian ethic of "Love thy neighbor." Our children are urged to compete, to win, to succeed at all costs, and yet they are told that this should not be a dog-eat-dog world and that they should be good Samaritans.

Reactions to Conflict

In the course of these and many more assorted conflicts, individuals react differently. Some children, and adults too, seem to thrive in times of motivational crisis, while others simply fold up and perhaps develop a whole series of psychological symptoms. As Allport once said, "The same fire that melts the butter hardens the egg."

Teachers must be made aware that the manifestations of emotional symptoms may not always be obvious. The teacher usually devotes much time and attention to the rebellious child. Thus, by "acting out" conflicts, the overtly aggressive child receives the attention and recognition of the teacher. However, a more serious psychological symptom, that of withdrawal, may easily escape the attention of the teacher (and parent, too). The child who withdraws, perhaps into a make-believe world of fantasy, does not upset the school routine and therefore does not seem to present a problem. Some teachers—at times, perhaps all—actually wish they had more withdrawn children, more "little angels," in their classes. This syndrome, however, can be serious since the withdrawn child who does not get needed attention and recognition may slip into a vicious circle that may result in further withdrawal and even a complete loss of contact with reality.

MOTIVATION AND DEVELOPMENT

In general we can say that broad types of motivational systems will vary according to both age and stage. This means that with younger children in the preschool and elementary grades, the predominant motivators will be extrinsically determined. Young pupils may become "interested" in learning because the teacher is much bigger and more physically powerful, or because they can win a candy bar, a gold star, a smiling face on a paper, or personal recognition and approval from the teacher or the other children. Such motivators are largely extrinsic or separate from the learning material itself.

This does not mean that intrinsic motivation is impossible at this age. However, to expect that elementary-age children will focus on basic skill learning (the three R's) solely for intrinsic reasons may be unrealistic. The romantic notion that teachers can constantly reveal the mysteries of academic disciplines so ingeniously that pupils will be filled with a gnawing, devouring compulsion to learn results in frustration

for the teacher and puzzlement for the pupil. Thus, the teacher's role at that level is to employ a variety of extrinsic motivators in addition to finding material that is intrinsically interesting. In this way, the likelihood of shaping the attention and time on task of the pupils will be increased.

During adolescence, of course, there is a greater likelihood for intrinsic motivation to become a major factor in pupil learning because of the adolescent's ability to perform formal operations. Thus, with the increased ability for self-direction and abstract reasoning, secondary school pupils can, for greater time periods, enjoy learning for its own sake. On their own, pupils can now seek out new ideas, new sources, and new concepts. Intrinsic motivation then becomes self-reinforcing.

However, this does not mean that the problems of motivation and learning are fully solved as a result of the onset of formal operations. In the first place, as we noted in Chapter 5, the majority of secondary school pupils do not employ formal operations even though that potential exists. In the second place, pupils may become intrinsically motivated to study material totally unrelated to the required school topics. Thus, there is no guarantee at all that adolescents will be bursting with enthusiasm to find out what the reasons are behind the Triangle of Trade or why the Tigris and Euphrates were so important or how English poetry changed with Wordsworth's "Tintern Abbey" or what the Pythagorean theorem means. Also it is apparent that the "time bomb" effect will not work as a motivational device unless the students are at extremely high levels of intrinsic motivation. If a teacher simply resorts to the plea, "Twenty years from now, class, you'll be glad that you learned about gerunds, the ablative case, and parsing," the class may react with glazed eyes, slouched postures, and puzzled expressions. The nonverbal message back to the teacher will be loud and clear—"Oh yeah? Why?"

Thus, from a developmental point of view, the continuum of motivational factors from extrinsic to intrinsic presents the teacher with an array of strategies to be matched with the pupil's age, stage, and interest level. It is most important to remember both White's and Allport's concepts. A teacher can employ a variety of extrinsic rewards as motivators, such as learning to please, to earn "tokens," to work for extra recess time, and so on. Such methods do not necessarily mean that the pupils will always be dependent on these specific external and extrinsic motivators. There can be, as we have seen, an intrinsic drive toward self-directed competence as well as toward functional autonomy. Students may start out learning to please the teacher and to earn material rewards and then find that the means (learning) becomes an end in itself. In the long run, of course, this is what is truly wanted—students capable of the enjoyment and stimulation that intrinsic learning experiences provide.

THE TEACHER'S ROLE

The teacher is in an especially advantageous position regarding a child's motivational conflicts, because outside of the parents, perhaps nobody else has the unique opportunity of being able to observe the child for so many hours and in such a variety of situations. The teacher can observe how the child relates to adults, to the peer group, or to frustration, and can detect when these reactions seem at all deviant. This is not to suggest that teachers must all become profes-

sional psychologists, but like it or not, we do "psychologize" whenever we make inferences about how or why people behave as they do.

The study of motivation in the classroom, especially as it relates to academic achievement, is indeed fascinating. As people come to better understand themselves, master themselves, and free themselves, all of humankind will be the beneficiaries. To paraphrase the late Lawrence K. Frank, the fundamental motives of the individual are precisely the same as the fundamental motives of society (Frank, 1969). Ideally, the school and the learning tasks in school should be organized in such a way as to promote the growth of personal competence and self-mastery. Therefore, important goals of the school should include fostering, nurturing, and facilitating personal growth in a learning context, thus counteracting debilitating effects and enhancing the full realization of human potential.

SUMMARY

Thorndike was the first psychologist to document experimentally the link between learning and motivation. He called this link the law of effect. Motivation has since become a firmly established concept in psychology and education. Motivation never acts in a vacuum but is always acting on and being acted on by both learning and perception.

Motives are composed of needs (deficits within the person) and drives (needs that cause the person to act). The whole sequence is called motivational when the drive is goal-directed. Although all people have physiological motives based on physical needs for food, sex, warmth, and so on, of more importance to the educational psychologist are the acquired motives. Allport's concept of functional autonomy suggests one way by which motives are acquired—when a means to an end becomes an end in itself.

Various emotional states may act to influence motivated activity. People will respond differently, despite similar motivations, when under different emotional sets. The physiological arousal associated with an emotion may even transfer from one motive to another. When the arousal activates motives, especially acquired motives, that are in opposition to one another, psychologists explain this phenomenon on the basis of what is called the opponent process theory of acquired motivation.

A distinction is made between intrinsic and extrinsic motives, or between those motives that can be satisfied from within and those that demand external satisfaction. In addition, Maslow has suggested a universal order in which people try to satisfy their needs—from physiological and safety needs to love, esteem, and self-actualizing needs.

Self-regulated learning occurs when the student achieves an intrinsic motivational set and is able to postpone gratification and rely on inner resources. Self-regulated learning and motivation are seen as interactive processes, with the learner's perception of personal academic self-worth as both the cause of a strengthened motivation for further learning as well as the effect of past outcomes. Techniques have been proposed, especially by the cognitive psychologists, for the teaching of self-regulation to those who don't seem able to achieve it on their own.

One of the most potent acquired motives is for social approval—from one's parents, one's teachers, and one's peer group. The skilled teacher takes advantage of this need and uses it to help nourish a genuine love of learning in his or her students.

Another important motive is based on the need for achievement. This need may become autonomous and function as an intrinsic drive to succeed. McClelland has conducted a great deal of research in the area of achievement. Sex differences in achievement are seen as culturally determined. Certain studies have shown that some women fail to achieve because they have learned to fear success.

White suggests the importance of competence motivation, an intrinsic drive to master one's environment. This motive is even thought to have had survival value for the human race.

Harlow shows the significance of the curiosity motive, an intrinsic and self-reinforcing motive to discover how things work. Bruner's discovery learning takes advantage of this motive.

Cooperative and competitive motives are acquired by the developing child, and these, too, can be brought into action in the classroom. Cooperativeness—especially in the older child—can be manipulated to create a less anxious classroom atmosphere. The competitive motive is not instinctive and is just

as culturally determined as is an acquired taste for certain foods.

Freud pointed out the importance of unconscious motivation and insisted that most human behavior is so determined. One example of unconscious motivation is repression—a form of motivated forgetting. The Zeigarnik effect, in contrast, is a kind of motivated remembering of those tasks which have not yet been completed.

Humans are beset by many motivational conflicts, such as needs for both dependence and independence. The way in which these conflicts are resolved depends on a host of cultural and personality factors. People may react to motivational conflicts by procrastinating—putting off for tomorrow (or forever) whatever produces the conflicts and anxiety.

The school is best organized when it promotes the growth of personal competence and self-mastery. The teacher's role is crucial in this process.

KEY TERMS AND NAMES

achievement motivation
acquired motives
approval, motive for social
Morton Deutch
drives
extrinsic motives
functional autonomy
Harry F. Harlow
   curiosity motivation
Matina S. Horner
   fear of success
intrinsic motives

D. C. McClelland
motivational conflicts
motives
need hierarchy
needs
opponent process theory
physiological motives
self-regulated learning
unconscious motivation
Robert White
Zeigarnik effect

THEORY INTO PRACTICE: MOTIVATION AND PROCRASTINATION

Of all the threats to achievement motivation, perhaps one of the most damaging is that of procrastination. The child who constantly puts off assignments soon begins to lag so far behind that new material becomes virtually impossible to understand. The teacher may sequence the topics in elegantly logical steps, but the child who hasn't attempted to take step one will find step five to be all but incomprehensible.

Obviously, everyone at one time or another becomes involved in procrastination, but the underachieving student may be making an absolute fetish

of this self-defeating trap. Research has shown that habitual procrastinators typically use one or all of three basic delaying tactics for allowing themselves the apparent luxury of putting things off.

Mañana   In this first case the student is convinced that what is perceived to be an unpleasant task will be done . . . but later. Homework is not done during study-hall time but will be done later, at home. Studying cannot be done at home during the afternoon because a "break" is needed after a long, tiring school day. Studying cannot be done that evening because the parents have the TV on and sister is listening to records—"But I'll catch up on the weekend, and if not this weekend, then the next one."

Contingency mañana   This method is used when the student sets up contingent conditions for completing a task, such as "I can't start writing my essay until my room is properly set up for studying." An entire term may pass before the room conditions become just right—pencil sharpener installed, new lights put in, cross-ventilation worked out, soundproof doors set up—the contingencies may be endless. And even then, "I can't write this essay until I've read all the books in the library on the topic, and I haven't gone to the library yet because I missed the session early in the term when they explained the card system."

Catch-22   The two previous methods allowed the student to retain the blissful hope that someday the job would be done—maybe not today, maybe not tomorrow, but sometime in the distant future. Catch-22, however, typically leads to the feeling that the job will never be done, "but it's not my fault." In this situation, circumstances are perceived as conspiring against the student so that whatever way the child turns, the goal of finishing the task is blocked. "Since the teacher doesn't like me I'll flunk anyway, even if I do my homework." "I can't ask Sally to the dance because my teeth aren't straight, and my family can't afford big dental bills." While this type of excuse often may bring on gloomy and depressed moods, the logic of the excuse seems to be so airtight that giving up becomes easy and even rewarding. The situation may even progress to the extent that the student begins assuming the role of a self-declared martyr, while still feeling good because he or she is so noble in facing impossible conditions. The motive, of course, is to fail, but also to enjoy the failure.

Select someone you know who has obviously been using one of these tactics (this search will not be difficult) and work with that person, using the following guidelines.

1. Ask the person to make a list of at least six things currently being put off: term paper, diet, exercise, whatever. Having the reality of a definite list helps prevent allowing the student to just forget about the various goals.

2. Establish an objective, limited as it might at first be, for each of the delayed plans: write at least one paragraph of the term paper, take off one pound of weight.

3. Slowly increase the rate and strength of the goals.

4. Ask the student to verbalize aloud several key phrases: It's just as hard to start tomorrow as today. If I can take the first step, I can take the second. Even if I don't yet have the ability to complete the task, I will develop my skills as I go along.

5. Indicate to the student that using cop-outs such as "I'm basically lazy" is itself simply a diversionary tactic.

6. Finally, convince the student that all the smoke screens and diversions being used are indeed very creative and that these creative powers can be channeled toward solid academic gains.

We are indebted to William Knaus, an expert in the field of motivational conflict, for providing us with the ideas for the preceding material. For a more complete coverage of the procrastination syndrome, read Knaus's *Do It Now*, published by Prentice-Hall in 1979.

Postscript

We should acknowledge that even with a carefully sequenced approach to the problem of procrastination, success may not always be ensured. One of the authors recently tested out the model on an advanced graduate student who was a notorious procrastinator: late assignments, papers always delayed, urgent requests for recommendations always at the eleventh hour, thesis topics in constant flux, and so forth. Finally, an action plan was developed. The student made out the list, established manageable objectives, and slowly increased the rate of accomplishments. She was also told to verbalize key phrases and *very directly* told to stop using her favorite cop-out phrase, "I'm overwhelmed and overworked, and I want my work to be the best you've ever seen." Shortly after these sessions ended, a Christmas card arrived from the grateful student. Along with the traditional greetings of the season she had penned a note of thanks, saying how well the new system was working. The Christmas card's envelope was postmarked January 9.

REFERENCES

Allport, G. W. (1967). Functional autonomy. In J. F. Perez and others, *General psychology: Selected readings* (pp. 157–159). New York: Van Nostrand.

Aronson, E. (1986). *Teaching students things they think they know all about.* Paper presented at the meeting of the American Psychological Association, Washington, August.

Aronson, E., Blaney, N., Stephan, C., Sikes, J., and Snapp, M. (1978). *The jigsaw classroom.* Beverly Hills, Calif.: Sage.

Bandura, A. (1989). Human agency in social cognitive theory. *American Psychologist, 44,* 1179–1184.

Bennett, W., and Gurin, J. (1982). *The dieter's dilemma.* New York: Basic Books.

Berlyne, D. E. (1960). *Conflict, arousal and curiosity.* New York: McGraw-Hill.

Bornstein, P. H. (1985). Self-instructional training: A commentary and state of the art. *Journal of Applied Behavior Analysis, 18,* 69–72.

Bruner, J. S. (1966). *Toward a theory of instruction.* Cambridge: Harvard University Press.

Callero, P. L., and Piliavin, J. A. (1983). Developing a commitment to blood donation: The impact of one's first experience. *Journal of Applied Psychology, 13,* 1–16.

Coleman, J. S., and associates (1966, *Equality of educational opportunity.* Washington: U.S. Department of Health, Education, and Welfare.

Cronbach, L. J. (1977). *Educational psychology* (3d ed.). New York: Harcourt Brace Jovanovich.

Davis, C. (1967). Results of the self-selection of diets by young children. In J. F. Perez, R. C. Sprinthall, G. S. Grosser, and P. J. Anastasiou (Eds.), *General psychology: Selected readings* (pp. 166–171). New York: Van Nostrand.

Deci, E. L., and Ryan, R. M. (1980). The empirical exploration of intrinsic motivational processes. In L. Berkowitz (Ed.), *Advances in experimental social psychology,* vol. 13. Orlando, Fla.: Academic Press.

Deci, E. L., Vallerand, R. J., Pelletier, L. G., and Ryan R. M. (1991). Motivation and education: The self-determination perspective. *Educational Psychologist, 26,* 3,4), 325–346.

Deutch, M. (1949). The effects of cooperation and competition upon group process. *Human Relations, 2,* 199–231.

Deutch, M. (1979). Education and distributive justice. *American Psychologist, 34*(5), 391–401.

Deutch, M. (1988). Use of innovative educational techniques with dropouts. In *William T. Grant Foundation Annual Report.* New York.

Ebel, R. L. (1980). The failure of schools without failure. *Phi Delta Kappan* (February), 386–388.

Frank, L. K. (1969). The fundamental needs of the child. In R. C. Sprinthall and N. A. Sprinthall (Eds.), *Educational psychology: Selected readings* (pp. 70–74). New York: Van Nostrand-Reinhold.

Garber, J., Kriss, M. R., Koch, M., and Lindholm, L. (1988). Recurrent depression in adolescents: A follow-up study. *Journal of the American Academy of Child and Adolescent Psychiatry, 27,* 49–54.

Goodenow, C. (1992). Strengthening the links between educational psychology and the study of social contexts. *Educational Psychologist, 27,* 177–196.

Gottfried, A. E. (1983). Intrinsic motivation in young children. *Young Children, 39*(1), 64–73.

Gottfried, A. E. (1985). Academic intrinsic motivation in elementary and junior high school students. *Journal of Educational Psychology, 77,* 631–645.

Hallahan, D. P., and Kauffman, J. M. (1988). *Exceptional children.* Englewood Cliffs, N.J.: Prentice-Hall.

Harlow, H. F., McGaugh, J. L., and Thompson, R. F. (1971). *Psychology* (p. 271). San Francisco: Albion.

Harvey, A. L. (1975). Goal setting as compensator for fear of success. *Adolescence, 10,* 137–142.

Hechinger, F. M. (1979). The principal is the secret to better schools. *The New York Times* (May 29), D34.

Horner, M. S. (1968). Women's will to fail. *Psychology Today, 3,* 36–38.

Horner, M. S. (1969). Fail: Bright women. *Psychology Today, 3,* 46–48.

Hummel, R., and Sprinthall, N. (1965). Under-achievement related to interests, attitudes and values. *Personnel and Guidance Journal, 44,* 388–395.

Kagan, J. (1984). *The nature of the child.* New York: Basic Books.

Knight, C. J. (1982). Cooperative learning: A new approach to an old idea. *Teaching Exceptional Children* (May), 233–238.

Kounin, J. (1970). *Discipline and group management in classrooms.* New York: Holt, Rinehart & Winston.

Krebs, D. (1979). Reconsiderations. *Human Nature, 2*(1), 93–95.

Laner, M. R. (1979). Sex and the single check. *Psychology Today, 12,* 45.

Lepper, M. R. (1985). Microcomputers in education: Motivational and social issues. *American Psychologist, 40,* 1–18.

Maccoby, E., and Jacklin, C. (1974). *The psychology of sex differences.* Stanford, Calif.: Stanford University Press.

Maehr, M. L., and Kleiber, D. A. (1981). The graying of achievement motivation. *American Psychologist, 36,* 787–793.

Maslow, A. H. (1954). *Motivation and personality.* New York: Harper & Row.

McClelland, D. C. (1965). Toward a theory of motive acquisition. *American Psychologist, 20*(2), 321–333.

McDougall, W. (1908). *Social psychology.* London: Methuen.

Minas, J. S., Scodel, A., Marlowe, D., and Rawson, H.

(1960). Some descriptive aspects of two-person non-zero-sum games. *Journal of Conflict Resolution, 4,* 193–197.

Nelson, L., and Kagan, S. (1972). Competition: The star-spangled scramble. *Psychology Today, 6,* 53–91.

Nelson, S., and Dweck, C. (1977). Motivation, competence, and reward allocation. *Developmental Psychology, 13*(3), 192–197.

Nicholls, J. G. (1984). Achievement motivation: Conceptions of ability, subjective experience, task choice, and performance. *Psychological Review, 9,* 328–346.

Nolan, T. (1991). Self-questioning and prediction: Combining metacognitive strategies. *Journal of Reading, 35*(2), 132–138.

Paris, S. G., Cross, D. R., and Lipson, M. Y. (1984). Informed strategies for learning: A program to improve children's reading awareness and comprehension. *Journal of Educational Psychology, 76,* 1239–1252.

Paris, S. G., and Newman, R. S. (1990). Developmental aspects of self-regulated learning. *Educational Psychologist, 25,* 87–102.

Parker, J. G., and Asher, S. R. (1987). Peer relations and later personal adjustment: Are low-accepted children at risk? *Psychological Bulletin, 102,* 357–389.

Parlee, M. B. (1979). Conversational politics. *Psychology Today, 12,* 48–56.

Piaget, J. (1932). *The mortal judgment of the child.* New York: Harcourt, Brace.

Postman, L., Bruner, J. S., and McGinnies, E. M. (1948). Personal values as selective factors in perception. *Journal of Abnormal and Social Psychology, 43,* 142–154.

Riesenzein, R. (1983). The Schachter theory of emotion: Two decades later. *Psychological Bulletin, 94,* 239–264.

Rofe, Y. (1984). Stress and affiliation: A utility theory. *Psychological Review, 91,* 235–250.

Rohles, F. H. (1980). Temperature or temperament: A psychologist looks at thermal comfort. *ASHRAE Transactions, 86,* 541–551.

Rosehan, D. L., and Seligman, M. E. P. (1989). *Abnormal psychology,* (2d ed.). New York: Norton.

Rosenshine, B. V. (1980). How time is spent in elementary classrooms. In C. Denham and A. Liberman (Eds.), *Time to learn* (pp. 107–126). Washington: National Institute of Education.

Sanford, R. N. (1936). The effects of abstinence from food upon imaginal processes. *Journal of Psychology, 2,* 129–136.

Schunk, D. H. (1991). Self-efficacy and motivation. *Educational Psychologist, 26,* (3,4), 207–231.

Slavin, R. E. (1983). *Cooperative learning.* New York: Longmans.

Solomon, R. L. (1980). The opponent process theory of acquired motivation. *American Psychologist, 35,* 691–712.

Sprinthall, R. C., and Bennett, B. (1978). Conformity and non-conformity among married women: The Reisman typologies. *Psychological Reports, 42,* 1195–1201.

Swartz, K. B., and Rosenblum, L. A. (1980). Operant responding by bonnet macaques for color videotape recordings of social stimuli. *Animal Learning Behavior, 8,* 322–331.

Tannen, D. (1990). *You just don't understand: Women and men in conversation.* New York: Morrow.

Thorndike, E. L. (1913). *Educational psychology: The psychology of learning* (p. 2). New York: Teachers College Press.

Webb, N. (1983). Predicting learning from student interactions: Defining the interaction variables. *Educational Psychologist, 18,* 33–41.

White, R. (1959). Motivation reconsidered: The concept of competence. *Psychological Review, 66,* 197–233.

Zeigarnik, B. (1927). *Uber das behalten von erledigten und unerledigten handlugen. Psychologische Forschung, 9,* 1–85.

Zimmerman, B. J. (1989). A social cognitive view of self-regulated learning. *Journal of Educational Psychology, 81,* 329–339.

Zimmerman, B. J. (1991). Self-regulated learning and academic achievement: An overview. *Educational Psychologist, 25,* 3–17.

Zimmerman, B. J., and Martinez-Pons, M. (1990). Student differences in self-regulated learning: Relating grade, sex and giftedness of self-efficacy and strategy use. *Journal of Educational Psychology, 82,* 51–59.

STUDENT DISCIPLINE: A DEVELOPMENTAL MODEL

Ask almost any teacher or adult to identify the most difficult problem of education and childrearing and he or she will usually mention discipline. In this chapter, we provide some historical background, showing the timeless nature of the problem and looking at some of the old theories and beliefs about character formation. We then outline the developmental approach to discipline, largely based on Lawrence Kohlberg's theory and illustrated with positive and negative modes of discipline at each stage. A chart outlines the answers to four related discipline questions: who makes the rules, who keeps them, how are the rules enforced, and why do the students obey? The chapter concludes with some case studies illustrating different methods of humane control according to developmental level.

HISTORICAL BACKGROUND

An archaeologist reportedly found evidence of the antiquity of the problem of discipline in the ruins of ancient Sumeria. He is supposed to have dug up some clay tablets recording a conversation between an adult and a teenager. According to the archaeologist's translation, the adult harangued the teenager as follows, "Grow up. Stop hanging around the public square and wandering up and down the street. Go

to school. Night and day you torture me. Night and day you waste your time having fun" (1968).

These words were spoken some 4,000 years ago; the problem—lack of discipline, unruliness, wasting time. The more recently discovered memoirs of President Edward Everett of Harvard suggest that he spent the most miserable three years of his life (1846–1849) dealing with problems of student discipline. As a scholar, Everett was regarded as equal to Pericles in Athens, yet he complained bitterly about his students:

> Hateful duties in the morning to question three students about beckoning to loose women in the College Yard on Sunday afternoon; to two others about whistling in the passage; to another about smoking in the College Yard. Is this all I am fit for?. . .The life I am now leading must end, or it will end me.
> . . .My time taken up all day with the most disgusting details of discipline, such as make the heart perfectly sick—fraud, deception, falsehood, unhandsome conduct, parents and friends harassing me all the time and foolishly believing the lies their children tell them (1965, p. 583).

If we turn to fiction we find similar sentiments. The tragic figure of the father in John Updike's novel, *The Centaur*, is likewise upset and in despair concerning student behavior and discipline. Mr. Caldwell, perhaps overstating the problem for effect, turns to a particularly "slow-witted" pupil, Deifendorf:

> "The Founding Fathers," he explained, "in their wisdom decided that children were all an unnatural strain on parents. So they provided jails called schools, equipped with tortures called an education. . . . I am a paid keeper of society's unusables—the lame, the halt, the insane and the ignorant. The only incentive I can give you, kid, to behave yourself is this: if you don't buckle down and learn something, you'll be as dumb as I am and you'll have to teach school to earn a living" (Updike, 1963, pp. 80–81).

It seems safe to conclude that problems of student behavior and discipline have been with us for a long time and will probably be with us for a long time to come. Studies of teachers' attitudes toward children's behavior have revealed concerns exactly like those revealed by the ruins of ancient Sumeria, by President Everett of Harvard, and by Updike's Mr. Caldwell. In 1928, for example, a study found that the greatest concern of most teachers was acting-out, loud, disruptive children (Wickman, 1928). Some thirty years later, in a replication, another researcher came to very much the same conclusion (Beilin, 1959). A particularly tragic effect of this preoccupation is that teachers may fail to recognize one of the most common mental-health problems—excessive inhibition—because their attention is diverted by the noisy, aggressive pupils. Even though educational psychologists have been trying to convince teachers to look beyond the obvious and recognize that withdrawn children may be a more serious problem than loud, active children, there is still a very strong tendency to equate activity and noise with a discipline problem and to ignore passivity.

STUDENT DISCIPLINE AND THE FALLACY OF CHARACTER EDUCATION

A general assumption we all tend to make about discipline is that pupils learn best when they are quiet. When we say, "Learn with your eyes and ears but not with your mouth," we are assuming that we can't learn anything if we are talking, making noise, or moving around. When all the students are sitting quietly, listening in rapt attention to the teacher, it does look as if they are learning. However, as we have already noted, appearances are deceiving.

If we accept the idea that a quiet atmosphere promotes learning, it follows that any breach of that atmosphere is not to be tolerated. In fact, to carry this logic a step further, it becomes the teacher's moral duty to keep peace in the classroom, because it is by this means that pupils develop the proper moral character. Thus, the teacher's role is seen in terms of simple-minded **character training,** or moral education.

Because of the seriousness with which moral education is viewed, no latitude or flexibility can be allowed. Student behavior is an indication of character, and so teachers may react strongly to noncompliant behavior: There is no room for give-and-take when we are dealing with issues of character.

Finally, to make matters even worse, this view assumes that by forcing obedience and conformity on children in school, self-directing and self-controlled adults will result. To many, however, it seems strangely paradoxical to teach self-control, personal independence, and responsibility by forcing students to be dependent and controlled. The discontinuity between demanding one set of behaviors when people are young and expecting a completely opposite set when they are older strikes some as counterproductive. Education will simply not promote personal independence if dependence and conformity are insisted on during the formative years. We noted earlier in this volume the almost indelible effect of early experience on later behavior. Teaching dependence and conformity will tend to enhance those behaviors rather than promote independence, inquiry, and self-direction. Or, as Horace Mann, an eminent educator of the nineteenth century, put it, "We cannot educate for freedom with the methods of slavery."

DISCIPLINE: A DEVELOPMENTAL METHOD

Although the problems of classroom discipline have been with us from the beginning of formal instruction, solutions have been elusive. Generally, most approaches to classroom discipline have been too singular. Each school of thought, so to speak, recommends a single procedure almost regardless of the age of the pupil or the situation. It's like writing a single prescription to be used in any emergency situation. For example, it is common to find a particular dictum or discipline law promoted as *the* answer. There is a view that strongly suggests that a teacher

Teachers often assume that silent attention is a sign of learning and that orderly obedience is a sign of character building. The teacher must face the conflict between the need for classroom control and the encouragement of self-reliance and responsibility.

can never permit any departure from a policy of strict obedience. Even the most minor breach of classroom peace is to be met with instant punishment. With this **authoritarian approach to discipline,** there is no room for variation or negotiation, regardless of circumstances. The dictum states, "Lay down the rules." In other words, permit no deviation, or chaos and anarchy will reign. Such a single-variable solution to interactions as complex as teaching inevitably fails. Either the teacher gets so caught up with enforcement that there is little time for teaching, or the pupils get so caught up with the game that their energy is spent in constantly testing the limits.

As if in reaction to the absolute obedience approach, an opposite extreme is often employed. Again, a single solution is proposed, only in this case

the recommendation is to ignore misbehavior. We have all had teachers who seemed studiously indifferent to our antics. They seemed to be busy organizing activities and were literally unaware of the noise, confusion, spitballs, and paper airplanes all about. This permissive, **laissez-faire approach** somehow assumes that a classroom group on its own will always be so interested in the learning activities that teacher sanctions and reminders are unnecessary. In either case, however, whether the recommendation is for strict obedience or the permissive approach, the solutions are really bound to fail. The assumption is that one method is best since consistency is important.

A developmental approach to discipline in the classroom rests on a different set of assumptions. As we have stressed throughout this work, pupils process and make meaning from their own experiences in qualitatively different methods. We have stressed the importance of tailoring or matching curriculum materials and teaching strategies to the developmental levels of the pupils. Thus, it will certainly come as no surprise to find that we recommend a similar approach to pupil discipline.

Stages of Development and Discipline

In order to avoid the trap of single prescriptions, the **developmental method of discipline** requires that

we view the problem from a complex perspective. We have made the point that the way in which a pupil understands intellectual or academic material (Piaget), value questions (Kohlberg), and personal issues (Erikson) depends on the child's stage. The same is true for discipline. Therefore, if we apply Kohlberg's framework of general value judgment to the question of how pupils understand rules and or-

der, we'll have a more appropriate scheme for discipline. Essentially, the question becomes: Which sanctions should I use as a teacher? What procedures may be more effective with which children? What is the repertoire of methods I should use as opposed to an exclusive reliance on any single type?

Table 19.1 outlines stages of moral development in relation to disciplinary methods. Most important,

TABLE 19.1   STAGES OF DEVELOPMENT: PUPIL DISCIPLINE

DESCRIPTION	POSITIVE	NEGATIVE
STAGE I		
Use of physical means to require compliance. Obedience because of unequal power. Generally effective only in short-term.	Helen Keller's teacher in *The Miracle Worker*. Placing an out-of-control child in a time-out room. Holding the arms of a child in the middle of a temper tantrum. Walking up to a child, standing over him or her. Making eye contact. Nonverbally indicating that the behavior is unacceptable.	Punching, kicking, breaking bones to teach a child a lesson. Locking a child in a dark closet. Punching the child with fists.
STAGE II		
Use of materialistic consequences such as rewards or withdrawal of privileges for acceptable or unacceptable behavior. Generally effective in the short run while the reinforcers are in effect (either positive or negative).	The Premack principle (see Chapter 10). Use of Skinnerian positive reinforcers such as a token economy. A balance between positive reinforcers and negative reinforcers (withdrawing privileges). Selective positive reinforcers. Positive teacher comments exceeding negative by 2:1. Positive reminders and cues on classroom rules.	Exclusive use of aversive conditioning. Exclusive use of negative reinforcers (withholding food or restricting rations, e.g., bread and water; use of criticism, sarcasm). Predominant use of negative verbal statements.
STAGE III		
Use of social group (peer and adult pressure) to promote individual conformity to group norms and classroom rules. Concern for feelings of the group. Can be highly effective for significant time periods as long as the individual remains in the group.	Setting classroom rules with group participation. Running classroom meetings to discuss general effects of misbehavior. Use of positive peer pressure. Rewarding the group as a whole to promote cooperative learning. Promoting group cohesiveness: "Our class—our team—our group." Cooperative learning materials. Using I-messages.	Turning the class members into a collective to scapegoat an individual child. Using the group to shame or shun a pupil publicly. Using a group to make individual pupils feel like outcasts (making a pupil sit in a "dunce chair"; standing the child in the wastebasket and having others throw trash in, etc.)

TABLE 19.1 *(cont.)*

DESCRIPTION	POSITIVE	NEGATIVE
STAGE IV		
Governance and sanctions according to legal standards. Individual responsibility and choice are stressed. Inner direction and individual decision making toward rules and laws. Can be highly effective over long time periods.	Careful observance by both adults and other pupils of each person's individual rights. Clear understanding of reasons for school laws. A point and contract system for grading. Understandable and reasonable consequences known to all for misbehavior. Teaching children self-management skills, such as self-directed behavior modification. Assertiveness training.	Excessive reliance on individual competition for grades. Exclusive stress on individual achievement. Narrow interpretation of laws and rules without regard to principles behind them.
STAGE V		
Governance and sanctions based on general democratic principles; fairness, equity, toleration, freedom of thought, and the like.	Rules and laws developed democratically by open participation of adults and pupils. Sanctions imposed by student and teacher councils. Due process followed. Town meeting procedures; each person has one vote. Individual autonomy *and* responsibility to the group stressed. Interdependence a focus. Only appropriate for secondary-age or older students.	

Note: In applying sanctions, the same developmental rules apply. Usually it is most appropriate to use methods that are one stage *up* from the learner.

the table includes examples of what can be considered to be positive disciplinary techniques versus negative disciplinary techniques within each stage. For example, at Stage I, the basic approach involves superior physical force. This can be manifested as brutality in such forms as whipping, breaking bones, bludgeoning, or maiming. A gym teacher instructing a class in sit-ups places his foot on the back of an overweight pupil and pushes his neck hard enough to force the boys' chin to his knee, all the while making the sarcastic comment, "Gee kid, you bend easy!"

Compare that approach to the technique used by the teacher in the movie *The Miracle Worker*. Anne Bancroft portrayed Annie Sullivan, a young Irish teacher-companion to Helen Keller. Helen, stricken with several physical handicaps, had been raised from birth with almost no limits set on her behavior. During the initial phase of the relationship, Sullivan literally had to use physical force to restrain Helen. She would not allow Helen to hit her and ended up in exhausting wrestling matches, holding Helen's arms until finally her reluctant pupil was willing to start the process of growth and self-development.

In the life of any teacher, there may be times when physical force is the only appropriate solution. A young child in a temper tantrum, beating up a peer, may need to be physically removed, gently yet firmly, and placed in a time-out room. A teenager, out of

Annie Sullivan (as portrayed by Anne Bancroft) used humane physical constraints to start Helen Keller's learning process.

control on drugs, may have to be physically restrained from doing harm to himself or herself as well as to others.

Thus, the old adage "Spare the rod and spoil the child" does not ring true. In fact, the use of aversive physical force does not achieve positive results, even with highly motivated persons. A series of studies reviewed by Roger Brown and Richard Herrnstien (1974) indicated that even with a variety of novel techniques (a cigarette case that electrically shocks the would-be smoker, a remotely controlled "bug in the ear" device by which an out-of-sight therapist could shock a patient up to 300 feet away), the outcomes were not positive. As soon as the aversive stimulus was removed, the individuals reverted to their normal behavioral patterns. Physical punishment produced no long-lasting changes. Thus, when

the Old Woman who lived in the shoe soundly whipped her too many children, it had no positive impact on the children. The more up-to-date recommendations suggesting that teachers use physical punishment have no supportive research base.

Rather, in particular situations there may be little choice except the application of physical force. The key is the choice between brutality and humane control. There are basically two questions to answer. First, is Stage I the appropriate level on which to base the sanction? Second, is the pupil in such a state that more complex methods will not work? For a variety of psychological reasons there are times when a child may be, literally, out of control. If that seems to be the case, then the second choice is most important, that is, between negative and positive applications of physical force. The amount of physical force employed should be just enough to restore control to the child or to the teenager. There is no point in massive retaliation. Also, it is important to remember that such physical control is effective only in the short run and in the immediate situation. Naturally, the educator's goal is to employ more complex methods that will aid the pupil in the development of self-control. Reaching such a goal, however, is a gradual process; it is not achievable overnight (Hart, 1991).

At the second stage, positive discipline involves the use of extrinsic or materialistic rewards to aid in the shaping of pupil behavior. Pupils at Stage II are still egocentric in the sense of "What's in it for me?" The great variety of so-called Skinnerian techniques fit here. Since we have described these in more detail in Chapter 10, we will not repeat them. The key is to use generally positive reinforcers such as extra recess time, special trips, or treats as rewards. Point systems and token economies are further extensions of that same approach.

Skinner is convinced that his operant conditioning works most effectively when the teacher uses rewards rather than relying exclusively on aversive conditioning. For example, studies of teacher-pupil verbal interaction show ratios as high as eight negative teacher comments for every positive one. A balance of teacher comments, in which the positive exceeds or at least equals the negative-critical, would improve classroom control. This recommendation does not mean, however, that the teacher should never make negative evaluative comments. To praise uncritically every activity of every child does not improve learning outcomes. However, a balance is clearly appropriate.

Thus, in selecting goals for reinforcement, choose

the positive. If you set up a token economy (so many points for handing in homework on time, for doing seatwork, for listening to directions, etc.), the goal could be special reading time or it could be avoiding detention. The more that teachers and principals use the latter category, the more schools become like prisons. As Skinner says, aversive measures and goals teach the child to seek a psychological escape, to learn not to learn.

It is clear that the Stage II positive approach is more effective as well as easier on both teacher and pupil than Stage I. Using behavioral principles to reinforce positive behavior is a powerful educational strategy. However, it does require extreme consistency on the part of the teacher. Therein lies the weakness, namely, that the teacher must remain absolutely consistent in providing immediate reinforcement for positive behavior. He or she must never (even inadvertently) reinforce negative behavior. For example, if a teacher mistakenly yells at loud, noisy children, the yelling reinforces the children's noise rather than achieving the opposite effect. Thus, for the system to work, the teacher has to monitor reinforcers with vigilance.

As in Stage I, the major responsibility for control is still with the adult. The system will work as long as the adult applies the contingencies with humane goals. Naturally, the system can be employed in the service of out-and-out demeaning manipulation. A most graphic example is found in the movie (and novel) *One Flew Over the Cuckoo's Nest.* Nurse Rachett, stunningly played by Louise Fletcher, expertly manipulates the patients. She controls all of the activities of the ward, allowing no individuality or choice. Like an absolute despot, she employs behavioral principles to prevent human growth. The importance for teaching is obvious. The choice of goals is critical. The means, that is, the disciplinary strategies, should be consistent with educative and growth goals.

At the Stage III level, the overall objective is to begin sharing the responsibility for control and discipline with the children as a group. The power of the social group as a community can be an extremely strong influence on class effort and behavior. The ability to experience how the group feels about individuals and vice versa means that control and direction no longer need to be exclusively determined by the adult. The group can participate in setting classroom norms and rules. Classroom meetings, in William Glasser's sense, are now possible for discussions on content as well as on feelings about appropriate and inappropriate behavior. The procedures recommended by Glasser (1975) are useful at this level. Also, the use of so-called I-messages by the teacher can now be effective. When children have the ability to understand their own emotions as well as the feelings of adults, the system of I-messages developed by Thomas Gordon (1974) becomes an important technique. There are three components of I-messages:

1. A nonjudgmental, precise, objective statement of the pupil's behavior: "When you interrupt Nancy..." *not* "When you rudely/inconsiderately/thoughtlessly blurt out/shout out/scream out at the answers Nancy is giving..."

2. A statement explaining why the behavior is troublesome: "The class can't hear what Nancy is trying to say..." *not* "I cannot let you steamroller your classmates/cut people off/have your own way/be so self-centered..."

3. A statement of how you feel: "I feel frustrated trying to listen to two people at once..." *not* "I feel ashamed to have such an unproductive student in my class who casts such a terrible reflection on the rest of us. How do you ever expect not to end up on welfare when you grow up?"

Thus an I-message has three parts—an objective description of troublesome behavior, an explanation of consequences to the teacher and the rest of the class, and a personal statement of the teacher's feelings. It may sound very awkward as a procedure, especially since it may appear that you are leading with your chin, so to speak. To be sure, an I-message will not always work, but teachers trained in Gordon's method report that it has a very substantial probability of success, especially if the teacher pauses and waits through the silence that usually follows.

In addition to classroom meetings and I-messages, the use of cooperative groups is a third important procedure at this level. Students can be taught to think and act in accordance with the welfare of the group as a whole. The decline in egocentric materialism of Stage II means that pupils can be enlisted as peer-teachers and that they can benefit from small group-learning activities. Rewards such as grades or treats can be granted to groups rather than to individuals. Loyalty and cooperation to one's own class or small group act as powerful motivators.

Procedures outlined by Robert Slavin (1990) are most appropriate for setting up small groups to enhance such cooperative learning. Under such conditions, children can monitor the members of their group who may not be positive contributors. "Come on, Henry and Althea, help the rest of us finish the project so we can all go on the museum trip!" or "You know you're leaving us holding the bag because you haven't learned your part yet for the play." The approval as well as the disapproval of the group are powerful conditioners of individual behavior. Also, it is obvious that the direction is more shared than at Stage I or II. The cohesiveness and group togetherness act as a bond. Children are no longer completely at one end of the classroom with the teacher at the other. There is more interaction, more colleagueship, and more mutual decision making. Classroom norms, written on the blackboard, are derived with student input and participation.

There is, however, a negative aspect of the general Stage III approach. It is relatively easy for a teacher, if he or she desires, to use the system to effect a kind of totalitarian approach. With manipulation, a teacher can use the class group to squelch any kind of individuality. In the educational system of the former Soviet Union the purpose was exactly that—to promote loyalty to the state at the expense of individuality. It is possible in any classroom to use group process toward such ends. Any pupil deviation or individual initiative (even relatively mild acting up) can be subject to public shaming. Group punishment for individual misdeeds is another way to turn members of a group against one of their colleagues. In the novel and movie *Lord of the Flies,* there was a dramatic example of how far a group of children can go to enforce absolute conformity. Adults can mastermind such activities through scapegoating and forcing individual confessions in kangaroo-court atmospheres.

Thus, as is the case at the two earlier stages, the procedures for discipline at Stage III are not fail-safe. The overall goals and learning activities as well as the methods help to determine if the techniques are educationally sound. However, at Stage III the effects can be longer-lasting than at either Stage I or II. The system is no longer exclusively directed by a single adult. The group is more pervasive and more powerful.

At Stage IV, the overall goal is to move the major responsibility for discipline from the group to the individual. This goal is clearly a democratic ethic. Self-governance and direction provide scope for individuality and autonomy. The shift is from social conformity and other-directedness to individual con-

science and inner direction. The laws that govern behavior are applied equally to teachers and pupils. There is clear public knowledge and acceptance of consequences.

At this level, the teacher may instruct pupils in so-called self-management techniques. There is a difference between this instruction and the control exercised by the teacher at Stage II. At the lower level the teacher regulated the reinforcers. At this higher level the teacher essentially gives the psychology of behavior modification away to the pupils. They are helped in setting up their own schedules of reinforcement in certain problem areas, in monitoring the outcomes, and in setting their own rewards. Thus, rather than punish a pupil for not handing in a term paper, the teacher and pupil (together) could work out a schedule, keep track of study time, and provide short-term and longer-term positive reinforcers. Ultimately, only the pupil can learn how to apply behavioral principles to his or her own problem areas.

A second approach involves what is called *assertiveness training.* Individuals are taught to speak up for themselves, to exercise their right of choice, and most important, to negotiate solutions to conflict situations. There is an important distinction here between assertiveness and aggression. These procedures are not designed to encourage a kind of Stage II egocentric aggressiveness. Rather, pupils are helped to develop the ability to speak up for themselves, quietly yet firmly.

With these abilities in the hands of the students, the overall teaching role naturally shifts more to that of a manager and consultant. Instruction and projects can be highly individualized. Learning contracts between teacher and pupil can be negotiated *and* renegotiated. In fact, at this level even the choice of consequences can be mutually determined. Goal setting can vary in accordance with pupils' differential abilities. Thus, for a particular pupil in a physical education class, improving from five to fifteen push-ups may be just as valued as a Mary Lou Retton type of performance by the star female gymnast in the class. Joint decision making and monitoring increase the likelihood of individual commitment and motivation.

Naturally, there is another side to Stage IV. Essentially, the possible difficulty of this system is that it can lead to excessive individualism. Any particular pupil can become so achievement-oriented that there is almost no concern for anyone else. Unmoderated competition can become so intense, the rugged individualism so rugged, that pupils may drive themselves to the brink of psychological breakdown. The achiever may become the overachiever. A pupil's life can become organized in the exclusive pursuit of grades or test scores. Highly "competitive" high schools with public class rankings, published college admission results, and posted SAT score profiles can create personal nightmares for those pupils who are already highly achievement-oriented. The same is true at the college and graduate levels. The signs are all too familiar, such as cheating, bribing, hiding assigned library books, or tearing out critical passages from them.

When the individual loses sight of the overall purposes of education and confuses grades as ends in themselves rather than as means, then negative consequences follow. Part of the challenge for the teacher is that much of this problem may remain hidden. The student who is overly achievement-oriented is hardly a discipline problem in the usual sense. Thus, it is important to monitor the level of individual competition in the classroom and to keep in mind that the goal of Stage IV is to promote self-management and self-direction and not rampant self-aggrandizement.

One further point at this level: since law becomes a reference point for decisions, it is possible to stick too closely to literal interpretations. Schools and state departments of education publish the legal aspects of students' rights, which call for highly detailed procedures. Access to file information (under the so-called Buckley amendment); the steps that must be followed before searching student lockers; liberalized court rulings on matters of suspension, hair length, dress codes, and legitimate student protests—all these areas are now regulated at the Stage IV due-process level. Such legal codes provide for more stability and equality in how schools and teachers may apply sanctions. Before these changes, children and teenagers could literally be pushed out more on the basis of their social class or ethnic background than on anything else.

There is, however, a possible danger in reliance on legalism. It can lead to a narrow interpretation of law. In this view, the rules must always be obeyed. Under no circumstances can a teacher, principal, or pupil change or adjust the rule. The reasons for the laws can be forgotten almost too easily. Stage IV has its limits, particularly because in exceptional cases the principles and reasons for the law may be ignored. Thus, there may be unique and admittedly rare occasions when exact recourse to the letter of the law is not appropriate. For example, a school nurse noticing an incoherent pupil in the midst of an extremely "bad" drug trip may need to know what drug has been taken in order to make a decision on an antidote. Obviously, examining the contents of the locker may be crucial for speedy action. In this case, as in some others, strict adherence to the letter of the law may have to be set aside.

At the Stage V level, the teachers, administrators, and pupils essentially form a democratic community. Each person participates in the creation of sanctions, laws, and rules that include all aspects of schooling. The organization that is set up is much like the town meeting; there is literally no difference between adults and pupils. Through parliamentary-style debate, rules are established and enforced across the board—honor codes, homework assignments, grading practices, attendance requirements, social-service obligations, and so on. Governance by students and teachers is according to majority rule. Arbitrary decisions by either teachers or students are not permitted. All issues are debatable and all consequences carefully examined. The overall concept is that of a community of teachers and pupils based on **democratic** principles of justice and equality—a kind of Jeffersonian, grass-roots, direct democracy.

The Stage V level of discipline does sound somewhat idealized as a goal and is perhaps unattainable. A basic assumption is that all members of any such community are far enough along developmentally to process at a Stage V level. In other words, such a plan simply will not work unless the participants are capable of understanding issues at a level of principled thought.

There are a few examples of such procedures actually working at the eleventh- and twelfth-grade level in public schools as well as at the college level. Such experiments suggest that this level of discipline may be possible but that it is also extremely difficult to achieve. The system demands a very high level of commitment on the part of teachers and pupils, huge amounts of goodwill, and high levels of cognitive ability. Genuine democracy is an extraordinarily fragile commodity. It is well to bear this in mind. Such procedures should be applied only after the most careful examination of the assumptions and required procedures. Ralph Mosher, this country's leading innovator in democratic high school organization, wryly sums up four years of experience with a quote from democratic theorist D. W. Brogan: "Non-democratic government is like a splendid ship, with all its sails set; it moves majestically on, then it hits a rock and sinks forever. Democracy is like a raft. It never sinks, but damn it, your feet are always in the water" (Mosher, 1979, p. 497).

Matching Discipline Levels and Pupils

With this five-stage scheme in mind, we can now turn to the question of specific application. We haven't outlined a Stage VI approach for two reasons--one theoretical and one practical. At the theoretical level, Stage VI individuals would always follow universal principles; therefore, any system would be unnecessary and clearly redundant. At the practical level, so few persons operate at Stage VI that the school itself might be the size of a phone booth.

As we noted at the outset, the role of the teacher in discipline is to discern in a general way the approximate range of levels within the class. Table 19.2 presents the overall trends by school grades (obviously a very general framework).

The table provides a guideline for choice and expectation. Remember: There is individual variation within any class, yet in general the class as a group will function at these levels. Also remember that even though the children cluster at a particular level, there is the plus-one concept. They are capable of understanding and being attracted to a slightly more complex level of discipline. Thus, even if you find yourself confronted with a prekindergarten class with everyone at the collective-monologue stage, you can still use some Stage II rewards and treats. In other words, the **matching of discipline to stage** can be a slight mismatch in which you try to use some techniques

TABLE 19.2   STAGE OF REASONING ABOUT DISCIPLINE AND GENERAL AGE LEVELS

AGE	PREDOMINANT REASONING LEVEL	NEXT MODEL STAGE UP
Preschool (3–4 years)	I	I (II)
Kindergarten to grade 3	I (II)	II
Elementary grades 4 to 8	II (III)	III
Grades 9 through 12	III (IV)	IV–V*

*Under special circumstances.

and strategies from the next level up. If there are occasions when that does not work, then you can still employ the humane or positive strategies precisely at the level of the pupils. The overall choice is to select the least restrictive alternative, given the age and stage of the pupils.

In addition to the plus-one idea, a second aspect of the discipline system is important to remember. Each stage is slightly more complex and more effective than the prior level. At the higher levels, more of the responsibility is shared with the pupils. They require less monitoring by you. Thus, the overall goal of discipline is not simply to keep the peace so that children will all sit still and listen. Essentially, the old approaches to discipline aimed at just that—a negative goal—with teachers applying power to control recalcitrant pupils. The developmental approach employs sanctions in the service of general growth. Pupils can gradually take over some of the responsibility and learn the process of self-management. In other words, it's like a creative abdication. The teacher gradually shifts some power, control, and responsibility to the pupils in accordance with their stage of development and readiness.

Certainly, the major procedure to avoid is gross mismatching either way by the teacher. Using procedures way over the heads of the pupils will simply confuse them and frustrate you. To expect second- or third-graders, for example, to understand the principles of participatory democracy is obviously unrealistic. Similarly, to expect pupils at straight Stage II levels to understand and to behave in accordance with a Stage IV "honor code" is to invite noncompliance. Finally (and perhaps this need not be mentioned), the teacher should not use methods substantially below the stage levels of the pupils. It would be clearly unnecessary and humiliating for a teacher consistently to employ initial-stage sanctions on children already capable of processing at higher levels. Such a procedure would clearly be regressive.

DISCIPLINE LEVELS: FOUR QUESTIONS

With the stage characteristics in mind, it is possible to organize classroom **discipline strategies** based on the following **four questions:**

1. Who makes the rules?

2. Who keeps the rules?

3. How are the rules enforced?

4. Why do students obey the rules?

Strategies at Stage I

At Stage I, the teacher sets the rules: "During seat-work time, students are expected to remain at their desks," or "Please raise your hands if you know the correct answer," or "In this class we will all line up by twos before we go out to recess." The teacher has carefully selected a minimum yet essential basic number of rules to preserve the classroom as an orderly, humane workplace for children. Understanding the developmental stage of the pupils means that the teacher does not expect the pupils to figure out what kind of learning environment is most appropriate to their needs. Thus, the answer to the first question is that the teacher makes the rules.

For similar reasons the teacher also monitors compliance. This means keeping careful track of pupil behavior. If a rule is broken a number of times without a response by the teacher, such silence actually encourages further testing of the limits. At the same time it is important to remember that positive monitoring is more effective than negative and/or aversive control. So praise for those who remain seated not only increases their obedience but also is a message quickly heard by the others. In addition, positive, nonverbal body language such as smiles, pats on the back, and nods of the head are other means of humane physical control. At this level, then, in answer to the question, who keeps the rules, the answer is that it is mostly the teacher and through a positive mode.

For the third question of how the rules are enforced, it is important to remember the system of judgment that the child uses. For those still reasoning at Stage I, what makes the rules effective is the physical presence of the teacher. Children during preschool and early elementary grades vary quite substantially in their ability to monitor their own behavior without an adult actually visible, or at least within earshot. Research has indicated that some (a few) preschool children can monitor their own behavior and delay gratification even without an adult present and with a tempting choice at hand (Mischel and Peake, 1982). While it is certainly a positive sign that children even at this early age possess some internal self-control, the researchers also found that young children make life most difficult for themselves in such tempting situations. They focus on what they cannot have, making the "forbidden fruit" even more attractive.

By the third grade, however, most children are fully capable of resisting temptation without an adult monitor. This means that the idea of a positive reward is strong enough in the student's mind that the pupil can postpone the immediate temptation. Yet even in this instance, remember that the findings come from studies of children one at a time and thus indicate a potential. Placing children in group situations, such as a classroom, can lower the ability to resist temptations. As we pointed out both in Chapters 5–7 and Chapter 18, children, like adults (unfortunately), can be swayed quite substantially by pressure to conform to the peer group. Thus, the teacher in preschool and the early elementary grades needs to proceed slowly toward a more complex and humane system at Stage II. This means that outside physical force is still a strong "reason" why children this age will keep the rules. Desire for physical approval or fear of punishment is the answer to the fourth question in our scheme.

One final point: Remember that children can process reasons at different levels. Some children, especially those reared by parents who follow the model of effective parenting outlined in Chapter 6, will show an ability to verbalize and exhibit a higher level of self-control. Not so with other children: If parents of kindergarten children regularly use negative physical force (severe corporal punishment), then children will most likely show very little capacity for self-control without an adult close at hand. In this case much patience and support is needed to prepare the child for discipline based on material rewards rather than physical presence (Likona, 1991).

Strategies at Stage II

At Stage II during the first part of elementary school the teacher still makes and keeps the rules. The big change, however, occurs with the pupil's ability to delay gratification and to work for concrete rewards instead. This means that the answers are the same for the first two questions but different for the last two.

Rules can be enforced through material rewards simply because that method fits the reasoning level of the children. This does not mean that the children are not capable of working and learning for intrinsic reasons. As we pointed out in Chapter 5, there is an innate drive to learn, a motivation for competence. However, new learning is not universally pleasant. We as educators have sometimes painted a picture of each child just dying to know whatever we are about to teach them—a classroom filled to the brim with eager learners, all waiting breathlessly for the next great moment of insight.

We know that such a view is both romantic and unrealistic. Instead, a part of each person's learning and processing stage likes the present "just fine, thank you." We all have a way of thinking and behaving that is comfortable and habitual. As William James's son noted, the pupils are in part "old fogeys," conservatives who like to keep in touch with the past. Certainly, if students have difficulty learning new material (and we all do at some point), then discouragement can set in and out-of-seat behavior increases. Thus, especially with elementary-age children, the teacher who does not use a systematic approach in dispensing concrete rewards is giving up a powerful ally. Discipline problems and pupil anxieties can be addressed simultaneously through a careful sequence of positive reinforcers. It is not manipulative if, in a humane way, you help children give up a reliance on outside physical control and replace it with reliance on point systems, a token economy, gold stars, "smiling faces," special time to work on puzzles and games, and the like. You are then aiding the children in the process of growth toward self-control. The Stage II methods help students gain a level of self-control and as a result facilitate the process of learning new and difficult material.

Strategies at Stage III

Not until the pupils begin to reason at a Stage III level can further shifts be made toward greater student participation. There is some potential for discipline in this mode by the late elementary and middle school years. Interaction in both rule making and rule keeping can increase. The teacher can use much more discussion in formulating rules and deciding on appropriately positive group sanctions. The reason that both making and monitoring rules needs to be "managed" by the teacher is that Stage III reasoning can be overscrupulous. We noted a concern about scapegoating. Other research has shown that junior high students can be little short of draconian in their ideas of fair punishment (Sprinthall, 1985). The Greek despot Draco set up a system of excessively harsh and downright cruel sanctions. Students at this age apparently quite easily suggest similarly fearful punishments even for minor misdeeds. As they emerge from childhood, it's almost as if they immediately identify with adults as authoritarians rather than as authorities. Thus, teacher monitoring is needed to ensure that mercy is mixed with their conception of justice.

As we have pointed out elsewhere in detail, junior high students often exhibit open streaks of racism and sexism. This is part of the Stage III social conformist mode. Students show little tolerance, often outright

Discussing classroom rules through a play activity reduces discipline problems.

Using a contract approach sets clear guidelines for student projects.

intolerance, toward anyone obviously different in ethnic background or social class.

Strategies at Stage IV

At the high school level students are developmentally ready to participate more fully in making, keeping, and participating in the sanctions when the rules are broken. They have reached the point of initial individuality and identity as autonomous people. To be sure, there are still strong aspects of social conformity, but the students now have a real potential for reasoning for and by themselves.

Perhaps the most important aspect of this stage is the rational or abstract understanding of what are sometimes called "natural consequences." It is true that younger children can learn about concrete consequences. Yet by high school, students have a greater depth of understanding. Thus, in setting up a learning contract for, say, a term paper, the student can learn the importance of doing each step in sequence and, most of all, that he or she can't wait until the night before the project's due to start on it. The wise teacher sets up the contract with a series of checkpoints: "After two weeks, list the references used and the key points of each reference. . . . After four weeks prepare the first draft in outline form." By dividing a large task

into manageable pieces developed with the student, there is a much greater chance for compliance. Similarly, in contracting for homework assignments, students can discuss how many points toward their final grade each assignment is worth, whether make-up homework counts, and if so, how much.

In preparing for and taking "chapter" tests, students and teacher can work out a comparable system of points. Then comes the most important part of the contract approach: failure. You must be firm but not harsh in dealing with failure. Students (and parents) need to know quite clearly that failure to study, to submit homework, and to prepare long-term assignments does have consequences such as not passing the course. At this point each classroom teacher needs the support of the school administration, so that failing one or a number of required courses will have a real consequence—to repeat the class, to attend summer school, to be ineligible for extracurricular activities, or even to receive in-school suspensions. Such negative sanctions are sometimes necessary even though, as with the other stages, the positive aspects of the contract system yield better and more cooperative results. For the slow or handicapped learner, the contract specifies a reachable level of improvement through an individualized education plan (to be discussed in more detail in Chapter 20).

SPOTLIGHT ON TRUANCY

The Strategy of a "Just Community"

In the "just community" approach to discipline, high school students and staff meet regularly to deal with student problems such as cheating, truancy, stealing, and similar difficulties. Beverly Noia, chair of the English department of the Garland Country Day School in Denver, visited such a school in Scarsdale, New York, and describes the process below.[a] A student called Martha cut classes regularly, was rude, exhibited temper tantrums when corrected, and rarely did her academic work. The "usual" approaches, such as detention, conferences with the parents, warnings, and the like, had failed. Instead of a faculty decision to expel her (in-school suspension), however, the community as a whole deliberated on what would be best for the school and for Martha. Noia's account of the meeting follows:

The student moderators called the community meeting to order, and Martha's advisor, a teacher, presented the facts to the community. It was made clear that while there were some bright moments in Martha's time at the A-school, they did not offset the fact that she seemed intransigent, or perhaps unable to improve. The faculty consensus that Martha should be expelled was announced. Martha was asked to present her "defense": she had very little to say. Her main point was

that although she recognized that she cut classes too often, still she felt that she had made some improvement since coming to the A-School, for in fact the previous year she had been in full attendance at her school for only six days. She expressed a desire to stay at the A-School, and a willingness to try harder to meet her responsibilities.

Perhaps if they had lowered the boom earlier, I thought to myself, she would have seen the seriousness of the matter sooner, and have taken herself in hand with much less suffering all around. This—the facing of expulsion— seemed to be the first time she had been forced to do some deep thinking and make some hard decisions and commitments. Would it have been more helpful, for her moral development, to have acted sooner?

The members of the community, students and teachers alike, began to ask Martha questions, seeking to understand why she had behaved as she had. It became clear that Martha saw that what she had been doing was not good for the community, and that it was hurting her as well. She seemed genuinely to want to change, but also to recognize that she had what she called "sort of an addiction." The more she cut classes, the less she could do the work; and the less she could work successfully, the more she cut classes. But she was convinced that she had the capabil-

ity of doing the academic work expected of her, if she could only break that vicious cycle. How might she? She had tried before, and failed. What was there to suggest that another chance to try would end any differently? "I've never been so scared before," she answered. "Now I know I have to do it."

Again I wondered whether this child had been done a disservice by being given too much freedom—too much rope to hang herself, some would put it. The primary motivations seemed to be fear (of being sent back to her former school— where she would have been freer to do the things she was now in trouble for doing!) and desire (to remain at the A-School—even though it asked of her behavior she found so difficult). Shouldn't these motivations have been brought to bear earlier, and have spared the child, the faculty, and the whole community much stress and this current distress?

As the discussion continued, something I had not anticipated began to occur: the community drew together seeking not simply justice (which would have been served had the student been expelled) but something else: the good of the student and of the wider community. One student suggested that interested students might volunteer to be a "support group" for Martha: call her at home in the evenings to see if she'd done her homework, and offer to

Strategies at Stage V

Finally, with some high school students, some teachers, and some administrators, it may be possible to go to the last step. The community as a whole handles

all three aspects of the rules (who makes them, who keeps them, and how they are kept), and the group can reason through discipline dilemmas on the basis of principles of justice. There are some ongoing **school-within-a-school** programs in which this proc-

help if she needed that; say, "Hey, you coming to class?" when they might see her lounging outside just before class; or simply be around to offer encouragement and appreciation. There was enthusiasm evident among Martha's peers as they realized they might be able to help her, and she herself seemed somewhat surprised at their caring, and grateful to accept their involvement. She wisely, though, would not pretend that her fate would be in their hands. "I've got to do this myself," she said repeatedly. She also knew that her tendency to flare up at adults when they "nagged" her might also apply to her peers, and she asked that the support group "not be on my back all the time."

What I was witnessing here was, to me, something both remarkable and beautiful: some sort of transformation was happening, not only for the student but for the whole community. The metaphor of antibodies rushing to a wound to help both cure it and restore the health of the whole organism seemed somehow appropriate. In my prejudice, I had anticipated some sort of "Crucify her!" scene; but I had underestimated the degree of caring, of maturity, and of willingness to share responsibility that existed in this group of adolescents.

The time came for making a decision. Four alternatives were proposed. (1) Martha could stay on, with no conditions. (2) She could stay at the A-School but on probation, with realistic terms to be set by a group including herself, the school director, and her advisor. (3) She could be sent back to her original school; and if her behavior improved there, she could return to the A-School the next fall. (4) Or, she could simply be expelled, with no opportunity to return. Martha asked permission to leave while the vote was taken, but the director convinced her to remain.

Should a fragile youngster be asked to stay while her fate is decided? Should adolescents be asked to vote on the fate of a peer, in her presence? The secret ballot is a longstanding tradition—why submit this girl to further suffering, or her classmates and teachers to the pressure of showing her exactly how they judged her? I was most uneasy.

The vote was taken: No one voted that she stay at the A-School unconditionally. No one voted that she be expelled with no chance to return. Roughly 95 percent of the community (including the *entire faculty*) voted that she be permitted to remain on probation. A few hands were raised for the expulsion-on-probation option. The mood was immediately one of rejoicing—faculty and students alike seemed to share some sense

that goodness had been done: they hadn't given up on one of their community members, nor had they ignored inappropriate behavior, and most of all everyone had come together to find a way to make things good.

I was glad Martha had seen the vote; it had to say something very important to her about the community's caring for her, and that in itself might be the key to her finally freeing herself from her "addiction." The overwhelming statement of support from her community was surely as important as the actual outcome (not being expelled), both for her development and for theirs.

Where the qualities of care, responsibility and general moral maturity in this community higher than they would have been in a school not run on the "Just Community" model? I do not feel qualified to judge that, but I do believe that their experience in expressing their values and judgments and their opportunity to make decisions that mattered, played a vital role in their capacity to handle this issue of truancy and potential expulsion with such moral maturity.

aNoia, B. Cheating and truancy: Discipline and locus of control in a "just community." *Moral Education Forum* (1983), 8(3), 8–10. Reprinted by permission.

ess is actually followed. A town meeting format is employed, and all major disciplinary decisions are made after full debate. Careful examination is made of alternatives, and consensus is achieved through voting. Such a program cannot work overnight, however. Democratic governance needs to be cultivated slowly. Otherwise, as soon as the first real crisis comes along, students will move quickly to their prior levels and either become excessive sticklers for the letter of the law or conform to their friendship groups.

Nevertheless, as the discussion in the spotlight on the "just community" indicates, it is possible for students at this age to act responsibly. Decision making can be based on Stage V principles.

From a preventive approach the democratic high school model is the comprehensive solution. Recent studies have shown that the atmosphere is significantly more positive than in the usual secondary school format. It is the quality of both the peer relationships on one hand and the student-to-teacher relationships on the other that make a major difference. In other words, discipline problems are reduced to such a minimal level that they almost disappear. In the studies that were made, cheating and stealing ceased altogether. Fighting was reduced to one incident in five years. Drug and alcohol abuse virtually disappeared, and racial integration increased. The program worked in a variety of public settings such as a school for gifted and talented, a suburban district, a "blue collar" school, and a school for high-risk students in the "Fort Apache" district of New York City (Kuhmerker, 1991). Research also illustrated that the students not only learned their academic lessons, but also learned to care for one another. Such students were very likely to offer help to a member of their school even though the student was not from their "clique." In contrast, students from regular schools generally ignored peers who were in some way different. Also, as a result of participation in the democratic format, students were more likely to behave proactively in activities in the surrounding community. It is an old-fashioned word, but they were better "citizens" both in and out of school—they were better informed and more likely to read about public affairs, and they had a greater respect for society's laws. Finally their assessed level of value development on the Kohlberg system (see Chapter 7) also improved (Sprinthall, Collins, and Edwall, 1994).

At the college level similar approaches to this democratic community milieu have been successfully implemented. The management of college dormitory rules and regulations can be turned over to the students and staff as a community (Sprinthall, Collins, and Edwall, 1994). Such a process promotes the development of greater maturity and responsibility. Just think what life would have been like for President Everett if such a method had been tried earlier.

Table 19.3 summarizes the answers to the four questions as an approach to discipline at the various stages.

TABLE 19.3   PREDOMINANT STAGE OF PUPIL'S REASONING AND APPROACHES TO DISCIPLINE

	STAGE I	STAGE II	STAGE III	STAGE IV	STAGE V
1. Who makes the rules?	Teacher	Teacher	Teacher and pupils	Teacher and pupils	Pupils and teacher
2. Who keeps the rules?	Teacher	Teacher	Teacher and pupils	Pupils and teacher	Pupils and teacher
3. How are the rules enforced?	Physical methods	Concrete rewards	Group discussion and class meetings	Pupils monitor own "contracts"	Town meetings and student-controlled discipline committees
4. Why do students obey the rules?	Out of fear of punishment or to seek physical approval	To gain some materialistic rewards or to avoid losing rewards	To belong to the class as a group (social conformity) or to avoid being isolated	To develop individual responsibility or to avoid an identity only as a member of a group	Out of an understanding of principles of justice and the meaning of democratic community of rights and responsibilities

At Stage V, a democratic approach to school discipline is a workable option.

Discipline: Effects of Discussion

The more you discuss reasons for rules of discipline and engage students in these discussions, the greater the likelihood of improvement in their level of understanding. In fact, one study has shown that the discussion approach helped even first-graders become somewhat more reflective and less impulsive in classroom behavior. There was a reduction in Stage I behavior, in kids hitting other kids and in other acts of physical violence (Enright, 1981). The teacher, of course, still set the rules and monitored compliance. Discussions about the reasons for rules, conducted at the child's level of understanding, can aid in promoting growth. In addition, you should not accept the current level of stage-linked reasoning about discipline problems as a permanent classification. Instead, always be on the watch for evidence of higher and more complex reasoning as you provide the opportunity for classroom discussion about rules and reasons.

The final and most positive point to remember is that students do have potential for developmental growth even in the worst-case discipline situations. They may behave at times in a manner approaching the level of Mr. Caldwell's students or the children in the movie *Lord of the Flies*. There still is some part of each student, as the assimilation-accommodation balance makes clear, that is attracted to a more complex and more humane system of controls. The advantage to you as a teacher is obvious. The greater the growth, the less time you must spend setting, keeping, and monitoring the rules. Then there is more time for learning.

Discipline Stage and Individual Differences

It is important to remember that developmental stages should be considered as general rules of thumb for students at different age groupings. It is obvious that not every student fits neatly into his or her appropriate modal stage. There are **individual differences.** In fact anyone who has worked with children or teenagers in any capacity such as a teacher, camp counselor, coach, or den leader can quickly relate examples of students who don't quite fit. Such students are the ones who clearly do not respond well to the average prescriptions matched to stage. It works both ways. Some students, developmentally advanced, may show signs of boredom or acting-up behavior, whereas others, for a variety of reasons, may be mismatched the other way, displaying an inability to attend to the material and methods you are employing.

The first step, then, is to review the student interaction with your teaching. How many different models are you using? Do you vary the assignments and promote a positive classroom atmosphere? For example, an eighth-grade honor student began acting up when a teacher assigned the same rotelike homework exercise for three days in a row: "Look up and identify the following fifty names of people and places from today's newspaper." Each day a new list. In another case an otherwise attentive student started an underground newspaper as a reaction to a classroom taught exclusively through a didactic high-structure method. Thus, as everyone's grandmother has always said, prevention is always better than a cure. Preventing discipline problems by modifying the classroom environment should always be the first line of defense (Wolfgang and Glickman, 1986; Charles, 1992).

After such a review of methods and materials, the next step is to deal with the misbehavior by individualizing your discipline strategies. There is always a debate between psychologists and educational psychologists as to how much time and effort should be directed at finding the psychological causes of misbehavior through family history. Naturally, it is helpful to understand any unusual circumstances which may be affecting a student (divorce, family abuse, loss of a grandparent), yet such "causes" cannot be used to overlook behavior which is truly disruptive and in fact which prevents not only the student in question but peers as well from learning.

Initiating and Preventive Teacher Behaviors

Robert MacDonald (1991) has provided a useful list of what he calls *initiating* and *preventive* teacher behaviors to deal with students who are disrupting the classroom atmospheres. Under **initiating** he suggests the following:

1. *Nonverbal cues:* Body posture position in the room, hand signals, and eye contact

2. *Tuning:* Verbal cues to start the discussion and reminders about taking turns

3. *Pausing:* Waiting quietly for extra comments to gradually subside

4. *Restarting:* Pausing halfway through giving directions and then restating the instructions

For **preventive** strategies he suggests a parallel set of teacher behaviors also designed to structure and remind in a low-keyed manner what the appropriate classroom behaviors are for those out of phase with the general procedures. This includes teacher activities such as

1. *Scanning:* To be able to spot possible trouble in advance

2. *Synchronizing:* To manage common tasks such as passing out or collecting homework, editing a particular page in an assignment, or shifting from lecture to small groups by guiding such transitions quickly

3. *Prepping:* To provide very clear and understandable directions for new classroom activities, including having students restate their understanding of the required tasks (especially important when using small cooperative learning activities)

4. *Renewing:* To review at both the beginning and end of each class the progress that the class is making toward the learning goals

5. *Positive framing:* To use positive reinforcement statements (remember the Walberg meta-analysis finding discussed in Chapter 12—avoid sarcastic comments; an old song of the 1940s serves as the model: "accentuate the positive, eliminate the negative")

In dealing with minor classroom management problems, then, from callouts to inattention, an array of initiating and preventive procedures will usually smooth out the learning process.

Transition to Corrective Methods: I-Messages

Generally, as MacDonald points out, when students feel treated fairly though firmly, the possible antagonism and hostility will subside and cooperation will increase. This is a reminder of the Flanders research on classroom atmosphere (see Chapter 12) which demonstrated both an increase in achievement and pupil self-concept as a learner in a democratic atmosphere. There still may be a student or two who doesn't respond to the initiating and preventive methods. At this point we recommend, at least for upper elementary and older pupils, the use of I-messages in an individual conference. The approach can be an effective confrontation yet must not be used in front of the entire class. If you do so, you run the risk of a "secondary gain," undue notoriety as well as the cornering of the student in front of his or her peers. The advantage of the individual conference is that you can calmly describe the annoying behavior, express your feelings and disappointment, and describe the adverse effects upon the teaching process and your role. In many cases such a meeting and "I-message" will be enough to curb the disrupting behavior. If it doesn't, then you'll need to consider corrective measures.

Corrective Techniques

Here MacDonald recommends a series of more deliberate low-profile methods followed by higher-profile disciplinary strategies. **Corrective low-profile methods** include

1. Stern eye contact
2. Gestures, including moving toward the student
3. Relocating the student
4. The "broken record" (e.g., repeating the instructions: "I said raise your hand first. . .I said to raise your hand. . .)
5. Defusing potentially explosive situations by coolly redirecting the challenge: "Your question on my personal plans is not relevant to the causes of WWI; now back to August 1914. . ."

Corrective high-profile methods include

1. Individual conferences with the student and the parent
2. Referral to other school procedures such as "time-out" rooms, or for more serious misbehaviors, to in-school suspension

Unfortunately the more you move to high-profile measures, the less effective will be the outcome, especially with adolescents. Such last-resort measures because of their punitive nature are relatively ineffective. As you can see, physically removing a student from the class may be necessary in some extreme cases. Yet the older the student, the less likely it will really produce positive behavior. With young children a short time-out is generally sufficient for them to regain enough self-control to return to the classroom. With the onset of adolescence such an exclusion policy takes on a different meaning. Thus it is a difficult trade-off.

To provide you with some specific examples of how to deal with more serious behavior problems, we now outline two common difficulties, cheating and acting-out behavior, and describe the various procedures you may wish to follow.

Dealing with Cheating

You may recall from the value development chapter that research has shown the two subgroups of adolescents most likely to cheat were either (1) the high-IQ/low-moral-judgment students or (2) the low-IQ/low-moral-judgment group. This sends an important message. Do not assume that either high IQs or for that matter high GPAs are also functioning at an average or above-average level in value development. In reality, both of the subgroups cheated over 80 percent of the time when given the opportunity. In this case, then, a preventive strategy is clearly the best choice. However, it will also take skill to create an atmosphere which reduces cheating but does not end as a punitive or prisonlike environment. This means that you must take positive action such as reinforcing the importance of students doing their own work. With adolescents you can even lighten up the situation a bit by reminding them that you were a teenager once and observed many of the common techniques, for example, formulas behind a watch crystal, hand signals for true-false tests, "gifted" peripheral vision by students reading other's answers two seats away. Such "friendly" reminders indicate in the Kounin sense that you are "with-it." You might even comment that you know the "Woody Allen story." Allen has said he got thrown out of college for cheating: on a metaphysics exam he peered into the soul of a classmate.

A second procedure is to be sure that the exam or the paper assignment is structured to minimize temptation. For example, if the students' chairs are close together and the room crowded, use alternate forms of the exam by row and be sure to scan the room to prevent test swapping. A second method is to use broader questions, or an open-book exam. For such a method to work you'll need to raise the level of the questions by asking the higher-order problems on Bloom's taxonomy. You could present the students with some material from the text and then ask them to either defend or criticize the position together with their reasons for such a view. Or you could present a case study based on the lessons and require a critical analysis.

A third method is to have the students read and sign an "honesty" pledge. By itself this doesn't work, but it does serve as a reminder of the importance of doing one's own work. In elementary and secondary schools it is, however, not recommended that students act as "radar" detectors for their peers. Some colleges with honor codes require peer monitoring. The written and signed pledge then is a verbal reminder to all the students but does not require peer enforcement—that is still your responsibility. From a developmental stage perspective, requiring peers to report cheating places students who blow the whistle in a near-impossible situation.

> I___(name)___pledge to use my own effort exclusively on the examination. I will not use notes or any other outside source for my answers.

When prevention fails then as in the previous case, you'll need to be prepared for corrective action. For example, as you are reading answers you may note that two papers are almost exactly alike. In fact years ago there was a now-famous example of two such papers, perhaps apocryphal. One student on the final question wrote, "This one has me stumped. No matter which formula I try I can't compute the answer." The next paper commented on the question more typically, "I couldn't do it, either." While this scenario is very unlikely, you will see less fanciful examples of extremely suspicious similarities. Thus, following our format, you start by holding a conference with the two students and send a straightforward I-message.

1. "When I read your papers and saw that they were almost exactly alike..." (*describe the situation*)

2. "I felt upset and discouraged" (*the impact on you at a feeling level*)

3. "I realized that you hadn't learned what I've been trying to teach you" (*effect on you*)

At this point you stop and wait for their responses which obviously can vary widely from denial to admission. It is important to remain somewhat dispassionate, allowing some of your feelings to show but not to the point of really "unloading." Then you can restate your disappointment, namely, that they failed to live up to their agreement. Of course you can't really tell who helped whom, and helping in this case is as bad as receiving. As a result, whatever grade the exam is worth should be divided in half. For

example, if the grade on one was 80, they both receive a 40. At the conclusion of the meeting, which should be relatively brief and brisk, indicate that the event is over. There will be no further penalties so they can start now with a clean slate on future classroom interactions, papers, and exams. Obviously, it is important not to over- or underreact to the situation. As the data on stages indicated, even persons reasoning at principled levels (Stage V) do not always resist temptations. On the other hand, with appropriate use of sanctions, students at all levels of development can learn from such a cheating experience that there are serious consequences. Probably the most difficult lesson of all (and certainly this was the case for one of the authors during his adolescence) is that helping a peer is also cheating. Not helping a friend seems to run counter to much of the Stage Three social conformity ethic and a definition of friendship. It does take a more mature perspective to understand just what the cheater has learned by being helped, that is, to avoid the normal consequences of one's own behavior. Such issues can be discussed individually with the students involved or in general with the class as a whole. A specific incident, however, should not be used as an object lesson in front of the classroom as a whole. Such public shaming is inappropriate, a miseducative experience.

When All Else Fails: Behavioral Contract Form

The final set of examples concerns more serious behavior problems in the classroom such as fighting, disrespectful racist and sexist comments, and displays of genuinely antisocial and antiacademic behavior such as truancy, repeated lateness, and homework either never done or done carelessly. In fact the test of severity is the repetitive nature of the behaviors. It means that the usual stage-appropriate methods, plus initiating, preventive, and corrective activities have failed. In such instances, the next procedure is the use of a contract, monitored by you, regardless of the age of the student. If behavior improves, the emphasis can be shifted to the student, but not at the outset. An example is found in Spotlight on Behavioral Contracting. The first step is to assess the level of mismatch between the student and the modal strategy for that age and then calibrate down until you find a match between current behavior and strategy. Also, it may be necessary to create both positive re-

SPOTLIGHT ON BEHAVIORAL CONTRACTING

Extremely Inattentive in Class

The hypothetical example here focuses on either middle school or high school. (Since behavioral contracting is commonly employed and is stage-appropriate in elementary schools, we haven't included an example for this level here.)

The problem behavior, one student's extreme inattention, has continued in this classroom in spite of your use of stage-appropriate methods (Stages III and IV), effective teaching methods (use of a variety of models), and appropriate subject matter (of general interest to most students). You conference with the student. Send an I-message, listen to his or her comments, and then set up the contract. You outline the behaviors necessary for positive points. Then add one or two of the "worst" inattentive behaviors commonly used. In this case it is either sleeping or poking classmates.

The reward was selected by the student from your list, and in this case you had already approached the local arcade owner for help in improving the academic achievement of certain students who were falling behind in their work.

After a week you notice a steady improvement, and after two weeks the student begins to show a genuine interest in the material. You conference, congratulate, and discontinue, explaining that the improvement in grades is now the indicator of real progress. You also call the parents to indicate how well things are going as the student brings home the first B ever. You suggest, if they haven't already mentioned it, their continued verbal approval and perhaps the giving of a special treat.

Remember, however, that the system of behavior shaping through extrinsic rewards has genuine limits. Recall the raccoon study (Chapter 9). The animals dutifully followed the system of picking up coins at the outset for a food reinforcer, but soon the system decayed when the animals began to rub the coins together in a washing ritual. Similarly the high-speed photos of pigeons shows that the birds were trying to *eat* the key that was to be pecked. Thus to avoid decay, do not employ such a system for lengthy periods. Instead, view it as a short-term procedure to get the student back on the learning track. The signs of decay will be obvious: a return of the original nonlearning behavior. On the other hand, the signs of success will be the emergence of genuine interest in the learning material as you switch to generic methods appropriate to the entire class.

POSITIVE ACTIVITIES	POINTS	DAYS				
		1	2	3	4	5
1. Takes notes without reminding	5					
2. Notes are organized	10					
3. Positive contributions to classroom discussions	5					
4. Attends to instructions	5					
5. Brings necessary materials to class	5					
		(Maximum in 1 week = +175)				
DISRUPTIVE ACTIVITIES						
1. Sleeps in class	−10					
2. Pokes classmates	−5					
		(Maximum in 1 week = −75)				
Goal for the first week	150 or 125					
Reward: Coupons for the video arcade	10 or 5					

wards and aversive consequences in order for some students to really understand the importance of giving up their disruptive behaviors. However, the *ratio* of positive to aversive rewards must greatly favor the positive. Thus, if the contract specifies points gained for attending behavior, the list should be long. You'll need to provide many examples of behavior which can earn points; for example, be on time for class and ready to start (5 points), bring books and writing material (5 points), listen to directions quietly (5 points), use an "inside" voice (5 points), keep hands and feet to self (5 points), turn in homework on time (5 points), etc. Then give a few examples of behavior which will cost points or "fines"; for example, antagonizes other students (minus 5 points) or leaves the seat constantly (minus 5 points). In the latter instance, carefully select only one or two of the most annoying behaviors. You simply cannot extinguish multiple behaviors simultaneously.

Also, you'll need to assess the general developmental level as to the type of activities which will gain points. If the student is still very concrete in orientation even though an adolescent, then an array of extrinsic/materialistic rewards may be the only effective rewards. Remember the examples of Stage II reinforcers. Sprick (1985) suggests that points can be earned for rewards like:

1. Free time
2. Food treats
3. A no-homework day
4. Computer game time
5. Free time in the shop, art, or weight room
6. Tickets to the roller rink, video arcade, or movies
7. Free time to read magazines or, for teenagers, a driver's manual

As you can see the rewards have no direct connection to the learning experiences. If you have difficulty in developing such a list you can ask the student for ideas as long as you reserve the right to veto the dangerous or the illegal. For example, in a camp for early adolescents, points were gained for a wide variety of positive behaviors, such as early preparation, at reveille, hands washed *before* eating, quiet at table, neat bunks. Small monetary fines were instituted for foul language. By the third day the language had improved and the positive behaviors increased substantially. The camper with the worst record at the

end of the first day turned completely around and won the Camper of the Week award and the largest share of the "fine" pot.

You probably cannot fine students in dollars and cents in public schools but you can devise some system of small penalties. The problem, of course, is that the system will fail if the penalties get too large and the student loses hope from the realization that he or she "owes" more points than could ever be earned. Also realize that you can "shape" only relatively small amounts of behavior, but this may be enough to get the student back on track for classroom learning.

For students who function at a higher and less concrete level you can use more intrinsic or learning-related activities. Again set up the system so that there are multiple behaviors for earning points and a few ways to lose or "owe" points. Then develop, perhaps with student input, a list of rewards:

1. Special lessons
2. An educational field trip
3. Extra time in some school activity
4. Extra help in some activity
5. Special recognition
6. Informal reading
7. Extra time with the computer

Otherwise the procedure is the same. The only difference is that with more advanced students, providing intrinsically interesting learning experiences is more likely to shape behavior. The reward is closer to their level of development.

Every so often educational practice seeks a quick-and-easy solution to the problems of classroom management, especially with the growing concern over delinquency, fighting, and the appearance of guns in the classroom. Teachers, counselors, and principals despair and yet hope there is a simple solution. Such was the case a few years ago with the famous Scared Straight program in Rahway, New Jersey. The idea was to send the worst offenders for a day at the state prison to receive lectures from hardened "lifers." Surely that would make the point. Stay in school, behave, or face a future in crime and ultimately land in the "slammer." In spite of all the favorable publicity, a follow-up study showed that the plan backfired. First, it had no effect on reducing delinquent behavior and, secondly, visiting the prison became a badge of distinction, desired by both delinquent and nondelinquent students. Needless to add, the program was suspended (Finenauer and Kuhmerker, 1979). A more systematic study on the effects of different approaches to discipline will be described from the work of Damon to which we now turn.

DISCIPLINE AND PARENTING: DAMON'S IMPLICATIONS FOR TEACHING

William Damon, of Brown University (1990) recently summarized much of the research on parenting styles and discipline. His analysis illustrates some important general issues for teachers. In the past, it has been common to classify parenting in three separate categories: (1) democratic-authoritative, (2) authoritarian, and (3) permissive. Damon finds, however, that the authoritarian and permissive styles are not really different from the point of view of the child. Both approaches have the same negative outcomes since both approaches meet the parent's needs, not the child's. Thus, authoritarian parents confront the child in a harsh and arbitrary manner when they *feel* like it, not when the child needs it. Similarly, the permissive (laissez-faire) parent uses sentimental overindulgence to protect the child from consequences in order to make the parent feel good. However, when such an overindulged child's behavior directly affects the parent, then severe punishment may be suddenly invoked.

Thus, according to Damon, both the authoritarian and the permissive parents make the same error, and it leads to arbitrary intrusions into the child's life. The paths are different but lead to the same outcome. On the one hand, authoritarian parents fail to confront the child on a regular basis so as to provide direction, but rather confront the child in response to their own moods and temper. This clearly limits the child's opportunities for exploration since the child doesn't really know when the hammer will come down but only that it will come down at some seemingly arbitrary point. On the other hand, permissive parents, by not setting reasonable, evenly enforced limits, shelters the child from the natural consequences of inappropriate behavior. At such points, the parents interfere and intrude. In both the authoritarian and the permissive cases, the adverse effects on self-control and initiative are the same since it is the parental power that is at issue.

The real difficulty with power as the exclusive means of control is that the effectiveness is very short-lived. In stage developmental terms, this means that discipline at Stage I is extremely limited. An observational study demonstrated that major use of power may actually reduce compliance with adult directives. One group of children threatened with severe punishment for playing with one specific toy actually played with the forbidden toy much more frequently than a second group who were only mildly admonished.

These studies then show that the definition of the humane application of a stage approach actually implies an authoritative method. According to Diana Baumrind's findings, the authoritative parent, or in our case the authoritative teacher, combines kindness and control with clear communication. Authoritative parents support the natural empathy in children by helping them understand when their actions hurt others. The parental commands are direct and honest rather than deceitful or manipulative. The demands imposed are realistically moderate and tuned to the child's developmental abilities. The parents also expect growth toward maturity and increasing amounts of independence with self-control. Thus, the pattern is clear as well as the effects. Baumrind finds that such children move toward social responsibility and are friendly, facilitative, and cooperative with adults (1989).

Children of authoritarian and/or permissive parents behave similarly, but their behavior is quite different from that of the children of authoritative parents. The former have difficulties in developing self-reliance, appropriate assertiveness, and a sense of social responsibility. One somewhat surprising finding is that both the authoritarian and permissive pattern produced children low in impulse control. Neither group could tolerate normal ups and downs. From a developmental viewpoint, then, we can now say that at any stage, discipline models that are administered in either an authoritarian or permissive manner will fail. Authoritative implementation, however, will help induce growth toward higher stages and more self-control. In fact, almost all studies of family discipline come to the same conclusion, namely, that adult modeling is important. What you do as well as how you do it will make lasting impressions on the pupils. In a Kenyan tribe, parents chose to actively discourage aggression in children by severe beatings. You can guess what the observer noticed when the children played alone (Edwards, 1987).

Thus, we can return to the overall framework as

a reminder of the importance of the different stages as well as the process of managing. Stage sets some broad limits as to how far "up" the scale you can proceed. For example, direct attempts to train elementary students in empathy (being able to understand how another child feels) did not generalize (Damon, 1990). However, empathy training at the high school level by means of programs such as peer counseling have been shown to generalize in follow-up. The developmental map then outlines the general reasoning levels that are most typical of the different age groups. The authoritative process is clearly the most effective means of getting the messages across at each level and of inducing maturity.

SUMMARY

One of the most potentially stressful aspects of teaching involves student discipline. Policing, monitoring, and keeping the peace often seem like the most unpleasant aspects of the role of the teacher. Individuals who choose teaching generally are not authoritarian personalities who enjoy and seek power and control over others.

Too often the most common approach has been to enforce a kind of "might-makes-right" dictum. Teachers are expected to enforce obedience and mold character almost at any cost. Failing that, teachers can be expected to rely on a series of tricks and games to bring about order. These may range from studied indifference (the head in the sand) to constant classroom entertainment (the teacher as Mary Poppins). There is no particular theory to guide the choice of disciplinary techniques. An alternative, however, is the developmental model. In using this framework, teachers must ask: (1) Who makes the rules? (2) Who keeps the rules? (3) How are the rules enforced? (4) Why do students obey? Answering these questions requires an application of stage theory: The choice of technique depends on the stage of reasoning of students. Very young pupils at Stage I may require the humane use of physical constraint. In the early elementary grades, pupils at Stage II may respond best to extrinsic behavior modification; in the later elementary grades, pupils at Stage III can be disciplined by peer pressure. In junior high and beyond, students (at Stages IV and V) are ready for more self-governance. Contract systems can be effective in those years.

There are humane and inhumane applications of methods within each stage, which involve carrying the approach too far or using it too literally. For example, harsh physical punishment versus firm physical constraint for an out-of-control child represent the wrong and right ways to approach discipline at Stage I. Excessively zealous application of stage-appropriate methods is a problem at all stages.

At the most complex level, teachers and pupils can form a democratic community along the lines of the old New England town meeting. This form of democratic citizenship training, while rare, can nonetheless serve as an ideal goal for student discipline.

When the developmental approaches do not work, the teacher may follow a series of steps to individualize the process. In our outline of these steps, we included a continuum of preventive, initiating, and corrective methods from MacDonald as well as a system for behavioral contracting.

The chapter closed with a discussion relating effective parental discipline to models for teacher strategies. The democratic-authoritative system was shown to have clear advantages over either the permissive or authoritarian models.

KEY TERMS AND NAMES

character training
William Damon
democratic versus laissez-faire or authoritarian
    methods
developmental method of discipline
discipline levels: four questions

individual differences
Robert MacDonald
matching stage to strategy
preventive, initiating, and corrective methods
the school within-a-school

THEORY INTO PRACTICE: MATCHING DISCIPLINARY STRATEGIES

We present a series of case studies in this application section. Your role is to read through each case carefully. List some of the main characteristics of the children in question and then review each of the four suggested disciplinary strategies. Next, make your selection and list the reasons for your choice. Also, for practice, identify the stage strategies in the other choices as well as your reasons for rejecting those choices. Finally, check out your answers in the last section to clear up any possible misunderstandings.

Case Study One: Elementary School

You are a third-grade teacher. Your pupils are just beginning their year with you. You notice, in the lunch room and playground, that the boys and girls are beginning to square off at each other. The amount of shoving, pushing, and name calling is on the increase. Also, during class itself, you begin to spot "little" incidents—a girl accidently shoves her spelling book into the ribs of a boy nearby; a boy just happens to slip his foot into the aisle and trips a girl on her way to your desk. What are possible solutions within a stage framework?

As you read the four suggestions that follow, try to assess the approximate developmental level of the strategy, whether it seems humane, and whether it would be appropriate to the level of development of third-graders, who are probably mostly Stage II with some mix of Stage III. Which would seem most effective and which least effective as discipline strategies?

1. I'd set an example so that they would know how such abuse physically feels. Every time I'd catch a culprit, I'd make the kid take punishment in kind. For example, I'd take the book and shove it into the ribs, not hard enough to leave a mark, but enough so she'd remember what it feels like! I'd teach her a lesson—it's called "an eye for an eye."

2. I'd approach it through the use of positive reinforcement. I'd explain that there is too much fighting at recess, in the lunchroom, and in class. As a class we would discuss some rewards for not fighting—a class field trip, a special movie, extra time for special projects, or things like that. Then we'd set up a chart to keep track of the amount of fighting, shoving, hair pulling, etc. I

would show them the chart I kept on them last week. Then we would keep track of misbehaviors next week and compare.

3. I'd try using some classroom discussions and some of the semistructured materials like Robert Selman's filmstrips on interpersonal problem solving and Henry DuPont's units on affective development. These materials are like case studies showing difficulties that children have in getting along with each other. We'd also have a chance to talk about alternative methods besides hitting back. Then I'd stress the importance of understanding each other's feelings and that as a class we will have to learn to work together. If this began to help, then I'd put in a few small-group cooperative learning games.

4. I'd talk to the class as a whole. I'd explain that they were acting like different countries in the world—fighting all the time. I would show them the need for a United Nations as a means of governance. Each person, like each country in the world, would have to learn that we are interdependent. I would demonstrate that our classroom is like our planet and that we are all on the same spaceship as a unit. In order to survive we all must pull together. I would show them a brief film on Eric Toffler's *Future Shock* and have them read about the Mayflower Compact and then the UN Charter.

Case Study Two: The Middle School

You are an eighth-grade English and a social studies teacher who also heads a guidance "bloc." You notice that most of your students seem to be social outcasts. There is a small group of ten or so (out of thirty-five) who form a clique. They dominate the discussion sessions in class, deliberately exclude most of their classmates from extracurricular activities, and even determine the mode of dress. Recently, the clique (about half boys and half girls) decided to wear good clothes to school—boys in suits and ties, girls in dresses and stockings. Pretty soon the others did the same. Then the "leading crowd" reverted to jeans and laughed among themselves at the "sheep." The clique tends to do well on exams, but there is a strong trend toward "white superiority" in their comments. They also put down the kids who have to work after class as know-nothing "hard hats." Tension in the class is increasing. You overhear some of the working kids and a few of the black kids talking about getting even.

1. I would get the class together and talk about the need for brotherhood and sisterhood. I'd explain that the world is full of hatred and prejudice. I would point out that it is up to each of us to live according to the "Golden Rule." Then I'd show excerpts from the film *Brian's Song* and have each student write an essay on Donne's meditation "No Man Is an Island."

2. I would excuse the clique early one day and talk to the rest of the class. I would indicate that I heard rumors of a possible fight. I would point out that fighting is against the school rules and that anyone caught would be put on detention or suspended, with the assistant principal's approval. I would make sure that they all knew that fighting, for whatever reason, was wrong and that we would not tolerate that kind of behavior.

3. I would develop a unit on cross-age teaching and counseling. This would involve classroom practice units in listening to feelings (communication exercises), sending I-messages, and learning to lead open-ended value-dilemma discussions. The values-clarification material, some Kohlberg-type dilemmas, and similar units would lead to an overall focus on values and relationships. We would include some material on the nature of prejudice, including some role-taking exercises. When the students, as teams, started teaching in the fifth- and sixth-grade classes, I'd be sure to assign team membership to prevent the clique from remaining together.

4. I would simply ignore the whole thing. My job as teacher is to teach the standard curriculum. We cover the material that the school board requires. If fighting occurs during class, I'd punish the class as a whole. All students would stay after school. If that didn't work, then I'd cancel the field trips and so forth.

Case Study Three: Secondary School

You are a twelfth-grade social studies teacher. It is the first week of the second semester. One of the immediate problems is the students' lack of initiative and independence. It isn't really a disciplinary problem in the usual sense. The students don't throw erasers or drop books, and most of them are on time

for class. The problem is more hidden but just as troubling. There is a kind of passivity tinged with hostility. They do the assignments and with some urging will answer questions reasonably well. The atmosphere is closer to boredom than anything else. There is very little volunteering. The feeling is one of going through the motions. They have let you know somewhat subtly that this is how they behave in their other senior classes. They will put their time in, do enough to pass, and don't want to be hassled by a lot of work. Their college applications are in and their SATs completed.

1. I would develop a unit on the value of hard work and stress the importance of high achievement. I would try to persuade them that though the college decisions would be made before the term ends, the colleges would still be interested in their senior semester. For those not going to college, the work in the senior semester would still be important for job recommendations. I would also talk about the importance of self-respect and how good they will feel to do well in the last semester even though it wouldn't really count for much.

2. I'm really not sure of the best way to handle this situation. My inclination would be to set up a reward schedule for playing their favorite rock videos at the end of each week if they were willing to put out more effort. I would rate their performance as a class each day. If they achieved three "outstandings" each week, they would earn a fifteen-minute video during the last period. If they earned no outstandings in a week, then I would assign extra homework or make them stay after school.

3. In order to promote more independence in learning, I would set up a series of assignments on key topics to be covered. I would indicate that my own role would be to serve as a resource person and that I could direct them to material in the library. I would provide a handout detailing how to use the new computerized catalog system. We would have group discussions on how to find and select resources. Each student would be given a topic and an outline of activities. The grades would be earned according to the number of points assigned for completing each section. Initially each student would write an outline on the topic and be prepared to present the information to the class as a whole on a first trial. Then after class discussion and more comment, the student would refine the topic and turn it into

a complete project to be presented to the class at the end of the semester. The information from all the topics would be collected and published in "desktop" form and filed in the library.

4. I would show a film of the "just community" approach as a demonstration of how high school students their age can set up their own classroom rules and norms. I would assign some readings on the topics to four small groups. The task of each group would be to develop sections of the overall plan. Included would be (1) participation rules, (2) means of protecting the rights of those holding minority opinions, (3) disciplinary strategies, and (4) responsibilities to others. By mid-semester, the goal would be to start functioning as a just community in discussing the key concepts of democratic governance. The community meetings would be chaired by different students. At the end, each student would write a paper detailing his or her own experience in the town meeting. Their weekly journals would form the raw material for their end-of-semester synthesis paper. The overall program, complete with video excerpts of the classroom just-community meetings, would also be presented to a local conference on innovations in education.

Suggested Answers

The elementary school strategies are quite straightforward. Suggestion 1 represents Stage I negative, the use of force to teach a lesson. Suggestion 2 illustrates the use of reinforcement principles (Stage II positive) to create a significant positive reward for "attending behavior." Suggestion 3 demonstrates a Stage III positive method of helping the children begin to experience and to reflect on issues of relationships and feelings. Suggestion 4 is essentially a Stage V approach and would be far too abstract and ideal for elementary school students to understand. One teacher, in fact, tried the "UN Day" method and the fighting on the playground increased. "Don't countries go to war all the time?" was the children's comment. The most appropriate methods, given the stage of the children, would probably be either suggestion 2 or suggestion 3, or maybe both in combination.

The middle school strategies cover a broad range. Suggestion 1, outlining a Stage V strategy, would probably go almost totally over the heads of junior high adolescents. Suggestion 2 represents a Stage IV negative method, since the solution, although legally correct, in essence misses the point of the problem.

Suggestion 3 details the most complicated response since, in order to be effective, the unit would require considerable time. In the long run, however, this would be the most effective approach. The actual role-taking experiences of "helping" others in small groups would aid in breaking down some of the barriers. This solution is essentially a combination of Stage III positive and Stage IV positive. The pupils learn to identify feelings in themselves and others (III), to send I-messages (III), and to speak up for themselves (IV). Suggestion 4 is a combination of Stage IV negative (a narrow legal definition of teaching) and Stage II negative (the use of aversive techniques to control behavior).

At the secondary level, suggestion 1 outlines a Stage III strategy of trying to gain compliance with the norm of hard work through exhortation. The students have all heard these exhortations before and would probably listen, agree with the substance of your comments, and not change their behavior at all. There might be some small change in the next day or two, but soon they would lapse back into semipassivity.

Suggestion 2 represents a humane Stage II positive reinforcement strategy. You are not changing the teaching-learning interaction or content but rather you are attempting to shape their behavior by an extrinsic reward system. The strategy may work in the short run but given the age of the students, it is really an example of undermatching. The use of punishment at the end changes the strategy from Stage II authoritative (or humane) to Stage II authoritarian. Compliance would likely to be low.

Suggestion 3 is basically a positive Stage IV method based on individualized learning contracts. You are providing some structure intended to wean them from dependence and tasks that require greater independence on the students' part. The requirements that they make a presentation before the class and eventually create a product will also help to promote responsibility. In teaching them the skills of finding, compiling, and presenting the information, your role is more that of a coach or supervisor. Developmentally, they are ready for such independence as learners, and it is what they'll need either in college or in their career.

Suggestion 4 is quite clearly a Stage V positive. You are providing the background and steps to move the class into a just community. Small-group and leadership experience through participatory decision making will help to promote both individuality and a caring community, a microcosm of a democratic ideal. As indicated in connection with the discussion of suggestion 3, the students are developmentally

ready for a guided and gradual transition to such a community.

REFERENCES

Baumrind, D. (1989). Rearing competent children. In W. Damon (Ed.), *Child development today and tomorrow*. San Francisco: Jossey-Bass.

Beilin, H. (1959). Teachers' and clinicians' attitudes toward the behavior problems of children: A reappraisal. *Child Development, 30*, 9–25.

Brown, R., and Herrnstien, R. (1974). *Psychology*. Boston: Little, Brown.

Charles, C. M. (1992) *Building classroom discipline*. New York: Longman.

Damon, W. (1990). *The moral child*. New York: MacMillan.

Edwards, C. P. (1987). Socialization in Kenya. In J. Kagan and S. Lamb (Eds.), *The emergence of morality in young children*. Chicago: University of Chicago Press.

Enright, R. D. (1981). A classroom discipline model for promoting social cognitive development in early childhood. *Journal of Moral Education, 11*(1), 47–60.

Finkenauer, J. O., and Kuhmerker, L. (1979). "Scared straight." *Moral Educational Forum, 4*, 1–7.

Glasser, W. (1975). *Schools without failure*. New York: Perennial Library. (Glasser's method of classroom meetings allows the teacher and the students to develop group rules and norms for appropriate behavior.)

Gordon, T. (1974). *Teacher effectiveness training*. New York: Longman.

Hart, S. (1991). From property to person status: Respect for the dignity of children. *American Psychologist, 46*, 66–71.

Harvard Alumni Bulletin, (May 1965), Cambridge: Harvard University.

Kuhmerker, L. (1991). *The Kohlberg legacy*. Birmingham, Ala.: REP.

Lickona, T. (1991). *Educating for character*. New York: Bantam.

MacDonald, R. E. (1991). *A handbook of basic skills and strategies for beginning teachers*. New York: Longman.

Mischel, W., and Peake, P. (1982). Beyond "déjà vu" in the search for cross-situational consistency. *Psychological Review, 89*, 730–755.

Mosher, R. L. (1979). *Adolescents' development and education*. Berkeley, Calif.: McCutchan.

National Geographic Society. (1968). *Everyday life in Bible times*. Washington: National Geographic Society.

Slavin, R. (1990). *Cooperative learning: Theory research and practice*. Needham Heights, Mass.: Allyn & Bacon.

Sprick, R. S. (1985). *Discipline in the secondary classroom*. West Nyack, N.Y.: Center for Applied Research in Education.

Sprinthall, N. A. (1985). Early adolescence and opportunities for growth in the 1980s: Ships passing in the night, again. *Journal of Early Adolescence, 5*(4), 533–547.

Sprinthall, N. A., Collins, W. A., and Edwall, G. (1994). *Adolescent Psychology: A developmental view*. New York: McGraw-Hill.

Updike, J. (1963). *The centaur*. New York: Knopf.

Wickman, E. K. (1928). *Children's behavior and teachers' attitudes*. New York: Commonwealth Fund.

Wolfgang, C., and Glickman, C. (1986). *Solving discipline problems*. Newton, Mass.: Allyn & Bacon.

20

MAINSTREAMING: STUDENTS WITH SPECIAL NEEDS

As a result of both a gradual revision of educational theory and a series of milestone legal decisions, special education for so-called atypical and exceptional children is undergoing a period of major formulation. Traditionally, societies have followed one of three practices with regard to children and teenagers labeled handicapped or difficult: (1) **remolding**, (2) **exclusion**, or (3) deviate-status placement (**segregation**). Different civilizations, and the same societies at different times, have naturally used a variety of methods to achieve each policy goal. In this chapter we describe these methods and discuss their shortcomings in view of both our current psychological understanding of such children and the emergence of a series of new "right-to-education" laws. We follow this with a discussion of current policy in special education, called **mainstreaming**, and its implications for classroom teachers.

TRADITIONAL PRACTICES REGARDING PLACEMENT

Remolding

As noted in Chapter 6 practically all societies have practiced remolding and reshaping their children during the early formative years, utilizing methods that vary from the somewhat benign to the most grotesque. For example, one old wives' tale suggests that it is important to play soft music to very young children to soothe the beast within their breasts; at the other extreme might be the medieval practice of exorcism, popularized in a movie.

The objective of all remolding methods is essentially to fit the child to the society. This means that, at least to some degree, the process of socialization was and is designed to eliminate individual variation or difference. Remolding can take the form of physically reshaping a child (binding the feet, elongating the neck, etc.), alteration of the physiological characteristics (such as conditioning feeding patterns—recall the old debate of demand versus scheduled eating), or psychological reshaping (for example, brainwashing). Thus, societies have attempted through physical, physiological, and psychological means to remake children.

Of course, not every society seeks to rebuild each child completely in its own adult image. It is clear, however, that a major goal of the practice is to eliminate some real or imagined negative attributes in children. Thus, in general, we should take a careful look at some of the procedures in early education to ensure that the programs are in the child's best interests and reflect effective methods toward promoting individual development. We have certainly stressed this view throughout this volume: Children are not miniature adults. For our purpose here, however, the critical questions are: What happens when children do not fit, when the procedures for remolding and reshaping do not work? What policies have societies followed when some children remain different? One policy is obvious—simply exclude such children from the rest of society.

Exclusion

The implementation of exclusionary policies can vary from an extreme—for example, murder—to psychological avoidance and exile. Ancient Sparta placed physically handicapped children on a mountainside; in seventeenth-century Salem, Massachusetts, teenaged girls and boys were put to death because they were thought to be witches. David Bakan has provided a detailed account of such bloodcurdling procedures in his appropriately titled work, *The Slaughter of the Innocents* (1971).

Of course, not all exclusionary policies necessarily result in death. In some instances a society simply pretends that the atypical or different child doesn't really exist. Thus, it is not unusual to find children who are labeled as retarded living a marginal existence, hidden from view most of the time or, even if they do appear in public, generally not acknowledged. Such "different" children are spoken of only in hushed voices, in the hope that they will soon return to attic rooms, cellars, or garages. Every so often newspaper stories announce the "discovery" of such children in a headline story; the famous case of the "wild boy" of Aveyron may be an instance of this exclusion.* It goes without saying that such children have literally no chance to grow and develop; they suffer either actual physical or, perhaps even worse, psychological death at an early age.

Segregation

Deviate-status placement   A more common policy, at least recently, has been the system of categorizing some children as deviate and placing children so des-

ignated in segregated environments. Various societies employ literally hundreds of different methods of classification—physical handicaps, racial characteristics, ancestry, intelligence testing, degrees of skin color, and so on. Naturally, a critical question here is the validity of the assessment procedures so employed, and we will discuss this issue more fully in a later section. At this point, we wish to emphasize that the effect of the overall policy is to exclude, separate, and segregate such children from the mainstream of society.

Sometimes the segregation policy is referred to as *warehousing:* States and nations build human warehouses, usually in remote areas, and place designated children within those walls for safekeeping. This policy is, of course, almost the same as deportation. So-called undesirables are literally shipped out and thus are effectively removed from citizenship roles in a manner similar to sending the French Emperor Napoleon to the island of St. Helena. The obvious natural tendency is for a society then to feel it has solved the problem; the education and growth of such children are now taken care of and we can all turn our attention to other concerns. The exclusionary policy eliminates designated children from society while the deviate-status-placement procedure segregates. "Out of sight, out of mind" is the hoped-for result.

To show that such a segregated approach has not totally disappeared, we need only recall a recent study of multihandicapped adolescents. The teenagers were placed in a rural residential facility. Besides the professional staff, they had contact with persons from the "outside" world on an average of less than one visitor per month. The isolation was so substantial that the teenagers' psychological development appeared halted (Dormer, 1975). In such a barren interpersonal environment, those adolescents would hardly have had a chance to develop any kind of identity in the Eriksonian sense. Without interaction, growth does not occur. Today fewer handicapped children are kept in such isolated residential units, but there are some. To be sure, such children may require medical assistance, yet they also have genuine interpersonal needs.

Segregation policies: A mockingbird   One scene in the Pulitzer Prize–winning novel *To Kill a Mockingbird* depicts the first day of school for a new second-grade teacher, Miss Caroline Fisher, in a small rural southern community. In the middle of a lesson a small "cootie" jumps out of Burris Ewell's hair, scaring Miss

---

* An eleven-year-old boy was found living like an animal in the woods in southern France in 1799. He had been left there some years earlier. He was subsequently cared for and educated by a famous French special educator, Jean Marc Gaspard Itard.

Caroline half to death. In the process of examining the youngster more closely, Miss Caroline concludes that he should be sent home to wash his hair with lye soap and the rest of himself with soap and water. As the novel's little-girl heroine "Scout" remarks, Burris "was the filthiest human I had ever seen. His neck was dark grey, the back of his hands were rusty and his fingernails were black deep into the quick. He peered at miss Caroline from a fist-sized clean space on his face." Miss Caroline emphatically comments then that Burris is to go home immediately and return "tomorrow" for the second day of school, clean as a whistle and ready to learn. But the boy balks:

> The boy laughed rudely. "You ain't sendin' me home, Missus. I was on the verge of leaving. I done done my time for this year."
>
> Miss Caroline looked puzzled. "What do you mean by that?"
>
> The boy did not answer. He gave a short contemptuous snort.
>
> One of the elderly members of the class answered her. "He's one of the Ewells, Ma'am—Whole school's full of 'em. They come the first day every year and then leave. The truant lady gets 'om here cause she threatens 'em with the sheriff, but she gives up trying to hold 'em. She reckons she's carried out the law just gettin' their names on the roll and running 'em here the first day. You're supposed to mark 'em absent the rest of the year" (Lee, 1962, 31–32).

The Ewell children, then, were deviates and segregated from the other pupils. The letter of the law in this case was honored, but the educational future of the children was ignored. The school itself could then avoid having to cope with the special problems of the Ewell children, cooties and all. In a less humorous vein, unfortunately, many of the segregated special-class placements for children have had the same effect. For the past forty years or so, the common educational policy has been to place children classified as mild to moderately educationally handicapped (IQ scores roughly in the 50 to 70 range) in special classes, separated from the other school-children. This practice has continued until recently, even though a long series of studies, beginning in the 1930s, has consistently indicated that such special-class placements are not superior to regular-class placements. In fact, no research evidence supports such special-class placements for "mild to moderately" retarded children; there are no academic gains for children placed in these classes and only equivocal

social gains. A comprehensive review suggests that the pupils placed in segregated classes suffer negative psychological consequences—namely, a lowered self concept—as a result of separation (Baroff, 1974).

A NEW POLICY: MAINSTREAMING

An alternative policy for children and teenagers classified as exceptional and/or handicapped is called mainstreaming. Essentially, the goal here is to expand the boundaries and reduce the barriers that have segregated such children from the mainstream of society. For many centuries this country legally sanctioned a segregated public school system that prevented black children from attending our society's mainstream white schools. The famous *Brown v. Board of Education* decision by the Supreme Court in 1954 ruled that separate facilities were inherently *not* equal. Thus, even if black children attended schools in new buildings filled with books, new carpets, and well-trained teachers, their schooling experience would still not be equal to that of mainstream white children. "Segregation equals second class citizenship" was the dictum of the Court. At a philosophical and psychological level, equal educational opportunity means that each child should have access to the same educational experience. To rule otherwise is a logical absurdity. A public school is for the public's children.* Segregation is inherently separate and *not* equal

In a manner similar to the 1954 *Brown* decision, a number of legal rulings have struck down the segregation of so-called retarded children. Following the reasoning of the Supreme Court decision of 1954, legislation such as the Pennsylvania Right to Education Law (1971) clearly commits educational policy to a goal of integrated education. The schools in Pennsylvania as well as other states are to provide public education for all children, regardless of the "label," "condition," "potential," or any other characteristic of the child.

Public Law 94-142

In 1975 a landmark federal law was enacted—**Public Law 94-142**, The Education for All Handicapped Chil-

---

* We are emphasizing the legal grounds on which the segregation laws were changed. This still doesn't touch the issue of so-called de facto segregation—a system of housing patterns, school-district lines, and the like—that produces a separate, segregated educational system in spite of the legal sanctions.

dren Act—which requires that all public school systems in all states meet the following regulations:

1. Identification of all handicapped children, aged four to twenty-one
2. Assessment of their educational needs
3. Individualized program planning
4. Procedural (due-process) safeguards for students and their parents
5. Education in the least restrictive alternative that meets the child's needs
6. Nondiscrimination

Public Law 94-142 has been referred to as an educational Magna Carta for all those children who have been excluded from regular classes by reason of any handicapping condition. Thus, the definition of the law is broad. Included are children and adolescents who may be classified in one or more of the following **handicapping conditions:**

> Learning disabled
> Speech impaired
> Mentally retarded
> Emotionally disturbed
> Deaf and hard of hearing
> Multihandicapped
> Orthopedically impaired
> Other health impaired
> Visually handicapped
> Deaf-blind

These ten types of handicapping conditions are deliberately broad so as to include practically all exceptional children and teenagers. It is no longer optional for schools to educate or not. The law is clear. Provision must be made from age four until graduation from high school (or its equivalent) or to the age of twenty-one.

The 94-142 law was then extended to include three-year-olds and was complemented by a new law (99-457) which now includes infants and toddlers, birth to two years, and which was fully implemented in 1991. Thus in the relatively short space of sixteen years, all special-needs children from birth to twenty-one years are now covered by the law. In the early 1970s as many as fifteen states had no legislation at all for such children (Ysseldyke and Algozzine, 1990). Thus the sheer scope of the legal changes is nothing short of enormous.

The "Least Restrictive" Dictum

The most far-reaching and controversial aspect of the legislation is the phrase "least restrictive alternative." This means that each pupil must be educated in an environment that is as normal as possible. The intention of the law is clear. Schools must include rather than exclude. Regular classroom environments must be expanded both physically and psychologically so that exceptional children can function in the mainstream. This aspect of the law may translate into such changes as barrier-free classrooms for wheelchairs and special apparatus for the hearing- and sight-impaired as well as a greater variety of curriculum materials.

The controversy arises from the so-called due-process provision. Before the school system can move a child out of the mainstream, it must prove its case. If parents disagree with the school's plan to place a child elsewhere than in the regular class, they have the right to a hearing, representation by a lawyer, and access to all the assessment information. Finally, they have the right to appeal the decision. In everyday language, this means that the burden of proof is on the school for every decision to exclude handicapped children from regular classes. It does not mean, however, that all children, including those with major and multiple-handicapping conditions, must be in regular classrooms all the time. When special services, and even special residential schools, may be required, the school needs to be able to demonstrate that such a facility is indeed the least restrictive alternative for that particular child. However, the boundary line is much broader. As a result of the legislation, literally thousands of segregated special classes have been closed, special-school enrollments have declined sharply, and special residential schools have dramatically reduced their populations.

The legal requirement then has created a bias toward mainstream placement as **Maynard Reynolds** (1990) has pointed out. The key concept, however, is the word *appropriate* which can create an ambiguous loophole as a barrier to mainstream inclusion. Certainly any observer of public schools will be struck by the increase in children with special needs attending regular classes. The movement is not without controversy since to a large degree the assessment of the learning potential of such children has not been achieved. Thus, how can we as educators decide what is an appropriate learning environment if the basis for diagnosis and placement is less than valid? We consider this question first and follow with a discussion of effective educational programming.

THE DIAGNOSTIC PROBLEM

IQ Testing: Is It Valid?

The traditional system of classifying children or teenagers as "retarded" or "deviate" has been criticized on at least two grounds: (1) The system of assessment is too narrowly based, and (2) the labels become permanent. The traditional method was based on an attempt to group children by degree of retardation, using an IQ test as the major assessment procedure. This resulted in three major categories:

1. *Educable mentally retarded (EMR):* IQ score is generally between 50 and 80 on standard tests. The child is usually classed as a slow learner and a "concrete" thinker but can be successfully employed later in life.

2. *Trainable mentally retarded (TMR):* IQ score is generally between 25 and 50 on standard tests. The child is considered not capable of "ordinary" academic learning but can learn self-care and safety rules. "Sheltered" workshops can provide an employment environment. The child can learn social adjustment.

3. *Profoundly retarded:* IQ score is between 0 and 25. The child requires constant supervision. Many children are bedridden.

As you can immediately see, the IQ score becomes extraordinarily important in deciding on the assignment of children to the EMR, TMR, or profoundly retarded groupings. Also, you may notice that these three labels can easily become euphemisms, or "softer" words replacing the older categories of moron, idiot, and imbecile. The primary difficulty, of course, is the effect of such a global classification based on a somewhat singular method of assessment. The major criticism is that we are overgeneralizing from a limited evaluation system. Maynard Reynolds has provided an incisive critique of this issue. He notes the following:

1. There is no sharp discontinuity in mental ability between people with IQs of 79 and 81, or 49 and 51, yet the tests can lend themselves to such absurd assumptions.

2. The test scores are also subject to the limitations of examiner influence and culture bias. Examiners either consciously or unconsciously do influence the scores achieved by their pupils. Also, few if any tests can claim to be completely culturally fair.

3. The tests themselves are not assessing the complete range of the child's functioning. For example, a "blind" child is usually not completely blind, nor is he or she necessarily incapable of functioning well in other areas. In the same way, a low-scoring-IQ child is not necessarily without school achievement potential, nor is he or she necessarily incapable of functioning well in other areas.

4. The tests themselves are virtually useless for making educational decisions with regard to placement. Educational classifications for special education only make sense when the classification is related to programs.

5. We should spend far less time in predicting how children with special needs may perform in "traditional" classrooms as a result of an IQ score. Instead, we should develop more effective instructional procedures that will reach more children—that is, increase the educational potential of each classroom to teach almost all children.

6. Special education should talk less about dysfunction, low IQs, deficits, impairments, and disabilities. Instead, school offerings should be differentiated sufficiently so that all children receive the help they need to develop maximally.

Reynolds sums up the generic assessment problem as one of "remote dispositional analysis" (1990, p. 427). By this he means that there is a great distance between a static concept like an IQ and the way children actually learn in the classroom. Such a distance is further removed since an IQ score has no relationship to effective teaching strategies or to what he calls "the level of the lesson" (1990, p. 427).

The most trenchant examination of the failures of diagnostic testing for special-education pupils has been provided by John Salvia of Pennsylvania State University and James Ysseldyke of the University of Minnesota. Their recent work clearly details how most common normative tests discriminate against such children (1991). Essentially, they literally indict almost all tests as having entirely inadequate norm groups. They point out that the test items themselves have been selected, in most cases, after excluding all so-called retarded pupils. In a sense, this is the same

Dr. James Ysseldyke

students of equivalent ability, one labeled and the other not, the results favored the nonlabeled group. The difference in academic achievement was half a standard deviation, an effect size approximately equal to the difference between a C− and a C+. Apparently, the combination of the label and the lowered teacher expectation interacts to reduce achievement. Can there be a special-education label without a stigma? The labels so developed become in the careful and somewhat arcane language of scientific researchers, a "powerfully biasing stimuli" (Ysseldyke and Algozzine, 1990, p. 89).

Assessment: The Problematic Nature of the Learning-Disabled Category

The assessment of exceptional children, however, does not end with an IQ test. There are nine other categories, as noted earlier. If there are genuine validity problems with the EMR grouping, what of the others? To understand this problem more clearly, it is necessary to outline the difference between the so-called high-incidence and low-incidence groups. The high-incidence group lists the categories in which most exceptional children are placed. The latter group contains a relatively small number of the total population. Table 20.1 presents the percentage differences. As you can readily see, over 90 percent of all exceptional children are grouped in just four categories: (1) learning-disabled (LD), (2) speech-handicapped, (3) mentally retarded (MD), and (4) emotionally disturbed (ED). While there seems to be no major difficulty in identifying a speech handicap, there are grave problems with all the remaining high-incidence groups. We have already pointed out the problems with the EMR area. The greatest problem, however, concerns the largest single category, LD. Recent surveys have shown that the criteria are so slippery that almost all schoolchildren (80 percent) could be classified as LD according to the definitions now in use. Also, there is substantial variation in different states. For example, Maryland classifies 5.2 percent of pupils as LD while New York has "only" an 0.8 percent incidence (Gelb and Mizokawa, 1986). Follow-up research has shown, quite unfortunately, that even with such broad and variable definitions, many students who are clustered as LD do not, in fact, meet the criteria. In one state, over 45 percent of the students enrolled were erroneously classified (Reynolds, Wang and Walberg, 1987).

argument that was used against the early forms of intelligence tests, which systematically excluded black children from the norm groups and then used the unrepresentative norm-group scores to classify black children.

Salvia and Ysseldyke also note that most national tests of academic ability such as those for reading, arithmetic, and other primary mental abilities *do not* provide local schools or particular classroom teachers with any useful information on which to base an educational program. Thus, the authors appeal for great caution in the continued use of most of the common national assessment tests of ability. Those procedures too often misclassify and misdiagnose, to the detriment of pupils from special-education backgrounds.

A recent study by Penelope Peterson provides telling commentary on the negative effects of the special-education categories (1988). With two groups of

SPOTLIGHT ON ASSESSMENT

Teachers Don't Want to Be Labeled

Harry W. Forgan

When teaching a course on tests and measurements at Kent State University recently, I decided to administer an adult group intelligence test to the class. I wanted the students to "feel" what it was like to take such a test and realize what items we use to measure intelligence. I also thought they might be more aware of the short time it takes to obtain a number which is regarded as very important by many educators.

The students were told not to write their names on the test papers, but rather to use a code such as their house number, physical measurements, or any less obvious symbol. I explained that I really didn't have faith in IQ scores; therefore, I didn't want to know their IQs.

The administration of the test required only 50 minutes. The students seemed to enjoy taking it and chuckled at some of the tasks they were expected to perform. I had to laugh myself when I saw some of them looking at their hands and feet when responding to items concerning right and left.

Upon scoring the test I found that the lowest IQ was 87 and the highest 143. The mean IQ for the 48 students was 117. I was not astonished by the 87, even though all of the students had successfully completed the general education courses and student teaching at Kent State and were ready to graduate by the end of the term. After all, IQ tests have many limitations.

Then I got an idea. I decided to prepare a report for each student, writing his code on the outside and "IQ 87" on the inside of each. I folded and stapled each paper—after all, an IQ is confidential information!

At the next class period I arranged all of the folded papers on a table at the front of the room. I wrote the range and the average IQ on the chalkboard. Many students snickered at the thought of somebody getting an 87. The students were eager and afraid as I began by explaining the procedures for picking up their papers. I made a point of telling them not to tell others their IQ score, because this would make the other person feel as if he too had to divulge this "total endowment." The students were then directed to come up to the table, row by row, to find their coded paper. I stood sheepishly—ready to laugh out loud as I watched the students carefully open their papers and see "IQ 87." Many opened their mouths with astonishment and then smiled at their friends to indicate they were extremely happy with their scores. There was dead silence when I began to discuss the implications of the IQ scores. I explained that in some states a person who scores below 90 on an IQ test is classified as a slow learner. The fact that group intelligence tests should not be used to make such a classifica-

tion was stressed. I also emphasized the fact that *someone* in this class could have been classified as a slow learner and placed in a special class on the basis of this test.

I told how many guidance counselors would discourage a child with an 87 IQ from attending college. Again I emphasized the fact that one person in this room was ready to graduate from college having passed several courses in history, biology, English, and many other areas.

I then went on to explain that the majority of elementary and secondary school teachers believe in ability grouping. This is usually done on the basis of intelligence tests, so I explained that I would like to try ability grouping with this class—again to see "how it feels." Some students objected right away, saying that "I did not want to know their IQ scores." I calmed them by saying it would be a worthwhile learning experience and assured them that I really didn't believe in IQ scores.

I told the students not to move at this time, but I would like all of those with an IQ below 90 to come to the front so they could sit nearer to me for individual help. I told the students who had an average IQ (between 90–109) to go to the back of the room and then take the seats in the middle of the class. The students with an above average IQ were asked to go to the side of the room and take the seats in the back because they really didn't need much more extra help.

"O.K., all those who got an IQ below 90 come to the front of the room." The students looked around to find those who scored below 90. I said that I knew there was an 87 and maybe a couple of 89's. Again, there was dead silence.

"O.K., all those students whose IQ is between 90–109 go to the back of the room." Immediately, to my amazement, 8 or 10 students picked up their books and headed for the back of the room. Before they could get there I said, "Wait a minute! Sit down! I don't want to embarrass you, but you would lie and cheat—the same way we make our students lie and cheat—because you don't want to be classified as "slow." I wrote 'IQ 87' on every paper!"

The class erupted. It was in an uproar for about five minutes. Some of the women cried. Some indicated that they needed to use the restroom. All agreed it was a horrifying and yet valuable experience.

I asked them to do one thing for me: Please don't label kids. Because we are all "gifted," "average," and "slow," depending on the task at hand. They promised.

From *Phi Delta Kappan,* September 1973. Reprinted by permission

TABLE 20.1   FREQUENCY OF HANDICAPPING CONDITIONS IN SCHOOL-AGE POPULATIONS

HIGH INCIDENCE	PERCENTAGE	
Learning disabled	48	
Speech handicapped	23	
Mentally retarded	14	Total high incidence = 93%
Emotionally disturbed	9	
LOW INCIDENCE		
Multihandicapped	2	
Orthopedically impaired	1	Total low incidence = 6+%
Deaf	1	
Visually handicapped	0.5	
Deaf-Blind	0.05	
Other	3	

Source: Twelfth annual report to Congress on implementation of the education of the Handicapped Act (Washington, D.C.: U.S. Department of Education, 1990).

An even more telling problem with the LD category is that the incidence changes over relatively short time periods. As Figure 20.1 shows, during the period 1976–1989, the number of students so labeled increased 150 percent while the number grouped as EMR declined by 36 percent. In fact, it has been suggested that the amount of criticism leveled against IQ tests, especially with regard to their use with minority students, has encouraged schools to avoid the EMR category for fear of due-process litigation (Reschly, 1988). In actual numbers, this could suggest that 300,000 pupils who were originally EMR are no longer denoted as "retarded" while 1 million students who were "normal" are now "learning-disabled." The actual reason for the shift probably has little to do with the learning potential of the children. Instead it is, in all probability, a reflection of a major court case, as we note on page 595.

To summarize, then, we note that the validity of the LD label is extremely doubtful if most normal students fit the definition. Also, the incidence varies substantially from state to state; even more to the point, there is major variation over short time periods as a result of litigation. Maynard Reynolds has referred to this phenomenon as the **hydraulic model of assessment**, which reduces the number in one container and increases the number in the closest container regardless of the initial accuracy of the distribution. This could mean that children are simply moved from category to category regardless of their learning potential.

Assessment: The Problem with the Emotionally Disturbed Category

As is shown in Table 20.1, the fourth special-education category in the high-incidence area is that of the emotionally disturbed. Approximately 9 percent of the students are so grouped, yet there are serious shortcomings with these assessment procedures. Some estimates run from 50 to 80 percent of students misclassified. A recent summary noted, "Who is or is not labeled behaviorally disordered for a given educational program or research investigation is likely to depend as much on political and subjective factors as on objective behavioral criteria" (Nelson and Rutherford, 1988). Thus, the problem of accuracy remains as a major question.

Also, as was the case with LD, it makes a difference as to the time period of classification. Over the recent period, the number of children in the group has changed. While not as dramatic as for LD, none the less there was a 36 percent increase in the numbers of students categorized as ED. Note that we need to exercise great care in wording. Because of validity problems, we cannot say that there has been a 36 percent increase in emotionally disturbed students, but only that use of the category is becoming more frequent. In fact, one very alarming trend is that the total number of children grouped in the high-incidence categories is increasing—from 3.7 million for the period 1977–1978 to 4.5 million for the period 1988–1989. This means that not only is there a hydrau-

FIGURE 20.1   (a) Changes in special-education classification, 1976 to 1989; (b) growth in numbers of students classified in special-education categories.

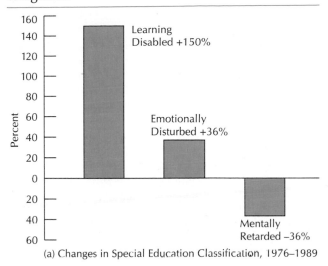

(a) Changes in Special Education Classification, 1976–1989

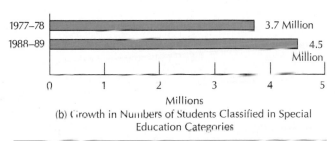

(b) Growth in Numbers of Students Classified in Special Education Categories

From *Twelfth annual report to Congress on implementation of the Education of the Handicapped Act,* Washington: U.S. Department of Education (1990).

lic system at work shifting identified pupils from one category to another, but there is also an increase in the population itself. It is difficult to accept the legitimacy of labeling ever more children with designations that are of doubtful validity. The two sets of changes are illustrated in Figure 20.1. Ysseldyke, Algozinne, and Thurlow refer to this as a problem of *categorical drift,* which looks more like a psychometric version of Dow Jones averages than accurate assessments (1992, p. 105).

Assessment: The Confounding Effects of Social Class, Ethnicity, and Gender

As if there weren't enough problems with the high-incidence categories, the effects of social class and ethnicity further complicate the issue. A major study

of all fifty states compared the use of the high-incidence and low-incidence groupings. The findings indicated that the low-incidence categories were not related to factors such as social class or ethnicity. Just the opposite was the case in the high-incidence categories, especially EMR and LD. Using a combined index of socioeconomic status (SES) the study reported a series of very strong correlations between SES and EMR, accounting for about 50 percent of a predicted relationship between SES and the EMR label. The actual correlations were + .70 and + .63, respectively, to indices of poverty, and infant mortality and − .60 to family income (the higher the income, the less likely the EMR classification) (Gelb and Mizokawa, 1986).

On ethnicity, there was a very strong correlation of + .65 between race and EMR for black students. There is every reason to believe that the overrepresentation of such minorities in special education is the result of faulty diagnosis. For example, in a very large urban system the rosters indicated that the system had three times more black students assigned to MR classes than any other school system in the country. For this to occur, either a huge concentration of retarded people all had to be living in a single city through some fluke or the method of assignment was at fault. Investigation has shown that the method was the cause. A major flaw in the use of MR, ED, and LD categories is that a disproportionate number of minority pupils are often classed as deviates. The label stigmatizes even when accurate; when inaccurate, it not only stigmatizes but leads to negative self-fulfilling prophecies. Research has shown consistently that minorities are the groups most often misclassified. In one study the MR label was applied to 16 percent of the school's minority population. A careful reassessment of the children indicated 2 percent were accurately classified. In the words of Maynard Reynolds, "Racial and ethnic minorities often deeply resent the high rates of classification of their children as 'retarded,' 'disturbed' or 'maladjusted' " (Reynolds, 1984, p. 77). In the cases cited, the resentment appears more than justified.

Unfortunately even the most recent evidence indicates further errors rather than effective solutions. It has been reported that the IQ testers favored middle-class children through positive feedback, a supportive environment, and a "lenient" (27 percent increase) scoring system. The reverse was true for children from working class and poverty backgrounds (Rothman and Semmel, 1990, p. 357).

SPOTLIGHT ON BIAS IN SPECIAL EDUCATION

Systemic Discrimination

Jim Ysseldyke, who leads a major assessment program at the University of Minnesota, and his colleague Bob Algozzine conducted a series of studies on the relation between parental social status and special-education placement.[a] For a sample of over 200 educational decision makers (teachers, counselors, and school administrators), they provided identical educational data for students referred for evaluation. They varied the parental background; for example, in half the cases the student had a father who was a bank vice president and a mother who was a real estate agent, and for the other half the father was a janitor and the mother a supermar-

ket clerk. The referrals for special education were substantially higher for the students from lower socioeconomic backgrounds even though there was no objective difference in academic performance, test scores, or classroom behavior for the students involved. Although unintentional, the educators were consistently biased in referring for special classes or resource room simply on the basis of family occupation. This is sometimes called *systemic discrimination*, a subjective prejudice that is built into the educational system. Although each decision maker would certainly claim that there was no bias on an individual basis, the Ysseldyke-Algozzine studies illus-

trated the opposite. This should remind all educators to become conscious of the effects of such prejudice on referral and placement particularly in the high-incidence areas of special-education categories.

Gaylord-Ross[b] points out the paradox: Public Law 94-142 calls for unbiased assessment; yet the single largest category (LD) is most strongly influenced by political, economic, and social factors rather than accuracy in classification.

---

[a] J. Ysseldyke, B. Algozzine, and M. Thurlow, *Critical issues in special education* (Boston: Houghton Mifflin, 1992).

[b] R. Gaylord-Ross, *Issues and research on special education*, Vol. 1 (New York: Teachers College Press, 1990).

Also, an extensive study by Shaywitz and associates (1990) has shown a bias against females in the classification of reading disability. It has long been a part of folklore that boys have more difficulty learning to read than girls. Shaywitz found that this view was apparently effecting a different referral rate for developmental or remedial reading assistance. Regular school referral procedures were compared to a careful reassessment method. The teachers in the early grades systematically overreferred boys and underreferred girls even though there were no objective differences between the groups in the extent of reading disability.

Currently about 4.4 million children are classified in some special-needs category, but unfortunately at present the view is that such a figure is grossly underestimated. Reynolds (1990) suggests that by the late 1990s the figure may well approach 8 million, almost double the current level. He sees four factors as "producing" children with special needs: (1) more school-age children, (2) more children living in poverty, (3) more low-birth-weight babies, and (4) more children victimized by drugs, alcoholism, neglect, and abuse.

Thus the sheer numerical increase is a cause for concern and adds to the urgency of solving the assessment problem.

ASSESSMENT: SOME NEW PROPOSALS

One recent attempt to improve testing has been termed *dynamic assessment*. The idea is based on the work of Vygotsky (see Chapter 5) to evaluate learning potential by a sequence of test-teach-test. The examiner through observation seeks to identify the child's "zone of proximal growth" as a first step. This is followed by direct instruction of learning material, for example, teaching the child how to solve a school problem. Then the child is tested again to see if he or she understood the problem. The early results of this approach are mixed since there is little evidence of increases in actual learning. Also the approach is both expensive and time-consuming since it is done on an individualized basis over extended time periods. The other difficulty is the problem of the relation between assessment and effective teaching strategies (Rothman and Semmel, 1990). Thus the theory for dynamic assessment may hold an important key to the problem of accuracy in classification, but current practice will need further revision.

A second method calls for a completely different sequence in the assessment procedures. The first step, when a child isn't keeping up, would be to assess the learning environment in the classroom, carefully reviewing the teaching methods, materials, and classroom atmosphere. Also, pupil achievement would not be measured by traditional nationally normed achievement tests, nor would pupil ability be assessed through the standard IQ method.

Nationally normed achievement tests measure only about one-third of the content of a given grade, which stacks the deck against a child if the test is used to measure current classroom learning. The problems with IQ tests have already been noted. In the words of Samuel Messick (then vice president of research for the Educational Testing Service), "An individual assessment of the pupil would be permitted only after deficiencies in the learning environment had been ruled out" (1984, p. 5). Thus, a careful look at the quality of instruction would become the first step. As a second step, a new method of assessment that emphasized actual problem solving or "work samples" would be followed. Basically, testing would be used only as a last resort; otherwise, the pupil would be unnecessarily "exposed to the risks of stigma and misclassification in referral and individual assessment" (Messick, 1984, p. 8). The final step, after ruling out the classroom environment and using a careful and comprehensive valid assessment of learning ability, would be to consider the special-class placement *temporary*, no more than one year at a time. The reason for such a time limit on assignment to segregated special classes is simply that the longer a pupil remains out of the mainstream, the less the probability of the pupil's returning. In the classes themselves, there is often "a sharply reduced curriculum and little cognitive demand" (Finn and Resnick, 1984, p. 11).

Judge Robert Peckham presided over a now-famous court case (*Riles v. Larry P.*, 1979). After an exhaustive examination of placement practice and the learning environments in a large urban district, he declared that the special classrooms were "dead-end classrooms." (*Riles v. Larry P.*, 1979). The doors, once closed, seemed permanently sealed.

To give you a greater personal sense of the effects of misdiagnosis, we present a brief case study drawn from the case files of a famous child psychotherapist.

Dibs: A case of misdiagnosis. Virginia Axline, a gifted child psychotherapist and author, has provided a dramatic case study of a little boy, Dibs. From parental description and nursery school behavior, it appeared that Dibs was grossly mentally defective. His parents reported that from birth on he was always remote, untouchable, slow to talk and walk, unable to play, and "striking out at people like a little wild animal."

The nursery school teachers were baffled by him. The school psychologist had been unable to test him. The pediatrician had concluded he was "strange," perhaps mentally retarded, psychotic, or brain-damaged. No one was apparently able to get close enough to Dibs to find out the causes of his difficulties.

The parents themselves were both brilliant and successful yet terribly ashamed, fearful, and anxiety-ridden over their "problem" child. Deep down they believed that the awful truth was that Dibs was an "idiot."

The mother related an incident at home to Axline, in which she described a terrible fight between Dibs and her husband. The four-year-old had apparently hurled a chair at his father, kicking and screaming all the while, "I hate you." This was in response to the husband's direct comment to Dibs that he was babbling like an idiot. The mother reported to the therapist the following scene with her husband.

> "Dibs wasn't babbling like an idiot now. 'He said he hated you.' Then, my husband sat down in a chair and actually wept! It was terrible; I had never seen a man cry before. I had never thought anything could cause my husband to shed a tear. I was afraid, suddenly terrified, because he seemed to be just as scared as I was. I think we were closer to each other than we have ever been. Suddenly, we were just two frightened, lonely, unhappy people with our defenses crumpled and deserted. It was terrible—and yet a relief to know that we could be human, and could fail and admit that we had failed! Finally, we pulled ourselves together and he said that maybe we had been wrong about Dibs. I said I would come and ask what you thought about Dibs."

Then Axline reported that the mother looked at her with an expression of fear and panic in her eyes. " 'Tell me,' she said. 'Do you think that Dibs is mentally defective?' " (Axline, 1967, p. 90).

FIGURE 20.2   Deno's Cascade—The "Cascade" classification system.

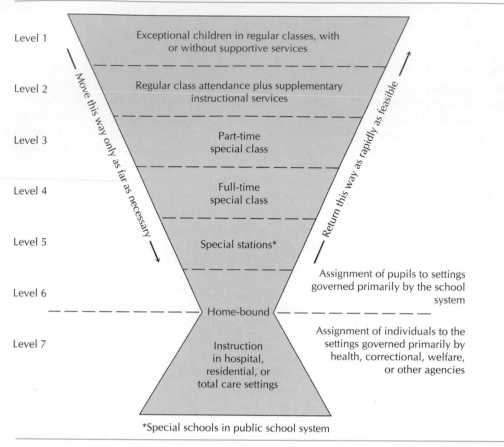

Level 1   Exceptional children in regular classes, with or without supportive services

Level 2   Regular class attendance plus supplementary instructional services

Level 3   Part-time special class

Level 4   Full-time special class

Level 5   Special stations*

Level 6   Home-bound

Level 7   Instruction in hospital, residential, or total care settings

Move this way only as far as necessary

Return this way as rapidly as feasible

Assignment of pupils to settings governed primarily by the school system

Assignment of individuals to the settings governed primarily by health, correctional, welfare, or other agencies

*Special schools in public school system

From Evelyn Deno: Special education as developmental capital. *Exceptional Children, 37* (1970), 229–237. Copyright by The Council for Exceptional Children. Reprinted with permission.

Dibs was "defective" only in the sense that he had suffered enormous emotional deprivation. For whatever reason, neither parent had been capable of forming a warm, supportive, nurturing early environment for him. In the language of a psychiatrist who interviewed the family, Dibs was "the most rejected and emotionally deprived child" he had ever seen.

In the case study itself, Axline describes the emotional reeducation she provided for Dibs, as well as the assistance to the parents so that they could maintain the gains. Dibs gradually yet dramatically emerged from his shell into the world of human relationships and, in the author's words, "was able to be a child." The work stands both as a moment of high drama and as a reminder of our basic human needs for supportive relationships to encourage healthy psychological development—an essential first step to becoming a person. The word "Dibs" is a common expression in England for "self."

An Alternative Classification Procedure

Test interpretation is a critical process, for it indicates how we make meaning and judgments. We certainly need a more comprehensive system of educational diagnosis for all children and particularly for those currently being classed as "special." Evelyn Deno (1970) an eminent theorist-practitioner in this field, developed a **cascade system** (see Figure 20.2) that respects both the complexity of the problem and the need to employ careful assessment in the service of the children. Rather than view the problem from society's perspective first, she suggests we start with the fundamental needs and rights of children. In this way we can keep our educational priorities in mind. The system is also based on a positive assessment concept designed to uncover the areas of positive educational potential. Thus, rather than generalize from one negative aspect of a child's functioning, the system seeks to differentiate general functioning into a series of elements. This helps prevent classifying children into negative categories. Instead, the children can be grouped into one of seven levels of educational environments, from regular classes to "total" care. The critical point, however, is the dynamic commitment in the plan to always move children upward in the system as far and as fast as possible. Thus, assignments are at first based on the level of activity the child brings to the environment. The educational goal of any particular level, then, is to prepare the child for the next level up, so to speak; none of the levels, two through seven, is regarded as a permanent placement.

Alternative Educational Environments: Promoting Development

Evelyn Deno's system clearly implies the need for differential service. The diagnostic problem, as we indicated, involves broad assessment procedures in all areas of functioning. The critical assumption, however, is not the initial prescription; instead, it's the developmental program. From this point of view, the various categories of handicapping conditions are, at best, only immediate and temporary stations for the child. Growth is determined by interaction. The labels are dangerous, since it's so easy to assume that the problems are safely locked up inside the child. The frameworks of Jean Piaget, Jerome Bruner, J. McV. Hunt, and Robert White suggest the following educational assumptions:

1. Special-education pupils develop through the same sequence of stages as "normal" pupils but at slower rates in the areas of their handicaps.

2. The growth of these children thus depends on the same set of principles applicable to "normal" children, namely, (a) a rich, stimulating, abundant early environment (Hunt); (b) an active rather than a passive learning environment, including a heavy emphasis on practice and participation from the early years onward (Piaget and Bruner).

3. Careful educational preparation is needed for stage growth and transition to the next stage up. This includes the process of *equilibration*, Piaget's term for a constructive match between the child's functioning stage and the learning environment— for example, a rich, stimulating sensory environment during the very early years. Developmental growth, as we have noted, depends on interaction

between the child and the environment. The opposite of this developmental assumption is the isomorphic view—that the learning problem is a deficit locked up inside the body of the designated child.

A number of studies, including a classic one by Maria Skodak and Harold Skeels (1949), the Perry Preschool Program (see Chapter 3), and one by Sandra Scarr-Salapatek and Richard Weinberg (1975), indicate rather clearly that intellectual functioning and general development can be positively influenced by a rich, stimulating early environment. Skodak and Skeels demonstrated that cognitive functioning could be dramatically increased for young children by modifying an extremely barren orphanage environment. The Perry Preschool Program showed the positive effects of a stimulating preschool environment, while Scarr and Weinberg showed the positive effects of modifying early-home-care environments. Whether the actual environment was an orphanage, a nursery school, or a home, the principles were the same— namely, that significant increases were found in cognitive functioning as a result of "active" learning, positive interaction, and developmental-stage equilibration. This is simply a means of placing the explanations for positive growth in developmental language. In all these studies, many preschool children were initially classified, on the basis of an IQ test, as retarded or as slow learners.

The Regular Education Initiative

As a result of a series of concerns over both the assessment problem and the ease with which children can be shunted from one category to another, a major new framework is under consideration for special education. Educator Madeline Will argued that as many as 20 to 30 percent of all schoolchildren were having academic difficulty. To address this challenge, she proposed a partnership between special and regular education to develop new instructional strategies in the mainstream—hence the term **regular education initiative** (REI) (Ysseldyke and Algozzine, 1990, p. 271). The regular education initiative seeks to increase the number of high-incidence children in regular classrooms. One of the difficulties with the Deno cascade system, which was discussed earlier in the chapter, has been the failure to maintain the movement toward levels 1 and 2 of her system. Use of the so-called pull-out programs, or resource rooms, has in-

SPOTLIGHT ON DYSLEXIA

A Case Study in Special Education

A lengthy debate has been waged over the question of word blindness in children and teenagers. Although given various labels such as **dyslexia** (word disability), *streptosymbolia* (twisting symbols), and *minimal brain dysfunction*, the symptoms of the syndrome are all the same. Essentially, children and teenagers afflicted with this disability reverse words and numbers and have enormous difficulty in spelling, remembering telephone numbers, looking up words in a dictionary, keeping number columns straight, and learning a foreign language—to name just a few of the most common symbol-processing areas.

The syndrome has a long history and has afflicted many famous people. Public figures such as Albert Einstein, George Patton, Woodrow Wilson, and Nelson Rockefeller have all described in the most poignant way what it was really like during these most difficult school days. They were being asked to perform activities that they literally could not understand. In math, for example, a child might be asked to add 783 and 227, but might actually read these numbers as 873 and 272 without realizing the reversal. Thus, when the answer was marked wrong, the reason for the failure would remain a mystery. Similarly,

in writing, *no* might become *on*, *god* might be seen as *dog*, and so on (or so no!).

In spite of the long history of personal accounts, systematic research studies, and a wide variety of documentation, there continues to be substantial opposition within educational circles to acknowledging the existence of the disability. Estimates run as high as one of seven pupils afflicted, with a large preponderance of males over females. There remains, however, on the part of too many teachers, a resistance to admitting that some pupils actually suffer from the disability. At an intuitive level, the common view is that it is just a

question of willfulness and motivation; somehow the dyslexic child isn't really working hard enough.

A second common misperception is that if dyslexia isn't a fancy psychological label for laziness, it's just a cover-up for mental retardation. The reason that Johnny can't read, or add, or spell is simple—he's stupid. Even though studies have shown that individually administered IQ scores do not correlate with dyslexia, this second myth continues.

If teachers have experienced difficulty in accepting the reality of dyslexia, psychologists and researchers have had difficulty in documenting the causes. In fact, for too long researchers have attempted to discover the single crucial factor. Some feel the problem is basically a physical-coordination deficiency. Others suggest a chemical basis, from bad reactions to artificial food coloring to hyperactivity due to a drug imbalance. Still others think of it as a psychoanalytic problem resulting from anal fixation, a lack of training during the formative preschool years, or a problem of birth order, of parental neglect, or of fatherlessness.

The physical-coordination school suggests solutions ranging from reliance on exercises, such as bouncing on trampolines, jumping rope, walking balance beams, and bouncing basketballs, to the extreme of surgical correction, such as removal of adenoids or altering eye muscles. The proponents of a chemical view suggest measures such as the careful supervision of diet, food without preservatives, and massive doses of vitamins,

tranquilizers, and seasickness pills. Theorists who attribute dyslexia to an intrapsychic problem suggest solutions ranging from individual counseling and play therapy to family analysis.

But human behavior cannot be reduced to a single cause. It is disheartening indeed to find parents, teachers, and educators first attempting to deny that dyslexia exists at all, and then reversing their stand and not only accepting the problem but seeking a single magical cure. Recently a somewhat cynical educational psychologist commented that, in the last decade, all the people who sold used cars, bait-and-switch real estate in Florida, and bust-development machines have moved into the dyslexia business. In fact, as a teacher you may be questioned in depth by anxious parents or school boards as to which single remedy is best—the "talking" typewriter, the sensory-deprivation booth, the color-coded alphabet, underwater swimming, behavior modification, organized crawling, or wall-to-wall trampolines?

Both theory and research evidence, however, strongly suggest that no single technique will produce cures. In fact, the remedies are something less than spectacular, consisting of multisensory tutoring and massive amounts of human support. If some pupils cannot employ the usual channels for processing symbols, than an educational program needs to include a broader array of techniques and experiences. Multisensory programs allow the child quite obviously to use all the

senses—see the letter, trace it in sand, cut it out of cardboard, say it out loud, pick it out of magazine ads and street signs, and touch it in block form.

The techniques really come down to "good" instruction—namely, an array of alternatives to help children learn the code. The same "solutions" apply to helping pupils learn to produce symbols. Since regular writing is difficult and at times torturous, other channels can be employed. In addition to paper and pencil, fat crayons, and chalk and chalkboard, pupils can also be "allowed" to tape-record reports, give oral reports in class, or use a typewriter.

Employing multiple techniques is, of course, not enough. In learning new and difficult tasks, any pupil will need extra human support and encouragement—and this support is especially crucial for the dyslexic child. Signs of impatience, despair, and discouragement by a teacher are quickly transmitted to a child afflicted with word blindness, and such a child will be hyperalert to teacher feelings. Positive human support is necessary to create a low-anxiety atmosphere that will help the pupil take risks and not feel it necessary to cover up his or her difficulty. Some dyslexic children learn magnificent social skills to prevent a teacher from finding out that they can't read or write. Probably the best tutoring in this instance would be from older children and adults who themselves have struggled with the problem. Given support, encouragement, and a multisensory approach, the word-blind children do learn to read.

Several studies conducted during the last thirty-five years all clearly indicate that intellectual functioning and general development can be positively influenced by a rich, stimulating early environment.

FIGURE 20.3   Special-education services.

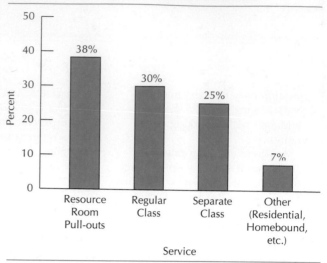

From Twelfth annual report to Congress on implementation of the Education of the Handicapped Act (Washington: U.S. Department of Education, 1990).

creased (see Figure 20.3). Exeptional children are removed from the mainstream for separate instruction for part of the day. While seemingly appropriate, new outcome reviews have shown that the pull-out system acts as a barrier to development. The criticism involves the following factors:

1. There is reduced cooperation between regular and special education.

2. The learning experiences of the students are fractionated.

3. The students fall further and further behind, increasing the likelihood that they will drop out.

4. Grouping low achievers together in the pull-out programs further reduces academic achievement.

5. The content of the pull-out curriculum takes precedence over the regular learning experiences.

6. The pull-out programs provide a less intense and reduced amount of instructional time (Hawkins, Doueck, and Lishner, 1988).

A major longitudinal study by Susan Osborne and her associates (1991) provides substantial cross-validation for these positions. Over a three-year span in elementary school, the team studied forty-two LD children from the standpoint of academic outcomes. The students were culturally diverse (62 percent Afri-

can American and 38 percent white) and the families were largely working class in background. Initially all the students were in a part-time, resource room (pull-out) program based on the same discrepancy between their intelligence score and their academic achievement. On an overall basis, the IQ scores averaged just below the 50th percentile, for example, 95.5, and academic achievement was in the vicinity of the 20th percentile. During the school years, a total of fourteen students were fully mainstreamed, twenty-five remained in the resource room program and three were moved to a self-contained room.

The outcomes are presented in Figure 20.4 according to math, reading recognition, and reading achievement. The results indicate most clearly that the mainstreamed LD students outperformed their resource room conterparts in all three areas. If that wasn't a very strong indicator of difference, the researchers also found that the resource room LD students experienced a *12-point drop* in verbal IQ score over the period of the study. Of course theories of intelligence are based on the concept of stability over such a time period (three to five years). Also it is relevant that such a drop is almost equal to a standard deviation of such a test. For both reasons the decline in learning potential (IQ) and the actual reduction in achievement creates a major cause for concern about the resource room model.

FIGURE 20.4 Mainstream versus resource room achievement (a three-year study).

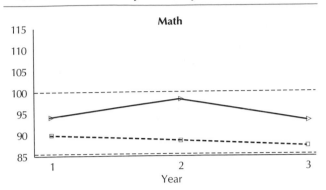

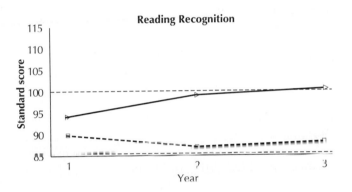

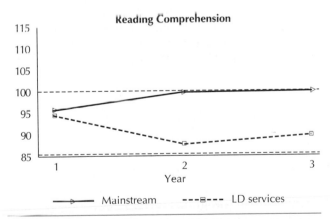

From S. Osborne, A. Schulte, and J. McKinney: A longitudinal study of students with learning disabilities in mainstream and resource programs. *Exceptionality*, 2 (1991), 81–95.

In searching for possible causal factors, Osborne noted that prior studies had found that such students were pulled out of the mainstream during academic instruction, particularly language arts. The same was true for the current study. Also, prior research had

indicated that there was very little interaction between special-education teachers and the mainstream instructors. This also proved true. Almost two-thirds of the mainstreamed LD students were never observed at all by the special-education teachers. On average, the teachers interacted about five minutes per month for the other students (Osborne et al., 1991). Thus the results seriously question the efficacy of the resource room approach. Another recent study (Hibbert, 1992) with three- and four-year-olds came to similar conclusions. In a study of emotionally disturbed (ED) preschoolers, those fully mainstreamed were assessed at higher levels of adjustment after one year versus a comparison group of resource room children, even though the control group received slightly higher initial ratings. These two studies provide a strong case for mainstream versus resource room approaches. "Stay put" appears more defensible than "pull out."

Unfortunately, a recent national review of pupil placement policies indicates a strong migration from the mainstream. Table 20.2 presents the recent survey of classroom assignments across three age groupings three to five years, six to eleven years, and twelve to seventeen years. There is a major reduction in the number of special-education pupils in regular classes from 40 to 18 percent and a major increase in resource room placement from 14 to 46 percent, whereas separate classes remain about the same. Figure 20.5 compares regular classes to resource rooms separately.

Naturally any such proposal as the REI is not without its critics. Naomi Zigmond and Janice Baker (1990) worry that regular-education teachers are not equipped by training to handle LD students. Their one-year study of thirteen students indicated some very positive outcomes compared to a previous year in a self-contained approach: improved behavior, more academic learning time, and general adjustment. The downside, however, showed no gain in academic achievement. The authors felt that the teachers reverted to "business-as-usual" (p. 185) and needed more variety in teaching techniques. Another criticism was voiced by Semmel and Gerber (1990) who suggested that REI will create yet another special-education category, namely, those who don't make it from within the REI group. Also they fear that teacher training will not be adequate. In any case the trend toward greater inclusion appears inevitable (Ysseldyke, Algozzine, and Thurlow, 1992), and a major step is the framework to eliminate the distinctions among three of the high-incidence categories.

TABLE 20.2   *SPECIAL-EDUCATION STUDENT PLACEMENT (SCHOOL YEAR 1987–1988)*

TYPE OF CLASS	AGE		
	3–5 YEARS, %	6–11 YEARS, %	12–17 YEARS, %
Regular	40 percent	40 percent	18 percent
Resource room	14 percent	35 percent	46 percent
Separate class	28 percent	20 percent	28 percent
Other	17 percent	4 percent	7 percent

From *Twelfth annual report to Congress on implementation of the Handicapped Act* (Washington: U.S. Department of Education, 1990).

We now turn to the issue of cross-categorical, or non-categorical, proposals.

Cross-Categorical, or Noncategorical, Systems

As a result of these difficulties, there is renewed interest in regular education, although it is clear that not all pull-out programs should be eliminated. The plan, however, is to reduce substantially the current reliance on separate teaching-learning experiences.

The first step will be to continue to move toward the elimination of the high-incidence categories, such as EMR, LD, and ED. The goal is to propose a single functional category of low achievement. It may sound confusing, but the creation of such a broad category is often referred to as a **cross-categorical,** or **noncategorical,** approach. What is really meant is that the new category is defined in terms of school achievement rather than some deficit within the child. Thus, the idea is to include the previously labeled students as part of a general educational continuum of learners. The "old" categories too easily became the cause of low achievement in spite of the problem of their virtual lack of validity.

The other major problem, never resolved with the old system, was the lack of relationship between the teaching strategy and the categories of deficit. As we will note, citing Haberman's work, effective teaching strategies for LD, EMR, and ED students are not that different from those for regular pupils. The specific prescriptions offered in the past as to special teaching methods for LD, EMR, or ED hardly varied at all from the general methods, again raising the question as to the utility of the labels in the first place. And, finally, research has shown that special teacher certification in these high-incidence catagories has no noticeable effect upon pupil achievement in those special areas (Ysseldyke, Algozzine, and Thurlow, 1992, p. 359).

FIGURE 20.5   Changes in special-education placement: Regular classes versus resource rooms.

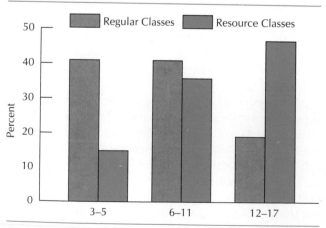

From Twelfth annual report to Congress on implementation of the Education of the Handicapped Act (Washington, D.C.: U.S. Department of Education, 1990).

INTERVENTION PROGRAMS

Increasing the Accommodative Capacity of Classrooms

As mainstream programs increase, it is obvious that the educational environments will need careful preparation, including attention to teacher attitudes and use of imaginative materials and methods. Studies have shown patterns of teacher behavior—namely, discomfort, anxiety, and stress—that teachers experience when dealing with children who are different. We noted earlier that in some urban classrooms white teachers were not responsive to the needs of black children: Teachers engaged in less eye contact, made more negative statements, displayed more punitive

Special-education studies have demonstrated the critical importance of positive teacher-child interaction in promoting intellectual growth.

behavior toward black children than toward white children. Whether mainstreaming succeeds, then, will depend on the ability to teach teachers to become more responsive to the fundamental needs of all children. In the special-education literature this is referred to as the need to increase the accommodative capacity of regular classrooms—to broaden the learning environment so that all pupils are genuinely included in positive learning activities. For example, it does little good to legalize racial integration in a school, only to have the school operate as a segregated institution, with students eating separately, occupying different spaces in the same building, participating in separate activities, being treated separately by school rules and teachers. In the same way, if previously separated special-education pupils are mainstreamed only to be resegregated once again, changing the form but not substance will produce a perpetuation of the status quo.

Jack Birch, of the University of Pittsburgh (1974), has summarized a series of studies in mainstreamed school districts. The cluster of positive attitudes of regular teachers was the most effective force for excellent special education.

1. Belief in the right to education for all children

2. Readiness of special-education and regular-class teachers to cooperate with each other

3. Willingness to share competencies as a team on behalf of pupils

4. Openness to including parents as well as other professional colleagues in planning for and working with children

5. Flexibility with respect to class size and teaching assignments

6. Recognition that social and personal development can be taught and that they are equally as important as academic achievement

He also noted that in the school districts that successfully "mainstreamed," including elementary and secondary levels and across disciplines, three factors stood out:

1. There was genuine appreciation of the team work with the special-education teachers, particularly the help the regular classroom teachers received with the children already in their rooms.

2. Regular classroom teachers found that special-education pupils were usually no more difficult to include in their classes than some children already there.

3. The spirit that all the children are in the same school system was expressed time after time.

Recent research by Stanley Deno and associates (1990) has shown that regular-education teachers can

MARIA MONTESSORI

Maria Montessori (1870–1952) was on the forefront of change and innovation throughout her entire life. She was raised in the small, conservative Italian town of Chiaravelle. Her aspirations, however, led her eventually to seek admission to the prestigious University of Rome for the study of medicine. It was literally unheard of at the time for a woman to pursue a medical career; there were simply no female physicians in the entire Italian nation. Such barriers, however, would not deter Montessori. Her brilliance of intellect, combined with personal drive and dedication, soon won the respect of the all-male college, and later, at the tender age of twenty-four, she became the first woman physician in the country.

Her interest in practicing general medicine, which at that time consisted largely of treating symptoms, soon waned. She began to ask larger questions about life and compassion, and her focus shifted toward the problems and needs of what at that time were called "idiot" or "insane" children. The streets of one section of Rome (the San Lorenzo district) were inhabited by gangs of unruly young delinquents, most of whom had been rejected by the traditional school system and all of whom were among the economically and culturally deprived. These roaming bands of street urchins were engaged in vandalism and aimless violence, and were generally destroying the neighborhood as an economically viable entity. To remedy this situation, a school was set up, called the *Casa dei Bambini* ("Home for Children"), and Maria Montessori, then aged twenty-nine, became its first director. At first, the school was considered to be more of a reform school than a real educational institution, and the authorities would have been happy if the school did nothing more than keep the children off the streets, making the area safe again. Her success, however, far surpassed the hopes of the sponsors. Using techniques originally inspired by her study of the works of Edouard Seguin (who had worked with retarded children) and Jean Marc Itard (who had worked with the "wild boy of Aveyron"), she soon taught these slum children how to read, write, and count, often before the age of five. As a by-product, delinquency in the area was greatly reduced, even on nonschool days. Montessori continued to create new learning materials, and always applied her theories to the classroom. Using her highly structured materials and multisensory procedures, she soon revolutionized the entire educational approach for these street urchins, who became perhaps the first generation of mainstreamed children with special needs.

Her work continued to expand in scope as she became increasingly interested in the general learning problems of all children, not just those of the disadvantaged or "disturbed." She began to suspect that learning was dependent on the interaction between the child and the environ-

work effectively with special-needs children and in fact that they often view the behavior of such students more positively than do the special-education teachers. It is also clear that the key to any successful mainstreaming continues to be the skill of the classroom teacher and the collaboration with special education.

Developing the Requisite Teaching Skills

In addition to the obvious importance of teacher attitudes, we also need to consider the other side of the coin, new teaching skills for the classroom itself. It would do the teacher little good to have highly positive attitudes toward exceptional children, but not have the requisite teaching skills to help them, as Zigmond and Baker (1990) as well as Semmel and Gerber (1990) have pointed out. We noted earlier the critical developmental assumptions:

1. Exceptional children can develop through the same Piagetian stages (especially sensorimotor, preoperational, and concrete), in a manner similar to regular children, yet at slower rates.

ment, between nature and nurture, an unpopular view at that time. David Elkind, a comtemporary American expert in cognitive-developmental theory, has noted that many of Montessori's concepts were highly similar to some of Piaget's later age-stage theories. She viewed development as occurring in a sequence of stages, or *sensitive periods*, as she called them, and she felt that such development proceeded by leaps and bounds and was followed by slower periods of integration. She used the phrase *growth explosions* to denote these qualitiative shifts to new cognitive stages.

Montessori's other obvious similarity to Piaget was her absolute genius for developing empathy with children. Without doubt, this sensitivity, which enabled her to understand both the thoughts and feelings of young children, was the central ingredient in her educational system.

Above all else, Maria Montessori throughout her entire life was committed to educational practice. Whereas Piaget focused mostly on discovering how children learn as an interesting theoretical question, Montessori always viewed every problem with an eye to practical application. She was a bridge between theory and practice; she both de-

scribed how children learn at a theoretical level and prescribed teaching methods to accomplish developmental goals. Thus, like Bruner many years later, she attempted to synthesize a theory of learning with a theory of instruction. From her naturalistic observations of how young children learn, she developed her now-famous "prepared environment." She wished not to accelerate growth or to force children to grow up overnight but rather to help children develop their own competencies maximally within each stage of growth. The environment, if carefully matched to the child, provides the nourishment for such growth. The child should not be overmatched, but provided with inputs that cause the child to "stretch." This notion was later picked up by both J. McV. Hunt (problem of the match) and L. S. Vygotsky (zone of proximal development)

Despite the true ring that Montessori's theories have for us today, she was long treated with a degree of disdain by psychology's inner circle of power figures, especially here in the United States. Part of the scorn was due to the fact that she was a woman, and she didn't fit the American stereotype of the woman's role. Secondly, her notions about child

development were too divergent from the dominant theories of psychoanalysis, behaviorism, and those of the IQ testers. After all, Montessori was insisting to everyone who would listen that intelligence was *not* fixed and *not* determined only by heredity and further that early experience *did* play a key role in the cognitive growth process

Naturally, as seems to be the case with all major innovators, a few of Montessori's "disciples" have misunderstood her intentions and have created some lockstep environments that do not always serve children well. For Montessori, development involved the matched environment of repetitive learning and multisensory materials, as well as spontaneity and empathy. Children do not learn best in prescriptive educational straitjackets.

Her long life was devoted to increasing our theoretical and practical knowledge of child development for both the normal and atypical child. In her lifetime she addressed many audiences: the teacher, the educational researchers, the curriculum-materials developer, and the parent. By the time of her death at eighty-two, Montessori had finally become accepted and had become a powerful voice for children.

2. Interaction with a rich, stimulating environment and active learning will promote growth.

Educational researcher David Hunt (1974) has shown repeatedly in a key series of studies that it is important to match the educational environment with the stage of development of the child. Pupils who are functioning at relatively low levels of conceptual thinking tend to learn most adequately in a highly structured teaching environment. Thus, in elementary schools, as pupils are attempting to master the initial stages of concrete thinking, Hunt's work would

definitely support carefully structured teaching. The educational tasks assigned should be (1) carefully explained, (2) relatively brief, (3) monitored quickly, (4) systematically varied, and (5) set up to achieve learning through multiple senses.

At first, this may strike you as overmanaging the child, shutting out the possibility of creativity and being too preplanned or programmed. If you view it from the child's position, however, Hunt's plan may not seem as negative. Children starting school at low conceptual levels can be confused easily by ambiguity. Also they may be afraid to ask for clarification, especially if they see that other children apparently understand the directions. Under such conditions children may revert to lower-stage thinking. If you were just on the threshold of learning to think concretely and became confused, anxious, and unsure of an educational task, you might understandably fall back into an earlier mode of thought, namely, preoperational thinking.

From an educational standpoint, the careful use of a structured approach to teaching is legitimate as a means of helping so-called slower, or lower-conceptual, children to master some initial tasks. However, we wish to avoid suggesting that all problems of retardation or other types of exceptionality can be "cured" through high-structured learning. Although there may be some individual cases of dramatic improvement within a group of children previously segregated in special classes, those will remain the exception. In the nineteenth century in this country an early pioneer in special education, Edouard Seguin, unfortunately suggested that slow learning and retardation could be stamped out. With training and responsive environments all children could be normalized. Such overly optimistic hopes, of course, created a backlash of disappointment when reality indicated that improvement was slow and limited. However, we need not expect that retarded or slow-learning children are capable of becoming geniuses. Instead, the goal of the educator is to stimulate development. Small gains, in the long run, may in fact be the most significant and long-lasting.

The differences in learning aptitudes between normal and mildly handicapped children—those in the high-incidence categories of LD, EMR, and ED—can be associated with stages of cognitive growth. This means that at any particular point, the latter may not process the teaching information as efficiently as their peers. Their cognitive strategies, or (as we outlined in Chapter 11) their system of information processing, may not be as well developed. Thus, one important variable is engaged learning time, its purpose being to provide extra experience as a means of catching on to the lesson at hand. While there are differences in the speed of acquisition between mildly handicapped children and their nonhandicapped peers, problem solving, information processing, and strategies of memorizing appear to be important additional factors in determining how much learning actually takes place. Certainly we have emphasized, throughout this book, that a goal of instruction is not so much rote repetition of answers as it is comprehension of both the content and the process. Thus, the aim for exceptional children is the same as for all others: to improve their cognition and problem-solving capacity (sometimes called *metacognitions*) as learners.

FROM DIAGNOSIS TO TEACHING

Assuming we develop a more valid base for classifying the handicapped, particularly in reducing the overassignment of minority children, what are the teaching implications for you? Just how different is it to teach a handicapped child? What knowledge of special education and teaching strategies do you need. What are the special learning characteristics of the child so designated? These questions are central to mainstream teaching. If there are nine handicapping conditions, are there nine different teaching strategies?

Martin Haberman (1980) former dean of the University of Wisconsin at Milwaukee, has done a careful

Dr. Martin Haberman

TABLE 20.3   EFFECTIVE TEACHING STRATEGIES FOR MAINSTREAMED PUPILS
(Summarized by Martin Haberman)

APPROXIMATE PERCENTAGES OF TIME SPENT IN ACTIVITY	TEACHING ACTIVITIES FOR WHICH "HELP" MAY BE SOUGHT BY CLASSROOM TEACHERS LEARNING TO MAINSTREAM
5–10%	Using special materials that are new to the teacher. This involves becoming familiar with materials and equipment and being shown how they operate.[*]
5–10%	Communicating with students who have special handicaps (e.g., hearing, visual). This involves receiving straightforward direction.[†]
5%	Special methods of teaching. There is a *very* small body of special teaching behaviors for working with handicapped students that teachers can learn through observation and develop through practice (i.e., usually supervisory procedures).[‡]
75–85%	Engaging in normal classroom teaching practices that are, in large part, effective with all children.[§]

[*]Maynard C. Reynolds and Jack W. Birch, *Teaching exceptional children in all America's schools* (Reston, Va.: The Council for Exceptional Children, 1977), pp. 569–571 and p. 632.
[†]Ibid., pp. 562–563 and pp. 630–631.
[‡]Ibid., pp. 565–569 and pp. 633–636.
[§]Ibid., pp. 303–304.

From M. Haberman, Principles of in-service training for implementation of mainstreaming in the public schools. In D. C. Corrigan and K. Howey (Eds.), *Concepts to guide the education of experienced teachers* (Reston, Va.: The Council for Exceptional Children, 1980), p. 60. Reprinted by permission of the Council for Exceptional Children.

examination of the mainstream problem, but from the teacher's point of view. He has reviewed both the variety of special-education techniques and the curriculum materials needed for special-education pupils who are now being mainstreamed. Also, he has examined the procedures and strategies that are common to all effective teachers. As a result he has presented a series of estimates as to how much special content and strategy you'll need, as well as general procedures for all children. When you look at Table 20.3, you may be quite surprised and, we hope, encouraged by his conclusions.

For example, the table estimates that from 5 to 10 percent of the time you will need to employ new materials and from 5 to 10 percent of the time, special methods of communication. With visually impaired students this would mean giving them access to books in braille, having them use a tape recorder for answering an essay exam, setting up the room to minimize changes in furniture placement, and having them sit close to the front of the room. Many visually impaired students have some residual vision. Hearing-impaired students would need a different set of materials, the use of a signer (a person adept at sign-

ing your words to the pupil), and similar accommodations to their special needs. For the orthopedically handicapped, the room would be set up to reduce barriers to mobility for a wheelchair, and the playground would have a lowered hoop for basketball. In one sense these are small changes, but they make a substantial difference to an individual student. Try maneuvering in the average school room or getting to the bathroom in a wheelchair, and you'll understand at an experiential level how different the world of a wheelchair user can be in activities we take for granted.

Consistent with these ideas, there has been a major shift in the training of special-education teachers themselves. Reynolds (1990) has shown that the fastest-growing speciality in teacher training is the noncategorical area. In one year in the 1980s, the number almost doubled from 16,000 to 26,000, further supporting the idea of generic teaching approaches especially in the high-incidence areas.

In the area of special teaching methods, as Haberman notes, there is a very small body of unique approaches, involving perhaps 5 percent of the teaching time. Many educators would argue that even these special methods are not that unique. In any case the special-education resource teacher or school psychologist can provide you with the current recommendations. The consistent use of a time-out room for a hyperactive child, the close monitoring of individualized seatwork with frequent positive reinforcement for an MR child, or the use of different standards in judging penmanship for palsied children represent some examples of somewhat specialized teaching methods. Probably the most significant special technique is more psychological than pedagogical—what psychologists call learned helplessness.

Learned Helplessness: A Common Characteristic

Some years ago a theorist, Martin Seligman, discovered a particular type of personality response that was common to many types of people who had been excluded from full participation in the mainstream of society (1975). Although Seligman originally focused on migrant workers and on economically poor or ethnically different people, his theory can also be applied to handicapped children, many of whom suffer from a similar kind of exclusion and resultant stigma. His central point is that such people learn to appear helpless. They acquire a set of behaviors intended to give an impression that they are not competent. Seligman stresses that these responses (giving up quickly, crying, refusing to try) have been *learned*—hence the term **learned helplessness.** Daniel Reschly (1988) has reviewed much of the literature on attitudes and motivation and finds that such pupils do not attribute success to themselves and show a dependence on other persons and on external reinforcement.

Research has also shown that parental attitudes and practices often impede growth for handicapped children. Although it is a complex story, reduced to its simplest terms, parents tend either to reject or overprotect such children. Parental anxiety and guilt result in the parents' quite unintentionally fostering dependency. However, do not make the mistake of simply blaming the parents, any more than you should blame teachers (remember Rosenthal's studies) for negative expectations. Remember that the syndrome is learned, and it can be unlearned. In fact Martin Seligman now makes that point most emphatically with the title of his new work, *Learned Optimism* (1991). The challenge is to turn feelings of helplessness into feelings of competence.

Unlearning Helplessness

In dealing with learned helplessness it is most important, especially at the outset, to employ a careful set of behavioral strategies. Find some positive behavior of the child that you can positively reinforce, and do not under any circumstances positively reinforce helplessness when an activity is well within the child's ability. These two rules go together; unless you follow both, you will quickly undo your gains. You will probably find this whole process extremely difficult at a personal level. The child has spent years learning the process. It is as if individual competence has been frustrated, so the child now becomes competent in getting others to wait on him or her. In some cases the act is very convincing, having been polished through many performances. Such children can make you feel guilty and perhaps even heartless. At such times it's important to review your own role. They need your support to nurture their growth, but that does not mean you should do for them those things they can learn to do for themselves. Dealing with your feelings of compassion and concern for a child struggling with a handicapping condition may well be your most difficult experience as a teacher. As your own experience grows, you will gain more confidence in your ability to identify areas of positive accomplishment to reinforce and become even more consistent in avoiding reinforcing the appearance of helplessness.

In the long run you will see the gradual emergence of the child's positive competence drive. The first sign may be most dramatic. The handicapped child lets you know, "Look here, I can do this myself." That's when you'll realize you have made progress—as an educator for all children.

TEACHING STRATEGIES FOR MAINSTREAMING

As clearly suggested, the greatest need in mainstreaming is the development of competent general teaching strategies. In this realm certain approaches need emphasis. These procedures are not unique to special-education pupils; they are useful with all children. Yet they are not used often enough in general and so must be underlined here as a system of instruction.

Also, by way of background, one of the major difficulties in developing teaching strategies for mainstreamed pupils has been the lack of diversity in teaching methods employed in the separate special-education classes prior to passage of the new law. In fact, criticism of the profession of special education itself has increased substantially in the past decade. As more research is done, the weaknesses in the old methods of classification become more apparent, thus emphasizing the need for better and more valid classifications, especially in the high-incidence areas. So too with teaching. There has been almost a complete reliance on behavior modification as the only method for such high-incidence areas. The difficulty from our view is simply the exclusion of other methods for teachers. A highly structured and simple-task approach is helpful (indeed the next section will provide an extensive outline of a behavior modification system that is most appropriate), but effective teaching for special-education children cannot begin and end there. Richard Snow, one of the originators of ATI (attribute-treatment interaction), has commented on the weakness of a singular approach: "A truly adaptive instructional system is needed, not a new blanket panacea chosen because it produces some average improvements" (Snow, 1984, p. 14).

As you read these recommendations, keep in mind that the various elements can become a system. We do not advocate any one as a "blanket panacea," a single and final solution. The system includes (1) precise teaching, (2) cooperative learning, (3) tutoring, (4) social skills training, (5) matching and gradual mismatching.

Precise Teaching

Substantial work has been done in a method of **precise teaching** as a means of providing high structure for children newly mainstreamed. Essentially, the method is derived almost directly from learning theory and Skinnerian principles. The specific advantages of the method are that it allows the learner to focus on a structured task, proceed at his or her own pace, receive positive reinforcement for accomplishments, and build up feelings of being a successful learner. The overall process, then, represents a method of tailoring educational tasks to fit each child, or, as it's sometimes called, individualizing instruction. A discussion of the key elements involved in setting up this process follows.

Select a manageable task The task to be learned by the child needs to be very specifically defined.

Thus, the educational objective should not be too cosmic. To become more human, to appreciate American civilization, to be spontaneous, and so on are all too ambiguous as manageable tasks for precise teaching (see Chapter 10). Instead—and this may sound hopelessly pedestrian to you—it is important to identify a highly specific task: learning to count from one to ten, to recognize vowels, to read ten single words without an error, or similar highly structured learning activities. We should also note that this approach is useful not just in special-education classes but in almost any new learning situation, especially where the ambiguity of a task may generate anxiety. Thus, the first problem is to pinpoint the specific area. Some examples of specific areas are:

1. *Subject areas:* Multiple mistakes in oral reading, faulty knowledge of the multiplication table, erratic completion of homework assignments, not enough divergent products in art work, and so on. (These must be described in behavioral terms—that is, in terms of something you can see and count with a very low level of inferences.)

2. *Deportment areas:* Hitting others, out-of-seat behavior, shouting out, not talking, never volunteering, excessive profanity, poor attendance, too much staring out of the window, and so on. (Be careful in picking out topics here. We don't want to turn all pupils into "Goody Two Shoes.")

3. *Personal areas:* Negative feelings toward self, putting self down, overly apologetic, hostile feelings, not speaking up for self, never trying a new activity, and so on.

Set up a contract with the pupil The contract should specify who will keep track of the counting, how the chart is to be set up, and how the count is to be kept. Contracts can be developed in almost any area and can even employ pictures to describe the activities for nonreaders. For example, in the contracts depicted in Figures 20.6 and 20.7 the positive behavior and desired reinforcements are described pictorially.

Other, more sophisticated contracts naturally are possible and may specify more complex behaviors. Also, other methods of keeping track of the counting are available. The important point is that the record be visible to the pupil so that he or she can see on a cumulative basis how the score is mounting. This feedback is essential to the system. You could have pupils keep paper charts and graphs, use a plastic grocery-store counter, or have them make a leather

FIGURE 20.6 Behavioral contracts for pupils who are not yet readers.

Contract		
What I Do	My Count	What Happens
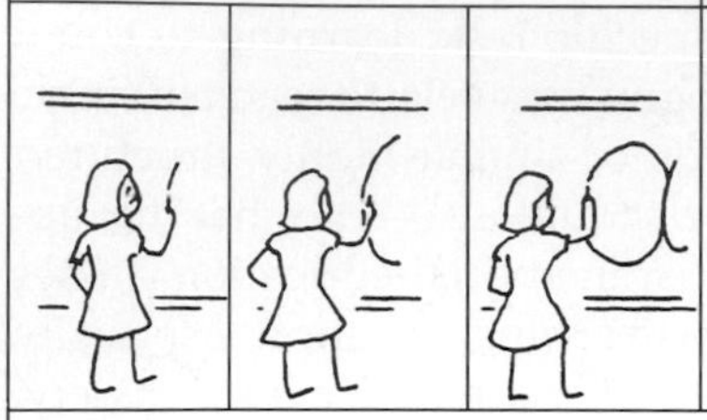	1 2 3 4 5 6 7 8 9 10 11 12 13 14 15 16 17 18	5 = ☆ 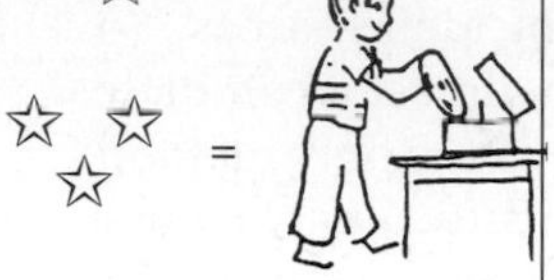
Teacher: ____ Student: ____ Dates: ____		

Contract		
What I Do	My Count	What Happens
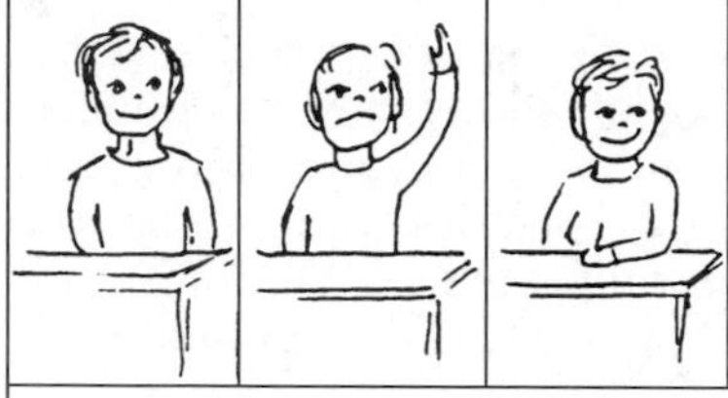	1 2 3 4 5 6 7 8 9 10 11 12 13 14 15 16 17 18 19 20	Each day = get 00000 Lose 0 for each talk out. End of day Ⓛ 00 = 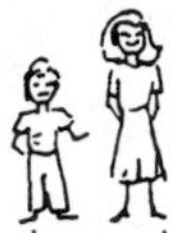 help teacher
Teacher: ____ Student: ____ Dates: ____		

From B. Dollar, Leadership Training Institute, University of Minnesota, Minneapolis. Used with permission.

bracelet containing small movable beads on strings of pipe cleaners. The one thing to avoid is asking them to keep track of the behaviors in their heads.*

Negotiate a significant "award" There is a debate among behavioral theorists as to whether just seeing a line on a chart "improve" is sufficient. In general, with younger pupils the more concrete the reinforcer, the better. There are thousands of funny stories about erroneous choices of reinforcers. For example, one teacher had pupils collect red chips for not speaking out of turn, then exchange five red for one blue, collect two blues and exchange for one gray, and exchange one gray for extra recess time. The children wouldn't exchange blue for gray. They didn't like the color.

It is certainly permissible to discuss the choice of reinforcers with the children. Also realize that you don't have to select conventional reinforcers, like a candy bar, gold stars, or extra recess time. Other possibilities might include open discussion time with you—setting aside a few moments of "special time" between an adult and a child can be an unusually powerful reinforcement. Remember that the quality of time, not the quantity, is the crucial aspect. A few

*The classic research of George Miller has shown that humans in general can keep about five to seven discrete pieces of "knowledge" in their consciousness at one time. After that point, unless we employ chunking, we become easily confused (see Chapter 11).

FIGURE 20.7 A behavioral contract for pupils who can read.

Contract

Date: _____

I will earn checks√ each day for

√ raising hand to speak …

√√√ helping others …

√√ working at each center …

I will lose checks√ each day for

√ talking out …

√√√ fighting …

√√ not working …

At the end of each week … I may …

√√√√√√√
√√√√√√
1. extra recess time
2. "good" note home
3. extra art time
4. Hershey bar

Teacher: _____

Student: _____

M   T   W   TH   F   M   T   W   TH   F

From B. Dollar, Leadership Training Institute, University of Minnesota, Minneapolis. Used with permission.

moments of focused individual attention can be most meaningful to a child, and for that matter to an adult, too!

In setting up the contract, specify rewards for positive behavior. For example, if a student is in constant motion, the contract should reward time spent at his or her desk. As we noted in the preceding chapter, positive reinforcement is both more effective and more humane than punishment. If you set up the contract so that the pupil loses privileges for disruptive behavior, you will find that the pupil will become less cooperative in general and more negative toward you in particular. Also it is important that the reward be offered for a genuine achievement. Special-needs children are similar to children in general in their ability to spot the real meaning of unsolicited help, sympathy, and overly generous praise (Graham and Barker, 1990).

A final point on the reinforcement schedule is to make sure that the reinforcement itself follows close on the heels of the desired contracted behavior. Long delays between accomplishment and reinforcement are ineffective, in spite of what we may think about building character through self-denial and discipline. B. F. Skinner has commented that a person would never learn to play the piano if he or she had to wait a week to hear the sound of the note. In baseball parks, electric scoreboards explode the very moment a home-run ball lands in the seats. The opera audience does not wait a month to reward the diva for an outstanding aria. A doctor is congratulated on the spot after a successful operation.

Don't employ the method too broadly   Try the method in single areas for relatively brief periods of time. It would be an obvious mistake to bombard a child with an endless series of contracts—too much of a good thing, so to speak. Thus, if we have children "charting" in all their subject areas, in a series of personal-management domains, and in extracurricular activities, the entire method of contracting may soon become aversive. The pupils will feel trapped, hemmed in, and rebellious. And that is not an invitation to ask them to keep track of that, too!

Naturally, the point of contracts is to help pupils become successful in mastering a variety of tasks. The contracts can provide positive motivation to help children focus their energies, receive positive feedback, and develop a sense of personal mastery in learning. The chart obviously should be used to help a child see how he or she is improving. Each child compares present performance only with his or her past performance. It would be destructive to have children compare themselves with each other, since the whole point of precise teaching to individualize instruction would be lost amid a flurry of competition. If I initially don't know how to read and then learn to recognize *cat, hat, bat,* and *sat,* that achievement should be regarded as significant in its own right. I should not be asked to compare my progress with that of another pupil who's learning to distinguish cases in Latin.

Cooperative Learning

We have provided a discussion on the use of the cooperative approach in Chapter 18, which will not be repeated here. It is important to remember that the cooperative method means mixing regular and special-education children together. For example, two researchers, Ray McDermott and Jeffrey Aron, set up a video recorder to examine teacher-pupil interaction in recently mainstreamed classes. Unfortunately, the teachers tended to isolate the four or five "new" special-education pupils in each class as a separate group in their classrooms. Thus, instead of four reading groups, there would be five, with similar groupings for math and other small-group activities. As you can see, almost from the start the new pupils were resegregated and clearly identified as different. To make matters worse, when the amount of teacher time was calculated from the video, it became apparent that the pupils in the segregated group had received almost no instruction. The special-education pupils were interrupted forty times in a thirty-minute reading group, whereas the top group of readers was interrupted only two times in the same interval. Thus, time-on-task virtually disappeared for the special-education pupils. The source of the interruptions was either the pupils in the top group or the teacher! The researchers observed, "Almost two-thirds of the time in the reading lesson is spent in either getting a turn or waiting for the teacher to attend to the group" (McDermott and Aron, 1978, p. 57).

Student Teams–Achievement Divisions   Robert Slavin, of Johns Hopkins University, has done a series of studies on actual classroom achievement when special-education children are mainstreamed. The learning tasks are set up as small-group activities with group problem solving. He calls one method the **student teams–achievement divisions (STAD).** The students are divided into groups of four or five, with high- and low-achieving students in each. After introducing the lesson content for the week through either direct or indirect teaching methods, the teacher hands out worksheets to each group. The students then quiz each other on the material, have a small-group discussion, and engage in a variety of activities. The final quiz scores within each small group are averaged and extra points are assigned during the semester for "improving" students in each small group. Slavin finds that this protects the slow learner from becoming a dead weight, or in baseball terminology, "an automatic strikeout."

The advantage of this approach, according to Slavin, is that it reduces destructive competition. Conventional approaches to grading basically lead to an unequal distribution of positive reinforcers. A few excellent students receive all the positives; the rest

SPOTLIGHT ON SELF-CONCEPT:

A Down Syndrome Teenager Speaks

A direct method of learning what it has been like for a child or teenager to experience a handicapping condition is through an interview. First you will need to establish a positive atmosphere with any such student before he or she will feel comfortable enough to share some personal insights.

One such teenager, who has Down syndrome, related his thoughts and feelings about a summer camp experience which had been designed and staffed specifically to help such children. Even though in some ways the program might be considered ideal objectively, there were some perhaps unintentional yet none the less difficult experiences. He said most forcefully: "I don't like being called handicapped. They need to talk about what people can do, not what they can't. Treat me like a friend, not like a person who can't do for themselves. Forget my handicap, look at me as a friend."

Note: We thank Dr. Peg Hibbert, Raleigh, N.C., for relaying this information.

do not. This does not happen with the cooperative approach, even though the so-called top students are recognized individually as well as through the team efforts. Most important, of course, are the learning outcomes for the special-education students. Rather than being allowed simply to "be," the students show both academic and social acceptance gains. Also, and in some ways this may be the most important point of all, the achievement of the other students does not decline; it improves. "This is critical; few schools would use a program designed to aid mainstreamed students if it did not also improve (or at least not retard) the achievement of the rest of the class" (Slavin, 1983, p. 100).

Most recently, Slavin has shifted his focus from the use of cooperative learning programs as a supplement to their use in regular instruction. He has tested out a method of integrating the cooperative approach with some aspects of individualized instruction. The results are most promising. Academic achievement in mathematics and language arts at the elementary school level improved substantially (Slavin, 1990).

On an overall basis, recent meta-analyses of deliberately formed mixed groups of students engaged in cooperative learning activities supports the approach. Academic achievement improves on the average of about three-quarters of a standard deviation—almost one grade level higher, in everyday language (Reynolds, 1990, p. 430).

Currently there are multiple approaches to cooperative learning methods in addition to the student teams–achievement divisions of Slavin. A partial list (Furtwengler, 1991) includes:

1. Teams, games, tournament
2. Team-assisted individuation
3. Cooperative integrated reading
4. Jigsaw I and II
5. Learning together
6. Group investigation

Although it is beyond the scope of this volume to detail the system of integrating individual and cooperative learning, the main point is that these systems improve the achievement of everyone in a class. The so-called Matthew effect (see the Spotlight on Gifted Development: What's the Price? Chapter 13) does not hold. These approaches do not result in uneven benefits, that is, in a situation in which the more able students gain the most from an innovation while the less able fall further behind.

Tutoring

Individual tutoring has a long tradition as a teaching method. Studies have consistently found that effective tutoring is the single most valuable instructional tool in all of teaching. Benjamin Bloom has called it the "two sigma problem" (1984, p. 4). Tutoring yields achievement that is two standard deviations *above* the

Tutoring may prove to be mutually beneficial to this high schooler and her preschool student. The student will progress with his class, and the tutor may advance academically beyond her peers because of her participation in the tutoring program.

level of conventional group instruction. In Bloom's study, the average tutored student ranked above 98 percent of the students in the controlled classes.

Since most studies of tutoring were not done with exceptional children, we can't be sure whether the benefit for them would be as great. (Perhaps it would be greater.) We can say, however, that some overall benefit would accrue to mainstreamed children. We also need to note that the study was done with trained tutors. Placing an exceptional child with an untrained tutor does not guarantee success. Under appropriate conditions, however, working with students on an individual basis will promote their learning more effectively than any other technique or even combination of techniques.

But another question needs to be asked: How can teachers employ tutoring for mainstreamed students when they have to teach all the other students as well? The answer is that it's impossible if the teachers must do the tutoring. But if other students (or community volunteers) can be used as tutors, the problem is solved. Research quite clearly shows that children, teenagers, or volunteers can learn fundamental tutoring skills and that such tutoring improves the academic performance and attitudes toward school of the students helped (Sharpley, Irvin, and Sharpley, 1983). This means that regular students can participate as tutors for mainstreamed children to help such children learn and prevent them from falling behind.

Also, such tutoring programs are becoming widely available.

But are we short-changing regular students by having them spend time tutoring other students? Naturally, if students were expected to spend fifteen to twenty hours per week tutoring, it would reduce the time they have for their own tasks. But if the time involved is reasonable (one to four hours per week), tutoring does not adversely affect the student tutor; in fact, it has the opposite effect. Some studies have shown that student tutors actually improve their own level of achievement at a greater rate than those they tutor. Some students have shown psychological gains as well. Student tutors exhibit higher rates of maturity, leadership, and empathy (concern for others) than peers who did not tutor. A carefully run tutoring program, then, benefits both groups. For example, a program of high school females doing math tutoring with underachieving fifth-grade females resulted in two sets of benefits. The secondary students improved on measures of leadership and conceptual complexity. The fifth-graders made an 11-point gain on the California Achievement Test in math, and changed their attribution of success from others to self. Control groups showed no gain at either level on any measure (Sprinthall and Scott, 1989).

For those tutoring mainstreamed children, it is especially important to provide systematic training. Otherwise, volunteer student helpers may end up with more negative attitudes to exceptional children than they had prior to the experience (Sprinthall and Blum, 1980).

The objectives of tutoring are similar to those of cooperative learning, but the academic gains for tutoring are more clear-cut. Both methods reduce invidious competition. Neither method impairs the achievement of the normal-progress students. "Used expertly and in selected ways, peer teaching can have good effects on all participants and on both academic and social outcomes" (Reynolds, 1990, p. 430).

Social Skills Training

You may wonder why a section on teaching effectiveness in a mainstreaming context would focus on social skills training as a special objective. The problem is simply that handicapped children are different from their peers not only in learning achievement but even more so in social skills. Because of both past isolation and current lack of interaction with normal peers, exceptional children often lag behind in rudimentary social abilities. Numerous studies have found that mainstreamed children unfortunately are not necessarily accepted socially by their peers. The base rates of interaction are low. The exceptional child is often ignored, or allowed to just "be."

Social role-taking refers to a process central to Erik Erikson's concept of personality development in stages—namely, the ability to understand where another person is "coming from," or to practice a kind of interpersonal perspective taking. It is an ability that develops from interaction with other people. We aren't born understanding relationships; our role-taking ability grows slowly. Studies have shown that exceptional children lag behind peers on social role-taking (Perry and Krebs, 1980). During adolescence the difference increases. For example, prior to adolescence deaf children are approximately only 5 to 10 percent behind on estimates of social and emotional maturity; with the onset of adolescence that figure climbs to 20 percent (Dupont, 1978). Similar shifts are reported with other types of exceptionality. An important aspect of the exceptional child's interpersonal development, then, is being ignored.

The results also suggest something else. Without some planned programs, mixing regular and mainstreamed children produces negative effects on social interaction. Virginia Bruininks has shown that learning-disabled students received the lowest peer-status ratings of all groups in school. Perhaps the most up-

setting finding was that learning-disabled students were unaware of their low social status (Bruininks, 1978). They did not apparently "understand" that they were actually being ignored and thus weren't aware of the need to improve their social skills to gain some acceptance. For their part, the regular children were content to avoid the "others" as much as possible. We mentioned earlier that Public Law 94-142 was based on the concept of the least restrictive environment for such children. The irony is that, especially during adolescence, mainstreaming can result in a more restrictive social environment.

Although you obviously cannot alter the social environment of an entire school, by employing some techniques such as social skills training, cooperative learning groups, and individual tutoring, you can reduce some of the isolation. You can also search out counselors and support their efforts to improve the social skills of the children and teenagers. An extensive review points out that some methods are effective in helping exceptional children fit into the school environment. Also, programs such as peer counseling have been shown to be effective as a means of socialization (Sprinthall, Gerber, and Hall, 1992). In general, this aspect of development has been sadly neglected during the mainstreaming process (Gresham, 1981).

Henry Dupont, who reviewed the studies demonstrating the increasing gap in emotional development of special-education students, suggests quite accurately that nearly all such children desperately need more adequate and responsive teaching-learning environments. The vocational adjustment and job success of these pupils are most directly related to their social-emotional adjustment. Social skills and interpersonal competence apparently are central ingredients of success after school. As a result, Dupont draws this conclusion: "All exceptional children need more acceptance as persons of individual worth. They also need an education that helps them develop higher levels of emotional-social maturity" (Dupont, 1978). This is as true for the gifted as for the slow learners (Reynolds, 1990).

Matching and Gradual Mismatching

This strategy is mostly a reminder of Snow's point, presented at the outset of this section. Effective teaching for special children requires a variety of methods, not one "blanket." In Chapter 13 we suggested that matching and gradual mismatching were in fact central to the process—or the art—of teaching. In David

Hunt's sense, then, the same rules apply to mainstreamed students. Especially if you suspect that a particular student is functioning at a very concrete, or even preoperational, level in Piaget's scheme (low CL in Hunt's scheme), then it is clearly most appropriate to use high structure and all the elements of that approach. You also need to watch academic performance for signs of growth toward more independence as a learner. Watch for possible differences in levels of functioning in different subject areas or in different parts of the same subject. The major mistake to avoid is assuming that a child who may be classified as a slow learner is slow in all areas. Because none of the common assessment methods really taps all the different components of what we commonly call "intelligence," be alert to any variation in school performance. By adjusting the teaching strategy, then gradually mismatching, you will increase the probability of developmental growth. Stages of development are not permanent classifications.

It is important to remember that effective teaching does not remain singular in its approach. While the direct, concrete, and focused approach may be the appropriate match or starting point for most mildly handicapped children, it is not the only method. The debut does not have to become the finale. In fact, Penelope Peterson reminds us that attribute-treatment interaction is still the rule for all learners. If we retain the singular approach of high-structured teaching, which has been the hallmark of most pullout programs, then the possibility of ever developing higher-order thinking skills is reduced. She correctly notes that research in mathematics and reading points to the importance of teaching for meaning and understanding while also teaching the lower-order skills through drill and practice. She suggests that in math, for example, word problems should be introduced early, while the students are engaged in mastering computations skills ("If there are two horses in one yard and three horses next door, how many horses all together?" rather than "Two plus three equal?").

Also in reading, asking beginners to discuss the meaning of what they have just read is another example of going beyond the drill-and-practice system. If students are taught only to memorize, then transfer becomes most difficult. Peterson provided the following example of a student who had memorized the multiplication table without understanding the meaning.

The problem: Twenty-nine students are to go on a field trip. Each van holds eight students. How many vans are needed?

The response:

Student: You have to multiply 8 by 9, um, then you have to multiply 9 by 7. Then you have to multiply 8 by 2.

Interviewer: Tell me everything that you're thinking.

Student: Um, then you multiply 7 by 2. Then you add 2, um, and you add 6 and 3. Then you add 6 and 1.

Interviewer: OK. Are you done? Yes? What do you think the final answer is?

Student: 14,992.

Interviewer: OK. What were you thinking about besides the problem?

Student: Um, the answer (Peterson, 1988, p. 344).

The question of how twenty-nine students could fit on 14,992 buses had apparently not occurred to the student. The student's own experience of riding to school on a bus had not been brought to bear on the question. Such are the difficulties with an exclusive focus on drill and practice.

THE INDIVIDUALIZED EDUCATION PLAN

With these five strategies in mind, we now turn to the question of mainstreaming and lesson planning. In general, Madeline Hunter's system is the most effective method for instructional planning. However, as more and more special-education students enter the regular classroom, the range of individual differences increases. In order to ensure that the newly mainstreamed are not lost in the shuffle, the law includes a provision for an **individualized education plan (IEP),** which is basically a lesson plan for one child at a time.

The plan is created by a team made up of (1) the teacher, (2) the psychological assessment specialist, (3) the special-education resource consultant, and (4) a school administrator. Its purpose is to set out specific learning objectives in a timetable and to identify how the outcomes are to be evaluated. Perhaps the most unique feature of this approach is that the plan must be accepted and approved by the parent. When first proposed, this feature of the IEP met with some resistance from school professionals, since in effect they would have to share the authority for the plan with parents. Also, further underlining the importance of this new approach, the parents had the right to bring in their own specialists, such as an independent psychological consultant and even a lawyer. After an initial period, however, the IEP approach has been largely accepted. School personnel and parents have found common ground in working out realistic goals and strategies for specific children. The plan starts where the learner is currently functioning and outlines the details. Each plan is reviewed every six months and includes

1. Current academic performance level

2. Goals and objectives

3. Specific services to be provided

4. The designation of school personnel and their roles

5. Where and on what schedule the service will be provided

6. An evaluation plan

In the light of some fifteen years of experience, the IEP is no longer seen as a radical change in educational philosophy but rather as a useful method to prescribe manageable learning objectives for children who otherwise might be overlooked in the fast pace and complex environment of a regular class. The document does protect the child's interests and serves as a reminder of his or her individual needs. You may find it initially awkward to set up IEPs. With so many points of view represented, the first few conferences will be somewhat confusing and perhaps even frustrating. After a while, though, you will see that an IEP is just a lesson plan that is very concrete and specific. You will have a clearer sense of what you can accomplish plus access to a resource team to help with the implementation. You will also find that, as your confidence increases, you will provide more and more suggestions for goals and methods to improve classroom performance.

It will also be helpful for you to remember our discussion of the Concerns-Based Adoption Model (CBAM, chapter 14). Susan Loucks-Horsley and Deborah Roody (1990) have applied that framework to the issue of mainstreaming and the regular education initiative. They found that the phases of concern from phase 0, awareness, to phase 6, refocusing, can apply directly to the mainstream issue. As a result, each of you confronted with the need to improve the accommodative capacity of the classroom will probably experience these phases of concern in sequence. They point out that the personal agenda of how you feel

about these changes is critical. "Teachers may feel challenged, hopeful and desirous of what can be accomplished, but they also may feel frustration, burden, fear, lack of support and inadequacies about their ability to teach children with different kinds of problems. These feelings need to be resolved before teachers can energetically tackle the task of teaching difficult youngsters" (1990, p. 54).

To provide teachers with help, a new program is under development (Tindal, Parker, and Germann, 1990). The idea is that the responsibility for the IEP and its implementation should be shared between the regular and special-education teachers. We noted earlier in the Osborne study that the interaction was minimal at best. In an attempt to promote colleagueship and collaboration, a mainstream consultation agreement (MCA) was drawn up to define ongoing cooperation between such teachers. Although the initial research results were problematic, the idea still appears promising, namely, the need to increase fruitful and coequal collaboration between both sets of teachers. Perhaps if such a program were combined with the CBAM approach, greater collaboration would result from the change process.

We should add that it is a good idea to teach the children in regular classes more about children with special needs. There are a number of children's books accompanied by teacher guides which will help sensitize children to certain handicapping conditions. The Council for Exceptional Children is an excellent resource. Such readings help spread the word that exceptional children may have difficulties in one area but have many talents in other areas. Oftentimes adults forget this too. Simply observe an adult trying to communicate with a sightless person by shouting or simplifying the language by dropping all prepositions and qualifiers.

THE CASE FOR MAINSTREAMING

In 1975, just prior to his death, Nicholas Hobbes, an eminent educational psychologist and clinician, headed a national commission charged with the responsibility of examining the problems of special-education classification systems. In a work significantly titled *The Futures of Children* (1975) Hobbes advanced the thesis that a comprehensive educational plan is required to classify children according to the services they need rather than the capabilities they lack. Special education and regular education essentially need the same point of view—namely, to create and emphasize educational programs that start where the learner is and then stimualte and nurture positive development. Both new skills and positive attitudes are needed for educational success in this area. For too long we have been satisfied to follow policies that have too often been designed to exclude or segregate significant numbers of children not only from the mainstream of schooling but from life as well. When so-called retarded children are placed in regular classrooms containing effective accommodative capacities, the pupils make as much educational progress as they would if they remained in separate classes (sometimes more). In addition to "academic" learning, all such pupils gain socially: their self-concepts become more positive, less stigmatized, and less characterized by self-hatred and self-contempt (Gartner and Lipsky, 1987).

A key factor in the entire concept of mainstreaming is the phrase "increasing the accommodative capacity of all classrooms to respond to a broad range of individual differences."

Certainly a crucial element in all this is the regular education initiative. At the same time, many special educators worry (Baker and Zigmond, 1990; Kauffman and Hallahan, 1990; and Semmel and Gerber, 1990) that such an effort may dilute the educative experiences for such children particularly if the result is a reduction in overall funding. In other words there is concern that such a change could expose the most vulnerable students to a polluted mainstream. Thus the task is difficult yet extremely important. We must creat a responsive, humane environment with positive regard for all children and sets of manageable learning tasks providing an appropriate learning atmosphere for all children. In other words, we can either say that special education becomes less "special" or that all education becomes more special and significant for each child.

SUMMARY

Traditional educational practices for dealing with exceptional children involved remolding their characters so that they fitted into society, excluding them from a society into which they did not fit, or segregating them from other so-called normal children. Under a new policy, mainstreaming, legislation requires that previously excluded groups of children now enter regular classrooms under the dictum that children should be educated in the least restrictive environments possible.

Nine designations of exceptionality have been set up; however, problems of accurate diagnosis and effective placement are substantial. The rate of error in diagnosis is highest in the categories that include the most children—mental retardation, learning disability, and emotional disturbance. As a result, traditional methods of dealing with exceptional children cannot be relied on. New approaches, such as Deno's system of graded educational environments that stress movement up as far and as fast as possible and other educators' emphasis on active learning and short-term, temporary placements for the exceptional, offer more promising alternatives.

The question of teaching strategies for special-education students is also important. Haberman has demonstrated that teaching strategies that are effective with "regular" students are just as effective with exceptional children; only a few procedures are needed in addition. Teachers must especially guard against fostering and maintaining the sense of learned helplessness that is so common among handicapped students.

The most useful teaching methods that can also be employed with special-education students are (1) precise teaching, (2) cooperative learning, (3) tutoring, (4) social skills training, and (5) matching and gradual mismatching. These strategies, taken as a whole, would help increase the accommodative capacity of regular classrooms and hence increase the learning potential of all pupils.

In using these methods with exceptional children, teachers can benefit their pupils most by also employing an individualized education plan (IEP). The plan is formulated by a school services team and is then revised as the student progresses. Careful attention to teaching strategies can help the mainstreamed student progress both academically and socially, as he or she gains a more positive self-concept.

KEY TERMS AND NAMES

cascade system
cross-categorical special education
dyslexia
exclusion
Martin Haberman
handicapping condition
hydraulic model of assessment
individualized education plans (IEP)
learned helplessness

mainstreaming
Maria Montessori
precise teaching
Public Law 94-142
regular education initiative
remolding
Maynard Reynolds
segregation
student teams—achievement divisions (STAD)

THEORY INTO PRACTICE: PEER TUTORING

A very effective method of increasing the educational resources of schools is to create a student tutoring program. Generally, this involves selecting older and more psychologically mature pupils as helpers. There is no optimal age difference between tutor and tutee: however, some amount of difference is usually more effective such as fourth- or fifth-graders and tenth- or eleventh-graders with middle schoolers.

The second issue is to provide the helpers with careful and systematic training. Actually, in a tutoring program, this means that you as a teacher become a tutor trainer. You teach the helpers some fundamental elements of effective teaching, have them practice with each other, and then set up the actual tutoring. Basically, this involves a role shift for you from teaching to supervising. What follows is a sample series of tutor-training lessons that were used to teach fourth-grade students to serve as *buddies* to trainable mentally retarded children.

Because of space limitations we cannot provide a complete outline of a curriculum in tutoring. However, the activities do give enough of a framework to enable you to add specifics to our suggestions in working with student tutors.

Unit 1

Objective: To learn similarities and differences between themselves and the handicapped children.

Materials: Blindfolds, wooden blocks of varying shapes (ten for each pair of tutors).

Plan: Each pair of students is to take turns as a tutee and a tutor. To help the students experience the feelings of a handicapping condition, the "tutee" is blindfolded and then asked to build a block tower.

The tutor is to give verbal directions only and no other form of help. Then the students switch roles.

After each pair has experienced the role of teacher and of handicapped pupil, conduct a discussion with the group as a whole to promote reflection.

What was it like to tutor a handicapped person using only verbal directions?

What was it like to try to build a tower without being able to see?

How did it feel to be given only verbal help? Was it frustrating?

What do you have to do to give good directions to someone who has a hard time with blocks and puzzles? (Encourage many ideas for altering the style of communication: speaking more slowly, giving more verbal clues, using shorter phrases.)

Should you give more help than you did? What kind of help? (Encourage the students to talk about hands-on help.)

Then, help the students draw conclusions about effective helping. Remember to use wait-time in questioning and call on students by name for answers.

Note: Other simulations of a handicapping condition include a blindfolded "trust" walk. Arrange a pathway through a maze of chairs and have the helpers direct the blindfolded peer with verbal directions only. Or have all the students write their own name, address, and phone number either with the nondominant hand (left if right-handed) or while looking into a mirror. These experiences help the students learn more about how it feels to struggle over otherwise ordinary tasks.

Unit 2

Objective: To learn to give clear directions.

Materials: Games or puzzles that are typically used with low-functioning students.

Plan: Remind the students of the outcome of Unit 1. Ask for a summary. Outline effective direction-giving and model the behavior with the help of one of the students. (Deliberate talk—one- or two-syllable words; be prepared to help.)

Then, have the children pair up and use one of the games. After five minutes or so have everyone switch roles. (During this experience, be sure to circulate and provide lots of positive reinforcement to anyone using one of the four techniques.)

After the practice, conduct the discussion session with questions such as:

Did you hear your tutor give clear directions?

How did you feel when the directions weren't clear?

How does this experience relate to working with exceptional children?

Again, remember to call on specific children by name rather than address a general question to all. Also remember to use both wait-time for a response and cues to help students answer more completely.

Unit 3

Objective: Learn to give positive feedback.

Materials: Games from the special-educational resource room.

Plan: Form pairs for role-play and ask the tutor to give instructions to the tutee and then say nothing at all if the student does well. Repeat the same exercise but provide praise whenever the tutee succeeds.

Reconvene the group as a whole and ask questions such as:

How did you feel with silence?

How did you feel with praise?

How might you feel if instead of silence you were criticized?

Can you see yourself giving praise to the "buddy" from the special class?

Remember to review the guidelines for effective praise (Chapter 12) so that the students don't over-praise or "gush over" the tutees.

Unit 4

Objective: Never say no—or hardly ever: how to handle discipline. Sometimes special-class children have not learned to play games by the rules. This doesn't mean that they are "naughty" but rather that they sometimes need extra help and encouragement. The objective is to help the tutor learn constructive ways to redirect attention and teach the buddy to follow directions.

Materials: Blocks of different colors.

Plan: Start by modeling the techniques. The first technique is verbal redirection. Demonstrate with a student; for example, hold out two colored blocks, one red and one blue. Then say, "Mary, give me the red one." Mary chooses blue. "Mary, this is blue. Here is the red one. Now give me the red one." Then when Mary hands over the red one be sure to use positive reinforcement. This will often be sufficient to keep the tutee on task.

The second technique is behavior redirection. Demonstrate the previous scene with Mary, but in this case, Mary has no interest in that particular game and starts to poke a nearby student. Say, "Mary, let's go over to this corner (away from others) and do some drawing with crayons. Let's see if you can draw a red line for me." Take Mary by the hand and walk with her to the corner. Then use positive reinforcement for Mary's appropriate behavior.

The third technique is a combination of physical restraint and redirection. Demonstrate the first scene again, but in this case Mary is about to hit a nearby tutee with the wooden box holding the game. You say, "Oh, Mary, I can't let you do that." Then move quickly to grab the box and hold Mary's arm. Follow this with the steps in the second technique.

After completing the demonstrations, have the tutors pair off and practice the three techniques, again verbally reinforcing good examples.

Reconvene the group and ask questions such as:

How did you feel about using the different techniques?

Why do you suppose you should not hit the child when she (or he) was about to bop another tutee?

Do you find it difficult to distract and redirect?

Does it bother you to find out that sometimes the child might not follow the rules of the game?

It will be most important to conduct the above discussion at length. Many children either from their own experience or from observation of adults may feel that physical retaliation, spanking, the knuckle on the head, etc., are appropriate. These ideas need to be aired, but you must also firmly indicate that physical retaliation is not permitted while restraint is. Recall the discussion in the previous chapter on the differences between humane and inhumane control. Exceptional children may need firm external control at times; that is, positive methods suited to levels of Kohlberg stages I, II, and III. They do not need the negative methods.

A final point—the use of student tutors can be a positive educational resource for exceptional children. The student tutors, however, need systematic training and continuous monitoring. Without training, as we noted, the tutors may end up with more negative attitudes toward the handicapped peers. With training, the students learn some important lessons themselves while helping others.

For further information see Sprinthall and Blum (1980), Peer and cross-age training.

REFERENCES

Axline, V. (1967). *Dibs*. Boston: Houghton Mifflin.

Bakan, D. (1971). *The slaughter of the innocents*. San Francisco: Jossey-Bass.

Baker, J., and Zigmond, N. (1990). Are regular education classes equipped to accommodate students with learning disabilities? *Exceptional Children, 56*(6), 514–527.

Baroff, G. S. (1974). *Mental retardation: Nature, cause, and management*. New York: Wiley.

Birch, W. J. (1974). *Mainstreaming*. Reston, Va.: Council for Exceptional Children.

Bloom, B. S. (1984). The 2 sigma problem: The search for methods as effective as one-to-one tutoring. *Educational Researcher, 13*(6), 4–16.

Bruininks, V. (1978). Actual and perceived peer status of learning-disabled students in mainstream programs. *Journal of Special Education, 12*(1), 51–58.

Deno, E. (1970). Special education as developmental capital. *Exceptional Children, 37*, 229–237.

Deno, S., Maruyama, G., Espin, C., and Cohen, C. (1990). Educating students with mild disabilities in general education classrooms: Minnesota alternatives. *Exceptional Children, 57*(2), 150–161.

Dormer, S. (1975). The relationship of physical handicap to stress in families with an adolescent with spina bifida. *Developmental Medical Child Neurology, 17*, 765–776.

Dupont, H. (1978). Meeting the emotional-social needs of students in a mainstream environment. *Counseling and Human Development, 10*(9), 1–11.

Finn J. D. and Resnick, L. (1984). Issues in the instruction of mildly mentally retarded children. *Educational Researcher, 13*(3), 9–11.

Furtwengler, C. B. (1991). How to observe cooperative learning classrooms. *Educational Leadership, 49*(7), 59–62.

Gartner, A., and Lipsky, D. K. (1987). Beyond special education: Toward a quality system for all students. *Harvard Educational Review, 57*, 367–395.

Gaylord-Ross, R. (1990). *Issues and research in special education* (Vol. 1). New York: Teachers College Press.

Gelb, S. A., and Mizokawa, D. T. (1986). Special education and social structure: The commonality of "exceptionality." *American Educational Research Journal, 23*(4), 543–557.

Graham, S., and Barker, G. (1990). The down-side of help: An attributional-developmental analysis of helping behavior as a low-ability cue. *Journal of Educational Psychology, 82*, 7–14.

Gresham, F. M. (1981). Social skills training with handicapped children: A review. *Review of Educational Research, 51*(1), 139–176.

Haberman, M. (1980). Principles of inservice training for implementation of mainstreaming in the public schools. In D. C. Corrigan and K. Howey (Eds.), *Concepts to guide the education of experienced teachers* (pp. 53–64). Reston, Va.: Council for Exceptional Children.

Hawkins, J. D., Doueck, H. J., and Lishner, D. M. (1988). Changing teaching practices in mainstream classrooms to improve bonding and behavior of low achievers. *American Educational Research Journal, 25*(1), 31–50.

Hibbert, M. (1992). *Assessing the social and educational development of preschool children in two mainstreamed programs*. Unpublished doctoral dissertation, North Carolina State University.

Hobbs, N. (1975). *The futures of children*. San Francisco: Jossey-Bass.

Hunt, D. (1974). *Matching models in education*. Toronto, Canada: Ontario Institute for Studies in Education.

Kauffman, J., and Hallahan, D. (1990). What we want for children: A rejoinder to REI proponents. *Journal of Special Education, 24*(3), 340–345.

Lee, H. (1962). *To kill a mockingbird*. New York: Popular Library.

Loucks-Horsley, S., and Roody, D. S. (1990). Using what

is known about change to inform the Regular Education Initiative. *Remedial and Special Education, 11*, 51–56.

McDermott, R. P., and Aron, J. (1978). Pirandello in the classroom: On the possibility of equal educational opportunity in American culture. In M. C. Reynolds (Ed.), *Futures of education for exceptional students*. Reston, Va.: Council for Exceptional Children.

Messick, S. (1984). Assessment in context: Appraising performance in relation to instructional quality. *Educational Researcher, 13*(3), 5.

Nelson, C. M., and Rutherford, R. B. (1988). Research integration of cognitive-emotional interventions for behaviorally disordered children and youth. In M. C. Wang, M. C. Reynolds, and H. J. Walberg (Eds.), *The handbook of special education* (Vol. 2). Oxford, England: Pergamon.

Osborne, S., Schulte, A., and McKinney, J. (1991). A longitudinal study of students with learning disabilities in mainstream and resource programs. *Exceptionality, 2,* 81–95.

Perry, J., and Krebs, D. (1980). Role-taking, moral development and mental retardation. *Journal of Genetic Psychology, 136*, 95–108.

Peterson, P. L. (1988). Selecting students and services for compensatory education: Lessons for aptitude-treatment-interaction research. *Educational Psychologist, 23*(4), 313–352.

Reschly, D. (1988). Learning characteristics of mildly handicapped students: Implications for classification, placement and programming. In M. C. Wang, M. C. Reynolds, and H. J. Walberg (Eds.), *The handbook of special education* (Vol. 2). Oxford, England: Pergamon.

Reynolds, M. C. (1984). Classification of students with handicaps. In E. W. Gordon (Ed.), *Review of educational research* (pp. 63–92). Washington: American Educational Research Association.

Reynolds, M. C. (1990). Educating teachers for special education students. In R. Houston (Ed.), *Handbook of research in teacher education* (pp. 423–436). New York: Macmillan.

Reynolds, M. C., Wang, M. C., and Walberg, H. J. (1987). The necessary restructuring of special and regular education. *Exceptional Children, 53*(5), 391–398.

Riles v. Larry P., C-71-2270 RFP. (San Francisco District Court, 1979).

Rothman, H., and Semmel, M. (1990). Dynamic assessment: A comprehensive review of the literature. In R. Gaylord-Ross (Ed.), *Issues and research in special education* (Vol. 1), (pp. 355–386). New York: Teachers College Press.

Salvia, J., and Ysseldyke, J. (1991). *Assessment in special and remedial education*. Boston: Houghton Mifflin.

Scarr-Salapatek, S., and Weinberg, R. (1975). The war over race and IQ. *Psychology Today, 9*(7), 80–82.

Seligman, M. E. P. (1975). *Helplessness*. San Francisco: Freeman.

Seligman, M. E. P. (1991). *Learned optimism*. New York: Knopf.

Semmel, M., and Gerber, M. (1990). If at first you don't succeed, bye, bye again: A response to general educators' views on the REI. *Remedial and Special Education, 11*(4), 53–61.

Sharpley, A., Irvin, J., and Sharpley, C. (1983). An examination of the effectiveness of a cross-age tutoring program in mathematics for elementary school children. *American Educational Research Journal, 20*(1), 103–111.

Shaywitz, S., Shaywitz, B., Fletcher, J., and Escobar, M. (1990). Prevalence of reading disability in boys and girls. *Journal of the American Medical Association, 264*(3), 998–1002.

Skodak, M., and Skeels, H. M. (1949). A final follow-up study on one hundred adopted children. *Journal of Genetic Psychology, 75*, 85–125.

Slavin, R. E. (1983). *Cooperative learning*. New York: Longman.

Slavin, R. E. (1990). *Cooperative learning: Theory, research and practice*. Englewood Cliffs, N.J.: Prentice-Hall.

Snow, R. (1984). Placing children in special education. *Educational Researcher, 13*(3), 12–14.

Sprinthall, N. A., and Blum, M. (1980). Peer and cross age teaching: Promoting social and psychological development in mainstream classes. In M. C. Reynolds (Ed.), *Social environment of the schools*. Reston, Va.: Council for Exceptional Children.

Sprinthall, N. A., Gerber, E. R., and Hall, J. S. (1992). Peer helping. *The Peer Facilitator, 9*(4), 11–15.

Sprinthall, N. A., and Scott, J. (1989). Promoting psychological development, math achievement and success attribution of female students through deliberate psychological education. *Journal of Counseling Psychology, 36*, 440–446.

Tindal, G., Parker, R., and Germann, G. (1990). An analysis of mainstream consultation outcomes for secondary students identified as learning disabled. *Learning Disability Quarterly, 13*, 220–228.

U.S. Department of Education (1990). *Twelfth annual report to Congress on the implementation of the Education of the Handicapped Act*. Washington, D.C.

Ysseldyke, J., and Algozzine, B. (1990). *Introduction to special education*. Boston: Houghton Mifflin.

Ysseldyke, J., Algozzine, B., and Thurlow, M. (1992). *Critical issues in special education*. Boston: Houghton Mifflin.

Zigmond, N., and Baker, J. (1990). Mainstream experience for learning disabled students (Project meld): Preliminary report. *Exceptional Children, 57*(2), 176–185.

GLOSSARY– STUDY GUIDE

This glossary–study guide has been prepared in order to help you develop familiarity with the key concepts and contributions of the major theories and theorists described in the book. A good way to use this guide is to review the key concepts and names just as you finish each chapter. Then, on notepaper, jot down a brief paragraph or two for each concept or person on the list. Try to figure out one or two main reasons why the person or idea is important to educational psychology. After you've given that activity your best effort, turn to this glossary–study guide and review your answers by comparing them with the ones provided. Then, since the concepts and names are keyed to the chapter numbers (in parentheses) for easy cross-referencing, clarify any possible ambiguities by going back to the chapter and rereading the appropriate section.

Of course, all this also means that it is important to understand the reasons behind the concepts. Jerome Bruner once said that a student needs to have a background of facts, what he called "the stuff of learning," before understanding and discovery learning can take place. The glossary–study guide will help provide you with the "stuff" for creative thinking in educational psychology. Just listening to lectures or reading text material, the student new to the field often becomes dismayed over the number of technical terms and the seemingly endless jargon. But what at first may seem like forbidding language is really an attempt to be precise. In order to understand the more global concepts in educational psychology, the student should master the tools of the trade, that is, the methods and terms used by educational psychologists in presenting their views.

The items in the guide define specific terms, outline broad theoretical positions, or provide brief biographies of some of the significant individuals in educational psychology. Although each entry is essentially a self-contained unit, in some cases you will be directed to one or two additional entries in order to develop a more complete thought. The number in parentheses at the end of each entry indicates the chapter in which the concept has been discussed.

Rote memorization will not serve you well, since if you don't have an underlying understanding, you may easily fall into the trap of repeating "nearly accurate" phrases that may, unfortunately, signify nothing. On an exam given by one instructor in educational psychology, it is alleged that a student wrote a brief essay that included a discussion of means and medians as well as a section on the standard devotions. So to avoid being caught without a prayer (sorry), study for understanding, not just for mere memorization.

Accommodation

Concept used by Piaget in his discussion of cognitive development. Accommodation is the adjustment the individual makes when incorporating external reality. Piaget uses this concept in conjunction with *assimilation*, which is the individual's ability to internalize and conceptualize his or her environmental experiences. Accommodation is the individual's response to the immediate and compelling environmental demands that have been and are being assimilated. *See also* Assimilation. (5)

Achievement Motivation

A possibly intrinsic motive to achieve just for the sake of achieving, rather than the achievement being in the service of some other motive. Research shows that the most important single ingredient in achievement motivation is a feeling of self-directed competence. (18)

Acquired Motives

Motives that are based on the activation of psychological needs, such as approval, affection, power, and prestige. Such motives are said to have been learned. (18)

Active School

Based on Jean Piaget's ideas, the concept suggests that learning will be enhanced through active, or hands-on, experiences in combination with thoughtful reflection. Piaget's dictum states, "To know by heart is not to know." Passive memorization does not necessarily mean that the pupil has really learned or understood the concepts. (5)

American Question

According to Jean Piaget, any question about how to accelerate cognitive-stage growth. Piaget suggests that Americans may be preoccupied with a concern for developmental teaching programs that are designed to speed up the naturally unfolding stages of cognitive growth. Some recent programs of infant stimulation are examples of Piaget's concern. (5)

Anal Stage

Second of Freud's psychosexual stages of development. During this stage, the child takes great pleasure, first in the act of defecating, and later in the act of withholding the feces. This stage usually takes place between the ages of eighteen months and three years. The first part of this stage is called the *anal expulsive* stage, which later develops into the *anal retentive* stage. Freud says that the way in which the child is treated during this stage (toilet training, etc.) makes a permanent imprint on the later adult personality. (6)

Anastasi, Anne

A past president (1971) of the American Psychological Association, Anne Anastasi has written on a wide variety of subjects in the field, ranging from the psychology of art to the nature-nurture controversy. She is best known, however, for her work in statistics and test construction. A firm believer in IQ tests, she feels that discontinuing the IQ test would be like asking a physician to throw away the thermometer just because children who are ill register an undesirable deviation from the norm. In her 1958 paper "Heredity, Environment and the Question 'How?'" Anastasi put the nature-nurture controversy in perspective. Instead of asking which component, heredity or environment, contributes more to the child's development, the better question is *how* heredity and environment interact in the development of behavioral differences. She also cites the importance of early experience on intellectual growth and development. (15)

Approval (Need for)

A social or acquired need for being accepted and positively evaluated by other persons. The need for approval is thought to be based on the individual's desire, learned in infancy, to be loved by his or her mother or primary caregiver. (18)

Archer, Sally

Developmental psychologist who has shown the importance of identity formation for teenage females, especially with regard to career development. Archer found that these females do not receive sufficient help and guidance to balance the problems of family responsibilities and careers. Too often females suffer from the costs of invisibility and the resultant delay in reaching an achieved identity. (6)

Arlin, Patricia

Developmental psychologist who has investigated the relationship between Piaget's stages and adult development. She suggests that there may be a fifth stage called *postformal operations,* which is characterized by abstract thought and problem finding. (5)

Artificial Intelligence

The simulation of human thinking by the use of a computer program. Programs attempt to parallel the human thought process. Artificial intelligence is based not only on our current understanding of how humans think but also on the fond hope that through the use of the program as a model our current understanding of thought processes will be increased. (11)

A/S Ratio

The A/S ratio is a concept developed by D. O. Hebb, the Canadian physiological psychologist. Hebb developed the ratio by comparing the amount of brain space devoted to association areas with the amount devoted to sensory areas. As he went up the phylogenetic ladder from rat to monkey to humans, Hebb found an ever-increasing A/S ratio. Rats, with their lower A/S ratio, are more sensory-bound, whereas humans, with a higher A/S ratio, are capable of far more varied and greater amounts of learning. (4)

Assimilation

Concept used by Jean Piaget in his theory of cognitive development. Assimilation is the process of taking within, or internalizing, one's environmental experience. Assimilation is used by Piaget in conjunction with the concept of accommodation. Piaget believes that assimilation is a spontaneous process on the part of the child. *See also* Accommodation. (5)

Attention Deficits

A syndrome that results in an inability to focus attention or concentrate for an extended period of time. This condition is often, but not always, accompanied by hyperactivity. (11)

Attention Deficit–Hyperactivity Disorder (ADHD)

A form of attention deficit characterized by a child who is easily distracted and unable to sustain focused attention and who shows high levels of restlessness, fidgeting, and squirming. (11)

Attitudes

A *learned* predisposition to respond either positively or negatively to persons, situations, or things. Attitudes carry a strong emotional component and therefore can never be neutral. When a negative attitude is generalized to include an entire group of people, it is called a *stereotype*. This can be destructive to the holder of the stereotype as well as to the group about which it is held. It can be especially destructive to the minority group member's self-image. (17)

Attribute-Treatment Interaction (ATI)

Framework, devised by David Hunt, that suggests that effective teaching should be a match between the developmental stage characteristics of the learner and both the process and content of the teaching program. At different conceptual levels (CLs), students have different needs regarding the amount of structure a teacher should employ and how concrete or abstract concepts being presented should be. Effectiveness requires starting where the learner is, then gradually removing the structure and increasing the abstractness of the concepts being taught. The term *stage* in Hunt's system refers to the currently preferred

learning style rather than any sort of permanent classification. (13)

Attribution Theory

The term *attribution* refers to the explanation a person gives for his or her own or another person's actions or beliefs. An attribution based on internal factors is called a dispositional attribution, and one based on external factors is called a situational attribution. The fundamental attribution error occurs when we assign dispositional factors to the actions of others and situational factors to our own actions. (17)

Ausubel, David

Educational theorist who has contributed, among other things, the concept of advance organizers to a model of teaching. His system involves providing learners with a clear set of objectives in advance of the presentation in order that the learners become oriented to the planned goals of the lesson. This model forms the basis for much of what is called the *direct instruction* approach. (12)

Authoritarian Leadership

Style of leadership in which the individual holding the leadership position retains all the decision-making power. (17)

Autokinetic Effect

A visual effect produced when a small but stationary pinpoint of light in an otherwise darkened room *appears* to move. Since the light remains physically stationary and since the perceived movement is only apparent, the autokinetic effect has been used to further our understanding of how group norms emerge. Experiments using the autokinetic effect have been performed by social psychologist Muzafer Sherif. (17)

Bandura, Albert

Orginator of social learning theory, which suggests that learning may take place not just on the basis of straight reinforcement principles, but also as a result of a process called *modeling*. Bandura insists that people may learn new responses simply by observing the behavior of others. (10)

Bayley, Nancy

Developmental psychologist and author of the famous Berkeley Growth Study. Bayley was the first woman ever to win the American Psychological Association's Distinguished Scientific Contribution award. Bayley's major findings have been that

1. IQs are not constant.

2. IQ variability is greatest during the first few years of life.

3. Intellectual growth may continue throughout life.

4. The components of intellect change with age level. (4)

Becker, Howard

Investigator of the relationship between the social class of the teacher and pupil attitudes. He found that many teachers from the lower middle class had difficulty accepting students from either lower or higher socioeconomic levels.

Behavior Genetics

A fairly new discipline within the field of animal psychology, concerned with the effects of genotype on behavior. Specifically, the behavior geneticist studies the effect of genetic differences on behavioral differences *within a population*. The method of study typically used is that of selective breeding and/or the use of inbred animal strains. An example would be Robert Tryon's study (1940) in which maze-bright and maze-dull rats were selectively bred and then compared over several generations according to their ability to run a maze. It must be pointed out that behavior genetics is *not* allied with the now-discredited instinct theory. (3)

Behavior Modification

A system for changing behavior based on the principles of conditioning. The term *behavior modification*, or *behavior mod*, is usually applied either to the classroom or to a patient undergoing therapy. When desirable behavior is exhibited, it is followed by a reinforcing stimulus; when undesirable behavior is emitted, it is followed either by no reinforcement (extinction) or, less commonly, by punishment. It is important when using this system that (1) goals be defined precisely *and in behavioral terms* and that (2) the conditioning schedule be followed with absolute consistency. (10)

Behaviorism

A school of thought in psychology usually considered to have originated in the work and writings of John B. Watson. In 1913 Watson outlined the behaviorist position in his paper "Psychology as the Behaviorist Views It." Watson argued there against the use of introspection in gathering psychological data. He considered observable behavior the only valid data in psychology. According to Watson, any concepts, like mind or consciousness, that have mentalistic overtones must be purged from the field of psychology. The most famous recent representative of this tradition was Harvard University's B. F. Skinner. (8)

Berkowitz, Marvin

One of Kohlberg's students, who examined different methods of leading value dilemma discussions. He found that effective discussion leaders combined support and challenge as well as indirect teaching methods. (7)

Binet, Alfred (1857–1911)

Orginator of psychology's first modern intelligence test (1905). In assembling his test, this French psychologist set up a series of intellectual tasks, as opposed to the sensorimotor tasks previously used by Sir Frances Galton. Binet also introduced the concept of mental age as the basis for scoring his later tests (1908). The original Binet test items were later used as the basis for the famous Stanford-Binet intelligence test (1916), published in the United States by Lewis M. Terman. The test was scored on the basis of the ratio between the test taker's mental age and chronological age. This ratio, multiplied by 100, is known as the *intelligence quotient*, or IQ. *See also Intelligence Quotient; Stanford-Binet Test. (16)*

Bloom, Benjamin S.

American educational psychologist and professor at the University of Chicago and Northwestern. He is most widely known for his work in two important areas in educational psychology:

1. Bloom sought to describe systematically the classroom teacher's educational goals, and methods for achieving those goals. This work is called his *taxonomy for educational objectives.*

2. Bloom also published the now-classic *Stability and Change in Human Characteristics* (1964), which outlined an early-experience position regarding intellectual growth. Bloom maintained that the positive effect of a beneficial environment on intellectual growth decreases as the children get older. Three-year-old children profit far more from enriching experiences than do seven- or eight-year-old children. (4)

Bonding

A process occurring between mother and child, seen by some to be similar to imprinting. Bonding requires direct physical contact between the mother and child and must occur within the baby's first three days of life. It produces a strong emotional attachment between the two. Failure to form this bond has been hypothesized as the cause for later episodes of child neglect and even abuse. (3)

Bornstein's Infant Intelligence Test

Intelligence test used on six-month-old babies and based on how long it takes a baby to process information about moving stimuli. Marc Bornstein discovered significant correlations between infant test scores and the IQ scores on Wechsler scales taken four years later. (16)

Brainstorming

A technique for generating new ideas in which individuals get together in a group and are urged to interact freely and call out any idea, no matter how seemingly bizarre. Brainstorming is used in many businesses, especially in areas in which creativity is important, as in an advertising agency's mapping out a new campaign. The actual research on brainstorming, however, casts some doubt on its effectiveness with regard to both the number of new ideas and the quality of the ideas produced by the group. (17)

Bruner, Jerome S.

Researcher of such varied subjects as propaganda techniques, the effect of need on perception, and most important, how people obtain knowledge and how they develop intellectually. In 1960, Bruner founded Harvard's Center for Cognitive Studies, and although he didn't invent cognitive psychology, he went a long way toward making it systematic and consistent with the rules of science. Perhaps Bruner's most famous statement is that any subject can be taught effectively in some intellectually honest form to any child at any stage of development. He stresses discovery learning and communication at three levels: enactive, iconic, and symbolic. (9)

Cascade System

A dynamic system used to group special-education services on a continuum with the aim of providing handicapped children with an environment that incorporates the fewest possible restrictions. The ultimate goal of this system is to move special-education children toward regular services. The cascade system has seven different levels and was created by teaching expert Evelyn Deno. (20)

Case, Robbie

Developmental psychologist who has become the major contemporary researcher in cross-validating and extending

the work of Piaget (through his research team at Stanford). His research includes cross-cultural studies, comparisons by gender, giftedness, and special education—all of which cut across intellectual, interpersonal, and social domains. (5)

Cattell, James McKeen (1860–1944)

A pioneer in the field of intelligence testing. Cattell, an American, studied both in Germany under Wilhelm Wundt and in England under Sir Francis Galton. He brought the message of European psychology back to the United States, and in 1888 he was appointed to the first professorship in psychology anywhere in the world. As Galton had done previously, Cattell devised a series of sensorimotor tests (auditory range, visual range, reaction time, etc.) designed to measure human intellectual potential by testing people's sensorimotor equipment. Cattell taught for many years at Columbia University, and on his illustrious list of students are the names E. L. Thorndike, R. S. Woodworth, and E. K. Strong.

Cattell is credited with fathering the mental-testing movement in the United States, and in fact it was Cattell, in 1890, who first used the term *mental test*. (2)

Cell Assembly

Concept used by D. O. Hebb in describing cognitive growth. The cell assembly defines the action of a group of brain cells organized into a coherent unit and enabling the young child to learn at an ever-increasing rate. The child learns slowly and ploddingly when operating at the single-cell level, but after cell assemblies are formed in the brain, the child's learning speed increases dramatically. (4)

Character Education, or Training

Education to develop character through inculcation and brainwashing. Research has shown that such education is ineffective; rather, character appears to develop in stages as more democratic and humane values are incorporated. (19)

Charisma

Term used in describing a leader or a leadership trait or quality, as in a charismatic leader. An individual who has charisma is thought to possess a kind of animal magnetism or hypnotic appeal. The power of a charismatic leader is seen by some as being almost mystical in its spellbinding appeal. When a charismatic person enters a room, the room is supposed to be suddenly charged with excitement. (17)

Chomsky, Noam

American psychologist interested in cognitive growth through language development. Chomsky has severely criticized the typical American learning theory explanation of language as the result of straight conditioning. Chomsky insists that the conditioning model of language development simply doesn't fit with the facts. Children learn the use of language far more quickly than the conditioning theory can explain. Chomsky explains this rapid rate of language development on the basis of a built-in capacity for language acquisition. That is, a baby enters the world genetically prewired, or born with a biological readiness that directs the course of language development. (9)

Chromosome

Long, threadlike bits of protein. Each cell of the human body contains twenty-three pairs. Egg and sperm cells, however, carry only twenty-three individual chromosomes, or just half the number contained in other body cells. An infant receives half of its chromosomes from each parent at conception, twenty-three from the sperm cell and twenty-three from the egg cell, thus achieving the full complement of twenty-three pairs. (3)

Chunking

The grouping together of several separate items in order to aid in their recall. Remembering digits that have been grouped in threes is an example of chunking. It is easier to retrieve the number 103 than the separate numbers one, zero, and three. (11)

Clark, Kenneth B.

Noted black educator, psychologist, and profesor at City College of New York. Clark's 1950 report on the effects of segregation in the schools was used extensively by the Supreme Court justices in their historic 1954 decision declaring segregation in public schools unconstitutional. Clark has worked and written in a wide variety of areas within the fields of educational and social psychology. (17)

Classical Conditioning

Term used to describe conditioning techniques introduced by Ivan P. Pavlov. It is the pairing of a conditioned stimulus with an unconditioned stimulus over long numbers of trials until the conditioned stimulus alone has the power to elicit the conditioned response. During the conditioning trials, the conditioned stimulus acts as a signal that the unconditioned stimulus will follow, and the organism thus eventually learns to respond to the conditioned stimulus alone. In Pavlov's basic experiment, a dog was conditioned to salivate at the sound of a tone. The tone was presented (conditioned stimulus), followed by meat powder (uncon-

ditioned stimulus), until the dog began salivating just at the tone. (8)

Cognitive Dissonance

Concept introduced by social psychologist Leon Festinger. Individuals prefer to maintain a state of equilibrium among their various attitudes, beliefs, and behavior. Inconsistency between thoughts and actions sets up within the individual a state of cognitive dissonance, an uncomfortable state that the individual attempts to resolve by changing either his or her actions or beliefs. It is far more comfortable, and thus desirable, from the individual's point of view to attain cognitive consonance over cognitive dissonance. (17)

Cognitive Learning

The view that learning is based on a restructuring of perceptions and thoughts occurring within the organism. This restructuring allows the learner to perceive new relationships, solve new problems, and gain understanding of a subject area. Cognitive-learning theorists stress the reorganization of one's perceptions in order to achieve understanding, as opposed to the conditioning theorists, who stress the importance of associations formed between stimuli and responses. Gestalt psychology has been oriented toward the cognitive view of learning. (8)

Cohesiveness

A concept introduced by social psychologist Leon Festinger. Cohesiveness describes those positive forces that hold a group together and prevent its deterioration. Cohesiveness is one of the few truly group concepts in social psychology. It can be thought of as the cement that binds the group together, or the attraction of the group for its members. Group cohesiveness can be increased by (1) friendly interaction, (2) cooperation, (3) increased group status, (4) an outside threat, or (5) democratic rather than authoritarian leadership. (17)

Collaborative Action Research

An approach to research that takes place in actual classrooms, where the teacher becomes both a participant and an observer. When problems arise such as in management or course content, the teacher engages in a sequence of planning, acting, observing, and replanning steps to solve the specific problem at hand. Teachers often work with colleagues and share decision making. This is similar to the original John Dewey "project method" and scientific problem-solving methods in the natural setting of the classroom or school building. It has been shown to have beneficial effects on both teachers and their students by helping teachers become more reflective inquirers, e.g., theoretical practitioners. (14)

Competence Motivation

Theory developed by the personality theorist Robert White. White feels that all humans, and even some animals, have a basic drive to achieve competence as a way of developing control over their environments. People have a need to be competent in some area. Of course, as competence increases, so too does enjoyment. Competence is a key concept for many educators and is viewed as being synonymous with personal mastery and self-direction. (6, 18)

Computer-Assisted Instruction (CAI)

Use of the computer, especially the microcomputer, as a "private tutor" constantly monitoring a student's progress and allowing a student to proceed at his or her own rate. The program, or software tutorial, may take a student through a discrete lesson unit and during its running allow many choices. A student's error, if it occurs, automatically triggers a program review of the material not fully comprehended. (10)

Concept Formation

In the information-processing model, the processing of data by identifying certain characteristics of incoming information and then organizing the information in such a way as to provide encoded meaning. (11)

Conceptual Level

Applied to teachers, David Hunt's concept that teachers process experience at different levels according to their stage of conceptual development, and behave in the classroom accordingly. At the least complex level, stage A, teachers tend to view knowledge as fixed truth and pupils as passive memorizers of rote facts. At a more advanced level, stage B, teachers perceive their role as more interactive, and they emphasize a combination of goals, including promoting pupil development. Teachers functioning at the highest level, stage C, exhibit the broadest variety of teaching methods keyed specifically to pupil needs and their levels of understanding. *See also* Hunt, David. (13)

Concordance Rate

Term used in behavior genetics to denote the percentage of cotwins exhibiting a specific phenotypic trait. (3)

Concrete-Operations Stage

A stage of thinking, according to Jean Piaget, that is characteristic of the period from ages seven to eleven. At this stage thinking is based on specifics and literal-mindedness. The child using this mode of thought is objective and logical, but almost too literal-minded. The child wants facts and wants the facts to be specific, but cannot separate facts from hypotheses at this stage. (5)

Conditioned Reinforcement

Sometimes called *secondary reinforcement*, it describes the situation in which a previously neutral stimulus acquires reinforcing power by being repeatedly associated with a primary reinforcer. The sequence of events for establishing conditioned reinforcement is as follows: (1) response; (2) neutral stimulus, such as a light or buzzer; (3) primary reinforcer, such as a pellet of food. In the classroom, conditioned reinforcers might be good grades, prizes, promotions, and generalized social approval. The use of tokens by behavior-modification proponents is another example of conditioned reinforcement at work in the classroom. (9)

Conditioned Response

Term used both in classical conditioning and in operant conditioning. In classical conditioning, the conditioned response is the response being elicited by the conditioned stimulus. The stronger the conditioning, the greater the magnitude of the conditioned response and the shorter its latency. In Pavlov's experiment the conditioned response was the dog's salivation to the tone.

In operant conditioning, since the response must precede the reinforcer, the conditioned response is defined not in terms of magnitude or latency, but in terms of either the rate of the response or its resistance to extinction. For example, a strongly conditioned operant will occur far more rapidly than one that has been only weakly conditioned. Also, a strongly conditioned operant will be far more difficult to extinguish. (8)

Conditioned Stimulus

In classical conditioning, the previously neutral stimulus takes on the power to elicit the response through association with an unconditioned stimulus. For this to occur, the conditioned stimulus must precede the unconditioned stimulus on enough occasions to cause the conditioned stimulus to serve as a signal that the unconditioned stimulus will follow. In Pavlov's experiment on conditioning the dog, the tone was used as the conditioned stimulus. The tone was consistently followed by the meat powder, until the dog began salivating to the tone alone. (8)

Conditioning

Process of learning whereby stimuli and responses become associated through training. There are two general types of conditioning, classical and operant. In classical conditioning a conditioned stimulus is presented, followed by an unconditioned stimulus. Conditioning is exhibited when the organism learns to respond to the conditioned stimulus alone. In operant conditioning the operant is allowed to occur and then is followed by a reinforcing stimulus. Operant conditioning is exhibited when the rate of responding increases over the original, preconditioned rate. (8)

Confluence Model

A theory of intelligence proposed by R. B. Zajonc (rhymes with *science*) that proposes a strong relationship between the number of children in a family and the family's overall intellectual level. The model predicts that the more children there are in a family and the closer together they are in age, the lower the IQs of all the children. (16)

Conformity

Term used in social psychology to describe the fact that individuals in group situations tend to behave in a uniform way. Group pressure acts on the individual to force him or her into acting in accord with the rules and norms of the group. Important studies in this area include: (1) Muzafer Sherif's study, in which individuals formed a common estimate of how far (autokinetic effect) a light appeared to move; (2) Solomon Asch's study, in which a naive subject's estimate of the length of a line conformed to the group's estimate, even though the group was obviously wrong; and (3) Stanley Milgram's study, in which subjects who believed they were administering an electric shock to their lab partner were less apt to deliver high voltages when acting in a group situation than when acting alone. (17)

Congruence

One of the three necessary and sufficient conditions (the others being empathy and unconditional positive regard) for the promotion of learning, according to Carl Rogers. By congruence, Rogers means total and complete honesty. To promote learning, the teacher must be "real" and honest in dealing with students. Teachers can't go through the motions of liking students. A teacher without congruence should probably try a different line of work. (12)

Connected Teaching

Based largely on the work of Belenky, Clinchy, Goldberger, and Tarule, connected teaching emphasizes the importance of personal experience, cooperation, consensus, and a supportive classroom atmosphere as ways of enhancing growth. In many ways it is similar to the Carl Rogers model of teaching. (12)

Conservation

Term used by Jean Piaget in his theory of cognitive growth and illustrated by the idea that water from a tall, thin glass can be poured into a short, wide glass *without changing the amount of water involved*. According to Piaget, the concept of conservation is typically acquired by a child reaching the stage of concrete operations or operational thinking (at about the age of seven). (5)

Correlation

A numerical statement as to the relationship among two or more variables. A correlation is said to be positive when high scores on one variable are associated with high scores on another variable, and low scores on the first variable are associated with low scores on the second. A correlation is said to be negative when high scores on the first variable are associated with low scores on the second, and vice versa. Correlations range in value from + 1.00 to − 1.00. Correlations that fall around zero indicate no consistent relationship among the measured variables. In psychological research a correlation is usually based on taking several response measures of *one group of subjects*. (15)

Criterion-Referenced Test

A test scored on the basis of how an individual's performance compares to an arbitrarily fixed standard of performance. Most teacher-made tests are criterion-referenced. (15)

Critical Periods

Concept used by Konrad Lorenz and other ethologists to define certain age periods in the organism's life in which learning can occur more easily than in any other age period. For example, Lorenz found that goslings imprint on moving stimuli only between hatching and an age of about thirty hours.

The concept of critical periods was also used in describing human growth and development by Myrtle McGraw in her study of the twins Johnny and Jimmy. The critical period hypothesis is usually used by those psychologists who favor an early-experience position on growth and development. *See also* Imprinting. (4)

Cross-Categorical Special Education

Because most of the categories in the high-incidence areas of special education, particularly LD, ED, and EMR, are so problematic and also because there are few unique teaching strategies (ATIs) for students in these high-incidence areas, a new system of classification has emerged. Instead of separate designations, a single broad category is now being used which includes all students experiencing low levels of achievement. It is now one of the fastest-growing specialties in the training of special educators. (20)

Curiosity Motivation

An inborn motive that is satisfied not by food, drink, or praise but simply by getting the answer. Harry Harlow feels the curiosity drive is fundamental and primary in monkeys and humans. (Why else would a child take apart a watch just to find out what makes it tick?) Daniel Berlyne, another theorist who posits the existence of curiosity motivation, believes that there is an optimum level of curiosity arousal that is a function of brain excitation. (18)

Damon, William

Educational psychologist who has studied the process of peer interactions, particularly at the elementary school level. He suggests that these relationships are important foundations to the development of empathy and moral judgment. This work forms an important basis for understanding the teacher's role in promoting such growth through *authoritative discipline*. (7, 19)

Deciles

Points that divide a distribution into tenths. Each decile represents ten percentiles, such that the 1st decile represents the 10th percentile and the 9th decile the 90th percentile. (15)

Declarative Memory

Storage of LTM information about names, dates, and past events—anything that can be put into words and "declared." Declarative memory is made up of both semantic and episodic components. (11)

Democratic Leadership

Style of leadership in which the decision-making power is shared by members of a group. (17)

Democratic versus Laissez-Faire and Authoritarian Methods

William Damon, a developmental psychologist at Brown University, has translated much of the research on parental styles into an overall framework for understanding and implementing classroom discipline. Laissez-faire and authoritarian methods, although seemingly different on the surface, both typically lead to the same outcome, namely, a lack of self-control by the pupil. (18, 19)

Deoxyribonucleic Acid (DNA)

Rather large organic molecules located in the chromosomes (which lie in the nucleus of every one of the body's cells). These molecules act to direct the body's growth and development. DNA has been called the building block of genetic organization and, along with RNA, makes up the chemical composition of the gene. Geneticists say that DNA acts as a blueprint for the formation of certain enzymes that guide the development of the organism. The coded information stored in the DNA molecule is transmitted to other parts of the cell by the RNA molecules. (3)

Deutch, Morton

Social psychologist who has studied, among other things, the issue of cooperation versus competition. Deutch believes that schools should be less competitively organized and that students will reap significant benefits from more cooperatively managed classrooms. (18)

Developmental Method of Discipline

A method of classroom control that matches discipline to the developmental stage of the pupils. Depending upon the stage, the teacher may use physical restraint, behavior modification, peer pressure, contracts, or democratic decision making. There are humane as well as inhumane aspects to how each of these techniques can be implemented. (19)

Developmental Model

In teaching, the model that suggests that the teacher's role is to stimulate the natural growth process of all pupils. The developmental framework assumes that each child has a basic learning potential and that the teacher's role is to arrange the most appropriate learning environment in order to nurture that growth. Since by definition teaching cannot be value-free, a goal for the professional development of each teacher is to become increasingly reflective about teaching while "doing." Teachers can then reduce the amount of pupils stereotyping and improve their attitudes. (14)

Developmental Stage

A growth and/or behavior organization category that satisfies the following four criteria:

1. It is qualitatively different from the preceding stage.

2. It represents a new and more comprehensive system of organization.

3. It occurs in a maturationally fixed sequence.

4. It is age-related within general confines. (5)

Deviation IQ

A technique for measuring intelligence based on calculating the percentage of individuals in each age category achieving a given score and then assessing how far a certain individual's score deviates from the mean score for the age group in which he or she belongs. The IQ score is thus determined on the basis of age standards and is considered to be norm-referenced. (16)

Dewey, John (1859–1952)

The philosopher and psychologist best known for his educational philosophy of "learning by doing." At the time of this pronouncement by Dewey, American education was still in the grip of the formal-discipline theorists, educators who were convinced that children should sit quietly in a classroom and "strengthen their minds" through the study of a classical curriculum. Dewey attempted to change this traditional method of education by creating learning environments in which children engaged actively in learning. To some extent, Dewey anticipated the ideas of Jean Piaget and the open classroom. Dewey's curriculum came to be known as *progressive education* and was incorrectly translated by many into meaning totally unguided education.

Before moving to Columbia University, where he spent most of his professional career, Dewey was involved with the functionalist school of psychology at the University of Chicago. (1)

Discipline Levels: The Four Questions

In assessing the different levels of discipline used in the classroom, it has been suggested that four basic questions should be asked: who makes the rules, who keeps the rules, how are the rules enforced, and what are the reasons for student compliance? (19)

Discovery Learning

Term used by Jerome Bruner to describe a form of learning that results not from rote memorization or conditioning but from the active exploration of alternatives on the part of the learner. Bruner maintains that the learning attained through discovery is more meaningful and long-lasting than that from memorization. (9)

Discrimination

A term used by learning theorists to describe the ability of an organism to respond to one stimulus and not to respond to another similar stimulus. Ivan Pavlov first demonstrated this phenomenon by conditioning dogs to salivate to a given conditioned stimulus—say, a 2,000-cycle tone—while not salivating to a similar stimulus—say, a 1,900-cycle tone. This was accomplished by continuing to reinforce (with the unconditioned stimulus) the presentation of the 2,000-cycle tone, while withholding reinforcement of responses following presentation of the 1,900-cycle tone.

B. F. Skinner has identified essentially the same phenomenon in the area of operant conditioning. Skinner reinforces a response that occurs in the presence of a given stimulus (S^D), while extinguishing the response when it occurs in the presence of the similar stimulus (S^Δ). (9)

Dispositions of Thoughtfulness

A major recent effort in educational goals has been to improve the thinking skills of students. From a developmental perspective, such skills can be conceptualized as representing higher-order dispositions of thoughtfulness. They can be seen as a synthesis of formal operations (Piaget), understanding democratic principles (Kohlberg), constructed knowledge (Belenky), and critical thinking (Glaser). The dispositions are generic and involve problem solving and problem posing. (13)

Distribution

A statistical term defined as the arrangement of measured scores in order of magnitude. Listing scores in distribution form allows the researcher to notice general trends more readily than the unordered set of raw scores would allow. A frequency distribution is a listing of each score achieved, together with the number of individuals receiving each score. In graphs of frequency distributions, the scores appear on the horizontal axis (abscissa) and the frequency of occurrence appears on the vertical axis (ordinate). (15)

Divided Attention

The ability to attend to more than one source of incoming information, such as when a child studies with the radio on. (11)

Dizygotic (DZ) Twins

Fraternal twins resulting from eggs that are fertilized at the same time but that are not identical. Thus, DZ twins are no more alike genetically than any set of brothers and sisters. (3)

Dominant Gene

Gregor Mendel's term for the unit of heredity whose characteristics are expressed when paired with a like gene or with a recessive gene. Recessive gene characteristics are not expressed unless paired with a like gene. (3)

Drives

Parts of the motivational cycle that are really just activated needs. Drives always result in some observable change in behavior. (18)

Dual-Code Theory

The information-processing theory that suggests that information in long-term memory may be encoded both verbally and visually. Verbal representations, however, play the major role. (11)

Dyslexia

A form of learning disability characterized by what is literally *word blindness*, which prevents the child from developing a reading level that would by typical for his/her IQ level and age. Dyslexia may be acquired, for example, either from a brain injury or from poor educational experiences, or it may possibly be inherited. (11, 20)

Early-Experience Position

A position taken by those researchers and theorists who stress the crucial importance of an individual's early environmental experiences in determining later adult characteristics. The early-experience proponents typically argue that the child goes through various time periods when certain cognitive and other skills can best be learned. Attempting to develop these skills either too early or too late can result in wasted effort on the part of the teacher and possible permanent damage to the student. (4)

Ebbinghaus, Hermann (1850–1909)

The father of the experimental study of learning. Ebbinghaus spent many hours memorizing long lists of nonsense syllables. Later he would relearn the lists, and he measured his retention capacity on the basis of how much more quickly he could learn the lists the second time. This technique is known as the method of savings. He drew two major conclusions from this work:

1. Forgetting occurs at an uneven rate, most of what is forgotten being lost very quickly.

2. In learning new material it is more efficient to space the practice sessions rather than mass them together. (8)

Elaborative Rehearsal

Technique used for consolidating LTM information based on expanding, embellishing, and/or relating new information to other items or concepts already stored. (11)

Elkind, David

Researcher who has demonstrated the difference between concrete and formal operations in thinking. In discussing Stonehenge, for example, concrete thinkers are more impressed by a long list of facts than a theory in deciding whether Stonehenge was a fort or a temple. Elkind has also described the extreme forms of egocentric thinking, such as the imaginary audience and the personal fable that young adolescents often use. (5)

Embryo

The second stage of prenatal development, which for the human begins at two weeks after conception and lasts until about eight weeks after conception. During this stage the heart begins beating and sex organs, hands and feet, and all the internal organs are formed. At the end of the embryonic stage, the organism may be clearly identified as human. (3)

Empathy

The ability to realize, understand, and appreciate another person's feelings, or the ability to experience and "feel" the world through another person's eyes. Also, one of the three necessary and sufficient conditions for the promotion of learning, according to Carl Rogers. The other two are unconditional positive regard and congruence. (12)

Enactive Representation

Stage of congitive development and method of communication introduced by Jerome Bruner. During this, Bruner's first, stage of development, the child thinks and communicates with "wordless messages." Young children understand things best at the action level: A chair is to sit on, a spoon is to eat with, and so on. Even adults may, and perhaps should, revert to this level of thinking when learning a new skill, especially a motor skill. An adept ski or tennis instructor often will ask the student (child or adult) to imitate his or her actions physically, rather than just teach at the verbal level. (9)

Encoding

In the information processing model, the creation of memory traces, or abstractions, based on the salient features of the incoming information. The encoded information, which represents the external object or event, can thus be used for storage. (11)

Engram

Term used, usually by the physiological psychologists, to denote the hypothesized physical location of memory. (11)

Epigenetic Principle

Erik Erikson's notion that human beings have an inherent or inborn tendency to grow. It represents the ground plan for personality development through the psychosexual stages he describes. Each stage involves the resolution of opposite tendencies; successful resolution involves acquisition of a sequence of virtues—hope, will, purpose, competence, and fidelity—from birth through adolescence. (6)

Episodic Memory

Information contained in LTM that holds past episodes in one's life and is stored in the form of images. (11)

Equilibration

Term used by Jean Piaget to describe the motivational force for arriving at an adjustment between the twin concepts of assimilation and accommodation. Equilibration makes it possible for the child to go on to new, higher-level assimilation and accommodation. (5)

Erikson, Erik H.

German-born personality theorist who studied under Sigmund Freud at the Psychoanalytic Institute in Vienna. Erikson has been in the United States since 1936, and he has taught human development at Harvard University. Although his theory of personality development has its obvious roots in psychoanalytic theory, it is definitely not just "warmed over" Freud. His theory describes stages of personality development extending throughout life, though there is special emphasis on childhood. The focus is always on the normal and healthy personality. Erikson sees development progressing through eight stages, each typifying a particular crisis. Through the attempt to resolve these crises, the healthy personality emerges. (The stages are sequential, and when a healthy adjustment to a particular crisis does not occur, it is even more difficult to resolve a similar crisis

at a later stage.) The mature personality should have a sense of identity, and although the climax of this search occurs during adolescence (identity crisis), residues of the conflict can emerge throughout life. (6)

Ethology

The study of the behavior of organisms in the organism's natural habitat. Unlike experimental psychologists, who often study animal behavior in artificial, laboratory situations, ethologists (like Konrad Lorenz) study behavior in the animal's natural environment. Ethologists have introduced such terms as *innate releasing mechanism* and *imprinting* into the working vocabulary of psychologists. *See also* Lorenz, Konrad. (2)

Exclusion

Method of dealing with those who do not conform to social expectations of normalcy by exile, physical avoidance, or even murder. (20)

Extinction

Term used by conditioning theorists to describe a forgetting process in which the stimulus-response associations are eroded. In classical conditioning, extinction occurs when the conditioned stimulus is presented without being followed by the unconditioned stimulus. Extinction is then defined as occurring when the magnitude of the conditioned response returns to zero. In operant conditioning extinction occurs when the conditioned operant is allowed to occur without being followed by a reinforcing stimulus. Extinction is defined as occurring when the rate of responding returns to its preconditioned level (operant level). (8)

Extrinsic Motives

Those motives that are driven by the push of external reinforcers. Such motives are often considered necessary in order to initiate the learning process. *See also* Intrinsic motives. (18)

Factor Approach

A mathematically based model of intelligence in which correlational statistical methods are used for determining the components of intelligence. Among the most widely known factor approaches are those of Charles Spearman (two factors), Louis Thurstone (seven factors), and J. P. Guilford (120 factors). (16)

Fear of Success

A basic fear that may be due to the perceived unpleasant side effects brought about by being overly successful. Women appear to be especially prone to this condition due to a conscious or unconscious belief that success may make them appear to lose their femininity. (18)

Fetus

The third stage of prenatal development, lasting from the eighth week after conception until birth. The fetus is definitely a behaving organism, and its behavior can be studied. (3)

Flanders, Ned

American educational psychologist known primarily for his work on defining teacher effectiveness. Using the concepts of direct and indirect teaching, Flanders found that despite various subject matters, different grade levels, and different school settings, teachers using indirect teaching styles were producing higher levels of student learning than were direct teachers. (12)

Flashbulb Memory

A person's extremely vivid recollection of an event or situation that was etched into long-term memory because the individual was in a highly charged emotional state. (11)

Formal Discipline (Theory)

Early educational theory that stressed a curriculum designed to discipline the mind. The theory rested on the assumption that the mind was like a muscle and must be systematically exercised until it became so strong it could learn and understand almost any new material. Subjects such as logic, Latin, and Greek were included in the curriculum not because they were thought to have any immediate practical use, but because they were thought to strengthen the mind. The theory of formal discipline originated in ancient Greece and remained in vogue until the early twentieth century. It was finally challenged by three psychologists, William James, E. L. Thorndike, and Charles Judd, whose independent studies in the area of positive transfer refuted the formal discipline position. *See also* Transfer. (1)

Formal-Operations Stage

A stage of cognitive development, according to Jean Piaget, occurring during early adolescence. The period of formal operations (eleven to sixteen years) is the last of Piaget's stages and is characterized by the youth's ability to develop full, formal patterns of thinking based on abstract symbolism. The youth is able to reason things out logically at the abstract level, develop symbolic meanings, and generalize to other situations. This is the highest level of thinking and, according to Piaget, must await the maturation of certain structures in the brain for its full development. (5)

Four-Way Agenda of Teaching

The four elements that are always interacting during the process of education. They include (1) student characteristics, (2) the subject matter, (3) teaching strategies, and (4) teacher characteristics. (1)

Frank, Lawrence K. (1890–1968)

The researcher who reviewed a wide variety of cross-cultural methods of childrearing and found that too often adults attempt to remold children as if they are midget-sized adults. (6)

Freud, Sigmund (1856–1939)

Perhaps psychology's single most famous figure, he originated the school of thought called *psychoanalysis*. A physician in Vienna, Freud treated patients with "nervous disorders" during the day and wrote down his thoughts and observations at night. From these observations and his own genius for speculating came the theory of psychoanalysis. It stated that all behavior is motivated and that the motives are usually hidden from the individual, thus causing much behavior to appear to be irrational. The basic source of energy for these motives is the libido, or pleasure-seeking drive. Freud described the personality as being composed of three structural components: id, ego, and superego. Most human anxiety results from inner conflict among these three components. Adult personality disorders can always be traced to and found to be directly caused by childhood trauma and anxiety. *See also* Psychoanalytic theory. (6)

Frustration-Aggression Hypothesis

Neil Miller and John Dollard's theory to explain aggressive behavior. The hypothesis states that aggression results from environmental causes. When a person is frustrated, or experiences goal blockage, aggressive behavior results. (17)

Fuller, Frances (1918–1975)

Educational researcher who created a framework for tracing the type and level of personal concern exhibited by teachers during their early experiences in the classroom.

Among other things, she outlined three general levels of concern: self, management, and impact. (14)

Functional Autonomy

Concept introduced by Gordon Allport and used to explain the great number of human motives for which no biological needs seem present. A means to an end becomes an end in itself, and an acquired motive comes to function independently (autonomously). The resulting motive comes to have a life of its own and is no longer dependent on its biological base. (18)

Furth, Hans

A leading contemporary Piagetian theorist interested in the interaction between "new" learning and "old" learning. He used the example of the young German boy and the church that looked like a house to point to what he called a *knowledge disturbance*. He traced the process of such knowledge disturbances to show how a child gradually develops more complex cognitive structures to take in new and strange information. (5)

Gage, Nate

One of the first educational researchers to accumulate a series of studies on teacher effectiveness. He was able to create the first scientific basis for the art of teaching and to show that different modes work better at the secondary than at the elementary level. (12)

Galloway, Charles

One of the first researchers to study teaching from the nonverbal perspective of body language. He demonstrated that clusters of teacher nonverbal behaviors either facilitate or impair student learning so that teacher actions in the classroom may speak louder than words. (12)

Galton, Francis (1822–1911)

Considered to be the "father of intelligence testing." Galton put together the first series of tests designed to measure intellectual ability. Although his tests seem somewhat naive by modern standards, his emphasis on the relationship between sensory ability and intellect foreshadows much of today's research on the importance of sensory stimulation in determining cognitive growth. Galton assumed that intelligence was dependent on the quality of the human sensory apparatus, and so his tests measured such abilities as reaction time, visual and auditory range, and sensory acuity. Galton firmly believed that one's sensory apparatus was largely inherited. Thus, the testing movement, from its very inception, sided with nature in the nature-nurture debate. Galton emphasized individual differences and, more than any other person, set psychology on the road to quantifying its data. (2)

Gardner, Howard

Psychologist and intelligence expert who has proposed that intelligence, rather than being made up of a single, underlying factor, is really composed of a variety of different traits. He suggests that there are at least seven different types of intelligence: linguistic, logicomathematical, spatial, musical, bodily kinesthetic, interpersonal, and intrapersonal. (16)

Gene

The fundamental unit of analysis in genetics. The gene is a tiny particle that contains hereditary information. Genes are located in the chromosomes of each of the body's cells and are composed of rather large organic molecules called *nucleic acids*. (3)

Genetics

The study of the rules and lawful relationships of heredity. Geneticists are interested in how inherited characteristics are transmitted from generation to generation. They study both the continuity and the variation of traits across generations. The first studies in genetics were those of Gregor Mendel (1860s), who determined that the color of flowers could be predicted from one generation to the next. Thomas Hunt Morgan (1910s) studied the fruit fly and suggested that genes are arranged in the chromosomes in an ordered sequence. James Watson and Francis Crick won the Nobel prize in 1962 for their pioneering work on genetic composition. A subfield in genetics, called *behavior genetics*, is of special interest to psychologists since it studies the effects of genotype on behavior. *See also* Behavior genetics. (3)

Genotype

The genetic properties of the organism, often latent (as opposed to the phenotype, which is always expressed). A brown-eye individual may carry a gene for blue eyes (genotype), but since the gene for brown eyes is dominant over the gene for blue eyes, that particular genotype would not be expressed. (3)

Gestalt Psychology

A school of thought maintaining that the organized whole, configuration, or totality of psychological experience should be the proper object of study. Founded in Germany by Max Wertheimer in the early 1900s, gestalt psychology's first interest was in the field of perception. Later, under Wolfgang Kohler's direction, studies were done in the area of learning, and, under Kurt Lewin's direction, in the area of motivation. Gestalt psychologists tend to emphasize cognitive processes in the study of learning. They stress that true understanding occurs only through the reorganization of ideas and perceptions, not through memorization or conditioning. *See also* Wertheimer, Max. (8)

Gilligan, Carol

Researcher who has charged that Lawrence Kohlberg's stage theory of moral development and his scoring system are biased against women. Extensive reviews of the research literature, however, have cast some doubt on her position. (7)

Goddard, Henry H. (1866–1957)

Early psychologist and strong hereditarian who researched the Kallikak family and concluded that intelligence was as directly controlled by heredity as was eye color. Goddard studied at Clark University under the tutelage of G. Stanley Hall and was the first psychologist to translate the Binet intelligence test into English. (2)

Great-Leader Theory

Theory that leadership is a function of personal traits rather than the social situation. Great leaders possess just the right blend of looks, personality traits, and intellect to be almost automatically thrust into power roles, regardless of the times in which they live. (17)

Greene, Maxine

A philosopher of education who conceptualizes the teacher's role as a "stranger"—that is, he or she is to be with pupils in the classroom but also apart from them in order to nurture their growth toward freedom. Greene is the leading exponent for the positive existential theory of educational practice. Self-direction and democratic values represent her dual goals for teaching and learning. (1)

Group Dynamics

A subfield of social psychology that studies the processes that create and maintain group life. Group dynamics has as its goal the systematic understanding of group functioning, the discovery of general laws concerning group properties, and the application of those laws to enhance group life. Generally, there are two broad positions within the field of group dynamics—the basic research wing and the applied wing. (17)

Group Tests of Intelligence

Tests sometimes called "paper-and-pencil tests" and designed to measure large groups of individuals at a single sitting. Originally devised during World War I and called the Army Alpha test, the group test became immediately popular, both because of its ease of administration and low cost. Many psychologists believe the group tests to have less validity than the individually administered tests. (16)

Guilford, J. P.

A specialist in the area of statistics and measurement theory, Guilford has constructed, through the use of factor analysis, a model of the "structure of intellect." Guilford concluded that intelligence is not just a single trait but is made up of a series of distinctly different modes of thought. He has grouped similar modes together into appropriate categories, and his famous phrase "the three faces of intellect" suggests that intelligence can be separated into three categories: operation, content, and product. Each of these three categories contains a further series of dimensions. So far, he has identified a total of seventy separate traits of intelligence (out of a possible 120 traits provided for by his model). Among the traits identified so far are those responsible for what is usually called creativity. (16)

Guthrie, Edwin R. (1886–1959)

Behaviorist and learning theorist in the tradition of John B. Watson. Guthrie believed that all learning could be explained on the basis of a single law—the law of contiguity: Learning resulted from the contiguous association of stimuli and responses. He also believed that forgetting was entirely the result of retroactive inhibition. (8)

Haberman, Martin

Investigator who examined the variety of teaching strategies that research has found to be effective with mainstreamed children. Surprisingly, he concluded that between 75 to 85 percent of the time, teachers should use regular teaching strategies that are effective with all children. There is only a very small body of highly specialized teaching methods specifically appropriate for special-education children. (20)

Handicapping Conditions

A physical, mental, emotional, or other condition recognized by Public Law 94–142. The law specifies nine categories and says that education must be provided for all those in these categories until graduation from high school or until the age of twenty-one. Recent study has shown that about 92 percent of the handicapping conditions are grouped into four high-incidence types: (1) learning disability, (2) speech problems (e.g., stuttering), (3) mental retardation, and (4) emotional disturbance. All other handicapping conditions total just over 6 percent and include multiple handicaps, physical impairment, deafness, visual impairment, and deaf-blind conditions. The main difficulty with this classification is that the validity and accuracy of the diagnosis is lowest in the areas of high incidence and vice versa. (20)

Harlow, Harry F.

An American psychologist who has spent most of his professional career at the primate lab of the University of Wisconsin. Harlow's research, usually on rhesus monkeys, has shed light on many important topics in psychology. Perhaps his three most famous studies were on (1) surrogate mothers—in which frightened young monkey's preferred cloth-covered, cuddly surrogates rather than wire-framed surrogates that delivered food; (2) learning sets—in which monkeys solved oddity problems by developing solution rules or strategies rather than on the basis of either insight or the slow accumulation of stimulus-response associations; and (3) curiosity drive—in which monkeys exhibited a motive to manipulate novel items in their environment despite the fact that no primary reinforcement was presented. (18)

Hartshorne, Hugh (1885–1967)

Researcher who, together with Mark May, studied the process of value inculcation with a large sample of children in the 1920s. The results exploded the myth that values could be ingrained in children. Hartshorne and May found almost no relationship between character-training programs and how children behaved in tempting situations. (7)

Head Start: Perry Preschool Program

A longitudinal study of the effects of Head Start, a government-funded preschool program designed to enhance the intellectual potential of disadvantaged children. Measures were taken on nineteen-year-old youths who as children had been in the Head Start program, and these were compared with measures taken on a control group of youths who had not attended Head Start. In virtually every measurement category, Head Start was found to have produced positive effects, ranging from an increase in academic achievement to a decrease in criminal activity. (4)

Hebb, Donald O. (1904–1985)

Canadian physiological psychologist Hebb who, in *Organization of Behavior* (1949), revolutionized psychological thought, especially in the United States. In this work Hebb dared to infer the existence of some possible physiological correlates of behavior. He stated that there was a relationship between intelligence and the way brain cells are organized. This organization occurs first at the level of cell assemblies, then as phase sequences, and finally in the total organization of the brain cells. Hebb also proposed a distinction between Intelligence A and Intelligence B, the former being one's innate potential, and the latter, one's present ability level on the intellectual growth continuum. *See also* A/S ratio; Cell assembly. (4)

Heritability

The proportion of the total variability of a given trait in a population that is due to genetic as opposed to environmental factors. Heritability is expressed as a value running between 1.00 and zero. Thus, regarding measured intelligence, if all the variation in IQ scores in a given population was due to genetic factors, the heritability of IQ would be 1.00. If all the variability was due to environmental factors, the heritability would be zero. The concept of heritability applies only to a particular population of a single generation under one set of environmental conditions. (16)

Herrnstein, Richard

Harvard psychologist who has been critical of the environmental explanation of intellectual growth. Herrnstein insists that American psychology has overlooked the importance of genetic factors in determining intelligence. He has also expressed reservations about the value of early-intervention programs such as Head Start. (4)

Hidden Agenda

Basic teacher attitudes toward the instructional process, perceptions of students, and self-knowledge that have been found to have a major influence on student learning. The influence can be either positive or negative. (14)

Homozygosity

An organism (diploid) that carries identical alleles at one or several genetic sites. (3)

Horner, Matina

Professor at Harvard University and, since 1972, president of Radcliffe College. Horner achieved almost instant recognition in the area of the psychology of women's attitudes and motives. She contends that society often conditions women both to expect and want to fail. Since motivational differences between the sexes are a result of social pressures, educators must revise their ideas, practices, and policies concerning young women in schools and colleges. Horner's own career is a model of academic achievement. (18)

Hunt, David

Researcher who, in applying developmental concepts to teachers and pupils, classified both groups according to conceptual level of development (CL). Hunt found that pupils' learning styles varied by CL stage according to preferences for the amount of structure provided. He also found certain teaching patterns (labeled A, B, and C) that were reflective of the CL stages of teachers. Teaching effectiveness was partly defined as the ability to "read and flex" with pupils and was correlated particularly with the higher conceptual levels. (13)

Hunter, Madeline

Theorist who outlined a systematic approach to lesson planning. Hunter suggested a sequence of (1) anticipatory set, (2) stated objectives, (3) input, (4) modeling, (5) checking, (6) guided practice, and (7) independent practice. It is not necessary to use all these steps, but independent practice should be used as a guide to assessing the quality of the final product and modifying a plan. (13)

Hydraulic Assessment

Term used by Maynard Reynolds to refer to shifts in special-education classifications for political or economic reasons rather than on the basis of any valid assessment. The students labeled as emotionally disturbed increased by 36 percent over a thirteen-year span, while those labeled mentally retarded declined by exactly the same percentage. (20)

Icon

The visual image of a stimulus held in the sensory register for only a brief duration. (11)

Iconic Representation

Jerome Bruner's second stage of cognitive growth and mode of communication, the first stage being the enactive level. At the iconic level, objects become conceivable without resorting to muscular action. The child can now visualize

an object or concept. He or she possesses an image that no longer depends on action. The use of pictures and diagrams illustrates the iconic mode of communication. (9)

Imprinting

A special form of learning that is acquired early in life, usually during a very specific time interval; that is triggered by a releasing stimulus; and that is not reversible. Konrad Lorenz demonstrated this phenomenon by presenting himself as a moving stimulus to a group of newly hatched goslings. The goslings then imprinted on Lorenz himself and followed him around as though he were the mother goose. *See also* Critical periods; Lorenz, Konrad. (2)

Individual Differences

The fact, first noted scientifically by Sir Francis Galton, that people tend to differ on a whole host of measured traits. Investigators disagree regarding the causes of these variations in abilities, traits, and performance measures, but there is no question as to their existence. (15)

Individualized Education Plan (IEP)

A plan of instruction mandated by Public Law 94-142 for all children classified in any category of special education. A team establishes a series of educational goals and time tables for each child. The plan is reviewed on a regular basis. At each point in the child's schooling, he or she must be placed in the least restrictive environment that is consistent with achievable educational attainments. This may vary from a regular classroom to other environments that offer much greater structure, such as a self-contained special class or even a special residence. (20)

Inductive Fallacy

An error in logic resulting from overgeneralizing on the basis of too few observations. The inductive fallacy results when one assumes that all members of a class have a certain characteristic because one member of that class has it. It would be fallacious to assume that all Mongolians are liars on the basis of having met one Mongolian who was a liar. (15)

Information Processing

Theory of learning and remembering that is based on the computer as a model. Information is seen as flowing into and within the organism. The sense organs respond to incoming information, and it is passed along and encoded in the memory and nervous system. The encoded information may then be stored and processed and finally retrieved and acted on. As with the computer, there is information input, storage and/or processing, and output. (11)

Innate Releasing Mechanism (IRM)

Reflexive stimulus-response mechanism in which responses react to certain specific environmental stimuli. Used currently instead of the discredited term "instinct." Environmental inputs are said to automatically trigger a certain response or series of related responses. (2)

Insight

A suddenly realized solution to a problem, sometimes called the "A-ha! phenomenon." Introduced by Wolfgang Kohler, the concept of insight is used to explain the apparently spontaneous appearance of a solution to a problem. Insight results from the reorganization of ideas and perceptions rather than from simple trial-and-error behavior. The concept of insight is used typically by gestalt psychologists. (8)

Instinct Theory

A now-discredited theory that attempted to explain behavior by simply describing it and then calling it "instinctive." For example, humans were seen as going to war because of an "aggressive instinct," or forming groups because of a "gregarious instinct," or even twiddling thumbs because of a "thumb-twiddling instinct." Instinct theorists committed a logical error called the *nominal fallacy. See* Nominal fallacy. (2)

Intelligence

Widely varying definitions—from Wechsler's "global capacity of the individual to act purposefully, to think rationally, and to deal effectively with his environment" to E. G. Boring's positivistic definition of intelligence as simply that which an intelligence test measures. The problem with intelligence as a concept is that it cannot be directly observed. It must be inferred from behavior. Rather than *being intelligent,* one can be viewed as acting intelligently.

As a hypothetical construct, intelligence has come to mean higher-level thought processes, or intellectual abilities, as opposed to Francis Galton's original notion of acute sensory powers. Statistical studies of intelligence utilize the concept of measured intelligence, which is the score received on a standardized intelligence test. *See also* Intelligence quotient. (16)

Intelligence Quotient (IQ)

Originally, a measure of intelligence calculated by dividing a subject's mental age by the chronological age and multiplying by 100. That is, $IQ = MA/CA \times 100$. This is called the *ratio method* of obtaining an IQ.

More recently, IQ has been computed by the deviation method. One's deviation IQ is defined by one's relative standing among peers. The deviation IQ is computed on the basis of how far one's score deviates from the mean score obtained for the entire group of individuals of the same chronological age. This technique is based on the standard, or z-score, concept and assumes a normal distribution for each age group. (16)

Intrinsic Motives

Those motives that are sustained by internal factors—for example, the need for self-satisfaction. Learning that is based on intrinsic motivation has been found to be longer-lasting than that based on the more transitory push of external reinforcers. *See* Extrinsic motives. (18)

Introspection

A technique used for ferreting out psychology's data by having a subject look within himself or herself and then report all feelings, sensations, and images. This technique was the basic method for obtaining data in the days of Wilhelm Wundt and the structuralist school of psychology. J. B. Watson, the founder of behaviorism, attacked the use of introspection as being too subjective for an objective, scientific discipline like psychology. The technique is rarely used in psychology today. (8)

Invariant Sequence

The notion in developmental theories that development occurs in stages arranged in a sequence that moves in only one direction. Further, these stages cannot be skipped. The growth process is thus seen as a sequence of steps that must be taken one at a time. (7)

James, William (1842–1910)

America's first, and probably most revered, psychologist. James spent his entire academic lifetime at Harvard University, first as a student and later as a professor. Though he received an M.D. degree, James carved out his career in academe, being a professor of both psychology and philosophy. In 1876 he created and taught the first psychology course ever offered in the United States. In 1890 he published *Principles of Psychology*, a book that still provides today's reader with a relatively modern version of psychology, so great was his vision. Later, in his famous "Talks with Teachers," James turned his attention to the classroom teacher and pointed out that the entire enterprise of education is determined by the performance of the teacher in the classroom. James is credited with originating the school of functionalism in psychology, a school of thought interested not so much in what the elements of consciousness are but in what they are for. (1)

Jensen, Arthur R.

Researcher and professor of educational psychology whose special interest is IQ. Jensen's 1969 article "How Much Can We Boost IQ and Scholastic Achievement?" created a big stir in educational psychology because of its pronounced emphasis on genetic factors in the development of intellect. Jensen has been especially criticized for one of the implications of his article, namely, that the difference between the tested IQs of black and white children is a result of the genetic inferiority of the black children. (16)

Joyce, Bruce

Theorist who conceptualizes effective teaching methods as a repertoire of different teaching models. Joyce suggests that teachers should deliberately employ a variety of modes. Exclusive reliance on any one mode will lead to boredom for both pupils and teachers. (12)

Just Community

System, developed by Lawrence Kohlberg and Ralph Mosher, in which a subgroup of high school students is organized on the basis of Stage V principles. The students and staff jointly determine and carry out all school rules. Research indicates that such communities have had some success in dealing with the usual problems of discipline and that levels of academic achievement increase while drug use and absenteeism decrease. (19)

Kallikak Family

Case name (taken from the Greek words for good and bad) for a family that was studied in great detail by Henry Goddard during the early years of this century. Goddard traced back two branches of the Kallikak family, both branches having originally been created by the Revolutionary War soldier Martin Kallikak. One branch, the "good Kallikaks," resulted from Martin Kallikak's marriage, while the "bad Kallikaks" were a result of Martin's affair with a barmaid. Goddard found that the two branches were significantly different in virtually every way, especially in

regard to intelligence: Most good Kallikaks were superior and most bad Kallikaks retarded. This "good seed-bad seed" account is regarded as totally fanciful by today's students of genetics. (2)

Kohlberg, Lawrence (1927–1987)

Psychologist whose Ph.D. thesis, written at the University of Chicago, outlined a theory of how moral reasoning develops in children. His theory of moral development states that children proceed through a series of developmental stages—preconventional, conventional, and postconventional. Like Jean Piaget's theory of cognitive development, Kohlberg's theory sees moral development occurring in an invariant sequence, with each stage qualitatively different from the preceding stage. *See also* Moral development. (7)

Kohler, Wolfgang, (1887–1967)

One of the founders of gestalt psychology. Having been a student of Max Wertheimer's at the University of Frankfurt, just before World War I, Kohler spent the war years in the Canary Islands, where he performed gestalt psychology's most famous animal learning study. He discovered, while studying apes, that some learning occurs on the basis of insight rather than solely on the basis of the slow accumulation of specific associations. Insight, or the "A-ha!" phenomenon, is learning that occurs suddenly as a new relationship among perceptions is discovered. *See also* Insight. (8)

Law of Effect

One of E. L. Thorndike's main laws of learning. It states that when an association between a stimulus and response is followed by a satisfying state of affairs, the association (or connection) is strengthened. When the association is followed by an annoying state of affairs, it is weakened. In brief, reward strengthens and punishment weakens any connection between stimuli and responses. In a later version of the law, Thorndike soft-pedaled the importance of punishment as a weakening agent. Thorndike's law of effect is considered by many psychologists to be the cornerstone on which B. F. Skinner built his system of operant conditioning. (8)

Law of Exercise

One of E. L. Thorndike's three main laws of learning. It states that the more frequently a stimulus-response connection occurs, the stronger the resulting association and, hence, the stronger the learning. The law was later amended to incorporate the importance of the consequences of the action; thus, practice without knowledge of results is not nearly as effective as when the consequences become known to the learner. (8)

Law of Readiness

One of E. L. Thorndike's three main laws of learning. It states that learning occurs when neurological conduction units are primed or ready to conduct. The reference here is to momentary readiness rather than maturational readiness. (8)

Learned Helplessness

The appearance of helplessness that is characteristic of some handicapped children. The term, from Martin Seligman, suggests the need for teachers to pay careful attention to such children in order to prevent them from being caught in the syndrome, especially since some of the children can be expert performers. Setting reasonable objectives in a firm yet supportive atmosphere will avoid reinforcing learned helplessness. (20)

Learning

A very general term referring to a process that leads to a relatively permanent change in behavior resulting from past experience. Thus, such activities as accquiring physical skills, memorizing poems, acquiring attitudes and prejudices, or even tics and mannerisms are all examples of learning. Learning may be conscious or unconscious, adaptive or maladaptive, overt or covert. Although the learning process is typically measured on the basis of a change in performance, most psychologists agree that an accompanying change occurs within the nervous system. Though there are a great many theories and explanations concerning learning, there is general agreement regarding its definition. (8)

Learning Curve

A graphic presentation of learning performance, with the measure of learning being plotted on the vertical axis and the amount of practice on the horizontal axis. Though learning curves take many shapes, depending on what is being learned and under what conditions, the classical, or ideal, curve is negatively accelerating. That is, acceleration (improved performance) becomes less and less as the amount of practice increases. When there is no further increase in performance, the curve levels off into a plateau. (10)

Learning Sets

Concept developed by Harry Harlow and used as a modern explanation for the gestalt term *insight*. Harlow insists that what the gestaltists had viewed as insight does not come about as a sudden reorganization of perceptions but rather occurs on the basis of learning how to learn, or the learning of general rules. The learning set does not occur "in a flash" but takes many trials and much experience in which to develop. The concept of learning sets is also in opposition to the straight stimulus-response learning model in that the learning set involves the development of a learning strategy rather than the slow accumulation of stimulus-response associations. A learning set is a form of nonspecific transfer. (10)

Locus of Control

Concept that identifies the type of personal control used by an individual. When the locus of control is internal, individuals view themselves as personally in charge of their own destinies. When the locus of control is external, the person feels he or she is at the mercy of external circumstances. (17)

Logicomathematical (LM) Learning

Concept developed by Jean Piaget to describe a form of learning that results not from the physical environment's acting on the learner but from the actions of the learner on the environment. LM learning is the result of an individual's continuous experience of organizing and reorganizing actions—a process that leads to the goal of understanding. Piaget says that LM learning is internally motivated. The discovery of a new relationship is self-rewarding. *See also* Physical (P) learning. (9)

Long-Term Memory (LTM)

In the information processing model, the second of the two main storage systems. Information that is in short-term memory may, under certain conditions, be passed along for processing and consolidation into a more permanent storage site, long-term memory. Long-term memory has the potential for holding encoded information for a lifetime. (11)

Lorenz, Konrad (1903–1989)

Austrian ethologist and winner of the Nobel Prize in medicine in 1973. Lorenz insisted that to understand animal behavior one must study the animal in its natural habitat, not in the artificial confines of the laboratory. In 1937 Lorenz first described the phenomenon of imprinting, a form of learning that dramatically illustrates the interaction of heredity, environment, and time in the determination of behavioral characteristics. Lorenz was able to revive the long-discredited instinct theory and, by carefully analyzing the biological mechanisms involved, to make the theory scientifically respectable. *See also* Imprinting. (2)

MacDonald, Robert

Educational specialist and teacher trainer who has outlined several new techniques for dealing with individual differences in classroom discipline. He particularly emphasizes *initiating* and *preventive* methods, with *corrective* techniques as a last resort. (19)

Mainstreaming

Placement of persons who might be classified as handicapped within the "mainstream" of society. Exceptional and/or retarded children are not placed in special classes but are kept in regular classrooms. Mainstreaming has been the policy since passage of Public Law 94-142. (20)

Maintenance Rehearsal

Technique used for consolidating LTM information based on rote memorization and repetition. (11)

Marcia, James

Educational psychologist who analyzed the process of identity formation during late adolescence by identifying four separate and distinct identity "statuses": foreclosure, diffusion, moratorium, and achievement. (6)

Massed Learning

Learning that occurs in massive doses, without a break, as opposed to spaced learning. Studies show that for many activities, especially motor activities, massed learning is less efficient than spaced learning. (10)

Matching and Mismatching

Method of teaching that involves discovering a student's cognitive stage of development, matching content and structure to that stage, and gradually introducing mismatches to stimulate development one stage up. Teachers should be alert, though, to the fact that some pupils may experience anxiety when new material is introduced or when going through developmental transitions. Also, some pupils may be "advanced thinkers" in certain subjects, though not in others. Watching for such variability in pupil responses can guide teachers in changing the level of structure when necessary. (13)

May, Mark (1891–1973)

See Hartshorne, Hugh

McClelland, David

Harvard psychologist interested in achievement motivation. McClelland has studied the problems of underachievement from the point of view of both the individual and the entire society. His studies indicate that the achievement motive, or "achievement syndrome," is composed of three major factors:

1. The ability to compete with some standard of excellence in mind
2. The ability to take moderate risks
3. The ability to make use of concrete feedback

Mean

A statistical measure of central tendency, found by adding all the scores in a distribution and dividing by the number of scores. It is also called the *arithmetic average*. (15)

Measurement

The assigning of numbers to observations according to certain rules. The rule used to assign the numbers determines which scale of measurement is being employed—nominal, ordinal, interval, or ratio. (15)

Measures of Central Tendency

A statistical term used for describing the typical, middle, or central score in a distribution of scores. Measures of central tendency are used when the researcher wants to describe a group as a whole with a view toward characterizing that group on the basis of its most common measurement. The researcher wishes to know what score best represents a group of differing scores. The three measures of central tendency are the mean (or arithmetic average), the median (or the midpoint of the distribution), and the mode (the most frequently occurring score in the distribution). (15)

Median

A statistical measure of central tendency found by identifying the middlemost point in a distribution of ordered values. (15)

Menarche

The time of the first menstruation, which signals the onset of puberty and/or adolescence among females. The girl who is secure in her sexual identity and has had adult support and guidance is less likely to feel anxiety when reaching this important developmental milestone. (3)

Mendel, Gregor (1822–1884)

Austrian monk whose work with the flower color of garden peas led to the theory of genetics that states that some genes are dominant and some recessive. When paired with a recessive gene, the dominant gene is the one whose characteristics will be expressed. (3)

Mental Age

Term first used by Alfred Binet as the unit for measuring intelligence. Binet defined mental age in terms of the age at which a given number of test items are passed by an average child. If, for example, the average six-year-old could correctly answer a certain number of items, then any other child correctly answering the same number of items would be assigned at least a mental age of six. (16)

Metacognition

Internal awareness of cognitive abilities, including self-awareness of both learning and retrieval strategies. If cognition is learning's pilot, then metacognition is the copilot. (11)

Milgram, Stanley (1933–1986)

Researcher who studied, among other subjects, human aggression and conformity. In one series of studies, Milgram asked subjects to deliver increasing amounts of electric shock to another person. He found that almost two-thirds of those tested were willing to risk killing someone they perceived to be a fellow subject. When tested in groups, however, only about 10 percent of the subjects pushed the shock lever all the way. Milgram interepreted this behavior on the basis of the liberating effects of conformity and group pressure on individual behavior. Milgram was professor of social psychology at the City University of New York. Milgram's experiments also demonstrated the relationships between Kohlberg's stages and moral development. Most subjects at the conventional and preconventional levels were willing to follow orders and administer seemingly painful electric shocks. (7)

Miller, Alan

Researcher who has reviewed a large number of studies that support the idea that pupils at more complex conceptual levels benefit from indirect instruction while those at lower levels need more direct methods. Thus, teacher methods and content should vary in accord with pupils' attributes. (13)

Milwaukee Project

A program directed by Rick Heber whose aim was to increase the intellectual abilities of slum-raised children born of low-IQ parents. Working with the children almost from the day of birth, Heber's staff at the Infant Education Center was able to increase the IQs of these culturally deprived children by what appear to be significant amounts. (4)

Mnemonic Devices

Memory aids used to increase retention powers. Mnemonic devices typically utilize one of the following learning strategies: (1) visual imagery, (2) rhyming, and (3) associations with past learning. Using the word *homes* for recalling the names of the Great Lakes (Huron, Ontario, Michigan, Erie, and Superior) is an example of a mnemonic device based on association with past learning. (11)

Mode

A statistical measure of central tendency found by identifying the most frequently occurring score in a distribution of scores. (15)

Modeling

Concept used in Bandura's social learning theory. Learning can occur not only through response conditioning but also through modeling, which is the imitation of the behavior of others. Learning by modeling can occur even when the imitative responses are not themelves being directly reinforced. *See also* Social learning theory. (10)

Monozygotic (MZ) Twins

Identical twins that have identical genetic backgrounds. They result from the fertilization of a single egg, which then divides. This provides for two individuals having precisely the same genetic makeup (3).

Montessori, Maria (1870–1952)

Italian educator, psychologist, and physician. Montessori was one of the first theorists to stress the developmental nature of humans in an evolutionary setting. Her approach to education was based on her work first with mentally retarded children and later with culturally deprived children living in the slums of Rome. Her educational technique, now called the Montessori method, stressed sensory training in a prepared environment. She insisted on the importance of early experience in cognitive development, and although her approach was rejected by most American behaviorists, it is now receiving renewed attention by serious educational psychologists. (20)

Moral Development

The process whereby children come to adopt guiding principles of right and wrong and achieve the ability to resist the temptations of unacceptable conduct. The view that morality develops in a series of growth stages originated in the work of Jean Piaget, who believed the development of moral stages was similar to cognitive development. One of the leading representatives of this view was Lawrence Kohlberg, who saw moral development occurring in a series of stages: preconventional, conventional, and postconventional. Like Piaget, Kohlberg described moral development as occurring in an invariant sequence, with each stage qualitatively different from the preceding stage. *See also* Kohlberg, Lawrence. (7)

Moratorium

Erik Erikson's term for a stage of identity formation during late adolescence. It is thought to be a time for possible experimentation, which precedes a commitment to an adult career. (6)

Motivation

A general psychological term used to explain behavior initiated by needs and directed toward a goal. Motives may be biogenic (that is, stemming from tissue needs within the organism) or acquired (that is, learned through interaction with the environment, especially the social environment). Almost all personality theorists have developed their own lists of important human motives, and great debates have occurred over which motives are of greatest importance or which can rightfully be called universal. Among learning theorists, Jerome Bruner makes much of the principle of motivation, assuming that almost all children have a built-in "will to learn." (18)

Motivational Conflicts

Conflicts that result when individuals seek a number of goals, one (or some) of which may be antagonistic to others. Those conflicts that most affect the lives of school-age children are (1) the need for independence versus the need for dependence, (2) internal sexual needs versus society's demand to leave those needs unsatisfied, and (3) internal feelings of aggression versus society's rule that such feelings not be directly expressed. (18)

Motives

Activated needs (drives) that are directed toward or away from some specified goal. (18)

Nature-Nurture Controversy

Debate over which component, nature (heredity) or nurture (environment), is more influential in determining behavior. In psychology the behaviorists consistently argued on behalf of nurture, and the intelligence testers favored nature. Educational psychology has long been the battleground on which this issue has been fought, since the psychologists primarily concerned with the issue were the learning theorists (largely behaviorists) and measurement practitioners. (2)

Need Hierarchy

Theory proposed by Abraham Maslow that suggests that humans place their needs on the following universal, order-of-importance scale: (1) physiological needs, (2) safety needs, (3) love needs, (4) esteem needs, and (5) self-actualizing needs. (18)

Needs

The part of the motivational cycle seen as deficits that lie within the individual. These may be physiological (e.g., the need for food) or psychological (e.g., the need for approval). (18)

Negative Discipline Techniques

Inhumane methods of classroom discipline, such as brute physical force, aversive conditioning, and scapegoating, that do not generally produce longlasting results of a positive nature. (19)

Negative Reinforcement

Any stimulus whose *removal* increases the rate of responding. If a rat is in a cage with an electrified floor grid and the electricity is turned off only after the rat presses a lever, the rate of the lever-pressing responses will tend to increase dramatically. Unlike punishment, which reduces response rates, negative reinforcement often increases response rates even more quickly than positive reinforcement. (9)

Negative Transfer

When the learning of A inhibits the learning and retention of B. For example, learning to type by the hunt-and-peck method may create bad habits that make the later learning of touch typing more difficult. (10)

Negatively Accelerated (Intellectual) Growth Curve

A graph of the relationship between intellectual growth and age. Benjamin S. Bloom suggests that this relationship is negative—that is, as a child increases in age his or her potential for continued intellectual growth decreases. (4)

Nieto, Sonia

Educational psychologist who investigated the relationship between teacher expectations and racial or sexual bias. She advocates that schools and teachers set goals of increasing racial diversity in the staff and that the curriculum be restructured to include a specific focus on valuing diversity and pointing out the negative effects of racism and discrimination. (14)

Nominal Fallacy

A logical error resulting from the attempt to explain an event on the basis of a redescription of that same event. Saying that sleeping pills work because they have dormative power or maintaining that people fight because they have aggressive instincts are examples of the nominal fallacy. The instinct theorists of the early 1900s built an entire system on the soft sands of the nominal fallacy. (2)

Nonverbal Behavior

Body language. Based largely on the theory of Charles Galloway and some research by Robert Rosenthal, the teacher's nonverbal behavior represents an important avenue for the transmission of teacher expectations. Galloway has shown how nonverbal behavior can promote or reduce pupil learning. Rosenthal has shown how his test (Profile of Nonverbal Sensitivity) can identify the channels for communicating how teachers really feel about their pupils. (12)

Normal Curve

A frequency distribution curve in which scores are plotted on the horizontal axis (X), and frequency of occurrence is plotted on the vertical axis (Y). The normal curve is a theoretical curve shaped like a bell, on which (1) most of the scores cluster around the center, and as we move away from the center in either direction there are fewer and fewer scores; (2) the scores fall into a symmetrical shape, each half of the curve being a mirror image of the other; (3) the mean, median, and mode all fall at precisely the same point, the center; and (4) there are constant area characteristics regarding the standard deviation. (15)

Normal Curve Equivalents (NCE)

A standardized set of scores (based on the normal curve) in which the mean is set at 50 and the standard deviation at approximately 21. (15)

Norm-Referenced Test

A test scored on the basis of how an individual's performance compares to the average performance of the group to which the individual is being compared. Most of the nationally standardized tests are norm-referenced. (15)

$O = H \leftrightarrow E \leftrightarrow T$

One of psychology's basic principles, which states that the organism is a product of heredity interacting with the environment interacting with time. (3)

Occam, William of (1300–1349)

British-born philosopher and Franciscan monk who warned that explanations are dangerous when they carry excess meaning. He believed that unnecessary assumptions should be avoided in order that explanations be kept as simple and straightforward as possible. This principle is now called the *law of parsimony*, and the concept of "shaving away" excess meaning is now referred to as using *Occam's razor*. Although primarily an empiricist, Occam tried to guide theorizing toward an objective approach that avoided both "wooly-headed" rationalism and "narrow-minded" empiricism. (1)

Ogbu, John

Educational anthropologist who documented the negative effects of the job ceiling upon the motivation for achievement by devalued groups such as African Americans, Native Americans, and Latinos. The program was set up by a successful entrepreneur, Eugene Land, in a New York City ghetto school. The results validated Ogbu's contention that removing the ceiling can dramatically increase academic motivation and achievement. (14)

Operant Conditioning

Form of conditioning, described by B. F. Skinner, in which the free operant is allowed to occur and is followed by a reinforcing stimulus that is, in turn, followed by an increased likelihood of the operant's occurring again. For optimum conditioning the reinforcing stimulus should follow the operant immediately. The rate of responding for a conditioned operant may jump dramatically over the preconditioned rate (operant level). (9)

Operant Level

The original, or preconditioned, rate of operant responding before any reinforcing stimuli have been introduced. If a rat happens to press the lever in a Skinner box four times an hour (without being reinforced), the operant level for that response is established at four per hour. Thus, the operant level is the rate at which the free operant is typically emitted prior to conditioning. (9)

Operants

Responses, according to B. F. Skinner, for which the original stimuli are either unidentified or nonexistent. The consequences of operant behavior can be observed even though the stimulus is not known. For example, if a rat presses the lever in a Skinner box and this results in reinforcement, an increase in operant rate will be observed despite the fact that no stimulus could be identified as initiating the original lever-pressing. In operant conditioning, reinforcement is contingent on the operant's first being emitted. The organism must in some way "operate" on the environment in order that the reinforcement will follow. Operant responding at one time was called *instrumental responding* by some psychologists. (9)

Oral Stage

First of Freud's psychosexual stages of development. During this stage, the baby lives through and loves through its mouth. This stage occurs between birth and about age eighteen months and permanently affects the child's later feelings of independence and trust. (6)

Paired-Associate Learning

A method used in the study of verbal learning and memory. A subject is presented with a list of word pairs (blue-moon, red-dog, play-toy, etc.) and is then tested by being asked to repeat the second word of the pair (response) each time the first word (stimulus) is introduced. This is one of the most common technique employed in the study of verbal learning, since many psychologists believe the learning of item pairs is a fundamental process in thinking and memory. (9)

Pavlov, Ivan (1849–1936)

Russian physiologist who won the Nobel Prize in medicine in 1904 for his work on digestive activity in dogs. His lasting fame, however, resulted from his observation that dogs salivated not only when meat powder was placed in their mouths but also when stimuli occurred well ahead of time (for example, when they heard Pavlov's footsteps coming down the stairs to the laboratory). Pavlov coined the phrase *conditioned reflex* to describe this phenomenon. Pavlov attempted to relate these behavioral observations to neural activity in the brain; for example, he introduced the concept of *cortical inhibition*, which he believed important in producing sleep. Though most modern psychologists consider his theory of neurological activity as something of a historical curio, his laboratory findings on conditioning are still of great importance. Pavlov's system of conditioning is now generally called *classical conditioning*. (8)

Pearson Product-Moment Correlation (Pearson *r*)

Statistical test introduced by Karl Pearson for showing the degree of relationship between two variables. It is used to test the hypothesis of association, that is, whether or not there is a linear relationship between two sets of measurements. The Pearson *r* can be calculated as follows:

$$r = \frac{\Sigma \, XY/N - (\overline{X})(\overline{Y})}{SD_x \, SD_y}$$

Computed correlations range from + 1.00 (perfect positive correlation) through zero to − 1.00 (perfect negative correlation). The further the Pearson *r* is from zero, whether in a positive or negative direction, the stronger the relationship. The Pearson *r* may be used for making better-than-chance predictions but may not be used for directly isolating causal factors. (15)

Percentile

The percentage of cases falling at or below a given score. Thus, if an individual were to score at the 95th percentile, that individual's score would exceed 95 percent of the scores of all persons taking that particular test. If test scores are normally distributed, and if the standard deviation of the distribution is known, percentile scores can easily be converted from the resulting *z* scores. (15)

Performance IQ

Term used by David Wechsler to describe the nonverbal component of intelligence. Wechsler believed that the Stanford-Binet test was too heavily loaded with verbal items, and thus when constructing his own test, Wechsler included a section designed to tap visual-motor abilities. The Wechsler IQ tests are scored on the basis of verbal IQ, performance IQ, and full-scale IQ. Scores in each of the three categories are computed. (16)

Periodization

Stages through which the brain passes in developing. This growth appears to parallel the Piagetian stages of cognitive development. As yet, there is no evidence to support the idea that learning cannot take place during the transitional phases of periodization. (5)

Permastore

That part of LTM, both semantic and episodic, which is said to be permanently stored. (11)

Peterson, Penelope

Researcher who has investigated attribute-treatment interaction (ATI). Peterson has shown the positive effects of systematically varying the amount of structure in teaching according to levels of pupil ability, anxiety, and attitudes toward learning. (13)

Phallic Stage

Third stage of personality development in Freud's theory of psychosexual development. During the phallic stage (ages three to seven years) the child focuses on the genital area. Conflict results as the child projects its sexual desires on the opposite-sexed parent and feels the fear of retaliation from the like-sexed parent. The conflict is resolved, at about age seven, when the child identifies with the like-sexed parent. The major crisis for the child during this stage centers on the struggle for sexual identification. (6)

Phenotype

The observable properties or the inherited traits that are expressed in the organism. (3)

Physical (P) Learning

Form of learning described by Jean Piaget that results from the action of the physical environment on the child rather than the actions of the child on the environment. Piaget's P learning (physical event acting on the learner) is very similar to B. F. Skinner's concept of operant conditioning. *See also* Logicomathematical (LM) learning. (9)

Physiological Motives

Motives that are based on the activation of physical needs, such as the need for food, water, sleep, sex, and warmth. (18)

Piaget, Jean (1896–1980)

Swiss psychologist who spent most of his adult life studying cognitive development. Through carefully detailed, hour-by-hour observations of the developing child, Piaget formulated a theory of how children learn to know or form concepts. Piaget stated that children learn concepts only as they go through a series of developmental stages that are sequential in nature and biologically based. Thinking processes are a biological extension of newborn motor processes. Piaget's developmental stages are (1) sensorimotor (birth to two years), (2) preoperational or intuitive (two to seven years), (3) concrete operations (seven to eleven years), and (4) formal operations (eleven to sixteen years). (5)

Plus One

The concept that students can understand reasoning keyed to their present stage and can also gradually be attracted to reasoning that is slightly more complex than their current level (one stage higher, or plus one). They show almost no understanding of reasoning two or more stages higher, however. (7)

Polygenic Inheritance

Inherited traits that result from the combination of large numbers of genes, as opposed to traits, such as eye and hair color, determined by a single pair of genes. (3)

Portfolio Approach

A system for evaluating student progress that is based on selected examples of a student's best work over a term or even an entire year of study. It is said that the portfolio approach places more emphasis on a student's overall accomplishments than on the ability merely to score well on a battery of tests. Typical portfolios include original poetry, plays, short stories, essays, and art projects. At the end of the term, the student hands over the portfolio to the teacher for evaluation. (15)

Positive Discipline Techniques

Humane methods for classroom discipline that are geared to the developmental stage of pupils. (19)

Positive Reinforcement

Any stimulus that, when added to the situation, increases the likelihood of the response's recurring. A pellet of food may be a positive reinforcer to a hungry rat only if it can be observed that the rat emits the same response (pressing the lever in the Skinner box) in order to get another pellet. In the classroom positive reinforcement may be provided by primary reinforcers, such as milk, cereal, or candy, or by conditioned reinforcers, such as gold stars, high grades, or social approval. (9)

Positive Transfer

When the learning of A aids in the learning and retention of B. For example, learning the rules of algebra makes the later learning of the principles of physics more efficient. (10)

Precise Teaching

Teaching technique used with newly mainstreamed children. Precise teaching provides maximum structure in the learning environment and utilizes behavior modification in order to aid students in mastering a variety of educational tasks. (20)

Preferred Style of Learning

The current system of problem solving preferred by a student at his or her stage of conceptual development. David Hunt believes that this learning mode is not fixed, nor is it a permanent classification. With appropriate matching and mismatching of material and methods, pupils can be encouraged to grow conceptually and increase the complexity of their thinking. (13)

Premack Principle

A principle of behavior modification introduced by David Premack. Premack states that behavior that occurs at a naturally high rate of frequency may be used to reinforce behavior that occurs at a naturally low rate. The establishment of high- and low-frequency responses must be done through careful observation. (10)

Preoperational Stage

The second of Jean Piaget's stages of cognitive growth (from ages two to seven). It is really the beginning of symbolic thinking and frees the child from the thinking of the sensorimotor period that is so directly tied to immediate experience. Oral vocabulary increases by a huge amount, and the child exhibits little concern over the accuracy or even the reality of perception. Imaginary friends, animals that talk, and very "tall" stories mark the period as one of free-wheeling creativity. (5)

Proactive Inhibition (PI)

The disruption of information retrieval due to interference from other encoded and stored information. When learning task A and then later learning task B, the encoded information of A works forward to disturb efforts to retrieve the encoded information of B. In effect, old learning is preventing the recall of new learning. (11)

Procedural Memory

Storage of LTM information concerning motoric patterns and conditionings. Procedural memory allows us to remember how to tie our shoes, ride a bike, or play scales on the piano. (11)

Profile of Nonverbal Sensitivity (PONS)

Robert Rosenthal's measuring instrument to assess the ability to identify aspects of nonverbal communications. The PONS measurement results have indicated that most adults in this culture are not aware of their own nonverbal behavior. The correlation between self-awareness and accuracy was zero. (14)

Programmed Instruction

An arrangement of instructional material in a step-by-step sequence designed to lead the student to a specified goal. The material being presented is broken down into small units called *frames*. There are two general approaches to programming: (1) *linear* programs, in which all students go through the entire program and the frames gradually increase in difficulty, and (2) *branched* programs, in which the student skips forward or backward in the program (the order of the frame presentation varies) as a result of the success or failure experienced in responding.

Programmed instruction can be in book form, or it can be presented through the use of a teaching machine and/or computer. The concept of programmed instruction is credited to B. F. Skinner. (10)

Protein Synthesis (in memory)

Part of a physiological memory theory that sees permanent memory as the result of RNA's role in synthesizing new brain protein. The new protein is assumed to contain the memory and is thus seen as the ultimate engram. *See also* Engram. (11)

Psychoanalytic Theory

Theory of human behavior and method of treating mental illness presented by Sigmund Freud at the turn of the century. The theory attempts to give a rational explanation for irrational thoughts and responses. Psychoanalytic theory states (1) that all behavior is determined by specific motives; (2) that most human motives lie at the unconscious level, and therefore people are unaware of the reasons for most of their own behavior; (3) that neurotic symptoms result from an individual's inner conflicts; and (4) that inner conflicts are a product of childhood trauma and anxiety. The technique is based on the therapist's revealing to the patient the source of his or her anxiety and helping the patient to thus achieve insight and emotional release. *See also* Freud, Sigmund. (6)

Psychological Defenses

Anna Freud's concept that adolescents employ various mechanisms, such as displacement, reversal of affect, and withdrawal, to ward off threats to their developing sense of self. These are considered relatively normal methods, while regression, asceticism, and being uncompromising may indicate serious psychological problems of adjustment. (6)

Punishment

A method for controlling behavior through the use of aversive stimulation. Punishment, though not itself causing the extinction of a conditioned response, does severely reduce that rate of responding *while the punishment is in force*. Punishment should not be confused with negative reinforcement. *See also* Negative reinforcement. (10)

Qualitative Development

The notion in stage theory that cognitive growth and maturation occur in a sequence of qualitative transformations in a manner similar to the change from an egg to caterpillar to butterfly. Each change leads to a major shift to a more complex system of thinking. (5)

Quantitative Development

Theory of intellectual development that sees growth occurring in a linear fashion. Cognitive growth is assumed to be based on steady additions to the intellect, not on any changes in the structure of thought. (5)

Quartiles

Points that divide a distribution into quarters. Each quartile represents twenty-five percentiles: the 1st quartile is equal to the 25th percentile, the 2d quartile to the 50th percentile, and the 3d quartile to the 75th percentile. (15)

Racial Identity Stages

Based on the work of Janet Helms, racial identity among whites can be considered as progressing through a series of six stages, from *contact* to *autonomy*. In a parallel sense, the work of Cross has focused on the same process among devalued groups, such as African Americans. The process for majority whites and for devalued groups suggests a gradual movement toward genuine understanding and respect among all such groups as the highest stage of racial identity development. (14)

Random Sample

A selection in which everyone in a population that is being researched has an equal chance of being selected. This helps to ensure that the sample will be representative of the population from which it was selected. (15)

Range

A statistical measure of variability found by subtracting the lowest score from the highest score. It measures the entire width of a distribution. (15)

Recessive Gene

Gregor Mendel's term for the unit of heredity whose characteristics are expressed only when paired with a like gene; those characteristics are not expressed when paired with dissimilar (dominant) genes. (3)

Regular Education Initiative (REI)

An approach for providing services for most high-incidence special-education children. Since the typical special-education categories seem to lack both reliability and validity, especially those of educable mentally retarded (EMR), learning disabled (LD), and emotionally disturbed (ED), REI has proposed to term such children as low achievers and therefore broaden the services provided in regular classes to meet those children's needs. (20)

Rehearsal

In the information processing model, the critical component of intentional learning. It consists of practice or repetition and is perhaps the key method whereby incoming information may become permanently encoded and stored. (11)

Reinforcement

Any stimulus that increases the likelihood of a response's recurring. Reinforcement, as a Skinnerian concept, should not be confused with reward, feelings of pleasure, or any other concept with subjective or mentalistic overtones. Reinforcement may be used in either classical (respondent) or operant conditioning. In respondent conditioning the unconditioned stimulus serves as the reinforcement. In operant conditioning the presentation of any stimulus following the emitted response can be considered a reinforcement *if it results in a higher response rate. See also* Positive reinforcement; Negative reinforcement. (9)

Reliability

The consistency of a measuring instrument over time. A reliable test, for example, tends to produce roughly the same results when used repeatedly under the same conditions. (15)

Remolding

An early method of dealing with children who did not fit in with adult perceptions of normalcy by physically transforming them. (20)

Respondent Conditioning

B. F. Skinner's term for classical conditioning, in which a conditioned stimulus that has been paired several times with an unconditioned stimulus comes to evoke the conditioned response. (9)

Respondents

Name given by B. F. Skinner to those responses that are sometimes called *reflexes*. Respondents are those responses that may be automatically elicited by a specific unconditioned or unlearned stimulus. Respondents are also called *unconditioned responses. See also* Unconditioned response. (9)

Retrieval

In the information-processing model, the output end of the memory process. Retrieval is the utilization of stored information and must be not only available but also accessible to the individual. (11)

Retroactive Inhibition (RI)

The disruption of information retrieval due to interference from other encoded and stored information. RI occurs when the learning of new material (task B), works backward to prevent the recall of older material (task A). Encoding new information thus hampers efforts to retrieve information already in storage. (11)

Retrograde Amnesia

The loss of memory for recent events as a result of head injuries accompanied by a loss of consciousness. (11)

Reynolds, Maynard

A national leader in the mainstreaming movement who has been critical of the use of a single IQ test for diagnosis and placement of retarded pupils. Reynolds has also shown how the common approaches to special-education classification often penalize students from minority backgrounds and lead to negative self-fulfilling prophecies. (20)

Ribonucleic Acid (RNA)

Molecules, located in the chromosomes, that carry the hereditary instructions contained in the DNA to other parts of the cell. RNA can be thought of as the "builder" that translates the DNA "blueprint" into a finished product. (3)

Risky Shift

Concept from social psychology suggesting that persons in a group situation are less cautious and more prone to risk taking than are persons who are alone. The group situation apparently allows individuals to become less conservative and more willing to take chances regarding both attitudes and behavior. (17)

RNA Theory (of memory)

Theory of memory based on chemical changes occurring within the organism. The life-controlling nucleic acid RNA (ribonucleic acid) is seen as being, if not the physical site of memory itself, at least part of the chain of events leading to the physiological formation of memory. (11)

Rogers, Carl (1902–1987)

Founder of the client-centered, or nondirective, approach to personality. Rogers challenged the orthodox psychiatric and psychological treatment techniques in vogue when he started practice. He felt that psychiatrists often harmed more than helped their patients. Rogers insisted that all persons have a natural tendency to grow in healthy directions and that the role of the therapist is to provide conditions whereby the patient (or client) can fulfill his or her destiny of self-actualization. The famous Rogerian triad of unconditional positive regard, empathy, and congruence became the crucial ingredients in the helping process. Good teaching, like good counseling, is based on this same triad. Classroom interaction should be based on the development of equal and genuine relationships. (12)

Role

Term used by social psychologists to denote the dynamic aspect of status. Role is the behavioral repertoire associated with an individual's status—the bundle of responses available to a person as a result of his or her niche in society's prestige hierarchy. Society *expects* individuals of a given status to act in certain ways, and the individual feels obliged to act according to society's expectations. *See also* Status. (17)

Rosenthal Effect

Concept introduced by Robert Rosenthal, who found that teachers often form expectations about the performance of students, and the students then respond on the basis of a self-fulfilling prophecy. If a teacher assumes a child to be intellectually inferior, the teacher treats the child in such a way as to reinforce inferiority. The child thus begins to act in accordance with the teacher's expectations. (14)

Saber-Tooth Curriculum

An educational spoof that clearly points out the current debate over educational goals: Should we teach specific skills (how to scare away fierce tigers with firebrands) or general abilities (how to be courageous)? Educational leaders often take extreme positions on teaching goals that fit the examples taken by the tribal elders in this mock history. (13)

Schedules of Reinforcement

According to B. F. Skinner, the arrangement of reinforcers on the basis of either time elapsed or number of responses emitted. Responses that are reinforced periodically, rather than each time they are emitted, tend to be conditioned more strongly and are thus more resistant to extinction. The major schedules of reinforcement are (1) continuous, (2) fixed ratio, (3) fixed interval, (4) variable ratio, and (5) variable interval. (9)

Segregation

A method of dealing with children who do not conform to societal perceptions of normalcy by providing separate facilities, such as residential schools in remote areas. (20)

Selective Attention

The ability to focus on one source of incoming information while ignoring possible distractions. This ability is developmental and increases with age. (11)

Self-Regulated Learning

Occurs when the learner achieves an intrinsic motivational set and is able to postpone gratification and rely on inner resources. The self-regulated learner is said to have an internal locus of control. (18)

Semantic Memory

Information in LTM that is based on language (words and the meaning of words), including names, dates, and facts. (11)

Sensitive Period

A time period when an organism is susceptible to a change in behavior due to certain kinds of environmental stimulation. The sensitive periods typically occur early in the organism's life and tend to produce behavior changes that are relatively long-lasting. The process of mother-infant bonding is said to occur only during the baby's first three days of life. (2)

Sensorimotor Stage

First stage of cognitive development, according to Jean Piaget, in which the child learns to distinguish himself or herself from the external environment, begins to notice and follow objects in the environment, and develops the rudiments of trial-and-error learning. This stage lasts from birth to age two years, and the child operates at the level of raw, immediate stimulation as experienced through the senses. An important milestone during this stage is the development of the concept of object permanence, the thought that objects still exist even though they are not, at the moment, being seen. Piaget insists that mental processes are developed directly from inborn motor processes. The child's ability at birth to make certain motor responses forms the basis for the cognitive processes that come later. (5)

Sensory Register

In the information processing model, the first stop for incoming information. When information first impinges on sensory receptors, there is a brief moment when it is held as raw, unprocessed information in the sensory register. It is the "buffer" or "way station" situated between the external environment and internal memory. (11)

Shaping (Successive Approximations)

Technique used by B. F. Skinner to encourage the acquisition of new conditioned operants. The learner is differentially reinforced for making ever-closer approximations of the behavior being conditioned. (10)

Short-Term Memory (STM)

In the information processing model, the first of two main storage systems. Sometimes called "working" or "active" memory, it may encode only about seven separate items. Estimates of how long information may be retained in short-term memory vary from about twenty seconds to over a minute. (11)

Sissy-Boy Syndrome

That there may be growth trends in the development of adult male homosexuality has been suggested by the psychiatrist Richard Green. Green asserts that he has identified a pattern of early male development, called the *sissy-boy syndrome*, which he claims can be used to predict the later onset of homosexuality. (3)

Skinner, B. F. (1904–1991)

Psychology's most important and honored behaviorist, Skinner is the originator of the system of operant conditioning. Using E. L. Thorndike's law of effect as a starting point, Skinner has shown that conditioning can take place when responses are allowed to occur and are then followed by reinforcing stimuli. Reinforcement is thus contingent on the fact that the response (operant) has been emitted. Skinner's emphasis is on response analysis. He is not concerned with what goes on inside the organism but is concerned with specifying the environmental conditions associated with and affecting the organism's response repertoire. Skinner's most notable contributions to education are the techniques of programmed instruction and behavior modification. (9)

Snarey, John

Investigator who used cross-cultural studies to determine whether Lawrence Kohlberg's system of classifying moral development was as universal as originally claimed. He found that western and nonwestern urban cultures were similar in the sequence of stages Kohlberg described, but tribal and/or feudal cultures exhibited a different pattern. (7)

Snow, C. P. (1905–1980)

Popularizer of the idea that science and the humanities are separate cultures, or distinct worldviews. The differences are often found in how the objective psychological scientist and the subjective educational practitioner view the world of schools and classrooms. (1)

Social Facilitation

A concept from the field of social psychology used to explain the fact that in some circumstances individuals perform more quickly when in a group situation than when alone. Social facilitation is most pronounced in the case of fairly simple mechanical tasks. The more difficult and the more intellectual the task, the less the effect of social facilitation. (17)

Social Inhibition

The fact that individuals, in some circumstances, perform less well when in the presence of other people. This is especially true when the tasks being performed are perceived as being difficult by the individual being measured. The opposite of social inhibition is called *social facilitation*. (17)

Social Learning Theory

Theory, proposed by Albert Bandura, suggesting that a large part of what a person learns occurs through imitation or modeling. Bandura's major concern is with learning that takes place in the context of a social situation in which individuals come to modify behavior as a result of how others in the group respond. Social learning *does not* require primary reinforcement. (10)

Social Psychology

The study of individual behavior in the context of the social situation. Social psychology analyzes the ways in which people affect and are affected by other people. Major topics in the field include conformity, cohesiveness, status and role, attitudes and attitudinal change, social perception, and group structure and leadership. (17)

Socialization

Process by which an individual learns and internalizes society's rules and norms, thought by social psychologists to be brought about through societal pressures to conform. (17)

Spacing Effect

The efficiency of spaced learning over massed learning is now called the *spacing effect*, and its documentation as a valid phenomenon goes back at least to the seminal work of Hermann Ebbinghaus in about 1905–1909. Hermann Ebbinghaus had stated that given a number of repetitions in which to learn something, spreading these sessions over a period of time is decidedly more advantageous than completing them all at a single time. *See also* Massed learning. (10)

Spearman, Charles E. (1863–1945)

English psychometrician and psychologist who proposed that intelligence was not a simple unitary process but could be separated into an underlying general factor (*g*) and a series of very specific factors (*s*). Among the *s* factors were such things as verbal ability, math ability, and even musical ability. Spearman used a statistical approach, mainly correlational, to segregate these components of intelligence. (16)

Spontaneous Recovery

The fact that a conditioned response that has been extinguished will, after a brief time, tend to recur on its own. The conditioned response returns, despite having been extinguished, with no additional conditioning trials. (9)

Standard Deviation (SD)

A statistical measure of variability that is based on how fall *all the scores* in a distribution vary from the mean. A large SD indicates a group of heterogeneous measures, whereas a small SD indicates homogeneity. (15)

Stanford-Binet Test

Intelligence test developed by Lewis M. Terman in 1916 while he was at Stanford University. The Stanford-Binet test was an American revision of the original Binet test, first published in France in 1905. It has since gone through numerous updates and revisions but is still considered to be more "verbally loaded" than its Wechsler counterparts. The Stanford-Binet, like the Wechsler, is an individual test of intelligence. (16)

Stanines

A set of standardized scores (based on the normal curve) arranged across nine intervals. The mean is set at 5, and the standard deviation at approximately 2. (15)

Status

Term used in social psychology to define an individual's niche in society's prestige hierarchy, or the individual's standing in a social system. The behavior expected of an individual of a given status is called his or her "role." *See also* Role. (17)

Stem and Leaf

A technique for graphing data in which the first digit is displayed in the first column, the stem, and the trailing digits in the second column, the leaf. (15)

Sternberg, Robert

Yale psychologist who has created a view of intelligence that is based on an information processing model and is called the *triarchic model*. The three major constituents are metacomponents, performance components, and knowledge-acquisition components. (5)(11)(16)

Stimulus Generalization

Term used in conditioning to describe a situation in which a previously neutral stimulus similar to the actual stimulus used in the training procedure takes on the power to elicit the response. In classical conditioning the neutral stimulus is similar to the conditioned stimulus, whereas in operant conditioning the neutral stimulus is similar to the discriminated stimulus S^D. (9)

Stimulus-Response Theory

A theory that stresses the importance of the buildup of stimulus-response *associations* in defining learning. Most behaviorists adhere to stimulus-response learning theories, the major exception being E. C. Tolman. The leading stimulus-response theorists are E. L. Thorndike, Ivan Pavlov, J. B. Watson, Edwin Guthrie, C. L. Hull, and B. F. Skinner. Stimulus-response theorists stress the importance of nurture in the nature-nurture debate. Most theories of learning during the first half of the twentieth century, especially in the United States, were stimulus-response theories. The cognitive-gestalt position, however, was *not* based on a stimulus-response theory. (8)

Stimulus Variety

Variation, at all sensory modes, of stimulus inputs. Stimulus variety was seen by many early-experience theorists as the crucial ingredient in intellectual development. J. McV. Hunt states that the more the child hears, sees, and touches, the more he or she will want to hear, see, and touch, and the more intellectual growth will occur. (4)

Storage

In the information processing model the organism's internal memory. When information is stored, it may persist over time. Currently, theorists refer to at least two storage components, short-term and long-term. (11)

Structure

Part of Jerome Bruner's theory of instruction, which states that any given subject area can be organized in an optimal fashion (structured) so that it can be transmitted to and understood by almost any student. Bruner feels that if a subject area is properly structured, then "any idea or problem or body of knowledge can be presented in a form simple enough so that any particular learner can understand it in a recognizable form." (9)

Student Crushes

A common problem for secondary school teachers, involving an inappropriate emotional attachment on the part of a student for a teacher. Using Anna Freud's framework, teachers can understand the need to handle such feelings without encouraging the fantasy. (6)

Student Teams–Achievement Divisions

A system created by Robert Slavin to promote mainstreaming. He integrates special-education and regular-class children and sets up achievement groups (teams) composed of a mix of students. By offering a variety of rewards, the system increases both group and individual achievement. It does not drain resources from the "regular" pupils to meet the needs of special-education children. (20)

Summerhill School

English boarding school whose curriculum and way of life is based on the permissive orientation of its founder, A. S. Neill. The school stresses the free expression of ideas without the rigors of required exams or the demands of required class attendance. (4)

Symbolic Representation

The third stage of cognitive development and method of communication introduced by Jerome Bruner, the first two being the enactive and iconic levels. At the symbolic level, the child is able to translate experience into language. Words can then be used for communication and for representing ideas. Symbolic representation allows us to make logical connections between ideas and to think more compactly. (9)

T Score

A standardized score (based on the normal curve) in which the mean is set at 50 and the standard deviation at 10. *T* scores range from a low of 20 to a high of 80. (15)

Teacher Enthusiasm

According to research by Jacob Kounin and Barak Rosenshine, the characteristic of being "with it" and alert that has been shown to have a consistent, positive relationship with student behavior. (12)

Teacher Expectations

A teacher's attitude toward student learning and achievement. Numerous factors have been found to influence teacher acceptance of pupils, including social class, ethnicity, gender, rearing in a single-parent home, personality, and academic achievement. Some estimates suggest that as much as 50 percent of current teachers harbor one or more stereotypes and as a result provide children with less than optimal learning opportunities in the classroom. (14)

Teaching Machine

A device used to present an instructional program one step (or frame) at a time. The student either writes in answers or presses a button corresponding to the correct alternative. The advantages of the teaching machine are that (1) the student can proceed at his or her own pace; (2) the student receives immediate feedback; (3) for many students the machines are intrinsically motivating. *See also* Programmed instruction. (10)

Terman, Lewis M. (1877–1956)

Professor of psychology at Stanford University (1910–1942) and deviser of the Stanford-Binet IQ test. The American revision of the original Binet intelligence test was published in 1916. Terman standardized the test on American schoolchildren, and he introduced so many new items that it was virtually a new test. He scored the test on the basis of IQ (intelligence quotient), rather than mental age as Binet had done. Terman is also noted for his long-term study of intellectually gifted children (IQs of 140 or higher), which proved that a high IQ does correlate with many traditional measures of success, both in school and in later life. (16)

Terminal Behavior

Concept used by experts in the field of behavior modification. Terminal behavior defines the educational goals for the class as a whole or for individual students. It defines these goals in objective, behavioral terms. Rather than use what they consider to be vaguely stated goals like "understanding," the behaviorists insist that the goals describe specific behaviors that will result when the objective is attained. For example, students can be said to have learned how to multiply when they can recite the multiplication table with no errors. (10)

Theory and Practice

The twin pillars of educational psychology. The discipline represents a bridge, or connector, between psychology as the science of human behavior and the profession of education. (1)

Thinking Skills

An effort to teach children strategies of thinking that will increase their abilities to comprehend and understand. The thinking-skills approach has been adopted as a result of outcome studies indicating that even though students may be mastering basic skills, they still show reduced levels of comprehension. The goals of this approach are similar to those previously proposed at the higher levels of Bloom's taxonomy. (13)

Thorndike, Edward L. (1874–1949)

One of America's most renowned educational psychologists. Thorndike studied at Harvard under William James and later taught at Columbia University's Teachers College. Early in his career, Thorndike did important laboratory studies of learning, using animals as subjects. From the results of these studies he constructed the first internally consistent learning theory. He created three major laws of learning (the law of readiness, the law of exercise, and the law of effect) and many subordinate laws. Thorndike believed learning occurs in a trial-and-error fashion and thought of learning itself as the result of a buildup of connections between stimuli and responses. He insisted that educational psychology must utilize the scientific method in establishing its own "book of knowledge." (8)

Thurstone, Louis L. (1887–1955)

One of the developers of the factor approach to the understanding of intelligence. Thurstone originally gave sixty different tests of special abilities to large groups of children and then separated out those test scores that correlated highly with each other. He discovered that out of the original list of seemingly separate tests, there were only seven underlying correlated groupings (or *primary abilities*): verbal comprehension, word fluency, numerical ability, spatial visualizations, associative memory, perceptual speed, and reasoning. (16)

Time-Out Room

A separate room for handling extremely difficult children by segregating them from other students for a relatively short period. Excessive use of such a room can become aversive, making the technique ineffective. (19)

Tip-of-the-Tongue (TOT) Phenomenon

Momentary retrieval problem that occurs when trying to access semantic information from LTM. Can be especially embarrassing when one stumbles in midsentence while introducing a friend or family member and the name gets stuck on your, well, uh, tip of the tongue. (11)

Token System

A system of reinforcement used by proponents of behavior modification, in which tokens of varying point values are awarded to students for fulfilling specific behavioral objectives. The tokens (conditioned reinforcers) may be cardboard or poker chips of various colors that the student may earn to achieve some desired prize or privilege. The system is said to have two main advantages: (1) It maintains a high daily rate of desirable responses, and (2) it teaches delayed gratification. (10)

Tolman, E. C. (1886–1959)

Creator of *purposive behaviorism*, a bridge between rigid behaviorism and doctrinaire gestaltism. Tolman was a behaviorist to the extent that he accepted observable responses as psychology's basic data, but he insisted that, far from being random or based on trial and error, learning was purposive, or goal-directed. He agreed with the gestaltists that people learn by forming cognitive maps of their environment. People can form hypotheses, see relationships, and then respond on the basis of these cognitive maps, rather than respond solely on the basis of a conditioned stimulus-response connection. Tolman's system is called an S-S (sign-significate) theory rather than an S-R (stimulus-response) psychology. (8)

Transactional Model

The interplay between individuals, especially the parent and child, where each, in effect, shapes the other's environment. This has given rise to a view of general development called the *transactional model*. These reciprocal influences affect not only the child's cognitive growth, but also the formation of the child's temperament, attitudes, and general personality. And, of course, the actions of the child also affect the future actions of the parent. Bruner has been using a variant of the transactional model to describe language acquisition, which he feels depends strongly on the myriad of small but continuing interactions between parent and child. (9, 16)

Transfer

That which occurs when the learning of one activity influences the learning of a second ability. If the learning of *A* facilitates the learning of *B*, it is called *positive* transfer. If the learning of *A* inhibits the learning of *B*, it is called *negative* transfer. (10)

Trivia in the Classroom

A teacher's rapid-fire series of questions to students, calling for rote-memory answers. A series of classroom observation studies dating back as far as the beginning of this century and extending to the 1980s has indicated that too often this is the common mode of teacher-pupil interaction. (1)

Two-Stage Memory Theory

In the information processing model, the theory that memories are encoded and stored in at least two stages—in short-term memory, which lasts from about a few seconds to up to a minute, and in long-term memory, which may last a lifetime. (11)

Unconditional Positive Regard

Concept used by Carl Rogers in dealing both with clients in therapy and with students in the classroom. Unconditional positive regard means accepting people for what they are, without passing judgment, and without exacting any condition for full acceptance. According to Rogers, this is one of the three necessary and sufficient conditions for the promotion of learning, the other two being empathy and congruence. (12)

Unconditioned Response

A reflex response or, in Skinnerian terms, a respondent. An unconditioned response is any response that can be elicited automatically by the presentation of a certain stimulus, without any training or learning. The term is used in classical conditioning, and in Ivan Pavlov's original experiment the unconditioned response was salivation to the stimulus of meat powder being placed in the dog's mouth. (8)

Unconditioned Stimulus

Any stimulus that will elicit a given response automatically, without any training or learning. The term is used in classical conditioning, and in the case of Ivan Pavlov's own experiment, the unconditioned stimulus was meat powder placed in the dog's mouth. (8)

Unconscious Motivation

Freudian view that most of a person's behavior is motivated by forces of which the person is unaware—irrational needs that lurk beneath the level of conscious awareness. (18)

Validity

The extent to which test instruments are true indicators of what they purport to measure. A valid history test, for example, should measure a person's knowledge of history, not his or her neatness, penmanship, or spelling ability. (15)

Variability Measures

Measures that give information regarding individual differences, or how individuals vary in their measured scores. The two most important measures of variability are the range and the standard deviation. (15)

Visual Cliff

The perceived dropoff at the edge of any steep place. Research has shown that the newborn of many species, including human babies, will avoid the "deep" side of a specially built platform. This seems to show that depth perception is innate rather than learned. (3)

Vygotsky, Lev S. (1896–1934)

A major Russian cognitive psychologist, educator, and researcher who primarily added two important concepts to stage theory: (1) the zone of proximal development and (2) the importance of peer and teacher interaction to "tow" cognitive development through stages. Vygotsky insisted that the child should be stretched into new areas of learning that are just beyond that child's comfort level. His work was considered too controversial by the Communist regime of Stalin and was banned for many years. (4, 5, 18)

Walberg, Herbert

A leading educational researcher who has applied the technique of meta-analysis to the study of teaching effectiveness. Walberg has been able to outline the relative importance of a variety of teaching strategies. Most important is providing positive reinforcement, followed by other methods such as giving cues and feedback, promoting cooperative learning, and establishing a positive classroom atmosphere. Other relevant factors are time on task, the incidence of higher-order questions, and use of advance organizers. (12)

Waterman, Alan

Working within the identity-formation framework of James Marcia, Waterman traced the pathways of identity development and demonstrated the number of multiple directions that were possible. Waterman asserts that the moratorium stage cannot be maintained indefinitely. *See also* Moratorium. (16)

Watson, John B. (1878–1958)

Founder of behaviorism, and, at one time, psychology's most vocal critic of subjectivism, mentalism, and especially the technique of introspection. Watson was a strong believer in the importance of environment (as opposed to heredity) in shaping virtually all human behavior. He also believed that learning resulted from a buildup of stimulus-response connections, or what he called "habits." He was a strong advocate of Ivan Pavlov's concept of classical conditioning and utilized this method in his study of the acquisition of fear in the baby Albert. Watson taught psychology at Johns Hopkins and later spent many years working for an advertising agency in New York. *See also* Behaviorism. (2)

Wechsler, David (1896–1981)

America's premier psychologist in the area of intelligence testing and test construction. Beginning in 1939 with the publication of the Wechsler-Bellevue test, David Wechsler spent his life creating, standardizing, and refining a long list of individual IQ tests (see below). He defined *intelligence* as "the global capacity of an individual to think rationally, act purposefully and deal effectively with the environment." All the Wechsler tests report three separate IQ scores: a verbal IQ, a performance IQ, and a full-scale IQ. (16)

Wechsler Tests

Individual IQ tests, developed by David Wechsler, currently including the Wechsler Intelligence Scale for Children (WISC III), the Wechsler Adult Intelligence Scale (WAIS-R), and the Wechsler Preschool and Primary Scale of Intelligence (WPPSI). All the Wechsler tests are administered by a trained examiner to one person at a time. All the tests yield three scores: a verbal IQ, a performance IQ, and a full-scale IQ. Wechsler believed that many of the intelligence tests of the day were too heavily laden with verbal items, and, to correct for that, the Wechsler tests all include a performance section that tests an individual's visual-motor abilities. Wechsler tests use the deviation IQ method of scoring. In the hands of a skilled examiner, the Wechsler test can be used as a projective test for ferreting out a subject's personality traits. *See also* Intelligence quotient. (16)

Wertheimer, Max (1880–1943)

Founder of the gestalt school of psychology (in the early 1900s). Wertheimer had criticized the structuralists and their insistence that all psychological phenomena should be analyzed into the smallest possible parts. He felt that the whole was more than just the sum of its parts. In order to understand psychological phenomena, one had to study all the parts together in their particular *Gestalt*, a German word meaning whole, or totality of configuration. Wertheimer's first studies were in the area of perception, especially the perception of apparent movement. Later he became interested in education and the principles of learning. He insisted that educators should teach for "understanding" rather than rely on repetition and rote memorization. *See also* Gestalt psychology. (8)

White, Robert

Harvard psychologist who has suggested that one of humankind's most fundamental motives is based on a strong personal desire to master the environment. White calls this the "competence" motive and believes it to be an intrinsic one that may even have survival value for the species. (18)

Wundt, Wilhelm (1832–1920)

German psychologist and founder of the structuralist school of thought. Wundt created the world's first laboratory of psychology at the University of Leipzig in 1879. He believed that psychology should devote itself to the study of the basic elements that make up conscious experience. To ferret out these individual elements, Wundt used trained subjects who looked within themselves and reported all their most fleeting and minute thoughts, feelings, and sensations. This technique of looking within the self is called *introspection*. Wundt's goal was to take psychology out of the field of philosophy and give it a sense of scientific respectability. (8)

z Score (Standard Score)

A number that results from the transformation of a raw score into units of standard deviation. The z score specifies how far above or below the mean a given score is in these standard deviation units. The normal deviate, z, has a mean equal to 0 and a standard deviation equal to 1.00. (15)

Zeigarnik Effect

The fact that in some situations, people are more apt to remember unfinished tasks than those they have completed. Memory is enhanced by the thought of the job still left undone. (18)

Zygote

First of the prenatal stages of development. The zygote is formed at conception and results from the fertilization of an egg by a sperm cell. The zygote floats freely within the uterus for about two weeks and finally attaches itself to the uterine wall. (3)

PHOTO CREDITS

Chapter 14

384: Susan Lapides/Design Conceptions. 387: Susie Fitzhugh/Stock, Boston. 389: Wally Huntington. 393: Courtesy Harvard Office of News & Public Affairs. 395: Jean-Claude Lejeune. 407: Bob Daemmrich/Stock, Boston. 408: Courtesy BBC Picture Publicity.

Chapter 15

424: Jean-Claude Lejeune. 426: Marie Geggis. 442: Elizabeth Crews/Stock, Boston. 447: Brown Brothers. 449: Courtesy Duane Library Archives, Fordham University, photo by Tom Weber.

Chapter 16

456: Jean-Claude Lejeune. 460: Historical Picture Service. 461: Courtesy National Library of Medicine. 463: Courtesy National Library of Medicine. 465: Wally Huntington. 466: Courtesy David Wechsler. 467: Psychological Corporation, New York. 470: Rosemary Good. 471: Jean-Claude Lejeune. 472: Jean Speiser. 473: Roger Dollarhide/Monkmeyer. 478: Courtesy Sandra Scarr.

Chapter 17

492: Elizabeth Crews/Stock, Boston. 494: Marshall Henrichs. 495: Bob Kramer/Picture Cube. 498: Shirley Zeiberg. 501: Marshall Hen-richs. 502: Jean-Claude Lejeune. 516: Wally Huntington. 517: Courtesy Clark, Phipps, Clark & Harris, Inc., photo by Raimondo Borea.

Chapter 18

526: Karen R. Preuss/Image Works. 531: Thad R. Wisehart. 539: Courtesy Harvard Office of News & Public Affairs. 541: Thad R. Wisehart. 542: Harry F. Harlow, University of Wisconsin Primate Laboratory. 544: Jim Carroll.

Chapter 19

544: Elizabeth Crews/Image Works. 557: Elizabeth Crews/Image Works. 560: Bob Henriques/Magnum. 566: Instructional Materials Production Center, North Carolina State University. 567: Jean-Claude Lejeune/Stock, Boston. 571: David Strickler.

Chapter 20

584: Bob Daemmrich/Image Works. 590: Courtesy James Ysseldyke. 598: *Left and right*, State Historical Society of Wisconsin. 600: The Boston Globe. 603: Paul Conklin/Monkmeyer. 604: Reverend William J. Codd, S. J. 606: Courtesy Photographic Services, University of Wisconsin. 614: Paul Conklin/Monkmeyer.

INDEX

Page numbers in **boldface** indicate illustrations, tables or boxes.

663

Locurto, C., 458, 459, 471
Locus of control, 500, 642
Lodico, M. G., 308
Loehlin, J. C., 52
Loevinger, J., 158, 163
Logicomathematical learning (LM), 249, 636, 642
Lohman, D., 362, 370, 378
Long-term memory (LTM), 289, 642
  retrieval from, 292–294
Lonky, E., **190**
Looks, expectations and, **510**
Lorayne, 302
Lorenz, Konrad, 38, 39, 82, 505, 630, 634, 639, 642
  biography of, **39**
Loucks-Horsley, Susan, 617
Love needs, 532, 645
Lubchenco, L. O., 47
Lucas, 302
Luehrmann, A., **277**
Luria, Alfred, 121, 127
Luther, Martin, 153, 162
Lyman, H. B., 441
Lynch, Gary, 311–313
Lynn, Richard, **482**
Lyons, N., 195, 366, 411

McCarthy, Mary, 194
McCartney, K., 475
McClelland, D., **478**, 536, 548–549, 643
Maccoby, E., 402, 476, 511, 537
McConnell, James V., 310–312
McCormick, J., 334
McCullough, G., 193
McDermott, Ray, 612
McDonald, F. J., 259
MacDonald, R., 572, 573, 578, 643
McDougall, William, **449**, 534
Mace, F. C., **269**
McGaugh, J. L., 295
McGraw, Myrtle, 78, 91–93, 215, 630
McKean, K., 458
Mackenzie, B., 477
McKinney, C. W., **347**
McKinney, J., **307, 601**
McKinnon, G., 441
McKinnon, J. W., 135
McLuhan, Marshall, 387–388
McMahon, F. B., 238
McMahon, J. W., 238
McNamee, Shari, 192, 193, 204
McPherson, M. W., **31**
McShane, J., 286
McTaggart, R., 411
MacWhinney, B., **248**
Madsen, Charles, 263, 264, 268
Madsen, Clifford, 263, 264, 268
Maehr, M. L., 536
Mainstreaming, 585, 587–589, 643
  case for, 617–618
Maintenance rehearsal, 290, 643
Malcolm X, 162, **164**
Malina, R. M., 59
Man Meets Dog, **39**
Mand, 240

Mandl, H., **248**
Manic depression, heredity and, 50
Mann, A., 167
Mann, Horace, 175, 556
Manson, Charles, 512
Marano, H. E., 60
Maratsos, M., 60, 62
Marcia, James, 160–162, 166, 170, 171, 643, 658
Marconi, 249
Margano, R., 371
Marijuana, 157
Marks, G., 501
Markstrom-Adams, C., 164
Martin, J., 476
Martinez Pons, M., 532
Masculine theme, 195
Masculinity-femininity score, **64**
Maslach, C., 500
Maslow, Abraham, 532, 534, 548, 645
Mass media, aggression and, 506–508
Mass-to-specific-action progression, 56
Massed learning, 257, 643
Masters, William, 65–67, 69
Mastery smile, 540
Mastery test, 441
Mastery versus inferiority, **146,** 155–157
Mastropieri, M., **347**
Matching of discipline to stage, 564
Matching and mismatching method of teaching, 363, 643
Maternal infant bonding, **60**
Mathematics, **64–65, 118,** 271, 487
  testing of, on WISC-III, 467
  tutors for, 167
Maturation, 68, 70
  (*See also* Early maturation; Late maturation)
Maturation rates for girls, **63**
Maurer, A., 267
Maurer, D., 59
May, Mark, 175–177, 189, 638, 643
Mayer, R. E., 362
Maze, 51, **64**
  Hebb-Williams, 84
Maze-bright animal, 36, 52
Meacham, M. F., 269, 273
Mead, Margaret, 36, 196, 534
Mean, 432–433, 435, 643
Measurement (technique), 13, 425–434, 643
  of central tendency, 432, 643
  of variability, 434
Median, 433–434, 643
Meichenbaum, D., 250
Meister, Carla, 374–375
Memory, **222**
  emotions and, 295
  flashbulb, 635
  procedural, 649
  protein synthesis in, 649–650
  RNA theory of, 651
  semantic, 652
  short-term (STM), 653
Memory enhancement, 546
Memory performance, 308
Men, sexual activity of, 66
Menarche, 63, 64, 643–644

Mendel, Gregor, 50, 633, 636, 644, 650
Mendelian explanation, 30
Mental age, 438, 462, **463,** 644
Mental life, 12
Mental retardation, **51,** 52, 97, **472,** 638
Mental test, 34, 627
Mentored small group, **123**
Mercer, Jane, **428–429**
Mesoderm, 53
Messick, S., 459, 595
Meta-analysis, **118,** 274, 658
Metacognition, 114, 305, **308, 309,** 644
Metamemory, 305
Metareflection, 417
Method of loci, 301
Metrazol, 84
Meyer, W. J., 402
Michaels, J. W., 494
Microgenetic method, **81**
Microneuron, 85
Microteaching, 350–352
Middle school, 579–580
Milgram, Stanley, 190–193, 204, 500, 507, 520, 630, 644
Military, intelligence testing of, 34
Miller, Alan, 362, 391, 644
Miller, G., 288, **610**
Miller, N., 501, 505, 635
Milton, 256
Milwaukee Project, 89, 92, 644
Minas, J. S., 544
Mind, **30,** 241
Minority (status), 2, 396, 397
  identity formation and, 163–165
Mischel, W., 110, 565
Mistrust, trust versus, 146–148, **151**
Mitchison, G., 298
Mizokawa, D. T., 590, 593
Mnemonics, 301–302, 316, 644
Modal stage plus one, 188
Mode, 434, 644
Modeling, 259, 625, 644
Mohatt, G., 328
Monkey(s), **105**
  Harlow's studies of, 147
  working on puzzles by, 119
Monozygotic (MZ) twins, 52, 471, **472,** 480, 644
Montessori, Maria, **604–605,** 644–645
Moore, B. R., 242
Moore, C. H., **510**
Moral development, 177, 645
Moral judgment, IQ and, 189
Moral reasoning, percentage of, at each stage, **187**
Moratorium, **152,** 161–163, 171–172, 643, 645
Morgan, Thomas Hunt, 36, 636
Morine, G., 342
Morine-Dershimer, Greta, 342
Morphological differences between male and female, **65**
Morris, C., 505
Morrow, Chen, 328
Morrow, James, 328
Morse, Frances, **386**
Mosher, Ralph, 563, 564, 641
Mother, day care versus, **150–151**